Public Budgeting and Finance

Fourth Edition, Revised and Expanded

PUBLIC ADMINISTRATION AND PUBLIC POLICY

A Comprehensive Publication Program

Executive Editor

JACK RABIN
Professor of Public Administration and Public Policy
Division of Public Affairs
The Capital College
The Pennsylvania State University—Harrisburg
Middletown, Pennsylvania

63. *Handbook of Administrative Communication*, edited by James L. Garnett and Alexander Kouzmin
64. *Public Budgeting and Finance: Fourth Edition, Revised and Expanded*, edited by Robert T. Golembiewski and Jack Rabin

Additional Volumes in Preparation

Handbook of Public Administration: Second Edition, edited by Jack Rabin, W. Bartley Hildreth, and Gerald J. Miller

Handbook of Organizational Theory and Management, edited by Thomas D. Lynch and Todd J. Dicker

ANNALS OF PUBLIC ADMINISTRATION

1. *Public Administration: History and Theory in Contemporary Perspective*, edited by Joseph A. Uveges, Jr.
2. *Public Administration Education in Transition*, edited by Thomas Vocino and Richard Heimovics
3. *Centenary Issues of the Pendleton Act of 1883*, edited by David H. Rosenbloom with the assistance of Mark A. Emmert
4. *Intergovernmental Relations in the 1980s*, edited by Richard H. Leach
5. *Criminal Justice Administration: Linking Practice and Research*, edited by William A. Jones, Jr.

Public Budgeting and Finance

Fourth Edition, Revised and Expanded

edited by

Robert T. Golembiewski
The University of Georgia
Athens, Georgia

Jack Rabin
The Pennsylvania State University—Harrisburg
Middletown, Pennsylvania

MARCEL DEKKER, INC.   NEW YORK · BASEL · HONG KONG

Library of Congress Cataloging-in-Publication Data

Public budgeting and finance / edited by Robert T. Golembiewski, Jack
    Rabin. — 4th ed., rev. and exp.
        p. cm. — (Public administration and public policy; 64)
    Includes bibliographical references and index.
    ISBN 0-8247-9389-7 (alk. paper)
    1. Budget—United States. 2. Budget. I. Golembiewski, Robert T.
II. Rabin, Jack. III. Series.
HJ2051.P795 1997
352.4—dc21

                                                            97-13943
                                                                CIP

The publisher offers discounts on this book when ordered in bulk quantities. For more information, write to Special Sales/Professional Marketing at the address below.

This book is printed on acid-free paper.

MARCEL DEKKER, INC.
270 Madison Avenue, New York, New York 10016
http://www.dekker.com

Current printing (last digit):
10 9 8 7 6 5 4 3 2 1

PRINTED IN THE UNITED STATES OF AMERICA

Preface to the Fourth Edition

This fourth edition of *Public Budgeting and Finance* offers 54 selections—several of them newly written—and runs over 1000 pages.

The basic course in public budgeting and finance *is* maturing, but it requires that more be known, in greater detail, and early in the student's program. We attempt to meet that need here.

How, specifically, do we go about doing it? The book is organized in terms of nine "units"—historical, conceptual, institutional, economic, strategic, administrative, behavioral, organizational, and technical contexts. The verbal circumscriptions of these several core units of public budgeting and finance will be substantially familiar to readers of the other volumes in this series. By structuring this book around these familiar units, we invoke a practical, tested framework.

These units constitute a basic structure for the content, which comes from many sources: about one-quarter are essays written especially for this volume, another quarter are adapted from one of the three previous editions of this volume, and about one-half are republished from other sources.

The contributions of many are reflected in the pages that follow. Obviously, our contributors deserve special thanks, and our students over the years have provided valuable tutelage in what works, and why. In addition, special thanks go to many whose skills and commitment underlay the preparation of this complex volume, including Sandra Daniel and Margaret DeGrange.

Robert T. Golembiewski
Jack Rabin

Preface to the Third Edition

The 13 years intervening between this edition and its first predecessor make this series seem a very good prophet indeed. Work in public administration has burgeoned; no other area has experienced more need for teaching/learning resources than public budgeting and finance. All three editions rest on those two basic propositions, and this edition does so even more than the others.

This third edition also seeks to change with the times in at least four significant ways. First and paramount, this edition does not have to do the job that faced the first edition. Fortunately so. An almost total lack of teaching/learning resources characterized those early days—few texts, no readers, no workbooks. Today those elemental deficiencies no longer exist.

So this third edition need not be—indeed, cannot be—that which the times required of the first edition. What did those times require? The first edition sought to be all and do all, for all users, and unattractive challenges, failures, and egregious compromises could not be avoided.

The third edition can count on other resources—especially the now numerous introductory texts—as a takeoff point. Those sources do many things well. Thus, they describe the various institutions relevant in budgetary processes; such sources document well historical changes in concepts of budgeting and approaches to it. They also tend to do an especially thorough job—even verging on overkill, at times—of sensitizing their readers to the political nature of budgetary processes, and so on. These constitute valuable components toward a reasonable working knowledge of public budgeting and finance.

Second, given these new riches, important questions come to mind. What remains undone for this third edition? And why not simply allow the second edition to go quietly out of print? Well, plenty still needs to be done. Specifically, the third edition seeks to complement and reinforce the available resources in three broad areas:

- *Behavioral*, via a focus on how and why individuals or groups respond in budgeting and financial settings.
- *Theoretical*, by enriching the operating models relevant to budgeting and finance, so that readers will have better "handles" for describing reality and can work toward more specific predictions about what is likely to happen under specific circumstances, and,

- *Technical*, by emphasis on both systemic and subsystemic approaches to the "how to" of budgeting and finance.

In this sense, then, this third edition is at once much less *broad* than its predecessors and yet very much *deeper*.

How do the other available teaching/learning resources fare in these three critical areas? Judgments will vary concerning one resource or another. However, approximate judgments safely can be made. Let us summarize.

- On *behavioral* materials, the other resources typically do little, sometimes even nothing.
- On *theoretical* materials, the record is better, but only a little, except for selected foci such as "incrementalism," concerning which we have talk, in general, and too much of it.
- On *technical* materials, the other resources no doubt provide the best coverage of the three broad areas considered here, but that "best" typically still falls far short of what is practically necessary, not to mention ideally desirable.

Third, over 75% of the selections reprinted here were published after the publication date carried by the second edition. That obviously reflects a major change in the contents of successive editions.

Fourth, this third edition seeks to preserve a substantial sense of the introductory sections of earlier editions. Readers of earlier editions seemed to profit from those introductions. Despite major changes in their substance, the present introductory notes retain much of the flavor of their predecessors.

Let us make one final note. Again, special thanks go to Mrs. Sandra Daniel, who contributed much of the detailed work on which this volume rests.

Robert T. Golembiewski
Jack Rabin

Preface to the Second Edition

It is pleasurable to see one's expectations being realized. And this second edition basically testifies to the soundness of the confidence in 1967 that training in public administration was about ready to increase in both quality and quantity. Without such a takeoff, simply, there would be no second edition.

This volume has three major motivations. First, the readings and the editorial introductions have been substantially updated and revised. As one measure of these changes, about one-half of the selections in this volume appeared after the publication date of the first edition. A number of classic pieces have been retained, so previous users of the volume no doubt also will see some old friends.

A number of classes and seminars contributed to this revision by evaluating the selections in the first edition. Drs. Augustus Turnbull, Jerry McCaffery, and Jack Rabin fielded those courses. Their efforts, and especially those of their students, are gratefully acknowledged

Second, the focus of the second edition has been changed substantially. From one perspective, this volume reflects more concern with issues and techniques applicable at all levels of government. The first edition, while saying the same things, had a definite bias on federal institutions and practices.

Third, the present volume has an added emphasis on the description and evaluation of alternative techniques or approaches relevant to budgeting and finance activities.

Patently, such a volume rests on many talents and contributions, and our role as editors is minor among them. Special thanks to Mrs. Sandra Daniel, an experienced hand in such matters, who managed the preparation and assembly of the finished effort.

Robert T. Golembiewski
Jack Rabin

Preface to the First Edition

It is a useful administrative truism that where one sits often determines what one sees and how one reacts. Thus it was for me. I had long been concerned with the lack of useful teaching materials in public administration. Rather than doing much about this basic need, I indulged my own long-run romance with theoretical and applied behavioral analysis relevant to organizations. As Academic Director of the MPA Program at the University of Georgia for the last several years, however, I found the lack of teaching materials of far more immediate concern. At U. of G. we are attempting to provide up-to-date training—what I fancy as the training of "professional generalists" with broad and deep competencies—and we are providing that training for students at the university center and throughout the state. We see ourselves concerned not only with quality training, but also with training in large numbers. The ready availability of teaching materials is vital to achieving such ambitions.

Public Budgeting and Finance is one of several attempts to provide teaching materials for our use and, hopefully, for the use of others. There seems no question that the need exists. Consider only a single point. Derived from the same motivation as the present collection, a comprehensive set of readings suitable for graduate and undergraduate courses in public administration has already appeared [1]. The wide acceptance of that publication reinforces three beliefs underlying this volume. First, I feel public administration as an area of specialization gives every indication of rising beyond its "topping-out" point reached after World War II. Second, I feel that unparalleled demands for professional training in public administration will be increasingly made on those of us in our nation's colleges and universities. My friend Dean Stephen Bailey, of Syracuse, foresees at least a tenfold multiplier at work; I agree with his prediction. Third, I feel that conveniently available teaching materials can serve as a valuable catalyst for the present ferment affecting research and teaching in the arts and sciences of public management.

At least two other aids to teaching in Public Administration will appear. A reader in public personnel is still some time off [2]. However, *Perspectives on Public Management: Cases and Learning Designs* will be published about the same time as the present volume [3].

Such an effort patently rests on diverse research and publishing talents. It is at once humbling and challenging to attempt to give some pattern to the products of these many talents. I have tried to act as a cutter and setter of gems in this case, selecting among the richness of voluminous literatures and striving to bring out the particular features of individual pieces by providing appropriate settings.

However successful my efforts at craftmanship, meeting the present challenge was at least eased for me in several senses. Thus I took advantage of early conversations with my colleagues, Drs. Frank Gibson and Ira Sharkansky, in developing the general format and coverage of the volume. In addition, Mrs. Sigrid Saunders was an invaluable aid in giving tangible order and form to my editorial decisions. Carol Holcomb, Lane Howell, and Mrs. Jennie Rogers provided the massive clerical and typing skills necessary for any such effort. The efforts of Philip Rosenberg also deserve note.

NOTES AND REFERENCES

1. Robert T. Golembiewski, Frank Gibson, and Geoffrey Y. Cornog (eds.), *Public Administration: Readings in Institutions, Processes, and Behavior*, Rand McNally, Chicago (1966).
2. The volume now has been published. Robert T. Golembiewski and Michael Cohen (eds.), *People in Public Service: A Reader in Public Personnel Administration*, F. E. Peacock, Itasca, Illinois (1970).
3. Robert T. Golembiewski (ed.), *Perspectives on Public Management: Cases and Learning Designs*, F. E. Peacock, Itasca, Illinois (1968).

Robert T. Golembiewski

Contents

I
HISTORICAL CONTEXTS OF BUDGETING AND FINANCE

EDITORIAL INTRODUCTION

Unit I advertises a focus on historical contexts, and the plural is used deliberately. Perhaps the most common simplification—and usually a flat-out mistake—involves seeing "wholes" where "particularities" or complex and even chaotic "mosaics" exist. These common simplifications involve *a* nation state, *a* public agency, even *a* family. In many cases, the singular usages constitute a version of the fallacy of misplaced concreteness.

Rather than a homogeneous entity, that is, we editors urge a view of public budgeting and finance (PBF) as a mosaic, at best. Thus, PBF components developed at specific points along a long time line, which is still extending itself even as the readers work their ways through this text. And, no one needs reminding, times can and do change. So any arena like PBF tends to be "lumpy": Various times and themes are reflected in different developments and—even though they differ in focal problems, approaches, and philosophies—these developments exist cheek-by-jowl within PBF conceived as a mosaic. These developments can fit uncomfortably with others that appeared earlier on the time line, and at times two or more developments can constitute poor fits or might even be antagonistic. So essential reality as well as convenience encourage the simplification of seeing PBF as *a* mosaic whose components often have specific and even contrasting histories.

On occasion, of course, a new conceptual broom may sweep an arena clean of the past. We now often call this a "paradigmatic change," a new and comprehensive way of viewing a particular area of study or practice.

PBF has not yet seen its paradigmatic revolution, or even a real beginning of one. Hence, the selections that follow introduce readers to developments from multiple and only partially overlapping historical contexts, whose loosely integrated products now eat out of the same trough, as it were. These developments represent different historical contexts and they often are substantially different kinds of "animals," even as they all constitute "parts" of the present PBF "mosaic."

PBF's Time Line

Jack Rabin's introductory essay does a take-off for PBF on the old axiom: Demography is destiny. Readers need only a little reminder of why that orienting perspective is so powerful.

1

For example, if the birth rate shows a major up-tick in 1996, rest assured that this will have downstream public and private consequences that we can anticipate but cannot avoid. Thus, 6 or so years later, more kindergarten spaces will be required; and so on through the full human life cycle.

Much the same is true in PBF—the past is a major influence on the present as well as on the future, as Rabin elaborates in his "The Budgetary Time Line," which he subtitles, "History Is Destiny." Rabin goes back to the beginnings, with attention to both American and English experience. This retrospective is telling. For example, readers who complain that so much of contemporary PBF is fragmented and even grid-locked will get historical perspective on why those characteristics were reasonable enough responses in early representative governments experiencing different days and times. Fragmentation and even the possibility of grid-lock were designed into the cores of our various institutional systems to inhibit a skilled and determined faction from stealing sovereignty from its true owners. The basic problem? Policies, approaches, and techniques reasonably tailored to earlier problems and technologies now may fall considerably short of today's requirements and potentialities.

In sum, today's basic PBF mosaic contains many elements designed to be responsive to very different days and times. In that basic sense, and given much illustrative detail, Rabin establishes how and why PBF's history *is* its destiny. History cannot be rejected as we might step out of last year's fashionable clothes. It is tenaciously with us, and the only question is whether it helps or hinders our ability to respond quickly to new imperatives, real or imagined.

An Early Attack on History's Shackles

Of course, on occasion, human effort can transmute its history, or even substantially transcend it. In the heroic view, for example, humankind need only break the shackles of the past. That can happen, but not frequently. More useful is a general view: that progress in updating PBF concepts and tools to new times is better seen as, at best, a slow and selective dissolving of the iron shackles of ideas developed during earlier intervals along PBF's time line.

Fittingly, then, our second selection introduces a major PBF effort at catching up with a new day's demands while struggling against the inventions of an earlier day. Specifically, the focus is on the major movement toward presidential leadership during the Franklin D. Roosevelt era. The Report of the President's Committee on Administrative Management was issued in the mid-stages of the evolution of an activist role for the U.S. federal government, as manifested in the New Deal under President Franklin Roosevelt. We here reprint "Fiscal Management," one part of that report.

While radical and even revolutionary in its day, "Fiscal Management" reflects the essentials of one version of the now-orthodox solution to the problems of executive control over public expenditures. This excerpt, and the report in which it is found, have numerous predecessors and successors, but "Fiscal Management" constitutes the most influential statement of how the problems of PBF should be dealt with at the highest level of responsibility. The excerpt thus represents an important milestone in the historical contexts that students of U.S. PBF need to take into account.

"Fiscal Management" is dated as a document, of course, but its main thrust is as current as today's newspaper. The report's basic purpose is the same one that motivates most thought about PBF practice: to assure, in the words of "Fiscal Management," that the Chief Executive can "fulfill the responsibility of his [sic!] office under the Constitution." In the orthodox opinion, this means that the elected Chief Executive "must possess individual executive powers and adequate means with which to exercise them."

Deficits as the Presenting Problem

Depending on the historic interval under consideration, major PBF issues vary. Opinions on the subject certainly differ, but today deficits seem to be on almost everyone's short list of major presenting problems that require attention. Obviously, much of the 1995 contention between the presidency and the Congress can be traced to different reactions to our pattern of chronic budgetary deficits.

Chapter 3, from the U.S. General Accounting Office, "The Deficit and Long-Term Damage to the Economy," provides stereophonic perspective on the how and why of U.S. budgetary deficits. That selection introduces some useful vocabulary, looks at income sources, establishes trends in various areas of mandated spending, downplays the contributing effects of defense and other discretionary outlays to the profile of growing deficits, and then assigns only a reinforcing role to economic cycles.

What causes deficits, then? Chapter 3 details a range of policies that contribute to deficits, and that list deserves careful attention.

Aggressive readers will find that this third selection not only provides needed knowledge, but also that it stands in real need of updating. Thus, today's and tomorrow's federal budgetary history can be reviewed to provide a more current view of relevant institutional arrangements than does the third selection. For example, the puniness of the Gramm–Rudman–Hollings bill introduced in Chapter 3 became clear only after the publication date of this selection. And readers can even test this adequacy of the several estimates made throughout the third selection to see how well they compare with actual experience in postpublication years.

Overview of a Recession

Many macroeconomic events clearly constitute important points on PBF's time line, and a fourth selection in Unit I describes how and why this truism applies in the specific case of a major event that most readers have directly experienced. Stephen K. McNees does the honors here in his "The 1990–91 Recession in Historical Perspective."

Why give attention to such macroeconomic events as a recession? That is a bit like asking why students of behavior should take notice of emotional depression! In both cases, obviously, we learn much about the coping capabilities of institutions and individuals by observing how they respond to downturns as well as up-ticks in the economy. But let us do a bit more than note that the relevance of Chapter 4 is obvious. For openers, recessions provide both fore-and-aft perspective useful for generalizing insight about PBF. That is to say, recessions can be seen as an outcome to which inept PBF policies and practices variously contributed. In addition, recessions constitute one of the major events to which PBF policies and practices must respond, whether constructively or maladroitly. Viewed either way, McNees's selection can well serve PPF students.

More basically, perhaps, McNees provides a unique focus, and hence generates especially revealing results. His text urges that the 1990–91 recession is not only noteworthy, but may be the precursor of a new type of recession that will be common in our futures. The text highlights the novelty of the 1990–91 recession, and McNees concludes that some people worry that "We are sailing on unchartered [sic] waters." Those people would be better to worry about sailing on *uncharted* waters! We get his meaning, that is to say, but only by neglecting his malapropism. Either way, one can expect a rough ride, about which the fourth selection warns as well as informs.

Focus on the Income Side

The mosaic of public budgeting and finance—conveniently, as before, labeled PBF—obviously involves both incomes as well as pay-outs, and here Glenn W. Fisher helps us get a historical sense of one major form of income generation by public authorities. His contribution, Chapter 5, is entitled "The Evolution of the American Property Tax."

The general property tax was an American innovation, consistent with the populist or Jacksoninan tradition that is so much a part of the U.S. scene. In detailing how that aspect of our political culture affected the development of the property tax, Fisher details legal and constitutional issues, political dynamics, and the organizational arrangements suitable for collecting property taxes. Fisher also emphasizes state-to-state differences on the common theme. In sum, federalism adds both distinguishing texture as well as great complexity to the PBF mosaic.

Fisher's combination constitutes a useful model for the analysis of the range of PBF policies and practices, broadly viewed. Typically, they involve legal, political, and organizational features interacting in a political culture or cultures. Moreover, given its attention to the diversity of our country and its traditions, Fisher's analysis leaves no doubts about how and why PBF differences will exist—between local, state, and federal levels of government, as well as between historic periods.

Stages of Reform

Given PBF's long and twisting timeline, no wonder that developmental phases can be distinguished. No paradigmatic change has occurred, but some shifting fashions have had wide and deep influence. Allen Schick does us the good service of describing the developmental coming and going of one major approach to root-and-branch change in PBF policies and practices. His selection is "The Road to PPB: The Stages of Budget Reform," and we editors leave to Schick the job of developing the details of the substance of the label "PPB."

The concept of "factoring" provides a useful backdrop for Schick's contribution. All budgetary decisions require factoring of some sort, so factoring problems there must be. However, different approaches to budgeting raise different factoring problems. Hence, no one can avoid all problems, but, to a degree, we can influence the kind of problems we will face.

Traditionally, the chief executive issues a call for estimates, which are generated from below. Thus a strict line-item budget might list "10 stenographers at $4,500 each." This line item is a product of many factorings beginning at low levels of organization whose requests are aggregated, massaged, and perhaps trimmed as they rise through a hierarchy. An overhead authority seeking control might well attempt to control the number of stenographers. Even if the executive did control this final factoring, the victory would be a slim one indeed, for that executive must be more concerned with what the stenographers do than with how many there are. Checking the validity and specifics of decisions made in early factorings poses a difficult problem for the traditional executive. Moreover, in these early factorings, agencies develop internal consensus about, and commitments to, specific programs. This consensus and its associated commitments often are difficult for any executive to change. Each additional lower level factoring further restricts the top executive's convenient and meaningful control. As Schick shows, the line-item budget makes it difficult for the top executive to influence those early factorings that he or she must control, sooner or later. This is an awkward combination.

Under a "program budget," in contrast, the executive can and must influence early factorings. This may enhance control, for this kind of budget in the first factoring deals with decisions made by the executive about the priorities of various programs—that is, with major objectives developed in a planning stage, which are intended to direct later factorings by lower level officials who deal with programming and then budgeting the activities appropriate to implement the basic planning. Hence the common designation "PPB" (planning–programming–budgeting) for the common replacement for the line-item budget. In PPB, later factorings must refine how program objectives will be achieved and which specific mix of resources will be used. These later factorings are difficult for the top executives to control, but, in a program budget, they also have less interest in them. Again, Schick provides much rich detail about how different PBF phases or stages influence or determine which problems are faced, when, and how.

This basic contrast about two kinds of budgets simplifies recalcitrant realities, but Allen Schick's contribution remedies this simplicism. Schick provides a detailed look at planning–programming–budgeting, which most broadly attempts to increase top executive control over early factorings. Schick carefully illustrates the arguments supporting program budgeting, speculates on its probable advantages, and makes some educated guesses about what changes in the processes of public spending are implied by PPB. Overall, the implied changes are significant. Thus, they require that clear plans be made before budget estimates are solicited. The premium is on doing—from the top, down—the planning and programming on which budgets are based.

Note also that history permits some firm generalizations about which Schick, when he wrote, could only make informed judgments or even guesses. Hence, a reader might well select an agency of government, and trace the history of PPB in it after the publication date of Schick's central contribution. Hindsight might not provide 20/20 vision, but such mini-analyses will help readers make judgments about the serviceability of Schick's stages

Diffusion of an Innovation

History is made by people, of course, as they variously respond to perceived situational demands as well as to stakeholder preferences. Whence came the PPB for which Schick provides such useful context? Robert T. Golembiewski and Patrick Scott, in "A Micro-political Perspective on Rational Budgeting: A Conjectural Footnote on the Dissemination of PPBS," hazard an informed guess about how and why PPB became the major development in PBF in the 1960s and 1970s.

Golembiewski and Scott detail which persons, and even which of their idiosyncracies, may have complemented historical forces in the sudden emergence—first at the federal level, and then later in state as well as local government—of a major approach to PBF that dominated a major portion of our recent history. You will never read such an account in the available textbooks, but perhaps, so much the worse for them! The sparse descriptions there of PPB amount to an analog of human birth as involving delivery by a stork. Golembiewski and Scott try to do better, adopting a best-evidence rule in a case where any evidence—let alone "hard" evidence—is hard to come by.

1

The Budgetary Time Line: History Is Destiny

Jack Rabin

Nothing creates itself, and this idea is seen best in the field of public budgeting, for in this area "history is destiny"—what occurred in an earlier time, sometimes one or two hundred years ago, can have a great effect on the practice of public budgeting today. These are the reasons underlying the creation of "The Budgetary Time Line."

Tracing the history of public budgeting back before the Revolutionary War, the time line identifies for the reader the major events. In addition, in order to provide further perspective, the time line also provides information about simultaneous occurrences in England, in the American private sector, and in the public administration literature.

Thus, one notes that the national debt of the United States was not something created by Franklin Delano Roosevelt in the 1930s, but rather started during the first years of the country's existence. Moreover, consider at what point in time the line-item budget was used.

The line-item budget format, nothing more than an organization unit's "shopping list" for the next year, also is traced back to the country's first years. Essentially, because the branches of government were *separated*, this situation left the Congress with a dilemma: being the most important and most powerful branch of the national government, making the laws and policies, but composed of legislators who were *part-time*, *non-specialists* in what the executive did. Furthermore, though the Congress could *make* the laws, it was not empowered by the Constitution to *implement* them. Consequently, the Congress had to find solutions to this dilemma, one of which was the requirement that all executive departments come under the "doctrine of specific appropriations"—itemization.

By having to list all objects of expenditure a department wished to purchase the next year, the administrators—those government officials who were full-time specialists responsible for the implementation (and interpretation) of the laws—came under great political control by the Congress. Finally, though the line-item budget gives us very little useful

Source: "Public Budget's History: The Budgetary Time Line," *Public Budgeting and Financial Management*, vol. 2, no. 1 (1990), pp. 65–143.

information about a department and its effectiveness, it has lasted in one form or another for over 200 years.

Citing the appearance of the line-item budget in the time line is a way of encouraging the reader to use this information source as a means for obtaining an historical perspective on the many influences on public budgeting. As Aaron Wildavsky also noted, budgets and the traditions and methods surrounding their creation are the results of historical processes, or, in other words, in public budgeting, "history is destiny."

Date	English developments	American developments		Dates in PA history
		Private sector	Public sector	
1215	Magna Carta			
1225	Magna Carta reissued for third time in definitive terms.			
1233	Coal mined for first time in New Castle.			
1253	Linen first manufactured.			1350–1500–Development of the unitary state in Europe.
1543–1588	Three works on double entry bookkeeping are published in English.			
1635		Plymouth Colony engaged Mr. Morton to teach children to teach children to read, write and cast accounts (commercial arithmetic).		1650–1750–Boston Post Road built.
1659		The earliest evidence of the use of double entry bookkeeping by colonial, Puritan merchants is found in "The Apologia of Robert Keayne."		
1677		The Boston "Town Record" reveals the availability of account-keeping education and the practice of auditing the town accounts.		
1688	British institute legislative system of appropriations.			
1689	Bill of Rights.			
1694	Founding of the Bank of England. Salt tax doubled in England.			

Date	English developments	American developments		Dates in PA history
		Private sector	Public sector	
1696	First English property insurance company founded.			
1698		Paper manufacturing beings.		
1700–1900		"Barter Accounting." Lack of sound monetary system. Different monies.		
1718	First Bank Notes.	Browne Thymms of Boston advertises public accounting practice. Thymms is an early public accountant, the earliest known to have practiced in America.		
1720		Early public stock ventures. The South Sea Company "bubble."		
1721	Regular postal service between London and New England.			
1729		Benjamin and James Franklin publish "The Pennsylvania Gazette."		
1731		George Brownell of New York advertises as a teacher of "merchants accounts."		
1747	Carriage Tax.			
1750	Cabinet system in place			
1751	British calendar altered by Act of Parliament; Jan. 1 henceforth to be beginning of New Year.			

Date	English developments	American developments		Dates in PA history
		Private sector	Public sector	
1752		Parliament enacts that the first day of January was to be acknowledged as the beginning of the year; thereby a basis was established for the annualizations of accounts.		
1755			Continental Congress creates committee of accounts to audit all accounts to be paid.	
1759	*The Public Ledger*, London daily paper appears. British gain Quebec from French.			
1763		First Chambers of Commerce in New York and New Jersey.		
1765	British Parliament passes Stamp Act to tax American colonies.	Virginia Assembly challenges right of Great Britain to enact the stamp tax; at Stamp Act Congress in New York delegates from nine colonies draw up a declaration of rights and liberties.		
1770	Civil Liberties, international free trade, textile machines, and steam power lead to an industrial revolution which slowly spreads all over the world.			
1774		Byerley and Day of New York advertise to teach "bookkeeping after the Italian method and the practice of the most regular counting houses."		

Date	English developments	American developments		Dates in PA history
		Private sector	Public sector	
1776–1781		Adam Smith's economic theory sets the pattern and direction for economic progress. The counting house supplies a central environment for early accounting functions and was the "record center" of the merchants. The close of this era marked the end of the age of colonial merchant accounts and the dawn of the era of corporate accounting.	American Revolution begins. Start of the U.S. Government debt.	1776—Adam Smith, *The Wealth of Nations*
1779	Spanish declare war on Britain.			1780–1825–Early development of U.S. postal system.
1783	Bank of Ireland founded.			
1785	*Daly Universal Register* (becomes *The Times* in 1788) is begun by John Walter.			
1787		Dollar currency introduced. New York Assembly imposes duties on foreign goods.		

Date	English developments	American developments		Dates in PA history
		Private sector	Public sector	
1789		The first American text on accounting by double entry is published: "The American Accountant; or Schoolmaster New Assistant" by Benjamin Workman. Pennsylvania State University formed (founded in 1749 as Philadelphia Academy).	U.S. Constitution ratified; Congress establishes U.S. Office of Controller General and Department of the Treasury; three Congressional Appropriations Acts inaugurate practice of making specific appropriations (itemization) for executive agencies. Act of September 2, 1789, requires Secretary of the Treasury "to prepare and report estimates of the public revenue and the public expenditures." President Washington (April) suggests ways of raising revenues to House of Representatives. Plan approved in September with Washington signing first appropriation act on September 29, 1789.	
1790–1800s		Several hundred business incorporations take place. Americans expand their holdings of new lands. Technical innovations reduce costs. Industry and commerce become rooted in the midst of a predominantly rural society.		
1790	First steam powered rolling mill built. John Sinclair, "The Statistical Account of Scotland," published.	Funding bill introduced by Alexander Hamilton. First patent law in United States.		

Date	English developments	American developments		Dates in PA history
		Private sector	Public sector	
1791			The first ten amendments to U.S. Constitution (Bill of Rights) ratified. Bank of United States founded. First instance of Congress investigating expenditure of funds by executive at the time when new approrpiations bill considered by Congress. Also, in 1791, House orders that an annual statement of receipts and expenditures be prepared and published. Continued until 1894. Total Federal revenues collected between 1789 and 1791 are $4.4 million.	
1792		A group of merchants and auctioneers gathers on Wall Street to fix a daily meeting time to carry on the trading of a heretofore scattered market for government securities, as well as the shares for banks and insurance companies.	Dollar coinage minted. Two political parties formed: The Republicans under Thomas Jefferson and the Federalists under Alexander Hamilton.	1792–"Political conformity" becomes hiring qualification for federal government jobs.
1789– 1800			Administrations of George Washington and John Adams; use of itemization in national budget; federal budget around $1.4 million.	

Date	English developments	American developments		Dates in PA history
		Private sector	Public sector	
1792–1812		Initial development of a transport network; turnpike companies chartered in Pennsylvania, New York and Massachusetts. Canal from South Carolina through Maryland and Virginia and up through New York was built.	Period of existence of the first Bank of the United States.	
1793	Board of Agriculture established in Britain.		Last attempt by Congress, until 1950, to pass "omnibus" appropriations bill, wrapping all federal spending into one bill; Congress debates Giles' resolution that "laws making specific appropriations of money should be strictly observed by the administrator of the finances thereof"; Congress advances President money with no appropriation to cover the expense.	
1794			11th Amendment to U.S. Constitution. U.S. Navy established.	

| Date | English developments | American developments | | Dates in PA history |
		Private sector	Public sector	
1795			Hamilton resigns as Secretary of Treasury; Wolcott succeeds, making doctrine that application of appropriated funds depends on Treasury Secretary's interpretation. Rep. Albert Gallatin opposes Wolcott and urges Congressional specificity in appropriations; Wolcott, by 1796, forced to itemize certain expenditures for the War Department; Congress also enacts provisions that "any sum remaining unexpended upon any appropriation for more than two years after the expiration of the calendar year in which the appropriation act was passed, was to go to the surplus fund."	
1796– 1806		The ledgers of Robert Oliver, a merchant of Baltimore, indicated that periodic trial balances were used, not for the purpose of disclosure, but solely for compiling the balances of all open accounts in order to determine bookkeeping accuracy.		

Date	English developments	American developments		Dates in PA history
		Private sector	Public sector	
1796	Spain declares war on Britain.		Congress establishes temporary Ways and Means Committee to deal with expenditures and revenues. It becomes permanent in 1802.	
1797	England begins to export iron. First copper pennies minted and first one-pound notes issued.			1798–Political affiliation determines who will be commissioned in the U.S. Army.
1800		Washington, D.C., is the new Capital City. Free inhabitants, 2464; slaves, 623.	Jefferson elected President; Congress (May 10) requires Secretary of Treasury to prepare, for the beginning of each session of Congress, a digest of estimates of revenues and expenditure, and suggestions on how to increase revenues.	
1801	Total population (U.K.), 10.4 million. London population, 864,000. First iron trolley tracks.			
1802			Congress passes act "that every distinct sum appropriated by any law for an object distinctly specified in the law should be applicable only to that object."	
1803			Louisiana Purchase; Thomas Jefferson first President to use impoundment power.	

Date	English developments	American developments		Dates in PA history
		Private sector	Public sector	
1804		The pioneering management controls in te DuPont Power Company suggest that there are many important uses of accounting data for operational control throughout this vertically integrated company.		
1805	Total state expenditure of Great Britain 62.8 million. Break between Britain and U.S. over trade with the West Indies.			
1806	Cotton industry employs 90,000 factory workers and 184,000 handloom weavers.			
1807	Street lighting by gas.		U.S. Embargo Act against Britain and France. Jefferson purchases military stores without congressional appropriation.	
1809			Congress enacts legislation authorizing the transfer of balances in agency accounts from one head of appropriation to another while Congress is in recess; debate to this day if Congress in 1802 or in 1809 Acts adopted doctrine of specific appropriations. If it did, agency practices of transfer through Civil War did much to nullify doctrine.	
1810		Total population (U.S.), 7,239,881.		

Date	English developments	American developments		Dates in PA history
		Private sector	Public sector	
1812	Gas, Light and Coke Company developed by F. A. Winsor.		United States declares was on Britain.	
1813	Last gold guinea coins issued.			
1814	The *London Times* printed by steam operated press.			
1815	Income tax ended (revived, 1842).		The first steam warship: *U.S.S. Fulton* (38 tons).	
1816	Economic crisis causes large scale emigration to Canada and United States.	Construction of Erie Canal between Buffalo and Albany begins.	U.S. House of Representatives establishes six standing committees to scrutinize expenditures of six executive departments.	
1818–1836			Period of existence of the second Bank of the United States.	
1819		A U.S. Supreme Court decision provides a legal foundation for modern corporate capitalism, recognizing the distinct quasipersonal legal attributes of the corporate form.	1819, U.S. agencies got around doctrine of specific appropriations by spending enacted appropriations at whatever rate they desired and, thus, having to come back to Congress for more funds ("coercive deficiency").	

Date	English developments	American developments		Dates in PA history
		Private sector	Public sector	
1820	Total population (U.K.), 20.8 million.	Land law fixes land price at a minimum of $1.25 per acre.	Act of 1820 is Congressional attempt to administer the surplus fund transfers and incurring of expenditures without appropriation. Act did not prevent deficiencies. Also, in 1820, Congress requires Secretary of the Treasury to present Congress with imformation on continuing appropriations and unexpended balances in agency accounts from past years.	
1824	Workers are allowed to unionize.			
1825	Expansion of trade union movement.			
1826	First railroad tunnel, Liverpool–Manchester.			
1820–1860			Various Congressional enactments permit or limit Presidential mingling of appropriations.	
1828		Charles Carroll of Carrollton, the richest American of his time, inaugurates construction of the Baltimore and Ohio, first railroad built for the transportation of passengers and freight.		

Date	English developments	American developments		Dates in PA history
		Private sector	Public sector	
1829	Economist Thomas Atlwood (1783–1856) founds the Birmingham Political Union to demand parliamentary reform. The omnibuses designed by George Shillebaer become part of London public transport. Centralized Metropolitan Police force installed in London.	The Delaware and Hudson's gravity railroad opens (constructed with locomotive operation in view). The first cooperative stores, Philadelphia and New York. The first patent on a typewriter granted to William B. Burt of Detroit.		
1830	26 steam cars on London streets.			
1831	Total population (U.K.), 13.9 million.	Total population (U.S.), 12.8 million.		
1832	The first Reform Act to enfranchise the upper-middle classes passed by the House of Lords; number of voters increased from 500,000 to 1,000,000.	The first horsedrawn trolleys in New York.		
1833	The Factory Act provides a system for factory inspection. Charity bazaars become popular.	General Trades Union in New York.	President Jackson moves against the Bank of U.S. (withdrawal of all governmental deposits).	
1834	Poor Law Amendment Act decrees that no able-bodied man in Great Britain shall receive assistance unless he enters a workhouse.	Grand National Consolidated Trade Union led by Robert Owne, formed January, collapses October.	President Jackson censured by Senate for removing deposits from the Bank of U.S.	
1837			U.S. agencies get around itemization by borrowing in anticipation of appropriations. This is replaced after 1828 with practice of deferred payment.	

Date	English developments	American developments		Dates in PA history
		Private sector	Public sector	
1840		Dozens of railroad securities being traded in the New York stock market, although the center of international finance remains in London.		1840–Office seekers take President William Henry Harrison prisoner in the White House and refuse to release him until he had reviewed their claims to office.
1841		Early railroad accounts, such as Utica and Schenectady, were cash basis summaries with statistical operating information.		
1842			Congressional Act gives agency heads nearly unlimited power to transfer funds among items; repealed in 1860. Also, in 1842, Congress passes law establishing the fiscal year.	
1844				1844–Jules Depuit, a French engineer, champions use of benefit-cost analysis in public works programs.
1850	British Civil Service System developed.		U.S. House requires that appropriations must have been previously authorized by law.	

Date	English developments	American developments		Dates in PA history
		Private sector	Public sector	
1851		E. G. Folsom, professor of the science of accounts, incorporates his Mercantile College to be opened in Cleveland. Among Folsom's first students were H.B. Bryant and H.D. Stratton, who later acquired the Folsom College and developed an international chain of more than fifty commercial colleges, leading the growth movement in business education from 1853 to 1866.		
1854		John Fleming's "Bookkeeping by Double Entry," published in Pittsburgh, includes several changes to reflect cost accounting considerations.		
1857			First U.S. public pension program started, for New York City Police Department.	

Date	English developments	American developments		Dates in PA history
		Private sector	Public sector	
1860–1865			Civil War; institution of income tax and large usage of paper money ("Green-backs") during war by national government; War cost $800 million; President Lincoln, during war, "for the defense and support of the Government," makes unauthorized and unbudgeted expenditure of $2 million for munitions.	
1865			U.S. House breaks up Ways and Means Committee and decentralizes budget responsibility among various committees; House creates Appropriations Committees; Congress stops considering both revenue and expenditure sides of budget at the same time.	
1866–1896		Start of American "Industrial Revolution." Prelude to the Modern Age.		
1867		Railroad merger movement. The creation of the New York Central System.		
1868–1874			Congress reinstates doctrine of specific appropriations.	

Date	English developments	American developments		Dates in PA history
		Private sector	Public sector	
1868			Congress passes law that ". . . no money appropriated for one purpose shall hereafter be used for any other purpose than that for which it is appropriated." Transfers, thus, made illegal.	
1869		The completion of the transcontinental railroad. The opening of the West.		
1870			Congressional Act mandates return of unexpended balances in agency budgets if not expended within two years; Attorney General opinion nullifies this enactment, however. Agencies permitted to draw upon monies before two-year period elapsed, thus allowing two additional years before money had to be surrendered.	
1874			Congress passes law again mandating return of appropriated funds to surplus fund if not expended within two years. This time provision sticks.	
1875			U.S. House of Representatives adopts rule permitting Appropriations Committee to propose amendments to substantive legislation.	

Date	English developments	American developments		Dates in PA history
		Private sector	Public sector	
1876			U.S. House of Representatives expands powers and functions of Committees in scrutinizing actions of government departments; Grant becomes first President after Jefferson and last before Franklin Roosevelt to impound funds.	
1877		The end of the period of reconstruction following the Civil War. The start of the era of big cities and big business.		
1880–1920			Stress on economy and efficiency in both business and government. Era of great immigration into country, placing a strain on public services.	
1880–1890		F.W. Taylor conducts time and motion studies at the Midvale Steel works in Philadelphia.		
1880–1905			U.S. agencies at national level habitually use "coercive deficiency" tactic to avoid itemization. Use appropriated funds quickly, and then ask Congress for additional monies (deficiency appropriation) to cover balance of the year.	

| Date | English developments | American developments | | Dates in PA history |
		Private sector	Public sector	
1880		The United States enters into a metropolitan style economy characterized by the growth and significance of industrial, urban areas as key points of demand, distribution and political influence.		
1882		The Standard Oil Trust is formed and a new vehicle for consolidating corporate operations initiated. Railroads, oil, and steel companies are organized along the lines of the trust. The Institute of Accountants and Bookkeepers is formed in New York and is the first professional accounting organization in the United States.		
1883		The first course in accounting to be given at the collegiate level is offered at the Wharton School of the University of Pennsylvania, which has started only two years earlier.		1883–Civil Service Reform (Pendleton) Act passed by Congress.
1885			U.S. House Appropriations Committee stripped of powers; appropriations to be considered by Substantive Committees.	1885–Woodrow Wilson, *Congressional Government*

| Date | English developments | American developments | | Dates in PA history |
		Private sector	Public sector	
mid- 1880s		The consolidated holding corporation begins to emerge as an alternative to the trust as an operating and control mechanism.		
1886		The first consolidated accounts are prepared for the American Cotton Oil Trust.		
1887				1887–Woodrow Wilson article, "The Study of Administration"
1888		The creation of the Interstate Commerce Commission.		
1889		The daily *Wall Street Journal* begins publication, a source of investment news.		
1890s		Public accounting profession begins to take root. J. Slatter Lewis's, *The Commerical Organization of Facilities*, stresses the use of staff and line techniques which have become formalized as part of overall management systems.		
1890		Tickers and telephones commonplace. It is possible to instantaneously transmit stock trading data to points far beyond Wall Street. There are more than a million individual stock investors.		

Date	English developments	American developments		Dates in PA history
		Private sector	Public sector	
		The passage of the Sherman Anti-Trust Act. The days of *laissez faire* are coming to a close. The first cost controls appear.		
				1891–W. F. Willoughby and W. W. Willoughby, *Government and Administration in the United States.*
1893		Severe Depression. Unemployment in manufacturing and transportation in 9% of the work force.		1893–Emile Durkheim, *The Division of Labor in Society.*
1894		The Interstate Commerce Commission establishes a system of accounts entitled, "The Classification of Operating Expenses."	U.S. House of Representatives rescinds its 1791 order that an annual statement of receipts and expenditures be prepared and published; Congress, in the Cockerell-Dockery Act, maintains functions of Secretary of Treasury in account settlement, accounting and auditing.	1894–National Municipal League founded.
		Frederick W. Taylor suggests the introduction of the piece rate system. This is the start of what is to be scientific labor time and motion efficiency in manufacturing.		

		American developments		
Date	English developments	Private sector	Public sector	Dates in PA history
1896		The State of New York passes the first accounting law and establishes certified accountants as members of a legally constituted profession. This represents the birth of the accounting profession in America.		
1898		The formation of accounting profession. Rise of financial capitalism. Managmeent becomes divorced from ownership. Increasing involvement of bankers and outside promoters in the operations of American corporations. Securities become the vehicles for accumulating wealth.		
1897–1918		60% of the listings on the New York Stock Exchange are railroad securities. The Industrial Commerce Commission is established to investigate and to report on questions relating to immigration, labor, agriculture, manufacturing and business		
1899		The New York Stock Exchange takes definite steps to require financial statements on a regular basis from listed companies.	National debt (June 30) $1.4 billion; National Municipal League drafts modern municipal corporation act.	

Date	English developments	American developments		Dates in PA history
		Private sector	Public sector	
1900	British Labor party founded.	Gold standard established.	Federal budget around $521 million. Total revenues collected by federal government from 1789–1900 was $15 billion; at this time, national government has few fiscal controls; agencies still prepare their own budget requests; no standardized accounting system.	1900–F. W. Taylor, *Scientific Management*; F.J. Goodnow, *Politics and Administration*.
1901		The first billion dollar "super consolidation," The United States Steel Corporation, comes into existence.		
1903		Anti-trust law reinforced. Henry Ford, with capital of $100.00, founds the Ford Motor Company.		
1905–1906			Anti-Deficiency Acts allow President to accelerate or decelerate spending due to "unforeseen circumstances." Yet, 1905 Act forbids coercive deficiencies, and requires agencies to divide appropriation into quarterly allotments.	
1905	London Automobile Association founded. Austin Motor Company formed; first motor buses in London.			

Date	English developments	American developments		Dates in PA history
		Private sector	Public sector	
1906	London population: 4.5 million.	New York City population: 4 million	New York Bureau of Municipal Research established; City of New York adopts "historical method" of analyzing past expenditures.	
1907	New Zealand becomes a dominion within te British Empire.	Panic of 1907 causes run on banks, stopped by J. P. Morgan's importation of $100 million in gold from Europe.	New York Bureau of Municipal Research publishes sample "program memorandum" for data on New York City Health Department; New York City reorganizes its financial procedures; Appropriations Act provides that U.S. Secretary of Treasury include revenue estimates in his annual report to Congress.	
1908		General Motors Corporation formed. The Ford Motor Company produces the first Model "T": 15 million eventually sold.		1908–New Jersey adopts state merit system.
1909			Appropriations Act provides that if national agency estimates exceed estimated revenue, Secretary of Treasury to inform President who, in State of the Union message, would provide recommendations for making up the difference.	

Date	English developments	American developments		Dates in PA history
		Private sector	Public sector	
1910	First labour exchanges open.	U.S. Postal Savings program established. Manhattan Bridge completed.	Ohio requires governor to draft a budget for submission to legislature (first state to do so); Chicago, Illinois, adopts new budget system.	1910–U.S. House of Representatives strips Speaker of powers.
1910–1914				1910–1914–Max Weber publishes ideas on organization and bureaucracy.
1911	Lloyd George introduces National Health Insurance Bill in Parliament.	Charles F. Kettering develops the first practical electric self-starter for automobiles.	State of California creates Board of Control to supervise state financial matters; State of Massachusetts places budget control in hands of governor; City of Philadelphia establishes accounting system "to analyze expenditures by fund, organization unit, function (or activity), character and object."	
1912		F. W. Woolworth Company founded.	U.S. (Taft) President's Comission on Economy and Efficiency recommends executive budget system. Commission also challenges the practice of itemization; State of Wisconsin provides methods for legislature and administration to develop budget as a joint measure. City of Cleveland, Ohio, adopts city charter consolidating all financial administration into one department under the director of finance.	

Date	English developments	American developments Private sector	American developments Public sector	Dates in PA history
1913–1915			Borough of Richmond, New York City, experiments with cost data budget, similar to performance budget system.	
1913		The advent of federal income tax had an immediate effect on accounting practices. It stimulates the growth of the public accounting profession by providing a whole new area of services, and it begins to divert attention from the balance sheet to the income statement. Henry Ford pioneers new assembly line techniques in his car factory. John D. Rockefeller founds Rockefeller Institute with initial grant of $100 million. Grand Central Terminal, New York City, completed.	State of Illinois provides for a budget; in April 1913, State of Ohio brings all state departments and offices under budget requirements. Sixteenth Amendment (Income Tax) adopted to U.S. Constitution. State of New York creates Board of Estimate to act as a means of central, budget control. Federal Reserve System established.	
1914	World War I. Bank of England authorized by government to issue money in excess of statutory limit.	Almost 10.5 million immigrants enter United States from southern and eastern Europe in period 1905–1914.	World War I. Federal Trade Commission established to police business practices in interstate commerce. City of Dayton, Ohio, adopts commission manager form of government and budget system. Wilsonian Reform Era.	

| Date | English developments | American developments | | Dates in PA history |
		Private sector	Public sector	
1915		Henry Ford develops a farm tractor. First transcontinental telephone call. Wireless service established between U.S. and Japan. Ford produces one millionth car.	State of New York Constitutional Convention provides for state budget system.	
1916	National Savings movement founded.	Law establishing eight hour work day for railroad workers prevents nationwide strike.	Congress, in Appropriation Act of 1916, creates Division of Efficiency; Maryland adopts system of executive budget-making.	
1917			United States enters World War I; Congress appropriates funds for war "in gross" (lump sums) following practice in earlier wars. Bureau of Municipal Research has developed a budget for New York City. Recommends a budget having line items organized by "function" and "work program" (performance budget)—fails in its attempt.	
1918	Food shortage leads to the establishment of national food kitchens and rationing.	Regular airmail service established between New York and Washington; first airmail postage. First Chicago-New York airmail delivered.		1918–W. F. Willoughy, *The Problem of a National Budget*.

Date	English developments	American developments		Dates in PA history
		Private sector	Public sector	
1919–1936		The beginning of the debate over business responsibility to society. Accounting theory and practice makes emphasis on the balance sheet. "Historical cost allocation model" becomes the dominant theory of accounting.		
1919	War between British, Indian, and Afghan forces. Lady Astor, First British woman member of parliament, elected.	International Labor Conference in Washington endorses eight hour workday. Railroad lines operate total of 265,000 miles.	National debt at $25.5 billion.	
1920	Marconi opens first public broadcasting station at Writtle, Britain. Coal production, 229 million tons. Motor vehicles licensed, 663,000. Unemployment insurance introduced	18th Amendment to U.S. Constitution goes into effect: Prohibition throughout United States. 19th Amendment gives American women the vote. Results of the census of 1920: population 117,823,165. Coal production: 645 million tons. Petroleum production: 443 million barrels. Motor vehicles licensed: 8,890,000. New York population: 5,620,000; Los Angeles: 576,000. Westinghouse Company opens first broadcasting station in Pittsburgh, Pennsylvania. First airmail flight from New York to San Francisco.	Both Houses of Congress give Appropriations Committee control over appropriations legislation.	

Date	English developments	American developments		Dates in PA history
		Private sector	Public sector	
1921	National Institute for Industrial Psychology founded in London.		Budget and Accounting Act passed at national level: enacting an executive budget; assistance for President in developing the executive budget (Bureau of the Budget); and, national government audit agency (General Accounting Office); agencies of national government re-adopt use of coercive deficiencies, nullifying Anti-Deficiency Act of 1905. Also, in 1921, the Bureau of the Budget (BOB) establishes itself as a "legislative clearing house," all legislation from agencies requiring money must be submitted first to the BOB, which would make recommendations to the President.	
1922		John Harwood invents a self-winding wristwatch (patented, 1924). Stockmarket "boom" starts after depression.	Protectionist tariff established. U.S. Government revenues: $4,919 million; expenditures: $4,068 million. Governor of Georgia appoints first woman, Mrs. W. H. Felton, to U.S. Senate to fill vacancy left by death of Thomas E. Watson; term is one day.	

| Date | English developments | American developments | | Dates in PA history |
		Private sector	Public sector	
1923	Registered trade union membership: 4,369,000	Briton Hadden and Henry R. Luce found the weekly news magazine, *Time*. Registered trade union membership: 3,600,000.	Congress passes the Classification Act of 1923 which establishes a system of personnel grades and pay rates.	
1924	Ramsay MacDonald forms first Labour government. British Imperial Airways begins operation.	General Motors adopts Planning-Programming-Budgeting System budget. Ford Motor Company produces 10 millionth car. German airship pioneer, Hugo Eckener, flies his Z-R-3 across the Atlantic to Lakehurst, New Jersey. Tax law, which creates the Board of Tax Appeals, gives both lawyers and CPAs the right to represent clients; thus, accountants become advocates.		
1925–1929		Public enthusiasm for securities trading reaches new heights. Rising stock market prices encourage corporations to issue shares to a public that is eager to buy them.		
1925	Unemployment Insurance Act enacted.	The Chrysler Corporation founded by Walter P. Chrysler.	Nellie Taylor Ross of Wyoming becomes the first woman governor.	

Date	English developments	American developments		Dates in PA history
		Private sector	Public sector	
1926	General strike called. British General Electricity Board established. Alan Cobham flies from Croydon, England, to Capetown and back to investigate the feasibility of long-distance air routes. Population (in millions): 45.	New York Stock Exchange (NYSE), recognizing the need for more effective surveillance of financial reporting by listed companies, names J.M.B. Hoxsey to the new, full time position of Executive Assistant to the Committee on Stock List. Population (in millions): 115. Petroleum production: 771 million barrels. Kodak produces the first 16 mm film.		1926–Leonard D. White, *Introduction to the Study of Public Administration.*
1927	British Broadcasting Corporation takes over from Britain Broadcasting Company.	15 millionth Model "T" Ford produced. Holland Tunnel opens as first vehicular tunnel linking New York and New Jersey.	Congress requires statement of final disbursement of appropriated funds.	1927–W. F. Willoughby, *The National Budget System*; W.F. Willoughby, *The Legal Status and Functions of the General Accounting Office.*
1928	Woman's suffrage in Britain reduced from age 30 to 21.	Teleprinters and teletypewriters come into restricted use in United States, Britain, and Germany. First scheduled television broadcast by WGY, Schenectady, N.Y. First color motion pictures exhibited by George Eastman in Rochester, N.Y.		

Date	English developments	American developments		Dates in PA history
		Private sector	Public sector	
1929	Margaret Bondfield becomes first British Woman Privy Councellor. U.K. percentage of worldwide industrial production: 10.4%. Picture telegraphy service begins between Britain and Germany. Pilgrim Trust: E. S. Harkness, American railroad magnate, places 2 million pounds sterling in the hands of Prime Minister Baldwin "for the benefit of Britain." Britain, United States, Japan, France, and Italy sign treaty on naval disarmament.	Cataclysmic stock market crash ends the speculative boom, and the end of the laissez faire era of financial accounting. Consequences: 1) the enactment of federal securities laws; 2) voluntary actions by the accounting profession to improve financial reporting. "Black Friday" in New York; U.S. Stock Exchange collapses on Oct. 28; world economic crisis begins; U.S. securities lost $26 billion in value. Bell Laboratories experiments with color television. U.S. percentage of worldwide industrial production: 34.4%		1929–A. E. Buck, *Public Budgeting.*
1930		U.S. population: 122 million.	Aggregate amount of coercive deficiency funds reaches 10% of national budget.	1930–Mabel L. Walker, *Municipal Expenditures.*
1931	Britain abandons gold standard; pound sterling falls from $4.86 to $3.49.	George Washington Bridge, New York, completed. Hattie T. Caraway becomes the first woman to be elected to the U.S. Senate.	U.S. Senate passes Veterans Compensation Act over President Hoover's veto. President Hoover suggests a one-year moratorium for reparations and war debts.	

Date	English developments	American developments		Dates in PA history
		Private sector	Public sector	
1932	BBC (London) takes over responsibility for developing television from the Baird Company. Unemployment: 2.8 million.	Unemployment: 13.7 million. Work begins on San Francisco-Oakland Bay Bridge (Golden Gate Bridge).	Congress permits Reconstruction Finance Corporation to borrow money directly from the Treasury. Reconstruction Finance Corporation, established for rebuilding of U.S. economy, provides $1.5 billion by year's end.	1932–Carl J. Friedrich and Taylor Cole, *Responsible Bureaucracy*.
1933		Security Act of 1933, "Truth in Securities Law." The Securities and Exchange Commission established and disclosure rules required for companies that make public offering of securities. NYSE announces that henceforth it will require independent audits of companies seeking a listing. Frances Perkins, appointed Secretary of Labor by President Roosevelt, becomes first woman cabinet member. First aircraft carrier, "Ranger," is launched.	First unemployment insurance law enacted in Wisconsin. Federal Reserve System reorganized. Start of the New Deal; U.S. goes off gold standard; era of "looseness" in doctrine of specific appropriations. Bank crisis. Congress grants Roosevelt broad powers over credit and currency. Congress passes Agriculture Adjustment and Federal Emergency Relief Acts. Tennessee Valley Authority created. National Industrial Recovery Act and Farm Credit Act made law. Public Works Administration created.	

| Date | English developments | American developments | | Dates in PA history |
		Private sector	Public sector	
1934	Depressed areas bill introduced. Road Traffic Act introduces driving tests. Iron and Steel Federation established	Enactment of the "Securities Exchange Act" which requires the filing of periodic reports by companies. The American Institute of Accountants (AIA) adopts five rules of accepted accounting principles.	Gold Reserve Act authorizes the president to revalue the dollar. Federal Farm Mortgage Corporation organized.	1934–A.E. Buck, *The Budget in Government Today.*
1935			Roosevelt signs Social Security Act. Wealth Tax Act passed.	1935–Social Security Act passed.
1936	BBC London inaugurates television service.	AIA Committee issues "Examination of Financial Statements," a document principally oriented to auditing procedures, but which also discusses accounting, and for the first time employs the term "generally accepted accounting principles." Ford Foundation established. Boulder (Hoover) Dam on Colorado River in Nevada and Arizona is completed, creating Lake Mead, largest reservoir in the world.		1936–O. Glenn Stahl, *Public Personnel Administration*; Harold Lasswell, *Politics: Who Gets What, When, How*; John Maynard Keynes, *The General Theory of Employment, Interest and Money.*

Date	English developments	American developments		Dates in PA history
		Private sector	Public sector	
1937	London bus strike. London *Daily Telegraph* and *Morning Post* merge.	SEC Chief Accountant issues first Accounting Series Release (ASR). Wall Street stock market decline signals serious economic recession. Government statistics show that one half-million Americans were involved in sit down strikes between September 1936 and May 1937. Lincoln Tunnel provides second major vehicular tunnel between New York and New Jersey. Golden Gate Bridge, San Francisco, opens. Supreme Court rules in favor of minimum wage law for women.	Report of "President's Committee on Administrative Management"; State of Oregon uses benefit-cost analysis in highway development program.	1937–Gulick and Urwick's *Papers on the Science of Administration.*
1938		40 hour work week established. 20,000 TV sets are in service in New York City.	Congress passes Wages and Hours Bill. Fair Labor Standards Act becomes effective.	1938–Chester Barnard, *The Functions of the Executive*; J. Wilner Sundelson, *Budgetary Methods in National and State Government.*
1939	World War II. Britain and France declare war on Germany, September 3. Conscription adopted.	After 1938 recession, the economy begins to recover; by autumn is blooming from orders of European countries for arms and war equipment. U.S. Supreme Court rules sit down strikes are illegal. Coal strike by United Mine Workers demonstrates power of John L. Lewis.	Reorganization Act; creates the Executive Office of the President, with Bureau of the Budget in Executive Office. Total federal budget is about $9 billion. Roosevelt asks Congress for $522 million for defense.	1939–Operations Research originates in England; American Society for Public Administration formed; F. J. Roethlisberger and William J. Dickson, *Management and the Worker*; James D. Mooney, *The Principles of Organization.*

Date	English developments	American developments		Dates in PA history
		Private sector	Public sector	
1940	Bacon, butter and sugar rationed.	Giant cyclotron built at the University of California for producing mesotrons from atomic nuclei. First successful helicopter flight in United States by Vought-Sikorsky Corporation. Population: 132 million; Alien Registration Act shows presence of 5 million aliens; average life expectancy: 64; 30 million homes have radios.	Roosevelt impounds $9 billion.	1940–V. O. Key article, "The Lack of a Budgetary Theory."
1941	Air Training Corps established. "Mosquito" fighter aircraft in use. A.R.P. (Air Raid Precaution) reorganized as Civil Defense.	U.S. Savings Bonds and Stamps go on sale. Office of Price Administration (OPA) established to regulate prices. OPA freezes price of steel; rubber rationing instituted.	Roosevelt impounds $13 billion.	
1942		The first electronic brain or automatic computer developed. Magnetic recording tape invented. Sugar rationing begins. Bell Aircraft tests first jetplane. Henry J. Kaiser develops techniques for building 10,000-ton Liberty Ships in four days. OPA freezes rents; gasoline and coffee rationing.	Congress passes the Federal Reports Act requiring the Director of BOB to coordinate federal reporting and statistical services.	1942–Avery Leiserson, *Administrative Regulation.*

Date	English developments	American developments		Dates in PA history
		Private sector	Public sector	
1943		Penicillin successfully used in the treatment of chronic diseases. 1300-mile-long "Big Inch" oil pipeline, from Texas to Pennsylvania, begins operation. President Roosevelt freezes wages, salaries, and prices to forestall inflation. Shoes, meat, cheese, fats, and all canned food rationing begins. Pay-as-you-go income tax system instituted in U.S.		
1944	Ministry of National Insurance established. First nonstop flight from London to Canada.	Cost of living rises almost 30%.		1944–John Von Neumann and O. Morgenstern, *Theory of Games and Economic Behavior.*
1945	"Black Markets" for food, clothing and cigarettes develop. Family allowances introduced. Japan surrenders; end of World War II. War dead estimated at 35 million, plus 10 million in Nazi concentration camps. Atomic Research Centers established at Harwell, England.	First atomic bomb detonated near Alamogordo, New Mexico, July 16. United States drops atomic bomb on Hiroshima, Aug. 9.		

Date	English developments	American developments		Dates in PA history
		Private sector	Public sector	
1946	Bank of England nationalized. Population (in millions): 46. UN General Assembly holds its first session in London.	Population (in millions): 140. John D. Rockefeller, Jr. donates $8.5 million to UN for site of permanent headquarters in New York City. Electronic brain built at Pennsylvania State University.	Employment Act of 1946; Council of Economic Advisors set up; Congress creates Joint Economic Committee to study the economy and government's impact on it. Congress enacts Legislative Reorganization Act, which creates a legislative budget, and (sec. 206) authorizes Comptroller General to make expenditure analyses of agency budgets; after several tries, attempt is abandoned. Truman budget in 1946 is $60.4 billion, the largest peacetime budget in history.	
1947	British coal mines nationalized. India is proclaimed independent and partitioned into India and Pakistan. Establishment of the first atomic pile at Harwell.	Bell Laboratories scientists invent the transistor. Airplane first flown at supersonic speeds. More than one million war veterans enroll in colleges under U.S. "G.I. Bill of Rights."	Congress establishes the Joint Financial Management Improvement Program.	1947 Herbert Simon, *Administrative Behavior.* Foreign Assistance.

Date	English developments	American developments		Dates in PA history
		Private sector	Public sector	
1948	First port radar system introduced in Liverpool. British railroads nationalized. Electricity industry nationalized; British Electricity Authority established. National health Service comes into operation. Bread rationing ends.	Month-long strike by soft coal miners; injunction prevents nationwide rail strike; first escalator clause, basing wage increases on cost-of-living index, in General Motors-United Auto Workers contract. Long-playing record invented by Peter Goldmark. 200-inch Mount Palomar reflecting telescope dedicated.		
1949	Britain devalues the pound sterling from $4.03 to 2.80; most European nations follow. British Gas Industry nationalized. Clothes rationing ends.	Guided missile launched 250 miles; highest altitude ever reached by humankind.	U.S. (Hoover) Commission on Organization of the Executive Branch of the Government recommends performance budget for national government. Bill grants $5.43 billion to Europe.	1949–National Security Act recommends separation of capital and operating costs in defense budget; Philip Selznick, *TVA and the Grass Roots*; Edward C. Banfield article, "Congress and the Budget: A Planner's Criticism."
1950	Britain recognizes Communist China and Israel. London dock strikes. London population (in millions): 8.3.	Einstein, "General Field Theory" (attempt to expand Theory of Relativity). Antihistamines become remedy for colds and allergies. Population: 150,697,999; illiteracy is 3.2%. New York population (in millions): 7.8. 1.5 million TV sets (one year later, approx. 15 million).	Congress resurrects "Omnibus" appropriations legislation; Congress passes Budget and Accounting Procedures Act, requiring all agencies to establish and maintain system of accounting and internal control.	1950–PAR "Symposium on Budget Theory."

Date	English developments	American developments		Dates in PA history
		Private sector	Public sector	
1951	46 percent of the population works in commerce and industry.	Electric power produced from atomic energy at Acron, Idaho. J. Andre-Thomas devises a heart-lung machine for heart operations. 30 percent of the population works in commerce and industry. Color television is first introduced.	General Appropriation Act (sec. 1211) amends Anti-Deficiency Act of 1905, giving President authority to establish reserves of appropriated funds after date when appropriations made available.	1951–David Truman, *The Governmental Process*; Talcott Parsons, *Structure and Process in Modern Societies*; Joel Dean, *Capital Budgeting*.
1952	Churchill announces that Britain has produced an atomic bomb. The last London trams are retired.	Truman announces H-bomb test in the Pacific.	Maryland adopts performance budget system.	
1953	London Stock Exchange opens public galleries.	Controls on wages, salaries, and on some consumer goods are lifted (February 6); all price controls removed (March 17). Lung cancer reported attributable to cigarette smoking.	Congress creates new cabinet post of Secretary of Health, Education and Welfare.	
1954–1960			Planning–Programming–Budgeting System (P.P.B.S.) "developed." David Novick ("Which Program Do We Mean in Program Budgeting?") urges program format in RAND paper.	1954–Abraham Maslow, *Motivation and Personality*; Alvin Gouldner, *Patterns of Industrial Democracy*; Frederick C. Mosher, *Program Budgeting*; *Brown v. Board of Education* case.

Date	English developments	American developments Private sector	American developments Public sector	Dates in PA history
1954	Independent Television Authority established.	Submarine "Nautilus" converted to nuclear power. Antipolo serum inoculation starts for schoolchildren. 29 million homes have TV. America contains 6% of all cars, 58% of all telephones, 45% of all radio sets, and 34% of all railroads.		
1955	Railroad and dock strikes. Commercial TV begins broadcasting.	Ultra high frequency produced at the Massachusetts Institute of Technology. Atomically generated power first used.	"Second Hoover Commission" recommends broadened use of "cost" in U.S. Government.	
1956	"DIDO" reactor opened at Harwell. Bank interest raised to 5.5%, the highest since 1932.	Bell Telephone Company begins to develop "visual telephone." Transatlantic cable telephone service inaugurated. Oral vaccine against polio.	Public Law 863 implements some Hoover Commission recommendations with respect to requiring the accrual method of accounting and the use of cost-based budgets in the U.S. government.	1956–Jesse Burkhead, *Government Budgeting*.
1957	Thermonuclear bomb in central Pacific explodes. Bank interest rate raised to 7%. Regular London-Moscow air service inaugurated.			1957–Fritz Morstein-Marx, *The Administrative State*; C. Northcote Parkinson, *Parkinson's Law and Other Studies in Administration*.

Date	English developments	American developments		Dates in PA history
		Private sector	Public sector	
1958	First parking meters appear in London.	Unemployment in United States reaches almost 5.2%.	PERT introduced into Polaris Missile development program. Artificial earth satellite, Explorer I, is launched from Cape Canaveral. United States establishes National Aeronautics and Space Administration (NASA) to administer scientific exploration of space.	1958–J.K. Galbraith, *The Affluent Society*: Roland N. McKean, *Efficiency in Government Through Systems Analysis.*
1959	TV coverage of General Election.		Hawaii becomes 50th state. First nuclear-powered merchant vessel, "Savannah," is launched.	1959–Frederick Herzberg, *The Motivation to Work*; Gladys M. Kammerer, *Program Budgeting: An Aid to Understanding.*
1960		First weather satellite, Tiros I. launched to transmit TV images of cloud cover around the world.	Gross National Product: $502.6 billion.	1960–Douglas McGregor, *The Human Side of Enterprise*; Wallace Sayre and Herbert Kaufman, *Governing New York City*; Andrew L. Stedry, *Budget Control and Cost Behavior*; E.E. Schattschneider, *The Semisovereign People.*
1961	Farthings no longer legal tender.	Alan Shepard makes first U.S. space flight. Population (in millions): 179. United States breaks off diplomatic relations with Cuba.	PPBS installed in the Defense Department.	1961–Bay of Pigs fiasco; Robert Dahl, *Who Governs?* William F. Whyte, *Men at Work.*

		American developments		
Date	English developments	Private sector	Public sector	Dates in PA history
1962	39 atomic reactors in operation.	U.S. military council established in Vietnam. 200 atomic reactors in operation. *The Sunday Times* issues its first color supplement. Nine New York daily newspapers are struck from December 1962 until April 1963.	"Comprehensive, zerobase" budgeting inaugurated in U.S. Department of Agriculture; Pay comparability with Federal Salary Reform Act of 1962.	1962–Harold Guetzkow, *Simulation in Social Science.*
1963	Britain rejected in entry into the Common Market.	Unemployment reaches 6.1%; Dr. Michael DeBakey first uses an artificial heart to take over the circulation of a patient's blood during heart surgery.		1963–Richard M. Cyert and James G. March, *A Theory of the Firm*; David Braybrooke and Charles Lindblom, *A Strategy of Decision*; Karl Deutsch, *Nerves of Government.*
1964	"Brain Drain": scientists emigrate to United States in great numbers. Britain grants licenses to drill for oil and gas in the North Sea. Bank interest increased to 7%.	Verrazano Narrows Bridge, the world's longest suspension bridge, opens to traffic in New York. Race riots erupt in Harlem, New York, and in many other cities.	State of New York adopts PPBS. 24th Amendment to the U.S. Constitution is ratified, abolishing the poll tax.	Chris Argyris, *Integrating the Individual and the Organization.* Robert T. Golembiewski, *Public Budgeting and Finance.*

| Date | English developments | American developments | | Dates in PA history |
		Private sector	Public sector	
1965	750th anniversary of Magna Carta; 700th anniversary of British Parliament.	Medicare bill becomes law upon President Johnson's signing; it was first proposed by President Kennedy in 1960. Legislative momentum gains for anti-pollution laws on a national scale. New immigration law classifies applicants by family condition, refugee status, and skills, replacing 1921 law based on nationality. More than $26.2 billion spent for public school education: $654 per student.	President requires nearly all federal agencies to adopt PPBS.	1965–Charles Lindblom, *The Intelligence of Democracy*; George S. Odiorne, *Management by Objectives*; Robert T. Golembiewski, *Men, Management and Morality*; William Hamovitch, *The Federal Deficit*.
1966	Prime Minister announces "standstill" in wages and prices. The "Times" of London changes its format, printing news instead of advertisements on the front page.	International Days of Protest (against U.S. policy in Vietnam). Michael E. De Bakey implants plastic arteries leading to an artificial heart which functions throughout 3.5 hour valve replacement operation: Population: 195,827,000. Car registrations total 78 million passenger cars and 16 million truck and buses. Color TV becomes popular.	California State government adopts P.P.B.S. (as "Programming and Budgeting" — "PAS"); Philadelphia adopts PPB system.	1966–Richard Fenno, *The Power of the Purse*; David Easton, *Varieties of Political Theory*.

Date	English developments	American developments		Dates in PA history
		Private sector	Public sector	
1967	Britain and Soviet Union pledge to make every possible effort to obtain peace in Vietnam.	50,000 persons demonstrate against Vietnam War at Lincoln Memorial, Washington, D.C. 100 million telephones are in service. United States has 74 nuclear powered submarines in commission. U.S. manned space flights are suspended after death of three astronauts in fire on launching pad.	President's Commission on Budget Concepts rules against the use of a capital budget by U.S. government.	1967–Anthony Downs, *Inside Bureaucracy*; Peter Drucker, *The Effective Executive*; Fred E. Fiedler, *A Theory of Leadership Effectiveness*.
1968	British government restricts immigration from India, Pakistan, and the West Indies. 19 million TV sets.	Apollo 7 spacecraft with three astronauts aboard, launched on flight orbiting 11 days. Apollo 8, with three astronauts aboard, launched on flight to the moon. 78 million TV sets.	Last year Congress was able to enact on appropriations bill before the start of the new fiscal year (July 1); Congress passes the Revenue and Expenditure Control Act which imposes ceilings on both outlays and new obligational authority; State of Arkansas adopts PPBS. Gross National Product almost $861 billion.	1968–C. West Churchman, *The Systems Approach*; Donald C. Rowat, *The Ombudsman*; Yehezkel Dror, *Public Policymaking Reexamined*.

		American developments		
Date	English developments	Private sector	Public sector	Dates in PA history
1969		First U.S. troops withdrawn from Vietnam. Apollo 10 and 11 launched. Neil Armstrong, from Apollo 11, steps out on the moon. U.S. government, heeding the results of laboratory experiments linking food additives to cancer, removes cyclamates from the market and limits use of monosodium glutamate. Also, the government takes steps to ban use of the insecticide, DDT.	Reorganization Act: consolidates different types of methods for keeping track of U.S. funds and expenditures; changes beginning and ending of fiscal year; creates Office of Management and Budget (OMB).	1969–Warren G. Bennis, *Organization Development*; Lawrence J. Peter, *The Peter Principle.*
1970	In Britain and France nuclear power heart pacemakers are successfully implanted in three patients to correct a condition called "heart block."	U.S. strength in Vietnam is reduced to below 400,000 men. Student protest against Vietnam war. 448 universities and colleges are closed or on strike. Dow-Jones Industrial Average drops to 631.	Congress passes Legislative Reorganization Act, calling on GAO to perform cost-benefit studies of federal programs; Jimmy Carter institutes zero-base budgeting for Georgia State government; President's Reorganization Plan No. 2 establishes Domestic Council and reorganizes BOB as OMB in Executive Office.	1970–Charles Perrow, *Organizational Analysis*; Robert H. Haveman and Julius Margolis, *Public Expenditures and Policy Analysis*; Percival Brundage, *The Bureau of the Budget*; Brookings Institution, first issue of *Setting National Priorities.*

Date	English developments	American developments Private sector	Public sector	Dates in PA history
1971	Postal strike leaves Britons without mail for 47 days.	The 26th Amendment to the U.S. Constitution allowing 18-year-olds to vote, ratified. President Nixon orders 90-day freeze on wages and prices and announces other economic measures designed to curb domestic inflation and strengthen the U.S. balance of payments position. Congress votes to end funding of the supersonic transport project. Apollo 14 launched. Amtrak begins to operate passenger railroads Legalized offtrack betting introduced in New York.		1971–Frank Marini, *Towards a New Public Administration*; *Griggs v. Duke Power Company* case; Lawrence C. Pierce, *The Politics of Fiscal Policy Formation*.
1972	A 47-day coal strike cripples Great Britain.	Phase II economic measures to control wages, prices and profits. U.S. petroleum products shortage first becomes apparent. Hurricane Agnes causes an estimated $1.7 billion damage to the eastern United States. The Dow-Jones Index for industrial stocks closes above the 1000 mark for the first time. Apollo 16 launched.	President Nixon increases use of impoundment power to stop spending off appropriated funds; Congress approves raising of national debt limit to $250 billion.	1972–Equal Employment Opportunity Act.

Date	English developments	American developments		Dates in PA history
		Private sector	Public sector	
1973	Great Britain formally joins the Common Market. The government orders three-day work week to conserve electricity following coal-workers overtime ban.	President Nixon ends wage-price controls except in the food, health care, and building industries. Vietnam cease-fire agreement signed January 23. Skylab I, II, III space missions completed successfully. Energy crisis: a petroleum products shortage of undetermined magnitude, coupled with Arab oil embargo, forces cutback in American, Western European, and Japanese home heating and transportation services and fuel-consuming industries. The Financial Accounting Standards Board (FASB) commences operation.		1973–Peter Phyrr, *Zero-Base Budgeting*; William H. Anderson, *Financing Modern Government*; Comprehensive Employment and Training Act (CETA) passed.

Date	English developments	American developments		Dates in PA history
		Private sector	Public sector	
1974		Worldwide inflation helps to cause dramatic increases in the cost of fuel, food and materials; oil-producing nations boost prices, heightening inflation; economic growth slows to nearly zero in most industrialized nations; Dow Jones stock exchange index falls to 663, the lowest level since the 1970 recession. All price and wage controls, in effect since 1971, end. A U.S. Air Force jet plane flies from New York to London, reaching speeds of 2000 m.p.h.	Congressional Budget and Impoundment Control Act passed; creates "legislative budget" and Congressional Budget Office (CBO); disallows President from impounding permanently appropriated funds, and gives President powers of rescission and deferral.	1974–Studs Terkel, *Working*; Edward Banfield, *The Unheavenly City Revisited.*
1975	Inflation rate jumps 25%.	New York City, needing cash to avert default, appeals to federal government. Unemployment rate reaches 9.2%, highest since 1941. U.S. Apollo and Soviet Soyuz 19 spacecrafts link up 140 miles above earth, the first international manned space flight. First Women's bank opens in New York City.	Congressional Budget Office presents to Congress its first economic report; U.S. Supreme Court holds presidential impoundment power illegal; Wilmington, Delaware, implements ZBB budget.	1975–Harry Hatry, *Program Analysis for State and Local Government*; E.S. Quade, *Analysis for Public Decisions*; Nathan Glazer, *Affirmative Discrimination*; Lennox L. Moak and Albert M. Hillhouse, *Concepts and Practices in Local Government Finance.*

| | | American developments | | |
Date	English developments	Private sector	Public sector	Dates in PA history
1976	World's first scheduled supersonic passenger service is inaugurated when two Concorde jets take off simultaneously from London and Paris; Britain and France begin trans-Atlantic supersonic service to Washington.	Scientists at M.I.T. announce construction of a functional synthetic gene, complete with regulatory mechanisms. U.S. Air Force Academy admits 155 women, ending the all-male tradition at the U.S. military academy.	Inspector General Act passed.	1976–Clark Abt, *The Evaluation of Social Programs.*
1977	Scientists report they have determined for the first time the complete genetic structure of a living organism.	President Carter warns that the energy crisis in the US could bring on a "national catastrophe"; Americans must respond with the "moral equivalent of war" making "profound" changes in their oil consumption. Two spacecrafts are launched to probe the atmosphere of Venus; spacecrafts Voyager I and III begin journeys to explore outer solar system. Scientists announce the discovery of primitive microorganisms called methanogens, a separate life distinct from bacteria, plants, and animals. Scientists confirm testing of neutron bomb which kills with massive radiation leaving most buildings intact. Population reaches 216 million.	Department of Energy is established.	1977–Charles L. Schultze, *The Public Use of Private Interest*; Hugh Heclo, *A Government of Strangers.*

Date	English developments	American developments		Dates in PA history
		Private sector	Public sector	
1977–1980			Zero-Base Budgeting (ZZB) attempted at national level; era of taxpayer revolts in the states.	1978–Civil Service Reform Act passed.
1978	"Test-tube baby" born in England; first human baby conceived outside the body of a woman. Gold in London rises to record $243.65 an ounce.	U.S. dollar plunges to record low against the Japanese yen; Canadian dollar falls to a 45-year low against U.S. dollar. Trading on the New York Exchange has record single day volume of 63.5 million shares on April 17; the Dow Jones industrial average soars 35.34 points on Nov. 1, a record breaking single-day advance. Congress extends the ratification of the Equal Rights Amendment from March 22, 1979, to June 30, 1982. Oil drilling begins in the Baltimore Canyon region off the New Jersey shore. Longest U.S. coal strike ends on 110th day after miners approve agreement.		

Date	English developments	American developments		Dates in PA history
		Private sector	Public sector	
1979	Conservatives win British parliamentary elections. Margaret Thatcher becomes first woman Prime Minister. Trucker's strike threatens the economy: more than 50,000 drivers on strike. Government announces abolition of all remaining exchange controls. Britain and China sign agreement on economic cooperation setting target of 7,000 million pound sterling for total trade over six years. Employment Bill, aimed at trade union reform, published.	Auto use threatened due to the scarcity of petroleum and sharply higher prices. ITT cleared for competition with AT&T to provide domestic long distance telephone service. Energy crisis develops; job gains in solar energy. Unemployment rate: 6.0% (August). Prime interest rate: 13% (August). Federal Aviation Administration grounds all McDonnell-Douglas DC-10 airplanes for safety checks. Serious accident at Three Mile Island nuclear reactor at Harrisburg, Pennsylvania.	President Carter announces energy and economic policy to curb U.S. imported oil; war on inflation is his number one priority. United States and China establish diplomatic relations for first time since foundation of People's Republic.	1979–Thomas D. Lynch, *Public Budgeting in America.*
1980	First national steel strike since 1926 (January 2–April 2). Budget: PSBR set at 8,500 million pound sterling; increased spending on defense, police, and pensions; aid for small businesses; short term social security benefits to be taxable. Government announces package of measures to cut public expenditures and increase taxation. Unemployment figures reach postwar record 2,133,000 (836,000 more than a year ago).	Grain embargo of USSR because of invasion of Afghanistan. Mt. St. Helens volcano erupts; 32 people dead, 98 missing. 25,000 Cuban refugees recently arrived in Florida. New York bus and underground rail workers stage first strike in 14 years, bringing service to a standstill. Space rocket, Voyager I, sends back first close-up pictures of Planet Saturn.	President Carter presents record $142,700 million defense budget. Government announces package of measures to contain inflation.	1980–Allen Schick, *Congress and Money.*

Date	English developments	American developments		Dates in PA history
		Private sector	Public sector	
1981	Unemployment rate: 11.1% (July). Inflation: 11.7%, dropped from 21.9% in 1980.	Auto sales fall sharply. OPEC freezes oil prices. Coal strike (March 27–June 6), 160,000 workers. Grain embargo lifted. Unemployment reaches 8.4%. Production of neutron weapons. First Space Shuttle launched. Voyager II scans Saturn. Sandra Day O'Connor becomes first female Justice of the U.S. Supreme Court.	Ronald Reagan assumes U.S. presidency. Omnibus Reconciliation Act of 1981, and Economic Recovery Tax Act of 1981: reduction in the budget and cut of taxes. U.S. government debt reaches $1 trillion.	
1983	Margaret Thatcher and her Conservative Party win a resounding victory.	OPEC forced to cut oil prices. Agreement of U.S. to export high technology items to China. Also, Textile Pact signed between U.S. and China. Flights on the space shuttle.	President Reagan signs Social Security Bill; increases in Social Security taxes. Reduction of welfare expenses. "Privatization" a growing public sector alternative.	

		American developments		
Date	English developments	Private sector	Public sector	Dates in PA history
1984	Britain's budget incorporates new tax structure; economy slows down. Fiscal and monetary policy has three principal objectives: to control public expenditure, to guard against the emergence of domestic inflationary pressures, and to accommodate the recovery begun in previous years. Unemployment rate: 12.7%. Cuts in price of oil. Government signs Hong Kong Accord that guarantees the return of Hong Kong to Chinese sovereignty in 1997.	Divestiture of AT&T takes effect. Japan agrees to increase U.S. imports. Repair of orbiting satellite. The National Heart, Lung, and Blood Institute publishes the results of 10-year study: all Americans should reduce their blood cholesterol levels. World responds to Ethiopian famine.	President Reagan wins reelection. Fiscal policy expansionary despite a modest reduction in the federal budget. Faster than expected growth in the economy. Single Audit Act provides single audit approach to states and localities receiving federal assistance.	Government Accounting Standards Board (GASB) established to set accounting standards for state and local governments; GAO establishes generally accepted accounting principles (GAAP) for federal government.
1985			Balanced Budget and Emergency Deficit Reduction Act (Gramm-Rudman Hollings) passed by Congress to control large national debt.	1985–*Garcia v Antonio Metropolitan Transit Authority* holds that provisions of the Fair Labor Standards Act of 1938 can be applied to state and local government.

| Date | English developments | American developments | | Dates in PA history |
		Private sector	Public sector	
				Bowsher, Comptroller General of the U.S. v. Synar, Member of Congress, case invalidates Gramm-Rudman-Hollings provision authorizing the Comptroller General to have executive functions; allows Congress to use "fallback" provisions in the Act in which the Directors of O.M.B. and C.B.O. prepare a report submitted to a specially-created, Temporary Joint Committee on Deficit Reduction, which must report to both Houses of Congress in five days a joint resolution regarding the Directors' recommendations.
1986	United Kingdom Finance Act—new rules drawn up to force companies to shed some of the large surpluses they had been able to stockpile. United Kingdom Insolvency Act—brought in a system of administrative receivership, imitating Chapter 11 legislation in the United States, enabling companies to file for protection from creditors at an earlier stage.		1986 Tax Reform Act—has mixed effects. Raises cost of capital, lowers top corporate tax rate, and diminishes the distortion between investments. Former President's Act of 1987.	

Date	English developments	American developments		Dates in PA history
		Private sector	Public sector	
1987			Omnibus Budget Reconciliation Act of 1987—major provisions of Act mainly affect corporations and wealthy individuals: extension of telephone excise tax and temporary Federal Unemployment Tax Act (FUTA) tax; initiation of IRS fees; modification of customs user fee; repeal of vacation pay reserve; change in the taxation of partnerships; distribution of income by mutual funds; and miscellaneous taxes.	
1987		Stock Market Crash—big decline in stock market from August to October 1987. As a result, economic growth slows in 1988 and unemployment rate stops falling.	Historic drop in Federal deficit, which declines from $221.2 billion in 1986 to $150.4 billion in 1987.	

Date	English developments	American developments		Dates in PA history
		Private sector	Public sector	
1988			George Bush is elected U.S. President. Medicare Catastrophic Coverage Act of 1988. Family Support Act of 1988. Technical and Miscellaneous Revenue Act of 1988 (TAMRA). Omnibus Trade and Competitiveness Act of 1988 requires that the Office of Management and Budget prepare an analysis of the budget's impact on the international competitiveness of U.S. business and the U.S. balance of payments position.	
1989			Resolution Trust Corporation (RTC) hearing on procedures to be established so that the assets of failed thrifts can be sold in a fair and open basis.	
1990			Budget Process Reform Act amends the Congressional Budget Act of 1974 to provide for budget process reform, to repeal sequestration under the Balanced Budget and Emergency Deficit Control Act of 1985, and to establish a pay-as-you-go basis for federal budgeting.	

		American developments		
Date	English developments	Private sector	Public sector	Dates in PA history
			Omnibus Budget Reconciliation Act of 1990 (OBRA)—agreement between the President and the Congress to reduce the federal deficit by about half a trillion dollars, compared to what it would have been, from 1991 to 1995. Budget Enforcement Act of 1990 (BEA) enforces deficit reduction agreement of the Omnibus Budget Reconciliation Act of 1990. BEA divides budget into two categories—discretionary programs and direct spending and receipts.	
1991		1991 budget recommends that the Food and Drug Administration (FDA) establish a system of user fees for the review of drugs and medical devices, including products that use techniques developed through biotechnology. Gross Domestic Product (GDP) increases at an average 1.6 percent annual rate. April 1991: President Bush announces America 2000 education reform strategy to help communities achieve National Education Goals by the year 2000.	Tax Extension Act of 1991 speeds up the timing of estimated tax payments by corporations and extends for six months twelve tax provisions that were originally scheduled to expire on December 31, 1991. Emergency Unemployment Compensation Act of 1991 provides over $5 billion in temporary emergency unemployment benefits to almost 3 million jobless workers.	

| | | American developments | | |
		Private sector	Public sector	
Date	English developments			Dates in PA history
1992	The United Kingdom savings ratio more than doubles, from a low of 5.4 percent in 1988 to a peak of 11.5 percent in 1992.		Anti-Recession Infrastructure Jobs Act of 1992 authorizes Secretary of Commerce to make grants to state and local governments for infrastructure projects in distressed areas. Resolution Trust Corporation Funding Act of 1992 requests additional funding to complete the savings and loan bailout. The Regulatory Sunshine Act of 1992 ensures that all oral and written communications concerning a regulatory action are publicly disclosed and authorizes appropriations for the Office of Information and Regulatory Affairs of the OMB. Bill Clinton is elected U.S. President.	
1993		August 1993–President Clinton's health care reform debates. Job Training 2000 replaces fragmentation of Federal job training programs with a new, coordinated, market-driven system.	The Fair Trade in Financial Services Act of 1993 gives U.S. negotiators new leverage to obtain the same equality of competitive opportunity for United States' financial firms operating in foreign markets than is extended to foreign firms in U.S. markets.	

BIBLIOGRAPHY

P. F. Brundage, *The Bureau of the Budget*, Praeger, New York, pp. 3–39 (1970).

A. E. Buck, *Public Budgeting*, Harper and Brothers, New York, pp. 10–19, 61–63 (1929).

A. G. Buehler, *Public Finance*, McGraw-Hill, New York, pp. 176–185 (1948).

J. Burkhead, *Government Budgeting*, John Wiley and Sons, New York, pp. 2–28 (1956).

F. A. Cleveland and A. E. Buck, *The Budget and Responsible Government*, Macmillan, New York, pp. 72–88 (1920).

"Executive Office of the President, Office of Management and Budget: What It is—What It Does," Executive Office of the President, Washington, D.C. (1976).

"Fiscal Management: President's Committee on Administrative Management," *Public Budgeting and Finance* (ed. R. T. Golembiewski), Peacock, Itasca, Ill., pp. 49–65 (1968).

W. Hamovitch, *The Federal Deficit: Fiscal Imprudence or Policy Weapon?*, D.C. Heath, Boston (1965).

J. Haveman, *Congress and the Budget*, Indiana University Press, Bloomington, Ind., pp. 3–37, 100–122, 174–188 (1978).

J. L. Herbert, *Experiences in Zero-Base Budgeting*, Petrocelli, New York (1977).

J. O. McKinsey, *Budgetary Control*, Ronald Press, New York, (1923).

L. Merewitz and S. H. Sosnick, *The Budget's New Clothes: A Critique of Planning-Programming-Budgeting and Benefit-Cost Analysis*, Markham, Chicago, pp. 1–12 (1971).

F. C. Mosher, *The GAO: The Quest for Accountability in American Government*, Westview Press, Boulder, Colo., pp. 13–63 (1979).

National Council on Governmental Accounting, "Budgetary Reporting in State and Local Governments: Discussion Memorandum," September 16, 1982.

D. Novick, "The Origin and History of Program Budgeting," *Calif. Manage. Rev.*, 11:7–12.

"Outline of History of the Bureau of the Budget and the Office of Management and Budget," *Federal Accountant*, December: 94–97 (1981).

"Public Budgets," *The Annals*, 62 (November 1915).

J. Rabin, *Planning, Programming and Budgeting for State and Local Governments*, Bureau of Public Administration, Tuscaloosa, Ala. (1973).

A. Schick, *Congress and Money*, The Urban Institute, Washington, D.C., pp. 17–81 (1980).

A. Schick, "The Road to PPB. The Stages of Budget Reform," *Public Admin. Rev.*, 26.243–258 (1966).

C. Seckler-Hudson, "Performance Budgeting in Government," *Adv. Manage.*, March: 5–9, 30–32 (1953).

A. Smithies, *The Budgetary Process in the United States*, McGraw-Hill, New York, pp. 3–89 (1955).

T. C. Stanton, "Conceptual Underpinnings of the Federal Budget Process," *Federal Accountant*, December: 44–51 (1975).

L. D. White, *The Federalists: A Study in Administrative History—1789–1801*, Free Press, New York, pp. 323–347 (1948).

L. D. White, *Introduction to the Study of Public Administration*, 4th ed. Macmillan, New York, pp. 232, 234–236, 240–241, 255, 279, 289–291 (1955).

A. Wildavsky and A. Hammond, "Comprehensive Versus Incremental Budgeting in the Department of Agriculture," *Admin. Sci. Q.*, 10:321–346 (1965).

W. F. Willoughby, *The Legal Status and Functions of the General Accounting Office of the National Government*, John Hopkins Press, Baltimore, pp. 1–24 (1927).

W. F. Willoughby, W. W. Willoughby, and S. Mc. Lindsay, *The System of Financial Management of Great Britain*, D. Appleton, New York, pp. 23–35 (1917).

L. Wilmerding, Jr., *The Spending Power: A History of the Efforts of Congress to Control Expenditures*, Yale University Press, New Haven, Conn. (1943); reprinted by Archon Books (1971).

2

Fiscal Management

President's Committee on Administrative Management

Sound fiscal management is a prime requisite of good administration. The responsibility of the Executive for the preparation of a fiscal program in the form of a budget for submission to the Congress and for the direction and control of expenditures under the appropriation acts must be carried on faithfully, effectively, and under clear-cut authority. To establish strict accountability of the Executive Branch for the faithful execution of the laws enacted by the Congress, there must be an independent audit of financial transactions by an independent officer reporting directly to the Congress and who does not exercise any executive authority.

From the standpoint of overall control the system of fiscal management of the Government now has four major defects, namely, (1) the inadequate staffing of the Bureau of the Budget; (2) the vesting in the Office of the Comptroller General, which is not responsible to the President, of the settlement of claims, the final determination concerning the uses of appropriations, and the prescribing of administrative accounting systems; (3) the absence of a truly independent and prompt audit of the financial transactions of the Government, whereby the Congress may hold the Executive Branch strictly accountable; and (4) the failure to devise and install a modern system of accounts and records.

Our recommendations for improvement of the fiscal administration of the Government are designed to correct these major faults, to return executive functions to the Executive Branch, and to make it accountable to the Congress.

Before taking up these recommendations in detail, we may review briefly the division of authority and responsibility between the Congress and the Executive Branch for the determination and execution of fiscal policies. The general theory underlying the Constitution is that the Congress shall be responsible for the determination and approval of the fiscal policies of the Nation and that the Executive shall be responsible for their faithful execution. The right of the legislative body to control the purse was a well-established principle prior to the American Revolution and was incorporated in the Constitution. The

---

Source: The Committee's *Report,* U.S. Government Printing Office, Washington, D.C., pp. 15–24 (1937).

Congress, as representative of the people, enacts the laws; the duty of executing them is placed by the Constitution upon the President.

This division of authority under our constitutional system was well stated by President Wilson in a message to the Congress on May 13, 1920.

> The Congress and the Executive should function within their respective spheres. Otherwise efficient and responsible management will be impossible and progress impeded by wasteful forces of disorganization and obstruction. The Congress has the power and the right to grant or deny an appropriation is made or a law is passed, the appropriation should be administered or the law executed by the executive branch of the Government. In no other way can the Government be efficiently managed and responsibility definitely fixed.

The Congress enacts the necessary revenue laws, authorizes activities which require the expenditure of public funds, and makes the appropriations. But the trust residing in the Congress does not end with the enactment of appropriation measures; its responsibility requires also that it possess suitable means with which to hold the Executive accountable for the faithful and effective execution of revenue and appropriation laws. Likewise the responsibility of the Executive Branch can be established only if it is given undivided executive powers. If the Chief Executive is to fulfill the responsibility of his office under the Constitution, he must possess undivided executive powers and adequate means with which to exercise them.

BUDGETING AND ADMINISTRATIVE CONTROL

The creation in 1921 of the Bureau of the Budget was a major step in the direction of effective administrative management in the Federal Government. It placed upon the President responsibility for the preparation of a comprehensive annual budget and recognized the need for executive discretion and leadership in preparing and submitting to the Congress a program of revenue and expenditure. At the same time it provided the President with one of the primary instruments needed for effective overall management of the executive establishment. The Director at the head of the Bureau is appointed by the President and, though within the Department of the Treasury, reports directly to the President. Through him the President can review and control the effectiveness of governmental agencies.

Purpose of the Budget System

It is the purpose of the budget system to provide in financial terms for planning, information, and control. Through the budget the spending agencies are required to translate their work programs in advance into fiscal terms, so that each activity may be brought into balance and proportion with all other activities, and with the revenues and resources of the Government, and in harmony with long-range and general economic policies. The budget not only serves as the basis of information for the Congress and the public with regard to the past work and future plans of the Administration, but also as the means of control of the general policy of the Government by the Legislative Branch and of the details of administration by the Executive. The Bureau of the Budget was therefore set up as the right arm of the President for the central fiscal management of the vast administrative machine and to enable him to submit regularly to the Congress a complete report on past activities and a future program for advance approval by the Legislative Branch.

In addition to its duties in the preparation of the annual budget, the Bureau of the Budget was given administrative research functions of outstanding importance. It was charged with the responsibility of making a continuous study of the organization, operation, and efficiency of the Executive Branch of the Government. Through its control over budgeting the Bureau is in a key position to detect weaknesses in the organization and functioning of the various departments and agencies and is the appropriate agency continuously to investigate administrative problems and to make recommendations to the President and the departments in the interest of economy and efficiency.

Substantial progress has been achieved through the Bureau of the Budget during its 15 years of operation. A spotlight has been thrown on national fiscal problems. The Executive has been placed in a better position to plan and control the fiscal program, for which he is held responsible in the public mind. It has been possible to scrutinize departmental needs in detail, and the departments have been assisted in improving their budgetary practices. The Congress has been presented not only with a more intelligible picture of the Nation's finances and financial problems but with a clear comparison between estimates and actual expenditures for the particular governmental activities. Substantial advances in improving governmental operation and in coordinating activities have been effected through the agency of the Bureau. Its staff has aided the President in the performance of many difficult administrative duties. The technical phases of budget making have been constantly improved and refined.

At no time, however, has the Bureau of the Budget achieved or even approximated its maximum possible usefulness and effectiveness as an instrument of administrative management. Because of its small operating appropriation, the Bureau has failed to develop an adequate staff of the highest attainable competence. Such a staff is necessary if it is to cope with the problems raised by a rapid growth in the magnitude and complexity of governmental organization and expenditures. It has not perfected its own organization and methods as a directing and controlling agency of the President. Rather, the Bureau has emphasized the task of preparing the Budget to the distinct disadvantage of its important complementary functions. It has only partially developed supervision over the execution of the Budget by the spending agencies.

The administrative research functions placed upon the Bureau are practically undeveloped; it is in this respect that the Bureau has missed its greatest opportunity. The Budget and Accounting Act of 1921 specifically authorized the Bureau to make detailed studies of the administrative departments and establishments for the purpose of advising the President intelligently as to changes that should be made in their organization and methods, in the grouping of services, and in the appropriations for various activities. The Bureau of Efficiency was abolished by an act of Congress, approved March 3, 1933, mainly on the grounds that it duplicated work that the law required the Bureau of the Budget to do. Its records and files were transferred to the Bureau of the Budget, but adequate provisions for carrying on its work are still to be made. Research in administrative organization has been negligible. Recommendations for reorganization have been conspicuously absent.

Staffing of the Bureau of the Budget

One obtains a vivid realization of the inadequate staff of the Bureau of the Budget from the fact that its appropriation for the current fiscal year (ending June 30, 1937) amounted to only $187,000—a sum considerably less than is spent by a single finance and accounting division of some of the great Government departments, and less than 3 percent of the amount required to audit the expenditures. It has a total personnel of only 45, and aside from the statutory positions of Director and Assistant Director, has only two positions compensated in excess of $6,000 per annum. Only $18,700 was provided for "research, surveys, and assistance." Yet this small staff is charged with preparing a budget of billions and with aiding the President in the exercise of his vast responsibility for the overall management of the huge and intricate Federal administrative machine.

If the Bureau of the Budget is to be developed into a serviceable tool for administrative management to aid the President in the exercise of overall control, it needs greater resources and better techniques. If continuing power is given the President to transfer and consolidate executive establishments, he will need adequate information, based on analyses of the greatest competence, as a guide to action. The Bureau of the Budget is the logical staff agency for the performance of this service. It should be given appropriations and a staff commensurate with the magnitude of the assignment. A relatively small sum invested in strengthening the Bureau of the Budget as a staff agency of the President will yield enormous returns in the increased efficiency of Government operation. It is with this in mind that recommendations regarding the Bureau of the Budget are presented.

The Director of the Bureau of the Budget is one of the few Government officers in a position to advise the President from an overall, as opposed to a bureau or departmental, point of view. He should therefore be relieved to the greatest possible extent from the minor details of administration. He should be released for duties of maximum importance to the President and freed so that he may attend important conferences of Cabinet officers and planning groups, where programs are being considered that may eventually result in appropriation requests or in changes in governmental organization or procedure. In accordance with suggestions made elsewhere in this report, the salary of the Director should be increased. It should be possible for the President to select a Director from the career service, though he should continue, of course, to have the right to appoint a man of his own choosing.

The position of Assistant Director of the Bureau of the Budget should be filled under civil-service rules, preferably by promotion from the career service. It should be a high permanent post to which career men should be encouraged to aspire. Continuity in office is important if the Assistant Director is to have the necessary background from which to advise a new Director concerning the techniques of budget making and the intricacies of Government machinery and if he is to be skilled in the execution of policies and programs. Breadth of experience, depth of knowledge, and broad vision are needed in this office; these can be obtained only through intensive training and long experience in the Government itself. The Assistant Director should maintain the ordinary contacts with the administrative and budget officers of the departments as well as with the heads of other overall management agencies such as the civil-service establishment. He should direct the activities of the several divisions of the Bureau of the Budget and in every possible way should assume responsibilities that would leave the Director free to concern himself with matters of major policy and program.

If the Bureau of the Budget is to perform effectively its functions of fiscal and overall management it must be staffed with an adequate personnel. Division chiefs of high competence should be appointed from the career service. It should continue to have a career man as administrative assistant to attend to the institutional needs of the Bureau, such as personnel, appropriations, organization, financial records, and general services. The Director should have the authority to appoint a number of special assistants from inside or outside the service for special assignments and to retain consultants from business and the professions on a temporary basis for investigations or conferences in technical fields. The right to transfer or detail personnel from other Government agencies is of particular importance to the Bureau of the Budget and this should be authorized. For long-term periods the Bureau should reimburse the departments from which the personnel are borrowed. In turn, the

Bureau should be permitted to accept reimbursement from Government agencies when it undertakes studies of organization and procedure at their request.

Activities of the Bureau: Estimates

The preparation and execution of the Budget are essentially executive tasks. The Bureau of the Budget as a managerial agency of the President should therefore be made responsible for the execution, as well as the formulation, of the budget as a national fiscal plan. The task of scrutinizing and passing upon departmental estimates and of exercising some measure of continuing direction over the execution of the budget should be assigned to a special division in the Bureau. The highly important task of budgeting requires a staff of unusual competence, breadth of vision, keen insight into governmental problems, and long acquaintance with the work of the Government. Only a staff having these qualifications can be of assistance to the President, the Congress, and the departments in the preparation and consideration of a budget. Well-considered and informed central direction of budgeting is essential; arbitrary, uninformed, and undiscriminating decisions must be avoided.

The staff in charge of budget estimates must keep in constant touch with the entire administrative machine for the purpose of developing and executing both short-term and long-term fiscal plans. Through this staff the President may exercise effective control over the formulation and execution of fiscal plans and policies and may review carefully and wisely the departmental estimates. In this manner fiscal planning may assume its proper relationship to the economic and social planning for which the Nation holds the President responsible.

Administrative Research and Other Managerial Activities

The President needs a research agency to investigate the broad problems involved in the administrative management of the Government—problems of administrative organization, finance, coordination, procedures and methods of work, and the many technical aspects of management. The function of investigation and research into administrative problems should be developed as an aid to overall executive management.

Economy and efficiency in government require constant investigation and reorganization of the administrative structure. It is a mistake to assume that the Government can be reorganized once and for all. Continuous study of the administrative organization of the huge Federal machine is necessary; new activities are constantly emerging and old activities are constantly changing, increasing, decreasing, or disappearing. Unless there is a special agency equipped to investigate problems of organization, new activities are set up without careful attention to where they should be located and what kind of organization is required. This results in costly mistakes and confusion. On the other hand, when the need for certain governmental activities declines or disappears, unless there is a special agency constantly studying the organizational requirements, adjustments are made late or not at all.

A division of administrative research in the Bureau of the Budget is the logical place to develop these functions which were authorized in the act of 1921. It should stimulate the continuous study of organization, methods, and procedures at the departmental or bureau level by the departments and bureaus themselves. It should engage in such studies on its own initiative where necessary, but should follow the policy of aiding and encouraging the departments to study their own organizational and procedural problems. It should endeavor to develop principles of organization that have general applicability and to act as a clearing house and consultation center for administrative research carried on in the departments. It should not undertake studies in fields in which other agencies of the Government are more competent or for which they are better equipped. Above all, persons engaged in administrative research should be freed from detailed routine duties involved in handling budget estimates.

The administrative research activities should be concentrated in a separate division of the Bureau of the Budget. It should be headed by a permanent chief possessing in unusual degree imagination, vision, creativeness, and analytical insight, as well as intimate acquaintanceship with both the practices of government and the principles of public administration. The research division must be staffed with persons of unusually high competence. Important research assignments upon administrative problems can be carried out successfully only by highly trained and experienced persons familiar with the organization and techniques of public administration. Flexible staff arrangements are necessary to permit the use of specialists drawn from the Government and from business for temporary periods.

A division of information should be established to serve as a central clearing house for the correlation and coordination of the administrative policies of the several departments in the operation of their own informational services, and to perform related duties. The United States Information Service might well be transferred to this division. It might also develop into a service which would supervise and foster regional associations of executive officers of the Government and other activities for coordination of the field services. The Director of the Bureau has been authorized by law to approve the use of printing and binding appropriations for the periodicals and journals published by Government agencies; the chief of the division of information could assist him in carrying out this duty.

The President has turned to the Bureau of the Budget for assistance in carrying out a number of important executive duties placed upon him. By reason of its close contact with the operating departments and with the President as a managerial agency, the Bureau is better able to perform these activities than are other administrative units.

One of the most important of these activities is the preparation, consideration, and clearance of Executive orders. Executive orders have been used since the early days of the Government, and, with the great increase in size and complexity of the governmental machine, have been utilized to an ever-increasing extent. They are particularly necessary in periods of emergency when there is rapid change in governmental policies and organization. Executive direction and control of national administration would be impossible without the use of this device. The activity of the Bureau of the Budget as a clearing agency in the issuance and amendment of Executive orders should be continued and strengthened by the development of a more adequate and expert staff. It should be equipped to aid the President in the consideration of administrative problems and to draft the necessary Executive orders.

Wider use could be made of Executive orders to establish uniform codes regulating management throughout the Government. These codes might well cover such matters as budgetary and other financial practices and controls, personnel, supplies, coordination, and other matters related to general organization and management. Such regulations should be promulgated after careful consideration by the departments. They could be arranged in suitable codes and would be of material assistance in guiding administrative officers.

Departmental regulations governing internal organization and management might also be cleared with the Bureau of the Budget. The purpose would not be formal approval or disapproval, but to give to the departments such assistance as the experts of the Bureau might be able to render and to enable the Bureau to inform the President upon any matters which should be brought to his attention. This clearance would result in the establishment of a greater degree of uniformity in the departmental management practices in matters in which uniformity is desirable. It would provide a desirable pooling of the experience of the several departments in many management activities. The Bureau of the Budget should be equipped to assist the departments, at their request, in preparing regulations relating to their internal management.

Another important activity of the Bureau of the Budget as a staff aid to the President is in connection with proposed legislation arising within the executive departments and establishments. In addition to his position as the head of the Executive Branch, the President is charged by the Constitution with important legislative duties, including the duty to advise the Congress "from time to time" of such "Measures as he shall judge necessary and expedient." As Chief Executive he may require "the principal Officer in each of the executive Departments" to give him an "Opinion, in writing, * * * upon any subject relating to the Duties of their respective Offices." Though the final authority for all legislative acts rests with the Congress and the President, it is the duty of the executive departments to supply the Congress with information and advise concerning the laws which they administer.

Inasmuch as a large part of all legislation is concerned with the structure and functioning of administrative departments and the creation and modification of administrative powers, the Congress is entitled, in the consideration of such legislation, to have from the administrative departments the benefit of their experience and special knowledge. All legislation recommended by the Executive Branch of the Government should be carefully considered before presentation to the Congress. The administrative, financial, legal, international, and other effects and implications of all such proposals should be thoroughly examined and the proposed legislation should be carefully drafted. Conflicts and differences between administrative departments concerning proposed legislation, whether of major policies or details, should, so far as possible, be adjusted before such bills are presented to the Congress. Though the ultimate decision in all such conflicts rests with the Congress, its work is hindered by differences between departments. These ordinarily should be adjusted within the Executive Branch of the Government in accordance with the constitutional concept of a single, and not a plural, Executive.

During recent years the Bureau of the Budget has functioned as an agency for the President in the clearance of the fiscal aspects of legislative measures proposed by the executive departments. This clearance is of value to the Congress and to the departments and is essential to the exercise of the authority and responsibility of the President. It should be applied to all legislation proposed by the executive departments and agencies and should not be limited to fiscal considerations. The Bureau of the Budget could well take over the present duties of the National Emergency Council in this respect.

To aid the President in carrying out this responsibility the Bureau of the Budget should develop a staff equipped to act as a clearance agency on all aspects of proposed legislation and to provide the departments with expert and technical assistance. This would enable the Administration to prepare more expertly proposed legislative measures and to insure that ill-considered measures are not submitted to the Congress.

Recommendations

Our recommendations regarding budgeting and administrative control may be briefly summarized as follows:

1. The Director of the Bureau of the Budget should be relieved from routine duties and thus enabled to devote himself to problems of fiscal policy and planning. Provision should be made for an adequate permanent staff of the highest competence, implemented by special assistants on assignments from the operating agen-

cies and by temporary consultants and specialists recruited from business and industry for special assignments.

2. The execution, as well as the preparation, of the budget should be supervised by the Bureau of the Budget and should be closely correlated with fiscal programs and plans.

3. The administrative research function of the Bureau of the Budget should be adequately developed to aid the President in his duties as head of the executive establishment. The Bureau should carry on constructive studies in public administration for the constant improvement of Government organization and procedure and should also stimulate continuous study of these problems by departments and bureaus.

4. The information function of the Bureau of the Budget should be developed and improved. The United States Information Service should be transferred to it, as should other appropriate activities in the coordination of the field services of the Government.

5. The Bureau of the Budget should serve in various ways as an agency of the President. Improvement should be made in its facilities for the clearance of Executive orders and the establishment of uniform codes of management in the Government. It should assist the departments in their regulation governing internal organization. It could render important service to the President and to the Congress in coordinating and clearing legislative recommendations which originate in the Executive Branch.

DIRECTION AND CONTROL OF ACCOUNTING AND EXPENDITURES

A second important phase of fiscal management is the direction and control of expenditures through the system of accounting. The present accounting system of the Government is badly scattered and presents a rather incongruous mixture of antique and modern practices. Essential parts of the system are now found in the Treasury Department, divided among three or four important Treasury units, in the General Accounting Office, and in the various operating bureaus, departments, and establishments. At the same time, the warrant procedure that dates back to Alexander Hamilton's day pursues its plodding way alongside the latest machine bookkeeping. Financial reporting from the various accounts is far from being systematized, is generally lacking in telling information for administrative purposes, and is often delayed beyond the point of any practical value.

Although the Budget and Accounting Act of 1921 had as one of its main objects the improvement of Government's accounting system, very little of real and lasting value has as yet resulted. The Comptroller General was vested with authority under this act to prescribe a system of administrative appropriation and fund accounting in the several departments and establishments. Fifteen years have since elapsed, and still no comprehensive and adequate system of general accounts has been developed by the Comptroller General's office.

The authority which the Comptroller General has exercised over departmental accounting procedures has, in many cases, improved the accounts in the departments and establishments. But these procedures have continually stressed the bringing of accounting information into the General Accounting Office, with little consideration for the informational needs of the Bureau of the Budget, of the Treasury Department, and ultimately of the

President. The tendency, therefore, has been to deprive the Executive of adequate accounting machinery, or even authority to develop this important instrument of financial direction. Because of the lack of interest in administration little effort has been made, for example, toward the development of unit or cost accounts. It is very doubtful if the Congress intended that the accounting provision of the 1921 Act should work in this way. Certainly it is inconsistent with Executive responsibility and efficient administration.

The time is ripe for a return to the basic notion that served as the groundwork for the original accounting system of the Government. There should now be installed in the Treasury Department a modern system of general accounting and reporting that would produce accurate information quickly and easily concerning expenditure obligations, appropriation and allotment balances, revenue estimates and accruals, and actual collections, as well as cash disbursements and receipts. Not only should the accounting methods be standardized throughout the governmental agencies, but there should be a complete revamping of the accounting procedure which would enable the Treasury Department to secure reliable information at a moment's notice on the status of all revenues and expenditures of the Government. There is abundant evidence that these accounting improvements are greatly needed, and that they can now be properly made.

Current Control of Expenditures

Through the accounting system current control over expenditures is exercised. This function is often confused with the function of audit. Current control involves final decisions as to proposed expenditures and the availability of funds. An audit is an examination and verification of the accounts after transactions are completed in order to discover and report to the legislative body any unauthorized, illegal, or irregular expenditures, any financial practices that are unsound, and whether the administration has faithfully discharged its responsibility.

A true audit can be conducted only by other officers than those charged with the making of decisions upon expenditures. No public officer should be authorized to audit his own accounts or financial acts and decisions. The maximum safeguard is provided when the auditor is entirely independent of the administration and exercises no executive authority. The control of expenditures is essentially an executive function, whereas the audit of such expenditures should be independent of executive authority or direction.

Although the title of the Budget and Accounting Act indicates that the principal purpose was to provide a budget system and "an independent audit of public accounts," the distinction between "control" and "audit" was confused in the act. It placed certain control functions, as well as the auditing function, in the Office of the Comptroller General, who was thus made both a "comptroller" and an "auditor." This has created an undesirable and anomalous situation: As an auditor the Comptroller General properly performs his function without the direction of any executive officer; but as a comptroller, exercising the executive authority to determine the uses of appropriations, to settle accounts and claims, and to prescribe administrative accounting systems—functions which are universally recognized as executive in character—he is improperly removed from any executive direction and responsibility.

Furthermore, the Comptroller General, as a comptroller, determines in advance the legality of expenditures and issues rules and regulations which govern the administrative procedures and practices of the executive establishments; later, as an auditor, he reviews and audits the action taken under his own previous decisions. The more the Comptroller General exercises control over expenditures through advance decisions, approval of contracts, preaudits, and otherwise, the less competent he becomes to audit them. This system results in divided authority and responsibility for the proper expenditure of public funds and the accounting therefore; it deprives the President of essential power needed to discharge his major executive responsibility. Equally important, it deprives the Congress of a really independent audit and review of the fiscal affairs of the Government by an official who has no voice in administrative determinations, which audit is necessary to hold the Administration accountable.

The removal from the Executive of the final authority to determine the uses of appropriations, conditions of employment, the letting of contracts, and the control over administrative decisions, as well as the prescribing of accounting procedures and the vesting of such authority in an officer independent of direct responsibility to the President for his acts, is clearly in violation of the constitutional principle of the division of authority between the Legislative and Executive Branches of the Government. It is contrary to article II, section 3, of the Constitution, which provides that the President "shall take Care that the Laws be faithfully executed."

In the recent case of *Springer* v. *Philippine Islands* (277 U.S. 189), which involved an attempt to vest executive powers in a legislative body, the Supreme Court declared:

> Legislative power, as distinguished from executive power, is the authority to make laws, but not to enforce them or appoint the agents charged with the duty of such enforcement. The latter are executive functions.

The settlement of accounts and the supervision of administrative accounting systems are executive functions; under the Constitution they belong to the Executive Branch of the Government. The audit, by the same reasoning, should operate under legislative direction. The Comptroller General today straddles both positions.

Prior to the adoption of the Budget and Accounting Act of 1921, accounts and claims were settled by the auditors, all of whom were Treasury officials, and the accounting procedures were prescribed by the Comptroller of the Treasury. Strictly speaking, there was no independent audit. When the Congress adopted legislation providing for a National Budget system in 1921, it also provided for an independent auditing office. The hearings on the act, as well as the language of the act itself, indicate clearly that the purpose in creating an independent auditing office was to enable the Congress to secure adequate and full information upon the finances of the Government. Members of the special committees of the House and the Senate complained that the auditors and the Comptroller of the Treasury, being a part of the administration and subject to removal, would not come before congressional committees and criticize the existing financial practices.

Major attention at that time was focused upon the provisions of the act relating to the creation of a National Budget; the far-reaching implications involved in placing the accounting and controlling authority in an auditing officer independent of the Executive were not clearly realized. There was, however, no lack of warning on this point. During the hearings on the act, in 1919, a number of outstanding witnesses who advocated the creation of an independent auditor stated that he should be charged with the sole task of auditing expenditures after they were made and reporting the results of the audit to the Congress. These witnesses expressed grave doubt as to the wisdom of giving to this independent auditing officer the controlling function as well, for this they regarded as unquestionably executive in character. Among those who called attention to this important distinction were men like former Governor Frank O. Lowden of Illinois, Senator Carter Glass (then Secretary of the Treasury), President Frank J. Goodnow of the Johns Hopkins University, President Nicholas Murray Butler of Columbia University, Mr. John T. Pratt, President of the National

Budget Committee, Mr. Henry L. Stimson, later Secretary of State, and Dr. Frederick A. Cleveland.

At various times in the hearings, members of both the House and the Senate committees expressed their own doubts concerning the wisdom of granting controlling and accounting authority to an independent auditor. But the final act transferred to the Comptroller General all the powers formerly exercised by the auditors and by the Comptroller of the Treasury.

Results of Independent Control

The results of placing executive powers of control in an independent auditing office may be reviewed briefly. Before 1921, when the head of a department questioned a ruling of the Comptroller of the Treasury, or when the President requested it, the ruling was referred to the Attorney General for a legal opinion. Since 1921 this practice has been discontinued. An impasse has resulted. The first Comptroller General of the United States consistently refused to submit any disputed question to the Attorney General or to modify any of his rulings in conformance with the opinions of the Attorney General. It is significant that the Attorney General has been sustained repeatedly when the issues were taken to courts of law.

Both the Attorney General and the Comptroller General are directed by the Congress to render opinions or decisions interpreting the meaning of congressional acts. Executive officers customarily turn to the Attorney General when there is any question about the authority or the legality of an action which they are contemplating. The present conflict of authority between these two officers leads to a great deal of uncertainty, delay, and expense, and at times reaches almost to the point of administrative paralysis. Speed, decision, vigor, and common sense in the conduct of national affairs have been subordinated to technical rulings on doubtful questions.

The virtual discontinuance of the practice of referring disputed rulings to the Attorney General for an opinion upon legal issues results in the Comptroller General interpreting his own jurisdiction and the scope of his authority through his own rulings. This is an extraordinary principle, clearly contrary to our political institutions and constitutional theory.

Before 1921 there was comparatively little complaint that the rulings of the Comptroller of the Treasury, precursor of the Comptroller General, encroached upon administrative discretion. This was probably because the Comptroller of the Treasury was a part of the administration itself, even though he had semi-independent status, and because of the practice of referring disputed questions to the Attorney General. From 1921 on, however, the Comptroller General, through numerous rulings, has carried his authority into areas which are clearly in the realm of executive decision. Any volume of the published rulings of the Comptroller General affords a wide variety of examples of this invasion of administrative responsibility. Many of his rulings go far beyond the terms of any statute.

Rulings by an independent auditing officer in the realm of executive action and methods, even when they seem wise and salutary, have a profoundly harmful effect. They dissipate executive responsibility and precipitate executive uncertainty. Many of the rulings of the Comptroller General, though issued in the belief that they are in the interest of strict legality, undoubtedly impede the work of the departments and add to their operating costs. Administrative officers have found it necessary to go not merely to their superior officers for the approval of legality, form, and procedure. This division of authority destroys responsibility and produces delays and uncertainty. It has become increasingly difficult, and at times simply impossible, for the Government to manage its business with dispatch, with efficiency, and with economic sagacity.

An effective continuing executive control over the administration of the Government to insure economy, legality, and expedition is impossible so long as such wide authority over plans, forms, and procedures is exercised by the General Accounting Office. The Comptroller General has also extended his authority into administrative matters by the expansion of the preaudit (i.e., audit before payment), by the increased use of advance decisions, and by his rulings all of which have constantly brought more and more administrative questions to him for final determination. The operating plans of the administration are greatly affected, and sometimes controlled, by his rulings. Fiscal practices are to a large extent governed by his decisions. These are areas of control that are customarily entrusted to executive officers, both in Government and in private business administration.

Numerous delays in administration are inevitable under the current procedures and routines of the General Accounting Office. Every voucher must be examined and passed upon in a single office at the seat of the Government. Final settlements are delayed from a period of 3 months to as long as 3 years after the original transaction has been consummated. Of what value to the Congress or to the administration is an audit which is not completed until after 3 years? Executive officers are unable to obtain accurate current reports on the financial status of their own departments or bureaus. The delay in the audit has also created much uncertainty as to the action. Delays are often expensive. Promptness is essential to vigorous, decisive, and efficient public administration.

Audit of Expenditures

The General Accounting Office has failed to achieve an independent audit of national expenditures. It has not supplied the Congress with the comprehensive information concerning the financial administration of the Government which an audit should render. The Budget and Accounting Act provides that the Comptroller General shall report to the Congress the results of his audit and his investigations into the financial transactions of the Government and states that he "shall specifically report to Congress every expenditure or contract made by any department or establishment in any year in violation of law." Except in a few isolated cases the Comptroller General has not carried out this provision of the act. He has rarely called attention to unwise expenditures or unsound fiscal practices. Since the present arrangement delays the final settlement of accounts, in some cases for as long as 3 years, it is impossible for the Controller General even to complete his audit of any fiscal year in time for it to be of any material value to the Congress.

The fundamental reason why the Comptroller General has failed to provide the Congress with a complete, detailed, and critical audit of the fiscal accounts of the Government, however, is the anomalous and inconsistent position of his office.

The results of the vesting of important executive authority in the Comptroller General, an independent officer, who is not responsible to the Chief Executive, nor, in fact, to the Congress or to the courts, are serious. Effective and responsible management of the executive departments is impossible as long as this unsound and unconstitutional division of executive authority continues. At the same time, the Congress is unable to secure a truly independent audit, which is essential if it is to hold the administration to a strict accountability.

Recommendations

Our recommendations regarding the direction and control of accounting and expenditures are as follows:

1. For the purpose of providing the Chief Executive with the essential vehicles for current financial management and administrative control, the authority to prescribe and supervise accounting systems, forms, and procedures in the Federal establishments should be transferred to and vested in the Secretary of the Treasury. This recommendation is not new. In 1932 President Hoover recommended to the Congress that the power to prescribe accounting systems be transferred to the Executive Branch, stating:

    > It is not, however, a proper function of an establishment created primarily for the purpose of auditing Government accounts to make the necessary studies and to develop and prescribe accounting systems involving the entire field of Government accounting. Neither is it a proper function of such an establishment to prescribe the procedure for nor to determine the effectiveness of the administrative examination of accounts. Accounting is an essential element of effective administration, and it should be developed with the primary objective of serving this purpose.

    In 1934 a special committee of the United States Chamber of Commerce on Federal expenditures, headed by Mr. Matthew S. Sloan, recommended that all accounting activities be removed from the Comptroller General and placed in a General Accounting Office directly responsible to the President. This committee stated in its report:

    > Since the Comptroller General is not under Executive control, as he reports to Congress and is responsible only to that body, the Executive is deprived of one of the most essential means of establishing effective supervision over expenditures, namely, a satisfactory accounting system directly under Executive control. Moreover, the Comptroller General is now in the anomalous position of auditing his own accounting.
    >
    > The Committee is convinced that accounting should be segregated from auditing, and that accounting should be centralized in an agency under the control of the President. Such a system would provide the administration with machinery necessary to establish control over expenditures and also afford Congress an independent agency for checking the fiscal operations of the administration.

2. For the purpose of fixing responsibility for the fiscal management of the Government establishment on the Chief Executive in conformity with the constitutional principle that the President "shall take Care that the Laws be faithfully executed," claims and demands by the Government of the United States or against it and accounts in which the Government of the United States is concerned, either as debtor or as creditor, should be settled and adjusted in the Treasury Department.

3. To avoid conflict and dispute between the Secretary of the Treasury and the departments as to the jurisdiction of the Secretary to settle public accounts, which conflicts and disputes have so marred the relationship between the Comptroller General and the departments in the past, and to make it impossible for the Secretary of the Treasury to usurp any of the powers vested in the heads of departments by the Congress, the Attorney General should be authorized to render opinions on such questions of jurisdiction (but not on the merits of the case) upon the request of the head of the department or upon the request of the Secretary of the Treasury,

and the opinion of the Attorney General on such questions of jurisdiction should be final and binding.

4. In order to conform to the limitations in the functions remaining within the jurisdiction of the Comptroller General, the titles of the Comptroller General and the Assistant Comptroller General should be changed to Auditor General and Assistant Auditor General, respectively, and the name of the General Accounting Office should be changed to the General Auditing Office.

5. The Auditor General should be authorized and required to assign representatives of his office to such stations in the District of Columbia and the field as will enable them currently to audit the accounts of the accountable officers, and they should be required to certify forthwith such exceptions as may be taken to the transactions involved (a) to the officer whose account is involved; (b) to the Auditor General; and (c) to the Secretary of the Treasury.

   The auditing work would thus proceed in a decentralized manner independent of, but practically simultaneous with, disbursement. Duplication of effort and delays due to centralization in Washington could be reduced to a minimum. It would not be necessary for the Treasury Department to duplicate the field audit of the General Auditing Office. Exceptions would be promptly reported to the Treasury. Prompt, efficient service could be afforded in the scrutiny of questioned vouchers and in the review of accounts of disbursing officers.

6. In the event of the failure of the Secretary of the Treasury and the Auditor General to reach an agreement with respect to any exception reported by representatives of the Auditor General concerning any expenditure, it should be the duty of the Auditor General to report such exception to the Congress through such committees or joint committees as the Congress may choose to designate.

3

The Deficit and Long-Term Damage to the Economy

U.S. General Accounting Office

THE DEFICIT OUTLOOK

Federal budget deficits have grown in the decades since World War II. They remain imbedded in the budget as a result of rapidly rising mandated spending supported by relatively flat revenue growth. Understanding the definition and measurement of deficits, their components, and their resistance to reduction measures is critical to the process of eliminating them.

Deficits Have Increased Rapidly Since the 1950s

During the 1950s, the federal deficit averaged less than 1 percent of GNP. By the 1970s, the average was 2.3 percent. Then in the 1980s it doubled to 4.1 percent. This year—fiscal year 1992—the deficit is expected to reach 6.3 percent of GNP before dropping back. CBO projects 1990s deficits averaging 4.0 percent over the decade. (See Fig. 1.)[1]

Although at its simplest the deficit is the gap between outlays and receipts, identifying its causes requires disaggregation of the two sides of the deficit. (See Fig. 2.) Revenues have grown slightly—from 17.6 percent of GNP in the 1950s to 18.9 percent in the 1990s—but the nature of the revenue stream has changed significantly. Outlays have not only increased—from 18.1 percent to 22.9 percent—but also have changed in composition. These composition changes have major implications for attempts to reduce the deficit.

Growth in Social Insurance Receipts Masks Decline in Other Revenues

Total receipts remained stable as a share of GNP because the increase in social insurance receipts—from 2.1 percent of GNP in the 1950s to 7.2 percent of GNP in the 1990s—was nearly matched by a decline in corporate income and excise tax revenues (from 7.3 percent to 2.4 percent). (See Fig. 3.)

Source: GAO/OCG-92-2 Budget Policy.

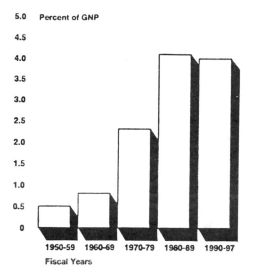

Figure 1 Average deficit by decade (1950–1997). (From *Budget of the U.S. Government*, 1950–91; CBO projections, 1992–97).

The decline in corporate income tax receipts as a share of GNP largely reflects the contraction of corporate profit as a component of national income. Over the 40-year period from 1950 to 1990, corporate profits, as measured in the national income accounts, dropped from 14.9 percent of GNP to 5.5 percent. Several factors are advanced as explanations for this drop in the corporate tax base:[2] rising interest rates and, more recently, increasing debt-to-equity ratios reduced corporate profits. Rate reductions and increased business investment tax preferences also contributed to the relative decline in revenue from the corporate profits tax.

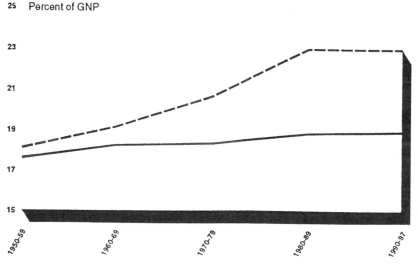

Figure 2 Total revenues (——) and outlays (- - - -) (1950–1997). (From *Budget of the U.S. Government*, 1950–91; CBO projections, 1992–97.)

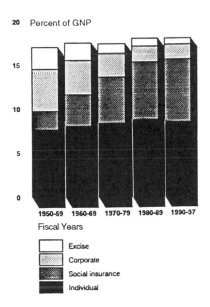

Figure 3   Revenues by source (1950–1997). Excludes other receipts that do not exceed 1 percent of GNP. Receipts for Medicare in 1996. (From *Budget of the U.S. Government,* 1950–91; CBO projections, 1992–97.)

The decline in excise tax revenues may be largely attributable to the excise tax structure. Instead of a percentage of the item's price, excise taxes tend to be set at a fixed dollar amount, and these amounts have not kept up with inflation.[3]

Although personal income tax receipts have been relatively stable since the 1950s, the design of that tax has changed. Rates were lowered in the 1980s, but the tax base was broadened as part of the tax reform package of 1986. In addition, the 1981 tax law's indexing of tax brackets, the standard deduction, and the personal exemption have meant that inflation no longer causes receipts to rise automatically as a percent of GNP. Although rate reductions thus far account for greater revenue losses than bracket indexing, the latter may exert more long-range effects on personal income tax receipts.

The growth in social insurance receipts—which take the form of payroll taxes—has been driven by Social Security. (See Fig. 4.) Social Security payroll tax revenues have grown from 1.4 percent of GNP during the 1950s to a projected 5.3 percent in the 1990s. This in turn is largely a function of rising payroll tax rates which have quadrupled in 40 years—from 3.0 percent of taxable wages in 1950 to 12.6 percent in 1991.[4]

Medicare has been a lesser contributor to the growth in social insurance receipts. Since its inception in 1966, Medicare's dedicated payroll tax has provided the majority of the program's funding. The tax is projected to equal 1.4 percent of GNP in the 1990s.

Defense and Other Discretionary Outlays Declined While Mandatory Outlays Grew Rapidly

Nondefense outlays increased from 7.4 percent of GNP in the 1950s to 18.5 percent in the 1990s. (See Fig. 5.)

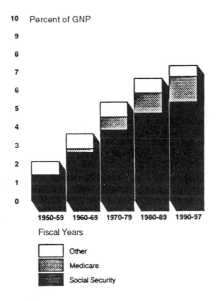

Figure 4 Social insurance revenues (1950–1997). Receipts for Medicare began in 1966. (From *Budget of the U.S. Government*, 1950–91; CBO projections, 1992–97.)

It is informative to further divide these outlays into discretionary and mandatory outlays. Since 1962,[5] mandatory outlays have risen from an average of 5.9 percent of GNP in the 1960s to 12.8 percent in the 1980s, and to 14.4 percent in the early 1990s. (See Fig. 6.) In contrast, discretionary outlays have fallen from 13.2 percent of GNP in the 1960s to 10.1 percent of GNP in the 1980s, and 9.3 percent in 1990–1992.

The programs contributing most to the mandatory growth include Social Security, Medicare, Medicaid, net interest, and, most recently, the costs associated with thrift and banking failures.

The nonmedical Social Security programs (Old Age Survivors and Disability Insurance [OASDI]) dominated this trend, increasing from 1.2 percent of GNP in the 1950s to 4.8 percent in the 1980s. OASDI is projected to remain stable as a share of GNP in the 1990s and beyond, and will not resume its growth until the baby boom begins to retire in 2010.

Medicare has become the fastest growing large program in the budget; it has gone from 0.2 percent at its inception in 1966 to a projected 2.2 percent of GNP in the 1990s. (See Fig. 7.)

Medicaid, although a small proportion of mandatory outlays, grew from 0.1 percent of GNP in 1966 to 0.9 percent in 1991. Much of this growth occurred in the late 1980s and shows no signs of abating in the future. With the slowing of Social Security's growth in the 1980s, Medicare and Medicaid have become two of the primary drivers of the recent growth in outlays.

Net interest costs have also played a large role in recent outlay growth. As a share of GNP, interest payments have grown from 1.3 percent in the 1950s to a projected 3.5 percent in the 1990s. Interest has absorbed an ever greater share of federal spending, growing from an average of 7.3 percent of federal outlays in the 1950s to 13.8 percent in 1992.

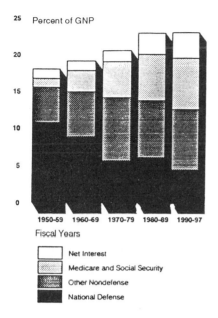

Figure 5 Outlays by function (1950–1997). Outlays for Medicare began in 1966. (From *Budget of the U.S. Government*, 1950–91; CBO projections, 1992–97.)

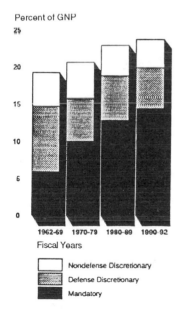

Figure 6 Mandatory and discretionary outlays (1962–1992). (From *Budget of the U.S. Government*, 1950–91; CBO projections, 1992–97.)

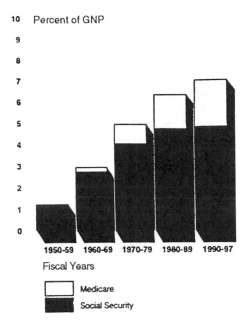

Figure 7 Medicare and Social Security outlays (1950–1997). Outlays for Medicare began in 1966. (From *Budget of the U.S. Government*, 1950–91; CBO projections, 1992–97.)

Growth of public debt is responsible in part for the steep rise in interest costs over the last decade. From the 1950s through the 1960s, even as the average deficit was increasing from 0.4 percent to 0.8 percent of GNP, federal debt held by the public fell from 82 percent to 30 percent of GNP. Although the average deficit more than doubled again in the 1970s, the debt-to-GNP ratio continued dropping to 26 percent in 1979, as the economy grew more rapidly than the debt. By the end of the 1980s, however, these trends reversed and the debt-to-GNP ratio grew to almost 43 percent of GNP. That, coupled with the high real interest rates of the 1980s, created the sharp increase in interest costs.

Given the rapid outlay growth in entitlements and mandatory programs, only the sharp decline in discretionary outlays prevented even larger deficits. Defense discretionary outlays dropped from 8.8 percent of GNP in the 1960s to 5.5 percent in the early 1990s, accounting for most of the 3.9 percentage point drop in discretionary outlays as a percentage of GNP.

The message from these budget trends is ominous. The only area of real revenue growth—social insurance receipts—supports primarily trust fund activities. General revenues have in fact declined as a percent of GNP. Meanwhile, mandatory costs financed from general revenues—interest, Medicaid, and the general fund subsidy for Medicare—have grown such that they have overwhelmed offsetting discretionary reductions and placed a growing demand on slower-growing receipts. Deficits become embedded in such a fiscal system.

The Structural Deficit Shows Cyclical Economic Change Is Not to Blame

In the short term, the deficit is highly sensitive to economic conditions. In other words, the deficit increases or decreases with changes in economic activity. This cyclical deficit—the deficit that is a function of the business cycle—should be less of a cause for concern than the structural deficit, the deficit remaining after removing the effects of cyclical factors. Focusing on the structural deficit allows us to separate out the impact of the economic downturn on the budget deficit.

Trends in the structural deficit show a growing problem. CBO estimates of that deficit have been rising. Even excluding deposit insurance outlays, which can be viewed as one-time needs, the structural deficit has risen from 2.8 percent of GNP in 1989 to 3.6 percent in 1992. Although the increase is not as steep as that of the total cash deficit, the structural deficit figures demonstrate that not all the recent growth in the cash deficit can be attributed to economic conditions and deposit insurance outlays.

Trust Fund Surpluses Mask the Full Extent of the Federal Funds Deficit

The unified budget[6] measures the cash position of the U.S. government. It is a fairly accurate measure of the economic impact of the deficit, but it masks the composition of that deficit and hence—in today's budget—understates the need for action. Separating trust funds financed by dedicated taxes or contributions from activities financed by general revenues and borrowing—the federal funds portion—gives a clearer picture of the source of the problem.

Social Security and other retirement trust funds have run large surpluses. Inclusion of the trust funds in deficit calculations has therefore masked the federal funds deficit. For example, in 1991, the reported total deficit of $268.7 billion actually represented the net effect of a $112.3 billion trust fund surplus and a $381.0 billion deficit in the rest of government. The federal funds deficit has also grown much faster than the unified deficit, mushrooming from less than 1 percent of GNP in 1960 to about 7 percent of GNP in 1985. (See Fig. 8.)

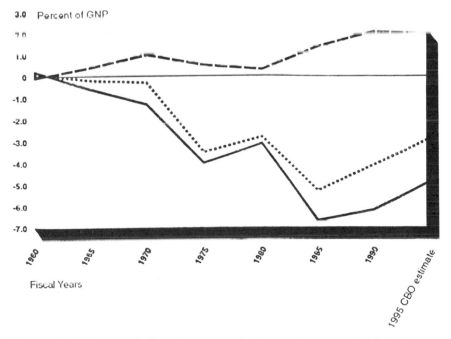

Figure 8 Federal funds (———), trust funds (– – – –), and total deficits/surpluses (- - - - - - - -) (1960–1995). (From *Budget of the U.S. Government,* 1950–91; CBO projections, 1992–97.)

Previous GAO reports[7] have discussed this issue in greater detail, demonstrating that federal fiscal problems are a manifestation of the large and growing federal fund deficits. Unless the imbalance in this part of the budget is addressed, real progress on the deficit will be unlikely in the immediate future.

Recent Legislative Attempts to Control the Deficit

Gramm–Rudman–Hollings Legislation Proved Ineffective

The Balanced Budget and Emergency Deficit Control Act of 1985, Public Law 99-177, also known as Gramm–Rudman–Hollings (GRH), attempted to eliminate the deficit by setting declining annual deficit targets. GRH provided for automatic, across-the-board spending reductions—sequestration—if the deficit targets were exceeded. GAO has criticized the GRH procedures for leading not to meaningful deficit reduction, but rather to a whole new generation of off-budget and other misleading practices that hid the true magnitude of the deficit problem. When even these practices failed to avoid sequestration, the deficit targets were simply revised, and the date for achieving a balanced budget was postponed. Thus, instead of the government reaching a balanced budget in fiscal year 1991, the original GRH target, the deficit reached record levels.

GRH not only failed to reduce the deficit, its enforcement measures were incapable of controlling those areas responsible for deficit growth. Most of the increases in the deficit under GRH were a function of the costs of savings and loan failures, rising interest costs, and a weakening economy, which led to much lower revenues and somewhat higher spending on mandatory programs. GRH had exempted major entitlement programs (for example, Social Security and Medicaid) from sequestration and limited the cuts that could be imposed on others, such as Medicare. Under GRH, the sequester "axe" thus fell most heavily on annually appropriated discretionary spending. This relatively narrow "sequestrable base" (about 28 percent of the budget) meant that, as the deficit grew, the rate of sequester required to reach the GRH target exceeded levels deemed acceptable (or even possible) and did not address the underlying causes of deficit growth.

OBRA Changes Focus of Budget Control

Passage of the Omnibus Budget Reconciliation Act of 1990 (OBRA), Public Law 101-508, changed the focus of budget control from the overall deficit level to current spending and tax decisions. In doing so it both increased the complexity of the budget process and offered what appeared to be a more effective approach to deficit reduction. OBRA put into law an agreement between the legislative and executive branches to achieve $482 billion in budgetary savings over a 5-year period. The Budget Enforcement Act of 1990 (BEA), Title XIII of OBRA, constrains appropriations to comply with established limits and prevents most new legislation from adding to the deficit. Although BEA has tempered spending growth, deficits have grown nonetheless.

BEA modified budget enforcement procedures to ensure future fiscal discipline. In contrast to the previous GRH enforcement procedure, BEA is not designed to control the deficit directly, at least through fiscal year 1993. Instead, BEA sets caps on discretionary spending (both budget authority and outlays) for defense, international, and domestic appropriations.[8] In addition, BEA requires that legislated increases in mandatory spending authorized in substantive law or cuts in taxes be offset by reductions in other mandatory programs or by revenue increases.

However, BEA attempts to control only the effects of annual appropriations and legislated changes or additions to mandatory programs. It does not require offsets for mandatory program increases or revenue decreases driven by inflation, recession, growth in the numbers of people eligible for a program, or the other external factors that influence mandatory spending programs and revenues under existing law. Thus, BEA shares with GRH the lack of a mechanism for controlling or reducing deficits embedded in the system because of the combination of past decisions—existing program design for mandatory programs, tax rates and coverage, or interest on the existing debt.

For fiscal years 1994 and 1995, BEA establishes a single cap on *total* discretionary spending. The distribution of discretionary spending among categories, and hence the distribution of the spending cuts required, has been left for the President and the Congress to determine.[9]

According to CBO's March 1992 estimates,[10] in nominal dollars, achieving the 1993 discretionary spending limits require budget authority cuts of an estimated $13.2 billion in defense programs and $6.5 billion in domestic programs. Total cuts in discretionary budget authority required to comply with the spending limits are estimated to be $58.6 billion in 1995. Figure 9 illustrates the growing gap between BEA limits and baseline projections.

Budget authority cuts of this magnitude will be difficult, whatever the distribution among the categories and programs. If the President and the Congress cannot make the cuts required to conform to BEA spending limits, sequestration would be mandated.

BEA therefore restricts fiscal policy options. If policymakers abide by BEA's enforcement procedures, and do not invoke provisions allowing emergency spending increases or tax cuts, they forego the option of providing new, short-term economic stimulus in response to recession. However, they would also avoid adding to the already huge federal deficit. This dilemma illustrates one of the negative effects of large federal deficits. Without the current deficit problem, policymakers would have much more flexibility to pursue anti-recession fiscal policies or meet other, currently unfunded public needs.

Deficits Could Explode In the Next Century

The negotiations that led to OBRA were aimed at significant deficit reduction. However, a weakening economy and increasing expenditures to protect the depositors of failed thrift institutions eroded the effect of the legislated savings. Other factors such as technical reestimates and some legislation have increased the deficit as well. Table 1 compared CBO's estimates of the deficit prepared shortly after OBRA was enacted with current CBO and OMB baseline projections. CBO's most recent baseline projections show deficits declining from 1992 levels to approximately $200 billion by 1995, around 3 percent of GNP. Although OBRA will not produce deficits as low as the authors of the law anticipated, its implementation constrains what might otherwise have been much larger deficits.

For the remainder of the 1990s, CBO projects baseline deficits of approximately 3 percent of GNP. Longer-run CBO baseline projections suggest deficits will rise to around 4 percent of GNP by the year 2002.

Because CBO baseline projections reflect the continuation of current policies under current law, the results unsurprisingly suggest no dramatic change. Baseline projections show significant change only when analysts anticipate large irregular expenditures within current legal authority or significant economic swings. Such conditions are relatively rare—the results of outlays covering losses by thrift institutions, for a recent example—and are especially difficult to quantify. Current CBO projections do not foresee any other swings of this sort in the next decade.

GAO analysis, however, identifies a danger that, if current policies continue, federal expenditures could exceed 40 percent of GNP and deficits could explode to 20 percent of GNP by the year 2020. These projections, which, like CBO baselines, assume current

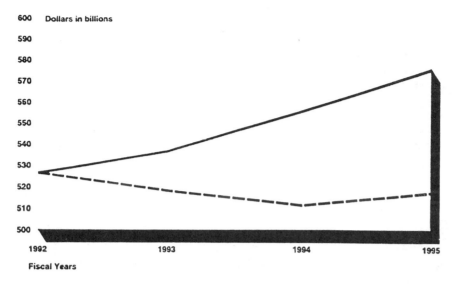

Figure 9 Total discretionary budget authority (1992–1995): CBO baseline (——) and spending caps (- - - -). (From CBO projections.)

policies under current law, differ from CBO figures in that they extend for almost 30 years and they incorporate the negative effect of deficit spending on long-term economic performance. The deficit's steep increase after 2010 (see Fig. 10) reflects the symbiotic relationship of the growing debt and the increased interest costs associated with financing it, as well as rising retirement and health care costs. In the GAO model, however, this is happening in the environment of an economy which is growing ever more slowly due to the debilitating effect of the deficits on national saving and investment, and which actually contracts in the final years of the projection period.

Although these projections present what some would consider an economic extreme, they do represent the logical extension of current tax and spending policies. The model assumes no policy reaction, however, even as rapidly increasing debt begins to cripple the economy. This is unlikely. Heightened sensitivity to the implications of rising deficits, as evidenced most recently by the passage of OBRA, suggests that policymakers might not allow this to happen. Furthermore, external events, for example, the international reaction to a deteriorating U.S. economy and rapidly rising international debt, would be likely to force action before 2020. Nevertheless's GAO's projections illustrate that preventing eco-

Table 1 CBO and OMB Deficit Baseline Projections, Dollars in Billions

	Fiscal Year				
	1991	1992	1993	1994	1995
CBO December 1990 estimates	−253	−252	−170	−56	−29
CBO February 1992 estimates[a]	−269	−368	−336	−267	−203
OMB February 1992 estimates[a]	−269	−400	−350	−212	−194

[a]OMB and CBO figures represent actual 1991 results.

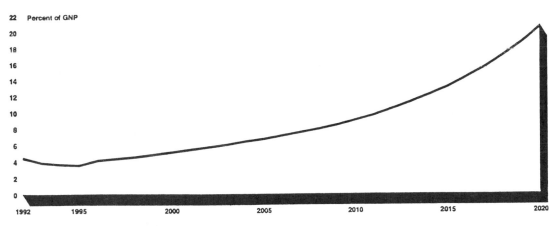

Figure 10 No action scenario budget deficits (1992–2020).

nomic and fiscal catastrophe will require significant and continuing deficit reduction well into the next century.

ECONOMIC POLICY CONSIDERATIONS

There are continuing discussions on the budget deficit, its effect on the economy, and how to measure it. The issue is not a simple one. The deficit is the net result of many transactions that affect receipts and outlays. The economic impact of those transactions may vary and the composition of them may change. Other economic factors, such as private saving and the availability of foreign capital may affect the impact of the deficit on the economy. Nevertheless, in our view, large and continued deficits are likely to seriously inhibit the growth of the economy under current and presently foreseeable economic conditions.

In this section, we discuss the sources of economic growth to provide a context for understanding why deficits matter. We then review evidence on the recent history of saving, investment, and productivity growth in the U.S. economy and identify points at which the budget deficit may have shaped that history.

Sources of Economic Growth

Economic growth is not a simple matter. Numerous factors contribute to growth, and the relationships among them are complex and not fully understood. Ultimately, no action available at the federal level can guarantee success in the quest for improved economic performance; the economy is simply too big and there are too many decision makers involved for that to be possible. The task for federal policy in promoting growth is to provide a supportive context in which other actors—including individuals, business firms, state and local governments, and nonprofit organizations—can identify and pursue opportunities for economic advance.

To accomplish this, the federal government must first seek to adhere to the old medical maxim, "first of all, do no harm." This is a nontrivial challenge in view of the complexity and unpredictability of the economic system, the many ways in which the system's performance falls short of what might be desired, and the wealth of ideas advanced for attempting to improve that performance in one way or another. The second challenge for the federal government is to perform efficiently and effectively the many important tasks that other parts of the system cannot do, such as providing macroeconomic stability, assuring national security, and dealing with a wide range of problems where effective policies are possible only at the national level. In carrying out these tasks, federal activity sometimes affects economic growth directly, and almost always affects it indirectly.

In the following discussion, we address in turn the main sources of economic growth that have been identified in the economics literature.[11]

Increased Labor Input

Over extended periods, the nation's total output tends to rise with its population. This is because a larger population can generally provide greater labor input to production. The correspondence between population and labor input is not, however, precise. In projecting labor input, it is necessary to take account of changing demographic patterns that affect the relative proportions of potential workers and other groups in the population. For example, the growing proportion of women in the work force has been a major factor since the end of World War II. The long-run outlook for the American economy now includes a marked rise in the ratio of the retired population to the working population beginning in about 2010. A number of factors besides demographics also affect overall rates of participation in the labor force. Unemployment and other sources of change in hours worked per member of the labor force also enter the picture. Finally, the economy's ability to translate increased hours worked into increased output is affected by its ability to provide the other sources of growth identified below. Sufficiently serious deficiencies in these other areas can mean that output trends down as population trends up.

Although the ability to maintain standards of living for an ever-rising population is not something that should be taken for granted, most of the discussion of economic growth has been concerned with the sources of growth in output per capita, or, more precisely, per hour worked. Growth in these terms is much more directly related to rising standards of living than is growth in total output. Achieving such growth means increasing the productivity of labor—getting more output per hour worked.

Capital Accumulation

Workers produce more per hour when they have more and better equipment to work with—and also more and better skills to permit them to work that equipment effectively. This general point can be well illustrated by mundane examples: Consider the transformation of ditch-digging from a relatively slow and somewhat imprecise process involving several ordinary shovels, much human energy, and low skill levels to a faster and more precise process often involving a single power digger controlled by an appropriately skilled operator. The difference between an advanced industrial economy with a high standard of living and a less developed country with a low standard of living can be largely described in terms of the elements of this example, varied in the details and repeated across millions of individual tasks.

Publicly owned capital can play a vital role in economic growth, increasing the productivity of private capital and labor. The classic example is transportation infrastructure. It is generally recognized, for example, that the development of our national highway system made a substantial contribution to the growth of productivity in the United States in this century.

If standards of living are to advance, the economy must meet some minimum standards in terms of its levels of investment in physical and human capital. Equipment that wears out must be replaced; younger workers entering the labor force have the time but need also the skills to replace what is being lost as older workers retire. If the labor force itself is growing—as it has for all but brief intervals in American economic history—a more demanding requirement is implied. Not only must depreciation be made good, but the additional workers of the new generation must be trained and equipped to a standard comparable to that of the old. Otherwise, output per worker, and living standards, may fall.

Improved Products and Processes

As just noted, the accumulation of physical capital provides workers with more and *better* equipment. The availability of better equipment is a reflection of the advance of technological knowledge that underlies the ability to design and produce such equipment. The growth of technology also makes possible the development of better products generally—better materials and better consumer goods, for example.

Since the late 18th century, economic possibilities have been expanded enormously through interacting advances in technology, science, and economic organization. This fundamental dynamic continues to transform the economies of the advanced industrial countries at what seems to be an ever-increasing rate. From the viewpoint of consumers around the world, this fierce international competition in the creation of new products and processes is almost always beneficial.

To producers, it poses a major challenge. Success and prosperity go to those individuals, business firms, and national economies that remain at or near the leading edge of technological and organizational advance. Maintaining such a position requires sustained and effective action by government at all levels, as well as by the private sector. It can be impaired by allowing primary and secondary education to deteriorate, or by neglecting to invest research and development effort in areas that do not attract private investors but nevertheless provide crucially important foundations for future economic growth.

Improved Resource Allocation

Economic growth typically involves extended periods in which labor and capital inputs are shifted out of some categories of use and into others where they are more productive or the need for them is more urgent. In American economic history, two great episodes of this type stand out: the settling of the continent with the westward movement of the frontier and the subsequent decline in the farm population as improved productivity in agriculture freed labor and capital for other uses. This sort of redeployment of productive resources is going on all the time, though not on the same grand scale. It is a vitally important process in economic growth and one that can be stalemated by faulty public policies that inappropriately interfere with the mobility of labor and capital.

Adequate Physical and Social Infrastructure

In economically advanced countries, private economic activity goes forward in an environment of services and resources that are largely provided by units of government or by regulated enterprises. Examples include not only elements of physical infrastructure such as highways, airports, air traffic control, and water and sewer systems but also elements of the social infrastructure that provide public safety, adjudication of disputes, regulation of financial institutions for safety and soundness, control of environmental hazards, and many other services.

The facilities and systems that provide these services are subject to deterioration and breakdown as a result of congestion, overload, and neglect. They typically come to the forefront in discussions of economic growth only when these stress conditions arise, and they are then perceived as obstacles to growth because they are inadequate or malfunctioning. Growth proceeds smoothly with adequate infrastructure as its unobtrusive backdrop.

Improved Organization and Management

The underlying relationships that determine the output obtainable from a given collection of inputs are partly matters of technology, but they are also matters of organization and management. In recent years, it has become increasingly clear that differing approaches to the tasks of management are a key determinant of differences in the effectiveness of business firms and other organizations.[12] An economy that lags in the adoption of demonstrably effective management approaches is as much disadvantaged in international competition as one that lags in the adoption of advanced technology.

Role of Expectations

Although "wishing will not make it so," the prospects for economic growth are enhanced when expectations regarding the future are favorable and encouraging to investors. Conversely, there is a real possibility that fear of the economic future can close off paths to economic advance that would otherwise be available. When the economies of cities, regions, or nations fall into distress, a self-reinforcing cycle of pessimism can set in. Initial distress erodes the tax base, causing governments to cut services and raise taxes. This directly reduces the profitability of investment and prompts fears of further policy moves of the same sort. The unfavorable outlook for investment then further erodes the tax base, renewing the cycle. For this reason, strong early action that lends credibility to a claim that "the worst is behind us" may yield results superior to those generated by the message "we will try to muddle through on the basis of current policy." The latter stance may lead investors to hedge their bets against the possibility that the promised narrow escape from policy change cannot be delivered—thus increasing the chance that it cannot in fact be delivered.

From this discussion it is apparent that government at all levels plays an important role in economic growth, from the education and training of the work force to the support of basic research, to the provision of the public infrastructure within which the private sector operates. The federal government has major responsibilities in each of these areas. . . . In addition, the federal government has unique responsibilities for assuring economic stability and an overall economic climate conducive to growth and development. It is in this arena that the federal budget deficit is of vital importance.

Why Deficits Matter

Deficits are likely to reduce long-run growth primarily because they consume private domestic savings that otherwise would be available to finance productive investment. The more the federal government borrows to finance the deficit, the lower the national saving rate is likely to be.

The federal government is simply one of the many entities in the economy that can add to or draw from the national savings pool. If the total savings of all the other entities in the economy is assumed constant, a federal budget deficit absorbs national savings as a matter of simple arithmetic. We believe that this simple proposition is generally a reliable guide to the economic impact of budget deficits in the long term. The statement must be qualified, however, by a recognition that there are circumstances in which the savings of other entities might *not* remain constant when the federal deficit changes. For example, when the economy is in recession and its productive capacity is underutilized, a reduction in the budget deficit may depress economic activity generally, causing other actors to save less. In the macroeconomic simulations presented in our previous report,[13] we found indications that deficit reduction induced some offsetting reduction in private savings. In the short term, the private saving decline offset as much as a third of the federal saving increase.

It is sometimes argued that, in response to increased government deficits, private saving will increase in anticipation of future taxes that will be imposed to pay the interest on increased government debt. While an effect of this type might occur in some circumstances, it appears unlikely that the effect would be of substantial magnitude under typical conditions. Casual examination of the experience of the 1980s provides no support for the view that deficits are offset by private saving, and academic research on the question has reached the same conclusion.

Finally, the impact of saving on economic growth depends critically on what is done with the savings. If the particular investments financed are not chosen by sound economic criteria, the benefits in terms of economic growth may not be realized. If the overall social, political, and economic environment is not conducive to investment, the savings may flow abroad to finance investment opportunities elsewhere.

Review of Recent Experience

Since the 1960s, the federal deficit has absorbed an increasing proportion of net national savings. (See Fig. 11.) During the 1960s, the budget deficit absorbed approximately 2 percent of net national savings generated by the private sector and state and local governments. During the 1970s, the federal deficit absorbed 19 percent of the net saving of other sectors. By the 1980s, nearly one-half (48 percent) of that savings was needed to finance the budget deficit. This trend continues: In 1990 the deficit absorbed 58 percent of net national savings from the rest of the economy.

Foreign savings can also finance domestic investment. This takes place not only through direct investment by foreigners in U.S. assets, but also when foreigners increase their holdings of U.S. securities and other financial investments. For example, when foreigners help

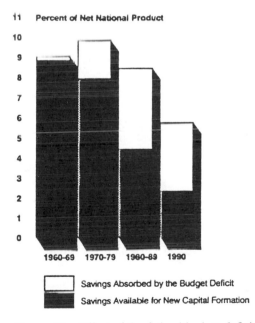

11   **Percent of Net National Product**

Savings Absorbed by the Budget Deficit

Savings Available for New Capital Formation

Figure 11   Effect of the federal budget deficit on net national savings (1960–1990). (From *Economic Report of the President*, February 1992.)

finance the budget deficit through purchase of government securities, some net national savings is freed up for investment in physical capital.

Foreign savings have been an important source of funds during the past decade, and without them U.S. investment would have experienced a greater decline. The problem with investment financed from abroad is that the United States must ultimately pay dividends or interest to the foreign owners of the assets involved. Nevertheless, if net national savings are insufficient to take full advantage of the investment opportunities in the economy, it is helpful to have foreign investment fill the gap. Activities financed by such investment bid for U.S. labor, land, and other resources. In that process, some of the returns from foreign-financed activity accrue to U.S. citizens.

Investment

Since 1984, U.S. domestic investment has been relatively weak. In 1990, gross private domestic investment was only 14.5 percent of GNP, compared to 19 percent in 1984. But even this low level of investment was not being met by gross saving. In fact, gross saving has been insufficient to finance domestic investment in every year since 1983. Figure 12 shows this trend. The gap between gross saving and private domestic investment since 1982 represents capital inflows from abroad. Foreign capital bridged the gap between investment and savings, and allowed domestic investment to remain above the level that gross saving alone would have permitted.

Figure 13 shows the effect of recent U.S. reliance on foreign capital on the balance of debt and equity claims between the United States and the rest of the world.[14] The net international investment position of the United States deteriorated between 1982 and 1989. A slight improvement occurred in 1990, but the balance remained adverse to the United States to the sum of approximately $412 billion.

The budget deficit and low saving appear to have contributed to high real interest rates. Figure 14 shows the historical pattern of real interest rates.[15] Real rates have fallen since 1984 and particularly in response to the current recession; however, longer-term rates have remained above historical norms. High real rates increase the cost of investment, decrease

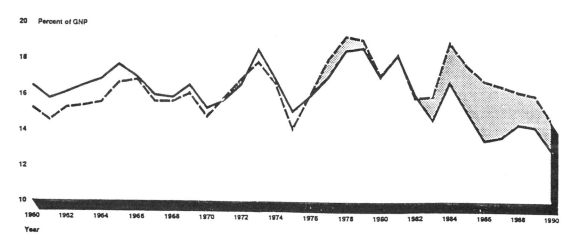

Figure 12   Gross saving (———) and gross domestic investment (- - - -) (1960–1990). (From *Economic Report of the President,* February 1992.)

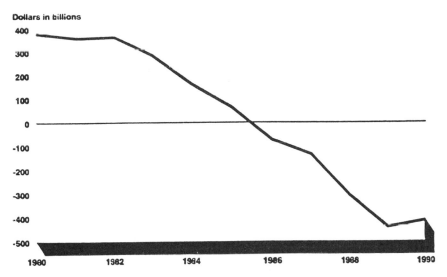

Figure 13 U.S. net international investment position (1980–1990). (From *Survey of Current Business,* June 1991.)

the accumulation of capital, inhibit economic growth, and ultimately reduce the standard of living.

The continued U.S. reliance on foreign capital also raises concerns about future real interest rates. Recent studies have pointed to a current worldwide shortage of saving.[16] The competing demands of the industrial and developing world, reconstruction of Kuwait, German reunification, and reform in Eastern Europe and the Commonwealth of Independent States are not likely to be met by the current rate of saving in the international community. Without a commensurate rise in the availability of global savings, real interest rates are predicted to rise further. These new demands could draw foreign capital away from the United States unless checked by a further increase in U.S. interest rates.

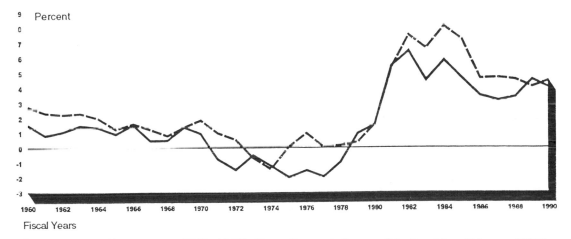

Figure 14 Real interest rates (1960–1990). (From *Economic Report of the President,* February 1992.)

Productivity Growth

Figure 15 examines trends in real wages between 1951 and 1991. The steady rise in average hourly earnings between 1951 and 1973 coincides with high productivity growth of 2.3 percent.[17] The stagnation in real average hourly earnings that began in 1973 correlates to the slowdown in productivity growth that occurred at the same time. In 1991, a recession year, real wages dipped slightly below their 1964 level. A somewhat more favorable picture is presented by trends in total compensation, which includes fringe benefits. However, the rise in fringe benefits is partly associated with rising costs of health care.

In the 1980s, U.S. saving and productivity growth were lower than during the period 1960 and 1973. Compared to seven large industrialized countries in the Organization for Economic Cooperation and Development (OECD),[18] the United States had the lowest average labor productivity growth and the lowest saving rate during 1960 through 1988. Figure 16 shows this comparison and suggests that those countries which grow are those which save.[19] While the very long-term relationship between saving and productivity growth remains controversial among economists, there is little reason to doubt that a rise in the U.S. saving rate will yield significant productivity gains over a span of a few decades. . . .

WEIGHING THE ALTERNATIVES

Some action to address the deficit problem is required. Action that is stronger and taken sooner yields greater long-range benefits in a number of dimensions of economic performance and fiscal soundness. But such action also involves a larger measure of difficult choices and sacrifices in the near term. . . .

Demographics argue for action early. Today, the baby boom generation is in its prime working years. Forty-nine percent of the population is in the labor force. By the year 2020 that share will have fallen to 44 percent. Most of the baby boom generation will have retired. . . . These trends increase pressures on the budget and on the next generation to finance the Social Security benefits for a larger population of elderly. The pain of deficit reduction can be more easily borne if spread across a large working population. Furthermore, action taken early pays benefits in terms of economic growth. A strongly growing

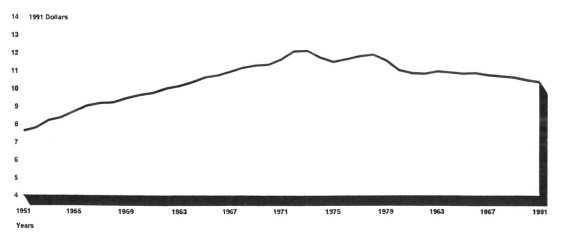

Figure 15 Average hourly earnings (1951–1991). (From *Economic Report of the President,* February 1992.)

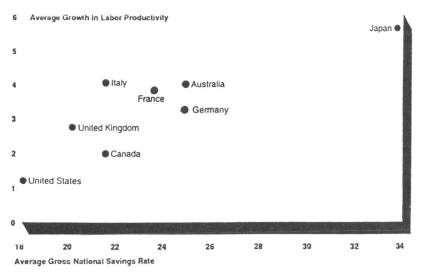

Figure 16 Relationship between gross national saving rate and productivity growth (1960–1988). (From Organization for Economic Cooperation and Development.)

economy can support both present commitments to a growing elderly population and a rising living standard for the future working population.

NOTES

1. Averages for the 1990s in Fig. 1 represent budget actuals for 1990 and 1991, and CBO projections for 1992 through 1997.
2. See, for example, C. Eugene Steuerle, *The Tax Decade: How Taxes Came to Dominate the Public Agenda* (Washington, D.C.: The Urban Institute Press, 1992) and James M. Poterba, "Why Didn't the Tax Reform Act of 1986 Raise Corporate Taxes?" National Bureau of Economic Research, Inc., Working Paper No. 3940, December 1991.
3. For a more detailed discussion of excise tax trends, see *Tax Policy: Revenue Potential of Restoring Excise Taxes to Past Levels* (GAO/GGD-89-52, May 1989).
4. Payroll tax rates include both employer and employee shares.
5. OMB reports mandatory and discretionary outlay categories only as far back as 1962.
6. The unified budget defines the deficit as the difference between total cash revenues and cash outlays for the federal government.
7. *The Budget Deficit: Outlook, Implications, and Choices* (GAO/OCG-90-5, September 12, 1990) and *Social Security: The Trust Fund Reserve Accumulation, the Economy, and the Federal Budget* (GAO/HRD-89-44, January 19, 1989).
8. Discretionary programs are funded through appropriation acts.
9. For the purposes of BEA, the three separate categories cease to exist after fiscal year 1993. We use the term category in regard to fiscal years 1994 and 1995 to refer to the set of programs included previously in each category by BEA.
10. Congressional Budget Office, *An Analysis of the President's Budgetary Proposals for Fiscal Year 1993*, p. 145.
11. The discussion here draws on various sources in the scholarly literature on economic growth, but particularly on Nicholas Stern, "The Determinants of Growth," *The Economic Journal*, vol. 101 (January 1991), pp. 122–133.

12. For a discussion of recent developments in this area, see *Management Practices: U.S. Companies Improve Performance Through Quality Efforts* (GAO/NSIAD-91-190, May 2, 1991).
13. See appendix I in *Budget Deficit: Appendixes on Outlook, Implications, and Choices* (GAO/OCG-90-5A, September 28, 1990).
14. Data reflected in this figure show U.S. investment abroad and foreign investment in the United Sates stated at current cost, or replacement cost, consistent with data from the Bureau of Economic Analysis (Department of Commerce) and the Federal Reserve Board on U.S. reproducible wealth and U.S. domestic wealth, respectively. The prior measurement problem of undervaluation of older U.S. owned assets versus recent foreign investment was rectified in 1991.
15. Real interest rates are nominal rates adjusted for inflation. The real interest rate for a given year is calculated as that year's average nominal rate deflated by the average annual change in the GDP deflator between the years before and after the one for which the interest rate applies.
16. International Monetary Fund, *World Economic Outlook, 1991.*
17. The recent comprehensive revision of the National Income and Product Accounts by the Department of Commerce has not been completed for the period 1951 through 1959.
18. The OECD includes Japan, Australia, New Zealand, and most industrialized countries in Western Europe and North America.
19. OECD's definition of saving (shown here) differs in its treatment of government capital from the NIPA definition. . . .

4

The 1990–91 Recession in Historical Perspective

Stephen K. McNees

The recession that began in mid 1990 has become perhaps the most noteworthy macroeconomic event of recent years. It coincided with, and was influenced by, several unusual events—the Persian Gulf War, the "credit crunch," and the "restructuring" phenomenon. Many contemporary observers regard the 1990–91 recession as wholly unique, suggesting "We are sailing in unchartered [sic] waters."

History never repeats itself exactly, so every recession is, of course, unique. But for the term "unique" to take on meaning, one needs to have some conception of what "normal times" are and what a "normal recession" might be. Nearly a decade has passed since the last U.S. recession ended, and memories of prior recessionary experiences may now have grown dim. The objective of this chapter is twofold: to provide a concise review of post-World War II recessions, with an eye to identifying their most distinctive features as well as their common elements; and to investigate the extent to which knowledge of a recessionary period provides insight into the subsequent expansion.

The chapter's conclusions are necessary tentative as the date the recession ended was not officially designated at the time of its writing. Even though the 1990–91 recession was characterized by several distinctive and still puzzling features, this is not uncommon for recessions. Virtually all recessions have occurred around the time of some highly distinctive, not purely economic event such as a war, a massive change in the price of imported oil, a major strike, or wage, price, and credit controls. Recessions almost always come as a surprise even though they seem easy to "explain" after the fact. This chapter finds that, contrary to common assertion, the severity of a recession provides little guidance to the course of the subsequent expansion.

A BRIEF OVERVIEW OF POST-WORLD WAR II RECESSION

Table 1 presents some of the salient features of the recessions since World War II. (Data or earlier recessions are sparse and less reliable.) The information is grouped according to

The author gratefully acknowledges the research assistance of Kim Gilbo.
Source: *New England Economic Review*, (January/February 1992), pp. 3–22.

Table 1 A Brief History of Post-World War II Recessions

Recession	Duration (months) (1)	Diffusion: industries with declining employment (maximum %) (2)	Depth						
			Real GNP (% change) (1982$) (3)	Real GNP (% change) (current weights[a]) (4)	Coincident indicators (% change) (5)	Payroll employment (% change) (6)	Unemployment rate (maximum change) (7)	Unemployment rate (maximum) (8)	Capacity utilization rate, manufacturing (minimum) (9)
Nov. 1948–Oct. 1949	11	90	−2.0	−1.6	−11.9	−5.2	4.4	7.9	71.7
July 1953–May 1954	10	87	−3.0	−3.4	−9.5	−3.5	3.6	6.1	78.8
Aug. 1957–Apr. 1958	8	88	−3.5	−3.9	−12.7	−4.3	3.8	7.5	71.3
Apr. 1960–Feb. 1961	10	80	−1.0	−1.6	−7.1	−2.2	2.3	7.1	73.5
Dec. 1969–Nov. 1970	11	80	−1.1	−1.0	−6.7	−1.5	2.7	6.1	75.8
Nov. 1973–Mar. 1975	16	88	−4.3	−4.9	−14.1	−2.9	4.4	9.0	70.8
Jan. 1980–July 1980	6	63	−2.4	−2.4	−6.6	−1.4	2.2	7.8	76.9
July 1981–Nov. 1982	16	72	−3.4	−3.4	−10.6	−3.1	3.6	10.8	70.0
Average of eight prior recessions	11	81	−2.6	−2.8	−9.9	−3.0	3.4	7.8	73.6
Standard deviation	3.5	9	1.2	1.3	2.9	1.3	9	1.5	3.2
Current recession (July 1990–April 1991(?))	9	73	−1.2	−1.3	−6.9	−1.5	1.9	7.1	77.2

[a]The 1948, 1953, 1957 and 1960 recession declines are in 1958 dollars; the 1969 and 1973 recessions are in 1972 dollars; the 1980 and 1981 recessions are in 1982 dollars; the 1990 recession is in 1987 dollars.

Source: Board of Governors of the Federal Reserve System: Ref. 1; National Bureau of Economic Research: Refs. 2–6.

what Geoffrey Moore [1] has called the three Ds, the three major criteria used to define a recession: duration, diffusion, and depth. Column (1) shows that postwar recessions have lasted as little as six months and as long as 16 months and have had an average duration of 11 months. Column (2) shows that the percent of industries experiencing employment declines has ranged from 90 in the 1948–49 recession to a low of 63 in the brief 1980 recession. Columns (3) through (9) illustrate two aspects of the depth of a recession: columns (3) through (7) show the maximum declines in several measures of economic activity, whereas columns (8) and (9) provide proxies for the maximum difference or gap between the actual and the "potential" or "normal" level of economic activity.

The distinction between these two aspects can be illustrated by considering which was the most severe recession in the postwar period. Based on the maximum decline in real GNP, final sales, or the index of coincident indicators, or on the increase in the unemployment rate, the answer is clearly the 1973–75 recession. However, because the major 1981–82 recession came only a year after the 1980 recession, the capacity utilization rate in manufacturing fell to a postwar low (70 percent) and the unemployment rate rose to a postwar high (10.8 percent), well above its 1975 peak. Thus, even though economic activity clearly declined more in 1973–75, one could easily argue that a maximum proportion of productive resources was idled in 1982, because the 1981–82 recession started from a much lower level of utilization.

Consider next the question of choosing the mildest recession in the postwar period. The 1980 recession is probably the most logical choice. It was the shortest since the records start in 1854, was the mildest in terms of duration, the decline in coincident indicators, and the diffusion and magnitude of employment declines. One could also make a case for either the 1953–54 or the 1969–70 recession. The 1953–54 recession was the mildest by the gap measures—the rates of manufacturing capacity utilization and unemployment—because it started from abnormally high rates of resource utilization during the Korean War. The declines in real GNP, employment, and coincident indicators in 1969–70 were among the smallest despite their reflecting a major strike.[1]

Assuming that the 1990 recession ended in the second quarter of 1991 (alternative assumptions are discussed later), it was clearly milder than the postwar average. The declines in real GNP and employment were about half as large as the average declines in prior postwar recessions. The rise in the unemployment rate was smaller than in any of the eight prior recessions, although it reached a higher maximum level than in the 1953 and 1969–70 recessions.

A THUMBNAIL CHRONOLOGY OF POSTWAR RECESSIONS

This section attempts to place each recession in its broader historical context by providing more information on the composition of real GNP, inflation and interest rates, and macroeconomic policy.

The 1948–49 Recession: Postwar Investment Adjustment

The 1948–49 recession was entirely an inventory recession—final sales increased 1.7 percent despite a sharp decline in business fixed investment. Personal consumption expenditures, consumer durable goods, residential investment, and state and local government purchases all rose more strongly than in any subsequent recession (Table 2).

Following the removal of wartime wage (in 1945) and price (in 1946) controls, the rate of inflation rose sharply, peaking at 20 percent in the year ending in March 1946 (Fig. 1).

Table 2 Components of Real GNP During Recessions: Percentage Changes from Reference Peak to Trough

Component	49:4 48:4 (58$) (1)	54:2 53:2 (58$) (2)	58:2 57:3 (58$) (3)	61:1 60:2 (58$) (4)	70:4 69:4 (72$) (5)	75:1 73:4 (72$) (6)	80:3 80:1 (82$) (7)	82:4 81:3 (82$) (8)	Average of eight prior recessions (9)	91:2 90:3 (87$) (10)
GNC	-1.6	-3.4	-3.4	-1.4	-0.1	-4.9	-2.3	-3.2	-2.6	-1.3
Change in business inventories	-3.3	-1.7	-1.7	-1.4	-0.5	-3.0	-1.0	-2.9	-2.0	-1.0
Final sales	1.7	-1.7	-1.7	0	0.4	-1.9	-1.3	-0.3	-0.6	-0.3
Personal consumption expenditures	3.2	.7	-0.6	-0.5	1.5	-0.4	-1.0	2.3	0.7	-0.9
Durable goods	16.4	-1.1	-9.8	-8.6	-7.1	-9.1	-6.9	2.5	-3.0	-7.1
Nondurable goods	1.5	-0.7	-0.9	0.1	2.9	-1.0	-1.0	1.8	0.3	-0.7
Services	1.3	3.3	3.2	1.9	2.9	3.1	0.7	2.6	2.4	0.6
Residential fixed investment	17.9	6.0	-1.0	-5.0	9.9	-31.4	-18.1	-5.3	-3.4	-9.9
Business fixed investment	-15.1	-2.2	-14.0	-5.7	-6.0	-14.2	-6.9	-12.5	-9.6	-7.3
Equipment	-17.1	-4.7	-17.4	-10.5	-6.9	-11.5	-8.0	-14.3	-11.3	-5.2
Structures	-11.7	2.0	-8.2	2.3	-4.6	-19.4	-4.8	-9.6	-6.8	-11.7
Total government purchases	6.1	-11.1	5.1	3.1	-1.6	2.6	0.5	4.7	1.2	1.8
Federal government	-0.7	-19.2	4.1	2.4	-9.7	0.5	2.0	10.2	-1.3	3.8
State and local government	14.6	8.6	6.1	3.9	5.5	3.8	-0.4	0.8	5.4	0.5
Net exports	-0.5	0.5	-0.7	0.5	0.2	1.0	1.0	-0.9	0.1	1.1
Exports	-9.8	8.4	-10.8	2.9	3.1	1.6	-3.8	-14.1	-2.8	3.0
Imports	-0.8	-4.1	3.0	-7.2	0.5	-11.5	-12.9	-7.1	-5.0	-5.2
Auto production	13.7	-6.4	-35.0	-32.4	-42.7	-32.1	-12.1	-14.5	-20.2	-23.1

Note: The change in business inventories is the difference between the change in real GNP and the change in final sales.
Source: Ref. 2, Tables 1.2, 1.5, and 1.16; Ref. 4, Tables 1.2, 1.4, and 1.15; Ref. 5, Tables 1.2, 1.4, and 1.18; Ref. 6, 1991; and author's calculations.

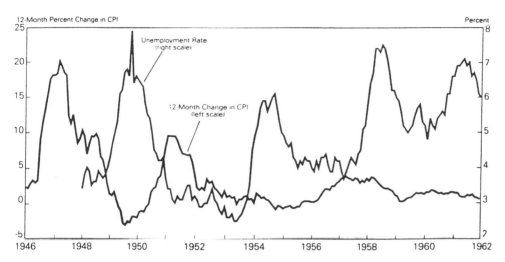

Figure 1   Inflation and unemployment rates, 1946–1961. (From U.S. Bureau of Labor Statistics.)

After decelerating steadily over the next year and a half, the level of the CPI peaked near the peak of the business cycle and declined more than 4 percent thereafter.

Since the war, monetary policy had been devoted primarily to supporting the price of government securities. Nevertheless, in 1948 reserve requirements were increased three times and the discount rate raised from 1 percent to 1.5 percent. These policy actions were greatly magnified by the sharp reversal from inflation to deflation. Real rates of interest swung quickly from large negative to large positive values.

Romer and Romer [1] have identified October 1947 as one of six times that monetary policy sought to reduce economic activity to curb inflation. Monetary restraint undoubtedly contributed to an inevitable winding down of pent-up demand from World War II. The fact that the declines were confined solely to business fixed and inventory investment suggests the slowdown in sales was propagated by a multiplier-accelerator interaction of the type that had already been described [8–10].

The 1953–54 Recession: The End of the Korean War

The 1953–54 recession was characterized by a sharp cutback in government spending, associated primarily with the end of the Korean War. Federal government purchases had nearly tripled between the outbreak of the war in June 1950 and the signing of an armistice in July 1953. Government spending had slowed and defense orders had slowed even earlier, as the prospect of an end to the war became clearer. The drop of nearly 20 percent in federal purchases, along with the decline in inventory investment, exceeded the decline in real GNP during the recession. State and local government purchases and exports rose briskly during the recession, and both residential investment and personal consumption expenditures increased. If any postwar recession can be attributed to reduced government spending, it would be this post-Korean War experience.

It is of some current interest to note that the early recovery from the 1953–54 recession is the slowest on record. Ordinarily, at a cyclical trough, economic activity not only stops declining but immediately starts to rise faster than its trend. This normal sequence was delayed in 1954 when, for example, payroll employment declined for three months after the May trough and did not exceed the May level until November. This is the only precedent for the extremely weak early recovery, or "L-shaped" recession, in 1991.

The 1957–58 Recession: Accelerating Inflation and Policy Restraint

The 1957–58 recession was preceded by an acceleration of the inflation rate from 0 in early 1956 to nearly 4 percent in early 1957 (Fig. 1). The unemployment rate had been below $4\frac{1}{2}$ percent since mid 1955 and below 4 percent in early 1957, just prior to the peak. Over the course of the expansion, short-term interest rates rose slowly but steadily from less than 1 percent to $3\frac{1}{2}$ percent at the peak, while M1 growth steadily decelerated from a peak of $4\frac{1}{2}$ percent to about 0 (Fig. 2).

The size of the decline in real GNP and final sales was about the same as in the prior recession but the composition differed greatly. Whereas the 1953–54 recession was dominated by a drop in federal spending, government spending increased strongly in the 1957–58 recession. Whereas capital spending hardly declined in 1953–54, it collapsed in 1957–58. Producers' durable equipment declined less in 1953–54 (less than 5 percent) than in any postwar recession but declined more in 1957–58 (17.4 percent) than in any postwar recession. Consumer durables, nearly flat in the previous recession, dropped nearly 10 percent in 1957–58. Except for the initial stability of residential investment, which had declined more or less continually from 1954 to 1957, the 1957–58 recession exhibits the signs of credit restraints.

The 1960–61 Recession: False Expectations?

In contrast to most other recessions, no one dominant factor characterizes the relatively mild 1960–61 recession. It is perhaps best viewed as the net result of a combination of several factors, their only common thread a mistaken reading of the strength of the real economy and the threat of inflation. Indeed, the 1960–61 recession may be the first and perhaps clearest postwar example of a recession due to a forecast error.

For this and earlier recessions, the record of explicit forecasts is rather sparse and not particularly helpful, because most forecasts were in nominal rather than real units and at

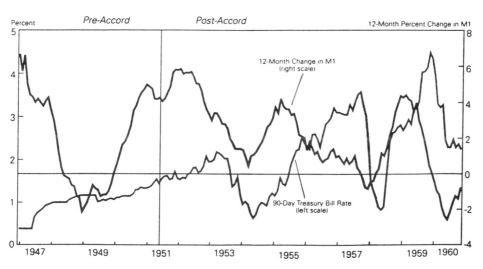

Figure 2 Measures of monetary policy, 1947–1960. (From Board of Governors of the Federal Reserve System and Ref. 12.)

annual rather than quarterly or monthly frequencies [11]. The impression that the state of the economy was misconstrued comes rather from qualitative, more contemporary accounts [12,13].

Note first that the 1958 recession had been relatively deep and that the recovery had not progressed far—for example, producers' durable equipment did not regain its earlier peaks during the 1950s. Throughout 1959, the unemployment rate held above 5 percent, a relatively high level for that time.

The underlying strength of the economy was obscured by the effects of the steel strike from July 15 to November 7, 1959, including the anticipatory buildup to it as well as the subsequent rebound from it. "It was widely believed that the drop [in activity attributable to the strike] was purely temporary and that, once the strike was settled, economic activity would continue at something like the vigorous pace it had displayed in 1958 and 1959" [Ref. 12, p. 618]. Thus, "Private forecasts at the end of 1959 and in early 1960 consistently pictured rising levels of economic activity during 1960" [Ref. 13, p. 241]. Even after it had begun, "The recession received little public discussion during the summer and fall of 1960. It was conspicuously ignored in public statements by presidential candidates of both parties, until late in the campaign, as well as by the incumbent administration" [Ref. 13, p. 243].

In view of this inability to recognize, let alone anticipate, the 1960–61 recession, it is not surprising that the focus of macroeconomic policy was inflation. Yet, in stark contrast to the acceleration of inflation that preceded the 1957–58 recession, the inflation rate held fairly steady throughout the brief 1958–60 expansion. The 12-month change in the CPI did increase from 0.1 percent in April 1959 to 1.9 percent in April 1960, but the corresponding rate excluding food and energy held constant at about 2 percent throughout that period. Nevertheless, despite the relatively stable inflation rate, both fiscal and monetary policy switched from highly expansionary in 1958 to restrictive in 1959.

Lewis describes in detail the "sharp tightening of budget policy in fiscal 1960," consisting of both expenditure cuts and tax increases [Ref. 13, pp. 240–241]. In 1959, short-term rose to their highest levels since 1929. Friedman and Schwartz attribute this "sharp reversal" of monetary policy to three factors: first, the brevity of the 1957–58 recession and the vigor of the early recovery; second, concerns about the outflow of gold in 1958; and "third, retrospective examination of its earlier policy persuaded the [Federal] Reserve System that it had erred during the 1954–57 expansion by continuing 'ease' for too long; that, while an easy-money policy was justified in 1954 and perhaps early 1955, the System should have taken severely restrictive measures in mid 1955 at the latest. It was determined not to repeat the error" [Ref. 12, pp. 617–618]. Thus, an acceleration of inflation in the mid '50s may have been the source of two recessions, the 1957–58 recession born of the necessity to roll back an actual acceleration in inflation, and the 1960–61 recession born out of fear of having to repeat that experience.

The 1970 Recession: Guns, Butter, and a Strike

The late 1960s present a classic example of an excess demand inflation. Prior to the 1970 recession, the unemployment rate had been below 4 percent for four years and below 3.5 percent from September 1968 through May 1969. This rate was lower than any serious estimate of "full" employment, particularly in light of the rapid influx of young and inexperienced workers. With aggregate demand overtaxing the economy's productive capacity, the inflation rate (as measured by the 12-month change in the CPI excluding food and energy) accelerated slowly but steadily from 1.2 percent in 1965 to 6.0 percent at the December 1969 cyclical peak.

The 1968 income tax surcharge and suspension of the investment tax credit had not succeeded in arresting the acceleration of inflation. The federal funds rate, below 4 percent in 1967, was gradually increased to its peak level of 9.2 percent in August 1969.

The 1970 recession unfolded in two fairly distinct phases—an initial, fairly mild downturn in activity until September and a second leg associated with the 68-day strike at General Motors from September 15 to November 23, 1970. Owing to the strike, the cycle reached a clear trough in November, but it is virtually impossible to guess exactly when the trough would have been if no strike had occurred.

The unusual 1970 recession illustrates clearly why real GNP is not a sufficient statistic for measuring recessions and expansions. One issue is the distinction between business cycle turning points (the reference cycle) and the high and low values of an individual economic time series (its specific cycle). The high and low of real GNP (or any other series) are not necessarily the cycle peak and trough. In addition, both the magnitude and the timing of changes in real GNP in the 1970 recession depend greatly on which version of the data is used (or more precisely, which benchmarking or base year's weights are used).

Both these points are illustrated in Table 3. All versions of the data show real GNP reached a local maximum in 1969:III (the quarter before the business cycle peak in December 1969). The contemporaneous data, with 1958-base weights, show real GNP declining in 1969:IV and 1970:I, rising in 1970:II and III, and falling in 1970:IV, a decline attributable entirely to the strike. These data suggest a 1.4 percent decline in real GNP, followed by an expansion starting in the spring of 1970, interrupted by an auto strike. When the GNP accounts were rebenchmarked using 1972-base weights, the recession appears far milder, a 1 percent decline from 1969:III to 1970:I and only a 0.1 percent decline over the business cycle. The next rebenchmarking, using 1982 weights, was the first to show a decline in 1970:II; this version of the data also shows a small (1.1 percent) decline from 1969:IV to 1970:II and a trivial (0.4 percent) decline between the cyclical peak and trough

Table 3 The 1970 Recession, Using Various Base Year Weights

	Real GNP (1958 weights)	Real GNP (1972 weights)	Real GNP (1982 weights)	Real GNP (1987 weights)
High	1969:III	1969:III	1969:III	1969:III
Low	1970:IV	1970:I	1970:II	1970:II
Specific cycle (% change, high to low)	−1.4	−1.0	−1.1	−0.9
Business cycle (% change, 1969:IV to 1970:IV)	−0.8	−0.1	−0.4	−0.2
Change from previous quarter (% change, annual rate)				
1969:IV	−2.2	−2.3	−1.6	−1.0
1970:I	−2.1	−1.5	−2.4	−1.1
1970:II	0.5	0.6	−0.4	−1.7
1970:III	2.9	3.9	5.0	5.2
1970:IV	−4.3	−3.1	−3.6	−3.1

Source: Data in 1958$ were taken from Ref. 3, July 1973; data in 1972$ were taken from Ref. 3, Sept. 1981; data in 1982$ were taken from Ref. 3, Sept. 1986.

quarters. Using the official NBER turning point dates, the 1970 recession would appear to be solely a reflection of the GM strike. But all versions of the data confirm a minor (1 to 1.4) percent decline in real GNP from 1969:III to some time in the first half of 1970, an increase in real GNP in 1970:III, and a strike-induced decline in 1970:IV and rebound in 1971:I.

In light of the difficulty in measuring even retrospectively what actually happened in 1970, it is hardly surprising that economic forecasters had difficulty predicting the 1970 recession. Before the peak, none of the median forecasts of real GNP from the ASA/NBER survey showed any declines in real GNP. The forecasts released in December 1969 and February 1970 showed small declines in 1969:IV but an increase in 1970:I, certainly not a recession call. It was not until the May 1970 survey that the median forecast anticipated two small quarterly declines in real GNP.

These forecasts were much more successful, however, in anticipating the increase in the unemployment rate. Since the first survey in late 1968, the median forecast had anticipated small increases in unemployment. In the December 1969 survey, the median forecast foresaw sizable increases in the unemployment rate in the first half of 1970. All postwar cyclical turning points have occurred in the quarter prior to "sizable" changes in the unemployment rate [Ref. 14, Table 1, p. 33]. Based on this criterion for predicting a recession, the median forecast released in December 1969 correctly anticipated the 1970 recession just as it began.

The 1973–75 Recession: Decontrol and Oil Inflation

As noted earlier, the 1973–75 recession produced the largest decline in economic activity in the postwar period. The recession was preceded by a sharp increase in inflation in 1973 (Fig. 3). The year opened with a phased dismantling of the wage and price controls that had been in effect since August 1971. In addition, most industrialized countries were experiencing a synchronous boom which, along with a large sale of U.S. grain to the Soviet Union, generated a worldwide explosion in commodities prices [15]. The inflation rate, as measured by the 12-month change in the overall CPI, rose from 3.4 percent in 1972 to 7.4

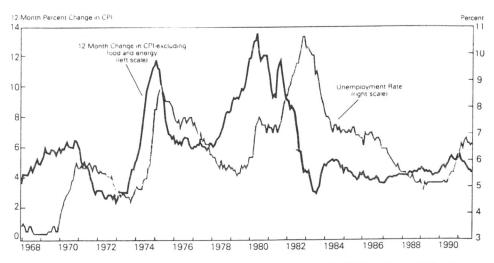

Figure 3 "Core" inflation and unemployment rates, 1968–1991. (From U.S. Bureau of Labor Statistics.)

percent in September 1973. Over the same period, the federal funds rate increased even more sharply, from less than 5 percent to 10.8 percent (Fig. 4). The outbreak of the Yom Kippur War on October 6, 1973, resulted in an embargo on oil shipments from the Middle East and a quadrupling of the price of imported oil. Analysts at the time understood this as an aggregate supply shift that would raise the price level and lower the pace of economic activity, but were uncertain of the magnitude and timing of these changes.

Like the previous recession, the 1973–75 recession can be divided into two fairly distinct phases: the first phase, the 10-month period from the peak until September 1974, during which employment continued to grow, industrial production declined only slightly, and the unemployment rate remained below 6 percent, was at the time dubbed an "energy spasm." The phrase was used to dismiss the idea that this episode was a genuine recession and call attention to the double-digit rate of inflation. The acceptance of this interpretation fostered a further increase in short-term interest rates and culminated in the Whip Inflation Now (WIN) conference in September 1974.

The second phase of the recession started in September 1974 and lasted six months. In these six months, employment dropped 2.7 percent, the unemployment rate rose 2.7 percentage points, and industrial production dropped 13 percent. Notwithstanding this virtual collapse in economic activity, inflation continued to rise. Thanks to a leveling-off in energy prices, the CPI peaked at 12.2 percent in November 1974 but the CPI excluding food and energy did not peak until February 1975, one month prior to the low point of the recession.

The 1980 Recession: Credit Controls

The 1980 recession was unusual in several regards. First, it was the shortest (six months) recession on record and in several respects the mildest of the postwar period. It was preceded by the longest peacetime expansion on record at that time, another sharp increase in the price of imported oil following the Iranian revolution, and a dramatic change in the Federal Reserve's operating procedures on October 6, 1979. Consequently, a recession had

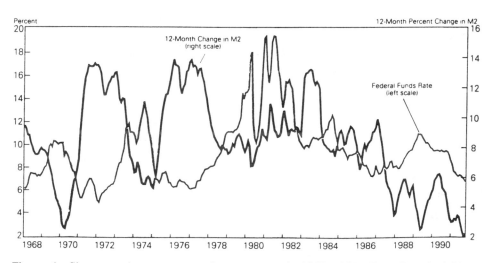

Figure 4 Short-term interest rates and money growth, 1968–1991. (From Board of Governors of the Federal Reserve System.)

been widely expected for at least a year before it actually began. Despite its having been widely predicted, the recession was exacerbated by restrictive macroeconomic policies, most notably the imposition of credit controls on March 14, 1980.

The short, mild recession slowed inflation only temporarily. It was followed by the shortest expansion since 1919–20. This episode is thus the only postwar example of a double-dip recession or "W-shaped" business cycle. It is even plausible to view the 1980 and 1981–82 recessions as a single episode of subpar growth.

The inflation rate had accelerated steadily but fairly slowly from 1976 to mid 1978. The revolution in Iran led to cutbacks in oil production which, along with the phased decontrol of domestic oil prices, more than doubled the world price of oil. Rising energy prices added directly about $2\frac{1}{4}$ percentage points to the overall rate of consumer price inflation in 1979, considerably more than they added during the previous oil shock in 1974. By the fall of 1979, consumer prices, excluding food and energy, were again rising at double-digit rates and the foreign exchange value of the dollar was plummeting.

During the acceleration of inflation, the federal funds rate had risen gradually from 4.6 percent in early 1977 to 11.4 percent in September 1979. In early October, the Federal Reserve changed its operating procedures in order to put more emphasis on the monetary aggregates and permit greater changes in the short-term money market conditions. The federal funds rate rose to 14 percent in October, where it stayed until March 1980.

Predictions of a mild recession were heard as early as late 1978. When gas lines appeared and it became clear that real GNP would decline over the first half of 1979, the recession call became unanimous. All prior half-year declines in real GNP had been associated with cyclical peaks. Nevertheless, real GNP rose in the third quarter and inflation continued to rise.

Virtually all forecasters continued to expect a recession. In January 1980, the President's Council of Economic Advisers pointed to

a number of reasons for expecting a mild recession in the first half of this year. . . . In most past periods of economic regression both fiscal and monetary policy have been eased significantly. At the present time, however, recession is still only a forecast; it has not appeared in overall measures of economic performance. Moreover the economy has recently withstood recessionary pressures far better than most analysts expected. These facts, together with the seriousness of our inflation problem, argue against an easing of policy at this time. [Ref. 16, 1980, p. 66]

Indeed, the original budget proposal was quickly replaced by a more restrictive budget, the federal funds rate rose to 17.6 percent, and on March 14, 1980, credit controls were imposed.

The public reaction to credit controls was far stronger than most contemporary analysts expected based on a literal reading of the regulations. Perhaps people thought use of credit was illegal or unpatriotic, but for whatever reason, personal consumption expenditures and final sales declined more rapidly in 1980:II than in any other quarter in the postwar period. In response, the federal funds rate fell from nearly 20 percent in late March and early April to under 9 percent in early July, when the credit controls program was terminated.

The 1981–82 Recession: Stubborn Inflation and the Double-Dip

The 1981–82 recession can be interpreted as a consequence of the continuing effort to reduce inflation that started in 1979. Its severity also reflected poor forecasts, which overestimated the short-term efficacy of tax cuts and failed to foresee the collapse in the income velocity of money.

The short 1980 recession only temporarily arrested the acceleration of inflation. In the last four months of 1980, consumer prices excluding food and energy were again rising at double-digit rates. Accordingly, the federal funds rate rose from 9 percent at the July 1980 trough to more than 19 percent, six months into the recovery.

In 1981, monthly increases in consumer prices temporarily receded but by summer, double-digit annual rates had returned. About the same time, several forecasters started to predict a short, mild recession. They were relatively quick to recognize that a recession had begun but far too optimistic about its ultimate severity.

The 1981–82 recession lasted 16 months, the same length as the 1973–75 recession. Unlike the 1973–74 experience, the decline was fairly steady: payroll employment, industrial production, and the coincident indicator index fell every month (except February 1982) and the unemployment rate rose every month (except August 1982) for nearly a year and a half. The declines were concentrated in the investment and export sectors, as personal consumption and government purchases increased fairly rapidly (Table 2).

Short-term interest rates fell in the second half of 1981 and monetary growth accelerated sharply. This easing of monetary policy, along with the recently enacted tax cuts that became effective in October, reinforced the expectation that the recession would be mild. One of the four basic elements in the Reagan Administration's economic recovery program had been a gradual but steady reduction in monetary growth. Large increases in December 1981 and January 1982 had brought M1 well above the top of its target range. "Consequently, the Federal Reserve slowed the growth of nonborrowed reserves during the first half of the year, with a view to gradually bringing M1 and M2 back to their target ranges. By June, M1 was within its target range, while M2 remained somewhat above the top of its range" [Ref. 16, 1983, p. 139]. Unfortunately, this deceleration of money growth coincided with the largest decline in the income velocity of money on record under the current definition. The sharp deceleration in nominal GNP exceeded the median contemporaneous forecast by a huge 6 percentage points. After mid year, both the inflation rate and the federal funds rate declined sharply and money growth soared, thanks in part to the introduction of interest-bearing NOW and MMDA accounts.

A BRIEF OVERVIEW OF POST-WORLD WAR II EXPANSIONS

Table 4 provides a brief description of the postwar economic expansions. In contrast to recessions, whose durations have been fairly uniform with a standard deviation of only 3.5 months, the duration of expansions (column 1) has ranged from 12 months to 106 months with a standard deviation of 33 months. It is not surprising, then, that the cumulative change in real GNP over the course of expansions has also varied widely—from a low of 3.3 percent in the 1980–81 expansion to an increase of more than 50 percent during the longest expansion in U.S. history, which took place throughout most of the 1960s (column 5).

Despite the variety in their overall dimensions, postwar expressions have been roughly similar in the pace of economic growth, especially in their early stages. The 1949:IV to 1953:II expansion, which included the Korean War, was by far the fastest expansion in the postwar period, even though it was fairly normal in duration and cumulative change. Clearly the weakest was the one-year expansion between the 1980 and the 1981–82 recessions, the only postwar example of a double-dip recession or "W-shaped" business cycle. Excluding these extreme cases, whose abnormality is easy to understand, the average rate of growth over the first two years of the remaining six postwar expansions has been extremely uniform

Table 4 Business Cycle Expansions, 1949–1990

Expansion		(1)	(2)	(3)	(4)	(5)
			Real GNP growth, annual percent rate			Cumulative % Δ to peak
Trough quarter	Peak quarter	Duration in months	First year	First 2 years	To peak	
1949:IV	1953:II	45	14.5	9.6	7.5	28.8
1954:II	1957:III	39	8.3	5.3	3.9	13.2
1958:II	1960:II	24	9.2	5.6	5.6	11.4
1961:I	1969:IV	106	7.6	5.9	4.8	50.2
1970:IV	1973:IV	36	4.7	5.8	5.3	16.7
1975:I	1980:I	58	6.7	5.5	4.4	24.3
1980:III	1981:III	12	3.3	n.a.	3.3	3.3
1982:IV	1990:III	92	6.5	5.8	3.6	32.0
Average		52	7.6	6.2	4.8	22.5
Standard deviation		33	3.4	1.5	1.4	14.7

Note: 1949, 1954, 1958 and 1961 expansions are in constant 1958 dollars; 1970 and 1975 expansions are in constant 1972 dollars; 1980 and 1982 expansions are in constant 1982 dollars; n.a. = not applicable.
Source: Ref. 2, Table 1.2; Ref. 4, Table 1.2; Ref. 5, Table 1.2; Ref. 3, Aug. 1991; and author's calculations.

(column 3), ranging only from a low of 5.3 in 1954–57 to a high of 5.9 in 1961–69. Slow growth in the first year (such as in 1971) was followed by a pickup in the second year of the expansion; rapid first-year growth (such as occurred in the 1950s) has been followed by a tapering down in the second year. The 1949–53 and 1980–81 experiences clearly illustrate, however, that this uniform pattern is simply a regularity and not an inevitability. An extraordinary source of demand (such as was associated with the outbreak of the Korean War) or an extraordinarily restrictive policy (such as the successful attempt to combat double-digit inflation in 1980–81) can alter the "normal" tendency for economic expansions to proceed at a 5½ to 6 percent annual rate during their first two years.

DO RECESSIONS CONTAIN THE SEEDS OF RECOVERIES?

It has literally become a cliché to say that the recovery from the 1990–91 recession will be weak because the preceding recession itself was mild. Table 5 shows that the history of postwar recessions and recoveries provides little support for that alleged relationship. Both the simple (numerical) and rank (ordering) correlations show little relationship between the severity of recessions and the strength of the first year, of the first two years, and of the total length of the following expansion.

The top panel uses the percent decline in real GNP as the measure of a recession's severity; this measure shows no correlation with the increase in real GNP in the first year of the expansion, a small negative relationship with the increase over the first two years, and a negative, insignificant relationship with the total increase in real GNP. (See also the left half of Fig. 5.)

The second panel of the table measures the severity of the recession by its duration. The duration of recession is also not associated with the subsequent expansion.

Table 5 Correlations of Recessions and Recoveries

	Recession measure	Expansion measure	Simple correlation	Rank correlation	Standard error
Real GNP	GNP	GNP1	.03	.24	.40
	GNP	GNP2	−.34	−.75[b]	.30
	GNP	GNPT	−.16	−.31	.39
Duration	DUR	GNP1	.07	−.02	.42
	DUR	GNP2	−.08	.06	.46
	DUR	GNPT	.46	.65[b]	.32
Employment	E	GNP1	.92	.83[a]	.23
	E	GNP2	.66	.21	.44
	E	GNPT	.16	.24	.40
	E	E1	.90	.95[a]	.12
	E	E2	.81	.82[b]	.26
	E	ET	.11	.12	.41

Note: GNP is the percent change in real GNP from reference peak to trough; GNP1 from the trough to the first year of the expansion; GNP2 from the trough to the second year of the expansion; GNPT from the trough to the next cyclical peak. DUR is the duration of the decline from reference peak to trough in months. E is the percent change in payroll employment from reference peak to trough; E1 from the trough to the first year of the expansion; E2 from the trough to the second year of the expansion; ET from the trough to the next cyclical peak. The 12-month 1980–81 expansion is excluded from GNP2 and E2.
[a]Significant at the .01 level.
[b]Significant at the .05 level.
Source: Author's calculations.

The next two panels measure the severity of recessions by the peak to trough decline in payroll employment. The conventional view, that weak recessions spawn weak expansions, receives partial support only when the recession is proxied by employment declines. Employment declines during a recession have been positively associated with real growth during the first year, but not the first two years, and not the total duration of the following economic expansion. Employment declines are also associated with employment growth during the first year and first two years of the following expansion. (See the right half of Fig. 5.)

THE 1990–91 RECESSION TO DATE

This section examines the recession that began in 1990. Because the trough date has not been designated, this description must be less a definitive history than a tentative forecast. Most of the economic series that measure economic activity reached at least local low points in the first half of 1991. Because a recession is defined as a period of declining economic activity, it is difficult to resist declaring that the recession has ended. Yet, most postwar recessions have been interrupted by one quarter of positive growth, although none by two consecutive quarters. The changes in economic activity to date have been so small—and so unlike the early stage of previous expansions—that they probably would not qualify as an economic expansion *if* economic activity were now to start to decline. In

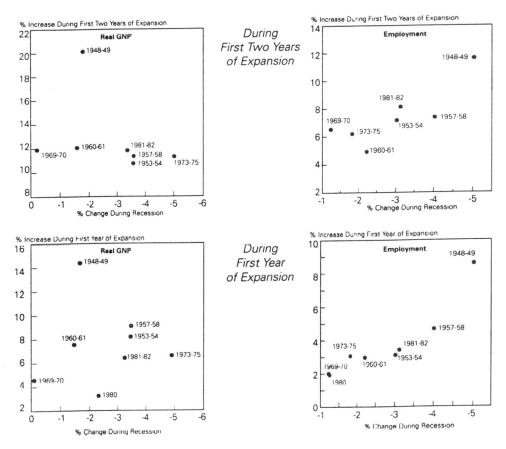

Figure 5 Real GNP and payroll employment during recessions and expansions. (From author's calculations.)

that event, a description of what would be the longest recession in the postwar period must await the evolution of its second phase. Any attempt to categorize this recession this early must necessarily assume that it has ended. This account is, therefore, subject to future revision.

Based on the assumption that economic activity continues to rise, the 1990–91 recession was clearly one of the mildest, though probably not the mildest, in the postwar era. Owing to slower growth in the working-age population and declines in the participation rate, the increase in the unemployment rate has been smaller than in any previous postwar recession. This relative mildness of the recession seems to run counter to fears that have been raised about the fragility of the financial system, the massive debt overhang, the wave of restructuring, and the record collapse in consumer confidence. These issues may yet emerge during the recovery or in the next recession.

One reason is that the current state of the economy is perceived to be worse than it appears when compared to previous recessions by a long period of slow growth. The Center for International Business Cycle Research at Columbia University has designated February 1989 as the start of a period of "below-trend" increases in economic activity—the onset of a "growth recession" (Table 6) [Ref. 1, Ch. 5, pp. 61–64]. This designation is consistent with the fact that nonfarm business productivity peaked at the end of 1988. Thus, the mild

Table 6 Business Cycle Expansions and Contractions and High- and Low-Growth Phases, 1948–1990

Business cycle reference dates		Duration in months		Growth cycle reference dates		Duration in months	
Trough (T) (1)	Peak (P) (2)	Contraction (T from previous P) (3)	Expansion (T to P) (4)	Upturn (U) (5)	Downturn (D) (6)	Low-growth phase (U from previous D) (7)	High-growth phase (U to next D) (8)
	Nov. 1948				July 1948		
Oct. 1949		11		Oct. 1949	Mar. 1951	15	17
	July 1953		45	July 1952	Mar. 1953	16	8
May 1954	Aug. 1957	10	39	Aug. 1954	Feb. 1957	17	30
Apr. 1958	Apr. 1960	8	24	Apr. 1958	Feb. 1960	14	22
Feb. 1961		10		Feb. 1961	May 1962	12	15
				Oct. 1964	Jun. 1966	29	20
	Dec. 1969		106	Oct. 1967	Mar. 1969	16	17
Nov. 1970	Nov. 1973	11	36	Nov. 1970	Mar. 1973	20	28
Mar. 1975	Jan. 1980	16	58	Mar. 1975	Dec. 1978	24	45
July 1980	July 1981	6	12				
Nov. 1982		16		Dec. 1982	Jun. 1984	48	18
	July 1990		92	Jan. 1987	Feb. 1989	31	25
Average		11	52			22	22
Standard deviation		3.5	32.5			10.6	9.8

Source: National Bureau of Economic Research, Inc. and the Center for International Business Cycle Research.

recession was preceded by 17 months of substandard growth, the longest of any postwar recession.

The first concerns about the longevity of the economic expansion that began in November 1982 arose after the 30 percent drop in stock prices on October 19, 1987. Such precipitous declines had often preceded periods of slower economic growth, if not actual recessions [17]. Despite those concerns, most analysts correctly anticipated that economic growth would remain strong in 1988. (Real GNP did slow down from its rapid 5.4 percent rate in 1987 but the decline was in large part due to the serious drought in 1988, which was presumably unrelated to the collapse of equity prices.) During 1988, nonfarm production grew 3.3 percent and the unemployment rate declined from 6 percent in October 1987 to 5.3 percent a year later. The economy was clearly running close to, if not beyond, its full productive capacity.

Slower real growth did materialize in 1989 along with fears that the slowdown would turn into a "hard landing" (that is, a recession). Despite an evident deceleration, real economic activity did increase fast enough to hold the unemployment rate below 5.5 percent until the cyclical peak in July 1990. This combination of small but positive real growth and steady unemployment was heralded as the achievement of a "soft landing."

The term "soft landing," however, had taken on the connotation not only of sustainable, positive growth but also of a deceleration of inflation. Unfortunately, starting in late 1989, the "core" rate of inflation started to accelerate: the 12-month change rose fairly steadily from the 4 to $4\frac{1}{2}$ percent range, where it had stayed through much of the 1980s, to 5.1

percent in the year ending in July 1990, while the more volatile three-month rate rose sharply from 3.8 percent in September 1989 to 6.5 percent in March 1990.

Recent recessions have generally been preceded by a sharp acceleration of inflation and followed by a sharp deceleration (Fig. 3). This pattern is not as universal as is commonly thought, as is clear from Fig. 1. The rate of inflation was clearly decelerating in the year before the 1948–49 and the 1953–54 recessions and fairly stable prior to the 1960–61 recession. The 1957–58 recession was the only early postwar recession immediately preceded by accelerating inflation. The 1990–91 recession falls roughly in the middle, relative to prior postwar experience: the acceleration of inflation prior to the cyclical peak was not nearly so pronounced as before the peaks in 1957, 1973, and 1980, though obviously much different from the decelerations in the year before the 1948 and the 1953 peaks. The experience mirrored the gradual yet distinct increases in the inflation rate that preceded the relatively mild recessions of 1960–61 and 1969–70 (Table 7).

In late July 1990, the other leg of the "soft landing" scenario was also called into question. Instead of expanding at a 2.2 percent annual rate, enough to hold the unemployment rate steady, revised data showed that real GNP had grown only 1 percent at an annual rate in the second quarter and had been growing at $1\frac{1}{2}$ percent or less for five consecutive quarters. These downward revisions cast the "soft landing" and its sustainability in an entirely new light. Instead of converging toward roughly the growth of productive capacity, the deceleration of economic growth had been sharper (Fig. 6). Some new source of strength would have to emerge to break the deceleration momentum.

Rising inflation, weakening real growth, and the threat of war in the Persian Gulf combined to generate a precipitous drop in consumer sentiment—the University of Michigan's index dropped an unprecedented 32 percent from its April peak to its October low. This drop, along with sharp increases in gasoline prices, brought about sharp declines in auto production. From 1990:III to 1991:I, the production of autos and light trucks dropped

Table 7 Inflation and Changes in Inflation Rate Near Cyclical Peaks

Peak date	CPI, 12-month % change	Change in 12-month rate from year earlier	CPI, 3-month % change	Change in 3-month rate from 3 months earlier	Change in 3-month rate from 12 months earlier
Nov. 1948	4.8	−3.7	−4.3	−11.5	−16.7
July 1953	0.4	−2.6	1.5	0.8	−1.9
Aug. 1957	3.5	1.3	4.1	1.2	−0.2
Apr. 1960	2.0	0.3	1.3	0	0
Dec. 1969	5.9	0.8	5.2	−1.2	−0.3
Nov. 1973	4.7	1.9	7.2	3.6	6.3
Jan. 1980	12.0	3.4	15.4	3.2	7.4
July 1981	11.1	−1.2	13.5	5.8	6.8
July 1990	5.1	0.6	5.2	−1.0	0.7
Average of nine recessions	5.5	0.1	5.5	0.1	0.2
Standard deviation	3.8	2.2	6.1	4.9	7.3

Note: CPI prior to 1960; CPI excluding food and energy thereafter.
Source: U.S. Bureau of Labor Statistics.

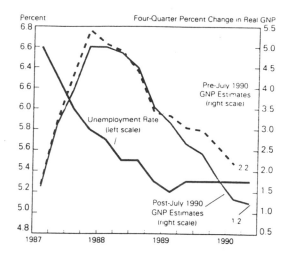

Figure 6 Changes in real GNP before and after July 1990 data revision, and the unemployment rate. (From U.S. Bureau of Labor Statistics and U.S. Bureau of Economic Analysis.)

28 percent, or nearly $50 billion in 1982 dollars, nearly as much as the decline in real GNP over the entire 1990–91 recession.

Although the record drop in consumer sentiment did not portend a severe recession by postwar standards, it was associated with a disproportionate decline in personal consumption expenditures. As noted in Table 2, consumption expenditures had increased 0.7 percent on average in previous postwar recessions. The largest previous drop had been the 1.0 percent decline in 1980, which was also associated with a large deterioration in measures of consumer sentiment. Relative to the decline in real GNP during the 1990–91 recession, the 0.9 percent decline in total consumption expenditures was disproportionately large. This abnormally large decline in consumption was offset by stronger than normal performances in exports, federal purchases, and producers' durable equipment. The 0.3 percent decline in final sales from 1990:III to 1991:II was close to the average of postwar recessions. The 1990–91 recession was milder than average, mainly because the inventory cycle was more muted than in most previous postwar recessions.

FORECASTING THE TIMING AND SEVERITY OF THE 1990–91 RECESSION

At the time of the July 1990 peak, few of the normal signs of a recession were visible. A substantial increase in the May index of leading indicators had been announced in late June; the first decline in the index for the month of August was not reported until late September. Similarly, stock prices reached new highs in mid July and did not decline precipitously until after Iraq's invasion of Kuwait (Table 8). Thus, it is not surprising that, in an early July *Wall Street Journal* roundup [18], only two of 40 forecasters anticipated a decline in real GNP: one predicted a very mild, "borderline" recession at worst, a 0.7 percent decline in the second half of 1990 followed by a 1.0 percent increase in the first half of 1991. The only clear recession call was made by a forecaster who had been expecting a recession ever since the 1987 stock market crash.

A primary reason for the belated recognition of the 1990–91 recession was the unusual behavior of financial variables. Watson [25] attributes the failure of NBER's Experimental

Table 8 Precursors of Peaks

| Peak date | Lead time (months) | | | |
	Downturn	Peak in short rate[a]	Index of leading indicators	S&P500
Nov. 1948	−4	−2	−5	−5
July 1953	−4	−3	−5	−6
Aug. 1957	−6	+2	−20	−13
Apr. 1960	−2	−4	−10	−9
Dec. 1969	−9	−4	−8	−12
Nov. 1973	−8	+8	−8	−10
Jan. 1980	−13	+3	−15	NST[b]
July 1981	n.a.[c]	1	−8	−8
Mean of eight prior recessions	−7	4	−10	−9
Standard deviation	4	4	5	3
Current recession July 1990	−17	−16	0	−1
Mean of nine prior recessions	−8	−1	−9	−8
Standard deviation	5	7	6	4

[a]The short rate is defined as the rate on 90-Day Treasury bills through 1961 and the effective rate on federal funds thereafter.
[b]NST = no specific turning point.
[c]n.a. = not applicable.
Source: Board of Governors of the Federal Reserve System; Standard & Poor's Corporation; U.S. Bureau of Economic Analysis.

Recession Index to anticipate the recession to the perverse behavior of the financial variables in the Index, arguing that real indicators "behaved qualitatively as they had in earlier recessions" (pp. 21–22). The same observation can be made about the behavior of short-term interest rates. Short-term interest rates are considered a roughly coincident indicator—they generally rise, often sharply, prior to cyclical peaks and typically fall once the recession has begun. Two clear exceptions—the increases in short-term rates during the 1973–75 and 1981–82 recessions—occurred in the midst of the longest, more severe recessions in the postwar period (Fig. 4).

The period leading up to the 1990–91 recession was a clear exception to previous postwar experience. Whereas the average lead time had been only one month and the *longest* prior lead time only four months (in 1960 and 1969), short-term interest rates peaked in the spring of 1989, 16 months before the business cycle peak. Prior to the 1990–91 recession, analysts could have correctly reasoned that no postwar recession had ever occurred after an extended period of declining short-term interest rates. It would seem a mistake to attribute the 1990–91 recession to rising interest rates; the proximate cause seems more likely to lie elsewhere. Even though a sharper decline in rates might have offset that unidentified "causal" factor, it is difficult to image that a much larger decline would have been feasible at the time, in the environment of low unemployment and rising inflation.

A follow-up survey of 34 of these same forecasters was conducted in August 1990, after the downward revision of the path of real GNP, the release of the actual data for 1990: II, and the invasion of Kuwait. Although the August forecasts were distinctly more pessimistic than those one month earlier—the average forecast for the second half of 1990 was revised down 1.3 percentage points to 0.3 percent and that for the first half of 1991 down 0.8 percentage points to 1.0 percent—two-thirds of the forecasters still expected real GNP to rise in both periods. Four did expect a brief, mild recession in 1990 but a resumption of growth in 1991; four others expected small but positive growth in the second half of 1990 followed by a decline in the first half of 1991; three expected negative growth in both periods. Of the nine forecasters who expected negative growth during the next year, all but one expected the decline in real GNP to be less than the actual decline of 0.9 percent (in 1982 dollars). It was not until their October forecasts that a clear majority of the eight prominent forecasters surveyed monthly in the Conference Board's *Economic Times* [20] anticipated the correct contours of the 1990–91 recession.

Although forecasters took longer to recognize that a recession had begun than in 1973 or 1981, and far longer than in 1980, they were much more accurate in gauging its severity and duration, if this recession did end in the spring of 1991, as has been assumed here. With the possible exception of the 1980 recession, forecasts made near the peak tend to underestimate its severity. The underestimation of the 1990–91 recession was trivial, however, especially when compared to forecasts of the severe recessions in 1973–75 and 1981–82.

SUMMARY AND CONCLUSIONS

The recession that began in mid 1990 and apparently ended in the spring of 1991 was milder than the average recession since World War II. The declines in production and employment were only about half as large as "normal"; the increase in the unemployment rate was the smallest in any postwar recession. The relatively small decline was due to a damped inventory cycle, as final sales fell by roughly an average amount. The declines were disproportionately concentrated in consumption of nondurable goods, the production of automobiles and light trucks, and the construction sector.

Perhaps the most unusual feature of the 1990–91 recession is the periods of slow growth both before and after the recession itself. A slowdown began a year and a half before the recession began. Real growth in the year prior to any postwar recession has never been lower than the 1.3 percent prior to the 1990–91 recession (Table 9). At the time, the slowdown was disguised by continuing employment growth—the level of nonfarm productivity had peaked in late 1988—and by the preliminary GNP data, which understated the degree of slowdown eventually revealed in the July 1990 revisions. This period of slow growth may have been attributable in part to the economy's operating at, or beyond, its productive capacity; the unemployment rate held below most estimates of "full employment" and the rate of inflation was slowly but steadily accelerating.

During this period, the index of leading indicators and stock prices were rising and short-term interest rates were generally declining. These were all highly unusual precursors for a recession. Consequently, even after Iraq had invaded Kuwait in early August, the majority of economic forecasters did not expect a recession. By the fall, after the record drop in consumer sentiment, most forecasters expected a mild recession, one of roughly the order of magnitude that did occur.

It is still too soon to write the history of the 1990 recession, let alone of even the early stages of the subsequent expansion. If the recession ended in the spring of 1991, the early recovery has been far weaker than previous recoveries. In other recoveries, economic activity has started to increase rapidly at about the same time that the recession ended (except for the expansion that began in 1954, when the lag was only a few months). In contrast, most of the monthly measures of economic activity, such as payroll employment, have

Table 9 Real GNP and Its Components: Percentage Changes from 1 Year Prior to Peaks

	48:4 (58$) (1)	53:2 (58$) (2)	57:3 (58$) (3)	60:2 (58$) (4)	69:4 (72$) (5)	73:4 (72$) (6)	80:1 (82$) (7)	81:3 (82$) (8)	Average of eight prior recessions (9)	90:3 (87$) (10)
GNP	4.5	6.0	2.4	2.0	1.3	2.2	1.6	3.3	3.3	1.3
Change in business inventories	0.7	1.5	-0.3	-1.2	-0.1	1.1	-0.7	2.0	0.4	-0.1
Final sales	3.8	5.3	2.7	3.2	1.4	3.1	2.3	1.3	2.9	1.4
Personal consumption expenditures	2.7	5.6	3.0	3.5	3.0	1.3	0.9	1.8	2.7	1.2
Durable goods	0	15.0	2.0	2.9	1.0	-0.3	-3.1	5.3	2.8	-3.1
Nondurable goods	1.7	4.0	3.1	2.9	2.0	-0.3	0.2	0.6	1.8	0.2
Services	4.9	4.7	3.3	4.5	4.6	3.5	2.5	1.8	3.7	3.0
Residential fixed investment	-8.7	5.3	-9.1	-13.4	-8.0	-12.6	-11.3	-3.5	-7.7	-9.9
Business fixed investment	5.5	2.0	0	7.4	4.5	10.6	3.6	8.7	5.3	2.0
Equipment	3.2	-2.5	2.1	8.5	4.8	13.2	-1.3	5.4	4.2	2.5
Structures	12.3	9.6	-3.2	6.2	4.1	6.0	14.3	14.6	8.0	0.9
Total government purchases	25.8	8.8	5.7	-.4	-2.3	1.7	1.8	1.5	5.3	2.2
Federal government	45.2	12.0	5.3	-3.0	-5.8	-1.8	2.9	5.8	7.6	-0.7
State and local government	8.4	1.7	6.2	2.8	1.0	4.0	1.1	-1.4	3.0	4.3
Net exports	-1.6	-0.8	0.1	1.0	0.1	1.5	1.5	-1.1	0.1	0.4
Exports	-15.1	-2.2	3.6	19.6	9.6	24.1	17.2	2.0	7.3	4.5
Imports	11.1	18.1	1.5	-.4	8.8	2.0	3.0	12.7	7.1	1.4
Auto production	10.7	41.7	25.9	2.9	-10.3	-6.3	-21.3	16.9	7.5	6.1

Note: The change in business inventories is the difference between the change in real GNP and the change in final sales. n.a. = not available.
Source: Ref. 2. Tables 1.2, 1.5, and 1.16; Ref. 4, Tables 1.2, 1.5, Tables 1.2, 1.4, and 1.15; Ref. 5, Tables 1.2, 1.4, and 1.18; Ref. 6, 1991; and author's calculations.

increased very little since their decline ended in the spring of 1991. The composite indexes of both leading and coincident indicators have increased far less at this stage of the cycle than in all earlier expansions. The most unusual feature of the 1990–91 recession may well be that it was both preceded and followed by periods of subpar growth, so that the "growth recession" that began in early 1989 has persisted for nearly three years.

NOTE

It is a mistake to attribute much significance to small differences in economic series drawn from very different time periods, as the data are not strictly comparable. For example, to combine all goods and services to arrive at an aggregate measure of GNP, one must adopt a set of fixed weights, typically the composition of output in a given base year. But the economic relevance of real GNP in 1953 measured with weights based on the composition of output in 1987 is far from clear. Many 1987 products did not even exist in 1953. To minimize this problem, this article uses weights from the base year closest to each recession (Table 1, column 4), even though this makes strict statistical comparisons impossible. Similarly, one cannot measure the gap between actual and potential resource utilization by the level of the unemployment rate or the capacity utilization rate, if their "full utilization" rates vary significantly over time. For example, a 6.1 percent unemployment rate in 1970, when the labor force had grown rapidly with an influx of young and inexperienced workers, probably represents less slack than the same rate in 1954, when the labor force was more experienced and had grown more slowly.

REFERENCES

1. G. H. Moore, "Businss Cycles, Inflation, and Forecasting," NBER Studies in Business Cycles No. 24, Ballinger, Cambridge, Mass. (1983).
2. U.S. Bureau of Economic Analysis, *The National Income and Product Accounts of the United States, 1929–65: Statistical Tables*, August (1966).
3. U.S. Bureau of Economic Analysis, "The National Income and Product Accounts: Revised Estimates," *Survey of Current Business*, April, July and August (1968–1991).
4. U.S. Bureau of Economic Analysis, *The National Income and Products Accounts of the United States, 1929–76: Statistical Tables*, September (1981).
5. U.S. Bureau of Economic Analysis, *The National Income and Product Accounts of the United States, 1929–82: Statistical Tables*, September (1986).
6. U.S. Bureau of Labor Statistics, "Prices, A Chartbook, 1953–62," Bulletin No. 1351 (1962).
7. C. D. Romer and D. H. Romer, "Does Monetary Policy Matter? A New Test in the Spirit of Friedman and Schwartz, " In *NBER Macroeconomics Annual 1989* (O.J. Blanchard and S. Fischer, eds.), MIT Press, Cambridge, Mass. pp. 121–183 (1989).
8. P. A. Samuelson, "Interactions Between the Multiplier Analysis and the Principle of Acceleration," *Review of Economics and Statistics, 21*(2):75–78 (1939).
9. L. A. Metzler, "The Nature and Stability of Inventory Cycles," *Review of Economics and Statistics, 23*(3):113–129 (1941).
10. J. R. Hicks, "Mr. Keynes and the Classics: A Suggested Interpretation," *Econometrica, 5*(2): 147–159 (1937).
11. V. Zarnowitz, "An Appraisal of Short-Term Economic Forecasts," National Bureau of Economic Research, Occasional Paper No. 104 (1967).
12. M. Friedman and A.J. Schwartz, *A Monetary History of the United States, 1867–1960*, Princeton University Press, Princeton, N.J. (1963).
13. W. Lewis, Jr., *Federal Fiscal Policy in the Postwar Recessions*, The Brookings Institution, Washington, D.C. (1962).

14. S. K. McNees, "Forecasting Cyclical Turning Points: The Record in the Past Three Recessions," *New England Economic Review*, March/April: 31–40 (1987).
15. B. P. Bosworth and R.Z. Lawrence, *Commodity Prices and the New Inflation*, The Brookings Institution, Washington, D.C. (1982).
16. Council of Economic Advisers, *Economic Report of the President*, Government Printing Office, Washington, D.C., Various years.
17. J. Peek and E.S. Rosengren, "The Stock Market and Economic Activity," *New England Economic Review*, May/June: 39–50 (1988).
18. T. Herman, "Lower Interest Rates Will Aid Economy, Help Avert Recession, But Growth Will Be Very Weak, Says Survey of 40 Economists," *Wall Street Journal*, July 5 (1990).
19. M. W. Watson, "Using Econometric Models to Predict Recessions," *Economic Perspectives*, *XV*(6) (1991).
20. Conference Board, *Economic Times*, Vols. 1 and 2, various issues (1990–1991).

5

The Evolution of the American Property Tax

Glenn W. Fisher

INTRODUCTION

The uniform tax upon all wealth, known as a general property tax, was an American innovation. In the nineteenth century, most of the constitutions adopted in the newly forming states on the frontier contained provisions mandating this tax as the principal form of taxation for state and local governments. Older states adopted uniform taxation by statute.

There was little systematic analysis of the general property tax prior to adoption, but the idea was consistent with the concepts of equality often identified as Jacksonian democracy. The administrative apparatus established to administer the tax was reflective of Jacksonian ideas and the conditions that existed on the frontier. Local officers were assigned specific duties by state statutes, but there was no provision for supervising or coordinating their work, even though the states were dependent upon the locally administered tax for the bulk of their revenue.

This type of organization was very different from the Weberian bureaucratic organization which has since been established to administer income and sales taxes. It proved inadequate for administering a true general property tax. This became more evident as property rights became more complex and tangible personal property more mobile.

The basic inconsistency between the desire to tax all wealth uniformly and the decentralized administrative structure resulted in a series of evolutionary changes. Legislatures enacted a variety of provisions designed to facilitate or encourage the accurate listing and valuing of property, but few of them were successful. Attempts to strengthen state control over local administration, especially assessment, were made. Some success was achieved, but there was, and is, strong resistance to state control. In most states, local assessors are still locally chosen and owe their primary loyalty to local governing bodies or local electorates. Often, administrative practices are adapted to local conditions or local political forces.

As a result of the failure of the states to clearly define the concept of uniform taxation of wealth and to establish an administrative organization capable of administering such a

Source: Public Budgeting and Financial Management, vol. 2, no. 1 (1990), pp. 279–309.

tax, the general property tax failed. It has been gradually replaced by a local property tax that is remarkably well adapted to financing the unusual system of numerous, overlapping, relatively autonomous units which characterize local government in the United States.

Among the most important characteristics of the tax is the growing importance of real estate in the tax base. The visibility and immobility of real estate and the *in rem* character of the property tax makes real estate taxation ideal for financing American local governments.

In response to political pressures, state legislatures have made other modifications, such as classification or exemption of property, and local authorities continue to make other, little publicized *de facto* changes. Assessment quality continues to be irregular and the tax is unpopular. Calls for eliminating it or reducing its role are frequent, but in the absence of major reorganization of local government the property tax will continue to be an important revenue source.

Political systems and tax systems are the result of long evolutionary processes. States and localities have traditions which carry over into current eras, and many kinds of shocks bring about changes which persist long after the conditions which brought them into being have disappeared [1]. For these reasons historical analysis can provide useful insights into the nature of the tax structure that are not revealed by cross section analysis.

This chapter explores the historical development of property taxation in the United States. It is argued that a strong symbiotic relationship exists between the structure of local government and the property tax, and that this relationship exists between the structure of local government and the property tax, and that this relationship results from interactions among constitutional, political, and administrative factors that date from the beginning of the country. Demands for equal taxation of wealth came into conflict with demands for local self government, creating political stress that resulted in system transformations and the evolution of a peculiarly American system of local government supported by a particularly American system of property taxation [2].

Property has been a subject of taxation for many centuries, but the idea of taxing all property at a uniform percentage of its value, sometimes called general property taxation, is arguably an American innovation [3]. Property taxes were an element in the colonial tax system; they did not apply to all kinds of property and often were based upon a statutory schedule of tax rates rather than upon the value of taxable property. To strengthen support for the revolutionary cause some colonial governments moved toward greater usage of broadly based, *ad valorem* taxation. The idea did not die despite some retreat from this concept after the war. Instead, it spread slowly until the beginning of the constitutional uniformity movement in the nineteenth century, when the idea received almost universal acceptance among political leaders [4].

CONSTITUTIONAL UNIFORMITY IN THE NINETEENTH CENTURY

In the nineteenth century uniformity clauses were written into the constitutions of most of the new states on the frontier. Illinois adopted a uniformity clause in 1818, although no attempt to implement it was made for several years. Missouri followed in 1820. In 1834 Tennessee replaced a unique clause requiring that land be taxed at a uniform amount per acre with an *ad valorem* uniformity clause. After that the practice spread rapidly. By the end of the century 32 states had adopted constitutions containing uniformity clauses or had revised constitutions to include such clauses. Several post Civil War constitutions of the Confederate states contained uniformity clauses. New Jersey was the only eastern seaboard state, other than former Confederate states, to adopt a uniformity clause, but several adopted uniformity by statute [5].

Twenty-two constitutional provisions adopted in the nineteenth century also contained universality clauses requiring that all property except designated kinds of religious, charitable, and government property be taxed.

Intellectual Roots of Uniformity

The origins of the uniformity movement are unclear. There are few records of debates over the issue and no evidence of any detailed evaluation of the merits of the tax. However, the concept is consistent with important intellectual and political sentiments of the period.

Adam Smith's canons of taxation were widely quoted. Early leaders, including James Madison, Alexander Hamilton, Albert Gallatin, James Monroe, and Thomas Jefferson, knew and quoted his work [6]. Some 2000 copies of *The Wealth of Nations* had been sold in the United States by 1820 [7]. Albert Gallatin wrote that the distinction between direct and indirect taxes found in the U.S. Constitution was borrowed from *The Wealth of Nations* [8].

Smith made no mention of a general or *ad valorem* property tax, but focused his analysis upon taxation of rent, profits and labor. His discussion of the tax on rents assumed a tax on annual, rather than capital, value. The only references to taxes based upon capital value were a brief, unfavorable, mention of tax on housing in Holland and a discussion of succession or transfer taxes based upon the value of the estate transferred [9]. Despite Smith's failure to discuss a property tax based on capital value, his first maxim was often cited in support of a general property tax. This reads, in part:

> I. The subjects of every state ought to contribute towards the support of government, as nearly as possible, in proportion to their respective abilities; that is, in proportion to the revenue which they respectively enjoy under the protection of the state. The expence of government to the individuals of a great nation, is like the expence of management to the joint tenants of a great estate, who are all obliged to contribute in proportion to their respective interests in the estate. In the observation or neglect of this maxim consists, what is called the equality or inequality of taxation. [10]

In light of a modern understanding of the difference between wealth and income, or even in light of Smith's discussion of the English tax on land rents, it is reasonable to argue that this maxim supports a proportional income tax, rather than a property tax. In the light of the conditions which existed when uniformity clauses were adopted, its use to support a general property tax was plausible. Many of the expenses of state and local government in newly opened territories were related to the settlers' attempts to establish their "estates" by acquiring and developing raw lands. The prevalence of land speculation focused attention upon capital value rather than upon the annual value.

In any case there was surprisingly little scholarly discussion of the general property tax during the time uniformity provisions were being adopted. There was much discussion of the protective tariff, but the scattered discussions of other kinds of taxation merely paraphrased Adam Smith or other classical English economists.

Political Roots of Uniformity

However weak the intellectual foundations of the general property tax, there was clearly important political support for the concept of uniform taxation. A loosely defined set of concepts sometimes called Jacksonian democracy, populism, or frontier democracy has been important throughout much of American history, but was especially important in the nineteenth century. The spread of the general property tax and elimination of property qualifications for voting and office holding were important manifestations of these concepts.

The Jacksonians depended upon experience, not theory. They dealt with problems as practical men on the basis of common sense [11]. Apparently they accepted the equality and justice of general property tax as an obvious truth. Robert J. Walker, President Polk's Secretary of the Treasury, in his classic statement of the democratic case against protectionism remarked, "It is deemed that taxation, whether direct or indirect, should be as nearly as practicable in proportion to property" [12]. Many workingmen's newspapers included among the slogans on their mastheads, "Equal Taxation of Property" [13]. In 1888 Francis A. Walker, a leading American economist, quotes an earlier writer as saying the system of taxation which the great mass of Americans instinctively accept is the equal taxation of property and the nontaxation of labor. Walker adds:

> . . . it is unquestionably true that the American of the period immediately preceding the Civil War did look upon wealth as the proper subject of taxation for the imposition of taxes to the full extent, or nearly so, of the needs of government. [14]

There seems to have been very little debate about property tax uniformity in the constitutional conventions, but some statements on the subject have been recorded. In 1849, the year the California constitution was written, the governor said:

> The law protects every man in his person and property. for the protection it gives his person he ought to pay a capitation or poll tax; and for the protection it gives his property, he ought to pay a tax in proportion to its amount and value. [15]

A member of the West Virginia constitutional convention of 1861–63 is quoted as saying:

> I look on this principle of the equality of property in regard to taxation as second only to the great principle which we have adopted, the equality of persons regarding representation. [16]

Constitutional Uniformity as Legislative Limitation

The uniformity requirement was consistent not only with Jacksonian concepts of uniformity, but also with the concept of limited government that lies deep in American political tradition. Early American constitution writers, reacting against the powers granted colonial governors, were careful to limit the power of the executive branch. The Articles of Confederation carried this to the extreme of not providing an executive branch. This proved unworkable and was remedied in the Philadelphia Constitutional Convention, but the separation of power among the branches of government was designed to avoid concentrating power in any branch of government. State constitutions were modeled after the federal constitution, but those adopted in the first years after the revolution generally provided for strong legislative branches and limited executive power. Later, when concern shifted to limiting the power of legislatures, constitutional provisions prescribing the form of taxation seemed an effective way of accomplishing this. Thus, uniformity clauses served a dual purpose—insuring that taxation would be in line with prevailing concepts of equitable taxation and limiting the power of the legislative branch of state government.

Decentralized Administration

Property tax administrative systems were established by state legislatures. They differed from state to state depending upon the conditions and the traditions with which the settlers in a given area were familiar. In some, the New England pattern of strong local government was influential. Others were influenced by the Southern tradition of more centralized government, but for the most part, the structures were in harmony with the Jacksonian desire for many elected officials and the belief that no special expertise was needed to hold government jobs.

In most of the states outside New England the county was the principal administrative unit for state law. Goodnow has referred to the result as legislative centralization/administrative decentralization. State legislatures passed laws but enforcement was left largely to officials elected by the counties [17].

The responsibilities for administering the property tax were divided among a large number of local officials. Often the county clerk was directed by the statutes to prepare assessment books according to a specified format. These were to be delivered to the assessors. Most commonly the assessors were elected township officials, but sometimes the law provided for city, ward, or county assessors and sometimes they were appointed by a local board. It was expected that assessment would require only a few days and compensation was on a per diem basis. The assessment books were returned to the county clerk and assessments were reviewed by the township or county board (or both) sitting as a board of equalization. Tax levies were made by the governing boards of the tax levying bodies and the tax bills were computed by the county clerk. County, city, or school district treasurers were designated as tax collectors. Typically, they were compensated by a percentage of taxes collected. Taxes due the state or other local government bodies were transmitted according to prescribed procedures and on prescribed dates. Uncollectible taxes were certified to the sheriff and, if his efforts failed, the sheriff, county attorney, and county clerk carried out the additional steps to bring about a tax sale. Often the statutory instructions for carrying out the duties were detailed, but supervision by the state was minimal, if not nonexistent.

The failure to develop statewide administrative structures needs to be understood in the context of the traditions, history, and the legal status of local government. The origins of local government structure in the United States are complex. Some features can be traced to English origins, but many modifications resulted from frontier conditions [18]. Except in the states which had been colonies, state or territorial governments were usually created before local governments so that local governments were historically as well as legally "creatures of the state." The state, a sovereign body, retained the authority to make laws but delegated the administration of those laws to officials elected by and responsible to a local electorate. Aside from any philosophical or political arguments for local government, there was a practical one. In most cases the newly forming states lacked the capacity to establish a state-wide administrative system. Enforcement of criminal laws, registering of land titles, and the collection of state and local taxes, all essential functions in a frontier area, were left to local officials sworn to uphold the state constitution and statutes.

The courts firmly upheld the legal supremacy of the state. Judge Thomas Colley's view that local governments were miniature polities with a measure of sovereignty received short-lived support in a few states, but Dillon's Rule, upholding the supremacy of the state over local governments, prevailed [19]. The legal doctrine is not the whole story, however. From a practical viewpoint, local units of government and local officials always held a great deal of political power. Then, as now, people developed intense loyalties to local communities and felt strongly about state "interference" in local affairs. This created an administratively complex situation. Property tax laws were enacted by the state, but administered by locally elected officials who were both administrative agents of the state and officials of the local government. These local officials normally felt more loyalty to local government and to the local electorate than to the state.

FAILURE OF THE GENERAL PROPERTY TAX

By the beginning of the twentieth century, the general property tax was recognized as a failure. Several articles condemning it had appeared in scholarly journals, and the National Tax Association, organized in 1906, devoted its first several annual conferences largely to condemnation of the tax. Papers delivered at those meetings included phrases such as "worst tax ever devised" and "it's impossible to speak of the failures of the tax in temperate terms" to describe the tax [20].

Reasons for failure of the tax were of three kinds. Some were related to failure of legislative bodies and tax administrators to properly conceptualize the concept of wealth as a tax base. Others were related to administrative structure and administrative techniques, while a third group involved the legal complexities of jurisdiction to tax property.

Conceptual Problems

Conceptual problems arose from the failure to define what was meant by "uniform taxation of property." Advocates of uniformity failed to deal with the problems resulting from the differences between property as a legal term referring to a bundle of rights and wealth as an economic concept. The rights to a particular item of wealth can be separated by the creation of mortgages or leases or by the separation of mineral from surface rights. Modern forms of business organizations, such as corporations, create complex property rights over a variety of tangible and intangible assets.

It is clear from examining the legislative history of the property tax that early legislators were aware of these problems, if unsure of the solutions. Numerous changes were made in the statutes regarding the taxation of such intangibles as mortgages, bank notes and bank stock, but there is no evidence that the attempted solutions were based upon a clear understanding of the problem. It was not until 1931 that Professor Jens Jensen clarified the issue by making a distinction between representative and nonrepresentative intangible property rights. Representative property, he said, is a right to an item of tangible wealth. Double taxation results if both the tangible wealth and representative intangible are taxed. Nonrepresentative intangible property, such as the going concern value of a business, is wealth and should be taxed. Jensen had some doubts as to the practical usefulness of this distinction, but in any case, it came much too late in the history of property taxation to have much influence [21].

Jurisdictional Problems

Problems arose from the relatively small areas covered by the jurisdiction administering the tax—township, county, or municipality—and from legal limits on the ability of states to tax property outside their borders. Certain kinds of tangible personal property are easily moveable. Cattle were driven from jurisdiction to jurisdiction to avoid assessment dates, and merchants' inventories were manipulated so that stocks were low on assessment day. Railroad rolling stock passed through many local jurisdictions on assessment day, but often could not be identified in any.

Intangible property presented even more difficult problems. A corporation many have tangible property in hundreds of local jurisdictions and security holders in thousands. Any system for taxing all the wealth of a large corporation would require the coordinated effort of many state and local jurisdictions. Even attempts to uniformly tax relatively simple property interests, such as real estate mortgages, ran into jurisdictional problems. Efforts to separately tax the interest of mortgagee and mortgagor were difficult if the mortgagee lived in another state. When the effort was successful, out-of-state lenders refused to lend or raised the interest rate to compensate for the tax.

Administrative Problems

If the conceptual and jurisdictional problems could have been solved, there would still have been need for sophisticated administrative organizations and procedures. The weakness of the organizations that existed can be understood by comparing administration as it existed in the nineteenth century with the features of a well structured government bureaucracy as outlined by Max Weber [22]:

1. *Division of labor and functional specialization.* This feature of Weber's model was found in nineteenth century property tax administration. The tasks involved in property tax administration were divided among several local officers and the statutes spelled out the responsibilities of each local official in considerable detail. There was very little duplication or overlapping of responsibilities.

2. *Hierarchy—a clear vertical "chain of command" in which each unit is subordinate to the one above it and superior to the one below it.* This feature of an effective governmental bureaucracy was almost completely lacking in nineteenth century property tax administration. The elected local officers were responsible only to the electorate, although their budgetary dependency on a county commission or other governing body may have created something of a subordinate–superior relationship. The principal instrument of enforcing performance of duty by local administrative officers was the judiciary. Taxpayers or other local officials could ask for a mandamus or an injunction to force an official to take or abstain from an action, but this was a blunt instrument. Courts occasionally invalidated tax titles because of procedural irregularities, or ruled on the taxability of claims for tax exemptions, but in the absence of obvious fraud, they rarely undertook to reassess property and almost never invalidated an entire tax levy.

3. *Formal framework of rules and procedures.* Complicated administrative procedures are normally governed by administrative regulations which supplement statutory provisions. Formal rules are needed to insure stability, predictability, and impersonality in bureaucratic organizations and thus bring about equal treatment for all who deal with the organization. Such regulations were rare at both state and local levels.

    One of the principal reasons for prizing small-scale local government is that it is personal—not impersonal bureaucratic. Assessors often ignored the statutes to benefit "poor widows," friends, or political allies. A quotation concerning centralization in English government could be equally well applied to America:

In every question of government, the fact of the Englishman's inbred opposition to centralization must not be forgotten. It is by no means unreasonable to say that had the central authority held the local authorities to the very letter of the law, public opinion would have demanded the removal of this central control, the far inferior results would have been secured than in reality have been. [23]

4. *Maintenance of files and other records.* State laws usually spelled out the format of the assessment rolls, tax rolls and other official documents, but supporting and procedural records were probably not common.

5. *Professionalism.* To meet Weber's criteria of professionalism, employees have to be appointed on the basis of job-related skills, be full-time career-oriented persons, and be paid a regular salary. It is safe to say that very few nineteenth century property tax administrators met this criterion. The exceptions were in metropolitan areas, but it was in other metropolitan areas that control of assessment was an important element in the power of political machines.

Lack of expertise was especially significant in the assessment process. Perhaps the part time farmer-assessor did have knowledge of the value of the land, farm machinery, and livestock which made up the bulk of property in the earliest days of statehood, but if so, that period soon passed. Tangible property became more complex and specialized, and values fluctuated as prices and economic conditions changed. The profession of appraisal was in it infancy. Value theory was central to the writing of economists, but at the end of the nineteenth century attempts to apply this theory to appraisal problems were just beginning. Few attempts had been made to provide training for assessors, and those few were confined largely to instructions in law rather than to appraisal methods.

EVOLUTION OF THE MODERN PROPERTY TAX

The need for an adequate, operational definition of property existed from the beginning of property taxation, but became increasingly important with the growth of the corporate form of business organization and the development of new kinds of property interests. It is not clear whether or not the problem was solvable. Very little attention was devoted to the problem by economists, and analysis of specific problems, such as the taxation of mortgages, was largely divorced from any general theory of wealth.

The reasons for a lack of adequate administrative structures are clearer. Such structures did not exist because they would have been incompatible with political and constitutional realities. The apportionment clause of the U.S. Constitution effectively prevented federal property taxation, insuring that the tax would be state or local. Thus, the administrative structure reflected the political ideology and the frontier conditions under which state constitutions and early statutes were written. Citizen legislators passed detailed statutes to be administered by locally elected officials sworn to support the law, but subject to no supervision by an administrative superior. Faced with the difficult problem of determining the market value of a variety of kind of property, it is not surprising that local officials were often influenced by local sentiment or the demands of politically important taxpayers.

Modification of the tax was not confined to local administrative actions. Legislatures, too, responded to complaints and pressures from taxpayers. Many of those who complained were advancing their own interest in lower taxes, but appeals to ideals such as equality or home rule often were used.

The demand for lower taxes had to be balanced with the need for local government revenue. Local government supplied essential services to American communities. Public safety, transportation facilities, public health service, and education were provided by a complex network of overlapping local governments. This created a network of people who as beneficiaries, officials, or employees of these governmental units accepted the property tax because it was necessary to finance local government. The political system responded to demands for lower taxes in ways which did not seriously endanger financial support for local government, even if principles of tax equality had to be sacrificed.

Although the evolution of the tax did not follow the same course in every state or locality, there seems to be one constant. The features of the tax which made it especially effective in producing revenue for local governments were preserved. The tax which evolved was not a general property tax, it did not produce equal taxation, but it financed a system of local government characterized by a large number of overlapping, relatively autonomous units. A leading student of public administration observed in the 1930s that in no important country of the world was local government so free of central administrative supervision as in the United States [24].

The evolutionary process was complex. It took a slightly different form in every state, but there were some general trends that are evident in many states. Only a brief recital of these is possible here [25].

Improving Administration

The conflict of interest between state governments and local administrators of the tax was revealed early in the history of the tax when local assessors discovered that underassessment of property would benefit the taxpayers of the district by reducing their share of the tax levied by the state or other overlapping taxing districts. To combat competitive undervaluation, state boards of equalization were created to equalize assessments among counties or other areas. Such boards existed in colonial days and by 1900 approximately two-thirds of the states had such boards [26]. Usually they were composed of elected state officials meeting for a few days per year. They rarely had staff or adequate data to carry out effective equalization. Typically they were provided with average assessed values per acre of land and per lot and, sometimes, with the average values assigned to items of personal property such as cows, horses, or particular items of machinery. Equalization was a politically unpopular task, and the lack of data regarding actual values made defending decisions difficult.

The early focus upon inequalities among geographic areas is explained by several different factors: (1) Political representation was by area. Securing or defending lower assessments for an area had obvious political payoffs for both local assessors and legislators. (2) There was often greater loyalty to local communities than to larger entities such as state or nation. (3) Inequalities were obvious, especially in frontier areas oriented toward land acquisition and speculation.

It soon became apparent that blanket changes in the assessment of particular kinds of property or property located in particular assessment districts could not correct poor original assessment. Attention turned toward inequities with assessing districts, and well before the end of the nineteenth century a variety of methods of improving intradistrict assessment equality were tried. Local boards of review were given authority to change individual assessments. Self-assessment schemes, backed by stringent oaths, were tried, as was a system of monetary awards to tax ferrets for reporting omitted or underassessed property. Methods of measuring intradistrict equality were developed. Usually these involved comparing assessed values with sales prices or with mortgage amounts, but early statistical methods were crude.

Expansion of the study of public administration and the governmental reform movements early in the twentieth century directed attention to the need to professionalize the assessment process. In a number of states, study commissions suggested that assessors be full-time professionals and that assessment personnel be trained in assessment methods. A number of states followed Indiana's 1891 lead by establishing tax commissions to take over equalization duties, to supervise local assessors, and to assess railroads and public utilities. The author of a comprehensive history of this movement reported in 1918 that the results were mixed. Forces opposing this move were strong [27]. This is well illustrated in Kansas, where an assessment reform law was passed in 1907 during a progressive Republican administration. A tax commission was established and given wide power to train and supervise county assessors. County assessors, in turn, were given power to choose and supervise deputy assessors who were to do the actual work of assessment. But, before the law was fully effective a special session of the legislature added a provision requiring that township trustees be appointed as deputy assessors. Further weakening of the law by legislative action occurred periodically thereafter. Even so, the Kansas commission was widely cited as a model, and the energetic chairman was elected president of the National Tax Association.

There were gradual improvements in appraisal methodology. Wide publicity was given to the "Somers" method of assessment developed in St. Paul, Minnesota. W. A. Somers, a former city engineer who had taken up the real estate business, became county assessor in 1891. He developed a system based upon using the opinion of builders and real estate experts to value lots and improvements. Corner influence and depth tables were developed to help value unusually sized or shaped lots, and buildings were classified by grade as an aid to determining the reproduction cost. Although somewhat deficient in terms of modern appraisal theory, this widely copied method met the Weberian criteria of professionalism and impersonality [28].

Separation of Sources

Early property tax reformers advocated separation of sources as a way of alleviating property tax problems. Most states took over the assessment of railroad and other utilities in the nineteenth century, but values were allocated back to local units for tax purposes. Advocates of separation of sources sometimes proposed that these values be taxed by the state. Some went further and proposed that the state take over the assessment and taxation of all complex properties such as manufacturing or intangible properties. Others advocated state use of nonproperty taxes such as inheritance or income taxes. The first suggestion was not acceptable to local governments and made little progress, but there was movement toward state adoption of nonproperty taxes in the early part of the twentieth century. The movement was greatly accelerated in the depression of the 1930s when states virtually abandoned the property tax in favor of income and sales taxes. Today, separation of sources is a fact. The property tax is almost entirely a local tax.

Administrative factors were important in the success of separation of sources. Income tax laws had been on the books in several states, but until Wisconsin centralized administration in 1911 they had produced little revenue. Centralized state tax administration systems were much closer to the Weberian model of bureaucratic organization. The feasibility of the retail sales tax was enhanced when the compensating use tax was held to be constitutional. This greatly reduced problems caused by the constitutional prohibition of state taxation of interstate sales.

Modification of the Base

One of the most important evolutionary changes has been the progressive exemption of personal property, both tangible and intangible. This evolution is still under way. *Ad valorem* taxation of intangibles has almost disappeared, but some taxes on intangible property or on the income from intangible property levied in lieu of *ad valorem* taxes are still in effect.

The difficulties experienced by local assessors in locating intangible property and in establishing jurisdiction to tax property, once found, were great, often insurmountable. In some cases it was not clear that intangibles should be taxed. Jensen's distinction between representative and nonrepresentative intangibles did not provide a practical answer, especially when the values involved were scattered among many taxing jurisdictions. In spite of the problems, some ingenious efforts to tax intangibles were made. The attempts to tax the difference between the value of the tangible assets of a corporation and its value as a going concern, sometimes known as corporate excess, is a case in point. The corporate excess tax laws provided that the value of the corporation as a going concern was to be calculated and the corporate excess derived by subtracting the assessed value of tangible assets. This had the merit of correcting for any under- or overassessment of tangible property. A combination of jurisdictional and constitutional problems compounded the difficulty of educating assessors and the general public as to the validity of the approach [29].

Taxation of tangible personal property continues in many states, but the trend is toward its elimination. A few states exempt all personal property. Very few attempt to tax household goods and personal effects. Inventories and many kinds of machinery are exempted in many states.

The interaction between administrative and political factors in the evolution of the property tax is well illustrated by the politics of property tax exemptions. Interest groups have made good use of the argument that the taxation of personal property is administratively difficult and adverse to economic development. Subtle or overt threats to move productive personal property from the state unless exempted from taxation have often played a role in political battles over exemption of personal property.

Another change in the nature of the tax base resulted from the adoption of property tax classification in several states. Early advocates of classification argued that property differs in its ability to pay taxes and that "scientific" classification would take account of those differences, but it is apparent that political power, rather than scientific principles, determines the level at which different classes of property are taxed. Most classification systems have been adopted as part of a reassessment or assessment reform effort. Fear of the political consequences of the shift in taxes that would result from reappraisal sometimes leads states to adopt a classification system reducing the shift. For example, the recently adopted classification amendment in Kansas was intended to reduce the shift of taxation from commercial, industrial, and utility property to residential and farm property that would have occurred if property had been reappraised under the uniformity requirement.

Although the modifications in the tax base have varied in detail and timing, there is one constant. Real estate makes up an increasingly large part of the total tax base. This is perhaps the clearest evidence of the interaction between tax structure and the survival of local government. Real estate taxation, as it developed in the United States, has three great advantages as a source of local taxation. It is visible, it is immobile, and it is levied *in rem* (against the property).

Visibility means that only simple procedures are required to identify the taxable object. In small rural jurisdictions the assessor can personally see all the potential tax base. Even in larger cities it is a rather simple clerical task to locate untaxed property using available city maps or aerial photographs.

The land portion of real estate is immobile. The building portion can change only slowly as the result of new building or the deterioration of existing buildings. This means that the tax base will not be quickly affected by changes in the tax rate. It also means that jurisdiction to tax is fixed and easily determinable.

In rem taxation means that the tax is levied against the property, not against the owner. This simplifies both the levy and the collection of the tax. The tax may be levied against the property, even if the owner is unknown or the ownership of the property is in dispute. If local officials fail to carry out the statutory directions to sell real estate on which taxes are delinquent, taxes remain a lien against the property. Taxes plus penalty and interest will continue to accumulate. Any attempt to transfer or mortgage the property will result in a title search that will reveal a lien that must be removed before good title can pass. Only in instances of severe contraction of real estate values, as in an economic depression or in blighted areas, are real estate taxes likely to go unpaid for long.

The self-collecting aspect of real estate taxation is an especially important characteristic of a local tax. Vigorous tax collection is an unpleasant duty which few officials enjoy performing. It is doubly unpleasant when carried out against one's friends and neighbors, and it may be political suicide when those friends and neighbors are also the electorate. The *in rem* character of the property tax results in the process being largely automatic and much less personal.

THE PROPERTY TAX TODAY

The hope that a general property tax, uniform and equal upon all kinds of property, would be the perfect tax system died long ago, but the property tax is still very much alive. It is the major source of local tax revenue in the United States. The case for the tax on the grounds of equity is weak, but a strong case for it can be made by those who want to preserve and strengthen local government. There is evidence for this not only in the historical record, but also in comparative tax literature [30].

It is beyond the scope of this chapter to describe or analyze the tax as it exists today, but it is important to extend the historical account by pointing out a few important characteristics. . . .

The Property Tax as Source of Local Government Revenue

There is no doubt that the fiscal importance of the property tax has declined. In 1986 it provided less than 1 percent of state government revenue and, as shown in Table 1, only 28.2 percent of local government revenue.

On the other hand, the property tax provided 74.0 percent of local *tax* revenue. To those who are concerned about local governments retaining some degree of fiscal independence this is a significant figure. Despite state property tax limits and controls over local expenditure of property tax funds, localities usually have more control over the levy and expenditure of property tax funds than over state aid funds, or even over locally levied, state-collected sales or income taxes.

There are, of course, many variations hidden in these total figures. Generally, local governments in the New England states with their strong tradition of local government depend more heavily upon the property tax than do local governments in the Southern states with a tradition of greater centralization. School districts and townships depend more heavily upon property taxes than do counties and municipalities. This observation seems to fit the conclusion that the property tax is an especially valuable revenue source for small, overlapping governments.

Table 1 Distribution of Local Government
Revenue, 1986

Federal aid	5.4%
State aid	33.3%
Property taxes	28.2%
General sales tax	4.2%
Individual income tax	1.8%
Corporate income tax	0.4%
Other taxes	3.5%
All use charges	13.2%
Miscellaneous general revenue	10.0%
Total local general revenue	100.0%

Source: Ref. 32.

State-to-State Variation

Abandonment of the general property tax ideal and repeal or modification of uniformity clauses in the state constitutions allowed state legislatures more freedom to shape tax policy to the ideology, needs, and political realities within the state. The result is that state-to-state variations in the property tax are probably greater than at any time since the beginning of the uniformity movement. In a departure from the *in rem* concept, property tax statues have been personalized by the addition of homestead exemptions, circuit breakers, and other provisions which take into account the needs of the property owner. These provisions differ considerably from state to state [31]. Homestead exemption frees a certain amount of the value of owner occupied homes from taxation. Circuit breakers are much more flexible and may take into account the income, age, dependents, and other characteristics of the owner or occupier. Circuit-breaker legislation in most states recognized the importance the property tax to local governments and provides rebates from the state rather than a reduction in the property tax paid local governments. Interestingly, circuit breakers formalize a practice that has been common, but illegal, throughout much of the history of property taxation. Perusal of the property tax literature, including proceedings of assessor conferences, will yield ample evidence that local assessors' judgment of the value of property was often tempered by their judgment as to how much tax the owner should or could pay.

Classification of property into different classes for purposes of taxation continued to spread. Originally classification applied only to intangible property and often resulted in lower rates in intangible property or the substitution of nonproperty taxes in lieu of property taxation. Today a number of states classify real estate as well.

Another major source of variation results from exemptions granted to encourage industrial development. Some states have statewide policies; others grant a good deal of freedom to local units of government. Often exemption policies are related to other economic development policies such as the issue of tax exempt bonds for industrial development purposes.

Most states have departed from *ad valorem* taxation of agricultural lands. There are a large variety of use-value provisions which purport to base taxation upon the value of land in agricultural use rather than on the basis of market value in the highest and best use. Some include recapture provisions, some involve contracts between the land owner and the government, and some simply provide a different method of assessing land classified as agricultural.

Administrative Arrangements

The attempt to improve assessment of the property tax has never ceased. Private appraisal organizations, the International Association of Assessing Officers, and other groups were instrumental in developing and disseminating appraisal methodologies based upon the three approaches to value: comparative sales, income, and cost. Recently, emphasis has been upon developing approaches to mass appraisal that are more suitable for the task facing appraisers and take advantage of low cost, easy to use computers. Computer-assisted mass appraisal (CAMA) systems utilize econometric methodology to make much better use of the data available to assessors.

Software packages have been developed that require only moderate statistical and computer skills. These packages are not only helpful in determining values, but also contain programs for testing the quality of assessment and for providing detailed information about the tax base. The new methodologies offer interesting possibilities for changing state–local relationships. Perhaps it will be possible for state agencies to monitor local assessment procedures in less obtrusive ways. This may involve state prescription of computer software and the application of standard statistical tests of assessment quality rather than day-to-day state supervision or state acquisition of large amounts of data.

The Future

Many predictions about the future of the property tax, especially those that predicted its rapid demise, have proved wrong. The current author has no desire to add to the list, but it does seem reasonable to suggest that the future of the property tax will be closely bound up with the future of local government in the United States. Economic analysis of taxation has its place, but any analysis of the property tax that does not give ample attention to administrative factors and to the political system in which both policy and administrative decisions are made is apt to miss several very important parts of the picture.

NOTES AND REFERENCES

1. J. M. Stonecash, "Fiscal Centralization in the American States: Findings from Another Perspective," *Public Budgeting & Finance*, 8:81–89 (1988).
2. The model of political systems developed by David Easton provides many insights into the way that political systems evolve and persist in the face of changing circumstances and conflicting demands. D. Easton, *A Framework for Political Analysis*, Prentice-Hall, Englewood Cliffs, N.J. (1965).
3. Professor E. R. A. Seligman traced the history of the property tax from ancient times and concluded that, once direct taxation is accepted, it assumes the shape of a land tax and then develops into a general tax. Various kinds of personal property escape taxation until the tax reverts to its original form as a real estate tax. E. R. A. Seligman, *Essays in Taxation*, 10th ed., Macmillan, New York, p. 56 (1928). A late historian of the property tax concluded that the general property tax is largely indigenous and never existed in Europe: J. P. Jensen, *Property Taxation in the United States*, University of Chicago Press, Chicago, pp. 19–26 (1931).
4. R. A. Becker, *Revolution, Reform and the Politics of American Taxation*, Louisiana State University Press, Baton Rouge (1980).
5. G. W. Fisher, "The General Property Tax in the Nineteenth Century: The Search for Equality," *Property Tax Journal*, 6:99–117 (1987).
6. H. C. Adams, *Taxation in the United States, 1789–1816*, Burt Franklin, New York, p. 21 (1884).

7. C. P. Neil and D. Raymond, *An Early Chapter in the History of Economic Theory in the United States*, John Hopkins University Studies, John Hopkins University Press, Baltimore (June 1987).

8. H. C. Adams [6], p. 21.

9. A. Smith, *An Inquiry into the Nature and Causes of the Wealth of Nations*, Cannan ed., Modern Library, New York, pp. 797, 809–814 (1937).

10. A. Smith, [10], p. 777.

11. L. D. White, *The Jacksonians: A Study in Administrative History*, Macmillan Company, New York, p. 551 (1954).

12. A. W. Schlesinger, Jr. *The Age of Jackson*, Little, Brown, Boston, p. 443 (1945). Walker was later the first territorial governor of Kansas.

13. A. W. Schlesinger, Jr.: [12], p. 134.

14. F. A. Walker, "The Bases of Taxation," *Political Science Quarterly*, *III*(March):1–16 (1888).

15. California, "Governor's Annual Message," *Journal of the Senate*, December 21, p. 35 (1849).

16. *Debates and Proceedings of the First Constitutional Convention of West Virginia, 1861–63*, III, Gentry Bros., p. 88 (n.d.).

17. F. J. Godnow, *City Government in the United States*, Century, New York, pp. 71–72 (1908).

18. The first local governments in every part of what is now the United States were established under frontier conditions. There were differences in time and space between frontier Virginia or Massachusetts and frontier Wyoming, but there were important similarities, such as the lack of established governmental and social institutions and sparse population.

19. D. S. Wright, *Understanding Intergovernmental Relations*, 3rd ed., Brooks/Cole, Pacific Grove, Calif., pp. 310–312 (1988).

20. The first national conference was held in 1907. National Tax Association, *Conference on State and Local Taxation, 1907*, Columbus, Ohio (1908). The proceedings of the second conference was published under the title *Second International Conference on State and Local Taxation*, but after a few years the term "national" was restored, even though Canadian participants took an active part.

21. J. P. Jensen, *Property Taxation in the United States*, University of Chicago Press, Chicago, pp. 48–53 (1931).

22. Based on an outline of Weber's model found in G. J. Gordon, *Public Administration in America*, St. Martin's Press, New York, pp. 58–60 (1978). At the end of the nineteenth century the discipline of public administration was in its infancy in the United States, but many of the principles that Weber articulated had been common in the military and ecclesiastical organizations for many centuries.

23. M. R. Malthie, "English Local Government of Today. A Study of the Relations of Central and Local Government," *Studies in History, Economics and Public Law*, *IX*(1):241 (1897).

24. L. D. White, *Trends in Public Administration*, McGraw-Hill, New York, pp. 49, 69 (1933).

25. The account that follows is based upon wide reading of state statutes and constitutions as well as numerous commission reports and scholarly articles. Much research is needed to quantify and date the changes.

26. L. D. White, [24], pp. 57–61.

27. H. L. Lutz, *The State Tax Commission*, Harvard University Press, Cambridge, Mass., pp. 33–39 (1918).

28. W. A. Somers, "Valuation of City Real Estate for Taxation," *Municipal Affairs*, Reform Club, Committee on Municipal Administration, New York, pp. 401–18 (1901).

29. G. W. Fisher, *Taxes and Politics: A Study of Public Finance*, University of Illinois Press, Urbana, Ill., pp. 129–133 (1969).

30. G. W. Fisher, "Four Challenging Hypotheses on the Property Tax," paper delivered at the International Symposium on the Property Tax, Seville, Spain, November 1988. Published in *Property Tax Journal*, June 1989.

31. Advisory Commission on Intergovernmental Relations, *Significant Features of Fiscal Federalism*, Washington, D.C., I (January): 74–89 (1989).

32. Advisory Commission on Intergovernmental Relations, *Significant Features of Fiscal Federalism*, Washington, D.C., 2(July): 70 (1988).

6

The Road to PPB: The Stages of Budget Reform

Allen Schick

Among the new men in the nascent PPB (Program Planning Budgeting) staffs and the fellow travelers who have joined the bandwagon, the mood is of "a revolutionary development in the history of government management." There is excited talk about the differences between what has been and what will be; of the benefits that will accrue from an explicit and "hard" appraisal of objectives and alternatives; of the merits of multiyear budget forecasts and plans; of the divergence between the skills and role of the analyst and the job of the examiner; of the realignments in government structure that might result from changes in the budget process.

This is not the only version, however. The closer one gets to the nerve centers of budget life—the Divisions in the Bureau of the Budget and the budget offices in the departments and agencies—the more one is likely to hear that "there's nothing very new in PPB; it's hardly different from what we've been doing until now." Some old-timers interpret PPB as a revival of the performance budgeting venture of the early 1950s. Others belittle the claim that—before PPB—decisions on how much to spend for personnel or supplies were made without real consideration of the purposes for which these inputs were to be invested. They point to previous changes that have been in line with PPB, albeit without PPB's distinctive package of techniques and nomenclature: such things as the waning role of the "green sheets" in the central budget process, the redesign of the appropriation structure and the development of activity classifications, refinements in work measurement, productivity analysis, and other types of output measurement, and the utilization of the Spring Preview for a broad look at programs and major issues.

Between the uncertain protests of the traditional budgeteer and the uncertain expectations of the avant garde, there is a third version. The PPB system that is being developed portends a radical change in the central function of budgeting, but it is anchored to half a century of tradition and evolution. The budget system of the future will be a product of

---

The author is indebted to Henry S. Rowen and Paul Feldman of the Bureau of the Budget and to the many Federal officials who guided him during a summer's sojourn along the road to PPB.

Source: *Public Administration Review*, vol. 26 (December, 1966), pp. 243–258. Used with permission of publisher.

past and emerging developments; that is, it will embrace both the budgetary functions introduced during earlier stages of reform as well as the planning function which is highlighted by PPB. PPB is the first budget system *designed* to accommodate the multiple functions of budgeting.

THE FUNCTIONS OF BUDGETING

Budgeting always has been conceived as a process for systematically relating the expenditure of funds to the accomplishment of planned objectives. In this important sense, there is a bit of PPB in every budget system. Even in the initial stirrings of the budget reform more than 50 years ago, there were cogent statements on the need for a budget system to plan the objectives and activities of government and to furnish reliable data on what was to be accomplished with public funds. In 1907, for example, the New York Bureau of Municipal Research published a sample "program memorandum" that contained some 125 pages of functional accounts and data for the New York City Health Department [1].

However, this orientation was not *explicitly* reflected in the budget systems—national, state, or local—that were introduced during the first decades of this century, nor is it *explicitly* reflected in the budget systems that exist today. The plain fact is that planning is not the only function that must be served by a budget system. The *management* of ongoing activities and the *control* of spending are functions which, in the past, have been given priority over the planning function. Robert Anthony identifies three distinct administrative processes, strategic planning, management control, and operational control.

> *Strategic planning* is the process of deciding on objectives of the organization, on changes in these objectives, on the resources used to attain these objectives, and on the policies that are to govern the acquisition, use, and disposition of these resources.
>
> *Management control* is the process by which managers assure that resources are obtained and used effectively and efficiently in the accomplishment of the organization's objectives.
>
> *Operational control* is the process of assuring that specific tasks are carried out effectively and efficiently [2].

Every budget system, even rudimentary ones, comprises planning, management, and control processes. Operationally, these processes often are indivisible, but for analytic purposes they are distinguished here. In the context of budgeting, *planning* involves the determination of objectives, the evaluation of alternative courses of action, and the authorization of select programs. Planning is linked most closely to budget preparation, but it would be a mistake to disregard the management and control elements in budget preparation or the possibilities for planning during other phases of the budget year. Clearly, one of the major aims of PPB is to convert the annual routine of preparing a budget into a conscious appraisal and formulation of future goals and policies. Management involves the programming of approved goals into specific projects and activities, the design of organizational units to carry out approved programs, and the staffing of these units and the procurement of necessary resources. The management process is spread over the entire budget cycle; ideally, it is the link between goals made and activities undertaken. *Control* refers to the process of binding operating officials to the policies and plans set by their superiors. Control is predominant during the execution and audit stages, although the form of budget estimates and appropriations often is determined by control considerations. The assorted controls and reporting procedures that are associated with budge execution—position controls, restrictions on transfers, requisition procedures, and travel regulations, to mention the more prominent ones—have the purpose of securing compliance with policies made by central authorities.

Very rarely are planning, management, and control given equal attention in the operation of budget systems. As a practical matter, planning, management, and control have tended to be competing processes in budgeting with no neat division of functions among the various participants. Because time is scarce, central authorities must be selective in the things they do. Although this scarcity counsels the devolution of control responsibilities to operating levels, the lack of reliable and relied-on internal control systems has loaded central authorities with control functions at the expense of the planning function. Moreover, these processes often require different skills and generate different ways of handling the budget mission, so that one type of perspective tends to predominate over the others. Thus, in the staffing of the budget offices, there has been a shift from accountants to administrators as budgeting has moved from a control to a management posture. The initial experience with PPB suggests that the next transition might be from administrators to economists as budgeting takes on more of the planning function.

Most important, perhaps, are the differential informational requirements of planning, control, and management processes. Informational needs differ in terms of time spans, levels of aggregation, linkages with organizational and operating units, and input–output foci. The apparent solution is to design a system that serves the multiple needs of budgeting. Historically, however, there has been a strong tendency to homogenize informational structures and to rely on a single classification scheme to serve all budgetary purposes. For the most part, the informational system has been structured to meet the purposes of control. As a result, the type of multiple-purpose budget system envisioned by PPB has been avoided.

An examination of budget systems should reveal whether greater emphasis is placed *at the central levels* on planning, management, or control. A *planning orientation* focuses on the broadest range of issues: What are the long-range goals and policies of the government and how are these related to particular expenditure choices? What criteria should be used in appraising the requests of the agencies? Which programs should be initiated or terminated, and which expanded or curtailed? A *management orientation* deals with less fundamental issues: What is the best way to organize for the accomplishment of a prescribed task? Which of several staffing alternatives achieves the most effective relationship between the central and field offices? Of the various grants and projects proposed, which should be approved? A *control orientation* deals with a relatively narrow range of concerns: How can agencies be held to the expenditure ceilings established by the legislature and chief executive? What reporting procedures should be used to enforce propriety in expenditures? What limits should be placed on agency spending for personnel and equipment?

It should be clear that every budget system contains planning, management, and control features. A control orientation means the subordination, not the absence, of planning and management functions. In the matter of orientations, we are dealing with relative emphases, not with pure dichotomies. The germane issue is the balance among these vital functions at the central level. Viewed centrally, what weight does each have in the design and operation of the budget system?

THE STAGES OF BUDGET REFORM

The framework outlined above suggests a useful approach to the study of budget reform. Every reform alters the planning–management–control balance, sometimes inadvertently, usually deliberately. Accordingly, it is possible to identify three successive stages of reform.

In the first stage, dating roughly from 1920 to 1935, the dominant emphasis was on developing an adequate system of expenditure control. Although planning and management considerations were not altogether absent (and indeed occupied a prominent role in the debates leading to the Budget and Accounting Act of 1921), they were pushed to the side by what was regarded as the first priority, a reliable system of expenditure accounts. The second stage came into the open during the New Deal and reached its zenith more than a decade later in the movement for performance budgeting. The management orientation, paramount during this period, made its mark in the reform of the appropriation structure, development of management improvement and work measurement programs, and the focusing of budget preparation on the work and activities of the agencies. The third stage, the full emergence of which must await the institutionalization of PPB, can be traced to earlier efforts to link planning and budgeting as well as to the analytic criteria of welfare economics, but its recent development is a product of modern informational and decisional technologies such as those pioneered in the Department of Defense.

PPB is predicated on the primacy of the planning function, yet is strives for a multipurpose budget system that gives adequate and necessary attention to the control and management areas. Even in embryonic stage, PPB envisions the development of crosswalk grids for the conversion of data from a planning to a management and control framework, and back again. PPB treats the three basic functions as compatible and complementary elements of a budget system, though not as coequal aspects of central budgeting. In ideal form, PPB would centralize the planning function and delegate *primary* managerial and control responsibilities to the supervisory and operating levels respectively.

In the modern genesis of budgeting, efforts to improve planning, management, and control made common cause under the popular banner of the executive budget concept. In the goals and lexicon of the first reformers, budgeting meant executive budgeting. The two were inseparable. There was virtually no dissent from Cleveland's dictum that "to be a budget it must be prepared and submitted by a responsible executive" [3]. Whether from the standpoint of planning, management, or control, the executive was deemed in the best position to prepare and execute the budget. As Cleveland argued in 1915, only the executive "could think in terms of the institution as a whole," and, therefore, he "is the only one who can be made responsible for leadership" [4].

The executive budget idea also took root in the administrative integration movement, and here was allied with such reforms as functional consolidation of agencies, elimination of independent boards and commissions, the short ballot, and strengthening the chief executive's appointive and removal powers. The chief executive often was likened to the general manager of a corporation, the Budget Bureau serving as his general staff.

Finally, the executive budget was intended to strengthen honesty and efficiency by restricting the discretion of administrators in this role. It was associated with such innovations as centralized purchasing and competitive bidding, civil service reform, uniform accounting procedures, and expenditure audits.

THE CONTROL ORIENTATION

In the drive for executive budgeting, the various goals converged. There was a radical parting of the ways, however, in the conversion of the budget idea into an operational reality. Hard choices had to be made in the design of expenditure accounts and in the orientation of the budget office. On both counts, the control orientation was predominant.

In varying degrees of itemization, the expenditure classifications established during the first wave of reform were based on objects-of-expenditure, with detailed tabulations of the myriad items required to operate an administrative unit—personnel, fuel, rent, office supplies, and other inputs. On these "line itemizations" were built technical routines for the compilation and review of estimates and the disbursement of funds. The leaders in the movement for executive budgeting, however, envisioned a system of functional classifications focusing on the work to be accomplished. They regarded objects-of-expenditure as subsidiary data to be included for informational purposes. Their preference for functional accounts derived from their conception of the budget as a planning instrument, their disdain for objects from the contemporary division between politics and administration [5]. The Taft Commission vigorously opposed object-of-expenditure appropriations and recommended that expenditures be classified by class of work, organizational unit, character of expense, and method of financing. In its model budget, the Commission included several functional classifications [6].

In the establishment of a budget system for New York City by the Bureau of Municipal Research, there was a historic confrontation between diverse conceptions of budgeting.

In evolving suitable techniques, the Bureau soon faced a conflict between functional and object budgeting. Unlike almost all other budget systems, which began on a control footing with object classifications, the Bureau turned to control (and the itemization of objects) only after trial-and-error experimentation with program methods.

When confronted with an urgent need for effective control over administration, the Bureau was compelled to conclude that this need was more critical than the need for a planning-functional emphasis. "Budget reform," Charles Beard once wrote, "bears the imprint of the age in which it originated" [7]. In an age when personnel and purchasing controls were unreliable, the first consideration was how to prevent administrative improprieties.

> In the opinion of those who were in charge of the development of a budget procedure, the most important service to rendered was the establishing of central controls so that responsibility could be located and enforced through elected executives. . . . The view was, therefore, accepted, that questions of administration and niceties of adjustment must be left in abeyance until central control has been effectively established and the basis has been laid for careful scrutiny of departmental contracts and purchases as well as departmental work [8].

Functional accounts had been designed to facilitate rational program decisions, not to deter officials from misfeasance. "The classification by 'functions' affords no protection; it only operates as a restriction on the use which may be made of the services" [9]. The detailed itemization of objects was regarded as desirable not only "because it provides for the utilization of all the machinery of control which has been provided, but it also admits to a much higher degree of perfection than it has at present attained" [10].

With the introduction of object accounts, New York City had a threefold classification of expenditures: (1) by organizational units; (2) by functions; and (3) by objects. In a sense, the Bureau of Municipal Research was striving to develop a budget system that would serve the multiple purposes of budgeting simultaneously. To the Bureau, the inclusion of more varied and detailed data in the budget was a salutary trend; all purposes would be served and the public would have a more complete picture of government spending. Thus, the Bureau "urged from the beginning a classification of costs in as many different ways as there are stories to be told" [11]. But the Bureau did not anticipate the practical difficulties which would ensue from the multiple classification scheme. In the 1913 appropriations act,

> there were 3992 distinct items of appropriation. . . . Each constituted a distinct appropriation, besides which there was a further itemization of positions and salaries of personnel that multiplied this number several times, each of which operated as limitations on administrative discretion [12].

This predicament confronted the Bureau with a direct choice between the itemization of objects and a functional classification. As a solution, the Bureau recommended retention of object accounts and the total "defunctionalization" of the budget; in other words, it gave priority to the objects and the control orientation they manifested. Once installed, object controls rapidly gained stature as an indispensable deterrent to administrative misbehavior. Amelioration of the adverse effects of multiple classifications was to be accomplished in a different manor, one which would strengthen the planning and management processes. The Bureau postulated a fundamental distinction between the purposes of budgets and appropriations, and between the types of classification suitable for each.

> An act of appropriation has a single purpose—that of putting a limitation on the amount of obligations which may be incurred and the amount of vouchers which may be drawn to pay for personal services, supplies, etc. The only significant classification of appropriation items, therefore, is according to persons to whom drawing accounts are given and the classes of things to be bought [13].

Appropriations, in sum, were to be used as statutory controls on spending. In its "Next Steps" proposals, the Bureau recommended that appropriations retain "exactly the same itemization so far as specifications of positions and compensations are concerned and, therefore, the same protection" [14].

Budgets, on the other hand, were regarded as instruments of planning and publicity. They should include "all the details of the work plans and specifications of cost of work" [15]. In addition to the regular object and organization classifications, the budget would report the "total cost incurred, classified by *functions*—for determining questions of policy having to do with service rendered as well as to be rendered, and laying a foundation for appraisal of results" [16]. The Bureau also recommended a new instrument, a *work program*, which would furnish "a detailed schedule or analysis of each function, activity, or process within each organization unit. This analysis would give the total cost and the unit cost wherever standards were established" [17].

Truly a far-sighted conception of budgeting! There would be three documents for the three basic functions of budgeting. Although the Bureau did not use the analytic framework suggested above, it seems that the appropriations were intended for control purposes, the budget for planning purposes, and the work program for management purposes. Each of the three documents would have its specialized information scheme, but jointly they would comprise a multipurpose budget system not very different from PPB, even though the language of crosswalking or systems analysis was not used.

Yet the plan failed, for in the end the Bureau was left with object accounts pegged to a control orientation. The Bureau's distinction between budgets and appropriations was not well understood, and the work-program idea was rejected by New York City on the ground that adequate accounting backup was lacking. The Bureau had failed to recognize that the conceptual distinction between budgets and appropriations tends to break down under the stress of informational demands. If the legislature appropriates by objects, the budget very likely will be classified by objects. Conversely, if there are no functional accounts, the prospects for including such data in the budget are diminished substantially. As has almost always been the case, the budget came to mirror the appropriations act; in each, objects were paramount. It remains to be seen whether PPB will be able to break this interlocking informational pattern.

By the early 1920s the basic functions of planning and management were overlooked by those who carried the gospel of budget reform across the nation. First-generation budget workers concentrated on perfecting and spreading the widely approved object-of-expenditure approach, and budget writers settled into a nearly complete preoccupation with forms and with factual descriptions of actual and recommended procedures. Although ideas about the use of the budget for planning and management purposes were retained in Buck's catalogs of "approved" practices [18], they did not have sufficient priority to challenge tradition.

From the start, federal budgeting was placed on a control, object-of-expenditure footing, the full flavor of which can be perceived in reading Charles G. Dawes' documentary on *The First Year of the Budget of the United States.* According to Dawes,

> the Bureau of the Budget is concerned only with the humbler and routine business of Government. Unlike cabinet officers, it is concerned with no question of policy, save that of economy and efficiency [19].

This distinction fitted neatly with object classifications that provided a firm accounting base for the routine conduct of government business, but no information on policy implications of public expenditures. Furthermore, in its first decade, the Bureau's tiny staff (40 or fewer) had to coordinate a multitude of well-advertised economy drives which shaped the job of the examiner as being that of reviewing itemized estimates to pare them down. Although Section 209 of the Budget and Accounting Act had authorized the Bureau to study and recommend improvements in the organization and administrative practices of federal agencies, the Bureau was overwhelmingly preoccupied with the business of control.

THE MANAGEMENT ORIENTATION

Although no single action represents the shift from a control to a management orientation, the turning point in this evolution probably came with the New Deal's broadening perspective of government responsibilities.

During the 1920s and 1930s, occasional voices urged a return to the conceptions of budgeting advocated by the early reformers. In a notable 1924 article, Lent D. Upson argued vigorously that "budget procedure had stopped halfway in its development," and he proposed six modifications in the form of the budget, the net effect being a shift in emphasis from accounting control to functional accounting [20]. A similar position was taken a decade later by Wylie Kilpatrick, who insisted that "the one fundamental basis of expenditure is functional, an accounting of payments for the services performed by government" [21].

Meanwhile, gradual changes were preparing the way for a reorientation of budgeting to a management mission. Many of the administrative abuses that had given rise to object controls were curbed by statutes and regulations and by a general upgrading of the public service. Reliable accounting systems were installed and personnel and purchasing reforms introduced, thereby freeing budgeting from some of its watchdog chores. The rapid growth of government activities and expenditures made it more difficult and costly for central officials to keep track of the myriad objects in the budget. With expansion, the bits and pieces into which the objects were itemized became less and less significant, while the aggregate of activities performed became more significant, With expansion, there was heightened need for central management of the incohesive sprawl of administrative agencies.

The climb in activities and expenditures also signaled radical changes in the role of the budget system. As long as government was considered a "necessary evil," and there was little recognition of the social value of public expenditures, the main function of budgeting was to keep the spending in check. Because the outputs were deemed to be of limited and fixed value, it made sense to use the budget for central control over inputs. However, as the work and accomplishments of public agencies came to be regarded as benefits, the task of budgeting was redefined as the effective marshalling of fiscal and organizational resources for the attainment of benefits. This new posture focused attention on the problems of managing large programs and organizations, and on the opportunities for using the budget to extend executive hegemony over the dispersed administrative structure.

All these factors converged in the New Deal years. Federal expenditures rose rapidly from $4.2 billion in 1932 to $10 billion in 1940. Keynesian economics (the full budgetary implications of which are emerging only now in PPB) stressed the relationship between public spending and the condition of the economy. The President's Committee on Administrative Management (1937) castigated the routinized, control-minded approach to the Bureau of the Budget and urged that budgeting be used to coordinate federal activities under presidential leadership. With its transfer in 1939 from the Treasury to the newly-created Executive Office of the President, the Bureau was on its way to becoming the leading management arm of the Federal Government. The Bureau's own staff was increased tenfold; it developed the administrative management and statistical coordination functions that it still possesses; and it installed apportionment procedures for budget execution. More and more, the Bureau was staffed from the ranks of public administration rather than from accounting, and it was during the Directorship of Harold D. Smith (1939–46) that the Bureau substantially embraced the management orientation [22]. Executive Order 8248 placed the President's imprimatur on the management philosophy. It directed the Bureau:

> to keep the President informed of the progress of activities by agencies of the Government with respect to work proposed, work actually initiated, and work completed, together with the relative timing of work between the several agencies of the Government; all to the end that the work programs of the several agencies of the executive branch of the Government may be coordinated and that the monies appropriated by the Congress may be expended in the most economical manner possible to prevent overlapping and duplication of effort.

Accompanying the growing management use of the budget process for the appraisal and improvement of administrative performance and the scientific management movement with its historical linkage to public administration were far more relevant applications of managerial cost accounting to governmental operations. Government agencies sought to devise performance standards and the rudimentary techniques of work measurement were introduced in several agencies including the Forest Service, the Census Bureau, and the Bureau of Reclamation [23]. Various professional associations developed grading systems to assess administrative performance as well as the need for public services. These crude and unscientific methods were the forerunners of more sophisticated and objective techniques. At the apogee of these efforts, Clarence Ridley and Herbert Simon published *Measuring Municipal Activities: A Survey of Suggested Criteria for Appraising Administration*, in which they identified five kinds of measurement—(1) needs, (2) results, (3) costs, (4) efforts, and (5) performance—and surveyed the obstacles to the measurement of needs and results. The latter three categories they combined into a measure of administrative efficiency. This study provides an excellent inventory of the state of the technology prior to the breakthrough made by cost-benefit and systems analysis.

At the close of World War II, the management orientation was entrenched in all but one aspect of federal budgeting—the classification of expenditures. Except for isolated cases (such as TVA's activity accounts and the project structure in the Department of Agriculture), the traditional object accounts were retained though the control function had receded in importance. In 1949 the Hoover Commission called for alterations in budget classifications consonant with the management orientation. It recommended "that the whole budgetary concept of the Federal Government should be refashioned by the adoption of a budget based upon functions, activities, and projects" [24]. To create a sense of novelty, the Commission gave a new label—peformance budgeting—to what had long been known as functional or activity budgeting. Because its task force had used still another term—program budgeting—there were two new terms to denote the budget innovations of that period. Among writers there was no uniformity in usage, some preferring the "program budgeting" label, others "performance budgeting," to describe the same things. The level of confusion has been increased recently by the association of the term "program budgeting" (also the title of the RAND publication edited by David Novick) with the PPB movement.

Although a variety of factors and expectations influenced the Hoover Commission, and the Commission's proposals have been interpreted in many ways, including some that closely approximate the PPB concept, for purposes of clarity, and in accord with the control–management–planning framework, performance budgeting *as it was generally understood and applied* must be distinguished from the emergent PPB idea. The term "performance budgeting" is hereafter used in reference to reforms set in motion by the Hoover Commission, and the term "program budgeting" is used in conjunction with PPB.

Performance budgeting is management oriented; its principal thrust is to help administrators to assess the work-efficiency of operating units by (1) casting budget categories in functional terms, and (2) providing work-cost measurements to facilitate the efficient performance of prescribed activities. Generally, its method is particularistic, the reduction of work-cost data into discrete, measurable units. Program budgeting (PPB) is planning oriented; its main goal is to rationalize policymaking by providing (1) data on the costs and benefits of alternative ways of attaining proposed public objectives, and (2) output measurements to facilitate the effective attainment of chosen objectives. As a policy device, program budgeting departs from simple engineering models of efficiency in which the objective is fixed and the quantity of inputs and outputs is adjusted an optimal relationship. In PPB, the objective itself is variable; analysis may lead to a new statement of objectives. In order to enable budget makers to evaluate the costs and benefits of alternative expenditure options, program budgeting focuses on expenditure aggregates; the details come into play only as they contribute to an analysis of the total (the system) or of marginal trade-offs among competing proposals. Thus, in this macroanalytic approach, the accent is on comprehensiveness and on grouping data into categories that allow comparisons among alternative expenditure mixes.

Performance budgeting derived its ethos and much of its technique from cost accounting and scientific management; program budgeting has drawn its core ideas from economics and systems analysis. In the performance budgeting literature, budgeting is described as a "tool of management" and the budget as a "work program." In PPB, budgeting is an allocative process among competing claims, and the budget is a statement of policy. Chronologically, there was a gap of several years between the bloom of performance budgeting and the first articulated conceptions of program budgeting. In the aftermath of the first Hoover report, and especially during the early 1950s, there was a plethora of writings of the administrative advantages of the performance budget. Substantial interest in program budgeting did not emerge until the mid-1950s when a number of economists (including Smithies, Novick, and McKean) began to urge reform of the federal budget system. What the economists had in mind was not the same thing as the Hoover Commission.

In line with its management perspective, the Commission averred that "the all-important thing in budgeting is the work or service to be accomplished, and what the work or service will cost" [25]. Mosher followed this view closely in writing that "the central idea of the performance budget . . . is that the budget process be focused upon programs and functions—that is, accomplishments to be achieved, work to be done" [26]. But from the planning perspective, the all-important thing surely is not the work or service to be accomplished but the objectives or purposes to be fulfilled by the investment of public funds. Whereas in performance budgeting, work and activities are treated virtually as ends in themselves, in program budgeting work and services are regarded as intermediate aspects, the process of converting resources into outputs. Thus, in a 1954 RAND paper, Novick defined a program as "the sum of the steps or interdependent activities which enter into the attainment of a specified objective. The program, therefore, is the end objective and is developed or budgeted in terms of all the elements necessary to its execution" [27]. Novick goes on to add, "this is not the sense in which the government budget now uses the term."

Because the evaluation of performance and the evaluation of program are distinct budget functions, they call for different methods of classification which serve as an intermediate layer between objects and organizations. The activities relate to the functions and work of a distinct operating unit; hence their classification ordinarily conforms to organizational lines. This is the type of classification most useful for an administrator who has to schedule the procurement and utilization of resources for the production of goods and services. Activity classifications gather under a single rubric all the expenditure data needed by a manager to run their unit. The evaluation of programs, however, requires an end-product classification that is oriented to the mission and purposes of government. This type of classification may not be very useful for the manager, but it is of great value to the budget maker who has to decide how to allocate scarce funds among competing claims. Some of the difference between end-product and activity classifications can be gleaned by comparing the Coast Guard's existing activity schedule with the proposed program structure. The activity structure which was developed under the aegis of performance budgeting is geared to the operating responsibilities of the Coast Guard: Vessel Operations, Aviation Operations, Repair and Supply Facilities, and others. The proposed program structure is hinged to the large purposes sought through Coast Guard operations: Search and Rescue, Aids to Navigation, Law Enforcement, and so on.

It would be a mistake to assume that performance techniques presuppose program budgeting or that it is not possible to collect performance data without program classifications. Nevertheless, the view has gained hold that a program budget is "a transitional type of budget between the orthodox (traditional) character and object budget on the one hand and performance budget on the other" [28]. Kammerer and Shadoan stress a similar connection. The former writes that "a *performance* budget carries the program budget one step further: into *unit costs*" [29]. Shadoan "envisions 'performance budgeting' as an extension of . . . the program budget concept to which the element of unit work measurement has been added" [30]. These writers ignore the divergent functions served by performance and program budgets. It is possible to devise and apply performance techniques without relating them to, or having the use of, larger program aggregates. A cost accountant or work measurement specialist can measure the cost or effort required to perform a repetitive task without probing into the purpose of the work or its relationship to the mission of the organization. Work measurement—"a method of establishing an equitable relationship between the volume of work performed and manpower utilized" [31]—is only distantly and indirectly related to the process of determining governmental policy at the higher levels. Program classifications are vitally linked to the making and implementation of policy through the allocation of public resources. As a general rule, performance budgeting is concerned with the *process of work* (what methods should be used) while program budgeting is concerned with the *purpose of work* (what activities should be authorized).

Perhaps the most reliable way to describe this difference is to show what was tried and accomplished under performance budgeting. First of all, performance budgeting led to the introduction of activity classifications, the management orientation of which has already been discussed. Second, narrative descriptions of program and performance were added to the budget document. These statements give the budget-reader a general picture of the work that will be done by the organizational unit requesting funds. But unlike the analytic documents currently being developed under PPB, the narratives have a descriptive and justificatory function; they do not provide an objective basis for evaluating the cost-utility of an expenditure. Indeed, there hardly is any evidence that the narratives have been used for decision making; rather they seem best suited for giving the uninformed outsider some glimpses of what is going on inside.

Third, performance budgeting spawned a multitude of work-cost measurement explorations. Most used, but least useful, were the detailed workload statistics assembled by administrators to justify their requests for additional funds. On a higher level of sophistication were attempts to apply the techniques of scientific management and cost accounting to the development of work and productivity standards. In these efforts, the Bureau of the Budget had a long involvement, beginning with the issuance of the trilogy of work measurement handbooks in 1950 and reaching its highest development in the productivity-measurement studies that were published in 1964. All these applications were at a level of detail useful for managers with operating or supervisory responsibilities but of scant usefulness for top-level officials who have to determine organizational objectives and goals. Does it really help top officials if they know that it cost $0.07 to wash a pound of laundry or that the average postal employee processes 289 items of mail per hour? These are the main fruits of performance measurements, and they have an important place in the management of an organization. They are of great value to the operating official who has the limited function of getting a job done, but they would put a crushing burden on the policy-maker whose function is to map the future course of action.

Finally, the management viewpoint led to significant departures from PPB's principle that the expenditure accounts should show total systems cost. The 1949 National Security Act (possibly the first concrete result of the Hoover report) directed the segregation of capital and operating costs in the defense budget. New York State's performance-budgeting experiment for TB hospitals separated expenditures into cost centers (a concept derived from managerial cost accounting) and within each center into fixed and variable costs. In most manpower and work measurements, labor has been isolated from other inputs. Most important, in many states and localities (and implicitly in federal budgeting) the cost of continuing existing programs has been separated from the cost of new or expanded programs. This separation is useful for managers who build up a budget in terms of increments and decrements from the base, but it is a violation of program budgeting's working assumption that all claims must be pitted against one another in the competition for funds. Likewise, the forms of separation previously mentioned make sense from the standpoint of the manager, but impair the planner's capability to compare expenditure alternatives.

THE PLANNING ORIENTATION

The foregoing has revealed some of the factors leading to the emergence of the planning orientation. Three important developments influenced the evolution from a management to a planning orientation.

1. Economic analysis—macro and micro—has had an increasing part in the shaping of fiscal and budgetary policy.
2. The development of new informational and decisional technologies has enlarged the applicability of objective analysis to policy making.
3. There has been a gradual convergence of planning and budgetary processes.

Keynesian economics with its macroanalytic focus on the impact of governmental action on the private sector had its genesis in the underemployment economy of the Great Depression. In calling attention to the opportunities for attaining full employment by means of fiscal policy, the Keynesians set into motion a major restatement of the central budget function. From the utilization of fiscal policy to achieve economic objectives, it was but a few steps to the utilization of the budget process to achieve fiscal objectives. Nevertheless, between the emergence and the victory of the new economics, there was a lapse of a full generation, a delay due primarily to the entrenched balanced-budget ideology. But the full realization of the budget's economic potential was stymied on the revenue side by static tax policies and on the expenditure side by status spending policies.

If the recent tax policy of the federal government is evidence that the new economics has come of age, it also offers evidence of the long-standing failure of public officials to use the taxing power as a variable constraint on the economy. Previously, during normal times, the tax structure was accepted as given, and the task of fiscal analysis was to forecast future tax yields so as to ascertain how much would be available for expenditure. The new approach treats taxes as variable, to be altered periodically in accord with national policy and economic conditions. Changes in tax rates are not to be determined (as they still are in virtually all states and localities) by how much is needed to cover expenditures but by the projected impact of alternative tax structures on the economy.

It is more than coincidental that the advent of PPB has followed on the heels of the explicit utilization of tax policy to guide the economy. In macroeconomics, taxes and expenditures are mirror images of one another; a tax cut and an expenditure increase have comparable impacts. Hence, the hinging of tax policy to economic considerations inevitably led to the similar treatment of expenditures. But there were (and remain) a number of obstacles to the utilization of the budget as a fiscal tool. For one thing, the conversion of the budget process to an economic orientation probably was slowed by the Full Employment Act of 1946, which established the Council of Economic Advisers and transferred the Budget Bureau's fiscal analysis function to the Council. The institutional separation between the CEA and the BOB and between fiscal policy and budget making was not compensated by cooperative work relationships. Economic analysis had only a slight impact on expenditure policy. It offered a few guidelines (for example, that spending should be increased during recessions) and a few ideas (such as a shelf of public works projects), but it did not feed into the regular channels of budgeting. The business of preparing the budget was foremost a matter of responding to agency spending pressures, not of responding to economic conditions.

Moreover, expenditures (like taxes) have been treated virtually as givens, to be determined by the unconstrained claims of the spending units. In the absence of central policy instructions, the agencies have been allowed to vent their demands without prior restraints by central authorities and without an operational set of planning guidelines. By the time the Bureau gets into the act, it is faced with the overriding task of bringing estimates into line with projected resources. In other words, the Bureau has had a budget-cutting function, to reduce claims to an acceptable level. The President's role has been similarly restricted. He is the *gatekeeper* of federal budgeting. He directs the pace of spending increases by deciding which of the various expansions proposed by the agencies shall be included in the budget. But, as the gatekeeper, the President rarely has been able to look back at the items that have previously passed through the gate; his attention is riveted to those programs that are departures from the established base. In their limited roles, neither the Bureau nor the President has been able to inject fiscal and policy objectives into the forefront of budget preparation.

It will not be easy to wean budgeting from its utilization as an administrative procedure for financing ongoing programs to a decisional process for determining the range and direction of public objectives and the government's involvement in the economy. In the transition to a planning emphasis, an important step was the 1963 hearings of the Joint Economic Committee on *The Federal Budget as an Economic Document.* These hearings and the pursuant report of the JEC explored the latent policy opportunities in budget making. Another development was the expanded time horizons manifested by the multiyear expenditure projections introduced in the early 1960s. Something of a breakthrough was achieved via the revelation that the existing tax structure would yield cumulatively larger increments of uncommitted funds—estimated as much as $50 billion by 1970—which could be applied to a number of alternative uses. How much of the funds should be "returned" to the private sector through tax reductions and how much through expenditure increases? How much should go to the states and localities under a broadened system of federal grants? How much should be allocated to the rebuilding of cities, to the improvement of education, or to the eradication of racial injustices? The traditional budget system lacked the analytic tools to cope with these questions, though decisions ultimately would be made one way or another. The expansion of the time horizon from the single year to a multiyear frame enhances the opportunity for planning and analysis to have an impact on future expenditure decisions. With a one-year perspective, almost all options have been foreclosed by previous commitments; analysis is effective only for the increments provided by self-generating revenue increases or to the extent that it is feasible to convert funds from one use to another. With a longer time span, however, many more options are open, and economic analysis can have a prominent part in determining which course of action to pursue.

So much for the macroeconomic trends in budget reform. On the microeconomic side, PPB traces its lineage to the attempts of welfare economists to construct a science of finance predicated on the principle of marginal utility. Such a science, it was hoped, would furnish objective criteria for determining the optimal allocation of public funds among competing uses. By appraising the marginal costs and benefits of alternatives (poor relief versus battleships in Pigou's classic example), it would be possible to determine which combination of expenditures afforded maximum utility. The quest for a welfare function provided the conceptual underpinning for a 1940 article on "The Lack of a Budgetary Theory" in which V. O. Key noted the absence of a theory which would determine whether "to allocate x

dollars to activity A instead of activity B" [32]. In terms of its direct contribution to budgetary practice, welfare economics has been a failure. It has not been possible to distill the conflicts and complexities of political life into a welfare criterion or homogeneous distribution formula. But stripped of its normative and formal overtones, its principles have been applied to budgeting by economists such as Arthur Smithies. Smithies has formulated a budget rule that "expenditure proposals should be considered in the light of the objectives they are intended to further, and in general final expenditure decisions should not be made until all claims on the budget can be considered" [33]. PPB is the application of this rule to budget practice. By structuring expenditures so as to juxtapose substitutive elements within program categories, and by analyzing the costs and benefits of the various substitutes, PPB has opened the door to the use of marginal analysis in budgeting.

Actually, the door was opened somewhat by the development of new decisional and informational technologies, the second item on the list of influences in the evolution of the planning orientation. Without the availability of the decisional–informational capability provided by cost-benefit and systems analysis, it is doubtful that PPB would be part of the budgetary apparatus today. The new technologies make it possible to cope with the enormous informational and analytic burdens imposed by PPB. As aids to calculation, they furnish a methodology for the analysis of alternatives, thereby expanding the range of decision making in budgeting.

Operations research, the oldest of these technologies, grew out of complex World War II conditions that required the optimal coordination of manpower, material, and equipment to achieve defense objectives. Operations research is most applicable to those repetitive operations where the opportunity for qualification is highest. Another technology, cost-benefit analysis, was intensively adapted during the 1950s to large-scale water resource investments, and subsequently to many other governmental functions. Systems analysis is the most global of these technologies. It involves the skillful analysis of the major factors that go into the attainment of an interconnected set of objectives. Systems analysis has been applied in DOD to the choice of weapons systems, the location of military bases, and the determination of sealift-airlift requirements. Although the extension of these technologies across-the-board to government was urged repeatedly by members of the RAND Corporation during the 1950s, it was DOD's experience that set the stage for the current ferment. It cannot be doubted that the coming of PPB has been pushed ahead several years or more by the "success story" in DOD.

The third stream of influence in the transformation of the budget function has been a closing of the gap between planning and budgeting. Institutionally and operationally, planning and budgeting have run along separate tracks. The national government has been reluctant to embrace central planning of any sort because of identification with socialist management of the economy. The closest thing we have had to a central planning agency was the National Resources Planning Board in the 1939–1943 period. Currently, the National Security Council and the Council of Economic Advisors have planning responsibilities in the defense and fiscal areas. As far as the Bureau of the Budget is concerned, it has eschewed the planning function in favor of control and management. In many states and localities, planning and budgeting are handled by separate organizational units: in the states, because limitations on debt financing have encouraged the separation of the capital and operating budgets; in the cities, because the professional autonomy and land-use preoccupations of the planners have set them apart from the budgeteers.

In all governments, the appropriations cycle, rather than the anticipation of future objectives, tends to dictate the pace and posture of budgeting. Into the repetitive, one-year span of the budget is wedged all financial decisions, including those that have multiyear implications. As a result, planning, if it is done at all, "occurs independently of budgeting and with little relation to it" [34]. Budgeting and planning, moreover, invite disparate perspectives: the one is conservative and negativistic; the other, innovative and expansionist. As Mosher has noted, "budgeting and planning are apposite, if not opposite. In extreme form, the one means saving; the other, spending" [35].

Nevertheless, there has been some *rapprochement* of planning and budgeting. One factor is the long lead-time in the development and procurement of hardware and capital investments. The multiyear projections inaugurated several years ago were a partial response to this problem. Another factor has been the diversity of government agencies involved in related functions. This has given rise to various ad hoc coordinating devices, but it also has pointed to the need for permanent machinery to integrate dispersed activities. Still another factor has been the sheer growth of federal activities and expenditures and the need for a rational system of allocation. The operational code of planners contains three tenets relevant to these budgetary needs: (1) planning is future-oriented; it connects present decisions to the attainment of a desired future state of affairs; (2) planning, ideally, encompasses all resources involved in the attainment of future objectives. It strives for comprehensiveness. The *master plan* is the one that brings within its scope all relevant factors; (3) planning is means–ends oriented. The allocation of resources is strictly dictated by the ends that are to be accomplished. All this is to say that planning is an economizing process, though planners are more oriented to the future than economists. It is not surprising that planners have found the traditional budget system deficient [36], nor is it surprising that the major reforms entailed by PPB emphasize the planning function.

Having outlined the several trends in the emerging transition to a planning orientation, it remains to mention several qualifications. First, the planning emphasis is not predominant in federal budgeting at this time. Although PPB asserts the paramountcy of planning, PPB itself is not yet a truly operational part of the budget machinery. We are now at the dawn of a new era in budgeting; high noon is still a long way off. Second, this transition has not been preceded by a reorientation of the Bureau of the Budget. Unlike the earlier changeover from control to management in which the alteration of budgetary techniques *followed* the revision of the Bureau's role, the conversion from management to planning is taking a different course—first, the installation of new techniques; afterward, a reformulation of the Bureau's mission. Whether this sequence will hinder reform efforts is a matter that cannot be predicted, but it should be noted that in the present instance the Bureau cannot convert to a new mission by bringing in a wholly new staff, as was the case in the late 1930s and early 1940s.

WHAT DIFFERENCE DOES IT MAKE?

The starting point for the author was distinguishing the old from the new in budgeting. The interpretation has been framed in analytic terms, and budgeting has been viewed historically in three stages corresponding to the three basic functions of budgeting. In this analysis, an attempt has been made to identify the difference between the existing and the emerging as a difference between management and planning orientations.

In an operational sense, however, what difference does it make whether the central budget process is oriented toward planning rather than management? Does the change merely mean a new way of making decisions, or does it mean different decisions as well? These are not easy questions to answer, particularly since the budget system of the future will be a compound of all three functions. The case for PPB rests on the assumption that the form in which information is classified and used governs the actions of budget makers, and, conversely, that alterations in form will produce desired changes in behavior. Take away the assumption that behavior follows form, and the movement for PPB is reduced to a trivial manipulation of techniques—form for form's sake without any significant bearing on the conduct of budgetary affairs.

Yet this assumed connection between roles and information is a relatively uncharted facet of the PPB literature. The behavioral side of the equation has been neglected. PPB implies that each participant will behave as a sort of Budgetary Man, a counterpart of the classical Economic Man and Simon's Administrative Man [37]. Budgetary Man, whatever his station or role in the budget process, is assumed to be guided by an unwavering commitment to the rule of efficiency; in every instance he chooses that alternative that optimizes the allocation of public resources.

PPB probably takes an overly mechanistic view of the impact of form on behavior and underestimates the strategic and volitional aspects of budget making. In the political arena, data are used to influence the "who gets what" in budgets and appropriations. If information influences behavior, the reverse also is true. Indeed, data are more tractable than roles; participants are more likely to seek and use data which suit their preferences than to alter their behavior automatically in response to formal changes.

All this constrains, rather than negates, the impact of budget form. The advocates of PPB, probably in awareness of the above limitations, have imported into budgeting men with professional commitments to the types of analysis and norms required by the new techniques, men with a background in economics and systems analysis, rather than with general administrative training.

PPB aspires to create a different environment for choice. Traditionally, budgeting has defined its mission in terms of identifying the existing base and proposed departures from it—"This is where we are; where do we go from here?" PPB defines its mission in terms of budgetary objectives and purposes—"Where do we want to go? What do we do to get there?" The environment of choice under traditional circumstances is *incremental*; in PPB it is *teletic*. Presumably, these different processes will lead to different budgetary outcomes.

A budgeting process which accepts the base and examines only the increments will produce decisions to transfer the present into the future with a few small variations. The curve of government activities will be continuous, with few zigzags or breaks. A budget-making process which begins with objectives will require the base to compete on an equal footing with new proposals. The decisions will be more radical than those made under incremental conditions. This does not mean that each year's budget will lack continuity with the past. There are sunk costs that have to be reckoned, and the benefits of radical changes will have to outweigh the costs of terminating prior commitments. Furthermore, the extended time span of PPB will mean that big investment decisions will be made for a number of years, with each year being a partial installment of the plan. Most important, the political manifestations of sunk costs—vested interests—will bias decisions away from radical departures. The conservatism of the political system, therefore, will tend to minimize the decisional differences between traditional and PPB approaches. However, the very availability of analytic data will cause a shift in the balance of economic and political forces that go into the making of a budget.

Teletic and incremental conditions of choice lead to still another distinction. In budgeting, which is committed to the established base, the flow of budgetary decisions is upward and aggregative. Traditionally, the first step in budgeting, in anticipation of the call for estimates, is for each department to issue its own call to prepare and to submit a set of estimates. This call reaches to the lowest level capable of assembling its own estimates. Lowest level estimates form the building blocks for the next level where they are aggregated and reviewed and transmitted upward until the highest level is reached and the totality constitutes a department-wide budget. Since budgeting is tied to a base, the building-up-from-below approach is sensible; each building block estimates the cost of what it is already doing plus the cost of the increments it wants. (The building blocks, then, are decisional elements, not simply informational elements as is often assumed.)

PPB reverses the informational and decisional flow. Before the call for estimates is issued, top policy has to be made, and this policy constrains the estimates prepared below. For each lower level, the relevant policy instructions are issued by the superior level prior to the preparation of estimates. Accordingly, the critical decisional process—that of deciding on purposes and plans—has a downward and disaggregative flow.

In the making of policy is to be antecedent to the costing of estimates, there will have to be a shift in the distribution of budget responsibilities. The main energies of the Bureau of the Budget are now devoted to budget preparation; under PPB these energies will be centered on what we may term *prepreparation*—the stage of budget making that deals with policy and is prior to the preparation of the budget. One of the steps marking the advent of the planning orientation was the inauguration of the Spring Preview several years ago for the purpose of affording an advance look at departmental programs.

If budget making is to be oriented to the planning function, there probably will be a centralization of policymaking, both within and among departments. The DOD experience offers some precedent for predicting that greater budgetary authority will be vested in department heads than heretofore, but there is no firm basis for predicting the degree of centralization that may derive from the relatedness of objectives pursued by many departments. It is possible that the mantle of central budgetary policy will be assumed by the Bureau; indeed, this is the expectation in many agencies. On the other hand, the Bureau gives little indication at this time that it is willing or prepared to take this comprehensive role.

CONCLUSION

The various differences between the budgetary orientations are charted in Table 1. All the differences may be summed up in the statement that the ethos of budgeting will shift from

Table 1   Some Basic Differences Between Budget Orientations

Characteristic	Control	Management	Planning
Personnel skill	Accounting	Administration	Economics
Information focus	Objects	Activities	Purposes
Key budget stage (central)	Execution	Prepreparation	Preparation
Breadth of measurement	Discrete	Discrete/ activities	Comprehensive
Role of budget agency	Fiduciary	Efficiency	Policy
Decisional flow	Upward, aggregative	Upward, aggregative	Downward, disaggregative
Type of choice	Incremental	Incremental	Teletic
Control responsibility	Central	Operating	Operating
Management responsibility	Dispersed	Central	Supervisory
Planning responsibility	Dispersed	Dispersed	Central
Budget-appropriations classifications	Same	Same	Different
Appropriations organizational link	Direct	Direct	Crosswalk

justification to analysis. To far greater extent than heretofore, budget decisions will be influenced by explicit statements of objectives and by a formal weighing of the costs and benefits of alternatives.

NOTES AND REFERENCES

1. New York Bureau of Municipal Research, *Making a Municipal Budget*, New York, pp. 9–10 (1907).
2. Robert N. Anthony, *Planning and Control Systems: A Framework for Analysis*, Allyn and Bacon, Boston, pp. 16–18 (1965).
3. Frederick A. Cleveland, "Evolution of the Budget Idea in the United States," *Acad. Polit. Social Sci.*, *62*: 16 (1915).
4. Ibid., p. 17.
5. See Frank J. Goodnow, "The Limit of Budgetary Control," *Proc. Am. Polit. Sci. Assoc.*, Baltimore, p. 72, (1913); also William F. Willoughby, "Allotment of Funds by Executive Officials, An Essential Feature of Any Correct Budgetary System," *Proc. Am. Polit. Sci. Assoc.*, pp. 78–87 (1913).
6. U.S. President's Commission on Economy and Efficiency, *The Need for a National Budget*, U.S. Government Printing Office, Washington, D.C., pp. 210–213 (1912).
7. Charles A. Beard, "Prefatory Note," Ref. 6, p. vii.
8. New York Bureau of Municipal Research, "Some Results and Limitations of Central Financial Control in New York City," *Municipal Res. 81*: 10 (1917).
9. "Next Steps . . . ,"
10. Ref. 9, p. 67.
11. Ref. 8, p. 9.
12. Ref. 9, p. 35.
13. Ref. 9, p. 7.
14. Ref. 9, p. 39.
15. Ref. 8, p. 7.
16. Ref. 8, p. 9.
17. Ref. 9, p. 30.
18. See A. E. Buck, *Public Budgeting*, Macmillan, New York, pp. 181–188 (1929).
19. Charles G. Dawes, *The First Year of the Budget of the United States*, Harper & Row, New York, p. ii (1923).
20. Lent D. Upson, "Half-Time Budget Methods," *Ann. Am. Acad. Polit. Social Sci.*, *113*: 72 (1924).
21. Wylie Kilpatrick, "Classification and Measurement of Public Expenditure," *Ann. Am. Acad. Polit. Social Sci.*, *133*: 20 (1936).
22. See Harold D. Smith, *The Management of Your Government*, McGraw-Hill, New York (1945).
23. Public Administration Service, *The Work Unit in Federal Administration*, Chicago (1937).
24. U.S. Commission on Organization of the Executive Branch of the Government, *Budgeting and Accounting*, U.S. Government Printing Office, Washington, D.C., p. 8 (1949).
25. See Ref. 24.
26. Frederick C. Mosher, *Program Budgeting: Theory and Practice*, Public Administration Service, Chicago, p. 79 (1954).
27. David Novick, *Which Program Do We Mean in "Program Budgeting?,"* The RAND Corporation, Santa Monica, p. 17 (1954).
28. Lennox L. Moak and Kathryn W. Killian, *A Manual of Techniques for the Preparation, Consideration, Adoption, and Administration of Operating Budgets*, Public Administration Service, Chicago, p. 11 (1963).
29. Gladys M. Kammerer, *Program Budgeting: An Aid to Understanding*, University of Florida Press, Gainesville, p. 6 (1959).
30. Arlene Theuer Shadoan, *Preparation, Review, and Execution of the State Operating Budget*, University of Kentucky Press, Lexington, p. 13 (1963).

31. U.S. Bureau of the Budget, *A Work Measurement System*, U.S. Government Printing Office, Washington, D.C., p. 2 (1950).
32. V. O. Key, "The Lack of a Budgetary Theory," *Am. Polit. Sci. Rev. 34*: 1138 (1940).
33. Arthur Smithies, *The Budgetary Process in the United States*, McGraw-Hill, New York, p. 16 (1955).
34. Ref. 26, pp. 47–48.
35. Ref. 26, p. 48.
36. See Edward C. Banfield, "Congress and the Budget: A Planner's Criticism," *Am. Polit. Sci. Rev.*, *43*: 1217–1227 (1949).
37. Herbert A. Simon, *Administrative Behavior*, Macmillan, New York (1957).

7

A Micropolitical Perspective on Rational Budgeting: A Conjectural Footnote on the Dissemination of PPBS

Robert T. Golembiewski and Patrick Scott

> The use of Planning, Programming, Budgeting [System, or PPBS] as a device for achieving greater rationality in government decisions . . . has been almost a total failure and has been dropped . . . almost as fast as it was adopted after 1965 when President Lyndon Johnson ordered it installed throughout the federal government. Although long abandoned in fact, it was formally dropped by Washington only in 1971. (By the way, who is *responsible* for the billions of dollars and millions of man-hours wasted on this gimmick?) [1]
>
> —V.A. Thompson

Thompson asks a difficult question, which is most conveniently (if not very revealingly) answered: President Johnson is *responsible*.

This narrative cannot answer the tough question posed by Thompson, but it does contribute to a possible and partial answer while also implying the complexity and detail of any precise response to Thompson's query. This casual history focuses narrowly on several possible contributors to an explanation of why and how PPBS *may have come* to get presidential sanction.

THE USUAL VIEW OF PPBS

No problems exist with the common view of how PPBS came to prominence, *if* one does not look too closely. The official beginning of the federal-wide phenomenon known as PPBS came on August 25, 1965, when President Lyndon B. Johnson announced a "new and revolutionary system of planning, programming and budgeting throughout the [civilian agencies of] Government." This new system, Johnson notes, would use the "tools of modern management [to bring] the full promise of a finer life . . . to every American at the

Source: *Public Budgeting and Financial Management*, vol. 1, no. 3 (1989), pp. 327–370.

lowest possible cost" [2]. More specifically, Johnson told a meeting of his extended Cabinet that PPBS "will enable us to [3]"

1. Identify our national goals with precision and on a continuing basis.
2. Choose among these goals the ones that are most urgent.
3. Search for alternative means of reaching those goals most effectively at least cost.
4. Inform ourselves not merely on next year's costs, but on the second, and third, and subsequent years' cost of our programs.
5. Measure the performance of our programs to insure a dollar's worth of service for each dollar spent.

The announcement was not surprising, given President Johnson's public agenda. He had so many things that he wanted to bestow on the American people. But his frustration grew: He increasingly lacked the resources for working his will, what with "a war abroad and a war at home." Hence the PPBS announcement can be seen as another form of Johnson's War on Waste to stretch the available resources. Participants still recall with feeling President Johnson's dramatic acting-out in a meeting of the extended Cabinet his willingness to roll up his sleeves and to finish the work begun some 20 years earlier by such prophetic voices for a more efficiently humane polity as Rexford Tugwell and Henry Wallace. President Johnson dramatically tore off his coat to signal his readiness, and participants remember leaping to their feet in a standing ovation after his virtuoso performance.

The watershed PPBS announcement also derived from several clear lines of development that make Johnson's August 25, 1965, statement reasonable, and perhaps even inevitable. Consider here only four of these supporting developments. First, the Washington atmosphere was hooked on cost reduction or at least cost-effectiveness as *the* remedy for out-of-control spending on Great Society programs as well as a sharply expanding war in Vietnam, and President Johnson clearly desired greater centralization in his office. PPBS promised to give the chief executive more power over both political appointees and the permanent bureaucracy by replacing a percolate-up budgeting model. Priorities would be decided at the top, and lower levels would be constrained by those priorities.

Signally, programmatic cutbacks were resisted. In his PPBS proclamation, Johnson reflected both the basic resolve to continue the level of spending and yet an urgency to do jobs faster, to do jobs better, and to do jobs less expensively [4].

Second, PPBS can be seen as representing another phase of public budgetary reform and its underlying theory. Generally, reform involved changes in the type of information included in budgets, as well as in the organization of budgets. Specifically, early budget reforms concentrated on items or activities; later reforms sought to develop data about programs—or related major clusters of items of activities—and sought to link program and resource data in expanding networks [5], first for subsystemic control and then for larger system planning. In its most influential form, this view of phases of reform distinguishes three progressively expansive concepts of budgets—as expenditure control, management control, and planning control [6].

PPBS can be viewed as an evolutionary increase in the scope of budgeting theory complemented by a revolutionary expansion in scale. "Program budgets" for a few federal agencies—which sought to link major clusters of activities to resources—had existed for some time. Hence early information about Johnson's PPBS emphasized only the novelty of its application to all agencies of civilian government. In addition, news releases conveniently but misleadingly noted that the "basic principles" had been applied in McNamara's Department of Defense, and also emphasized the PPBS model had been approached "in some respects" in a gaggle of federal agencies—FAA, NASA, Interior, and the Forest Service, among others [7].

Third, PPBS basically rested on the then recent and well-regarded development of decisional techniques far outside the compass of budgeting theory. These techniques include operations research, cost-benefit analysis, systems analysis, and computer hardware/software [8], which cumulatively and suddenly permitted cloaking budgeting theory in the golden raiments of management science. The emphasis on these "recent developments" was in part well-founded, and some public-sector experience—most prominently in Defense—seemed generally transferrable to the bulk of government. In far larger part, however, the emphasis had shaky foundations: in reasonable but futuristic extensions of an existing technological base, in unsophisticated extrapolations from that base, and in just plain smoke-blowing.

Fourth, McNamara's Department of Defense is all but universally accorded a prominent place in disseminating PPBS. In some versions, McNamara himself is *the* active agent: for example, "The [Defense PPBS] system was judged so successful . . . that by 1965 Robert McNamara was able to convince President Johnson that the system could be profitably applied throughout the entire executive structure" [9]. The popular press had a field day: for example, *Business Week* proclaimed that "U.S. Agencies get Order to Join McNamara's Band." Other observers see a less direct but still potent role, as in Cronin's view that "McNamara's previous reputation and his subsequent performance as a talented manager of large complex organizations mesmerized . . . Johnson" [10]. McNamara needed to do no selling, in this view, and Johnson's own very general impressions [11] sufficed to motivate his announcement of August 25, 1965. Still others propose only a symbolic role for McNamara, in an attempt by the Johnson administration to capture the appearance of effective management with modest concern about either the validity of the claim or about how to achieve effective management. In this view, Donovan notes of the August 25 announcement: "In making the decision to universalize PPBS in Federal executive budget-making, the Johnson administration apparently assumed that a system which was performing so well in Defense matters ought to be applied across the vast range of public policy" [12]. Others go even further, suggesting a bare-faced presidential effort to capitalize on McNamara's novelty and popularity [13].

The immediate aftermath implies a fast-fading effect, whatever the real McNamara influence. Doh tells us that Johnson initially "had faith in PPBS," but adds that his "interest was not a sustained one." Doh concludes: "The support of PPBS during the remaining years of the Johnsonian era continued noisy and promotional rather than substantive" [14].

In sum, powerful forces supported the President's announcement of a "revolutionary system." Among other factors: the need for efficiency was great and growing; some experience could be marshaled in support of PPBS-like applications, and especially from such highly regarded agencies as Defense and NASA; and both the reality and reputation of the power of recent analytic and computational developments provided comforting if often-uninformed support for the great-leap-forward via PPBS.

PPBS AS SURPRISE

Despite the array of factors that support the PPBS application, Johnson's announcement of August 25, 1965, had major aspects of suddenness. Six features illustrate this broad characterization.

First, the very announcement of PPBS caught even close observers off guard. Hence the descriptors "startling" and "surprise" concerning the announcement, which apparently had been quickly made and tightly held. Secretary of Defense McNamara talked with Johnson "three or four times" on the topic, but McNamara now proposes that neither he nor other Defense officials had anything direct to do with the events that crescendoed in the announcement.

The pervasiveness of the surprise can be judged by some of the assumptions made by interested actors. One close observer even guesses that "Charlie Schultze was as surprised as almost everyone else," and Schultze was to guide the PPBS effort. In other versions, Schultze and President Johnson were won over to the view of certain PPBS advocates in the Bureau of the Budget, who are not identified, in the face of the opposite and strong wishes of other Bureau officials [15].

What seems clear? The PPBS announcement gives no evidence of careful staff work, and suggests that President Johnson was convinced, definitely but probably suddenly and vaguely—by someone or something—that PPBS would help reduce his frustration about not being able to do what he saw as necessary. Moreover, President Johnson "knew little about administration or management, and cared less," in the words of one close associate. So no exhaustive demonstration of PPBS's utility would have been necessary, or perhaps even tolerated by the President. Even had he sought it, technical opinion would have provided little support for President Johnson's sweeping decision. For example, PPBS was applied quite selectively in Defense [16] and, despite its star billing in Washington, that localized experience would provide no direct model for federal-wide installation. Nor would the technicians provide strong support, apparently. Thus one observer emphasizes the prevailing skepticism among many departmental budget officers who believed that PPBS was "waving a magic wand over matters not given to magical solutions" [17].

But somehow, somewhere, something got to President Johnson, convincing him that PPBS could do what Johnson felt needed to be done. As Mosher and Haar report [18]:

> The President's order came quickly, so suddenly that it was a surprise to many high officials in the government and even some in the Budget Bureau. In it he specifically used the Defense Department terminology of PPBS and referred to Defense as a model. The undertaking was to go into effect immediately and apply to almost the entire executive branch. The Director of the Budget was given responsibility to direct and supervise the new system.

Second, as late as mid-April 1965, President Johnson desired "less direct presidential identification" [19] with a similar program in the Department of State—the Executive Review of Overseas Programs, or EROP, about which more will be written at several points.

Four months later, no doubt existed that a similar "revolutionary system" had the president's backing. Did something of significance but not in the public eye occur between those dates?

Third, the immediate aftermath of the announcement does not encourage the view that the new planning system either had the benefit of much prior planning, or even informed thought. For example, on August 25, detailed instructions were promised within a month, but it was October 12 before even very sketchy instructions were released [20]. Moreover, the "government-wide effort" was scaled-down in the interval: The 21 largest departments and agencies "will come under the new budgeting system immediately," the October 12 instructions note, while 18 other agencies "will be encouraged" to adopt the system [21]. Personal recollections are consistent with the overall view of a kind of "dysjointed affirmation." One Cabinet official recalls: "We were called together one morning and after a brief summary by Budget Director Schultze, ordered to put it into effect promptly. There was no meaningful discussion of whether or not it would work" [22].

Fourth, the PPBS announcement fit poorly with other similar initiatives. Indeed, it undercut EROP, sanctioned by President Johnson only months before. in the Bureau of the Budget, moreover, PPBS can be traced back to 1964, albeit not by that name, but the Bureau's effort had been deliberately "selective and gradual." Indeed, this Budget posture of gradualism was affirmed decisively and publicly as late as June and July of 1965 [23] by the same Charles L. Schultze who shortly thereafter came to head Johnson's very broad PPBS program. It may be that Schultze changed his mind before August 25, but it appears that other Bureau officials retained their opinion beyond that date, after arguing against the announcement. Botner reports: "In issuing his sweeping across-the-board statement to implement PPBS, Johnson acted against the wishes of some BOB officials. They urged him to experiment first rather than applying it government wide" [24].

A similar sense of a precipitous and unsynchronized decision seems to extend to the U.S. Department of State. There, the 1965 announcement came as both surprise as well as poor fit with EROP, which involved joint leadership by State and Budget in all foreign affairs spending. EROP was a major initiative, mandated only a bit earlier on March 25, 1965, by President Johnson himself in a dramatic way, consistent with the widely held opinion that State should "take charge" in foreign affairs, albeit without a "unification reorganization" like that at Defense or HEW. The evidence suggests that PPBS took much of the wind from EROP's sail, variable and generally modest as its momentum had been [25].

Fifth, the August 25 announcement proposed a very tight schedule, if not an impossible one. Thus the PPBS schedule in effect disregarded the long developmental history underlying PPBS in Defense. Moreover, PPBS milestones gave unrealistically low weights to the advantages that an agency like Defense had in a similar but scaled-down venture. As Mosher and Haar observe [26]:

> The attempt to install PPB systems in most of the civil agencies of government in the course of a few months was a gigantic undertaking. Few if any of them enjoyed the advantages of the Defense Department . . . . : the background of study and experiment; the trained and sophisticated staff; the existing data base; the tremendous appropriation items; and the vigorous executive, already attuned to the techniques.

Sixth, President Johnson's announcement emphasized the general need for new "program analysis" staffs, but the proposed implementation schedule neglected supply-side issues [27]. Not only was PPBS fundamentally different than traditional budgeting, even program budgeting, but it also required analytic skills that were in short supply. Paramountly, perhaps, PPBS required relationships of substantial trust between financial officials and line officials that were rare. The ambiguities and the commonly perceived threat posed by Johnson's mandate would severely challenge existing relationships.

Again, the evidence suggests a precipitous decision with delayed and uncertain follow-up. Some efforts were made to develop small cadres with the requisite skills [28], and a few attempts at relationship-building did occur [29]. But the training constituted only catch-up efforts in 1966 through 1968 and, if of then-unprecedented scale, those efforts were too little and too late. Witness the program in systematic analysis fielded by selected universities. In its first year, 93 feds took part. Relationship-building had an even dimmer record. Some successes were attained within State, especially via Project ACORD [30], but other related efforts were stone-walled. One prominent change-agent left a top-level interdepartmental meeting sponsored by the Bureau of the Budget, for example, with departmental fears and rivalries inhibiting any significant exchanges of information and even restricting chitchat. "They had to check with their headquarters before going to the bathroom," this prominent notes in explaining his exit.

In short, these factors and others suggest a sudden executive decision, narrowly arrived at, with no strong sense of reasonable learning from available experience, and innocent of prudent extrapolations from experience to guide what required doing in the near future.

For limited purposes, at least, this record encourages reformulations of Thompson's trenchant question. Responsibility for PPBS is one thing. But why was Johnson's announcement made on August 25, 1965? And why was PPBS to be applied, in the original intent, to the entire federal establishment, given the breath-taking scope of the enterprise? And why were similar and ongoing efforts treated in such an apparently-cavalier fashion, with even some (many? most?) principals unaware of the announcement? These interrogatives sharpen the basic questions. Why PPBS? And how?

Hence this search for events compelling enough to induce President Johnson to make the fateful announcement of August 25, 1965.

A MICROVIEW OF POLICYMAKING

Compelling tethers restrict our analytic reach toward answers to the key questions. These constraints deal with the depths of the human soul and psyche, they relate to dim memories and to real motivations to manage history, and they also involve major actors known for silence concerning their public service. Paramountly, *the* major actor is now dead these several years, and left no known record of his PPBS thought processes.

Nonetheless, we look for some set of trigger events for the August 25 announcement which might credibly have inspired a great leap in the face of adverse situational features, against staggering odds, and with little attention to experience. The present contribution to how PPBS came to engage monumental energies is in part consistent with the common view, but extends far beyond it; and this contribution permits only alternative and even contradictory views of reality at several crucial points.

So several orienting caveats are in definite order. Paramountly, this counternarrative rests only in very small part on the written record. Even though a moderately determined search has been made of the published literature, only a few elements of the story below can be sustained in that way. Indeed, curiously, the literature is virtually mute about the specifics of the decision to go with federal-wide PPBS. For example, Johnson's biographers pay little or no attention to the issue [31]. Moreover, the memoirs and autobiographies of central actors provide little detail [32], and no critical actors have gone into print with their stories related to PPBS [33].

Basically, what follows is a bit of oral history. Variously formal interviews were held over the years with central actors, most of whom spoke off the record. The general policy is to include only materials that have independent corroboration, or (when identified as such) that seem reasonable inferences from corroborated accounts.

Some Fateful Internal Dynamics at State

The story below deals with a key set of incidents—serendipitous in large part, and even bizarre—that may have conspired to induce a huge and unprecedented investment of time and dollars in "modern approaches" to administration. Let us begin this narrative in a way that can be supported, and staunchly, by available records [34]. In the early 1960s, a number of zealous and determined State officials undertook an initiative unique in State, and generally unpopular in that agency as well as almost everywhere else in federal agencies interacting with State.

Manifestations of the central initiative became known by many acronyms, but they had a similar intent: to bring order into State via modern management methods, originally those associated with the computer but later also extended to the application of behavioral science methodologies [35]. In brief, a few State personnel in the 1960s developed a growing appreciation that successful installation of even the most profoundly useful rational/technical system vitally depends on behavioral factors; on an organization culture whose norms reinforce innovation and renewal; and on trusting relationships that will foster change not only by buffering its adverse consequences, but also by reducing the threat or suspicion that can undercut the best-designed systems.

William J. Crockett, Deputy Under Secretary of State for Administration, was the central and charismatic actor in these complex events. He had been a major critic of State practices and policies and, for his troubles, at mid-career found himself in State's "deep-freeze," which was agency jargon for being bypassed in ways that often led to termination. The story is told that Congressman John Rooney, a fearsome nemesis of State and chairman of a key subcommittee, came to learn of Crockett's fate. Rooney was so taken by Crockett's incisive criticisms as to buoy the latter's sudden resurrection as a mover-and-shaper in State.

Crockett's fall in State, in effect, gave him high stature in Rooney's eyes. Rooney himself placed great reliance on Crockett, and demanded as much from others. Rooney's patronage mated opportunity with Crockett's strong motivation to reform, in short.

Crockett and his energetic zealots developed a brand of middle-level advocacy. In general, indeed, almost all State officials preoccupied with policy and diplomacy did not much credit the new management initiatives: They did not value them, or understand them, or both. In any case, the State system-builders often involved willing lower level units and officials, not only insiders but outsiders as well. For example, the State system-builders had obtained data concerning expenditures in specific countries from field agents of several federal agencies that were generally very secretive about such matters, if not overtly involved in heated interdepartmental conflict with State in Washington. Friendly groups of neighbors in the field—lower level officials from various federal agencies in common geographic loci who saw a common need—provided data necessary to test the competence and integrity of the early computerized systems built by some State personnel. These databases rested on a high degree of trust between representatives of many federal agencies and State officials, and were truly remarkable for their time. One such database contributed a large matrix: all overseas spending by federal agencies, classified by such significant criteria as the purposes of expenditure, the point-of-spend, and so on. No similar data matrix existed at that time, anywhere else in the federal establishment. The acronym for the later versions of this database was CCPS, or Comprehensive Country Planning System. It will have a central place in later discussion.

In sum, some State personnel were involved in advocacy administration. And their developmental efforts were so far advanced—as with CCPS—that programmatic applications were needed not only to satisfy future ambitions, but also to justify past expenditures. As one State informant notes: "Getting CCPS data was one thing, and tough enough. Building those data into on-going budgeting is quite another matter."

The advocates also stimulated major counterreactions—often intense, and even fearsome. This reflects the tenor of the times in State, then still definitely recoiling from the McCarthy era. And it also reflects the growing social and political uneasiness that came to pervade Washington officialdom, in turn infuriating and inhibiting many of them.

These advocacy activities sought to balance the usual diplomatic emphasis in State with a professional and robust "management" emphasis [36]. This effort toward a new balance was profoundly political, even as its base rested in new analytic and behavioral technologies.

Hence the associated dynamics often took on an either/or character, and sometimes even the flavor of war. For "diplomacy" had long reigned supreme in State, and its prestigious proponents not only saw themselves as "agents of the president" but they also often stereotyped nondiplomats as "pants-pressers." State officials in administration, in retaliation, often categorized the diplomats as "cookie-pushers" or "striped-pants warriors." Their new emphasis on "administration" was often interpreted by those "in diplomatic service" as a mere power grab [37], if not a perversion of the right order of things.

This internal ferment had multiple roots, including the challenge (and the taunt!) to State by several prominents, including President Kennedy. State "should take charge" of our foreign affairs spending, lest duplication and overspending get further out of control. The ferment in State was generally interpreted as reflecting the complex pushes-and-pulls concerning whether and how that should/could/would be done. Some federal officials cheered because they saw the necessity of any form of integration of our foreign affairs initiatives; some were threatened and resisted what they perceived as tampering by State and Budget Bureau officials in their budgets for overseas activities; and perhaps most were situationally flexible, working along with State officials at times but also sensitive to the ebb-and-flow of specific initiatives [38]. Generally, State integrative efforts were seen in cost-reduction terms, and hence as possible reductions in budgets. This encouraged either wait-and-see postures, or overt resistance.

TWO PERSPECTIVES ON HOW STATE ADVOCACY GOT UNSTUCK

The portents did not favor State advocates breaking the logjam. State executives provided variable support, and had no enthusiasm for encountering the bureaucratic resistance and turf-protecting—especially from the Bureau of the Budget—they saw as the consequences of aggressive action concerning "management" initiatives. Ambassadors would in effect usually prefer to wait on specific executive direction in such matters, which was generally not forthcoming.

The dazzling approach to unstuckness involved getting President Johnson's support, given substantial differences of opinion about some of the details. Two basic versions exist of how this support came to be granted, specifically. They are not inconsistent versions of reality and, indeed, the fancy version fits quite nicely with the straight-vanilla view. But proponents of the latter view dismiss the former. Readers can decide for themselves as they review the three following sections, which, in turn, provide several scenarios of how President Johnson's support for State advocacy might have been induced.

Mutual Crying-in-the-Beer at the Mayflower?

One evening, goes the fancy view of reality, fate directed three parties to the Mayflower Hotel. They included a White House special assistant and two State officials. The duo from the State department were reflecting on how to make use of the results of an effort that had absorbed large amounts of time and dollars—CCPS, or Comprehensive Country Planning System. CCPS was the database described briefly above, and it was a major achievement. For a number of countries, by sponsoring agencies, it listed details about all foreign affairs spending for the current budget year.

But the CCPS was both misnamed and incomplete. CCPS was not a "system": It was a database in increasingly desperate search of a programmatic application. Without such an application, it constituted only a substantial investment, or even a potential embarrassment.

Also present in the Mayflower the same evening was a special assistant to President Johnson, Horace Busby, himself (in this first view of reality) predisposed to some crying in his professional brew. The term "alleged" is used because Busby was not available to corroborate this narrative, but independent evidence [39] does confirm the essential outcomes, whatever the details.

Let us focus on the details in doubt. "Problems," Busby in effect is said to have observed during his chance-meeting with the two men from State. "I've got them in spades." Among his other duties, Busby prepared agenda items for Cabinet meetings, and therein lay some of his concerns.

The State duo listened to Busby's litany of woe, first in friendly commiseration and then with a growing realization that *his* problem might be a major part of *their* solution.

Busby's problem derived from President Johnson's style of managing Cabinet meetings, the two men are said to have learned. After several false starts, a format evolved that the President found tolerable. The format demanded little of the President; and it had the effect of keeping Cabinet members on their toes, if not in fear of what requests might be forthcoming from their President in full view of their prestigious peers.

The format? For each Cabinet meeting, Busby would prepare a number of "agenda items" which were not to inspire discussion but to mandate action by a cabinet officer: Do this or that; or Report on such-and-so. The "items" often had supporting rationales, and could be a page or more long, but index-card length was more common. Several items typically were arrayed on the podium behind which the President stood if for the typically brief Cabinet meeting. Apparently, Johnson seldom saw Busby's materials prior to entering the Cabinet room. Typically, after making his entrance, Johnson would survey the items while a Cabinet member was reporting on an earlier charge. Sometimes brief discussion followed; and often President Johnson would choose a new item to direct at one of the attendees.

The processes underlying these mechanics typically followed a simple and direct pattern. Cabinet members arrived a bit on edge, concerned as to whether "their" topic would be the center of attention. Invariably, also, the Cabinet meeting would end abruptly after President Johnson had directed a new agenda item at the appropriate target. Presumably, the unscathed would be anxious to leave lest they got presidential attention; and the target-for-the-meeting presumably would hurriedly return to his or her office to begin a response to the new charge.

At first, this view continues, Busby was well stocked with alternatives. Some Cabinet members saw a good opportunity to introduce pet issues that way; and on occasion the device might be used (if carefully) to gain points in interdepartmental skirmishes by helping highlight the problems or embarassments of others.

Quickly, however, four points became clear, in this first view of reality. Paramountly, President Johnson had a very strong penchant for issues that would gig Cabinet attendees—to leave them gasping a big, if not seriously wounded. Relatedly, if the available agenda items did not directly raise such issues or problems, the President would reformulate them in suitable ways, but with obvious displeasure, of which Busby was the primary recipient. In addition, President Johnson had a very long memory when it came to "stale items," that is, those that had at any previous time been placed on his podium. Consequently, the supply of volunteered issues and problems quickly was falling behind the demand: Few new suggestions were forthcoming, and President Johnson's appetite for additional materials had increased, if anything.

In this first view of how PPBS came to be announced dramatically, the two State executives were delighted to supply Busby with perhaps two alternative ways of highlighting CCPS. One or more CCPS issues were put on President Johnson's podium, goes the story, along with three or four other non-State possibilities the President might choose.

Eventful Strategizing Between Friends?

A second version of reality has a straight-vanilla quality. Busby and Crockett here are old friends from Johnson's vice-presidential days when Crockett was variously involved in several overseas trips by the Vice President. So it was just understandable, in this second view, that the two men easily got involved in strategizing about how the President might be made aware of the management progress within State on CCPS, as well as about how the President might add impetus to State's initiative while serving his own interests in controlling spending.

President Johnson is in this view seen as "liking alternatives," and especially concerning the War on Waste, and the two men see direct ties between Johnson's growing frustration and the State effort on CCPS. It is not clear in this view when and in what form President Johnson decided to support the Crockett initiative, but presumably Busby's advice would have been more telling and direct than in the first view of reality sketched above.

DEFINITE PRESIDENTIAL SUPPORT

These two versions of reality can be viewed from several perspectives. Thus available evidence implies Busby could have played the role associated with either scenario. In available reports, for example, Busby is the good presidential friend and companion, at times even staying in the President's bedroom until sleep comes with difficulty to Johnson. Busby is also said to have exerted major influence on Johnson's decision not to seek a second term [40].

Whatever the preliminaries—view I or II of reality, or some combination thereof—President Johnson gave the explicit support of his office to the statement in Fig. 1, and State advocates got a program for their CCPS database. A statement was drafted—either in conversations or in a set of phone calls—and authorship seems to have been substantially or entirely Crockett's.

President Johnson read the statement in Fig. 1 at the Cabinet meeting of March 25, 1965. The resulting project was immediately christened PROP, for Presidential Review of Overseas Programs, apparently by State officials eager to ride Johnson's coattails, and shortly Programs, when Johnson expressed a disinclination for the direct identification with the effort implied by the first acronym.

SOME QUESTIONS OF SUBSTANCE AND DETAIL

There appears to have been no public discussion after Johnson read the statement in Fig. 1, and the Cabinet meeting adjourned quickly. Both were standard. But the statement did raise a number of serious questions, in fact, of which five get attention here.

What Did President Johnson Order?

Even a superficial grasp of Exhibit 1 implies EROP's substantial scope—"all U.S. agencies, all U.S. programs, and all U.S. policies related to people and programs" are to be reviewed in "10 or 15 countries." No more than 6 months would be available if the President's target were to be met—"before our next budget enters preparation."

ALL DEPARTMENTS—and virtually all agencies—have personnel and programs abroad. From time to time, I have expressed to you individually my views in regard to this. I do not believe it is necessary—or desirable—for the executive branch to duplicate globally the pattern of domestic responsibilities and operations at home.

I have recently been giving much thought to such matters. And today I want to share some observations—and make a recommendation—in this regard.

Our programs around the world are all important to the accomplishment of our foreign policy objectives. But our resources and money are always scarce. They are never plentiful enough to cover every need and to fulfill every objective.

For that reason, I am today asking the following:

That the Secretary of State, who is responsible for recommending our foreign policy objectives, and the Director of the Budget, who is responsible for recommending distribution of resources to accomplish those objectives, meet with all of you who have overseas programs to look at our operations in 10 or 15 countries.

This would be done on experimental basis—with all U.S. agencies, all U.S. policies related to people and programs being reviewed country by country. The object should be to determine that we are doing the things that are most essential for us to do, that there are no unnecessary programs—and that all our money is being well spent.

In countries where such reviews are conducted, I shall expect each agency to respect the levels established for each of the programs by Secretary Rusk, and Mr. Gordon in the allocation of funds—and in the projection of our plans . . .

[NOTE: The President read the statement at 1:15 p.m. in the Cabinet Room at the White House.]

Figure 1 Statement to the Cabinet on the Need for Economical Operations of Overseas Programs, March 25, 1965. (From *Public Papers of the President*, Vol. 1, Government Printing Office, Washington, D.C., p. 318 (1966).)

These basic features raise serious questions about President Johnson's expectations and interest. Certainly, he knew that federal agencies would not easily accept a determination of "the levels" established for each of our programs by Secretary Rusk and Mr. Gordon "in the allocation of funds and resources for the ensuing year," even if it were possible to gather and review data about all spending by all agencies. Congress and its subunits could be counted on to support determined foot-draggers, at the very least. And Johnson no doubt was aware of the already serious issues between Budget and State officials. And how much President Johnson believed could be accomplished in 6 months is not known. Indeed, in the first version of reality sketched above, the deadline deliberately would have been set so as to be out of reach, with the operative purpose being to remind Secretary of State Rusk and others who was in command.

Who Knew About CCPS?

It seems probable that most central actors did not understand that a database for EROP was already available in CCPS. Indeed, even central persons in State did not understand that EROP provided only a programmatic home for the CCPS data base [41].

So it is unlikely that President Johnson understood that a database already existed for the review that he mandated. Developing the CCPS database had taken years, although CCPS encompassed more than the 10–15 countries that EROP would consider.

Secretary of State Rusk may not have known about the CCPS/EROP linkage, in addition, and he probably knew little about the CCPS effort or the resources devoted to it. Rusk had been exposed to a "general briefing" on CCPS, and small staff meetings held three times a week were used to keeping the Secretary aware of developments. However—given the predictably negative reaction of Budget Bureau officials to EROP, and given Rusk's general aversion to bureaucratic in-fighting—it seems likely that his before-the-fact knowledge of EROP was slight. Rusk was a very busy person in Washington, not only on various matters central to his State responsibilities, but more especially with those of broad interest to President Johnson—civil rights, voter registration, and so on.

Who Drafted the Announcement, or Was Consulted About It?

The substance of the announcement came from Crockett, apparently by phone to Busby's secretary. And perhaps some additional writing or editing was done at the White House. But there seems to have been no prior clearance of the announcement outside the White House, or even outside Busby's office.

Far from encouraging prior consultation and clearance, indeed, the evidence suggests that several major actors and agencies would have used clearance only to obstruct CCPS/EROP. For example, Crockett's draft recognized Budget's role "in the allocation of funds and resources." However, as Crockett knew, Budget officials had not responded to his earlier letter suggesting a similar mutual effort, perhaps because the Bureau had launched its own PPBS-like effort. The failure to respond was not seen as a Budget oversight, in any case, and this raises serious doubt about any clearance of the March 25 announcement with Budget. This doubt is heightened by the lukewarm character of the subsequent involvement of Budget officials in the EROP reviews. Crockett feels certain that Budget officials had advance notice of the content of the announcement, however, if only as a matter of minimal courtesy.

Who Knew About the Announcement, and When?

Little confidence seems appropriate concerning the issue of who, if anyone, knew in advance that the March 25 statement would be made. Busby is said to have been confident that the item would be included *among* agenda items, sooner or later; and Crockett apparently told Rusk and Under Secretary George Ball that "the subject *might* appear" on a Cabinet agenda [42]. Moreover, Rusk and Crockett both are reported to have gone to the cabinet meeting of March 25, which is consistent with their foreknowledge. However, the source does not note whether they knew that the announcement would be made, and Crockett himself doubts seriously that he attended the meeting.

It is possible that even President Johnson did not know he would make *that* announcement, until he reviewed the several "agenda items" on the podium, *after* he walked into the meeting.

How Did Crockett Get the EROP Mandate?

Some doubts also exist about how Crockett's group received the charge to get cracking on the March 25 statement. In one published version, Rusk and Crockett attend the Cabinet session. Afterward, Rusk tells his Under Secretary: "It's your baby, Bill" [43]. Crockett feels certain he did not attend the meeting, however, as noted.

Another version has a surprised and troubled Rusk at the cabinet session alone. In this view, his shoulders slump at this new challenge from his President, which he eagerly but despairingly accepts—probably absent working knowledge of CCPS, and almost certainly unaware of the details of Crockett's now-successful effort to generate a programmatic application of the CCPS database.

While Rusk journeys back to Foggy Bottom, perhaps Crockett and an aide arrange to "just drop by." They had received word that the President had in fact gone on record, as they hoped. "What can anyone do about that, and in six months or so?," Rusk may have said, in effect. His two State aides just happened to have the answer—one precisely tailored to the presidential charge about which Rusk was fretting.

EROP AS ABORT, COMPETITIVE STIMULUS, OR TRANSCENDANT?

These micro-unknowns introduce and impact on a mega-issue. What were the effects of EROP's limited effort to provide a programmatic application of the CCPS database?

Three views of reality contest here. Some observers see no notable effect; others see an indirect effect; and some see EROP at once as a program that motivated its own demise and yet experienced a self-transcendance in federal-wide PPBS.

EROP as Well-Intended Abort?

Some observers see no notable EROP products beyond a flurry of meetings and some paper. Despite direct presidential authorization, one observer notes, "EROP still had to deal with the clerks of the world." And EROP lost—in part due to problems internal to State, in part because the Presidency had bigger fish to fry, and also due to the magnitude of the task as well as the resistances it induced.

Consistent with this view, federal PPBS developed quite independently of EROP, and any similarity of objectives is merely coincidental and reflects the multiple streams of activity in complex government. PPBS came in its own good time, then, with a key factor in its timing being President Johnson's landslide victory over Senator Goldwater in the election of November 1964.

EROP as Competitive Stimulus?

In a second view, EROP is seen as a surprising stimulus that located Bureau of the Budget activity re PPBS, resulting in the President's August 25 announcement of system-wide PPBS. In this view, Budget did not expect EROP, feared the loss of initiative it represented, and counterattacked by impelling President Johnson toward the PPBS announcement. This proposes a view of PPBS as a consequence of bureaucratic in-fighting, with Budget having the better access to President Johnson's ear, EROP notwithstanding. In this view, Budget lost a skirmish but won the right to direct a war.

Speculation supporting such a bureaucratic view has compelling features, in fact. A kind of natural point of tension existed between Budget and any agency that sought to rationalize the budget process outside of existing relationships with the Bureau—that had long been clear, although state officials acknowledge that they badly underestimated the Bureau's sensitivity on this basic issue. While they resisted initiatives by others, progress on Budget's own version of PPBS went at a measured pace. Indeed, in June and July 1965, Budget officials indicated their approach would remain "selective and gradual," and some officials remained staunch in that position even after August 25.

Other evidence also supports the preeminent role of the Bureau of the Budget. Although no "smoking gun" yet exists, most central informants attribute decisive influence to Budget. Weighty also are the two recollections of senior Defense officials. Despite the media's association of Defense with PPBS, they argue, McNamara's role was limited to discussing the technology with President Johnson "three or four times." Moreover, they declare that the naive features of the August 25 PPBS announcement would not have survived strong inputs from Defense. Finally, the announcement determinedly focused on what might be called "intra-agency PPBS." Both Defense and EROP initiatives had self-consciously systemic ambitions, in contrast, and focused on "interagency PPBS"—with its numerous "crosswalks" and comparisons of priorities at the broadest possible levels. The agency focus of the PPBS announcement fit more comfortably with the way Budget did its budget examining—beginning with several levels of subsystemic review, *before* any attempt was made at systemic analysis, and where "examining" usually served *in place* of systemic analysis. These dynamics reflect the Budget view that any budgetary applications would have to develop a supporting culture in each agency, consistent with local traditions, clientele, and ways of doing business [44].

One major open question especially troubles this view of EROP as competitive stimulus, however. The sudden and surprising August 25 announcement does not sit well with Budget going public in June and July with the news that their emphasis on PPBS would continue to be "selective and gradual." Of course, something may have occurred later that changed the minds of Budget officials. But what? The following section offers one possibility.

EROP as Curiously Transcendant?

A third and colorful version of reality proposes EROP's direct and visual impact on President Johnson. Several settings have been proposed. One source puts it in the Cabinet room itself, with stacks of computer printout piled a foot high on the large table. The occasion and date also are in doubt. One source maintains it was at a Cabinet meeting, but that has not been confirmed. In any case, the setting was a progress report on EROP, some time between the EROP announcement on March 25 and the implicit presidential deadline of September 25 or thereabouts.

This view of reality dwells on a picture of a preoccupied president, zooming into the briefing, and visibly startled by the stacks of printout, some 3 or 4 months after State had accepted what many—and perhaps even the President—considered a mission impossible. During the early dog days of Washington's 1965 summer, the President is said to have been startled to learn that, from a mass of materials, State analysis could tell how much the U.S. government was spending (let us say) for nails in Mexico—by which agency, for what purposes, and so on. The surprise would have been greatest, of course, if Johnson had intended the EROP announcement only as a way of getting the attention of State and other agencies, of reminding them of their responsibility to him and stirring them up by mandating a task the President saw as beyond anyone's reach. Readers of minutiae may here remember that EROP began its life as a presidential review but soon became an executive review, apparently at Johnson's insistence.

This third view of EROP impact seems correct to some observers, while others consider it a picture of what should have happened, perhaps, but probably did not. The something that got to President Johnson or to his Bureau of the Budget advisors, in this view, was a startlingly unexpected review of progress on CCPS/EROP. That quick review of progress was dramatic enough to trigger sudden (even precipitous) action.

At the very least, this view is consistent with the dominant presidential style: The review of unexpected progress on CCPS/EROP—in a dramatic setting featuring mountains of printout—might have inspired sudden presidential visions of the reasonableness of far broader PPBS initiatives, and also may have seemed a way out of the President's burgeoning frustration derived from vaulting ambitions and ever-tighter resources. Rusk's great concern about being responsive to presidential directions also is consistent with some proud demonstration of quick progress.

Proponents of the fancy version of how and why EROP received presidential sanction also point to the delicious irony of such a review of CCPS/EROP success. Consider that irony. President Johnson impulsively selects the EROP agenda item, intending it as a mission impossible, but nonetheless relishing its practical effect—putting some fear of God in State and other public officials, and in the "management" he did not understand but which he believed needed stirring up. If it occurred, the presidential confrontation with CCPS/EROP products would have been dramatic, and might have triggered a quick decision to extend the approach to the entire federal government, in the disjointed ways described above.

CONJECTURES SUPPORTING AN EROP IMPACT

Several close observers doubt that CCPS/EROP products impressed the President in any dramatic way, but consider one fact and an extended conjecture. The PPBS effort was authorized on August 25. This was 5 months after EROP was blessed by President Johnson, if in a hedged way; it was 2 or 3 months after Budget reaffirmed its long-standing gradualist approach to PPBS; and it was 1 or 2 months after the perhaps apocryphal sharing of State progress with the President and/or Budget officials.

Did EROP directly or indirectly influence the PPBS announcement? Conjecture must dominate, but it provides support for a substantial effect. Here consider only three major points.

1.   President Johnson and/or Budget Bureau officials could have been impressed by State's work, which extended far beyond the reach-and-grasp of other similar systems, such as that in Defense. The CCPS database was *sui generis* in critical regards, and might well have generated very high hopes about the even greater comprehensiveness that firm presidential support could induce in federal-wide effort. Moreover, the CCPS/EROP output was generated in what seemed to Johnson a very short time, given his probable lack of appreciation of the effort that had gone into the prior preparation of the CCPS database which underlay the EROP country reviews. Again, this possibility could have encouraged the unrestrained exuberance reflected in the August 25 PPBS announcement. Budget officials also might have been surprised at EROP's apparently sudden progress.

Why might Johnson have been especially impressed by the State progress? Primarily, the CCPS/EROP data involve many federal departments, some of them quite antagonistic to State as well as to each other. And their aggregate spending had been comprehensively and conveniently catalogued and variously cross-classified in CCPS, in stacks of printout that might well have left observers impressed by the power of the then newfangled computer, as well as with the drive and competence of the bright and ambitious people at State. This kind of central overview had seldom, if ever, been possible for clusters of federal agencies. And the possibilities for analysis—as well as for overhead political control—permitted by the data arrays would no doubt strike Johnson as being great.

2.   There is no evidence that President Johnson or Budget officials ever were briefed on the years of significant effort that underlay the CCPS/EROP output, and especially about the psychological and cultural forces that had been mobilized—consciously and serendipitously—as a behavioral foundation for the data-processing effort. Five points illustrate major features of CCPS/EROP that were given little attention:

- Personal relations between representatives of numerous federal agencies in the field had been developed that overcame political barriers that existed or even towered at higher levels, and especially in the Washington environment.
- Field agents of various federal agencies shared data that was in common practice closely held in most other loci, if not kept secret by explicit orders of Washington superiors or by long-standing custom.
- In part, geographical isolation induced these warm and supportive relationships, reinforced by distance from headquarters as well as by the low priority assigned to some overseas assignments by many federal agencies in countries in the CCPS panel.
- In part, the CCPS process reflected the growing appreciation by some State officials of the organizational centrality of interpersonal and intergroup trust, and especially of the developing behavioral science technologies for inducing trust: sensitivity training, team building, conflict resolution by third-party intervention, on so on [45].
- Resistance to the State effort was not high: The low-profile CCPS effort finessed resistance at senior levels (even within State!), and the impact of multiple constituencies and organization loyalities was blunted by trusting relationships in the field.

In behavioral science jargon, the "host was culturally prepared" for the CCPS data-gathering intervention, and this critical preparatory work was neither generally appreciated nor provided for in the federal PPBS application. Indeed, that lesson did not become manifest even in the several-year hustle and bustle to implement the August 25 announcement. For example, in the 2 or 3 years following the 1965 announcement, several universities contracted to run workshops to train federal employees in PPBS philosophy and techniques. Several programs of study have been consulted and, despite sparse documentation and memories that can be vague at crucial points, little or no explicit attention was given to "cultural preparedness" in the substantial but underpowered effort to spread the PPBS gospel.

3.   The President and others also may have been impressed by the apparently quick appearance of CCPS/EROP products, especially in the context of the vigorous (even savage) differences that existed within State. Battles between "managers" and "diplomats" ravaged State for years. For example, these unresolved battles were significant in the demise of Project ACORD, or Action for Organization Development. ACORD failed in its proximate objective of inducing a new organization culture at State, but it succeeded in various specific areas, and its long-run consequences were felt for years in the efforts to adjust State operations and norms to dramatically changing environments [45].

DISCUSSION

Two facts stand out, and one assumption seems reasonable. PPBS took off like a rushing wind in the federal government, but with little awareness of, and guidance from the State or Defense experiences. Moreover, generally unrecognized events may have helped that rushing wind along, if they did not supply the crucial momentum that set the federal bureaucracy in pursuit of the PPBS ideal.

NOTES AND REFERENCES

1.   V. A. Thompson, *Without Sympathy or Enthusiasm*, University of Alabama Press, University, Ala., pp. 95–96 (1975).

2. "Transcript of President's News Conference," *Washington Post*, August 26, A18 (1965).
3. F. C. Mosher and J. E. Haar, *Programming Systems and Foreign Affairs Leadership*, Oxford University Press, New York, p. 92 (1970).
4. Ref. 2, p. A18.
5. R. D. Lee, Jr., R. W. Johnson, *Public Budgeting Systems*, University Park Press, Baltimore, Md., p. 66 (1983).
6. A. Schick, "The Road to PPBS: The Stages of Budget Reform," *Public Admin. Rev.*, *26*: 243–258 (1966).
7. "Johnson Altering U.S. Cost Control," *New York Times*, August 25, p. 6 (1965).
8. Ref. 5, p. 82.
9. K. L. Handa, *Program and Performance Budgeting*, Uppal Publishing House, New Delhi, p. 96 (1979).
10. T. E. Cronin, "An Examination of White House-Departmental Relations," p. 178, in *The Institutionalized Presidency*, (N. C. Thomas and H. W. Baade, eds.), Oceana Publications, Dobbs Ferry, N.Y. (1972).
11. F. J. Lyden and M. Lindenberg, *Public Budgeting in Theory and Practice*, Longman, New York, pp. 89–98 (1983).
12. J. C. Donovan, *The Policy Makers*, Western Publishing, New York, p. 113 (1970).
13. Ref. 12, esp. p. 113, encouraged this reader to that interpretation.
14. J. C. Doh, *The Planning Programming Budgeting System in Three Federal Agencies*, Praeger, New York, p. 165 (1971).
15. S. B. Botner, "Four Years of PPBS," *Public Admin. Rev.*, *30*:426 (1970).
16. For example, Ref. 12.
17. Ref. 12, p. 113.
18. Ref. 3, p. 92.
19. Ref. 3, pp. 76–77.
20. Bureau of the Budget Bulletin No. 66-3, October 12 (1965).
21. Information Office, Bureau of the Budget, OD-185, p. 2.
22. Quoted in Ref. 15, p. 424.
23. Ref. 3, pp. 91–92.
24. Ref. 15, p. 424.
25. Ref. 15, p. 123–124.
26. Ref. 15, p. 97.
27. H. Margolis, "President Orders 'Revolutionary' Budgeting System," *Washington Post*, August 26, p. A17 (1965).
28. Ref. 3, p. 93.
29. State had instituted a relationship-building effort in connection with its efforts at planned change, and that leaked into the broader PPBS effort. A few other federal agencies had similar programs, but their association with the PPBS initiative was unusual and uneven when it occurred. See Ref. 15, p. 424.
30. For example, see R. D. Walton, *Interpersonal Peacemaking*, Addison-Wesley, Reading, Mass. (1969). ACORD is the acronym for Action for Organization Development.
31. The corpus of Johnson's presidential papers in the Austin archives have *not* been searched, but such works were consulted:
J. M. Blum, *The Progressive Presidents*, W. W. Norton, New York (1980).
R. A. Caro, *The Years of Lyndon Johnson: The Path to Power*, Alfred A. Knopf, New York (1982).
F. Corimer, *LBJ: The Way He Was*, Doubleday, New York (1977).
H. Druks, *From Truman Through Johnson: A Documentary History*, Robert Speller and Sons, New York (1971).
R. Evans and R. Novak, *Lyndon B. Johnson: The Exercise of Power*, New American Library, New York (1966).
E. F. Goldman, *The Tragedy of Lyndon Johnson*, Alfred A. Knopf, New York (1969).

R. Harwood and H. Johnson, *Lyndon*, Praeger, New York (1973).

L. B. Johnson, *The Vantage Point*, Holt, Rinehart, and Winston, New York (1971).

M. Miller, *Lyndon*, Putnam's Sons, New York (1975).

B. Mooney, *LBJ: An Irreverent Chronicle*, Thomas Crowell, New York (1976).

G. Reedy, *Lyndon B. Johnson: A Memoir*, Andrews and McMeel, New York (1982).

C. Roberts, *LBJ's Inner Circle*, Delacorte Press, New York (1960).

P. R. Rulon, *The Compassionate Samaritan*, Nelson-Hall, Chicago (1981).

H. Sidney, *A Very Personal Presidency*, Atheneum Press, New York (1968).

A. Steinberg, *Sam Johnson's Boy*, Mcmillan, New York (1968).

J. Valenti, *A Very Human President*, W. W. Norton, New York (1975).

32. See, for example, R. S. McNamara, *The Essence of Security*, Harper and Row, New York (1968); and C. L. Schultze, *The Politics and Economics of Public Spending*, Brookings Institution, Washington, D.C. (1968).

33. Among the probable central actors, to judge from a bibliographic search, these individuals have not written for publication about the target events: Richard W. Barrett, Horace Busby, William N. Capron, William J. Crockett, Kermit Gordon, Charles Hitch, and Dean Rusk.

34. The major exception is Ref. 3.

35. For useful summary, see M. M. Harmon, "Organization Development in the State Department: A Case Study of the ACORD Program," in *High Performance and Human Costs*, (R. T. Golembiewski and A. Kiepper, eds.), Praeger, New York, pp. 179–196 (1988).

36. A. J. Marrow, *Making Waves on Foggy Bottom*, NTL Institute, Washington, D.C., (1974); and D. P. Warwick, *A Theory of Bureaucracy*, Harvard University, Cambridge, Mass. (1975).

37. J. Alsop and S. Alsop, "Let the Poor Old Foreign Service Alone," *Saturday Evening Post*, June, p. 14 (1966).

38. For example, Ref. 3, pp. 77–92.

39. Ref. 3, pp. 74–75.

40. M. Miller, *Lyndon*, Putnam's Sons, New York, p. 508 (1975).

41. Ref. 40, p. 77.

42. Ref. 40, p. 75.

43. Ref. 40, p. 76.

44. See Ref. 14.

45. See Harmon, Ref. 35; Marrow, Ref. 36; and Warwick, Ref. 36.

II
CONCEPTUAL CONTEXTS OF BUDGETING AND FINANCE

EDITORIAL INTRODUCTION

However inadequate it must be, we cannot avoid the attempt here to indicate in conceptual terms some of what is meant by the term "public budgeting and finance." Three focal questions preoccupy this attempt:

- What arenas does PBF encompass?
- How can PBF products be used by management?
- What are major constraints on PBF policies and practices?

The first two selections in this unit deal with the "what" of PBF. The views there are intentionally broad, and subsequent chapters will add much detail.

A third selection, by Simon and his associates, focuses on the use of basic budgeting and finance procedures. This illustrates the "how" of PBF, of course.

The final three selections—Chapters 10–12, to be specific—focus on ethics, culture, and comparative contexts, in turn. In effect, these last three selections illustrate possible constraints in PBF. To put it oversimply, the "what" and the "how" of PBF are always applied under *some* conditions. The last three selections in this chapter describe three sets of such conditions that, in effect, serve as constraints on the "what" and "how" of PBF—ethical positions, cultural features, and comparative differences between micro- as well as macro-loci hosts of PBF approaches, policies, and techniques.

An Overview of Budgeting

In Chapter 8, Irene S. Rubin's "Budgeting: Theory and Concepts" provides a useful start for Unit II. To begin, she highlights the centrality of "theory" for any field of inquiry. Basically, theory provides coherence for the efforts of many observers, as by highlighting assumptions made and by spotlighting major issues. In no full sense of the term, Rubin adds, can PBF be said to have a "theory." So much the worse for PBF, she implies.

This basic judgment motivates Rubin, but it does not deter her. That is, she begins to lay some of the groundwork on which an increasingly comprehensive theory can be built. Rubin's scope is broad. Thus, she begins by associating PBF directly with "society." This basic conceptual linkage implies a vast range for inquiry. For example, some PBF manifestations could be built on Marxist or Neo-Marxist values and orientations, as those are embodied in specific social contexts. At the same time, Rubin goes into detail to suggest the distinctive character of the values and orientations that underlay what might be called U.S. PBF.

And so it goes with Rubin's contribution, in one particular after another. Clearly, no PBF theory exists to serve readers of this text, largely American. No less clearly, Rubin indicates many of the components that will become part of that theory.

However, one important component of an eventually satisfactory theory will emphasize the themes of budgets as an instrument of control as well as a plan of action [e.g., 1, esp. pp. 17–91]. Basically, in this view, the focus is on levels of aspiration, and the practical tasks involve inspiring appropriate levels as well as responding to variances between performance, aspiration, and budgetary requirements. One central question: Should budgets be "tight"—that is, difficult or impossible to achieve, given one's aspirations—or "loose"? The "discrepancy" is a crucial element, with most opinion agreeing with Stedry [1] that most individuals will try to reduce discrepancies between their aspiration level and the budget target "at a rate which depends on the size of the discrepancy." This implies "tight" budgets. But the related issues seem more complex [2, pp. 61–84].

Stedry's discussion of "standards" and "standard costs" also is useful, for to "plan" and "control" require some estimate of how much of which resources are required for specific objectives. Thus, budgets require commitment to some total figure as well as to its component standards. "Standards" or "standard costs" imply what work is expected from some sum of dollars. For example, a department in a university may have a large budget for salaries, but if the faculty–student ratio is also high, this implies a standard that many professors may find unattractive even though their salaries are quite pleasing. Directly, budgeting and finance must motivate individuals to strive appropriately—that is, to meet a total budget as well as to induce them to accept its component standards.

Despite the brevity of these introductory notes, PBF's "what" clearly encompasses many phenomena at the heart of the management of people and the coordination of cooperative behavior. Only a little interpretation makes the matter clear. Thus, the "plan" aspects of budgeting and finance require that their processes must lean toward the future, and embody and reflect some idealized sense of things as they might be better. The "plan," however, cannot command total attention. The "control" aspects imply that PBF processes also must rest upon a strong sense of things as they are, or as they might be at their worst. Avoiding the worst, while attempting to permit the best, is a human challenge of heroic dimensions. Just that challenge rests very near the heart of PBF.

Uses of PBF Products

To expand the sense of the "what" of PBF, Simon and his associates provide some additional conceptual detail in Chapter 9, "Management Uses of Figures," which is excerpted from their book *Centralization vs. Decentralization in Organizing the Controller's Department*. Basically, they argue that three types of questions must be considered by any comprehensive program of the "internal reporting" of financial data. The authors distinguish:

- Score-card questions, such as "Am I doing well or badly?"
- Attention-directing questions, such as "What problems should I look into?"
- Problem-solving questions, such as "Of the several ways of doing the job, which is the best?"

Score-card questions patently must play a crucial role in every organization. That is, organizations have as their basic purpose the efficient and effective utilization of collective resources. "Are we doing well or badly?" consequently must be of central organizational concern. The processes of providing those answers are very delicate ones indeed. Directly, PBF personnel could easily come to be seen as punitive because of one of their major traditional roles. They develop answers to score-card questions, and they provide those answers to top management to control those at lower levels.

Hence, also, the especial importance of giving extensive attention to attention-directing questions as well as problem-solving questions, which can be more helpful to lower level operatives. Answering these two kinds of questions requires working closely with officials at all levels, which can help balance PBF's typically close identifications with top management. In addition, officials at various management levels who have been disciplined via answers to score-card questions might be reticent to accept help, or ask for it. That is, to ask for or to accept help potentially risks providing to budgeting and finance officials "inside information," which in turn may be used against the manager. Useful responses to attention-getting and problem-solving questions can help rectify awkward inclinations to go it alone.

Ethics as Constraint

Elementally, as the title of Carol W. Lewis' contribution (Chapter 10) reflects, PBF always deals with delicate balances between what is and what should be: "Power Without Privilege: Ethics in Public Budgeting and Financial Management." In effect, normative fingerprints are all over the preceding selections, and will seldom be absent from the numerous selections to follow. And that should be the case, as Lewis proposes for reasons she explains. Indeed, she adds, the salience of valuable issues in PBF is—if anything—greater than ever in the context of today's troubled financial situations, where budgets are tighter and demands are greater.

The attractions of Lewis' contribution can only be suggested here. Conceptually, to illustrate, her analysis urges that normative choice-making is ubiquitous in PBF: in making reasoned and reasonable judgments about right and wrong; in taking ethical positions consistent with law, good practice, or professional guides; and especially in connection with the common cross-pressures associated with accountability and responsibility. In more practical terms, again only to illustrate, Lewis draws useful attention to the professional standards of the Government Finance Officers Association, which provides ethical guidance for PBF in Canada as well as in the United States.

Culture as Constraint

Aaron Wildavsky introduces yet another major constraint on PBF policies and practices in Chapter 11, "Budgeting and Culture." This selection puts us all on important notice. Some observers, like Woodrow Wilson, believe that PBF policies and practices are in some sense applicable in any and all contexts, and Wildavsky warns us about making that convenient assumption.

Wildavsky's argument is significant enough to encourage the following outline, even though he is quite straightforward in making that argument in his own terms. Basically, he identifies four kinds of "primary political cultures": fatalist, individualist, collectivist, and egalitarian. In subsequent detail, Wildavsky then makes the compound point that various PBF policies and practices variously fit those four political cultures. For example, collectivist cultures may be better able to manage revenues, but expenditures tend to balloon in those settings because of the operating bias toward equal outcomes for all across a broadening front of goods and services. Alternatively, Wildavsky proposes, fatalist cultures tend to be ineffective managers of both revenues and expenditures.

Wildavsky's basic point is a simple but significant one. Just as PBF policies and practices have to be judged by their fit with prevailing ethical standards, so also must that fit be judged against specific political cultures.

The application of Wildavsky's basic notion presents major challenges. Thus, political cultures need to be distinguished at each point in time, and as actual as well as ideal. The two versions can overlap, but they also can be widely discrepant. The degree of that overlap can make a very big difference. In any large system, moreover, subsystems may differ as to their political cultures, both ideal and practical. The analytic challenge is profound in federal systems like ours, because major differences in political cultures might well characterize all three levels of government—federal, state, and local. Moreover, differences also might exist between actors at any one level, as between several federal departments or between bureaus within a single department. Or differences in political cultures also might exist between the levels of government. So the issue of degree of fit can pose issues requiring not only subtlety to isolate them, but also skill as well as wisdom to manage them.

Comparative PBF Aspects as Constraint

In Chapter 12 George M. Guess extends the considerations of goodness of fit to the question of the transfer of PBF policies and practices, between localities, states, federal agencies, and even nation states. The key questions are direct: Does policy/practice A work here? Is there a reasonable probability that policy/practice A also will work there?" "Comparative Government Budgeting" summarizes our limited but growing theory and experience with such core questions.

Guess is clearly no true believer in the adequacy of our existing theory and practice. He details a number of major difficulties facing any relevant research. And he implies the need for care and even cunning in interpreting that research.

At the same time, Guess does not seem to represent a cynical view, even as he provides useful ammunition for the skeptic. Rather, his selection reflects two generalizations. Thus, transfer of technology constitutes a major challenge at all stages of development, in all arenas. And our success in making effective transfers of technology will be a major factor in approaching the full life in the just state.

8

Budgeting: Theory and Concepts

Irene S. Rubin

The function of a theory is to provide an orientation to a field, to state assumptions, to point to certain problems as of key significance, and to come up with some hypotheses about what causes what. In public administration, theory has the additional responsibility of culling practical problems and suggesting solutions. Budget theory in particular should be able to answer questions about why particular practices should be adopted, the importance of particular tasks, and the location of particular tasks in a larger process.

Budgeting does not currently have a theory in this sense. Writers on budgeting do not agree on common assumptions or recommendations. While there are some common questions that have long stirred interest in budgeters, there is no widely accepted set of linked hypotheses concerning cause and effect in budgeting. One paradigm—a set of hypotheses and a methodological approach—dominated the field for a while, but that dominance is now over.

Budget theory today is fragmented and incomplete. In some areas the field seems to be moving toward a consensus, while in others the level of disagreement is acute. Budget theory is in the process of being invented. Studying public budgeting is therefore exciting, but a little confusing. The purpose of this chapter is to organize and reduce the confusion by outlining some of the key assumptions and concepts in public budgeting.

BUDGET THEORIES AND ASSUMPTIONS

One function of a theory is to provide an overall orientation to a field. Of what is public budgeting a part? Why is it important? Who might want to study it, to find out what kinds of things? How is budgeting conceived?

At the broadest level, theory links public budgeting to the study of society. One reason to study budgeting is to learn about a society by looking at the way the government spends public funds, both in terms of the processes used and the priorities expressed. Budgeting

---

Source: Budgeting: Theory, Concepts, Methods, and Issues, *Handbook of Public Budgeting*, Marcel Dekker, New York, N.Y. (1992).

varies enormously across time and across jurisdictions. It matters whether the public budgeting is being carried out in a capitalist, democratic, federal society, or in a socialist, authoritarian, national state. It matters whether the form of government is parliamentary or presidential. In the United States, state and local budgeting differs in significant ways from federal budgeting. The size of the budget, the scope and variety of functions performed by the public sector, the openness of the budget process, and the distribution of costs and benefits vary from society to society and from community to community.

Although in recent years observers have agreed that variations in budgeting from place to place and from time to time are significant, when the relationships of budgeting to society are examined for the United States, there has been little agreement as to what budgeting reveals about the society. Each theoretical school makes its own assumptions.

Neo-Marxists have argued that class interests dominate budgeting and allocation choices. Several different schools argue that government itself, as represented by the bureaucrats or agency heads, determine allocations, while some scholars have argued that interest groups dominate or even determine budgeting [1].

The Neo-Marxists, who form only a loose kind of school, generally argue that government is controlled by capitalists, or those who own the means of production, and that they determine spending priorities to serve their own needs. Those needs include particular programs and funds that aid in the accumulation of capital. Social welfare programs in this theory are used to buy off opposition from the poor who would otherwise protest the system and possibly overturn it. Neo-Marxists call attention to military spending as enriching arms manufacturers, to increases in spending for economic development, much of which is a transfer payment from the average citizen to the relatively well-to-do, and to a variety of tax breaks that have benefited the well-to-do more than the poor. In a Neo-Marxian perspective, maintaining markets abroad has been the reason for both imperialism and wars, and preserving bond markets has been a major reason for much of state and local fiscal policy.

Neo-Marxists have usefully called attention to phenomena that might otherwise be ignored, but their models are still incomplete. Some, especially the older ones, tend to be structural and deterministic, with little ability to explain variation over time and between geographic locations [2]. Studies looking for evidence of capitalist domination have found more variability than uniformity. Business groups sometimes do have disproportionate influence, but they are sometimes split, sometimes badly organized, and there are a variety of issues in which they have little interest. The Neo-Marxist model does not explain why one business group wins out over others, or when and why they sometimes lose. A theory that utilized differentiated interest groups would probably be more effective at capturing and describing business impact and would undoubtedly be better at outlining the impacts of other interests on the budget.

A second theoretical approach to linking budgeting and society is the public choice school. Individual theorists have taken widely varied positions, but what they share is the assumption that human behavior is based on individual economic rationality and the maximization of individual benefits, or what economists call utility. Their model of the ideal government is an extension of the marketplace where citizens can buy exactly the amount of services they want in the combinations they prefer. They deplore any departure from this model that provides people with more government services than they would choose on their own. They argue that a combination of majority voting and the ability of individuals and groups to share the cost of what they want with other taxpayers makes the costs of many benefits to individuals too cheap and inflates the demand for public goods and services. Government thus tends to overprovide services in comparison to a true market. In addition, the expansion of bureaucracy benefits the bureaucrats, so they always push for expansion, causing a second impetus to oversupply.

Public choice theorists emphasize the very important issue of the relationship between what the citizen taxpayers want government to do and spend and what it actually does and spends. There is no doubt that in a democracy this is a crucial linkage. This school emphasizes several mechanisms for achieving that linkage, including voting, suburbanization, and making budgeting, and especially taxation, more visible to the public.

The voting mechanism posits that citizens can choose among candidates those that best reflect their own spending priorities. Since there may be no candidate who matches their individual preferences, and those preferences may not be clearly stated, and candidates are chosen sometimes in primaries by less than a majority of voters, the level of control actually exerted by this mechanism may be tenuous.

The mechanism of suburbanization suggests that citizens choose their residences based on their preference for public service packages—they move to communities whose residents are people like themselves who want the same things from government and who are willing to pay similar amounts of taxes to get them. After a number of studies, however, it is not clear that people generally do this. The choice of where to live may be affected by many other factors, including cost of housing, proximity to work, closeness to relatives, and absence of crime.

The third mechanism, the openness of taxation, implies that the scope of government and the expense would be controlled if people clearly saw how much they were paying in taxes. People would then insist on receiving only those services most crucial to themselves, and would be unwilling to pay for more. The problem with this part of the theory (called fiscal illusion) is that obscured taxes are not just a plot hatched by government officials to expand government, but they are generally preferred by the public. The government is doing what the citizens want when it imposes taxes in less visible, small doses. This leaves the public choice theorists with the apparent contradiction that to bring about a tighter relationship between the public and government, government should go against the wishes of the public.

Despite some obvious strengths, public choice theory also has some weaknesses. This theory tends to be deterministic, and has difficulty explaining change over time. It postulates nearly continuous government growth, for example, although government growth has not been continuous, but jerky and stepwise. The theory cannot explain and does not deal with why government has not expanded further, taken on more functions, or why some functions have been added rather than others. On the one hand, public choice theorists see government as performing tasks the market has failed to perform, but on the other, they try to make government as much like a market as possible. They assume that all individuals, including bureaucrats and legislators, are interested only in maximizing their own utilities. A summary function of citizens' individual utilities should determine government spending, but the individual utilities of bureaucrats and legislators are viewed as narrow, self-interested, and thwarting of the public will. The theory ignores the existence and importance of altruism and the existence of group goals that are different from individual goals. As one might expect, these theorists sometimes have difficulty figuring out how to aggregate individual utilities, since simple majorities may dominate minorities, and more complex voting patterns may contain contradictions.

The third major theory that relates budgeting to society is incrementalism, and its related theory of interest-group pluralism. Incrementalism argues that budgeting occurs virtually exclusively inside government; by inference, government is not directly controllable or controlled by society. Interest groups exist, but there are many interest groups, they represent a variety of interests, and none determines the outcomes. Writers in this school observed budgeting, and emphasized the process they saw, of agency request and legislative review, with stable actors over time, strategies of agency heads and responses by legislators, and norms worked out over time because the same actors remained in place and dealt with each other over time. The observers did not see the public, and so assumed they played little role; they did not see much of the interest groups, who often work behind the scenes, and so assumed they played little role.

The incrementalists watched too small a part of the public budgeting process, and at times just looked at the outcomes and tried to figure out what the process was that led to the outcomes. Their ability to perceive indirect effects, such as how politicians felt constrained by voters, was minimal. They did not observe the constraints that executive branch superiors put on budget requests, and they did not fully realize that the agency requests they saw were not the first step in the process. Consequently, they underestimated the relationship between the society and budgeting, and overestimated the autonomy of agencies in determining budgets.

Incrementalists saw budgeting as a formal process, based on bargaining and technical needs, but fairly devoid of policy concerns. Money had to be appropriated to run the agencies, the fiscal year had to begin, and divisive policy matters were decided elsewhere. As a result, the incrementalists did not envision the budget process as responding to perceived societal problems, emerging situations, or environmental changes. They assumed budgets would continue to be allocated pretty much the same way from year to year. Thus incrementalism was unable to theorize about changing budgets or budget process. As interest groups became more visible in the budget process, and consequently the process became less one of insiders working with each other developing their own norms of constraint, the theory could not cope [3]. As budgeting in Congress became more centralized, and the dominance of the agencies in determining outcomes clearly was reduced, the theory could not cope and became less descriptive. As entitlements became a more important part of the federal budget, the theory could not cope. It had no mechanism for explaining change other than major external events like a new president of a different party.

More recent theories of budgeting have not coalesced into a single school, but they have moved toward a common understanding of how budgeting relates to the society more broadly, and how seemingly technical internal decision making is influenced by actors who seldom seem to appear. The mechanisms for integrating budgets with the society are described in hierarchy theory [4], which focuses more on the executive branch, and by the macro-micro budget theorists [5], who focus more on Congress. The idea is similar in both cases.

Hierarchy theory says that the top levels of the executive branch make decisions about broad policy issues, and judge the environment, and pass that information down through the budget office to the agencies before they make their requests. Thus the identification of current problems and the selection of which ones will be addressed in the current budget are made early and frame the decisions of subordinates. Perceptions of interest group power may enter at this level or at the level of the budget office when it is judging requests from the agencies. The budget offices judge the requests based to some extent on knowledge of and performance of the agencies, and to some extent on the priorities given to them by the chief executive.

The macro–micro budgeting theory argues that bargaining still goes on over budget strategies, but broader policy issues are also explicitly dealt with and frame the choices and outcomes of the bargaining. On the congressional side, economic policies, priorities, spending ceilings, and assumptions about the growth of the economy are made by the budget committees, and to some extent guide or determine the decisions of the other committees as they work on parts of the budget.

The integration of budget policy and consideration of the environment and its constraints go on at federal, state, and local levels, regardless of the structure or degree of independence of the executive and legislative branches. At the city level, a city manager (chief executive) and the city council may meet at the beginning of the budget process, with the manager laying out the technical constraints and environmental problems, and the council laying out priorities, before the departments put in their budget requests. Both the manager's technical constraints and the council's priorities often appear in budget prefaces.

The current consensus is that budgeting is linked to the society and to the environment by both technical constraints and policy, and that interest groups are sometimes important in determining outcomes, although their role has not been well specified. Sometimes coalitions of interest groups form that approximate class boundaries, but there is no evidence of continuing class dominance. None of the deterministic models has survived well, and their inability to predict or explain change has been a major factor in their obsolescence. Current theory has drifted toward a consensus that allows for both direct and indirect influence of the environment over budgeting, and hence builds in the possibility of continuous change and adaptation.

The theories just summarized deal with why budgeting is important and provide an overall orientation to the field. Budget theory can also be helpful in explaining what budgeting is and how it operates. Much of this literature has taken the perspective that budgeting is decision making, and the task of theory is to describe the decision making that occurs during budgeting. Key issues have been how rational budgeting has been, how much effort has there been to get the best possible results, how much comparison of alternatives has there been, and what criteria are used to make decisions.

The theory has developed in a dialectical fashion. First, theory strongly emphasized rationality and getting the most from each dollar; then a second school grew up to refute the maximizers, arguing that very little rational decision making went on; the current literature argues for a variety of positions in between. Despite the emerging consensus on the middle ground, all three views continue to influence the literature.

The first position, characterized as the finance economists' position, emphasizes the need to allocate according to standards that will maximize the benefits to everyone. Among the standards often used is Pareto optimality, which means that budget increases should be allocated so that some individuals or groups are better off and none are worse off. This criterion would exclude any reallocation. Another standard that economists often allow is welfare economics, which means that government programs can make up for or change the market distribution of income to create greater equality. Under this standard, some reallocation would be acceptable.

Finance economists may disagree about the desirability of reallocation, but they generally agree that each new dollar of a public budget should be allocated to create the maximum of return in desired goods or services. This standard implies both efficiency and comparison of alternative spending choices, especially at the margins. So, to take a local example, the first hundred dollars of revenue we may wish to spend on roads, but the next hundred we may prefer to spend on public health. Once a minimum level of public health is achieved, we may wish to spend additional money on more roads. Presumably there is a limit, and the public would not desire more and more roads until they covered all available ground. Finance economists ask at the same time how much service will one more dollar provide, and how badly does the public want that additional service compared to what a dollar would provide in some other service area. Finance economists today often emphasize a variety of cost-benefit analysis techniques that combine analysis of how much a dollar will provide and compare projects in terms of the desirability to the community.

If finance economics is the thesis, incrementalism presented the theoretical opposite, or antithesis. Based on the theory of bounded rationality in decision making, incrementalism suggested that no one could make the comparisons necessary to make rational decisions. It would take too much time, and would require more information and more intelligence than people could normally bring to decision making. Moreover, the making of explicit choices between spending alternatives would sharpen controversy, increase the level of participation in budgeting, and generally slow it down if not stop it altogether. So rational decision making was neither possible nor desirable. Some of the incrementalists went further and argued that political decisions would be based on what projects benefited the voters in whose districts, and any attempt to impose other, supposedly more rational criteria on top of that crucial political choice, would fail. Decision makers avoid comparisons by making across-the-board decisions, such as a 3% increase for all units, or a 2% productivity reduction across the board.

The current synthesis—synthesis may be too strong a word for the variety of positions—is part way between the two extremes. Without arguing that all projects are indeed subject to cost-benefit analysis, scholars no longer argue that budgets are reviewed by legislators concerned only with benefits for their districts [6]; similarly, while scholars do not argue that all expenditures are compared against each other to achieve the maximum benefit from each dollar of revenue, neither do they argue that all new spending decisions are made without examination or across the board.

Studies at the national level emphasize that while pork barrel distributive projects still exist, they are a small and shrinking portion of the budget [7]. One author argues that decisions to cut requests are not made all at the same time, in an across-the-board fashion, but in sequence, that requests are cut a bit, one at a time, and then added up to see if they come under the limit; if not, a second round of cuts is begun [8]. Sometimes, across-the-board rules may begin a budget trimming process, but these estimates are then adjusted up or down on a case-by-case basis.

Arguments from the budget maximizers have always assumed that comparisons between programs would be fairly complete, even if only at the margins, and that programs that were found less worthy would be cut or eliminated. It has become increasingly evident that the structure of the budget and the type of expenditure limit the ability of budget trimmers to cut some programs; some are mandated, some have restricted funding, or matching funding, some programs actually generate revenue, and some are long term and contractual and cannot be readily adjusted except at fixed intervals. The decision about what kind of program to offer and whether to earmark money is also a budgetary decision; it locks a particular comparison of alternatives into the budget for a period of time. So comparisons do occur, but not necessarily annually, and some programs may be left out of the comparisons. The result is not rational budgeting in the sense of the finance economists, but neither is it the simple decision rules of the incrementalists.

The discussion to this point has summarized some of the key budgeting theories, suggested some of the assumptions they make concerning the relationship of budgeting to the broader society, and indicated that budget theory generally conceptualizes budgeting as a decision-making process. Each of the major historical theories has contributed some important truths, but has often been unable to explain change or has been too one-sided. Current budget theory accepts key themes from each major school, but also emphasizes the existence and meaning of change in budgeting, and has staked out, but not fully explored, a middle ground on the nature of budgetary decision making.

An understanding of budgeting requires not only an overview of the development of the broad theories, but also an understanding of the key concepts of budgeting.

BUDGET CONCEPTS

The most important of budget concepts is the concept of *budgeting* itself. What is a budget, and how does a public budget differ from that of a corporation or a family? "A budget links tasks to be performed to the amount of resources necessary to accomplish those tasks, ensuring that money will be available to wage war, provide housing, or maintain streets" [9]. Budgets limit spending to the amount of income, ensuring balance and preventing overspending. Budgeting allocates scarce resources, and implies choice between potential objects of expenditure. The decision of what to spend the money on involves a process, in which individuals or groups are assigned parts of the decision, the parts are coordinated and timed, and resources are allocated.

In public budgeting, people and groups with different goals and points of view are always vying to get what they want out of government. There is often little consensus about what should be accomplished or for whom. In public budgeting, there is a separation between those who pay the bill, and those who make the decisions about how the money will be spent. The decisions makers are ultimately *accountable* to those who pay the bills. Budgets are an important link between taxpayers and public officials. Budgets tell citizens what their taxes are being spent on, and in a general way how well their money is being spent. If taxpayers do not approve the government's choices, they can, and sometimes do, refuse to approve additional taxes.

Public budgeting is both political and technical, influenced by interest groups and by agency heads. Budgeting has its routine parts, and its almost unpredictable and nonroutine parts. Public budgeting is *open to the environment*, in the sense that it is influenced by the economy, by public opinion, by other levels of government, by interest groups, by the press, and by politicians.

Budgeting is a decision-making process. That means that who makes the decisions, or parts of decisions, influences the distribution of power over outcomes. To get an accurate picture of who makes budget decisions, one needs to look across types of budgeting decisions. Some types of budget decisions, such as those setting limits on the growth of government or making tradeoffs between defense and social services, attract large coalitions of interest groups that approximate class interests, the rich, the middle classes, and the poor, or workers and owners. Other kinds of budget decisions attract specific narrow interest groups. The allocation of tax breaks often involves a single industry or company, sometimes even a single individual. Budget decisions involving the implementation of the budget normally involve no interest groups at all. An evaluation of the *distribution of budget-making power* must weigh these different types of decisions.

Budget processes vary, both between jurisdiction and across time. Some are more open to interest groups and the public than others. Some cities, for example, actively solicit public opinion about budget priorities, and keep citizens informed about budget choices; others virtually never solicit public opinion and seldom communicate about the budget except at tax increase time. Congress has sometimes organized budgeting decisions in a way that was open to interest groups, and sometimes locked up the decision making in privacy to keep the interest groups out.

Some literature argues that when resources were relatively more plentiful and the decision had been made to expand spending, Congress reorganized itself to be more open to interest group and beneficiary demands. *There is a relationship between the allocation of decision-making power and budgetary outcomes*. Not only does this formulation begin to provide an explanation for changes over time, but it also suggests that budget process reflects societal conditions including the economy and public need, and that budget processes in turn influence both access of interest groups and spending levels [10].

Descriptions of budget processes have not been simply a list of decisions, actors, and due dates, but descriptions of the shifting location of power. Discussion of budget process has often focused on the implications of these different arrangements. Two major dichotomies have been used to describe the shifts in location of power: *executive versus legislative*, and *top-down versus bottom-up*. Executive budgeting means that the chief executive and his staff have responsibility for putting together a budget proposal, and presenting it to the legislature for approval. Legislative budgeting means that the agencies make their proposals for spending directly to the legislature, without being evaluated first by the executive. Top-down budgeting means that budgeting is centralized, in either the executive branch or the legislative branch or both. An individual, a committee, or an office is responsible for setting overall targets, and evaluating requests in light of these targets. By contrast, bottom-up budgeting means there is no prior central policy control over the budget. Budgets are created as the aggregates of individual requests from agencies and from committees or subcommittees. The requests are put together with decision rules that avoid comparative consideration of the merits of programs.

There are positions between a pure executive and legislative budget. Even those that are considered executive budgets are in fact often in between the extremes of executive and legislative budgets. For example, most cities have executive budgets, but they are not pure types. Cities' budgets are normally drawn up by the mayor or manager, and his or her budget staff, and then approved by the council, which makes the process an executive budget. But the mayor may be a member of the council (the legislature), chosen by the council members to be mayor; the city manager, if there is one, is chosen by and may be fired by the city council. In effect, the manager is the staff of the council—the legislative branch. Where cities still budget with a legislative budget process, the finance committee of the council receives budget requests from the departments and holds hearings with each department, and makes recommendations to the council. Sometimes, however, the mayor sits in on these meetings, or actually makes the recommended cuts to the council, creating a hybrid that defies easy categorization. These examples suggest that for cities the budget process is often somewhere between the poles of the legislative-executive distinction.

Typically budgets are neither completely top-down nor completely bottom-up, but some combination of the two. Departments or agencies may have more or less freedom in putting together their budget proposals; chief executives sometimes give lots of advice in advance, and sometimes give very little. Sometimes top-down budget reviews are thorough and sometimes superficial.

Budget process describes not only who has power over budget decisions, but also how those decisions are actually made—how much information is provided, what kinds of decision rules are used, how much comparison there is between proposed expenditures.

The kind of information that is used for budget decision making is highly variable. Revenue projections may be the result of complex econometric models, modified by experience as the budget year commences or they may result from linear projection from previous years' experience plus an informed guess. Information about programs may be minimal or may include accounting data, performance evaluations, and other data. The budget format, which provides most of the data for the budget reviewers, is variable from jurisdiction to jurisdiction and from time to time. Sometimes information is presented one year and not in the following years, but still remains active in the minds of the decision makers. Sometimes extra information is made available when an issue is particularly salient or a key increase or decrease is being considered.

One of the ways that information about departments, agencies and programs is conveyed to decision makers is through the budget request form that the agencies fill out. How do agencies *justify* their requests? Sometimes the information required is technical, almost arithmetical. For example, there are so many staff members, their salary is so much, their benefits cost so much, so many of them receive so much for longevity (the number of years they have been working in that position), and so many dollars are for salary increases. The agency is planning so many trips to such a place at so many dollars a trip. If there are no changes to the program or the way of managing it, a *constant services budget*, it will cost so many dollars for this agency next year. Budget justifications sometimes include descriptions of new programs requested or new equipment or staff needed. These may be justified in terms of workload data, community need, or future savings, or other arguments that agency heads think will be convincing.

In an executive budget process, this information from the agencies is collected, reviewed, altered, and put together in a recommended package for the legislature to review. The format of this proposal is also variable. One format is called a *line-item budget*. Expenditures are broken into accounting categories, and each line of the budget represents one such accounting category or item. For example, a budget request might include $2000 for travel, $500,000 for salaries, $25,000 for insurance, and $75,000 for office supplies. How detailed or general the line items are is highly variable even within jurisdictions that use primarily line-item budgets.

Line-item budgets seem almost deterministic. They tell little if anything about the cost or efficiency of programs provided (they provide the costs for departments and administrative units, not for the programs that the units provide). They provide almost no information that might help decision makers choose which budget proposals to cut or which to increase. This format encourages budget officials to make cuts that are across the board, because they cannot make intelligent decisions between programs.

Straight line-item budgets that provide almost no other information are becoming relatively rare. Most public budgets today are in a program format, which emphasizes less the administrative unit of the department or agency and more the programs that each such unit provides, listing the costs for each one. While decision makers can still trim or increase budgets across the board if they choose, the allocational impacts of cutting one program or another are much more obvious, and the ability of decision makers to increase popular programs and decrease less popular ones is enhanced. *Program budgeting* makes it more obvious to the public what their tax dollars are buying, and whether their money is being spent for the programs they want. The level of controversy can be toned down or tuned up. With this budget format the policy decisions being made through the budget process are clearer to all the participants, and *trade-offs* between programs are more obvious when they are being made.

Program budgets allow public officials to clearly choose between priorities and express them in the budget, but they do not provide a way of evaluating the relative efficiency or effectiveness of programs. Implicit in much of budgeting is that there is a technical component, requiring the administrators to get the most from each dollar and to put each additional dollar where it will get the maximum return of desired goods and services. This concept has led to the idea of a *performance budget*, in which program information is related in terms of the costs per unit of services delivered, and this information is included in the budget. Presumably decision makers would then allocate new or additional funds to those agencies operating at the peak of efficiency, and take funds away from those whose operations were less efficient or were decreasing the level of their efficiency.

Performance budgeting has had many difficulties, and while sometimes implemented has seldom worked as billed, and has often been modified. One problem with it is that it is easier to measure the costs per unit of service delivered in some programs than in others; second, for the concept to work, the quality of performance must be held constant, but we seldom measure the quality of service and program outputs over time; third, cost per unit of service delivered can vary independent of the agency's efforts, so an agency head may be held responsible for outcomes over which he or she has only limited control. Dollar losses due to fires, for example, depend on events and conditions over which the fire department has little control, such as the level of wind or rain, the number and age of wooden dwellings, how quickly a fire is called in, the time of day fires occur, and the existence of active arsonists. In addition, costs per unit of service delivered tend to go up, with everything else held constant, because inflation pushes up the costs of salaries and material. Even if employees work just as hard as they always have, unless they can continually introduce higher productivity, their programs will look worse. All these factors, plus a natural dislike of being continually evaluated, make performance budgeting difficult to sell and even harder to make work. The process of designing performance measures and maintaining records about them is time consuming, which creates both a reason and an excuse for agency heads and staff to slight the tasks.

Budget formats implicitly or explicitly define the range within which policy and allocational decisions will take place. Incremental budgets of the line item format provide comparisons between last year, this year, and the proposal for next year; this is about the only information that gives a clue that decision makers might latch onto. So they tend to focus on changes at the margins and what they mean. What is already in the budget is assumed to have been examined in previous years, and is at least in theory not examined further. But if budgets were formatted differently, they could focus attention not only on the differences between recent years, but also on some items from previous years that were once considered important but that now are less important than new proposed spending or program expansion. The format that allows for such reconsideration is called *zero-base budgeting*.

Zero-base budgeting in its full-blown form requires the agencies to put all their budget requests into decision packages, and rank order them in importance. A decision package is usually a program at a particular level of service and its associated cost. A department might have three programs and be able to offer them at three levels of service, good, fair, and poor. That would make nine decision units for the department to rank order. Then the rankings of the agencies are gathered and arranged according to criteria that make sense at a government-wide level. At the national level, a moderate level of defense might be the nation's top priority, but a vastly expanded defense department might be lower in priority than a program to house three-fourths of the homeless. The formation of such lists requires a conscious attention to the criteria that should be used to rank programs, including measures of public need, popularity, the dependence of people on the program (whether alternatives are available), and whether life is endangered by reducing the program. When a complete list of priorities is formed, the decision packages are funded in the order ranked; if the money runs out before the bottom of the list, those items are not funded. Items at the top may already be being performed, or they may be new or expanded programs. Money can be *reallocated* from the lower priorities to the higher ones.

Complete zero-base budgets of the form just described are relatively rare, in part because they assume a knowledge of program costs that may not be present, in part because they open the whole budget, much of which is not really likely to change, to such prioritization. As a result, simplified zero-base budgets, called *target-based budgets*, have been more widely used. Such budgets create a pool of money for reallocation by taking new money and a percent of existing funds. Agencies cut themselves by a given percent (presumably their lowest priority items) and propose what they would do with new money and why. These proposals are rank ordered and funded as far down the list as the money available allows. This procedure forces a clear statement of priorities, and links the goals of the governmental unit with the budget presented. It allows for some reallocation without creating unnecessary chaos or insecurity.

For many people the only part of budgetary decision making that is important is this question of how the process allocates money, who wins and who loses. Various budget formats provide at least partial answers to this question. In line-item formatting, with incremental budgeting, programs are never compared, and the existing set of priorities is largely maintained. Change is slow. To some extent, those who have, get, and those who have not yet made a successful claim have a very difficult if not impossible time getting heard. This pattern of budgeting pits those who have already gained budgetary power against new claims, and weighs heavily in favor of the old timers. In program budgeting, programs more explicitly compete against each other for new or additional money, but there is no mechanism for reallocation from one program to another as priorities or technology changes. Only in zero-based and target-based budgeting is competition between programs paired with a mechanism for reallocation. The potential rate of change is faster in any form of zero-base budgeting than in simple program budgeting, and both program and zero-base budgets provide for more change than incremental budgeting.

While some people are most concerned with allocation and particularly reallocation decisions, others are most concerned with the relationship of budgeting to outcomes. How does public spending achieve public goals? How tightly are the two linked? The idea of planning, of choosing goals and devising and funding programs to achieve those goals, is implicit in the more modern forms of budgeting. The planning may be more or less formal, and more or less encompassing, but the idea of an activist government defining and attempting to resolve problems through the budget is inherent in these budget formats. On the one hand they are defended as more rational and less wasteful; on the other, they allow for more public participation, more controversy, and more goal-directed change.

Planning programming budgeting system was the most integrated and fullest statement of the linkage between planning and budgeting, but even when the full system is not adopted, budgets may state goals and link spending requests with those goals. Incrementalists implied that such goals could not be stated, because there would be so little agreement that a clear goals statement either would be impossible or would generate competing alternatives that would tear a community apart. At the local level, recent budget innovations suggest that this has not been that serious a problem; many of a city's competing goals are stated, and the programs in the budget that address each goal are listed, although often without the dollar amounts that might exacerbate controversy. Rather than suggest goallessness, these budgets suggest progress toward multiple goals, faster in some areas than others, and more in some years than others.

The emphasis on linking budgeting to goals has shown up in recent years with the linkage of *management by objectives* to budgets. Management by objectives (MBO) is a technique for specifying overall and intermediate goals and objectives, and getting employees to be responsible for the achievement of particular levels of achievement and particular tasks, so that the overall goal can be achieved. This kind of planning is formally linked to the reward system of employees. But it can and ultimately must also be linked to the budget to work; employees cannot promise to accomplish a particular level of work, and accept salary increments based on their success, unless they have sufficient resources in the budget to carry out that level of work. Thus MBO and budgets have been linked.

Underlying much of the discussion about budgets and allocations, planning and goals, is the question of *trade-offs*. Many of the early budget theorists simply assumed that there were budget trade-offs, because resources were limited, and money spent on one program or project could not be spent on another at the same time. Budgeting implied choices, and choices meant more of something equaled less of something else. But when the incrementalists went looking for such choices during the 1960s, they found instead relative stability of allocations, and they could not find allocation criteria, and often could not find programs, let alone a process that compared programs. They concluded that the limits of human intelligence and attention prevented budgeters from comparing all programs all the time, and the level of controversy that would be generated would be unacceptable, so that no comparison was in fact done.

The incrementalists gradually modified their position in two ways. One way was to argue that small incremental changes from year to year could accumulate over time to reflect changes in direction or priorities; the second way was to argue that allocational changes did occur at long intervals when some major external event occurred, like a major election that changed party and ideology or a war.

The idea of trade-offs at the national level was obscured both by the theory that said changes and comparisons did not occur and that budgets were aggregates of the demands of individual agencies, and by the fact that for many of those years the federal government ran deficits. It appeared, for example, that the country could have both guns and butter, both military buildup and social programs at the same time. The budget total did not look fixed. Increased spending in one area correlated with increases in other areas, while the theory of trade-offs suggested that there should be negative correlations. Even with deficits, total spending is limited, and trade-offs have to occur, but with a model that required a negative correlation to prove the existence of trade-offs, they were hard to find and prove [11].

On the state and local levels, where revenue totals were more clearly fixed and deficits generally illegal, even when budgets were line item and incremental, trade-offs were clearer. If one department is growing at 3% a year and another at 8% a year, within a few years the change in spending priorities is obvious. Thus after the urban riots of the 1960s, the federal and municipal response was to beef up local police departments. Over a period of years, relative spending on police departments with respect to other municipal departments was obvious [12]. When revenue sharing was eliminated in the mid 1980s, cities had to make explicit choices about which services would be maintained, or whether new revenue would have to be raised locally to replace the federal grant. There were clear issues of priorities and trade-offs that observers could detect.

After the 1974 budget reform act in Congress, trade-offs became more obvious at the federal level as well, not because the deficits were under better control, but because the budget process required an explicit guideline for each budget on how much to allocate to each major function in the budget. The early years of the Reagan presidency, with their emphasis on rapid military buildup and cutting back of social programs, made a dramatic statement about the existence of trade-offs, but suggested that they are more acute and visible in some years than in others.

Trade-offs are easier to see when they change, but they exist even in a stable and relatively unchanging budget. Any public budget reflects relative values placed on major categories of the budget. How much will be spent, relatively speaking, on prevention versus suppression in the fire department? Or on the State Department and negotiations versus the Defense Department and weapons? Or on covert operations versus overt operations? On attracting new businesses or maintaining existing ones? Even when these proportions do not change each year, they still represent trade-offs (unless one drops the assumption of relative scarcity). Sometimes these trade-offs are nested. For example, the first trade-off may be between the operating and the capital budget. The next may be within the capital budget between water projects, street projects, and drainage projects. At the next level, within the streets capital budget, there may be a trade-off between repair and replacement. Then the choices may be between concrete, brick, and blacktop streets, each of which are located in different parts of a city and have different wear characteristics. Within the operating budget there may be trade-offs between salary and benefits, between regular wages and overtime, and between administrative staff and line employees.

The structure of the decision making brackets trade-offs. That is, the decision-making process frames what the choices will be between, and what trades with what, and what does not trade with what. Generally, for example, cities do not trade off police and fire. The assumption is made that the city must have both. Rather, a category is devised called basic services, and basic services trade off against nonbasic services. What fits in basic and what fits in nonbasic may be variable, but what is often defined as basic is police, fire, streets, sanitation, and water; what is nonbasic is social services, planning and zoning, and other expenditures. Cities rather explicitly trade off capital and operating expenditures, but the federal government, which does not have a proper capital budget, cannot frame its trade-offs in the same way. Decision makers reveal these trade-offs in their conversations. Listening to them may help the quantitative modelers of trade-offs specify their models more appropriately.

Viewing the budget in terms of trade-offs emphasizes the policy aspect of budgeting, for example, the relative emphasis on regulation or on privatization, or on suppression and prevention. It also emphasizes, however, the narrower question of who benefits, who wins and who loses. The wins and losses may be viewed in terms of bureaucratic actors, and the winners ranked in terms of percentage of budget growth, but they may also be viewed in terms of class or interest groups. Looking at the allocation process in terms of the beneficiaries of government programs introduces several other budget concepts: equity, distribution, and redistribution.

Equity is a broad term that also applies to taxation, but in the context of spending choices it raises the topic of welfare economics. Does government have a role in making the distribution of income more equal than the market alone would create? Is the function of budget allocation more than getting the most out of every dollar and making services and programs efficient and effective? If so, how is this mission being carried out? Is the effect of spending (or taxing) to reallocate income from the rich to the poor? Or from the poor to the well to do? *Distribution* implies spending that does not affect the distribution of wealth, and *redistribution* suggests spending that does. Over the years, the word redistribution has picked up the connotation of taking money from the rich to give to the poor, but that leaves the reverse concept, taking from the poor to give to the rich, without its own word. Redistribution can be either up or down.

Distribution and redistribution have a second and related meaning in budgeting that suggests that some programs will create far more controversy than others. Distribution means that program beneficiaries are widespread, almost everyone benefits from a program, and there are few that define themselves as losers. Alternatively, it means that a few benefit, but that the losers either do not know that they are losers, or their loss is not politically salient to them. Redistribution means that some interests gain at the obvious expense of others.

Redistributive issues are highly contentious. It is much easier to maintain distributive and relatively peaceful politics when resources are reasonably plentiful. When money is particularly tight, what might have otherwise been defined as distributive may become redistributive and hence highly contentious. For example, as long as resources are reasonably plentiful, young people do not perceive programs to support the elderly as competitive with benefits to higher education, but with fiscal restraints and social services lumped together to compete for funding, the young may perceive themselves as in direct competition with the elderly. Then the young may be interested not only in what they themselves receive but also in what others receive.

If budget allocations restricted themselves to providing only goods and services that were widely desired and widely distributed, the public that pays the taxes would probably be quite content (assuming minimal waste, fraud, and abuse) that their priorities had been realized in the budget. They would be in essence buying services from the government that the government chose to provide and that were generally unavailable elsewhere or were much more expensive in the private sector. Even when goods and services are delivered to particular groups rather than to the population as a whole, most taxpayers accept this use of their money as long as they can get what they want from government at especially cheap prices. But when taxpayers perceive that their money is being spent on some other group instead of on themselves, they are likely to get angry at government.

The issue of allocation and reallocation thus raises the broader issue of *accountability*. Is government doing what the taxpayers want it to do? Do the priorities of the government, as reflected in the budget, reflect the priorities of the taxpayers? The idea of accountability in a democracy means that government is not a dictatorship, extracting taxes from the public and spending it at will; taxpayers are the ultimate bosses, and government's role is to serve, and to reflect the demands and desires of the taxpayers. The budget is one of the key vehicles for making government accountable to the people, by making the policy choices in the budget numbers clear. Government is also accountable to the public for spending tax money with as little waste as possible and without fraud or abuse.

Some public budgets provide more accountability than others, but overall they do a pretty good job of explaining how public money was spent and linking public priorities with public spending. There are a variety of techniques for achieving accountability, with some aimed more toward stating priorities and others more toward demonstrating that money was spent honestly and efficiently.

One of the key techniques for providing budgetary accountability is called *fund accounting*. It means that a budget is not one piggy bank, out of which expenditures come, but many smaller piggy banks, each of which has its own revenues and expenditures. Each piggy bank has its own purpose, and no one can spend more from any piggy bank than the piggy bank has in it (balance). These metaphorical piggy banks are called funds. These funds play several functions, but one of the most important of them is to see that money that has been earmarked for a particular purpose is indeed spent for that particular purpose and no other. The earmarked money is put into its own fund, and not mixed with other money for other purposes. If it is transferred to other funds, it leaves a paper trail describing how much money was transferred and for what purpose. If user fees are collected, for example, airport landing fees, these are put into a special account, which can be spent only on airports.

Inside a fund, money can be reasonably freely traded across categories of spending [13], but transfers between funds are carefully monitored. That means that not all expenditures can in fact be traded off against all other expenditures. If a trust fund is set up for airports or highways, airport or highway spending is no longer competing with other expenditures for the same dollars. It has its own earmarked dollars that no other program can get. That means that a budget may be structured to make some trade-offs easier and others more difficult or impossible to make in the short run. As a government sets up its fund structures it is often deciding also on what trades for what, and what may not be traded for what.

One key element of accountability is the completeness of the public record. If only some items are included in the budget, but others are decided on and paid for with tax dollars, the budget may be very misleading. The more fragmented budgets are, that is, the more separate jurisdictions publish their own separate budgets, the harder it is for citizens to find out how their money is being spent. Especially at the local level where numerous units of government may perform one or two functions each, and not have the staff time or expertise to put together a budget that explains how much money was spent on what priority, *fragmentation reduces accountability*.

At all levels of government, when some functions are on budget and others are off budget (that is, have separate budgets) it becomes confusing how money is being spent. On the other hand, when budgets are consolidated, they may contain many different kinds of programs and many different kinds of resources. These may not reasonably be added together. For example, a loan is not the same thing as a grant, since the loan should be returned over time, with interest. When a percentage is subtracted for expected defaults, the net cost of a loan program may be zero. A grant, by contrast, is money spent without expectation that it will come back. One cannot add grants and loans and expect the total to convey any meaning. How one can best report different types of resources in a public budget to maximize accountability is a problem yet to be fully worked out.

Accountability requires *financial control* during the budget implementation stage. The budget that is passed in full public view, and is the representative to the public of how public money is being spent, should be very similar to the budget that is actually implemented. There should be as few changes as possible, and those that are made should be technical, not policy-laden. That means that cuts made during the year, as opposed to at budget time, should be across the board (such cuts minimize the policy implications); increases in revenue during the year should normally be either allocated according to a preset list of priorities, or put in an annual fund balance to be allocated as part of the following year's budget process. Departments and agencies must be prevented from seriously overspending their budgets, not only because such overspending presents the possibility of deficits, but also because it may change the priorities implicit in the budget that was legally approved.

One of the most fundamental concepts in budgeting is *balance*. Sometimes other goals of budgeting, such as trying to use public spending to stabilize the economy, seem to overrule balance and create deficits, but the concept of balance remains even during deficit budgeting. Balance means that total income has to match total outgo, with or without borrowing. If it has no concept of balance, if there is no attempt to match income and outgo, there is no budget. Balance means agreement over time between revenues and expenditures, not necessarily balance every minute or every week.

Balance can be defined more or less constrictively. For example, one could say that the budget had to be balanced when presented to the legislature. That is a fairly weak form of balance requirement, since the budget proposal is based on estimates of revenues and expenditures. To make a budget look balanced requires only a slightly higher estimate of revenue or a slightly lower estimate of expenditures. A more restrictive definition would require the budget to balance at the end of the year. Balance requirements can be more or less inclusive of the budget. That is, the requirement for balance may apply only to the operating budget, or even only to the general fund, or only to an enterprise fund. It may apply to any items on budget but not any items off budget. There may be in addition to the requirement for balance a restriction on the level of borrowing, or on the level of revenue. Some school districts have been borrowing by selling bonds to provide operating funds; under some laws they may be balancing their budgets—getting enough revenue to cover expenditures—while under other laws they would be operating with unbalanced budgets.

Throughout this chapter, the idea has been emphasized that budgets and budgeting change. Some of this change is in response to changes in the environment, and some is in response to campaigns of *reform*. Reform means change in a direction advocated by some groups or individuals. It does not necessarily mean improvement. Over the years, major campaigns to reform budgeting have focused around increasing the power of the executive in forming and reviewing departments' and agencies' proposals, making decision making more open and accountable, making comparisons between programs more explicit and more rational, and changing the budget format and process to allow for at least some flexibility and possible reallocation. Current efforts at reform are focused on reducing the size of the federal deficit, strengthening the legislature, and cutting the size of government.

NOTES

1. One seminal Neo-Marxist work is that of J. O'Connor, *The Fiscal Crisis of the State*, St. Martin's, New York (1973). A second useful work in this school is F. Block's "The ruling class does not rule: Notes on the Marxist theory of the state," *Socialist Revolution*, *33*(May/June): 6–27 (1977), reprinted in T. Ferguson and J. Rogers, eds., *The Political Economy: Readings in the Politics and Economics of American Public Policy*, M. E. Sharpe, Armonk, N.Y. (1984). Both incrementalists and public choice theorists have often argued that the bureaucracy has disproportionate influence on spending levels. The key incrementalist study outlining the influence of the bureaucracy is A. Wildavsky's *The Politics of the Budgetary Process*, Little, Brown, Boston, (1964). One of the seminal public choice studies that outline the importance of bureaucratic agencies in increasing expenditures is W. Niskanen's *Bureaucracy and Representative Government*, Aldine, Chicago (1970). Those who argue for interest-group determination of budget levels fall into a less cohesive or recognizable school. Some argue that the provision of pork to local districts drives much of the budget. See for example M. Fiorina, *Congress: Keystone of the Washington Establishment*, Yale University Press, New Haven, Conn. (1977). Others argue that interest groups rather than geographic areas drive the budget. Much of this latter argument has gone on in the context of whether interest group pluralism works as billed. Opponents of interest group pluralism or what Lowi calls interest-group liberalism argue that the influence of interest groups is conditional, and sometimes, in some policy areas, is dominant. See T. Lowi, *The End of Liberalism*, 2nd ed., W. W. Norton, New York (1979), and M. Hayes, "The semi-sovereign pressure groups: A critique of current theory and an alternative typology," *J. Politics*, *40*(February): 134–161 (1978).

2. An excellent discussion of Neo-Marxist approaches to urban analysis is presented in M. Gottdiener and J. Feagin, "The paradigm shift in urban sociology," *Urban Affairs Q.*, *24*(December): 163–187 (1988). The authors refer to some of these older models in passing, on the way to describing more current and dynamic models that describe the urban outcomes as products of continuing struggles between capital and labor.

3. For a discussion of the inability of incrementalism to cope with these developments, written by a leading exponent of the theory, see A. Wildavsky, *The Politics of the Budgetary Process*, Little, Brown, Boston (1984), especially the preface and prologue to the fourth edition. Wildavsky later dropped his incrementalism in favor of more timely descriptions of the changes in budgeting.

4. Hierarchy theory is the product of John Padgett. Key elements in the theory are outlined in "Hierarchy and ecological control in federal budgetary decision making," *Am. J. Sociol.*, *87*(1): 75–129 (1981).

5. See for example L. LeLoup, "From micro budgeting to macro budgeting: Evolution in theory and practice," in *New Directions in Budget Theory* (I. Rubin, ed.), SUNY Press, Albany, N.Y. (1988). Actually both hierarchy and the macro–micro theories are intended to apply to both the legislative and the executive branches. I make the distinction here because of the expertise of the writers who originated each concept, and the greater organizational integrity of the executive branch, so that the word hierarchy fits more naturally with the commonsense understanding of bureaucracy.

6. Anton, one of the leading incrementalists for many years, had argued that the legislative budget review in Illinois in the 1960s was limited to their concern for the geographic distribution of projects. No more in-depth review took place. See T. Anton, *The Politics of State Expenditure in Illinois*, University of Illinois Press, Urbana (1966).

7. See R. D. Arnold, "The local roots of domestic policy," in *The New Congress* (T. Mann and N. Ornstein, eds.), American Enterprise Institute, Washington, D.C., pp. 250–287 (1981).

8. John Padgett makes this argument in "Bounded rationality in budgetary research," *Am. Polit. Sci. Rev.*, *74*(June): 334–372 (1980).

9. I. Rubin, *The Politics of Public Budgeting*: *Getting and Spending, Borrowing and Balancing*, Chatham House, Chatham, N.J., chapter 1 (1990).

10. See A. Schick, "The distributive congress," *Making Economic Policy in Congress*, American Enterprise Institute, Washington, D.C. (1983), and C. Stewart III, *The Design of the Appropriation Process in the House of Representatives, 1865–1921*, Cambridge University Press, Cambridge (1989).

11. There has been an extensive literature on budget trade offs, but the results have been highly variable depending on the methodology used. For example, Bruce Russett, one of the key writers in this area, was unable to find major trade-offs in his 1982 study of defense and domestic spending, "Defense expenditures and national well being," *Am. J. Polit. Sci.*, *76*(December): 767–777 (1982). But he argued that his lack of results does not mean that the trade-offs do not occur. Rather, getting good data is a problem, and devising good theoretical specifications is difficult (p. 774).

12. S. Welch, "The impact of urban riots on urban expenditures," *Am. J. Polit. Sci.*, *19*(November): 741–760 (1975).

13. There are often limits within funds, too, if specific legislation mandates spending on a particular program.

9

Management Uses of Figures

Herbert Simon, George Kozmetsky, Harold Guetzkow,
and Gordon Tyndall

In the seven companies studied, accounting information is used at various executive levels to answer three different kinds of questions:

Score-card questions: "Am I doing well or badly?"
Attention-directing questions: "What problems should I look into?"
Problem-solving questions: "Of the several ways of doing the job, which is the best?"

The organizational problems of providing effective service to management in the score-card and attention directing areas were usually quite different from those of providing services in the area of special studies. Different sets of operating executives are generally involved in the two areas, and the kinds of data and analyses used may be quite different. Because of these differences, a controller's department which is well organized to provide the one type of service may or may not be well organized to provide the other.

SCORE-CARD AND ATTENTION-DIRECTING USES

In a factory the total departmental variance from standard or from budget would be an example of an item of score-card significance and use for the supervisor of the department concerned.

To the factory manager, the cost variances of individual departments would be attention-directing items—they would be one of the pieces of information which would direct his attention to departments requiring more careful review.

Source: *Centralization vs. Decentralization in Organizing the Controller's Department*, Controllership Foundation, New York, pp. 2–4, 22–24, 26–27, 28–30, and 32–33 (1954). Reprinted with permission.

Acceptance of standards and the constructive use of accounting data for score-card and attention-directing purposes requires that the operating executives have confidence in the standards and in the performance reports that go to their superiors. In all cases, a close and direct relationship between accounting personnel and operating personnel appeared to be the most important factor in producing this confidence. This relationship needed to be close in the standards-setting procedure so that the operating man might have an opportunity to negotiate a standard which he could regard as a reasonable and attainable forecast of his operations. The relationship needed to be close in the reporting process so that the operating man might have help in interpreting his variances, and might have a part in developing the explanations of off-standard performance that were presented to his superior. Hence, for effective attention-directing service, *it is essential for the controller's department to develop direct and active channels of communication with the operating executives at those points in the organization where operations are being measured.*

PROBLEM-SOLVING USES

When data are used for problem-solving purposes—to choose among alternative processes, to decide whether to buy new equipment, to help in policy decisions—a special study is usually required. This commonly draws upon engineering estimates and industrial engineering standards as well as accounting information and usually means going back into the basic records of the accounting system.

There are two principal ways in which accounting data may come into the problem-solving process:

Executives may turn to the regular accounting and statistical reports for help.
The controller's department may make special studies for particular problems.

In which of these directions does the greatest promise lie for improving the aspect of controllership service? In the direction of more elaborate periodic reports or in strengthening the special studies services? This study indicates that *further development of staff and facilities for special studies is a more promising direction of progress than elaboration of periodic accounting reports.*

In one company, an annual calculation is made for each factory of the ratio of profit earned by that factory to investment in factory facilities. For the plant manager this has a *score-card* value. If he earns a high percentage of profit, or if his profit goes up from one year to the next, he is likely to feel that he is doing a good job. If the profit is low or goes down, he is likely to be encouraged to additional effort. In some cases, the use of the accounting results as the basis for a supervisory bonus emphasizes the score-card function. Note that in these cases, the accounting figures act as a stimulus, but do not help the manager decide what can or should be done.

This very same figure, the factory's rate of return on investment, is used by top management in this company as an *attention director*. Those factories which consistently turn up with low or declining profit percentages are regarded as trouble spots requiring special attention from the company executives. In those factories where the rate of return is regarded as satisfactory, the manager is left rather free to run his own show. For the company management, therefore, the return figure is more than a score-card record. It also directs attention to operating units which need special analysis and review. Thus, the same item of information may be an attention director for one executive but primarily a score card for others, or it may have both score-card and attention-directing utility for the same person.

For example, take a factory general foreman or department head. His job consists in considerable part in "pushing" the work. He generally spends a large part of his time on the factory floor where he can actually observe the work being performed. He is concerned with seeing that jobs are filled, but that superfluous men are not on the payroll; that emergencies are met quickly and effectively, and delays minimized; that short-run, day-to-day problems of all sorts are handled promptly. His direct face-to-face contact with his subordinates and their work gives him many sources of information about what is going on, and he regards accounting information as only a supplement—and, in many instances, a not too important one—to the other sources. Accounting data are useful to him mainly in giving him a score card, summarizing for longer periods his day-to-day impressions. They also are useful in directing his attention to matters that are not visible and tangible—say, the rate of consumption of expendable tools, or of operating supplies.

In most of the companies, any appropriation for major new equipment has to be justified by an economy study or savings statement. This is an example of the "problem-solving" uses of accounting data. These uses go beyond the case where out-of-line accounting figures call attention to a problem or show in what area the problem lies. In problem-solving uses, the actual accounting data are inserted in the equation, so to speak, in order to solve the problem. Apart from plant and equipment studies, the most common examples of the problem-solving use of accounting data are in the comparison of profitability of product lines as a basis for a selective selling program, and the use of accounting data to forecast working capital requirements.

At higher levels of management the problem-solving uses of accounting data appear more commonly. For the vice-president for manufacturing there are policy problems—developing and putting into production new products, plant location decisions, installation of new equipment and replacement of old, make-or-buy decisions, and so on. In many of these areas of decision, accounting data are used for problem-solving purposes. Sometimes they apparently are not used where they *could* be. They are used in preparation of special analyses or studies usually prepared by the executive's own assistants or by "staff" departments [1] An equipment study, for example, would be most often made by the industrial engineering department. Sometimes, special studies are assigned to the controller's department and, even more frequently, that department is called on by other special-study units to supply the accounting data or dollar statistics needed for an analysis. Hence, the extent to which accounting data are used for problem-solving purposes depends very much on the kinds of staff assistance available to the vice-president and on how much he is accustomed to use them.

Another concern of the manufacturing vice-president is the evaluation and development of men. He needs to learn how his subordinates are doing, their strengths and their weaknesses. Moreover, the vice-president has far less opportunity than the factory department head to observe his subordinates on the job. Hence, he is more dependent on reports as a basis for evaluating their progress and problems. He often uses accounting data and reports of internal auditors as a score card for his subordinates, and as a means of directing his attention to the areas where he needs to apply pressure or raise questions.

Observations made on this survey indicate that the score-card and attention-directing uses are apt to be more frequent than the problem-solving uses at all levels of management. First-line supervisors tend to use such data primarily as a fill-in on aspects of the work that they cannot appraise from actual contact. At higher levels, the data are used as a means of judging subordinates and as an independent check on what is happening at the operating level. Problem-solving uses of accounting data occur primarily in administrative units (staff units) for making analyses or special studies, for use by general management.

SCORE-CARD AND ATTENTION-DIRECTING USES OF DATA

It has been pointed out that no sharp line can be drawn between the score-card and the attention-directing uses of accounting data. What is a score card for the factory manager may be an attention director for the vice-president for manufacturing; what is a score card for the regional sales manager may be an attention director for the general sales manager.

Illustrations of Score-Card and Attention-Directing Uses of Data

Here are some typical interview replies that illustrate the relation of the two uses:

> A general sales manager was asked:
> "How do you tell when your regional managers are doing a good job?"
> "The main things are the sales figures. Then, we've got to watch their expenses. Let's look at our weekly summary statistics. I see that the sales report of X product are low compared to the quota. I go back to the regional sales report and see that New England is the low region, also which of the sales branches in the region are low. Then I know to whom to write a letter to follow it up."
>
> One of the regional sales managers in the same company was asked: "How do you tell when you are doing a good job?" He replied: "I have a sales quota and an expense budget. I try to operate my region so that I will meet the quota or surpass it; and at the same time, I try to do the job in the most economical manner."

Attention Directing and the "Principle of Exceptions"

The use of accounting data to call attention to problems is closely related to what is usually called "the principle of exceptions." For this procedure to work, the operating man must accept the validity of the standards for determining what is "out of line." Moreover, effective attention-directing uses of accounting data imply that it is through such data that problems are called to the attention of operating executives or general management.

Persons interviewed consistently reported that, in many instances where the production and sales executives *might* have had their attention directed to problems by accounting data, they had already learned of the problems from other sources before the accounting reports appeared. For example, delays due to equipment breakdown or material shortages are almost immediately brought to the attention of the foreman and usually the department head. If the problem is a serious one, the news travels upward rapidly, even to vice presidential and presidential levels. On these matters, accounting reports usually provide the supervisors with history but not with news.

On the other hand, in the course of his daily work, even a first-line supervisor may find it difficult to learn that a particular machine logs excessive down-time because of mechanical failure. Here, a monthly summary of machine down-time with notation as to causes can be a valuable attention-directing report.

Interview data show conclusively that supervisors up to factory department heads use accounting reports for attention-directing purposes largely in areas that are not easily visible in the course of day-to-day supervision. The following comment of a factory department head is typical:

> "Every day when I go out through the departments, I know the standard number of men who should be working on each operation. If I see more than the standard number working on a job, I check up to see why the extra people are there." "Couldn't you get that from the daily variance report?" "Yes, but I'd have to wait two days."

Operating supervisors were seldom able to cite other types of examples of the attention-directing services of the accounting system. On other items—direct labor, material usage, yield—the common reaction was: "We know all about that before the accounting reports come."

The following conclusions validly generalize survey information about attention-directing uses of accounting data by supervisors and executives who have direct contact with the factory floor or the sales market.

A large part of an operating executive's knowledge about his operation comes by direct observation and informal reports. These reports are frequently verbal and come to him through the regular supervisory channels. Accounting reports are only one, and not always the most important, of his sources of information, although they may be of considerable use in confirming his observations.

The operating executive has special needs for periodic accounting reports on items that are not "visible" from direct, day-to-day supervision. In manufacturing, machine performance and consumption of operating supplies are examples of such items.

For executives further removed from actual operations, the greatest significance of attention directing accounting data lies in the information they transmit independently of operating supervisors. The existence of this independent source and channel of information has important consequences for the relations between executives at lower and higher levels.

THE ROLE OF STANDARDS [2]

When accounting data are used for score-card or for attention-directing purposes, a comparison of the actual data with some kind of standard or norm is always involved. This need not be a deliberately designed and established standard of the sort involved in a standard cost system, but may be any figure that is regarded as a "normal," "expected," "reasonable," or "satisfactory" value for the figure in question.

If an operating department head has become accustomed to "red" variances of $50,000 a month measured against the standard cost of his operation, then he is likely to regard a month in which his "red" variance is only $25,000 as a good one, even though the performance is still below standard. Similarly, a considerable number of executives were encountered whose real concern was not how they were making out with reference to the accounting standard, but how well they were doing in relation to historical records of past performance, or comparison with other plants in the same company.

Acceptance of Standards

Interview results show that a particular figure does not operate as a norm, in either a score-card or attention-directing sense, simply because the controller's department calls it a standard. It operates as a norm only to the extent that the executives and supervisors, whose activity it measures, accept it as a fair and attainable yardstick of their performance. Generally, operating executives were inclined to accept a standard to the extent that they were satisfied that the data were *accurately recorded*, that the standard level was *reasonably attainable*, and that the variables it measured were *controllable* by them. When there were doubts as to the accuracy of recording or classification of data, when the factors causing variances were thought to be beyond their own control, the executives simply did not believe that the standard validly measured their performance. Then they were influenced by it only to the extent that they were forced to think about the reactions of their superiors.

The degree of acceptance of standards was not the same, of course, in all the factories visited, nor even among different departments in the same factory. Some of the reasons for this are technical, and these will be discussed in the following paragraphs. In addition to these technical reasons, the length of time a cost system has been in operation has an important bearing on the validity and acceptability of standards. In all the companies studied, several years were required after the installation of a cost system before it was "shaken down" and a reasonably acceptable system of cost determinants arrived at. The same thing was observed in a case where a new processing department had recently been introduced in a factory which had a long-established cost system in its other departments.

It is not necessary to report on the degree to which standards were accepted in these various factories. As already mentioned, the range in level of acceptance was great. It is important, however, to learn what conditions have to be met so that accounting standards have a constructive influence upon operations, and how these conditions can be brought about through proper organizational relationships between the controller's department and the operating departments. For these reasons, the objections to existing accounting standards will be examined in some detail.

Two kinds of objections to standards were most frequently encountered. Some were criticisms of oversimplified determinants that failed to account for important external factors causing variability in costs. Thus, in several cases a cost that was only incurred during one season of the year received the same budget allowance per unit of output throughout the year. The fact that monthly variances in these cases were virtually meaningless tended to discredit the accounting standards and reports based on them.

In many instances the nature of the manufacturing operation practically precludes the establishment of adequate budget determinants. One problem frequently encountered is variation in the quality of raw materials. Food processing companies have continual difficulties of this kind, but similar troubles are found in other concerns. In companies like Westinghouse, where a standard cost often has to be estimated on each order, the task of arriving at acceptable and accepted standards is equally difficult [3].

The recalculation of indirect costs was the second major source of distrust of accounting standards—and this on two scores. Almost all operating men stated their dislike at having on their statements items they did not regard as within their control. The objections were particularly strong when the items were not shown as standard, but caused variances on the statements.

Moreover, in the case of indirect items that were admitted to be partially controllable— maintenance expenditures, for example—doubts were frequently expressed as to the accuracy of the charges. In almost all companies there was a widespread belief (not entirely without foundation) that maintenance foremen inflated their time estimates to absorb idle time. As a matter of fact, at least one maintenance department head stated that he did just that: "Suppose the charges don't balance—there's $1,000 unallocated. Well, we know in X department they have some rough edges, so we shove that charge off on them." When clerical errors occur in charging supplies and maintenance to the proper accounts, they also feed this distrust.

In addition, there were frequent objections to the "lumpiness" of indirect charges. "You go along for months with favorable variances and then one month you'll take a licking." This sometimes led to the uneconomical ordering of small quantities of supplies, and pressure was often felt (and, fortunately, frequently resisted) to postpone necessary maintenance: "The machine was still not fixed and we were running out of our budget expense, but I didn't stop. They came around afterwards and said, 'You're way over your budget.' I said, 'Look out there. The machine is running, isn't it? Isn't that what the boss wants?' "

But a department head in another factory said, "I will sometimes pull back on some repairs when I think I can get along without them, especially toward the end of the month."

Finally, supervisors could not always predict which month's budget would be charged with an expenditure. "When they throw charges in, they don't throw them in until the end of the month. I think I'm going along pretty well and then—bang—they hit me with some charges."

Reactions to Unacceptable Standards

Now, what occurs when an operating executive is placed in a situation where he fundamentally mistrusts the standards for any of the reasons discussed above, but where his superiors hold him responsible for unfavorable variances and expect explanations from him? There were frequent opportunities to observe how operating men reacted to such situations. The answer was always the same. When the operating man is placed in the position of justifying his performance in terms of a standard that he doesn't regard as fair he has two choices: to change the performance, or to change the measurement of it. And since he regards the measurement of his performance as unfair, he almost inevitably chooses the second alternative. The following two comments are typical of many made during the interviews:

> "If you find a variance that's way out, it's either a poor budget or it's not set up properly."
>
> "My boss comes around and asks me about my variance once in a while. This is often a good opportunity to point out things which are wrong with the accounting reports. If I say the standards are off, he should go back and see why the standards are off."

The first reaction of a supervisor who is confronted with an unfavorable variance in an account is to suspect that something has been charged to the account which should not have been charged. Hence, in a situation where the cost accounting is not completely trusted, a great deal of energy of accounting and operating personnel goes into discussion and debate about the correctness of the charges.

The second reaction of the operating man is to look for uncontrollable external circumstances that can explain the unfavorable variance. Thus, in the case of the seasonal item mentioned before, the operating man explains his unfavorable variances by pointing out that they will be balanced by favorable variances the next summer.

Distrust of standards coupled with pressure to eliminate variances leads to preoccupation with "wooden money" savings—to use a term that was current in one factory. When attention is directed by accounting data to an uneconomical operating practice and the practice is corrected, this leads to a real saving for the company that will ultimately be reflected in its profits. When the concern with variances is centered on detecting wrong charges and getting these shifted to the proper account, only "wooden money" is saved and company profits are not increased. Here are typical reports by operating men of their use of accounting data to produce "wooden money" savings:

> "The foreman keeps a running total of what he has spent. When the report comes back from accounting, he checks his total. It is important to analyze the charges slip by slip. We find that saves us five to six thousand dollars a month on incorrect charges by accounting or some other department."
>
> "There's a good example of another reason why I think these reports are good. If I hadn't had that report, I would never have known this was charged against me."

In the interviews, the relative amount of emphasis on "wooden money" savings proved to be a sensitive index of distrust of standards. In situations where confidence in standards was lowest, the examples given by respondents of their use of accounting data almost all involved reclassification of charges, and not instances where accounting showed opportunities for improving operations.

NOTES

1. As is well known, "staff" is a slippery word that is perhaps best avoided altogether. In this chapter the term is used simply as a shorthand way of referring to all the departments of a company other than manufacturing, sales, and engineering; and to all the departments of a factory other than the manufacturing and maintenance departments.
2. Findings with respect to standards are in close agreement with other previous studies. See especially J. D. Glover and F. J. Roethlisberger, "Human Reactions to Standards and Controls," *Controllership in Modern Management* (T. F. Bradshaw and C. C. Hull, eds.), Richard D. Irwin, Chicago, chapter vii (1949); and C. Argyris, *The Impact of Budgets on People*, Controllership Foundation, New York (1952).
3. These problems, of course, go beyond the controller's department to the other departments, like industrial engineering, that establish the physical determinants of standards. Nevertheless, even when the controller's responsibility is limited to "dollarizing" physical standards established by other departments, the variances appear on accounting reports and the accounting personnel are the ones principally criticized for unacceptable standards.

10

Power Without Privilege: Ethics in Public Budgeting and Financial Management

Carol W. Lewis
University of Connecticut, Storrs, Connecticut

INTRODUCTION

Impelled by severe financial straits, the municipal council agonizes and by majority vote stops funding the community alliance that runs the homeless shelter. You are sincerely distressed on three counts: the homeless have nowhere else to turn; you believe you are in public service to help people, not hurt them; and the administration publicly is committed to being responsive to community projects like the shelter. As a budget professional, it is your job to see that council decisions are implemented, but you think this one is a disgrace. How should you handle this?

This chapter examines ethical challenges that professionals in public and nonprofit budgeting and financial management (hereafter, B&FM) are likely to face in the near future. Ethics entails:

Making systematic, reasoned judgments about right and wrong (moral judgment, which draws upon moral character)

Taking ethical action (moral choice, or the practice of virtue)

Taking responsibility for both

When coupled with accountability in a democracy, taking responsibility means being willing and able take a stand that is publicly and personally defensible in authentic ethical terms. Given the topic, this chapter says very little about corruption and other issues made unambiguous in terms of ethical reasoning because one or more of the three elements is missing and/or are treated at length elsewhere.

Central Themes

This chapter builds on two underlying arguments. First, B&FM is *not* distinguished by special ethical values and perspectives; the basics among these commonly are shared by others in public service, the general American public, and many other cultures. It is often said that public service is marked by a "higher standard"; this is best understood not as a different morality but rather as the public's expectation that general ethical standards be fulfilled meticulously by public servants exhibiting unassailable personal integrity. Moreover, claims to a special morality all too frequently degenerate into attempts to evade general ethical precepts, rather than uphold higher ones.

Second, the discussion presumes *ethical* rational decision makers attempt to maximize a complex sex of values—among them, ethical values—instead of, for example, an exclusive or paramount concern with personal economic interests. The working assumption is that most practitioners in public and nonprofit agencies bring moral character to the job and are motivated at least in part by wanting to make a positive difference in the community or society; otherwise, why not more lucrative work, perhaps on Wall Street?

Conflict of Interest

In fact, the ban against using public office to advance personal interests is precisely the definition of conflict-of-interest prohibitions, the cornerstone of governmental and professional codes of conduct. (According to the Council on Governmental Ethics Laws' *Blue Book* [1]; many specific forms of conflict of interest are restrained by a majority of the states, with using public position for personal benefit, bribery, and misuse of confidential government information among the most common prohibitions.) In its positive form, the prohibition against conflict of interest translates into "pursue the public interest."

Public Interest

Pursuit of the public interest need is not always a clear-cut or easy task. Because shared but numerous and often contending moral values, duties, and principles may be assigned different weights in different situations by different decision makers (and the same decision maker at different cognitive stages), there often is no single, simple, and incontestable resolution to a given predicament. What is the right thing to do? No single set of rules handily substitutes for ethical reasoning; no set of rewards and punishments displaces ethical responsibility. Decision makers form their own judgments, take action and responsibility, and thereby safeguard both their personal integrity and public accountability. Nonetheless, because guidelines are helpful, the discussion briefly acquaints readers with professional standards of conduct and models of ethical decision making.

THE MEANING IS IN THE DOING

Firsthand experience is helpful as well (and explains the pedagogical popularity of case studies). In ethics, the meaning is in the doing. It is an applied subject, a practical field according to Aristotle in his *Nicomachean Ethics*. Therefore, prior exposure to ethical dilemmas under conditions allowing for reflection usefully engages practitioners destined to work in demanding, ever-changing professional and technical environments. Case studies and exercises (all field-tested by the author with B&FM professionals and other public managers) in this chapter simulate such exposure and stimulate the exercise of moral judgment. To enable the reader to examine timely, core issues, the chapter emphasizes five broad issues, including legal, fiduciary, and substantive responsibilities; information integrity; and accountability. The exercise "Cutbacks and Priorities," shown in Fig. 1 introduces these concerns. (The reader should complete Fig. 1 before reading further.)

In one form or another, the problem described in Fig. 1 is probably familiar to most practitioners. In this example, the task is to recommend immediate steps to counter an impending budget shortfall, and targeting programs to eliminate amounts to withdrawing or denying help. Although individuals opposing certain steps mistakenly or cynically may confuse not helping with purposefully doing harm, it is in fact a very different matter: Avoiding doing harm is the customary minimum ethical duty. But it is also true that someone or something is going to lose help or get less of it. The first option illustrates how moral duty often is seen as especially forceful and urgent in matters of life and death or acute, immediate need. Disaster relief therefore may be assigned an "A" or "B" and ranked a "5," meaning that many decision makers will not tolerate this option.

Cutback . . . retrenchment . . . downsizing . . . this technical jargon actually translates into withholding help--someone or something is going to lose help or get less. The challenge is to choose in a way that is (1) ethically principled, (2) legal, (3) accountable, (4) publicly and personally defensible, (5) professionally credible, and (6) fiscally and managerially prudent.

PROBLEM. An unexpected drop in state revenue dictates taking immediate steps toward a positive year-end fund balance. In a strategy session, legislative leadership develops guidelines and asks you to use them to rank several programs and recommend cuts.

PRIORITIES. These are leadership's priorities for evaluating programs.
A. Essential to preserving life in long or short run   E. Contribute to state's fiscal health or revenue
B. Provide for health and safety   F. Maintain or enhance quality of life
C. Avoid significant future harm   G. Obsolete, duplicative, ineffective
D. Prevent more costly services in future   (alternatives are available or better)

    Step #1. Evaluate policies using priorities A to G (may be used more than once).
    Step #2. Rank policies from critical (5) to worthy (3) to good target for cut (1).

A-H   1-5 *(Letters and numbers may be used more than once.)*
___ ___ 1. Disaster relief (food, water) program for immediate use by victims
___ ___ 2. Support for water quality inspection teams
___ ___ 3. Computer link to speed processing of vendor and third-party payments
               (and avoid charges for late payment)
___ ___ 4. Funding of ambulance and rescue services at subsidized charge to user
___ ___ 5. Scheduled pay increases for government employees
___ ___ 6. Computer security to protect confidentiality of personal records
               (client, employee)
___ ___ 7. Servicing general obligation bonds
___ ___ 8. Upkeep of parks and recreational areas

❶ Assume funding is zero or 100 percent.
  Select two programs to be cut (from among programs you ranked "1")
  #___   #___
  Reason for choice: Reason for choice:

❷ Are you willing to defend these choices publicly?

❸ Is something important missing? What else should we think about?

Figure 1 Cutbacks and priorities. (Priorities adapted from letter of December 4, 1990, from Connecticut Office of Policy and Management's Secretary-designate Wm. J. Cibes, Jr., to agency heads.)

Ethical Analysis of Options

Budgetary measures and fiscal policies through which scarce resources are allocated and costs distributed carry moral content. They pronounce the moral judgments that are very much a part of the answer to V. O. Key, Jr.'s (1940) classic question [2]; "On what basis shall it be decided to allocate X dollars to activity A instead of activity B?" (Key opted for an efficiency criterion.) Working through this exercise, decision makers may find themselves thinking about who would be affected, and how. Can they survive the cut? Are we breaking a law or a promise?

The options Fig. 1 lays out speak to ethical issues and claims. The third option of the computer link illustrates how economy so often crowds out efficiency when moral imperatives come into play. Similar reasoning may affect the eighth item, which also carries a substantial future price tag.

The eighth and second options raise questions of stewardship—for whom is the B&FM a fiduciary? Should anyone speak for the voiceless, future stakeholders[1]—and thereby moderate immediate democratic responsiveness and accountability? If so, who should? The eighth option also stands for the familiar choice of deferred maintenance, perhaps made relatively palatable by the arguable proposition that current damage can be undone and the harm is temporary at worst.

The fifth option illustrates two main lines of ethical thought—one duty-based (deontological), the other grounded in consequences (teleological). Because denying the salary increase, the fifth option, is not itself life-threatening, it may be preferred by decision makers who value consequences; others, more influenced by principles or duties, may reject it because of the implied broken promise. (The promise-breaking suggests why like choices tend to trigger a sense of betrayal and moral outrage.)

The seventh choice in Fig. 1 evokes another promise—implicit or explicitly sworn—to comply with the law when acting in one's official capacity. Legal compliance, with constitutional obligations at its core, affects both procedural and substantive responsibilities. Long-term bonded indebtedness represents a legally binding commitment but also prompts consideration of intergenerational equity.

The sixth option points to the concern with information integrity and confidentiality. Considerations of privacy and confidentiality are especially productive sources of ethical dilemmas today because of accelerating technological capacity, but also and more fundamentally because they stand as a first line of defense against using people as objects, or instrumentally.

Decision-Making Models

Assuming professionals in B&FM ordinarily try to make decisions in a thoughtful, scrupulous, and principled way, one anticipates the selection of options deemed to be the least damaging, most defensible cuts. In many decision-making models developed for public service as well as the business sphere, core, ethical duties often are framed in terms of not doing harm; reducing harm and repairing injury; taking care of those depending upon the decision maker; and taking into account ethical claims such as legal compliance and promises made. (See Recommended Readings.) Many models also emphasize sufficient information and feedback so that genuine ethical claims are not overlooked and error can be avoided or corrected.

To meet these multiple elements, decision makers concerned with integrity, responsiveness, and accountability often are encouraged to provide moral, democratic leadership (use the "moral imagination") by proposing principled, creative resolutions to ethical dilemmas that threaten personal or community ethical gridlock or damaging exclusion of ethical claims. The considerations enumerated here serve to alert the ethical professional to the central issues raised in the case that opens this chapter.

Special Obligations, Not Special Privileges

The cutback exercise also suggests the power B&FM practitioners wield. With access to and responsibility for resources well in excess of one-third the national economy, B&FM professionals in the public and nonprofit realm exercise substantial discretion. Still, decisions are made under conditions of ambiguity, uncertainty, and complexity; decision makers experience sharp work stresses, urgent deadlines, and forceful cross-pressures flowing from legal, political, professional, and personal obligations, expectations, and attachments.[2]

Paradoxically, practitioners in this core administrative function oversee a large part of any jurisdiction's control system, yet themselves face extraordinary opportunity to realize potential gain from wrongdoing. The public's and profession's long-standing concern with ethics is understandable and fitting, given the nexus of power, opportunity, and public and professional duties.[3]

"Who guards the guardians?" has been a central issue since at least the second century, when Juvenal formulated the question ("Quis custodiet ipsos custodes?"). A later rendition of this question comes from Federalist no. 51, in which James Madison wrote (in the gender-exclusive terminology of his day), "If men were angels, no government would be necessary. If angels were to govern men, neither external nor internal controls on government would be necessary. In framing a government which is to be administered by men over men, the great difficulty lies in this: you must first enable the government to control the governed; and in the next place oblige it to control itself." Michigan's House Fiscal Agency provides a contemporary version, allegedly involving $2 million. Governor John Engler responded that the "failure to provide proper management and oversight to the House Fiscal Agency has allowed the questionable conversion of public funds for private purposes and alleged kickbacks—the result of a system fraught with nepotism, secrecy and no accountability" (quoted in Ref. 8, p. 25).

Standard practice answers the question along two dimensions. First, standards of conduct rely upon enforcement (e.g., criminal statutes, administrative sanctions) and/or exhortation and counsel to deter corruption and block the use of public position for private gain or conflict of interest. Second, the exercise of reasoned judgment rooted in moral values and principles seeks to safeguard personal integrity in the face of contending ethical claims and opposing pressures. From either and both perspectives and also in light of personal and jurisdictional liability, ethics is a critical survival tool for practicing professionals in B&FM.[4]

The cutback exercise demonstrates that there is an ethical core to public service. Given the resources, power, and uneven sharing of benefit and harm in the B&FM enterprise, practitioners cannot afford to lose sight of what is right. Their power compared to those they serve is behind the idea that, as Thomas Jefferson wrote, "Public service is a public trust." The bottom line is clear: B&FM professionals exercise public power, but without privilege; their power is cut off from personal benefits and perks, so that *public* interest dominates. Ethics checks self-serving and arbitrary behavior and substitutes instead the obligation to adhere scrupulously to ethical standards. Special obligations—not special privileges—are the payoff from unequal power and the exercise of public authority.

STANDARDS OF CONDUCT

Governmental and professional codes lay out formal obligations (See Recommended Readings.) A profession is defined in part by its advocating a set of behavioral standards. Figures 2 and 3 show respectively the professional codes of the Government Finance Officers Association (GFOA) and the National Association of State Budget Officers (NASBO). Other

Government Finance Officers Association

Code of Professional Ethics

The Government Finance Officers Association of the United States and Canada is a professional organization of public officials united to enhance and promote the professional management of governmental financial resources by identifying, developing and advancing fiscal strategies, policies and practices for the public benefit.

To further these objectives, all government finance officers are enjoined to adhere to legal, moral and professional standards of conduct in the fulfillment of their professional responsibilities. Standards of professional conduct as set forth in this code are promulgated in order to enhance the performance of all persons engaged in public finance.

I. Personal Standards
Government finance officers shall demonstrate and be dedicated to the highest ideals of honor and integrity in all public and personal relationships to merit the respect, trust and confidence of governing officials, other public officials, employees, and of the public.
- They shall devote their time, skills and energies to their office both independently and in cooperation with other professionals.
- They shall abide by approved professional practices and recommended standards.

II. Responsibility as Public Officials
Government finance officers shall recognize and be accountable for their responsibilities as officials in the public sector.
- They shall be sensitive and responsive to the rights of the public and its changing needs.
- They shall strive to provide the highest quality of performance and counsel.
- They shall exercise prudence and integrity in the management of funds in their custody and in all financial transactions.
- They shall uphold both the letter and the spirit of the constitution, legislation and regulations governing their actions and report violations of the law to the appropriate authorities.

III. Professional Development
Government finance officers shall be responsible for maintaining their own competence, for enhancing the competence of their colleagues, and for providing encouragement to those seeking to enter the field of government finance. Finance officers shall promote excellence in the public service.

IV. Professional Integrity-Information
Government finance officers shall demonstrate professional integrity in the issuance and management of information.
- They shall not knowingly sign, subscribe to, or permit the issuance of any statement or report which contains any misstatement or which omits any material fact.
- They shall prepare and present statements and financial information pursuant to applicable law and generally accepted practices and guidelines.
- They shall respect and protect privileged information to which they have access by virtue of their office.
- They shall be sensitive and responsive to inquiries from the public and the media, within the framework of state or local government policy.

V. Professional Integrity-Relationships
Government finance officers shall act with honor, integrity and virtue in all professional relationships.
- They shall exhibit loyalty and trust in the affairs and interests of the government they serve, within the confines of this Code of Ethics.
- They shall not knowingly be a party to or condone any illegal or improper activity.
- They shall respect the rights, responsibilities and integrity of their colleagues and other public officials with whom they work and associate.
- They shall manage all matters of personnel within the scope of their authority so that fairness and impartiality govern their decisions.
- They shall promote equal employment opportunities, and in doing so, oppose any discrimination, harassment or other unfair practices.

VI. Conflict of Interest
Government finance officers shall actively avoid the appearance of or the fact of conflicting interests.
- They shall discharge their duties without favor and shall refrain from engaging in any outside matters of financial or personal interest incompatible with the impartial and objective performance of their duties.
- They shall not, directly or indirectly, seek or accept personal gain which would influence, or appear to influence, the conduct of their official duties.
- They shall not use public property or resources for personal or political gain.

Figure 2 Government Finance Officers Association Code of Professional Ethics.

NATIONAL ASSOCIATION OF STATE BUDGET OFFICERS

STANDARDS OF PROFESSIONAL CONDUCT

The National Association of State budget Officers is an independent, professional organization of public officials affiliated with the National Governors' Association united to assist the Governors in developing and implementing fiscal, budgetary and central management policies and to encourage professional development and expertise in state budget offices.

To further these objectives, the standards of professional conduct as set forth in this code are promulgated in order to enhance the performance of all persons engaged in public budgeting. NASBO adapted this code from materials developed by the Josephson Institute of Ethics.

1. **HONESTY.** Be scrupulously and consistently honest by being truthful, sincere, forthright, and candid where professional duties requiring confidentiality permit, so that persons are not misled or deceived.

2. **INTEGRITY.** Demonstrate integrity by: (1) exhibiting conduct consistent with core beliefs and assuring that practices are congruent with principles; (2) honoring and adhering to the general principles of public service ethics, the mission and values of the organization; (3) expressing and fighting for your concept of what is right and upholding your convictions to the best of your ability.

3. **COMMITMENT.** Demonstrate promise-keeping by: (1) fulfilling commitments by making your word your bond; (2) discharging commitments in a fair and reasonable manner; (3) exercising prudence and caution in making commitments, considering that unknown or future factors might arise which could make fulfillment of them impossible, difficult or undesirable; (4) assuring that commitments made are clear to all parties.

4. **FAIRNESS.** Demonstrate fairness by: (1) making decisions with impartiality based on consistent and appropriate standards; (2) demonstrating a commitment to justice, the equitable treatment of individuals in all actions including recruiting, hiring and promoting employees; (3) exercising authority with open mindedness and seeking all relevant information, including opposing perspectives; (4) voluntarily correcting personal or institutional mistakes and improprieties and refusing to take unfair advantage of mistakes or ignorance of citizens; (5) scrupulously employing open, equitable, and impartial processes to gather and evaluate information necessary for decisions.

5. **RESPECT FOR OTHERS.** Respect others by: (1) acknowledging and honoring the right of those affected by official and managerial decisions to privacy and dignity; (2) treating others with courtesy and decency; (3) exercising authority in a way that provides others with the information they need to make informed decisions about matters within the scope of their professional duties.

Figure 3 National Association of State Budget Officers Standards of Professional Conduct.

organizations such as the Institute of Internal Auditors and American Institute of Certified Public Accountants also have adopted codes that oblige members to conform to specified standards of professional conduct.

All codes have two characteristic limitations. First, given our definition of ethics, codes can neither substitute for personal integrity nor supplant individual responsibility. (The same must be said about organizational norms and supervisor's orders.) Second, not even an encyclopedic compilation could cover all possible permutations and nuances. Although no blueprint, codes do articulate peer expectations, alert decision makers to core professional concerns, and provide useful guidelines. For example, GFOA (Fig. 2), NASBO (Fig. 3),

6. **PURSUIT OF EXCELLENCE.** Perform your duties with excellence by: (1) being diligent, reliable, careful, prepared, and informed; (2) continuing to develop knowledge, skills and judgment necessary to the performance of your duties.

7. **PERSONAL ACCOUNTABILITY.** Be accountable by: (1) accepting personal responsibility for the foreseeable consequences of actions and inactions; (2) recognizing your special opportunities and obligations to lead by example; (3) making decisions that take into account long term interest and the need to exercise leadership for posterity.

8. **LOYALTY.** Demonstrate loyalty by: (1) advancing and protecting the interests of those with legitimate moral claims arising from personal and institutional relationships; (2) safeguarding confidential information without violating professional duties; (3) resolving conflicting loyalties to various parties by placing obligations to the constitution, the institution of government and fundamental principles of representative democracy above your duty to individuals; (4) refusing to subordinate other ethical obligations in the name of loyalty such as honesty, integrity, fairness and subordinate other ethical obligations in the name of loyalty such as honesty, integrity, fairness and the obligation to make decisions on the merits, without favoritism, in the name of loyalty.

9. **PUBLIC OFFICE AS PUBLIC TRUST.** Treat your office as a public trust by using your powers and resources to advance the public interest.

10. **INDEPENDENT OBJECTIVE JUDGMENT.** Employ independent objective judgment in performing your duties, deciding all matters on the merits, free from conflicts of interest and both real and apparent improper influences while discharging lawful discretionary authority to the public/taxpayers best interest.

11. **PUBLIC ACCOUNTABILITY.** Assure that government is conducted openly, efficiently, equitably and honorably in a manner that permits the citizenry to make informed judgments and hold government officials accountable.

12. **DEMOCRATIC LEADERSHIP.** With a positive attitude, honor and respect the principles and spirit of representative democracy and set a positive example of good citizenship by scrupulously observing the letter and spirit of laws and rules.

13. **RESPECTABILITY AND FITNESS FOR PUBLIC OFFICE.** Safeguard public confidence in the integrity of government by being honest, fair, caring and respectful and by avoiding conduct creating the appearance of impropriety, which is unbefitting a public official.

Adopted July 19, 1992

Figure 3   Continued.

and the Institute of Internal Auditors emphasize maintaining professional competence. Note also GFOA's and NASBO's accent on obligations relating to managing and disclosing information; candor and comprehensibility (or *transparency*) constitute NASBO's first standard and relate to the eleventh, assuring public accountability.

New Twists

Organizational and technological complexity or new twists to familiar problems sometimes complicate a decision or mask underlying ethical issues. The very "rules of the game" in B&FM routinely demand discretion, prudence, judgment, and personal integrity. B&FM staff experts soon discover the inherent tensions among executive leadership, expert analysis, and public accountability. The tension stimulates some hard questions about virtue and duty, as the excerpt in Fig. 4 from OMB's Circular A-11 illustrates at the federal level. What is the difference between candor and telling the truth, which is to be preferred and when, and is lack of candor tantamount to lying? What is prudence? Is it really any different from self-protection? What is loyalty in complex settings like the federal government, and to whom is loyalty owed? How far should it go?

Analogous questions arise at the state level. NASBO's code (the eighth standard in Fig. 3) obliges members to advance and protect "the interests of those with legitimate moral claims arising from personal and institutional relationships." It goes on to require that conflicting loyalties be resolved "by placing obligations to the constitution, the institution of government and fundamental principles of representative democracy" above personal loyalties.

12.9. Responsibilities for disclosure with respect to the budget.

(a) **Agency testimony before and communications with Congress on budgetary matters.**--The nature and amounts of the President's decisions are confidential and will not be released until the budget is transmitted formally to Congress. The executive branch communications that have led to the budget will not be disclosed either by the agencies or by those who have prepared the budget. . . .

Following formal transmittal of the budget, an amendment, or a supplemental appropriation request, agency representatives will be guided by the following policies pertaining to budgetary matters when testifying before any congressional committee or communicating with Members of Congress:

(1) Witnesses will give frank and complete answers to all questions.

(2) Witnesses will avoid volunteering personal opinions that reflect positions inconsistent with the program or appropriations request the President has transmitted to Congress.

(3) If statutory provisions exist for the direct submission of agency budget estimates to Congress, OMB may provide agencies with additional materials supporting the President's budget request to be forwarded by the agency to Congress with agency testimony., Witnesses for such agencies will be prepared to explain the agency submission, the request in the President's budget, and any justification material.

(4) In responding to specific questions on program and appropriations requests, witnesses will refrain from providing the agency request to OMB as well as plans for the use of appropriations that exceed the President's request. Witnesses typically bear responsibility for the conduct of one or a few programs, whereas the President must weigh carefully all of the needs of the Federal Government, and compare them against each other and against the revenues available to meet such needs. Where appropriate witnesses should call attention to this difference in scope of responsibility in explaining why it is not proper to them to support efforts to raise appropriations above the amounts requested by the President. . . .

(b) **Clearance of budget-related materials for Congress and the media.**--Policy consistency is essential among the various sections of the President's budget , and the budget-related materials prepared by the agencies for Congress and the media. Agencies are responsible for ensuring that these budget-related materials are consistent with the President's budget and are submitted for clearance to OMB, unless a specific exemption from clearance is approved by OMB.

Agencies will submit all proposed budget justification materials to OMB for clearance prior to transmittal to congressional committees or individual Members of Congress or their staff. Agencies also will submit to OMB for clearance budget-related oversight materials. . . .

Figure 4 Excerpt from OMB Circular A-11. (From OMB Circular No. A-11, 1994, Washington, D.C., pp. 22–23.)

Professionally Speaking

The case study in Fig. 5 suggests that B&FM at the local level also operates in a complex, sometimes ambiguous context and summons multiple, often competing values and duties. This case calls on many professional standards and ethical responsibilities that may pull and push a thoughtful professional in different directions. (The reader should complete Fig. 5 before reading further.)

The "gag rule" raises considerations of access to public records, public disclosure, transparency, professional credibility, and multifaceted accountability, all issues with serious ethical content or implications. The first question in Fig. 5 solicits ethical concerns such as

---

In a particularly bitter budget battle, the chief executive officer (CEO) cut several departments' original budget requests, then ordered all municipal department heads not to discuss any budgetary matters with council members, except in formal session. The edict also orders all department heads to advocate the CEO's recommendation before the council (the town's fiscal authority), the press, and public.

One municipal department head protests what he calls a "gag rule" and claims that he has the legal right and professional duty to discuss the budget under all circumstances and to address responsibly questions from council members and the public whether at public hearings or not. In fact, he has just updated the spreadsheet on his office PC to submit to the CEO and prepare for the annual budget ritual.

Objecting to "blind" decision making and the "back-room politics" that cut into his doing his job, a municipal council member requests the preliminary budget estimates that department heads routinely bring to the informal budget meetings with the CEO. The CEO, who uses these estimates to prepare the executive recommendation, responds that preliminary papers were discarded after they were no longer needed.

The council member then discovers that the finance and other departments' documentation procedures do not include maintaining background papers or draft worksheets. The finance head explains that too many numbers confuse the public and approvingly points to the CEO's gag rule.

❶ What issues does this case raise?

- •   •
- •   •

❷ What is accomplished by presenting departmental estimates to the council and public?

❸ Is the department head correct about his "legal right and professional duty"? How should he handle the issues raised in the first question?

❹ Under what conditions would/should a department head temper program advocacy? Is the department head a team player? Whose team? Is this an *ethical* issue?

❺ Would/should a department head inform the council member about having the preliminary estimate on the PC?

❻ Do any laws apply in this situation? Is the department head ethically bound to comply? Why? The CEO?

❼ How do professional standards of conduct offer guidance here?

Figure 5 The "gag rule."

contending loyalties, telling the truth, and legal compliance. GFOA's Code of Professional Ethics (Fig. 2, Standard II) enjoins members to "uphold both the letter and the spirit of the constitution, legislation and regulations governing their actions." Because members assent to "maintaining their own competence" (Standard III) and promise-keeping is a conventional ethical value, knowing the law as it applies to public records and specifically to computerized budget estimates is a useful starting point for thinking through this case. Many decision-making models begin with accurate fact-finding.

For example, Connecticut General Statutes Sec. 1-19(c) states that "disclosure shall be required of (1) interagency or intra-agency memoranda or letters, advisory opinions, recommendations or any report comprising part of the process by which governmental decisions and policies are formulated, except disclosure shall not be required of a preliminary draft of a memorandum, prepared by a member of the staff of a public agency, which is subject to revision prior to submission to or among the members of such agency." When a Connecticut mayor denied access to estimates that had been discarded, the state's Freedom of Information Commission noted in its notice of final decision (February 11, 1993) that "estimates are used in the . . . budget process to determine the operating budgets for each municipal department" and found that "the estimates comprise part of the process by which governmental decisions and financial policies are formulated." The commission found that "the estimates are public records . . . and are subject to disclosure." Furthermore, the commission warned that failing to maintain copies of budget estimates might violate Connecticut's Records Retention Act.

The Public Record

Truth-telling, as any virtue, is valued for its own sake. Playing a central role in democracy, it is necessary to public confidence and trust, and to informed participation by citizens. But accountability demands more than telling the truth when pressed to do so. Figures 2 and 3 indicate that disclosure is a core professional obligation. It requires full exposure of all information material and available or attainable for decision makers to make informed, responsible decisions. It is the very basis of building the public record. Disclosure puts into play the many values, virtues, and duties such as candor, truth-telling, keeping promises, accountability, information integrity, legal compliance, and more. It is no wonder, then, that many decision models include a step for fact-finding and that many, many practitioners have suggested that the demands of disclosure, a core ethical obligation in B&FM, are key to resolving the "gag rule."

PROFESSIONAL RESPONSIBILITY

A profession is marked by its expert knowledge and members' behavioral norms. The latter may be articulated formally, as in codes of professional conduct, or informally through routine practices on the job. The definition of ethics includes taking responsibility and, for professionals, that extends to professional norms and customs. In some formulations, professional responsibility also includes enhancing colleagues' competence and organizational performance on which one's own competence and performance depend (e.g., GFOA's Standard III). Focusing on this professional responsibility, "Drawing the Line," shown in Fig. 6, exposes selected behaviors to ethical appraisal. (The reader should complete the exercise in Fig. 6 before reading further.)

The objective is to polish principled thinking about the ethical dimensions of on-the-job behaviors and to take personal responsibility for everyday practices. The first step asks

Working proposition: the more unethical we judge a behavior,
the less willing we are to practice it, or tolerate it when others do it.

Please do each step quickly, spontaneously, using common sense and gut feel.

STEP #1. Call it as you see it.
In the spaces below, write the letter that best describes each action.

    a = highly unethical   c = not especially wrong
    b = moderately unethical   d = not at all wrong

___ 1. Anticipating usual cuts, pad budget requests to protect efficient programs
___ 2. Hold back bad news on budget shortfall so it does not influence the election
___ 3. Prove inflation and intergovernmental mandates eat up the tax increase
___ 4. Cover for a decent colleague's erroneous estimate
___ 5. Try to neutralize lowered bond rating by cynically blaming predecessor
___ 6. Duplicate copyrighted software to take home to learn
___ 7. Prepare for negotiations by adding throw-away items to trade
___ 8. Blame subordinate for office's submitting muddled cost analysis to meet deadline
___ 9. Meet with a supportive reporter, put an unreleased document on your desk,
       and leave the office momentarily
___ 10. _____
              (a practice you identify)

⇨ Some people see ethics as a toggle switch--on or off, right or wrong--and refuse
  to consider any moderating factors in an assessment or reaction. Do you agree?
              Did you select only "a" and "d" categories?   ☐ yes   ☐ no

STEP #2. Draw the line in a principled way.
       Looking only at your "a" choices, star three you see as most serious wrongs.

⇨ Why are starred items so offensive? Check all that apply.
  ☐ purposefully causes harm to innocent parties   ☐ indulges conflict of interest
  ☐ fails to remedy a problem one directly caused   ☐ fails to help weak or needy
  ☐ voids accountability (*via* deception or irresponsibility)   ☐ injures or neglects public interest

STEP #3. Circle the "a" and "b" choices that, in your experience, commonly occur.

***As a professional committed to the highest standards of integrity,
what is your responsibility for starred practices? For circled practices?***

Figure 6 Drawing the line.

for an assessment of the practice; the "b" and "c" choices allow for wiggle room, for judgment. Even when upstanding people agree on right versus wrong, they may weigh ethical claims differently and sort offenses by discounting for the hat one wears and place in the organization; imputed motive, intent, and the action's likely impact; and norms, habits, and customs in the community. Some decision makers may justify some of the practices listed in Fig. 6 on the grounds that they are common and more or less necessary tactics to accomplish a greater good. For example, the sixth item represents theft (of intellectual property, but theft nonetheless), which some may try to justify because it benefits the organization rather than the individual. Padding the budget, the first choice, relies on purposeful misrepresentation to accomplish organizational objectives, but here the professional is substituting expertise for authoritative, accountable decision-making processes.

Different from virtue (the practice of which is valued in and of itself), a tactic by definition is instrumental, something employed in order to accomplish something else. But does that mean that anything goes? The arrow under Step 1 asks whether you designated all behaviors as "highly unethical" and "not at all wrong." Working though analogues of this exercise, the overwhelming majority of many hundreds of public leaders, including B&FM professionals, report using "b" and "c," the middle ground that reflects assessing degree or gradation of ethical offense. Given this, a key to keeping personal integrity intact is to draw the line *in a principled, ethically defensible way.*

Like public service generally, B&FM tends to use the widely accepted boundaries shown in Step 2 to constrain behavior and filter action in a principled way. These boundaries are rooted deeply in ethical ground. The fifth item, for example, is starred very often. It is a common choice because it implies purposefully causing harm to an innocent party and, in this way, denies the minimum ethical duty of not doing harm. Also, it neglects correcting the underlying problem. Numbers 5 and 8 suggest that self-protection is more important than competence, loyalty, truth, and more. What kind of an organization is this? What makes the second item so offensive that it has been starred by many elected officials in numerous forums? This action not only hurts the opposition candidate and fails to help the voters, it also prevents accountability and informed citizen participation. The blank (number 10) asks, "Where do *you* draw the line?"

The third step asks for the identification of more or less common practices. A B&FM professional recently suggested that we rename all government agencies "other department." The reason, he explained, is that it is always so easy to cut other departments. While amusing, the remark reflects his expectation of irresponsibility and inauthenticity as standard practice in budgeting.

A profession's development depends upon members' self-conscious distinction between customary behaviors and professional practices grounded in ethical values and principles. Here the words of the American revolutionary Tom Paine are worth remembering: "A long habit of not thinking something wrong gives it the superficial appearance of being right." The concluding question in Fig. 6 about responsibility is a critical component in this continual development. It was answered in the nineteenth century by answered by Ralph Waldo Emerson: "We must hold a man amenable to reason for the choice of his daily craft or profession. It is not an excuse any longer for his deeds that they are the custom of his trade. What business has he with an evil trade?"

PURPOSES AND PROSPECTS

Professional responsibility moves beyond practice and includes purpose. The case that opens this chapter captures this substantive responsibility. Aaron Wildavksy [9, p. 787], one of the most influential scholars in the field, wrote that "the second question is how well you accomplish objectives; the first is which objectives it is right to try to accomplish. Answers to the second question matter, but only after the first is settled."

A conclusion to a chapter on professional ethics is inappropriate for at least two reasons. First, an individual's moral development and a profession's ethical evolution are ongoing, and symbolic space makes room for the optimism on which professionalism depends. Second, the definition of ethics demands that responsible, ethical decision makers make the judgment, have the final word. They daily answer a core ethical question in B&FM: Given the actual prospect of exceeding legal authority, budget, energy, credibility, and more, what do you do when you can't do it all?

NOTES

1. On stewardship responsibilities in public service, see especially Refs. 3–5.
2. For impact of political agenda on budget professionals, see Ref. 6. On political pressure or intimidation, see Ref. 7.
3. The 1994 conference, The Ethics of Accounting and Finance, sponsored by Bentley College's Conference on Business Ethics, is just one instance reflecting the parallel concern in the business world.
4. Illustratively, the Chief Financial Officers Council and Joint Financial Management Improvement Program identify ethics as among the learning objectives of core competencies of curricula for federal budget officers, accountants, and others. Note that the JFMIP compendium of courses describes a content largely linked to federal laws and regulations.

RECOMMENDED READINGS

S. Bok, *Lying: Moral Choice in Public and Private life*, Vintage Books, New York (1978).

T. Cooper, *The Responsible Administrator. An Approach to Ethics for the Administrative Role*, 3rd ed., Jossey-Bass, San Francisco (1990).

A. H. Hayes, Jr. "Fraud Happens: A Primer on Lying, Cheating, and Stealing," *Govern. Finance Rev.*, *11*(December): 7–11 (1995).

S. Garment, *Scandal, The Culture of Mistrust in American Politics*, Anchor Books, New York (1992).

R. A. Gorlin, ed., *Codes of Professional Responsibility*, 2nd ed., Bureau of National Affairs, Washington, D.C. (1990).

C. W. Lewis, *The Ethics Challenge in Public Service. A Problem-Solving Guide*, Jossey-Bass, San Francisco (1991).

C. W. Lewis and B. L. Catron, "Professional Standards and Ethics," *Handbook of Public Administration*, 2nd ed. (J. L. Perry, ed.), Jossey-Bass, San Francisco, pp. 699–712 (1996).

P. Madsen and J. M. Shafritz, eds., *Essentials of Government Ethics*, Meridian, Penguin Books, New York (1992).

L. L. Nash, *Good Intentions Aside, A Manager's Guide to Resolving Ethical Problems*, Harvard Business School Press, Boston (1990).

J. A. Rohr, *Ethics for Bureaucrats: An Essay on Law and Values*, 2nd ed., Marcel Decker, New York (1989).

D. Rosenbloom, "The Constitution as a Basis for Public Administrative Ethics," *Essentials of Government Ethics*, (P. Madsen and J. M. Shafritz, eds., Meridian, Penguin Books, New York, pp. 48–64 (1992).

D. F. Thompson, "Mediated Corruption: The Case of the Keating Five," *Am. Polit. Sci. Rev.*, *87*(June): 369–381 (1993).

D. F. Thompson, "The Possibility of Administrative Ethics," *Public Admin. Rev.*, *45*: 5–561 (1985).

U.S. Office of Government Ethics, *Standards of Ethical Conduct for Employees of the Executive Branch*, Washington, D.C. (1993).

REFERENCES

1. Council of State Governments, COGEL Blue Book, 9th ed., Lexington, Ky. (1993).
2. V. O. Key, Jr., "The Lack of a Budgetary Theory," *Am. Polit. Sci. Rev.*, *34*: 1137–1144 (1940).
3. B. L. Catron, "Principles and Strategies for Intergenerational Equity, Balancing Risks, Costs and Benefits Fairly Across Generations," paper presented to National Academy of Public Administration, Washington D.C., November (1994).

4. H. G. Frederickson, "Can Public Officials Correctly Be Said to Have Obligations to Future Generations?", *Public Admin. Rev.*, *54*: 457–464 (1994).

5. H. D. Kass, "Stewardship as a Fundamental Element in Images of Public Administration," *Images and Identities in Public Administration* (H. D. Kass and L. Catron, eds.), Sage, Newbury Park, Calif., pp. 113–131 (1990).

6. K. Thurmaier, "Decisive Decision Making in the Executive Budget Process: Analyzing the Political and Economic Propensities of Central Budget Bureau Analysts," *Public Admin. Rev.*, *55*(5): 448–460 (1995).

7. J. Fritsach, "Senate Aide Uses Budget Threat to Intervene in a Pollution Case," *New York Times*, August 24: A1, B15 (1995).

8. G. Weeks, "Leaders Act Quickly in Fiscal Agency Scandal," State Legislatures, *19*(July): 25–26 (1993).

9. A. Wildavsky, "What Is Permissible So That His People May Survive? Joseph the Administrator. The 1989 John Gaus Lecture," *PS: Polit. Sci. Politics*, *22*: 779–788 (1989).

11

Budgeting and Culture

Aaron Wildavsky†

A state of nature, as commonly conceived, is prior to society. There are individuals but they are presumably not connected to one another. Obviously, no society means no government and, hence, no budget. I reject this antisocial (worse still, this unbudgetary) view of the world. Without some sort of society, there can be no individuality. Budgets and social life imply one another. Ask how budgets ought to be made and you will hear also how social life ought to be lived.

Social organization requires social support. People have to be able to do things for other people. They have to be able to make demands in support of their way of life, and to hold each other accountable for things that go wrong. Mobilizing, allocating, and controlling resources is another expression for budgeting.

Budgets are promises. If agency proposals are approved, they will get the money the treasury promised them. Commitments made to certain classes of people—the elderly, the handicapped, the sick—will be kept no matter what. Different types of spending devices—annual appropriations, indefinite "no-year" entitlements, indexed entitlements—grade the degree of certainty that government promises will be kept. Making too many promises means that not all may be able to be kept to the same degree at the same time.

Budgets are social orders. A moral order regulating relations among people specifies commands and prohibitions. So does a budget. "There is no money" may not be the saddest sentence of them all, but it is one of the most conclusive. It is equivalent to the other great classes of prohibitions—there is no time, it is unnatural, and God forbids it [1]. Even the architecture of budgets, as in the family practice of providing envelopes for this or that expenditure, suggests an order of priorities. Students of the subject are used to ferreting out the implicit preferences of those who rule from the patterns of resource mobilization

Source: This is a revised and updated version of "A Cultural Theory of Budgeting," *Int. J. Public Admin.*, *11*(6): 651–677 (1988).
†Deceased.

and resource allocation. Similarly, it should be possible to relate patterns of budgeting to regimes of rule through which political power is exercised in a society.

POLITICAL CULTURE

This comparison of political cultures (Fig. 1) is based on the proposition that what matters most to people is other people [2, 3]. Two questions are basic: Who am I—a member of a strong group that takes collective action or an individual able to transact freely with whomever I wish? What should I do? Should I do as I am told, being bound by numerous prescriptions, or should I do as I please, the only norm being the absence of physical coercion? The strength of commitment to the group or institution and the extent to which norms of everyday behavior are prescribed are the basic dimensions of political cultures from which other combinations are constructed.

Political culture provides motivation for the uses of resources. As soon as physical survival is assured, there is room to mobilize and allocate resources so as to do what matters most—support one's way of life. By invoking political culture, we bring back into budgeting the values and preferences that contain the differing motives for the particular use of resources in a given society.

Strong groups with numerous prescriptions combine to form a hierarchical regime. Strong group boundaries with few prescriptions form an equitable regime—a life of voluntary consent without inequality. By uniting few prescriptions with weak group boundaries and thereby encouraging endless new combinations, the bidding and bargaining of market regimes creates a self-regulating substitute for hierarchical authority. When boundaries are weak and prescriptions strong, so that decisions are made by people outside the group, such a controlled regime is fatalistic.

Just as an act is socially rational if it supports one's way of life, governmental budgeting is politically rational if it maintains the political regimes existing in that place and time. In regimes organized on a market basis, for instance, budgets reflect opportunity for gain by bidding and bargaining. Under hierarchical regimes in which the binding rules of social organization differentiate people and their activities by rank and status, budgets reflect that detailed division of labor. And when an equitable regime emphasizes equality of condition, budgets are devoted to (re)distributing equal shares.

My cultural hypothesis is that hierarchical regimes that strive to exert authority spend and tax high in order to maintain their rank and status. Market regimes, preferring to reduce

Group strength

		Weak	Strong
Number and variety of prescriptions	**Many**	Fatalism (apathetic regime)	Collectivism (hierarchical regime)
	Few	Individualism (market regime)	Egalitarianism (equitable regime)

Figure 1   The primary political cultures.

the need for authority, spend and tax as little as possible. Equitable regimes spend as much as possible to redistribute resources, but their desire to reject authority leaves them unable to collect sufficient revenues.

When rich nations mimic the poor ones by coming close to repetitive budgeting—remaking the budget several times a year—or when poor ones achieve the certitude that used to be obtained only by the rich, governments have transcended their material conditions. When, outside the grip of compulsion, governments make more or less of the circumstances in which they find themselves, the way is open for cultural explanations based not only on potential resources but also on what they prefer to do with them.

My task is not merely to set up models of rule in regimes but to relate them to budgetary behavior. Each regime, I hypothesize, is accompanied by a process of budgeting, not all the time but most of the time, not entirely but largely. The social relationships epitomized by these four regimes are supported by characteristic modes of budgetary behavior.

If social order and hence political regimes are congruent with budgetary processes, this symmetry should show up in the standard topics of the subject. Thus I shall deal with the form of budgeting, auditing, budgetary balance, and deficits (the distance between expenditure and revenue). I shall also examine the place of the budgetary base—agreed understandings on totals and items—among the political cultures. Finally, I shall provide a cultural explanation for the growth of government. It is best to begin with budgetary control because it shows power relationships most clearly: Is budgeting made from the top down or the bottom up? How is control exercised—by following the forms, or by producing the right results? How are errors detected and corrected? Is information avidly sought after or suppressed? How are sanctions and rewards applied?

FORMS OF BUDGETING

Every form of budgeting is supposed to produce results. The question is, what kind? Under the *exploitative budgeting* of apathetic regimes, the rulers seek to maximize the surplus of revenue over cost produced by the ruled. In the *productivity budgeting* of market regimes, it is the ability of money to make money, or to spend least for a given objective, that counts. The *redistributive budgeting* of equitable regimes aims at the redistribution of whatever goods there are. And the *procedural budgeting* of hierarchical regimes aims at the correct form. Who has the right to do what is as (or more) important than what is done.

Market value autonomy: each unit, ideally, would be responsible for its own budget. Failure is to be unproductive and is punished by competitors bidding resources away. Success is performing well as measured by the productivity standards of the time. Reward is being able to use the gain for new and expanded enterprises, constructing ever-larger networks.

Social orders governed by hierarchical regimes penalize budgeters who disobey the rules (for limits on spending, for assessment of taxes, for transfers among categories). As long as officials allow the required forms, they expect to be protected. Suppose the economic or technical results, despite the good form, are unfortunate: Who pays the penalty? No one or everyone. Insofar as possible, the error will not be recognized, for otherwise procedure might not be accepted as perfect. If error has to be recognized, the blame will be shared throughout the hierarchy as a collective, so no one in particular is responsible, or it will be pinned upon deviants who ostensibly did not do the right thing. The offending parties will be subject to reeducation in the moral desirability of the rules, hopefully strengthening their attachment to the regime. Should that fail, should the offenders prove incorrigible, they will not receive promotion up the ladder and will lose the privileges that go with rank. Where the offender in an equity might be expelled, and in a market lose autonomy to invest resources, the deviant in a budgetary hierarchy suffers the worst fate—he is released from the rules on the grounds that he is out of his head.

When misfortune occurs, adherents of an egalitarian regime blame the system, the coercive hierarchies and inegalitarian markets that oppress the populace. Success is reducing disparities in reward and in status.

AUDITING AS A FUNCTION OF REGIME

Budgetary control requires budgetary information, and the quality of information depends on the degree of uncertainty perceived to be present in the situation. It is not information per se but the part of the budgetary process to which these competing cultures direct their members that is important. Markets and equities assess performance, the former's criterion being productivity of revenue and expenditure, the latter's equal assessment and distribution. Hierarchies are interested in outcomes, but it is not only the substance but the form that concerns them, for they care about maintaining the proper divisions of roles among the participants. Budget rituals, such as the rite of the exchecquer, with its minuet-like moves, reinforce the rightfulness of the regime by encapsulating its principles.

Hierarchies are interested both in budgetary promises (preaudit in modern parlance), so as to assess good legal intentions, and in retrodictions (postaudit), so as to determine whether there has been adherence to rules. Equities, begin collectives, also care about pre- and postaudit but for a quite different purpose: They want assurance that egalitarian purposes and egalitarian results are being obtained. Market regimes could not care less about the past or future but only about present productivity, or the bottom line, as they call it.

Placing a high value on stability, hierarchies are, by their very structure, uncertainty-absorbing mechanisms. Uncertainty exists, of course, since knowledge of the future is woefully limited, but it is absorbed into the division of labor and its accompanying specialization: Each level has to act as if it knew what it was doing. There has to be trust among levels, so each accepts the data provided by the others, provided only it is presented in the right way. Equities exist to oppose hierarchies and markets; they seek, in Marxist jargon, to "unmask" the power relationships underlying the unequal allocation of burdens and benefits.

It is market regimes that specialize in uncertainty. Their members are supposed to take risks in order to reap rewards. But social trust is in short supply. So market regimes accept uncertainty, judging expenditures by the degree to which objectives are achieved. Unlike hierarchies, budgetary procedures in markets are flexible but the demand for productivity is not. "What have you done for me lately?" is its perennial query. Where the equity insists on auditing for equality and the hierarchy on auditing for legality, the anarchy is in perpetual audit for results.

Budgetary boundaries are of three kinds—the total size of the enterprise in regard to the size of the economy, the balance between revenue and expenditure, and the demarcations among sources of income and items of spending. Let us begin with items of spending because the dividing lines are clear, written in, as it were, since mankind first learned to write.

Line-Item, Program, and Zero-Base Budgeting

The most prevalent modern form of expenditure budgeting is called line-item budgeting. Exactly. There are lines with sums attached and these lines separate items specifying the spending involved. The main criticism of this form is that the items are related to organizational needs, such as operations, maintenance, and personnel, rather than the broad purposes the spending is supposed to serve. Precisely. Line-item budgeting is the form par excellence of the hierarchy. The more lines there are, the finer the differentiation among them, the better they mirror the division of labor within the bureaucracy and, by extension, the roles and statuses the society is trying to maintain.

Program budgeting and zero-base budgeting, by contrast, reflect different social orders. By erasing lines of authority in favor of activities supporting broad objectives, program budgeting is designed to facilitate competition. The costs and benefits of alternative programs are arranged, and hopefully the most effective in terms of return is chosen. It is not the mix of resources that matters—any combination is acceptable—but only their effectiveness. Resources have no intrinsic merit, either in themselves or their forms, but only an instrumental value—the rate of return. It is no secret, indeed it is its avowed rationale, that program budgeting is based on economic models embodying market processes. Program budgeting is part of the rationale for a society of competitive individualism (programs compete instead of or in addition to people) whose political manifestation is in the market regime.

Similarly, if a society organized entirely on an egalitarian basis were to choose its form of budgeting, it would have to reject the line-item variety as redolent of hierarchy. Program budgeting would be anathema because it suggests that everything is negotiable through the common currency of market transactions. If an ideal form were devised for equities, it would have to be zero-base budgeting. For one thing, the zero-base approach, taking nothing for granted as if the budget were born yesterday, is perfectly suited for attacking existing relationships. All these, the product of social understandings reached over long periods of time, are, in concept, to be swept away. No base, no carryover of the dead hand of the past imposing its distinctions (read "line items") on the future, no social order. What could be better suited to an equity than a budgetary form presupposing that the world was to be made anew every year?

THE BUDGETARY BASE AS A MANIFESTATION OF SOCIAL ORDER

If a budget both reflects and rationalizes a social order, as I contend, then the boundaries of budgeting should guard that order. This is the significance of the budgetary base, the largest part of the budget, the bulk of which is protected from serious scrutiny, so it remains unchallenged. Inside the base, excepting only small additions or subtractions, all is protected; outside the base, everything is up for grabs. On the stability of the budgetary base, therefore, rests the stability of the political pillars of society. An across-the-board attack on the budgetary base is equivalent to a revolution. Governments, therefore, seek to invest major sources of revenue and items of expenditures with some sort of sanctity. Each source or item becomes a minibudget with its own priorities. Breaching the budget is equivalent to opening up the boundaries of the social contract to renegotiation.

The base is nondiscretionary spending. It is a manifestation of social agreement on essentials. But if that is all there is, no more and no less, budgets would be predetermined. For there to be resource allocation, there must be discretionary income and expenditures, monies that might be raised or spent, or not, depending on circumstances. It is this slack, as resources in excess of immediate needs are called in the organizational literature, that has to be given relative ranking. These increments up or down are the stuff of ordinary budgetary dispute.

There is a regime, however, whose members lack discretionary income, and who, there-fore, do not budget in the ordinary sense of acquiring or allocating resources. In apathetic regimes, the rules are not made by the people but for them. Just as there are no social boundaries for them to maintain, there are no boxes or niches or line items of revenue or expenditure. The culture is fatalistic; the people take what comes. The culture is timeless; there is no marked separation between the days and years, no past or future, only the present. There is no saving, no anticipation of tomorrow. The social experience necessary to make a budget, that is, to periodically relate income to outgo or to divide each into component parts, is missing.

From no real budgeting in apathetic regimes, we move to the flexible budgets of market regimes. Their form is to be formless: Their rule is that all transactions among consenting adults are permissible. The base shifts with the next bargain. Budgetary totals may not shift much, but the programs that make them up do. Programs are in competition. The winners attract more discretionary resources. The budgetary process is extremely flexible—there are only a few general heads of taxing and spending, among which transfers are readily arranged—and experimental—new combinations are continuously being devised and discarded. Budgeting is like riding a roller coaster—fun if you stay on, awful if you fall off.

Boundaries make good budgets, I might say with apologies to Robert Frost, but lack of internal rules does not. Because the division of labor is suspect as elevating some people above others, and specialization is suspect because it suggests that some people know more than others, equities are ambiguous about role performance. Equities are for diminishing past distinctions, so they take on their political color by opposing the inequalities of the existing establishment, the usual alliance of hierarchies and markets. Because accumulation of resources is held suspect, economic development is held down. Thus the demand for equality leads to requirements for redistribution that are difficult to meet. The result is an all-or-nothing approach to budgeting in which no change alternates with radical change.

Hierarchy is the home of the budgetary base. Interaction in society establishes a base that is as well defined as its social structure. There ought to be and there are categories corresponding to a hierarchically organized list of priorities for taxing and spending. Very nice, providing only that social rigidity does not lead to rigor mortis of the budgetary process. Everything is dependent on mechanisms for evaluating revenues and expenditures so as to help make incremental adjustments. Each unit or status resists change. Absent adaptation, the economy runs down. Conflict accumulates. The budget becomes petrified.

When the budgetary base is widely accepted, conflict is limited both because there is an agreed starting point and because the increments are small. When the budgetary base is unacceptable, calculation becomes more complex and conflict rises. This is exactly what has happened in the United States federal government since the late 1970s. The president's budget is treated as "dead on arrival." Dispute immediately ensues over whether the base is last year's spending, the current services budget (the prior year adjusted for price changes), the Senate or House budget resolution, a continuing resolution (last year's ap-propriation plus some special provisions), on and on. Disputes over where to begin exac-erbate those over where to end.

The growing dissensus over the federal budget is not reflected in disagreement over the desirability of budget balance, for everyone claims to want that; rather, the conflict occurs over whether budgets are to be balanced at higher or lower levels of taxing and spending. It is the size of government, involving as this does the kind of government, that is at issue.

BUDGETARY BALANCE

The Micawber principle—it is not the level of income and outgo but their relationship that matters—is essential to budgeting. It is important, therefore, in deriving the form of budgeting in each regime, to ask how expenditure and revenue are related to one another. Which regimes run deficits and surpluses? Which spend more than they take in or take in more than they spend? Which regimes are likely to have what kind of problems—too low revenues, too high expenditure, inability to vary either one?[1]

The potential expenditures and revenues of regimes exhibit a diversity so vast as to be unhandleable, but the number of ways in which governments can manage spending in relation to their management of resources is quite limited. The following possibilities exist:

1. Governments can manage neither their expenditures nor their revenues.
2. Governments can manage their expenditures but not their revenues.
3. Governments can manage their revenues but not their expenditures.
4. Governments can manage both their expenditures and their revenues.

These logical possibilities are drawn on the assumption that governments either can or cannot manage expenditures and revenues. But, of course, these are not all-or-nothing conditions: Government may be able to manage a little or a lot. The significance of these all-or-nothing conditions is that they map out the various extremes that it is possible for governments to attain. There are two different ways in which governments may get the chance to choose: They can choose in one way if they have scope to manage their spending, and they can choose in another way if they have scope to manage their resources. If governments can manage both, they can also manage the overlap. Depending upon how they simultaneously mix increases or decreases in revenue and expenditures, they can vary the size of the balance or imbalance.

There are five strategies for relating revenues and expenditures so that these are kept within hailing distance of one another

1. Do nothing.
2. Decrease spending.
3. Increase revenues.
4. Increase revenues and increase spending.
5. Decrease revenues and decrease spending.

My hypothesis is that the five alternative strategies generated by the ability or inability of governments to manage income and outgo are related to their cultures. Translated into political terms, this means that the essential relationships between revenue and expenditure vary with the kind of regime. Table 1 predicts that fatalists will vary neither revenue nor expenditures. Their life is assumed to be beyond their control. Budget balance is achieved at very low levels.

To understand budgeting by competitive individualists, it is necessary to go from private to public budgeting. In the private sphere, each competes with the other for goods, for credit, and for followers. Competition for resources increases spending. If their investments bear fruit, individualists are able to pay off; if not, competitors take their place. Both revenues and expenditures are high. At the governmental level, however, there is little desire for spending that does not directly benefit a particular entrepreneur. The state is kept poor as ostentation is reserved for rich individuals. Budget control assumes importance insofar

Table 1 Budgetary Strategies Under Political Regimes

Culture: Fatalism	Culture: Collectivism
Regime: Apathy—cannot manage expenditure or revenue	Regime: Hierarchy—can manage revenues but not expenditures
Economic growth: Low	Economic growth: Medium
Strategy: Do nothing	Strategy: Maximize revenue
Balance: Spending equals revenue at low levels	Balance: Spending exceeds revenue at high levels
Culture: Individualism	Culture: Egalitarianism
Regime: Market—can manage both expenditure and revenue at low levels	Regime: Equity—can manage expenditure but not revenue
Economic growth: High	Economic growth: Low
Strategy: Minimize expenditure and revenue	Strategy: Minimize expenditure
Balance: Deficit varies at low levels	Balance: Spending exceeds revenue at low levels

as market regimes spend the minimum amount congruent with providing essential services. Consequently, very low spending is overtaken by even less revenue, so that deficits still arise. But these deficits have a different meaning, for they are revenue-led deficits designed to increase the size of the private sector.

Taxation, which involves getting some people to pay for others, is tricky. Since the benefits are collective but the costs are individual, market regimes find assessment difficult. Each participant has an incentive to pass the burden on to others. That is why market regimes are tempted to use tax farmers, individuals who bid for the right to collect a certain tax. Not only is this method congruent with individualism, but it avoids a direct determination of who should pay how much. Much the same can be said of consumption taxes. Alternatively, market regimes prefer "earmarked revenues" so that there is congruence between the cost and the benefit. For equities, earmarking is outrageous because it limits redistribution. Special funds would be acceptable, however, if they are explicitly devoted to redressing wrongs (to the poor, to nature) by redistribution. Equities obviously prefer steeply graduated income taxes and disfavor consumption taxes as repressive. In the name of equity, of course, they will use any tax. Hierarchies are ambivalent about earmarked taxes because segregation of funds is a principle of demarcation, but a jumble of funds resists central allocation. Hierarchies like all kinds of taxes because they need as much revenues as they can get.

The egalitarian collectives I call equities try to keep personal consumption to a minimum. Wealth is regarded as both a sign and a temptation to inequality. By abjuring wealth, they implicitly criticize the market regimes to which they are opposed and whose wealth they cannot, in any event, match, for equities find accumulation difficult. Lacking internal authority, they cannot make large revenue demands on members. Because accumulation of capital is a source of inequality, it is rejected. Whatever there is soon gets redistributed. Low levels of spending, avoidance of the conspicuous consumption of individualism, or of the public display that goes with hierarchical authority, justifies low levels of revenue.

A hierarchical regime is able to expand its revenues. Collective investment through forced saving enables past commitments to be made good in the future. Taxes, like other rules, are imposed from the top and punctiliously collected. But spending is not as easily controlled. Each role and status within the hierarchy has its prescribed duties, including the kinds of display that are required. New rules limiting display (sumptuary laws, as they are called) are not easily formulated or accepted because they upset prevailing distinctions. It is easier for hierarchies to raise money than to decrease spending. Hence their budgets are unbalanced, with high levels of expenditure being exceeded by even higher revenues.

The careful reader will observe that one of the available budgetary strategies—increase both revenues and expenditure—has not been attributed to any of the four regimes. Perhaps this strategy represents a logical possibility, though not an empirical actuality. But I think not. The reason for the omission is that heretofore I have considered only basic types (primary colors, if you will) and not the hybrid regimes that may be formed among them. In a social democracy composed of hierarchy and equity, for instance, the impulses toward equality of result are strengthened, thus leading to greater redistribution of income by the state. Social democracies, therefore, both tax and spend at maximal levels, thus fitting the fourth budgetary strategy.

How can hierarchies make sure that the public spends its money for collective purposes? How can equities make sure that goods are not used to create invidious distinctions? The solution to this dilemma (there is no telling what people will do with money) is to take it from the populace in cash and give it back in services. In this way the state can determine that income is used for what it considers good causes (the hierarchical preference), and it can also regulate the degree of display (the equity preference). In the seemingly simple act of shopping, for instance, the individual is likely to pay less for certain foods, because they are subsidized; pay more for others, because they are heavily taxed; and to pay a sales tax to boot, so that even experts find it difficult to calculate real prices. It is this sucking in and spitting out of resources that leads to the churning between taxation and expenditure that is so pronounced a feature of the modern welfare state. It might well be cheaper to calculate the gross effects of all these subsidies and sanctions (hence the complaints), but this is to miss the point or, rather, the objective, which is to increase state direction of private spending.

All Western nations are pluralist democracies. In these terms, that means they have elements of the three primary political cultures; they differ in the proportions of each, and it is the differing shapes of these hybrid regimes that create the kinds of imbalances experienced in recent decades. In the United States, as hierarchy becomes even weaker than it has been, the ever-strong market elements combine with a renascent egalitarianism to produce deficits fueled from rising social entitlements (the egalitarian contribution) and lower tax rates (a product of the market mentality). With stronger hierarchical and equitable political regimes—as in Sweden and the Netherlands—and weaker market forces, we find a combination of very high taxation and still higher expenditure. Where market forces are stronger and egalitarian elements weaker and hierarchy is still dominant (as in Germany, England, France, and Japan), spending, though still high, diminishes, and deficits are not quite so large. The difference between the administration of Prime Minister Thatcher and President Reagan, both avowed adherents of market relationships, is that she was also part of a strong hierarchy, interested in balance among the whole and the parts. President Reagan, however, far less restrained by hierarchy, was able to pursue the goal of limited government in a more single-minded manner.

What, if anything, can I predict about budget imbalance in the future from this analysis? First I would have to know what the future balance of power among political cultures will be. This would be tantamount to understanding the sources and operation of social change in the world, and I make no such claim. Rather, mine is an "as, if, and when" theory: When, as, or if various combinations of political cultures appear in the world, I predict patterns of expenditures, revenues, and deficits (rarely surpluses) that will be associated with them.

Balance in budgets depends on balance on society—a proposition in its general import at least as old as Aristotle. The budgets we get depend on the kind of people we are. We people in the Western world would not be experiencing unbalanced budgets unless we preferred political regimes that produce that outcome. If once we had something like balanced budgets and now we do not, this is not due to the conjurer's art (now you see it, now you don't) but because the balance among our ways of life has changed. As individualism has grown weaker and egalitarianism stronger, norms regulating budgetary behavior have been transformed from those justifying balance at low levels of spending to norms that encourage imbalance at higher levels of spending. How we choose to budget and how we like to live are different facets of the same question.

I have posed the question of balanced and unbalanced budgets in a different way: What sorts of people, organized into what ways of life, sharing which values, legitimating which social and political practices, would act as to balance or unbalance their budgets? What combinations of political regimes lead to patterns of taxing and spending that produce (un)balanced budgets? Thus, the focus in budgetary theory changes from the resource position of nations to the ways in which they choose to make use of what they have.

WHY THE RICH MAY BE UNCERTAIN

The spur to cultural analysis was my inability in the first edition of *Budgeting* [4] to account for the coexistence of wealth with uncertainty. Why would nations with high per capita gross national products (GNPs), large amounts of resources, more than enough to get by, and the ability to withstand adversity for long periods of time, end up budgeting like banana republics? Why would these governments fail to fund all or most of their agencies by the end of the fiscal year? Why would their spending budget have to be redone several times a year? Why could agencies no longer count on receiving all the money specified in the budget? This is another way of asking why central control agencies felt it necessary to "claw back" funds previously allocated.

Wealth does provide protection against adversity. Redundancy of resources enables governments to fill in whatever is needed. Wealth is an advantage in gaining greater wealth, as it provides the wherewithal for a diversity of investments, some of which are bound to pay off. But wealth by itself is not certain barrier to its eventual dissipation. Wealth itself does not guarantee it will grow faster than it is used. There is a strong element of preference here that I shall try to tap through political culture.

If market cultures were dominant, they would spend low, tax less, and invest all over the place. If hierarchies were dominant, they would tax high and spend higher, investing enough so that each generation could pay off its promise to the future, that is, to abide by the structured inequalities of the hierarchical way of life so each generation will be better off than the last. Should the typical alliance we call the establishment be formed between hierarchy and markets, the balance between them should assure moderate taxing and spending. Egalitarians, however, combine these tendencies leading to financial instability: (1) high spending in the service of equality of condition, (2) inability to collect revenues due to lack of authority, and (3) rejection of the authority exercised by others. When egalitarianism combines with hierarchy, the balance between them may be stable, the high taxing ability of the one supporting the redistributive proclivities of the other. But as the passion for equality grows, the phenomenon Scandinavians call "the scissors crisis" manifests itself: the rate of expenditure increase exceeds the rate of economic growth even in the best years. It is not the absolute decrease of revenues, however, but the rapid increase in spending, coupled with the resistance to reduction, that is responsible for the growing difficulty of responding to hard economic times. For it is the purpose of existing programs, especially entitlements, to keep individuals stable while government has to scramble to maintain itself. The budgetary instability of Western nations, far from being something imposed by external forces or a product of unfortunate circumstances, is built into the warp and woof of their public policies. Of course, they do not desire the collective consequences of the programs they have so willingly adopted. They do not want, but they may nevertheless get, the formula—the security of the citizen equals the insecurity of the government.

The United States has a little different problem, though the results are similar. It still spends and taxes considerably less than European social democracies. Therefore, it has more room to raise taxes or reduce spending. But the United States lacks one thing the social democracies possess—agreement on spending to support the welfare state. The inability to decide whether to raise taxes or to create a new tax, like the value-added tax, to reduce entitlements, to cut taxes to compel lower spending, or to increase spending and thereby insist on more taxes, leads to a continual stalemate. It is political conflict, not economic decline, that leads to the appearance of repetitive budgeting in the United States federal government.

The great question, I think, is not whether the budget will be balanced but how it will come closer to balance. Will there be a government of high taxes and substantial services or a government of low taxes and fewer services? The deep ideological dissensus that stultifies efforts to choose one or another solution, a conflict between Democratic Party egalitarians and Republican hierarchists and individualists, has made agreement difficult. Why, then, was it possible to agree on deficit reduction amounting to something like $490 billion over 5 years in a law called OBRA (the Omnibus Budget Reconciliation Act of 1990)? The decline of the Cold War made it possible to reduce the defense budget further than in the past. And the replacement of a strong, economically conservative president, Ronald Reagan, with a hierarchically inclined social conservative, George Bush, disposed to compromise, made a big difference. And the desertion of the President by House of Representatives Republicans, dismayed at his disavowal of his "no-new-tax" pledge, made it necessary for the president to rely on Democratic majorities. Hence OBRA has a moderately progressive egalitarian cast.

GROWTH OF GOVERNMENT

The question of why government budgets grow may usefully be decomposed into several smaller queries:

1. Why does government spending in Western democracies grow in small steps or large leaps but hardly ever decline as a proportion of gross national product?

2. Why do government budgets in some nations grow faster than others? Why does the United States "lag behind" yet also gradually increase the size of government? Why do the other "Anglo-Saxon" democracies, such as Canada and Australia, fit the general trend of growth but still spend less than the Western European nations? Why do the Swiss spend so much less proportionately than the Swedes? If there is a "logic of industrialization," why does it not operate equally on all industrial nations?

3. Why is most of the growth of government budgets attributable to programs—pensions, health, education—that contain a significant redistributive component?

The rising proportion of national product spent through governments in the twentieth century, I contend, cannot primarily be explained by growing wealth or industrialization. Nor can it be attributed, as recent authors do, to the political changes that follow from modernization. On the contrary, the very wealth and technological capacity of these countries would make it possible, were they so inclined, to diminish the proportion of state activity in national economies.

Which political cultures (shared values legitimating social practices), I ask, would reject ever-greater governmental growth and which ones would perpetuate it? My hypothesis is that the size of government in any given society is a function (consequence, if you prefer) of its combination of political cultures. This cultural theory also explains the tendencies of political regimes to balance or unbalance their budgets.

The rise of equities, which view government as a force for equality against inegalitarian markets, has impelled the United States part way toward large government. European nations, which share strong hierarchies and moderate to strong egalitarianism, all have stepped up spending, and some (i.e., Sweden and the Netherlands), being more egalitarian, spend more than others (i.e., Switzerland). Canada is in between because while hierarchy remains strong, so do market relationships [5, 6].

An empirical test of this cultural theory I have been propounding would have to include the reverse causal sequences to that postulated by the numerous camp followers of Wagner's law: Increased equality would have to *precede* growth in proportion of public expenditure to national product. The rise of egalitarian regimes would lead to an increased desire for redistribution through government. Soon (say, in a generation) government spending on welfare and in total would rise significantly. Fortunately, Sam Peltzman has provided exactly the kind of test we require. Peltzman's Law, as I will call it, states that "reduced inequality of income stimulates growth of government" [7, p. 263]. The greater the inequality between taxpayers in a prior period, Peltzman contends, the less inclined they are to support redistributive spending in a later period [7, pp. 285–286]. Peltzman's Law may be broadened to say that cultural change precedes and dominates budgetary change: The size of the state today is a function of its political culture yesterday.

If cultural theory is superior to alternatives, expenditure should not merely have increased as a proportion of national product; its most egalitarian components should have gone up far more quickly and the least egalitarian (say, military spending) much more slowly. This, too, has taken place.

Looking at the programs that dominate budgets in Western nations from 1954 to 1980, Richard Rose finds that although the overall increase in the share of national product taken by government was 22%, the growth rates of major programs differed substantially from one another, and only economic infrastructure (i.e., roads and housing) increased at the average rate. Everywhere spending on defense fell as a proportion of national product, whereas income maintenance, education, health, and interest on the debt greatly increased. In the United States, for instance, spending on health rose 213%, whereas defense declined by 59% [8]. Leaving out debt interest (which is a product of increasing deficits), programs concerned with income transfers, health (another form of equalizing income), and education (which tends, though not so strongly, in the same direction) have risen sharply.

Let us remind ourselves of what we wish to explain: (1) the continuous rise of public spending as a proportion of national product among industrial democracies; (2) the resistance to downward movement, that is, the absence of countervailing forces; and (3) despite the applicability of (1) and (2), the large difference in state spending that still separates the United States from other nations. In posing the grand question, I would associate myself with Harley Hinrichs's formulation (except that today his upper bound might well be doubled):

> A complex democratic industrialized state could function with a public sector, say, between 20 and 40 percent. The point where it settles within (or above) this range is most likely to be determined not by structural needs (which would demand, say only 20 percent) but by ideological commitments, toward a "welfare state" and/or toward the "security and defense" of an existing ideological system. [9, pp. 9–10]

Since up to the present, "welfare" continues to dominate "warfare" spending in the democracies by more than two to one, it is to their "ideological systems," their values and practices, that I would look for explanations of the growth of government.

Spending could have increased absolutely by following the trend rate of increase in national product. Some programs could have gone beyond the rate if others were reduced by a similar amount. But that did not happen. More for one major program did not signify less for another. More for all is possible only if economic growth rises at the same rate, which did not happen, or if an implicit choice is made, not merely once but repeatedly, to increase the share government takes of national product. When movement toward equality of result is at stake—as in income maintenance, health, and education—one major program may be favored more than another, but all rise absolutely and relatively in regard to proportion of national income. It is this trend toward equalization—a steady increase in spending for redistributive programs—that is best explained by a cultural hypothesis.

Why has budgetary control in the West collapsed? The obvious answer—because governments and their constituents want to spend more—should not be ignored. On what do they want to spend? Largely, on egalitarian measures. We have come full circle in explaining the consequences of the rise of regimes favoring that budgetary outcome. The tendencies of political regimes to tax and spend in different ways are summarized in Table 2.

BRINGING PREFERENCES BACK INTO BUDGETING

My aim has been to bring together various strands of thought about the relationship between cultures and budgets, expressed at different times and places [4, 10–13], into a single essay. I would like to end by stating what I conceive to be the advantages of taking a cultural approach to budgeting. First, a word about what cultural theory is not.

Cultural theory is not about the influence of ideas alone. Ideas are not disembodied, free to float anywhere, discarded like an old coat, any more than different arrays of taxes and expenditures may be rearranged at will. Always ideas are attached to the different kinds of social relations they justify, modify, or attack. Nor is this a theory of social determination in which a place in the social structure fixes one's position on budgets. Always, diverse sets of social relations are attached to ideas that legitimate or undermine them. No explanation, no legitimacy.

Cultural theory is a theory of multiequilibria; it does not provide optimum solutions. The reason is that the theory tells us in what sorts of direction adherents of a particular culture will want to go, say, toward greater or lesser equality. It does not tell us what instruments of policy, under the historical circumstances being studied, lead adherents of a particular culture to want to do. If egalitarians in the early days of the American republic thought that the central government was a source of inequality, and therefore wanted to limit it severely, and their spiritual (I should say, cultural) successors, liberal Democrats,

Table 2 Budgeting in Political Regimes

	Culture		
	Individualism	Egalitarianism	Collectivism
Structure	Self-regulation	Voluntarism	Authority
Trust	Low	Low	High
Equality of	Opportunity	Result	Law
Roles	Shifting	Ambiguous	Clear
Economic growth	High	Low	Medium
Regime	Market	Equity	Hierarchy
Power	Noncentralized	Shared	Centralized
Authority	Avoided	Rejected	Accepted
Blame	Internalized	Externalized (hidden hierarchies)	Collectivized (the system)
The good citizen	Competes	Reduces distinctions	Maintains distinctions
Private vs. public sectors	Minimal public, maximal private	Moderate public, minimal private	Maximal public, minimal private
Taxes	Very low	Very high	High
Collection	Low	Low	High
Process			
Criterion	Productivity	Redistribution	Procedural
Agreement on base	High on totals, low on items	Low on totals and items	High on totals and items
Procedures	Flexible	Rigid	Rigid
Spending	Low	Low	High
Responsibility	By program	By system	By position
Accounting	Results	Preaudit	Postaudit
Form	Program budgeting	Zero-base budgeting	Line-item budgeting

want to use the central government to decrease inequality, they are both egalitarians but life has taught them different lessons.

Cultural theory is about how individuals who identify with rival cultures (sets of social relations and their accompanying rationalizations) seek to strengthen their preferred ways of life (assuming, of course, they have a choice) and to weaken others. Cultural theory, as I conceive it, is a form of functionalism, but the functions are performed for cultures not for societies.

The advantage of a cultural theory of budgeting is that it relates resource accumulation and resource allocation to many other aspects of life. Especially important is bringing people's preferences for the good life into budgeting. Thus we can hopefully give a more satisfactory answer to the perennial question of what difference it makes which way budgeting is carried on. For rational choice theorists, there is a suggestion: in addition to whatever participants are trying to get due to their local circumstances, they are also trying to act in a way that is globally rational, that is, to defend their way of life. Thus it is not sufficient to say that everyone is motivated by self-interest, because adherents of different ways of life define self-interest differently. Because cultural theory connects preferred ways of life to budgetary behavior, moreover, we are able to generate many falsifiable propositions. Cultural theory, in short, is a way to bring what different people want and why they want it into budgeting.

NOTE

1. This section is adopted from joint work with Michael Thompson.

REFERENCES

1. M. Douglas, "Environments at Risk," *Implicit Meanings*, Routledge & Kegan Paul, London, pp. 230–248 (1975).
2. M. Thompson, R. Ellis, and A. Wildavsky, *Cultural Theory*, Westview Press, Boulder, Colo. (1990).
3. M. Douglas, "Cultural Bias," *In the Active Voice*, Routledge & Kegan Paul, London, pp. 183–254 (1982).
4. A. Wildavsky, *Budgeting: A Comparative Theory of Budgetary Processes*, Transaction Books, New Brunswick, N.J. (1986).
5. R. T. Kudrle and T. Marmor, "The Development of Welfare States in North America," (P. Flora and A. J. Heidenheimer, eds.), Transaction Books, New Brunswick, N.J., pp. 81–121 (1981).
6. S. M. Lipset, *Agrarian Socialism: The Cooperative Commonwealth Federation in Saskatchewan*, Anchor Books, Garden City, N.Y. (1968).
7. S. Peltzman, "The Growth of Government," *J. Law Econ.*, *23*: 209–287 (1980).
8. R. Rose, "The Programme Approach to the Growth of Government," *Br. J. Polit. Sci.*, *15*: 1–28 (1985).
9. H. H. Hinrichs, *A General Theory of Tax Structure Change During Economic Development*, Harvard University Press, Cambridge, Mass. (1966).
10. A. Wildavsky, "The Budget as New Social Contract," *J. Contemp. Studies*, *5*: 3–19 (1982).
11. A. Wildavsky, "Budgets as Social Orders," *Res. Urban Policy*, *1*: 183–197 (1985).
12. A. Wildavsky, "A Cultural Theory of Expenditure Growth and (Un)Balanced Budgets," *J. Public Econ.*, *28*: 349–357 (1985).
13. A. Wildavsky, "The Logic of Public Sector Growth," *State and Market* (J. E. Lane, ed.), Sage, London, pp. 231–270 (1985).

12

Comparative Government Budgeting

George M. Guess
Development Alternatives, Inc., Bethesda, Maryland

INTRODUCTION

Over the last two decades, as part of major efforts to improve governance in particular regions of the globe, we have witnessed an outpouring of applied work, technical assistance, and training in the broad field of public financial management. These efforts have led to a broad consensus on what works and what does not to improve budgetary processes and fiscal management. The accumulation of such experience could not have occurred without the support of international donors, university research offices, international research and exchange programs, and the willingness of host country, often ministry of finance, officials to reveal problems and take personal risks in applying new solutions.

This chapter reviews some of these experiences and suggests new avenues for future work. It is divided into three sections. The first section examines the rationale for public budgeting assistance in improved "governance." As now commonly used, this is a general term that combines administrative and political considerations of the executive and legislative branches. The role of government is not just an ideological issue. At some point the scope and size of government must correspond to fiscal policy realities. The efficacy of government is inextricably linked to its capacity to formulate and implement budgets, and to allocate resources to programs that serve its development objectives. The second section reviews some of the major problems in the transfer of public financial management tools and techniques abroad. For instance, many of the concepts and systems do not travel well. They are plagued by terminological confusion and the tendency in practice to transfer them in isolation.

The last section reviews experiences in applying available financial management tools and techniques. Conditions must be ripe for transfer of public budgeting tools and systems from one region to another. Perhaps recent challenges in the transitional economies of Eastern Europe have brought home the earlier failures to consider context and culture in Latin America and Africa. In dealing with Eastern European problems similar to those in Latin America, it is clear that the systems can and must be made adaptable to local values and habits. This means targeting assistance to the right level of the organization and the right function. It is also clear that many of the fundamental problems of planning and budgeting across regions are similar despite apparent differences. This raises the issue of which systems are appropriate. Finally, successful selection and transfer of comparable tools and systems requires attention to differences in political culture. This is a much-maligned concept that in reality still intrudes between problem and solution.

USE OF THE COMPARATIVE METHOD FOR PUBLIC BUDGETING

Comparative budgeting issues have been raised with increasing frequency by scholars and practitioners. The need for tested models and systems have never been greater than at present. This is a major change from the past when comparative budgeting was largely an outgrowth of comparative politics, an academic field questing for theory. In this initial phase, skepticism was voiced over the relevance of applications to host country contexts [1, 2]. The collapse of the Soviet Union unintentionally created a new market for tested solutions in the field of public financial management. Transition to Western-style economic management required governmental policymaking strength, the foundation of which is the financial management system. This major political event also challenged many of the solutions proposed in the past, perhaps because they and the rest of public administration systems were never viewed as life or death matters to society. Whether Honduras managed its fiscal affairs was always important. But revelations of total financial chaos only meant that donors would have to throw in more funds to cover earlier investments. It was not a matter of whole-systems transformation and the need to build Western public fiscal systems out of the wreckage of conceptually different systems. It is now evident that for many of the transitional societies, the ability to politically survive will depend upon delivering goods and services (especially social benefits), which will require immediate reforms in public finance and public sector management systems. Eventually, this will require tested, falsified and modified propositions on comparative public budgeting.

Much of the "comparative" work in budgeting has in fact been case study analysis based on unrepresentative interviews and time-series data of often limited reliability and validity. This is hardly unexpected given the difficulty of gaining access to data, or generating new sets (in the case of transitional societies). The good case studies [see Ref. 3] produced are still only case studies. The inability to test the impact of budgetary tools in different conditions and at the margins has been largely due to the action nature of much of this work: short-term missions from international donors to solve obvious problems of expenditure control and fiscal deficit. For example, Wildavsky and Jones [4] offered norms and rules from the U.S. experience to assist budgeting at the European Union. A major finding from their study is that "command and control" rules fail to "incentivate" managers to achieve expenditure control [4, p. 10]. Such studies are valuable in that they link institutional behavior and power variables to budgetary process. But in most cases, there has not been much incentive to move from immersion in the particular to generalized hypotheses about institutions or system performance. Nor do such studies falsify existing findings in any systematic way (command and control works under the following conditions . . .). The interest has largely been to put out fires with a few tools at hands and to move onto the next problem.

The "comparative" component of most budgetary field work remains at the preliminary stage of applying the correct tool(s). This does not mean that it is "soft" or ad hoc work. Zola once described his literary comparative method in speaking of the woes and fatalities of the French miners: "to get the broad effect, I must have my two sides as clearly contrasted as possible and carried to the extreme of intensity" [5, p. 5]. This is comparison for effect. What we refer to here is selection of the appropriate financial management tools derived from different contexts. Ideally, this should be based on formal research and analysis. Instead, it is based on nuts-and-bolts applications and experiences of success and failure handed down through meetings and memos. Much technical assistance in this area is even called "budget plumbing" by the World Bank.

In short, most of the work so far is not formal in the sense of applying the comparative method to empirically identify and measure the impact of exogenous variables [6, p. 42]. Formal work can be done by falsification of comparative explanatory propositions by specification of those generic attributes of the system that cause it to be an exception to proposed theory [6, p. 46]. Or it may build theory by formal addition of variables through incremental analyses to account for deviant cases. For instance, despite general consensus against earmarking and for budgetary flexibility to manage programs in the West, 80% of the Swiss annual budget is mandated by law and the budget is extremely inflexible [7, p. 30]. The Swiss still achieve admirable control over fiscal deficits and annual expenditures. If this deviant case can be explained by interagency mutual respect and competence, what does this case suggest for exceptions to the general findings of good budgetary practice?

Further, in public budgeting, formal research means measuring the impact of institutional variables and budget systems on such dependent variables as expenditure control or performance and fiscal deficits. The attribution of fiscal deficits to institutional and process problems is obviously much more difficult than linkage to specific failures of tools such as cash management and accounting systems reports. Much of the "knowledge" gained so far has been through incremental additions by mission work compiling case studies of tool performance.

So, for example, we know that value for money reforms work only with accounting support and institutional incentives. But the kinds of incentives and accounting systems that work under particular country conditions have not been specified. We know also that devolution of authority to line managers for funds provided in broad line items and for which they are accountable for program targets "incentivates" managers and makes the budget a realistic tool of management. This works in Australia and New Zealand. But what are the conditions under which this "budgetment" system is transferable? We know that in the new transitional economies, techniques such as cash limits, have worked to achieve macro fiscal targets (mostly from IMF). But what have been the micro costs to programs of these successes? What kind of forecasting capacity is required before cash limits function other than to crudely turn off the funding spigot, producing long-term arrears to suppliers and other downstream costs? How can cash limits be designed to serve both micro program objectives and the attainment of macro limits? In the area of budget support, we know that commitment accounting systems are essential to ensure proper reporting of budget execution and to prevent expenditure overruns. But what kind of monitoring is included to ensure that the formal systems will be used by personnel in line ministries? In short, much of the knowledge we have in this field is broadly conceived, untested, and unlinked to institutional contexts in a systematic way. In much of the comparative budget literature, the problems are treated as mere opportunities for diffusion of Western systems and skills. The field has a decidedly technocratic air despite evidence that operational glue is needed to bind systems with which country hosts are intimately familiar (usually from other consultants) with institutional roles and systems that are not. For example, bureaucracy in transitional socialist systems was a largely passive affair, and budgeting simply reflected administration of the physical plan. Financial management was not a major consideration in policymaking or implementation. Public budgeting has had to be introduced from scratch, relying heavily upon the considerable existing accounting and statistical skills exercised by officials in these systems. Despite weaknesses in selection of tools, and major obstacles to reform, the effects of past and ongoing international transfer of public budgeting and finance seem to have been generally positive. Those countries adopting recommended budget tools and systems have been able to improve their fiscal policy performance.

BUDGETING AND GOVERNANCE

The field of comparative budgeting is guided by the working premise that the allocation of public resources affects policy results. Progress toward socioeconomic development can often be traced to how many and how well resources are allocated between sectors (primary health care vs. defense) and within sectors (roads vs. rail transport; construction vs. maintenance). In principle, budgeting facilitates this by providing the singular opportunity to analyze results and attach price tags to public programs. The budgetary component of the policy process permits consideration of trade-offs for the purpose of expenditure control, management efficiency, and planning effectiveness. In reality, project and program failures are regularly strewn about the developing and transitional world. They are characterized not just by the favorite observation of excessive "politics." All public undertakings involve disagreements, and the only question is whether institutions can structure the conflict into decisions that are acceptable. What we find instead are more specific problems, like weak management controls, underfunding, improperly designed projects, and institutional disincentives for proper performance that lead to overruns. The budget process itself in many cases impedes fiscal and policy performance. This means that more resources provided to governments would often be wasted without changes in the process that allocates them.

Financial problems of scarcity and misallocation then reflect general failures of governance and public sector management. Public budgeting cannot by itself reform government, make public policy, or change public administration. But budget processes are the foundation for all such reforms. The budgetary process determines expenditure allocations and guides program implementation during a fiscal year [8, p. 9]. Budgeting is the central incentive structure for the global financial management system. Governance failures often can be traced to the more common problems of financial management. These can be divided into issues of (1) analytic methods, (2) organizational levels, and (3) resource allocation stages. The problem might be in the method of budget formulation or payroll cutback. Formulation may discourage expenditure analysis; personnel cutbacks can lead to short-term savings at the cost of needed corporate experience and morale. Or, allocation of institutional authority might be such that budgetary issues are handled by inappropriate levels. Senior staff time might be consistently wasted on daily operational matters like timesheets instead of engaging in strategic planning and oversight of management control systems. More commonly, operational people might have authority to impede management efficiency and inhibit the attainment of strategic plans. Allocating division of labor is critical to avoid building in the wrong incentives. This requires devoting resources to the design and implementation of a management control system that integrates planning, budgeting, accounting and evaluation [9]. Finally, failure to engage in real expenditure planning can push budgeting into the implementation phase when plans should be executed and evaluations should be fed back into the formulation phase. Much of public budgeting in the developing world occurs (wrongly) during the implementation phase. Very little actual planning and analysis of priorities actually occurs as scheduled. Predictably under these conditions, implementation is haphazard and costly. Budgets are not really modified—they are created and remade during the year by a system that favors short-term planning decisions (termed "repetitive budgeting" or "disappearing budgets" by Caiden and Wildavsky [10]).

One nagging question at this point in the story is, with such an obvious link between budgeting, policy results and governance, why has it taken so long to work up solutions? Comparative budgeting has passed through three historical phases, and it may be useful to review them briefly. In the first phase, dating roughly from the 1960s to the 1970s, interest centered on development planning at the national or sectoral levels (e.g. agricultural development). Despite the early observations of LaPalombara [11, 12], field work ignored institutional issues of budgeting and civil service performance of particular tasks and functions. Public budgeting courses heavily emphasized investment planning through quantitative techniques such as benefit-cost analysis. Such techniques as planning, programming, and budgeting (PPBS) were expected to rationalize the current budget and make services efficient and effective both in the United States and elsewhere. Foreign assistance stressed planning techniques; public administration programs focused on formal-legal structures, and debates continued over the meaning of such terms as development and modernization [13]. More innovative thinkers such as Hirschman [14] worked on improving development project performance by focusing on micro institutional distortions in the local environment, including processes of allocating project funds.

In the mid-1970s, scholars began to link financial management problems with general failures of governance and of foreign assistance funding processes. The classic text in this field by Caiden and Wildavsky [10] pointed to institutional problems that caused fiscal uncertainty and meaningless budgets. The U.S. General Accounting Office (GAO) [15] noted the cause-and-effect linkage between weak financial management capacity of host governments and the repeated failure of foreign aid programs. About this time, USAID began a financial management reform project in Latin America focusing on the core areas of accounting, auditing, purchasing, treasury management, cash management, and budgeting. The goal was to integrate these functions into one system with budgeting as simply one of several functions. A problem here that surfaced in later projects was the tendency to ignore the central power function of budget offices in controlling not only formulation but implementation as well. Budgeting in practice does not end after the document is approved but continues throughout the year. Nevertheless, before budgeting can perform this central guidance function, financial management system must be linked together. An emphasis on broader financial management is necessary for this purpose. Functions and offices must be wired together and information must be compatible and useful. In many countries, such as Honduras, virtually none of the core functional offices exchange information within the ministry of finance (SHCP) [16]. In the District of Columbia, 80 agencies are fed by 6 streams of funds, which overwhelm absorptive capacity under the best of circumstances. In other cases, managers use the slippage to bypass systems for purchasing and payments. They cannot enter commitments into the overloaded computer system, and thus available revenues still exist in the budget and deficit is hidden. Similarly, the personnel system is separated from payroll, which allows extra employees to be entered into the system and paid before it becomes clear that departments have exceeded budgeted payrolls [17]. In short, in many governments, financial management system are not integrated.

The current stage of comparative budgeting began around 1990 and might be termed the emphasis on "public expenditure management". The focus here by agencies such as the International Monetary Fund's Fiscal Affairs Department and the various public sector management units within the World Bank has been on strengthening the institutions involved in budgeting to prevent them from diminishing the intended benefits of public expenditure. This involves improvements in such basics as budget coverage and classification, expenditure control devices, cash forecasting and management systems, linkages between treasury and central bank systems, and program evaluation capacity. Public expenditure management also links into civil service reform via the payroll function and the need to budget for efficient and effective personnel performance. Technical assistance and training missions have drawn upon materials and systems from around the world to improve expenditure management practices. The efficacy of results often depends upon proper selection of tools and systems for the particular context. It also depends upon the skill of experts in combining flexibility and patience with opportunities for knowledge transfer. More than a few missions have been derailed by the arrogance and impatience of international experts in host countries.

Two forces combined to focus interest in the 1990s on public expenditure management. First, widespread interest in democratization encouraged devolution of authority to autonomous municipal governments as counterweights to the centralized governments of the past, and in holding regularly scheduled elections to transfer power from traditional national level ruling elites to accountable elected officials. Transition from centrally planned systems to democracies leads to a demand for greater accountability, and this requires a transparent financial management system. The problem, of course, is that many local governments lacked capacity to raise revenues, design programs responsive to local citizens, and to manage them effectively [18, p. 11]. At the same time, the opposite danger had to be avoided of enfeebling governments with too many interest groups in the name of creating accountability and responsiveness. Second, widespread constituencies exist in many countries for scaling back the role and size of governments. In part, support derives from the realization that contracting-out and privatization of services can save public funds that, and that with retention of proper governmental monitoring authority, such strategies can ensure similar or even improved service delivery. The driving force is resource scarcity, born of real aversion to taxes and ostensible revulsion against fiscal deficits. The positive thrust of this movement could translate into systems that ensure hard review of budget proposals. Under these conditions, governments will have to work to make existing services operate better with fewer resources available. This will require improved financial management.

PROBLEMS IN TRANSFER OF PUBLIC BUDGETING SYSTEMS AND SKILLS

Prior to specific discussion of the tools and systems themselves, several historical problems in transferring them should be noted. There are four main difficulties that suggest strongly that just as host country budget processes determine much of its own outcome, the process of aid transfer largely determines the operational success of its tool and systems. Put another way, the problems of exchanging and adapting cross-border budgetary tools may have less to do with selection of inappropriate systems that are rejected by the host country than with individualized working repertoires of consultants, and the institutional rules and processes which transfer them overseas.

Transfer of financial management tools is often fragmented. Acting on scopes of work drawn up by aid missions, field experts bring isolated tools in public budgeting, personnel administration, and intergovernmental fiscal transfers. While they may be related to larger project frameworks, in the ministry or department, it is often unclear how these tools fit together to improve public sector operations. For instance, budgeting, program evaluation, and public management remain separate areas despite the need for integration in practice [19, p. 54–55]. Central governments are slated for installation of new fiscal transfer systems that rely on formulae and performance incentives. But they are often weakly linked to actual local government operations. Current efforts focus on "reinvention" of governments through cutbacks and redirection of incentives for improved performance. But field experts offer only isolated methods (if at all) to put this strategy into practice. Needed are methods to (1) review essential functions that should be performed by government first, (2) clarify roles and chains of command to coordinate activities, (3) create or strengthen particular management information systems, and (4) develop the necessary skills to administer public sector reform.

Tools are often not adapted to existing local reform strategies. This is not a reference to the subtleties of political culture or even to use of the wrong tools. Experts often simply forget that old governance systems persist. The attempt to transfer in public budgeting tools is often just the latest in a long line of reforms, many of which have not been fully implemented. The layers of reform in many countries could stimulate development of a political archeology discipline. Experts often have a difficult time sorting them out, especially in reviewing local laws and regulations. For instance, many governments are still implementing planning, programming, and budgeting systems when the lessons are clear that frozen program categories actually impede analysis and have never penetrated legislative appropriation routines. Nevertheless, old budget laws and even constitutions of particular Latin American countries still require program budgets. Needed are methods that adapt existing structures, such as program accounting systems, to new systems of service-level and results-oriented budgeting. Comparative budgeting work has not been effective at designing incentives to get rid of or to adapt old systems to new ones. Needed also are means of stimulating local thinking with new models that combine public management incentives, forward expenditure planning, and decentralized ministry controls, such as in Australia and New Zealand. At the same time, experts need to specify the institutional preconditions for the successful operation of such models abroad. In many developing countries, the preconditions do not yet exist.

Third, the specialized jargon of public budgeting has often been challenged for its terminological confusion and abstruseness. A recent edition of the *Washington Post* spelled "rescission" three different ways. Current budgets are made in current terms. Encumbrances, commitments, and obligations are often used interchangeably, even though their meaning may differ slightly between levels of government. Apportionments are often used to mean allotments and vice versa. But use of this language has actually become dangerous now that it clashes with the old jargon of central planning. Host-country people are confused by the jargon and the legions of different consultants using different terms to describe the same concept. For instance, the World Bank's budget "norms" referred to quantitative benchmarks against which expenditures for operations and maintenance could be compared. Budget "norms" under central planning were physical output mandates unlinked to cost. "Payments" systems differ in the French, Spanish, and United Kingdom contexts according to stage. Use of the term "payment" may be referring to the request, commitments, verification, or actual payment stage. This creates confusion.

Expenditure "planning" and macroeconomic "planning" terms have caused a lot of trouble in Eastern Europe and the former Soviet Union. Planning in the Western notion is use of forecasting techniques to predict the behavior of costs and benefits subject to specified variables. The purpose is to adjust budgets and plans to meet targets. In many cases, planning leads to rejection of projects altogether. Western planning is some combination of expert judgment and formal technique. Under socialism, planning meant placement of physical structures according to nonfinancial "scientific" criteria that often boiled down to elite preferences. Planning was viewed as the privilege of the nomenklatura and elite members of the planning ministry. Plans directed budgeting, and the budget was simply a passive, formal exercise to finance the plan. In the West, the budget process actively feeds into planning of both current services and capital projects. For instance, the DAI public administration project in Poland, initiated in 1995 and funded by USAID, proposed a new financial management system to strengthen fiscal policymaking and implementation. Despite elaborate clarifications both in the proposal and during the assessment team visit to the country, members of the Polish Council of Ministers interpreted this to mean central planning revisited. The U.S. Embassy in Warsaw viewed this component to be excessively radical, and too politically hot for a public administration project. The result: The project now quietly focuses on local government training and reform. If possible under these conditions, experts need to clarify existing use of budgetary and financial terms before introducing new ones.

Finally, training and technical assistance itself may be resisted by local officials. Under central planning, training was viewed as a form of brainwashing to produce ideological correctness. Experienced nomenklatura scoff at the "greenhorn" preservice graduates entering government with their new Western concepts. Trainers often take offense and arrogantly push ahead despite the belief by officials that they already know what they are hearing. In the process of implementing the current USAID-funded DAI public administration project targeting five Estonian cities, this has been a problem so far in conducting effective public budgeting training. The irony is that officials under central planning systems did in fact gain considerable experience in use of statistical and accounting data. In a World Bank training session in Bulgaria, trainees refused to believe that they already knew about unit cost measurement of services until it was spelled out for them. Such training revealed that Bulgarian officials were actually far ahead of developing country officials and need only to learn more about Western cost concepts to strengthen their capacities. But in other contexts, trainers often refuse to admit that trainees already know the materials. Thus, needed are training exercises and methods that reveal the limitations of nonfinancial budgeting and planning. Western experts can contribute here by developing action-forcing cases, simulations, and innovative exercises from their technical assistance experiences in host countries.

THE EFFECTS OF POLITICAL CULTURE ON BUDGETING

The question of culture comes into the equation to the extent that there must be an adjustment between local values, attitudes, and customs and the tools and training techniques to be transferred. Important questions for the field expert include: How can relevant features of political culture be maximized to serve local budgeting (e.g., experience with statistics and accounting data for central planning)? Conversely, how can unwanted behavioral elements be modified to make systems efficient and effective? More commonly mentioned negative features include interpersonal distrust at official levels, and command and control public management styles. The broader comparative issue is whether the solutions from Western cultural systems are applicable to non-Western systems.

Answers will often turn on whether one believes the driving force of culture to be values and attitudes (anthropology/sociology) or political and economic institutions (economists and political scientists). The first perspective often leads into a trap. For instance, the question of whether a cultural practice is "productive" or "unproductive" turns on how much one values it and its mutability. Anthropologists tend to reify local values and attitudes despite evidence that they are often unproductive and even uncivilized. Values and attitudes in India, for instance, become manifest in the caste system, which often impedes operation of efficient hierarchy for public management. Can such attitudes and behavior be changed? How is it unproductive? Is this cultural behavior, or something else? One of the definitional problems of culture is that if clusters of values and attitudes constitute culture, this means that culture varies by culture, leading into tautology and the use of a content-free explanatory concept. Are we talking about the effects of cultures, history, or simply idiosyncratic behavior that has been mislabeled as culture?

By contrast, the political economist views culture (and we agree) as matrices of incentives and stimuli to which people predictably respond. By this perspective, Americans do not culturally overconsume gas but simply respond to long-standing gas policies that ensure cheap pump prices. This perspective suggests that persistent, short-term systemic changes can produce deep cultural values that reinforce systems and further deepen cultures. Cultures are variables, not constants. For instance the strength of existing Costa Rican democratic participation and tolerance is largely explicable by incremental reinforcement of institutional changes that began with the so-called "revolution" of 1948. Despite the surface plausibility of what has been said, political scientists are extremely skeptical of the explanatory value of this concept. It has been recently criticized for its failure to deliver—for inability to specify mechanisms linking culture to structure, and for including ever more lines of causal influence, rather than specifying more precisely the parameters of a cultural model of politics [20, p. 168]. The political economy perspective on culture has also been criticized for simple overdetermination. For example, a recent study concluded that modern German federalism and low birth rates are products of centralized Nazi rule, which is a bit far-fetched [21].

However, viewed as a response to institutional forces, political culture can be useful in explaining such budgetary problems as lack of analysis, and resistance to devolution of authority to line managers. Analysis of programs and expenditure items is important for good budgeting in any system. To the extent that cultural features can be linked in as a determinant of constructive criticism, the concept can be said to have explanatory power. For example, Cash [22] traces the general taboo of the U.S. South on general criticism to the lack of systemic complexity born of the plantation system, its associated indifference to public education systems, and predictable features of rural religious literalism. Lack of analysis and rigid conformity were cultural features of simple and static political and economic structures that began in the antebellum era and were not radically modified afterward. Based on the needs of this simple system, there was no need for government beyond the plantation. The needs of the plantation system conditioned behavior, silenced critics, and restricted the reach of government services. Blocked by customs of individual posturing that rewarded rhetorical flourish and unreal oratory (storytelling), frontier political institutions, and in particular, budget processes did not function to raise open conflicts over expenditure priorities to the agenda or to resolve them. By this thesis, a charming but authoritarian Southern culture would explain the rigidity and lack of incentives for constructive criticism in contemporary public budgeting. Such uses of political culture are largely hypothetical and have not been tested empirically. More empirical uses have been made of the concept to explain U.S. state expenditures in various policy arenas [23, 24].

Further, use of political culture can help explain lack of decentralization and management discretion in many developing countries. Centralization of power is reflected in budget priorities of ruling elites and retention of administrative controls at the center. At the same time, it is often puzzling when fiscal decentralization occurs under authoritarian regimes instead of previously elected democratic governments, such as in Chile [18, p. 11]. It is also well known that decentralization to local elites may not improve program performance or service delivery. It is recognized that some functions, such as purchasing and payments, may need to remain centralized to ensure against waste and fraud by localities incapable of expenditure control. Countries that have engaged in major fiscal decentralization, such as Brazil, have had major problems controlling commitments made by state and local units for which the national treasury has been responsible. Fiscal deficits have soared. But the general trend is against command and control from the capital city and toward delivery of more efficient service delivery with fewer resources. Expenditure controls can be applied to prevent abuse by local units. But in the administrative structures of West Asia and much of Latin America, long-standing formalistic practices, reinforced by caste and disciplinary measures, have solidified into authoritarian cultures that have had little effect on local fiscal abuse.

Control measures must be designed to be consistent with administrative cultures. The technicalities of designing control systems must ensure correspondence with the key figure to sustaining proper organizational cultures: the leader. The norms, rules, and styles of the organizational leader need to be reflected in the structure, human resource management systems, management styles and fiscal control systems. Ensuring this consistency allows the organizational culture to serve as a counterforce to parochial interests [25, p. 680]. In many cases, ignoring the values of leadership and parochial interests through simple command and control dictates from the center is self-defeating. It can be said that often the threat of control imposition is more effective than actual use of them to interfere with local affairs [4, p. 9].

Some centralized cultures are perceptibly thick, with highly formalistic, top-down relationships. Managers exercise authority in peremptory, almost rude style. Underlings are berated in public and occasionally flogged for minor indiscretions. Chains of command are rigid, and authority lies only with senior officials. In Nepal, for instance, an administrative practice described as *tippani* moves files endlessly between desks, up and down the hierarchy for months and even years for receipt of signatures. Use of forms with multiple signature blanks reinforces diffusion of responsibility and ensures delay. This is an elaborate delay tactic since in few cases are there final signatures. Senior officials (elite lords) control most decisions and delegate authority for only the most minor transactions to midlevel staff [26, p.6]. Similarly, Latin American and Eastern European midlevel staff have little authority to even make minor transfers of budget funds between items (*traspasos*) without approvals from senior officials [27]. Even systems that provide strong controls from the Ministry of Finance and Parliament give only limited flexibility in redeploying resources across categories to respond to changing needs and prices [28, p. 92]. Political culture thus limits installation of more modern performance-based systems, where output standards are clearly set and managers are allowed to reallocate resources within their total budgets to attain these performance goals. In short, as endlessly repeated by the development literature over the last thirty years, systems and skills need to be designed with extreme sensitivity to local values and attitudes.

Ultimately, the question of the degree of mutability of a political culture is critical for technical assistance in the budget field. As noted, anthropologists tend to find that values, attitudes, and habits are functional, rational, and changeable only to the detriment of indigenous peoples. As applied to public administration and budgeting, this would suggest that work habits and values take years to change. The more optimistic or perhaps naive public administration specialists believe and have found that work habits and administrative practices that have persisted for 50 years can in fact be changed by management in the short term. As noted by Thurmaier [29, p. 84], for example, Polish *gmina* councils are "beginning to see the potential for using the budget as a policy and management tool. The evolutionary transformation of budgeting, which took 50 years in the U.S., may take only five years in

Poland." This confirms the thesis that cultural practices that have arrested state development and impeded public sector performance can be changed by self-correction and adoption of modern public administration norms [30]. More importantly, systems that reinforce the negative features of existing cultures (e.g., rigid program structures and legalistic internal controls enforced through reporting requirements to the central government) should be avoided. Reforms should be designed with existing norms and practices in mind, and managers should work to maximize positive features of local cultures.

PUBLIC EXPENDITURE PROBLEMS AND AVAILABLE SOLUTIONS

We turn now to the actual field problems in public budgeting and finance and attempts to import solutions to them from other systems. As indicated, in many cases this is an informal selection process. An IMF mission to Costa Rica might be staffed with Spanish experts who would then recommend many of the features of the Spanish public financial management system. This is not the policy of IMF. Nor is it the collective intention of the mission in many cases. It simply works out that way because its members judge that these solutions will best meet the problems at hand. Where missions are composed of multiple nationalities, debate can arise over the best available methods and systems (e.g., French vs. United Kingdom treasury management system), and this may confuse local officials. If the mission is from a bilateral donor such as USAID, there is a high probability that recommended systems will be from some level of the U.S. federal system (usually local or county). Thus, field experts do not go in armed with the results of any comparative budgetary research, but rather rely upon their instincts and best judgments from past work. Some of these have been flawed, it must be admitted, precisely because their experiences has been parochial. For example, I once served on a mission to an Eastern European country with a midlevel accountant from the British civil service. He had never been out of England professionally or for travel and simply recommended to the host country what he knew about that system.

Assessment of Public Budgeting Systems

Field experts are often faced with the problem of assessing governmental capacity to revise budget laws, formulate budgets, control expenditures and evaluate program and project expenditures. They have no time for full-fledged management audits and must instead engage in action research to focus on immediate problems that can be remedied through technical assistance and training in the short and medium term. They must martial their resources to define the problems and establish baselines for improvement. Frequently existing fiscal administration systems are dilapidated, having passed through economic crises, political changes, and even wars. Here, expert experiences in multiple settings facilitate the task of where to look and how to narrow the scope of problems to actionable dimensions. The budget expert begins by analyzing institutional arrangements, meaning rule systems and the incentives and disincentives they create for officials. This also requires examination of the information available to officials and their incentives to use it. For example, the annual budget document in Saudi Arabia is a closely guarded state secret, and its distribution is quite limited even within the government. Under such extreme conditions, the expert has to figure out how changes in the working rules can alter incentives and produce better financial management decisions.

More common public expenditure management problems found in developing and transitional societies include formulated budget unrelated to that executed, insufficient funding for operations and maintenance, unreliable flow of budgeted funds to programs and lower levels of government, inadequate accounting systems, poor management of external aid, lack of attention to cash management, and poorly motivated staff. Comparative experience so far suggests that budget systems need to work within given contexts. But experts also need to know what the overall recommended system should look like. They need a general blueprint. The ultimate budgetary system should (1) build on existing practices that may even be corrupt or dysfunctional, (2) rely on midlevel managers for inputs to ensure ownership, (3) utilize the existing line-item classification and accounting categories to strengthen the foundation of the annual budget, and (4) provide incentives for ministries to budget and manage for results and for ministries of finance to provide stable funding [31].

Budget Laws

The subject of budget legislation has traditionally been raised on narrow questions of compliance with appropriations. Line-item formats with detailed inputs have been used consistently to plan and monitor expenditures to ensure compliance in the strict auditing sense of that term. But public budgeting reforms in recent years have emphasized broader issues of macroeconomic management, and the efficiency and effectiveness of resource use to achieve program objectives. In most cases, these additional emphases have been pursued through administrative and supporting regulatory reforms without major changes in budget legislation.

The technical question then is, what subjects should be covered by budget legislation? To answer this, comparative legal practices must be examined. Confusion often occurs over the fact that provisions in budget legislation are separate from those in the constitution or in annual budget laws (appropriations) and financial regulations. Budget legislation should refer to the organic law that guides and regulates budget management, accounting, and auditing. Based on work in this area, it is generally agreed that the following elements should be contained in a budget law: (1) comprehensive coverage of financial operations, including definition of the deficit, and provisions for extrabudgetary funds, (2) the management role of the ministry of finance, particularly budget execution, cash management, and public borrowing, and (3) procedures for presentation of the annual budget within a macroeconomic framework, development of deficit ceilings, and provisions for deficit financing by the banking system [32].

Clearly, the laws of many countries do not include all these topics. Nor do provisions govern them in the same ways. Some countries deal with such matters as annual budget preparation administratively rather than by law. This allows for more management flexibility in reviewing requests and squaring departmental reporting rules with analysis techniques. To discern the best approach, the field expert should be versed in comparative practices. For example, one problem noted earlier is the unreliable flow of funds to programs from ministries of finance (the release process). What do budget laws require in the area of fund release and how might a provision be designed to ensure flow of funds consistent with managerial program needs and accounting needs for control? Among OECD countries, according to Allan [32, pp. 21–22], the Ministry of Finance and/or Treasury must approve warrants before release in Australia, France, New Zealand, Portugal, Sweden, the United Kingdom, and the United States. In Germany, the MOF may block expenditures if economic development requires it. Thus, laws protect ministries from legislative intrusions.

Can ministries move funds about freely to compensate for releases withheld because of revenue scarcity or economic downturns? Comparison of legal provision reveals that transfers (virement) between votes or programs generally requires legislative approval. Sweden permits transfer between programs only with MOF approval. New Zealand permits such major transfers providing the total appropriation is increased by no more than 5%. In general, laws still restrict management fiscal discretion in the name of compliance, especially in Latin America. In New Zealand, management discretion has been expanded by regulations providing incentives for use of allocations to purchase outputs from departments rather than to simply control the costs of inputs [32, p. 8]. The efficacy of such regulatory streamlining depends upon prior development of standards of fund control. Most developing and transitional societies lack such preconditions.

Budgetary Coverage

In order to ensure that budgets measure fiscal deficits accurately, the budget must be unified and comprehensive. This means that all relevant fiscal funds and expenditures of the general government sector should be registered in the budget. Budgets in developing and transitional societies are riddled with off-budget funds and hidden special accounts which destroy budgetary unity and weaken both expenditure planning and control. Latin American governments are famous for incomplete and fragmented budgets. In China, extrabudgetary funds are used for capital construction projects. This is inflationary and creates liabilities for future maintenance and operational responsibilities on the current budget [33, p. 17]. In addition, incomplete coverage obscures mobilization of credit and financing requirements. The Chinese government (and many others) routes budgetary loans through specialized institutions, and the debt servicing from these institutions is not reflected clearly in the budget. Limited information about fiscal extrabudgetary accounts hinders assessment of the financial needs of government units and their repayment capacities. In most cases, the reason for such practices is not ignorance of how to design accounts. Rather, off-budget funds allow the appearance of fiscal rectitude. While operating deficits are superficially decreased and management discretion increased, such practices increase treasury commitments. Fiscal sustainability is weakened, and this makes it harder to achieve development objectives.

The public expenditure management goal should be transparent registration of all government fund transactions—general fund, debt service, and capital projects. Government funds generally include revenues and expenditures of (1) full budgetary units (spending ministries), (2) differentiated budget units (e.g., government print shops), and (3) self-reliant units or nonfinancial public enterprises (utilities). In many countries, transactions of these types of units are pushed off-budget, which, as noted, obscures fiscal operations. More importantly, the accounts of state enterprises (units that receive subsidies and are subject to taxes) are often mixed up with those of government units. This is particularly the case in China [33, p. 17]. In general, because they are not in the nature of government transactions, state enterprises should be treated off-budget with only net flows or net effects in terms of subsidies and profit remittances reported in one or two line items in the annual budget. Comparative experience suggests that state enterprise budgets should not be consolidated into the government budget, since this invites intervention into the details of enterprise planning, forces managers to get ministerial permission for even minor changes, and leads to rigidities and costly delays in decision making by the enterprise. Since enterprises have different objectives, they should be held to account for profitability and efficiency, not simply compliance with appropriations through comparisons of actual with budgeted expenditures [34, p. 29]. In short, any interfund transfers, and future obligations of the general fund created by extrabudgetary fund losses should be made transparent.

The treasury function is linked to budget execution through the backbone of accounting information [35, p. 1]. The treasury should be the central source of all information on fiscal flows horizontally from the central bank to the ministry of finance and vertically from spending ministries to the ministry of finance. This function should operate to smooth out the mismatch between revenues and expenditures during the year (cash management), and provide financing for short- and long-term needs (debt management). A properly designed treasury system requires accurate and timely information regarding cash on hand, outstanding commitments against cash, and anticipated revenues and expenditures. The major sources of information for this system are operating and capital budgets with which to control expenditures and revenues. It is critical therefore that budgets include all revenues and expenditures, and that the accounting system keep daily cash balances by fund and account.

In Costa Rica, the existence of many separate accounts weakens the budget as a tool of treasury management. The question is what to do about this. Currently, programs such as Social Security and Asignaciones Familiares are reflected as special funds that are not presented with the rest of the budget. One option in such cases would be to include all transactions within the general fund. But this would obscure the fact that the general fund subsidizes or is subsidized by other funds. A second option would be to maintain separate balances in special funds. But this weakens budget comprehensiveness, inhibits expenditure planning, and complicates calculation of fiscal deficits. The third option would be to maintain separate funds and integrate accounts and budgets. To prevent excessive amounts of raw data from inundating the treasury, state enterprise funds would need only to provide line items on debt and cash flow. This is consistent with the idea of presenting only useful data on net effects and net flows in order to maintain budgetary unity.

A distinction should be made between programmatic independence and the needs of treasury management. In the United States, local government budgets control large sums of money (up to $10 billion) through the use of special funds whose balances are maintained in the overall fund structure. Governmental funds include general, debt service, and capital project funds. Proprietary funds include general, debt service, and capital project funds. Proprietary funds include enterprise and debt service funds. Fiduciary funds include trust and agency funds.

In the United States and elsewhere, transactions within and between these funds are recorded in the regular expenditure and revenue accounts. The chart of accounts coding structure reflects at minimum the funds, department, and objects of expenditure. The treasury therefore is aware of movements between and within funds, while the fund programs maintain managerial independence. Resistance to showing transactions between the budget and units, particularly extrabudgetary units, can be severe. Such units have substantial freedom from controls required by a unitary budget. One method of restoring unity is to maintain earmarking of previous funds to reassure agencies, units, and local governments that they will not lose resources or control over them when funds are grouped with other general budgetary funds.

Classification of Expenditures

The capacity to plan and control expenditures depends upon their presentation in the budget (coverage) and use of a classification with clearly defined and discrete categories. Failure to do so impedes performance analysis and supervision of revenues and expenditures to strengthen financial control. Overbroad categories weaken accountability; narrow categories multiply line items into an accounting nightmare.

In transitional countries of the former Soviet Union, such as Armenia, budgets have been classified mostly according to inconsistent rules and definitions. Expenditures were classified by purpose of financing (functional categories) rather than by nature of transaction (economic classification, such as salaries). Categories were often overbroad, such as "national economy," which included both current and capital expenditures and items from several functions. No systematic distinction was made between current and capital expenditures. Budgets were a hodgepodge of above (current consumption) and below the line (capital formation), salary and nonwage items. This made it impossible to conduct any kind of variance analysis of planned versus actual expenditures, or to evaluate expenditure performance.

In some cases, functional expenditures boiled down to those of one organization; that is, the budget was simply an administrative classification. Under central planning, productive expenditures were simply expected to increase societal resources. Much of the information to MOFs from spending ministries therefore related to physical production rather than financial expenditures, which would have been more useful for management purposes. "Nonproductive" expenditures were considered services. But under a single budget system, no distinction was made between current and capital items. Similar problems existed in China, where substantial capital expenditures were classified in the vague category of "technical transformation" in the construction budget, while maintenance outlays appeared in the construction budget. A common category used under central planning systems was "geological prospecting." This appears in construction budgets. But whether the predominant nature of the transaction was acquisition of capital assets or investment in a developmental activity involving current expenditures was not clear [33].

Revised budget classification is usually not considered a structural reform. Structural reforms require deeper revision of charts of accounts and reconciliation of accounting categories with the budget. Nevertheless, clearer categories and definitions can provide incentives to generate appropriate data for budget improvements. For example, classification can help move budgeting from emphasis on input measurement to output performance. But this requires often costly financial systems that generate unit cost and performance data. Clarifying current, capital, and development budget definitions, and allocating objects of expenditure by cost center are the first steps toward this objective. In many developing countries, overlapping current and capital categories are compounded by the addition of "development" budgets in which such items as education (salaries and investments) are included because they represent asset creation. But this weakens the distinction between current and capital needed to identify operating deficits and financing requirements, while allowing current items to be financed with loans. Failure to maintain this distinction creates downstream pressures on current budgets that diminish options for those items left in the current budget.

Similarly, classifying expenditures by cost center can encourage accountability through incentives for management performance. That is, standard international categories classify expenditures by (1) wages and salaries, (2) fringe benefits, (3) operations and maintenance, (4) subsidies, (5) interest payments, (6) transfers, and (7) public investments and equipment [36]. These are common to the annual object of expenditure budget, often scoffed at by reformers eager to get to performance. But there is no reason that inputs and outputs for each of these categories cannot be related by departmental analyses derived from cost accounting. For instance, the productivity of the wage and salary budget can be presented in narratives and cost centers in either a line-item or program budget. A prerequisite is installation of often expensive cost accounting infrastructure to assess unit costs and distinguish fixed and variable costs of particular expenditures. Some OECD countries cannot afford this, despite their constant support for multiannual expenditure planning and value for money budgeting. Still using annual budgets arrayed in line items, departments can employ workload measures to show how variations in funds relate to variations in work performed and results achieved. The intermediary step is to allocate line-item expenditures (particularly salaries) to indirect (administration and overhead) and direct costs (expenditures for service delivery thorough facilities and activities). The final step is to link these costs to activities (cost/client served), developing unit cost measures regularly through the financial management system. As stated, the foundation of this effort is clarifying the classification system.

Budget Reform, Analysis, and Evaluation

Past budget reforms tended to emphasize expenditure programming across functions, projects, and programs, often at the expense of accountability for controls over all expenditures. The econometric reforms such as program budgeting have usually foundered from excessive quantification, inability to control allocations for broad multiple-objective purposes, and semantic debates about the distinctive meanings of program, projects, and policies. It was politically difficult to budget across organizational boundaries, and this presented major control problems where expenditures served more than one objective (e.g., policing) [37, 96]. Program budget systems were also top-down reforms, usually designed around categories that were both rigid and insufficiently transparent. Program budgeting ignored the need for management discretion to shift expenditures despite long-range projections, or the political need to satisfy constituents first.

With most budgets dominated by fixed costs in salaries, debt service, and operations, the latest thinking in "budget reform" seeks to make the annual budget work first, then integrate management interest in program results, with control over the downstream cost implications to present investments. Newer reforms to induce budget analysis thus attempt to integrate public management and budgeting.

A major lesson of past budget reforms is that to improve expenditure results, internal controls must be in place to account for allocations that should be made in broad line-items to encourage line manager responsibility and accountability. Internal control systems safeguard against unauthorized expenditures and ensure reliability of financial records. Internal control units normally operate within ministries. Broad functional or program categories that deviate from traditional line items cause internal control problems that must be remedied by either redesign of accounting systems (very expensive and few successful examples anywhere) or shifting back to more discrete categories such as activities or services. The line-item or object-of-expenditure classification still serves the goal of improving expenditure performance.

Consistent with this, service-level or performance-based budget systems [38, pp. 46–49] are now recommended as the predominant U.S.-style reform. The rest of the OECD emphasizes systemic reforms to integrate macroeconomic planning and budgeting, or multi-year expenditure planning type systems. In practice, there may not be a major difference between the two regional reform examples. The blending of budget reforms across the OECD (including the United States) is increasingly common. For example, a recent World Bank recommendation to the Government of Nicaragua identified the following (rather typical) budget reform objectives:

1. Ultimately serve as the basis for full medium-term expenditure planning within decentralized ministry responsibilities.
2. Ensure that resources will be identified and allocated on the basis of past results and probable future results (derived from unit cost and performance data).
3. Serve as a tool of management for allocation of resources, and provide incentives for performance evaluations that will be fed back into budget formulation.
4. Provide a framework for rethinking the means and ends of agency actions, by questioning the current structure of ministry responsibility centers, the effect of existing regulations on personnel incentives, patterns of budget allocations, and

program and personnel performance results. The annual budget formulation phase will thus serve as a vehicle to analyze the institutional environment of service delivery.

5. Provide ministries with the capacities to utilize performance data to predict and assess the costs and consequences on service performance of different levels of budget allocations.

6. Ensure expenditure control by allocating resources for activities and services in objects of expenditures to management responsibility centers. Consistent with development of a new chart of accounts to improve classification, expenditures can then be crosswalked between line items and activities to measure results and assess expenditure performance.

Budget reforms have historically attempted to provide policymakers with sufficient information to link expenditures and results. The goal has been to improve implementation by using the budget as a policy tool. By this broad perspective, U.S.-style reforms have included executive budgeting, unified budgets (complete coverage of expenditures), line-item classifications, performance budgets, and program budgets. All attempted to permit budgetmakers to anticipate behavior of revenues and expenditures and to control outlays accordingly. Most of these reforms have targeted the formulation and implementation activities of the executive branch. Legislative approval processes were largely outside earlier reforms. To the extent that the legislative process has been included in later reforms (Gramm–Rudman–Hollings bills of 1985 and 1987, the Omnibus Budget Reconciliation Act of 1990, and the Budget Enforcement Act of 1991), the emphasis has been on procedural changes to force deficit control and reduction, and less on managerial incentives to link input–output relationships [39, p. 11]. This "messy" democratic feature accounts for the much of the disjointed nature of U.S. federal budgeting. International observers are amazed at the sophisticated, technocratic planning and implementation of executive budgets that are regularly derailed by congressional intrusions through such practices as pork-barrel politics and earmarking.

Value-for-money reforms, such as program budgeting, called for such logical actions as identification of program objectives (mission statements), analysis of alternatives, and development of multiyear financial plans. Information was to be improved by analysis, program structures, and transparency. Program budgeting was designed to link input–output information. It was largely triggered by poor reporting from spending ministries [19, p. 261] and stressed efficiency and effectiveness of expenditures. Where such reforms have worked, such as zero-based budgeting and performance budgeting at the state and local government levels in the United States, they have engaged the legislatures and councils to participate in more rational planning and cutting of expenditures.

European Commonwealth-style reforms have attempted to move beyond emphasis on formal information structures to an approach to managing expenditures that utilizes decentralized authority, multiyear budgets, and macroeconomic planning. Such reforms recognize the core role of institutional incentives in successful actions. Australian budgeting, for example, emphasizes the management discretion needed to get the job done through provision of multiyear budget authority for "running costs" (operations and maintenance). Budgets are allocated in broad lump-sum line items to ministries according to totals developed in the forward expenditure estimate. Given potential rewards in budget savings and individual merit increases, departments have every incentive to utilize analysis to perform the work efficiently and effectively.

The case of Australia suggests that elimination of the line-item budget and its replacement with program formats was a misplaced reform objective. The line-item accountability and control "reform" is retained; ministries conduct input–output analyses of expenditures with whatever tools they need. There was nothing magic in "programs." As many have written, the program structure and its elaborate technical baggage caused considerable confusion [19, p. 261] and may have actually set the cause of budget reform back. In Australia and other Commonwealth countries, line managers are given fixed limits based on macroeconomically derived ceilings that cannot easily be changed. The presumption is against supplemental appropriations and deviations from annual plans [40]. There is less legislative intrusion, and this gives managers the financial stability needed to manage programs. Multiyear budget plans are "reconciled" every 6 months on a rolling basis with new planning estimates. This ensures that planning and budgeting processes are inextricably linked.

Tight fiscal planning and budgeting is not unusual in the OECD, or with selected U.S. federal expenditures. Canada integrates bottom-up management with top-down multiyear policy ceilings through its Policy and Expenditure Management System (PEMS). Agreements are forged out on cutbacks, new initiatives, and inflation forecasts and translated into allocations across functional "envelopes" [41]. Similar to Australia and Canada, Denmark modernized its public sector by decentralizing fiscal responsibilities through block appropriations and abolishing the requirements of central approval of all new positions [42, p. 530].

The key to success in all three cases has been maintenance of limited access points to pressure for changing plans. The U.S. system is politically porous, and this restricts the ability to focus budgeting on purely efficiency aspects. More recently, the Canadian system has suffered some of the same problems. Nevertheless, the United States uses multiyear expenditure planning for entitlements, construction (advance appropriations for airports and mass transit projects), carryover authority for multiyear programs, and forward funding provisions that allow current obligations for future use. These provide managerial flexibility, stability, and expenditure control (avoiding piecemeal decision making and the annual budget maximization game). Linking budgeting with management incentives serves macroeconomic as well as program objectives.

Thus, even European Commonwealth reforms retain the line-item budget for control and maximize results by devolving authority and responsibility to line managers for attaining targets. In contrast with U.S. reforms, which largely tried to eliminate the annual line-item framework, budgeting is linked at the source into legislative routine (for adoption of ceilings) and incentives for management productivity. Institutionally, the Australian system combines tight internal controls from the Department of Finance over ministry expenditures, with broad manager discretion, and program audits. This reduces risk aversion and allows use of the budget as a management tool.

The Commonwealth reform model has much to offer for budget reform in specific regions. For example, in Eastern Europe and Latin America, creating a culture of analysis where official criticism has been discouraged for decades will require modification of incentives. This means basic improvements in budget structures, followed by emphasis on expenditure controls during budget implementation. Some have argued that implementation capacity should precede formulation capacity on the grounds that uncontrolled expenditures will simply waste resources. But basic budget structures–proper budget classification into controllable categories like "operations" and "teaching," extrabudgetary fund coverage, accounting consistency, mission and activity statements, and cost analysis capabilities in finance and spending ministries—are required first. Proper budget formulation is essential to prevent budgeting from occurring during the implementation phase, when managers should be implementing plans made during the formulation phase. Eastern European governments lack formulation capacities, and this is a major constraint to encouraging critical analysis of expenditure items [8, p. 12].

As noted, past attempts were made to induce budget analysis by changing budget formats and systems from inputs to outputs. But this ignored disincentives to evaluation and the overriding resource constraint that ensured distorted analyses as part of ministry competition for its fair share of the pie. Faced with the twin problems of policy incoherence and line agency budget maximization games, like other Commonwealth countries, the Canadian government combined basic reforms in budget preparation with modifications of incentives. The Canadians combined the apparently inconsistent forces of budget centralization (tighter controls over policy and expenditures by the MOF) with management decentralization (greater discretion by departmental heads to reallocate funds and manage human resources). This was done through introduction of a management appraisal system that created a common corporate culture among top bureaucrats [43]. Such comparative examples are transferrable to similar contexts. In Estonia, the government introduced a program allocation budget that targets disincentives for analysis and performance by spending ministries. For FY 1995, the focus is on the amount of resources that will be given to each unit and not on the allocation of these resources by expenditure category [28, p. 81]. This introduces incentives for line managers to be accountable for ensuring that spending is within prescribed allotments, and that programs are implemented with commensurate savings.

Accounting and Control Systems

Well-designed and well-managed accounting systems that record, classify, and summarize financial transactions are necessary for proper stewardship over public funds. Solid accounting systems are necessary for financial control and to serve management needs. The accounting system is the foundation and the backbone of all financial management functions. In particular, timely and accurate information is necessary to prepare and administer both operating and capital budgets, and to purchase goods and services [44, pp. 6-7] A review of 21 structural adjustment facilities between the IMF and host countries found major budget implementation problems caused by accounting system weaknesses. In particular, there were problems of failure to link charts of accounts to useful expenditure codes, absence of commitment accounting systems, incongruent reporting between financial and physical results of expenditures, and arrears without solid information on exact levels [45].

Accounting is the "bedrock" of good budgeting [19, p. 229]. But the budget function allocates and controls execution based on accounting inputs. The budget function is responsible for monitoring and controlling execution. To do this, fiscal managers require information from the treasury, accounting, purchasing, cash management, and payroll systems. When the accounting foundation deteriorates, the rest of the body politic suffers. This is as true of poor as rich countries. For example, according to the U.S. General Accounting Office, the District of Columbia government "does not know how many bills it owes, is allowing millions of dollars of obligations to occur without required written contracts, and does not know its cash status on a daily basis" [46]. Dilapidated accounting and budget systems reinforce cultures of carelessness.

All public transactions quantifiable in monetary terms should be recorded in the accounting system and reported on, including those which are off-budget. According to Wesberry [47, p.10], the most problematic area in creating an integrated financial management system (in which a common, single database links the core subsystems) is the segregation of budgetary execution data from other financial data and/or maintenance of ad hoc budgetary records outside the accounting system. This is illustrated fictionally by the African road clerk, Mr. Johnson, who posted entries for various debts in his own set of source books (e.g., beer cash book) for a road construction project. In creating his own "road treasury," he created a set of plausible but illegal accounting rules (e.g., borrowing from the current uniforms line item to pay for construction materials next year; recording live cows as exports because of their hides) and never posted them to general journals or ledgers [48]. This creativity violated nearly every accepted canon of accounting practice and expenditure control. Unfortunately, in a political culture based on personal trust rather than impersonal systems, his actions also led to completion of the project!

Thus, accounting and control systems need to be designed into local values and attitudes. Colonial systems obviously had little interest in this. But local behavior can be modified through properly designed training and technical assistance to install appropriate norms of control and discretion. Training efforts in Eastern Europe to modify net material product systems linked into accounting and statistical systems, have such objectives in mind. But in the past, to manage the common problems of annual cash flow, governments often instituted draconian measures, such as narrow line-item restrictions, and cash rationing. Damaging enough in themselves, they have often been applied without underlying control systems. In effect, the government cannot tell if the controls are working as planned, or if changes in cash flow are due to poor reporting systems and practices. In such cases, field experts should encourage two reforms: (1) commitment accounting systems, and (2) cash management systems.

To ensure proper expenditure control, experience suggests that governments need to move beyond cash recording to mixed accrual systems that measure revenues on a cash basis and expenditures by commitments or encumbrances. In many transitional and developing countries, purchase orders can be placed without incurring obligations or debiting appropriations; transactions are recorded on a cash basis. When payment is made, the ministry account would be debited and the treasury would have to find the money to pay. This obscures the growth of fiscal deficits during the year. Systems that record commitments, such as statutory payments like public debt, staff salaries and allowances, unpaid bills, and existing contractual obligations, ensure that the available balance of appropriation is not overstated. Such systems, it should be noted, prevent overcommitment of budgeted funds. They also act perversely to discourage underspending, lapsed apportionments, and any budget savings! Nevertheless, they are an essential accounting tool to support good budgeting. One problem for field analysis is that systems may not be fully cash or commitment (obligational). The spending ministries may maintain accounts on a commitments basis while the central treasury of finance ministry maintains cash accounts. This was found to be true in such diverse countries as Armenia and Ghana.

One solution to the problem of weak central control of outlay accounts, is to decentralize payments authorization and accounting to spending ministries. Malawi did this in 1987. Checks were issued by cost centers in order to speed up the flow of cash to programs and projects. But failure of ministries to monitor their commitments against budget allocations resulted in overdrawn accounts. At the same time, the central bank honored all checks to sustain the appearance of sovereignty. This encouraged fraud and more overdrafts and progressive loss of expenditure control by the center. The problem of decentralizing payments is that it is heavily dependent upon financial management will and capacity at the ministry level. It also leaves MOFs vulnerable to ministry reporting vagaries. In particular, the Malawi ministry of finance had no idea of the actual volume of claims against funds arising from checks issued, cleared or cashed. A solution to the earlier "solution" would be to utilize an accounting program that integrates appropriation accounts, payments, commitments, and treasury releases. Accounting software programs are available that would prevent check issuance if funds are committed or exhausted. This would ensure that the treasury was aware of and could manage the actual amount of cash needed for the year. In short, installation of commitment accounting systems need to be accompanied by training to ensure accurate and timely use of them [49].

Cash management is the process of conserving cash and optimizing its flow so that specified levels of deficit are not exceeded [50, p. 75]. Recall that this is part of the treasury function discussed earlier. Metering the flow of resources to coincide with revenue and expenditure schedules allows ministries of finance (MOFs) to maintain cash flows, minimize borrowing costs and even to invest idle funds. Based on reliable accounting data, cash management permits MOFs to avoid liquidity crises and collections arrears. But many countries impose cash limits across the board or through detailed line-item restrictions. This often translates into monthly budgets that have to be revised by managers based on estimates of probable releases. Service delivery and contractor payments accordingly suffer. In Bulgaria, cash was at one point rationed to ministries by the MOF on a weekly basis. In Estonia, balanced budgets have been assured by restricting expenditures to cash available. But the requirement of matching cash inflows–outflows makes it hard for ministries to plan expenditures in orderly fashion. Since cash is often not on hand to pay bills, the system encourages rent-seeking behavior by ministries and provision of "inducements" to those in the MOF controlling releases of funds [28, p. 92].

The cash limit system effectively replaces the approved budget, reinforcing skepticism and uncertainty in the ministries about allocations to come in the future. Cash limits encourage short-term decision making, and program implementation usually suffers. If MOFs expect ministries to rationally adjust their budgets to inflation and fewer revenues, and to balance resources against a modified volumes of services, the usual result is to delay payments and run up arrears. In many countries, cash limits are an indication that the macro stabilization goal is being pursued without due regard to economy and efficiency [50, p. 76].

As noted, one solution to cash flow problems during implementation is to build up the "treasury function" to smooth out seasonal mismatches between revenues and expenditures. This means management of finances and programs with timely and accurate information on the unified cash position. The advantage of this approach is that it provides centralized information on fiscal flows through a unified account while facilitating a more decentralized approach to cash management at the spending ministry level that can include programmatic considerations. Agreed budgets rather than daily cash flow should determine the amount released to ministries each month.

CONCLUSION

Improvements in public expenditure management are necessary to strengthen governmental institutions. According to the *Economist* in an editorial on Mexico, "Economic reform will mean little now and will always remain vulnerable in the future as long as it is not accompanied by political and institutional reform" [51]. In this context, the transfer of tools and models to strengthen institutions via public budgeting reforms will always depend less upon the results of empirical research than on the portfolio of experiences brought by field experts.

Thus, several conclusions can be reached on the needs of field experts themselves. First, it is critical that the experts have the depth and breadth of knowledge to recommend feasible changes in systems and workable training programs. Next, it is important that the field expert be able to assess whether "culture" is a constant or variable in particular settings. Local habits may be so thoroughly grounded in strict religious codes, for example, that the practice is in fact a constant and a complete barrier to systemic change. On the other hand, institutional practices may be variables, changeable at the margin, to be treated with correctly designed incentive packages. Expert judgment will depend here upon field experiences, fed to some extent by comparative findings from reports and observations of other field experts.

Finally, to gain the confidence of host officials and others, experts need to be able to present comprehensive critiques of the failings of those systems and skills that they intend to transfer. Locals have often learned from their experiences, or other field technicians, the defects of this or that law, budget reform, accounting and control system, or classification scheme. They know that it is not as simple as following the manual or cookbook to success in public expenditure management. The only question they have is whether the expert, the immediate "salesperson" of this system or skill, recognizes the contradictions and problems with such systems in other country applications, and in his or her own country. Providing such insights in order to conduct proper fieldwork remains one of the key purposes of comparative budgetary analysis. As we move further into the data-gathering and analysis stages of this field toward theory building, it is probably useful to remember that the ultimate users of our works will be practitioners.

REFERENCES

1. G. M. Guess, "Comparative Government Budgeting," *Handbook on Public Budgeting and Financial Management* (T. D. Lynch and J. Rabin, eds.), Marcel Dekker, New York, pp. 161–191 (1983).
2. G. M. Guess, "Comparative Government Budgeting," *Handbook of Public Budgeting* (J. Rabin, ed.), Marcel Dekker, New York, pp. 95–124 (1992).
3. L. R. Jones, "Symposium on International Budgeting and Fiscal Policy," *Public Budgeting and Finance, 14*(4) (1994).
4. A. Wildavsky and Jones (1994).
5. L. Tancock, *Introduction to Emile Zola's* Germinal, Penguin, Middlesex (1954).
6. L. C. Mayer, *Redefining Comparative Politics, Promise Versus Performance*, Sage, Newbury Park, Calif. (1989).
7. P. Urio and L. R. Jones, "Public Finance Issues and Problems in Switzerland," *Public Budgeting and Finance, 14*(4): 23–36 (1994).
8. G. M. Guess, "Budgeting and Administrative Reform in Eastern Europe," *Developing Alternatives, 4*(2): 9–14 (1994).
9. R. Anthony and D. Young, *Management Control in Nonprofit Organizations*, 4th ed., Irwin, Homewood, Ill. (1984); see Hoagland Hospital A Case.
10. N. Caiden and A. Wildavsky, *Planning and Budgeting in Poor Countries*, John Wiley, New York (1974).
11. LaPalombara, "Bureaucracy and Political Development: Notes, Queries and Dilemmas," *Bureaucracy and Political Development*, Princeton University Press, Princeton, N.J. (1967).
12. J. LaPalombara, *Bureaucracy and Political Development*, Princeton University Press, Princeton, N.J. (1967).
13. J. A. Bill and R. L. Hardgrave, *Comparative Politics: The Quest for Theory*, Merrill, Columbus, Ohio (1974).
14. A. O. Hirschman, *Development Projects Observed*, Brookings Institution, Washington, D.C. (1967).
15. U.S. General Accounting Office, "Training and Related Efforts Needed to Improve Financial Management in the Third World," Washington, D.C. (1979).

16. World Bank, "Honduras: Public Sector Expenditure Review," IBRD, Washington, D.C. (1995).

17. M. P. Flaherty, "Failure to Compute Adds to D.C.'s Bills, Disparate Systems Fall Short of Needs," *Washington Post*, May 15, p. 1 (1995).

18. D. R. Winkler, "The Design and Administration of Intergovernmental Transfers, Fiscal Decentralization in Latin America," World Bank, Washington, D.C. (1994).

19. D. Axelrod, *Budgeting for Modern Government*, St. Martins, New York (1988).

20. D. D. Laitin, "The Civic Culture at 30" *Am. Polit. Sci. Rev.*, *89*(1): 168–173 (1995).

21. *Economist*, August 12, p. 72 (1995).

22. W. J. Cash, *The Mind of the South*, Vintage, New York (1941).

23. J. C. Clingermayer and B. D. Wood, "Disentangling Patterns of State Debt Financing," *Am. Polit. Sci. Rev.*, *89*(1): 168–173 (1995).

24. J. Lieske, "Regional Subcultures of the United States," *J. Politics*, *55*: 888–913 (1993).

25. P. S. Kim, W. Pindur, and K. Reynolds, "Creating a New Organizational Culture: The Key to Total Quality Management in the Public Sector," *Int. J. Public Admin.*, *18*(4): 675–711 (1995).

26. I. G. Somali, *Fancy Footwork: Entrapment in and Coping With the Nepali Management Model*, Kathmandu (1992).

27. G. M. Guess, "Centralization of Expenditure Controls in Latin America," *Public Admin. Q.*, *16*(3): 376–394 (1992).

28. World Bank, "Estonia: Public Expenditure Review," IBRD, Washington, D.C. (1994).

29. K. Thurmaier, "The Evolution of Local Government Budgeting in Poland: From Accounting to Policy in a Leap and a Bound," *Public Budgeting and Finance*, *14*(4): 84–97 (1994).

30. L. Harrison, "Voodoo Politics in Haiti," *Atlantic Monthly*, June: 101–107 (1993).

31. M. Holmes, "Improving Budgetary Capacity," background paper for "Government Expenditure and Financial Management" seminar, November 15–16, World Bank, Washington, D.C. (1994).

32. B. Allan, "Public Expenditure Management and Budget Law: Toward a Framework for a Budget Law for Economics in Transition," Discussion Paper K39, H61, International Monetary Fund, Washington, D.C. (1994).

33. World Bank, "China: Budgetary Policy and Intergovernmental Fiscal Relations," IBRD, Washington, D.C. (1993).

34. M. Shirley and J. Nellis, *Public Enterprise Reform: The Lessons of Experience*, World Bank, Washington, D.C. (1991).

35. T. Ter-Minassian, P. P. Parente, and P. Martinez-Mendez, "Setting Up a Treasury in Economics in Transition," Working Paper H60, International Monetary Fund, Washington, D.C. (1995).

36. K. Y. Chu and R. Hemming, *Public Expenditure Handbook, A Guide to Public Policy Issues in Developing Countries*, International Monetary Fund, Washington, D.C. (1991).

37. J. McMaster, *Urban Financial Management, A Training Manual*, World Bank, Washington, D.C. (1991).

38. D. Stachota, *The Best of Governmental Budgeting, A Guide to Preparing Budget Documents*, Government Finance Officers Association), Chicago (1994).

39. D. S. Ippolito, "The Budget Process and Budget Policy: Resolving the Mismatch," *Public Admin. Rev.*, *53*(1): 8–13 (1993).

40. M. Keating and D. Rosalky, "Rolling Expenditure Plans: Australian Experience and Prognosis," *Governmental Financial Management, Issues and Country Studies* (A. Premchand, ed.), International Montery Fund, Washington, D.C. (1990).

41. Organization for Economic Cooperation and Development, *The Control and Management of Government Expenditure*, Paris (1987).

42. A. Schick, "Micro-Budgetary Adaptations to Fiscal Stress in Industrialized Democracies," *Public Admin. Rev.*, *48*(1): 523–534 (1988).

43. J. Bourgault, S. Dion, and M. Lemay, "Creating a Corporate Culture: Lessons from the Canadian Federal Government," *Public Admin. Rev.*, *53*(1): 73–80 (1993).

44. C. K. Coe, *Public Financial Management*, Prentice Hall, Englewood Cliffs, N.J. (1989).

45. A. Premchand, *Government Financial Management, Issues and Country Studies*, International Monetary Fund, Washington, D.C. (1990).

46. *Economist*, "An Unexpected Guardian Angel," August 19, p. 23 (1995).
47. J. P. Wesberry, "Integrated Financial Management in Government," background paper for "Government Expenditure and Financial Management" seminar, November 15–16, World Bank, Washington, D.C. (1994).
48. J. Cary, *Mr. Johnson*, New Directions, New York (1989).
49. M. Stevens, "Expenditure Control in Malawi" (draft), World Bank, Washington, D.C. (1994).
50. A. Premchand, *Public Expenditure Management*, International Monetary Fund, Washington, D.C. (1993).
51. *Economist*, "Mexico Starts Again," August 26, pp. 12–13 (1995).

III

INSTITUTIONAL CONTEXTS OF BUDGETING AND FINANCE

EDITORIAL INTRODUCTION

An old saying proposes that wise persons put all their eggs in one basket, and then *watch that basket.* Given due attention and strength, or lack of thieves, that person can conveniently protect all the eggs.

But this strategy has its clear limits. If the egg watcher's attention wavers, or if defenses are inadequate, all of the eggs may be lost in one fell swoop. Alas, the strategy of minimizing the probability of partial losses also maximizes the risk of a total loss.

Perhaps because of this awkward feature, the shapers of our original political institutions followed a multiple-basket strategy. In sum, those institution builders deliberately decided to distribute our political eggs among several baskets. The negative root belief is that the electorate cannot be expected to be either eternally vigilant or broadly informed. The positive root belief is that the interests of the electorate can, will, and should be engaged in enough significant cases to make their impact felt, in the long run and if the need *really* exists. Both root beliefs encourage the strategy of multiple baskets. They cannot all be stolen at once, and a theft or two will rouse even a disinterested citizenry before it is too late.

This general working accommodation in America has been the despair of doctrinaire thinkers, having as it does dual goals: the control of necessary (but potentially dangerous) political elites, and the reliance on a vital (but often lethargic) mass electorate. Native cunning, therefore, called for political institutions set against one another so that some degree of mutual surveillance was built into the system, without rigidifying the total system while providing an opportunity for the broad electorate to mobilize, when necessary.

As a result, our political eggs are scattered, with dual expectations, in several institutional baskets. Thus, the chances are increased that no faction can steal all of our political eggs, even as we risk the vulnerability of some of them. Relatedly, any really ambitious egg snatchers are more likely to be balanced by other ambitious individuals or factions, or will receive the multidirectional attention that sooner or later will motivate the electorate to turn the rascals out. The underlying strategy minimizes the chance of maximum loss, and is prepared to absorb smaller losses as a cost. Even gridlock may be an attractive alternative to jeopardizing the sovereignty of the people.

How American political institutions put their eggs in several baskets may be suggested via the late Mort Grodzins' fecund image of a "marble layer cake." Grodzins described the "vertical" sharing of power in our federal system between the central government, the states, and local government in terms of the several multicolored strata of a political layer cake. The differing widths of the various strata of the cake reflect the differing power of the several levels of government in various issue areas. Further, the several strata of a layer cake subtly blend into one another in some places, while they stand boldly distinct at others. Just so is power usually shared in our federal system—usually in complex blends, although at times in some area one level or another may exercise a virtual monopoly.

Putting our political eggs in several baskets has had profound PBF effects. Indeed, perhaps *the* central issue of all public administration today concerns the basic redefinition of the scope of the powers of the various levels of governments. The "perhaps" requires emphasis, for the point oozes controversy. Thus, the scope of power has been a recurring problem, and observers may differ widely about whether the issue is as central today as it was (for example) during the 1860s. Some will argue, beyond this point, that the present pattern of shared powers prevents creative adaptations to new conditions. Others thank their lucky stars for countervailing governmental powers, "vertically" as well as "horizontally." In some eyes, these countervailing assignments are the major defense against making public policy a vehicle for incautious social experimentation.

The six selections in Unit III illustrate how the basic American bias toward divided authority influences PBF. Many other readings in this volume add substance and detail to the six selections in Unit III that often give prominence to "the politics" of PBF.

Reforms Highlight Diffuse Causal Texture

Joseph C. Pilegge performs a kind of experiment to reveal the basic character of the American political cultures and the institutions that have developed in them. His intent is clear. Focus on PBF reforms, and see how the political cultures and their institutions respond. What reforms are generally accepted, and which are resisted, will reveal much about the cultural and institutional contexts into which the reforms are introduced.

Pilegge's "Budget Reforms" (Chapter 13) does not leave much doubt about the basic point, while he also provides a useful historical review about how and why things came to be as they are. Basically, PBF reforms have struggled to put more eggs into one basket, or into fewer baskets. Also, those reforms were generally resisted by powerful interests, which suggests the dominance of divided and shifting powers in prevailing American political cultures and institutional systems. Put in another way, the causal texture within which American PBF is imbedded can be described as "diffuse" or "loosely linked." Hence, its resistance to one-basket strategies.

The Federal Budget Cycle

To simplify, two major purposes are served by Chapter 14. "The Budget System and Concepts of the United States Government" is a publication of the U.S. Office of Management and Budget, which, in turn, is an arm of the Executive Office of the President. First, on the general principle that a picture is worth a thousand words, or more, Chapter 14 provides an overall view of the U.S. budget cycle in a single graphic. Substantial text adds substance to that chronological outline.

Second, the selection also provides valuable guidance about numerous concepts and categories necessary for a working sense of American PBF. Thus, among other topics, attention gets directed at the coverage of budget totals and classifications, various budgetary transactions, and the characteristics of federal credit, among other relevant themes.

A Focus on Congress

As preceding readings suggest, and especially Chapter 13, the American institutional framework tends toward diffusion, with several factions deliberately set in opposition to contend for centrality. In Chapter 15, we focus only on what will be called presidential and congressional factions, even though that grievously simplifies.

Over the past few decades, the trend line for the institutionalized presidency has been up, quite definitely. In sum, the presidency permits the focusing of great and growing resources and prestige to influence PBF. Illustratively, the Office of Management and Budget (once the Bureau of the Budget) occasionally before 1974 used the ultimate presidential weapon, the power to "impound" funds whose expenditures Congress had authorized. The presidency's power of impounding—an "implied power," at best—was a super item veto. That is, the executive used it to negate total bills or individual items of both legislative authorization and appropriation, and without the possibility of the action being formally overridden by the legislature as is the case with the constitutional power of veto. Of course, use of impounding by the executive ran the risk of stirring up countermeasures by legislators. Less ultimately, OMB's influence over allotments for spending by executive agencies also reflected the substantial power of the presidency.

Congress has been at a substantial disadvantage over most of the post-World War II interval and, as Chapter 15 highlights concerning the several phases or stages of the budget cycle, legislative institutions, practices, and history are such as to reduce the ability of Congress to provide comprehensive financial oversight. This is the case even when the presidency has come on hard times, as in post-Watergate times, and when Congress has sought to gain the initiative. What factors constrain Congressional ambitions? For example, the very existence of *two* houses of Congress—with different terms, constituencies, personalities, and styles of decision making—generates powerful centrifugal forces that fragment legislative consideration and oversight of financial matters, for good or ill. Legislative–executive relations are not simply a "direct and inevitable outgrowth of the separation of powers." In massive reinforcement, Congress and its electoral systems "foster localism" and provide multiple points of access for diverse, organized interests that seek to get their concept of public or private advantage embodied in legal principle or in actual practice. These "organized interests" include both executive agencies and multifarious associations representing industries, many of the professions, veterans, and so on.

Granted that Congress may be characterized as relatively "diffuse" and the presidency as relatively "focused" in making budget and financial decisions, one need not make a judgment that the legislature can be only a poor institutional cousin of the institutionalized presidency. That issue was up for grabs in the 1995–1996 controversy involving President Clinton, Speaker of the House Newt Gingrich, Senate Majority Leader Robert Dole, and their many minions. At the extremes, both "executive leadership" and "legislative leadership" have their patent costs, and it is perhaps the guiding genius of our institutions that we can peacefully maintain the two strategies in confusing and ever-changing sets of balances in various issue arenas at different times.

A clear sense of this relative diffusion of institutional powers gets bold relief in Linda K. Kowalcky and Lance T. LeLoup's "Congress and the Politics of Statutory Debt Limitation." In sum, they focus on another case of whether something is better than nothing. In outline, Kowalcky and LeLoup draw attention to four central features: to how debt limitation came to be, to its subsequent history, to the partisan coalitions that get reflected in it, and to the uses/limits of debt limitations as a tool of Congressional control.

Depending on their political criteria, observers will differ as to how much better than nothing they see debt limitation. Congress has a central role in the control of the purse strings, of course, and hence the relevance of tools such as debt limitation. On the other hand, there are real senses in which the tool can be a paper tiger. Kowalcky and LeLoup provide useful ammunition for cases across a broad range of stance-taking about how much better than nothing debt limitation is seen as being. The authors also argue that some of the usefulness members of Congress see in debt limitation is based on more subtle considerations than are acknowledged by those who see little in the periodic squabbles over debt limitation in the federal legislative halls.

A Focus on Fiscal Federalism

Political power is shared, and fought over, vertically as well as horizontally between the three branches of the federal government. Kenneth T. Palmer and Matthew C. Moen direct useful attention to the horizontal dimension of federalism in Chapter 16, "Intergovernmental Fiscal Relations in the 1980s."

This horizontal dimension has been the target of both substantial conflict and some experimentation over the decades. Palmer and Moen sketch some of the major features of alternative policies and practices, and estimate their impacts on state and local governments. As the authors observe, devolving authority or budgets to nonfederal levels may have an intuitive appeal, but what serves the states may come at the expense of the local governments. As the authors observe, moreover, "delegation" may in point of fact be "relegation," where the shifts involve assigning unwelcome costs and unwanted responsibilities to the state or local authorities. This may be convenient to the relegating authority, but it constitutes no constitutional principle.

While today's political tides are running strong toward delegation or relegation to nonfederal authorities, one point needs to be kept in mind. Much of the concentration of federal power has come directly from the inability or failure of nonfederal levels. This was clearly true in providing for national defense during the Cold War, for example, as well as in attacking racial segregation. So enthusiasm reasonably should be limited when it comes to delegation, and certainly when relegation is at issue.

Toward Integration: U.S. General Accounting Office

Various institutional arrangements have been developed to swim against the currents generated by the complexities, scales, and self-interests encompassed by PBF. James A. Stever provides us with a useful overview of one such development in Chapter 17, "The General Accounting Office: Its Origin, Expansion, and Dilemma." In its development, the GAO brings to mind the evolutionary stages sketched by Allen Schick in Chapter 6. In its essence, GAO reflects another example of the multiple-baskets view of handling power and responsibility. Although intended as a curb on executive action in one sense, the GAO also was institutionalized in ways that encourage its relative "independence" from both executive and legislative, as in the long term of the GAO's head. The goal seems to be that of creating an honest, capable "third party," more or less.

Stever's task is a complex one, if only because the GAO constitutes a moving target, as it were. In its earliest forms, the GAO sought to establish the integrity of the paper trail linking legislative enactment to disbursement. The key question in those early days was, does the authority for the expenditure exist? Later, GAO took a broader view of its responsibilities, focusing on the effectiveness as well as the efficiency with which federal agencies (in Stever's terms) "managed their resources and implemented policy."

The evolutionary end is nowhere in sight, as Stever reminds us. Even as we editors write in early 1996, the GAO may well be poised for yet another round of reform. And so it goes.

Toward Integration: Congressional Budget Office

In Chapter 18, R. Phillips Twogood provides a kind of mirror image of institutional developments toward integration, this time from a strictly legislative point of view. He focuses on the technical and substantive duality that often characterizes the upper reaches of all U.S. government. Twogood's selection is titled "Reconciling Politics and Budget Analysis: The Case of the Congressional Budget Office."

Twogood develops a picture of high expectations that have been ratcheted downward over two decades of experience. The CBO is directly on the politics/administration interface at the federal level and, as in the case of the budgetary dispute of 1995–1996, technical advice is located at the very center of a very heated political process. In effect, CBO became "our guys" for Congress, which served as a counterweight to the Office of Management and Budget, which over the past several decades has become "our guys" for the presidency and the executive.

13
Budget Reforms

Joseph C. Pilegge

Born in the turmoil of turn-of-the-century municipal reform movements, budgeting in the United States emerged as a key part of the "good-government" package of that period. During the near century since, no aspect of public administration has been more frequently subjected to the reformist zeal. Every change in the process or format of budgeting, however minor, has been labeled "reform." The literature on budgeting and financial management is filled with accounts of the aspirations and complications, the successes and failures of budgetary reform. It is the purpose of this essay to explore this long-running phenomenon and its legacy.

INTRODUCTION: THE HISTORICAL RECORD

The idea and practice of an executive budget system came late to the United States. Usually associated with the development of representative political institutions, some have traced the roots of Britain's budgetary system back to the Magna Carta in 1215 [1]. Although primarily concerned with the control of taxation rather than expenditures, rudimentary "budgets" appeared in Austria as early as 1766 and in France following the Revolution in 1789. But a national executive budget would not come into being in the United States until 1921.

Early Municipal Reform

Not only did budgeting come late to the United States, but unlike most subsequent budgetary reforms, it began at the lowest (local) level of government and gradually worked its way upward. At the time Congress decreed a national executive budget system, numerous municipalities and nearly one-half of the states already had put similar systems in place.

The innovation owed much to the existence of municipal corruption and its disclosure by the so-called "muckrakers," such as Lincoln Steffens and Ida M. Tarbell [1]. Like its companion reforms in the areas of personnel management and administrative reorganization,

Source: *Handbook of Public Budgeting*, Marcel Dekker, Inc., New York, N.Y. (1992).

the executive budget was designed to empower and thus hold accountable municipal executives who were, in financial matters, formally subordinate to powerful councils. Spearheaded by two influential reform groups and with strong support from the business community, budgeting was well established in most major American cities by the early 1920s [2, p. 40]. The New York Bureau of Municipal Research, founded in 1906, and the National Municipal League are usually credited with the groundwork necessary to establish the need for a municipal budget system.

Burkhead [1] credits the New York Bureau with having had the greatest impact. Its work followed on the heels of the National Municipal League's first model municipal corporation act, which provided for a city budget process dominated by the mayor. In 1907, the New York Bureau's staff issued its first report entitled "Making a Municipal Budget" with specific recommendations for budgeting the city's health program [3, p. 13]. Referring to the leadership of the Bureau, Waldo [4, p. 32] described them as being "fired with the moral fervor of humanitarianism and secularized Christianity." Supportive of the new wave of scientific management, they "verged upon the ideas of a planned and managed society" and looked to the business organization and the "efficiency idea" as models for the conduct of public business.

If government was irresponsible, the corrective was to be found in executive leadership. And the budget was viewed as a formidable weapon in the arsenal of true executive power. In addition, the budget system would focus the spotlight of public attention on the city's political leadership, ending the long era of what the reformers described as "invisible government." Party bosses no longer would be able to divert public funds to private purposes without being held accountable [5].

Because budgeting was viewed by its advocates as well as its opponents as part of an overall plan to strengthen the executive, legislative hostility had to be overcome at all levels of government.

The Taft Commission

During most of the post-Civil War period, national government finances were characterized by annual budgetary surpluses. Beginning in 1894, however, the government experienced 6 consecutive years of deficits. In 1899, the deficit of $89 million was equal to 12.9% of expenditures [6]. (This compares with an average deficit/expenditure ratio of 14.8% for the 1977–1988 period.) Following a brief return to budget surpluses, deficits were again recorded in 3 of Theodore Roosevelt's 7 years in the presidency. Most importantly, deficits accrued during the first 2 years of the Taft administration, prompting the portly Ohio Republican to create the Commission on Economy and Efficiency, which produced in 1912 a report entitled "The Need for a National Budget."

The Commission's report, carrying the President's endorsement, fell on deaf ears in Congress. The procedures recommended, including systematic review by the president of estimates prepared by the agencies and the consolidation of those estimates into a single unified budget document to be presented to Congress, would not be adopted until a decade later. As Shuman [7] has noted, there were political reasons going beyond mere executive-legislative conflict that led to the proposal's rejection.

Small budget surpluses in 1911 and 1912 had eased concerns about the deficit problem. Further, 1912 was an election year and Democrats controlled the House of Representatives where budget reform legislation would have to be initiated. Taft, of course, was defeated in his bid for reelection by the Democrat Woodrow Wilson, who had other reforms on his agenda. Undeterred, even in defeat, Taft unilaterally submitted a presidential budget to Congress for fiscal 1913. It was ignored.

The wheels of major budgetary reform had been set in motion, however. The so-called Taft Commission's recommendations would provide the basis for continuing discussion of the merits of an executive budget. Those recommendations, which would be incorporated in the Budget and Accounting Act of 1921, included the following: (1) the President, as the constitutional head of the executive branch, would submit to Congress, annually, a budget; (2) the budget would contain a budgetary message setting forth "the significance of the proposals to which attention is invited" as well as a summary financial statement to include an account of the revenues and expenditures for the last completed fiscal year, as well as (3) a summary of proposed expenditures, "classified by objects," and (4) a summary of proposed changes in legislation "to enable the administration to transact public business with greater economy and efficiency." The commission also recommended submission to Congress by the Treasury Department of a consolidated financial report showing revenues and expenditures, by departments, covering the past 5 years. It proposed that a uniform system of accounts be established under the President's authority and that the President clearly be responsible for recommending the content of appropriations bills.[1]

The Nineteenth Century

In the context of America's historical experience, the Taft Commission's recommendations represented a radical departure from "business as usual." While the conventional picture of earlier presidents being almost totally isolated from the budget process has been brought into question [9], none could be said to have enjoyed the central role proposed in 1912. One of the earliest arguments in the running battle between president and Congress was over the question of presidential involvement in budget preparation [10]. Fisher has described the efforts of early presidents such as Jefferson, John Quincy Adams, Van Buren, and Tyler, usually acting through their Treasury secretaries, to influence the budgetary actions of Congress.

Granting the point that at least some nineteenth century presidents did seek to intervene, with varying degrees of success, in the budgetary process, the pre-1921 arrangements were clearly designed to enable Congress to exert control. The Constitution of 1787 says little about the subject, providing only that "no money shall be drawn from the Treasury but in consequence of appropriations be made by law," and requiring the publication "from time to time" of an account of all receipts and expenditures (U.S. Constitution, art. 1, sec. 9).

From 1802 to 1865, control over both revenues and appropriations was concentrated in the House Committee on Ways and Means. This centralization within Congress enabled some presidents to influence appropriations through their role as leader of a political party. Otherwise, executive input was largely limited to the annual report of the Secretary of the Treasury, who also submitted to Congress at the outset of each session a Book of Estimates containing the expenditure requirements of the various departments and agencies, a function characterized by Burkhead [2, p. 10] as "primarily clerical."

Such internal unity within the Congress broke down after the Civil War with the creation of a separate House Appropriations Committee. Before the end of the century, no fewer than 10 standing committees in the House and eight in the Senate had been given authority to recommend appropriations bills. The system of funding government operations at this time consisted essentially of agencies dealing more-or-less directly with particular committees of Congress. No one was responsible for formulating a coordinated budgetary program for the entire government [11]. Agency spending officers submitted their needs to the particular congressional committee authorized to appropriate funds for that agency. Neither the agencies nor the individual committees were in a position to weigh the relative merits of these requests. Lacking any means of coordination or planning, it is not surprising that problems arose, including the much-criticized practice of incurring "coercive deficiencies."

This practice, common as well among state governments, broke down budgetary control. As Buck [3, p. 486] described it, spending agencies were permitted to obligate themselves to expenditures in excess of their appropriations. Having done so, they then presented these claims to the legislature, which had no choice other than to provide the additional funds. Under this system of congressional finance, late nineteenth century presidents were largely limited to exhorting Congress toward fiscal prudence. Fortunately, most of the period was characterized by revenue surpluses, allowing nearly half of the Civil War debt to be paid off by 1884 [12].

But the age of innocence and of limited government was coming to a close. By the turn of the century the activities and accompanying expenditures of the federal government were expanding visibly. The first twentieth century president, Theodore Roosevelt, could openly discuss the responsibilities of an "affirmative kind" of administration. It would be left to his immediate successors, however, especially the otherwise phlegmatic Taft, to trigger the public debate that would lead ultimately to the adoption of an executive budget for the nation.

The Wilson–Harding Years

Taft, defeated for reelection in 1912, left office without having convinced Congress of the need for an executive budget. But the work of his commission in pointing out the deficiencies of the existing arrangements transformed budgeting into an "issue of national significance" [3, p. 21]. Several factors had contributed to the deferral of action on the matter. First, of course, the fiscal needs of the government remained modest until the nation's entry into World War I. In addition, adoption of the sixteenth amendment and the subsequent enactment in 1913 of legislation imposing a national income tax promised relief on the revenue front. Within a year after the income tax went into effect, however, war broke out in Europe, with adverse consequences for the U.S. economy [13, p. 32]. Government revenues plummeted in the wake of a near-cessation of imports, a bank crisis, stock market failure, and drastic reductions in industrial production. Congress reacted with emergency revenue legislation focused mainly on raising excise taxes. Political attention again was riveted on the need for obtaining adequate revenues, rather than designing a method for rationalizing government expenditures. But that was a minor distraction compared with the advent of American involvement in the war.

Presiding over this sequence of events was Taft's successor, Woodrow Wilson, a reform-oriented executive whose long list of ideas for improving government did not include budgetary reform. Described as having only a "passing interest" in such matters, he relied heavily upon his Secretary of the Treasury William G. McAdoo [13, p. 33]. Also, Wilson was less committed than his predecessors to a balanced budget. In any event, no further action to establish a budget system would be taken until after the war. A single exception, largely the work of Congress and suggesting some support for greater executive involvement in the process, was the creation in 1916 of the Bureau of Efficiency, which was made directly responsible to the president [11, p. 101].

With bipartisan legislative support and Wilson's endorsement, Congress in 1920 passed a budget and accounting act embodying most of the recommendations of the Taft Commission. But Wilson surprisingly vetoed the measure, citing constitutionally based objections to a provision in the bill that exempted the chief accounting officer from the president's removal power. No further attempt at enactment of the legislation was made until after the election of 1920, which brought Warren Harding to the White House.

Harding, subsequently to be labeled the nation's least distinguished chief executive, signed a new Budget and Accounting Act into law within 3 months after assuming office and almost 1 year to the day from Wilson's veto of a virtually identical bill. Harding's campaign rhetoric had stressed the need for a "return to normalcy" and he apparently saw the budget bill as a vehicle for restoring a balanced federal budget and reducing the war-incurred national debt. Inadvertently, perhaps, he had simultaneously provided a major weapon in the development of the strong executive through the concentration of budget initiative in the hands of the president.

The Budget and Accounting Act

The Budget and Accounting Act of 1921 has been described by one historian of American public administration as "the watershed in the pursuit of executive budgetary efficiency" [10, p. 361]. The bill (42 Stat. 18, 1921) required the president to transmit to Congress annually "the Budget" and to assist him in this task created the Bureau of the Budget to be located in the Department of the Treasury. The Bureau (BOB), headed by a director appointed by and responsible to the president, was authorized to "assemble, correlate, revise, reduce, or increase" departmental budget estimates (Section 207). The act further required each department of the government to appoint a budget officer and to submit its spending estimates to the Bureau, thus ending the old practice of transmitting uncoordinated requests to Congress.

The legislation also created the General Accounting Office, to be headed by the Comptroller General of the United States, and transferred to the GAO the auditing functions previously carried out by the Treasury Department. The Comptroller General, appointed by the president to a 15-year nonrenewable term, was made subject to removal only by joint resolution of Congress (Section 303). It was this provision that had led Wilson to veto the earlier act. Along with reporting requirements, it was made clear that the government's principal auditing agency was accountable directly to Congress. As part of the budget reform, the House of Representatives in 1920 changed its rules to reduce to one the number of committees authorized to deal with appropriations. The Senate followed suit 2 years later [14].

The Bureau of the Budget

Located in the Treasury Department for the first two decades of its existence, the Bureau of the Budget was in fact directly responsible to the President from the outset [3, p. 295]. This arrangement was formalized in 1939 when the Bureau was transferred to the newly created Executive Office of the President. At the outset, however, Harding had the good fortune to select as BOB's first director the energetic and capable Charles G. Dawes, a former Army general who later would become vice-president under Coolidge. Dawes, committed to the notion that the Bureau was a presidential staff agency, was given wide discretion in dealing with administrative matters [15, p. 6]. Obsessed with imposing efficiency and economy on departmental operations, he is credited with establishing the Bureau's key role and influence throughout the government [3, p. 450].

With his attention focused on the single task of reducing spending, however, Dawes neglected the broader issues of administrative management and reform [15, p. 7]. Although the 1921 act clearly authorized the Bureau to concern itself with such matters (Section 209), neither Dawes nor his successors in the Coolidge and Hoover administrations showed much interest. Under Roosevelt, the Bureau would institutionalize its long-developing role as the clearing house for legislative requests, strengthening White House control over agency relationships with Congress [14].

It would fall to the report of Roosevelt's Committee on Administrative Management, the famous Brownlow Committee, to point out the Bureau's major failing as an instrument of administrative management [15, p. 12]. Implementation of this report led to the creation of the Executive Office of the President (EOP) in 1939. As a first step in reorganization, the Bureau of the Budget was transferred from the Treasury Department to the EOP. Its newly expanded functions, elaborated in Executive Order 8248, gave high priority to "the development of improved plans of administrative management." Henceforth, in addition to its budgetary functions, the Bureau would be charged with advising the executive departments and agencies on improved administrative organization and practices.

As Berman [15, p. 14] has noted, this "born-again Budget Bureau needed leadership of far greater vision and administrative ability than it had received since 1921." To this end, Roosevelt named Harold D. Smith as director, and it was he who created the "modern" Budget Bureau as "an indispensable presidential managerial staff." It was Smith's view that the budget reflects the President's program, and, when enacted, it becomes the work program of the government [16]. In its new form and under new leadership, the Bureau was launched on a course, which it would follow to the present time, as the principal staff aide to the President. As Sorensen [17, p. 29] would later note in discussing presidential decision making, "the official most often likely to loom largest in his thinking when he makes a key decision is not the Secretary of State or the Secretary of Defense but the Director of the Budget." More importantly, for our purposes, no important executive branch budget reform attempted over the next half century would stand a chance of succeeding without the active support of the BOB or, as it was later to be renamed, the Office of Management and Budget.

THE "MODERN" ERA

Adoption of the new executive budget system in 1921 was followed by a period of budgetary tranquility that spanned nearly three decades. During that long period, the federal budget was "an immensely detailed document that provided surprisingly little information about the programs government carried out" [18, p. 5]. A traditional line-item format was employed in which an agency's request was broken down on the basis of things to be purchased and people to be employed, the "inputs" of the governmental process. The most significant portion of such a budget, then as now, focused on personnel costs. Separate lines spelled out in detail requests for funds with which to pay for supplies, equipment, utilities, and travel, among other items. This standard format also was found in most state and local jurisdictions, where it is still dominant [19, 20].

Allen Schick [21], in a piece now regarded as a classic, linked the functions or purposes of budgeting to the forms of budgets. Drawing, in part, from the earlier work of Robert Anthony [22], Schick posited three basic orientations of any budget system: control, management, and planning. While elements of each purpose are present in all budget types, one will typically predominate in any single system. Of the three, control was (and, I would argue, still is) primary. Control was the dominant aim of early line-item budgets with their hundreds—even thousands—of distinct items, each subject to individual scrutiny by reviewing authorities and ultimately incorporated into the language of appropriation bills.

The line-item or "object" classification was a product of an era in which legislators and the general public distrusted administrators [1, p. 128]. By establishing detailed listings of things for which public funds were being spent and then linking each category of spending to a specific account, tight control could be exerted over the bureaucracy. That was the principal purpose of the system: to control expenditures at the agency and departmental levels and to hold public officials accountable after the fact through an extensive auditing process. This type of budget and accounting system, by detailing the objects of expenditure, greatly reduced the discretionary power of administrators [23].

Cursed by its critics as mindless, irrational, short-sighted, fragmented, and conservative [24], it nevertheless fulfilled the need of legislative bodies to control public spending. In spite of its detractors, the structure and process of budgeting changed remarkably little until, with the distractions of the Great Depression and World War II out of the way, administrative reform movements resurfaced in the late 1940s. The ensuing 40-year period brought a succession of reforms, both structural and procedural, executive and legislative. It is these to which we now turn.

Performance Budgeting

Dissatisfaction with the standard line-item format appeared early. Lacking information regarding program goals or achievements, it was considered a poor instrument for relating public expenditures to public accomplishments. It might be interesting, even important, to know the salaries of clerk-typists in the engineering department, but that in itself was no clue as to what those employees were doing. Beyond providing year-to-year comparisons of costs and indicating the maximum amount of funds available, the budget was of limited usefulness to managers or policymakers in arriving at programmatic decisions. Nor was it helpful in explaining or justifying government programs to citizens.

Credit for introducing a performance-type budget into the federal government is usually awarded to the first Hoover Commission.[2] This report [25], issued in 1949, recommended that the "whole budgetary concept of the Federal Government should be refashioned by the adoption of a budget based on functions, activities, and projects" (p. 8). The idea was not new. Under a variety of different labels, performance budgeting had appeared in several cities across the country prior to World War II. Indeed, the Taft Commission on Economy and Efficiency in 1912 had stressed the importance of presenting the budget in accordance with the subjects of work to be done [1, p. 134]. While its adoption was not widespread, some federal agencies, notably the Department of Agriculture and the Tennessee Valley Authority, experimented with what was called "project" budgeting in the mid 1930s. A similar format was employed by the Department of the Navy in preparing its fiscal 1948 budget request. It was to these early efforts that the Hoover Commission looked in formulating its recommendations in 1949.

Under the traditional line-item or "object" budget, the legislative body provided funds to acquire the resources necessary to conduct the business of government. In short, the focus was on the amounts needed to pay for things: personnel, equipment, supplies, etc. Such a presentation revealed little about what was accomplished as a result of such expenditures. Policies, programs, and activities of the spending units of government were not incorporated into the budget document. The question of efficiency was not answerable based on the information available in the traditional budget. It should not be surprising, then, that the first major reform effort was directed toward the design of a budget format that would enable program managers, agency heads, elected officials, and citizens to gain some insight into the costs associated with the various activities of government. As the Hoover Commission report put it, "the all-important thing in budgeting is the work or service to be accomplished, and what that work or service will cost" (p. 8).

Performance budgeting, then, is an attempt to go beyond the dollars alone and the mere objects being bought and paid for, to look at the services being provided, the activities being carried out. Further, it seeks to attach cost figures to those programs and activities. Budgets take on a different appearance in response to the need to present information in a different context. Tied to cost-accounting techniques, performance budgets presented managers and policymakers with detailed breakdowns of the unit costs of agency outputs. Examples would include, at the local level of government, such things as the cost per mile of streets resurfaced, or the cost per ton of garbage collected. Such data made cost and performance comparisons possible across years or between one jurisdiction and another. A fully developed performance budget became, in effect, the work program for the budgeting unit. As such, it required more involvement on the part of program managers.

Congress, through the Budget and Accounting Procedures Act of 1950, provided for government-wide presentation of the national budget on a performance basis. Without using the term "performance budget," the Act specified that

> The Budget shall set forth in such form and detail as the President may determine—(a) functions and activities of the Government; (b) any other desirable classification of data; (c) a reconciliation of the summary of expenditures with proposed appropriations. (64 Stat. 832, Title I, Section 102)

Commenting on the innovation shortly thereafter, Seckler-Hudson [36] pointed out that the new concept "basically means a focus of attention on the ends to be served by the government rather than the dollars to be spent." In constructing a performance budget, she added, the most important single task would be "the precise definition of the work to be done and a careful estimate of what the work would cost" [26, p. 5].

While performance budgeting suffered from indifference and neglect in Washington, it caught on in municipal governments across the country. Labeled "management budgeting" by the International City Management Association [27, p. 103], the performance budget fit comfortably into a climate where increased attention was being focused on improving the efficiency of operations. It was also the case that many local government functions lent themselves to the kind of quantification demanded by the performance budget format. Activities such as solid waste collection, street maintenance, and fire protection have measurable outputs in terms of end results. Cost accounting enables these outputs (e.g., lane miles resurfaced) to be stated in terms of unit costs. Aggregating those costs produces a budget estimate of expenditures for that particular activity in a given year.

During this first wave of serious budgetary reform, many local governments adapted their financial presentations to the performance format, with or without cost-accounting techniques [27]. Some, such as Los Angeles, received high marks [28]. Others got an "E" for effort, but were credited with doing less than might have been possible [30]. Some, when placed under a more demanding microscope, were found to have fallen well short of providing accurate cost estimates of city services [31]. Still, as an instrument for providing both managers and policymakers with detailed service performance-cost data, the performance budget represented a major step forward. Its usefulness is attested to by the relatively few cities that, having adopted it, later discarded the performance budget.

Program Budgeting

Performance budgeting, never fully accepted at the federal level of government, was swept aside in the early 1960s by a new development in budgetary technology: program budgeting. Entering the government by way of the Defense Department where it was hailed as an instant success, the Planning-Programming-Budgeting System, (PPBS) was made mandatory for all federal agencies by President Johnson in 1965.[3] Like many budgetary reforms introduced into government, this one also had its roots in private industry. According to David Novick [33], one of its earliest advocates, program budgeting actually made its governmental debut in 1942 when the War Production Board employed a version of it to assign priorities and control production of war materials. But it was the adoption of PPBS under the direction of Defense Secretary Robert McNamara that led to a decade of dominance of this approach throughout the 1960s.

The basic idea underlying program budgeting, including PPBS, is that budgetary decisions should be based on output categories (objectives and end products) rather than inputs (personnel and equipment costs). Charles J. Hitch, former Comptroller of the Defense Department and the man usually credited with installing PPBS there, described it as combining two management techniques: program forecasting and system analysis. Program forecasting means focusing on goal-oriented programs rather than on expenditure objects and projecting both inputs and outputs into the future [34]. Systems analysis seeks to study outputs by means of quantitative methods and a model where possible to enable policymakers to compare alternative courses of action.

Program budgeting goes beyond performance budgeting and its narrow concern with carrying out specific tasks efficiently. It asks, first of all, what the goals are of a government and its various agencies and institutions.

Program budgeting, especially as manifested in PPBS, was largely the contribution of economists. It introduced into the budget-making process certain concepts previously ignored, except in rare and short-lived experiments. These included the systematic consideration of alternative means to accomplish a given task, the comparison at the margins of both program costs and benefits, and the idea of "trade-offs" of substitutions in arriving at policy choices.

Basically there were five crucial elements involved in the program budgeting process:

1. A focus on the objectives or purposes of government. Once these fundamental objectives were identified, then all activities of the government—regardless of their organizational location—could be assigned to broad program categories (i.e., education, national security, health, etc.).

2. An across-the-board program structure, linking all the activities and their costs to those common programs. The total cost figures would then represent the "budget."

3. A multiyear program and financial plan. Employing an extended time horizon—usually 5 years—the future implications of present decisions could be projected, in terms of both costs and benefits.

4. Program analysis. At the heart of PPBS was the use of cost–benefit and cost-effectiveness studies to compare the various programs and projects being considered as alternative means to achieve a given objective or carry out a stated purpose.

5. Budget aggregation. Summing the total costs of program decisions resulted in the creation of the budget.

One of the claimed strengths of program budgeting and, ultimately, one of its weaknesses—was that it pretended to ignore organizational boundries. Because, as Novick [35] put it, program structures rarely conform to either the appropriation structure or the organizational structure, crosswalks had to be created to convert program based data into the necessary line-item, object-class, organizationally based budget. Neither Congress nor state legislatures exhibited a willingness to alter the traditional language of their appropriation bills to match the program format.

While budget theory may have no difficulty in abrogating agency and departmental jurisdictional boundaries, neither the bureaucracy nor the legislatures that oversee them are similarly inclined. In program budgeting, "organization gives way to program" [36]. In the real world, it is usually the other way around. One of the most obvious revelations contained in program budgeting is the dispersed, overlapping, and sometimes conflicting organizational arrangements devised to house similar programs. The thought that immediately arises is, why shouldn't organization reflect program distributions? Why should public health programs be dispersed among more than 30 agencies, departments, boards, and commissions, as is the case in Alabama? In short, program budgeting encourages administrative reorganization. But few states—Kentucky and Washington come to mind—were willing to accompany the introduction of program budgeting with the restructuring of the executive branch of government. At the federal level, McNamara's success is using PPBS to overcome service boundary (and rivalry) problems in the Department of Defense was not matched elsewhere in the government. Instead, each department had its own program structure, and no coordinating authority emerged to integrate programs across organizational lines [37].

If performance budgeting was efficiency oriented, program budgeting fixed its sights on effectiveness. Given a set of agreed-upon goals, it presented policymakers with available alternatives, both in terms of objectives and the means by which to achieve them. Cost–benefit analysis (or cost-effectiveness analysis) was employed to cast alternative policy choices in quantitative terms. By displaying both the long-term benefits as well as the total costs of various proposals, this form of marginal analysis was intended to produce "new ways of thinking about policy making" [38].

Program budgeting, in its various manifestations, has its intellectual roots in economics and management science. Its underlying rationale is to improve rationality in the making of resource allocation decisions. In this, it adopts an anti-incrementalist posture. Unsurprisingly, its principal critics have been those political scientists [39–43] who viewed program budgeting as an attack on cherished principles of pluralist democracy and individualism. To the critics, bargaining is the essential element in policy making. Program budgeting, at least as practiced in PPBS, was seen as flawed by its omission of explicit consideration of political factors [39]. Schick [21] suggested that PPBS took "an overly mechanistic view of the impact of form on behavior." He questioned the existence of "Budgetary Man" as a counterpart to the classical "Economic Man."

PPBS, nevertheless, shifted the thinking of budget officials from a concentration on the means of government to consideration of the ends and successfully introduced into the budgetary process both analysis and planning. The language and techniques of program analysis spread swiftly throughout the federal bureaucracy and filtered down to state and local governments as well. When the method was formally abandoned in 1971, it left behind a residue of disciplines and practices that continue, in some places to this day [44].

As an idea, program budgeting was both attractive and logical. It suggested that the government should plan what to do rather than blindly meander along [45]. Still, by 1971, this innovation in budgeting had come to the end of its rope. The reasons for its demise have been catalogued by Allen Schick [37]. Imposed from above by the Bureau of the Budget, PPBS analysts remained outsiders, unable to penetrate the routines of agency budgeting. The Budget Bureau, itself, seemed less than enthusiastically committed to the reform. The new routines were imposed without accompanying increases in resources, and the centralizing tendencies associated with PPBS did not sit well with middle-level managers in the agencies. By highlighting duplication in service delivery functions and posing the threat of administrative reorganizations, the new system introduced additional conflict into the bureaucratic arena. Finally, like most budgetary reforms, PPBS was an instrument of executive branch origins. It was installed without taking into account congressional reactions. And that reaction, generally, was not favorable. What a bureaucrat wants from a budget may not be identical with what a legislator wants [46, p. 105]. In any event, Congress declined to alter its notions as to what it expected to find in a budget submission. Neither did the reform appear to result in noticeably different outcomes in Congressional budgetary decisions [47].

Management by Objectives

Although it was a product of the Kennedy–Johnson years, PPBS continued in use through the early days of the Nixon administration. In 1971, however, the technique was formally abandoned as a requirement for federal agencies. In its wake, reflecting a new emphasis on management at OMB, came another approach borrowed from the private sector: management by objectives (MBO). Conceptually, "the Nixon Administration sought to shift attention from problems of choice to problems of management" [48]. By 1973, spurred by OMB deputy director Frederic V. Malek, management by objectives had been implemented widely throughout the federal government.

Reacting to one of the chronic complaints levied against PPBS—that it generated too much paperwork—management by objectives advocates in OMB played down the new system's manpower and paperwork requirements. The major federal agencies involved were allowed considerable discretion in defining objectives. It became, whatever the original intentions, a much less comprehensive approach than PPBS. With its primary focus on managerial aspects of program implementation, MBO placed less emphasis on long-range planning and program evaluation. Where PPBS tried to force the comparison of programs across organizational boundaries, MBO respected those jurisdictional lines. Where PPBS had had a centralizing, top-down orientation, MBO promised a more participative approach, with line managers heavily involved in the setting of agency objectives.

Operationally, management by objectives consists of a three-part cycle [49]: First, managers and subordinates agree on a list of measurable, results-oriented objectives and link these to the departmental budget request. Second, milestones to be achieved en route to the objectives are established and periodic progress reviews are scheduled. These management conferences, scheduled bimonthly or quarterly throughout the year, assess the status of each objective and, if necessary, permit the objectives themselves to be changed to conform to new initiatives. Third, the results are evaluated, each manager submitting to the department head a year-end report describing successes and failures in meeting the objectives set earlier.

Like PPBS, management by objectives relied for success on the ability to clearly define goals and objectives. Like performance budgeting, it demanded an ability to measure performance against specific, quantifiable standards. Unlike its two predecessors, however, MBO failed to establish itself as an activity essential to budgeting. While a few agencies made an attempt to link MBO to the budget process, most were unable to make the connection. As Lynch [2] explains, such linkage can be accomplished by using a matrix table juxtaposing agency objectives and budget activities. In this way, the amount of money needed to carry out a given objective during the budget year would be highlighted. Implementation of such a process encountered two related problems. First, since most programs have multiple objectives, it was difficult to isolate funds in mutually exclusive categories. Second, not all program activities were covered by MBO objectives. Worse, managers became fixated on identifying objectives, a process that became self-defeating since long lists of objectives were not accompanied by resources sufficient to carry out any but the first few [50, p. 184].

Budgeting, it has been said, is a schizophrenic enterprise, trying simultaneously to accommodate both political choices and managerial decisions [51]. The emphasis in PPBS was on the former, in MBO on the latter. Some saw the possibility that the two approaches could be combined into one that would offer more than either alone [52]. It was not to be. When Richard Nixon flew west into temporary exile in California, management by objec tives lost its champion in the White House. Gerald Ford, inheriting the whirlwind, undertook a "megamanagement" effort spanning a broad spectrum of administrative reforms in 1976. An avalanche of management improvement directives emanating from OMB buried management by objectives in its path [48]. Instituted informally at the outset, MBO "evaporated" slowly and by 1979 remained viable only in scattered outposts of the federal government.

Zero-Base Budgeting

Since government began, whenever politicians could find nothing better to do with their time and energy, and whenever they confronted the need to demonstrate concern for a public problem, they reorganized the public bureaucracy. [53]

Or they reformed the budget process. The winding down of PPBS and management by objectives created only a momentary vacuum in budget styles. This time, the winds of change blew out of Texas and Georgia in the form of zero-base budgeting (ZBB). With a newly-elected President of the United States as its leading advocate, ZBB took hold in Washington in 1977. As with its predecessors, this budgetary innovation made its way to the nation's capital via the private sector and state and local government experiments [54, 55]. At the time of its introduction into the federal government, an even dozen states already had taken steps to implement a similar process [56].

Whatever else may have been claimed for this new approach—and much was claimed—it would, its advocates insisted, make possible the reallocation of funds from lower to higher level priorities and put an end to the much-condemned practice of incrementalism. It would, in President Jimmy Carter's words, make it possible to "plan and allocate resources more rationally" [57, p. 26]. Scattered early reports from the field raised questions about the applicability of zero-base budgeting in state government [58, 59]. But Carter, as governor of Georgia, had been impressed by the technique and promised during the 1976 campaign that, if elected to the presidency, he would bring the reform to Washington with him. He was, and he did. Three months after his inauguration, the heads of executive branch departments were instructed to prepare their fiscal year 1979 budgets according to the zero-base format.

Developed in the private sector, notably for Texas Instruments, zero-base budgeting was sold to governments largely on the basis of the oldest promise contained in campaigns for budget reform. As a candidate for presidency, Carter had declared the federal budget process to be "inefficient, chaotic, and uncontrollable." ZBB, he argued, would "reduce costs and make the federal government more efficient and effective" [57]. This would be accomplished by improving the quality of budgetary information, involving line managers in the decision process, and emphasizing the kind of analysis that would shed greater light on the cost-effectiveness of programs.

Theoretically, zero-base budgeting drew on the insight of Verne B. Lewis [60] and others who had argued that decision makers should consider more than a single recommended level of spending for various programs. In this sense, ZBB was a form of "alternative budgeting." It required managers to consider not only alternative levels of funding and service output, but alternative means for achieving objectives. In this, it shared some of the conceptual ground previously occupied by PPBS and management by objectives.

While not applied uniformly in every organization, ZBB basically involved a four-step process. First, organizational objectives were determined and "decision units" were defined. These were simply those units at which budgetary and programmatic decisions were made.

Frequently, they were coterminous with existing organizational substructures, although they could be defined along broader program lines. Second, each decision unit was analyzed within the framework of a "decision package." This was the "building block" of the zero-base approach [54]. Each decision package consisted of a cluster of activities related to the accomplishment of the unit's objectives. At this point, managers were required to consider alternative means of achieving the objectives as well as different levels of services and resources. Also included at this stage of analysis were such factors as work loads, performance measures, and the costs and benefits associated with each level of service and expenditure. Ultimately, each activity contained in the package had to be considered in terms of reduced, current, and increased levels of effort and funding. In this way, managers presented higher level decision makers with several choices to select from, rather than a single set of recommended figures. Based on such information, decision units could be compared with each other and decisions could be made to approve or disapprove competing claims on the budget. This ranking of decision packages constituted the third step in the process, frequently referred to as "prioritizing." Finally, at the highest level, the organization's budget request was formulated based on the funding needs associated with each adopted level of program activity.

A principal advantage claimed for ZBB was that it generated previously unavailable information that could be used in both managerial decision making and broader, higher level policymaking. By offering decision makers multiple options it broke with the traditional "one best way" of presenting agency requests. To the extent that legislative bodies accepted the zero-base format—and acceptance was far from universal—it allowed them to view the probable consequences of providing different incremental levels of funding for various programs.

In the sense that budget formats determine how budgets are viewed, the information presented, and the kinds of questions asked, ZBB had an impact. Specifically, this approach shifted attention away from what is to be added to the current year program and focused upon increases to the minimum level of support [2, p. 53]. But an impact on the process is not the same thing as an impact on outcomes. On this point, ZBB produced its share of "rational skeptics." Even before the ink was dry on the FY 1979 federal budget, a study of ZBB's performance in Georgia raised pertinent questions as to whether it made a difference. Lauth [59] found that, contrary to former Governor Carter's impression, ZBB had had relatively little impact on budgeting in Georgia. Its use in that state had failed to reduce incrementalism, reallocate budget shares, or change significantly the way in which agencies prepared their budgets. Schick [61] rendered a similar verdict on federal ZBB, observing that it had "changed the terminology of budgeting, but little more."

Introduced by President Carter, zero-base budgeting departed Washington with him. The Reagan administration dropped the label, but decision units, variable funding level documentation, and priority rankings continued to be employed [62, 155]. Indeed, in preparing the FY 1986 budget, the Reagan OMB literally zero-based (requested no funding) for several programs, including Amtrack and the Appalachian Regional Commission. Congress, as it had on several occasions with Carter, restored the funds.

Zero-base budgeting suffered from some of the same difficulties that had plagued its predecessors. It assumed an ability to clearly define the goals and objectives of each activity being budgeted, as well as the goals and objectives of the entire organization [63, p. 426]. In addition, the process generated a massive amount of paperwork. In Georgia, there were 11,000 decision packages accompanied by 33 pages of instructions and 24 different forms. It was estimated that if the governor allotted 4 hours every day for 2 months he could spend about 1 minute on each decision package, not enough time to read it, let alone analyze it [64].

Like PPBS and management by objectives, zero-base budgeting, to use Richard Rose's term, has "evaporated." Gone but not forgotten, it survives in pockets of the federal bureaucracy and, in altered form, in some 20 states. What all three of these executive branch budgetary reforms had in common was an emphasis on analysis. But analysis was either unwelcome or unnecessary.

The age of analysis may not be dead, but it is at least sleeping. Wildavsky [65] had raised the question whether analysis had been driven from the field by "political dissensus." That is, when partisan and policy polarization have reached the levels currently seen in Congress, the nature of the important questions changes. V. O. Key [66] had pondered whether analysis could inform the decision where the choice was between allocating marginal dollars to battleships or poor relief. He was skeptical. Wildavsky [39, 65] argued that such questions are too "aggregated" and too philosophical to be subjected to analysis. He added that when the critical questions center around the size of the deficit and the size of government and the parties cannot agree on either, stalemate results. "When size matters more than content, there is no need for analysis" [65].

CONGRESSIONAL REFORMS

The budgetary reforms discussed thus far have been executive centered, technical, and geared toward improving the ways in which budgets are prepared. They have focused on the budget document itself, with minimal impact on the broader "process" by which spending decisions are finally arrived. One often-cited cause of the failure of these reforms was their inability to alter significantly the way in which budgets were dealt with by the legislative branch of government. At the national level, Congress throughout most of the nation's history gave only sporadic attention to how it handled one of its principal responsibilities. The enactment of appropriation bills that confer legal authority on executive branch agencies to commit the government to certain expenditures has remained a largely haphazard process. Efforts to link revenues and expenditures were seldom attempted and short-lived.

Early Reforms

Prior to passage of the Budget and Accounting Act of 1921, congressional control of the budget process was sufficiently strong that little need for reform was evident. Agencies dealt directly with congressional committees, and presidential involvement was minor. The 1921 act, however, shifted the balance toward the executive. The Bureau of the Budget provided the President with staff expertise not available on Capitol Hill. The contrast "between executive management and congressional aimlessness" became clear [63, p. 417]. The legislative branch, running contrary to the trend toward centralization of executive budget authority, maintained a decentralized approach to budget making. The arrangements, entrenched for more than a half century, are familiar. Authorization, revenue, and appropriation responsibilities were dispersed among separate committees in both houses. Nowhere did Congress attempt to pull the whole picture together [66].

Periodically, in recognition of its deteriorating position, Congress would entertain proposals designed to remedy the situation. But it would be 1974 before serious reform of the legislative budget process would emerge. Before examining that still-in-place modification, a brief look at a few of the earlier efforts might set the stage.

Joint Committee on the Budget

In 1952, Senator John L. McClellan of Arkansas introduced a bill to create a joint committee of Congress to deal with the budget. The measure, which would have provided the committee with a staff of budget analysts to rival the executive branch's Budget Bureau, passed the Senate but was defeated in the House. The proposed committee would have included 14 members from the House and Senate Appropriations Committees. It was opposed in the House by the Chairman and ranking minority member of that body's Appropriations Committee, who contended that the proposed committee would encroach on the functions of their committee. After defeating the bill, the House added $500,000 to increase the staffs of the appropriations committees [67].

More than 50 years ago, A. E. Buck [68] had recommended the consolidation of the appropriations committees in the two houses into a single joint committee on the budget. One supporting argument was that it would eliminate the need for duplicate hearings.

Inherent in the proposal for a joint legislative committee on the budget was the notion of a congressional counterpart to the Bureau of the Budget. Congress simply did not have access to the analytical data about the budget that was available to the executive branch [69]. As McClellan put it, Congress had "no authentic source of information to refute or contradict the claims of need and justification made by the spending agenices" [67]. Proposals for correcting this imbalance usually centered on an expanded role for the General Accounting Office, a congressional agency. A more extreme suggestion would have transferred the Bureau of the Budget to Congress [66]. Questions of legislative interference in executive administration and the fear of possible partisan manipulation of congressional budget staff halted this reform in its tracks, at least temporarily.

The Legislative Budget

The provision for a so-called legislative budget has been called the least successful feature of the Legislative Reorganization Act of 1946 [79]. The act provided that the four congressional financial committees (House Ways and Means, Senate Finance, and House and Senate Appropriations) would recommend at the outset of each session the maximum limit on appropriations for the next fiscal year. The figure arrived at was to be based on consideration of the President's recommendations, including estimates of overall federal revenues and expenditures. If estimated receipts exceeded estimated expenditures, the act called for recommendations for reducing the national debt. It projected expenditures were greater than expected receipts, the concurrent resolution was to recommend an increase in the public debt sufficient to cover the expected deficit [70, p. 93].

It was a noble attempt to make Congress take some responsibility for keeping revenues and expenditures in balance. But, as Smithies noted, it was doomed from the start. The antideficiency provision imposed no obligation on the Congress but affected only the President. There was no arrangement for recommending increases or decreases in taxation. The only way to eliminate a presidential deficit was through a reduction in spending. The attempt by Congress to impose a ceiling on appropriations was motivated by a zeal for retrenchment [1, p. 328]. Efforts to implement the legislative budget in 1947 and 1948 failed and the process was abandoned.

This effort at reform revealed that Congress is in no position early in a session to set spending and revenue ceilings, a lesson that would have to be relearned 30 year later. As one observer noted, however, the ill-fated effort at reform reflected a congressional distaste for the system of considering the budget piecemeal. It showed "a desire for some means whereby Congress may at one time pass upon the total budget, revenues as well as expenditures" [67].

The Omnibus Bill

The Budget and Accounting Act of 1921 was designed, in part, to enable Congress to deal more effectively with the budget. It proved to be an elusive target. The President's budget, on arrival in Congress, was promptly divided into 12 or 15 parts and scattered among a like number of subcommittees in each house. (Since 1968, there have been 13 subcommittees and 13 appropriations bills in each chamber.) The Congress, therefore, never considered the budget as a whole or weighed the relative merits of all programs. Decisions made in the various subcommittees of the appropriations committees tended then, as now, to be relatively binding. Thus, the locus of power in budgetary matters was highly decentralized and the end product a fragmented whole.

One attempt to remedy this situation was the one-time use of something called the omnibus appropriation bill. This device, employed only in 1950, consolidated all appropriation bills into a single omnibus bill. The results were unsatisfactory and the experiment was not repeated.

There were numerous drawbacks to the omnibus approach. Most dissatisfaction arose from the fact that delay in the House of Representatives kept the bill from moving to the Senate until May 10, during a time when the fiscal year began on July 1. The Senate did not complete action until August 4, and subsequent conferences delayed signing by the President until September 6, 1950, 2 months after the start of the fiscal year [1, p. 330]. In the apparent belief that the procedure conferred too much power on the chairmen of the appropriations committees, members of the House Appropriations Committee voted against their chairman and killed an effort to use the omnibus bill the following year. It was never revived.

Budget and Impoundment Act

As the size of government increased markedly in the years following mid-century, so did the federal budget. It grew in many ways unanticipated by earlier reformers, not only in size but in complexity. The congressional budget process, however, remained decentralized, fragmented, and uncoordinated. Other problems, always lurking in the background, came to a head. Linda Smith [71] identified four major factors that combined to produce the Congressional Budget and Impoundment Control Act of 1974, the single most comprehensive reform of the legislative budget process ever undertaken. The major problem and the one that triggered congressional action was that of impoundment [72]. This device, traceable back to the Jefferson administration, enabled the President to withhold spending authority already approved by Congress. Traditionally, it had been used only when further spending on a project was unnecessary because of cost savings, early completion, or where the need for economizing was shared by Congress and the President. The practice became controversial only when, beginning with the presidency of Franklin D. Roosevelt, appropriated funds were withheld from the spending agencies for budgetary or political purposes [73]. Post-World War II impoundments by Truman, Eisenhower, and Kennedy were concentrated in the defense area. Lyndon Johnson extended the use of impoundments to curtail spending for domestic programs, although most were merely deferrals, the funds being released later.

The issue came to a boil during the Nixon administration when the President impounded upward of $20 billion in more than 100 programs, nearly all of them domestic and most involving grant-in-aid monies appropriated to assist state and local governments. The action, spread over a 4-year period, prompted more than 60 court cases as state and local public officials and interest groups sued the appropriate cabinet officers to obtain release of the funds [74]. In all but a handful of cases, the plaintiffs were victorious. But Congress was not content to rely upon the courts to uphold the allocation of appropriated funds. The courts, in any event, had not addressed the issue of constitutionality but had relied upon language in the various statutes in ordering the funds released. Language severely restricting the President's impoundment authority would be included in the 1974 Budget Act.

In addition to impoundments, three other factors combined to prompt the 1974 reform legislation [71]. First among these was the problem of "uncontrollable" spending. These were expenditure items locked into existing laws, which could not be changed merely as a result of the annual appropriations process. Entitlement programs such as Social Security and other trust-fund-based spending accounted for much of the total, which by 1970 had reached more than 50% of total federal outlays.

Another problem related to the increasing inability of Congress to pass appropriation bills by the beginning of the fiscal year. In each year between 1948 and 1974, Congress had failed to enact all 13 appropriation bills prior to the start of the fiscal year, in those days July 1 [75, p. 67]. As a result, most agencies of the government were forced to operate under continuing resolutions for at least part of the year. These measures usually allow agencies to continue spending at levels provided in the preceding year, thus curtailing program improvements and playing havoc with agency planning.

A third problem contributing to the fragmentation and loss of control over the budget process was so-called backdoor spending. Closely related to, indeed the cause of, much of the "uncontrollability" problem, this form of off-budget financing accounted for more than $30 billion of federal spending by the early 1970s. Its principal forms included contract authority granted by the authorizing committees, which enabled some agencies to enter into contracts in advance of appropriations, thereby committing the government to pay the bills when they subsequently became due. In addition, some agencies were authorized to spend debt receipts as a result of selling their own bonds or by borrowing from the Treasury, all without action by the appropriations committees. Finally, certain agencies derive income from leases, rents, fees, or sale of government assets. These proprietary receipts (oil leases, grazing fees, military sales, etc.) show up as offsets to agency expenditures rather than income and outlays.

All of these matters, along with a general assertiveness on the part of Congress in the wake of the Vietnam War and the Watergate scandal, combined to spur 2 years of study culminating in the Budget Act of 1974. In short, Congress was determined to discipline itself and retrieve budgetary powers ceded to the President during the previous half-century [6].

Major Provisions of the 1974 Act

Structurally, procedurally, and politically, the 1974 act wrought changes in the way Congress deals with the budget. A political document, it reflects a host of compromises necessary to win acceptance. The act did not, for example, do away with any existing institutions, nor did it create something that might be called a congressional budget along the lines of the executive budget submitted by the President [6, p. 217ff.]. Essentially, and in summary form, the Act did the following:

1. It sharply curtailed the President's impoundment powers by creating procedures whereby Congress could block such measures. No longer could the executive, relying on OMB's apportionment power, unilaterally withhold from the agencies spending authority granted in congressional appropriation bills. Instead, the act prescribed two new procedures for presidents to follow in cases where the executive sought to delay or cancel authorized spending. Basically, the legislation (Title X) amended the Anti-Deficiency Acts of 1905 and 1950, which had conferred upon the President the power to limit or cancel spending

under certain conditions. Henceforth, the executive would be required to notify Congress of any intent to impound funds or delay their use. Two new categories were established: deferrals and rescissions. In the case of the former, where the President wishes to delay the timing of obligations or reserve funds for future use, either house can block the action by passage of an "impoundment resolution." The provision fell victim to a 1983 Supreme Court decision in an unrelated case that declared unconstitutional the one-house veto. With regard to a rescission, the effort to cancel spending authority altogether, both House and Senate must approve within 45 days after it is submitted or the President is forced to release the money. This provision has survived, and congressional approval has been granted sparingly. The usual practice employed to deny presidential rescission requests has been for Congress to refuse to vote on them, effectively killing them. During Ronald Reagan's second term, not a single rescission request was brought to a vote in Congress.

2. While the 1974 act did not abolish the existing taxing and spending committees of Congress, it did create a standing Committee on the Budget in each house, each with its own staff. In a move to provide Congress with more resources and expertise, the act also established the Congressional Budget Office, whose director is appointed by the Speaker of the House and the President pro tempore of the Senate. The principal function of the budget committees is to conduct hearings and present to their respective houses a budget resolution setting spending limits for about 20 functional categories (defense, agriculture, transportation, etc.) along with an aggregate total spending figure. This activity, taken early in the legislative phase of the process, is supposed to guide the future actions of the appropriations committees. It represents, to the extent that it is honored by subsequent actions, a congressional "budget." Initially, a second resolution, adopted 2 weeks prior to the start of the fiscal year, was designed to be binding and, in effect, to adjust differences created by appropriations actions taken after passage of the first resolution. However, the second resolution was subsequently abandoned and the first resolution has become the "binding" resolution [6, p. 237]. As for the Congressional Budget Office (CBO), its large professional staff was meant to serve Congress as a counterbalance to the analytical capacity available to the executive branch through OMB, the Council of Economic Advisers, and the Treasury Department [73]. In addition to formulating a congressional alternative to executive branch economic forecasts and budgetary proposals, CBO is also charged with providing the Budget Committees with information and assistance as requested. It also serves a similar function for the House Ways and Means and Senate Finance Committees as well as the appropriations committees in each house.

3. In addition to dealing with the impoundment problem and making internal structural changes, the Budget Act of 1974 altered the legislative budget process in substantial ways. First, it created a new fiscal year in an attempt to give Congress additional time to pass appropriations bills. The old fiscal year, which began on July 1 and ran through June 30 of the following year, was changed to an October 1–September 30 year. With an additional 3 months to consider the budget proposals, it was hoped—forlornly, as it turned out—that the appropriation bills would be enacted prior to the beginning of the fiscal year. In addition, the President was now required to submit something called the current services budget on November 10, prior to sending up his official budget request in January. The current services budget assumes no new programs or policy changes and simply estimates what it will cost next year to continue in place, with adjustments for inflation, those programs already authorized. Delivered to the Joint Economic Committee of Congress, it languishes there. Not taken seriously by OMB, which prepares it, or by members of Congress who prefer to await the arrival of "the real thing" in January, the current services budget remains an

ornamental ritual lacking in impact [6, 59]. The act set forth a rigid timetable designed to keep congressional budget action on a fixed track. The schedule has fallen into disuse as Congress, utilizing easily adopted rules, has repeatedly ignored or bypassed its self-imposed deadlines.

Gramm–Rudman–Hollings

The principal failure of the 1974 Budget Act has been its inability to stem the flow of red ink in the federal budget. By the mid 1980s, a combination of tax reductions and increased outlays had produced annual deficits in excess of $200 billion. The budget process created in 1974 had been designed to revise congressional procedures to create a framework for more systematic consideration of federal fiscal policies and to enhance accountability in Congress for budget decisions [76, p. 14]. Reducing the deficit and balancing the budget were secondary considerations. The Balanced Budget and Emergency Deficit Control Act of 1985, on the other hand, was almost single-minded in its focus on those matters. Known popularly as Gramm–Rudman–Hollings, in recognition of its principal authors in the Senate, this legislation, amended in 1987, built upon the 1974 act with the stated objective of reducing the annual deficit to zero by 1991 (later extended to 1993).

THE FUTURE OF BUDGET REFORM

> The budget is a mythical beanbag. Congress votes mythical beans into it, and then tries to reach in and pull real beans out.—Will Rogers

Cynicism about the way governments finance their operations has provided a stimulus for and been a result of budget reform. Constantly disappointed by their efforts, reformers of the budget process reach back and try again.

Focusing reform efforts on the budget document and process may be aiming at the wrong target. If off budget spending, the government's numerous credit activities, offsetting business-type revenues, and various forms of quasi-governmental spending mandated by statute are counted, probably more than one-half of public-purpose expenditure is not included in the budget. The federal budget, according to Michael Boskin [77], is no longer a very comprehensive report or forecast of government involvement in the economy.

In spite of such concerns, or perhaps because of them, the calls for budget reform still echo across the fiscal landscape. Caiden [78] has argued the case for yet another try at bringing the budget process into line with the nation's changing economic environment. Further, she suggests that the search for new approaches to budgeting is a task for each generation as it confronts changing economic and fiscal conditions.

The future will undoubtedly see continued and renewed efforts at budgetary innovation. As in the past, most will likely be aimed at finding technical procedural—not policy—solutions.

NOTES

1. U.S. House of Representatives Document No. 854 (June 27, 1912), reprinted in Ref. 8.
2. Commission on the Organization of the Executive Branch of the Government (1949).
3. President Johnson's reasons for imposing PPBS on a government-wide scale remain unclear. On this point, see Golembiewski and Scott [32].

REFERENCES

1. J. Burkhead, *Government Budgeting*, John Wiley & Sons, New York (1956).
2. T. D. Lynch, *Public Budgeting in America*, 3rd ed., Prentice-Hall, Englewood Cliffs, N.J. (1990).
3. A. E. Buch, *Public Budgeting*, Harper & Brothers, New York (1929).
4. D. Waldo, *The Administrative State*, Ronald Press, New York (1948).
5. F. A. Cleveland and A. E. Buck, *The Budget and Responsible Government*, Macmillan, New York (1920).
6. U.S. Bureau of the Census, *Historical Statistics of the United States, 1789–1945*, Department of Commerce, Washington, D.C. (1949).
7. H. E. Shuman, *Politics and the Budget: The Struggle Between the President and the Congress*, Prentice-Hall, Englewood Cliffs, N.J. (1988).
8. A. C. Hyde and J. M. Shafritz, eds., *Government Budgeting: Theory, Process, Politics*, Moore Publishing, Oak Park, Ill. (1978).
9. L. Fisher, *Presidential Spending Power*, Princeton University Press, Princeton, N.J. (1975).
10. R. C. Chandler, *A Centennial History of the American Administration State*, Free Press, New York (1987).
11. D. T. Selko, *The Federal Financial System*, Brookings Institution, Washington, D.C. (1940).
12. L. H. Kimmel, *Federal Budget and Fiscal Policy, 1789–1958*, Brookings Institution, Washington, D.C. (1959).
13. J. L. Waltman, *Political Origins of the U.S. Income Tax*, University Press of Mississippi, Jackson, Miss. (1985).
14. R. E. Neustadt, "Presidency and Legislation: The Growth of Central Clearance," *Am. Polit. Sci. Rev. 48*: 641–671 (1954).
15. L. Berman, *The Office of Management and Budget and the Presidency, 1921–1979*, Princeton University Press, Princeton, N.J. (1979).
16. H. D. Smith, *The Management of Your Government*, McGraw-Hill, New York (1945).
17. T. C. Sorensen, *Decision-Making in the White House*, Columbia University Press, New York (1963).
18. B. T. Pitsvada and F. D. Draper, "Is It Time for a New Executive Budget System?" *Federal Manage.*, 2: 5–9 (1989).
19. D. M. Daley, "Control, Management, and Planning: A State-Level Replication of the Friedman Study of Budget Practices," *Int. J. Public Admin.*, 7: 291–304 (1985).
20. L. Friedman, "Control, Management, and Planning: An Empirical Examination," *Public Admin. Rev.*, 35: 625–628 (1975).
21. A. Schick, "The Road to PPB: The Stages of Budget Reform," *Public Admin. Rev.*, 26: 243–258 (1966).
22. R. N. Anthony, *Planning and Control Systems: A Framework for Analysis*, Harvard University, Graduate School of Business Administration, Boston (1965).
23. A. Schick, "Control Patterns in State Budget Execution," *Public Admin. Rev.*, 24: 97–106 (1964).
24. A. Wildavsky, "Budgetary Reform in an Age of Big Government," *Contemporary Public Administration* (T. Vocino and J. Rabin, eds.), Harcourt Brace Jovanovich, New York (1981).
25. Commission on Organization of the Executive Branch of Government, *Budgeting and Accounting*, U.S. Government Printing Office, Washington, D.C. (1949).
26. C. Seckler-Hudson, "Performance Budgeting in Government," *Adv. Manage.*, 18: 4–9, 30–32 (1953).
27. ICMA, *Management Policies in Local Government Finance* (J. R. Aronson and E. Schwartz, eds.), International City Management Association, Washington, D.C. (1981).
28. F. Sherwood, "Some Non-Cost Accounting Approaches to Performance Budgeting," *Public Manage.*, 36: 9–12 (1954).
29. A. Eghtedari and F. Sherwood, "Performance Budgeting: Has the Theory Worked?" *Public Admin. Rev.*, 30: 63–85 (1960).

30. C. W. Binford, "Reflections on the Performance Budget: Past, Present and Future," *Govern. Finance 1*: 30–32 (1972).
31. E. S. Savas, "How Much Do Government Services Really Cost?" *Urban Affairs Q., 15*: 23–42.
32. R. T. Golembiewski and P. Scott, "A Micro-Political Perspective on Rational Budgeting: A Conjectural Footnote on the Dissemination of PPBS," *Public Budgeting and Financial Manage., 1*: 327–370 (1989).
33. D. Novick, "The Origin and History of Program Budgeting," *Government Budgeting: Theory, Process, Politics* (A. C. Hyde and J. M. Shafritz eds.), Moore Publishing, Oak Park, Il. (1968).
34. R. H. Jones, "Program Budgeting: Fiscal Facts and Federal Fancy," *Q. J. Econ. Business, 9*: 45–57 (1969).
35. D. Novick, "What Program Budgeting Is and Is Not," *Contemporary Approaches to Public Budgeting* (F. A. Kramer, ed.), Winthrop Publishers, Cambridge, Mass. (1979).
36. D. Novick, *Current Practice in Program Budgeting (PPBS)*, Rand Corp., Crane, Russak and Company, New York (1973).
37. A. Schick, "A Death in the Bureaucracy: The Demise of Federal PPB," *Public Admin. Rev, 33*: 146–156 (1973).
38. M. J. White, "The Impact of Management Science on Political Decision Making," *Public Budgeting: Program Planning and Implementation* (F. J. Lyden and E. G. Miller, eds.), Prentice-Hall, Englewood, N.J. (1982).
39. A. Wildavsky, "The Political Economy of Efficiency: Cost-Benefit Analysis, Systems Analysis, and Program Budgeting," *Public Admin. Rev., 26*: 292–310 (1966).
40. A. Wildavsky, "Rescuing Policy Analysis from PPBS," *Public Admin. Rev., 29*: 189–202 (1969).
41. B. M. Gross, "The New Systems Budgeting," *Public Admin. Rev. 29*: 113–137 (1969).
42. C. E. Lindblom, "The Science of Muddling Through," *Public Admin. Rev., 19*: 79–88 (1959).
43. C. E. Lindblom, "Still Muddling, Not Yet Through," *Public Admin. Rev., 39*: 517–526 (1979).
44. M. Foster, ed., *The Greener Side of Air Force Blue*, Air University, Maxwell Air Force Base, Ala. (1985).
45. L. T. LeLoup, *Budgetary Politics*, 2nd ed., King's Court Communications, Brunswick, Ohio (1980).
46. J. Wanat, *Introduction to Budgeting*, Duxbury Press, North Scituate, Mass. (1978).
47. J. E. Jernberg, "Information Change and Congressional Behavior: A Caveat for PPB Reformers," *J. Politics, 35*: 722–740 (1969).
48. R. Rose, "Implementation and Evaporation: The Record of MBO," *Public Admin. Rev., 37*: 64–71 (1977).
49. R. H. Brady, "MBO Goes to Work in the Public Sector," *Harvard Business Rev., 51*: 65–74 (1973).
50. A. Wildavsky, *The Politics of the Budgetary Process*, 4th ed., Little, Brown, Boston (1984).
51. J. McCaffery, "MBO and the Federal Budgetary Process," *Public Admin. Rev., 36*: 33–39 (1976).
52. B. H. Woolfson, "Public Sector MBO and PPB: Cross Fertilization in Management Systems," *Public Admin. Rev., 35*: 387–395 (1975).
53. B. G. Peters, *Comparing Public Bureaucracies: Problems of Theory and Method*, University of Alabama Press, Tuscaloosa, Ala. (1988).
54. P. A. Pyhrr, "The Zero-Base Approach to Government Budgeting," *Public Admin. Rev., 37*: 1–8.
55. A. Schick and R. Keith, *Zero-Base Budgeting in the States*, Congressional Research Service, Washington, D.C. (1976).
56. U.S. Congress, Senate Committee on Government Operations, *Compendium of Materials on Zero-Base Budgeting in the States*, 95th Congress, First Session (1977).
57. J. Carter, "Jimmy Carter Tells Why He Will Use Zero-Base Budgeting," *Nation's Business, 65*: 24–26 (1977).
58. J. D. LaFaver, "Zero-Base Budgeting in New Mexico," *State Govern., 47*: 108–112 (1974).
59. M. J. Scheiring, "Zero-Base Budgeting in New Jersey," *State Govern., 49*: 174–179 (1976).
60. V. B. Lewis, "Toward a Theory of Budgeting," *Public Admin. Rev., 12*: 42–54 (1952).

61. A. Schick, "The Road from ZBB," *Public Admin. Rev.*, *38*: 177–180 (1978).
62. J. L. Mikesell, *Fiscal Administration: Analysis and Applications for the Public Sector*, 2nd ed., Dorsey Press, Chicago (1986).
63. G. Starling, *The Politics and Economics of Public Policy*, Dorsey Press, Homewood, Ill. (1979).
64. R. N. Anthony, Zero-base budgeting is a fraud. *Wall Street Journal* (27 April), reprinted in Ref. 62 (1977).
65. A. Wildavsky, "The Political Economy of Efficiency Has Not Changed But the World Has and So Have I," *Public Budgeting and Financial Manage.*, *1*: 43–53 (1989).
66. V. O. Key, "The Lack of a Budgetary Theory," *Am. Polit. Sci. Rev.*, *34*: 1137–1144 (1940).
66. F. J. Lawton, "Legislative-Executive Relationships in Budgeting as Viewed by the Executive," *Public Admin. Rev. 13*: 169–176 (1953).
67. J. P. Harris, "Needed Reforms in the Federal Budget System," *Public Admin. Rev.*, *12*: 242–250 (1952).
68. A. E. Buck, *The Budget in Governments of Today*, Macmillan, New York (1934).
69. R. A. Wallace, "Congressional Control of the Budget," *Midwest J. Polit. Sci.*, *3*: 151–167 (1959).
70. A. Smithies, *The Budgetary Process in the United States*, McGraw-Hill, New York (1955).
71. L. L. Smith, "The Congressional Budget Process: Why It Worked This Time," *Bureaucrat 6*: 88–111 (1977).
72. J. P. Pfiffner, *The President, the Budget, and Congress: Impoundment and the 1974 Budget Act*, Westview Press, Boulder, Colo. (1979).
73. D. S. Ippolito, *The Budget and National Politics*, W. H. Freeman, San Francisco (1978).
74. D. Axelrod, *A Budget Quartet: Critical Policy and Management Issues*, St. Martin's Press, New York (1989).
75. J. Cranford, *Budgeting for America.*, Congressional Quarterly, Washington, D.C. (1989).
76. S. E. Collender, *The Guide to the Federal Budget: Fiscal 1990*, Urban Institute Press, Washington, D.C. (1989).
77. M. J. Boskin, "Macroeconomic Versus Microeconomic Issues in the Federal Budget," *The Federal Budget: Economics and Politics* (M. J. Boskin and A. Wildavsky, eds.), Institute for Contemporary Studies, San Francisco (1982).
78. N. Caiden, "Public Budgeting Amidst Uncertainty and Instability," *Public Budgeting and Finance*, *1*: 6–19 (1981).

14

The Budget System and Concepts of the United States Government

U.S. Office of Management and Budget, Executive Office of the President

The budget system of the U.S. government provides the framework within which federal decisions on resource allocation and program management are made. These decisions are made in relation to the requirements of the nation, the availability of resources, effective financial control, and accountability for use of the resources.

This chapter provides an overview of the budget process and explains some of the more important budget concepts. Citations to the principal laws pertaining to the budget, which are referred to by title, are provided at the end. The President's budget document itself, the *Budget of the United States Government*, provides a fuller explanation of some concepts in the context of the related budget data.

THE BUDGET PROCESS

The budget process has three main phases: (1) executive formulation and transmittal; (2) congressional action; and (3) budget execution and control. Each of these is interrelated with the others (see Table 1).

Executive Formulation and Transmittal

The *Budget of the United States Government* sets forth the President's financial plan and indicates his priorities for the federal government. The primary focus of the budget is on the budget year—the next fiscal year for which Congress needs to make appropriations. However, the budget is developed in the context of a multiyear budget planning system that includes coverage of the 4 years following the budget year in order to integrate longer-range planning into the executive budget process. The system requires that broad fiscal goals and agency spending and employment levels be established beyond the budget year.

Source: A publication of the Executive Office of the President, Office of Management and Budget, dated January 1992.

Table 1 Overview of the Budget Process

Executive budget process	Timing	Congressional budget process
Agencies subject to executive branch review submit initial budget request materials.	September 1	
Fiscal year begins.	October 1	Fiscal year begins.
Agencies not subject to executive branch review submit budget request materials.	October 15	
OMB issues its final sequestration report;[a] President issues sequestration order, if necessary.	10 days after end of session 15 days after end of session	CBO issues its final sequester report.
	30 days later	Comptroller General issues compliance report.
Legislative branch and the judiciary submit budget request materials.	November–December	
	5 days before President's budget transmittal	CBO issues its sequestration preview report
President transmits the budget to Congress, including OMB sequestration preview report. OMB sends allowance letters to agencies.	Not later than the first Monday in February February–March	
	February 15	Congressional Budget Office reports to the Budget Committees on the President's budget.
	Within 6 weeks of President's budget transmittal	Committees submit views and estimates to Budget Committees.
	April 1	Senate Budget Committee reports concurrent resolution on the budget.

Date		
April 15		Congress completes action on concurrent resolution.
May 15		House may consider appropriations bills in the absence of a concurrent resolution on the budget.
June 10		House Appropriations Committee reports last appropriations bill.
June 15		Congress completes action on reconcilliation legislation.
June 30		House completes action on annual appropriations bills.
After completion of action on discretionary, direct spending, or receipts legislation.		CBO provides estimate of the impact of legislation as soon as practicable.
July 15	President transmits the Mid-Session Review, updating the budget estimates.	
July–August	OMB provides agencies with policy guidance for the upcoming budget.	
August 15		CBO issues its sequestration update report.
August 20	OMB issues sequestration update report	

Note: OMB also reports to Congress on the impact of enacted legislation and provides an explanation of any differences between OMB and CBO estimates, within 5 calendar days of enactment of legislation.

[a] A "within session" sequestration is triggered within 15 days after enactment of appropriations that are enacted after the end of a session for the budget year and before July 1, if they breach the category spending limit for that fiscal year. A "lookback" reduction to a category limit is applied for appropriations enacted after June 30th for the fiscal year in progress that breach a category limit for that fiscal year and is applied to the next fiscal year.

The President transmits his budget to Congress early in each calendar year, 8 to 9 months before the next fiscal year begins on October 1 [1].

The process of formulating the budget begins not later than the spring of each year, at least 9 months before the budget is transmitted and at least 18 months before the fiscal year begins.

During the formulation of the budget, there is a continual exchange of information, proposals, evaluations, and policy decisions among the President, the Office of Management and Budget (OMB), other Executive Office units, and the various government agencies. Decisions concerning the upcoming budget are influenced by the results of previously enacted budgets, including the one being executed by the agencies, and reactions to the last proposed budget, which is being considered by Congress. Decisions are influenced also by projections of the economic outlook that are prepared jointly by the Council of Economic Advisers, OMB, and the Treasury Department.

The President establishes general budget and fiscal policy guidelines. Based on his decisions, OMB issues general policy directions and planning levels to the agencies, both for the budget year and for the following 4 years, to guide the preparation of their budget requests.

In September, agencies submit budget requests to OMB, where they are reviewed in detail, and decisions are made. These decisions may be revised as a result of presidential review. Fiscal policy issues, which affect outlays and receipts, are reexamined. The effects of budget decisions on outlays and receipts in the years that follow are also considered and are explicitly taken into account, in the form of multiyear budget planning estimates. Decisions must also take into account any statutory limitations on spending and the deficit. Thus, the budget formulation process involves the simultaneous consideration of the resource needs of individual programs, the total outlays and receipts that are appropriate in relation to current and prospective economic conditions, and statutory constraints. For 1991 through 1995, certain categories of spending and the maximum deficit amount are constrained by law. The President's budget proposals must be consistent with these constraints, which are discussed below under "Budget Enforcement."

Congressional Action

Congress considers the President's budget proposals and approves, modifies, or disapproves them. It can change funding levels, eliminate programs, or add programs not requested by the President. It can add or eliminate taxes and other sources of receipts, or make other changes that affect the amount of receipts collected.

Congress does not enact a budget as such. It enacts appropriations bills that provide authority to spend for specified purposes and other legislation that affects outlays or receipts, such as legislation to amend eligibility requirements for benefit payments or to amend revenue laws. However, most receipts collected and most outlays made in any year are not the result of laws enacted specifically for that year. Therefore, Congress has only a limited ability to reduce a deficit in a given year through legislation passed in that year.

Prior to making appropriations, Congress usually enacts legislation that authorizes an agency to carry out a particular program and, in some cases, includes limits on the amount that can be appropriated for the program. Some programs require annual authorizing legislation. Others are authorized for a specified number of years or indefinitely.

In making appropriations, Congress does not vote on the level of outlays directly, but rather on *budget authority*, which is the authority to incur obligations that will result in immediate or future outlays. For the majority of federal programs, budget authority becomes available each year only as voted by Congress in appropriations acts. However, in many cases Congress has voted permanent budget authority, under which funds become available annually without further congressional action. Many trust fund appropriations are permanent, as are a number of federal fund appropriations, such as the appropriation to pay interest on the public debt. In recent years, more budget authority has become available under permanent appropriations than by current actions of Congress. The outlays from permanent appropriations, together with the outlays from obligations incurred in previous years, account for the majority of the outlay total for any year. Therefore, most outlays in any year are not controlled through appropriations actions for that year. The types of budget authority, their control by Congress, and the relation of outlays to budget authority are discussed in more detail in later sections.

Congressional review of the budget begins shortly after the President transmits his budget estimates to Congress. Under standing law, the budget is required to be transmitted not later than the first Monday in February of each year.

Under the procedures established by the Congressional Budget Act, Congress considers budget totals before completing action on individual appropriations. The Act requires each standing committee of Congress to report on budget estimates to the House and Senate Budget Committees within six weeks after the President's budget is transmitted. Congress adopts a concurrent *budget resolution* as a guide in its subsequent consideration of appropriations and receipt measures. The budget resolution, which is scheduled to be adopted by April 15, sets targets for total receipts and for budget authority and outlays, in total and by functional category. Like the President's budget, the budget resolution is subject to spending limitations imposed in law for 1991 through 1995.

Budget resolutions are not laws and, therefore, do not require the President's approval. However, there is consultation between the congressional leadership and the Administration, because legislation developed to meet congressional budget targets must be sent to the President for his approval. For some budgets prior to 1991, the President and the joint leadership of Congress formally agreed on the framework of a deficit reduction plan. These agreements, known as Bipartisan Budget Agreements, were reflected in the budget legislation passed for those years. A similar agreement process led to the enactment of the Budget Enforcement Act, which is designed to constrain spending for 1991 through 1995.

Congressional consideration of requests for appropriations and changes in revenue laws occurs first in the House of Representatives. The Appropriations Committee, through its subcommittees, studies the request for appropriations and examines in detail each agency's performance. The Ways and Means Committee reviews proposed revenue measures. Each committee then recommends the action to be taken by the House of Representatives. After passage of the budget resolution, a point of order can be raised to block consideration of bills that would cause a committee's targets, as set by the resolution, to be breached.

When the appropriations and tax bills are approved by the House, they are forwarded to the Senate, where a similar review follows. In case of disagreement between the two houses of Congress, a conference committee (consisting of members of both bodies) meets to resolve the differences. The report of the conference committee is returned to both houses for approval. When the measure is agreed to, first in the House and then in the Senate, it is ready to be transmitted to the President as an enrolled bill, for his approval or veto.

When action on appropriations is not completed by the beginning of the fiscal year, Congress enacts a joint *continuing resolution* to provide authority for the affected agencies to continue financing operations up to a specified date or until their regular appropriations are enacted. In some years, a portion or all of the government has been funded for the entire year by a continuing resolution. Continuing resolutions must be presented to the President for approval or veto.

In each of the last several years, Congress has enacted omnibus budget reconciliation acts, which combine many amendments to authorizing legislation that affect outlays and receipts. For example, these acts may change benefit formulas or eligibility requirements, the spending for which is often not controlled through appropriations acts.

Budget Enforcement

Limits on expenditures, receipts, and the deficit are established in law for 1991 through 1995, as are procedures for enforcing the limits throughout the budget process each year. These limits and procedures are determined by the Balanced Budget and Emergency Deficit Control Act (commonly known as the Gramm–Rudman–Hollings Act), which was extended and amended extensively by the Budget Enforcement Act. The latter also affected the President's budget and the congressional budget process.

The law divides spending into two types—*discretionary appropriations* and *direct spending*. These definitions are designed to distinguish spending that is generally controlled through annual appropriations acts from that which is generally provided in other, more permanent laws (most entitlement and other so-called mandatory spending). The law specifies processes, called *sequesters*, for reducing spending. Different sequester procedures are prescribed for reducing the excess spending resulting from discretionary appropriations and for eliminating increases in the deficit resulting from legislation affecting direct spending or receipts. A third type of sequester applies to all types of spending if, after application of the discretionary and direct spending procedures, the deficit exceeds specified maximum deficit amounts.

The sequester processes for discretionary appropriations and direct spending are designed to apply uniform reductions to the same kind of spending that caused the sequester. Discretionary appropriations are subdivided into three categories for 1991 through 1993—*defense*, *international*, and *domestic*. Spending limits for budget authority and outlays are specified for each category for each of those years. For 1994 and 1995, the limits apply to the total of discretionary spending. From adjournment of a session of Congress (usually in the fall of each year) through the following June 30 of a fiscal year, discretionary sequesters take place whenever an appropriation bill causes the limit in a category to be breached. Under a sequester, spending for most nonexempt programs in the category is reduced by a uniform percentage. Special rules apply in reducing some programs and some programs are exempt from sequester by law. Between June 30 and the end of a fiscal year, for practical reasons, the sequester is accomplished by reducing the limit for the category for the next fiscal year.

Sequesters of direct spending, called *pay-as-you-go* sequesters, occur following the end of a session of Congress if there is estimated to be a net increase in the deficit caused by laws enacted that affect direct spending and receipts. Under a pay-as-you-go sequester, spending for most nonexempt programs in the category is reduced by a uniform percentage. Special rules apply in reducing some programs and some programs are exempt from sequester by law.

A deficit sequester occurs if it is calculated that estimated spending in all categories and estimated receipts will result in a deficit that exceeds the maximum deficit amount for the year by more than the allowed margin (zero in 1992 and 1993, $15 billion in 1994 and 1995). Under a deficit sequester, half of any excess must be taken from defense programs and half from nonexempt nondefense programs. Spending for most programs is reduced by a uniform percentage that is calculated (separately for defense and nondefense programs) to eliminate the increase in the deficit. Special rules apply in reducing some programs, and some programs are exempt from sequester.

The law provides that the estimates and calculations that determine whether there is to be a sequester are to be made by the OMB and reported to the President and Congress. The Congressional Budget Office (CBO) is required to make the same estimates and calculations, and the Director of OMB is required to explain any differences between the OMB estimates and the estimates prepared by CBO. The estimates and calculation by OMB are the basis for sequester orders issued by the President. The President's orders may not change any of the particulars the OMB report. The General Accounting Office is required to prepare compliance reports.

Budget Execution and Control

The President's budget, as approved or modified through appropriations acts and other laws, becomes the basis for the financial plan for the operations of each agency during the fiscal year. Under the Antideficiency Act, most budget authority and other budgetary resources are made available to the agencies of the executive branch through an apportionment system. The Director of OMB apportions (distributes) appropriations and other budgetary resources to each agency by time periods and by activities, in order to ensure the effective use of available resources and to avoid the need for additional appropriations.

Changes in laws or other factors may indicate the need for additional appropriations during the year, and supplemental requests may have to be sent to Congress. On the other hand, amounts appropriated may be withheld temporarily from obligation under certain limited circumstances in order to provide for contingencies, to achieve savings made possible through changes in requirements or greater efficiency of operations, or as specifically provided in law. The Impoundment Control Act provides that the executive branch, in regulating the rate of spending, must report to Congress any effort through administrative action to postpone or eliminate spending provided by law. Deferrals, which are temporary withholdings of budget authority, take effect immediately unless overturned by an act of Congress. Rescissions, which permanently cancel budget authority, do not take effect unless passed by Congress within 45 days of continuous session. Otherwise, the withheld funds must be made available for spending.

Budget Calendar

No later than the 1st Monday in February	President transmits the budget, including a sequester preview report.
Six weeks later	Congressional committees report budget estimates to Budget Committees.
April 15	Action to be completed on congressional budget resolution.
May 15	House consideration of annual appropriations bills may begin.
June 15	Action to be completed on reconcilliation.
June 30	Action on appropriations to be completed by House.
July 15	President transmits Mid-Session Review of the budget.
August 20	OMB updates the sequester preview.
October 1	Fiscal year begins.
15 Days after the end of a session of Congress	OMB issues final sequester report, and the President issues a sequester order, if necessary.

COVERAGE OF THE BUDGET TOTALS

Agencies and Programs

The budget document provides information on all federal agencies and programs, including trust funds and government corporations. The total receipts and outlays of the federal government are composed of both on-budget receipts and outlays and off-budget receipts and outlays. By law, the receipts and outlays of social security (the federal Old-Age and Survivors Insurance and the federal Disability Insurance trust funds) and the Postal Service Fund are excluded from the budget totals and from the calculation of the deficit for Gramm–Rudman–Hollings Act purposes. The off-budget transactions are separately identified in the budget. The on-budget and off-budget amounts are added together to derive totals for the federal government.

Neither the on-budget nor the off-budget totals include transactions of private, government-sponsored enterprises, such as the federal National Mortgage Association and federal home loan banks. However, because of their relationship to the government, these enterprises are discussed in several parts of the budget.

A presentation for the board of governors of the Federal Reserve System is included in the budget for information only. The amounts are not included in either the on-budget or off-budget totals because of the independent status of the system.

Functional Classification

The functional classification arrays budget authority, outlays, and other budget data according to the major purpose served—such as agriculture. There are 19 major functions, most of which are divided into subfunctions. For example, the *Agriculture* function is divided into *Farm Income Stabilization* and *Agricultural and Research Services*. The functional array meets the Congressional Budget Act requirement for a presentation in the budget by national needs and agency missions and programs. That Act also requires an annual concurrent resolution on the budget to establish limits for the budget in total and for each functional category, and to allocate amounts within the limits to the congressional committees that have jurisdiction over the programs in the functions. For 1991 through 1995, the budget resolution also will allocate resources under the limits imposed on discretionary spending categories.

The following criteria are used in the establishment of functional categories and the assignment of activities to them:

- A function comprises activities with similar purposes addressing an important national need. The emphasis is on what the federal government seeks to accomplish rather than the means of accomplishment, the objects purchased, or the clientele or geographic area served.
- A function must be of continuing national importance, and the amounts attributable to it must be significant.
- Each basic unit being classified (generally the appropriation or fund account) usually is classified according to its predominant purpose and assigned to only one subfunction. However, some large accounts that serve more than one major purpose are subdivided into two or more subfunctions.
- Activities and programs are normally classified according to their primary purpose (or function) regardless of which agencies conduct the activities.

Types of Funds

Agency activities are financed through federal funds and trust funds.

Federal funds are of several types. The *general fund* is credited with receipts not earmarked by law for a specific purpose and is also financed by the proceeds of general borrowing. General fund appropriation accounts record general fund expenditures. *Special funds* account for federal fund receipts earmarked for specific purposes, other than for carrying out a cycle of operations, and the associated expenditures. *Public enterprise* (revolving) *funds* conduct a cycle of business-type operations in which outlays generate collections, primarily from the public, which are credited directly to the fund. *Intragovernmental funds*, including revolving and management funds, conduct business-type operations primarily within and between government agencies and are financed by collections, which are credited directly to the fund.

Trust funds are established to account for the receipt and expenditure of monies by the government for carrying out specific purposes and programs in accordance with the terms of a statute that designates the fund as a trust fund (e.g., the Highway Trust Fund) or for carrying out the stipulations of a trust agreement (e.g., any of several trust funds for gifts and donations for specific purposes). These monies are not available for other purposes of the government. *Trust revolving funds* are credited with collections earmarked by law to carry out a cycle of business-type operations.

There is no substantive difference between a trust fund and a special fund or between a trust revolving fund and a public enterprise revolving fund.

Current Expenses and Capital Investment

The budget includes spending for both current operating expenses and capital investment, such as the purchase of land, structures, and equipment. It also includes subsidies for capital investment provided by direct loans and loan guarantees; the purchase of other financial assets; and the conduct of research, development, education, and training.

BUDGETARY RESOURCES AND RELATED TRANSACTIONS

Budgetary Resources

Government agencies are permitted to enter into *obligations* requiring either immediate or future payment of money only when they have been granted authority to do so by law. This authority is called *budget authority*. Unobligated balances of budget authority remaining available from previous years are not recorded as budget authority again in subsequent years, but they constitute a budgetary resource that is available for obligation. The use of budgetary resources may be restrained by the imposition of legally binding limitations on obligations (for example, obligations for administrative expenses of benefit programs). Such limitations substitute for budget authority, for some purposes, and are treated as a budgetary resource.

Budget authority and other budgetary resources permit obligations to be incurred. The amounts of budget authority requested are determined by the nature of the programs or projects being financed and the amounts of unobligated balances available for the purpose. For activities such as operation and maintenance, for which the cost depends upon the program level during the fiscal year, the amount of budget authority requested usually is the amount estimated to be needed to cover the obligations to be incurred during the year.

For most major procurement programs and construction projects, an amount adequate to complete the procurement or project generally is requested to be appropriated in the first year, even though it may be obligated over several years. This policy, sometimes referred to as "full funding," is intended to avoid piecemeal funding of programs and projects that cannot be used until they have been completed.

Budget authority takes several forms. It is usually provided in the form of *appropriations*, which permit obligations to be incurred and payments to be made. Appropriations include the authority to spend offsetting collections that are specifically authorized to be credited to appropriation and fund accounts (e.g., Postal Service collections from the sale of stamps). The Budget Enforcement Act redefined budget authority to include the authority to spend offsetting collections. Another form of budget authority is *contract authority*, which, when specifically authorized by law, permits obligations in advance of appropriations but requires a subsequent appropriation or the collection of receipts to liquidate (pay) these obligations. Another form of budget authority is *borrowing authority*, which permits obligations to be incurred but requires that funds be borrowed, generally from the Treasury, to liquidate these obligations.

With certain exceptions, it is not in order for either house of Congress to consider any bill that provides new borrowing or contract authority unless that bill also provides that such new spending authority will be effective only to the extent or in such amounts as provided in appropriations acts.

Appropriations are available for obligation only during the fiscal year for which they are enacted, unless the appropriation language specifies that an appropriation is available for a longer period. Typically, appropriations for current operations are made available for obligation in only one year. Some appropriations are made available for a specified number of years. Others, including most of those for construction, some for research, and many for trust funds, are made available for obligation until the amount appropriated has been expended or until the program objectives have been attained.

Usually Congress makes budget authority available on the first day of the fiscal year for which the appropriations act is passed. Occasionally, the appropriations language specifies a different timing. The language may provide an *advance appropriation*—budget authority that does not become available until one year or more beyond the fiscal year for which the appropriations act is passed. To meet the special timing requirements of many education programs, the appropriations for them provide for *forward funding*—budget authority that is made available for obligation beginning in the last quarter of the fiscal year for the financing of ongoing grant programs during the next fiscal year. For certain benefit programs funded by annual appropriations, the appropriation provides for *advance funding*—budget authority that is to be charged to the appropriation in the succeeding year but which authorizes obligations to be incurred in the last quarter of the fiscal year if necessary to meet higher than anticipated benefit payments in excess of the specific amount appropriated for the year.

When budget authority is made available by law for a specific period of time, any part that is not obligated during that period expires (lapses) and cannot be used later. Congressional actions that extend the availability of unobligated amounts that have expired or would otherwise expire are known as *reappropriations*. Reappropriations are counted as new budget authority in the fiscal year in which the balances become newly available.

A *rescission* is a legislative action that cancels new budget authority or the availability of unobligated balances of budget authority prior to the time the authority would otherwise have expired. Rescissions of both new budget authority and unobligated balances of budget authority are recorded as decreases in new budget authority for that year. Accordingly, it is possible that some accounts show negative budget authority because an amount of unobligated balances was rescinded that was greater than the amount of new budget authority made available.

A *deferral* is an executive branch action or inaction permitted in limited situations (such as the establishment of legally authorized reserves) that delays the obligation or expenditure of funds within the year that the action is taken. Deferrals are not identified separately in the budget.

Budget authority is classified and labeled in the budget as *current* or *permanent*. Generally, budget authority is current if it is provided by annual appropriations acts and permanent if it becomes available pursuant to standing authorizing legislation. Advance appropriations of budget authority are classified as permanent, even though they are provided in annual appropriations acts, because they become available a year or more following the year to which the act pertains. The authority to spend offsetting collections credited to appropriation and revolving fund accounts usually is provided by authorizing legislation and, therefore, is usually a form of permanent budget authority.

Obligations and outlays resulting from permanent budget authority, including the authority to spend offsetting collections credited to appropriation and revolving fund accounts, account for more than half of the budget totals. Put another way, less than half of the obligations and outlays in the budget result from current actions by the Congress. Most permanent budget authority, other than the authority to spend offsetting collections, arises from the authority to spend trust fund receipts and the authority to pay interest on the public debt. Most authority to spend offsetting collections occurs in public enterprise revolving funds.

Budget authority also is classified and labeled in the budget as *definite* or *indefinite*. Budget authority is definite if the legislation that provides it specifies a definite amount or an amount not to be exceeded. Budget authority is indefinite if the legislation providing it permits the amount to be determined by subsequent circumstances. Examples of indefinite authority are authority to borrow that is limited only to the amount of debt that may be outstanding at any time, the appropriation for interest on the public debt, and trust fund appropriations that make all of the receipts collected in the fund immediately available for expenditure. Indefinite budget authority is the amount needed to finance obligations incurred or estimated to be incurred in the case of certain appropriations, contract authority, and borrowing authority, and the amount of receipts collected or estimated to be collected each year in the case of many special and trust funds. The Congressional Budget and Impoundment Control Act, as it was amended by the Budget Enforcement Act, specifies that for four trust funds—the Federal Hospital Insurance Trust Fund, the Supplementary Medical Insurance Trust Fund, the Unemployment Trust Fund, and the railroad retirement account—the indefinite budget authority is the amount needed to finance obligations incurred or estimated to be incurred under legal limitations on obligations or benefit formulas, not the amount of the receipts collected. This treatment has been adopted for most other special and trust funds.

Obligations Incurred

Following the enactment of budget authority and the completion of required apportionment action, government agencies incur obligations. Such obligations include the current liabilities for salaries, wages, and interest; contracts for the purchase of supplies and equipment, construction, and the acquisition of office space, buildings, and land; and other arrangements requiring the payment of money. Beginning in 1992, obligations are recorded in an amount equal to the estimated subsidy cost of direct loans and loan guarantees (see "Federal Credit").

Outlays

When obligations are liquidated (paid), outlays are recorded. Outlays usually are in the form of checks, cash, or electronic fund transfers. Obligations also may be liquidated (and outlays recorded) by the accrual of interest on public issues of Treasury debt securities (including an increase in the redemption value of bonds outstanding), or by the issuance of bonds, debentures, notes, or monetary credits. Refunds of receipts are treated as reductions of receipts, rather than as outlays. Payments for earned income tax credits in excess of tax liabilities are treated as outlays rather than as a reduction to receipts. Outlays during a fiscal year may be for the payment of obligations incurred in prior years or in the same year. Outlays, therefore, flow in part from unexpended balances of prior year budget authority and in part from budget authority provided for the year in which the money is spent. Beginning in 1992, outlays for the subsidy cost of direct loans and loan guarantees are recorded as the underlying loans are disbursed. Outlays are stated both gross and net of offsetting collections for an account, but totals are only stated net. Total outlays for the federal government include both on-budget and off-budget outlays.

Balances of Budget Authority

Not all budget authority enacted for a fiscal year results in obligations and outlays in the same year. In the case of budget authority that is available for more than one year, the *unobligated balance* of budget authority that is still available may be carried forward for obligation in the following year. The *obligated balance* is that portion of the budget authority that has been obligated but not yet paid. For example, in the case of salaries and wages, 1 to 3 weeks elapse between the time of obligation and the time of payment. In the case of major procurement and construction, payment may occur over several years. Obligated balances of budget authority are carried forward until the obligations are subsequently paid [2]. The ratio of the outlays resulting from budget authority enacted in any year to the amount of that budget authority is referred to as the spendout rate.

A change in the amount of obligations incurred from one year to the next is not necessarily accompanied by an equal change in either the budget authority or the outlays of that same year. Conversely, a change in budget authority in any one year may cause changes in the level of obligations and outlays for several years.

FEDERAL CREDIT

Government programs may be carried out through federally supported credit in the form of *direct loans* or *loan guarantees*. A direct loan is a disbursement of funds by the government to a nonfederal borrower under a contract that requires the repayment of such funds with or without interest. A loan guarantee is any guarantee, insurance, or other pledge with respect to the payment of all or a part of the principal or interest on any debt obligation of a nonfederal borrower to a nonfederal lender. The Federal Credit Reform Act made significant changes in the method of budgeting and accounting for federal credit programs beginning in 1992. The revised method (described below) is designed to measure the effect on the budget of direct loan programs and guaranteed loan programs so that they can be compared to each other and to other methods of delivering benefits, such as grants, on an equivalent basis.

The estimated *subsidy costs* arising from the direct loans and loan guarantees of a program must be calculated on a net present value basis. For most programs, direct loan obligations and loan guarantee commitments cannot be made unless Congress has appropriated funds for the subsidy cost in advance in annual appropriations acts. In addition, the budget proposes annual limitations in appropriations language on the amount of obligations for direct loans and commitments for guaranteed loans.

Subsidy appropriations are recorded as budget authority in *credit program accounts*. All cash flows arising from direct loan obligations and loan guarantee commitments are recorded in separate *financing accounts*. The transactions of the financing accounts are not included in the budget totals. The program accounts make subsidy payments, recorded as on-budget outlays, to the financing accounts at the time of the disbursement of the direct or guaranteed loans.

The transactions associated with direct loan obligations and loan guarantee commitments made prior to 1992 continue to be accounted for on a cash flow basis and are recorded in *liquidating accounts*. In most cases, the liquidating account is the account that was used for the program prior to credit reform.

COLLECTIONS

In General

Money collected by the government is classified into two major categories:

- *Governmental receipts*, which are compared to outlays in calculating the surplus or deficit
- *Offsetting collections*, which are deducted from gross disbursements in calculating outlays.

Governmental Receipts

These are collections from the public that result primarily from the exercise of the government's sovereign or governmental powers. Governmental receipts consist primarily of tax receipts (including social insurance taxes), but also include compulsory user charges, receipts from customs duties, court fines, certain licenses, and deposits of earnings by the Federal Reserve System. Gifts and contributions (as distinguished from payments for services or cost-sharing deposits by state and local governments) are also counted as governmental receipts. Total receipts for the federal government include both on-budget and off-budget receipts.

Offsetting Collections

These are amounts received from the public that result from business-like or market-oriented activities (e.g., the sale of a product or service) or amounts collected from other government accounts. They are classified into two major categories: *offsetting collections credited to appropriation or fund accounts*, and *offsetting receipts* (that is, offsetting collections deposited in receipt accounts). The offset is applied differently for each type.

Offsetting Collections Credited to Appropriation or Fund Accounts

For all revolving funds and some appropriation accounts, laws authorize collections to be credited directly to expenditure accounts and, usually make the collections available to spend for the purpose of the account without further action by the Congress. The authority to spend the offsetting collections is recorded as budget authority. It is not unusual for the Congress to enact limitations in annual appropriations acts on the obligations that can be financed by such budget authority. The budget authority and outlays of the appropriation or fund account are shown both gross (that is, before deducting offsetting collections) and net (that is, after deducting offsetting collections). Totals for the agency, subfunction, and budget are net of such offsetting collections, except where specified otherwise.

Offsetting Receipts

Offsetting collections are called offsetting receipts and credited to general fund, special fund, or trust fund receipt accounts unless laws authorize them to be credited to expenditure accounts. Offsetting receipts are deducted from budget authority and outlays in arriving at total budget authority and outlays. In most cases, such deductions are made at the subfunction and agency levels. Offsetting receipts are subdivided into two categories as follows:

- *Proprietary receipts from the public.* These are collections from the public, deposited in receipt accounts, that arise out of the business-type or market-oriented activities of the government. Most proprietary receipts are deducted from the budget authority and outlay totals of the agency that conducts the activity generating the receipt and of the subfunction to which the activity is assigned. For example, fees for using national parks are deducted from the totals for the Department of Interior, which has responsibility for the parks, and the Recreational Resources subfunction. Some proprietary receipts, however, are not offset against any specific agency or function and are classified as undistributed offsetting receipts. They are deducted from the government-wide totals for budget authority and outlays. For example, the collections of rent and royalties from Outer Continental Shelf lands are undistributed because the amounts are large and do not arise in significant measure from the spending of the agency and subfunction that administers the transactions.

- *Intragovernmental transactions.* These are collections from governmental appropriation or fund accounts, deposited into receipt accounts. Most intragovernmental transactions are deducted from the budget authority and outlays of the agency that conducts the activity generating the receipts and of the subfunction to which the activity is assigned. In two cases, however, intragovernmental transactions appear as special deductions in computing total budget authority and outlays for the government rather than as offsets at the agency level—agencies' payments as employers into employee retirement trust funds, and interest received by trust funds. The special treatment for these receipts is necessary because the amounts are large and would result in distortions in the agency totals.

There are several categories of intragovernmental transactions. *Intrabudgetary transactions* include all payments from on-budget expenditure accounts to on-budget receipt accounts. These are subdivided into three categories: (1) *interfund transactions*, where the payment is from one fund group (either federal funds or trust funds) to a receipt account in the other fund group; (2) *federal intrafund transactions*, where the payment and receipt both occur within the federal fund group; and (3) *trust intrafund transactions*, where the payment and receipt both occur within the trust fund group. In addition, there are intragovernmental payments from on-budget expenditure accounts to off-budget receipt accounts, and from off-budget expenditure accounts to on-budget receipt accounts.

MEANS OF FINANCING

Deficits are financed by borrowing and, to a limited extent, the other items discussed under this heading. Surpluses are used to reduce debt and, to a limited extent, may be absorbed by the other items.

Borrowing and Repayment

Borrowing and debt repayment are not treated as receipts or outlays. If they were, the budget would be balanced by definition. This rule applies both to borrowing in the form of public debt securities and to specialized borrowing in the form of agency securities, including the issuance of debt securities to liquidate an obligation and the sale of certificates representing participation in a pool of loans.

Exercise of Monetary Power

Seigniorage is the profit from coining money. It is the difference between the value of coins as money and their cost of production. Seigniorage on coins arises from the exercise of the government's monetary powers and differs from receipts coming from the public, since there is no corresponding payment by another party. Therefore, seigniorage is excluded from receipts and treated as a means of financing the deficit other than borrowing from the public. The increment (profit) resulting from the sale of gold as a monetary asset also is treated as a means of financing, since the value of gold is determined by its value as a monetary asset rather than as a commodity.

Credit Financing Account Balances

Credit financing accounts are established outside the budget to record the nonsubsidy cash flows (mainly direct loan disbursements and repayments and guaranteed loan default payments) for new credit transactions beginning in 1992. These accounts will have balances of assets and liabilities. The financing accounts for guaranteed loans will hold subsidy cost payments from on-budget accounts against the need to make future default claim payments; the financing accounts for direct loans will have balances of debt owed to Treasury. Changes in these balances affect Treasury's need for cash, even though the transactions are not a part of the budget. Such changes are treated as a means of financing the deficit other than borrowing from the public.

Deposit Fund Account Balances

Certain accounts outside the budget, known as deposit funds, are established to record amounts held temporarily until ownership is determined (for example, earnest money paid by bidders for mineral leases) or held by the government as agent for others (for example, state and local income taxes withheld from federal employees' salaries and payroll deductions for the purchase of savings bonds by federal employees). Deposit fund balances may be held in the form of either invested or uninvested balances. Changes in deposit fund balances, if they are not invested in private securities, affect Treasury's cash balances, even though the transactions are not a part of the budget. To the extent that deposit fund balances are not invested, changes in the balances are reflected as a means of financing the deficit other than borrowing from the public. To the extent that the balances are invested in federal debt, changes in the balances are reflected as borrowing from the public or a means of financing the deficit other than borrowing from the public, depending on whether the deposit funds are classified as part of the public or the government, respectively.

Exchange of Cash

The government's deposits with the International Monetary Fund (IMF) are considered to be monetary assets. Therefore, the movement of money between the IMF and the Treasury is not considered in itself a receipt or an outlay, borrowing, or lending. However, interest paid by the IMF on those deposits is an offsetting collection. In a similar manner, the holdings of foreign currency by the Exchange Stabilization Fund are considered to be cash assets. Changes in these holdings are outlays only to the extent there is a realized loss of dollars on the exchange and are offsetting collections only to the extent there is a realized dollar profit.

BASIS FOR BUDGET FIGURES

In General

Outlays usually are stated in terms of payments (in the form of checks, cash, and electronic fund transfers) net of offsetting collections received. When a cash-equivalent financial instrument is developed to use as a substitute for cash or checks, the monetary value of the instrument is normally counted as outlays in the budget in order to record the transaction in the same manner regardless of the means of effecting it. In particular, the acquisition of physical assets through certain types of lease-purchase arrangements are treated as though they were outright purchases.

The accrual basis is used for interest on the public issues of Treasury debt securities. Interest on special issues of the debt securities held by trust funds and other government accounts is normally stated on a cash basis. When a government account invests in federal debt securities, the purchase price is usually close or identical to the par (face) value of the security. The budget records the investment at par value and adjusts the interest paid by Treasury and collected by the account by the difference between purchase price and par, if any. However, in the case of two trust funds in the Department of Defense, the Military Retirement Trust Fund and the Education Benefits Trust Fund, the differences between purchase price and par are routinely relatively large. For these funds, the budget records the holdings of debt at par but records the differences between purchase price and par as adjustments of the assets of the funds that are amortized over the life of the security.

Data for the Past Year

The past year (budget year minus 2) column of the budget generally presents the actual transactions and balances as recorded in agency accounts and as summarized in the central financial reports prepared by the Treasury Department for the most recently completed fiscal year. Occasionally the budget reports corrections to data reported erroneously to Treasury but not discovered in time to be reflected in Treasury's published data. The budget usually notes the sources of such differences.

Data for the Current Year

The current year (budget year minus 1) column of the budget includes estimates of transactions and balances based on the amounts of budgetary resources that were available when the budget was transmitted, including amounts provided as appropriations for the year, and that are expected to become available during the year.

Data for the Budget Year

The budget year column of the budget includes estimates of transactions and balances based on the amounts of budgetary resources that are expected to be available, including amounts proposed to be appropriated. The budget generally includes the appropriations language for the amounts proposed to be appropriated. Where the estimates represent amounts that will be requested under proposed legislation, the appropriation language usually is not included; it is transmitted later, usually after the legislation is enacted. In a few cases, proposed language for appropriations to be requested under existing legislation is transmitted later because the exact requirements are not known at the time the budget is transmitted. In certain tables of the budget, the items for later transmittal and the related outlays are identified separately. Estimates of the total requirements for the budget year include both the amounts requested with the transmission of the budget and the amounts planned for later transmittal.

Multiyear Budget Planning Data

The budget presents estimates for each of the 4 years beyond the budget year in order to reflect the effect of budget year decisions on longer term objectives and plans. These data often reflect specific presidential policy determinations and are shown in many budget tables.

Allowances

Lump-sum allowances are included in the budget to cover certain forms of budgetary transactions that are expected to increase or decrease budget authority or outlays but are not reflected in the program details. Budget authority and outlays included in the allowance section are never appropriated as allowances, but rather indicate the estimated budget authority and outlays that may be requested for specific programs.

Principal Budget Laws

The following are the basic laws pertaining to the federal budget process:

- *Article 1, section 9, clause 7 of the Constitution*, which requires appropriations in law before money may be spent from the Treasury.
- *Chapter 11 of Title 31, United States Code*, which prescribes procedures for submission of the President's budget and information to be contained in it.
- *Congressional Budget and Impoundment Control Act of 1974* (Public Law 93-344), as amended. This Act comprises the Congressional Budget Act of 1974, as amended, which prescribes the congressional budget process; and the Impoundment Control Act of 1974, which controls certain aspects of budget execution.
- *Balanced Budget and Emergency Deficit Control Act of 1985* (Public Law 99-177), as amended, which prescribes rules and procedures (including "sequestration") designed to eliminate excess deficits. This Act is commonly known as the Gramm–Rudman–Hollings Act.
- *Budget Enforcement Act of 1990* (Title XIII, Public Law 101-508), which significantly amended the laws pertaining to the budget process, including the Congressional Budget Act and the Balanced Budget and Emergency Deficit Control Act.
- *Federal Credit Reform Act of 1990*, a part of the Budget Enforcement Act of 1990, which prescribes the accounting for federal credit programs.

- *Antideficiency Act* (codified in Chapters 13 and 15 of Title 31, United States Code), which prescribes rules and procedures for budget execution.

NOTES

1. All years referred to are fiscal years, unless otherwise noted.
2. Additional information is provided in a separate report, "Balances of Budget Authority," which is available from the National Technical Information Service, Department of Commerce, shortly after the budget is transmitted.

15

Congress and the Politics of Statutory Debt Limitation

Linda K. Kowalcky and Lance T. LeLoup

Most analysts view the statutory limit of federal debt as archaic. . . . Voting separately on the debt is hardly effective as a means of controlling deficits, since the decisions that necessitate borrowing are made elsewhere. By the time the debt ceiling comes up for a vote, it is too late to balk at paying the government's bills. . . . [1].

Statutory debt limits enacted by Congress have not only failed to curtail the government's growing tide of red ink, but, ironically, they have become a favorite vehicle for expanding federal programs and expenditures. Nonetheless, debt limitation legislation has long been a congressional ritual. Even in the face of the obvious political difficulties associated with sanctioning trillions of dollars of debt, members of Congress cling to the tradition. Perhaps because enacting statutory limits on federal borrowing is perceived as a hollow exercise, it has attracted little scholarly attention. Yet since 1917, statutory debt limits have played a role in federal borrowing, congressional oversight, and the legislative process. In this chapter, we examine the politics and policy consequences of statutory debt limitation and explore the complex member goals that help explain why Congress has doggedly maintained the practice.

At first glance, the practice seems anomalous, given the growing importance of electoral incentives in explaining congressional behavior [2]. For the majority who must vote for it, the debt-limit vote allows little credit taking and is potential fodder for the negative campaign of an opponent. Contemporary theories of legislative politics stress the reciprocal nature of the structure and procedures of the U.S. Congress and the needs of its members [3–5]. The conventional wisdom about congressional behavior would lead one to expect members to seek protection from these votes, particularly in the House of Representatives, where limited floor debate and amendment restrictions can shield members [6,7].

Source: *Public Administration Review*, Vol. 53 No. 1 (January/February 1993), pp. 14–27. Reprinted with permission from *Public Administration Review* (c) by the American Society for Public Administration (ASPA), 1120 G Street NW, Suite 700, Washington, D.C. 20005. All rights reserved.

The periodic but inevitable need to increase the debt ceiling has long provoked a partisan political response. As federal debt ballooned in the 1980s and 1990s, the debate has become more politicized than ever. Instead of becoming less frequent, debt-limit votes have increased in number and controversy in recent years. We believe that, despite the apparently unattractive and politically risky aspects of debt-limit votes, they serve member needs in other ways. Our analysis suggests three general types of member goals that may be achieved.

Borrowing Restraint and Oversight of the Executive Branch

Despite the fact that outside experts have consistently reported to Congress that the debt limit is ineffective at curbing borrowing, many members believe that it serves a useful function. This argument appeared to be especially powerful with fiscal conservatives through the 1970s. Some members claim, at least publicly, that the debt limit acts as a real check on borrowing. Others believe that, even if it does not act as a constraint, it has symbolic importance in demonstrating congressional attentiveness and concern with burgeoning debt.

In addition, the debt limitation bills have provided Congress with an opportunity to review and comment on administration economic policy and to oversee the Department of the Treasury. The committee hearings have given members the opportunity to examine and question specific practices dealing with Treasury borrowing, to hear administration budget and fiscal policy directly from Treasury officials, and to put their statements on record. Oversight was more important in the early years of this study; prior to the enactment of the Budget and Impoundment Control Act of 1974, the debt-limit bill was one of the few opportunities for reviewing and debating administration economic plans for the forthcoming fiscal year. Before 1974, congressional budgets were no more than an aggregate of individual appropriations and revenue bills. Committee hearings and floor debates on debt-limit extensions partially filled that gap.

Partisan and Ideological Goals

The debt bill has for decades provided an unparalleled opportunity for political opportunism, the articulation of conservative economic values, and clarifying partisan differences. A substantial number of legislators in both houses may speak and vote against the debt limit with the knowledge that it will ultimately pass. Over the years, a consistent ideological theme has appeared in the debate and votes, especially among Republicans and fiscal conservatives. Some members based their congressional reputation on balancing the budget and the evil of government borrowing. Self-proclaimed "watchdogs" like H. R. Gross (R-Iowa) made a career of denouncing government waste and prolificacy, particularly relishing opposing the debt bills. Fiscal moderates and liberals, usually Democrats, accepting Keynesian precepts and the inevitability of extending borrowing authority, often found themselves on the defensive and soft-pedaled their support.

Party control of Congress and the presidency, as we shall see, is the crucial variable in explaining voting alignments on debt legislation. The majority party in Congress—particularly under unified party control of government—is responsible for governing, including the obligation to pay the nation's bills. In contrast, the minority party has no such obligation and instead has an opportunity to score political points and establish a public record against government borrowing. Historically, this was particularly true of the House Republicans, who, as a "permanent" minority with little influence on budget outcomes, used the floor debate and debt vote as policy platforms [8]. Party control of the White House is also important, as members are likely to be less critical when the proposal comes from a President of their party.

"Must-Pass" Legislation

Finally, debt limitation bills also can achieve certain procedural objectives by facilitating the passage of controversial legislation. The bills have become increasingly attractive in recent years as a way to overcome the legislative logjam in Congress. Because failure to extend borrowing authority ultimately results in government default and the failure to make benefit payments such as Social Security, the legislation must pass. As divided government and legislative gridlock have increased, debt-limit bills accordingly have become more important. They have attracted not only germane amendments dealing with the budget and debt but a host of nongermane amendments as well. At times, however, the relationship may be reversed, with attractive amendments- such as increases in Social Security benefits -added to make the debt extension vote more palatable to reluctant members.

FISCAL NORMS AND THE EVOLUTION OF THE DEBT LIMIT

Hostility to borrowing by the federal government and the ideal of a balanced budget go back to the beginning of the Republic. While government borrowing and federal debt have always had economic consequences, their political symbolism has been equally important. The meaning of the symbolism has changed significantly over the years, however. Issues surrounding federal debt were most sharply framed in the 1790s by Alexander Hamilton and Thomas Jefferson, reflecting their very different visions of the powers and responsibilities of the federal government. Behind Jefferson's opposition to Hamilton's sanctioning of federal debt was the notion of "corruption," meaning not merely graft, but an undermining of the basic republican nature of government [9, Chapter 4]. In Jefferson's view, a government saddled with debt would weaken its constitutional foundations because of the resulting social and economic inequality; the wealthy aristocracy, speculators, and bankers who financed the debt would gain financial leverage on the government. In 1798, Jefferson proposed a balanced budget amendment to the Constitution to eliminate the federal government's ability to borrow [9, p. 106]. Two generations later, Andrew Jackson echoed the same themes, urging the reduction of debt and limits on the sources of federal revenues, particularly through tariffs.

The symbolic importance of federal debt and a balanced budget shifted after the Civil War, a deficit-financed war fought to defend, not undermine, the Constitution. During the next 70 years of Republican dominance, federal spending was significantly expanded to support capitalism and industry. These expenditures were financed through a system of high tariffs that were justified as necessary to prevent deficits and to retire debt [9, p. 122]. In reality, expanded federal spending was also needed to prevent budget surpluses, which were considered as undesirable as deficits. By the turn of the century, as a result of the Progressive movement, balancing the budget became an important symbol of efficiency and integrity in government. As revenues became more dependent on income taxes rather than tariffs, Republican opposition to federal borrowing solidified.

Congress first enacted legislation to statutorily limit the borrowing authority of the U.S. Treasury as part of the Second Liberty Loan Act in 1917, as a means of consolidating Treasury borrowing following the United States's entry into World War I [10, Sept. 24, pp.

A991–A993; 11]. Until 1940, the borrowing authority of the Treasury remained remarkably stable; between 1921 and 1931, it stayed unchanged at $43.5 billion. In the years that followed, however, the exigencies of the Great Depression and the United States' entry into the Second World War sharply increased the need for public borrowing. This required the Democrats to attempt to alter the political symbolism of deficits and debt, a difficult and uncomfortable task. Keynesian theories legitimized deficit spending but confronted the powerful balanced budget norm. Republican opponents of Roosevelt attacked the New Deal and the deficits associated with it, establishing the foundations of partisan conflict over federal borrowing that continue through the present day.

In 1945, Congress overwhelmingly approved a permanent debt ceiling of $300 billion. The seven years following 1945 provided little opportunity for partisan politics over the debt ceiling. Between 1945 and 1953, only one amendment was made to the Second Liberty Loan Act—in 1946 to decrease the debt-limit ceiling from $300 billion to $275 billion. Although the Employment Act of 1946 justified borrowing to counter downturns in the business cycle, fiscal orthodoxy opposing deficit spending and the accumulation of government debt remained strong [12].

Equally important were congressional norms and institutional arrangements that gave conservatives firm control of the authorizing and appropriations process. Indeed, the appropriations committees, especially in the House, took pride in their role as the "guardians of the Treasury" and regularly appropriated funds below the levels requested in the President's budget [13]. Other important committees, such as the tax-writing House Ways and Means and Senate Finance Committees, were guided by powerful and conservative chairmen. The norms and structures that favored conservative approaches to government finance would eventually prove inconsistent with majority preferences in Congress.

The symbolic importance of federal debt remains central to understanding Congress's role and performance. Over the past 40 years, extending the federal government's borrowing authority has become necessary more frequently and has become increasingly contentious. Today, the national debt is rising faster, borrowing limits are reached sooner and must be raised by larger and larger amounts. Table 1 shows the expansion of debt subject to statutory limit over the past 50 years, increasing from $43 billion in 1940 to nearly $4 trillion today. Table 2 compares 5-year periods since 1950, showing the number of times the debt limit had to be increased, the average duration of the limit, and the percentage increase over five years. The limit increased only 2% between 1951 and 1955; between 1986 and 1990, it increased by nearly 120%. In the early 1950s, the limit was adjusted twice for an average duration of 30 months. In the last 5 years of the 1980s, it had to be raised 15 times for an average duration of only 4 months.

In the pages that follow, we trace the politics of statutory debt limitation, focusing on its managerial, partisan, and procedural implications We divide our analysis into the years before and after the adoption of the congressional budget process in 1974. Many important procedural changes occurred after 1974, but until 1990, at least, the statutory debt-limit votes remained important. By examining these changes over the past four decades, we hope to explain why Congress continues to engage in the difficult and seemingly unpalatable task of raising the debt ceiling when it has a negligible effect on fiscal discipline. Congressional debates, voting patterns, amendments, and rule changes within the House and Senate will help us draw some conclusions about the relationship between Congress and the public debt. Finally, we assess the prospects for debt limitation legislation in the future.

Table 1 Debt Subject to Statutory Limit, End of Fiscal Year, 1940–1996 (in millions of dollars)

End of fiscal year	Debt subject to limit	End of fiscal year	Debt subject to limit
1940	43,219	1969	356,107
1941	49,494	1970	372,600
1942	74,154	1971	398,650
1943	140,469	1972	427,751
1944	208,077	1974	458,264
1945	268,671	1975	475,181
1946	268,932	1975	534,207
1947	255,767	1976	621,556
1948	250,381	TQ	635,822
1949	250,965	1977	699,963
1950	255,382	1978	772,691
1951	253,284	1979	827,615
1952	257,233	1980	908,723
1953	264,220	1981	998,818
1954	269,379	1982	1,142,913
1955	272,348	1983	1,377,953
1956	270,619	1984	1,572,975
1957	269,120	1985	1,823,775
1958	275,395	1986	2,110,975
1959	282,419	1987	2,366,014
1960	283,827	1988	2,586,869
1961	286,308	1989	2,829,770
1962	295,374	1990	3,161,223
1963	302,923	1991 estimate	3,583,342
1964	308,583	1992 estimate	3,986,360
1965	314,126	1993 estimate	4,327,897
1966	316,293	1994 estimate	4,548,462
1967	323,143	1995 estimate	4,736,441
1968	348,534	1996 estimate	4,912,801

Source: *Budget of the United States FY1992*, part 7, pp. 74–77.

Table 2 Comparison of Increases in the Debt Limit in 5-Year Periods, 1951–1990

Year	Number of times debt limit increased	Percentage increase in borrowing authority over 5 years	Average number of months before limit was reached
1951–55	2	2.2	30.0
1956–60	5	4.3	12.0
1961–65	8	11.9	7.5
1966–70	5	20.4	12.0
1971–75	10	50.6	6.0
1976–80	11	55.4	5.5
1981–85	12	105.7	5.0
1986–90	15	117.8	4.0

Source: *Budget of the United States FY1992*, part 7, pp. 74–77.

STATUTORY DEBT LEGISLATION: 1953–1975

The Debt Limit as Managerial Oversight: The Eisenhower Era, 1953–1960

President Dwight Eisenhower took office in 1953 as a fiscal conservative, having run on a platform that unequivocally stressed a reduction in federal spending and the goal of balancing the federal budget. In his first State of the Union Address, his commitment to "reduce the planned deficits and then balance the budget" headed Eisenhower's list of domestic initiatives [14, p. 19]. Nonetheless, Eisenhower was the first Republican President to feel the tension between the balanced budget ideal and the prescriptions of compensatory fiscal policy during an economic downturn. Although Herbert Stein [12] argues that Eisenhower helped legitimize Keynesian economics, Ike remained firmly committed to the fundamental moral correctness of a balanced budget. In a study of economic policy making during the Eisenhower years, John Sloan [15] shows that the balanced budget norm ultimately gained ascendancy over compensatory fiscal policy.

Underscoring Eisenhower's interpretation that the 1952 election carried a mandate for conservative fiscal policies were the congressional election results that established narrow Republican majorities in the House and Senate. However, shared party affiliation and commitment to reducing the federal debt did not ensure cooperation between Congress and the White House. In 1953, the Eisenhower administration requested an increase in the debt limit, citing the costs of the Korean War and the cold war defense buildup as the reason for the increase. The House acted promptly on the request, but floor debate made it clear that Republican members were not entirely comfortable in their positions as supporters of an increased debt limit. Although House Republicans overwhelmingly approved the administration's request on the final vote, their floor comments were peppered with rhetoric calling for the President to put the nation's "fiscal house in order" [16, July 31, p. 10704]. House Democrats voted nearly two to one against the increase. Apparent in many of the speeches was the members' belief that the debt ceiling should be used as a congressional instrument of oversight and control over the executive branch. Two comments by Republicans are illustrative.

> The purpose of the debt limit is to discourage the bureaucrats, Republican and Democrat, from wasting the money appropriated by the Congress [16, Rep. Richard Poff, R-Va., July 31, p. 10704].

> One of the reasons for the [debt] limit was so that we could reexamine the operations of the Secretary of the Treasury as far as management of the debt is concerned . . . [16, Rep. Daniel Reed, R-N.Y., July 31, p. 10705].

On the other side of the capitol, the Senate Finance Committee refused to report legislation for the request, despite presidential threats that Congress would have to be called into a special session if necessary. After an 11–4 vote to table the request, the Republican committee chairman noted "that the Treasury could get by until the first of the year as is" [17, 1953, p. 409]. The Treasury did just that, in part as a result of revised budget estimates and through the sale of gold reserves. The Eisenhower administration had confronted a Republican Congress on an important component of the nation's financial management and lost. Moreover, it signaled the start of a pattern that made debt ceiling legislation a component of the broader efforts by fiscal conservatives to control government spending.

Ironically, Eisenhower had greater success in extending the government's borrowing limit after losing his Republican majorities in Congress in 1954. Table 3 examines House roll call votes on the debt-limit bills between 1953 and 1960.[1] Although support from

Table 3 Roll-Call Voting on Debt-Limit Bills in U.S. House of Representatives, Selected Years, 1953–1960 (Vote on Final Passage)

Year	Bills	Vote		Democrats		Republicans	
		For	Against	For	Against	For	Against
1953	HR6672	239	158	69	125	169	33
1955	HR6992	267	56	134	43	133	13
1958	HR9955	328	71	186	29	142	42
	HR13580	286	109	166	44	120	65
1959	HR7749	256	117	168	69	88	48
1960	HR12381	223	174	140	114	83	60

Source: Ref. 17, 1953–1960.

members of his own party declined steadily throughout his term, from 1955 on a majority of Democrats supported administration requests to increase the ceiling. Democrats opposed the debt limit only in 1953 while they were in the minority. As Republican support waned, Democrat support increased.

Failure to respond to administration requests in a timely fashion sometimes forced stop-gap measures to avoid default. The Treasury's ability to work under the previous limit despite the Senate's refusal to grant the Eisenhower administration's request in 1953 weakened the President's case. Moreover, the belief that the debt ceiling reflected a set of discretionary choices by the administration was buttressed by the apparent flexibility of the administration when Congress raised the debt ceiling by an amount less than that requested.

Congress's view that the statutory debt limit could curb borrowing was manifest in the dubious distinction it drew between "temporary" and "permanent" debt limits. Enacting temporary rather than permanent increases in the debt ceiling reflected the hope that the debt would eventually decrease. It was viewed as a means of checking further spending by forcing presidents and members of Congress to pay regular attention to the size and growth rate of the debt. During one debate, Senator Harry Byrd (D-Va.) noted that "this additional temporary extension should be regarded by the Administration as an indication of Congressional notice that it should not be repeated again" [18, June 30, p. 9573]. As confidence in the statutory debt limit as an oversight tool declined, members' frustration grew. When the Democrats recaptured the White House, partisan divisions over statutory borrowing authority became even sharper.

The Debt Limit as Partisan Ideology: The Kennedy–Johnson Era, 1961–1969

The Democratic victory in the 1960 presidential election heralded a change in economic policy making as well as a shift in party control of the White House. President Kennedy brought with him a cadre of economists eager to implement policies reflecting the "new economics" of the Keynesian school, which included increased federal spending during recessions as a means of stimulating the economy. They introduced the concept of the "full-employment" budget that rationalized government borrowing if the economy were not operating at full capacity [19]. In testimony before the Senate Finance Committee on the FY62 budget, Budget Director David Bell told members that the projected deficit was "deliberately planned as an antirecession measure" [20, June 28, p. 12154].

The administration gained some Republican support at first because many believed that the restraint of the Eisenhower administration during its last 2 years had let the economy stagnate. Keynesian economics was made more palatable by being presented in the form of a tax cut for individuals and businesses, the latter appealing to an important Republican political base—the business community. These factors made it possible to attract 40 of 153 House Republican votes in 1961 and 60 of 158 Republican votes in 1962 for the debt extensions (Table 4).

James Sundquist [21, p. 49] suggests that Republican votes for the tax cut and the concomitant higher deficits meant that "they joined the Democrats in abandoning the notion that the budget should be balanced." The evidence suggests, however, that after the first two debt-limit votes, ideological lines and Republican opposition to extending borrowing authority stiffened, most notably in the House. The Democrats' new economic perspective was of limited success in changing the perception of the deficit and the debt. According to many accounts, members of Congress and even the President himself were sometimes dubious [12, 21, 22]. In its advocacy of Keynesian-based policies, the Kennedy administration made no secret about the effect on federal deficits but made a point of insisting that the full-employment budget would be in balance. Nonetheless, fiscal conservatives in Con-

Table 4 Roll-Call Voting on Debt-Limit Bills in Congress, 1961–1967 (Vote on Final Passage)

Year	Bill	Vote		Democrats		Republicans	
		For	Against	For	Against	For	Against
			House				
1961	HR7677	231	148	191	35	40	113
1962	HR10050	251	144	191	46	60	98
	HR11990	211	192	202	39	9	153
1963	HR6009	213	204	212	32	1	172
	HR7824	221	175	219	17	2	158
	HR8969	187	179	187	32	0	147
1964	HR11375	203	182	203	58	0	154
1965	HR8464	229	165	223	43	6	122
1966	HR15202	199	165	198	44	1	121
1967	HR4573	215	199	213	26	2	173
	HR10328	197	211	197	35	0	176
	HR10867	217	196	217	20	0	176
			Senate				
1962	HR11990	55	34	43	14	12	20
1963	HR6009	60	24	45	11	15	13
	HR7824	57	31	45	12	12	19
	HR8969	50	26	39	13	11	13
1964	HR11375	48	21	36	9	12	12
1965	HR8464	61	26	49	10	12	16
1966	HR15202	50	17	40	8	10	9
1967	HR4573	54	23	42	11	12	12
	HR10867	60	30	45	15	15	15

Source: Ref. 17, 1961–1968.

gress professed "astonishment" and "shock," complaining that the administration "seems to regard the federal budget as a tool for testing economic theories" [20, June 28, p. 12163].

Voting patterns through the 1960s revealed pronounced House-Senate differences among Republicans. Nearly half of the Senate Republicans supported legislation to extend borrowing authority. The bills tended to pass easily since approximately 80% of the Senate Democrats also supported the legislation. In the House, however, with members facing reelection every 2 years, Republican opposition became nearly unanimous, and with 30 to 40 defections among Democrats, debt increase measures passed only by narrow margins. As a result, the administration and House leadership had some difficulty putting together majorities sufficient to pass the necessary increase. In order to gain support at all, congressional leaders were forced to keep the increases low and the duration of the increase short, which resulted in more frequent votes.

Floor debate reveals that many members viewed a vote to increase the statutory debt limit as a referendum on the nation's economic policy and the different positions of the two parties. The link between debt ceiling votes and administration budget policy served to intensify partisan ideological attacks. Many Republican members argued that having voted for reduced appropriations during the prior year, they had no obligation to support the current proposal for increasing the debt limit. Illinois Republican Harold Collier's comments on the House floor were typical:

> Because I have personally voted in a responsible manner on all authorization and appropriation bills since I have been a member of this body . . . , I refuse to be a rubberstamp for any administration when the debt limit legislation has been brought before us . . . [23, June 18, p. 14360].

Political alignments changed little during Lyndon Johnson's presidency, despite his legendary legislative skills. Proposed increases in the statutory debt limits evoked the same united Republican opposition in the House, made increasingly rancorous by Republican perceptions that Johnson was using Vietnam War costs to cover borrowing for domestic programs. The administration's attempt to sell government securities, which were exempt from the debt limit, was viewed as a gimmick designed to disguise the actual levels of federal spending. It only increased Republican perceptions that the administration could not be trusted.[2]

Two significant events occurred in 1967: the first outright defeat of debt-limit legislation and the first permanent increase in the debt ceiling since 1959. Not surprisingly, after years of clinging to the fantasy that borrowing was only temporary and would soon fall to lower levels, the increase in the permanent debt ceiling was highly contentious. Opponents portrayed the permanent nature of the increase as an admission of defeat in efforts to curb federal spending. Furthermore, it was evident that the belief in the ceiling as a means of controlling the deficit was slowly being put to rest. Representative Joe Skubitz (R-Kans.) spoke for most Republicans:

> Mr. Chairman, I resent most strongly the very fact that for the ninth time since I entered Congress in 1963, the Members of this body are considering another raise of the public debt limit. . . . Today, every member must surely realize how meaningless we have made this "permanent" debt figure. I would further question how any of us can believe that we will today be voting on any debt dollar limit which will be realized other than on paper [24, June 7, p. 15055].

The Debt Limit as Must-Pass Legislation: The Nixon–Ford Era, 1969–1976

Richard Nixon was elected to office during a period of intensified political conflict resulting from the sharpened debate in Congress over the war in Vietnam. Members had become accustomed to using partisan arguments in debates on debt limits; divided government and growing interbranch conflict would do nothing to curb that practice. Additionally, during this period, the genesis of a pattern developed that would eventually become full-blown in the mid-1970s and 1980s: the use of the debt ceiling vote as a vehicle for other legislative matters.

The pattern of Republican support that existed under Eisenhower reappeared under Nixon and his successor, Gerald Ford. The President received initial support for his requests to extend borrowing authority before Republican support waned, causing Nixon and Ford to depend on support from House Democrats to supply the necessary votes (Table 5). In

Table 5 Roll-Call Voting on Debt-Limit Bills in Congress, 1969–1976 (Vote on Final Passage)

		Vote		Democrats		Republicans	
Year	Bill	For	Against	For	Against	For	Against
House							
1969	HR8508	313	9	173	52	140	41
1970	HR17802	236	127	129	68	107	59
1971	HR4690	238	162	123	100	105	62
1972	HR12910	247	147	155	78	92	69
	HR15390	211	168	113	109	98	59
	HR16810	221	163	80	142	141	21
1973	HR8410	261	152	134	97	127	55
	HR11104	253	153	160	65	93	88
1974	HR14832	191	190	116	97	75	93
1975	HR2634	248	170	186	94	62	76
	HR7545	175	225	129	137	46	88
	HR8030	223	196	163	115	60	81
	HR10049	178	217	136	130	42	87
	HR10585	213	198	200	76	13	122
1976	HR11893	212	189	166	97	46	92
	HR14114	184	177	147	92	37	85
Senate							
1969	HR8508	67	18	36	14	31	4
1970	HR17802	64	19	33	12	31	7
1971	HR4690	80	0	43	0	37	0
1972	HR12910	53	29	25	17	28	12
	HR15390	78	3	42	2	36	1
	HR16810	61	11	33	8	28	3
1973	HR8410	72	19	48	3	24	16
	HR11104	58	34	44	10	14	24
1974	HR14832	58	38	35	21	23	17
1975	HR2634	70	20	46	10	24	10
	HR8030	72	21	43	11	26	10

Source: Ref. 17, 1961–1968.

the meantime, members discovered that debt-ceiling legislation was a useful vehicle for other legislative matters. Proposed amendments were not new to debt limit legislation; the difference was in their germaneness to the issue. Previously, amendments had been primarily concerned with the mechanics of debt management: the interest rates on government bonds, sales of government-owned certificates, or more often reduction of the size of the increase itself. In the House Ways and Means Committee, Democrat Charles Vanik (D-Ohio) unsuccessfully attempted to offer two amendments to the 1970 debt ceiling bill: one to reduce the debt limit increase and another to cut the military budget by $6 billion. Two amendments were offered in the Senate to the same bill: one to postpone a congressional pay raise until the federal budget was balanced and the other to establish an overall ceiling on federal expenditures.

The issue that became most closely associated with debt-limit legislation during the Nixon administration was Social Security. Senate debate on the 1971 debt bill was dominated by discussion of the Social Security provisions, overshadowing the original purpose of the bill. It was the first of three instances when the Senate would attach popular Social Security legislation to a debt ceiling bill. Controversial amendments, such as one suspending bombing in Cambodia, became more common. Delay in enacting debt limits increasingly threatened to disrupt government operations; a filibuster against a campaign finance reform amendment delayed the approval of a 1973 debt ceiling bill until 2 days after the expiration the previous "temporary" limit.

The strategy of using essential debt-ceiling extensions for legislative purposes was adopted by the President as well. In the debt-ceiling bill he sent to Congress in 1972, President Nixon included a controversial spending ceiling and provisions to give the President broad impoundment powers with which to meet that limit. Although the provisions were later deleted altogether in conference, it is a telling example of the potential of the "must-pass" bill for both ends of Pennsylvania Avenue.[3]

Despite the changes in the politics of statutory debt limitation, a consistent theme from earlier periods remained: the attempt to cut proposed debt limit increases linked with the expressed need to curb federal spending. By this time, however, many members recognized the need for additional tools for Congress to exert greater control over spending and borrowing. Support grew for creating an entirely new congressional budget process.

STATUTORY DEBT LIMITATION AFTER BUDGET REFORM, 1976–1990

The Budget and Impoundment Control Act of 1974

Frustration with growing debt, the piecemeal appropriations process in Congress, and antipathy towards the Nixon administration helped forge a bipartisan coalition in support of budget reform. Expectations of reform were high. In reporting in 1974 the last debt ceiling extension before the enactment of the budget act, the Ways and Means Committee noted that the debt bill would provide "some overall congressional control over the budget until Congress enacts legislation creating a legislative system for examining and controlling budget totals and budget components" [25, May 25, p. 1402]. The Joint Study Committee on Budget Control [26, p. 8] concluded that "the failure to arrive at congressional budgetary decisions on an overall basis has been a contributory factor in the size of these deficits." Members were also concerned about the disintegration of the appropriations process. By 1974, only 45% of outlays were under the jurisdiction of the appropriations committees [26, p. 10]. Backdoor spending and rapid growth in entitlements undermined the more traditional means of legislative control [27]. Increasingly, Congress failed to pass spending bills by the start of the fiscal year. Between 1972 and 1975, not a single appropriation bill was passed on time, and in several instances, no spending bill was ever passed [28, 310–311]. Rather than eliminating the old authorization-appropriations process, the Budget and Impoundment Control Act of 1974 superimposed a new budget process over the old system. The House and Senate budget committees, the Congressional Budget Office, and a strict timetable were all created by the act [29, 30]. The budget act made no specific changes or references to the Second Liberty Loan Act, but section 310 of the act provided that the budget resolution would "specify the amount by which the statutory limit on the public debt is to be changed and to direct the committees having jurisdiction to recommend such change" (Public Law 93-344, Title III, Section 310 (3)).

It was generally believed that the process would help reduce federal borrowing by requiring a majority of members to go on record supporting a deficit and an increase in the national debt *before* the fact. Under the old system, when congressional taxing and spending decisions produced a deficit, the statutory debt ceiling had to be raised *after* the fact. With the required votes on first and second concurrent resolutions on the budget, reformers believed that Congress would be less likely to allow a deficit or expand the national debt. Such optimism would prove unfounded as budgets remained unbalanced, and the politics of statutory debt limitation was left largely unchanged by budget reform.

Looking at the patterns of debt growth before and after the implementation of budget reform suggests it had little effect on debt limitation. The debt continued to accumulate at approximately the same pace in the 5 years after budget reform as it had in the previous 5 years. The debt expanded even more rapidly in the 1980s, tripling in less than ten years. Budget reform also had no noticeable impact on the growing frequency of debt extensions (Table 2). In 1976, congressional leaders attempted to synchronize the statutory debt limit with the government's new fiscal year. A 15-month extension running through September 30, 1977, was adopted. This effort proved unsuccessful, however, since the ceiling was either reached sooner than expected or a majority would only support an extension of shorter duration. Nor was there any new "realism" about the exercise, despite expert testimony that separate statutory limitations now made even less sense from a policy perspective. In addition, the fiction of the temporary versus the permanent extension was continued after budget reform. The permanent debt limit stayed at $400 billion for almost a decade as the government's actual borrowing needs grew to $925 billion. Not until 1983 did Congress eliminate the distinction between the permanent and temporary debt limits.

Elimination of the Separate House Vote

In 1979, 4 years after the implementation of the congressional budget process, the House of Representatives adopted an amendment by Richard Gephardt (D-Mo.), eliminating the requirement that the House have a separate vote on the statutory debt limitation. As the budget process became more time consuming and difficult, particularly in the House, pressure grew to reduce the number of these highly contentious votes. This had been tried once before. In 1978, the Ways and Means Committee had unsuccessfully attempted to link the debt extension to the budget resolution. Many worried that adding another burden to the already controversial budget resolution might make it impossible to enact.

There was also a constitutional problem: The congressional budget was enacted through a concurrent resolution binding only on Congress and did not need the signature of the President. The debt, however, had to be limited by statute, signed by the President. Members were not anxious to involve the President in the congressional budget process, so the two procedures remained separate. The Ways and Means Committee attempted to link the two actions informally by enacting debt-ceiling legislation immediately after the adoption of the budget resolution.

By 1979, however, a majority of House members were ready to eliminate the troublesome debt limitation vote. Gephardt devised an approach that avoided the constitutional problem. His amendment provided that the debt limit, approved as part of the concurrent budget resolution, would be inserted in a joint resolution deemed to be passed by the House. It would then automatically be sent to the Senate to await action and final approval, and then the signature of the President (HR 5369, H Rept. 96-472). Support for the change was solid; the House defeated a motion to strike the amendment from the bill by a vote of 132-283 [31, Sept. 26, p. H26349].

The change in the process did not eliminate separate votes on the debt ceiling in the House, although it reduced them. If the joint resolution sent to the Senate was amended in any way, the House had to vote on the conference report. In instances where the limit was reached before a budget resolution had been approved, or in years where the House could not approve a budget resolution on time, separate votes would have to be taken. Table 6 compares the number of roll-call votes on debt-limitation amendments and final passage from 1976 to 1990. It clearly shows the increase in the number of votes in recent years. It also indicates that the House continued to be embroiled in controversial debt votes, including 12 separate votes in 1981. Since the adoption of the Gephardt amendment, however, the Senate has had significantly more roll calls on debt legislation, a total of 81 votes compared to 48 for the House. Although the Gephardt amendment has not eliminated voting on controversial statutory debt limits in the House, it has reduced them.

Borrowing Restraint and Executive Oversight

Despite the economic, political, and institutional changes that occurred during this period, some members still insisted that the debt limit could be used as a tool of fiscal discipline. This argument resurfaced during a 1976 debate when Representative William Ketchum (R Calif.) claimed that if the Ways and Means Committee, "had refused to accommodate the big spenders and kept a lid on the debt, Congress would have to come to grips with its own profligacy" [17, 1976, p. 87]. During the 1979 House debate over the Gephardt amendment, Representative Delbert Latta (R-Ohio), ranking minority member of the Budget Committee, expressed the view of those who wished to retain the separate votes as an instrument of fiscal control.

Table 6 Debt Limitation Votes in Congress, 1976–1990 (Amendments and Final Passage)

Year	House	Senate	Year	House	Senate
1976	4	0	1984	6	7
1977	4	1	1985	6	13
1978	9	1	1986	4	14
1979	12	10	1987	5	16
1980	7	6	1988	0	0
1981	12	2	1989	3	0
1982	0	7	1990	3	1
1983	3	15			

Source: Authors' calculations from records in Ref. 17, 1976–1990.

This is not budgeting, it is flim flam to cover the growth of big government. Unless this House acts today the flim flam will be made worse by allowing this House to duck the entire issue of the debt. Unless the provision relating to future debt increases is removed from the bill there will be a built-in escalator for future expansions of the debt [31, Sept. 26, p. H23669].

Even if frequent voting did not actually serve to reduce borrowing, some believed that at least the process helped publicize the problem. John Ashbrook (R-Ohio) explained that

In the consideration of the debt limit bills, our attention is focused solely on the amount of debt this country has accumulated. We need to do this from time to time. In budget resolutions, the debt limit tends to disappear in a morass of other figures. At least every once in a while we should stop and realize what we are doing to this country by burdening it with an ever escalating national debt [31, Sept. 26, p. H23669].

Although more frequently a claim by Republicans, some Democrats, when in the minority, also asserted that the statutory debt limit leads to more borrowing. In 1983, when federal deficits were heading for an all-time record, a coalition of Republicans and Democrats succeeded in defeating President Reagan's request for a $225 billion increase in borrowing authority. Led by William Armstrong (R-Colo.) and Russell Long (D-La.), the Senate refused to go along. In urging defeat, Long warned his colleagues that "when you vote for this motion, you are voting to continue the biggest deficits in the history of this country as far as anybody can see" [17, 1983, p. 241].

The debt limit continued to serve as a means for Congress to oversee Treasury operations after the adoption of the new budget process. As in previous years, Congress consistently reduced the duration of the new borrowing authority to make the amount of the debt smaller than that requested by the President. Debt-limit bills were also still used to make specific changes in Treasury policy. For example, in 1976, Congress set a minimum of 4% interest on Series E savings bonds, increased by 20% the amount of long-term bonds that the Treasury could sell above the statutory interest rate ceiling, and extended the maximum maturity of Treasury notes from 7 to 10 years (PL 94-232). Similar specific changes in Treasury department actions were adopted throughout the 1970s and 1980s.

Congress has also indirectly affected Treasury Department policy by waiting until the last possible hour to extend the debt ceiling or actually letting it expire, something that has occurred on numerous occasions since 1976. Congressional delays have resulted in underinvesting in trust funds, delays of Treasury auctions, borrowing from Social Security, and other actions to meet the government's obligations. Perhaps the most serious consequences came during the fall of 1985 when Congress was deadlocked over the Gramm–Rudman–Hollings mandatory deficit reduction plan (see below). To keep up the pressure on negotiators, Senate leaders refused to consider temporary extensions of borrowing authority for nearly a month after it expired. The Treasury was required to take several stopgap actions, including disinvesting from the Social Security and other federal retirement funds [17, 1985, pp. 457–458]. More than any other Treasury action, this spurred a strong congressional response, and the final budget agreement in 1985 barred the practice in the future.

Treasury Department actions taken in response to congressional delays or the expiration of borrowing authority are summarized in Table 7. As the table indicates, the administration had to adopt defensive measure throughout the 1980s to allow the government to keep paying its bills. One of Treasury's problems is that their transactions are seasonal and "lumpy," not evenly spaced over the year. Heavy borrowing takes place in the fourth quarter

Table 7 Treasury Department Responses to Debt Limitation Expiration, Debt-Limit Increases from September 1982 to October 1990 (billions of dollars)

Date of increase	Amount of limit	Expiration date	Treasury actions at close[a]
Sept. 30, 1982	1,290.2	Sept. 30, 1983	More or less timely increase (followed Social Security bailout)
May 26, 1983	1,389.0	Permanent	Delayed auctions, underinvested trust funds; cash crunch gradual
Nov. 21, 1983	1,490.0	Permanent	Postponed auctions, underinvested Social Security
May 25, 1984	1,520.0	Permanent	Cut back auctions, underinvested Social Security
July 6, 1984	1,573.0	Permanent	Delayed auctions, underinvested trust funds; cash not critical
Oct. 13, 1984	1,823.8	Permanent	Gramm–Rudman interruption: cut late-Sept. auctions to force crisis; borrowed through FFB; actively disinvested trust funds
Nov. 14, 1985	1,903.8	Dec. 6, 1985	More or less timely increase
Dec. 12, 1985	2,078.7	Permanent	Used FFB temporarily to credit Social Security; otherwise timely
Aug. 21, 1986	2,111.0	Permanent	Used FFB authority; underinvested trust funds; cash not critical
Oct. 21, 1986	2,300.0	May 15, 1987	Postponed some auctions; cash ample
May 15, 1987	2,320.0	July 17, 1987	Postponed some auctions; cash not critical
July 30, 1987	2,320.0	Aug. 6, 1987	Postponed auctions (quarterly refunding)
Aug. 10, 1987	2,352.0	Sept. 23, 1987	Rescheduled some auctions; otherwise timely; cash ample
Sept. 29, 1987	2,800.0	Permanent	More or less timely increase associated with S&L bill
Aug. 7, 1989	2,870.0	Oct. 31, 1989	Increased cash balances to buy another week
Nov. 8, 1989	3,122.7	Permanent	More or less timely increase before congressional recess
Aug. 9, 1990	3,195.0	Oct. 2, 1990	More or less timely increase as part of budget summit weekend
Sept. 30, 1990	3,195.0	Oct. 6, 1990	Increased as part of continuing resolution after summit rejected
Oct. 9, 1990	3,195.0	Oct. 19, 1990	Borrowed up to limit on Oct. 19 pending next increase
Oct. 19, 1990	3,195.0	Oct. 24, 1990	Delayed several auctions
Oct. 25, 1990	3,195.0	Oct. 27, 1990	Compressed auctions and settlements into this time period
Oct. 28, 1990	3,230.0	Nov. 5, 1990	Temporary limit until reconciliation bill ($4,145.0) signed

[a]Actions listed do not include suspension of savings bond and state and local government series (SLGs) sales, which are more or less routine responses to a debt-ceiling interruption (especially after expiration of a temporary ceiling).
Source: Ref. 38.

because no major income tax deadlines occur. Although we found no systematic accounting, it is generally believed that delays in extending an allowing borrowing authority to expire has cost the government hundreds of millions of dollars.[4]

Clarifying Partisan and Ideological Differences

Patterns of partisanship that appeared in the 1960s have continued in recent years. As the debt has grown more rapidly and debt legislation has come to the floor more often, political opportunism has not diminished. Congressman Ed Jenkins (D-Ga.) concluded that opposition to the debt extension boiled down to nothing more than politics.

> First of all, there is always the political aspect of it. I do not think anyone in this House has anyone writing them asking them to vote to extend the debt limit. There is no constituency for this type of legislation, obviously. . . . We really play a game with ourselves. When we have a Republican President in the White House, then many of the Democrats do not feel obligated to vote for the debt limit legislation. When we have a Democrat in the White House, few, if any, Republicans feel any obligation whatsoever to vote for this legislation . . . [(yet)] all of us in private agree that this has to be done if the Government is going to continue to operate [31, Sept. 26, p. H26342].

Representative Barber Conable (R-N.Y.) explained in clear political terms what was behind the partisan strategy.

> I do not see any reason why on an issue of this sort, given its comparative lack of significance in terms of controlling the fiscal policy of the country, why the minority should be required to let those majority Members who are from marginal districts have the benefit of voting against this bill politically, which you would have us deny to ourselves [31, Sept. 26, p. H26343].

Roll-call voting since 1976 shows patterns consistent with earlier periods. Tables 8 and 9 show roll-call votes on the passage of statutory debt extensions since 1976. With Democrat Jimmy Carter in the White House, House Republicans voted as a bloc against the bills. They were usually joined by anywhere from 50 to 80 Democrats, often making the final margin close or actually defeating the bill. Also consistent with earlier patterns, partisanship was much more restrained in the Senate, where Republicans generally split evenly and Democrats generally supported the President. These party divisions also correspond closely to House and Senate voting patterns on budget resolution votes in the 1970s and 1980s [32].

Voting alignments changed in the 1980s with the election of a Republican Senate and President. In a purely political move following the 1980 elections, congressional Democrats made sure that the debt ceiling would be reached only weeks after Reagan's inauguration, assuring that the unpleasant task of extending the government's borrowing authority would be one of his administration's first legislative actions. One of the few benefits accruing to the Senate Democrats from their newly acquired minority status was the ability to force Senate Republicans to provide the votes to extend borrowing authority. Between 1981 and 1987, when they regained a majority, only once did a majority of Senate Democrats vote for the debt limit. In many instances, they opposed it by margins of greater than 3 to 1. Even these numbers do not reveal the full extent of their efforts to hold Republican senators' feet to the fire, particularly those Republicans who had voted against the debt measures for years. In a number of instances, Democratic senators would withhold their vote, standing

Table 8 Roll-Call Voting on Debt-Limit Bills in U.S. House of Representatives, 1977–1990 (Vote on Final Passage)

Year	Bill	Vote		Democrats		Republicans	
		For	Against	For	Against	For	Against
			Carter				
1977	HR8655	180	201	164	87	16	114
	HR9290	213	202	194	81	19	121
1978	HR11180	165	248	157	115	8	133
	HR11518	233	172	206	59	27	113
	HR12641	167	228	162	99	5	129
	HR13385	205	202	196	74	9	128
1979	HR1894	194	222	191	73	3	149
	HR2534	212	195	209	53	3	145
	HR5229	200	215	197	70	3	142
	HR5369	219	198	214	52	5	146
1980	HR7428	208	198	208	44	0	154
			Reagan				
1981	HR1553	305	104	155	68	150	36
1984	HR5665	150	263	104	148	46	115
	HR5692	211	198	142	108	69	90
	HR5927	138	282	79	178	59	104
	HR5953	208	202	124	130	84	72
1985	HR3721	300	121	212	31	88	90
1986	HR5395	216	199	197	44	19	155
1987	HR2360	296	124	219	28	77	96
	HR3022	263	155	222	21	41	134
			Bush				
1989	HR3024	231	185	181	63	50	122
1990	HR5355	221	205	175	76	46	129

Source: Ref. 17, 1977–1990.

around the chamber with their arms folded, waiting until a sufficient number of Republicans voted in the affirmative.

In the House, the pattern changed less dramatically, even with a Republican in the White House. Because the Democrats remained the majority party in the House, Republicans still had the ability to oppose the measures. Only in 1981, the first extension of the debt ceiling after Reagan became President, did a majority of House Republicans vote for the legislation. In every subsequent vote, they opposed it by substantial margins. The presence of a Republican in the White House, however, did have a measurable effect. The number of House Republicans voting for the debt extension, while still a minority, was significantly greater than those who supported it during the later years of the Carter administration and earlier Democratic administrations (Table 8). This was despite the fact that federal borrowing grew much more rapidly under Reagan than Carter.

Amendments to Debt-Limit Legislation

In the face of a growing deadlock between the Republican President and the Democratic Congress, the statutory debt limit became increasingly popular as a means to move bills

Table 9 Roll-Call Voting on Debt-Limit Bills in U.S. Senate, 1977–1987 (Vote on Final Passage)

Year	Bill	Vote		Democrats		Republicans	
		For	Against	For	Against	For	Against
Carter							
1977	HR9290	58	30	41	12	17	18
1978	HR11518	62	31	40	16	22	15
1979	HR2534	62	33	48	10	14	23
	HR5369	49	29	34	10	15	19
1980	HR7482	67	20	43	6	24	14
	HJR569	54	39	46	9	8	30
Reagan							
1981	HR1553	73	18	27	15	46	3
	HJR265	64	34	18	28	46	6
1982	HJR519	49	41	8	33	41	8
	HJR520	50	41	14	26	36	15
1983	HJR2990	51	41	12	31	39	10
	HJR308	39	56	11	31	28	25
	HJR308	58	40	20	24	38	16
1984	HJR654	14	46	1	28	13	18
	HJR654	37	30	0	26	37	4
1985	HJR372	51	37	13	29	38	8
1986	HJR668	47	40	18	24	29	16
	HR5395	34	47	11	29	23	18
	HR5395	36	35	10	26	26	9
1987	HR2360	58	36	33	18	25	18
	HR3190	51	39	33	14	18	25
	HJR324	54	31	25	21	29	10

Source: Ref. 17, 1977–1990.

through the legislative process during the 1980s. The increased centralization of authority in Congress during the 1980s was associated with the so-called "four bill system" that included the statutory debt limitation [33, pp. 48–51]. The ability of the leaders to control access to these bills, particularly in the House, significantly strengthened their power. Amendments to the debt limitation legislation in the past two decades encompassed both germane and nongermane amendments. Notable differences existed between the House and the Senate, largely because of the Gephardt amendment in 1979 and the ability of the House leadership to control the rules. After 1979, virtually all nongermane amendments originated in the Senate.

Nongermane Amendments

Major nongermane amendments to the statutory debt limitation from the late 1970s to the present are given in Table 10. Throughout the 1980s especially, the statutory debt limitation attracted a wide range of amendments. These included an attempt to invoke the War Powers Act concerning military action in Grenada, votes on a nuclear freeze, and congressional instructions to negotiators in the strategic arms reduction talks. Domestic issues often dealt with taxes, including attempts to alter Reagan's 1981 Economic Recovery Tax Act (ERTA) reduction in income taxes, gasoline taxes, real estate taxes, windfall profits tax, and tariffs

Table 10 Major Nongermane Amendments to Statutory Debt-Limit Bills in the Senate, 1978–1987

1978	To require equal per capita spending by state
1979	Presidential veto repeal of oil import fee[a]
	Indexing personal income tax rates
	Across-the-board income tax cut
1981	Reduce tax deduction for business meals
	To order Fed to lower interest rates
	To modify ERTA tax cut
1982	Reduce period for long-term capital gains
	To allow voluntary school prayer
	To ban busing to achieve integration
1983	To invoke War Powers Act to force withdrawal from Grenada
	To order Japan to eliminate nontariff barriers on beef
	To instruct START negotiators on nuclear arms reductions
1984	Nuclear freeze proposal
	To limit tax on imputed interest
	To exempt certain real estate sales from taxation
1985	To increase federal gas tax
	To reduce spending of Commodity Credit Corporation
1986	Deficiency payments to farmers
	To repeal windfall profits tax
	To increase tariff on imported oil
	Drought aid to farmers
	Insurance for AIDS victims
	To create new federal crime of money laundering
1987	Repeal congressional and federal pay raises

[a]Senate and House.
Source: Authors' compilation from Ref. 17, 1978–1990.

on imported oil. One of the more dramatic legislative battles involving the debt limitation occurred in 1980 when Congress included a repeal of President Carter's imported oil fee as part of the bill. Carter's veto was crushed by override votes of 355–34 in the House and 68–10 in the Senate in what was a low point in his legislative record [17, 1980, pp. 273–274].

What had once been only a tacit legislative strategy was now openly exploited by congressional leaders. One of the more extreme examples of this was seen in 1982, when Majority Leader Howard Baker made the dubious promise to senators that they could use the debt-limit bill as a vehicle for pet legislation that had been bottled up all session. The result was over 1,400 proposed amendments on nongermane issues [17, 1982, pp. 44–45]. The Senate spent 5 weeks debating scores of amendments with most of the time consumed by Senator Jesse Helms (R N.C.), who was determined to limit federal court jurisdiction over school prayer and busing. It became clear that the amendments would topple the bill, and Baker was forced to renege on his promise. A bipartisan agreement that no amendments whatsoever would be allowed on the bill, including those already adopted, facilitated final passage.

Despite the range of amendments offered to debt-limit legislation, the record of success was not impressive; few of the amendments were enacted. Although the potential of the debt limitation as "must-pass" legislation appears high, it has not proved an effective means in practice for adopting nongermane legislation. It has, however, been much more important as a vehicle for budget and deficit-related measures.

Budget and Deficit-Related Amendments

Major germane amendments from the late 1970s to the present are summarized in Table 11. In 1978, as we have seen, the House attempted to eliminate separate votes on the debt limit. This effort was successful in 1979 with the adoption of the Gephardt amendment. The same year, an amendment was offered in the Senate to instruct the budget committee to submit a budget resolution providing for a balanced budget in the coming years. Other budget-related amendments included limiting federal revenues as a proportion of GNP, a spending freeze, support for a line-item veto, and a requirement that amendments to increase spending be offset by tax increases or spending cuts. The most important budget-related rider was the Gramm–Rudman–Hollings mandatory deficit reduction law that was adopted in 1985 and amended in 1987 and 1990.

As frustration with exploding deficits and ballooning federal debt came to a head, a scheme for mandatory deficit reduction became the dominant issue in Congress in late 1985 [34]. The Balanced Budget and Emergency Deficit Control Act of 1985, better known by the name of its sponsors as Gramm–Rudman–Hollings, was offered as an amendment to that year's debt limitation legislation. Its success was propelled by the political concerns members had with voting against anything that purported to reduce deficits. Over a period of 3 months, delicate negotiations between the Democratic House and the Republican Senate produced a compromise that was unpopular, but in the words of one cosponsor, was a "bad idea whose time had come" [24, p. 85]. Pressure was maintained on negotiators by

Table 11 Major Budget Process and Deficit-Related Amendments to Statutory Debt-Limit Bills, 1978–1987

1978	House: To eliminate separate vote on debt ceiling
1979	House: To eliminate separate vote on debt ceiling
	Balanced budget amendment
	Senate: Requiring Budget Committee to submit balanced budget
	Senate: Limit federal revenues to 20.5 percent of GNP
1980	Senate: To enhance President's rescission powers
1982	Senate: Eliminate distinction between temporary and permanent debt limit
1983	Senate: Eliminate distinction between temporary and permanent debt limit
	Senate: Express support for line-item veto amendment
	Senate: To require that amendments to debt bills be deficit neutral
1984	Senate: Federal spending freeze
1985	House: Order Treasury to restore disinvested Social Security funds
	House and Senate: Gramm–Rudman–Hollings mandatory deficit reduction
	Senate: Require spending increases be offset with spending cuts, not tax increases
1986	Senate and House: To reinstate Gramm–Rudman–Hollings mandatory provisions
	Senate: To exempt Social Security administrative expenses from sequester
1987	Senate and House: Gramm–Rudman–Hollings II, reinstating mandatory provisions and amending targets
	Senate: To provide President with line-item veto

Source: Authors' compilation from Ref. 17, 1978–1990.

successfully blocking any attempt to enact stopgap borrowing authority. When Social Security and other benefit checks were in jeopardy in November, temporary authority was finally extended. The key compromise that allowed the bill to pass involved an agreement that any across-the-board cuts (sequesters) would fall equally on domestic and defense programs. The bill set deficit targets for 5 years and required automatic cuts in nonexempt programs unless Congress met the targets.

The statutory debt limit would prove critical in 1987 as well. When the Supreme Court struck down the automatic across-the-board cuts in Gramm–Rudman–Hollings because of the role of the Comptroller General, proponents set out to restore them [35]. Although efforts failed in 1986, they succeeded in 1987 by holding the debt limitation hostage until a Gramm–Rudman–Hollings "fix" was adopted. Others attempted to use the debt-limit bill to force President Reagan to a budget summit with Congress. Once again, the debt bill was the focal point of the partisan battle between Reagan and the Democratic House and Senate. Conferees finally agreed in September on Gramm–Rudman–Hollings II, which fixed the constitutional flaw and revised the deficit targets. Perhaps the greatest accomplishment of the bill was the extension of the debt limitation from $2.1 trillion to $2.8 trillion, the largest increase in history and enough to last through early 1989, after the presidential election. The compromise, however, did little to restore confidence in the ability of Congress and the President to curb growing deficits. Several weeks later, U.S. stock markets suffered their worse decline in history.

After nearly half a century, there are signs that the debt limitation may finally be receding in prominence and importance. The statutory debt limit did not play a critical role in 1990 during the adoption of the Omnibus Budget Reconciliation Act, which included the Budget Enforcement Act [36, pp. 43–57]. In fact, members seem increasingly willing to forego voting on the controversial measures. No significant amendments have been adopted since 1987. In 1990, the debt limit held a low profile among the larger budget issues: extensions were simply rolled into the stopgap continuing resolutions until a final agreement was reached [37, Oct. 6, p. 3187]. At one point, negotiators made an effort to extend the debt limitation for the full term of the agreement, which would have eliminated such votes for 5 years. Finally, in compromise, negotiators agreed to extend the debt limit to an amount that they believed would last until early 1993, after the presidential election.

SUMMARY AND CONCLUSIONS

Although congressional responses have changed over time, many themes have remained consistent, including the high degree of significance attached to statutory debt ceiling votes. The practice of periodically increasing the debt ceiling appears to be something of a puzzle. Each vote calls attention to the increased size of the debt, a pattern about which members have been clearly uncomfortable. Treasury officials have repeatedly made plain to Congress that the ritual serves no useful function and that a one-time vote to remove the statutory debt ceiling altogether would put an end to these votes. Yet despite the disagreeable position the vote puts them in, and despite its limited utility as a management tool, Congress has maintained the practice.

We believe the puzzle is, in part, explained by the way in which the votes have served members' needs in other ways. Our examination of the 57 debt ceiling increases since 1945 show that such motivations do exist. Member goals have evolved to reflect changes in legislative institutions, the relationship between Congress and the executive, and norms within Congress. Yet it has not been the case that the emergence of one purpose has replaced those before it. Rather, new goals have been encompassed within former practices.

The member goals we identified include (1) managerial concerns: control of spending and oversight of the executive branch, (2) clarifying partisan and ideological differences on economic policy, and (3) exploitation of debt ceiling's must-pass status as a vehicle for other legislation. The earliest period of the study seemed to be dominated by debt management concerns. Given the conservative nature of Congress and the executive at the time, balanced budgets were valued as a goal by executive and legislature alike. As a result, member debate focused predominantly on the Treasury Department's explanation for the request and with admonitions about the rate of spending.

Once those values became less hegemonic, congressional debate became increasingly focused on the different positions of the two major parties. The minority was motivated primarily by electoral concerns and the majority with governing needs. This fissure was widened by the Kennedy administration's attempt to alter fiscal norms with its embrace of the "new economics." When Richard Nixon took office, partisanship in debate on the debt ceiling had become the rule rather the exception. This pattern of partisanship has been remarkably resilient over the past 40 years. The patterns of Republican and Democratic support for debt limitation bills since 1950 are shown in Figures 1 and 2. Republican opposition in the House was nearly unanimous under Democratic administrations, and after initial support, declined sharply throughout Republican administrations. On the other hand, House Democrats were either divided or tended to support the President regardless of his party and, except during Republican control in the 1980s, Senate Democrats tended to support raising the limit.

The Nixon presidency also marked the advent of what was to be a long period—interrupted by only the Carter administration—of divided government. Partisan disagreements between Congress and the executive inevitably slowed the policymaking process. As a result, members searched for alternative ways to accomplish legislative policy goals. Its must-pass nature made legislation increasing the statutory debt ceiling the perfect choice for riders. The increased frequency of these votes, spurred by rapidly rising debt, only increased their attraction. By the 1980s, the debt ceiling bill as a vehicle for amendments had become the norm. Legislative deadlock and the constraint of deficits elevated

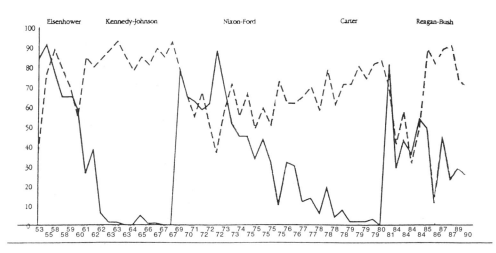

Figure 1 Party support for debt-ceiling extensions, House, 1945–1990. Republicans (——), Democrats (---).

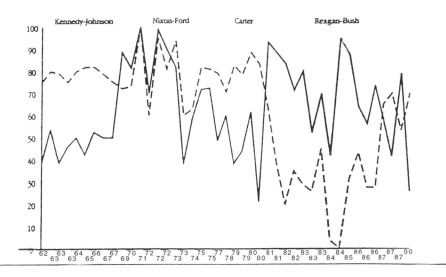

Figure 2 Party support for debt-ceiling extensions, Senate, 1960–1990. Republicans (———), Democrats (---).

their political salience and convenience, but were still no guarantee that the proposals would be adopted.

What of the future? After nearly half a century, the importance of debt legislation may have reached its peak in the late 1980s. The institution of budget summits and the Budget Enforcement Act may have reduced the debt ceiling to a minor issue in comparison with long-term taxing and spending decisions. Those same long-term agreements will not only diminish the frequency of the votes but also their potency as a partisan tool and a legislative device as well. Until new precedents are clearly established, it is too soon to draw the final curtain on the importance of statutory debt limitation.

NOTES

Acknowledgment: The authors wish to acknowledge Patrick Taylor, graduate research assistant at UM-St. Louis, and Kathy Ruffing of the Congressional Budget Office for their invaluable assistance in this project.

1. All the Senate votes taken during this period were voice votes with the exception of a vote in 1960 on HR 12381, which was passed 84–0.
2. For a discussion of the issues and controversy surrounding the sale of Participation Certificates (PC's), see *Congressional Quarterly Almanac* [17, 1967, p. 317].
3. The provisions were actually deleted in a second House–Senate conference on the measure. The first conference report granted the President considerable leeway in this regard, and it was rejected by the Senate, 27–39.
4. In 1978, for example, it was estimated that a lapse in the statutory authority cost the Treasury approximately $15 million. In 1984, Treasury Secretary Regan wrote Congress that postponements of two October auctions would cost $400 million in higher interest.

REFERENCES

1. J. L. Blum, Congressional Budget Office Testimony, Statement before the Subcommittee on Taxation and Debt Management, Committee on Finance, U.S. Senate, July 31 (1990).

2. D. Mayhew, *Congress: The Electoral Connection*, Yale University Press, New Haven, Conn. (1974).
3. J. Cooper, *The House at Work* (J. Cooper and G. C. Mackenzie, eds.), University of Texas Press, Austin, pp. 319–355 (1981).
4. R. Davidson and W. Oleszek, "Adaptation and Evolution in the U.S. House of Representatives," *Legislative Studies Quarterly*, *1*(1): 37–65 (1976).
5. B. Sinclair, "The Transformation of the U.S. Senate: Towards a Rational Choice Explanation of Institutional Change," *Home Style and Washington Work* (M. P. Fiorina and D. Rohde, eds.), University of Michigan Press, Ann Arbor, pp. 119–136 (1991).
6. R. C. Fenno, *Homestyle: House Members in Their Districts*, Little Brown, Boston (1978).
7. R. K. Weaver, "The Politics of Blame Avoidance," *Journal of Public Policy*, *6*: 386–398 (1986).
8. C. Jones, *The Minority Party in Congress*, Little Brown, Boston (1970).
9. J. D. Savage, *Balanced Budgets and American Politics*, Cornell University Press, Ithaca, N.Y. (1988).
10. *Congressional Record*, 65th Cong., 1st sess. (1917).
11. J. A. Cantor and D. R. Stabile, *A History of the Bureau of the Public Debt, 1940–1990*, Government Printing Office, Washington, D.C. (1990).
12. H. Stein, *The Fiscal Revolution in America*, University of Chicago Press, Chicago (1969).
13. R. C. Fenno, *Power of the Purse*, Little Brown, Boston (1966).
14. *Public Papers of the President*, Dwight D. Eisenhower, (1953).
15. J. W. Sloan, *Eisenhower and the Management of Prosperity*, University of Kansas Press, Lawrence (1991).
16. *Congressional Record*, 83rd Cong., 1st sess. (1953).
17. *Congressional Quarterly Almanac*, Congressional Quarterly Service, Washington, D.C.
18. *Congressional Record*, 84th Cong., 1st sess. (1955).
19. W. Heller, *New Dimensions of Political Economy*, Harvard University Press, Cambridge, MA (1967).
20. *Congressional Record*, 87th Cong., 2nd sess. (1962).
21. J. Sundquist, *Politics and Policy*, Brookings Institution, Washington, D.C. (1968).
22. S. Harris, *Economics of the Kennedy Years*, Harper and Row, New York (1964).
23. *Congressional Record*, 88th Cong., 2nd sess. (1964).
24. *Congressional Record*, 90th Cong., 1st sess. (1967).
25. *Congressional Quarterly Weekly Report* (1974).
26. Joint Study Committee on Budget Control, *Recommendations for Improving Congressional Control over Budgetary Outlay and Receipt Totals*, April 18, 93d Cong., 1st sess. (1973).
27. R. K. Weaver, *Automatic Government*, Brookings Institution, Washington, D.C. (1988).
28. A. Schick, "Budget Reform Legislation: Reorganizing Congressional Centers of Fiscal Power," *Harvard Journal on Legislation*, *11*(2): 307–326 (1974).
29. L. T. Leloup, *The Fiscal Congress*, Greenwood Press, Westport, Conn. (1980).
30. A. Schick, *Congress and Money*, Urban Institute, Washington, D.C. (1980).
31. *Congressional Record*, 96th Cong., 1st sess. (1979).
32. L. T. LeLoup, "Process Versus Policy: The House Committee on the Budget," *Legislative Studies Quarterly*, *4*(2):227–254 (1979).
33. L. Dodd and B. Oppenheimer, "Consolidating Power in the House," *Congress Reconsidered*, 4th ed., CQ Press, Washington, D. C., pp. 39–64 (1989).
34. L. T. LeLoup, B. L. Graham, and S. Barwick, "Deficit Politics and Constitutional Government: The Impact of Gramm–Rudman–Hollings," *Public Budgeting and Finance*, *7*(Spring): 83–103 (1987).
35. *Bowsher* v. *Synar*. 1986, 106 S. Ct. 3181.
36. Congressional Budget Office, *The Economic and Budget Outlook FY 1992–96*, Government Printing Office, Washington, D.C., January (1991).
37. *Congressional Quarterly Weekly Report* (1990).
38. K. A. Ruffing, Congressional Budget Office (1991).

16

Intergovernmental Fiscal Relations in the 1980s

Kenneth T. Palmer and Matthew C. Moen

INTRODUCTION

No goal of the Reagan administration was more central than the reordering of relationships between the federal government and the states. President Reagan entered office with a pledge to reduce the presence of the federal government in subnational affairs, as part of an overall effort to shrink the size of the national government. Much of the drama in the 1981 session of Congress centered on reductions of grants-in-aid to state and local governments. In fact, despite many other initiatives to modify the existing system, the Reagan administration's main legacy concerning federalism was fiscal. As John Shannon [1] has written: "The creation of a fiscal environment that forces state and local officials to become more self-reliant stands out as the primary impact the Reagan administration has had on our federal system." This chapter outlines the policies under which fiscal federalism changed so sharply in the 1980s, and how subnational governments in general coped with the changes.

REAGAN ADMINISTRATION INITIATIVES

The 97th Congress (1981–1982)

President Reagan wasted no time striving to reorder federal and state relations. Only a month after taking office, he outlined a program of economic recovery that was driven by $53.9 billion in tax cuts and $41.4 billion in budget cuts for the next fiscal year [2]. Part of the budget cuts were to be achieved by changing categorical grants to block grants, which Reagan argued would save $24 billion over 5 years by consolidating programs "scattered throughout the federal bureaucracy" [3]. Several months later, Reagan reiterated those themes in a major address before the National Conference of State Legislatures, adding that: "This nation has never fully debated the fact that over the past forty years, federalism—one of the underlying principles of our Constitution—has nearly disappeared

Source: *Public Budgeting and Financial Management*, vol. 4, no. 3 (1992), pp. 529–550.

as a guiding force in American politics and government . . . . My administration intends to initiate such a debate . . . . " [4].

Interestingly, Reagan's rhetoric was somewhat incongruous with the proposals his administration transmitted to Capitol Hill in 1981. Despite a call for $41.4 billion in budget cuts, for instance, only $34.8 billion (a 16% reduction) was formally requested [5]. Perhaps even more interesting, though, was Reagan's willingness to compromise. He accepted modest reductions in Medicaid spending, for instance, in lieu of the cap on spending increases that he proposed, as well as acceded to Democratic wishes to remove the Elementary and Secondary Education Act and the Education for All Handicapped Children Act—two pillars of the "war on poverty"—from block grant consolidation [6]. That pattern was repeated in other tussles over block grants. The Administration advocated the conversion of 88 categorical grants into seven major block grants, but ultimately settled for consolidation of 76 categorical grants into nine block grants [7]. Most of the work was done in the 1981 budget reconciliation bill (PL 97-35), which lumped 19 health programs into four health block grants (preventive health and health services; alcohol, drug abuse, and mental health services; primary care; maternal and child health); consolidated 13 minor education programs into a single block grant; established a nutrition block grant for Puerto Rico to replace Food Stamps and other programs; and established a community services block grant program to replace an array of antipoverty programs administered by the Community Services Administration [8].

In 1982, Reagan offered another wave of federalism proposals. These centered around the transfer of $47 billion in federal programs to the states over a 10-year period, and a "financial swap" in which the federal government would assume full responsibility for Medicare/Medicaid, in return for the states' assumption of Food Stamps and Aid to Families with Dependent Children (AFDC). The proposals encountered stiff resistance from state officials, who met with Administration representatives 25 times over the next 6 months [9]. During those meetings, the White House agreed to scale back the proposed transfer of funds from $47 billion to $30 billion, and to drop food stamps from the proposed "swap" of functions [10]. Despite those concessions, though, Reagan's "New Federalism" proposals met with such hostility on Capitol Hill that Reagan never even bothered to transmit a formal proposal during 1982. He did so in early 1983, but it proceeded no further than hearings in the Joint Economic Committee [11].

The 98th Congress (1983–1984)

In February 1983, Reagan unveiled yet another major federalism initiative. He called for consolidating 34 programs into four "mega-block" grants: State Block Grant; Federal-Local Block Grant; Transportation Block Grant; and Rural Housing Block Grant [12]. Like the New Federalism proposals of the preceding year, though, Congress mostly ignored the initiative, focusing instead on reauthorizing general revenue sharing, set to expire in September.

Action began in the House Government Operations Committee, which reauthorized general revenue sharing for five years, with annual funding increases of $730 million [13]. The full House dropped that reauthorization to 3 years and scaled back increases to $450 million; the time frame met with Administration approval, but it sought flat funding at the fiscal 1983 level of $4.6 billion. The Senate passed the 3-year, $4.6 billion plan Reagan sought, and used the threat of a presidential veto to prevail upon the House to accept its version. Revenue sharing was kept alive, but at reduced levels, since inflation eroded the flat annual amount. In any case, reauthorization of general revenue sharing would be the last major federalism proposal approved during the Reagan presidency. Major initiatives like New Federalism and mega-block grants never resurfaced, and more minor items like urban enterprise zones received only sporadic attention.

The Second Term (1985–1989)

Throughout his second term, President Reagan served mostly as a "cheerleader" of sorts, extolling the virtues of federalism, but ceasing to transmit serious legislative proposals. He resigned himself to reminding Americans, as in his 1985 inaugural address and in messages to Congress in 1986 and 1987, that state and local governments were "closer to the people" [14]. Apart from those rhetorical flourishes, though, federalism was basically off the congressional agenda, with one exception: the reauthorization of general revenue sharing in 1986. President Reagan weighed in early on that issue, saying in 1985 that general revenue sharing was a luxury the nation could not afford in the midst of record budget deficits [15]. Despite the warning, House members tried to keep the program alive. With assistance from lobbyists for local governments, proponents passed the reauthorization request out of the Government Operations Committee, and over the objections of its chairman, Jack Brooks (D., Tex.). The leadership refused to schedule the measure for floor action, however, forcing proponents to graft it onto a budget or appropriations bill. In the final days of the session, Appropriations Committee Chairman Jamie Whitten (D., Miss.) tried to add $3.4 billion in general revenue sharing monies to a continuing appropriations bill, but his effort was rebuffed by the Rules Committee, which refused to report the bill for floor action so long as it contained the revenue sharing provisions. Whitten reluctantly withdrew his proposal, marking the end of a program that had disbursed a total of $83 billion from 1972 to 1986 [16]. The conflict over general revenue sharing was the last major battle over federal and state relations in the Reagan presidency.

FISCAL IMPACTS

The early impact of the Reagan policies on federal assistance was dramatic. In 1981 when President Carter left office, federal grants to state and local governments amounted to $94.8 billion [17]. The next year they dropped to $88.0 billion, and rose in 1983 to $93.0. This leveling off in overall dollars contrasted sharply with the steady rise of federal expenditures for subnational governments that had taken place in the Johnson, Nixon, Ford, and Carter administrations. Under those presidents, grants generally increased at a faster rate than most other portions of the federal budget (in the Johnson budgets, for instance, grant assistance rose at a level of nearly 25% per year). Between 1981 and 1983 federal grants to states and cities decreased from 19.5% of federal domestic outlays to 16.1% and from 25.1% of state and local expenditures to 21.8% [18]. In fiscal 1983 grants to those governments made up the smallest percentage of federal domestic budget since the early 1960s.

Accompanying that trend was a shift in the distribution of funds among program areas. Health programs amounted to 17% of all grants in 1980, but grew to 28% in 1988 largely because of increases in Medicaid. Income security programs moved from 20% to 27% of the total grant package during the same period. In contrast, community development, education, social services, training, and employment grants decreased from 31% to 21% in the 1980–88 period.

The significance of those shifts was that transfer payments, that is, grants that have individuals as recipients, made up a rising share of the total package. Transfer payments composed 31.9% of all grants in 1980, but an estimated 67.3% in 1990. These programs are usually more difficult to cut in the federal budget process than other types of grants, such as ones directed to state and local governments to carry out a function or to provide for physical capital investment. The "grants to governments" category sustained major reductions during the Reagan years, especially with the demise of revenue sharing in 1986. By the end of the 1980s its portion of the local grants package had decreased from two-thirds to one-third of all grants [19].

Diminishing Support for Localities

The new pattern found localities more sharply affected than the states. As Table 1 shows, Reagan administration policy sought to channel grant assistance through the states, and to phase out certain direct federal–local programs that had operated since the 1960s. As an example, the Job Training Partnership Act (1982), which replaced the Comprehensive Employment and Training Program, funneled aid to localities through state governments instead of through the U.S. Department of HUD. Federal revenue as a percentage of local government revenues dropped from 9.0% in 1978 to 4.2% in 1987. Federal support for the states declined more slowly, from 22.3% to 18.5%, during the same period [20].

The administration's approach to the distribution of funds among subnational governments differed sharply from that of the Carter period. An equalization or "targeting" strategy had been a critical part of President Carter's approach to grants-in-aid. Under the Anti-Recession Fiscal Assistance Act (enacted in 1976 over President Ford's veto and expanded with new funds in the early Carter years), cities with high levels of unemployment received added amounts of general revenue sharing. The goal was to incorporate subnational governments into a national policy of economic stabilization by discouraging localities from adopting strategies (such as raising taxes) that might counter national efforts.

Although the 1980s witnessed several severe downturns in regional economies, the Reagan administration opposed all efforts to utilize some form of ARFA (which had expired in 1978) to aid fiscally distressed areas. The administration's "hands off" approach also led to a diminution of the targeting features of some grant programs established in the 1970s. Under the Community Development Block Grant's "dual formula," which was set

Table 1   Distribution of Federal Aid Revenue to State and Local Governments, 1980–89 (millions of current dollars)

Year	Federal aid revenue	Percentage to states	Percentage to localities
1980	$ 83,029	74.5	24.5
1981	90,295	75.2	24.8
1982	86,945	75.9	24.0
1983	89,983	76.6	23.4
1984	97,052	78.5	21.5
1985	106,193	79.5	20.5
1986	113,099	81.9	18.1
1987	114,996	83.0	17.0
1988	117,602	85.4	14.6
1989	125,839	86.0	14.0

Source: U.S. Department of Commerce, Bureau of the Census, *Government Finances,* U.S. Government Printing Office, Washington, D.C. (1980–1989).

in 1977, all communities of 50,000 or more population were entitled to receive some funds, and added allotments were made to communities especially afflicted by poverty. Data from the 1980 census increased the number of entitlement communities by about 25%, many of which were relatively affluent [21]. As a result, the share of CDBG funds allocated to cities in greatest fiscal distress declined from 48.2% in 1980 to 44.4% in 1985.

Federalism as Tax and Fiscal Policy

An important change in the 1980s concerned how issues of fiscal federalism were debated. In earlier administrations, discussions over federal assistance to state and localities usually centered on broad political topics: how much discretion should be permitted to subnational jurisdictions and whether assistance should be confined to needy areas or spread among all towns, cities, and counties. In the 1980s, especially after the first 2 years, relatively little discussion of such federalism issues occurred. Instead, intergovernmental fiscal policy was made part of broader tax and fiscal policy. The leading example was the Tax Reform Act of 1986, which arguably was the most important piece of intergovernmental legislation enacted during the decade. Despite this, there was virtually no explicit discussion of its impact on national–state–local relations during its formulation [22].

The absorption of federalism issues into national fiscal debates was closely linked to federal budget discussions. The rapid growth of the federal deficit in the 1980s led to the federal budget's becoming the main determinant of intergovernmental policy. Earlier, a president's political philosophy often shaped debates on federal-state-local relations. The new tendency was reinforced by President Reagan's ability, after his successes in securing budget reductions in 1981, to keep the national agenda focused on questions of fiscal retrenchment. The trend can be noticed in comparing the tone of the presidential campaign of 1980, when federalism issues were highlighted, with that of 1988, when neither candidate gave more than passing reference to intergovernmental issues in campaign pronouncements.

Although changes in federal expenditures dramatically affected intergovernmental fiscal relations, it was the tax policy of the Reagan administration that probably had, and will continue to have, the greatest long-term effects. The federal income tax underwent revolutionary changes. The top marginal rate was cut from 70% to 50% in the Economic Recovery Tax Act of 1981 and again from 50% to 28% in the Tax Reform Act of 1986. As Timothy Conlan has written, the changes in the tax code amounted to no less than "a frontal assault on the revenue base of the modern welfare state, not only in Washington but also at the state and local levels" [23]. The attack was notably reflected in the 1981 tax reductions, which were huge in comparison with the budget reductions of that year, and permanently lowered the capacity of the federal government to undertake new spending programs, including new grants-in-aid.

STATE AND LOCAL REACTIONS

The Reagan fiscal revolution came at a critical time in the progress of state governments. The states had been undergoing political reform for approximately two decades by the beginning of the 1980s. About three-quarters of them had substantially revised their constitutions, and all states had found ways to strengthen their legislatures and executive departments. The states were no longer the "fallen arches" among the three levels of government. Instead, as Carl Van Horn has pointed out, they were on their way to becoming "arguably the most responsive, innovative, and effective level of government in the American federal system" [24]. Between 1964 and 1986, the states increased their spending from

$24 billion to $228 billion, nearly a 10-fold increase. During that period, state spending grew slightly more rapidly than federal spending and considerably faster than local spending.

States Decisions Differ

The greatest financial challenge the states faced in the 1980s took place during the 1981–82 recession. The states were asked to make up cuts in federal grants-in-aid at the same time that they struggled with the worst recession since World War II. How did they respond? Richard Nathan and his associates studied intensively 14 states at this time, and found that state actions varied significantly according to both specific grant programs and the characteristics of the states [25]. The states moved much more rapidly to replace federal funds in the Medicaid program, for example, than they did in the Aid for Dependent Children (AFDC) program. Both programs were open-ended, matching grants, and were often managed by the same state agencies. However, certain differences were crucial: For one thing, the Medicaid constituency was fairly strong, since it was composed disproportionately of elderly persons who as a group tended to be active politically. AFDC mothers, on the other hand, were generally a less vocal interest group. Further, Medicaid was less redistributive than AFDC, an important point since state politicians were inclined to regard highly redistributive programs such as AFDC with their targeted constituencies of low-income persons as "the federal government's" programs. States were often reluctant to replace federal funds in such programs. In contrast, they were more generous in dealing with long-established state and local functions such as health programs, which included Medicaid.

States with moderate or liberal political cultures usually made more generous overall responses to the federal government's budget curtailments than states where conservative values held sway [26]. In the Nathan study, New York and Massachusetts were prominent in finding replacement funds for human service programs. On the other hand, California's response to the Reagan budget policies was very limited. Conservatives in that state had succeeded in winning passage of several tax and spending limits in the late 1970s. Economic conditions also shaped state fiscal policies. Missouri, especially hard-pressed by the recession of 1981–82, was unable to commit funds to grant programs that it might otherwise have invested. In contrast, Oklahoma faced relatively little fiscal distress, and was a leader in replacing federal funds.

Local Budget Changes

How did localities react to the Reagan budget cuts? Generally, they forged greater fiscal independence. As shown in Table 2, between 1980–81 and 1987–88, the portion of local government revenues derived from federal sources fell from 8.7% to 3.9% [27]. That decline did not slow local governments' overall revenues, which grew from $257 billion to $434 billion in the same period, an increase of 41%, but it did require localities to look more intensively to their own revenue sources to maintain their programs. Between 1980–81 and 1987–88, taxes grew from 36.9% of local revenues to 39.5%, and charges during the same period rose from 19.8% to 23.0%.

Interesting variations appeared among different local governments in the way their revenues changed. Counties experienced major shifts. Their support from the federal government declined from 7.8% to 2.5% during that period, largely because of the end of federal revenue sharing. As a result, charges levied by counties grew from 16.7% of their budgets in 1980–81 to over one quarter (25.3%) of their revenues by 1987–88. In contrast, school districts, for which federal support had never amounted to more than 1–2% of their

Table 2 State Aid to Localities, 1980–89 (millions of current dollars)

Year	State aid	State aid as percent of state general expenditures	State aid as percent of local general revenues
1980	$ 82,758	36.3	63.6
1981	91,307	36.0	62.7
1982	96,950	36.0	59.4
1983	99,544	34.9	55.6
1984	106,651	34.4	54.3
1985	119,640	34.7	55.4
1986	129,828	34.5	55.6
1987	138,970	34.4	54.7
1988	148,803	34.4	54.9
1989	165,506	35.2	56.4

Source: U.S. Department of Commerce, Bureau of the Census, *Government Finances,* U.S. Government Printing Office, Washington, D.C. (1980–1989).

budgets, showed less change. Federal assistance dropped in percentage terms by nearly half between 1980–81 and 1987–88, but compensating funds were found through slight rises in local school taxes and additional state aid.

As Table 2 shows, the portion of state budgets committed to local assistance programs changed little during the 1980s. However, localities generally grew more dependent on their own revenue sources. The figures somewhat underestimate state involvement in local operations because some states took over entire functions, such as courts, corrections, health care, welfare, and transportation, instead of assisting localities to operate them with state funds. For instance, New York State's greater role in financing Medicaid was estimated to have reduced the state's intergovernmental aid by approximately $5 billion in 1986 [28].

In contrast to the federal government, state governments in the 1980s tended to intensify the targeting of fiscal assistance to financially distressed jurisdictions. The process mostly began in the 1970s. According to one study, central cities in large metropolitan areas received $123 per capita from their states in 1968, an amount virtually identical to the aid provided the generally wealthier jurisdictions outside of central cities ($122). By 1981, central cities were obtaining $441 per capita as contrasted to $377 for communities outside of central cities [29]. In 1985, New York and Massachusetts introduced sophisticated indicators of fiscal distress into their general aid formulas. Massachusetts sought, for instance, to take into account the costs of delivering various urban public services in different communities [30].

FROM FINANCE TO REGULATION

In the 1990s, federal policy toward states and localities is likely to focus on regulatory, not fiscal, tools. While its most visible efforts at intergovernmental reform were in the financial sphere, the Reagan administration also pursued changes in federal regulatory policy, some of which were highly centralizing. It successfully endorsed national product liability legislation, uniform standards for truck weights, and a federally set drinking age (21), all of which took power from the states [31]. Meanwhile, Congress was enacting various forms of statutory preemption, whereby the national government regulates an area of activity, but permits a certain degree of freedom for state action. In fact, more than half of all the preemption statutes enacted since 1789 were enacted in the 1970s and 1980s [32]. For its part, the U.S. Supreme Court encouraged federal regulatory efforts by providing Congress, in two important cases, with virtually unlimited powers to legislate in matters affecting state and local governments [33]. The federal budget deficit favors regulatory growth. As John Kincaid has written, "an avenue for action in a fiscally constrained but constitutionally unconstrained environment is to regulate something, in the private sector or state-local sector" [34].

Bush administration policy reflected a continuing retreat from financial assistance, and sought to shift new costs and responsibilities to the states. An example was the administration's transportation policy, announced by Secretary Thomas Skinner in late 1989. Skinner indicated he wanted to sort out responsibilities for road maintenance: the federal government would expand its funding of 160,000 miles of major arteries, including the interstate system, but states and localities would be expected to assume more of the financial obligation for the other 740,000 miles of federal-aid highways [35].

The evolving self-reliance that marked state–federal–local relations in the 1980s seems likely to remain in place in the 1990s. It has clearly replaced the cooperative federalism of the 1960s and 1970s, characterized by proliferating federal grants funded by an expanding federal domestic budget. Still, if state and local jurisdictions must now take greater responsibilities for raising their revenues, their capacity to govern well has never been greater.

NOTES AND REFERENCES

1. J. Shannon, "The Faces of Fiscal Federalism," *Intergovernmental Perspective, 14* (Winter): 17 (1988).

2. K. T. Palmer, "The Evolution of Grant Policies," (L. D. Brown, J. W. Fossett, and K. T. Palmer, eds.), Brookings Institution, Washington, D.C., p. 46 (1984); *Public Papers of the President: Ronald Reagan,* U.S. Government Printing Office, Washington, D.C., p. 109 (1982).

3. *Public Papers of the President: Ronald Reagan,* U.S. Government Printing Office, Washington, D.C., p. 111 (1982).

4. Ref. 3, p. 680.

5. H. E. Shuman, *Politics and the Budget,* 2nd ed, Prentice-Hall, Englewood Cliffs, N.J., pp. 251–252 (1988).

6. "Medicaid Spending Cut but 'Cap' Rejected," *Congressional Quarterly Almanac, 37*: 478–480 (1982); "Education Programs," *Congressional Quarterly Almanac, 37*: 499–501 (1982).

7. "Congress Adopts Some Reagan Block Grants," *Congressional Quarterly Almanac, 37*: 463 (1982); G. E. Peterson, "Federalism and the States," *The Reagan Record* (J. L. Palmer and I. V. Sawhill, eds.), Ballinger, Cambridge, MA, p. 229 (1984).

8. "Congress Adopts Some Reagan Block Grants," *Congressional Quarterly Almanac, 37*: 463 (1982).

9. See respectively: A. N. Pattakos, and K. T. Palmer, "Downcast But Not Down Under: Maine Responds to the Reagan Challenge," *Publius: The Journal of Federalism, 13*(Spring): 39–49 (1983); R. Williamson, "The 1982 New Federalism Negotiations," *Publius: The Journal of Federalism, 13*(Spring): 17 (1983).

10. "President's Budget Message," *Congressional Quarterly Almanac, 38*12E (1938); K. T. Palmer, in Ref. 2, p. 50.

11. K. T. Palmer, in Ref. 2, p. 51.

12. "Remarks to State and Local Officials on Proposed Federalism Legislation," *Public Papers of the President: Ronald Reagan,* Government Printing Office, Washington, D.C. p. 292 (1984).

13. The ensuing discussion draws heavily upon "Revenue Sharing Extended For Three Years," *Congressional Quarterly Almanac, 39*: 226–229 (1984).

14. See respectively, "Inaugural Address," *Public Papers of the President: Ronald Reagan*, Government Printing Office, Washington, D.C., p. 55 (1988); "Message to Congress Transmitting the Annual Management Report of the President," *Public Papers of the President: Ronald Reagan*, Government Printing Office, Washington, D.C., p. 138 (1988); "Message to Congress on a Quest for Excellence," *Public Papers of the President: Ronald Reagan*, Government Printing Office, Washington, D.C., p. 73 (1988).

15. "Housing/Community Development," *Congressional Quarterly Almanac, 41*: 22 (1986).

16. "Revenue Sharing Dies," *Congressional Quarterly Almanac*, 585 (1987).

17. Unless otherwise noted, statistics concerned with federal grants-in-aid are drawn from *Special Analysis, Budget of the United States Government*, Government Printing Office, Washington, D.C. (1980–1988).

18. See K. T. Palmer, in Ref. 2, p. 47.

19. See K. T. Palmer, in Ref. 2.

20. J. Kincaid, "Currents of Change in the Federal System," *Intergovernmental Perspective, 15*(Fall): 22 (1989).

21. P. R. Dommel and M. J. Rich, "The Rich Get Richer: The Attenuation of Targeting Effects of the Community Development Block Grant Program," *Urban Affairs Quarterly, 22*(June): 552–79 (1987).

22. T. Conlan, *The New Federalism: Intergovernmental Reform from Nixon to Reagan*, Brookings Institution, Washington, D.C., Chapter 7 (1988).

23. Ref. 22, p. 133

24. C. Van Horn, "The Quiet Revolution," *The State of the States*, Congressional Quarterly Press, Washington D.C., p. 1 (1989).

25. R. P. Nathan, F. C. Doolittle, and associates, *Reagan and the States*, Princeton University Press, Princeton, N.J., Chapter 4 (1987).

26. Ref. 25, Chapter 5.

27. Data are drawn from *Governmental Finances*, U.S. Government Printing Office, Washington, D.C. (1980 and 1987).

28. S. D. Gold and B. M. Erickson, "State Aid to Local Governments in the 1980s," *State and Local Government Review, 21*(Winter): 16 (1989). For a good discussion of emerging intergovernmental fiscal roles, see J. P. Nathan and J. R. Lago, "Intergovernmental Fiscal Roles and Relations," *Annals of the American Academy of Political and Social Science, 509*(May): 36–47 (1990).

29. D. Walker, "Intergovernmental Relations in the Well-Governed City: Cooperation, Confrontation, Clarification," *National Civic Review, 75*(March-April): 75 (1986).

30. See the articles in S. F. Liebschultz, "Targeting by the States: The Basis Issues," *Publius: The Journal of Federalism, 19*(Spring), especially P. D. Moore, "General-Purpose Aid in New York State: Targeting Issues and Measures," pp. 17–32.

31. See Ref. 22, pp. 213–217.

32. J. Kincaid, "From Cooperative to Coercive Federalism," *Annals of the American Academy of Political and Social Science*, 509(May): 148 (1990).

33. The cases are *Garcia v. San Antonio Metro Transit District*, 469 U.S. 528 (1985), which upheld Congress's power to bring state and local employees under the provisions of the Fair Labor Standards Act, and *South Carolina v. Baker*, 108 S. Ct. 1355 (1988), which strengthened Congress's power to determine the extent of federal tax exemption for state and local government bonds.

34. Ref. 32, p. 149.

35. A. O'M. and M. A. Pagana, "The State of American Federalism, 1988–1990," *Publius: The Journal of Federalism, 20*(Summer): 7–8 (1990).

17

The General Accounting Office: Its Origin, Expansion, and Dilemma

James A. Stever

University of Cincinnati, Cincinnati, Ohio

The General Accounting Office (GAO) located at 4th and G Street occupies an entire city block in Washington, D.C. At first glance, this agency of the federal government appears similar to many others. It has a limestone exterior, is seven stories tall, and is within walking distance of the nation's capitol. Yet the GAO stands apart from other federal agencies. Its mission is to evaluate and criticize the performance of other governmental agencies. In pursuit of this mission, the GAO aspires to mold a reputation for accurate, objective, careful work. Its original mission and reputation was focused on budgetary matters. Its first Comptroller General aspired to simply hold federal agencies accountable to the budget set for them by the U.S. Congress. However, as its mission broadened and its range of activity increased, the GAO itself became controversial. In addition to holding federal agencies accountable in a budgetary sense, the GAO attempted to evaluate how effectively and efficiently federal agencies managed their resources and implemented policy.

The old image of the GAO was that of a scrupulous accountant—examining the expense vouchers of federal agencies. In one now famous incident, a GAO auditor challenged the Interior Department's purchase of a camera by asking how it intended to use this equipment. Secretary of the Interior Harold Ickes responded, "To take pictures, you damned fool." The new GAO evaluator scarcely resembles this old stereotype. In contrast, the new evaluator, working under tight security, could be found examining the performance of a Polaris submarine, or conveying a classified report evaluating this performance to the House or Senate Armed Services Committees. In a variety of settings, it is customary for GAO evaluators to interview those who receive federal benefits in order to determine what level of service they receive. Hence, GAO evaluators come in contact with an array of people ranging from welfare mothers to military veterans to forest rangers. It is now common for career evaluators to spend time away from Washington, D.C. working in field offices or at audit sites located in the federal agency under examination.

This transition can be understood from a variety of perspectives. On one hand, change is normal and the GAO evolved in response to successive challenges that its original founders could not foresee. On the other hand, critics charge that the GAO is now attempting to evaluate things that cannot be objectively and precisely evaluated. As a result, the GAO has encountered the charge that it has become wasteful and inefficient, even nonobjective and political.

This chapter will first explore the history of the GAO. This history provides some explanation for why its mission not only changed but expanded. Historical analysis of the GAO reveals two major kinds of change. One kind of change can be categorized as willful, controlled change. New Comptroller Generals appointed by the Congress changed the organization by employing people other than traditional accountants. A second kind of change can be labeled as reactive change. This change was dictated by events beyond the control of either the Congress or the Comptroller Generals who led the agency. The GAO was often forced to change in response to unanticipated changes and crises encountered by the federal government. Subsequent sections will build upon this historical analysis by assessing the dilemmas and challenges faced by the GAO as it has attempted to adapt its services, personnel, policies, and structure to the changing needs of the federal government.

HISTORY OF THE GENERAL ACCOUNTING OFFICE

The history of the GAO is best explained by a "big bang" theory. Formally, this organization began with the Budget and Accounting Act of 1921. Yet this formal explanation does not tell the whole story. The GAO was formed by an explosive mixture of cultural and political forces that had simmered for 30 years within American government. Progressivism began in the 1880s at the local and state level as an attempt to convert America's corrupt political machines into sound administrative mechanisms. In 1904 the Progressives extended their influence to the federal government with the election of Theodore Roosevelt. Like the local and state activists, Progressives at the national level argued that the institutions of the federal government should become more efficient.

President William Howard Taft gave the Progressives a golden opportunity to change the federal government with the 1910 creation of the Taft Commission on Economy and Efficiency [1]. Members of the commission included well known administrative reformers such as Frederick A. Cleveland, W. F. Willoughby, and F. J. Goodnow. The original assumption of the commission was that the federal government would be improved by giving the executive branch of government, namely the President, enhanced power to develop and supervise the budged of various federal agencies. However, this approach raised fears among members of the Congress that their power within the federal government would be eclipsed by granting new budgetary power to the presidency. Hence, a decade of struggle ensued. On one hand were those who believed that the route to an efficient federal government could only be achieved by giving the President increased powers over the budget. On the other hand, supporters of the Congress argued that the traditional powers of the legislature over spending must be preserved.

This struggle was resolved during the presidency of Woodrow Wilson with the Budget and Accounting Act of 1921. Like so many convulsive governmental reforms, this 1921 act attempted to forge a Solomon-like solution. It created the Bureau of the Budget (BoB), which became the budgetary arm of the presidency [2]. The General Accounting Office was also created to preserve and enhance the traditional legislative role in the budget. Yet the creation of these two agencies did little to dampen the ongoing tensions between the executive and legislative branches. Progressive reformers who favored presidential dominance viewed the GAO as an agency that interfered with the natural development of the administrative power of the executive branch [3]. Conversely, congressional supporters argued that the legislature must have tools such as the GAO to insure that executive agencies were held accountable.

Prior to the creation of the GAO, an executive agency, the Department of the Treasury, was responsible for auditing the expenditures of federal agencies. The Budget and Accounting Act transferred this responsibility to the GAO. The head of this new agency, the "Comptroller General," was appointed by the president but approved by the Congress for a term of 15 years. Removed only by impeachment or by joint resolution, the new GAO Comptroller General was destined to be a powerful figure.

The term of the first Comptroller General, John McCarl, from 1921 to 1936 was known as the "voucher era." This was a period in which the agency's mission was narrowly interpreted. The GAO became under McCarl an agency consumed with the small details. It matched up government checks with expense vouchers—making sure that the check drew upon the appropriate account, and that the check was written and endorsed properly. Agency accountants also insisted that each government agency purchase only those items or services expressly authorized by congressional statute. During this period, the GAO also inserted itself into each federal agency's contracting process, insisting that each agency follow approved processes in developing its contracts and that each contract be worded correctly.

To understand the legalistic, detail orientation that characterized this founding period, one must understand the mind of McCarl himself, who was trained as a lawyer. His approach to the mission of the GAO was to insure that all federal agencies followed the rules for spending money established by the Congress. In his words:

> It is the duty and responsibility of the General Accounting Office to carefully scrutinize all expenditures to see whether the restrictions, limitations, and directions in the law have been observed in connection therewith. The yardstick of control is that stated by the Congress in the Law [4].

McCarl viewed the agency as a rule enforcer: one that checked each expense voucher against authorizing legislation to verify conformity to law. Thus, the GAO aspired to avoid independent judgment about specific expenditures. Its role was to ascertain whether expenditures were legal within the narrow confines of explicit congressional statutes.

Federal agencies reacted negatively to the new and narrow budgetary controls placed upon them. Powerful agencies such as the Department of War or the Department of the Treasury could ignore attempts by the GAO accountants to disallow their expenditures or to rescind their contracts [5]. Other agencies with less power to disregard the GAO disputed and protested instead. Clashes between GAO auditors and federal agencies escalated during President Roosevelt's New Deal. This was a period not only in which federal expenditures increased but also in which federal legislation began to address new domestic problems. Roosevelt came to regard the GAO as an obstruction to his agenda of expanding and reorienting the scope and scale of the federal government. It was hardly surprising that the agency heads appointed by Roosevelt were predisposed, like the President, to resist. In one well-publicized incident, Harry Hopkins, head of the Civil Works Administration, answered the GAO request for more information by depositing 15 barrels of the agency's checks on the GAO loading docks, and told McCarl, "Let me know if you find anything wrong" [6].

Such open challenges not only questioned the legitimacy and authority of the GAO, but suggested that the strategy of the agency itself was not synchronized with the growing needs of the federal government. By the end of McCarl's term as Comptroller General, the GAO was finding itself hard pressed to keep up with the mounting audit work load. Agencies were beginning to complain that their operation was impeded by the inability of auditors to keep pace. In the face of mounting agency dissatisfaction and presidential opposition, the legitimacy of GAO auditing methods was called into question.

The tensions between GAO and the executive branch were eased by external challenges to the federal government: that is, the growing realization that cooperation was essential to meet the external challenges of the Great Depression and World War II. The growth of the federal government in response to these two events gradually overwhelmed the auditing capacity of the GAO and it became increasingly apparent that a new approach would be necessary.

One alternative was that advanced by President Franklin Roosevelt, who convened a prestigious group of experts within an informal institution known as the President's Committee on Administrative Management, sometimes called the Brownlow Committee. Predictably, this committee was sternly critical of the voucher approach of the GAO to auditing and recommended increased presidential and executive agency control of budgeting and accounting. In opposition, some members of Congress, supported by the Brookings Institution, believed that the auditing powers of the GAO should be expanded. The resulting Executive Reorganization Act of 1939 was a compromise. It gave additional management and budgeting power to the President, but it did not address how federal agencies would be audited. The de facto solution came later with the appointment of Lindsay Warren as Comptroller General.

Warren, whose full formal term extended from 1945 to 1954, differed from John McCarl in two major ways. First, he was personally more inclined to cooperate with the executive branch. Second, he held a different philosophy of auditing [7]. One of his first decisions was to recruit broadly educated people for auditing tasks, rather than narrow technicians. Furthermore, as a concession to the growing administrative and budgetary sophistication of the executive branch, Warren shifted the more narrow auditing tasks to specific agencies, and delegated to them the flexibility to establish accounting systems that served their unique operational requirements. The new task of the GAO became that of establishing general accounting standards for agencies to follow. How they achieved these standards became a matter for each agency to decide.

Granting federal agencies more authority was a pragmatic move. Even with this decentralization, the GAO grew eventually to employ over 15,000 people by the end of World War II. Even with the additional personnel, its auditors were working on fiscal year 1941 when the war ended in 1945. Warren solved this workload with additional centralization—giving agencies even more auditing power, and reducing GAO employment. At his retirement in 1954, GAO personnel roles had been reduced to 6000.

In spite of the Warren reforms, the period between 1945 and 1966 is customarily known as "the GAO interregnum" [8]. The most striking reforms during this period were made within the executive branch. The Executive Office of the Presidency and the Bureau of the Budget emerged as the most innovative and dominant element of the federal government. In response, the GAO ceded authority and cooperated more. The changes it implemented were more incremental and reactive, and did not match the scale of institutional reform that transformed the executive branch.

The term of Joseph Campbell from 1954 to 1966 lends further credence to the argument that the GAO labored in an interregnum or transitional mode as opposed to making decisive reforms that had a significant, positive impact on the federal government. Campbell, appointed by President Eisenhower, was the first professional accountant to serve as Comptroller General. Sometimes autocratic, Campbell plunged the GAO back into a conflict mode with federal agencies. Stressing the independence of the GAO, even from Congressional supervision, Campbell defined the agency's mission as that of an independent agency within the federal government whose duty was to discover and then publicize malfeasance. Campbell transformed the organization into an aggressive, precise auditing agency where personnel were expected to be professional, loyal, and independent. This approach earned the GAO enemies both inside and outside the Congress. The Campbell regime ended in 1966 when defense contractors pressured Representative Chester Holifield to hold hearings on the nature of GAO audit procedures. The very existence of the hearings were a public rebuke to the agency, and these hearings forced Joseph Campbell to resign.

Elmer Staats was appointed Comptroller General in 1966 and served until 1981. His appointment inaugurated what is traditionally called the "second great transformation of GAO"—the first great transformation having occurred under Lindsay Warren during World War II [9]. This second transformation resulted from the confluence of Staats' leadership and external influences. The reforms that were initiated during this era continued during the term of Comptroller General Charles A. Bowsher, appointed in 1981.

One way to view the Second Great Transformation is to consider the background of Elmer Staats. In comparison to other comptroller generals, he was atypical. Unlike his predecessors, Staat's was a career civil servant with no party affiliation. He had worked at the Bureau of the Budget since 1939, serving as Deputy Director under four presidents: Truman, Eisenhower, Kennedy, and Johnson [10]. Staats was neither accountant nor lawyer. He was trained in public administration and had spent his life working to enhance not only the budgetary integrity of the executive branch, but its managerial integrity as well. Finally, Staats enjoyed a reputation as not only a planner and innovator, but one who understood the Congress and who worked well with the powerful committee chairmen of both parties. President Johnson, who had worked closely with Staats in the BoB, appointed him in the aftermath of the Holifield hearings that had displaced Joseph Campbell. With this background, it is hardly surprising that in the ensuing 15 years the BoB, the GAO, and the Congress cooperated on an wide array of projects without the conflict that had characterized their relationships during previous GAO eras.

Another way to understand the second great transformation of GAO is to consider the expansion of mission that occurred in this era. In previous periods, this agency struggled with new and innovative ways to financially audit federal agencies, moving from micro-oriented voucher audits in the McCarl term to system-oriented financial audits during the Warren years. During the Staats term, the GAO expanded the concept of "auditing" to include not only budgeting and finance, but auditing of programs, policies, and management practices and systems. Critics would later charge that this expansion distended and distorted the concept of auditing because the latter could not be audited with the same degree of precision and objectivity as budgets and finances.

The migration into these new areas began inconspicuously. Suspicious of President Johnson's War on Poverty, Republican Senator Winston Prouty of Vermont was able to insert into the Economic Opportunity Act of 1967 the requirement that the GAO review the effectiveness of poverty programs. In retrospect, Senator Prouty initiated a significant shift by asking the GAO to audit a program instead of a budget. Though auditing programs was a qualitatively new activity for the GAO, its 1969 report was considered successful [11]. Program analysis became an institutionalized fixture at GAO in 1970 with the creation of the Program Analysis Division. In 1983, it developed further into the Program Evaluation and Methodology Division.

The subsequent GAO migration into policy analysis and management analysis was also incremental and inconspicuous. Unlike program evaluation, which became an identifiable institutional unit, policy analysis and management analysis were gradually woven into the activity of GAO. By the mid 1970s, GAO reports delved into matters unthinkable during the 1950s and 1960s: immigration, breeder reactors, energy assistance to low-income families, family policy. Instead of focusing on the structure and design of financial systems, the agency began to consider the management systems of agencies: how they planned and set priorities, how they delivered services, how they made decisions. GAO began to ask new policy-oriented questions regarding the performance of federal agencies—questions that went beyond its traditional budgetary focus. For many of the new questions that it began to ask there were no factual, objective answers. Instead of objectively judging on the basis of numerical evidence, it had ventured into the world of evaluation where there were few clear-cut answers. This world of evaluation was, in many respects, quite similar to the world of politics. Whereas the early Comptroller Generals were quite careful to distinguish between the political activity of the Congress versus the objective, numerical focus of the GAO, Staats was not so committed to observing this distinction. One way to understand the magnitude of this shift is to consider that the occupational titles of those employed at the GAO shifted from auditor to "evaluator." By 1980, only 7% of its total work load revolved around the legal constraints affecting financial auditing. Economy and efficiency studies accounted for 29% of the workload. Program evaluation and policy analysis accounted for nearly 50% of the 1980 workload [12]. In 1993, the GAO labeled 57% of its employees as evaluators, and another 15% as evaluator related [13].

By 1993 the reconstituted GAO had organized itself into six divisions. These divisions were (1) the General Government Division, (2) Health, Education and Human Services, (3) National Security and International Affairs, (4) Resources, Community and Economic Development, (5) Accounting and Information Management, and (6) Program Evaluation and Methodology. Each division is further divided into approximately six issue areas. Once division leaders specify and issue area, that area becomes both an organizing focus and a priority within the division. In addition, the GAO operated 14 field offices, though it has closed some since. In 1993 there were 4500 GAO employees.

The second great transformation also changed the internal organizational culture at GAO. Whereas, prior to the Staats era, the GAO lunchroom would be filled with individuals with an accounting and finance background, the new GAO began to recruit the social scientist. The methods of social science began to displace the old auditor culture. This old culture was focused around numbers, dollars, expenses, and efficiency. In contrast, the new culture accepted the legitimacy and values of the social sciences, and it was more tolerant of relativity and ambiguity. Hence, psychologists, economists, public administrators, sociologists, and political scientists found a new home within the GAO for their methods and concerns. The initial route used by social scientists to enter GAO was through what is now the Program Evaluation and Methodology Division. In 1988 the GAO established a formal training institute to train personnel in evaluation methodology [14].

This transformation not only has expanded the scope of work performed by GAO, but also has shifted the nature and content of the work. One perspective on this expansion is to argue that the GAO has evolved—the result being new types of service available for the Congress. Another, however, is that the changes within GAO have compromised its integrity, reducing it to a politicized institution with an agenda. This controversy, like other defining controversies of the past, will likely result in significant reforms and changes within the internal organizational structure. Key members of Congress have entered the debate and the resolution will not be evident until the Congress selects a successor to Charles A. Bowsher in 1996. The following section considers the issues and dilemmas faced by both the Congress and the GAO as it faces an uncertain future.

ISSUES AND DILEMMAS

The issues and dilemmas resulting from the reforms of the GAO under Elmer Staats and Charles A. Bowsher can best be illustrated by considering two new areas of work into which the GAO has expanded: policy analysis and general management reviews. These are genuinely innovative and valuable tools that the GAO can use to provide information to the Congress and the nation about the performance of the federal government. However, their introduction has generated controversies and problems. Each deserves some elaboration and consideration.

Policy Analysis

Predictably, the GAO argues that the second great transformation and the use of policy analysis has been a success. Assistant Comptroller General Harry Havens states:

> As the world has changed around us, the work needed to satisfy that mandate has also changed, as has the institution of GAO. The work and the staff performing it have become more technically sophisticated, more policy oriented, and more closely attuned to the needs of the Congress [15].

Thus, Havens articulates the official position—arguing that the organization's increasing reliance on policy analysis is normal and that the institution is incrementally adding to the skills and services of the institution. In the same vein of thought, the head of the Program Evaluation and Methodology division, which performs a more narrowly focused form of policy analysis, also contends that the shift from auditing to evaluation has enhanced the General Accounting Office by adding new skills and new tools of analysis. Eleanor Chelimsky, Assistant Comptroller General, contends:

> Overall, our experience of the past nine years shows that it is entirely possible for auditors and social scientists not only to share the same workplace in reasonable harmony, but also to learn from each other and to work together productively [16].

In spite of this confidence, the incorporation of policy analysis into the services offered by GAO is a daunting task. It is an open question whether this portion of the second great transformation can be accomplished.

The full success of the second great transformation depends upon attaining two grand goals. On one hand, GAO leaders must reconcile the internal organizational tensions caused by the introduction of evaluators into the traditional GAO culture. On the other hand, these leaders must convince the Congress and federal agencies subject to its jurisdiction that the new methods employed by the evaluator can be used as effectively, objectively, and precisely as those employed by the traditional auditor. For this latter goal to be accomplished, the GAO must convince those that it audits that evaluation can be just as precise and objective as budgetary and financial examination. The legitimacy of the evaluation techniques used by the social sciences is the central issue surrounding the achievement of this second goal.

Developing policy analysis also continues to be the goal of professionals in the social science discipline. The late Aaron Wildavsky, who contributed to this development, acknowledged that much remained to be done. The following passage from his well-known book on policy analysis, *Speaking Truth to Power*, makes this point:

> The technical base of policy analysis is weak. In part its limitations are those of social science: innumerable discrete propositions of varying validity and uncertain

applicability, occasionally touching but not necessarily related, like beads on a string . . . Unlike social science, however, policy analysis must be prescriptive, arguments about correct policy, which deal with the future cannot help but be willful and therefore political [17].

Wildavsky's long career demonstrated that policy analysis is laced with politics. To use the techniques of policy analysis to demonstrate that any given policy works or does not work, is inefficient or efficient, or whether a given policy benefits one group at the expense of another.

The Congress has an ongoing interest on policy analysis. The fortunes of individual members depend on policy analysis favorable to the policies and programs they sponsor. To be sure, the Congress is also affected by a budgetary and financial analysis of the policies and programs that it authorizes. However, when the GAO included policy analysis among its activities, it added a significant new dimension to the feedback it gives to the Congress about its performance. In addition to informing the Congress about the cost of its policies, it could report on such things as client satisfaction and the efficiency and effectiveness of the agencies that were implementing the program, and provide a dizzying array of qualitative indicators that were completely outside the scope and capacity of the old GAO. In short, policy analysis profoundly affected the relationship between GAO and the Congress.

One way to understand this relationship is to consider the much-reported statistic about the shift in the independence of the GAO vis-à-vis the Congress. Even as late as the mid 1960s the GAO exercised substantial control over the work that it performed. Over 90% of the studies that it undertook were initiated within the GAO. By the early 1990s this control had waned to the point that nearly 80% of the work performed by the GAO was in response to requests from the Congress [18]. This shift, whatever its cause, is significant. When a Congressman requests work, the nature of the work is a product of negotiations between the GAO and a particular Congressional staff. This means that when such requests are levied upon the GAO, Congress exercises some influence over not only what is to be studied but the scope, design, and methodology of the study. The question is whether the ability of the Congress to request, then to interact with those who design the study compromises the objectivity of the GAO.

General Management Review

In many respects, the issues and dilemmas posed by the introduction of the general management review parallel those of policy analysis. Strictly speaking, one could argue that the original voucher audits undertaken by the original GAO were a form of management analysis in that negative judgments about an federal agency's expenditure were also implicit testimony to the other features of the agency such as the frugality of the agency's leaders or their fidelity to the spirit and letter of federal statutes. To be sure, it was common for federal agency heads to take offense at criticisms made by the GAO about the way that it handled its budgetary and financial affairs. Yet the key point here is that prior to the introduction of the general management review, any criticisms of federal management were restricted to the budgetary and financial decisions made by the management team in charge of a given federal agency. The general management review effectively lengthened the list of things about an agency's management that were fair game for GAO scrutiny: for example, its leadership, the organizational structure used by a federal agency, its personnel policy, its use of technology such as information management. In short, after general management reviews were introduced, secretaries of federal agencies were on notice that far more aspects of their agency would be scrutinized than simply the budgetary and financial.

The GAO began general management reviews in the early 1980s and created a staff within its General Government Division to conduct these general studies of agency management. Since then, it has completed approximately 48 of these studies. As is the case with policy analysis, the use of general management reviews by the GAO raises questions of technical precision and objectivity. On one hand, it is possible to precisely state that a given agency has overspent its authorized budget for office supplies. However, is it possible, through the use of management analysis, to precisely determine whether a federal agency has used sound strategic planning or whether the agency is appropriately structured?

Improving the technical base of the general management review has been a continuing GAO concern. In 1990, with strong support from Comptroller General Bowsher, the agency attempted to incorporate the technique of total quality management (TQM) into the general management review [19]. Despite such efforts, critics argue that the technical base of the general management review needs improvement and that the GAO needs more management expertise on its general management review staff [20].

Critics of the general management review argue that no matter how sound the technical base is, the GAO oversteps its authority in attempting to audit the general management practices of federal agencies in the same way that it audits an agency's budget or its finances. The executive branch began to consolidate its authority over the management and administration of federal agencies with the Executive Reorganization Act of 1939. It further strengthened its presence by making management a responsibility of the Bureau of the Budget when the Office of Management and Budget (OMB) was created in 1970. Though presidents since 1970 and successive OMB directors have not openly challenged the authority of GAO to conduct general management reviews, individual agency heads have expressed their opposition [21]. This resistance of the executive branch will likely increase as if the GAO further asserts its prerogative to review executive branch management.

Perhaps the most telling indicator of how controversial the expansion of GAO has become during the second great transformation is the opposition of the Republicans in the 1991 Congress. The Republicans, then a minority party, accused the GAO of collaboration with the Democratic majority and of skewing its research so as to favor the Democratic political agenda. Senator William V. Roth was one prominent critic who penned a lengthy letter, dated June 13, 1991, to Charles A. Bowsher containing the following paragraph:

> I think that I can best sum up the problems that have been reported to me by stating that when GAO is objectively fact finding there is none of us who finds fault with your role. However, when the GAO enters the arena of politics by selecting among alternative solutions which are charged with political electricity, you are in danger and we are in danger. If you select a solution that echoes the positions of one party, you may aid that party in the short run. But over the long term you damage your usefulness to both parties. When you adopt a party line, that party cannot long hold GAO up as nonpartisan before those of the other party will begin to distrust the results of other GAO studies [22].

Two weeks later, a group of powerful Republican senators underscored their support for the Roth letter by introducing a GAO Reform Act. This act proposed to restore the professional integrity of GAO by subjecting it to a battery of controls including a special inspector general whose responsibility would be to investigate complaints against the GAO.

This Republican revolt within the Congress underscores the thin line that separates both policy analysis and the general management review from becoming partisan enterprises. It also underscores the fact that the GAO has not convinced either federal agencies or many of those in Congress that these new social scientific techniques of research and analysis can be grafted on to its auditing tradition without sacrifices to its reputation for rigor and objectivity.

TOWARD THE THIRD GREAT TRANSFORMATION OF GAO

Identifying and certainly predicting periods of institutional history is a tenuous enterprise. Yet there are indications that the second great transformation has run its course. The original critics of the second transformation, Republicans, took control of both houses of Congress in the congressional elections of 1994. It is likely that these critics will forge a new relationship, though the nature of that relationship is not yet clear. A recent congressional review recommended that GAO retrench and retreat using only those forms of research and study that are less political, more factual:

> Congressional committees and other requesters of GAO work should not jeopardize GAO's role and reputation as objective and impartial auditor and evaluator, by selecting report topics and posing research questions that inevitably will place GAO in the midst of value-based debates and political controversies, detached from fact-based analysis [23].

In the face of these criticisms, it is likely that the GAO will be forced to reform, and the scope of these reforms will become clearer with the appointment of a new Comptroller General in 1996. In the near term, the organization, like all other federal agencies, is finding its own budget curtailed as the Congress struggles to balance the federal budget. In the longer term, the new Comptroller General will face hard choices. One alternative is to shore up the technical integrity of policy analysis and the general management review so that the Congress and the federal agencies are reassured that studies using these social science methods are nonpolitical, fact-based, and objective. The other choice is to return to the budgeting and financial roots of the agency. This would please the older auditors who feel that the GAO has strayed from the basics and who want the GAO to return to its auditing heritage in order to salvage its credibility. Pursuing either choice poses risks and considerable organizational commitment and adjustment. The next Comptroller General will struggle with these alternatives at least through the 1990s and probably beyond.

NOTES

1. For further information on the description of this commission, see H. Emmerich. *Federal Organization and Administrative Management*, University of Alabama Press, University, pp. 40–41 (1971).
2. The Bureau of the Budget was further reformed in 1970 and became the Office of Management and Budget. Frederick C. Mosher has written a fascinating history of both the Bureau of the Budget and the GAO in which he traces the tensions between these two agencies and draws fruitful comparisons. See F. C. Mosher, *A Tale of Two Agencies*: *A Comparative Analysis of the General Accounting Office and the Office of Management and Budget*, Louisiana State University Press, Baton Rouge (1984).
3. Hebert Emmerich (see note 1), p. 22.
4. Harvey Mansfield, *The Comptroller General*, Yale University Press, New Haven, Conn., p. 2 (1939).
5. W. E. Walker, *Changing Organizational Culture*: *Strategy, Structure, and Professionalism in the U.S. General Accounting Office*, University of Tennessee Press, Knoxville, p. 27 (1986).
6. "Full Check-up of Emergency Units Sought," *Washington Star*, June 6 (1934).
7. F. C. Mosher (see note 2), pp. 79–82, presents more information on Warren's philosophy.

8. H. S. Havens, *The Evolution of the General Accounting Office: From Voucher Audits to Program Evaluations*, U.S. General Accounting Office, Washington, D.C., GAO/OP-2-HP, pp. 4–6, (1990).

9. F. C. Mosher (see note 2), p. 143; H. S. Havens (see note 8), p. 6.

10. F. C. Mosher, (see note 2), pp. 145–151.

11. *Review of Economic Opportunity Programs*, B-130515, March 18 (1969).

12. F. C. Mosher (see note 2), pp. 145–146.

13. *The Roles, Mission and Operation of the U. S. General Accounting Office*, report prepared for the Committee on Governmental Affairs, U.S. Senate by the National Academy of Public Administration, 103d Congress, 1st Sess. (October), p. 7 (1994).

14. E. Chelimsky, "Expanding GAO's Capabilities in Program Evaluation," *GAO Journal, 8* (winter/spring): 50 (1990).

15. H. S. Havens (see note 8), p. 27.

16. E. Chelimsky (see note 14), p. 50.

17. A. Wildavsky, *Speaking Truth to Power, The Art and Craft of Policy Analysis*, Little, Brown, Boston, p. 16 (1979).

18. The Roles, Mission and Operation of the U.S. General Accounting Office (see note 13), p. 62.

19. One index of the magnitude of this effort is that the GAO invited the guru of total quality management, C. Edwards Deming, to speak to a number of its executives in June 1990. It also issued a scoping study that assessed how this technique of management analysis could be used to support the general management review process. See *Quality Management Scoping Study*, U.S. General Accounting Office, Washington, D.C., November (1990).

20. *The Roles, Mission and Operation of the U.S. General Accounting Office* (see note 13), pp. 53–57.

21. One conspicuous example of this opposition was the response of the executive branch administrators to GAO's general management review of the administration of Social Security. See *Social Security Administration: Stable Leadership and Better Management Needed to Improve Effectiveness*, General Accounting Office, Washington, D.C., March, pp. 52, 53, 69–72 (1987).

22. Letter to Charles A. Bowsher from Senator William V. Roth, Jr., dated June 13, 1991.

23. *The Roles, Mission and Operation of the U.S. General Accounting Office* (see note 13), p. 69.

18

Reconciling Politics and Budget Analysis:
The Case of the Congressional Budget Office

R. Philip Twogood

In 1974 the creation of the Congressional Budget Office was authorized as part of Congress' major budget process reform. As part of the political rhetoric which accompanied the office's birth, high expectations were expressed for an organization that would help to illuminate an often irrational and poorly informed budgetary system. Since those optimistic days of the mid-1970s, it has unfortunately become obvious that process reform and new analytical organizations have been unable to improve radically on budgetary decision making. In particular, the controversy-laden history of the Congressional Budget Office (CBO) has mirrored the rocky history of budget reform.

Study of the CBO is useful for a variety of reasons. Not only does the office's history illustrate the extent to which congressional budget reform has been institutionalized, but, more importantly here, CBO is a fascinating example of how professionalism, protected by an appropriate organizational structure, interacts with a heavily political environment. Furthermore, the case of the CBO is an excellent one in which to examine the uneasy relationship that often exists between the policy analyst and the political decision-making process.

In this chapter, I shall first discuss some of the organizational concepts that deal with leadership, the institutionalization of mission and goals, and protection of core technologies. Second, the concept of professionalism, especially as it applies to the economist, will be examined as a significant aspect of CBO's core technology. Their efforts to protect CBO's sense of mission and professional cohesiveness through organizational structure will be evaluated. Finally, CBO's success in protecting its professionalism and promoting itself as a nonpartisan source of budget and policy analysis will be considered. While the primary emphasis will be on the Rivlin years at CBO, some concluding comments will be made on CBO's current situation.

Research for this project was done primarily between 1977 and 1983. Scores of congressional hearings and other government documents were studied, and 56 interviews were

Source: *Public Budgeting and Financial Management*, vol. 3, no. 1 (1991), pp. 65–87.

conducted with CBO personnel (including Alice Rivlin), Budget, Appropriations, authorizing committee staff members, and a former OMB director. Except for Dr. Rivlin, all interviewees were promised anonymity.

Overall, this research is valuable not only as a case study of a highly visible and historically colorful office, but as further evidence of the uneasy relationship that exists between a professional group, struggling to maintain and promote professional standards, and a politically charged decision-making process. The CBO experience illustrates the possibilities for and limitations on the analyst, when the analyst is within the protection of a "friendly" organizational structure.

INSTITUTIONALIZATION AND ORGANIZATIONAL MISSION

The concept of "institutionalization," as discussed by Philip Selznick, involves the ways in which an organization evolves from a set of formal goals and design into a value-infused social structure, supported and prized by its members for its unique, distinctive identity. As Selznick writes,

> Institutionalization is a process. It is something that happens to an organization over time reflecting the organization's own distinctive history, the people who have been in it, the groups it embodies and the vested interests they have created, and the way it has adapted to its environment [1].

As an important part of the institutionalization process, Selznick emphasizes the need for effective leadership. Especially in situations where formal organizational goals are vague and conflicting, leadership provides a crucial service by defining organizational mission. This involves the recasting of "the general aims of the organization so as to adapt them without serious corruption, to the requirements of institutional survival" [2]. What will be examined in later sections of this paper is Alice Rivlin's role as an institutional leader.

Once this concept of institutional purpose is identified, it becomes necessary to protect the organizational mission and goals from the fluctuations and intrusions of environmental forces. As James D. Thompson has noted, this involves the attempt by an organization to balance the desire to operate as a closed system with the practical necessity of existing in an open, often unpredictable and uncontrollable, system. Thompson states that the goal is to "seal off their core technologies from environmental influences" [3].

Much of an organization's success in protecting its core technology depends upon the leadership's ability to encourage environmental acceptance of organizational domain (or its claim to a particular area of action), to use an appropriately designed organizational structure, and to scatter dependence so that no single client group can dictate organizational purpose [4].

When the ideas of these two authors are combined, a framework is suggested that emphasizes the friction between institutional goals, values, and norms and the pressures and uncertainties provided by environmental actors. Protection of core values and institutional mission through organizational design and prestige is an important leadership function, and the CBO case is an excellent example of these dynamics in action.

PROFESSIONALISM: ADDING DEFINITION TO INSTITUTIONAL MISSION

As government agencies have become more and more dominated by professional groups, the standards and norms of these groups have become an important component in the institutionalization process. The definition that I use for a profession comes from Frederick Mosher: a clearly defined occupational field, education at least through the bachelor's level, and lifetime career opportunities for members [5].

Fortunately, there is a wealth of literature on the importance of professionalism in government, and few have contributed as much to the field as Frederick Mosher. As Mosher notes, professions have their own unique approaches on how to address issues and problems:

> Each profession brings to its organization its own particularized view of the world and of the agency role and mission in it. The perspective and motivation of each profession are shaped, at least to some extent, by the lens provided by professional education, prior professional experience, and professional colleagues . . .
>
> . . . The climate of an organization as well as its view of mission and its effectiveness in carrying it out are in considerable part a product of the professional structure and professional value system [6].

Two further points from Mosher need to be noted. First, a profession that is dominant within a specific agency attempts to control the operations and hiring within the organization in order to protect and develop both professional standards and career opportunities for its members. Therefore, although an agency may be staffed by a variety of professional groups, one group will often be seen as the elite, and it will work to further its unique position through the use of organizational means. Second, professionalism and politics are often antagonistic since professionalism is based on "correct ways of solving problems and doing things" while "politics is seen as being engaged in the fuzzy areas of negotiation, elections, votes, compromises . . . ." As a result, "politics is to the professions . . . as heresy is to true belief" [7].

Mosher's ideas add an important component to the institutionalization framework by focusing on a key aspect of organizational cohesiveness and culture. If, as Selznick argues, an important part of institutional leadership requires the definition of mission, then professionalism is a logical tool for providing an organization with its sense of purpose.

CREATING A PROFESSIONAL CORE AT CBO

The importance of a professional perspective as a basis for CBO's institutionalization has been a dominant theme throughout the office's history, and that perspective has been centered on the economist.

A primary role in CBO for the professional economist was not necessarily a universally held congressional intention, and the roots of CBO's development can be seen in the original choice of an office director. The House of Representatives, envisioning a small, technical support staff, supported the selection of Phillip S. Hughes from the General Accounting Office [8]. The Senate Budget Committee, conceiving of a broader CBO mission and public policy analysis capabilities, pressed for the selection of Brookings Institution economist Alice Rivlin.

This choice, which had serious implications for the future of the office, can be seen as a contest between two professional orientations, the budgeteer's and the economist's, with two distinct understandings of nonpartisan service. Based upon interviews and the writings of Michael Malbin, some generalization's about differences between the two groups can be constructed.

The budgeteer is more apt to concentrate on the technical aspects of budget preparation, while the economist emphasizes more the analysis of broader policy issues. While the budgeteer is known as being more politically sensitive and better as a negotiator (as Sam

Hughes was), the economist is more inclined to ignore political considerations and to present "correct" analytical answers based on an allegiance to an outside standard of professionalism. Consequently, nonpartisanship is viewed differently by the two groups. Former House Budget Committee staff director Walter Kravitz's comments about the role of staff summarize the budgeteer's approach to nonpartisanship:

> Staff work for chairmen and chairmen have their own policies and ideologies. You are nonpartisan in the sense that you will work for any chairman who comes along, but you have got to work with the chairman you have.
>
> In the end, the job of the staff is to help the committee do what it wants to do . . . [9].

On the other hand, the role of the economist was expressed well by former House Budget Committee chief economist Nancy Teeters when she noted, "I view my job to be that of giving them the economic information and projections straight, without any partisan tinge" [10]. As Malbin states, Teeters' approach involved making projections and recommendations based on her best professional judgment, not her service to the political goals of the House Budget Committee [10]. The Teeters comments were certainly more in line with the Rivlin view.

When the two original Budget Committee chairs finally agreed on Alice Rivlin, the office was stamped with the economist's approach. Rivlin obviously accepted the directorship with high expectations about CBO's role, and the maintenance of a highly professional service organization with the independence to make its own hiring decisions, to select some of its own areas of study, to protect the integrity of its projections, and to publicize its findings was a crucial part of meeting these expectations. All of this was to be accomplished while maintaining an image of nonpartisanship and preventing what would appear to be recommendations to Congress. Consequently, the assumption that appears to have been made was that professional standards could be used to support the office's claims of nonpartisanship, even though CBO would be operating in a political environment where nonpartisanship was seen in different terms.

In her initial hiring decisions, Rivlin made it clear that the professional economist was to be the backbone of the organization. As William Capron wrote in his 1976 evaluation of the new office, "The CBO staff is said by some to have been created very much in Alice Rivlin's own image" [11]. What this meant was a staff strong in professional and academic credentials, but weak in congressional experience. The result was, as Frederick Mosher has noted,

> The CBO is the domain of analytical economists whose education and experience—and many of whose future careers—are not in Congress but in professional groups, in executive agencies of the government or in research institutions, policy analysis staffs, or universities. Their norms, standards, and aspirations are those of their professional peers, which are often in conflict with the pressing demands of Congress for quick analyses of proposed bills and their economic consequences [12].

The type of analyst that CBO attracted was consequently what Arnold Meltsner has tagged the "technician":

> The technician is an academic researcher—an intellectual—in bureaucratic residence. No admirer of bureaucratic flokways, he weaves around himself a protective

cocoon of computers, models, and statistical regressions . . . . Politics is somebody else's business. His main business is research which is linked to policymaking, and if left alone he will faithfully adhere to an internal standard of quality [13].

The CBO envisioned by Alice Rivlin was an institution that would rely on professional standards and technical excellence in order to maintain its independence and to become an influential Capitol Hill actor. As an institutional leader, Rivlin was successful in infusing her organization with a sense of mission and a feeling that a rare opportunity existed for contributing to the policymaking process. For many, there was a deep sense of institutional pride and excitement in being part of the CBO staff. Along with this excitement, however, came a naivete in dealing with a Congress that often saw CBO as an uncontrollable and unresponsive staff organization. As will be examined more thoroughly in a later section, Congress did not always agree that CBO's reliance on "professional" standards equaled office nonpartisanship.

PROTECTING THE PROFESSIONAL CORE

As is the case in many legislative compromises, CBO was given a broad set of duties based upon what a variety of congressional actors expected the office to accomplish. The new office was given specific responsibilities to serve the economic and budgetary analysis needs of the new congressional budget process while also receiving vague instructions on broader policy studies.

Many hours of congressional hearings have been consumed by discussions over CBO's work priorities, independence in study initiation, duplication with other agencies, and appropriate responsibilities, and this is certainly not the place to readdress those issues. Let it suffice to say at this point that Rivlin unquestionably wanted CBO to be more than a narrow budget analysis staff for the two Budget Committees.

The development of a broader policy analysis capability was an important part of her expectation for the office, and the requirements for producing a professionally acceptable work quality involved the need for isolation from day-to-day congressional demands. Consequently, Rivlin attempted to protect what she defined as an integral part of her office's core technology by organizationally separating budget and program analysis functions and by scattering the office's client relationship throughout Congress. Through these efforts, not only would policy analysts be insulated from the continuous demands of the budget process, but the CBO's analytical market would not be confined to the Budget, Appropriations, and tax committees. By serving all of Congress, CBO would have more flexibility in selecting its own research agenda and could assert greater institutional independence. These "strategies" would seem to indicate CBO's impression that congressional views of policy analysis (and CBO's right to include such a function) differed substantially from the professional standards expected by Rivlin and that without certain organizational buffering, these standards would be difficult to maintain.

SELLING CBO PROFESSIONALISM TO CONGRESS

To this point ideas regarding institutionalization, professionalism, and organizational protection of core technology have been applied to the early CBO. I have argued that Alice Rivlin's plans for CBO involved a certain perception of professionalism and a desired role for the office that may have been in conflict with traditional congressional policymaking norms. In this section of the chapter, I shall evaluate Rivlin's success in selling to Congress her views of professionalism and her vision for CBO. Two areas in particular will be examined: economic forecasting and policy analysis studies.

Economic Forecasting

Historically, one of the more controversial CBO work products has been the economic forecast, the assumptions on growth rates, unemployment, inflation, and interest rates that drive the budget numbers. In regard to these projections, Rivlin was placed in a difficult position. In order to be seen as a nonpartisan support for the entire Congress, Rivlin had to claim vigorously that CBO professionalism equaled objectivity and neutrality, even though that claim may have been unrealistic. Given the range of uncertainty involved in economic projections, and the corresponding uncertainty in outlay, revenue, and deficit figures, Congress will always have an incentive to ignore projections that reduce its program flexibility.

In addition to the problem of forecasting accuracy and the corresponding incentives for budgetary "flexibility," the challenge of trying to separate economic theory from partisan controversy complicated CBO's position. When disagreements over economic models were as intense as disputes over political goals, then CBO's claim to professional neutrality had little credibility.

A few examples from CBO's turbulent economic forecasting history will indicate the challenges faced by Rivlin. During the first years following the passage of the Budget Act, many of the disputes over CBO's economic projections involved the House Budget Committee. Although the Senate Budget Committee under Senator Edmund Muskie was more consistently supportive of CBO's economic assumptions, the House Budget Committee regularly asserted its forecasting independence.

One dramatic example of this occurred during conference action on the fiscal year 1978 fall budget resolution. CBO had projected a growth rate for the next fiscal year of 4.56%, and the Senate Budget Committee had basically concurred by using a 4.6% figure. The House Budget Committee and its chariman, Representative Robert Giaimo, pushed however for a 5% figure on the basis of the political implications of suggesting pessimistic economic trends. As Giaimo stated, "I would hesitate to send out a message to the people, to the economy in general, that the Congress thinks the economy is going to go down." Giaimo went on to argue that the projections involved a high degree of guesswork anyway: "We're all sitting around here like great sages saying its going to be a 5.4 or 5.3 growth rate. . . . I was never an economist. Who the heck knows what's going to happen in a $2 trillion economy?" [14].

In the final conference report, which contained a compromise figure of 4.8%, a final disclaimer on the ability to forecast accurately was presented: "The conferees recognize that it is not possible to predict the precise rate of economic growth; and that estimates of the rate of growth may change substantially over the coming months" [15].

Perhaps one of the most serious criticisms of CBO's economic forecasting expertise took place during the last years of the Carter Administration as the "supply-side" economists began to challenge the theoretical foundations of CBO's capabilities. In critiques such as Preston Miller and Arthur Rolnick's paper, "The CBO's Policy Analysis: An Unquestionable Misuse of Questionable Theory," and in numerous congressional committee hearings, CBO was attacked for its failure to incorporate new economic perspectives, for "ignoring the uncertainty implicit in its own model," and for "overstating the accuracy of its forecasts" [16].

The Miller and Rolnick arguments, coupled with the internal congressional questioning of CBO's forecasting capabilities, illustrated a number of enduring difficulties for the "nonpartisan" analytical office operating in a highly partisan policy area. First, although the limitations of the economic profession required an admittance of forecasting uncertainties, the budget process demanded greater precision. As William Beeman, director of CBO's Fiscal Analysis Division, wrote in response to Miller and Rolnick, clients

> object to the CBO's insistence on ranges rather than point estimates . . . . They complain about repeated qualifications and references to uncertainty and lengthy discussions on the sources of uncertainty in our economic reports.

Since the Budget Committees had to prepare budgets with specific targets, "we grit our teeth and do the best we can" [17]. Although not specifically writing about CBO, Robert Samuelson made a similar point in a *National Journal* article:

> The political process inherently stretches economists beyond their capabilities. Honest analysis admits to ambiguity and uncertainty; effective advocacy demands self assurance, the selective use of evidence, and slick presentation. The two exist uneasily, and often, not at all . . . . [While economic change is a long-term process,] politics turns the process on its head. What matters almost exclusively are short-term results. [18].

A second major point illustrated by CBO's difficulties was that economic forecasting is a very political exercise, and no attempt to hide behind claims of nonpartisanship could mask that reality. CBO Director Alice Rivlin was therefore placed in the precarious position of needing to maintain her office's integrity through an image of balance and distance from political pressures, while being forced into the middle of the ideological cleavages wracking Congress

At a time when political divisions were being expressed in terms of economic theory, CBO was indeed vulnerable to charges of political bias. As one Joint Economic Committee aide argued:

> The old models remain comfortable for CBO because the emphasis on government spending gives them the incentive to go to the liberal Budget Committee chairmen and tell them what they want to hear about program spending. The supply side models require them to learn new things. Their level of sophistication is not that great, but people on the Hill don't know that [19].

The office's position was not strengthened when a memo from "an undisclosed source" attributed to Rivlin the feeling that "critics of the models CBO uses for forecasting are an extreme right-wing clique who should not be given an audience, lest it legitimize their views" [20].

While criticism of CBO was certainly present during the last years of the Carter Administration, nothing could compare with the intensity of the attacks made during the first year of the Reagan presidency. Republicans in Congress vehemently argued that efforts to adhere to traditional economic theory were undercutting Reagan initiatives, and Alice Rivlin's CBO was seen by some as personifying this resistance. One particularly intense criticism occurred during the Senate Budget Committee's Fiscal year 1982 first resolution hearings when Senator Robert Kasten charged Rivlin:

You assured me that you were going to work in a strong bipartisan way, supporting the committee with the facts that we would need, and not biasing your assumptions for or against any set of political ideas.

I would like to say, then, can you think of anything you have done since February that has been anything but destructive? You are undercutting the administration's proposal with the economic assumptions you are making [21].

This and other attacks placed the office under siege during the first half of 1981, and there were even calls for Rivlin's resignation. Interestingly enough, when CBO's mid-year 1981 revised economic forecasting report appeared, it contained a substantially more optimistic assessment of the economy, and much of the credit for this upturn was attributed to Reagan policies. While previously skeptical Republicans, such as Rep. Lynn Martin, were apologizing to Rivlin for their previous harsh treatment, Democrats, such as Michigan Senator Donald Riegle, were disappointed that the report "masterfully evade [d] the seriousness of the problem that we face right now" [22]. Some whom I interviewed preferred to say that CBO had "trimmed its sails" in the face of hostile fire.

These examples of forecasting controversies should not suggest that CBO was without success in establishing itself on Capitol Hill. The Senate Budget Committee, especially under the chairmanship of Senator Muskie, relied heavily on CBO numbers, and, following the instability of the 1981 budget cycle and the threats in that year to Rivlin's job security, the Republican-dominated Senate Budget Committee returned in 1982 to a basic acceptance of CBO economic assumptions. Remarkably, Senate Budget Committee Chairman Domenici stated in a March 1982 hearing,

I believe that the economic forecast presented in CBO's annual report is a prudent basis for this committee to use in making budget decisions. It may be that the economy will perform better than CBO predicts, and I certainly hope so. But to be responsible, we must make our decisions based on cautious forecasts like the CBO's, and on overly optimistic forecasts . . . .

I do not need to tell you, Dr. Rivlin, how difficult is the task this committee faces. Your guidance this afternoon will be very important to us [23].

In regard to economic projections then, CBO's attempts to portray itself as nonpartisan and professional were limited by the highly political nature of the product. In her various dealings with Congress, Rivlin was forced to overstate her position in order to sustain the independent image of the office, but this same independence was often seen by Congress as politically threatening.

Policy Analysis

A second major aspect of Rivlin's mission concept was the production of economic policy analysis studies, which involved the evaluation of alternative policy choices. For many analysts in CBO, it was the perceived opportunity to influence congressional policymaking that made the organization an attractive employer. It was also another area in which Congress questioned the office's interpretation of professional standards.

Interviews with a variety of committee staff members indicated that the early CBO analysts were not sensitive to congressional needs. Work products were often described as uneven in quality and of questionable value to the legislative process. Committees that were concerned with specific legislation at a specific time found the broadly developed CBO alternatives to be outside of committee concerns, too "academic," and lacking in "nuts and bolts" issues. Staff members also complained that reports were overly dependent on the personal assumptions of the analysts and that CBO's poor, and sometimes politically insensitive, timing in the release of studies reinforced many committees' image of a politically disruptive, "loose cannon" organization. CBO's "ego problem" was raised by several staff members who felt that some CBO analysts saw their organization as *the* only independent, objective organization on Capitol Hill. Many committee staff members resented the implication that they were somehow not as expert as the CBO analysts and that their own work was inferior because it had been tainted by political considerations. Consequently, committee staff comments suggested that CBO reports were unpredictable, uncontrollable, and politically undesirable.

Many of the early CBO policy analysts seemed to resemble the "technician" described by Meltsner. They felt that their ability to provide the best analytical product depended upon being insulated from political pressures. The standard for quality was, therefore, geared in many cases toward a professional standard and an outside audience instead of toward the congressional client.

Did this mean that CBO had no success in gaining acceptance of its policy analysis role? No, not entirely. Although Congress did express some serious reservations about Rivlin's CBO and although CBO professionalism would not mean that the office's products would hold a positions of sacred dominance above a tainted, political legislature, there were some indicators of success. First, despite congressional pressures to combine the policy analysts and the budget analysts (a reorganization which would have reversed Rivlin's professional insulation efforts), the policy analysis division remained separate. Second, CBO was able to diversify its clientele and to receive requests from a variety of authorizing as well as budget-related committees. Finally, although CBO's program papers continued to be seen as inconsistent in relevance and quality, improved communications between analysts and committee staffs at least partially reversed some of the earlier trends. The general trends were toward higher quality products, improved CBO anticipation of important issues, and better timeliness. The office's ability to become involved in issues at an earlier stage and to "plug in" to the political environment was far from perfect, but it was improved.

Basically, advances in CBO's policy analysis role came as a result of greater willingness to serve client interests, and, as a result, there was more congressional tolerance of this CBO function. As Rivlin stated in 1982,

> Summarizing our work over just this past fiscal year, we responded to requests from 11 Senate committees and 9 House committees and for testimony from 11 Senate committees and 8 House committees. This broad spectrum of committees is representative of a trend we have seen developing since CBO began to provide such services . . . . I believe this shows an important contribution by CBO to the legislative process. Key budgetary decisions are often made by authorizing committees, which are increasingly relying on our assistance in analyzing both the programmatic impacts and the costs of various policy options as they develop legislative strategies [24].

SOME CONCLUSIONS ON CBO INSTITUTIONALIZATION

The Rivlin years at CBO provide a fascinating example of a new office, infused with professional values, that was struggling to maintain its sense of mission in an often hostile atmosphere. The arguments have been made that institutional leadership is an important factor in mission development and protection and that professionalism can be a crucial factor in institutionalization. These elements certainly can be seen in CBO's history as Rivlin worked to ensure the office's place on Capitol Hill.

While I have not claimed that Congress ever completely accepted the appropriateness of Rivlin's definition of "professionalism," her successes can be viewed as remarkable under the circumstances. Despite the controversies surrounding it, CBO became a highly respected Capitol Hill organization. Although there was congressional uneasiness caused by her public appearances and claims of independence and although there was a widely held opinion that Rivlin could be sorely lacking in political savvy, the CBO image was basically one of fairness and quality. It is questionable whether a director of less personal stature and integrity would have withstood the political pressures placed on the office. Rivlin's ability to survive during 1981 was a crucial part of maintaining office independence and demonstrating that Congress had come to accept, at least in part, many of the Rivlin values.

Some caveats should also be presented, however. First, this chapter has focused primarily on the more controversial aspects of CBO's mission. A large portion of its responsibilities, and a major reason for its positive reputation, was the office's budget analysis work. It is difficult then to say to what extent Congress tolerated CBO's policy analysis side because of its excellent budget analysis reputation.

Second, Rivlin was forced in some cases to revise CBO work priorities in the face of congressional pressure. For example, during the first years of CBO's existence, some personnel positions were shifted from the policy analysis divisions to the budget analysis division. Policy analysts also found that to have influence on Capitol Hill, it was necessary to develop better working relations with congressional committees. Work that was untainted by political contact was often unread and unwanted.

Finally, I would argue that, based on the Rivlin experience, the maintenance of CBO's sense of mission, as it applies both to internal institutionalization and to the office's projected image of professionalism requires the continued presence of strong leaders who enjoy career reputations beyond Capitol Hill. Internally, although the glue of professional standards can provide some common values, the two-audience approach of many CBO analysts may work against organizational cohesiveness unless strong leadership is exercised. In office relations with Congress, lack of strong leadership could certainly threaten the acceptance of a CBO mission that includes a concept of professionalism not easily understood by Congress.

More recent events indicate that CBO's independence can be threatened without strong leadership. After Rudolph Penner's departure in March 1987, Congress went through 2 years of acting CBO directors before finally making a permanent choice [25]. In March 1988, an episode concerning what appeared to be a politically forced revision of a CBO number raised fears in Congress that there may be a "politicization" of the office [26]. Finally, it is noteworthy that CBO's major role in the original Gramm–Rudman process was not reconstituted in Gramm–Rudman II.

The history of the Rivlin years at CBO and the analytical perspectives of professionalism and institutionalization do provide a fascinating way to examine the past, and possible future, role of this important organization. CBO was designed to provide Congress with a counterbalance to OMB numbers, and a weakened or politicized CBO would not serve well either the budget process or the Congress.

NOTES AND REFERENCES

1. P. Selznick, *Leadership in Administration: A Sociological Interpretation*, Row Peterson and Company, Evanston, Ill., p. 16 (1957).
2. Ref. 1, p. 16. For more on institutionalization see S. Maynard-Moody, D. Stull, and J. Mitchell, "Reorganization as Status Drama: Building, Maintaining, and Displacing Dominant Subcultures," *Public Administration Review*, 46(July/August): 301–310 (1986).
3. J. D. Thompson, *Organizations in Action*, McGraw-Hill, New York, p. 19 (1967).
4. Ref. 3, pp. 32–33.
5. F. C. Mosher, *Democracy and the Public Service*, 2nd edition, Oxford University Press, New York, pp. 115–116 (1982). For other research on the role of professionals in government see G. Benveniste, *Professionalizing the Organization: Reducing Bureaucracy to Enhance Effectiveness*, Jossey-Bass, San Francisco (1987). See also W. E. Walker, *Changing Organizational Culture; Strategy, Structure, and Professionalism in the U.S. General Accounting Office*, University of Tennessee Press, Knoxville (1986).
6. F. C. Mosher (see note 5), pp. 132–133.
7. F. C. Mosher (see note 5), pp. 118–119.
8. J. Havemann, "House, Senate Disagree on Director for New Budget Office," *National Journal*, December 28: 1960 (1974).
9. M. Malbin, *Unelected Representatives: Congressional Staff and the Future of Representative Government*, Basic Books, New York, p. 194 (1980).
10. Ref. 9, pp. 195–196.
11. W. Capron, "The Congressional Budget Office," in U.S. Congress, Senate Commission on the Operation of the Senate, *Congressional Support Agencies: A Compilation of Papers*, 94th Congress, 2nd Sess., p. 80 (1976). For another account of CBO's early period, see A. Schick, *Congress and Money: Budgeting, Spending, and Taxing*, Urban Institute, Washington, D.C. (1980).
12. F. C. Mosher, *The GAO: The Quest for Accountability in American Government*, Westview Press, Boulder, Colo., p. 275 (1979).
13. A. Meltsner, *Policy Analysis in the Bureaucracy*, University of California Press, Berkley, p. 18 (1976).
14. M. Rood, "Congress Sets Binding Fiscal 1978 Budget Levels," *Congressional Quarterly Weekly Report*, September 17, 1949 (1977).
15. Ref. 14, p. 1950.
16. P. Miller and A. Rolnick, "The CBO's Policy Analysis: An Unquestionable Misuse of a Questionable Theory," *The Congressional Budget Process After Five Years* (R. Penner, ed.), American Enterprise Institute, Washington, D.C., p. 52 (1981).
17. W. Beeman, "A Rebuttal to Miller and Rolnick," *The Congressional Budget Process After Five Years* (R. Penner, ed.), American Enterprise Institute, Washington, D.C., p. 71 (1981).
18. J. Samuelson, "Influence over Integrity," *National Journal*, April 23: 595 (1982).
19. R. Cohen, "The 'Numbers Crunchers' at CBO try to Steer Clear of Policy Disputes," *National Journal*, June 7: 941 (1980).
20. Ref. 19, p. 940.
21. United States Congress, Senate Committee on the Budget, *First Concurrent Resolution on the Budget, Fiscal Year 1982*, Hearings before the Committee on the Budget, vol. 2., 97th Congress, 1st Sess., p. 29 (1981).
22. United States Congress, Senate Committee on the Budget, *Second Concurrent Resolution on the Budget—Fiscal Year 1982*, Hearings before the Committee on the Budget, 97th Congress, 1st Sess., pp. 37–38 (1981).
23. United States Congress, Senate Committee on the Budget, *First Concurrent Resolution on the Budget—Fiscal Year 1983*, Hearings before the Committee on the Budget, 97th Congress, 2nd Sess., p. 304 (1982).

24. United States Congress, Senate Committee on the Budget, *Congressional Budget Office Oversight*, Hearings before the Committee on the Budget, 97th Congress, 2nd Sess., p. 54 (1982).
25. D. Cloud, "Budget Committee Leaders Battle over Top CBO Post," *Congressional Quarterly Weekly Report*, February 6, p. 246 (1988).
26. L. J. Haas, "Questions about CBO Independence," *National Journal*, May 28: 1419 (1988).

IV
ECONOMIC CONTEXTS OF BUDGETING AND FINANCE

EDITORIAL INTRODUCTION

At its heart, PBF involves marshaling economic and financial tools and skills relevant to who should, and who does, get which scarce resources, and when. This unit turns to four selections that bear on these core concerns. Their focus is basically on American contexts, but the final selection provides a bit of comparative perspective on how the political institutions of mainland China influence one aspect of their version of PBF.

Adequacy of PBF Arts and Sciences

Many observers, including those experienced in both politics as well as economics like Walter W. Heller [1], see a profile of incomplete but real contributions of economics to PBF. Heller focuses on the various economic functions of government; he indicates the tangled difficulties of attempting to use governmental controls or budgetary action where free-market dynamics cannot or should not determine outcomes; and he gives attention to the selection of alternative means for the effective performance of government functions or activities. Through it all, the themes of usefulness/incompleteness of economic and financial analysis appear prominently.

Heller's qualified optimism about the usefulness of tools of analysis gets ample support from the mixed record of success of coping with the major components of "public expenditure theory," as well as from areas developed more recently. Thomas Havrilesky provides one exemplar of the latter kind in his "The New Political Economy of Monetary Policy," reprinted as Chapter 19. Of late, "public choice" has been front and center in both economics and politics, and Havrilesky wishes to extend its reach and grasp to "the electorally adverse consequences of income redistributions." In developing how public choice can fill the need required for specificity about who gets how much, Havrilesky selectively surveys five presidential administrations to provide specific contexts for his recommended addition to the PBF arts and sciences.

More narrowly, but significantly, PBF as applied has "what" and "when" aspects. As for "what," several distinct if overlapping uses of PBF processes and products seem obvious. For example, PBF can relate to

- Program analysis, for example, for monitoring the current status and for designing future states of Program A.

- Financial analysis, for example, for determining whether debt management/cash flow policies are adequate to support some total mix of public goods and services.
- Economic analysis, for example, for attempting to manage the various types of "inflation" by fiscal policies and public spending.

As for the "when," to illustrate, Weidenbaum [2] highlights valuable insights about safeguards against worst coming to worst when timing the economic impact of public spending. He identifies four stages of the spending process:

- The sequence of events leading to, and including, legislative authorization of appropriations.
- The period during which contracts are placed.
- The complex processes of gearing up for production in private sectors of the economy.
- The completion of the processes leading to payments in private sectors of the economy.

In sum, Weidenbaum argues that government spending has variable impacts on private consumption and investment, depending upon the specific stages of the spending process. For example, public spending can have at least some impact almost as soon as the formal announcement is made.

Weidenbaum's analysis, however, rests on a crucial assumption—an underlying confidence in public decisions. If that confidence is lacking, less sanguine effects than Weidenbaum expects are probable. Hence, the pressure is really on for accuracy in economic analysis, as well as for the political will to be clearly expressed and acted on consistently.

Considering a second aspect of "when," the timing of government spending as a vehicle for economic stabilization still remains a central concern. Given the often substantial lead time between the decision to spend and the actual public outlays, real force gets marshaled behind a family of arguments against government attempts at stabilization by spending. These antispending arguments apply particularly where relatively full employment exists, where large number of employables are in the armed services, or where augmented public spending requires skills that are already in short supply. Timing is crucial under any conditions, however. Thus, public spending might come too late to keep the economy from "cooling down." More seriously, gearing up for public spending might be completed just as the economy somehow recovered, triggering a flood of private spending that had been deferred by economic warning signs. In such a case, increased public spending could "overheat" the economy and contribute to an inflationary spiral.

Clarity About Expenditures/Receipts

The rubber especially meets the road concerning the adequacy of the PBF arts and science when it comes to this bottom line: Who pays for public programs, and who profits from them? That issue is a politically volatile one nowadays: It always has been a tough issue, and no doubt it will remain so. Even if a broad-based consensus does support some program of public spending such as Social Security, it is not always clear who gets what at whose relative expense. The programs commonly are that complicated. Thus, some have argued that Social Security taxes are "regressive," that they "soak the poor." Others have argued that the taxes are "progressive" and, oppositely, "soak the rich."

Powerful motivators may underlay such ambiguity. It is easy to denigrate giving the impressions of simultaneously "soaking the rich" and "soaking the poor," but just such verbal "flexibility" may be necessary to preserve and perhaps enhance the "moving consensus" on which our political institutions often rest.

However, there are limits on even the strongest consensus. Perhaps the classical budgetary rule proposes: You cannot spend, not for long and certainly not indefinitely, more than you take in. Hence, the "balanced budget rule."

This rule seems reasonable but can be seriously counterproductive. For example, attempts to balance the public budget when the economy is faltering may only deepen the downswing. In fact, such false economies might paradoxically result in larger deficits (income minus spending) than policies less concerned with balanced budgets each year. Whatever the case, our once-deep national commitment expressed in the "full employment" legislation of 1946 in effect rejected the balanced budget rule. "No budget rule can be accepted," observers Colm and Wagner [3] prescribe "which is not compatible with a policy designed to support balanced economic expansion and stabilization."

What that means, however, is only imprecisely known, and the valid and reliable tools necessary for the required analysis are not all in-hand. At the very least, those sanguine days are gone forever when most persons in authority could support the simple "balanced budget rule" without serious reservations. The new age of working through and testing a budgetary rule and analytical techniques more congenial to "full employment" has only begun.

To be sure, and perhaps especially in recent times, many have come to place a low value on "full employment," however defined. For them, no sophisticated analytic tools are required. A meat cleaver will do the job for them.

All this is not to say that every issue is up in the air. In Chapter 20, for example, Jean Harris seeks to provide one approach to gaining a greater clarity about who pays for public programs and who profits from them. She introduces one relatively new approach to getting a firm handle on a small part of the issue in "Tax Expenditures, Concept and Oversight."

Harris's essay gives detailed attention to the conceptual twists and turns of various concepts of "tax expenditures," and reviews some of the associated history. Moreover, Harris also provides useful illustrations of the practical issues involved in making operational and concept of "tax expenditures."

Some Required Distinctions

One basic reason for shortfalls in applied economics and finance in PBF relates to the failure to make required distinctions. Here, we present two exemplars—one in outline form, and the other reinforced by a reprinted selection by Murray L. Weidenbaum.

A brief summary of one argument [4, pp. 1–28] reminds us of a crucial shortfall concerning distinctions, with special regard to two types of expenditures. The flavor of the argument is usefully sampled. As Bator [4] notes, merely "to add up all the money paid out each year by public agencies . . . is not a very revealing exercise." To do so would be to add the proverbial apples and oranges. Rather, Bator distinguishes two types of expenditures: "nonexhaustive" and "exhaustive." The former is spending that redistributes income or assets. In a direct sense, consequently, "nonexhaustive" spending does not absorb economic output. In contrast, such spending consists of "transfer payments" like unemployment compensation, old-age and retirement benefits, and so on. "Exhaustive" expenditures do absorb goods and services, oppositely. They are a measure of the public claims on resources that become unavailable for private consumption or investment.

The two types of spending raise different challenges to individual freedom, among numerous other implications for PBF. Thus, nonexhaustive spending requires a redistribution of income, with important implications for the individual freedom (however that is defined) of all parties. Assume that some citizens contribute more and others receive more than the average contribution. The former citizens might complain that their freedom has been restricted by the provision of unequal contributions, which was enacted only (they might argue) because of the effective lobbying of the officials in charge of the program. If the transfer payments have no "strings" attached to them, however, those individuals receiving more than they contributed may have their lives and freedom enhanced.

Individual freedom faces at least two other derivative challenges. The difficult decision, first, concerns the point at which the felt deprivation of the former people is so great as to require ceasing or postponing further need gratification of the latter people. There is no substantive rule for such a decision. Rather, our basic rule is procedural. When "enough" resistance is generated through our existing institutions and procedures, then the redistributing has tended to stop. To go further might endanger the "moving consensus" on which our relatively peaceful political life in part depends; and to stop short of "enough" resistance is to lose an opportunity to increase the commitment to their society of those who are net recipients of any transfers. In any case, second, both parties would have to develop controls to help assure the responsibility and responsiveness of the public officials monitoring transfer programs, a challenge that is always with us. Failure in this second challenge would negatively affect the individual freedom of all citizens, whatever their specific balances of transfer payments.

It requires no great insight to recognize that these two derivative challenges characterize today's times. History does not provide a standard solution for either case just illustrated, however. Perhaps that is the wisdom of our traditionally lesser concern with the kinds of decisions made. Rather, our concern is more with the processes used to make decisions and with the resulting consensus (or dissensus) about the decisions.

Exhaustive expenditures imply other and serious challenges for individual freedom. For example, failure to brake expenditures during an economic boom may contribute to inflation. This implies a broad challenge to individual freedom.

Bator [4] provides valuable data on the distribution of public spending of both kinds, and in various areas. These data should enlighten discussions of the impact on individual freedom of spending in the public sector. The sharp increase over time in nonexhaustive versus exhaustive expenditures, for example, has a significant place in any discussion about the growing "size" of our public budgets.

Murray L. Weidenbaum draws attention to a second major distinction that often is neglected in discussions about how to better target public resources. The burden of his contribution is clearly signaled in the title he chose for his essay—"Budget 'Uncontrollability' as an Obstacle to Improving the Allocation of Government Resources."

The dilemma should be obvious. The larger the uncontrollability, in brief, the shorter the leash on efforts to "rationally" allocate expenditures. Weidenbaum isolates controllable versus uncontrollable kinds of spending, associates them with specific agencies, and offers several suggestions for increasing the proportion of controllable expenditures. In effect, then, Weidenbaum at once acknowledges an "uncontrollable" zone while also seeking to detail how that zone can be reduced by human wit and will.

Another Place, A Familiar PBF Theme

The selections in Unit IV have a clear U.S. bias, and understandably so. But too much can be made of even the best things. Hence Chapter 22. It provides a bit of comparative perspective that shows how administrative and political contexts can be influenced by the locus in which they exist—this time a colossus-sized Asian nation-state. Huaping Luo and Robert T. Golembiewski review a common PBF theme as it gets worked on in a non-North

American setting. Luo was born on mainland China, and remains a citizen as he completes his graduate work. Golembiewski is a student of American public management who collaborated with Luo to extend the former's appreciation of PBF dynamics in the global setting.

Luo and Golembiewski detail important variations on a common theme in "Budget Deficits in China: Calculations, Causes, and Impacts." Readers will find familiar ground in the Chinese approach to problem solving via definition, whose convenience obviously does not respect national boundaries. At the same time, this selection introduces some new vocabulary to help describe a PBF system that has evolved in response to the specific national history and circumstances of a country half a world away.

REFERENCES

1. W. W. Heller, *Federal Expenditure Policy for Growth and Stability*, U.S. Government Printing Office, Washington, D.C. (1957).
2. M. L. Weidenbaum, The timing of the economic impact of government spending, *Natl. Tax J.*, *12*: 79–85 (1959).
3. G. Colm and P. Wagner, Some observations on the budget concept, *Rev. Econ. Stat.*, *65*(2): 122–126 (1963).
4. F. M. Bator, *The Question of Government Spending*, Harper and Brothers, New York, pp. 9–28 (1960).

19

The New Political Economy of Monetary Policy

Thomas Havrilesky

INTRODUCTION

Since the Treasury-Federal Reserve Accord of 1951 American monetary policy has pursued an ever-changing array of goals. At various times and in varying degrees it has been devoted to manipulating interest rates or exchange rates, to influencing the unemployment rate, and to controlling the rate of inflation. As a result, economists have had a rather difficult time discovering and verifying consistent patterns in the Federal Reserve's reactions to the state of the economy. For example, in the late 1960s and late 1970s, the monetary authority seemed most concerned with suppressing increases in interest rates, for short intervals in the mid 1970s and early 1980s inflation was Federal Reserve enemy number one, and in the mid 1980s the international value of the dollar became the central bank's bugaboo.

Economists have grown increasingly aware that monetary policy responds systematically to signals from the public and private sectors regarding a wide array of variables [1]. Therefore, they are not likely to be satisfied with the explanation that shifting Federal Reserve policy reactions are merely a random walk or reflect technical changes in its operating procedures.

In the past decade there have been several notable attempts to link Federal Reserve reactions (to unemployment and inflation) to a measurable political phenomenon—the proximity of elections. The original Nordhaus–Macrae theory of the political business cycle, PBC, claimed that the monetary authority tried to reduce unemployment prior to Presidential elections and fought inflation afterward [2]. Aside from being inconsonant with the assumption of forward-looking agent behavior, this predicted pattern has often been shown to be inconsistent with the facts.

In contrast to the original, the more recent theory of the political business cycle [e.g., 3] claims that election outcomes themselves constitute proper monetary surprises that necessarily change the expectations of market participants and, therefore, provoke cyclical swings. The new PBC theory has two shortcomings. First, it is rather narrow in its institutional focus, inasmuch as it depends on multiple political parties espousing, in regularly

Source: Public Budgeting and Financial Management, vol. 2, no. 3 (1990), pp. 431–451.

scheduled elections, significantly different policy objectives for only two variables, unemployment and inflation. Second, like the original PBC theory, it does not purport to explain interelection monetary surprises.

What is needed is a political economic theory of monetary policy that explains not only Federal Reserve behavior between elections but also its continual shifting across a wide array of monetary policy objectives. Ideally, such a theory would be complementary to but broader than the theories of the political business cycle, which focus only on unemployment and inflation and only around election periods.

A PUBLIC CHOICE THEORY OF MONETARY POLICY

I propose a public choice theory of monetary policy. In this theory monetary policy surprises are reactions to the electorally adverse consequences of income redistributions. Because promises to redistribute income have marked the advent of every presidential administration in the past 25 years and because monetary surprises are enacted between elections, when delivering on these promises is seen as having adverse electoral impacts on interest rates, exchange rates, effective tax rates, exports, import-sensitive output, unemployment, or productivity growth, an electoral pattern has emerged. The particulars of each promised redistribution—the groups favored, the variables and sectors subsequently impacted, and the related monetary surprises—depend on demographic considerations and the distribution of voting rights within the distribution of income as well as on existing financial regulatory and tax structures. Moreover, since these (income and voting rights) distributions and structures change over time, promised redistributions, the sectors and variables subsequently burdened by them, and related monetary surprises will also change over time. Therefore, economists should expect monetary policy reactions to the state of the economy to be neither countercyclical, stable, election-focused, nor limited to a few variables.[1] Instead, they should expect the Federal Reserve, because of its ever-shifting responses to conflicting sectoral pressures, to inject episodically procyclical swings to the business cycle.

This public choice theory of monetary policy is consistent with voter rationality. No matter how forward-looking voters are they will be imperfectly informed about future tax and financial regulatory environments. Therefore, when redistributive promises are made voters can anticipate neither the timing, magnitude, nor location of the subsequent sectoral impacts nor the timing and magnitude of the related future monetary surprises; neither can they easily filter credible signals for surprises from the often subtle, but continual, barrage of political and private pressures on monetary policymakers [1].

Support for this theory of the political economy of monetary policy is found in an examination of joint redistributive and monetary activism across the five presidential administrations from Lyndon Johnson's to George Bush's. Let us examine the historical record.

REDISTRIBUTIVE POLICY AND MONETARY POLICY ACROSS FIVE PRESIDENTIAL ADMINISTRATIONS

Lyndon Johnson

Explicit and implicit redistributive promises are the essence of every presidential campaign's economic platform. Such promises are typically motivated by demographic changes and changes in the distribution of voting rights within the distribution of income. In his 1964 State of the Union Address Lyndon Johnson pledged the highest level of federal support in history for health, education, and welfare. In so doing he was, of course, cognizant of the increased voting power and participation of lower income minorities, precipitated by the 1962 Supreme Court one-man one-vote decision and subsequent voting rights legislation. In the absence of a significant tax increase, Johnson's redistributive program, combined with Vietnam War expenditures, boosted the deficit from $8.6 billion in 1967 to $25.2 billion in 1968. As a consequence, interest rates rose.

Since the Glass–Steagall Act of 1933 the financial regulatory structure (e.g., deposit insurance and barriers to geographic, product-line, and price competition) has been deployed to protect the nation's depository institutions, particularly the smaller ones. Protected savings and loan associations financed a good portion of the demographically motivated housing boom of the 1950s and early 1960s. The political clout of these institutions and their clientele in the home construction industry became apparent when rising interest rates caused housing starts to fall from 1.47 million in 1965 to 1.17 million in 1966. The Federal Reserve responded by imposing ceilings on deposit interest rates that were lower for commercial banks than for S&L's. Ceilings on S&L deposit rates were difficult for the Federal Home Loan Bank Board to raise because doing so would have eroded S&L earnings. Thereafter, every time that market rates of interest rose above these ceilings, S&L's lost deposits and the Fed came under tremendous pressure from the home construction and home financing industries to lower interest rates. From the late 1960s until the late 1970s the political support of potential home buyers and these industries was far more important than that of creditor groups who favored higher rates.[2] It was in this decade that former Federal Reserve Governor Sherman Maisel called attention to the fact that trade-offs between the benefits and burdens visited on interest groups were the core of Federal Reserve policymaking [4]. Lyndon Johnson's politically savvy signals to the Fed to keep interest rates down were a legendary reflection of those trade-offs [5,6]. The money growth explosions of 1967 and 1968, shown in Fig. 1, were the result.

Richard Nixon

The Nixon campaign embraced the task of halting the inflation ignited by LBJ's monetary surprises, but refused to modify the warfare welfare state. The two goals were quickly to prove irreconcilable. In fact, in 1968, while pledging a war on inflation, Richard Nixon promised both a defense buildup and a cost-of-living Social Security adjustment. Once elected, his administration, attuned to demographic changes, that is, the growing percentage of older voters, became embroiled in an outbidding game with the Democrats over Social Security entitlements that continued right up to the 1972 election.

Nixon's anti-inflationary monetary policy thrust interest rates upward and produced dramatic deposit losses for S&L's in 1969 and 1970. By 1970 in the face of these impacts and the recession brought about by his anti-inflationary militance, Nixon, announcing that he was a Keynesian, gave up on his goal of an annually balanced budget and then asked for and received a rapid spurt in money growth, which peaked in 1971. In 1971, in an attempt to stifle the inflation that was sure to result, Nixon imposed price and wage controls. Ironically, by 1972 this set off pressures for even more rapid money growth, as evidenced in Fig. 1.

The absence of controls on interest rates was viewed as evidence that banks were not sharing the burden of Nixon's redistributive program. Many felt that the burden was being borne disproportionately by consumers and wage earners. As a result, extraordinary pressure was brought on the Federal Reserve to keep interest rates from rising above the levels prevailing at the time controls were imposed. This explains the money supply growth of 1972. Nixon, like LBJ, bowed out under a cloud of rising inflation and looming recession.

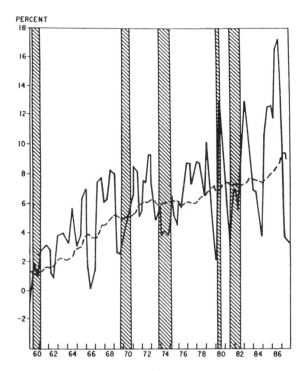

PERCENT

Figure 1 Rates of change of money stock (M1): (1) two-quarter rate of change and (2) 20-quarter rate of change; data prior to first quarter '64 are M1 on the old basis. Shaded areas represent periods of business recessions. (*Source*: Federal Reserve Bank of St. Louis.)

Jimmy Carter

The Carter Administration adhered faithfully to the redistributive promises that worked for LBJ in the mid 1960s but failed to perceive fully the electoral consequences of demographic changes and inflation's effect on the nation's financial regulatory and tax structures. As under the Johnson Administration, growth in expenditures was not impeded by calls for tax hikes or program cutbacks. The deficit rose from $53.2 billion in 1977 to $59.8 billion in 1978 and produced considerable pressure on interest rates. Spokespersons were adamant that interest rates not be permitted to rise and, in the jargon of the time, "abort the recovery." Therefore, as money growth soared in 1977 and 1978 there was palpable a lack of concern with inflationary pressures and a good deal of "cost push" scapegoating.

Because of bracket creep, the resulting rise in tax revenue financed a sizeable share of the Carter regime's expenditures. Despite the tax rate cut of 1975 and 1978, revenue from inflation had become the accepted way of dealing with fiscal imbalance. By neglecting to adjust fully marginal income tax rates while raising regressive Social Security levels, the Carter Administration alienated lower and middle income wage earners. In 1967 24.1% of taxpayers faced a marginal tax rate of 21% or higher. By 1979 this figure had risen to 60.2%. The taxpayers' revolts of the late 1970s signaled that it was no longer politically optimal to use inflation to raise revenue.

At the same time as the taxpayers' revolts were occurring, inflation was propelling financial deregulation. Under the influence of sustained high inflation, financial innovations, such as money market mutual funds, continually siphoned funds from depositary institutions and deprived their clientele of financing. Continued inflation would force a dismantling of the interest rate ceilings that had protected depository institutions and provided subsidized financing to home buyers.

However, the pivotal element in financial deregulation may have been demographic. The baby boom bulge of first-time home buyers, who were interest-rate-sensitive debtors, had subsided. The political clout of the home construction and home financing industries had ebbed. A growing demographic cohort was flexing its political muscle—the senior citizens. As creditors, seniors were delighted with high interest rates.

Demographics, deregulation, and the taxpayers' revolt shifted the political balance of power. No longer would it be politically advisable to suppress interest rate increases with inflationary monetary surprises. The Carter White House failed to realize this.

Following the second oil price shock of 1979, the Federal Reserve reined in money growth over the strenuous objections of the Carter team. In 1980 the Oval Office reasserted itself in a tragic replay of Nixon's 1972 game plan. Controls, on credit instead of prices, were imposed while money growth again soared, as seen in Fig. 1. Carter, like Johnson and Nixon, exited under the stigma of rising inflation and recession.

Ronald Reagan

The burgeoning popular demand for tax cuts combined with a growing tolerance of higher interest rates provided the essential common ground for the right-of-center Reagan coalition. The Reagan revolution sought support from middle-class wage earners, a backing it received in exchange for its *status quo ante* tax cut redistribution. However, unlike the Nixon experience, because of financial deregulation and the demographic shift in the debtor/creditor balance of power, the Reagan Administration could afford to be far more earnest in its embrace of the old-time religion of monetary moderation. Nevertheless, as with the Johnson, Nixon, and Carter Administrations before it, the Reagan regime would also find that politically favorable redistributions were ultimately irreconcilable with monetary moderation.

In 1981 a survey of informed opinion would have shown that virtually everyone believed that we would either have to grow our way out of the deficits caused by the Kemp–Roth tax cuts or cut federal expenditures or else experience crowding out in interest-sensitive sectors of the economy. No one foresaw that after 1982 changes in the financial regulatory and tax structures would shift the burden of the Reagan redistribution in an unexpected direction.

As deficits averaged about 5% of GNP and real interest rates were permitted to rise in the deregulated financial environment, foreign saving flows proved responsive. The repeal of the withholding tax on interest paid to foreigners, part of the Reagan tax reform package, stimulated the flow of funds from abroad. This helped drive the value of the dollar upward against foreign currencies and led to crowding out, not in interest-sensitive sectors, but in export-oriented and import-sensitive sectors.

In 1985 and 1986, because of mounting sectoral protests associated with the trade deficit, Farm Aid, and protectionist movements, the Reagan Administration, like each of its predecessors in the previous 20 years, abandoned its sound money catechism. Supply-side appointees inundated the Federal Reserve Board, intervention in international currency markets became the rule instead of the exception, and, as seen in Fig. 1, money growth exploded.

By 1987 interest rates had to rise in order to sustain the flow of foreign saving at the resulting falling value of the dollar and the higher expected rate of inflation. The stock market could not easily digest these interest-rate fundamentals. In 1988 the Reagan regime bowed out under the same penumbra of rising inflation that haunted its predecessors over the previous quarter century. Monetary surprise and inflation, once again, were symptoms of an administration's retreat from distributive.

George Bush

The relationship between the Federal Reserve and the Bush Administration reveals a strengthening of episodic pressures on the Fed for monetary ease whenever it becomes politically expedient for the Administration to retreat from distributive conflict. George Bush's career has been marked by strong personal, but minimal ideological, loyalties and a strong desire to be liked without espousing firm policy postures. His "a little something for everyone" approach to government seems to derive from the latter characteristic [7–9]. This approach strongly suggests that Bush will not hesitate to pressure the Fed whenever sectoral flak mounts. Federal Reserve officials play into the Administration's hands by publicly continuing to allow administrations to bequeath upon them "the divine right of interest rate selection." Whenever current Fed officials, in their rhetoric, announce that interest rates or exchange rates are "too high" or "too low," they set the stage for future Administration pressures on monetary policy. These pronouncements produce the widespread expectation that the Fed will be able to raise interest rates whenever economic growth or the deficit increases and to lower interest rates whenever economic growth or the deficit declines. Such expectations give the Administration useful leverage to press for lower interest rates whenever it is politically necessary, for example, whenever symbolic progress is made in reducing the budget deficit. The Administration unabashedly applied this leverage in the late summer of 1989. Given these proclivities, the anti-inflationary ardor of Fed Chairman Alan Greenspan notwithstanding, increased politicization of monetary policy under the Bush Administration can be expected to heighten the volatility of money supply growth.

CONCLUDING COMMENT

Between 1966 and 1979 the financing of politically favorable redistributions in favor of lower income groups placed politically unacceptable (high interest rate) burdens on debtor/first-time home owners, on the home construction and financing industries, and on their protective edifice of financial regulations. Monetary surprises and subsequent inflation simply "bought time" for politicians in their retreat from distributional conflict. Unfortunately for Jimmy Carter, sustained inflation resulted in bracket creep, which placed a politically unacceptable burden on middle-income taxpayers. Inflation also destroyed the financial regulatory edifice that was protective of debtor/first-time homeowners just as the political balance of power was tilting away from them and in favor of creditor/senior citizens. The Reagan revolution capitalized on the resulting desire for *status quo ante* tax cuts and tolerance of higher interest rates. However, when confronted with sectoral dissonance Reagan, like his predecessors, reverted to monetary ease. There is no reason to believe that George Bush will break with this pattern.

The political and economic record of the past 25 years supports the now widespread awareness that political decisions have macroeconomic antecedents and macroeconomic consequences. More particularly, the historical record reviewed here suggests that politically motivated redistributions will later have adverse electoral consequences that can be mitigated by inflationary monetary surprises, which help propel cyclical swings in economic activity. To build support for this new theory of the political economy of monetary policy requires the development of operational measures of redistributive promises, their demographic/electoral antecedents, and their effects on monetary policy.

There exists, of course, a comprehensive menu of fiscal and monetary reforms, any one of which would short circuit this inflationary mechanism. Fiscal reforms would, in general, forge stricter controls on spending, taxing, and the ability of special interests to extract benefits from government. Monetary reforms, such as the gold standard, a Friedman money supply growth rule, etc., would, in general, uncouple the management of the nation's money supply from (the consequences of) political decisions to spend, tax, and redistribute to special interests.

One reason that little headway has been made in implementing such reforms is that redistributive promises get politicians elected while monetary surprises allow them to retreat from the ensuing redistributional conflict. Another reason is that if effective fiscal and/or monetary reforms were implemented, redistributional conflict would probably lead to direct confrontation over distributive issues. Direct confrontations would probably be less acceptable than the pattern of episodic inflationary spirals followed by short intervals of monetary restraint that is facilitated by present institutional arrangements [10]. Moreover, with or without reforms, a genuine reduction in redistributional conflict would require either a social consensus on implementing a more equitable distribution of income or a shift in societal values away from the traditional obsession with material gain (see [11] for further suggestions on how redistributive pressures can be abated). As long as so many of our institutions and organizations legitimate themselves almost exclusively by pointing to our material abundance while, at the same time, we deny sizable segments of our population equal access to that abundance, distributional conflict is inevitable. Under current monetary and fiscal institutional arrangements, inflation is simply a reflection of that conflict.

BIBLIOGRAPHY

Cukierman, Alex, "Central Bank Behavior and Credibility: Some Recent Theoretical Developments," *Review* (Federal Reserve Bank of St. Louis, May, 1986).

Fellner, William, Kenneth W. Clarkson and John H. Moore. "Correcting Taxes for Inflation," Washington DC: American Enterprise Institute for Public Policy Research, 1975.

Gettleman, Marvin E., *The Great Society Reader*. Random House; New York, 1967.

Goldman, Eric F., *The Tragedy of Lyndon Johnson*. New York: Alfred A. Knopf, 1969.

Havrilesky, Thomas, "A Partisanship Theory of Monetary and Fiscal Policy Regimes," *Journal of Money Credit and Banking* (August, 1987).

Havrilesky, Thomas, "The Influence of the Federal Advisory Council on Monetary Policy," *Journal of Money, Credit and Banking* (1990).

Haywood, Charles F. and Charles M. Linke. *The Regulation of Deposit Interest Rates*, A Study Prepared for the Association of Reserve City Bankers, 1968.

Hetzel, Robert L. "The Political Economy of Monetary Policy," in Thomas Mayer, ed., *The Political Economy of American Monetary Policy*. New York: Cambridge Press, 1990.

Kane, Edward J. "Politicians against the Prime—The Dual Rate Fiasco," *The Bankers Magazine*, (Spring, 1974) 88–95.

Keech, William, "Politics and Macroeconomic Policy Optimization," *American Journal of Political Science* (May, 1980).

Zarefsky, David, *President Johnson's War on Poverty*. Tuscaloosa, Ala.: The University of Alabama Press, 1986.

NOTES

I am grateful to Woo Sik Jung for helpful comments.

1. Of course, to the extent that one could model the distribution of voting rights within the distribution of earned income, predict the resulting redistribution of income, and predict the impact of

that redistribution on interest rates, exchange rates, tax rates, unemployment, etc., one could theoretically specify the monetary policy reaction function.

2. The presence of interest rate arguments in empirical monetary policy reaction functions estimated for the 1964–1980 period as well as the dominance of interest rate targeting over the same timespan may be explained by this demographic–political fact.

REFERENCES

1. T. Havrilesky, "Monetary Policy Signaling from the Administration to the Federal Reserve," *Journal of Money, Credit and Banking*, February (1988).
2. W. Nordhaus, "The Political Business Cycle," *Review of Economic Studies*, April (1975).
3. A. Alesina and J. Sachs, "Political Parties and the Business Cycle in the United States, 1948–1984," *Journal of Money, Credit and Banking*, February (1988).
4. S. J. Maisel, *Managing the Dollar*, W. W. Norton, New York (1973).
5. J. T. Woolley, *Monetary Politics: The Federal Reserve and the Politics of Monetary Policy*, Cambridge University Press, New York (1984).
6. W. Greider, *Secrets of the Temple*, Simon and Schuster, New York (1988).
7. G. Sheehy, *Character: America's Search for Leadership*, William Morrow, New York (1988).
8. G. Wills, "The Ultimate Loyalist," *Time*, August 22 (1988).
9. J. D. Barber, "George Bush: In Search of Mission," *New York Times*, January 19 (1989).
10. T. Havrilesky, "Monetary Activism as Addiction," *Challenge*, May/June (1989).
11. T. Havrilesky, "A Compassionate Solution to Distributional Conflict," *Challenge*, March/April (1989).

20

Tax Expenditures: Concept and Oversight

Jean Harris
The Pennsylvania State University—Harrisburg, Middletown, Pennsylvania

INTRODUCTION

Billions of dollars of indirect spending occur each year via tax provisions. Concealed in tax code jargon and excluded from systematic oversight, indirect spending often escapes public scrutiny.

In 1967, Stanley Surrey, Assistant Secretary for Tax Policy in the U.S. Treasury Department, coined the term "tax expenditures" to describe tax provisions that are similar to direct outlays [1].

> The term "tax expenditures" refers to the fact that many of the provisions of the U.S. tax laws are intended, not as necessary structural parts of a normative tax, but rather as tax incentives or hardship relief provisions. These provisions are thus really spending measures [2, pp. 123–124].

The term *normative tax* refers to a set of norms for conceptualizing the design of a model tax from a theoretical perspective. Exceptions to the normative tax create tax expenditures. Other terms used to describe the tax expenditure concept are backdoor spending, hidden entitlements, hidden spending, off-budget spending, silent spending, tax incentive, tax preference, and tax subsidy.

A tax credit for energy conservation is an example of a tax expenditure. Incentives to encourage energy conservation could be structured as a direct expenditure, such as a grant, or as a tax expenditure, such as an energy credit. The grant represents an allocation of benefits from current resources. In contrast, the tax expenditure represents an allocation of benefits financed by foregoing the receipt of future resources.

Although similar economic effects result from the distribution of benefits via direct expenditures and via tax expenditures, control processes are dissimilar. Direct expenditures are subject to basic controls designed to achieve accountability for resources. These basic controls include institutionalized competition for resources, projection of the amount of spending, periodic authorization of spending, and monitoring of spending. The monitoring of spending entails collection of information about expenditures, public distribution of this information in financial reports, and comprehensive examination of efficiency and/or effectiveness of selected expenditures through performance audits. Each of the basic control procedure appears stronger for direct expenditures than for tax expenditures. However, Zelinsky [3] does argue that tax expenditures are subject to more intense political competition than are direct expenditures.

Increasing either tax expenditures or direct expenditures will consume resources. Direct expenditures reduce the stock of resources by increasing disbursements or present outflows. In contrast, tax expenditures reduce the flow of public resources by reducing collections or future inflows. Direct expenditures and tax expenditures when adopted share two attributes: (1) Each provides benefits to recipients and (2) each reduces the pool of public resources. It is these two attributes that support the characterization of a tax expenditure as a form of spending equivalent to a direct expenditure. Although tax expenditures are sometimes described as a form of silent spending, this description is a misnomer because what is silent is not the spending per se but records of the transaction in the traditional financial control system.

From an accounting perspective, a tax expenditure represents two separate constructive transactions between taxpayer and governmental entity that are offset and then reported as one net transaction. The first transaction is collection of a tax, and the second transaction is disbursement of a benefit via tax provision. Because the parties to both transactions are the same, collection and disbursement are offset. The result is one transaction between taxpayer and governmental entity, representing receipt of a net amount of revenue. If two separate transactions were reported, distinct records of collection and disbursement would exist. Instead, recording the net transaction conceals the amount of tax imposed and the amount of benefit distributed. Accordingly, it impairs the exercise of control over collections and over disbursements, and hampers the evaluation of tax and budget policies. Surrey and McDaniel [2] observe, "It is being increasingly recognized that unless attention is paid to tax expenditures, a country does not have either its tax policy or its budget policy under full control (p. 124).

Tax expenditure take many forms. McDaniel [4] provides a comprehensive list of the means of structuring tax expenditures. These include departures from:

1. A normative tax base such as exclusions, exemptions, deductions, and credits
2. Normal rate structures such as the granting of preferential rates on capital gains
3. Rules defining taxable units such as the rule that corporations and their shareholders are separate entities
4. Normal accounting period rules such as the authorization of accelerated depreciation
5. Normal international tax rules such as exclusion of income earned abroad

Tax expenditure controls lack the simplicity of straightforward controls over direct expenditures because offsetting violates the most basic principle of financial control, which is the maintenance of separate records of collection and disbursement. By converting two separate transactions into one net transaction, information is lost and straightforward controls are disabled. Thus using the revenue system to affect spending necessitates new controls because the alternative is no control.

This chapter is about the kinds of control procedures that are appropriate for a tax expenditure control system. Acceptance of the tax expenditure concept, identification of tax expenditure provisions, and the estimation of tax expenditure costs are necessary but not sufficient conditions for a control system. It is fundamental for a control system to generate information that is useful in evaluating tax expenditures.

OVERSIGHT CONSIDERATIONS

Tax expenditure control is grounded in the proposition that a tax expenditure is a form of spending that transfers significant benefit among different groups of stakeholders. If this proposition is accepted, the need to control tax expenditures is apparent, but the means for controlling tax expenditures are elusive.

By design, tax expenditures are structured as entitlements and therefore tend to be difficult to capture with pretransaction controls such as budgets and authorizations. The application of posttransaction controls is also challenging. Some governmental entities estimate and report tax expenditure costs, but these estimates lack precision. They are based on certain assumptions about taxpayer behavior that may not be valid. The estimates cannot be verified against a referent in the sense that projections of direct spending subsequently can be compared to actual spending. For the governments that do estimate and report tax expenditure costs, the systematic monitoring of tax expenditures is uncommon, and examination of the efficiency and/or effectiveness of tax expenditures is rare. Because the monitoring of tax expenditures is sporadic, excessive costs may be incurred for years before concerns about control arise. Several characteristics of tax expenditures intensify the need for financial control.

Magnitude and Growth [5–7]

The magnitude of federal tax expenditures is substantial, and the rate of increase in total tax expenditures is steady. For the U.S. Income Tax total estimated tax expenditures for 1995 is $453 billion [6]. This is almost as much as direct outlays for defense and interest combined and is more than double the budget deficit. The estimated cost for tax expenditures related to the U.S. Income Tax for the 5-year period 1995–1999 is $2.5 trillion [6]. These tax expenditures are slightly over 60% of the total income tax [7].

In real terms, tax expenditures have increased about 4% annually from 1974 to 1993 [5]. The trend of increasing tax expenditures was reversed with passage of the Tax Reform Act of 1986. However, growth in tax expenditure has resumed; in constant dollars tax expenditures are expected to increase almost 18% from 1993 to 1999 [6]. This increase in tax expenditures will occur over a period when discretionary spending is expected to decline by 13% in constant dollars [6].

Tax expenditures tend to be just as pervasive in state and local tax systems as in the federal tax system. It is common for state and local tax expenditures to represent 50% or more of revenue. Clearly tax expenditures are a source of major source resource outflows. Some tax expenditures are effective. Other tax expenditures are expensive failures. Almost no tax expenditures are subject to the same scrutiny that is applied to direct expenditures.

Costs Ignored

Tax expenditures are often advocated as a means of introducing individual choice and administrative efficiency. Decision making is decentralized. Each taxpayer decides whether to pursue beneficial behavior, and benefits are promptly disbursed through a reduction in tax liability. The cost of creating or expanding administrative agencies to administer a direct expenditure programs is avoided. But the tax expenditure solution is not without costs [8]. Although real, the costs of using tax expenditures may not be obvious.

Market Distortion

In 1995, $65 billion of tax expenditures will go to corporations [6]. A tax expenditure, such as accelerated cost recovery, can distort decisions to the point that investors are motivated more by tax benefit than by return from operations. Such policies not only consume public resources, but can shift the flow of private investment away from other activities [9]. Historically tax incentives have had a substantial effect on investment in real estate, natural resources, insurance, and financial institutions.

Impaired Analyses of Tax and Budget Policies

The failure to record separately collections and disbursements distorts the analyses of both tax and budget policies. Tax liability is reduced by a spending offset and thus net tax liability does not provide a true measure of tax. Additionally, budgets exclude indirect tax expenditures and thus do not provide a true measure of total spending.

The extent to which the analysis of tax policy is distorted by tax expenditures depends on one's concept of tax liability. If one adopts a net obligation concept, then tax liability is the amount of normative tax adjusted for tax expenditures [10]. From this perspective, tax expenditures may alter the net obligations of taxpayers. If one accepts that tax expenditures are a form of spending and adopts the concept of tax liability as gross obligation before adjustment for tax expenditures [11], tax equity is not affected by tax expenditures, but the equity of resource distributions may be affected significantly.

Concealment of Windfall Benefits

When tax expenditures are offered as incentives to alter behavior, many taxpayers receive a windfall benefit for actions they would have taken in the absence of an incentive. For example, if two-thirds of the taxpayers claiming an energy credit would have taken action to conserve energy without a tax incentive, the incentive motivated one-third of the beneficiaries and the remaining two-thirds of the beneficiaries received a windfall benefit. Individual Retirement Accounts (IRAs) provide a classic example of windfall benefits. As originally enacted, these provisions motivated many beneficiaries simply to switch savings from an account providing no tax benefit to an account that provided tax benefit.

Risks of Administration

The primary function of a tax agency is to collect revenue; it is not to administer operational programs. Shifting the administration of operational programs to a tax agency may increase tax compliance costs for taxpayers, burden the agencies with enforcement challenges that consume its resources, and contribute to ineffective program administration [12]. Each new tax expenditure increases the rules to which taxpayers are subject. Evaluating the application of those rules, will increase compliance costs for many taxpayers. Alternatively, the tax agency must enforce more rules. For it, the enforcement burden, if assumed, may necessitate shifting resources from other functions. If the enforcement burden is not assumed, extensive fraud and corruption within the program may be overlooked.

The effectiveness of having a tax agency administer operational programs, such as child care, energy conservation, and industrial development, is open to question. Personnel in a tax agency may be unaware of program goals and unable to evaluate program efficiency and/or effectiveness. Public policy objectives, such as avoiding the support of discriminatory activities, may be ignored. Although the administrative consequences are not measurable with any degree of precision, the long-term costs of having a tax agency administer operational programs may be substantial.

Inequities in the Distribution of Benefits and Extraction of Cost Savings

Tax expenditures tend to benefit middle and upper income taxpayers. The three largest tax expenditures in the U.S. Income Tax are (1) the exclusion from income of pension plan contributions including IRAs and Keogh plans, (2) the exclusion from income of employer-paid medical insurance and care, and (3) the deductibility of mortgage interest on owner-occupied homes. For 1996 the estimated costs of these tax expenditures respectively are $70 billion, $67 billion, and $54 billion [13]. In 1994, two-thirds of the benefits from the deductibility of home mortgage interest went to taxpayers with income in excess of $75,000 [6]. Because the income tax is progressive, higher income tax payers receive more benefit from a tax expenditure than lower income taxpayers. For example, in 1994 the average benefit of the deductibility of home mortgage interest for taxpayers earning $20,000 to $30,000 was $116. However, for taxpayers earning $200,000 or more the average benefit from the same provision was $5,968.

From a budget perspective, tax expenditures often are not viewed as spending. In periods of fiscal crisis there is a tendency to restrict direct expenditure, but to ignore tax expenditures [14]. Thus the burden of fiscal crises and deficit reduction fall disproportionately on stakeholders who benefit from direct expenditures.

THEORIES OF TAX EXPENDITURE USE AND REPORTING

Most of the tax expenditure literature either examines the concept of tax expenditures or applies the concept to evaluate specific tax expenditures. Two issues that have received much less attention are conditions that motivate (1) the use of expenditures and (2) the adoption of tax expenditure controls.

Tax Expenditures

Wildavsky [15] describes the tax expenditure mechanism as an "end run" around normal allocation procedures, and contends that its use does not result from an ignorance of economics. Senator Russell Long, in referring to tax expenditures, stated, "I have never been confused about it. I've always known that what we were doing was giving government money away" [16, p. 716]. Political scientists offer several explanations concerning the administration of programs by a tax agency and about the motivations for tax expenditure reporting.

Hansen [17] constructs a general theory to explain tax expenditure spending. The core of this theory posits that tax expenditures are encouraged by two significant advantages: (1) Benefits will be highly visible to beneficiaries but virtually invisible to nonbeneficiaries, and (2) costs will be obscured both for beneficiaries and for nonbeneficiaries.

King [18], Schick [19], and Steinmo [20] contribute to a social benefit theory by pointing to the desirability of using tax expenditures for intrusion into the private sector. Social benefit theory posits that mature democratic governments assume the primary role of redistributing income and purchasing services rather than providing services [19]. Schick [19] argues that this changed role has been accompanied by a shift from administrative budgeting, designed to exercise control over cash receipts and disbursements, to transfer budgeting. In the case of transfer budgeting, public and private sector boundaries are blurred; the primary purpose is to influence beneficiary behavior. Accordingly, tax expenditures are beneficial mechanisms because they enable government to influence private sector behaviors by supporting private-sector endeavors in a nonintrusive manner. Thus, tax expenditures are viewed as serving a unique function rather than merely substituting for direct expenditures.

King [18], Schick [19], and Steinmo [20] recognize the tendencies for democratic governments to transfer benefits from the public sector to the private sector through tax expenditures, and to finance traditional public services through direct expenditures. King [18] grouped U.S. tax and direct expenditures into 18 categories in relationship to their function with reference to budget. He found weak reliance on tax expenditures in military categories, moderate reliance in social welfare and product promotion categories, and strong reliance in intergovernmental fiscal assistance categories. Thus, tax expenditures seem to be more adaptable to transfer functions rather than to service functions.

Havemann [21] and Surrey and McDaniel [2] suggest an individual political benefit theory. Independent of the possible provision of social benefit, tax expenditures may enhance the political power of tax committee members. Operational issues become tax issues when drafted as tax expenditures [22]. Thus, tax committee members may exercise power over operational programs and appropriations by advocating tax expenditures [2,21]. This expansion of power fosters the ability of those who make tax policy to garner political contributions from new stakeholders.

Tax Expenditure Reporting

Tax expenditures are a target of control because tax expenditures are at the core of distributive policies concerning "who gets what." Havemann [21] documents, without exploring, the intensely partisan nature of national debate about reporting tax expenditures at the national level. In this debate, Democrats strongly favored reporting and Republicans strongly opposed to it. Possible explanations for the partisan nature of debate include: (1) Republicans are ideologically drawn to tax expenditures as a way of operating government without creating large administrative agencies; (2) tax expenditures for business development are commonly associated with the Republican agenda; and (3) the Republican spending agenda tend toward spending in the form of tax expenditures. Thus Republicans may be less supportive of tax expenditure disclosure and control.

Schick's analysis [19] lays the foundation for an explanation of motivations for tax expenditures reporting that is dependent on budgetary stress caused by fully utilizing revenue capacity. Schick [19] contend that budgetary stress which motivates efforts to reduce the growth in direct spending also leads to efforts to reduce indirect spending. He views the reporting of tax expenditure information as a response to budgetary stress and part of an effort to reduce indirect expenditures. Benker [10] also views reporting as a means of increasing options in times of fiscal need. She writes that reporting can "provide lawmakers with budget flexibility during economic downturns" [10, p. 25]. Both Benker [10] and Schick [19] cite high budgetary stress as a motivation for tax expenditure reporting. However, they attribute this stress to different sources. Schick [19] views this stress as a result of excessive growth in transfer spending, whereas Benker [10] suggests that this stress develops from poor economic conditions.

From an accountability perspective, neither direct expenditure control nor tax expenditure control is synonymous with expenditure reduction. Expenditure control provides relevant and reliable cost-related information to draw on for planning, for implementing, and for monitoring resource allocations. Such information is useful because it contributes to the reduction of uncertainty in decision making. However, depending upon the circumstances and issues, reducing costs may or may not be a priority concern for policymakers.

TAX EXPENDITURE REPORTING

Tax expenditure reports disclose estimates of the costs of various tax expenditure provisions. Reporting is the most basic control over tax expenditures because it is essential for other, potentially stronger controls to function.

Tax expenditure reporting evolves from the tax expenditure concept. The central aspect of the tax expenditure concept is that tax expenditures represent an allocation of benefit. Vickery [23] discussed the idea that a reduction in taxable income constituted a subsidy to taxpayers. McKenna [24] wrote a seminal paper about disclosing the opportunity cost involved in granting tax preferences. Wolfman noted that "tax support of science resembles a direct federal expenditure" [25, p. 171].

Surrey was the most influential person in gaining acceptance for the tax expenditure concept among policy makers in the U.S. and abroad. He led the academic debate concerning the validity of the tax expenditure concept [26–30] and authored or co-authored the three most comprehensive books on the subject of tax expenditures [31–33]. Griswold [34] lists a complete bibliography of Surrey's works. Among Surrey's achievements are the introduction in 1967 of the tax expenditure concept at the U.S. Treasury Department [1], overseeing research that produced in 1968 the first tax expenditure report for the U.S. [1,35], and promoting the adoption in 1974 of a requirement to publish estimates of tax expenditure costs in the annual budget of the U.S. [35].

Reporting Objectives

The primary objective of tax expenditure reporting is to facilitate tax expenditure control. Reporting contributes to the achievement of control in a number of ways [10]. Reporting promotes acceptance of the tax expenditure concept. Such acceptance is at the core of initiating tax expenditure controls. Additionally, reporting promotes understanding of a tax system. The systematic analysis of tax provisions results in a cataloging of tax expenditure provisions that prompts consideration of the normative nature of a tax and or original legislative intent. Reporting also provides helpful information for making decisions when a change in fiscal circumstances merits rapid adjustment

The literature on tax expenditure reporting supports the conclusion that reporting serves many functions relating to the evaluation of public policies in general and tax policies in particular. Furthermore, utility is not limited to a single objective. Reporting provides information that is relevant to (1) evaluating proposed and existing tax provisions in terms of revenue foregoing, and (2) evaluating direct and indirect tax expenditures as alternative means of financing. The availability of information alone does not result in the achievement of effective control. Effective control requires deliberate consideration and the taking of action in response to relevant and reliable information.

Arguments Against Reporting

The problem with tax expenditures is an absence of control. No one has argued that spending via tax provisions should be free of control because it is an insupportable argument. Instead, argument has focused on the feasibility of extending control mechanisms, such as disclosure and review, to tax expenditures.

Surrey describes tax expenditure as:

> deliberate departures from accepted concepts of net income . . . through various
> special exemptions, deductions and credits . . . to affect the private economy in

ways that are usually accomplished by expenditures in effect to produce an expenditure system described in tax language [28, p. 528].

Surrey's reference to "accepted concepts of net income" introduces the idea of a normative tax. Bittker also discusses the idea of a normative tax by referring to "a generally acceptable model, or set of principles" [26, p. 247], and "a standard or set of criteria for a 'proper' or 'correct' tax structure" [27, p. 528]. The Haig–Simons definition of income is referenced as such a model criterion [26]. The concept of normative tax is at the heart of the debate over the identification of tax expenditures.

When the tax expenditure concept originally was advanced, Surrey and Hellmuth debated with Bittker the merits of the general concept [26–28]. Many later discussions of the tax expenditure concept are grounded in Bittker's [27] two major criticisms, impossibility of identifying tax expenditures and of estimating tax expenditures. Bittker's [26] criticisms strike at two basic tax expenditure assumptions, the existence of a normative tax and the ability to measure tax expenditures. Thus Bittker [26] challenged the relevance of tax expenditure estimates by contending expenditures cannot be identified in the absence of an accepted normative standard and the reliability of tax expenditure estimates by contending their costs cannot be measured.

Impossibility of Identification

Bittker [27] argued that tax expenditures cannot be identified because there is no agreement about standard provisions that a normative tax would include. Thus, in the absence of agreement on the norms, departures from the norm, such as tax expenditures, cannot be identified. Bittker's [26,27] concern with defining normative tax was shared by Andrews [29] and Blum [30]. The Committee on Fiscal Affairs of the Organization for Economic Cooperation or OECD [36] also identified conceptual difficulty in defining a normative tax structure as the primary obstacle to adoption of reporting by OECD countries.

Surrey and Hellmuth responded that the purpose of tax expenditures is not to "show deviations from an 'ideal tax base,'" but "to represent the cost of special tax provisions . . . to allow decisions which make the most effective use of all budgetary resources" [28, p. 530]. As the discussion of this issue continued, it became apparent that Surrey and McDaniel were arguing for a more adaptable view of normative tax than Bittker. Surrey and McDaniel wrote:

> The tax expenditure concept posits that an income tax is composed of two distinct elements. The first element consists of structural provisions necessary to implement a normal income tax, such as the definition of net income, the specification of accounting rules, the determination of the rate schedules and exemption levels, and the application of the tax to international transactions. These provisions compose the revenue-raising aspects of the tax. The second element consists of the special preferences found in every income tax. These provisions, often called tax incentives or tax subsidies, are departures from the normal tax structure and are designed to favor a particular industry, activity, or class of persons [33, p. 3].

The New York State Department of Taxation and Finance [37] drew on the work of Surrey and McDaniel [33] to identify five elements of a normative tax: tax base, accounting methods, tax unit, tax rate schedule, and realization of income. In the federal budget tax expenditures are defined as "revenue losses due to preferential Provisions of the Federal tax laws, such as special exclusions, exemptions, deductions, credits, deferrals, or tax rates" [38, p. 39]. If one accepts the absence of normative tax attributes and structure, then tax policy is merely a matter of negotiation. The implication of this view extends beyond tax expenditure control to issues of equity and reinforces the need for tax expenditure analysis.

The debate over the need to define a normative tax reflects the most basic question, How may one identify tax expenditures? M. McIntyre [39] and Thuronyi [14] proposed identification approaches which avoid the concept of normative tax. Three proposed approaches are:

1. *Normative*—Costs are estimated for tax provisions that are departures from a normative model [26–31,33].
2. *Structural*—Costs are estimated for all structural provisions that could possibly be considered as tax expenditures [39].
3. *Substitute*—Costs are estimated for tax provisions for which a direct expenditure could achieve the same objective with no loss of efficiency [14,40].

Each approach just listed reflects a different emphasis. The normative approach emphasizes the logic of tax theory, the structural approach emphasizes the decision maker's need for revenue costs, and the substitute approach emphasizes the need for outlay costs. All three approaches include subjective elements. For an extensive discussion of definitional problems see Thuronyi [14]. At the federal level two agencies estimate tax expenditure costs, the legislative Congressional Budget Office (CBO) and the executive Office of Management and Budget (OMB). They produced virtually identical lists of tax expenditures until 1983 and continue to reflect general agreement.

The federal budget includes estimates for items classified as tax expenditures under the normal tax baseline or normative concept. It also indicates which of these items would not be classified as a tax expenditure using a reference tax law approach. Under the reference tax law approach, general deviations from a normative, comprehensive standard are excluded from tax expenditure classification. For example, graduated corporate income tax rates are excluded as a tax expenditure under the reference tax law baseline system.

Unreliability of Measurement

Bittker's [27] second criticism is that tax expenditures cannot be measured because no adjustment is made for the behavioral responses of taxpayers. Consider repeal of the deductibility of interest on loans for consumer purchases. Because interest on home mortgages continues to be deductible, the behavioral response of taxpayers has been to capture the same benefit by pursuing the alternative strategy of using home equity loans to finance consumer purchases [41]. Consequently, the estimated amount of revenue lost to the treasury from permitting consumer interest deduction does not represent the revenue gained from repeal of the same deduction. Other forms of secondary effects merit mention, such as structural, functional, and investment effects.

Structural effects result from alternative provisions being afforded by the tax structure. Assume home mortgage interest is the taxpayer's only item of itemized deduction. If the taxpayer did not itemize home mortgage home interest expense as a deduction, the taxpayer would be entitled to a standard deduction. Thus the revenue gain to the treasury would be reduced by the benefit resulting from the standard deduction.

Functional effects result from alternative resources being required to meet the same objective. If taxpayers were not entitled to a home interest deduction, perhaps a direct expenditure program would be funded to meet the objective of encouraging housing production and home ownership. The cost of the alternative direct expenditure program would reduce the gain to the treasury from repeal of the home mortgage interest expense deduction.

Investment effects result when the tax expenditure is intended as an incentive to stimulate economic growth, which in turn generates more revenue. Thus, one may argue that some "tax expenditures" may actually be "tax generators" when the secondary investment effect is considered. For example, if the home mortgage interest deduction were intended to stimulate housing construction and did so, the benefit of revenue generated from additional tax collections on construction industry income could be viewed as reducing the tax expenditures cost of the deduction. The theoretical potential of new revenues exceeding tax expenditure costs probably is remote because more taxpayers tend to benefit from a tax expenditure than respond to it. For example, the home mortgage interest deduction may influence the home purchase decision for one-third of new homeowners. For the other two-thirds of new homeowners, the mortgage interest deduction is a windfall benefit.

Surrey and Hellmuth 28], in responding to the exclusion of interactive effects from the measurement of tax expenditures, questioned why differing methodological standards should apply to tax expenditures and direct expenditures. The same procedure, excluding interactive effects, is used to estimate direct expenditures. They explain that secondary interactive effects reflecting beneficiary behavior are not incorporated into either estimates of tax expenditure costs or estimates of direct expenditure costs. McDaniel [42] argues that the problems of estimation are no different for tax expenditures than for direct expenditures. A change in either type of expenditure may trigger secondary interactive effects, increasing or decreasing another expenditure. Additionally, the estimation of tax expenditures and direct expenditures depends on assumptions pertaining to future economic conditions and behaviors of those beneficiaries affected by programs. McDaniel [42] concludes that methodological limitations do not invalidate the concept of estimating direct expenditures or tax expenditures.

Given the impossibility of incorporating the numerous potential secondary effects into the estimation of tax expenditure costs, it is reasonable to assume that no changes in taxpayer behavior will occur. The complication of secondary effects may be more of a problem of interpretation than of measurement. In using tax expenditure estimates, it is important to understand that because of secondary interactive effects, estimates of tax expenditure costs do not represent the amount of revenue which would result from repeal of a provision. Moreover, the almost certain occurrence of some secondary effects means that tax expenditures cannot be added together to produce a meaningful total measure of foregone revenues. However, the addition of tax expenditures may produce meaningful comparisons of the relative growth and distribution of tax expenditures by functional categories, tax, etc. [5,7].

Tax expenditure identification and computation issues underscore differences between tax expenditures and direct expenditures. There is less consensus about what constitutes a tax expenditure than a direct expenditure, and less precision in measuring their costs than in measuring costs of direct expenditures. This lack of consensus and precision exists because tax expenditures are a logical construct and not the historical reporting of a past transaction or event [14]. Despite inherent differences between tax expenditures and direct expenditures, the tax expenditure concept remains operative. A continuing interest in the amount of resources allocated by way of tax provisions is evidenced by the increasing number of governmental entities that are investing resources to estimate and to report tax expenditures.

Right to Income

The tax expenditure concept has been criticized as representing the idea that all income belongs to the government. Kristol [43] made this argument as follows:

So they [tax expenditure reporting advocates] come quickly to refer to all exemptions and allowances in our tax laws as "tax subsidies" or even "tax expenditures." But note what happens when you make this assumption and start using such terms. You are implicitly asserting that all income covered by the general provisions of the tax laws belongs of right to the government, and that what the government decides, by exemption or qualification, not to collect in taxes constitutes a subsidy. Whereas a subsidy used to mean a governmental expenditure for a certain purpose, it now acquires a quite another meaning—i.e., a generous decision by government not to take your money [43, p. 15].

The State of New York Legislative Commission on Public–Private Cooperation (LCPPC) [44] advanced three counterarguments.

1. The right of individuals to income is inherent in the concept of net income. Surrey and McDaniel made exactly this point when they wrote, "including all items of gross income and subtracting the costs of producing that income . . . does not in any way assert that all income belongs to the government" [16, p. 687].
2. A function of government is to set tax rate schedules. According to Surrey and McDaniel, the tax expenditure concept does not dictate adoption of a 100% rate necessary to support the argument that all income belongs to the government [16].
3. Tax expenditures are a form of subsidy that have the effect of altering the amount of tax paid by nonbeneficiaries. Senator Bradley (*Tax Notes Today*, LEXIS 95-TNT 16-140) argued that tax expenditures provide special exceptions to the rules that oblige taxpayers to share in the support of government. Senator Kennedy [45] wrote, "the amount of tax expenditure is a measure of how much more taxes the average citizen has to pay, because others pay too little."

Review Is Adequate

There are three components to the argument that review is adequate, each of which is discussed by Benker [10]

1. The review of each individual tax provision is subject to extensive examination and debate prior to adoption.
2. Most major tax expenditures are enshrined through massive public support in tax codes. The revenue loss from expenditures for which repeal is politically feasible is so marginal as to not justify the cost of review.
3. Tax expenditures, especially industrial development expenditures, are in reality investments to enhance the competitive position of states in attracting business. Additional scrutiny could create the image of a negative business climate.

The merit of each of these arguments is doubtful. Exhaustive examination of any expenditure on an individual basis at the time of adoption does not provide the scrutiny of comparative review as part of a total package of tax expenditures and direct expenditures. Nor does preadoption debate provide the scrutiny of ongoing oversight involved in monitoring the magnitude and distribution of benefits. No systematic procedures or inherent characteristics justify excluding tax expenditure from the periodic competition for resources applied to direct expenditures.

Repeal of tax expenditures is not the primary objective of reporting, any more than repeal of direct expenditures is the primary objective of direct expenditure reporting. The objective of reporting is to facilitate the management of public resources. Gregory and Morberg explained,

Examining only the direct spending side considerably distorts the view of winners and losers in the competition for public dollars, while also restricting the range of options available to decision-makers for resolving public issues [46, p. 5].

For example, tax expenditure support for housing far exceeds direct expenditure support for housing. Relying only on information about direct expenditures provides an extremely distorted accounting of the extent of public financial support for housing. Whether support should be provided and at what levels are two questions separate from investigation into whether complete cost information should be available for a complete accounting.

For those tax expenditures that are viewed as investments, the investment nature of the expenditure does not justify the absence of disclosure. Direct expenditure investments are disclosed. In fact, the need for information about the cost of investments is fundamental to evaluating return. The public relations effect of industrial development expenditures does not justify exempting tax expenditure investment from cost evaluation any more than it justifies exempting direct expenditure investment from cost evaluation.

Adverse Consequences

A final set of arguments against tax expenditure reporting predicts that various adverse consequences will result from this practice. Such consequences include a pejorative perception of provisions classified as tax expenditure, the elimination of tax expenditures, and increases in direct spending to replace tax expenditures [44]. Tax expenditures have been reported at the federal level for almost 30 years absent the occurrence of predicted consequences. Tax expenditure reporting does not assume that tax expenditures have no merit and should be terminated any more than direct expenditure reporting assumes direct expenditures have no merit and should be terminated. Tax expenditure classification is the beginning of a control process to subject tax expenditures to periodic, institutionalized scrutiny.

Arguments for Oversight and Reporting

The basic argument for reporting tax expenditures is the argument for control over tax and budget policies. A utilitarian argument for tax expenditure reporting is advanced in a report by The State of New York Department of Taxation and Finance.

The real question for tax expenditure reporting is whether such reports can be useful to policy makers. Tax expenditure reporting should be viewed as a practical, not philosophical matter. The structure of a state's tax system is a critical policy concern. The reporting of the revenue implications of the provisions of that system is a necessary element in any informed policy discussion [47, p. 7].

The core aspect of the tax expenditure concept is that tax expenditures represent an allocation of benefit. Absent the recognition of this concept, three standard controls are avoided by using the tax expenditures to encourage desired behaviors or relieve hardships.

1. Disclosure of the amount of public support for programs implemented via tax provision is avoided. Lack of disclosure contributes to ignorance about the identity of beneficiaries, distributional impacts, and effective tax rate.
2. Periodic scrutiny, which is characteristic of programs funded via direct expenditure, is avoided. Accordingly, tax expenditures do not compete with direct expenditures and are seldom held to the same standards of accountability.

3. The traditional control of separating responsibilities for revenue collections and disbursements is avoided. Thus the power of legislative tax committees is enhanced.

The Committee on Fiscal Affairs of the OECD [36] study listed three arguments in favor of reporting and of tax expenditure oversight:

(1) Tax expenditures are a route for governments to pursue policies and should be subject to the same evaluation and control procedures that are applied to government subsidies provided by direct expenditures.

(2) A review of government policies in any area will be more effective if all the different methods of government intervention . . . are taken into account and if similar budgetary techniques are used to evaluate the cost of tax and direct expenditures.

(3) Control of government expenditure will stand less chance of success if tax expenditures can be easily substituted for direct expenditures [36, p. 10].

Given acceptance of the tax expenditure concept, reporting is fundamental to tax expenditure control. By itself, reporting constitutes one form of control, disclosure. Although disclosure alone is a weak control, it is essential to instituting stronger controls such as periodic scrutiny, and to the integration of direct expenditure and tax expenditure control processes. However, by itself reporting can provide educational information about the extent of spending via tax provision, foster public discussion about tax system design, and provide information to facilitate cost–benefit analyses of tax expenditure programs.

Extent of Tax Expenditure Reporting

The tax expenditure concept has gained wide acceptance. The United States and most European countries have adopted some form of tax expenditure reporting. Following a slow but steady trend, 29 states in the United States have adopted periodic reporting of tax expenditures. Municipalities have joined the trend, by recording the costs of property tax abatements. The implementation of reporting forces consideration of (1) technical questions such as choice of tax expenditure definition, object of measurement, estimation method, and data to collect, and (2) report design questions relating to the classification of information and to the analysis of information.

National Level

West Germany was the first country to adopt tax expenditure reporting and published its first report in 1966 [48]. Shannon [49] compares development of the tax expenditure concept in Germany and in the United States. Benker [10] lists nine countries that report tax expenditure reports: Austria, Australia, Canada, France, West Germany, Japan, Spain, the United Kingdom, and the United States. In a 1983 study, the Committee on Fiscal Affairs of the OECD [36] described these reports and reviewed multinational use and implementation of reporting.

Among countries that report tax expenditures, Canada has adopted the most extensive structure for integrating control of tax expenditures and direct expenditures in a budget system [8,19,50,51]. In the Canadian system, cabinet committees are assigned responsibility for managing an "envelope" of resources that includes both tax expenditures and direct expenditures. Tax expenditure increases are charged to the envelope, reducing the resources available for direct expenditure. Reductions in tax expenditures are added to the envelope if the tax expenditure is judged equivalent to a direct expenditure. Otherwise, reductions in tax expenditures are added to general revenues. All changes to envelopes must be approved by the minister of finance and the minister responsible for the affected operating policy.

The first tax expenditure report for the United States was prepared in 1967 under the direction of Surrey, and was included in the *Annual Report of the Secretary of the Treasury for Fiscal 1968*. In 1974 Congress passed the Congressional Budget Act which mandated the Congressional Budget Office (CBO) to publish an annual report of tax expenditures for individual and corporate income taxes. The actual tax expenditure estimates are prepared by the staff of the Joint Committee on Taxation (JTC) for the CBO. The same 1974 law required the executive Office of Management and Budget (OMB) to include a tax expenditure analysis with the budget. This analysis has been published annually since 1976 as part of the President's budget. For additional discussion on the history of reporting in the United States, see Benker [10], Forman [1], and Edwards [52].

State Level

In 1971, California became the first state to adopt tax expenditure reporting, and issued its first report in 1976. Since 1980, the number of states publishing periodic reports has increased from four states to 29 states. Some states report annually and others report biennially. Table 1, shows the states that have adopted tax expenditure reporting.

Tax expenditure reporting at the state government level has been the subject of four studies [10,44,53,54]. Except for Harris, the authors of these studies were associated with organizations concerned with the promotion of reporting standards. Both the NCSL and New York LCPPC addressed issues pertaining to what processes and report content should characterize tax expenditure reports. Each of these groups recommended model reporting programs. Recommended models share some common attributes, but unique attributes of each are not in conflict.

At the state government level, tax expenditures reporting differs in three ways from reporting at the federal government level [53]. First, the general concept is broader than that adopted at the federal government level. Second, state tax expenditure analyses exclude more items of expenditure from estimation than federal tax expenditure analyses. And third, state tax expenditures are estimated using one object of measurement rather than two objects of measurement.

Table 1 States That Report Tax Expenditures

Arizona	Massachusetts	Ohio
California	Michigan	Pennsylvania
Connecticut	Minnesota	South Carolina
Delaware	Mississippi	Tennessee
Hawaii	Missouri	Texas
Illinois	Montana	Virginia
Kentucky	Nebraska	Washington
Louisiana	New Hampshire	West Virginia
Maine	New York	Wisconsin
Maryland	North Carolina	

Note: Arkanasa, and Indiana have issued special, nonperiodic reports. Alabama and Kentucky have prepared reports for internal use only. The reports of Hawaii, North Carolina, and Texas are limited in scope.

Gold and Nesbary [53] explain that the tax expenditure concept tends to be more complicated or broader at the state level because state analysts extend the concept to more types of taxes. The tax expenditure concept has been applied by Forman [55], Hudder [56], and Davie [57], respectively, to payroll taxes, sales taxes, and excise taxes. The extension of the concept to sales and other taxes is necessary because state governments rely less on income taxes than the federal government. However, extension of tax expenditure estimation is complicated because there is less general agreement about the normative tax structure of other taxes. For example, Gold and Nesbary [53] indicate that if a sales tax is viewed as a consumption tax, the exemption of services represents a tax expenditure; but if the sales tax is viewed as a tax on personal property, the exemption of services does not represent a tax expenditure.

State tax expenditure analyses may exclude more items from estimation than federal tax expenditure analyses. Some states exclude the effect of any provision required by the state's constitution or any provision adopted for conformity with federal tax structure [53]. These tax expenditures may be viewed either as part of a modified normative structure or practically beyond change. Furthermore, some states impose threshold values on expenditure estimates before reporting or restrict reporting to expenditures adopted after a base year [10]. The imposition of threshold values restricts the use of scarce analytical resources to significant tax expenditures, and reporting on expenditures adopted after a base year shifts the focus to the recently adopted, less entrenched tax expenditures.

State tax expenditures are estimated using the revenue foregone object of measurement [53]. In contrast, the OMB at the federal level uses both the revenue foregone and outlay equivalence objects of measurement. Each of these objects of measurement is discussed later in this chapter.

There has been a steady interest in tax expenditure reporting at the state level for the past 20 years. Organizations concerned with fiscal policy control have sponsored studies to describe state-level reporting and proposed model reports. These studies establish that (1) reporting as conducted by states differs from reporting as conducted by the federal government and (2) reporting as conducted by states is a highly diverse activity.

Local and Municipal Level

At the municipal level, interest has centered on the recording and uniform reporting of property tax abatements. Martin [58] defines a tax abatement as a temporary reduction in tax for a limited time period during which economic development is expected to occur. A 1986 survey of local governments found 25% of cities and 42% of counties report information on tax abatements and cancellations, a subset of tax expenditures [59]. The Government Finance Officers' Association (GFOA) has supported research calling for issuance of governmental accounting standards on the recording and reporting of tax abatements. In 1988, it published a research report by Regan [60] arguing for the issuance of tax expenditure reports for economic development incentives including tax abatements. Uniformity of reporting is an issue because numerous political subdivisions within a state may abate taxes. Local decisions to abate taxes, especially property taxes, may effect state-level obligations to finance services and state-level decisions to finance local economic development. In 1993, legislation was introduced in the New York State Assembly that would require tax expenditure reporting by cities, towns, and counties with populations exceeding 100,000 [61].

Hughes and Motekat [62] report that four out of seven presenters at a 1988 hearing on future governmental accounting issues encouraged the addition of tax expenditure recording and reporting standards to the agenda of the Governmental Accounting Standards Board

(GASB). Martin [58] reproduces correspondence asking that GASB address tax expenditure recording and reporting. GASB has not responded.

Literature about the extent of tax expenditure reporting supports the conclusion that the tax expenditure concept has broad applicability and has gained widespread acceptance. The tax expenditure concept has been adapted to a variety of taxes, and reporting has been adopted at multiple levels of government.

Implementation of Tax Expenditure Reporting

The implementation of reporting forces report preparers to consider questions of computation and presentation. Definition, object of measurement, estimation method, and data collection are issues that affect the computation of tax expenditures. These issues are relevant to control because of their potential to affect the interpretation of information. The absence of uniformity related to these matters makes it extremely difficult to compare tax expenditure reports issued by different entities. Besides this difficulty, changes over time, particularly improvements in data collection, affect the reliability of time-series analyses.

Definition

As previously discussed, tax expenditures may be defined as (1) departures from a normative tax, (2) items represented by structural components such as exemptions, deductions, credits, etc., or (3) costs for which a direct expenditure alternative may substitute. Basic definitional approaches may be modified by source of expenditure, statute or constitutional provision, amount of expenditure, data of expenditure adoption, etc. These modifications produce different lists of tax expenditures.

Object of Measurement

Three distinct theoretical objects of measurement exist: (1) revenue foregone, (2) revenue gain, and (3) outlay equivalence [36]. Most reporters use the revenue foregone object of measurement. The Office of Management and Budget (OMB) uses both the outlay equivalence and revenue foregone objects of measurement and provides two separate sets of estimated costs in the Budget of the United States.

The revenue foregone object of measurement is designed to measure the amount by which tax revenues are reduced because of the existence of a particular provision. It is an after-the-fact measure of the cost of a given provision. The foregone amount is the difference in revenue based on a comparison of existing legislation including the provision of interest and the same legislation without the provision of interest. Taxpayer behavior is accepted as observed for the period under consideration. No secondary interactive effects are considered.

The revenue gain object of measurement is designed to measure the amount by which tax revenues would increase if a given provision were repealed. In theory, use of this object of measurement requires consideration of secondary effects such as changes in taxpayer behavior, changes in the level of economic activity, and interactions among taxes. The difficulty of taking secondary effects into consideration is substantial. No reporters are known to use this object of measurement in actual practice.

The outlay equivalence object of measurement is designed to measure in pretax dollars the direct expenditure that would be required to achieve the same after-tax dollar benefit if a tax expenditure were replaced by a corresponding direct expenditure program. McDaniel and Surrey [63] describe the outlay equivalent cost as the cost of the direct expenditure that would be required to provide the same benefit to beneficiaries directly. The outlay equivalence object of measurement differs in perspective and objective from the revenue foregone and revenue gain objects of measurement [19]. The revenue foregone and revenue gain objects of measurement are directed to revenue management, while the outlay equivalence object of measurement is directed to benefit management. Leonard [64] discusses the relationship between management objective and object of measurement. For additional discussions of objects of measurement see Committee on Fiscal Affairs of the OECD [36], McDaniel and Surrey [32,63], Gold and Nesbary [53], Schick [19], and Richardson [65].

Estimation Methods

In preparing tax expenditure reports, one basic decision is whether to estimate historical tax expenditures, forecast current and future tax expenditures, or do both. Three approaches are discussed in a report prepared by the New York State Department of Taxation and Finance [37]. The three approaches are application of (1) historical data to historical tax law, (2) historical data to current tax law, and (3) trended data to current tax law. The first approach is methodologically sound, but may not be relevant to current and future years. The second approach provides for the estimation of new tax expenditures, but requires the assumption that taxpayers behave the same under old and new tax laws, which weakens the reliability of results. The third approach matches current data to current law. However, it is a technically complex, expensive approach, which by trending estimates increases the uncertainty associated with final estimates. All three approaches are used and may provide meaningful information about the relative magnitude of various tax expenditures.

Data Collection

Regardless of other production consideration, unless quality data can be obtained the reliability of reports will be impaired. The New York Department of Taxation and Finance [37] classifies data sources by degree of reliability. The most reliable source for developing estimates is data from tax returns filed with a reporting entity, followed by aggregate data such as Statistics on Income, federal estimates of tax expenditures, and self-constructed estimates from nontax data. The federal government and some states maintain databases developed from actual returns for statistical and reporting purposes. If a database is not available, development is an expensive endeavor. A return database, however, will not provide all the information one needs for estimating tax expenditures. For example, state returns may not provide specific information on benefits called passive tax expenditures, which flow through from federal provisions. Hildred and Pinto [66–68] have pursued a stream of research to evaluate the reliability of passive tax expenditures. Moreover, estimates of the costs of exemptions, particularly sales tax exemptions, may be extremely unreliable because of the lack of quality data.

Definition, object of measurement, estimation method, and data collection are issues to resolve in producing tax expenditure reports. Decisions related to these issues affect the interpretation of reports. Thus it is important that users understand the choice made and their implications.

Utility of Tax Expenditure Reporting

The tax expenditure literature presents reporting as a tool to aid in control of fiscal resources. Few states have developed any form of institutionalized tax expenditure oversight process. Precisely how control may be achieved has not received as much attention as explanations of the control problem. However, certain control objectives are discussed.

Improved Debate

The general overall objective of tax expenditure reporting is to contribute to an increased awareness of tax expenditure costs stimulating control over tax expenditures. Davenport

[69] argues that one of the primary benefits of the tax expenditure concept and reporting is improvement in the quality of debate, generating pressure on legislators to justify their actions. Although the tax expenditure concept is not accepted universally [70], the literature shows a general acceptance of the concept and of its utility for examining tax policy and a general exclusion of the concept from budget policy.

Improved Management

Four control objectives are related to the management of tax and spending policies. From the inception of reporting, cost comparison and revenue comparison were mentioned as objectives [28,71]. The earliest and most frequently mentioned objectives, cost comparison and revenue comparison, may be regarded as primary objectives. The first of these objectives, comparison of direct expenditure costs with indirect tax expenditure costs, is advocated as a means of encouraging adoption of the most cost beneficial means for administering operational programs [10,25,28,72]. A second objective is to protect revenue bases from erosion [10,53,60,71] by considering revenues foregone from tax expenditures. Erosion of revenue bases from increases in tax expenditures may have the same effect on public deficits as increases in direct expenditures [65]. A third objective is to achieve an equitable distribution of exchange by considering the distribution of normative tax liabilities and of tax expenditures [71,73,74]. A fourth objective is to contribute to the design of tax expenditures that operate in the most cost beneficial manner [60]. Given the recent and limited discussion by reporting advocates of distributional impact and efficient design of tax incentives, these objectives appear peripheral.

Policy Impact

The impact of tax expenditure information on policymakers is a subject that has not attracted much attention. Advocates of reporting, while supporting greater institutionalization of tax expenditure oversight, seem to assume (1) that cost-benefit comparisons are central to decision making and (2) that tax expenditure report information will be used as a management tool in preparing cost-benefit comparisons to guide fiscal decisions [75,76]. Neither of these assumptions has been verified.

Assessments of the utility of tax expenditure reporting tends to be based on personal accounts. Praising reporting, M. McIntyre makes this observation:

> It has induced Congress to alter its procedures for scrutinizing tax subsidies, now called tax expenditures, and it has focused public attention on the indefensible consequences that often result when Congress uses special deductions, exemptions and other tax mechanisms to achieve its spending goals [39, p. 79].

Salamone describes the Minnesota Tax Expenditure Report as "a key tax reference document used in tax committee discussions" [77, p. 32]. George Deukemejian, a former governor of California, was a critic of reporting. In 1984, he recommended its termination, stating, "the report seems to have little impact, since a number of tax expenditures have been adopted over the last decade" [10, p. 44]. However, California continues to report tax expenditures, and also has initiated the performance auditing of tax expenditures.

A few published references to tax expenditure report utility are inconsistent with the rational objectives advanced by reporting proponents. R. McIntyre [78] observes that the availability of tax expenditure analyses has supported the evaluation and adoption of new tax benefits on spending grounds while fairness and administrability have been ignored. Pomp [79] reports that tax expenditures data have been used by legislators to show the value of tax benefits enacted on behalf of their constituency and by special interest groups to show need for additional tax benefits.

Surrey and McDaniel [2], R. McIntyre [78], Richardson [79], and Thuronyi [14] compile case analyses of the influence of reporting on specific federal tax reform. Except for the Surrey and McDaniel [2] case report, each of the cited cases questions whether report information has a significant impact on policy making. Thuronyi observes, "institutional problems aside, evidence also indicates that Congress has not taken the tax expenditure concept fully to heart" [14, p. 1171]. Leonard [64] discusses the limitations of informational reporting as a control mechanism. Harris [54] conducted the only systematic study of tax expenditure report use by state legislators. She found over 75% of legislators who serve on tax committees view reports positively and consider report information when discussing tax policy.

Aggregate Analyses

Much of the literature about tax expenditure reporting centers around conceptual arguments about the classification of provisions as tax expenditures or about arguments related to reporting. The informational content of reports has received much less attention. Aggregate analysis offers valuable potential for understanding the impact of tax expenditures on the distribution of benefits to taxpayers and the modification of burden on taxpayers for support of the government.

Empirical analyses of report information in the aggregate are rare except for the evaluation of individual tax expenditures. King [18] identifies policies supported by federal tax expenditures. Noto [80] and Weinberg [74] estimate the distributional impact of federal tax expenditures; Joulfaian [81] estimates the distributional impact of Massachusetts tax expenditures. Hildred and Pinto [66] estimate the impact of federal tax expenditures on state revenues. The nonadditiveness of tax expenditure estimates resulting from the disregard of secondary effects is a major obstacle to aggregate studies. Other obstacles are the lack of comparability among state reports, the lack of comparability over time because of changing estimation models and classifications, and the absence of disclosure of data except by type of tax.

MEANS OF OVERSIGHT

Aside from tax expenditure reporting, other procedures have been proposed to strengthen control over tax expenditures.

Report Utilization

Report utilization includes such procedures as (1) preissuance and postissuance reviews and (2) extension of reporting to include report analysis and performance audits of selected expenditures.

Although report production is common, preissuance and postissuance review of report information is rare. Preissuance review refers to the review of report information prior to distribution by an agency external to the preparing agency. Such review may contribute to report quality by ensuring consideration of completeness, reliability, and relevance of report information.

Postissuance review refers to legislative review of report information after its distribution. At the state level, it is the exception rather than the rule to find responsibility assigned for reviewing tax expenditure costs. Absent the adoption of a review process, review is sporadic.

When postissuance reviews are undertaken, the analysis that some reports contain seems useful. A tax expenditure report may be nothing more than a catalog of tax expenditures with cost estimates attached. However, state reports are starting to aggregate and to classify data in ways to facilitate analysis [44,80]. For example, expenditure data may be disclosed by government function such as agriculture, education, etc., and include graphic displays. Some state reports estimate the effect of recent tax expenditure repeals and adoptions. Other state reports list tax expenditure which are scheduled to terminate in the next few years. For selected tax expenditures, a few states show the number of taxpayers benefiting from a provision, the distribution of beneficiaries by income groups, and/or the average benefit by income group. It is evident that an effort is being made to improve the presentation of report information.

Canada, the United States, and a few states have instituted reviews or performance audits to evaluate the effectiveness and/or efficiency of selected tax expenditures. Some of the issues associated with such an evaluation include determination of (1) criteria for selecting expenditures to review [79] and (2) criteria and procedures to apply in evaluating selected tax expenditures [8,10,72]. McIntyre [6] recommends that such reviews address five questions:

1. Is the subsidy designed to serve an important public purpose?
2. Is the subsidy actually helping to achieve its goals?
3. Are the benefits, if any, from the subsidy commensurate with its costs?
4. Are the benefits of the subsidy fairly distributed, or are they disproportionately targeted to those who do not need or deserve government assistance?
5. Is the subsidy well administered?

Performance auditing is a promising control procedure because it permits the comprehensive analysis of a limited number of tax expenditures where strong justification for evaluation exists. The New York State Department of Taxation and Finance [37] discusses the difficulties in evaluating tax expenditures. Elkin [8] describes the Canadian approach to tax expenditure auditing. The Office of Management and Budget (OMB) has commenced a pilot program of reviews under the Government Performance and Results Act of 1993 (GPRA), which requires that program goals and key indicators of performance be reported for selected tax expenditures [5].

Structural Integration

Structural integration controls are those that integrate tax expenditure controls into the appropriations process and the accounting system. The simplest form of structural integration would be to merge information about tax expenditure costs into the budget presentation of related direct expenditures. Other controls focus on defining acceptable levels of tax expenditure. In the United States, Senator Bradley has introduced legislation which would require that tax expenditure targets be established as part of the budget reconciliation process [82]. If adopted, this would result in the specification of tax expenditure saving targets analogous to direct expenditure saving targets and of formal justification of the adopted targets. At the state level, a legislator in Massachusetts proposed a somewhat similar control, a revenue loss cap [83]. As another mean of limiting tax expenditures, the U.S. Senate is considering legislation to give the President authority to exercise a line-item veto over both direct expenditures and tax expenditures [84].

The highest form of integration is to incorporate tax expenditures into the appropriations process by adopting joint review of direct spending and tax expenditures. Joint review could be achieved (1) by having revenue and appropriations committees hold joint hearings on tax expenditures, (2) by adopting a system of sequential jurisdiction over tax expenditures, or (3) by creating joint committee for the review of tax expenditures.

At the national level, Canada's "envelope" system explicitly submits tax expenditures to spending controls. Gregory and Morberg [46], writing for the Michigan House Fiscal Agency, argue for stronger process integration controls. Based on their analysis, Michigan faces structural deficits partially because the rate of increase in tax expenditures is larger than the rate of increase in direct expenditures. Gregory and Morberg [46] conclude that (1) structural deficits justify stronger tax expenditure control and (2) stronger tax expenditure control requires consideration of integrating the direct and tax expenditures control processes.

At the local level it has been proposed that the traditional accounting system incorporate tax expenditure transactions. The major local tax is often a property tax, which structurally may be quite simple in comparison to an income tax. For example, the base is the assessed value of property with a statutory rate applied. If taxes are abated, as an incentive to undertake a particular action, the revenue gain cost is easy to estimate as secondary interactive effects are few.

Hughes and Motekat [62] outline procedures for recording tax expenditures in an accounting system. They suggest recording the gross revenue before allowance for tax expenditures and then recording the expenditure as a deduction from revenue. In a research report to GFOA, Martin [58] recommends a similar accounting model for recording property tax abatements. The proposed treatment is analogous to the recording of tuition waivers by universities and insurance discounts by hospitals. The advancement of proposals to incorporate reporting of tax abatements into the traditional accounting system reflects acceptance of the tax expenditure concept and confidence in the measurement of tax abatements.

Although potentially helpful, the accounting treatment proposed by Hughes and Motekat [62] and Martin [58] may not be an adequate control. Schick cautions:

> Merely placing nonconventional transactions in the budget might be little more than a bookkeeping change; it might not significantly improve the capacity of government to control the allocation of resources through nonconventional financing instruments [19, p. 17].

The challenge is to create effective controls for nonconventional spending.

Design of Provisions

Controls over the design of legislation include procedures that limit the loss of revenue from tax expenditures. Examples of such controls are (1) restricting the amount of benefit that all taxpayers can receive by requiring advance application to receive a benefit, (2) restricting the amount of benefit that any single taxpayer can receive by restricting benefits to a maximum dollar amount, (3) excluding high income taxpayers from eligibility by adopting restrictions on eligibility, (4) limiting the value of tax expenditures to the lowest marginal tax rate, (5) structuring tax expenditures as credits rather than exclusions or deductions, and (6) sunsetting benefits by specifying a termination date for the tax provision. Sunsetting is intended to force a periodic review of the applicable tax expenditure.

Preadoption Analysis and Disclosure

A number of state legislatures now require that proposed legislation be reviewed for its potential impact on revenue and that fiscal notes be attached to proposed legislation estimating the impact of the legislation on revenue. Thus a fiscal note requirement compels the estimation and disclosure of tax expenditure costs prior to adoption of the expenditure provision. Since the analysis focuses on one specific proposal, the revenue gain object of measurement may be used.

Publication of Beneficiaries

Specific identification of corporate beneficiaries has been advocated as a disclosure control by Pomp [79]. This proposal equates the treatment of direct expenditures and tax expenditures. The beneficiaries of public spending are a matter of public record. Pomp [79] argues specific identification would stimulate public interest in tax expenditure control by giving a reality to statistics. This suggestion parallels other circumstances in which tax expenditures be treated as spending by the courts [85].

CONCLUSION

Aside from reporting, governmental entities have little experience with tax expenditure control procedures. McDaniel described tax expenditure reports as providing an "analytic tool to be used by practical legislators and government policy officials responsible for real budget and tax policy decisions" [4, p. 589]. Discussing the use of the federal tax expenditure budget or report, McDaniel [42] recommends regular review of tax expenditure programs, coordination of tax review of tax expenditure programs, coordination of tax expenditure programs with direct expenditure programs, and automatic termination or sunsetting of tax expenditures. The National Conference of State Legislatures [53] suggests submission of a tax expenditure report with the direct expenditure budget, assignment of review responsibilities to a specific committee, automatic termination of new tax expenditures, and review and disposal of the tax expenditure report in a manner analogous to the direct expenditure budget. Pomp [79] emphasizes the need for the state to institutionalize periodic comprehensive reviews of selected tax expenditures including the examination and disclosure of beneficiaries. Surrey and McDaniel [2,63] advocate dividing the tax expenditure report into functions in a manner similar to the direct expenditure budget. Each of these recommendations assumes the availability of the most fundamental control tool, tax expenditure report information.

   The institutionalization of tax expenditure oversight has been neglected at the federal level and haphazard at the state level [65,79]. A few states have put limits on some types of tax expenditures, adopting sunsetting laws, and/or assigned review responsibilities to specific legislative committees. But for the most part, coordination of tax expenditure programs with direct expenditure programs, limiting the overall amount of tax expenditures, and coordination between tax expenditures in a manner analogous to the direct expenditures has not occurred.

   Ladd [86] questions the contribution of tax expenditure accounting to tax reform and budgetary control. However, accounting alone, whether for direct expenditure or for tax expenditures, is not sufficient to establish budgetary control. When one looks at the history of direct expenditure accounting over a period of more than a century, tax expenditure accounting is quite new as an innovation. The rapid acceptance of tax expenditure accounting is perhaps more surprising than the incompleteness of control systems. In less than 35 years, most industrial countries and almost three-fifths of the states in the United States have adopted tax expenditure reporting. Although other controls are seldom adopted, the introduction of legislation to control tax expenditures is common. These legislative proposals signal the progression of efforts to control tax expenditures. As budgetary stress intensifies, it is likely that more attention will be given to tax expenditure control systems.

BIBLIOGRAPHY

Baumbusch, P. L. (March 9, 1981). Surrey And Tax Expenditures: Further Comments, *Tax Notes*, *12*: 500–502.

Benker, K. M. (1986). Tax Expenditure Reporting: Closing The Loophole In State Budget Oversight, *Nat. Tax J.*, *39*: 403–417.

Bennett, J. T., and DiLorenzo, T. J. (1983). *Underground Government: The Off-Budget Public Sector*, Cato Institute, Washington, D.C.

Bezdek, R. H. and Zampelli, E. M. (1986). State and Local Government Tax Expenditures Relating To The Federal Government, *Nat. Tax J.*, *39*: 533–538.

Bosworth, B. P. (1984). *Tax Incentives and Economic Growth*, The Bookings Institute, Washington, D.C.

Brannon, G. M. (1980). Tax Expenditures and Income Distribution: A Theoretical Analysis of the Upside-Down Subsidy Argument, *The Economics of Taxation*, (H. J. Aarons and M. J. Boskins, eds.), The Brookings Institution, Washington, D.C., pp. 87–98.

Break, G. F. (1985). The Tax Expenditure Budget—The Need For A Fuller Accounting, *Nat. Tax J.*, *38*: 261–265.

Brennan, G. and Buchanan, J. (1980). *The Power To Tax*, Cambridge Univ. Press, Cambridge, U.K.

Butler, J. R. G. and J. P. Smith (1992). Tax Expenditures on Health in Australia: 1960–61 to 1988–89, *Australian Economics Review*, *99*: 43–58.

Congressional Budget Office (CBO) (1995). *Reducing the Deficit: Spending and Revenue Options*, CBO, Washington, D.C.

Driessen, P. A. (1987). A Qualification Concerning The Efficiency of Tax Expenditures, *J. of Pub, Econ.*, *33*: 126–131.

Feldstein, M. (1980). A Contribution of the Theory of Tax Expenditures: The Case of Charitable Giving, *The Economics of Taxation* (H. J. Aarons and M. J. Boskins eds.), The Brookings Institution, Washington, D.C., pp. 99–122.

Fisher, P. S. (1985). Corporate Tax Incentives: The American Version of Industrial Policy, *J. of Econ. Issues*, *19*: 1–19.

Follain, J. R. and D. C. Ling, and G. A. McGill (1993). The Preferential Income Tax Treatment of Owner-Occupied Housing: Who Really Benefits? *Housing Policy Debate*, *4*: 1–24.

Freeman, R. A. (1983). *Tax Loopholes: The Legend and the Reality*, Am. Enterprise Institute-Hoover Policy Study, Washington, D.C.

Gold, S. D. ed. (1986). *Reforming State Tax Systems*, Nat. Conf. of State Legislatures, Denver, CO.

Gold, S. D. ed. (1988). *The Unfinished Agenda for State Tax Reform*, Nat. Conf. of State Legislatures, Denver, CO.

Grady, D. O. (1987). State Economic Development Incentives: Why Do States Compete?" *State and Local Govt. Rev.*, *19*: 86–94.

Greenwood, J. K. and Whybrow, J. A. (1982). Property Tax Treatment of Agricultural and Forestland in Canada: Implications for Land Use Policy. *Property Tax Journal*, *11*: 159–205.

Grigsby, W. G. (1993). Comment on James R. Follain, David C. Ling, and Gary A. McGill's 'The Preferential Income Tax Treatment of Owner-occupied Housing: Who Really Benefits?', *Housing Policy Debate*, *4*: 33–42.

Hamm, K. E. and Robertson, R. D. (1981). Factors Influencing the Adoption of New Methods of Legislative Oversight in the U.S. States, *Legislative Stud. Qtr.*, *6*: 133–150.

Harris, J. E. (1993). Factors Affecting Tax Expenditure Report Use, *Pub. Budgeting and Fin. Management*, 5: 387–416.

Harris, J. E. and Hicks, S. A. (1992). Tax Expenditure Accounting: Practice and Objective, *Accounting Enquiries*, 2: 126–167.

Harris, J. E. and Hicks, S. A. (1992). Tax Expenditures and Reporting: The Utilization of an Innovation, *Pub. Budgeting and Fin.*, 12: 32–39.

Harstad, P. F. (Dec. 21, 1981). Tax Expenditures Called "The Spending of the 1980s," *Tax Notes*, 13: 1532–1534.

Hedgespeth, G. and Moynihan, E. (1984). "Special Problems in Developing a State Tax Expenditure Budget," *Proceedings of 52d Annual Meeting of Nat. Assoc. of Tax Administrators*, pp. 123–129.

Helms, L. J. (1985). The Effect of State and Local Taxes on Economic Growth: A Time Series-Cross Section Approach, *The Rev. of Econ. and Statistics*: 574–582.

Hughes, J. W. (1981). The Tax Expenditure Concept: Its Interpretation and Measurement Plus an Evaluation, *The Nat. Pub. Accountant*, 26: 22–25.

Ingram, R. W., Robbins, W. A. and Stone, M. S. (1988). Financial Reporting Practices of Local Governments: An Overview, *Govt. Fin. Rev.*, 4: 17–21.

Jacobs, J. (1979). *Biding for Business: Corporate Auctions And The 50 Disunited States*, Public Interest Research Group, Washington, D.C.

Kaplow, L. (1991). The Income Tax as Insurance: The Casualty Loss and Medical Expense Deductions and The Exclusion of Medical Insurance Premiums. *California Law Review*, 79: 1485–1510.

Kettl, D. F. (1988). *Government by Proxy (Mis?) Managing Federal Programs*, Congressional Qtr. Press, Washington, D.C.

Kobrak, P. and Gregory, W. (1993). Expanding Budget Options: Tax Expenditures and the Michigan Legislative Process, *Pub. Budgeting and Fin. Management*, 5: 189–224.

Ledebur, L. C. and Hamilton W. W. (1986). The Failure of Tax Concessions as Economic Development Incentives, *Reforming State Tax Systems* (S. D. Gold, ed.), Nat. Conf. of State Legislatures, Denver, CO. pp. 101–118.

Lees, J. D. (1977). Legislative Oversight: A Review Article on a Neglected Area of Research, *Legislative Stud. Qtr.*, 2: 193–207.

Levitan, S. A. and E. I. Miller (May/June 1992). Enterprise Zones Are No Solution for Our Blighted Areas. *Challenge*: 4–8.

Lind, N. S. and Elder, E. H. (1986). Who Pays? Who Benefits? The Case of the Incentive Package Offered to the Diamond-Star Automotive Plant, *Govt. Fin. Rev.*, 2: 19–23.

Malan, R. M Jr., Martin, S. W., and Regan, E. V. (1988). The Cost of Tax Incentives, *Govt. Fin. Rev.*, 4: 3.

McDaniel, P. R. (1988). The Impact of the Tax Expenditure Concept on Tax Reform, *The Quest for Tax Reform* (N. W. Brooks, ed.), Carswell, Toronto, Canada, pp. 387–396.

McDonald, J. F. (1993). Tax Expenditures for Local Economic Growth: An Ecometric Evaluation of the Illinois Enterprise Zone Program, *Pub. Budgeting and Fin. Management*, 5: 477–506.

McGuire, T. J. (1986). Interstate Tax Differentials, Tax Competition, and Tax Policy, *Nat. Tax J.*, 39: 367–373.

McIntyre, M. J. (Aug. 9, 1976). The Sunset Bill: A Periodic Review for Tax Expenditures, *Tax Notes*, 4: 3–6, 9.

McIntyre, M. J. (March 9, 1981). Tax Incentives For Investment: A Review of A Study of Studies, *Tax Notes*, 12: 491–492.

McIntyre, R. S. and Tipps, D. C. (1985). Exploring the Investment-Incentive Myth, *Challenge*: 47–52.

Papke, J. A. and Papke, L. E. (1986). Measuring Differential State-Local Tax Liabilities And Their Implications For Business Investment Location, *Nat. Tax J.*, 39: 357–366.

Peretz, P. (1986). The Market for Industry: Where Angels Fear to Tread, *Policy Stud. Rev.*, 5: 624–633.

Peretz, P. (1988). Modelling the Provision of Industrial Development Incentives, *Market Based Public Policy* (R. Hula, ed.), MacMillan, London, U. K., pp., 150–180.

Plant, J. F., ed. (1986). Charles E. Lindblom's "Decision-Making in Taxation and Expenditures," *Pub. Budgeting & Fin.*, 6: 76–86.

Plaut, T. R. and Pluta, J. E. (1983). Business Climate, Taxes and Expenditures and State Industrial Growth in the United States, *Southern Econ. J.*: 99–119.

Pomp, R. (Aug. 1985a). A New York Perspective on Tax Incentives: The Role of Tax Incentives in Attracting and Retaining Business, *Multistate Tax Commission Rev.*: 1–9.

Pomp, R. (1985b). The Role of Tax Incentives in Attracting and Retaining Existing Business, *Tax Notes*, 29: 521.

Pomp, R. (1986). Simplicity and Complexity in the Context of a State Tax System, *Reforming State Tax Systems* (S. D. Gold, ed.), Nat. Conf. of State Legislatures, Denver, CO, pp. 119–142.

Pomp, R. (1989). Discussion: State Tax Expenditures—And Beyond, *1988 Proceedings* (F. Stocker, ed.), Nat. Tax Assoc.—Tax Institute of Am., Columbus, OH, pp. 33–36.

Pomp, R. D. (1993). Rethinking State Tax Expenditure Budgets, *Pub. Budgeting and Fin. Management*, 5: 337–354.

Premchand, A. (1983). *Government Budgeting and Expenditure Controls*, Internat. Monetary Fund, Washington, D.C.

Pressman, S. (1993). Tax Expenditures for Child Exemptions: A Poor Policy to Aid America's Children, *J. of Econ. Issues*, 27:699–719.

Regan, F. V., Fanshawe, H. M., Hadley, J. D., and Malan, R. M. (1993). Economic Development and Tax Expenditures Accountability and Control: The Problem and Some Proposed Solutions, *Pub. Budgeting and Fin. Management*, 5: 355–386.

Rogers, C. A. (1987). Expenditure Taxes, Income Taxes, and Time-Inconsistency, *J. of Pub. Econ.*, 32: 215–230.

Rosenbloom, D. H. (1987). Constitutional Perspectives on Public Policy Evaluation, *Policy Stud. J.*, 16: 233–241.

Rosenthal, A. (1981a). Legislative Behavior and Legislative Oversight, *Legislative Stud. Qtr.*, 6: 115–131.

Rosenthal, A. (1981b). *Legislative Life*, Harper & Row, New York, NY.

Ross, S. G. (Feb. 18, 1985). A Perspective On International Tax Policy, *Tax Notes*, 26: 101–106.

Schaatsma, P. W. and Vasche, J. D. (1993). Tax Expenditure Reporting and Fiscal Crises, *Pub. Budgeting and Fin. Management*, 5: 225–242.

Sheppard, L. A. (Feb. 13, 1984). Tax Expenditure Budget Revisited, *Tax Notes*, 22: 557–558.

Shoup, C. (1975). Surrey's Pathways to Tax Reform—A Review Article, *J. of Fin.*, 30: 1329.

Spicer, M. W. (1993). A Contractarian Approach: Rules Which Shape Tax Expenditure Decisions and Policies, *Pub. Budgeting and Fin. Management*, 5: 265–282.

Stephenson, S. C. and Hewett, R. S., (1985). Strategies For States In Fiscal Competition, *Nat. Tax J.*, 38: 219–226.

Surrey, S. S. (Nov. 17, 1980). *Our Troubled Tax Policy: False Routes And Proper Paths to Change*, Taxation with Representation Fund, Washington, D.C., 1980. (Speech to 73rd annual meeting of Nat. Tax Assoc., New Orleans, LA).

Suyderhoud, J. P., Pollock, R. L., and Singleton, W. R. (1993). Measuring State Income Tax Expenditures: A Pragmatic View of Income Tax Base Erosion, *Pub. Budgeting and Fin. Management*, 5: 417–442.

Taylor, D. C. (1993). Review and Analysis of Tax Exemptions in Washington State, *Pub. Budgeting and Fin. Management*, 5: 243–264.

Tax Notes (April 2, 1979). Oversight Subcommittee Hearings Initiate Tax Expenditure Review. *Tax Notes*, 8: 389–390.

Tax Notes (June 18, 1979). Halperin on Sunset for Tax Expenditures. *Tax Notes*, 8: 788.

Tax Notes (Oct. 26, 1981). The CBO on the Tax Expenditure Concept. *Tax Notes*, 13: 1011–1013.

Tax Notes (Dec. 21, 1981). Ture's Unreleased Testimony On Tax Expenditures. *Tax Notes*, 13: 1535–1539.

Teuber, J. (Feb. 14, 1994). Exclusion for Employer Health Payments Tops Tax Expenditure List, *Tax Notes*, 62: 796–798.

Ture, N. B. and Sanden, K. B. (1977). *The Effects of Tax Policy On Capital Formation*, Financial Executive Research Foundation, New York, NY.

U.S. Senate, Committee on the Budget, 95th Congress, 2d Session, (1978). *Tax Expenditures: Relationships to Spending Programs and Background Material on Individual Provisions*. Govt. Printing Office (Committee Print), Washington, D.C.

Vasche, J. D. (1987). Tax Expenditure Reporting—A Comment, *Nat. Tax J.*, *40*: 255–257.

Wildavsky, A. (1979b). *The Politics of the Budgetary Process* (3rd ed.), Little, Brown and Company, Boston, MA.

Wilson, R. (1989). *State Business Incentives and Economic Growth: Are They Effective? A Review of the Literature*, The Council of State Governments, Lexington, KY.

Wolfman, B. (1985). Tax Expenditures: From Idea To Ideology, *Harvard Law Rev.*, *99*: 491–498.

REFERENCES

1. J. B. Forman, "Origins of the Tax Expenditure Budget," *Tax Notes*, *30*: 537–545 (1986).
2. S. S. Surrey and P. R. McDaniel, "The Tax Expenditure Concept and the Legislative Process," *The Economics of Taxation* (H. J. Aarons and M. J. Boskins, eds.), Brookings Institution, Washington, D.C., pp. 123–144 (1980).
3. E. Zelinsky, "James Madison and Public Choice at Gucci Gulch: A Procedural Defense of Tax Expenditures," *Yale Law J.*, *102*: 1165–1207 (1993).
4. P. R. McDaniel, "The Tax Expenditure Concept: Theory and Practical Effects," *Tax Notes*, *8*: 587–592 (1979).
5. T. McCool, M. Brostek, S. Ragland, A. Stevens, E. White, and M. Wrightson, *Tax Policy, Tax Expenditures Deserve More Scrutiny*, U.S. General Accounting Office, Washington, D.C. (1994).
6. R. S. McIntyre, *The Hidden Entitlements*, Citizens for Tax Justice, Washington, D.C. (1995).
7. A. D. Manvel, "Tax Expenditures Rereviewed," *Tax Notes*, *67*: 293 (1995).
8. B. Elkin, "Auditing Tax Expenditures or Spending Through the Tax System," *Int. J. Govt. Auditing*, *10*: 7–16 (1989).
9. M. Daly, "The Role of Tax Expenditure Reporting In a Global Economy," *World Economy*, *18*: 87–111 (1995).
10. K. M. Benker, *Tax Expenditure Reporting: Closing The Loophole In State Budget Oversight*, National Association of State Budget Officers, Washington, D.C. (1985).
11. P. R. McDaniel, "Identification of the 'Tax' in 'Effective Tax Rates,' 'Tax Reform' and 'Tax Equity,'" *Natl. Tax J.*, *38*: 273–279 (1985).
12. S. S. Cohen, "Sheldon S. Cohen on Tax Expenditures," *Tax Notes*, Jan. 18 (1981).
13. "Fiscal '96 Budget: Exclusion of Health Premiums Tops Tax Expenditure List Again," *Tax Notes*, *66*: 921 (1995).
14. V. Thuronyi, "Tax Expenditures: A Reassessment," *Duke Law J.*, *1988*: 1155–1206 (1988).
15. A. Wildavsky, *How to Limit Government Spending*, University of California Press, Berkeley (1979).
16. S. S. Surrey and P. R. McDaniel, "The Tax Expenditure Concept and the Budget Reform Act of 1974," *Boston College Industrial and Commercial Law Rev.*, *17*: 679–738 (1976).
17. S. Hansen, *The Politics of Taxation*, Praeger, New York (1983).
18. R. F. King, "Tax Expenditures and Systematic Public Policy: An Essay on the Political Economy of the Federal Tax Code," *Public Budgeting Fin.*, *4*: 14–31 (1984).
19. A. Schick, "Controlling Nonconventional Expenditures: Tax Expenditures and Loans," *Pub. Budgeting Fin.*, *6*: 3–19 (1986).
20. S. Steinmo, "So What's Wrong with Tax Expenditures? A Reevaluation Based on Swedish Experience," *Public Budgeting Fin.*, *6*: 27–44 (1986).
21. J. Havemann, "Tax Expenditures—Spending Money Without Expenditures," *Natl. J.*, *9*: 1908–1911 (1977).
22. B. Kirchheimer, "Annual Tax Expenditures and Targets? Bill Bradley Says Yes," *Tax Notes*, *63*: 505–507 (1994).

23. W. Vickery, *Agenda for Progressive Taxation*, p. 18 (1947), quoted in B. Wolfman, "Tax Expenditures: From Idea to Ideology," *Harvard Law Rev.*, *99*: 493 (1985).

24. J. P. McKenna, "Tax Loopholes: A Procedural Proposal," *Natl. Tax J.*, *16*: 63–67 (1963).

25. B. Wolfman, "Federal Tax Policy and the Support of Science," *Univ. PA Law Rev.*, *114*: 171–186 (1965).

26. B. I. Bittker, "Accounting for Federal "Tax Subsidies" in the National Budget," *Natl. Tax J.*, *22*: 244–261 (1969).

27. B. I. Bittker, "The Tax Expenditure Budget—A Reply to Professors Surrey and Hellmuth," *Natl. Tax J.*, *22*: 538–542 (1969).

28. S. S. Surrey and W. F. Hellmuth, "The Tax Expenditure Budget—Response to Professor Bittker," *Natl. Tax J.*, *22*: 528–537 (1969).

29. W. D. Andrews, "Personal Deductions in an Ideal Income Tax," *Harvard Law Rev.*, *86*: 309–385 (1972).

30. W. J. Blum, Book Review, *J Corp. Tax.*, *1*: 486–490 (1975).

31. S. S. Surrey, *Pathways to Tax Reform*, Harvard University Press, Cambridge, MA (1973).

32. P. R. McDaniel and S. S. Surrey, eds., *International Aspects of Tax Expenditures: A Comparative Study*, Kluwer Law and Taxation Publishers, Seventer, The Netherlands (1985).

33. S. S. Surrey and P. R. McDaniel, *Tax Expenditures*, Harvard University Press, Cambridge, MA (1985).

34. E. N. Griswold, "Statesman, Scholar, Mentor," "In Memoriam: Stanley S. Surrey," *Harvard Law Rev.*, *98*: 329–350 (1984).

35. B. Wolfman, "Statesman, Scholar, Mentor," "In Memoriam: Staney S. Surrey," *Harvard Law Rev.*, *98*: 343–345 (1984).

36. Committee on Fiscal Affairs of Organization for Economic Cooperation and Development, *Tax Expenditures*, OECD, Paris (1984).

37. New York State Department of Taxation and Finance, *Issues In State Tax Expenditure Reporting: A Discussion Paper*, Office of Tax Policy Analysis, Albany, NY (1988).

38. "Tax Expenditures" (Chapter 5), *Analytical Perspectives, Budget of the United States Govt., Fiscal 1996*, Government Printing Office, Washington, D.C. (1995)

39. M. J. McIntyre, "A Solution to the Problem of Defining a Tax Expenditure," *U.C. Davis Law Rev.*, *14*: 79–103 (1980).

40. S. Fiekowsky, "The Relation of Tax Expenditures to the Distribution of the 'Fiscal Burden,'" *Canadian Taxation*, *2*: 213–216 (1980).

41. D. J. Shakow, "Tax Expenditures for Housing," *Tax Notes*, *59*: 1823–1828 (1993).

42. P. R. McDaniel, "Institutional Procedures for Congressional Review of Tax Expenditures," *Tax Notes*, *8*: 659–664 (1979).

43. I. Kristol, "Taxes, Poverty, and Equality," *Public Interest*, *33*: 15 (1974).

44. State of New York Legislative Commission on Public–Private Cooperation, *Tax Expenditure Reporting Requirements: An Effective Way to Monitor "Back Door" Spending*, State of New York, Albany, NY (1987).

45. E. M. Kennedy [Letter to the editor.] Senator Kennedy on the concept of tax expenditures. *Washington Post*, May 2 (1976).

46. W. C. Gregory and J. T. Morberg, *Silent Spending*, House Fiscal Agency, Lansing, MI (1990).

47. New York State Department of Taxation and Finance, *Issues in State Tax Expenditure Reporting: A Discussion Paper.* Office of Tax Policy Analysis, Albany, NY (1987).

48. P. R. McDaniel, "Federal Spending Limitations," *Tax Notes*, *10*: 475–479 (1980).

49. H. A. Shannon III, "The Tax Expenditure Concept in the United States and Germany: A Comparison, *Tax Notes*, *33*:201–213 (1986).

50. G. B. Doern, "Canada's Budgetary Dilemmas: Tax and Expenditure Reform," *Public Budgeting Fin.*, *3*: 28–46 (1983).

51. J. McCaffery, "Canada's Envelope Budget: A Strategic Management System," *Public Admin. Rev.*, *44*: 316–323 (1984).

52. K. K. Edwards, "Reporting for Tax Expenditures and Tax Abatements," *Govt. Fin. Rev.*, *4*: 13–17 (1988).

53. S. D. Gold and D. Nesbary, "State Tax Expenditure Review Mechanisms," *Tax Notes*, *30*: 883–891 (1986).

54. J. E. Harris, "Tax Expenditures: Report Utilization by State Policy Makers," Ph.D. diss., Virginia Polytechnic Institute and State University (1990).

55. J. B. Forman, "Would a Social Security Tax Expenditure Make Sense?," *Public Budgeting Fin. Manag.*, *5*: 311–336 (1993).

56. J. J. Hudder, "Sales Tax Expenditure Reporting: A State Problem," *Public Budgeting Fin. Manage.*, *5*: 283–310 (1993).

57. B. F. Davie, "Tax Expenditures in the Federal Excise Tax System," *Natl. Tax J.*, *47*: 39–62 (1994).

58. S. W. Martin, *Accounting and Reporting for Property Tax Abatements*, Grand Valley State University, Grand Rapids, MI (1989).

59. R. W. Ingram and W. A. Robbins, "*Financial Reporting Practices of Local Governments*," Govt. Accounting Standards Board (Research Report), Stamford, CT (1987).

60. E. V. Regan, *Government, Inc., Creating Accountability for Economic Development* (Monograph of Government Finance Research Center), Government Finance Officers Association, Washington, D.C. (1988).

61. State Tax Notes, New York Legislative Proposal Would Require Tax Expenditure Reporting by Local Governments. *State Tax Notes*, LEXIS 93-STN 54-17, March 22 (1993).

62. J. W. Hughes and J. Motekat, "Tax Expenditures for Local Governments," *Public Budgeting Fin.*, *8*: 68–73 (1988).

63. P. R. McDaniel and S. S. Surrey, "Tax Expenditures: How To Identify Them; How To Control Them," *Tax Notes*, *14*: 595–625 (1982).

64. H. B. Leonard, *Checks Unbalanced*, Basic Books, New York (1986).

65. P. Richardson, "Tax Expenditures and Tax Reform: The Federal Experience," *1988 Proceedings* (F. Stocker, ed.), National Tax Association–Tax Institute of America, Columbus, OH, pp. 23–28 (1989).

66. W. M. Hildred and J. V. Pinto, "Passive Tax Expenditures: Estimates of States' Revenue Losses Attributable to Federal Tax Expenditures," *J. Econ. Issues*, *20*: 941–952 (1986).

67. W. M. Hildred and J. V. Pinto, "Impact of the 1986 Federal Tax Reform on the Passive Tax Expenditures of States," *J. Econ. Issues*, *24*: 225–238 (1990).

68. W. Hildred and J. Pinto, "Approaches to Tax Expenditure Estimation: The Case of Passive Tax Expenditures," *Public Budgeting Fin. Manage.*, *5*: 443–476 (1993).

69. C. Davenport, "Tax Expenditure Analysis as a Tool for Policymakers," *Tax Notes*, *11*: 1051–1054 (1980).

70. D. A. Kahn and J. S. Lehman, "Tax Expenditure Budgets: A Critical View," *Tax Notes*, *54*: 1661–1665 (1992).

71. S. S. Surrey, "Tax Subsidies as a Device for Implementing Government Policy," *Tax Adviser*, *3*: 196–204 (1972).

72. P. R. McDaniel, "Evaluation of Particular Tax Expenditures," *Tax Notes*, *8*: 619–625 (1979).

73. P. R. McDaniel, "Identification of the 'tax' in effective 'tax rates,' 'tax reform' and 'tax equity,' " *Natl. Tax J.*, *38*:273–279 (1985).

74. D. H. Weinberg, "The Distributional Implications of Tax Expenditures and Comprehensive Income Taxation," *Natl. Tax J.*, *40*: 237–253 (1987).

75. A. E. Meyer, "Tax Policy and the Federal Budget," *Am. Economist*, *35*: 32–40 (1991).

76. M. Hill and E. L. Ranck, "Tax Expenditures or Tax Loopholes?," *J. State Taxation*, *11*: 15–21 (1992).

77. D. Salamone, "Minnesota's Experience with Tax Expenditure Reporting," *1988 Proceedings* (F. Stocker, ed.), National Tax Association–Tax Institute of America, Columbus, OH, pp. 28–33 (1989).

78. R. McIntyre, "Lessons for Tax Reformers from the History of the Energy Tax Incentives in the Windfall Profits Tax Act of 1980," *Boston College Law Rev.*, 22: 705–746 (1981).

79. R. Pomp, "State Tax Expenditure Budgets—And Beyond," *The Unfinished Agenda for State Tax Reform* (S. D. Gold, ed.), National Conference of State Legislators, Denver, CO, pp. 65–81 (1988).

79. P. Richardson, *The Effects of Tax Reform on Tax Expenditures*, Congressional Budget Office, Washington, D.C. (1988).

80. N. A. Noto, "Tax Expenditures: The Link Between Economic Intent and the Distribution of Benefits Among High, Middle, and Low Income Groups," *Studies in Taxation, Public Finance and Related Subjects (A Compendium)*, Vol. 5, Fund for Public Policy Research, Washington, D.C. (1981).

81. D. Joulfaian, "Revenue Estimation and Progressivity: The Case of the Massachusetts Income Tax," *Natl. Tax J.*, 38: 415–419 (1985).

82. "Bradley Calls for Tax Expenditure Controls," *Tax Notes*, 66: 708 (1995).

83. Massachusetts House of Representatives, "Massachusetts HB 4427 Would Control The Cost of Tax Expenditures," *State Tax Notes*, LEXIS 95-TNT 117-15 (1993).

84. "Senate Begins Work on Tax Expenditure Line-Item Veto," *Tax Notes*, 66: 479 (1995).

85. D. A. Adler, "The Internal Revenue Code, The Constitution and The Courts: The Use of Tax Expenditure Analysis in Judicial Decision Making," *Wake Forest Law Rev.*, 28: 855–917 (1993).

86. H. F. Ladd, "The Tax Expenditure Concept After 25 Years," *NAT Forum*, 20: 1–5 (1995).

21

Budget "Uncontrollability" as an Obstacle to Improving the Allocation of Government Resources[1]

Murray L. Weidenbaum

INTRODUCTION

The increased efforts that economists and others have been making in recent years to improve the concepts and procedures for allocating public resources make it especially necessary and desirable to focus greater attention on the obstacles to making these improvements operational. One major set of obstacles to improving public resource allocation is the legal and other institutional constraints that limit the discretion of governmental policymakers.

For example, under present law it is almost futile to perform benefit/cost or similar analyses which may demonstrate that the government obtains a lower return on its investments in highway transportation than in air transportation or some other alternative and, hence, that some shifting of funds might improve economic welfare. The futility arises from the simple fact that the major financial authorizations for highway programs are not contained in the authorization bills requested by the President and enacted by the Congress, but in the relatively long-term legislation which authorizes the federal-aid highway program. Thus, the Congress cannot, through the budget review and appropriations process, in practice effect a transfer of funds from surface to air transportation by reducing the appropriations for the Bureau of the Public Roads and increasing those for the Federal Aviation Agency, two component units of the Department of Transportation.

Similarly, these is no discretion through the budget process to shift funds from an income-maintenance program such as public assistance to aid to education, both functions of the Department of Health, Education, and Welfare—or to any other purpose whether it involves expenditures or tax reduction. This rigidity arises because the expenditures under

Source: U.S., Congress, Subcommittee on Economy in Government, Joint Economic Committee, *The Analysis and Evaluation of Public Expenditures: The PPB System. A Compendium of Papers*, Vol. I, U.S. Government Printing Office, Washington, D.C. (1969). Some footnote material has been omitted.

the public assistance program are in the nature of fixed charges; they are predetermined by statutory formulas governing federal matching of state disbursements for public assistance. Given the permanent statute on the books, the amount that the federal government spends on this income-maintenance activity each year is determined by the pattern of state welfare disbursements. Neither the President nor the Congress can much influence the amount of federal expenditures in this area within the confines of the budget process. Changes in the basic social security legislation would be necessary.

There are many other examples of these institutional obstacles to improving the allocation of public resources, as will be shown later on a more comprehensive basis. The end result of course is that the process of public resource allocation is hardly that deliberate and systematic choice among alternatives that economists try to envision. Rather, it is a fragmented and compartmentalized affair. Many of the key decisions are not made during the budget process or within the budgetary framework at all.

It is an earlier stage of the process which is the effective point of decision making on numerous government spending programs—the enactment of substantive and often permanent legislation. This is the birth stage, and rebirth and growth stages, of a substantial proportion of federal spending. This is the stage where many of the basic policy decisions are made—the nature of farm subsidies, the types of public assistance payments, and the level of highway grants. However, since it is the substantive committees of the Congress which handle enabling or authorizing legislation (e.g. Commerce or Foreign Relations or Public Works), rather than the appropriations committees, cost implications of the new programs often are relegated to secondary consideration or even ignored.

As will be demonstrated below in quantitative terms, the effectiveness of appropriations control over federal government expenditures is far less than it superficially appears to be.[2]

This study of the techniques of governmental budgeting may shed some light on the substantive issues involved in the allocation of government resources. It may help to explain, for example, why the military budget goes through cycles of alternative expansions and contractions, while the expenditures of domestic civilian activities—notably the welfare programs—continue to rise almost without interruption. The basic explanation presented here is in terms of the differences in the relative controllability, through the appropriations review process, of the different types of government spending programs.

TYPES OF BUDGET CONTROLLABILITY

This study focuses on the effectiveness of congressional power over the public purse, as measured by the degree to which the Presidential budgetary recommendations are subject to substantial modification through the appropriations process. In most cases, the discretion of the Executive Branch in preparing the budget estimates is also limited by similar institutional obstacles.

The rather narrow definition of controllability of government funding used here needs to be emphasized. The analysis is being made from the viewpoint of annual action by the Congress on the appropriation bills that finance the various government agencies. Given a long enough time span and the support of the Congress as a whole, virtually all federal spending programs are susceptible to modification, if not elimination. If it is so wished, the Congress could repeal the substantive, permanent legislation requiring public assistance grants or veterans pensions or farm price supports, or at least modify the statutes to make them more permissive. In time, it could conceivably retire the public debt and thus obviate the need for annual interest payments or at least reduce the size of the debt to be serviced.

Nevertheless, in practice the President and the Congress do not face each year's budget preparation and review cycle with a clean slate; they must take account of large accumulations of legal restraints within which they must operate.

From the viewpoint of appropriations review, there are thus numerous exogenous forces and factors which they must take account of and cannot effectively control: the number of eligible veterans who apply for pensions or compensation, the amount of public assistance payments made by the states and for which they must be partially reimbursed according to prescribed matching formulas, and so forth. The relatively controllable portion of the budget, from this viewpoint, consists of those government spending programs where the determining factors are endogenous to the appropriations process, which may modify them, at least to a considerable extent.

Four categories of exogenous institutional barriers to improving (or at least changing) the allocation of government resources are identified here: trust funds, permanent and indefinite appropriations, fixed charges, and ongoing projects. These categories are not mutually exclusive and thus individual programs have been assigned to them sequentially; that is, all federal government activities operated through trust funds have been assigned to that category, even though the great bulk is financed through permanent and indefinite appropriations. Thus the category of permanent or indefinite appropriations is limited to federal activities not operated though trust funds. Similarly, activities financed under permanent appropriations may be viewed as a fixed charge on the annual budget. Nevertheless, only programs which do not fall within the two categories mentioned previously (trust funds and permanent or indefinite appropriations) are shown as fixed charges. Thus, double counting is avoided.

Trust Funds

The first category of relatively uncontrollable items dealt with here is the so-called trust funds. These vary from the large social insurance type of mechanisms, such as the old-age, survivors', and disability insurance program, to the gift fund for the Library of Congress. The common characteristic of these trust funds which is relevant for the present inquiry is that they are generally financed through permanent appropriations which do not require annual action by the Congress. As stated in one recent Budget Document: "Most trust fund receipts are made available for use by permanent law, without requiring further action by Congress."[3]

Another clear indication of the relative uncontrollability of these trust funds through the budget process is that they generally do not even appear in the annual appropriation bills. In the case of the social insurance funds, the actual level of expenditures is determined by the number of eligible persons who apply for benefits during a given year.

For grants to states for highways, the Federal-aid Highway Act of 1954 and amendments to it not only authorize the program but also provide authority to enter into obligations, in this case to commit the federal government to make grants to the states at a later date. This bypassing of the appropriations process if often referred to as "backdoor spending." Technically, however, it is backdoor financing. The actual disbursements of the federal funds to the states require the Congress to enact so-called "appropriations to liquidate contract authorizations." The latter is a mere formality. There is virtually no Presidential or Congressional discretion over these liquidating appropriations—the government was financially committed at an earlier point, at the time the obligations were incurred.

In the federal budget for the fiscal year 1969, trust funds accounted for $55.1 billion or 27% of the total budget authorizations requested for the year.

Permanent and Indefinite Appropriations

In addition to the trust funds, there are numerous permanent appropriations which are contained in budget funds. The largest of these is the permanent and indefinite appropriation for the payment of interest on the national debt: "Such amounts are appropriated as may be necessary to pay the interest each year on the public debt" (31 U.S.C. 711 (2) and 732).

Other permanent accounts cover such items as the appropriations to the Department of Agriculture for removal of surplus farm commodities and to the Department of the Interior for range improvements. Thirty percent of gross customs receipts is automatically available to finance the agriculture program each year, regardless of estimated need or relative desirability vis-à-vis the changing mix of public sector activities. One-third of grazing revenues from Federal lands is similarly available for range improvement work.

A related category of funding is the "indefinite" appropriations. Although these are contained in the annual appropriation bills, they are in the nature of a blank check good for one year. Indefinite appropriations authorize a government agency to spend the sums necessary to meet a given specified requirement. For example, the Post Office department is financed through an annual indefinite appropriation. So is the retired pay of commissioned officers of the Public Health Service.

In the fiscal 1969 budget, permanent or indefinite appropriations (other than to trust funds) accounted for $20.2 billion or 10% of the total authorizations requested.

Other Fixed Charges

A third type of budget request which is relatively uncontrollable through the appropriations process is often term a "fixed charge." These are programs where the level of spending is determined effectively by basic statutes rather than through the review of annual appropriation requests. The largest programs in this category are the appropriations for public assistance and for veterans' compensation and pension payments. The Department of Health, Education, and Welfare makes grants to states to reimburse them for a fixed share of the public assistance payments that they make. Similarly, the Veterans' Administration provides statutorily determined benefits to all qualifying veterans or their widows and children who apply.

Although programs such as these are funded through annual definite appropriations, there is little effective control over the actual level of disbursements. Frequently, the initial appropriations turn out to be too low and supplemental appropriations are subsequently requested and routinely approved. There is considerable incentive for the Congress to appropriate less than the initial amount requested in the budget for these items. Thus, it gains some political benefit for supposedly "cutting" the budget. They then can later and much more quietly vote supplemental funds.

In the fiscal 1969 budget, fixed charges (other than those arising from trust funds and other permanent appropriations) amounted to $19.0 billion or 9% of budget requests.

Partially Completed Projects

The final type of relatively uncontrollable budget activity analyzed here is the amount of new funds requested to continue or complete construction and similar long-term projects started with money voted in the budgets of earlier years. The almost unassailable justification for these appropriations is the old question, "What is the value of just half a bridge?" Typically for government agencies with large construction programs, such as the Army Corps of Engineers and the Department of the Interior, each year's budget request is dominated by funds needed for projects begun under prior year budgets.

One indication of this influence of previous commitments is the fact that the Federal Budget for 1969 estimated that $2.4 billion would be spent in that year to carry on construction projects previously begun and for which a total of $28.8 billion already had been spent prior to the budget year. Even though these expenditure figures are not directly comparable to the appropriation or budget authority estimates used in the present study, the contrast between large amounts of what in effect are sunk costs and relatively small increments of additional funding is clear.[4]

The National Aeronautics and Space Administration (NASA) may constitute a special case at the present time [1969]. The great bulk of its current expenditures is devoted to completion of Project Apollo, the effort to land a man on the moon prior to 1970. Theoretically, the program can be reduced or stretched out and thus the President or the Congress could reduce the funds requested for Apollo. In practice, there is a very natural reluctance to interfere with the successful completion of an undertaking in which the nation already has invested such sizable funds (over $15 billion for Apollo during the fiscal years 1959–68 alone).

The data for funds requested to continue or complete ongoing projects, as shown in the tables that follow, are incomplete. In many cases it was not possible from publicly available information to identify the specific long-term projects of many agencies. Thus, the funds shown as relatively controllable are overstated, and the uncontrolled funds understated.

The Department of Defense (military functions) constitutes the major example of this gap in our knowledge and thus no military projects are shown in this category of relatively uncontrollable programs. On occasion individual weapon systems have been canceled after substantial investment of development and productions funds. Nevertheless, budget reviewers in both the executive and legislative branches often are reluctant to terminate a large project, even though the changing course of events indicates that the returns may not be as attractive as originally envisioned.

It may be that nonstatutory, implied commitments may be of overriding importance in military budgets from time to time. During the Vietnam War, for example, the Congress has appropriated virtually all of the funds requested in support of that specific and costly military endeavor. Formally, the $30 billion a year request for Vietnam was subject to substantial reduction by the appropriations committee, and is therefore included in the controllable portion of the budget in this analysis; in practice no substantial modifications of the Vietnam estimates were considered by the Congress. However, the Congress did critically review and modify the non-Vietnam portions of the budget of the Department of Defense.[5]

In essence, what is involved here is justifying this military situation, and comparable civil ones, in an implicit incremental benefit-cost analysis: Will the returns from the completion of the total project exceed the additional cost to be incurred in completing it? Clearly, many projects midway in the construction state may show incremental benefit-cost ratios substantially in excess of unity, whereas freshly computed total benefit-cost ratios would indicate far less attractive results. There may be substantial public onus attached to abandoning an effort after the investment of substantial public funds. The completion and operation of a public undertaking where the newly determined estimated costs are greater than the estimated benefits are hardly likely to attract great public attention.

ESTIMATES OF RELATIVE BUDGET CONTROLLABILITY

On the basis of the foregoing analysis, Table 1 was prepared in an effort to indicate the relative controllability of the budget request of the various federal departments and agencies. The data cover all of the recommended budget authority (new obligational authority as well as loan authority) contained in the Federal Budget for the fiscal year 1969. Table 1 includes both budget and trust funds and is based on the unified budget concept, the most comprehensive measure of federal finance available at the present time.

In the aggregate, the trust funds, the ongoing construction projects, and the other permanent and indefinite appropriations and fixed charges account for a major share of the budget—$97.5 billion or 48% of the total budget authority requested in the fiscal year 1969. It should be emphasized that where the budget document and available supporting materials did not provide sufficient detail, or where any doubtful cases existed, the items in question were treated as controllable. Hence, there may be some significant underesti-

Table 1 Controllability of Federal Government Budget Requests, Fiscal Year 1969 (in millions of dollars)

Department or Agency	Relatively uncontrollable				Relatively controllable	Total
	Trust funds	Permanents, indefinites	Fixed charges	Ongoing projects		
Funds Appropriated to the President	1,324	—	—	—	4,819	6,143
Agriculture	68	735	3,831	—	2,896	7,530
Commerce	134	214	—	—	679	1,027
Defense—military	7	—	2,313	—	76,796	79,116
Defense—civil	9	4	—	950	344	1,307
Health, Education, and Welfare	37,670	41	7,456	13	6,190	51,370
Housing and Urban Development	159	1,821	358	—	3,004	5,342
Interior	97	268	—	180	312	857
Justice	—	—	—	—	542	542
Labor	4,095	—	145	—	596	4,836
Post Office	—	920	—	—	—	920
State	12	2	—	—	414	428
Transportation	4,703	70	51	—	1,701	6,525
Treasury	39	15,425	—	—	−54	15,410
Civil Service Commission	3,626	—	42	—	131	3,799
General Services Administration	—	1	2	—	327	330
Railroad Retirement Board	1,064	—	18	—	—	1,082
Veterans' Administration	746	12	4,664	—	2,368	7,790
NASA	1	—	—	2,133	2,235	4,369
Export-Import Bank	—	608	—	—	—	608
Farm Credit Administration	535	—	—	—	—	535
All other	773	97	91	—	896	1,857
Total	55,062	20,218	18,971	3,276	104,196	201,723

Note: Includes requested new obligational authority and loan authority.
Source: Based on data contained in Budget of the United States Government, Fiscal Year 1969, and appendix.

mation of the relatively uncontrollable portion of the budget shown here. As mentioned earlier, there undoubtedly is an underestimation in the ongoing project category.[6]

Variations by Agency and Program

Were the fixed charges and other relatively uncontrollable items distributed proportionally to the size of the budgets of the various government agencies, the interference with the allocation of government resources might be less than is presently the case. However, as shown in Table 2, this is hardly the case. Some agency programs virtually escape the scrutiny of effective annual budgetary review—the Post Office, the Export-Import Bank, the Railroad Retirement Board, the Farm Credit Administration, and the great bulk of the Treasury Department.[7]

At the other end of the controllability spectrum, all or almost the entire annual budgets of the Department of Defense (excluding civil functions such as the Corps of Engineers' construction work), the Departments of Justice and State, and the General Services Administration are subject to effective control through the annual budget process.

An interesting contrast appears between the two departments with the largest budgets, one military and the other civilian. The Department of Defense—which received most of the funds appropriated for national defense purposes—operates with very few and very

Table 2 Relatively Controllable Portions of Agency Budgets—Fiscal Year 1969 Budget Requests

Justice	100
General Services Administration	99
Defense (military)	97
State	97
Funds Appropriated to the President	78
Commerce	66
Housing and Urban Development	56
NASA	51
All other	48
Agriculture	38
Interior	36
Veterans' Administration	30
Defense (civil)	26
Transportation	26
Health, Education, and Welfare	12
Labor	12
Civil Service Commission	3
Post Office	0
Treasury	0
Railroad Retirement Board	0
Export-Import Bank	0
Farm Credit Administration	0
Average for federal government	52

Source: Table 1.

small trust funds and other fixed charges. Almost all of its budget is subject to annual scrutiny.[8] In comparison, only one-tenth of the HEW budget can effectively be altered during the annual budget cycle. Most of the funds spent are insulated by permanent and indefinite appropriations and other long-term statutory commitments.

Upon further examination, it can be seen that a relatively small number of large programs account for the bulk of the funds which are relatively immune to effective budgetary control. The following 12 programs of over $1 billion each account for over $85 billion or 88% of the portion of the fiscal year 1969 budget, which is here estimated to be "relatively uncontrollable":

	In millions
Social security trust funds	$37,670
Interest on the public debt	15,200
Public assistance	5,765
Veterans' pensions and compensation	4,654
Highway grants to states	4,650
Unemployment insurance	4,095
Civil service retirement payments	3,626
CCC (farm price supports)	3,362
Military retired pay	2,275
Project Apollo	2,133
Medicare (Treasury contribution)	1,360
Railroad retirement payments	1,064

The Relatively Controllable Portion of the Federal Budget

Table 3 shows the distribution by agency of the relatively controllable portion of the federal budget authorizations requested for the fiscal year 1969. It is apparent that the Department of Defense accounts for the great bulk of the funds where the President and the Congress possess substantial discretion over the amounts initially requested (74%). For purposes of comparison, it can be noted that the DOD represents 38% of the total Federal Budget.

A handful of other departments and agencies—Agriculture, HEW, Transportation, NASA, and the Veterans' Administration—account for the bulk of the remainder of the relatively controlled portion of the budget.

REDUCING THE INSTITUTIONAL OBSTACLES

The data presented earlier lead to the rather striking conclusion that the great bulk of the expenditures for the domestic civilian agencies of the federal government is authorized virtually automatically as a result of the basic, continuing commitments previously enacted by the Congress, rather than through the deliberations of the annual budgetary process. Somewhat less conclusively, it appears that the military programs are susceptible to effective budgetary review to a far greater extent.

For most of the nondefense programs, the effective point of control appears to occur not at the time that the appropriations are voted, but at the earlier period where the Congress enacts the basic legislative commitments, that is, the rates of veterans' pensions or social security benefits.

Table 3 Distribution of Relatively Controllable
Budget Requests, Fiscal Year 1969 Budget
Requests

	Percent
Defense (military)	74
Health, Education, and Welfare	6
Funds Appropriated to the President	5
Agriculture	3
Housing and Urban Development	3
Transportation	2
Veterans' Administration	2
NASA	2
Commerce	1
Labor	1
All other	1
Defense (civil)	a
Interior	a
Justice	a
State	a
Civil Service Commission	a
General Services Administration	a
Post Office	0
Treasury	0
Railroad Retirement Board	0
Export-Import Bank	0
Farm Credit Administration	0
Total	100

[a]Less than one-half of 1%.
Source: Table 1.

For purposes of analysis, it may be helpful to divide the various uncontrollable items into two categories, "natural" and "artificial" (this attempt at labeling by no means exhausts the possibilities).

The "natural" type of uncontrollable item is exemplified by the permanent, indefinite appropriation for the payment of interest on the public debt. These payments arise directly from the amount and types of public debt issues which are currently outstanding. There is no discretion left at the disbursement phase of the process; the federal government simply must honor its promise to pay the interest on its obligations as its falls due. The natural uncontrollability of this item expense is acknowledged by the Congress in the form of a permanent appropriation to pay interest with no fixed dollar limit.

Similarly, the making of monthly compensation payments to veterans on account of service-connected disabilities is a program which is naturally uncontrollable within the confines of the budget process. The law requires monthly payments to all those certified by VA doctors as possessing a given percentage impairment of earnings. However, in this case the Congress insists on annually reviewing the appropriation for the payment of veterans' pensions and compensation. It is hard to characterize this congressional review as anything other than wheelspinning or having "fun and games" with the budget. Moreover, this exercise in futility diverts executive branch and congressional time and attention to the budget away from the areas where they can significantly alter the results.

In sharp contrast, there are numerous government programs which are artificially uncontrollable as a result of statutory law, but which lend themselves, through changes in substantive legislation, to effective annual budgetary review. For example, under section 32 of the act of August 24, 1935 (U.S.C. 612 C), an amount equal to 30% of annual customs receipts is automatically appropriated into a permanent, indefinite special fund for the "removal of surplus agricultural commodities." These amounts bear little relationship to the requirements for such funds. In fact, recent appropriation acts have authorized transfers of funds to the school lunch program and for related activities. Clearly, the amount of funds automatically appropriated exceeds the needs of the basic activity financed by the appropriation.

The annual grants of $50,000 paid to each state and Puerto Rico for A & M colleges similarly are made under a permanent appropriation act. Neither the Bureau of the Budget nor the President nor the Congress has any opportunity to review the annual appropriation request and thus annually redetermine the continued need for or desirability of these payments.

There are numerous other examples. Many permanent indefinite appropriations to the Department of the Interior are tied to a portion of revenues from sales or rentals of government assets and bear little relationship to the current requirements for federal expenditures for the activity to which they are earmarked. Thus, visitor fees at Yellowstone National Park are automatically used to provide educational expenses for dependents of park personnel, while visitor fees at Grand Teton National Park are used automatically as payments to the state of Wyoming, in effect in lieu of taxes.

CONCLUSIONS

Although the analysis of individual government programs presented here is incomplete (partly due to the lack of available data), it is clear that the effectiveness of appropriations control over federal government expenditures is far less than is generally appreciated. The following changes might be considered toward reducing these institutional obstacles to improve the allocation of public resources.

1. *A review of the necessity for the numerous trust funds that have been established.* Some of them—such as those for the financing of social security benefits—appear to somewhat approximate the general notion of funds held in trust. In many other cases—such as the federal-aid highway program—it is hard to make a case for segregating the activity from ordinary budget operations. In that particular case, the program of federal grants to the states did operate out of general revenues until 1954. In good measure, the highway-related excises which are now funneled through the highway trust fund may be viewed more properly as a form of earmarked taxes and treated as a special fund within the regular budget procedure.

2. *A reevaluation of the need for the various permanent and indefinite appropriations.* Some of them may have outlived their usefulness. However, there is no automatic or periodic review of their status and a clean slate examination might be useful.

3. *A reexamination of the "fixed charges" on the budget.* Some of them might usefully be converted into permanent or indefinite appropriations. In other cases, discretion might be restored to the appropriations committee to determine annually the

amount to be voted for the stipulated purpose, in the light of then current conditions and completing requirements. This latter action, of course, would require changing the substantive legislation governing the program.

4. *A focusing of greater attention on "new starts" of construction and other long-term projects.* It is a natural tendency to place greater emphasis in the budgetary review process on the items with the largest price tags. However, as has been shown, most of the appropriation requests in this category of long-term projects are to continue or complete projects already underway. The point of most effective control is at the outset, prior to the investment of public resources in the project. However, it is precisely at the starting-up stage where the appropriation requests are most modest and thus perhaps more readily approved. A careful weighing of the expected full or long-term costs and benefits is thus extremely important at the outset.[9]

The reduction of these institutional obstacles to maximizing the taxpayers' return on their investment will not of itself result in eliminating relatively low priority and less efficient government activity, but it should make efforts in that direction less difficult.

NOTES AND REFERENCES

1. An earlier version of this analysis appears in M. L. Weidenbaum, "On the Effectiveness of Congressional Control of the Public Purse," *National Tax Journal*, December 1965. The author is indebted to Mr. Suk Tai Suh for assistance in developing the statistical materials used here.
2. This substantive point is developed more fully in M. L. Weidenbaum, *Federal Budgeting: The Choice of Government Programs*, American Enterprise Institute for Public Policy Research, Washington, D.C. (1964).
3. *The Budget of the United States Government for the Fiscal Year Ending June 30, 1965*, Appendix, U.S. Government Printing Office, Washington, D.C., p. 898 (1964).
4. *Special Analyses, Budget of the United States, Fiscal Year 1969* U.S. Government Printing Office, Washington, D.C. p. 82 (1968).
5. See U.S. House of Representatives, Committee on Appropriations, *Department of Defense Appropriations for 1969*, U.S. Government Printing Office, Washington, D.C. (1968).
6. For what was perhaps the pioneering attempt to analyze the controllability of Federal spending, but limited to the administrative budget, see "Controllability of 1952 Budget Expenditures," in Joint Economic Committee Report, U.S. Congress, *January 1951 Economic Report of the President*, U.S. Government Printing Office, Washington, D.C., pp. 89–103 (1951).
7. Interfund adjustments complicate the Treasury figures. In practice, the budgets of the operating bureaus are generally subject to effective annual review.
8. As pointed out earlier, the Congress may be reluctant to exercise this potential control over the military budget during wartime and similar emergency periods.
9. In recent years, the budget requests for military and selected other areas have been prepared on the basis of "full funding" of proposed projects, that is of appropriating the entire estimated cost of a project at the time it is started. This procedure helps to enable the Congress to ascertain the total cost of a project before the work actually begins. However, water resource projects continue to be an important exception to this desirable change. See *Special Analyses, Budget of the United States, Fiscal Year 1970*, U.S. Government Printing Office, Washington, D.C., p. 81 (1969).

22

Budget Deficits in China: Calculations, Causes, and Impacts

Huaping Luo and Robert T. Golembiewski
University of Georgia, Athens, Georgia

This essay needs to acknowledge two deep debts. It sees itself in the perspective proposed by a leading report coauthored by the researcher to whom this chapter is dedicated in appreciation [1]. There, every public function—personnel, finance, and so on—is seen intimately linked with its cultural and constitutional contexts in developmental cycles whose understanding will challenge the best that is in practitioners and researchers. Ideally, re search can inform action; and action always helps set the agenda for research, whether that elemental fact is recognized or suffers neglect. Generalizations typically are dangerous, but we cannot here go far wrong in assigning a high priority to public budgeting and financial administration. This was true in the United States of the 1970s and 1980s; it remains appropriate for the 1990s; and one can even now raise reasonable claims for the continuing salience for financial administration as we move beyond the year 2000 A.D.—the Chinese year of the Dragon.

Cross-national studies on public budgeting and financial administration typically involve many challenges but, as a scholar points out, individual case studies and analyses constitute a key step in the right direction [2]. This essay deals only with selected aspects of China's financial administration that will inform later and full-blown comparative analysis. This essay does not hide its ambition, but it can now claim the label "comparative" only in the narrow sense of an early exploration of the synergy between the training, methods, and experiences of the two coauthors.

This essay also draws from Verma in another particular: Comparative methods and research designs have a special power. Although developmental phases often will differ, good comparative research is relevant for many governmental units. In sum, such research can inform policymakers about where their jurisdiction is, has been, or may be going.

Budget deficits are a main theme for disciplines like public administration, political science, and economics [3–7]. The People's Republic of China provides a window through which students of comparative and development administration can have a glimpse at how one developing country deals with budget deficits. This essay has four emphases: It discusses the calculations of deficits in China, analyzes the causes of budget deficits, assesses the impacts of deficits, and predicts the future of deficits in China.

CALCULATING BUDGET DEFICITS IN CHINA

Budget deficits are simply a fact of life for most of the countries in the world, and they are similarly understood. A budget deficit is simply the amount by which a government's expenditures exceed receipts. There are no important differences in the way oriental and western scholars generally define budget deficits [5, 8].

However, a general definition of deficits does not resolve the problem of how to estimate or calculate deficits [9, pp. 8–12]. To illustrate, the calculation of deficits by the Chinese government uniquely dealt with debt revenues before 1994.[1] In the Chinese calculation, a budget deficit equaled expenditures minus the sum of debt disbursements and current revenues. In other words, in China, debt disbursements constituted revenues rather than a means of financing deficits. As a result, the officially published deficits were much smaller than the ones calculated by the method accepted by most countries. For instance, suppose that in a fiscal year the government's expenditures were 500 billion yuan, debt revenues were 50 billion yuan, and nondebt revenues 400 billion yuan. For the Chinese government, the deficit was 50 billion yuan (500 billion − [400 billion + 50 billion]). But for most countries, the deficit would be 100 billion yuan (500 billion − 400 billion).[2]

Note another feature associated with this unique calculation. The official deficits were totally financed by "loans" or "overdrafts" from the central bank—the People's Bank of China. In China, up to now, the People's Bank cannot refuse overdrafts by the Ministry of Finance (MOF) because the government budget is approved by the top leaders. Of course, no one expected that such "loans" would be repaid by MOF to the People's Bank, and in fact such "loans" have never been repaid. The official or "hard" deficits were simply financed by printing money. Consequently, the financing of deficits in China was different from that in America where financing deficits through direct loans from the Federal Reserve is prohibited by law, although for the latter the Federal Reserve monetizes a small share of the government deficit through open market operation [5, p. 28; 9, p. 20; 11].

The Chinese official deficits were often called "hard" ones because of their great impact on the economy. They were financed by printing money, which increases the supply of money undesirably, and exert inflationary pressure on the economy [12]. Unlike the United States, where the money supply is controlled by the independent Federal Reserve, the Chinese money supply nominally is controlled by the People's Bank, which is very responsive to the commands of top party and government officials.

When judged from standard international practice, in China, "soft" deficits had also existed, although they were not reported by the government. Those deficits were "soft" because they were completely financed by the government's domestic and foreign debts, and exert less inflationary pressure on the economy than "hard" deficits. "Soft" deficits approximately equaled the net of debt revenues (new issuances minus repayments). This is not the place for details, but calculations suggest that about 58% of the actual deficits (calculated by international standards) from 1979 to 1993 are "soft."

The unique Chinese official calculation of deficits further encouraged an always tempting illusion—that the government can spend without discipline. On the maturity of government debts, and as debt repayments reach their peak, the government has simply but constantly increased the size of the new debt issuance. The illusion was a dangerous one, even if all stakeholders agreed to play that game.

The official calculation of deficits, although rather peculiar, had a major political advantage—it underestimated the size of deficits and hence overestimated the performance of the government. The Ministry of Finance (MOF) loved this definition because deficits were believed to be a negative indicator of MOF's performance. In addition, because Chinese "hard" deficits had an inherent linkage with inflation, when (as often happens) inflationary pressures became a concern of the society, the government and elites leaders tended to prefer underestimated if illusory deficits over a real but larger one because no one wanted to take the responsibility for inflation.

Note that, since the early 1980s, the government's attitude toward budget deficits has changed from complete rejection to limited acceptance. Prior to 1980, China's budgetary policy produced or even faked an annual balance between revenues and expenditures, plus a small surplus [13]. This budgetary policy was required by China's traditional command economy, in which the government controlled all economic activities. Microeconomically, the government specified what to produce and how much to produce by state-owned enterprises, which accounted for more than 80% of all goods and services. In this command economy, producer sovereignty reigned. Consumers had few choices other than purchasing whatever the state-owned enterprises produced: They could risk dilution of their funds by inflation, or go extralegal or illegal. Macroeconomically, the government tried to keep a balance, although illusory, between the quantity of money in circulation and quantity of commodities in order to avoid a "hidden" inflation—commodity shortages. This was a losing game. The planned economy inevitably more or less resulted in shortages because price signals did not play an effective role in allocating resources. A planned economy failed because no government, even aided by modern computers, had the capacity to predict individual consumers' demands and, accordingly, to plan production. Budget deficits were believed to be a factor aggravating shortages. When prices were controlled, an unduly expanding supply of money would demonstrate itself by creating shortages of supplies and commodities. Of course, it is incorrect to attribute all shortages to budget deficits.]

In addition, the Chinese government tried to avoid deficits because they were believed to symbolize government inadequacy. Since the government had tried to maintain a picture of being omnipotent, it had claimed the ability to balance its budget. Budget deficits would erode the credibility of the government.

Consequently, the government tried to avoid deficits, or at least to camouflage them. Although deficits actually existed in 10 of the 30 years from 1950 to 1979, all of them occurred as a result of overestimating revenues or underestimating expenditures due to uncontrollable factors such as natural disasters [15]. In other words, not even a single deficit was planned. Rather, expenditure controls were weak and/or arbitrary. In China, for example, supplemental appropriations needed no approvals from the legislature. Typically, when an agency faced an urgent unplanned demand, it could obtain extra appropriations if its request was approved by the main party and government leaders. If no revenues available could meet the agency's demand, the Ministry of Finance would overdraw from the People's Bank of China.

In the early 1980s, as noted, the Chinese government policy featured a limited acceptance of budget deficits, related to 1979's unprecedently large deficit—17.9 billion yuan, or 14% of expenditures. This resulted from several sources: a revenue decline caused by wage increases to state-owned enterprises' staff and workers; an increase in capital outlays resulting from the government's ambitious development programs; an increase in defense expense due to the Sino–Vietnam border conflict; and a one-time repayment to government employees of salaries postponed by the Cultural Revolution.[4] In FY 1979, while revenues decreased by 1.78 billion yuan, the wage bill, capital outlays and defense expenses increased by 6 billion yuan [16]. The 1979 deficit, due to its immensity, shook the government's confidence in its ability to balance its budget in the short run, given the demands for government investment to fund long-term development. In 1980, the government planned a deficit for its budget for the first time [17]. Ever since, all deficits have been planned rather than as a result of unexpected influences in the implementation process, except for those in 1981 and 1986 when planned balanced budgets ended with deficits. The correlation between budgeted and actual deficits seems both high and positive (see Figure 1).

This change in budgetary policy might be said to symbolize a shift in fiscal philosophy in China [19] but, to a greater degree, it reflected tough trade-offs between political and economic alternatives. Although accepting deficit budgets was hardly easy, it did have its economic and political advantages, given China's context at that time. Economically, the government's dominant role in economic development was inevitable, given the tiny non-public sector, and government capital spending had been the major engine for China's economic development. However, limited budget resources became a severe constraint on future development: It seemed impossible to further raise tax rates and profit contributions. Compared to slowing economic development, deficits were politically attractive. Rapid development is very helpful in building top leaders' credibility. Because of a lack of personal stature like Mao Zedong's, the Chinese leaders in the post-Mao period were eager to establish the trust of the people. People were tired of unfilled promises made by the government in the past. They strongly supported those who could help reduce poverty. As a result, development became a top priority. Selecting between reform and a balanced budget, the leaders chose economic reform. Hence, to post-Mao leaders, the political attractiveness of

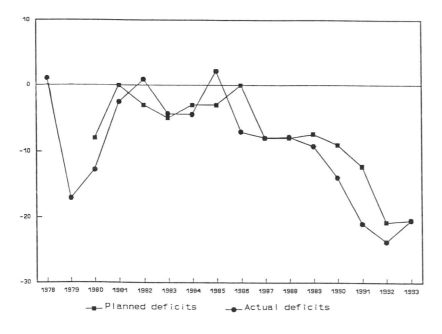

(in billions of yuan)

Figure 1 Planned and actual deficits (official definition), 1978–1993. (*Sources*: Ref. 18, Ref. 22, p. 20; Ref. 32; and Ref. 33, p. 20.)

reform even with unbalanced budgets was larger than that of no reform with balanced budgets.

As noted earlier, the official estimates underestimated the size of deficits in China because debt disbursements were counted as revenues. In order to have a clear picture of China's deficits, the official deficits need to be adjusted by a normal definition of deficits (see Table 1).[5] It should be pointed out that China's deficits were modest even adjusted according to internationally accepted practice. Table 1 shows that the ratio of adjusted deficits/GDP and the ratio of adjusted deficits/expenditures were 2–3% and about 10%. Those two ratios were only about half of the average levels for developing countries [11, pp. 29–31]. However, although declining in the mid-1980s, the deficits thereafter increased in absolute size. The causes for the sharp increases in deficits are analyzed in the next section.

CAUSES FOR SUSTAINED BUDGET DEFICITS

The growth of budget deficits was linked to market-oriented reforms and to the way they were carried out, but some political considerations were involved. In the post Mao period, especially during the late 1970s and early 1980s, competition continued between two political cliques: One favoring reform and development, and one insisting on maintaining the status quo [26].

The reform faction's chief asset was popular support because the people expected to live a better life through economic reform. It was very clear to those favoring reform that people were no longer satisfied with the planned economy because it led to serious commodity shortages. However, in the beginning, the reform lacked a strong power base. The status quo faction was dominated by conservatives, who objected to reform either because they feared losing their vested interests, or because they had a deep commitment to Mao's policies [27].

To counteract the conservatives, the reform faction had to obtain support from local bureaucrats at the provincial level and below, as well as from ordinary people. Those in this group proposed to decentralize or delegate as well as to increase profits retained by state-owned enterprises. Pro-reform leaders at the top won support from local bureaucrats because the latter gained power in the decentralization process. Besides its political advantage, decentralization was economically justified as improving efficiency in that the central government had never effectively controlled state-owned enterprises.[6]

Decentralization was implemented in two ways. The central government delegated to local governments discretion concerning planning, investing, and budgeting. In addition, reforms increased profits retained by state-owned enterprises and gave them more management discretion. The state-owned enterprises (SOEs) accounted for more than 80% of total output in China, and hence any improvement in their efficiency would trigger China's economic growth. Delegating management discretion was the first step to revitalize SOEs via increasing their responsiveness to markets. This discretion focused on input procurement, production decision making, pricing and marketing of products, and the use of retained profits.

Fiscal decentralization is another important dimension of decentralization. Under the new fiscal system, the fiscal contracting system, provinces were encouraged to develop their economies by keeping a large share of revenue increases, in sharp contrast with the previous fiscal system. Under the pre-reform intergovernmental fiscal relationship, the budgets of all provinces had to be approved by the central government, which dictated a specific percentage of the revenues that each province could retain for each new fiscal year (FY). The

Table 1 The Size of Actual Deficits in China 1979–1993

Fiscal year deficit	79	80	81	82	83	84	85	86	87	88	89	90	91	92	93
(in billions of yuan)	20.6	14.8	5.7	7.1	9.8	10.4	4.1	18.6	24.8	33.3	37.9	36.7	48.5	39.3	50.1
Deficit/GDP (%)	5.2	3.3	1.2	1.4	1.7	1.5	0.5	1.9	2.2	2.4	2.4	2.1	2.5	1.6	1.6
Deficit/expenditures (%)	14.0	10.1	4.0	4.3	5.8	5.4	1.8	7.1	8.8	10.6	10.4	9.5	11.7	8.8	10.6

Note: Deficits are calculated according to internationally accepted practice (see note 5).
Sources: Ref. 20, pp. 186, 245; and Refs. 21–24.

percentages varied from province to province. Some poor provinces, whose source revenues alone were insufficient to cover their expenditures, received grants from the central government.[7] Although this system was designed to reduce fiscal disparity among provinces, it often proved counterproductive because it encouraged provinces to spend money rather than save or boost revenues. Under this system, the more you spent relative to your own-source revenues (excluding grants) in FY_{t-1}, the higher the sharing ratio of retained revenues to total own-source revenues in FY_t. Of course, provinces' expenditures must be authorized, but the problem was that not all expenditures, once authorized, were justified. For example, even if some expenditures were no longer necessary due to unexpected changes after the budget was approved, provinces had no motivation to cut them. Under the fiscal contracting system, the sharing ratio for a province's own-source revenues was fixed for a 3- to 5-year period. This longer period was designed to stabilize the fiscal expectations of provinces and, hence, to reduce opportunistic behavior by them. In any case, the sharing ratio varied widely from province to province. Shanghai, the largest industrial city in China, was required to transfer three-quarters of its own-source revenues to the central government. In contrast, about 80% of Tibet's expenditures were funded by grants from the central government [28, p. 74].

The fiscal contracting system stimulated the development of local economies because it stabilized the expectations of local bureaucrats. Under the fiscal contract signed in 1979, for example, Guangdong province was required to transfer 1 billion yuan to the central government every year. Because it could keep 100% of marginal revenues beyond 1 billion yuan, it was motivated to develop revenue-producing industries, and in turn the increased revenues supported many development programs. As a result, Guangdong's economy has shown very rapid development for more than a decade.

However, the fiscal contracting system had reduced the growth of the central government's revenues since it was implemented more than decade ago. In the post-Mao period, provinces' interests and independence were strengthened and they gained opportunities to bargain with the central government. In the negotiations with provinces, the central government did not have as much leverage as in the pre-reform period. In fact, the central government often had to make concessions, with the major consequence that the growth rate of transferred revenues from provinces to the central government was low, as compared with both economic growth and inflation. According to the fiscal contracts for 1988–1990, the nominal growth rate of transferred revenues from provinces to the central government ranged from 3.5% to 9% while, in the same interval, GNP grew annually by 14% [28, p. 264]. Because fiscal contracts were fixed for 3–5 years, the central government could not adjust the sharing percentages annually, as it did before. When the economy grew rapidly, the central government's revenues did not increase at the same rate, and provinces got windfalls. As a result, the growth of local government's revenues was larger than that of the central government's revenues, and the ratio of the central government's revenues to consolidated revenues went down over time [29]. While local governments could always find items on which to spend, the central government had to fund its increasing expenditures even if its revenues grew slowly because it seemed to lag in transferring expenditure responsibilities to provincial governments. This inevitably led to an increase in national deficits.

Another negative impact of decentralization on balanced budgets was abuse of discretion, including the granting of tax reductions and exemptions by local governments. Although in China all taxes belong to the central government by law, provincial and county governments enjoy important discretion—for example, in granting tax reductions and exemptions to enterprises under their jurisdictions. Decentralization reinforced provincial motivation to seek their own interests. In the post-Mao period, performance on local economic development and popular support become more important than rewards from Beijing.

In order to protect their own interests, rich provinces used both illegitimate and legitimate methods to reduce the tax liabilities of their enterprises. Those provinces with a high revenue-remitting percentage would reduce the tax liabilities or profit remittances of their own enterprises rather than transfer revenues to the central government [30, p. 17], often excessively. In this way, revenues were kept in their own enterprises and later would be "voluntarily" donated for local expenditures. Ningbo, a city of Jiangsu Province but under fiscal contract with the central government, was required to remit 72.1% of its own source revenues [28, p. 74]. For instance, if it reduced the tax liability of one of its enterprises by 100 yuan, the central government's revenues would decrease by 72.1 yuan and Ningbo's government revenues would be reduced by 27.9 yuan. After that, the Ningbo government could ask those enterprises granted tax reductions to contribute 40 yuan to those programs financed by Ningbo's budget. In this game, the central government lost 72.1 yuan, but the Ningbo government and the hypothesized SOE "gained" that sum: 12.1 yuan to the Ningbo government, and 60 yuan to the SOE. Such abuses of tax reductions and exemptions contributed to the growth of central budget deficits [21].

Another factor contributing to the growth of budget deficits was the reform of state-owned enterprises (SOEs). In the pre-reform period, taxes and transferred profits from SOEs accounted for 85% of the consolidated government's revenues [31, p. 191]. However, SOEs operated inefficiently due to stifling management system. SOEs acted as a government agency in relationships with central or provincial or country governments. Besides paying taxes, SOEs transferred nearly all profits to the government. At the same time, almost all expenses—including working capital and investment—were financed by government budgets. Moreover, SOEs would receive subsidies from governments for their operating losses. The lack of linkage between SOEs' profit performance and the disposition of financial resources, although contributing to equal income distribution among workers, eroded the motivation of SOEs to seek efficiency. As a result, from the beginning of the reform, the government decided to strengthen the linkage between the amount of profits made by SOEs and their spending.

Since then, two major profit-contracting systems—the profit-retaining system (PRS) before 1986, and the contracting responsibility system (CRS) since 1987—have been carried out in SOEs. Under either system, if the actual profits made by an SOE are smaller than or equal to the target profits set by the government, the SOE retain profits up to 10%. If the actual profits were larger than the target profits, as much as 70% of the excess profits could be kept in the SOE. This put pressure on the negotiation of targets, but otherwise encouraged profit seeking.

A higher marginal retaining percentage for increased profits over targets was an incentive for SOEs to improve efficiency. As China's economy showed rapid growth due to the reform and flow-in of foreign investment, government revenues did not grow rapidly as expected due to low performance of SOEs and the weaknesses in the profit-sharing method. Furthermore, the more rapid the economic development, the lower the ratio of the government's revenues/GNP, as SOEs had a higher marginal retaining percentage for surpluses over the target profits [30, p. 16]. Consequently, both PRS and CRS tended to lower the growth of government revenues.

The profit-contracting systems sparked controversies between the players in the decision-making process, based on their conflicting interests. In general, the systems were welcomed by managers and workers of state-owned enterprises. With increased profits retained by SOEs, managers could control more funds and workers received more bonuses and improved welfare. In contrast, the Ministry of Finance (MOF) officials emphasized the importance of a balanced budget, and therefore opposed the profit-contracting systems. In the opinion of MOF, the systems were often titled in favor of SOEs at the expense of the government's revenues. MOF advocated implementing a tax-for-profit system, under which each SOE would pay taxes rather than remit profits to the central or local governments, because taxes are not subjects to negotiations. In contrast, other central industrial administration departments—for example, Oil, Railroad Transportation, Chemical, and Nonferrous Metal Industries—advocated the profit-contracting system. Under the profit-contracting systems, these ministries could play a role in setting ratios or quotas of remitted profits for enterprises under their supervision, and could even receive contributed funds from them.

MOF officials could generate a strong argument. Although fiscal decentralization and the profit-contracting systems provided institutional incentives for rapid economic growth, the government's revenues as a percentage of GNP declined from 34 in 1978 to 15.3 in 1993 (see Figure 2). Figure 2 shows that the consolidated government's revenues grew more slowly than GNP from 1978 to 1993, with the former growing at 9.7% and the latter at 15.3% [31, pp. 28–29].

As government revenues declined, budget deficits could have been moderated by reducing expenditures, but expenditure pressures were sustained. China's reforms were carried out in an incremental style because they had no precedents to follow [20]. Incremental reforms were intended to reduce risks and social shocks, but they had disadvantages—primarily, the failure of the decision makers to estimate in advance the fiscal impacts of reform programs and to integrate them into a comprehensive plan. More often than not, the government increased discretionary expenditures to compensate citizens for the increasing living costs arising from price adjustments and liberalizations, with the hope of mitigating

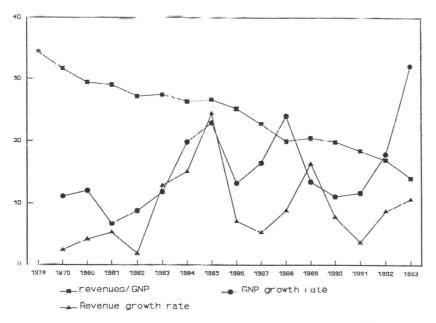

Figure 2 Government revenues (excluding debt revenues) and GNP (%) 1978–1993 (in constant dollars: 1980 = 100). (*Sources*: Ref. 20, p. 186 and 239; Ref. 21, Ref. 22, p. 20; Ref. 32; and Ref. 33, p. 20.)

Table 2 Structure of the Consolidated Government Expenditures (%), 1978–1993

Fiscal year	1978	1980	1985	1990	1991	1992	1993
Administrative	4.0	4.6	6.2	8.6	8.4	9.7	9.3
Defense	13.7	13.3	8.3	7.5	8.0	8.5	8.9
Education and science[a]	7.3	10.1	11.5	12.4	12.9	13.1	12.0
Culture, health and welfare	3.3	2.0	4.4	4.9	5.4	6.1	5.8
Economic services	14.6	13.1	9.6	9.8	10.2	11.2	11.4
Capital spending	43.5	32.3	27.7	21.0	20.1	21.3	18.6
Subsides	9.3	18.7	21.8	24.7	20.1	17.3	15.9
Other	4.2	5.9	10.5	11.1	13.8	12.8	14.7
Total	100.0	100.0	100.0	100.0	100.0	100.0	100.0

[a]Estimated by authors.
Sources: Ref. 29, p. 218; and Refs. 21, 22, 24, and 32.

popular discontent but with the reality of budget deficits. Main expenditure pressures have been from subsidies, education and technology expenses, and administrative spending (see Table 2). Expenditures as a whole increased a bit more rapidly than revenues, with the former growing at 10.1% and the latter at 9.7% [31, pp. 191–192].

The differing increases in revenues and expenditures resulted from a particular reform style, contextual factors, and development strategy. Since reforms were initiated in 1979, for example, the government's spending for subsidies has constituted a large share of total expenditures—from 9.3% in 1978 to 17% in 1993 (Figure 3). The subsidies included two categories: one for essential daily consumer goods, and the other for SOE operating losses.

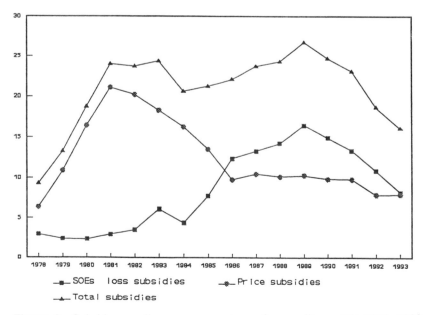

Figure 3 Subsidy spending as a percentage of expenditures (%) 1978–1993. (*Sources*: Ref. 20, p. 242; and Refs. 21 and 22.)

Subsidizing consumers for essential goods was a strategic choice for gaining popular support for the reform. It had been very clear to Deng Xiaoping and his supporters that even if a reform brought benefits to people in the long run, it would be doomed to fail if it were carried out at the cost of lowering the living standards of most people. A case-in-point, economic reforms in the East European socialist countries such as the former Yugoslavia were accompanied by inflation and increased living costs that led to social shocks. In order to reduce dissatisfaction with several redistributions arising from reform, essential consumer goods were subsidized. The subsidized consumer goods included food grains, edible oil, meat, vegetable, cotton, and household coal [34].

In sum, reform was often a matter of one step forward and then one backward. In order to stimulate agricultural development, for example, the government raised the purchasing prices of agricultural goods several times after 1979. Since an overall wage increase without efficiency improvement would reduce the profits of SOEs and probably also would induce inflation, wage increases were delayed. Consequently, in order to prevent the living standards of most citizens from going down due to inflation, essential agricultural products had to be sold to urban dwellers at prices lower than the purchasing prices paid to farmers.

The losses caused by the price gap between purchasing prices and reselling prices were subsidized from the government budget. Although price subsidies protected the vested interests of most citizens, they induced a perverse phenomenon: the greater the agricultural production, the more the government's spending on subsidies. If further reforms on marketing and pricing of agricultural goods are carried out, and if citizens accept upward adjustments of the prices of consumer goods, price subsidies will tend to decline (see Figure 3).

The other kind of substantial subsidy compensated for SOE losses during the course of market-oriented reform, and the bill is high. Overall, 45% of SOEs operate at losses [35]. In order to avoid serious unemployment and social riots due to the possible bankruptcies of SOEs, the government paid large subsidies to loss-making SOEs. A top leader even said that if all loss-making enterprises were allowed to go bankrupt, the resulting 20% unemployed might well hit the streets in demonstrations, and the government would be paralyzed.[8] The net contributions to government revenues from SOEs' profits decreased from 52.7% in 1978 to 5.0% in 1993 (see Table 3), a decrease due in part to the rapid expansion of the private economy. Recently, the government has made every effort—including passing the Bankruptcy Law and the Enterprise Law—to make SOEs responsible for their financial performance. These laws are designed to reduce government subsidies to SOEs, but their effects to date have been limited. Indeed, as Figure 3 shows, those subsidies have more or less stabilized at a historically high level.

Chinese leaders understood the positive relationship between increasing subsidies and deficits, but they preferred reform to a balanced budget. In 1985, when a price reform plan was discussed at a meeting of the top decision-making group, an MOF official argued that the country could not afford such an ambitious price reform program. Premier Zhao retorted fiercely, asking MOF not to use its budgetary problem to slow reform.[9]

Even if these subsidies to SOEs are unavoidable, they have serious consequences. Although increased government subsidies were not surprising given China's institutional context and reform strategy, ironically, administrative spending as a percentage of the government's total expenditures increased from 4% to 8.4% in 1992. While government has been reorienting from micromanagement to macromanagement, and as the tasks of government should have been reduced, the size of government employment also has increased by 8% from 1978 to 1990. This compares with the growth rate of 2.9% in the total social

Table 3 Net Contributions (in billions of yuan) from the Profits of SOEs to Consolidated Government Revenues, 1978–1993

Fiscal year	Profit tax and profit transfer	Loss subsidies	Net contribution (NC)	NC/revenue (%)
1978	68.6	3.6	65.0	52.7
1979	68.9	3.5	65.4	51.8
1980	70.9	3.4	67.5	51.3
1981	72.3	4.2	68.1	49.1
1982	66.8	5.2	61.6	43.6
1983	66.6	10.3	56.3	35.3
1984	71.8	8.5	63.3	34.5
1985	64.0	18.0	46.0	21.2
1986	63.8	32.5	31.3	12.8
1987	60.6	37.5	23.1	9.0
1988	64.2	44.6	19.6	7.0
1989	64.7	59.9	4.8	1.5
1990	68.2	57.9	10.3	2.9
1991	64.6	50.6	14.0	3.8
1992	60.8	44.6	16.2	4.1
1993	65.7	41.3	24.4	5.0

Sources: Ref. 20, p. 239; Ref. 21; and Ref. 33, p. 20.

labor force [31, p. 80]. Undoubtedly, this growth is counterproductive. It suggests that the government met difficulties in attempts at "streamlining." For example, government employees were reluctant about nongovernment employment because Chinese public bureaucrats enjoy high status, job security, and benefits such as public housing. Some top leaders also wanted to protect their pet ministries. For instance, two industrial departments—Machine Manufacture and Electronic—were merged in 1987, only to be separated in 1993, soon after Li Peng became Premier. Not incidently, Li Peng had worked in the Ministry of Electronic Industry.

The fast growth of spending for education and science as a percentage of expenditures—from 7.3% in 1978 to 13.1% in 1992—was supported by Deng's preference and China's economic development strategy. Unlike Mao, Deng studied abroad in the 1920s and accepted the significance of knowledge and technology to economic development. He walked that walk, rather than merely talking it. Indeed, when Deng was rehabilitated as Vice Premier for the second time, in 1977, he chose to take charge of national educational and science affairs. Virtually all Chinese leaders believed that it was impossible for China's economy to take off without major improvements in human capital. The economic objective is to make China a middle-income country in the next 50 to 70 years. Sustained economic growth based on quality human resources and technical progress is indispensable if this objective is to be achieved. Hence, increases in government's expenditures on education and science were inevitable strategic choices, and their short-run contribution to deficits intended to serve continued economic development.

THE IMPACTS OF BUDGET DEFICITS

In sum, the growth of deficits in China involved not only economic factors but also political dimensions. Politically, budget deficits supported the reform and hence strengthened the power of the pro-reform leaders. Realistically, few reform programs could have been implemented if China had stuck to the balanced-budget principle.

Nonetheless, conservative leaders often used budget deficits as a pretext to attack market-oriented reforms. Chen Yun, whose personal stature may be no lower than Deng's, is a stubborn proponent of balanced budgets. He attributed the growth of deficits to the reforms advocated by Deng, and saw them as a symptom of a deteriorating economy. Deng replied: "Why be afraid of small deficits? The United States has had large-sized deficits, yet its economy is still expanding." In November 1990, after the Tiananmen prodemocracy movement, conservative leaders—using budget deficits as evidence—tried to recentralize the fiscal system but failed due to strong resistance from local leaders.[10]

Despite the persistence of deficits, the political pressure has been strong enough to encourage certain flexibilities in economic reporting. In 1987, when many people complained about high inflation and attributed it to budget deficits, Premier Zhao ordered MOF to produce a phantom balance, a strategy often used in the American budgeting process [36]. MOF delayed reporting until expenses actually incurred in 1986.[11]

Budget deficits may have positive economic impacts under some conditions [37], and China's deficits as a whole contributed to the development of bottlenecked sectors such as energy, transportation, and communications. These arenas are very important to China's long-term economic growth, but they are underdeveloped, compared with other industries. The government has been the main investor in these sectors over an extended period, due to several deficiencies. Basically, capital markets are underdeveloped, and large investments in infrastructure are hard to obtain. In addition, nongovernment entities pour their capital into arenas producing high profits in the short run, but have far less interest in low-payback sectors, even if strategic. Although government investment has declined sharply, it concentrated on the bottlenecked sectors. If China balanced its budgets by cutting capital expenditures as it did in the past [38, 39], the investment in energy, transportation, and communications would bear the brunt, and their development would lag even more. Balancing budgets by cutting capital expenditures can be penny wise and pound foolish [40].

Seen from another point of view, China's deficits also have troubling impacts. Because most of China's deficits (adjusted for debt revenues) are financed by "loans" or overdrafts from the central bank, the deficits directly contribute to inflation (see Table 4). From 1979 to 1993, the correlation coefficient between the size of deficits and the rise in the retail price index is 0.93. This correlation is not perfect, but neither is it very distant from 1.0.

THE OUTLOOK FOR BUDGET DEFICITS IN CHINA

Will China's deficits continue into the foreseeable future? The answer is yes, probably.

Let us review the positive as well as negative impacts of possible future developments on both the revenue and expenditure sides of the government's budget. Positive developments include a higher growth rate of the government's revenues and a decline in subsidies. Here, the early signs seem favorable. Beginning in 1994, a new intergovernmental fiscal realtionship—a division of taxing power—came into effect [41]. Under the new framework, the central government divides taxing power between itself and the provinces in order to strengthen its fiscal position. Provinces are deprived of the right to grant tax exemptions or reductions if the tax in question is administered by the central government. Moreover, a new tax system, through which the central government tries to control most important taxes—such as profit taxes and value-added taxes—was implemented in 1994 [42]. According to this tax system, SOEs will no longer remit profits to the central or local governments. Instead, they will pay a profit tax, whose rate is 33%. All enterprises in a few

Table 4 Financing of Deficits (adjusted for debt revenues) and Inflation 1978–1993

Year	Deficits (−) (billions)	Percent of deficits financed by loans from the Central Bank	Retail price index (1980 = 100)
1979	−20.6	82.5	94.3
1980	−14.8	84.9	100.0
1981	−5.7	44.8	102.4
1982	−7.1	102.8	104.4
1983	−9.8	88.6	105.9
1984	−10.4	82.9	108.9
1985	−4.1	97.6	118.5
1986	−18.6	68.8	125.6
1987	−24.8	71.8	134.8
1988	−33.3	66.1	159.7
1989	−37.9	68.9	188.2
1990	−36.7	64.6	192.1
1991	−48.5	41.9	197.7
1992	−39.3	61.8	208.4
1993	−50.1	23.8	235.5

Note: Another source for funding deficits is foreign loans.
Sources: Ref. 20, p. 245; Ref. 31, p. 264; Ref. 22, p. 20; and Refs. 24 and 32.

industries have to pay a value-added tax. A consumption tax also exists. In addition, spending on price subsidies might be further reduced. In 1993, many provinces liberalized the prices of daily necessities and the government made no commitment to pay for possible increases in future living costs [43].

However, bad news concerning possible deficits also exists. Although the growth of the government's revenues may speed up in the coming years, expenditure pressures will remain. As noted earlier, it will be impossible to reduce capital outlays appreciably without negative effects. A study of deficits showed that in the pre-reform period the government tended to balance its budget by cutting capital outlays in FY_t, if the FY_{t-1} budget ended with a deficit [39]. However, this deficit-reduction strategy may result in more losses than gains over the long run. As analyzed earlier, investment in highly desirable sectors such as energy, transportation, and communications would be reduced sharply if the budget were to be balanced. A lag in the development of these sectors will constrain China's economic growth in the long run.

Another expenditure pressure on the government budget comes from pay increases to government employees. Since 1986, the pay level of staff and workers in the sectors of administration, education, science, health, and culture has been lower than the average wage level. It seems impossible in these sectors for the government to delay pay increases very much longer. The government increased pay by a small amount to government employees in 1994, a strong pressure for continuing increases to guarantee the salary gap in a reasonable range between the government and nongovernment sectors. Finally, SOE losses will continue to be a heavy burden, with nearly one-half of them reporting losses in recent months [35]. In short, deficits may increase rather than decrease. Revealingly, early predictions fear that the budget deficit in 1994 will be more than double 1993's deficit [24].

SUMMARY

China's deficits reflect serious conflicts in the course of market-oriented reform. The government had to retreat from overwhelming monopolization of resources, but its role in economic development was not assumed by other organizations. Due to decentralization in pursuit of market-oriented reforms, the government's revenues as a percentage of GNP went down, at least in the short run. An inherent weakness in the intergovernmental fiscal relationship—the abuse of tax reductions and exemptions by provinces—exaggerated the decline of revenues. At the same time, the government faces difficulties in shifting expenditures, and spending on subsidies increased at a high rate. Here, there is a serious dilemma: Reform has reduced the control of resources by the government, especially the central government, but sustaining development requires investment by government. Consequently, budget deficits became critical to the Chinese government. Political considerations are an important reason China abandoned the balanced budget principle and turned to budget deficits as a means of financing development. The political costs of deficit reductions will be prohibitive, and the probability of success seems small. People's expectations about living standards have escalated, and this implies a sustained and stable development. Slow development based on a balanced budget might lack support from the people.

Can China recentralize its fiscal system? That probably is doomed to be an exercise with high potential for civic unrest. Early reform empowered a particular interest group—local bureaucrats—and they would strongly oppose this attempt.

In sum, balanced budgets do not seem probable in China's future. This dour prediction has to be discounted a bit, however. Recently, the government initiated a series of reform programs concentrating on adjusting intergovernmental relationships, especially the tax system. Some of them are designed to increase the government's revenues as a percentage of GNP, as well as to increase the central government's revenues as a percentage of consolidated revenues. In addition, price reforms may reduce the government's spending on subsidies.

NOTES

1. The Minister of Finance reports a consolidated budget for all governments in China. Similarly, a province's budget consists of the budget of the provincial government and the budgets of all county governments. This budget practice is common in centrally planned economies [10].
2. Beginning with FY 1994, the government is changing the practice used since 1949: The government budget sees public debt as a means of financing deficits, but printing money is still an important source for funding deficits.
3. The famous economist Janos Kornai denied a linkage between budget deficits and shortage [14]. However, Kornai's conclusion is valid only when deficits are financed by debts, or when financing deficits by loans from the central bank does not lead to a simple increase in supply of money. Neither of the two conditions is satisfied in China.
4. Mao deprived hundreds of thousands of dissidents of their jobs from 1960s to 1970s. In 1979, Deng rehabilitated them and paid them salaries owed from the past years due to the deprivation of jobs.
5. In the Chinese context, adjusted deficit = (revenues + SOE's subsidies) + (expenditures + subsidies) + (debt disbursements − payments of principal and interest) [25].
6. State-owned enterprises are administered by either the central or local governments.
7. The percentage for FY_t is the ratio of authorized expenditures in FY_{t-1} (E_{t-1}) to provinces' own source revenues in FY_{t-1} (R_{t-1}). If the ratio for a province was larger than 1, it meant that the province received grants from the central government. If the ratio for a province was smaller

than 1, it indicated that the province remitted some of its own source revenues to the central government. For developed provinces, E_{t-1} is smaller than R_{t-1}, and the ratio of the retained revenues to the total own source revenues is E_{t-1}/R_{t-1}. Suppose that a province's own source revenues are 1,000 million yuan and the authorized expenditures are 650 million yuan in FY_{t-1}, and are 1,500 million yuan for FY_t. The retaining ratio for that province for FY_t would be 0.65, and retained revenues would be 975 million yuan (1,500 million $\times$ 0.65). The revenues transferred to the central government would be 525 million yuan [1,500 million $\times$ (1 − 0.65)]. For poor provinces whose E_{t-1} was larger than R_{t-1}, the gap was filled by grants from the central government.

8. Confidential source.
9. Confidential source.
10. Confidential source.
11. Confidential source.

REFERENCES

1. S. P. Verma and S. K. Sharma, *Managing Public Personnel Systems: A Comparative Perspective*, New Delhi: Indian Institute of Public Administration, p. 21 (1985).
2. G. M. Guess, "Comparative Government Budgeting," *Handbook of Public Budgeting* (J. Rabin, ed.), Marcel Dekker, New York, p. 95–124 (1992).
3. A. Wildavsky, *The New Politics of the Budgetary Process*, Scott Foresman, Glenview, Ill., pp. 205–209 (1988).
4. A. Schick, *The Capacity of Budget*, Urban Institute Press, Washington D.C., pp. 70–74 (1990).
5. D. Kettl, *Deficit Politics*: *Public Budgeting in its Institutional and Historical Context*, Macmillan, New York (1992).
6. J. D. Savage, *Balanced Budgets and American Politics*, Cornell University Press, Ithaca, N.Y., pp. 14–17 (1988).
7. R. Eisner and P. T. Pieper, "A New View of the Federal Debt and Budget Deficits," *Am. Econ. Rev.*, *74*(1): 11–29 (1984).
8. G. Chen, Gong, M. Hou, and Z. Yuan, *Public Finance*, China Financial and Economic Press, Beijing, pp. 123–135 (1984).
9. P. N. Courant and E. M. Gramlich, *Federal Budget Deficits*: *America's Great Consumption Binge*, Prentice-Hall, Englewood Cliffs, N.J., pp. 8–12 (1986).
10. A. Premchand, "A Cross-National Analysis of Financial Practices," *Handbook of Comparative Public Budgeting and Financial Management*, (T. D. Lynch and L. L. Martin, eds.), Marcel Dekker, New York, pp. 87–102 (1993).
11. W. N. Shahin, *Money Supply and Deficit Financing in Economic Development*, Quorum, Westport, Conn., p. 74 (1992).
12. "The Government's Revenues Exceeded the budget target," *People's Daily*, March 28: 3 (1993).
13. Z. Ge, "On the Issue of Balancing the State Budget," *Chinese Economic Studies*, *1*: 107–123 (1982–1983).
14. J. Kornai, *Economics of Shortage*, Institute for International Economics Studies, Stockholm University, Stockholm, pp. 931–935 (1979).
15. J. Shen and B. Chen, "China's Fiscal System," *Almanac of China's Economy* (Economic Research Center, the State Council of the People's Republic of China, eds.), Modern Cultural Company, Hong Kong, pp. 634–654 (1981).
16. Z. Zhang, "Introduction: China's Economy after the Culture Revolution," *China's Economic Reforms*. (L. Wei and A. Chao, eds.), University of Pennsylvania Press, Philadelphia, pp. 1–38 (1982).
17. B. Wang, "A Report on the Implementation of the 1979 State Budget and the 1980 Preliminary State Budget, *New China Monthly*, September: 11–18 (1988).
18. Ministry of Finance, Department of Comprehensive Planning, *China Fiscal Statistics*, Science Press, Beijing (1992).

19. K. H. Hsiao, *The Government Budget and Fiscal Policy in Mainland China*, Chunghua Institution for Economic Research, Taiwan, p. 46 (1987).

20. World Bank, *China: Reform and the Role of the Plan in the 1990s*, World Bank, Washington, D.C. pp. 37–42 (1992).

21. Z. Liu, "A Report on the Implementation of the 1992 State Budget and the 1993 Preliminary State Budget," *Beijing Review*, 3(1): 19–22 (1993).

22. Economic Intelligence Unit, *Country Report: China and Mongolia*, 2nd quarter, Business International, London, UK (1993).

23. "Guoqi Shangshi Nongtu Zhuoyong (State-Owned Enterprises Lose Their Dominance)," *World Journal*, April 23: 10 (1994).

24. "Jingnian Caizhengchizhi Jiangjin Qibaiyi (This Year's Deficit will Be Nearly 70 Billion Yuan)," *World Journal*, March 12: 11 (1994).

25. International Monetary Fund, *A Manual on Government Finance Statistics*, International Monetary Fund, Washington, D.C., pp. 91–92 (1986).

26. P. Short, *The Dragon and the Bear: China and Russia in the 80s*, William Morrow, New York, pp. 227–251 (1982).

27. S. L. Shirk, *The Political Logic of Economic Reform in China*, University of California Press, Berkeley, pp. 145–149 (1993).

28. R. Agarwala, *China: Reforming the Intergovernmental Fiscal Relationship*, World Bank, Washington, D.C. (1992).

29. P. W. Wong, "Central-Local Relations in an Era of Fiscal Decline: The Paradox of Fiscal Decentralization in Post-Mao China," *China Quarterly*, *128*: 691–714 (1991).

30. World Bank, *China: Revenue Mobilization and Tax Policy*. World Bank, Washington, D.C. (1990).

31. State Statistics Bureau, *China Statistical Yearbook*, China Statistics Publishing House, Beijing (1992).

32. "Xiaouchu Yingchizhi Jinnian Zhongtuxi (To Eliminate 'Hard' Deficits is a Challenge to the Implementation of this Year's Deficit)," *World Journal*, March 11: 11 (1994).

33. Economic Intelligence Unit, *Country Report: China and Mongolia*, 2nd quarter, Business International, UK (1994).

34. L. D. Wulf, *International Experience in Budgetary Trend During Economic Development and Its Relevance to China*, World Bank, Washington, D.C. (1986).

35. "State Enterprises Continue to Lose Money," *China News Digest* (Electronic News), October 28–29 (1994).

36. J. L. Mikesell, *Fiscal Administration: Analysis and Applications for Public Sector*, Brooks/Cole, Pacific Grove, Calif., pp. 84–94 (1991).

37. R. Heilbroner and P. Berstein, *The Debt and the Deficit: False Alarm/Real Possibility*, W. W. Norton, New York, p. 132 (1989).

38. H. Luo, "The Rigidity of and Control of Government Expenditures" (in Chinese), *Zhongqinnian Jingji Luntan* (Young Economist Forum), 3: 58–62 (1988).

39. H. Luo, "A Comparative Analysis of Fiscal Deficits in the Pre-Reform and Reform Periods" (in Chinese), *Caijing Lilun Yu Shijian* (Public Finance in Theory and Practice), 8(March): 17–20 (1988).

40. G. Colm and M. Young, "In Search of a New Budget Rule," *Public Budgeting and Finance: Readings in Theory and Practice* (R. T. Golembiewski, ed.), F. E. Peacok, Itasca, Ill., pp. 186–202 (1968).

41. "A New Plan for Reforming the Intergovernmental Fiscal Relationship Released," *People's Daily*, September 14: 1 (1993).

42. "China Adopts a New Tax System," *Beijing Review*, 37(11): 11 (1994).

43. "State to Ensure Steady Price Reform," *Beijing Review*, 36(33): 6 (1993).

V

STRATEGIC CONTEXTS OF BUDGETING AND FINANCE

EDITORIAL INTRODUCTION

Readers may have heard the one about the economist who dug himself into a deep hole. What to do? No problem! The economist simply assumed a ladder.

Such mind games are an elemental strategy, can be stimulating mind exercisers, and promise no great harm until you try to climb out of a real hole on an assumed ladder. Trouble will then follow, generally.

We editors tell this story not only because it is cute, but also because its moral is often neglected. Directly, many observers have tried to simplify PBF by making some convenient assumptions that simplify their mind-games, for good or ill. Consider this small handful of assumptions:

- Relatively complete and comparable knowledge by both voters and policymakers exists about what individuals and groups want, as well as about how to get it.
- Meaningful comparisons between alternative programs or agencies are available, so that scarce budget dollars can be assigned in terms of such criteria as the relative efficiency of attaining social ends of various orders of preference.
- Rational decision making characterizes both voters and policymakers.

PBF often has succumbed to the temptations and pitfalls of this assumptive strategy. Indeed, a central PBF point of debate—earlier, and even today—has polarized much of the literature. Witness the prevalence of opposing positions on several related polarities relevant to PBF logic, philosophy, and approaches—ideal versus actual, rational versus emotional, comprehensive versus incremental, certainty versus uncertainty, and so on. And some of the literature even warns about succumbing to the convenience of assuming what we should come to know only after much thought, experience, experimentation, and theory.

On balance, then, convenience has tended to overwhelm caution in PBF. But we editors and contributors try to do better here, or at least we do differently here. Five contributions provide detail about this intent to do better, and why it is necessary.

Decision Making Under Two Basic Conditions

Jeffrey Weber seems to be in the cautious camp, as he provides integrative oversight concerning a central point of contention in the PBF literature. Overall, his "Certainty and

Uncertainty in Decision Making: A Conceptualization" seeks to avoid either/or choices. That is, being comprehensive is a more reasonable goal when relative certainty prevails, while dominant uncertainty encourages more limited hunt-and-peck approaches. In effect, Weber poses a key question, perhaps even *the* question: Is it (A) Certainty or (B) Uncertainty in PBF? He responds: Either one or the other, or possibly even both, depending on the prevailing conditions.

The PBF literature has tended to be less restrained, as noted. Either A or B has tended to dominate in individual arguments, and often warfare, or some close approximation thereto, existing between proponents of A versus B. Weber does the reader the additional service of illustrating how three trends in the PBF literature can be informed by a deliberate effort to encompass both certainty and uncertainty, as the circumstances allow.

Exploring Polarities via Models

Perhaps the most intriguing approach to reconciling polarities is via "modeling," which typically relies on assumptions to build careful representations of parts of our worlds that can be subjected to rigorous tests. R. D. Specht helps us understand the why and how of this important potential in "The Nature of Models."

Careful model builders at once abstract from reality, and yet seek to provide a reasonable analog of some relevant portion of that reality. Consequently, a "good" model will help trainees learn how to fly complex airliners without risking lives or expensive airframes; and a "good" model will help "predict" what will happen in the economy if interest rates are increased by (let us say) 10%. In short, the assumptions of "good" models are either well tested or shrewd guesses, but in either case are supported by the model's ability to apply reasonably to relevant arenas of experience.

"Bad" models exist in large numbers. Typically, they rest on awkard assumptions, which, in the worst case, are unarticulated and perhaps even unconscious. Relying on them can cause much mischief.

Specht not only gives all of us fair warning, but he also helps us all to be better at differentiating "good" from "bad" models. That is a significant capability. For we all need models to live by, and we therefore unavoidably must increase the proportion of "good" models and decrease the proportion of the "bad," or we will suffer the consequences. Learning to separate the proverbial sheep from the goats is an important consequence of building this important competency.

Exploring Polarities via Two Models of Decision Making

Jack Rabin's "PPBS: Theory, Structure, and Limitations" provides oversight of one way in which a basic polarity engaged so much of our thought and action in the post-World War II period. With minor reservations, Rabin's analysis applies to the earlier and more pervasive emphasis on PPBS at the federal level. At all levels, the focus was on attempting to gain control over public spending, a challenge that remains front and center in our day.

Rabin provides much detail about how PPBS developed in policy and managerial ways, but central in his discussion is a basic polarity: rational versus incremental decision making. That focus is on two models that are known by many names and that, whatever their labels, have been central in much PBF thinking and practice. Thus, some prefer to think of rational-comprehensive versus successive-limited-approximations models.

We editors let Rabin and others unfold their analyses, while directing readers toward historic sources [e.g., 1], but here let us provide three introductory perspectives on rational-comprehensive versus incremental models, which apply to PPBS as well as much else in

PBF. First, the two views differ because their proponents are looking at somewhat different things in somewhat different ways. Incrementalists tend to emphasize how things actually are; in contrast, rational-comprehensive budgeters are given to emphasizing how they ought to be. Consequently, budgeters of the two persuasions are liable to find themselves at odds on a wide range of issues. Emphasis on the "is" and the "ought," in short, reflects different habits of mind and analytic approaches. The consequences are especially troublesome when those reliances are unreflective as well as unshakeable.

Second, political strategy and maneuvering are all-important to the incrementalist view, whereas they are distinctly secondary in any rational-comprehensive approach to budgeting. The rational-comprehensive approach implies an affinity to seek support for a program in terms of its consistency with national objectives. Its bias thus is toward articulating those objectives, and perhaps complaining if agreement about objectives is incomplete and movement toward them is sluggish. Although our present view admits of some exaggeration, the incrementalist seeks strategies that are acceptable enough even if agreement about their premises is in fact unlikely or impossible. Of course, agreement about objectives probably always is desirable. Failing that, this question remains: Is there some program we can agree is good enough, notwithstanding a lack of agreement about objectives or premises?

Third, deep philosophical differences may underlie the two approaches to PBF decisions. The incremental position is more at home with a pluralist concept of what the basic form of government is, or ought to be. The rational-comprehensive approach inclines more toward some form of elitism or authoritarianism as a descriptive or prescriptive guide for governance. Again, the point must not be pushed to extremes, for pluralism and elitism may have developmental ties. For example, "too much" pluralism may in practice lead to social and political chaos. In such a case, overexuberant pluralism may then lead to elitism, or even authoritarianism.

Denying One Polarity

As if matters were not complex enough, Lance T. LeLoup proposes that the rational-comprehensive versus incremental debate has been too much ado about too little. The title of LeLoup's contribution clearly indicates where he is coming from, as well as where he is going: "The Myth of Incrementalism: Analytical Choices in Budgetary Theory."

LeLoup takes on a big challenge. "Incrementalism" often constitutes the prevailing sense of what budgeting *is seen to be*, and many propose that incrementalism also prescribes how budgeting *ought to be*. As LeLoup sees it, incrementalism rests on a set of imprudently made analytic choices that lead to a "misleading view of budgeting." LeLoup concludes that its self-fulfilling character leaves incrementalism "nearly useless for social science theory." In making that case, LeLoup usefully contributes to the goals of this text.

Strategies for Fitting Political Dimensions

Steven Parker helps us understand why a single model has little chance of supplying all the needs related to PBF. His "Political Dimensions of Federal Budgeting in the United States" provides useful, overall perspective on the diverse quality of challenges to PBF over the years, in effect focusing on the kaleidoscopic political dimensions to which PBF strategies and tactics have to be fitted.

For those readers interested in a microview along the same theme, the recently deceased Aaron Wildavsky [2, pp. 64–84] provides useful guidance. He details a number of ways in which agencies can enhance their ability to influence multiple stakeholders. As it were, the father of incrementalism, Wildavsky, details in characteristically good form how agency officials can position themselves to be more than incremental in influencing budgetary processes. No doubt, Aaron enjoyed the irony and relished the paradox.

REFERENCES

1. C. E. Lindblom, Decision-making in taxation and expenditures. *National Bureau of Economic Research*, *Public Finances*, Princeton University Press, Princeton, New Jersey, pp. 295–323 (1961).
2. A. Wildavsky, *The Politics of the Budgetary Process*, Little, Brown, Boston (1964).

23

Certainty and Uncertainty in Decision Making: A Conceptualization

Jeffrey A. Weber

The Pennsylvania State University—Harrisburg, Middletown, Pennsylvania

INTRODUCTION

All of life is decision-making activity. From the time we wake up in the morning to the time we go to bed we are making decisions. Since our lives are consumed by the act of making decisions, it is not odd that decision making is the subject of an immense body of literature that spans several centuries, academic disciplines, and practitioner fields. It is studied in budgeting and finance, business administration, economics, history, management, organizational theory, philosophy, political science, psychology, public administration, and sociology, just to name a few. How a decision maker arrives at a "correct" decision has been a universal driving force behind this ongoing and possibly never-ending study.[1] The desire to be correct implies a need for certainty. Therefore we find implied in the majority, and the specific subject of a fraction of the literature, the concepts of certainty and uncertainty and their association with decision making, the decision maker, and the decision.

The purpose of this chapter is to introduce a broad generalizable conceptualization of certainty and uncertainty and then apply it to decision making and to three trends in the public budgeting and finance literature. Certainty and uncertainty are conceptualized as flowing from a knowledge paradigm and consisting of (1) temporal, (2) biological, (3) psychological, and (4) social components. To arrive at this conceptualization, a review of the literature is presented beginning with western philosophy and then moving to some specific decision-making literature of the past 50 years. This review helps identify a gap in the literature concerning the conceptualization of certainty and uncertainty. The next section responds to this gap by offering an alternate conceptualization. Next, the alternate conceptualization is applied to nine commonalties found in the decision-making literature. The final section explores the possible role of certainty and uncertainty within three broad trends that have been identified in the budget and finance literature: finance economist, incremental, and in-between [1].

A REVIEW OF THE LITERATURE

This literature review serves a twofold purpose: first, to introduce the concepts of certainty and uncertainty, and second, to identify a gap in the literature. The review begins with a brief survey of the thinking of several western philosophers and then examines a selection of the decision-making literature of the past 50 years. The philosophic survey combined with a review of current thinking shows the foundations and current conceptualization of certainty and uncertainty. It also reveals that this conceptualization has developed from a rational comprehensive paradigm, which has created a gap in the literature.

A rational comprehensive paradigm is defined as a focus on a decision maker's processes. Typically, this paradigm has been presented in a model that consists of (1) identification of the problem, (2) identification of alternative solutions to the problem, (3) establishment of criteria to evaluate the alternatives, (4) evaluation of the alternatives, and (5) choosing the alternative that best matches the evaluation criteria. The rational comprehensive paradigm has been presented in several different ways, but always with the same basic steps as just described. The primary focus of the paradigm is that all aspects of decision making are viewed from the perspective of the decision maker. This paradigm has been, and still is, dominating the decision-making literature's conceptualization of certainty and uncertainty.

Western Philosophy and Certainty and Uncertainty

Aristotle implies in *Nicomachean Ethics* [2] that certainty in choice is an attribute of one's knowledge of a subject (1139b.25–35). He explains that choice is "desire and reasoning with a view to an end." (1139a.30–34). "Intellect" and "a moral state" exist together in the making of the choice (1139a.30–34). Aristotle states that the intellect and the moral state acting together is the way one derives truth, which is knowledge that one is certain of (1139b.10–14).

Aristotle also contends there are five ways to reach truth (certainty) in choice: (1) scientific knowledge, (2) practical wisdom, (3) intuitive reason, (4) philosophical wisdom, and (5) art (1139b.15–18). Scientific knowledge begins with what is known and builds upon the known through inductive or deductive reasoning (1139b.22–35). Scientific knowledge is "judgment about things that are universal and necessary, and the conclusions of demonstration, and all scientific knowledge [, which] follow from first principles" (1140b.30). Practical wisdom is "the reasoned and true state of capacity to act with regard to human good" (1140b.20). Intuitive reasoning is the manner in which we grasp "first principles," which become the starting point of all knowledge and thus our certainty (1141a.1–10). "Philosophic wisdom is scientific knowledge combined with intuitive reason, of things that are highest by nature" (1141b.2). Finally, art is "a reasoned state of capacity to make" (1140a.7).

The basis of certainty for Aristotle was found in "intuitive reasoning" where a person establishes "first principles." Deductive or inductive reasoning was used to formulate logical propositions and arguments based on the first principles in the areas of scientific knowledge, practical wisdom, philosophical wisdom, or art.[2] Therefore, to Aristotle, certainty depended on the ability of an individual to (1) intuitively know the first principles, (2) gather information, and (3) apply inductive and/or deductive reasoning.

Thomas Aquinas in *The Summa Theologica* [3] examined Aristotle's assumption of our capability to reason and understand the facts in a subject area (I. Q1. Art. 5). Aquinas contended that certainty is limited by our intellect, human error, and error in previous knowledge (I. Q1. Art. 5). Aquinas argued that because of our limited ability to study and analyze a subject, our understanding of it is limited. He implied that reason and logic should be used in the pursuit of knowledge, but that any knowledge derived from such methods is uncertain, because of the "defect in our intellect" (I. Q1. Art. 5. Reply 2).

God, Aquinas contends, is the source of certainty, because he is the source of "wisdom above human wisdom" (I. Q1. Art. 6). God has provided "three grades of knowing powers:" (1) "the sense . . . the act of a corporeal organ," (2) "human intellect," the ability to reason; and (3) "angelic intellect," which provides divine revelation (I. Q85. Art. 1). Our ability to use these "knowing powers" proceeds from our physical and mental ability to act (I. Q85. Art. 3). One's knowledge moves from the simple to the complex depending on physical, mental, and spiritual abilities (I. Q85. Art. 3).

Like Aristotle, Aquinas implied that certainty is an attribute of one's abilities and knowledge. He also assumed human fallibility and limitations, the existence of an all-knowing and infallible God, and that one can have a direct linkage with God. Since one's certainty comes only from having accurate and factual knowledge, and since only God has infallible knowledge, then it is only through God that we can become certain. Aquinas implied that our certainty is a factor of allowing God to work through our rational processes. In essence, Aquinas argued for the use of spiritual intuition as a means of attaining certainty. This use of intuition is not being advocated by Aquinas as a substitute for thinking and reasoning, but instead as a means of making up for human limitations. The essence of Aquinas's thinking is that uncertainty is an established part of human nature and certainty can only be achieved through rational and spiritual methods.

Aquinas provided a division point in philosophic thought on uncertainty. One line of thought continued to expand on uncertainty as a part of human nature. The other line of thought saw limitations in our ability to be certain, but if the proper methods or techniques were applied, one could achieve a degree of certainty.

Thomas Hobbes in *Leviathan* [4] expanded on the belief that uncertainty is a part of human nature (pp. 49–61). He showed that our thinking occurs over time and that time serves as another mechanism for making us uncertain. Hobbes argued that:

> The discourse of the mind . . . is nothing but seeking. . . . We see something and we want to know its causes or we imagine something and we want to know how to bring it about. . . . The *present* only has being in nature; things *past* have a being in memory only; but things to come have no being at all, the *future* is only fiction of the mind. All our intellect is finite, therefore anything that man conceives, he must conceive in some place; and apply to that conception some finite determinable magnitude. (p. 53)

Because of the finite limits of the mind coupled with the effect of time, Hobbes implied that absolute certainty is impossible. Uncertainty, to Hobbes, appears to be a metaphysical attribute of our being.

Rene Descartes, in *Discourse on the Method of Rightly Conducting the Reason* [5], accepted the contention that one is always uncertain, but believed that it is possible to achieve amounts of certainty, thereby eliminating total uncertainty (Part III). Descartes explained that when studying a subject and seeking to understand it, or when making a decision, probabilities can be determined for the various explanations or alternatives (p. 49). Thus, probabilities serve as the basis for one's certainty. Probabilities are based on one's experience, others' experiences, and scientific method. He contended that when one can not determine a probability, then one should just randomly choose and act upon that choice. By just acting upon a randomly selected choice, the person is gaining experience that will later serve to help establish a probability for a similar situation (p. 49).

Continuing in the belief that limited certainty is possible, John Locke [6] and David Hume [7], in their respective works, both titled *Concerning Human Understanding*, contended that certainty is a measure of one's perception of things. Through demonstrative explanations, intuition, proofs, and probabilities it is possible for one to perceive certainty in an issue. From this point the two philosophers diverged.

Hume explained that reality is an attribute of the mind and of our existence (*Concerning Human Understanding* [7], pp. 458–459). He argued that certainty is beyond our ability to achieve, we merely believe we are absolutely certain, because the probability of an event occurring is so high that we discount any doubt (pp. 469–470). Probability is a function of quantity and number, but it does not deal with the interrelationship of matters of fact and existence (pp. 458–461). Matters of fact and existence are in the realm of cause and effect, which is discovered through experience (p. 459). Repetitious experience in an area provides us with the data to determine probabilities (p. 461). Hume contended that experience is what we draw our certainty from and probability is merely a limited predictor. Hume implied that absolute certainty is not possible and contended that all supposed matters of fact are really a combination of perception, customs, and experience (pp. 458–465).

Locke believed that there is a reality separate from one's consciousness, but there are no innate principles or ideas (*Concerning Human Understanding* [6], pp. 95–112, 119). Intuition is Locke's means of achieving certainty and he defines intuition as "the mind perceives the agreement or disagreement of two ideas *immediately by themselves*" (p. 309). Intuitive knowledge serves as the basis for Locke's definition of certainty: "the perception of the agreement or disagreement of our ideas, and demonstration nothing but the perception of such an agreement, by the intervention of other ideas or mediums" (p. 325). Certainty in simple ideas is achieved when the idea in one's mind is as one perceives it to be (pp. 324 and 331). Certainty in a complex proposition requires demonstrative or probability calculation, but each of these must still be broken down to the level where one can achieve certainty through intuition (pp. 310–312, 324). The intuitive process of certainty Locke called "certainty of knowledge," and the certainty achieved through demonstration or probability he called "certainty in truth" (p. 331). Locke thought that you can not have "certainty in truth" without "certainty in knowledge" (p. 331).

The elevation of perception and intuition by Locke serves as his method of counteracting the limitations of the mind, senses, and rational processes. The focus for Locke's conceptualization of certainty is found in the individual's perception of reality as measured against the knowledge that one has accumulated. The reliance on individual perceptions poses the dilemma of a highly subjective certainty, because individual perceptions may differ.

Immanual Kant in *Critique of Pure Reason* [8] categorized human cognition as philosophical or mathematical (p. 211). Mathematical cognition is empirical and can achieve demonstrable certainty (p. 211). Philosophical cognition is "the cognition of reason by means of conceptions" (p. 211). Kant contended that philosophical certainty is based on the construction of a general representation, which is derived from a priori intuition (p. 211). He explained that in this "nonempirical" cognition it is not possible to achieve certainty, but only to present what one perceives to be the concept of something based on experience (pp. 212–218).

Kant, by creating a division between the empirical and the nonempirical, appears to have brought the philosophic thought on certainty and uncertainty full circle to the thoughts of Aristotle. Kant, though, adds to the concepts of perception, intuition, and logical argument the dichotomy of empirically measured facts versus nonempirical values. To Kant, certainty in nonempirical areas is possible within the context of one's knowledge and experience (pp. 212–218). This certainty, though, is strictly a matter of individual perception.

The philosophical roots just described have served as the basis for defining certainty and uncertainty in the current decision-making literature. The limitations of the human mind and our inability to comprehend are the basis of the concept of "bounded rationality" [9,10]. The idea of determining the amount of certainty one has in an area (i.e., probabilities) is the subject of decision models and various statistical applications to decision making [11–16]. The belief that certainty is a matter of perception is being studied by multiple scholars [17–24]. In addition, it has also served as the basis for the development of attempts at measuring certainty and uncertainty in various decision-making environments [24,25].

Western philosophy established and institutionalized a rational comprehensive paradigm for conceptualizing certainty and uncertainty. A rational comprehensive paradigm is one that views certainty and uncertainty as a measure of the knowledge of the decision maker related to the decision, the alternatives, the consequences of the alternatives, and the choice. The next section shows that the rational comprehensive paradigm continues to serve as the basis for the conceptualization of certainty and uncertainty in the decision-making literature. Even when authors specifically seek to escape it, they continue to use it.

Decision-Making Literature of the Past 50 Years and Certainty and Uncertainty

The decision-making literature of the past 50 years consists of four branches that are derived from the decision maker's (1) ability to gather information, (2) ability to predict consequences of actions, (3) use of intuition, and (4) perception of environmental uncertainty.

The works of Herbert A. Simon dominate the first branch. Simon [9,10,26–33] implies in the majority of his works on decision making that certainty is based on the ability of the decision maker to gather information about the alternatives available and the consequences of those alternatives. He contends that "the function of knowledge in the decision making process is to determine which consequences follow upon which of the alternative strategies" [10, p. 68]. The desire to know alternatives and their consequences serves as the basis for the second branch of the decision-making literature.

The second branch seeks to apply statistical methods to the prediction of the alternatives consequences. Statistical models exist and are constantly being refined to aid the decision-maker in choosing the alternative with the highest probability of success. Within this branch, certainty is viewed as a continuum of probability. The higher the probability, the more the decision-maker is certain. This continuum was turned into a scale measuring the probability of the success of achievement [34]. This scale was later refined by defining the ends of the continuum as petty and severe uncertainty [14]. The emphasis that these first two branches place on a scientific process has spurred the creation of the third branch: the decision maker's intuitive ability.

The intuitive branch of the literature appears, at first notice, to be a counterreaction to the first two branches' dependency on the scientific process. The basic premise of the use of intuition is that the decision maker has a "way of knowing and recognizing possibilities in any situation" and that this way of knowing comes from within the decision-maker [18, p. 5]. Some see the way of knowing as a "gut feeling" or a "sensing" [18], while others see it as a spiritual guidance or an "inner compass" [35].

Though intuitive methods at first appear to be the opposite of the scientific method, in actuality they are similar. Intuitive models merely apply different search mechanisms to identify alternatives and different criteria to evaluate the consequences of those alternatives. Instead of using probabilities of success or failure to evaluate alternatives, intuitive models depend on how one feels about the alternatives either based on responsive judgment, gut feelings, or one's conscience. How the decision maker feels or perceives uncertainty serves as the premise for a fourth branch of the literature, the decision maker's perception of environmental uncertainty.

Environmental uncertainty is conceived as consisting of three components: effect, response, and state [36]. Effect uncertainty is "an inability to predict what the nature of the impact of a future state of the environment or environmental change will be on the organization" [36, p. 137]. Response uncertainty is "defined as a lack of knowledge of response options and/or an inability to predict the likely consequences of response choice" [36, p. 137]. State uncertainty "means that one does not understand how components of the environment might be changing" [36, p. 136].

The environmental uncertainty branch of the literature encompasses components of the other branches. It recognizes the bounded rationality of the decision maker to know the environment. Furthermore, the use of statistical and/or intuitive methods equally applies for understanding the environment.

This branch has gone the furthest in its attempts to understand certainty and uncertainty. Measurement scales have been constructed to further the research in environmental uncertainty [25, 37–39]. This research has been used to refine our understanding of certainty and uncertainty and to confirm the validity of previously used scales of measurement.

The conceptualization of certainty and uncertainty in the four branches of the recent decision-making literature also represents the current trends in the thinking and research. Each branch is developed from the rational comprehensive paradigm, because all four are from the perspective of the decision maker. The use of the rational comprehensive paradigm creates narrow boundaries for theory and research. The boundaries are narrow for they restrict the conceptualization of certainty and uncertainty. The conceptualization is limited to the decision maker's knowledge and perceptions of alternatives and consequences. This limitation has produced a gap in the decision-making literature, which is the lack of an adequate conceptualization of certainty and uncertainty that defines the entirety of the concepts. The move to a holistic conceptualization of certainty and uncertainty requires the use of a different paradigm.

CONCEPTUALIZING CERTAINTY AND UNCERTAINTY

This conceptualization of certainty and uncertainty begins by establishing a paradigm. Instead of the rational comprehensive paradigm, as previously described, a knowledge paradigm is used. The focus of the knowledge paradigm consists of three parts: (1) knowledge (independent of the decision maker), (2) the decision maker's ability to know and to act, and (3) the environment of knowledge and the decision maker.

Knowedge is viewed not only as an attribute of the decision maker but also as something that exists independently. The whole of what is known, unknown, and unknowable is the components of knowledge. The knowledge of the decision maker is considered in the second part of the paradigm by taking account of the decision maker's ability to search and integrate data and information. This part is similar to the previously discussed rational comprehensive paradigm. Moreover, the ability to act is also included because it directly relates to the ability of the decision maker to search and to integrate information. If the decision maker has some actual or perceived limitations in the ability to act, this will focus or skew the data, which are the searched and collected. The final aspect of the paradigm is the environment of knowledge and the environment of the decision maker. The environment of knowledge consists of what data and information has been kept and how it has been kept. This is a function of how data and information are recorded and the accuracy of their recording. The environment of the decision maker consists of social and organizational influences. Social influences include culture, norms, and technological and political factors. Organizational influences include structure, position, rules and procedures, and organizational culture.

This paradigm seeks to extend certainty and uncertainty beyond the bounds of the decision maker and to the bonds of knowledge. This broader boundary is useful because it improves the validity of the concepts for theorizing and research. The concepts now include their multiple attributes. This holistic conceptualization consists of four components: (1) time, (2) biological, (3) mental, and (4) social.

Time

Knowledge is affected by time.[3] Along the time line, knowledge can be conceived of consisting of the known, the unknown, and the unknowable (see Fig. 1). The known is all the data and information that we (humankind) have recorded and is presently retrievable. The unknown is all the data and information that exists but has not been recorded or was recorded, but the record, over time, has been lost. The unknowable is the data and information that have not occurred and therefore do not exist.

The known and the unknown exist in the present and the past. The unknowable exists in the future. Because of the effect of time on knowledge, uncertainty is not just the unknown, but also the unknowable. The unknown has the attribute of existing, but just is not known or understood by the decision maker and therefore could possibly become known. The unknowable is that which will never be known because it does not exist. The unknowable can be guessed, but because life consists of so many variables, the guess is never certain.

It is possible for the decision maker to search the past and the present to accumulate and integrate data and information. Theoretically, if the decision maker's search, filter, and integration mechanisms and abilities were good enough it would be possible to have knowledge of the exact events of the past and present. Currently, the mechanisms and abilities do not exist and it is only possible for someone to obtain partial data and information. Though the events have taken place in a certain manner, the discerning of those events is determined by the manner in which those events are recorded. The best that someone could

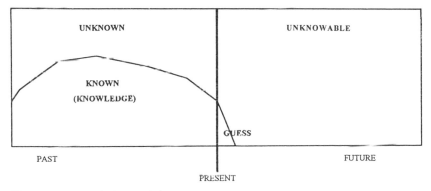

Figure 1 Knowledge and time.

hope for is a combination of multiple participants in the event, combined with detailed documentary evidence. The further back in time one goes, the more there is a decrease in the number of participants and the more chance there is that documentary evidence is lost. The closer one is to the actual event that took place, there are more participants available, but there is less complete documentary evidence that has been sorted, reviewed, and evaluated. There is a point, somewhere along the timeline for each event, where there is sufficient number of participants along with documentary evidence that allows for the potential of gaining the most knowledge possible.

The ability to guess the unknowable is a function of both time and complexity. The more variables are involved in an event, the more difficult it is to guess the future consequences. The further one gets into the future, the more variables interact with what one is trying to predict and, therefore, the less knowledge one has of an event. In the future there is no data to be searched for; therefore there is no information, and with no information one can not have knowledge of it. All that one can have is a guess, and "the ability to guess the future is extremely limited" [42, p. 333].

The ability to guess the future is a function of statistical probability, logic, and imagination. One can guess with some accuracy (probability) a limited number of events that will occur in the near future. By "some accuracy" we mean that the guess about the future event matches how the actual event occurs. The near future means within a year [42]. Logic also can be used to make a guess about a future event. Through inductive and deductive reasoning one could project into the future the most logical occurrence that could take place. Moreover, the imagination provides a unique mechanism for projecting into the future, because it creates a vision of what may be possible.

The primary limitation of a guess is that the guess may influence future behavior and thereby determine how the future will occur [43, p. 12]. This limitation appears to be lost on those who place much faith in trend projections and forecasting. Generally, it must be remembered that the future has not yet occurred and, therefore, there is no data or information yet to be searched and to be gathered. The future is, and always will remain, in the realm of the uncertain.

Biological

The biological component of certainty and uncertainty is the functioning of individual human organism(s) that is (are) the decision maker(s). The decision maker's ability to know and to understand consists of three components: searching mechanisms, filter mechanisms, and compiling and integration mechanisms [43, p. 27; 44, p. 14] (see Fig. 2).[4] The extent to which each of these mechanisms can gather and process data is dependent on the physical capabilities of the human organism(s) and on its (their) ability to use or create technology and processes.

Searching for data is a constant and directed activity. The five senses are bringing in data constantly, and data are being processed by the brain. Other data are brought in because they are searched for either purposively or by accident. The purposeful search for data implies a desire to get it for some end. The desire that produces the purposeful search is an area of overlap with the mental component. (The mental component is discussed in the next section.) How a decision maker searches for data determines the type and amount of data gained [20,43,45]. The search itself is an initial filtering of data, because the search is directed in a certain area and therefore gathers only a select amount of data or information [20,46].

Data and information are received and travel through filtering mechanisms in which some of them are discarded as irrelevant [44]. The data and information that remain go

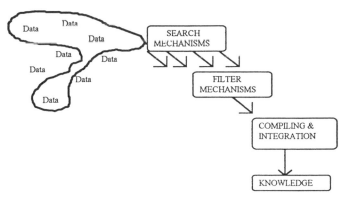

Figure 2 The accumulation of knowledge.

through compiling mechanisms that sort and categorize. Finally, the integration mechanisms interpret data, turning them into information; combine it with other information gathered; and place it in context with the existing knowledge of the decision maker. The sum of all integrated data and information equals the total knowledge of the decision maker.

Certainty and uncertainty are effected by the reliability of the biological search, filtering, compiling, and integrating mechanisms. If the mechanisms are of limited ability, then there is an increase in uncertainty. The ability to search may be misdirected and the wrong data are gathered. There is also the possibility of the search mechanism creating data that do not exist. The filter mechanisms may filter too much or not enough. Data or information that is irrelevant may be accepted as relevant, or relevant data could possibly be discarded. How everything is compiled produces uncertainty because it involves interpretation in order to sort and categorize the data and information. Finally, the integration of what is compiled can produce uncertainty, based on how it is evaluated and integrated.

The biological mechanisms produce uncertainty because of the subjective elements of interpretation and evaluation that are a part of it. The ability of a decision maker to understand its own biological limitations has not been explored. One possible conjecture is that it is a product of itself. In other words, a limited biological mechanism can only come to a limited understanding of itself. This produces an interesting dilemma, in that the decision maker may believe that it is certain because it does not understand its own limitations.

Mental

The mental component consists of the ability of the decision maker to perceive and reason. In essence, it is the decision maker's intelligence and those mental attributes that enhance or distract from it. The decision maker's intelligence poses limitations and boundaries to the acquisition of knowledge [9,10,43,47]. Intelligence is limited by the decision maker's biological capabilities (in terms of the functioning of the brain), existing integrated knowledge, and understanding [48,49]. This is true not only when the decision maker is an individual, but also when it is a group or organization [50–52].

The brain's abilities limit the decision maker in the pursuit and in interpreting the data and information. Common knowledge of the functioning of the brain reveals that the brain consists of three distinct regions: hind-, mid-, and forebrain. The hindbrain primarily transmits signals between the brain and the spinal cord and controls our automatic functions.

The midbrain serves as a connection between the hind- and forebrain. The forebrain consists of the two cerebral hemispheres, which are further divided into four sections: frontal, parietal, temporal, and occipital lobes. Each of these lobes deals with motor and sensory areas of the body. Another major functional area of the brain that has been identified is the association cortex, which appears to control the functioning of higher level activities.

Damage to any of these parts or various chemical imbalances in the body can alter the functioning of the brain. Along with influencing the gathering of data and information, the functioning of the brain also effects the decision maker's perception of uncertainty. A decision maker may perceive uncertainty where there is none or perceive certainty in areas that are totally uncertain.

Groups and organizations have the advantage of multiple individuals involved in decision making. Weakness in one individual may be offset by the abilities of another. The degree that this compensation occurs depends on the formal and informal structures and processes established within the group or organization [50,53]. Mental limitations in individuals, groups, and organizations can be partially negated by technology. Technology can only help to the degree that the user understands it and uses it properly.

Social

The social component of uncertainty and certainty is the interaction of individuals within groups or organizations and the interaction of the whole social unit with the decision maker [47, pp. 41–42]. These interactions, that are the "social" are viewed as having both nondeliberate [47, p. 42] and deliberate aspects [54, pp. 94–125].

Nondeliberate interactions are social norms and mores that subtly influence, direct, or limit the decision maker's searching and filtering mechanisms. Established beliefs and norms have long been viewed as one of the unconscious guides to individual and group action. The decision maker is unconciously directed by beliefs and norms to focus on certain data and information. Thus, some data and information will be overlooked. How those data are filtered and compiled will also be influenced by the customs and norms of the decision maker. The decision maker will be approaching the data and information from a perspective that has been established by the customs and norms. This perspective serves as the guide for the piecing together of the data and information. This is why different decision makers with different social backgrounds can arrive at different conclusions after examining the same data and information.

The deliberate social aspects are laws, regulations, rules, and procedures formally established to direct and control the decision maker's action. These affect the decision maker's ability to search by preventing access to possibly relevant data or information. Furthermore, the decision maker may decide that various data and information are irrelevant, because the deliberate social aspects make it unusable. An example of a deliberate social aspect affecting a decision maker's search and filtering mechanisms would be our laws and regulations concerning the conduct of medical research. Another would be the laws and regulations used to establish the conduct of research in space. The influence of laws and regulations on bureaucratic decision makers has been well established [11,55–60].

The deliberate and nondeliberate social aspects not only affect certainty and uncertainty by influencing the decision maker's searching, filtering, and compiling mechanisms, but also by influencing how data and information are recorded for future use. Social norms, customs, laws, and regulations direct what information will be preserved and saved and what information or data will be discarded. In essence they act as a social searching, filtering, and compiling mechanisms. This affects what it is possible to know and what will become unknown. Thus, the decision maker's search for data and information is already limited and directed from the very start.

We have conceptualized certainty and uncertainty from a knowledge paradigm and as consisting of the components of time, biological, mental, and social. The time component showed that certainty can only reside in the past and present, because the future does not exist and is unknowable. All that has occurred in the past and present is not known and a major part of it is unknown; therefore this limits the decision maker's ability to be certain even further. The biological and mental components further decrease the decision maker's ability to be certain, because of the limitations of the limitations of the searching, filtering, compiling, and integration mechanisms. The social component also decreases the ability of the decision maker to be certain because social customs, norms, laws, regulations, rules, and procedures act as biases that influence the decision maker. In the next section, we will examine how this conceptualization fits into decision making.

DECISION MAKING AND CERTAINTY AND UNCERTAINTY

The study of decision making has produced hundreds of models, processes, and techniques. A detailed accounting of all the decision-making models, processes, and techniques is beyond the scope of this chapter. Instead the focus is on the commonalties found in the decision-making literature. There are nine commonalties found throughout the decision-making literature:[5] (1) a definition of a decision, either implicit or explicit; (2) a decision maker; (3) a state of nature; (4) the ends or values being sought; (5) alternatives, known and unknown; (6) a relationship among the first five; (7) a choice; (8) the act of implementing that choice; and (9) a consequence, feedback, and interpretation of the feedback. By focusing on these commonalties we can see the relationship of the previously described conceptualization of certainty and uncertainty with decision making.

Definition of a Decision

One of the primary concepts in the study of decision making is a "decision." However, the literature is sparse defining explicitly the concept of "decision." Most of the literature implies a definition of a decision, and three definitions stand out in the literature: (1) a selection/choice [16,20,26,62,63]; (2) a mutual adjustment [64–68]; and (3) a chance combination of solutions, problems, and participants [69–71].

A decision as a selection or choice is the dominant definition in the literature.[6] Here a decision is a "practical activity" [62, p. 1]. This practical activity is viewed as an essential part of life where "All behavior involves conscious or unconscious selection of particular actions out of all those which are physically possible to the actor and to those persons over whom he exercises influence and authority" [62, p. 3].

This conceptualization of the concept of decision is prevalent in the public budgeting and finance and decision sciences literature. Moreover, an assumption of the selection/choice definition is that the decision is dependent on the decision maker. Another assumption is that there is a selection or choice to be made, and that the selection or choice was arrived at in a particular manner.

In addition it is assumed that through various procedures or techniques one should be able to improve one's ability to make a selection or choice. Examples of the selection or choice definition are cost-benefit analysis; planning, programming, budgeting system (PPBS); program evaluation review technique (PERT); and critical path method (CPM).

A decision also has been conceptualized as a mutual adjustment [64–68,72]. This mutual adjustment is a consensus among individuals who are participants in the decision-making process. This definition implies a group as the unit of analysis, and has been used to study group, organizational, and political decision making.

A chance combination of solutions, problems, and participants is the third conceptualization of a decision found in the literature [69–71]. This idea contends that decisions are not conscious or unconscious acts of choice, but actions that "just occur." It is argued that a decision rarely involves just an individual or group, but a myriad of other participants. Each of these participants have their ideas and interests and are influencing and affecting each other. Organizational structures and processes also influence the participants and affect the arrival and dissemination of information [69]. This disjointed combination of participants, interests, structures, processes and information is "loosely coupled" and determine (1) the arrival of information, (2) who becomes involved and when they become involved, (3) the amount of power or influence of each participant, and (4) how a decision is implemented [73, p. 17].

In applying certainty and uncertainty theory to the conceptualizations of a decision we see the importance of the time component. All decisions deal with action or thought yet to occur, so automatically uncertainty is involved. As a decision increases the use of what is known, there should be a corresponding increase in certainty.

A decision as a mutual adjustment maybe associated with the most certainty, because it relies on what has occurred and what is known. A decision as a selection or choice depends on the situation. It can be highly uncertain if it involves a projection far into the future based on little to no known data or information, or it can be as certain as decision making under mutual adjustment if it involves the near future and is heavily dependent on known data and information.

A decision as a chance combination of solutions, problems, and participants has the highest uncertainty because it focuses in the present (when the combination occurs). At the present, events and activities have occurred, but there has not been sufficient time to analyze and document them. A decision about a future action or activity, based on this little known data or information, will have elements of uncertainty.

Decision Maker

The decision-making literature views a decision maker as an individual, group, or an organization having one of two behaviors: (1) rational and/or value maximizing, or (2) participating in a loosely coupled system.

The dominant conceptualization of the decision maker is one who is rational and value maximizing [9,10,15,20,61]. This notion is commonly emphasizes the individual, but also focuses on group and organizational decision making. Moreover, this approach assumes that the decision maker is operating consistently with reason and logic and is seeking a course of action that will maximize the value(s) being sought.

A second conceptualization views the decision maker as a participant in a loosely coupled system [69–71]. Here the emphasis is not on the rationality of the individuals, but their activity and influence in the system. This conceptualization postulates that the decision maker's activity and influence in a system of participants, solutions, and problems are what determines the outcome of a decision, not rationality or value maximization.

The biological, mental, and social components of certainty and uncertainty are related to both these conceptualizations of a decision maker as rational value maximizer and a participant in a loosely coupled system. The biological, mental, and social components of certainty and uncertainty work together to determine the decision maker's conception of what is rational; the value(s) that is (are) being sought; and what constitutes maximization of those values. These components also influence the role one plays as a participant in a system. A part of a decision maker's certainty and uncertainty stems from how well the three components have worked together to define for the decision maker rationality, values, maximization, and participation role. When these terms are unclear in the mind of the decision maker, there probably will be an increase in the amount of uncertainty.

State of Nature

The state of nature is the environmental context within which exists decisions, decision making, and the decision maker [61]. The literature proposes two environments: (1) the decision environment, and (2) the decision-maker environment [9,20,24,25,30,43,47,61, 62,74,75].

The decision environment consists of certainty and uncertainty [14,24,36,61]. We have already discussed the idea of certainty and uncertainty found in the literature. The broader conceptualization of certainty and uncertainty can serve as a description of the decision environment. In this role, the components of certainty and uncertainty serve as linkages to all the other commonalties of decision making.

The environment of the decision consists of the attributes of the decision independent of the decision maker. For instance, is the decision that is to be made understandable and knowable or is the decision not able to be known fully? Furthermore, the environment of the decision contains of all the possible alternatives embodied in that decision and the consequences of those alternatives. Moreover, the environment of the decision exists independently of the consciousness of the decision maker, but at the same time it is affected by the actions of the decision maker.

The decision-maker environment is the knowledge, perceptions, biological conditions, socioeconomic influences, and motivations of the decision maker [47]. It is "an infinite complex of physical and usually social elements and systems in interaction with the organic individual" [43].

This use of a broader conceptualization of certainty and uncertainty brings together the decision environment and the decision maker's environment. It provides a useful way of understanding how the two environments overlap and interrelate, and also gives one a means of understanding the interrelationship of the commonalties in the decision-making literature.

The Ends or Value Being Sought

The decision maker has an end or some values that are desired. The clarity of the ends or goals is dependent on the ability of the decision-maker to define them. Nutt [20] defines ends or goals as the object of the decision, while others concentrate on the process used to determine direction and activity to accomplish an end or value [9,20,43].

Still others define the end or value as independent of the decision maker. Here the decision maker comes upon an end or value and then pursues it because it matches available solutions and the actions of the other participants [69]. Even in this view the ends or goals are dependent on the consciousness of the decision maker because they must be recognized or perceived to be used.

The ends, values, and goals being sought are the linking concepts that join the environment of the decision maker to the environment of the decision. At any single moment there are countless numbers of decisions to be made that exist totally independent of the decision maker.

Certainty and uncertainty influence the defining of the ends or values being sought. In addition, the location of the ends or values in time determines the certainty or uncertainty of their definition.

Furthermore, how concretely the ends or values are defined serves to focus the biological and mental mechanisms of the decision maker. Inadequately defined ends or values produce a broad focus, which increases the uncertainty of the decision maker. A concrete definition of the ends or values narrows the focus and increases certainty.

Alternatives

Commonly in the decision-making literature, and specifically in the rational comprehensive model, certainty and uncertainty are defined in terms of knowledge of the alternatives to accomplish an objective and the consequences of each alternative. Often, alternatives are viewed as solutions to a problem. Another view in the literature is that alternatives are solutions that already exist and converge with problems and participants to form a decision [69].

Two views regarding alternatives serve as the focus for much of the current study of certainty and uncertainty. On the one hand, alternatives are constructed or created to solve a problem. On the other, the alternatives already exist and are waiting for a problem. In either case, there must be a point where the decision maker becomes aware of the alternatives.

The broader conceptualization of certainty and uncertainty allows for a more complete understanding of how certain one can be of the alternatives chosen and their consequences. Knowing the uncertainty created by time, biological limitations, the working of the brain, and social influences allows for an understanding of where to focus effort and energy in exploring alternatives. Those alternatives, for instance, that are too far into the future should receive little effort because they will always remain uncertain. This knowing that alternatives can be affected by biological, mental, and social limitations places various uncertainties upon them and their consequences, which, in turn, can be used as criteria for consideration.

A Relationship Between the First Five Commonalties

All of the decision-making literature describes a relationship between the decision maker, the decision, the state of nature, the ends or values being pursued, and the alternatives; this relationship is at the heart of the decision-making process. The decision-making process can be divided into two major groupings: rational/intuitive comprehensive, and happenstance.

The rational/intuitive comprehensive grouping consists of all the techniques and models that make the decision making process dependent on the decision maker. In other words, according to this approach, the decision maker consciously or unconsciously follows a process and makes a decision. Various models and techniques in this grouping include the rational comprehensive model and all its variations [9,14,20,43,47,61,63,67,75–80]; incremental models [64–66,68]; and intuitive models [18,35].

The above happenstance grouping consists of all theories and models that contend that decisions result from a chance meeting of solutions, problems, and participants. Here, a decision is not dependent on the decision maker, but on solutions already available, problems that need to be solved, the various participants involved, and the time each of these is brought into the process. The best example of happenstance grouping in the literature is the garbage-can model [69,70].

The garbage-can model does not serve as a process, but as a description of reality and as a means of measuring it. The model contends that the rational process is not involved in making the decision, but rather that decision making is the blending of solution, problems, and participants. All the testing that has been done on the model has involved decision makers that were using a variation of rational comprehensive approach [70]. However, the question that has yet to be researched is, what brought the solution, problems, and participants together?

The relationship among the five decision-making commonalties also is connected with the certainty and uncertainty within each of these five areas. Possibly as each of these commonalties affect each other, the certainty and uncertainty that is a part of each of them also interacts. The result of this interaction is the overall certainty or uncertainty of the decision maker in a situation that manifests itself in the choice.

A Choice

The concept of a choice is a sixth commonalty in the decision-making literature and is the result of the relationship between a decision, a decision maker, a state of nature, the ends or values being pursued, and the alternatives. Choice is dependent on the clarity of the decision maker's definition of it and how close that definition comes to what was actually chosen. A decision maker may make a choice, but may not be conscious of the choice that was made or may believe that he or she made an entirely different choice. Thus, the definition of the choice affects how the choice is implemented.

High certainty in the definition of the choice produces high certainty in the means of implementation, whereas high uncertainty in the definition of the choice produces high uncertainty in the means of implementation. When the decision maker is certain of the choice, then the alternative that was chosen implies a means of achieving that choice. When the decision maker is uncertain of the choice, the means of implementation is also uncertain.

The Act of Implementing that Choice

The act of implementing the choice consists of putting the decision into action. Action produces consequence. How a choice is implemented will influence the consequences. The action part of implementing a choice consists of multiple decisions. Thus, within decisions are other decisions. With each implementation decision are the same effects of certainty and uncertainty that impacted the original decision. To determine if the consequence of the implementation of the choice is similar to the ends or the values originally being pursued, the decision-making literature provides a feedback loop.

A Consequence, Feedback, and Interpretation of the Feedback

The implementation of a choice will result in a consequence. The consequence, in turn, will be interpreted by the decision maker or others and will produce some feedback. How the decision maker searches for feedback and evaluates it are also decisions within the original decision process. Certainty and uncertainty have the same influence on this decision as on previous ones.

The feedback and interpretation decision influences the certainty and uncertainty in future decisions. The feedback, and evaluation of it, produces experience for the decision maker. As previously described, experience influences the biological mechanisms used by a decision maker and, thus, can affect the certainty and uncertainty involved in future decisions.

Thus far we have seen that certainty and uncertainty can be conceptualized as consisting of time, biological, mental, and social components. The relationship of this conceptualization to decision making was examined by focusing on six commonalties in the decision-making literature, and resulted in a rather broad notion of the concepts of certainty and uncertainty. A narrower focus will now be sought by applying the conceptualization of certainty and uncertainty to three previously identified trends in the public budgeting and finance literature: finance economist, incremental, and in-between [1].

APPLICATION TO PUBLIC BUDGETING

The public budgeting and finance literature consist of three schools of thought, two developed and one that is developing: (1) finance economist, (2) incremental, and (3) in-between [1]. This section examines each of these schools of thought from the perspective of the previous discussion on certainty and uncertainty. This examination should provide a general framework for an understanding of the influences of certainty and uncertainty on public budgeting and finance.

Finance Economists

The finance economist school of thought "emphasizes the need to allocate according to standards that will maximize the benefits to everyone" [1, p. 8]. The emphasis of this school of thought has been on rationalism and the ability to compare costs and benefits and achieve a Pareto optimality [1]. Flowing from this school of thought are numerous techniques and processes, such as line-item budgeting, cost-benefit analysis, program planning budgeting systems, zero-base budgeting, and performance-based budgeting. A common aspect of each of these budgeting techniques is the attempt to control uncertainty by the establishment of a plan for the future. By examining the line-item and planning programming budgeting systems we will briefly be able to see the influence of certainty and uncertainty on rational budgeting processes.

Line-item budgets seek only to fix a certain cost to a particular item. There are a limited number of variables that are active in a line-item budget, many of which can achieve certainty. The data that one must compile in this process are hard data and accessible. The items are knowable and they already exist, or the components of them exist. Uncertainty comes into play in the projection of the future cost of the items. A budget being drafted for the near future enables one to have certain probability of knowing that the item will cost the amount projected.

The planning programming budgeting system (PPBS) is a rational comprehensive budgeting system that was introduced by the RAND corporation. It seeks to integrate planning and budgeting. The budget is linked to goals and programs or plans to achieve them. The emphasis on future projections and trend analysis plays a major role in PPBS. Thus, PPBS is laden with uncertainty, because of its future orientation.

The PPBS, though, is a budget system that was designed to create certainty, because it allowed for rational and centralized control [56]. The centralization aspect of PPBS increases the uncertainty by enhancing the biological limitations. Centralization limits the search, filtering, compiling, and integration mechanisms involved in the process. Information and data are sent to a centralized location; because of the enormous amount of data involved in the process, the central location becomes the primary biological mechanism involved in the decision-making process. Thus, whatever biological and mental limitations exist in the centralized areas are the ones that will influence the degree of uncertainty.

Incremental

Incrementalism was presented as a superior process to the rational comprehensive methods [64,65]. Charles Lindblom [64,65] argued that real-world decision making was one of "successive limited comparisons." Incrementalism as a budgeting model was advocated by Aaron Wildavsky [81,82]. Wildavsky contended that the budget was a political document and that "the largest determining factor of the size and content of this year's budget is last year's budget." The keystone of incremental budgeting models, which was recognized by Wildavsky [83], was the consensus of the ends of goals. Incrementalism strives to eliminate uncertainty by limiting the context of the decision and the decision maker. It assumes a consensus of the goals or ends to be reached. Therefore, the focus of the decision and the decision maker is continuously on adjusting the implementation.

The incremental approach focuses in the past. It uses the past (the known) as the foundation for the decision. By focusing on the past the biological search mechanism of the decision maker is focused and directed to a concrete set of data. The incremental approach is argued as reflecting the reality of an open social discourse, but that discourse is focusing on known data sets. The primary uncertainty that is involved is in interpreting the known data. Psychologically, the decision maker is confronted with more certainty than uncertainty, which makes for a comprehensible decision situation.

In-Between

The in-between approach is a blending of rational comprehensive and incremental models. Rubin [1, p. 9] contends there is a trend in the public budgeting and finance literature that presents an approach in between the rational comprehensive and incremental. He contends that:

> It has become increasingly evident that the structure of the budget and the type of expenditure limit the ability of budget trimmers to cut some programs; some are mandated, some have restricted funding, or matching funding, some programs actually generate revenue, and some are long term and contractual and cannot be readily adjusted except at fixed intervals. The decision about what kind of program to offer and whether to earmark money is also a budgetary decision; it locks a particular comparison of alternatives into a budget for a period of time. So comparisons do occur, but not necessarily annually, and some programs may be left out of comparisons. The result is not rational budgeting in the sense of finance economists, but neither is it simple decision rules of the incrementalists. (p. 9)

Rubin does not fully explain the in-between approach, but merely identifies it as something that is presently occurring. Basically, Rubin is showing how the budget process limits the actions of the decision makers to the point that they fully apply neither incrementalism nor the rational methods of the finance economists. This is an example of the social component of certainty and uncertainty. The established social processes influence the searching, filtering, compiling, and integration mechanisms of the decision maker and create an increase in uncertainty.

Another variation of the in-between approach was offered earlier by Amitai Etzioni. Etzioni [84] argued for a "mixed scanning" approach to decision making. He saw rational comprehensive and incremental approaches being done simultaneously. The decision on the goals to be achieved (the direction) involved a rational comprehensive type of model. The implementation of achieving the goals involved an incremental approach.

Etzioni's in-between approach of rational for major goals and incremental for the implementation assumes that a goal consensus will be reached. From the standpoint of certainty and uncertainty there are possible problems with the mixture. The incremental approach is dependent on a long-term agreement of goals or ends to be achieved [83]. Without a long-term consensus on the end to be achieved it is not possible to be incremental. The rational approach to deciding long-term goals involves a feedback mechanism that may result in major adjustments to the goals or ends being sought, thus preventing the ability to be incremental.

With Etzioni's in-between approach, uncertainty is introduced in the determination of the long-term goals or ends. The incremental aspect of his approach involves only the decisions that are made within the implementation component of the original decision (which was the goal or end). The certainty in the incremental approach is countered by the high uncertainty of the long-term goals. The possible inability to do incrementalism, as previously explained, will negate that certainty, thereby causing an increase in uncertainty.

CONCLUSION

This chapter has offered a conceptualization of certainty and uncertainty as flowing from a theory of knowledge and consisting of four components: time, biological, mental, and social. To construct this conceptualization the philosophical roots of certainty and uncertainty were explored. A conceptualization, with an integrated review of the literature, was explained. This was followed by a brief overview of the application of this conceptualization to decision making and public budgeting and finance.

This chapter has served only as a means of introducing the concepts certainty and uncertainty. The conceptualization offered here is still rough and needs to be refined. It is hoped that this conceptualization is broad and generalizable enough to function in multiple disciplinary research efforts. Some of the areas open to exploratory research are: Does knowledge of uncertainty allow for the development of techniques and processes to limit it? Do we have to feel certain about actions, or is it possible to live with uncertainty? Does the existence of uncertainty make long-term budget projections meaningless guesses? What are the implications of uncertainty upon trend and forecast analysis? These are a few of the many possible research questions that can be explored.

This chapter began by stating that all of life is decision-making activity. Certainty and uncertainty are an integral part of decision making, the decision maker, and the knowledge that is used by both. Certainty and uncertainty should no longer be viewed as components within decision making and the decision maker, but as the primary concepts that decision making occurs within and that the decision maker acts in. Thus, we conclude as we began, but now stating that all of life is certainty and uncertainty.

BIBLIOGRAPHY

Allison, Graham. 1969. "Conceptual Models and the Cuban Missile Crisis." *American Political Science Review* 63 (September): 689–718.

Anderson, D., D. Sweeny, and T. Williams. 1985. *An Introduction to Management Science: Quantitative Approaches to Decision-making*, 4th ed. St. Paul, MN: West Publishing Co.

Asher, William. 1978. *Forecasting: An Appraisal for Policy Makers and Planners*. Baltimore, MD: Johns Hopkins University Press.

Ayres, Robert U. 1979. *Uncertain Futures*. New York, NY: John Wiley and Sons.

Axelrod, Robert, ed. 1976. *The Structure of Decision: The Cognitive Maps of Political Elites*. Princeton, NJ: Princeton University Press.

Baron, Jonathan. 1994. "Nonconsequentialist decisions." *Behavioral and Brain Sciences* 17 (1): 1–42.

Bazerman, Max H. and F. D. Schoorman. 1983. "A limited rationality model of interlocking directorates: An individual, organizational, and societal decision." *Academy of Management Review* 8: 206–217.

Becker, G. and McClintock, C. 1967. "Value: Behavioral Decision Theory." *Annual Review of Psychology* 18: 239–286.

Becker, S. W. and F. O. Brownson. 1964. "What price ambiguity? Or the role of ambiguity in decision-making." *Journal of Political Economy* 72: 62–73.

Bell, R. 1985. "Professional Values and Organizational Decision-making." *Administration and Society* 17: 21–60.

Berry, William D. 1990. "The Confusing Case of Budgetary Incrementalism: Too Many Meanings For A Single Concept." *Journal of Politics* 52(1): 167.

Bowman, E. H. 1963. "Consistency and optimality in managerial decision-making." *Management Science* 9: 310–321.

Braybrooke, David and Charles E. Lindblom, C. 1963. *A Strategy of Decision: Policy Evaluation as a Social Process*. New York, NY: Free Press.

Brock, Bernard, et al. 1973. *Public Policy Decision-Making: Systems Analysis and Comparative Advantages Debate*. New York, NY: Harper & Row.

Bronner, Rolf. 1993. "Decision-making in Complex Situations—Results of German Empirical Studies." *Management International Review* 33 (1): 7–25.

Bullard, James and Alison Butler. 1993. "Nonlinerity and Chaos in Economic Models: Implications For Policy Decision." *The Economic Journal* 103 (July): 849–867.

Campbell, Charles A. 1992. "A Decision Theory Model for Entrepreneurial Acts." *Entrepreneurship Theory and Practice* 17 (1): 21–28.

Churchman, C. West. 1961. *Prediction and Optimal Decision*. Englewood Cliffs, NJ: Prentice-Hall, Inc.

Conrad, Cynthia. 1993. "Binary Decision Analysis: An Empirical Approach to Predicting and Understanding Organizational Decisions." *International Journal of Public Administration* 16 (April): 527–626.

Daft, Richard L. 1992. "Decision-making." In *Organization Theory and Design*. New York, NY. West Publishing.

Davis, Fred D. and Jeffrey E. Kottemann. 1994. "User Perceptions of Decision Support Effectiveness: Two Production Planning Experiments." *Decision Sciences Journal* 25 (1). 57–78.

Dawes, R. M. 1979. "The robust beauty of improper linear models in decision-making." *American Psychologist* 34: 571–582.

Dean, James W. Jr. and Mark P. Sharfman. 1993. "The Relationship between Procedural Rationality and Political Behavior in Strategic Decision-making." *Decision Sciences Journal* 24 (6): 1069–1084.

Delbecq, Andre L., Andrew H. Van de Ven, and David H. Gusafson. 1975. *Group Techniques for Program Planning: A Guide to Nominal Group Delphi Processes*. Glenview, IL: Scott, Foresman and Co.

Deng, Pi-Sheng. 1993. "Automating Knowledge Acquisition and Refinement for Decision Support: A Connectionalist Inductive Inference Model." *Decision Sciences Journal* 24(2): 371–394.

Desai, Uday and Michael M. Crow. 1983. "Failures of Power and Intelligence: Use of Scientific Technical Information in Governmental Decision-making." *Administration and Society* 15 (August): 185–206.

Dubin, Robert. 1949. "Decision-Making by Management in Industrial Relations." *American Journal of Sociology* 54 (January): 292–297.

Drazen, Prelec and George Lowenstein. 1991. "Decision-making Over Time and Under Uncertainty: A Common Approach." *Management Science* 33 (7): 770–786.

Einhorn, H. J. and R. M. Hograth. 1985. "Ambiguity and Uncertainty in Probabilistic Inference." *Psychological Review* 92: 433–461.

————. 1978. "Confidence in Judgment: Persistence in the illusion of validity." *Psychological Review* 85: 395–416.

Eiselt, Horst A. and Ann Langley. 1990. "Some Extensions of Domain Criteria in Decision-making Under Uncertainty." *Decision Sciences Journal* 21(1): 138–153.

Enke, Stephen, ed. 1967. *Defense Management.* Englewood Cliffs, NJ: Prentice-Hall.

Erev, Ido. 1993. "The Negative Effect of Probability Assessments On Decision Quality." *Organizational Behavior and Human Decision Processes* 55 (June): 78–94.

————. 1967. The Active Society: A Theory of Societal and Political Processes. New York, NY: The Free Press.

Fishburn, Peter C. 1964. *Decision and Value Theory.* New York, NY: John Wiley & Sons.

Fischer, G. and M. Kamlet. 1984. "Explaining Presidential Priorities: The Competing Aspirations Levels Model of Macrobudgetary Decision-making." *American Political Science Review* 78: 356–371.

Gargan, John J. and Carl M. Moore. 1984. "Enhancing Local Government Capacity in Budget Decision-making: The Use of Group Process Techniques." *Public Administration Review* 44 (Nov): 504–511.

Ghosh, Dipankar and Terry L. Cain. 1993. "Structure of Uncertainty and Decision-making: An Experimental Investigation." *Decision Sciences Journal* 24 (4): 789–808.

Gist, John R. 1989. "Decision-making in Public Administration." In Jack Rabin, W. Bartley Hildreth, and Gerald J. Miller (eds) *Handbook of Public Administration,* New York, NY: Marcel Dekker, Inc.

————. 1982. "Stability and Competition In Budgetary Theory." *American Political Science Review* 76: 859–872.

————. 1978. *Mandatory Expenditures and the Defense Sector: Theory of Budgetary Incrementalism.* Beverly Hills, CA: Sage Publications.

————. 1956. "Administrative Decision-Making in Federal Offices." *Public Administration Review* 16 (Autumn): 281–291.

Gore, William and J. W. Dyson, eds. 1964. *The Making of Decisions: A Reader in Administrative Behavior* New York, NY: Free Press of Glencoe.

Gore, William and F. Silander. 1959. "A Bibliographical Essay on Decision-making." *Administrative Science Quarterly* 41: 97–121.

Hassebrock, Frank, Paul E. Johnson, Peter Bullemer, Paul W. Fox, and James H. Moller. 1993. "When Less is More: Representation and selective memory in expert problem solving." *American Journal of Psychology* 106 (2): 155–190.

Hunt, Raymond G. and John M. Magenau. 1984. "A Task Analysis Strategy for Research on Decision-making in Organizations." In Llyod G. Nigro, *Decision-making in the Public Sector,* New York, NY: Marcel Dekker, Inc.

Jamis, Irving L. and Leon. Mann. 1977. *Decision-making: A Psychological Analysis of Conflict, Choice and Commitment.* New York, NY: Free Press.

Johnson, Gerry. 1988. "Rethinking Incrementalism." *Strategic Management Journal* 9 (1): 75–91.

Kahn, B. E. and R. K. Sarin. 1988. "Modeling Ambiguity in Decisions Under Uncertainty." *Journal of Consumer Research* 15: 265–271.

Kottemann, Jeffrey E. and Fred D. Davis. 1991. "Decisional Conflict and User Acceptance of Multicriteria Decision-Making Aids." *Decision Sciences Journal* 22 (4): 918–926.

Landau, M. 1962. "Concept of Decision." In S. Mailick and E. Van Ness (eds) *Concepts and Issues in Administrative Behavior.* Englewood Cliffs, NJ: Prentice Hall, Inc.

Larson, J. R. 1980. "Exploring the External Validity of a Subjectively Weighted Utility Model of Decision-making." *Organizational Behavior and Human Performance* 26: 293–304.

LeLoup. L. 1978. "The Myth of Incrementalism: Analytical Choices in Budgetary Theory." *Polity.* 10: 488–509.

Lerner, A. 1982. "Decision-making by Organizations." *Micropolitics* 2: 123–151.

Lewis, Holly S. and Timothy W. Butler. 1993. "An Interactive Framework for Muti-Person, Multiobjective Decisions." *Decision Sciences Journal* 24 (1): 1–22.

————. 1980. *The Policy-Making Process*, 2nd ed. Englewood Cliffs, NJ: Prentice-Hall.

Mack, Ruth P. 1971. *Planning on Uncertainty: Decision-making in Business and Government Administration*. New York, NY: Wiley-Interscience.

Madansky, Albert. 1979. "Uncertainty." In E. S. Quade and W. I. Boucher, eds. *Systems Analysis and Policy Planning*. New York, NY: American Elsevier Publishing Co. Inc.

Mandell, Marvin B. 1984. "Strategies for Improving the Usefulness of Analytical Techniques for Public Sector Decision-making." In Lloyd G. Nigro, ed. *Decision-making in the Public Sector*, New York, NY: Marcel Dekker, Inc.

March, James G. 1962. "Some Recent Substantive and Methodological Developments in Theory of Organizational Decision-making." In A. Ranney (eds) *Essays on Behavioral Study of Politics*. Urbana, IL: University of Illinois Press.

McGowen, Robert P. 1989. "Five Great Issues in Decision-making." In Jack Rabin, W. Bartley Hidreth, and Gerald J. Miller (eds) *Handbook of Public Administration*. New York, NY: Marcel Dekker, Inc.

————. 1984. "The Limits of Cost-Benefit Analysis." In Llyod G. Nigro, ed. *Decision-making in the Public Sector*, New York, NY: Marcel Dekker, Inc.

Miller, David W. and Martin Starr. 1967. *The Structure of Human Decisions*. Englewood Cliffs, NJ: Prentice-Hall.

Mintzberg, Henry, Duru Raisinghani, and André Theoret. 1976. "The Structure of Unstructured Decision Processes." *Administrative Science Quarterly* 21 (2): 246.

Mishan, Edward J. 1976. *Cost-Benefit Analysis*, 2nd ed. New York, NY: Oxford University Press.

Mowitz, Robert J. 1980. *The Design of Public Decision Systems*. (Baltimore, MD: University Park Press.

Mumby, Dennis K. 1992. "The Politics of Emotion: A Feminist Reading of Bounded Rationality." *Academy of Management Review* 17 (July): 465–486.

Murray, Michael A. 1986. *Decisions: A Comparative Critique*. Marshfield, MA: Pitman Publishing Co.

Newell, Allen and Herbert Simon. 1972. *Human Problem Solving*. New York, NY: Prentice Hall.

Nigel, Howard. 1993. "The Role of Emotions in Multi-Organizational Decision-making" *Journal of Operational Research Society*. 44 (June): 613–623.

Nigro, Lloyd G., ed. 1984. *Decision-making in the Public Sector*. New York, NY: Marcel Dekker.

O'Leary Daniel E. 1993. "Determining Differences in Expert Judgment: Implications for Knowledge Acquisition and Validation." *Decision Sciences Journal* 24 (2): 395–408.

Quade, E. S. 1975. *Analysis for Public Decisions*. New York, NY: Elsevier.

————, ed. 1964. *Analysis for Military Decisions*. Santa Monica, CA: The Rand Corporation.

Quade, E. S. and W. I. Boucher, eds. *Systems Analysis and Policy Planning*. New York, NY: American Elsevier Publishing Company.

Raiffa, Howard. 1968. *Decision Analysis*. Reading, MA: Addison-Wesley.

Ripley, Randell B. and Grace A. Franklin. 1991. *Congress, The Bureaucracy, and Public Policy*, 5th ed. Pacific Grove, CA: Brooks/Cole Publishing Company.

Schoemaker, Paul J. H. 1993. "Strategic Decisions in Organizations: Rational and Behavioral Views." *Journal of Management Studies*. 30 (Jan): 107–129.

Schroeder, H. M. and P. Suefeld. 1971. *Personality Theory and Information Processing*. New York, NY: Ronald Press.

Simon, Herbert. 1980. "The New Science of Management Decision." In R. Cyert and L. Welsch, eds. *Management Decision-making*. New York, NY: Penguin Books.

————. 1977. *The Science of Management Decision* 3rd ed. Englewood Cliffs, NJ: Prentice Hall, Inc.

————. 1967. "Making Management Decisions: the Role of Intuition and Emotion." *Executive* (February): 57–64.

————. 1964. "On the Concept of Organizational Goal." *Administrative Science Quarterly* 9 (June): 1–22.

Smith, G. and D. May. 1980. "The Artificial Debate Between Rationalist and Incrementalist Models of Decision-making." *Policy and Politics.* 8: 147–162.

Springer, J. 1985. "Policy Analysis and Organizational Decisions." *Administration and Society* 16: 475–508.

Steinbruner, John D. 1974. *The Cybernetic Theory of Decision.* Princeton, NJ: Princeton University Press.

Stinchcombe, Arthur L. 1990. *Information and Organizations.* Berkely: University of California Press.

Sudgen, Robert and Alan H. Williams. 1978. *The Principles of Practical Cost-Benefit Analysis.* New York, NY: Oxford University Press.

Taylor, R. N. 1984. *Behavioral Decision-making.* Glenview, Ill.: Scott Foresman.

Taylor, R. N. and M. D. Dunnette. 1974. "Relative Contribution of Decision-maker Attributes to Decision Process." *Organization Behavior and Human Performance* 12: 286–298.

Thieranf, R. J. and Richard A. Grosse. 1970. *Decision-making Through Operations Research.* New York, NY: John Wiley & Sons.

Tversky, A. and D. Kahnemann. 1981. "The Framing of Decisions and the Psychology of Choice." *Science* 211: 453–458.

———, ———. 1974. "Judgment Under Uncertainty: Heuristics and Biases." *Science* 204: 1124–1131.

Vroom, Victor H. 1973. "A New Look at Managerial Decision-making." In Jack Rabin, ed., *Organizational Theory and Management,* (215–226) Lexington, MA: Ginn Custom Publishing.

Wall, Kent D. 1993. "A Model of Decision-making Under Bounded Rationality." *Journal of Economic Behavior and Organization.* 20 (April): 331–352.

Weiss, Andrew and Edward Woodhouse. 1992. "Reframing Incrementalism: A Constructive Response to the Critics." *Policy Sciences.* 25 (3): 255.

Wilensky, Harold L. 1967. *Organizational Intelligence: Knowledge and Policy in Government and Industry.* New York, NY: Basic Books.

NOTES

1. Throughout this chapter the term "decision maker" means the individual, group, organization, or institution making the decision.
2. Aristotle discusses his manner of reasoning in *Prior Analytics* and *Posterior Analytics*.
3. The effect of time on human knowledge is a common theme of philosophy. A few of the numerous sources are: Aristotle, *Metaphysics* (982a.30–b3); Thomas Hobbes, 1651. *Leviathan: Or, Matter, Form, and power of a Commonwealth Ecclesiastical and Civil* [4, p. 53]; Francis Bacon, *The Advancement of Learning* [40, pp. 32, 61–62]; John Locke, *Concerning Human Understanding* [6, pp. 165, 357]; William James, *Psychology* [41, pp. 421–427].
4. The searching, filtering, compiling, and integration mechanisms described in this section were developed by Chester Barnard [43] and William Pasmore [44]. The author has adapted their ideas to this chapter.
5. The search for commonalties began with Alexis and Wilson [61, p. 148]. They address the idea of commonalties in the decision-making literature and found six commonalties: (1) state of model; (2) the decision maker; (3) the goals or ends being served; (4) the relevant alternatives and set of actions from which a choice is made; (5) a relation that produces a preference ordering of alternatives; and (6) the choice itself.
6. Of the 234 books and articles surveyed, 194 or 83% used either explicitly or implicitly the definition of a decision as a selection or choice.

REFERENCES

1. Rubin, "Budgeting: Theory, Concepts, Methods, and Issues." *Handbook of Public Budgeting,* (Jack Rabin, ed.) Marcel Dekker, Inc., New York, pp. 3–22 (1992).

2. Aristotle, *Nicomachean Ethics*, transl. W. D. Ross, *Great Books of the Western World*. (R. M. Hutchins, ed.), vol 9, *Aristotle II*, University of Chicago, Chicago (1984).

3. T. Aquinas, *The Summa Theologica* (1272), transl. Fathers of English Domican Province, rev. by Daniel J. Sullivan, *Great Books of the Western World*. (R. M. Hutchins, ed.), vol. 19, *Thomas Aquinas I*, University of Chicago, Chicago (1984).

4. T. Hobbes, *Leviathan: Or, Matter, Form, and Power of a Commonwealth Ecclesiastical and Civil* (1651), *Great Books of the Western World* (R. M. Hutchins, ed.), vol. 23, *Machiavelli, Hobbes*, University of Chicago, Chicago (1984).

5. R. Descartes, *Discourse on the Method of Rightly Conducting the Reason* (1637), *Great Books of the Western World*. (R. M. Hutchins, ed.), vol. 31, *Descartes, Spinoza*, University of Chicago, Chicago (1984).

6. J. Locke, "Concerning Human Understanding" (1690), *Great Books of the Western World* (R. M. Hutchins, ed.), vol. 35, *Locke, Berkeley, Hume*, University of Chicago, Chicago (1984).

7. D. Hume, "An Enquiry Concerning Human Understanding," *Great Books of the Western World* (R. M. Hutchins, ed.), vol. 35, *Locke, Berkeley, Hume*, University of Chicago, Chicago (1984).

8. I. Kant, *The Critique of Pure Reason* (1788), transl. J. M. D. Mciklejohn, *Great Books of the Western World* (R. M. Hutchins, ed.), vol. 42, *Kant*, University of Chicago, Chicago (1984).

9. H. A. Simon, *Administrative Behavior*, Macmillan, New York (1947).

10. H. A. Simon, *Administrative Behavior*, 3rd Ed., The Free Press, New York (1976).

11. W. Gore, *Administrative Decision-making: A Heuristic Model*, John Wiley and Sons, New York (1964).

12. L. W. Hein, *Quantitative Approach to Managerial Decisions*, Prentice Hall, Englewood Cliffs, N.J.

13. E. S. Quade, *Analysis for Public Decisions*, Elsevier, New York (1975).

14. K. Aiginger, *Production and Decision Theory Under Uncertainty*, Basil Blackwell, Oxford (1987).

15. B. F. Baird, *Managerial Decisions Under Uncertainty*, John Wiley & Sons, New York (1989).

16. R. D. Badinelli and J. R. Baker, "Multiple Attribute Decision-making with Inexact Value-Function Assessment," *Decision Sciences Journal*, 21(2): 318-336 (1990).

17. M. H. Bazerman, *Judgment in Management Decision-Making*, John Wiley & Sons, New York (1986).

18. W. H. Agor, *The Logic of Intuitive Decision-making: A Research Based for Top Management* Quorum Books, Westport, CT (1986).

19. Beyer, "Idealogies, Values, and Decision Making in Organizatons," In *Handbook of Organization Design* (Paul C. Nystrom and William Starbuck, eds.) vol. 2, Oxford University Press, London (1981).

20. P. C. Nutt, *Making Tough Decisions: Tactics For Improving Managerial Decision-Making*, Jossey-Bass, San Francisco (1990).

21. W. G. Astley, "Organization Science, Managers, and Language Games," *Organization Science*, 3(4): 443-460 (1992).

22. R. B. McCalla, *Uncertain Perceptions: U.S. Cold War Crisis Decision-Making* (1992).

23. J. D. Hey, "Dynamic Decision-making Under Uncertainty: An Experimental Study Of the Dynamic Competitive Firm," *Oxford Econ. Papers*, 45(1): 58–82 (1993).

24. A. A. Buchko, "Conceptualization and Measurement of Environmental Uncertainty: An Assessment of Miles and Snow Environmental Uncertainty Scale," *Academy of Management Journal*, 37: 410–475 (1994).

25. R. E. Miles and C. C. Snow, *Organizational Strategy, Structure, and Process*, McGraw-Hill, New York (1978).

26. H. A. Simon, *Models of Man: Social and Rational*, John Wiley & Sons, New York (1957).

27. H. A. Simon, "Theories of Decision-Making in Economics and Behavioral Science," *Am. Econ. Rev.*, 49(June): 253–283 (1959).

28. H. A. Simon, *The New Science of Management Decision*, Prentice Hall, Englewood Cliffs, N.J. (1960).

29. H. A. Simon, "The Executive as Decision-maker," *The New Science of Management*, Harper and Row, New York (1960).

30. H. A. Simon, "Administrative Decision-Making," *Public Admin. Rev., 25*(March): 31–37 (1965).

31. H. A. Simon, *The Sciences of the Artificial*, Harvard University Press, Cambridge, Mass. (1969).

32. H. A. Simon, "The Structure of Ill-Structured Decision Process," *Artificial Intelligence, 4*: 181–201 (1973).

33. H. A. Simon, "Making Management Decisions: The Role of Intuition and Emotion," *Acad. Manage. Executive*, Feb.: 57–64 (1987).

34. L. D. Attaway, "Criteria and the Measurement of Effectiveness," *Systems Analysis and Policy Planning* (E. S. Quade and W. I. Boucher, eds.), American Evelsier, New York (1968).

35. S. R. Covey, A. R. Merrill, and R. R. Merrill, *First Thyings First*, Simon and Schuster, New York (1994).

36. Milliken, "Three Types of Perceived Uncertainty About the Environment: State, Effect, and Response Uncertainty," *Academy of Management Review, 12*(1): 133–143 (1987).

37. R. B. Duncan, "Characteristics of Organizational Environments and Perceived Environmental Uncertainty," *Administrative Science Quarterly, 17*:313–327 (1972).

38. R. L. Daft, J. Sormunen, and D. Parks, "Chief Executive Scanning, Environmental Characteristics, and Company Performance: An Empirical Study," *Strategic Management Journal, 9*: 123–139 (1988).

39. Gosh and Cain, "Structure of Uncertainty and Decision Making: An Experimental Investigation," *Decision Sciences Journal, 24*(4): 789–808 (1993).

40. F. Bacon, *The Advancement of Learning*, *Great Books of the Western World* (R. M. Hutchins, ed.) vol. 30, *Francis Bacon*, University of Chicago, Chicago (1984).

41. W. James, *The Principles of Psychology*, *Great Books of the Western World* (R. M. Hutchins, ed.), vol. 53, *William James*, University of Chicago, Chicago (1984).

42. A. Wildavsky, "A Budget for All Seasons? Why the Traditional Budget Lasts," *Public Management: The Essential Readings* (J. Steven Ott, A. C. Hyde, and J. M. Shafritz, (eds.), Nelson-Hall, Chicago, pp. 327–341 (1978).

43. C. Barnard, "The Significance of Decisive Behavior in Social Action," unpublished manuscript (1940).

44. Pasmore, *Designing Effective Organizations*, John Wiley & Sons, New York (1989).

45. March et al., *Ambiguity and Command*, Pitman Publishing, White Plains, NY (1986).

46. G. J. Cook, "An Empirical Investigation of Information Search Strategies with Implications for Decision Support System Design," *Decision Sci. J., 24*(3): 683–698 (1993).

47. C. Barnard, *The Functions of the Executive*, Harvard University Press, Cambridge, Mass. (1938).

48. W. Edwards, "The Theory of Decision-making," *Psychol. Rev., 51*(September): 380–471 (1954).

49. H. J. Einhorn and R. M. Hograth, "Behavioral Decision Theory: Processes of Judgment and Choice," *Ann. Rev. Psychol., 32*: 53–88 (1981).

50. J. G. March and A. Simon, *Organizations*, John Wiley & Sons, New York (1958).

51. A. Madansky and J. Olsen, *Ambiguity and Choice in Organizations*, Universitesforlaget, Bergen, Norway (1979).

52. R. H. Hall, "Decision-making," *Organizations: Structures, Processes, and Outcomes*, Prentice Hall, Englewood Cliffs, N.J. (1991).

53. Pasmore, *Designing Effective Organizations*, John Wiley & Sons, New York (1988).

54. A. Etzioni "Mixed Scanning: A Third Approach to Decision Making," *Public Admin. Rev., 27*: 385–392 (1967).

55. A. Downs, *Inside Bureaucracy*, Little, Brown, Boston (1967).

56. R. J. Art, *The TFX Decision: McNamara and the Military*, Little, Brown, Boston (1968).

57. T. D. Clark and W. A. Shrode, "Public Sector Decision Structures," *Public Admin. Rev., 39*: 343–354 (1979).

58. F. E. Rourke, *Bureaucracy, Politics, and Public Policy*, Harper Collins, New York (1984).

59. B. G. Peters, *The Politics of Bureaucracy*, 3rd ed., Longman, New York (1989).

60. K. J. Meier, *Politics and the Bureaucracy: Policymaking in the Fourth Branch of Government*, Brooks/Cole, Pacific Grove, Calif. (1993).

61. M. Alexis and C. Z. Wilson, *Organizational Decision-making*, Prentice-Hall, Englewood Cliffs, N.J. (1967).

62. H. A. Simon *Administrative Behavior*, *3rd Ed.*, The Free Press, New York (1978).

63. P. Bachrach and M. Baratz, "Decisions and Non-Decisions," *Am. Polit. Sci. Rev.*, *57*: 632–642 (1963).

64. C. E. Lindblom, "The Science of Muddling Through," *Public Admin. Rev.*, *19*: 298–312 (1959).

65. C. E. Lindblom, "Still Muddling, Not Through Yet," *Public Admin. Rev.*, *39*: 517–526 (1979).

66. J. J. Bailey and J. O'Connor, "Operationalizing Incrementalism: Measuring the Muddles," *Public Admin. Rev.*, *35*(January/February): 60–66 (1978).

67. A. Lerner, *The Politics of Decision-Making*, Sage, Beverly Hills, Calif. (1976).

68. W. H. Starbuck, "Organizations and Their Environments," In *Handbook of Industrial and Organizational Psychology* (M. D. Dunnette, ed.) Rand McNally, Chicago, pp. 1069–1124 (1983).

69. M. D. Cohen, J. G. March, and J. P. Olsen, "A Garbage-Can Model of Organizational Choice," *Admin. Sci. Q.*, *17*(March): 1–25 (1972).

70. R. Weissinger-Baylon, "Garbage Can Decision Processes in Naval Warfare," In *Ambiguity and Command: Organizational Perspectives on Military Decision-Making* (J. G. March and R. Weissinger-Baylon, eds.), Pitman, White Plains, N.Y., pp. 36–52 (1986).

71. R. M. Cyert and J. G. March, *A Behavioral Theory of the Firm*, 2nd ed., Prentice Hall, Englewood Cliffs, N.J. (1992).

72. C. E. Lindblom, *The Intelligence of Democracy: Decision-Making Through Mutual Adjustment*, Free Press, New York (1965).

73. J. G. March and J. P. Olsen, "Garbage Can Models of Decision Making in Organizations," In *Ambiguity and Command: Organizational Perspectives on Military Decision Making*, (J. G. March and R. Wesinger-Baylon, eds.) Pitman Publishing, White Plains, NY, pp. 11–29 (1986).

74. Beyer "Ideologies, Values, and Decision Making in Organizations," In *Handbook of Organization Design* (Paul C. Nystrom and William Starbuck, eds.), vol. 2, Oxford University Press, London (1981).

75. F. Heller, P. Drenth, P. Koopman, and V. Rus, *Decision in Organizations*. Sage, London (1988).

76. Knight (1921).

77. J. D. Thompson, *Organizations in Action*, McGraw Hill, New York (1967).

78. Pinefield (1968).

79. G. Allison, *Essence of Decision: Explaining the Cuban Missile Crisis*, Little, Brown, Boston (1971).

80. Hickson (1987).

81. A. Wildavsky *The Politics of the Budgetary Process*, Little, Brown, Boston (1964).

82. A. Wildavsky, *Budgeting*, Little, Brown, Boston (1975).

83. A. Wildavsky, *Searching for Safety*, Transaction Books, New Brunswick (1988).

84. A. Etzioni, "Mixed Scanning: A Third Approach to Decision Making," *Public Admin. Rev.*, *27*: 385–392 (1967).

24

The Nature of Models

R. D. Specht

WHAT IS A MODEL?

If this were a psychological test in which I give you a word and you respond by writing down your free association—the first thing that comes to your mind—and if I were to say "model," you might react by writing down "36-24-36."

Now you may think that this is irrelevant—that this is not a model in the sense that concerns us in this book. But if you think so, you are wrong. Our definition of "model" will include your "36-24-36." Our definition of "model" will be broad enough to cover even your guess.

Here, you will meet a surprising variety of things that we shall classify as "models"—a collection of mathematical equations, a scenario, a program for a high-speed computer, a war game. And the list of creatures that we could include in our model zoo is much longer yet. We could add an organization chart, a map, a set of questionnaires, a copy of Plato's *Republic*, a Link trainer, and a group of people and machines acting as if they were an air defense direction center.

What is it that all these have in common? Each is an idealization, an abstraction of a part of the real world. Each is an incomplete representation of the real thing. Each is an analog, an imitation of reality.

But why settle for an imitation? Because the real thing is not available for study or is too expensive to experiment with. Some of the things we contemplate are too expensive to allow to happen even once.

A model, then, is an analog of reality. It is made up of those factors that are relevant to a particular situation and the relations among them. We ask questions of the model and from the answers we get, hopefully, some clues, some hints, to guide us in dealing with that part of the real world to which the model corresponds.

We must not object that a model does not look like the real thing or that it does not represent all aspects of reality. It seldom does. The important thing is whether or not the

Source: R. D. Specht, "The Nature of Models," in E. S. Quade and W. I. Boucher, *Systems Analysis and Policy Planning*, American Elsevier Publishing Company, New York, pp. 211–227 (1968).

outputs of the model, the answers it gives to our questions, are reasonably appropriate and valid.

We would like to test the results of our analysis of a model and determine the correctness and relevance of these results for real-world decisions. Perhaps we could make this test if we lived in the best of all possible worlds. But, unfortunately, we live next door. We can never be certain, in this sinful world, that we have been wise. Perhaps the best that we can hope for is to be honest.

We must not object if the analyst changes models on us, if he produces different models for the same reality. The model depends not only on the thing being modeled, on the part of the real world with which we are concerned. The model also depends on the questions to be asked of it, the decisions to be affected by its results.

A trivial example: If you are driving from Santa Monica to San Francisco and have not yet decided on a route, then an adequate model of this part of California may be a road map. If you are a trucker concerned about maintaining a schedule between here and San Francisco, then an adequate model may be a timetable that tells you, among other things, when you are due to pass Pismo. If you are a highway planner who must recommend a freeway route between the two cities, then quite a different model or set of models is necessary—road maps, topographic maps, maps of land use and value, traffic charts showing origin and destination, and a model, implicit and subjective, of the behavior of a population surfeited with taxes, attached to their real estate, and not altogether enchanted with freeways. Each is unrealistic in its own way, but each is useful when shaken well and taken as directed.

. . . E. S. Quade defined a model in something like the following terms. Given a set of alternatives (including ones that the analyst may have invented in the course of studying the problem), a model is a "black box." The analyst has designed the particular box to deal with his particular problem, and he has constructed it to reflect the state of the world of which the alternatives are a part. Into this box as inputs the analyst feeds information about the alternatives, and from the box as outputs comes information about the effectivenesses, plural, and the costs of each of the alternatives. With the help of a criterion, the analyst or the decision maker can then rank the alternatives in order of desirability and can select the optimum.

The black box, of course, is simply a figure of speech to represent any device or process with which we can take into account, in a way as nearly logical as possible, the interrelations of the relevant factors. And the black box isn't really that color. If the analyst, the model builder, has done his work satisfactorily, the walls of the box will not be black; they will be transparent. The spectator and the user of the model will be able to see inside, will be able to understand and evaluate the structure of the model.

Now Quade's definition of a model—a means of producing measures of the costs and effectivenesses of various alternatives—is a handsome definition, and I can't improve on it. But you will soon discover, if you haven't already done so, that, unfortunately, the world is not this tidy.

For one thing, instead of a single model that produces information about both cost and effectiveness, it will often be convenient to have separate models—a cost model, for example, or a campaign effectiveness model. Indeed, more often than not, the analyst will use a collection of models for various parts of his problem, knitting these submodels together by means of verbal arguments.

There are other problems. For example, we said that a model interrelates the relevant factors; but, at least when he begins his study, the analyst probably does not know just which factors are the crucial ones, which may safely be neglected. Part of his job is to discover what is important, what is trivial. This means that the analyst may go several times around the cycle of building a model, experimenting with it, deducing its implications, building a better model, and so on.

But the major difficulty with this definition comes only if you misuse it, if you let it suggest that an analyst armed with model and criterion can arrive at an optimal course of action to recommend to the decisionmaker. In his wonderful address in May 1960 as retiring president of the Operations Research Society Charles Hitch laid this ghost to rest. The operations researcher, he said, is

> . . . faced by his fundamental difficulty. The future is uncertain. Nature is unpredictable, and the enemies and allies are even more so. He has no good general-purpose technique, neither maximizing expected somethings, nor *maximin*ing, nor gaming it, to reveal the preferred strategy. How can he find the optimal course of action to recommend to his decisionmaker?
>
> The simple answer is that he probably cannot. The same answer is also the beginning of wisdom in this business. There has been altogether too much obsession with optimizing on the part of operations researchers, and I include both grand optimizing and sub-optimizing. Most of our relations are so unpredictable that we do well to get the right sign and order of magnitude of first differentials. In most of our attempted optimizations we are kidding our customers or ourselves or both. If we can show our customer how to make a better decision than he would otherwise have made, we are doing well, and all that can reasonably be expected of us.[1]

And this much, said Hitch, we frequently can do.

If the analyst with his models is not computing optimal solutions, what is he about? Computation is not his most important business. His functions are to define alternative objectives, to design alternative solutions, to discover the critical uncertainties, to recommend ways of reducing them, and to explore the implications of alternative courses of action. And computations help do these things.

Let us leave generalities for a spell and look at a model, a real one.

DESIGN AND USE OF MODELS: AN EXAMPLE

This is a model a RAND analyst, T. F. Burke, devised to help him think about the problems of hard point defense of missile sites. To keep the explanation brief, I have simplified his model, but only slightly.

The problem, simply put, is whether or not to buy active defense for a land-based ICBM force. Should we buy an undefended missile force, or should we spend the same budget for a smaller defended missile force? It is obvious without either model or analysis that if ICBMs are expensive and defense is cheap, and if there is appreciable danger of attack, then we buy the defense system. But how expensive? How cheap? We set up a model that will quantify, even if crudely, some aspects of this problem.

We first need some definitions. Let

M = number of undefended missiles we can buy with a given budget

A = number of shots fired by an attacked at our missiles

p = probability that 1 shot kills an undefended missile

p_D = probability that 1 shot kills a defended missile

$\$_M$ = cost of 1 undefended missile

$\$_D$ = cost of defense for 1 missile

There are the factors that we have chosen as relevant—at least for our first cut at the problem. Later we shall call the role of factors that have been omitted from this model.

Consider first the attack upon the undefended missile force. There are A attacking shots against M targets or A/M shots per target. In order to simplify the arithmetic we assume that the number A/M is an integer, that the number of attacking shots fired at each missile is a whole number.

(Burke did not make this simplifying assumption.) Then:

p = the probability that a missile is killed by 1 shot

$1 - p$ = the probability that a missile survives 1 shot

$(1 - p)^{A/M}$ = the probability that a missile survives A/M shots

and the expected number of our missiles that survive the attack is this probability multiplied by the number of missiles in the force, all undefended:

$$M(1 - p)^{A/M}$$

Now the attack upon the defended missile force. First we calculate the size of the defended missile force:

$$\text{Total budget} = M\$_M = (\text{number of defended missiles})(\$_D + \$_M)$$

or

$$\text{number of defended missiles} = \frac{M\$_M}{\$_D + \$_M} = \frac{M}{\dfrac{\$_D}{\$_M} + 1}$$

There are again A attacking shots, but this time their kill probability P_D is lower and distributed over the smaller force just calculated, $M\$_M/(\$_D + \$_M)$ defended missiles. The number of shots per missile is then

$$A \div \frac{M\$_M}{\$_D + \$_M} = \frac{A(\$_D + \$_M)}{M\$_M} = \frac{A}{M}\left(\frac{\$_D}{\$_M} + 1\right)$$

Again we make the simplifying assumption (for this explanation, and not for the original analysis) that this number of attacking shots per missile is an integer. Then, as before,

p_D = the probability that a missile is killed by 1 shot

$1 - p_D$ = the probability that a missile survives 1 shot

$$(1 - p_D)^{\frac{A}{M}\left(\frac{\$_D}{\$_M} + 1\right)} = \text{the probability that a missile survives all shots}$$

and the expected number of our missiles that survive the attack is this probability multiplied by the number of missiles in the force, all defended:

$$\frac{M}{\dfrac{\$_D}{\$_M} + 1}(1 - p_D)^{(A/M)[(\$D/\$M)+1]}$$

We now choose a criterion. We recommend buying defense for the missile force if this leads to the expectation of a greater number of missiles surviving. That is, buy defense if

$$\frac{M}{\dfrac{\$_D}{\$_M} + 1}(1 - p_D)^{(A/M)[(\$D/\$M)+1]} > M(1 - p)^{(A/M)}$$

or, dividing both sides by M, buy defense if

$$\frac{(1 - p_D)^{(A/M)[(\$D/\$M)+1]}}{\dfrac{\$_D}{\$_M} + 1} > (1 - p)^{(A/M)}$$

We note, incidentally, that the missile defense model uses expected values—it is not what is called a Monte Carlo model. From the probability p that a missile target survives a single shot we computed the expected number of surviving missiles, neglecting the matter of fluctuations that may occur about this value. In some cases, the fluctuations may be important. If your employer offered to toss you double or nothing for your month's paycheck, you might develop an interest in such fluctuations, even though your expectation had not changed. But in most cases, these statistical uncertainties are not crucial when compared with such real uncertainties as future enemy capabilities and actions, not to mention our own costs and capabilities.

Where statistical fluctuations must be reckoned with, they can be handled sometimes by mathematical analysis. At other times, the situation is treated by drawing random samples from a carefully determined distribution. In a bombing campaign, for example, we may follow the airplanes by tail numbers and for each one draw random numbers to determine whether or not it aborted, made a navigation error, killed its target, and so on. Such a model is referred to as a *Monte Carlo* one, in contrast to an *expected-value* model; our missile defense model is an example of the latter kind. . . .

Now the analysis is not completed at this point. In fact, we have hardly begun. For example, we need to study the dependence of the kill probability p on the attacker's accuracy and the missile site hardness. Thus another model is introduced. With it we can study the worth of hardening, a competitor to active defense for promoting missile survival. Again, we can study the effect of varying the force ratio, M/A, of missile sites to attacking shots. We can fix the values of all the factors in the inequality above with the exception of the defended kill probability, p_D. We can then ask how small this inequality requires p_D to be—how effective the active defense must be before it is worth buying. Alternatively, we can fix the value of every factor except the unit cost of defense, $\$_D$, and ask how small it must be—how cheap defense must be before it is a good buy. How does this price depend on the other factors—the kill probabilities, the size of the attacking and attacked missile forces, the cost per missile?

Omissions in This Example

What have we omitted from the model? Many things, and I name a few:

We have not considered buying defense for only part of the missile force.

We have not considered the possibility of grouping several ICBMs at each defended point in order to decrease the cost of defense.

We have not let the attacker use a shoot-look-shoot policy.

We have not let the attacker saturate the defense by simultaneous penetration.

And you will think of other omissions. The ones I have mentioned could be taken care of by a more complex model and more costly analysis. (And Burke did this for some factors.) This model involves implicitly some simplifying assumptions:

All missile sites are equivalent in hardness, in cost, and in worth.

Unit costs of missiles and defenses are fixed, independent of the number procured. This means, for example, that we have neglected the research and development costs of an active defense system (or, alternatively, that we have estimated the number of missiles and have prorated the cost of research and development).

And others. These simplifications, too, could be removed by more extensive analysis, if it were thought worth the doing.

And finally, there are idealizations in the model that could not be removed easily, if at all, by more complex analysis. For example, we have neglected the values, military and political, that may come from owning a larger missile force, apart from survival in the attack considered. And so on.

I have spent some time on this model not because we are concerned in this chapter with hard point defense or with this particular study; not even because we have an undue concern with this type of mathematical model. Rather, this model furnishes a concrete example around which we can make some comments that, hopefully, will apply to other instances of analysis as well. The following remarks, then, are less comments upon this particular model and more in the nature of generalities draped for convenience around it.

The Problem of Selecting Criteria

To begin with, consider the matter of criteria. In our example we chose as the criterion the maximizing of surviving missiles. We recommended the alternative that led to the largest expected number of surviving missiles. But this, by itself, is not an adequate criterion (as Burke points out). Suppose, for example, that costs, attack size, and kill probabilities lead us to the conclusion that a small defended missile force is preferable to a larger undefended force because it has more surviving missiles; but suppose, further, that in neither case does the force survive in sufficient strength to be useful. In this case, we do not buy either of the two alternatives; we look for a third and more satisfactory one.

This suggests that in any study it may be hazardous to choose the first criterion that comes to mind, reasonable as it may seem—an observation that you will encounter more than once in this book. The problem of selecting a criterion is more difficult than we have just indicated. If the question at issue is whether or not to start the development of a new weapon system—an ABM system, say—then the decisionmaker will be interested in the analysis whose beginnings we have outlined. But he will have a host of additional questions. How effective might the system be in the damage-limiting role? What countermeasures can the enemy develop? How is he likely to react? What are the technical prospects for development to meet an advanced enemy threat? And so on. Some of these questions affect the choice of criterion; others determine the form of analysis that is appropriate; still others add qualitative factors that cannot be translated into elements of a mathematical analysis. It is unlikely that any quantitative model can do more here than throw light on some aspects of the problem.

The Problem of Deciding What Is Relevant

Another lesson from the missile defense model is that it is not an easy matter to decide which factors are relevant, which may be omitted. Are the results sensitive to a shoot-look-shoot capability and tactic on the part of the attacker? There is no firm guide here except the experience and intuition of the analyst as he devises his model, gains experience in working with it, and, as is likely, revises it.

The Necessity of Being Explicit

Again, the simplifying assumptions made in the model may not be readily apparent to the user of the model's results. This makes it all the more important that the analysis not be cast in the form of a black box with the user asked to take the analyst's word for it that all is well within. As E. S. Quade has said,

> All of the assumptions of a model must be made explicit. If they are not, this is a defect. A mark of a good systems analyst (or any wise person communicating with others) is that he state the basis on which he operates. This does not imply necessarily that he makes better assumptions, but only that his errors will be more evident.[2]

The Treatment of Nonquantitative Considerations

From the missile defense model we learn that most problems involve considerations that cannot be handled quantitatively—for example, any military and political values that may come from owning a larger missile force. If we were trying to assist in a decision on the initiation of a new weapon system development, and if we were trying to see whether or not the new development was justified on the basis of the damage limiting objective, then many intangible factors would become essential to the decision: What kind of war? Can we use superiority in surviving forces to coerce the enemy? And so on.

The Static Character of the Model

The missile defense model, like almost all models, is static. This is no criticism; one would always begin this way, and often it is sufficient for the problem at hand. On the other hand, force optimization studies have sometimes been carried out to assist decisions on new weapon system developments, and it is not enough in such cases merely to predict a future Soviet posture against which one then attempts to evaluate various U.S. force structures. It is necessary for the analyst to recognize the dynamic nature of the arms race. For example, development by one side of improved warheads and of an antiballistic missile system might stimulate subsequent work on mobile or hidden basing and on new warheads by the other side. Over the years each side acquires knowledge about its own major weaknesses and those of the enemy, and this knowledge is reflected in the sequence of decisions about advanced weapon systems. This does not mean that analysis is impossible. But it does suggest that simple arithmetic models have some limitations.

Other Observations

We can use the missile defense model as a hook on which to hang a few additional comments. We saw that a model may involve submodels—like the one that relates the kill probability p to an attacker's accuracy and the hardness of missile sites. We saw that building and working with a model constitute only part of a study. We saw that there is no experimental proof that a model is correct and appropriate. The physicist can test his models in the laboratory, but the systems analyst does not have access to an experimental war. And if he did, it might not help too much. Even a war might not resolve all doubts. I observe that the Civil War is still the subject of some dispute. And in some aspects, an actual war resembles a game played only once. So the analyst cannot test his models satisfactorily. The best he can do, as E. S. Quade has said, is to determine answers to the following questions:

> Can the model describe correctly and clearly the known facts and situations?
>
> When the principal parameters involved are varied, do the results remain consistent and plausible?
>
> Can the model handle special cases in which there is some indication as to what the outcome should be?
>
> Can it assign causes to known effects?

A few words about the role of judgment and intuition. The missile defense model gives the appearance of being coldly objective and free of the foibles of human intuition. We will indeed see examples of models in which human judgment plays no explicit and integral part. But in all models, including the missile defense one, human judgment and intuition enter, if not in an explicit fashion. In the first place, man designs the model, that is, he decides what factors are relevant to the problems and what the interrelations between these factors are to be in the model. In the second place, man decides the numerical values of the input variables fed into the model. And, finally, man inspects, analyzes, and interprets the results, the outputs of the model.

This fact—that judgment and intuition and guesswork are embedded in a model—should be remembered when we examine the results that come, with high precision, from a model.

I would like to think that all RAND analysts have always understood this. We haven't. I find in a 1947 document the following statement made with calm and impressive assurance: "In so far as practicable RAND attempts to eliminate intuitive thinking and comparisons from its evaluation work. Wherever possible, the optimum instrumentality is selected by precise mathematical methods."

The role of judgment and of objective analysis in present and future studies has been described by M. M. Lavin in an internal RAND memorandum:

> In the last 5 years, study technique has really taken a back-seat at RAND. For one reason, we've just gotten more thoughtful about the criterion problem and have admitted to its multi-dimensional and semi-qualitative nature. Good decision criteria just seem overwhelmingly more important in broad problems than do analytical models. For another reason, we've begun to face up to Air Force decision problems so broadly ramified, with so many intangible components that only the most naive analyst would attempt to deal with them by analytical models . . . I venture the following anticipation: For future broad studies, particularly those concerning Air Force posture and compositions and others involving the criterion problem in its most obtrusive form, we shall continue to use intuitive, subjective and *ad hoc* study schemes . . . No individual or organization can hope to be objective. They can, however, be honest in identifying and displaying their bias. The notion that big decisions can be an automatic consequence of the application of mathematical models, cost-effectiveness analysis, or computer simulation belongs to that dreadful era when science-fiction writers, including some on the editorial pages of

the N.Y. *Times*, were heralding the advent of "push-button" warfare (in some instances, with the buttons being pushed by computers).

TYPES OF MODELS

If we were to look at very many models it would be convenient to have some scheme of classification, some set of characteristics according to which we could group them. But there are many ways in which we can slice this cake, many characteristics by which we can organize our knowledge of models. For example, we can classify models according to

Purpose—training, study, and so on

Field of application—strategic, tactical, logistic, and so on

Level—from national policy to base operations

Time character—static or dynamic

Form—two-sided or one, conflict or not

Analytical development—degree to which mathematics is used

Use of computers—how much and how

Complexity—detailed or aggregated

Formalization—the degree to which the interactions have been planned for and their results predetermined.

And so on.

The classification scheme I shall use is as unsatisfactory as any other, but it will serve to suggest some of the relations between the models described elsewhere . . . as well as between many other models that we could describe.

We shall file our models in 10 pigeonholes (Fig. 1) arranged in five rows and two columns. The five rows of our filing scheme describe the form of the model: verbal, analytical, and so forth. Each of these five categories is broken into two according to whether or not an active opponent is involved and conflict is an essential part of the model.

Our five categories of model form are

   I.   Verbal

  II.   People—as an integral part of the model

III.   People and computers interacting as a part of the model

IV.   Computer

  V.   Analytical

If conflict is an essential element, then we shall speak of model types

   Ic, IIc, IIIc, IVc, Vc

(A conflict situation does not, of course, exclude the case of opponents who also have interests in common.) If conflict plays little or no role, then we shall speak of model types

   Inc, IInc, IIInc, IVnc, Vnc

When the "conflict" or "no conflict" subscript is lacking, both kinds of models are contemplated. Thus V includes all analytical models, both the game-theoretic ones dealing with conflict situations, and the host of analytical models used in operations research.

CONFLICT
LITTLE OR NONE   ESSENTIAL

	LITTLE OR NONE	ESSENTIAL
I. Verbal	Inc	Ic Some scenarios
II. People	IInc Command Post Exercise	IIc War game Crisis exercise
III. People and computers	IIInc Logistics Systems Laboratory	IIIc TAGS
IV. Computer	IVnc FLIOP SAMSOM	IVc STAGE
V. Analytical	Vnc Missile defense example	Vc Game theory

IV and V are bracketed as *Mathematical models*.

Figure 1 Categories of model forms.

If we wished to be complete, we would have to add a few more pigeonholes. At present our classification scheme excludes physical models—for example, wind tunnels. More important, it has no place for visual models like the organization chart or the blackboard chart that could be filled in as we describe the various categories and which would make the clumsy symbolism Vc unnecessary in this model of models.

Our five categories, from "verbal" to "analytical," constitute a scale that measures, roughly speaking, how broad or narrow a part of the real world can be satisfactorily treated. Let us take a look at each type of model, beginning at the narrow end.

Analytical Models

Our missile defense example fits into category Vnc here—as do most of the models built by operations researchers. In this pigeonhole are found the models that use the interesting techniques of linear and dynamic programming, queueing theory, network theory, and so on. A computer may be used in category V, but as an aid and after the mathematician has finished most of his work. It is characteristic of the models in V that they deal not with specificity, but with generality; not with a single play of a situation (game or otherwise), but with all possible plays of the situation.

Pigeonhole Vc contains the models of game theory. Here the analyst is concerned not with playing tic-tac-toe—that is done in box IIc or IIIc—but with the theory of optimal play. He is concerned not only with our decisions, as in the case of the missile defense example, but also with the decisions of our opponent. You may remember the cartoon which showed a high-level conference in Washington, with the speaker saying, "The way I see it, Russia thinks we think they think we're not willing to go to war." Game theory does not solve that problem, but it does furnish a framework in which one can think more clearly about the difficult problems of conflicting interests. . . .

Computer Models

In the missile defense example, the relevant factors were few enough in number, and the relations between them were simple enough, that we could trace out the interactions with pencil, paper, and a little mathematics. We arrived analytically at the relation which specified, for any value of the parameters, when the defense option was preferred. In the problems addressed by the models of category IV, the relevant factors are too numerous or their interrelations too complex to be handled analytically. Instead we must write our instructions for an electronic computer, and the model thus appears as a computer program. In contrast to category V, a particular run of a computer model deals with numerical values and hence with a specific play of a situation.

One example of the models found in pigeonhole IVnc is SAMSOM, a Monte Carlo model which simulates the capability of an aircraft organization to generate sorties and turn aircraft around to support peacetime flying-training programs, meet maximum effort readiness requirements, and provide combat capabilities. There are also the global air war model STAGE (which is used in the Air Force by the Office of the Assistant Chief of Staff for Studies and Analysis), the strategic planning tool FLIOP, and other models of category IV.

Categories IV and V together constitute the class of "mathematical models."

People Models

We skip, temporarily, category III. As we observed earlier, humans are involved in all models—as designers, and experimenters, and users. But in category II humans are an integral part of the model. In category IIc we find the war game, the business game, and the military and political crisis exercise. . . . A command post exercise in which the opponent is either absent or plays only a pro forma role is an example of a category IInc model.

People and Computer Models

Here both people and computers are embedded in the model. RAND's Logistics Systems Laboratory and the air defense simulations of RAND and the System Development Corporation are examples of type IIInc. The limited war game China-5 and the tactical air and ground support game TAGS, both played at RAND some years back, go into pigeonhole IIIc.

Categories IV, III, and II together make up the class of "simulation models."

Categories IVc, IIIc, and IIc together make up the class of "gaming models."

Verbal Models

As we have seen, the model builder decides what factors are relevant to his study, determines the relations between them, and traces out their interactions and implications. This activity is, more or less, what anyone does who thinks about a problem. (We have been speaking prose all our lives without realizing it.) The model builder merely does these things explicitly and, where possible, quantitatively—his assumptions laid out on the table for any person to inspect and criticize.

If a model has no quantitative content it goes, perforce, in category I. Note that the most common study is one that combines verbal and analytical models; it is a mixture of I and V.

The scenario, whether used alone or in conjunction with other models, is often cast in the form of a verbal model. . . .

All of us use models of various parts of the real world, though in most cases we do not make them explicit and, indeed, would probably have great difficulty in laying them out for others—or even ourselves—to see. And most of our decisions must be made on the basis of these implicit models.

When an ad hoc committee of experts addresses a problem around a table, it attempts to arrive at a consensus on the basis of whatever analysis may be done, together with the knowledge and intuition and the implicit models of each member of the committee. For some problems this may be a satisfactory approach in spite of the difficulties that can arise—"the hasty formulation of preconceived notions, an inclination to close one's mind to novel ideas, a tendency to defend a stand once taken, or, alternatively and sometimes alternately, a predisposition to be swayed by persuasively stated opinions of others."[3]

The search for better ways of making systematic use of expert judgment has led to various techniques, including Olaf Helmer's Delphi method, which exposes the experts' views to one another's critiques by a program of sequential individual interrogations interspersed with feedback of prior and preliminary consensus.

While verbal models often remain unstated and implicit, there are exceptions. For example, in a verbal model built by Anthony Downs, a bureaucracy is defined as an organization that has the following four characteristics:

1. It is large; that is, the highest ranking members know less than half of all the members personally. This means that bureaus face substantial administrative problems.

2. A majority of its members are full-time workers who depend upon their employment in the organization for most of their income. That is, the bureau members are not dilettantes but are seriously committed to their jobs. Also, the bureau must compete for their services in the labor market.

3. Hiring, promotion, and retention of personnel are at least theoretically based upon some type of assessment of the way in which they have performed or can be expected to perform their organizational roles (that is, rather than on some characteristics such as religion, race, or social class or periodic election).

4. The major portion of its output is not directly or indirectly evaluated in any markets external to the organization by means of voluntary tit-for-tat transactions.

Some typical examples of bureaus covered by the theory are the Roman Catholic Church (except for the Pope, who is elected), the University of California, the Soviet central planning agency, the U.S. State Department, the New York Port Authority, and the Chinese Communist Army. The theory has been designed to make practical predictions about the likely behavior of real-world bureaus. The theory generates specific propositions linking certain elements of the internal structure of bureaus with certain aspects of their functions and their external environments.[4]

CONCLUSION

As a RAND staff member, D. Ellsberg, has observed, those critics of analysis who object that it deals with an artificial and oversimplified version of the real world often have even more artificial, more highly simplified models of the world, although implicit. For example, they sometimes appear to think that the arms race may be summarized merely by referring to budgets or by counting warheads; that weapons are either invulnerable or vulnerable, first-strike or second-strike; that postures are characterized either by "superiority" or "stability"; that reliability is either perfect or impossible; that both U.S. and Soviet Union wartime objectives are simple; that many things can be assumed as certain: escalation, or all-out war, or spread of arms, Allied response, nuclear war; or that many things can be assumed impossible: thermonuclear war, big threats, big conventional war, bigger nonnuclear forces, a U.S. first strike.

Systems analysis and the use of logical models, Ellsberg argues, will not eliminate uncertainty or insure correctness; will not foresee all major problems, goals, contingencies, and alternatives; will not eliminate the necessity of judgment or the effect of bias and preconception. Hopefully, they will tend to increase the influence of the "best," most informed, judgments, both on component matters and in the final weighing of decisions; they can provide choices and a market of ideas. They can discover problems, stimulate relevant questions, and encourage people to face complexity and uncertainty explicitly and honestly.

NOTES AND REFERENCES

1. C. J. Hitch, "Uncertainties in Operations Research," *Operations Research,* 8(July-August): 443–444 (1960).
2. "Methods and Procedures," *Analysis for Military Decisions* (E. S. Quade, ed.), Rand McNally, Chicago, p. 168 (1964).
3. N. C. Dalkey and O. Helmer, *An Experimental Application of the Delphi Method to the Use of Experts,* RAND Corporation, RM-727-PR (Abr.), July, p. 2 (1962).
4. A. Downs, *Inside Bureaucracy,* RAND Corporation, P-2963, August (1964). For a full account of this theory, see A. Downs, *Inside Bureaucracy,* RAND Corporation Research Study, Little, Brown, Boston (1967).

25

PPBS: Theory, Structure, and Limitations

Jack Rabin

The planning, programming and budgeting system (PPBS) is an analytic tool which was adopted by many states and localities. It was originally developed by the Rand Corporation in Santa Monica, California, for use by the U.S. Air Force. The technique was adopted by the Department of Defense when Robert McNamara became Secretary of Defense in 1961. In 1965, President Lyndon Johnson, by Executive Order, instructed the executive departments to adopt PPBS, thus making this system the decision-making and financial tool for the federal government.

A number of states (e.g., Arkansas, California) adopted PPBS as their budget technique; moreover, many cities (e.g., Dayton, Ohio; Philadelphia) used a form of the technique. Therefore, an examination of what PPBS is and is not, a review of the major assumptions and techniques employed, and a look at the potential benefits and costs of adopting such a system are in order.

This chapter has two global objectives. We shall review (1) PPBS in theory and (2) PPBS in practice. Thus, our objectives will be accomplished if the reader can (1) gain an understanding of what theory underlay PPBS and (2) realize that PPBS's limitations hindered implementation and reduced its value.

PPBS IN THEORY

Considering the theoretical underpinnings behind a planning, programming, and budgeting system is a complicated and elusive task. The approach here seeks to answer three questions:

1. What is a useful working definition of PPBS?
2. What is the model of decision-making which underlies PPBS?
3. What is the specific structure of PPBS?

Source: Robert T. Golembiewski and Jack Rabin, *Public Budgeting and Finance*, *2nd Ed.*, Peacock Publishing Co., Itasca, Illinois, pp. 427–447 (1975). Chapter title was previously "State and Local PPBS."

A Useful Working Definition

The scholarly literature is muddled about defining PPBS, although the technique has been in existence for more than four decades. Consider only one reflection on the point in the journal *Public Administration Review*, which devoted two full issues to PPBS. In responding to the first PAR review, Frederick C. Mosher commented in a letter to the editor:

> Over the last few years and particularly the last few months, I have been searching for "satisficing" answers to two questions about PPBS. First, what is really new and distinctive about it? Second, in what directions is it really influencing governmental decision-making and the conduct of governmental operations?
>
> I was therefore particularly gratified to learn that PAR would devote a complete issue to PPBS, and I read all of it with unusual (for me) care and thoroughness. It was a very good and rewarding issue. Yet I cannot honestly say that these articles resolved my questions; indeed, I am somewhat more confused now than before. Most of your authors, like others before them, differ among each other as to what PPBS really is; few of them say or predict what its real effects are or will be—beyond the confident assurance that decisions will be more rational, governmental operations more efficient (excepting, of course, Mr. Wildavsky's alarums from the wilderness of political science). I am in sympathy with most of PPBS and its constituent elements insofar as I understand what they are. In fact, I have been a supporter for about thirty years—ever since I took a course in budgeting taught by Bob Steadman in 1936. But apparently I have been missing some things. These are what I am searching to identify. [1]

With appropriate caution, then, a working definition is hazarded here. The intent is not to force a standard usage, but to provide a base for elaboration and analysis.

Planning, programming, and budgeting system is a rational decision-making technique which may be used to make more systematic decisions, given a set of objectives and the information at hand. PPBS emphasizes the long-term benefits and costs of programs, rather than the short-term. PPBS is composed of program budgeting and systems analysis, which typically involves cost/benefit studies.

Program budgeting basically places into common categories all activities necessary to accomplish some broad end or "program."

Program budgeting thus contrasts with the line-item budget, which aggregates similar activities into common categories, without regard to the programs or goals to which they contribute.

There are three documents used in program budgeting: the multiyear program and financial plan; special analytic studies; and program memoranda. These documents are augmented by systematic analysis, forecasting long-term costs and benefits.

The PPB system should be considered as cyclical. That is, the results of the decisions of previous years provide data for decisions in any current year. The past, as it were, thus provides "feedback" for present and future decisions.

PPBS is only a tool for budgetary forecasting and programming. The tool never makes decisions; decision makers, choosing to use data derived from the tool, make decisions.

This working definition of PPBS—like all others—implies two levels of purpose. One level is explicit, and the other level of purpose is typically implied but is nonetheless real. Clarity about both levels of purpose is desirable.

Stated Purposes of PPBS

With basic unanimity, observers agree as to the stated purposes of PPBS. As Arthur Smithies explains:

> Planning, programming, and budgeting constitute the process by which objectives and resources, and the interrelations among them, are taken into account to achieve a coherent and comprehensive program of action for the government as a whole. Program budgeting involves the use of budgetary techniques that facilitate explicit consideration of the pursuit of policy objectives in terms of their economic costs, both at the present time and in the future [2].

Consequently, it can be said that PPBS served such stated purposes as:

1. "To improve the basis for major program decisions" [3].
2. "To subject decisions about resource allocation to systematic analysis, comparing alternative courses of action in a framework of national objectives clearly and specifically stated" [4].
3. To use "the rule of efficiency (in choosing) that alternative that optimizes the allocation of public resources" [5].
4. To help "responsible officials make decisions. It is *not* a mechanical substitute for the good judgments, political wisdom and leadership of those officials" [6].

The overall purpose of PPBS, then, was to serve as an aid to human judgment, not to supplant it. PPBS never "decides" an issue; the goal is to have the decision-maker use the data generated to make better decisions.

Derivatively, PPBS implied the existence of three crucial elements in pursuit of this concept of systematic and comprehensive approach to planning, action, and evaluation. In Charles Schultze's terms, PPBS implied:

1. The existence in each agency of an *analytic* capability, which carries out continuing in-depth analyses by permanent specialized staffs of the agency's objectives and its various programs to meet these objectives.
2. The existence of a multiyear *planning and programming* process, which incorporates and uses an information system to present data in meaningful categories essential to the making of major decisions by agency heads and by the President.
3. The existence of a *budgeting* process, which can take broad program decisions, translate them into more refined decisions in a budget context, and present the appropriate program and financial data for Presidential and Congressional action [7].

Overriding, If Often Implicit, Purposes of PPBS

Overall, PPBS reflected the basic if often implicit goal of reserving major and growing decision-making authority in the hands of the executive. In sum, PPBS had a strong "centralizing bias." As Thomas Schelling states:

> Any discussion of PPBS is unrealistic unless it is acknowledged that budgetary processes are a means of control, as well as a means of evaluation . . . Almost anyone concerned with administration sooner or later discovers that control of budgetary requests and disbursements is a powerful source of more general control. . . . Anything that makes budgeting more effective will add to the authority of those involved in the budgeting. Budgetary procedures provide invaluable opportunities for holding hearings, demanding justifications, spot-checking the quality of

planning, identifying objectives, and even enhancing competition among lethargic subgroups. Furthermore, the budgetary process being geared to an annual cycle, it provides a regular and systematic way of repeatedly examining these subjects [8].

This control orientation in PPBS may produce a lukewarm to hostile reaction on the part of legislators and lower level administrators, even when executive decision-makers are committed to PPBS. That is, adoption of PPBS may help to bring about "power redistribution" [9] effects which may not seem desirable to some decision-makers. For example, while top political decision-makers may embrace it, their career subordinates may treat the process as a threat. Thus, anyone embarking upon a program of implementing or "selling" PPBS must taken into account its centralizing and power-redistribution effects, and often be prepared for questions relating to both.

Some Underlying Models of Decision-Making

The theory of PPBS implied a specific model of decision-making and thereby generated substantial opposition. The point can be demonstrated by contrasting two broad models of human decision-making: the rational and the incremental models. PPBS rested on a rational decision-making model; opponents of PPBS usually favored the incremental model as their explanation as to how the process of human decision-making worked, and indeed how it should work [10].

Rational Decision-Making Model

In this model, objectives (ends, goals, etc.) are known and are accepted by the participants in the decision-making. The sole decision-making task becomes a search for (1) the alternative means to attain the end and (2) the specific approach which costs the least and gives the most benefit (or, in military terminology in use in the 1960s, the "most bang for a buck"). Some major properties of the rational model are sketched in Figure 1.

Early rational decision-making theorists gave the impression that people could know and predict all alternatives, all costs, and all benefits. Later, the *limits* of an individual's

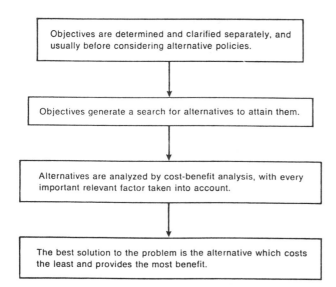

Figure 1 The rational model of decision-making. (*Source*: Ref. 10.)

rationality typically are taken into account. Illustratively, compare the contrasting but developmental views of Gene Fisher and Charles Schultze in Table 1. These men were a Rand analyst and the Director of the Bureau of the Budget, respectively, and both were intimately associated with the development and implementation of PPBS.

Incremental Decision-Making Model

In contrast to rational models, the several incremental varieties emphasize five factors: (1) people are assumed to have great and often overwhelming difficulties in foreseeing the consequences (costs and benefits) of decisions, (2) people do not agree about the goals of government, (3) many ends are means to other ends, (4) many problems are too complex and are related to so many other variables that people cannot fully understand them, and (5) a majority of decisions can be explained in terms of a kind of "domino theory," with one decision stimulating the need for another decision, ad infinitum, as opposed to the simultaneous consideration of all alternatives implied by rational models. Figure 2 sketches the major features of incremental models of decision-making.

A Modified Rational Model

The incrementalists made some telling points. Figure 3 represents an adjustment to both theories.

Basically, Figure 3 reflects a substantial dash of humility about what is inevitable, and perhaps even desirable, about public spending decisions. In sum: As long as one keeps in mind that he or she will not be able to know all alternatives to solving a problem, that analysis of costs and benefits will not be perfect, and that one will be dealing only with the information that one can get, then the rational approach to budgeting/decision-making can be a helpful, if limited, analytic tool.

Table 1 Major Characteristics of Cost-Utility Analysis

Gene H. Fisher: Cost-Utility Analysis (1964)	Charles Schultze: Cost-Effectiveness Analysis (1967)
1. Systematic examination and comparison of alternatives to achieve specified objectives.	1. Systematic examination and comparison of alternatives to achieve specified objectives.
2. Assessment of cost and utility of each alternative.	2. Assessment of cost and utility of each alternative under the following provisos: (a) one will never have "all the relevant information" so that (b) analysis is performed only with the information one "can get."
3. The time context is in the future.	
4. Quantitative methods should be used "as much as possible," with "uncertain" elements faced up to and treated explicitly in the analysis.	3. The time context is in the future.
	4. ". . . you can put into a cost-effectiveness PPB framework all of the information you can get (although not all of it can be expressed quantitatively)."

Source: Based on Gene H. Fisher, "The Role of Cost-Utility Analysis in Program Budgeting," in David Novick (ed.), *Program Budgeting*, 2nd ed, Holt, Rinehart & Winston, New York, pp. 66–67 (1969); Charles Schultze, in U.S., Congress, Senate, hearings before the Subcommittee on National Security and International Operations, Committee on Government Operations, 90th Cong., 1st Sess., August 23, p. 186 (1967).

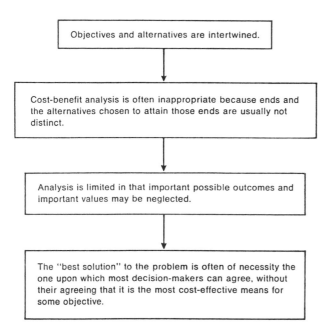

Figure 2   The incremental model of decision-making. (*Source*: Adapted from Ref. 10.)

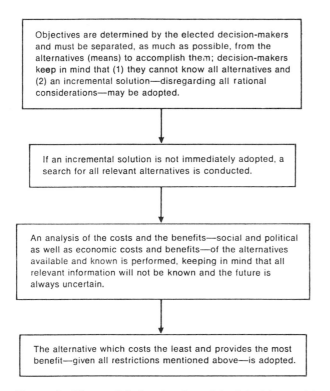

Figure 3   The modified rational model of decision-making.

Specific Structure of PPBS

In essence, PPBS builds toward program budgets, and the immediate purpose is to provide a flowchart of the major activities involved in the development of program budgets. The sections below will consider four major elements:

1. Goal definition
2. The development of a program structure
3. The major PPBS documents
4. Cost-benefit analysis

Goal Definition

Ideally, a planning, programming, and budgeting system begins with a definition of objectives and subobjectives and extends that emphasis as far as possible. This definition is usually accomplished by elected decision-makers and department heads in policy statements, legislation, and so on. For example, in 1961 President Kennedy stated that a national goal for the United States was to place a man on the moon before the end of the decade. In 1965, President Johnson launched a "war" on poverty, seeking to eradicate its causes and consequences in the United States. These are goals. Both were accepted by Congress. Once goals are defined, then program budgets can be developed.

However, the basic question in American government remains *who* should define goals. Are goals to be defined by the people at the "top" or by those at intermediate levels who must find ways of implementing the goals? Paul L. Brown grapples with this dilemma:

> What disturbs me about this broad approach (of goal definition) from the top down is that many of these definitions become almost truisms. They have to be refined through several levels before they become meaningful for immediate budgetary or operational purposes. These immediate purposes are areas in which we must make decisions today. . . . I see more of a payoff in concentrating initial attention at a lower level of activity than the goals and objectives of government.
>
> I am not convinced that a proper description of the objective cannot be started at an intermediate level, be properly evaluated, measured and combined with statements for higher levels to reach a unified goal which can then be evaluated and worked back down. In this way objectives and subobjectives could be formulated, and perhaps better measurements could be developed more rapidly [11].

Brown essentially argues for the factoring process involved in "suboptimization." Suboptimization is the process of breaking "problems of choice into manageable pieces or subproblems" [12] and then developing courses of action. As Roland McKean states:

> In a government or department, one man or one committee cannot possibly examine all problems of choice simultaneously and select each course of action in light of all the other decisions. The task is divided among various persons along hierarchical lines, some of the broader policy choices being made by high level officials or groups, and others being delegated to lower levels [13].

Thus, the process of suboptimization applies to the making of choices among alternative courses of action, and it also concerns the definition of government objectives. Subobjectives, defined by elected decision-makers and department heads, may be usefully handled in constructing a program budget even if the sum of the subobjectives only approximates the ultimate goals of government.

The Development of a Program Structure

A program structure consists of the program categories which are determined on the basis of objectives, but often the concept of the program structure is changed in practice. Here, we shall deal with the theory underlying programs and program structure; in "PPBS in Practice" we shall investigate how environmental and political variables may alter the concept.

The program structure is usually subdivided, based on subobjectives, into smaller components. Last (and definitely last), program categories, determined by top elected and appointed decision-makers, bring together activities (i.e., line items, objects of expenditure), regardless of agency location, so long as the activities contribute to the same program objective. Since agencies commonly share responsibilities for any specific program, "crosswalks" are required to link agency structures and program structures, as is illustrated in Figure 4.

Traditional budgeting procedures emphasize agency location rather than program, and line-item budgets thus emphasize agency, division, and activity (or similar labels), as in the right-hand portion of Figure 4. This common emphasis neglects the crucial fact that many activities of government cut across agency lines. For example, both the U.S. State Department, through the Agency for International Development, and the Defense Department engage in military-related foreign aid projects. However, these projects are rarely coordinated, due in part to their placement in the organization structure. Whatever the example, the conclusion is the same. A coordinated approach to social problems is often hampered or precluded by agency barriers.

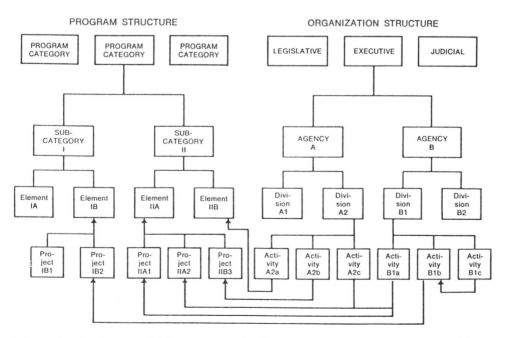

Figure 4 The "crosswalk" between organization structure and program structure. (*Source*: "Planning and Budgeting, A Seminar on Planning and Budgeting Concepts for Florida," presented to the state legislature and all operating departments and agencies by the Planning and Budget Commission and Legislative Auditor, State of Florida, p. 64.)

A rough contrast may be helpful. A line-item budget stresses the individual bits of public spending: positions, typewriters, etc. A program budget, on the other hand, stresses the broad product, or objective.

Reconciling the two approaches is easier said than done, but, in essence, program budgets seek to cluster activities necessary to achieve major objectives and consequently must seek coordination between government agencies. The left side of Figure 4 illustrates such a program structure clustering of diverse agency activities necessary to meet major objectives. Program structures are typically multileveled and can relate to:

1. The attainment of a major government objective, usually identified as a *program category*.
2. The accomplishment of narrower objectives, usually expressed in terms of *program subcategories*.
3. Specific products which are grouped under the heading of *program elements* [14].

In essence, then, program budgets create a new organizaton or structure of activities, based on broad government objectives, and two factorings of these objectives. Life would be simpler if the individual agencies themselves were organized around programs. Typically, however, a tension existed between the agency and program structures, with the crosswalks identifying which agencies contribute to which programs, in what specific senses, and in what degree.

The Major PPBS Documents

Several major documents derive from and add detail to the program structure. Three kinds of such documents will be considered here: (1) multiyear program and financial plans, (2) special analytic studies, and (3) program memoranda.

One of the important products of program budgeting is a compact document termed the *multiyear program and financial plan* (PFP). The PFP:

1. Is based on the program structure.
2. Usually covers a period of years (often 5 years).
3. Includes activities contemplated as well as authorized.
4. Indicates what the department head thinks will be appropriate over the period covered by the plan.
5. Translates projected costs and receipts into financial, quantitative terms.

A brief excerpt from one PFP is shown in Table 2. In reality, the plan may contain hundreds of categories.

Special analytic studies (SASs) are analytic efforts to examine in depth a specific topic at the request of a decision-maker. SASs typically have one or two time frames. One type is initiated and completed during one budget year. This one-year study usually is conducted in support of a budget request submitted in a program memorandum. Other SASs go beyond one budget year. To illustrate, one such continuing study was designed to develop "on a longer-run basis the conceptual understanding necessary to improve the data available, to evaluate the implications of agency objectives, and to provide an analytic basis for deciding future Major Program Issues" [15]. A major program issue is one requiring decision in a current budget cycle, with major implications in terms of either present or future costs, the direction of a program or group of programs, or a policy choice. Most centrally, a major program issue identifies specific alternative courses of action, and the costs and benefits of each. Pertinent legislative as well as budgetary considerations can also be emphasized [16].

Table 2 Excerpt from Sample PFP

Multiyear Program and Financial Plan, Fiscal Years 1972–78 (dollars in millions)

Program categories	FY 1972 Actual	FY 1973 Current estimate	FY 1974 Budget year estimate	FY 1975 Program estimate	FY 1976 Program estimate	FY 1977 Program estimate	FY 1978 Program estimate	Total costs '72–'78
I. Personal safety								
Civilian law enforcement								
Traffic safety								
Fire prevention & control								
Safety from animals								
Protection and control of natural and manmade disasters								
Total Program Area I								
II. Health								
Physical health								
Mental health								
Drug and alcohol addiction-prevention and control								
Total Program Area II								

Source: State-Local Finances Project, PPB Note 1, George Washington University, p. 5.

The *program memorandum* (PM) presents

a statement of the program issues, a comparison of the cost and effectiveness of alternatives for resolving those issues in relation to objectives, the agency head's recommendations on programs to be carried out, and the reasons for those decisions. PMs, therefore, provide the documentation for the strategic decisions recommended for the budget year [17].

In other words, the program memorandum:

1. Spells out specific programs recommended by the department for the multiyear period.
2. Demonstrates how the programs meet the objectives specified by the decision-making process.
3. Shows the total cost of programs recommended.
4. Indicates how recommended programs differ from current and past programs.
5. Describes recommended program objectives, expected benefits, and costs for several years into the future.
6. Describes recommended program objectives "insofar as possible" in quantitative physical terms.
7. Compares the effectiveness and cost of (a) alternative objectives, (b) alternative types of programs which may meet the same objectives, and (c) different levels within program categories.
8. Makes "explicit the assumptions and criteria which support recommended programs."
9. Identifies and analyzes the main uncertainties in assumptions, in costs and benefits [18].

Cost-Benefit Analysis

Cost-benefit analysis—which may also be called cost-effectiveness or cost-utility analysis—is a rational decision-making tool and a variety of systems analysis. The major goal in cost-benefit analysis is to determine the projected costs and benefits of different alternatives to the achievement of an objective or subobjective.

The inability to *meaningfully quantify* all relevant variables is a major limitation of cost-benefit analysis. According to Klaus Knorr, for example, cost-benefit analysis is most useful when "the objective or output is definitely fixed—that is, when there is only one dependent variable, and the sole task is to minimize the costs which are readily and accurately measured" [19]. However, "the usefulness of the technique is the more limited, the less the problem is capable of uniform quantification" [20].

Two other important limitations on cost-benefit analysis relate to the definition of "cost" and the availability of information. First, consider the depth of measurement involved in cost-benefit analyses. Many cost-benefit studies disregard all nonmonetary costs; that is, situations or alternatives may involve such costs as morale, "loss of face," and so forth. Since these costs cannot be easily quantified, the tendency is to ignore what may be important considerations. This can be a serious limitation which can seriously mislead incautious interpreters of specific cost-benefit analyses.

Second, applications of cost-benefit analysis are limited by "imperfect information." Many situations may be so uncertain or volatile that accurate information concerning alternative courses of action is either too expensive to obtain or too unreliable to use. Directly, the quality of the input information is critical in interpreting the results of any cost-benefit analysis.

However, given such limitations, the cost-benefit tool should not be hastily discarded. At its best, the technique can help to improve decision-making. Moreover, cost-benefit analysis can heighten the usefulness of a program budget. Pointedly, program budgets are meaningful more or less in direct proportion to the adequacy of their underlying cost-benefit analyses, whether they are implicit or explicit analyses.

PPBS IN PRACTICE: EXPERIENCE IN NEW YORK STATE

This section begins with a paradox. PPBS had major attractions, in principle. In practice, however, it often degenerated into an exercise taking all the items in the line-item budget and finding a place for them in the PPBS budget, with "crosswalks" considered more as colorful demonstrations than as reflections of cooperation and coordination between agencies providing activities to the same program or programs. This, of course, represented a perversion of the original concept of PPBS and helped to reinforce the status quo. Thus, the ideal program sought to reallocate or eliminate activities inconsistent with program needs. However, most actual programs were political compromises that, because of agency resistance, tended to aggregate all the existing activities of agencies into new "boxes."

PPBS did not have the success for which its proponents hoped. We shall consider one example of this mixed success. New York state exemplified a failure to implement a "true" PPBS budget due to agency resistance, rivalries, and so on.

PPBS in New York State

New York was the first state to adopt PPBS (in 1964) and the first to discard it [21]. The technique was hindered in implementation by a series of organizational and management problems. First, a jurisdictional fight occurred between the agencies which had been given operational control over PPBS implementation. Second, little effort was made in the beginning to overcome the agency tendency to use PPBS as a planning tool, with budgeting occupying a subordinate role. Third, the various "mini-wars" which affected PPBS implementation soon led to a general disillusionment with it. Finally, these problems contributed to the abandonment of PPBS and the adoption of program analysis and review (PAR), which was an attempt to gain firm executive control over the situation.

The Jurisdictional Fight

Three agencies were involved in PPBS implementation in New York: the Office of the Secretary to the Governor, the State Budget Division (which was the "traditional" budgeting agency), and the Office of Planning Coordination.

The development of PPBS programs was given to the Office of the Secretary to the Governor, which soon contained a staff of 100 analysts, many of whom served as staff people assigned to particular program functions. Placing program development in this agency led to the Secretary's Office becoming the center of policy formulation in the state and induced an unpublicized rivalry between that office and the State Budget Division.

A third agency soon entered the picture. The need for statewide comprehensive planning stimulated the creation of the Office of Planning Coordination. This agency was responsible for devising long-range resource plans. The State Budget Division, however, saw the creation of yet another agency as a further threat to its leadership in financial affairs [22].

This jurisdictional dispute between the State Budget Division and the two planning agencies affected PPBS implementation. When PPBS was adopted by the state, both the

State Budget Division and the Office of Planning Coordination established separate PPBS staffs, but neither agency treated PPBS as an important part of its work.

The PPBS staff in the State Budget Division—the program analysis unit—gradually became estranged from the budget director. Moreover, this staff was treated by members of the Budget Division—specifically the examination and the management units—as an outsider:

> This . . . (estrangement) . . . was due as much to the eagerness of the PPBers to be free from the constraints of the old-timers as to the desire of the old-timers to operate without PPB interference. By and large, the examiners were enemies of PPB. They were not really consulted. The PPBers had come to government out of nowhere or out of physical planning. Thriving on their separateness, the PPBers did not recognize that there are other decisional processes outside PPB. [23]

The Stress on Planning

Another constraint which limited PPBS almost from its inception was that the system was begun primarily as a statewide planning system, with budgeting in a *subordinate* role. It did not take agency officials very long to realize that the annual budget cycle was operating virtually independent of PPBS. Documents were consequently viewed as burdens and eventually were consigned for preparation to agency clerks.

After New York enlisted as one of the five states in the State-Local Finances Project in 1967, the State Budget Division was able to expand its PPBS apparatus and began to redirect the system toward budgeting. This move was accompanied by a waning interest in PPBS by the planners in the Office of Planning Coordination.

By 1968, new legislative budget guidelines had legitimized this move on the part of the State Budget Division and had firmly redirected the course of PPBS in New York into the financial management area. Furthermore, in the same year, the State Division was able to supplant the Office of Planning Coordination as the major PPBS agency in the state.

Disillusionment with PPBS

Although the attempt had been made in 1968 to overhaul the system, it was not enough to rescue PPBS from the ennui which had set in during its previous four years' practice. Interagency rivalry prevented the issuance of adequate guidelines for submitting PPBS documents. Furthermore, no attempt was made to inform the agencies why the information they were preparing was important or what would be done with it when submitted.

By 1969, the operation of PPBS in New York had come "to a virtual halt" [24]. Key PPBS personnel were looking for other positions. In the summer of 1969, the program analysis and coordination unit in the State Budget Division was abolished.

Conclusion

Implementation of PPBS in New York was similar to the federal experience in that no attempt was made to gain agency acceptance of a new form of budgetary decision-making, which was overlaid on the existing decision structure.

SUMMARY

The most important point to remember with regard to choosing PPBS and similar techniques is that this is a *political* decision involving the major budgetary decision-makers in the instrumentality. As was the case in New York, many planners become disillusioned because the political process is not systematic and decisions on important issues are not made rationally.

The decision to adopt PPBS has implications for vested interests, appropriations committee members in the legislature, the chief executive, and the bureaucracy. With its centralizing and power-redistribution effects, it can have substantial implications for any one of these groups. These implications must be kept in mind by anyone proposing any rational decision-making budgeting tool.

Furthermore, when PPBS or similar techniques are being considered, one should question whether the major budgetary decision-makers have a desire to plan and use the data provided by the system once the project is in operation. Statistical data can be used as justification or a "smokescreen" for virtually any alternative course of action. In fact, the likelihood and potential exists for (1) the utilization of machine data to "snow" decision-makers or (2) the production of meaningless data in the agencies if the assent of the bureaucracy is not obtained. Thus, one must be vigilant even after the technique has been installed.

NOTES AND REFERENCES

1. *Public Admin. Rev.*, *27* (March 1967): 67.
2. Arthur Smithies, "Conceptual Framework for the Program Budget," *Program Budgeting* (David Novick, ed.) 2d ed., Holt, Rinehart & Winston, New York, p. 24 (1969).
3. "Planning-Programming-Budgeting," Bulletin 68–2, Executive Office of the President, Bureau of the Budget, July 18, p. 1 (1967).
4. Charles J. Zwick, "Commentary on Recent Developments in the Planning, Programming, and Budgeting System," *Planning-Programming-Budgeting: Budget Bureau Guidelines of 1968*, Hearings before the Subcommittee on National Security and International Operations, Committee on Government Operations, U.S. Senate, 90th Cong., 2d sess. 1968. *Planning, Programming, and Budgeting*, U.S. Government Printing Office, Washington, D.C. p. 557 (1970).
5. Allen Schick, "The Road to PPB: The Stages of Budget Reform," *Public Admin. Rev.*, *26*: 243–258 (1966).
6. Hearings before the Subcommittee on National Security and International Operation, Committee on Government Operations, U.S. Senate, 90th Cong., 1st sess. August 23, *Planning, Programming, and Budgeting*, p. 172 (1967).
7. "Planning-Programming-Budgeting," Bulletin 66–3, Executive Office of the President, Bureau of the Budget, October 12, p. 1 (1965).
8. Thomas C. Schelling, "PPBS and Foreign Affairs," memorandum prepared at the request of the Subcommittee on National Security and International Operations, Committee on Government Operations, U.S. Senate, 90th Cong., 2d sess. *Planning, Programming and Budgeting*, p. 113 (1968).
9. See Aaron Wildavsky, "The Political Economy of Efficiency: Cost-Benefit Analysis, Systems Analysis, and Program Budgeting," paper presented at conference on public policy, Social Science Research Council.
10. For further information regarding the incremental model of decision-making, see Charles E. Lindblom, "The Science of Muddling Through," *Public Admin. Rev.*, *19*: 79–88 (1959).
11. Paul L. Brown, "Establishing a Program Structure," *Planning, Programming, Budgeting* (Freemont J. Lyden and Ernest G. Miller, eds.), 2d ed., Markham, Chicago, pp. 184–185 (1972).
12. Roland N. McKean, "Criteria of Efficiency in Government Expenditures," *Public Budgeting and Finance* (Robert T. Golembiewski, ed.), F. E. Peacock, Itasca, Illinois, p. 517 (1968).
13. Ibid., p. 517.
14. "Planning-Programming-Budgeting," BOB Bulletin 66–3, p. 5.

15. "Planning-Programming-Budgeting," Bulletin 68–9, Executive Office of the President, Bureau of the Budget, April 12, p. 542 (1968).
16. Ibid., p. 542.
17. Ibid., p. 542.
18. "Planning-Programming-Budgeting," BOB Bulletin 66–3.
19. Klaus Knorr, "On the Cost-Effectiveness Approach to Military Research and Development," *Bull. Atomic Scientist*, *22* (November 1966).
20. Ibid.
21. Allen Schick, *Budget Innovation in the States*, Brookings Institute, Washington, D.C., p. 117 (1971).
22. Ibid., pp. 119–120.
23. Ibid., p. 120.
24. Ibid., p. 126.

26

The Myth of Incrementalism: Analytic Choices in Budgetary Theory

Lance T. LeLoup

INTRODUCTION

Of all the subfields of political science, budgeting is most dominated by one theory to the exclusion of completing theories. For over a decade, *incrementalism* has dominated conceptualization, analysis, and description of the budgetary process. This chapter attempts to show that this dominance has been detrimental to an overall understanding of the dynamics and processes of budgeting. Incrementalism was developed as a fully articulated theory on the basis of a number of implicit analytic choices appearing so obvious as to preclude the consideration of alternatives; however, they were costly in that they provided a misleading view of budgeting [1].

A growing number of studies challenge the incremental theory of budgeting. The coherent integration of previously isolated challenges in terms of analytic and interpretive choices in the development of budgetary theory will be attempted here. This will not only help to clarify incrementalism but also suggest a number of alternative approaches and explanations. New directions refocusing budgetary theory on annual budgeting and multi-year budgetary decisions will be proposed as more promising for theoretical development. Finally, the conclusion will review the persistence of incrementalism and its relevance to budgeting.

INCREMENTALISM AS BUDGETARY THEORY

When V. O. Key lamented the lack of a budgetary theory, he was referring to the lack of normative theory to guide allocative decisions under conditions of scarcity [2]. Subsequently attempts were made, perhaps in response to Key, to specify a normative theory of budgeting [3], and the literature supporting planning/programming/budgeting (PPB) can be seen as a recent extension of such efforts [4]. While incrementalism has a normative foundation in

Source: *Polity*, *10*(4): 488–509 (1978).

pluralism [5], our analysis seeks to avoid the explicitly normative dimensions and instead concentrates on explanatory and descriptive aspects of budgetary theory.

The "incrementalists" are the authors of the most influential works on budgeting in the last two decades: Lindblom, Wildavsky, Fenno, Davis et al., and Sharkansky. In "The Science of Muddling Through," Lindblom suggests that in governmental decision making, successive limited comparison of policies is more feasible and rational than comprehensive analysis [6]. Limited, noncomprehensive, incremental change, representing mutual adjustment of participant groups, is portrayed as the most common method of policy formulation [7]. Muddling through is not only what is done, it is what *should* be done.

Incorporating Lindblom's thesis, the fully developed and most influential statement of incremental budgeting is found in Wildavsky's *The Politics of the Budgetary Process*, where he examines the interaction of agencies and Congress and the resulting appropriations decisions [8].

> Budgeting is incremental, not comprehensive. The beginning of wisdom about an agency budget is that it is almost never actively reviewed as a whole every year in the sense of reconsidering the value of all existing programs as compared to all possible alternatives. Instead, it is based on last year's budget with special attention given to a narrow range of increases or decreases [9].

Incrementalism explains the strategies and behavior of participants as well as the observed patterns of budgetary stability. The incremental process of mutual adjustment is built around the reinforcing roles and expectations of the participants; agencies attempt to establish a base and then gradually expand it. Their strategy is to ask for an increase, but a modest increase. While they expect to be cut back and take this into account in their calculations, too large a request might result in severe cutbacks. Congress, through the appropriations committee and subcommittees, makes incremental cuts in agency requests because it expects the agencies to request more than they need.

Focusing on the appropriations process in Congress, Richard Fenno detailed the roles assumed by the appropriations committees [10]. As "guardians of the public purse," subcommittees normalize their decision making by routinely making cuts in request [11]. As political subsystems, they develop stable relationships over time with the agencies. Looking at annual changes in agency appropriations, Fenno concludes:

> Committee decisions are primarily incremental ones. These kinds of decisions represent the logical outcome of incrementalism which appears in the agency's expectations about committee action and in the committee's perception of agency budgets [12].

It is apparent that incrementalism is used in at least two different senses: (a) to characterize the decision-making process of mutual adjustment and bargaining, and (2) to describe the budgetary outcomes that result from that process [13]. Using Fenno's data, Wildavsky interprets budgetary outcomes as incremental because in a majority of cases the final appropriation varies within a range of $\pm 10\%$ of the previous year's appropriation. This is the closest one gets to a firm definition of an incremental income. Fenno's conclusion that committee decisions reveal a basic incrementalism is similarly made without establishing the necessary criteria.

The work of Lindblom, Wildavsky, and Fenno was essentially descriptive of the process of calculation, decision, and the budgetary outcomes. The most important explanatory variable is the budget base, specifically, last year's appropriation.

From descriptive incrementalism, the theory was elevated to what Morcland has called "analytic incrementalism," that is, mathematical representation of the process using regression equations [14]. The empirical models of agency appropriations by Davis, Dempster, and Wildavsky are the most influential tests of the theory [15]. In the initial model (1966), eight equations were hypothesized to explain the decisions rules used by the participants. The dependent variable was the final appropriation voted by Congress. Using data from 56 domestic agencies from 1946 to 1963, Davis et al. found they could account for 86% of the appropriation decisions. One model each for Congress and the agencies best represented the decisions. The dominant agency decision rule in calculating requests was to take a fixed percentage increase over last year's appropriation. The dominant congressional decision rule in voting appropriations was to make a fixed percentage cut in the agency's request. These two simple calculations summarize the process and the results of incrementalism: the "striking regularities of the budgetary process" that are indicative of the stable decision rules employed by the participants [16]. Change in appropriation patterns are defined as "random shocks in an otherwise deterministic system," the result of "disturbances" and "special circumstances" [17]. The causes of disturbances, special circumstances, shift points, or changes in decision rules are left largely unexplained.

The final elevation of incrementalism was to a predictive theory using econometric modeling techniques [18]. This represented an effort to explain what were previously assumed to be random shift points. These shifts had been detected in years of partisan political change; added to this factor were a number of social, economic, administrative, and political explanatory variables. The inclusion of these environmental variables increased the explanatory power of the models, but since the R^2 were so high under the initial model, the improvement was only marginal [19]. Environmental factors were included as binary variables, "to model the abrupt changes in behavior in response to exogenous forces" [20]. Agencies performing services to the administration and population and in the natural resources areas were found to be most susceptible to environmental influences. The impact of the political, social, economic, and administrative variables was found to be evenly distributed among the categories [21]. The latest refinement, although recognizing for the first time the potential impact of external factors, is based on the same theoretical assumptions and reinforced the conclusions of earlier work.

The theory of budgetary incrementalism is not limited in application to the United States federal budget; subsequent studies have applied it to virtually every level of United States government as well as to other nations and international organizations. Separate studies by Sharkansky and Anton concluded that incrementalism explained budgeting in the American states [22]. John Crecine extended the focus to municipal budgeting with the important caveat that incremental calculations are constrained by revenue projections [23]. Gerwin found incrementalism in school district budgeting [24]. Cowart et al. extended the theory to Norway [25], and Hoole et al. found incremental decision rules in the United Nations, the World Health Organization, and the International Labor Organization [26]. Wildavsky's latest work, developing a comparative theory of budgeting, makes some important distinctions between governments on the basis of wealth and predictability [27]. The common basis of budgeting in his comparative theory, however, revolves around the concepts of incrementalism. Because of the tremendous scope of these studies, they cannot be examined here, and we shall therefore limit ourselves to United States federal budgeting. A final testament to the pervasive dominance of incrementalism, however, is found in secondary works. Incrementalism has filtered down and is heavily relied on in a range of basic texts on American government, state and local, Congress, the bureaucracy, public policy, etc. [28]. The range of different meanings applied to the term and to the theory has further confused the issue.

In spite of its widespread acceptance, some scholars have been critical of the theory. Some of the criticism is on the normative level; as an outgrowth of pluralism it is said to dignify an irrational, biased process with rational status [29]. More general criticism has objected to the view of budgeting it provided, producing as it does a uniform set of results in the face of political bargaining. The upshot is an almost apolitical, deterministic, mechanistic explanation of budgeting. Some have attacked the failure to account for the most important points: the bases from which incrementalism proceeds [30]. The present critique of incrementalism will focus on interpretative questions and the analytic framework itself.

INTERPRETIVE QUESTIONS

Are budgetary outcomes clearly incremental as Wildavsky, Fenno, and others have stated? Some suggest that the incrementalists did not interpret their descriptive data correctly. Bailey and O'Connor claim that this misinterpretation is a result of the confusion between incrementalism in the process and incrementalism in outcomes [31].

> When incremental is thus defined as bargaining, we are aware of no empirical case of a budgetary process which is nonincremental. Further, the working assumption has been that the products of bargaining are incremental outputs. If this is accepted as true by definition, then incrementalism as a descriptive concept is simply not useful. Indeed, the interesting question concerns the range of outputs from bargaining processes and the linkages between nonincremental outputs and the processes which generate them [32].

Reexamination of Fenno's data reveals a surprising amount of change, greater than 10%. Additional budgetary data reveal a similar diversity in budgetary outcomes. Looking at state, federal, and comparative foreign budgetary data, Bailey and O'Connor conclude that all reveal a broad range of results [33]. From 1960 to 1971 the Army Corps of Engineers had nine of eleven annual changes (82%) in the ±10% range; during the same period the United States Office of Education had only one of eleven changes (9%) in that range [34]. While there may be some question as to the exact definition of an incremental outcome, it seems clear that there exists a broader range of budgetary outcomes than the incrementalists have described.

A second major question concerns the interpretation of the regression equations. Both Moreland and Gist suggest that the high correlations found by Davis et al. are the direct result of not controlling for secular trends in the data [35]. Controlling for collinearity, Gist found that at least 50% of the variance in requests and appropriations is explained by the secular trend alone [36]. Examining the impact of administrative maturity on budget outcomes while controlling for collinearity, Moreland concluded that agencies in the Department of Agriculture could only count on receiving 44 cents of each dollar appropriated in the previous year [37]. Both found that when serial correlation is accounted for, the impact or existence of incrementalism is dramatically reduced.

A related criticism was made by John Wanat [38]. Using sensitivity analysis, he concluded that strategic interpretations of budgetary incrementalism are not warranted on the basis of the correlation analysis of Davis et al. He found that the magnitude of correlations in randomly generated data approximates those found by Davis et al. Therefore, one cannot validly support the existence of budgetary decision rules on the basis of high correlation coefficients.

Based on their request/appropriation figures the incrementalists concluded that there is a basic similarity in agency strategies, that is, requesting a moderate (incremental) increase. One of the first critics of this interpretation was Ira Sharkansky (who nonetheless remained supportive of the theory). He complained that this conclusion was reached without a comparison of individual agency strategies [39]. He suggested that some agencies are more assertive than others in that they ask for larger increases and concluded that different strategies exist in the form of varying degrees of assertiveness affecting budgetary outcomes. To get more, agencies need to ask for more. Examining the same phenomena, Sharkansky's interpretation ran counter to Wildavsky, Fenno, and Davis et al., who had argued that agencies asking for large increases are cut back more severely.

Changing requests in the President's budget for eight agencies revealed that agencies requesting larger increases tended to have significantly greater budget growth [40]. A recent study found a great deal of variation in agency strategies and outcomes [41]. The incrementalists make the assumption that agency requests contained in the President's budget reflect the goals and desires of agencies. In the study of agencies in the Department of Agriculture (DOA), data on initial agency estimates, department requests, and Office of Management and Budget (OMB) recommendations were all included in the analysis. The results indicated a much greater variation in agency behavior and demonstrated the error of assuming that requests in the President's budget are indicative of agency strategies. In two out of three cases the agencies requested an increase of more than 10%, and in one-quarter of the cases the agencies requested increases of more than 50% [42].

Additional findings in this study call in question the incremental dichotomy of "spenders" versus "savers." The budgetary roles assumed by the DOA and the OMB appeared to be significantly different. The DOA assumed what might be called a balancing role, tending to increase requests for agencies which requested a cut in funding while, concomitantly, severely cutting back agencies which requested the largest increases. The OMB, on the other hand, tended to make across-the-board cuts in agency requests regardless of the size of the increase asked for. The findings confirmed the existence of alternative strategies to the single incremental strategy of moderation and showed that assertiveness has an important impact on budgetary results and that further differentiation among roles is necessary.

Much of the theory of incremental budgeting rests on Wildavsky's and Fenno's interpretation of their extensive descriptive data and on empirical tests. Their work contains a great deal of interesting information on the appropriations process. It appears, however, that incremental assumptions structured their analysis and conclusions. Reanalyzed and reinterpreted, their empirical data could support a more differentiated set of conclusions.

ANALYTIC CHOICES AND ALTERNATIVES

In addition to its questionable interpretation of results, incrementalism as a theory of budgeting is built on a number of analytic choices that affect its forms of empirical validation and applicability. No attempt is made to delimit the application of incrementalism to only certain budgetary decisions; the clear implication is that it applies to the full range of phenomena. Their choices were not necessarily the wrong choices but strictly limit the applicability of the theory.

This section attempts to specify a number of interrelated analytic choices, their implications, critical responses, and some alternatives. Three main areas of analytic choice are

(1) level of aggregation, (2) time and object of analysis, (3) dependent and independent variables.

Level of Aggregation

The incrementalists chose to focus on domestic budget items aggregated at the agency level. This was an obvious choice for analysis; totals are available, agency officials and members of Congress are certainly concerned with the final appropriation, and it is commonly a visible figure. A number of recent studies have shown, however, the negative consequences of using this level of aggregation.

Aggregating at the agency level treats all components of an agency's request and appropriation as equal; the highest common denominator is dollars. But agency budgets can be disaggregated into different components. Gist asserts that agency budgets must be divided into mandatory and controllable components [43]. He suggests that mandatory spending items preclude any strategic manipulation in incremental strategies. If these decisions are previously determined, incrementalism cannot explain budget stability in such categories [44]. Gist further refines this point in a subsequent study. Because of the increase in uncontrollable spending, the budget base is not only reviewed but has become a fairly regular target for reductions [45].

> The contention of incrementalism that the budget base is not reviewed cannot be sustained. While attention to the annual increment may be the normal state of affairs . . . , it has not characterized congressional budget behavior over the past decade or so . . . , Congressional budgeting has become as often "basal" as "incremental" [46].

Wanat also differentiates between components of appropriations. Agency budgets consist of three parts: the base, mandatory needs, and programmatic desires [47]. Wanat's mandatory component has a different meaning from the conventional use of mandatory or uncontrollable spending [48]. It refers to the new costs required to keep the agency operating at the same level as last year: an inflation factor. The program component represents the desire for new programs or expansion of old ones. Examining the Department of Labor budget, he found that agencies differentiate between these components in their presentations to Congress. Results, according to Wanat, can be empirically explained on the basis of an agency's mandatory needs. His study makes the important point that agencies conceptualize components differently and that budgetary decisions are subject to external constraints (this theme will be pursued later).

Another alternative level of budget aggregation is the intraagency program level. Several studies have concluded that the agency level of aggregation used by the incrementalists leads to erroneous conclusions about policy stability. Natchez and Bupp argue that a stable appropriation pattern may belie substantial program shifts occurring at lower levels [49]. Looking at the Atomic Energy Commission, the authors show patterns of growth, decay, and fluctuation among AEC programs in nuclear rockets, high-energy physics, thermonuclear research, and nuclear weapons, all within the context of stable, apparently incremental budget totals [50]. They conclude that significant policy change is missed by the incremental perspective; the most interesting questions of social and political change require more extensive probing into the lower levels of the administrative process where key decisions are made:

> In this regard, Davis, Dempster, and Wildavsky's stochastic models perpetuate a fundamental error about the way the government operates. . . . We have seen that

real change does occur within this "massive stability," reflecting real conflicts over purpose and priority [51].

Arnold Kanter makes a similar observation by uncovering significant program variation in the Department of Defense [52]. The risk of a higher level of aggregation is that variation is often masked, gains and losses by competing programs cancel each other out in the totals, and it has a tendency to bias results toward incremental interpretations. Gist also breaks down the defense sector budgets into their major program components. Both Kanter and Gist find that after disaggregating totals, nonincremental patterns actually dominate. The rates of growth in procurement and research and development were significantly greater than growth in the overall defense budget [53]. Gist includes a similar disaggregation of the budgets of the National Aeronautics and Space Administration (NASA), the AEC, and the State Department. While the incremental model still predicts accurately in some cases (more frequently for Congress than the agencies), nonincremental decisions are evident in every budget item analyzed [54].

In choosing total agency budgets as the level of aggregation, the incrementalists made the assumption that all dollars in the budget were the same. Such a choice and concomitant assumptions helped to ensure finding incremental results. The alternative analytic choices discussed above facilitate a fuller understanding of underlying processes and policy changes in the budgetary process.

Time and Object of Analysis

Related to the choice of level of aggregation is time and object of analysis. Incremental theorists focus on annual appropriation decisions. This, too, is an apparently obvious choice since the yearly submission and review of appropriation requests are perhaps the most salient feature of the budgetary process. But annual appropriations are not the only important budgetary decisions and may not even be the most important.

The annual budget consists of a revenue as well as an expenditure side. Of critical importance to appropriation decisions are revenue estimates, taxation decisions, and decisions on the approximate size of the deficit (or surplus) and, most recently, expenditure ceilings. Based on these decisions, there is a certain maximum amount of change that can occur in a given year. While the tax structure in the United States is not reviewed in an orderly yearly fashion and has been relatively stable, some major changes have occurred in the past decade in the sources and nature of federal revenues [55]. Decisions on revenues, deficit, and outlays constrain the appropriations process. With the implementation of new budget procedures in Congress, decisions on these totals are made consciously, and they create tighter parameters for subsequent decisions [56]. Using appropriations as the sole object of analysis eliminates the possibility of detecting relationships between decisions on the whole and decisions on parts.

Along with annual decisions are a host of multiyear spending decisions that affect the budget. These include a number of substantive legislative and administrative decisions on the so-called uncontrollable spending items that are not reviewed every year [57]. The previous consideration of level aggregation referred to the need to separate out mandatory spending items. Yet the resolution of this problem by excluding these categories, estimated to be approximately 75% of the budget for fiscal year (FY) 1978 [58], from analysis is unsatisfactory. This is a point that has been ignored by the critics of incrementalism as well as by the incrementalists themselves. The analytic choice of single years as the time frame precludes theoretical explanation of three-quarters of the budget. The impact of long-term spending decisions has become so great that one cannot hope to understand budgeting without considering them. The next section discusses in more detail some suggestions for a nonannual perspective; it is important to recognize here that selection of annual appropriations represents an analytic choice that virtually excludes these other important budgetary decisions.

Dependent and Independent Variables

A third set of related analytic choices concerns specific dependent and independent variables. The selection of final appropriations as the variable to be explained has led the incrementalists to specify single important explanatory variables: last year's appropriation for agencies; this year's request for Congress. Certainly these are key variables in budgetary decision making. Alternative measures of budgetary results are available, however, and suggest a broader range of relevant independent variables. Changing the dependent variable from final appropriations to the percentage change in appropriations may suggest a new set of theoretical variables [59]. In one study, the level of presidential support for an agency was shown to relate to changes in requests and appropriation growth [60]. Priorities expressed in the public statements of the President affect changes in the rate and amount of change in agency budgets. At the same time, change in appropriations in the previous year had virtually no impact on percentage changes in agency requests or appropriations. This dependent variable does not preclude finding stability; if rates of change were constant, this would be reflected in the results. Davis, Dempster, and Wildavsky's 1974 study including a variety of environmental variables represents a substantial improvement. Their inclusion as binary variables in the model, however, only begins to suggest the potential impact of political, social, and economic factors on budgetary change. Shull has found that coalitions in Congress and the executive branch affect appropriation outcomes [61]. The partisan makeup of Congress and the presidency, the degree of congressional support for the President, and the level of conflict in Congress all have an impact on agency budgets [62].

As described earlier, Sharkansky, and LeLoup and Moreland found that variation in agency strategies affects budget results. Variations in the level of support from departments and the Budget Office also affect success and growth [63]. Moreland indicated that agency size and administrative experience of the agency staff correlate with greater appropriations. An additional analytic alternative is to use annual appropriation data with secular trends removed and examine the residuals [64]. As Gist has shown, analysis of residuals can confirm incremental conclusions, but it also reveals evidence of nonincremental decision rules.

THE VALIDITY AND APPLICABILITY OF INCREMENTALISM

It would be a simple task to debunk a theory if disconfirming evidence were obtained from a "straightforward" test. But with incrementalism, where empirical validation of the highest order continues to result, the nature of the tests themselves ensures something close to incremental results. There are several critical problems in dealing with the theory. Beyond the confusion between incremental decision making (mutual adjustment) and incremental results (small annual changes), there is a general confusion surrounding the term: it has taken on a host of nontheoretical meanings. In most secondary, casual treatments (introductory texts, for example), it simply refers to the truism that budgets (or governments) do not change radically from year to year. But why? Because most spending commitments are for periods of longer than a year, and in any given year there are externally determined parameters to the amount of change that can occur. Incrementalism takes no account of these critical factors, which must be included in budgetary theory. More serious than the general confusion associated with the term is the tautological nature of the theory itself and the self-confirming nature of the empirical tests. Wildavsky's barb at critics is suggestive:

> The huge increase in the size of the budget . . . should end the vacuous debate over the importance of making decisions in small increments as opposed to large proportions of the total. For one of the secrets of incrementalism is that the base is as important as the rate of increase.
>
> Another secret of incrementalism is that one can get a long way by rapid movements, if they continue long enough [65].

When a theory applies to all situations at all times without the possibility of disconfirming evidence, it is no longer a theory and is of little use for explanation or even description.

An additional problem related to the dominance of incrementalism is the tendency to characterize budgetary studies in either/or terms. A nonincremental approach does not necessarily have to assume that budgeting is unstable, that all components of the budget are reviewed from the ground up every year, or that budgeting conforms to the rational-comprehensive model.

In spite of this, it would not be accurate to say that incrementalism is totally wrong. It correctly describes some aspects of annual budgetary decision making in some agencies and some congressional subcommittees. However, its applicability is limited to a subset of annual appropriations decisions; it provides a misleading view and explanation of the overall budgetary process. To be sure, some of the underlying concepts of incremental budgeting are relevant, but they are in need of modification:

1. *Complexity*: Budgeting is complex, and participants employ aids to calculation. Yet some participants deal with the budget as a whole (president, OMB, budget committees) and are generalists, using aids in calculation required by the complexity of the process which are not mentioned by the incrementalists. Other participants may use nonincremental aids in making calculations at the agency level.

2. *Budget base*: Last year's appropriation may not be the only base for agency calculations, and the multiple components of the base itself are treated differently by the actors. Changes are made by reviewing bodies in the controllable base and the increment [66]. For those responsible for budget totals, last year's budget may be of less value than current policy estimates of a "standpat" budget [67].

3. *Roles*: The roles adopted by participants are more complex than the simple advocate/guardian dichotomy. Within the executive branch, agencies, departments, and the OMB differ in their behavior and may adopt multiple or mixed roles. In Congress, differing roles adopted by authorization, appropriations, and budget committees are apparent. For example, the authorization committees behave like advocates to the budget committees, but as guardians to the agencies.

4. *Bargaining*: The incrementalists correctly claim that budgeting is political; allocations cannot be and are not made "rationally" on the basis of a total view of the public interest. Yet some actors do bargain over the totals. The scope, object, and intensity of bargaining differs across policies, decision-making levels, and time. Conflict and its resolution shifts dramatically depending on the actors involved, partisan control of the presidency, economic conditions, and other external factors.

5. *Outcomes*: Bargaining matters; it does not always result in a deterministic pattern of stability. Change cannot be assessed without defining the time frame. Over the long run, significant reallocation can occur and has occurred. But even in the short run, budgeting produces a set of results that cannot simply be described as "incremental." Within the budget, at lower levels of aggregation, significant changes can occur within a pattern of overall stability.

The incremental theory of budgeting was formulated on the basis of a number of interrelated analytic choices. As has been shown, these choices played a critical role in determining what was found and what conclusions were drawn. Focusing on striking regularities, crucial changes were obscured; in a relatively simple explanation of budgetary decision making, complex alternatives were ignored. The history of incrementalism presents a dramatic example of the pitfalls of social science theory. What appeared to be an obvious and self-evident analytic approach actually involved numerous choices and excluded alternatives. The consequences of these choices are a set of findings highly skewed toward a single interpretation.

DEVELOPING BUDGETARY THEORY

Significant changes have occurred in the composition of the federal budget in the past 30 years. Income security increased its share of the budget 700%, health 2000%, and social service 2100% between 1946 and 1976. At the same time the defense share of the budget fell from 64 to 27% of the total. The most dramatic changes in the budget have occurred within the last decade. The growth in uncontrollable spending has aroused concern over the amount of annual discretion for decision makers. Changes have also taken place in the budgetary process. The Bureau of the Budget became the OMB in 1970 and, more significantly, Congress overhauled its procedures in 1974. The relevance of budgetary theory depends on its ability to comprehend the changing composition of the budget within the context of a set of external and internal constraints on the actions of key actors in the budgetary process.

In attempting to suggest new directions in developing budgetary theory, several key factors must be included. The shortcomings of incrementalism can be as instructive to the scholar as the observations and alternatives suggested in the many studies cited. Five key considerations should be recognized in attempting to advance our theoretical understanding of budgeting:

1. Perhaps the most important step is to expand the definition of relevant decisions. Besides the agencies and appropriations committees, many actors make decisions that affect the levels of revenues and expenditures. The authorization committees have become particularly important but are often excluded since their main function is not budgeting.

2. Time is essential in the reformulation. Most decisions are nonannual, having a duration of more or less than one year.

3. Budgetary decisions are made at different levels from different perspectives. Some actors are responsible for the whole budget, most for just a part of the budget. Budgetary decision making differs considerably depending on how general or specific the decisions themselves are.

4. Annual budgeting is not simply a one-way process, aggregating from small parts to the whole. One of the weaknesses of incrementalism is that budgeting is por-

trayed only as building increments on a base. This ignores the existence of external parameters, decisions on totals, that constrain the process. Budgeting can be seen as both an upward and downward process, with relevant theoretical questions focusing on the existence of parameters, their determination, and their impact.

5. Finally, budgetary theory must analyze discretion. How much flexibility do decision makers have in the shortrun? Even the distinction between controllable and uncontrollable spending does not provide an accurate determination of the actual range of discretion for decision makers.

Based on these key points, we are suggesting below a tentative framework for the analysis of national budgeting in the United States. While incrementalism has had a much wider application, our critique has focused on its application at this level. With appropriate modifications, some of the proposals may suggest new directions in other applications of budgetary theory.

"Levels" of Decisions

Budgetary decisions range from the broad and the general to the narrow and the specific. Decisions can be classified in terms of three categories:

- *Priority decisions*: These are a set of choices on budget totals for expenditures, revenues, deficit, and spending subtotals in functions such as defense, health, agriculture, etc. Priority decisions are macrobudgeting actions representing priorities in economic and fiscal policy. Such decisions are made annually and are the most general type of budgetary actions.

- *Program decisions*: These concern program authorizations, agency appropriations, entitlement programs, construction projects, and a variety of decisions concerning agencies and programs. Decisions made at the program level review the legal basis of programs, fund existing programs, and may initiate new programs. Decisions at this level may be annual, multiyear, or open ended.

- *Operations decisions*: These allocate and obligate funds to specific purposes. Included are decisions on the timing of spending, the amount of spending, carrying over balances, future funding, reprogramming, and transferring funds between accounts. Operations decisions are continual, occurring daily, weekly, monthly, quarterly, etc., and are the most specific type of budgetary actions.

Key Actors

Different sets of actors are most prominent in the decision-making processes on the three levels. Priority decision makers include the President and his advisors, Congress (the budget committees), and the OMB. Implementation of the Budget Control and Impoundment Act has made the decisions on totals more explicit in Congress and the bargaining between the president and Congress more visible. Program decisions involve the largest group of actors, and participants may vary depending on whether decisions are annual or multiyear. Appropriation decisions center on the familiar relationship between agencies and appropriations subcommittees. Key actors making authorization decisions (annual, multiyear, permanent) include agencies, standing committees, interest groups, and occasionally the President, OMB, and Congress. Specific entitlement programs and long-term construction projects involve combinations of these actors. Operations decisions are dominated by agencies, and include periodic interactions with appropriations committees and subcommittees and the OMB.

Key Relationships

Decisions at different levels are highly interrelated and interdependent. The most important limiting factors are the spending commitments made in previous years. Within the parameters imposed by these continuing commitments, it is possible to identify interrelationships between the general (higher level) and the specific (lower level) decisions. Higher level decisions establish *constraints* for lower level decisions; that is, priority decisions set boundaries for program and operations decisions. At the same time, budgeting involves combining smaller items into larger ones; *aggregation* may be defined as the process of successive combinations of lower level into higher level decisions. For example, priority decisions on totals may represent the aggregation of various program level decisions. Budgeting, then, is an interactive process combining constraint and aggregation. At any given time, one set of relationships may be ascendant. For example, prior to 1975, congressional budgeting was closer to an aggregative process, although presidential totals were sometimes used as reference points. The implementation of budget reform has increased the constraints imposed on authorization and appropriation decisions by totals agreed to in the concurrent budget resolutions.

Environmental Factors

Finally, decisions at all levels are affected by external factors, such as economic, social, and political trends. Economic changes may have the most significant direct impact. Rising unemployment, under existing statutory requirements, decreases tax collections and increases expenditures for unemployment, welfare, etc. Cost of living escalators translate general increases in price levels into larger expenditures for Social Security, federal retirement, etc. Other political and social trends have a less direct impact, but often affect changes in budgetary directions.

Figure 1 summarizes the concepts and relationships discussed above and suggests a variety of hypotheses. For example, one may speculate on the degree of constraint, the relative dominance of Congress or the executive at different levels, or the impact of external changes in the environment. Specific policies and actors may predominantly occupy a certain level; others cut across levels.

Discretion

It is not enough just to recognize that a large proportion of the budget is uncontrollable because controllability, as officially defined, does not translate into discretion [68]. Expenditures classified as "uncontrollable" are not equally uncontrollable. Fixed costs (such as interest on the national debt) constitute firmer commitments than long-term construction of weapons, dams, etc. These projects, in turn, offer less possibility for control than entitlement programs. Efforts made in 1975 and 1976 to tighten eligibility for Food Stamps, to restrict cost of living escalators, and to hold back mandated federal pay increases demonstrate that some potential for control exists. While the percentage that may change in a given year is small, the fact that these expenditures constitute just under half of the total budget allows more discretion than many "controllable" expenditures that make up only a small portion of the total.

Similarly, all expenditures categorized as controllable are not equally controllable. Since most of the controllable portion of the budget consists of personnel costs, civil service rules concerning severance pay, sick leave accumulation, etc., making large-scale changes is very difficult. It has been estimated that in 1976 only $5 to 7 billion could be cut from the

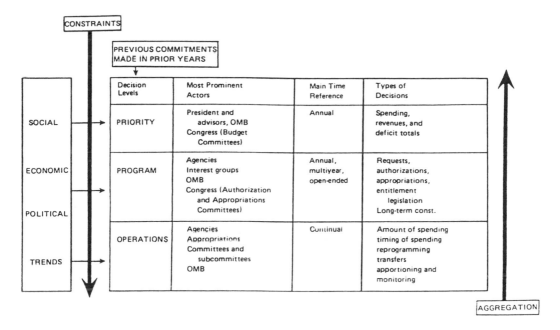

Figure 1   A framework for budgetary analysis.

controllable portion; this is approximately the same amount that could be cut from the uncontrollable portion [69].

The official controllable/uncontrollable dichotomy can be misleading; a continuum from most to least controllable expenditures would provide a more useful notion of discretion. The limits of annual discretion and the importance of multiyear decisions show that budgeting is a much more dynamic process than the correlation of consecutive appropriations patterns would indicate.

SUMMARY AND CONCLUSIONS

In all probability incrementalism will remain in prevalent use regardless of findings to the contrary; it is a truism that government changes only marginally from year to year. Even though the precise descriptive validity of the term has been challenged, many devotees of incrementalism will persist in the belief that government and budgeting will remain "incremental." Unfortunately, its self-fulfilling nature renders incrementalism nearly useless for social science theory. If it retains any validity after process is distinguished from outcomes, it is only in relation to a relatively narrow range of annual appropriations decisions.

This study has attempted to clarify the meaning of incrementalism as a theory of budgeting and integrate recent studies which challenge the theory. From the perspective of the social scientist, incrementalism appears predicated on a number of implicit analytical choices. Specification of these choices and alternatives clarifies the biases of incrementalism and suggests some of the difficulties encountered in the construction of theory.

The main bias of incrementalism is towards stability and against change. Analytical alternatives and the general suggestions for the development of budget theory presented here undoubtedly have their own biases. But in light of the experience of the previous decade, these alternatives may have greater promise for developing a balanced set of budget theories relevant to both the stability of budgeting and the mechanisms of change.

NOTES AND REFERENCES

1. This theme could logically be discussed in terms of paradigm dominance and change as suggested by T. Kuhn in *The Structure of Scientific Revolution*, University of Chicago Press, Chicago (1970). However, because of the controversy among philosophers of science and some highly problemmatic applications of Kuhn's ideas by political scientists, this approach is avoided. Also see Imre Lakatos and Alan Musgrave, *Criticism and the Growth of Knowledge*, Cambridge University Press, Cambridge (1970).
2. V. O. Key, The lack of a budgetary theory, *Am Polit. Sci. Rev.*, *34*(December): 1137–1144 (1940).
3. V. B. Lewis, Toward a theory of budgeting, *Public Admin. Rev.*, *12*(Winter): 42–54 (1952). A. Smithies, *The Budgetary Process in the United States*, McGraw-Hill, New York (1955).
4. F. J. Lyden and E. G. Miller (eds.), *Planning Programming Budgeting*, Markham, Chicago (1972). C. Schultz, *The Politics and Economics of Public Spending*, Brookings, Washington, D.C. (1968). D. Novick (ed.), *Program Budgeting*, Harvard University Press, Cambridge, Mass.: (1965).
5. A. Schick, Systems politics and system budgeting, *Public Admin. Rev.*, *29*(March-April): 137–151 (1969).
6. C. Lindblom, The science of muddling through, *Public Admin. Rev.*, *19*(Spring): 79–88 (1959).
7. Ref. 6, p. 88.
8. A. Wildavsky, *The Politics of the Budgetary Process*, Little, Brown, Boston (1964, 1974).
9. Ref. 8, p. 15.
10. R. Fenno, *The Power of the Purse*, Little, Brown, Boston, p. 15 (1966).
11. R. Fenno, *Congressmen in Committee*, Little, Brown, Boston, pp. 47–51 (1973).
12. Ref. 10, p. 354.
13. J. Bailey and R. O'Connor, Operationalizing incrementalism: Measuring the muddles, *Public Admin. Rev.*, *35*(January–February): 60–66 (1975).
14. W. Moreland, A nonincremental perspective on budgetary policy actions, *Policy Making in the Federal Executive Branch* (R. Ripley and G. Franklin, eds.), Free Press, New York, Chap. 3 (1975).
15. M. Davis, M. Dempster, and A. Wildavsky, A theory of the budgetary process, *Am. Polit. Sci. Rev.*, *60*(Sept.) p. 529, (1966). M. Davis, M. Dempster, and A. Wildavsky, On the process of budgeting II: An empirical study of congressional appropriations, *Studies in Budgeting* (Byrne et al., eds.), North-Holland, London (1971). M. Davis, M. Dempster, and A. Wildavsky, Toward a predictive theory of the Federal Budgetary Process, (paper delivered at the Annual Meeting of the American Political Science Association, New Orleans, Sept. (1973). M. Davis, M. Dempster, and A. Wildavsky, Towards a predictive theory of government expenditure: U.S. domestic appropriations, *Br. J. Polit. Sci.*, *4*(October): 419–452 (1974).
16. Davis et al., A theory of the budgetary process, p. 529 (see note 15).
17. Davis et al., A theory of the budgetary process, p. 531 (see note 15).
18. Davis et al., Towards a predictive theory of government expenditure (see note 15).
19. A. Wildavsky, *Budgeting*: *A Comparative Theory of Budgetary Processes*, Little, Brown, Boston, table 3-2, p. 52 (1975).
20. Ref. 19, p. 51.
21. Ref. 19, pp. 65–68.
22. I. Sharkansky, Four agencies and an appropriations subcommittee: A comparative study of budget strategies. *Midwest J. Polit. Sci.*, August: 254–281 (1965). I. Sharkansky, Agency requests, gubernatorial support and budget success in state legislatures, *Am. Polit. Sci. Rev.*, *62*(Dec.): (1968). T. Anton, *The Politics of State Expenditure in Illinois*, University of Illinois Press, Urbana (1966).

23. J. Crecine, A computer simulation model of municipal budgeting, *Manage. Sci.*, July: 786–815 (1967). I. Crecine, *Government Problem Solving, A Computer Simulation of Municipal Budgeting*, Rand McNally, Chicago (1969).

24. D. A. Gerwin, *Budgeting Public Funds: The Decision Process in an Urban School District*, University of Wisconsin Press, Madison (1969).

25. A. Cowart, T. Hansen, and K. E. Brofoss, Budgetary strategies and success at multiple decision levels in the Norwegian urban setting, *Am. Polit. Sci. Rev.*, *69*(June): 543–558 (1975).

26. F. Hoole, B. Job, and H. Tucker, Incremental budgeting and international organizations, *Am. J. Polit. Sci.*, *20*(May): 273–301 (1976).

27. Ref. 19.

28. Without undertaking a thorough survey of texts, readers are referred to familiar books used in classes.

29. Ref. 5, p. 95.

30. B. L. R. Smith, Letters to the editor, *Am. Polit. Sci. Rev.*, *61*(March): 150–152 (1967).

31. Ref. 13, p. 60.

32. Ref. 13, p. 65.

33. Ref. 13, p. 65.

34. L. T. LeLoup, Agency policy actions: Determinants of nonincremental change, *Policy Making in the Federal Executive* (R. Ripley and G. Franklin, eds.), Chap. 5, p. 76 (1975).

35. J. R. Gist, Mandatory expenditures and the defense sector: Theory of budgetary incrementalism, *Sage Professional Papers in American Politics*, Vol. 2, series (04-020, Sage, Beverly Hills, Calif., pp. 13–14 (19). Ref. 14, p. 49.

36. Ref. 35, p. 31.

37. Ref. 14, p. 61.

38. J. Wanat, The bases of budgetary incrementalism, *Am. Polit. Sci. Rev.*, *68*(Sept): 1221–1228 (1974).

39. Sharkansky, Four agencies, and Agency requests; see note 22.

40. L. T. LeLoup, *Explaining Agency Appropriations Change, Success and Legislative Support: A Comparative Study of Agency Budget Determination*, Ph.D. diss., Ohio State University (1973).

41. L. T. LeLoup and W. Moreland, Agency strategies and executive review: The hidden politics of budgeting, *Public Admin. Rev.* (1978).

42. Ref. 41.

43. Ref. 35, p. 15.

44. Ref. 35, p. 10.

45. J. Gist, "Increment" and "base" in the congressional appropriation process, *Am. J. Polit. Sci.*, *21*(May): 341–352 (1977).

46. Ref. 45, pp. 350–351.

47. Ref. 38, p. 1225.

48. B. M. Blechman, E. M. Gramlich, and R. W. Hartman, *Setting National Priorities, the 1976 Budget*, Brookings, Washington, D.C., pp. 191–192 (1975).

49. P. B. Natchez and I. C. Bupp, Policy and priority in the budgetary process, *Am. Polit. Sci. Rev.*, *67*(Sept): 951–963 (1973).

50. Ref. 49, p. 960.

51. Ref. 49, p. 963.

52. A. Kanter, Congress and the defense budget: 1960–1970, *Am. Polit. Sci. Rev.*, *66*(March): 129–143 (1972).

53. Ref. 35, p. 18. Ref. 52, p. 133.

54. Ref. 35, p. 36.

55. Ref. 48, Chap. 6.

56. Budget and Impoundment Control Act, 1974, Public Law 93-344.

57. M. Weidenbaum, Institutional obstacles to relocating government expenditures, *Public Expenditures and Policy Analysis* (R. Haveman and J. Margolis, eds.), Markham, Chicago, pp. 232–245 (1970).

58. U.S. Office of Management and Budget, *Budget of the United State Government, Fiscal Year 1978*, U.S. Government Printing Office, Washington, D.C. (1977).

59. R. Ripley and G. Franklin (eds.), *Policy Making in the Federal Executive Branch*, Free Press, New York (1976). Selections in this volume suggest several different sets of relevant variables.

60. Ref. 34, p. 83.

61. S. A. Shull, Coalitions and Budgeting, Paper presented at Annual Meeting of Midwest Political Science Association, Chicago, May (1975).

62. Refs. 34 and 61.

63. Ref. 41.

64. Ref. 35, pp. 30–36.

65. Ref. 8, Preface to the Second Edition, pp. xix, xx (1974).

66. John Crecine et al., Controllability of "Uncontrollable" Expenditures: Manipulation of Ambiguity in Budgetary Decision Making, Paper presented at Midwest Political Science Association, April 21, Chicago (1977). Preliminary findings suggest that uncontrollables are manipulated within the executive branch as are controllables.

67. Current policy estimates (Congressional Budget Office) and current services estimates (OMB) are projections of outlays in the next fiscal year if no programs are changed and services are maintained at a constant real level.

68. L. T. LeLoup, Discretion in national budgeting: Controlling the controllables, *Policy Anal.*, Fall (1978); see this for a detailed attempt to estimate discretion.

69. Ref. 48, pp. 192–194. See also Ref. 57, Institutional obstacles, pp. 234–238; J. Havemann, Ford, Congress seek handle on "uncontrollable" spending, *National J.*, 6(48) (1975).

27

Political Dimensions of Federal Budgeting in the United States

Steven Parker

This chapter will provide a discussion of the political dimensions of budgeting at the national level of American government. Vast change has transformed much of this process in the last decade and thus the field is in a state of considerable flux. Recognizing this fact, we will begin with a treatment of the rise and fall of the theory known as incrementalism. This will be followed by an examination of the literature on executive and congressional budgeting. We will close with attention to the politics of the federal deficit.

INCREMENTALISM—THE POLITICS OF MICROBUDGETING

The paradigm known as incrementalism still commands a prominent place in any discussion of the politics of budgeting. As a general theory of budgeting, it reigned for decades. However, the chapter needs to start with attention to it, since it is the very essence of politics.

For some analysts incrementalism remains the best way to explain the political reality of budgeting while for others it represents an old orthodoxy which must nonetheless be acknowledged before moving on to an examination of that which is more congruent with contemporary reality [1]. For years, of course, the classic elaboration of this approach was to be found in the works of Richard Fenno [2] and Aaron Wildavsky [3, 4]. Over the course of two decades and four editions of his *Politics of the Budgetary Process* Wildavsky chronicled a system that was highly decentralized and relied on a "bottom-up" bargaining process. This process began with a base and focused primarily on the increments to it. During any given budget-negotiation cycle the great bulk of an agency's appropriation thus already enjoyed a consensus, and conflict was held to a minimum. Department heads were among the main actors and the rules of the game spelled out various strategies that they could employ. In the book's final, 1984, edition, however, Wildavsky warned readers that the

Source: Jack Rabin, *Handbook of Public Budgeting*, Marcel Dekker, Inc., New York, pp. 23–49 (1992).

system was changing because its central premises—predictability, limits, and collectivity—were no longer tenable.

Nonetheless, the last decade did give us a number of defenses of incrementalism. For example, Malachowski et al. [5] argued that the old approach was still valid as long as certain modifications were made. The authors did this by updating Fenno's analysis with data from 1964–1984. These data focused on congressional changes of presidential spending requests, and they highlighted the significance of the concept of role flexibility. Specifically, the authors contended that the old roles (advocacy, guardianship, and appeals court) were not dead, but that their institutional homes had merely shifted. Thus, during the Carter and Reagan years the guardianship role was assumed by the executive branch while Congress took over appeals-court actions. Finally, the conclusion was presented that such a reinterpretation (stressing role flexibility and partisanship) made it premature to simply reject the incremental approach.

Accepting the validity of many of the model's criticisms, Ptisvada and Draper [6] stated a similar position. Yes, there were problems, they noted, but when compared to other interpretations, it still represented the best way to see budgets. This was held to be so because five basic factors are operating to make incrementalist analysis even more useful: indexing, multiyear budgeting, continuing resolutions, baseline reviews, and agency use of incremental and decremental display formats. Explaining the logic of this argument, they point out that indexing, for example, makes a budget more incremental since each year a small adjustment is made to the base using some guide like the CPI. Similarly, baseline reviews provide a current services budget whose emphasis is on stability. The authors see these conclusions as beneficial to democratic theory since social needs and wants (at least in this country) seem to change only by increments.

Numerous interpretations of democratic theory rely upon the notions of bargaining and compromise, and it is thus noteworthy that in 1986 just 2 years after the publication of the Pitsvada article, Jeremy Plant [7] gave us a condensation and updating of Charles Lindblom's thoughts on the subject of budgeting. Here again we see the relevance of incrementalism because of the near-permanence of two constraints: the human limited intellectual ability and the fact of limited information. Their reality means that partisan mutual adjustment will continue to function as a mainstay of politics in general and as a mainstay of the budget process in particular. Comprehensive management and planning via the appropriations route would be too abstract for either the executive or legislative branches to accept.

In a very real sense, however, articles like these have, together, constituted no more than a minority, rear-guard action, since most of the last decade's scholarly attention to incrementalism has focused on its passage from the scene. Intellectual positions here spread across a continuum from those heralding its death or irrelevance to those contending that it has merely been supplemented by, or overlaid with, a new kind of politics. Three currents will be identified as the demise school, the base-adjustment school, and the new politics school of thought.

Demise

Let us begin with the position that incrementalism is dead. One of the most succinct statements of this view was provided by Lance LeLoup [8] in a discussion of what he saw as incrementalism's analytical problems. His argument was essentially that the main phenomena selected for study are not the most appropriate ones. Specifically there are questions of (1) level of aggregation, (2) time and object of analysis, and (3) dependent and independent variables. The main burden of his argument is that the theory's choice of data in each of these areas (for example, agency-level aggregation and final appropriations) very nearly sets up a self-fulfilling prophesy. For example, if the aggregation does not distinguish between mandatory and controllable elements it will inevitably "discover" stability although such stability is not a result of budgetary bargaining. Because of problems such as these, hypotheses based on the theory are not verifiable and thus the theory is not really "theory."

While the foregoing indictment is epistomological in nature, one by Bozeman and Straussman [9] is essentially experiential. Written early in the Reagan era, it is based on the empirically verifiable fact that the administration had gone farther than any other in instituting a top-down budget process. Macrobudgeting sets priorities centrally and works within constraints set by an external environment. During this period, congressional spending resolutions and presidential taxation policy came to dominate the process. Bozeman and Straussman were thus arguing that the model no longer matched the reality: that incrementalism was ill-equipped to serve as a general theory of budgeting for the United States.

Regarding the concept of macrobudgeting, another article by LeLoup [10] is of relevance. In it he contends that incrementalism, or microbudgeting, tended to ignore the president's role in budgeting, while it was in fact central (and centralized) even in the paradigm's heyday—the 1950s and 1960s. To the extent that the Office of Management and Budget/Bureau of the Budget (OMB/BOB) was a subject of study it was conceived of as a mere bargaining agent, not as the packager of presidential priorities that it in fact was.

In other words, macrobudgeting has been with us for a long time, and it differs from microbudgeting in terms of the conceptualization of its key actors (authorization and appropriations committees versus budget committees), the dominant mode of legislation (individual bills versus budget resolutions), and its basic process (fragmented versus centralized).

Finally, Irene Rubin [1, 11] has written on what she terms "the demise of incrementalism." The first of these two works is her introduction to a fine volume on budget theory. The subject is treated almost at once because much of the book is focused on the subject of new directions. As she puts it, "The need for a new budget theory became urgent with the demise of incrementalism." She explains this demise by arguing that the paradigm was at once too global, too narrow, and too difficult to prove or disprove. While the latter contention is reminiscent of LeLoup's 1979 analysis, the first point seemingly stands Lindblom on his head. The theory is too global because it was based on perceived characteristics of human nature—exactly the idea that was supposed to make muddling through inevitable. Her contention that it has been too narrow is an amplification of Bozeman and Straussman, that is, that it does not fit with observed reality.

Her 1989 article, which was an extended review of two books by Wildavsky, elaborates further on this last point. Thus, here we are presented with a catalogue of empirical failings. It cannot account for entitlement programs, explain top-down budgeting, or deal with cutbacks, interest groups, or the external environment.

Base Adjustment

One of the most important critiques of incrementalism has come from the work of Kamlet and Mowery [12]. These researchers have argued persuasively that the concept of the base is not fixed and that it has varied considerably at least since the days of the Kennedy administration. They show how OMB formulates the base in several different ways and how these vary significantly during the life of the planning period. For example, base may be defined as current estimates, as the cost of the ongoing level of activities, or as the mandatory budget. If the base is not stable but is indeed open to interpretation and nego-tiation, then it is clear that the increment is not the sole focus of the process. Their analysis continues by pointing out that the selection of a definition can depend on at least three factors: the agency being considered, the context for use of the base, and the function it is intended to serve. If this is so, base is a highly volatile concept and one subject to the vaguaries of political and administrative discretion.

Another of their studies [13] has provided an in-depth examination of the pre-Reagan administrations of Eisenhower, Kennedy, and Johnson. Here we see that incrementalism probably put too much emphasis on Congress rather than the presidency. Focusing on the relationship between the White House, OMB and the federal agencies, they show a linkage between fiscal and budgetary policies. The interdependence between domestic budgetary policy, defense budgetary policy, and fiscal policy makes it clear that presidents have been using a top-down approach for years and that the idea of an agency base has not been stable.

The New Politics

Finally, there is another group of scholars who also recognize that substantial change has taken place in budgeting. For them, however, this has altered the process not by making incrementalism irrelevant, but by adding new elements to the mix. As one of the fathers of the old orthodoxy, Aaron Wildavsky [14] is fitting found in this camp. He begins his *New Politics of the Budgetary Process* with a recognition of the reality of the changes that have occurred in the last two decades. He quickly adds, however, that they have not actually replaced anything: "rather the new has been layered onto the old." The operation of top-down rules, entitlements, federal credit, and changes at OMB are, for him, merely new additions to many of the old incremental verities. For example, the guardianship role iden-tified by Fenno is still operative. It is just that today it is played primarily by the budget committees, not by the House Appropriations Committee. Yet he also recognizes that change runs deeper than this. Bowing to the evidence, he concedes that what makes the "new politics" new is precisely the fact of conflict over the base, and not just the increment.

If agreement about the base has eroded, then the fundamental hallmark of the new era is its loss of consensus. Regarding such a loss, he tells us that the central question concerns what has caused the budget process to become so "unsatisfactory." One of the reasons he offers concerns the growth of entitlement programs in conditions of growth, balance, and decline. The operation of backdoor spending through federal credit is another factor, and the subsidy activities of the Federal Financing Bank are detailed in chapter four.

Regarding the loss of consensus about the base, Donald Kettl [15] has argued that three changes in the budget process have caused participants to focus on protecting themselves and their clientele groups rather than on expanding further. These three are as follows: changes in federal spending (indexing, budget-balancing), changes in federal taxation (where the use of trust funds, etc. has cut down on flexibility), and what he calls the "budgetary twilight zone" (government loan and tax expenditure activities). Thus, for ex-ample, indexing has plunged us into a fiscal ice age in which the benefits for some are assured while other agencies have to scramble all the harder to minimize damage to their bases. He dates this "politics of protection" from 1970, while he claims the preceding two decades were characterized by a "politics of expansion."

Similarly, Lee Sigelman [16] has reexamined data from the American State Adminis-trator Project and found that in none of the 4 years for which figures were available did a majority of high-ranking state administrators pursue budget increases in excess of 15%. In fact in every year a substantial number called for little or no agency expansion (the politics of protection). Clearly the idea of the bureaucrat as budget maximizer [17] is no longer descriptive of reality.

A thoughtful essay by Naomi Caiden [18] is even more to the point. In "The politics of subtraction" she claims that the old rules invited incremental change but that the additional steps in today's process place the attention on conflict. Such conflict has generated new tactics, and she details the most significant ones: package splitting, leverage on essential matters, avoiding responsibility, negotiating alternatives, and brinksmanship. This, then, is another example of how the "new politics of the budgetary process" can be seen as an overlay—adding new dimensions to, rather than completely replacing, the old.

This section of the chapter has focused on the politics of incrementalism, examining defenses of the old orthodoxy and then three schools of thought regarding its current status. It is now time to turn our attention to research on how this, or some other, theory actually operates in the context of U.S. governmental institutions.

THE EXECUTIVE BRANCH

The President

Because ours is a system of separated institutions sharing power, it would be artificial to treat either the President or Congress in isolation. Like codependent spouses, the power of each is greatly affected by the power of the other. They interact constantly, and a sizeable body of literature has been produced focusing on budgetary relations between them. Basically there tend to be two overall positions: presidential dominance and congressional resurgence. Perhaps the best statement of the latter position is to be found in a book by James Sundquist [19]. He begins by tracing Congress's long-term loss of power during this century and then shifts to how it was reborn in the 1970s confrontations with Richard Nixon. While Sundquist considers many aspects of this confrontation, the one of greatest relevance here is treated in a chapter entitled "To Regain the Power of the Purse." Sundquist recounts the executive excesses that led to the passage of the Congressional Budget and Impoundment Control Act of 1974. Writing in 1981, he noted that the law's centralizing effects established a strong counter to presidential dominance. The significant idea here is that of institutionalization, and a report card from the first several years after the book's publication does not invalidate its insight. He refers to a new orderliness and to the fact that Congress established its own decision-making capacity (with the budget committees) and its own source of independent information (the Congressional Budget Office). Such structural changes created a countervailing power that was previously absent.

A variation on this theme is also presented by Dennis Ippolito [20] who claims that budget reform has not brought a basic realignment to the balance of power. Risking oversimplification, he writes that Congress' share of the spending power was not in danger earlier, and is not presently. Impoundment is no longer a problem, and presidential power has been further limited by the growth of uncontrollables.

The "congressional resurgence" position is, however, a minority phenomenon. Most authors who confront this question head-on tend to conclude that it is the President who dominates the budgetary process [21]. However, such a view was not always accurate, and for an appreciation of the cyclical nature of budgetary power the reader is referred to a work by Pfiffner [93]. During the nineteenth century, Congress was dominant in budgetary matters, but inefficiencies and abuses led to calls for reform. An excellent case for the initiation of an executive budget process can be found in the Taft Commission's original 1912 report [22]. While its recommendations were initially rejected, many of them became part of the Budget and Accounting Act of 1921. A 50-year period of executive dominance followed, but then the cycle renewed itself in 1974 with Congress' reactions to executive budgetary "excesses."

One of the best-known spokesman for the "presidential dominance" position is Howard Shuman [23]. In both the 1984 and 1988 editions of his book he informs the reader that the budget is the nation's most important statement of its priorities and that it is initiated and orchestrated by the president. He then proceeds to show us exactly why and how this is so. Not unexpectedly, he begins with a discussion of the Budget and Accounting Act of 1921, which introduced the practice of executive budgeting.

He also takes an informal and extralegal approach, stressing what he sees as the main principles of executive budgeting. These he covers with labels such as rolling history, implied blackmail, sacred cows, the unofficial leak, and politics of the bureaucracy. He next includes a chapter on the "Reagan Revolution" where he focuses on how the President was able to convert the 1974 act to his own uses and pursue a four-point program: (1) to change fiscal and budget priorities and to reprogram resources from the civilian to the military sector; (2) to shift financial burdens to state and local governments; (3) to privatize numerous other government activities; and (4) to shift the tax burden from the wealthy.

A useful treatment of the development of executive domination is contained in a book by Louis Fisher [24]. After a brief review of nineteenth-century spending powers, he clearly chronicles the reform movement and the growth of central control inherent in the adoption of executive budgeting. One of the best-known case studies of a president's attempts to consolidate both general and budgetary powers is the study of the Nixon presidency done by Richard Nathan [25].

Two general works on the subject of budgeting are also helpful because of the specific attention they devote to presidential budgetary power. Ippolito [26] analyzes the Johnson, Nixon, Ford, and Carter presidencies and finds an interesting trend. Congress and the President appear to have used their budgetary powers to different ends, with presidents emphasizing military expenditures and Congress using its power on behalf of social programs.

While Ippolito looks at goals, LeLoup [21] provides the reader with a concise typology of budgetary styles. The author examines the varying degrees of personal involvement that selected presidents have had in budgeting and presents the following set of categories: passive involvement, active involvement, and mixed involvement.

Discussing this typology, LeLoup accepts the widely held view of Eisenhower as essentially being passive and lacking in power. However, this interpretation has come under some attack. For an effective presentation of alternative evidence, the reader is referred to a fine analysis of Eisenhower's defense budget by Kinnard [27]. There one finds a picture of a strong president exercising power through the use of budget ceilings and active manipulation of the joint chiefs of staff.

Presidential budget power is also the subject of the book by Louis Fisher [24], which was mentioned earlier. The focus of Fisher's work is the spending side—rather than the formulation and adoption side—of the budget process, and in it the author argues that Congress has been thoroughly unable to control executive spending decisions. Detailed attention is given to various tools of administrative budgetary power: covert financing, impoundment, lump-sum appropriations, transfer of funds, reprogramming of funds, executive commitments, and timing of obligations. These vehicles enabled presidents and other executive-branch officials to get around congressional power by taking action after that branch's role was largely completed, that is, during the budget execution phase. Fisher [28–30] expanded this analysis with three shorter studies as well.

Today, of course, the subject of presidential budget power cannot be divorced from attention to Ronald Reagan's impact on it. This literature has boomed in recent years, and here we will consider a small sampling. Kamlet et al. [31] use simulation for one type of assessment of his impact. They show that budget priorities were relatively stable from Eisenhower through Carter, but that with Reagan they changed dramatically. This was most striking with regard to increased defense spending and lowered domestic outlays. They base their comparison on "what had been the case under pre-Reagan budget priorities."

Congressional scholar Allen Schick [32] has focused not on substantive policy like this but on Reagan's impact on processes. He argues that although Reagan moved budgeting more toward a top-down approach he did not really give us new budget institutions. Instead, he pursued such ad hoc tactics of control as packaging the budget and aggressively working the Hill. Because of such facts the Reagan legacy will likely consist of four developments: (1) centralized budgeting; (2) mulityear budgeting; (3) a more comprehensive resource allocation process; and (4) a more active role for the president in the legislative process.

This fourth point has also been addressed by Robert Reischauer [33] in a discursive essay on congressional budgeting. He concludes that neither house is capable of executing priority shifts or dealing with issues like retrenchment and deficit reduction without the cooperation and leadership of the president. He also suggests that this leadership is more important to the extent that the political parties have divided control of the two houses.

The effect of partisanship on presidential budgeting power during another era has been examined by Lowery et al. [34] in a reanalysis of Fenno's original data. The authors proceed by using the concept of "presidential advocacy" and show that Congress plays its budgetary roles with greater or lesser degrees of strength depending on the partisanship of the executive branch.

Continuing with the concept of "presidential advocacy," several investigators have provided analyses of the Reagan years. LeLoup and Hancock [35] use a chronological approach, dividing his administration into three time periods: 1981–1982, 1983–1986, and 1987–1988. During each of these periods three different elements of executive–legislative budgeting are considered:

1. Budgetary politics and issues—the extent to which conflict was based on ideological, economic or partisan differences.
2. Procedural changes—alterations in the budget process itself.
3. Policy results—the extent to which Reagan's budgets altered programs and priorities.

Assessments are then offered in each of these areas. For example, regarding policy, they conclude that "the Reagan revolution did not fail." The budgets achieved many of his goals: the growth in defense spending, the cut in discretionary domestic programs, and the shift in, or reduction of, the tax burden. In the area of procedures, however, they agree with Schick, concluding that the 1980s generated tremendous budgetary instability. They argue that such a condition resulted from three factors: (1) growing outlay inflexibility, (2) administration actions to limit congressional options, and (3) the increasing difficulty of making accurate economic and budget forecasts.

While the article just discussed analyzed three separate time periods, another study by one of the same authors focused exclusively on the early days of the Reagan administration [36]. In this instance LeLoup assessed the impact of the 1981 budget battle on the overall budget process, emphasizing that it did three things. First, it resulted in the entire committee system being set aside by a single vote. Further, it blurred the distinction between authorizing and appropriating committees, and finally it tended to weaken the overall committee system.

This theme of the reining in of decentralization is also taken up by Hartman [37]. In another early article he presents a preliminary conclusion about the increased power of the budget committees. Such a situation, of course, was not to remain unchanged.

A widely read, if somewhat undisciplined, account of the tension between centralization and decentralization, macro and micro, is provided by David Stockman [38]. This insider's narrative account of how he believes the Reagan Revolution failed takes its title from the author's diagnosis of the ills. It was a "triumph of politics" that thwarted the centralized working of the President's mandate and supply-side orthodoxy. Of course, this mildly self-serving portrayal focuses on the fact that it was Stockman's programming of the mandate that eventually was sacrificed to the winds of compromise, expediency, and failure. And it "failed" precisely for reasons having to do with microbudgeting politics—decentralization, vote trading, constituency service, interest-group activity, and the iron triangles of Theodore Lowi.

In the famous article by William Greider [39] we learn of the ideologue's lament as he confronted the realities of power and pork via programs such as the fast-breeder nuclear reactor at Clinch River, Tennessee. This is a fine, journalistic account of the rough and tumble of microbudget politics set against the background of flawed macrobudget estimates.

Perhaps it is difficult for a true believer to accept the idea of compromise, but a fascinating cross-national study of defense budgeting by Michael Hobkirk [40] concludes that it is inevitable here. This book-length, comparative analysis of budgetary institutions in the United States and Great Britain highlights the near impossibility of cleanly following a top-down approach in Washington. Hobkirk cites such factors as the ability of a service to take its case directly to Congress if it is dissatisfied with the priorities of the Secretary of Defense. In the absence of a tradition of party responsibility, neither the executive nor the legislative branches can eliminate the presence of interservice rivalries in the planning of defense expenditures. For Pitsvada and Draper [6], unlike Stockman, such evidence of the ongoing vitality of the iron triangles is a reassurance that democratic theory is still relevant.

The Office of Management and Budget (OMB)

For information about the OMB, there is no better place to start than with a book by Larry Berman [41]. Its first half is devoted to a history of the agency's predecessor, the Bureau of the Budget (BOB). Here we see an agency maturing in its sense of mission and analytical capability. In 1970, however, OMB was created as part of a Nixon reorganization, and it is doubtful that this change led to continued progress. Berman analyzes OMB's power decline in such areas as partisan politics, organizational requirements, and the growth of countervailing bodies, such as the Congressional Budget Office (CBO).

Another fine historical treatment is provided by Frederick Mosher [42], who has traced the evolution of both the OMB and the General Accounting Office (GAO) in a book rich in contextual information. After sketching each agency in considerable detail, he gives the reader a final chapter that offers a systematic overview and analytical comparison. Here one learns, for example, that since World War II the OMB and GAO have been becoming more alike, with OMB moving away from an exclusively managerial concern and more toward finance, while the GAO has simultaneously developed more interest in management. In addition, both are essentially conservative agencies, staffed by generalists. Because both are seen as being reactors and counterpunchers, they are similarly viewed as enemies by interest groups and bureaucrats. In other words, they work for an agency with power.

Attempting to analyze just what kind of power the office has, Hugh Heclo [43] concludes that it has too much political power and not enough analytical power. Throughout most of its history, its predecessor, the BOB, had been known for its "neutral competence." This impartial, nonpartisan expertise was the basis of its very real governmental authority. Richard Nixon "politicized" the OMB, turning its role away from neutral competence and toward political support for the president.

The reader can find this theme elaborated upon in two other articles [44, 45], which document related facets of decline. In addition, Zeidenstein [46] points out that the requirement that the director of the OMB by confirmed by the Senate is a direct consequence of the office's politicization.

Ultimately, assessments of the office's power must rest, of course, on the pivotal nature of its budget function, especially during the Reagan years [47]. However, other factors have been shown to be contributory. Cooper and West [48] focus on its central clearance of agency rules. While all rules must be submitted for review, the agencies are not bound to take OMB advice. Why do they usually comply, however? Cooper and West answer that OMB also has the power to review their budgets and "he who pays the fiddler calls the tune." Benda and Levine [49] also relate its power to its responsibility for setting personnel ceilings—a function intimately tied to the budget process.

An indication of the extent to which OMB's decision-making process has changed over the years is provided by comparing two articles. Relying on data from the late 1960s, Bromiley and Crecine [50] present a picture of the staff making budget decisions by balancing top-down and bottom-up approaches. In this model we see them relying both on agency-specific information and on aggregate economic and fiscal data. Hugh Heclo [51], on the other hand, provides us with an analysis of the Stockman era where a very different picture emerges. Not only do we see a decision process that became almost completely top-down, it was highly "personalized" as well. Decisions were made by Stockman after consultation with White House strategists. The OMB staff was then merely called upon to follow through on these choices rather than to independently analyze numerous policy options. Helco writes that the political leadership believed that it knew exactly what to do and then simply oriented to the OMB staff as though it were a congressional office. David Mathiasen [52] writes that other reasons for the agency's changed role include the 1982–1983 recession, the idea of "normal budget growth" coming under fire, and the concept of baselines.

This changed role, of course, raises the whole question of politicization again. Bruce Johnson [53, 54] is a former budget examiner who has provided first-hand accounts of the shift from neutral competence to advocacy. This shift involves three roles: formulating and enforcing the budget, negotiating with Congress, and practicing an advocacy mission with the media and interest groups. Wyszomirski [55] reminds us that the trend did not start with Reagan. What she sees as a deinstitutionalization set in with Nixon and has continued ever since, with the office's leadership becoming ever more inexpert and partisan. Such a trend has sacrificed the organization's credibility.

Mosher and Stephenson [56] are more skeptical of the charges of politicization. Relying on both interviews and the literature, they show that during the early Reagan years there was no increase in the number of the agency's political positions. Furthermore, they argue, OMB staff members have always had a predisposition to cut. Reagan's ideology merely provided them with an opportunity to "do what comes naturally" for budget examiners.

Agencies and Programs

The trend toward centralization that accelerated during the Reagan years had a major impact on the budgetary roles played by individual agencies and programs. Aaron Wildavsky [14] has shown, however, that these roles have very diverse elements, combining "bottom-up, top-down and in-between" components. Indeed, while he gives a great deal of attention to subjects like reconciliation and sequestration, he still writes about the agency's role as featuring "the dance of the dollars."

Lance LeLoup [21] also emphasizes many continuities when discussing agency advocacy during an era of retrenchment. One continuity involves the ongoing use of certain games and strategies. Several of these he labels as follows: calling out the troops, current fashion, the end run, and the foot in the door. Leonard Reed [57] also compiled a number of these strategies and showed how they can be used to augment bureaucratic power. Several examples will suffice to convey the flavor of his approach:

The king's pawn opening—overstating what a program will cost.

The shortfall game—underestimating costs on "uncontrollables," shifting funds and making up the difference through supplemental appropriations.

The Washington Monument game—resisting cuts by threatening to eliminate essential programs.

A statement of general principles by Irene Rubin [58] also sheds additional light on agency options. She claims that four characteristics of public budgeting help explain the politics of expenditures. These characteristics are multiple actors with different goals, decision making that is open to the environment, a separation between those who make spending decisions and those why pay taxes, and finally a budget process filled with constraints.

Regarding this last point, the Reagan years were, of course, a period of severe belt tightening for many federal agencies. The fact that some dealt with this phenomenon better than others is made clear in another book by Rubin [59]. Concerned with the shrinking federal government, it examines the effects of cutbacks on five different federal agencies: the Bureau of Health Planning, the Employment and Training Administration, the Urban Mass Transit Administration (UMTA), the Office of Personnel Management (OPM), and the Community Planning and Development Program. Among the five, those agencies with strong interest-group support were able to better resist the President and reverse cuts in funding levels. Remember David Stockman's lament? For example, UMTA had strong interest-group support and therefore cuts in its funding levels were reversed. In addition, the administration's proposed termination of operating subsidies was defeated. On the other hand, an agency like OPM with no real clientele was forced to take substantial cuts. The irony of Rubin's message is sobering. When it comes to retrenchment, agencies that have been colonized by their clientele groups are likely to be better off than their more professional counterparts that have held the interest groups at arm's length.

Joseph Wholey [60] has also given us a comparative analysis of executive agency retrenchment. Like Rubin, he examined five agencies from 1981 to 1983 in order to observe the processes and impacts of cuts: the Food and Nutrition Service, the Employment and Training Administration, the Health Resources and Services Administration, the National Institute of Mental Health, and the Administration of Aging (AoA). His basic approach was to set out a list of OMB objectives and then determine the operational impact of each one on each of the five agencies. The objectives included items such as the reduction of spending, the reduction of agency staffing, and the combining of categorical programs into block grants.

Once this assessment was completed, Wholey, again like Rubin, examined whether programs enjoying broader political support were better able to resist retrenchment than those with weak political bases. For example, during a time of recession the Unemployment Insurance Program fared better than the Food Stamp Program. The constituency of the latter, we are reminded, is much less politically visible. Senior citizens also make a very active clientele, and thus AoA programs of nutrition and social services experienced only marginal cuts.

Numerous examinations of agency budgeting in the pre-Reagan era are also still useful. Many of them appropriately tended to focus on incrementalism. Evidence of administrative budgetary power was found by Wanat [61]. In his historical examination (1968–1972) of the Labor Department's budget process, he demonstrated that most of the incremental increases dealt with mandatory expenditures. Substantial changes did occur, however, in the discretionary area. Thus he clearly showed that not all of the budget was dealt with in an incremental fashion.

Padgett [62] argued for a substitution of "serial judgment theory" in place of the Wildavsky/Lindblom approach. He argued that the latter is valid only if we confine our analysis to absolute dollar levels. When we shift to programmatic change, however, incrementalism simply becomes too rigid.

Less theoretical treatments of departmental budgetary power are also available. Korb [63] for example, took an intradepartmental focus in his analysis of procedures at the Department of Defense. He analyzes three basic budgetary processes used there and clearly shows the critical nature of ceilings in generating compliance. The decentralized system is also examined in considerable detail, but the most valuable contribution of the study is its insistence on the fact that budgeting is an inherently political process.

On a related plane, Davis and Ripley [64] examined interaction between executive agencies and the central budget staff. They conclude that agencies tend to see the budget staff as either hostile, neutral, or inclined to advocacy. The exact nature of each relationship will depend on such factors as presidential purposes, accessibility of information, past budgetary decisions, and the degree of need for support that both parties feel.

This agency/central budget staff relationship also has been treated by LeLoup and Moreland [65]. Theirs is a useful article for information on the amount of change that takes place in a budget before it ever gets to the Congress. Most studies focus on the changes that occur in the budget after it leaves the White House, but such analysis can tell only part of the story.

The statement made above about agency/congressional relations being the more usual focus of scholarly concern is perhaps best exemplified in a study done by Sharkansky [66]. Restricting himself to four agencies whose appropriations requests were heard by the same subcommittee allowed Sharkansky to introduce an element of control into his work. He analyzed the different ways in which the agencies dealt with the subcommittees—assertiveness, breaking of norms, use of promotional devices—and then sought to explain these strategies in terms of certain independent variables: public support, agency support, and the nature of the agency's programs. This last factor was found to be a critical element of agency power.

Today, of course, the politics of agency/congressional committee interaction frequently lack the urgency of Sharkansky's day. One reason for this is the fact that much of the discretion and uncertainty has been removed from the process by entitlement programs and indexation [14]. Currently 46% of the federal budget automatically goes to individuals and units of government meeting eligibility requirements established by statute. For a discussion of the magnitude and growth of this spending see Rivlin [67].

Jeffrey Straussman [68] has examined such programs not in terms of their aggregate impact on budget totals, but with an eye to their relationship to the political process. He presents entitlements as a type of rights-based budgeting and shows how the concept does not fit well with our traditional ideas about the appropriations process, since tradeoffs become impossible. This being so, he concludes that there are three broad lessons to be learned from studying the relationship between rights and budgets: (1) the need to extend our knowledge about the institutional character of the public budgeting process; (2) the need to further examine classic budgeting in rights-based environments; and (3) the impact of political change on rights-based budgeting.

One of the best studies of the politics of this subject is contained in a book by Kent Weaver [69]. His focus is indexation—the automatic adjustment of public policy outputs for inflation. This phenomenon, of course, involves officials' surrender of control over programs, and his study is an analysis of why they have been willing to do this. Three primary motivations are offered and discussed: credit claiming, good policy, and blame avoiding. The author then uses this framework in his treatment of a half-dozen indexing programs showing how decision makers weigh political costs and benefits.

The book concludes with an analysis of the consequences of indexation, consequences for the policy process, accountability, clientele groups, the economy, and the budget. Regarding the latter, both his case studies and overall data indicate that the combination of indexed and nonindexed programs increases federal deficits and that indexing tends to keep deficit-reduction plans off the agenda.

Another type of program change with direct political implications involves what is frequently called "off-budget budgeting" [70]. What is at issue here is the question of federal credit programs. These are not included in the unified budget and thus do not come under the same micro and macro political controls.

Two book-length studies of this phenomenon are worth noting. The first, by Dennis Ippolito [71], assesses the political and economic ramifications of a situation in which these credit programs can lay claims to funding without having to compete with direct spending. The book examines the sharp increase in loans and loan guarantees for housing, agriculture, education, and international affairs. There are also excellent case studies dealing with several big bailouts: Penn Central, Lockheed, New York City, and Chrysler Corporation. His central message is clear. Such programs provide well-defined and substantial benefits to important constituencies.

The second book, by Bennett and DiLorenzo [72], is less satisfying because it is less measured. Where Ippolito factually cites the problems created by hidden spending, these authors adopt an almost shrill tone as they rail against off-budget enterprises (OBEs). The book is not so much an analysis of the budgetary implications of OBEs as it is an attempt to characterize their use in conspiratorial terms. Public office-holders at all levels of government are portrayed as either sinister manipulators or cowardly fools who turn to these devices as a way to subvert the public interest. The book is a thinly veiled attempt to make a morality play out of this aspect of public spending.

Case studies focus on New York State under Nelson Rockefeller and on numerous off-budget activities of local government. A separate chapter entitled "The Underground Federal Government" focuses on the loan guarantee and other functions of the Federal Financing Bank. Data are also presented on overall, guaranteed loan transactions of the federal government. Here the book is more factual and less alarmist, allowing the reader to compare the government's off-budget priorities.

CONGRESS

The Classic Appropriations Process

During the late 1970s and most of the 1980s the Congressional appropriations process was in a state of great flux. Buffeted by deficits, reforms, and mandatory cuts, it sought to identify a new modus operandi. However, prior to this period there was a more stable time. It was characterized by a "classic appropriations process," one that operated largely from the bottom up, and scholars documented it with a substantial body of literature. Among the numerous works extant, one of the best known and most influential is that of Richard Fenno [73]. Written more than two decades ago, it is still cited as the definitive work on the classic appropriations process in general, and on the functioning of the appropriations committees and subcommittees in particular. Beginning with the House Appropriations Committee, Fenno found its power manifest in protecting the power of the purse and serving as a "guardian" of the federal treasury. Such a mission was seen as "the essential bulwark of congressional power." What this meant in practice was a role orientation that urged committee members to examine agency budgets in great detail and make cuts wherever possible.

The role of the Senate Appropriations Committee, on the other hand, was that of an appeals courts. Its deliberations were frequently concerned with agency requests for restoration of funds cut by the House, and Fenno found its record for the granting of such increases to be quite substantial.

Significant elaboration upon the Fenno thesis was provided by other sources [74, 75], one of the best being a study of congressional budgeting for eight agencies [76]. Comparing House and Senate actions on individual agencies over a 25-year period, the authors confirmed that the House Appropriations Committee in fact did reduce a greater proportion of agency requests than the Senate. However, they also found that highly constituency-oriented agencies were likely to receive favorable treatment from the appropriations committees of both houses.

The exercise of power through the cutting or restoring of funds characterized not only congressional-bureaucratic relations but also intracongressional relations. According to Fenno, the appropriations committees held a considerable amount of power over the substantive committees as well. These latter bodies frequently wanted higher appropriations for programs they backed, and this drive collided with the House Appropriations Committee's guardianship role. The result was a power confrontation—one that the Appropriations Committee could usually dominate.

The appropriations committees, of course, are divided into various subcommittees, and these are given considerable attention in the classic literature [2, 74, 77, 78]. One of the most insightful studies was published by John Gist [79]. An analysis of Senate appropriations subcommittees, it clearly documented the existence of a prestige hierarchy among the subcommittees. The author hypothesized that this hierarchy was based on the degree of actual power that the subcommittees had over their appropriations; and power, in turn, was based on controllability. For example, the budgets examined by certain subcommittees contained high proportions of uncontrollable expenditures. This resulted in a low subcommittee power and prestige rating. It might be concluded, therefore, that there was a relationship between subcommittee power and budget controllability.

In a related study, Fenno [2] claimed that the reason the appropriations committees functioned so effectively was that they were integrated so well. Such integration, in turn, was assured by five factors: consensus, the nature of the subject matter, the legislative orientation of committee members, the attractiveness of the committee for its members, and the stability of committee membership. Membership stability also was cited [80] as a key characteristic of the powerful Ways and Means Committee—another body intimately concerned with fiscal matters. Such factors, then, may be seen as bases of committee power.

Other works emphasized the impact of these and related variables. Joseph Harris [81], for example, placed much emphasis on the fact that appropriations committee members tended to come from safe districts. This ensured them a long tenure and the chance to develop real budgetary expertise. Jeffrey Pressman [82], in turn, took the logic one step further by highlighting the informal working relations that developed between these senior elected representatives and the budget officials in the executive branch. For the Ways and Means Committee, Catherine Rudder [83] also showed that similar working relations existed between committee members, administrative officials, and the representatives of various affected interest groups.

A final condition for committee budgetary power during the classic period concerned staff resources [78, 84]. An early recognition of the critical importance of this component may be found in the 1950 writing of Emmerich and McLean [85]. More than 40 years ago, they raised questions about the training, role orientations, and ethics of individuals functioning in this key capacity.

Nelson Polsby [77], one of Capitol Hill's most ardent defenders, wrote that although there are undoubtedly differences in the powers and processes of the Congress and the executive branch, these are outweighed by the similarities. For example, the budgetary decisions of both may be viewed not as reflecting differing levels of information and analysis but as responses to the demands of different groups. Thus, the fact that power is dispersed in Congress need not be a sign of weakness. Rather it may be a way of accommodating more and more groups and thus gaining more power. Such a theory is congruent with the work of David Truman [86]. In making classic budgetary allocations, therefore, both Congress and the President examined (1) what the agencies received last year, (2) external developments, (3) agency reputations for estimate accuracy, (4) previous programmatic commitments, and (5) interest group demands [77].

One of the most thorough studies documenting congressional budget power during this period was that of Arnold Kanter [87]. He clearly showed the impact of congressional initiative on the defense budget during the 1960s. An uncritical examination of Congress's aggregate changes in proposed defense spending for that period would have made it appear that the legislative branch had minimal impact on the Pentagon. However, Kanter proceeded by breaking the sums down into expenditure categories and discovered that most congressional changes in the defense budget were concentrated in procurement and in RDT & E (research, development, testing, and evaluation). These two categories are of extreme policy significance, and Kanter demonstrated that, with regard to them, Congress was able to enforce compliance to its wishes. Such key programmatic power is overlooked when the analyst concentrates on aggregate figures.

A similar conclusion was reached by John Gist [79] in his examination of the power prestige hierarchies of Senate subcommittees. One looking at modal changes in the executive budget made by the "average subcommittee" would have concluded that, in general, Congress had little power. However, such an approach hid a great deal of useful data. Thus, Gist argued that our analyses must distinguish between the various subcommittees. Clearly, some were very powerful vis-à-vis the executive branch while others were largely passive.

The "Reformed" Appropriations Process

The stability of the classic period was not to last indefinitely. In the mid 1970s Congress moved into its confrontation with Richard Nixon, and then later, as Carter was replaced by Reagan, the deficits began to mount. The literature of this later era, an era through which we are still groping, has tended to take as its starting point the passage of the Congressional Budget and Impoundment Control Act of 1974.

A very well written article by Thomas Wander [88] focuses on the forces that led to its adoption. Using March and Simon's [89] concept of the "occasions for innovation," he examines the internal and external factors that together created a need for change. Adaptive reforms are those generated by external variables, and here he cites the state of the economy and the President's abuse of impoundment. While these were undoubtedly significant causes they were not alone. The law also sought to create ameliorative changes in response to the internal problems of widespread decentralization and committee conflict that had led to turf disputes. Thus, right from the start we see that the law was an attempt to solve two very divergent kinds of problems with a single legislative stroke. Other analyses of the causes leading to reform are provided by Lynch [90], Penner and Abramson [91], Schick [92], and Pfiffner [93].

That Congress tried to do too much with a single piece of legislation may be the reason for its difficulties, contradictions, and failures in the judgment of many who have studied it. One of its strongest critics has been Louis Fisher [94, 95]; who has argued that the basic problem has been caused by the attempts to execute comprehensive budgeting via an institution based on decentralization and constituent service. This view sees it as doomed to inevitable failure from the beginning. Central to the reformed process is the passage of resolutions, and these, of course, are instruments of macroeconomic policy. However, Congress is designed so as to be able to best handle micropolicy. Cataloguing the resultant ills, Fisher notes that appropriations bills are now enacted in a less timely manner, that continuing resolutions have become more common, and that the deficits are larger than before the passage of the act.

A similar assessment is made by Kenneth Shepsle [96] who argues that the law's objectives were sabotaged by excessive accommodation to existing power centers in the House. He documents this charge by citing a reluctance on the part of the House Budget Committee to challenge the turf of other committees. In addition there are what he calls the "adding machine function" and the "substitution effect," for example, the trimming of the budget by merely requiring that other levels of government take over certain expenditures.

Accommodation, however, is a relative concept and not necessarily positive or negative in and of itself. Interestingly, then, this same phenomenon is cited by Congressional scholar Allen Schick in his assessment in a book edited by Penner [97]. Noting that during the act's first 5 years the budget committees avoided explicit trade-offs among functions, he merely reminds us that this is a disappointment only if the budget is to be seen as an outright contest over national priorities.

Five years later he gives us an even more measured critique [98]. Yes, there have been shortcomings, but we must consider these in terms of the conditions under which the law must operate. Here he refers specifically to the nation's economic predicament during the 1970s and to the fact that congressional budgeting takes place within a presidential context. Examining the Ford, Carter, and Reagan presidencies, he outlines how the chief executive takes the budgetary lead and thus leaves Congress dependent on negotiations with him. Schick's reference to these two factors, of course, dovetails nicely with Wander's [88] analysis of external factors, cited above. Regarding Wander's internal factors, he also notes that the act has had an impact on the role of party leaders, boosting their power.

The distinction between internal and external stresses is also made by Roger Davidson [99] who uses it to separate reform from mere change. Here we learn that the law has been more successful (a generator of reform) in helping Congress deal with the external environment, one concerned with macroeconomics and presidential leadership. With regard to internal problems, however, the law's consolidative thrust has led to a danger of simply overloading the process—a process that has become a target for committee leaders in both chambers.

Again, though, we encounter the problem of relativity and elasticity of terms. The law has been effective in helping Congress deal with its external world, yet Hebert [100] presents some interesting data regarding impoundment. This was, of course, prohibited and Congress was given the power to review rescissions and deferrals. However, his data indicate that presidents have been relatively free to exercise their deferral power and that even with rescissions they win most of the time.

Other scholars have taken a less evaluative approach to studying the law and have sought merely to assess its institutional impacts. Copeland [101] for one examines four types of changes in the House of Representatives: (1) the provision of expertise via the CBO; (2) the generation of jurisdictional jealousies between the budget and other committees; (3) the fact that it has increased partisanship; and (4) the strengthening of bargaining power that it has given to those on the ideological extremes of both parties.

A similar type of analysis by Ellwood [102] looks at the reform's impact on relations between the two chambers. Here the bottom line is found to be an increase in the power of the Senate. He demonstrates that the Senate tends to win more issues in conference than the House, due to the more stable membership on its Budget Committee and to its greater bipartisanship. He also has written [103] that the law's procedures have led to a shift from distributive to redistributive politics: from a politics designed to give something to everyone, to a politics of winners and losers.

During the reform period significant changes have also taken place in the nature and operations of congressional committees. These changes have produced a considerable new body of literature, but it is a literature best understood against the backdrop of the past. Before going further, it is worth noting that Bruce Oppenheimer [104] has provided us with an excellent bibliographic essay synthesizing 15 years' worth of scholarly research on Congress and budgeting. He presents his material using a six-part framework: legislative actions or functions, legislative actors, the stages of policymaking, legislative outputs, the influence of legislatures in different policy areas, and the differences among legislatures.

Earlier it was noted that three decades have passed since the publication of Richard Fenno's 1966 classic analysis of the congressional appropriations process [2]. His work focused on the role orientations of the two appropriations committees. In the House the committee played the role of "guardian" of the federal treasury, while in the Senate the analogous role was that of "appeals court." Thus he noted that while the House frequently cut agency requests, Senate deliberations were concerned with their restoration.

The 1974 rules changes and the creation of the budget committees in each chamber, of course, altered these roles dramatically. An excellent analysis of this transformation was provided by Allen Schick [92]. He characterized the appropriations committees as having adopted the role of claimants, while the budget committees have taken on the role of guardian. This is so, he argues, since the act prohibits appropriations decisions until after the passage of the first budget resolution. Given the context, spending decisions during the 1970s were made, he believes, on the basis of silent accommodation.

Schick [105] elaborated further on the idea of accommodation in another article assessing the act's first 5 years. Specifically, he writes that such a strategy deliberately avoided tradeoffs. Instead of prioritizing, the budget committees compartmentalized their spending decisions and avoided placing the functions in a zero-sum relationship to one another.

Obviously, however, this trend did not continue uninterrupted, changing quite dramatically in 1981 when Ronald Reagan managed to gain control of the congressional budgetary process. Lance LeLoup [21] provides a broad overview of the change as it affected the Senate. Buttressing Schick, he first demonstrates, a "dominance of accommodation" during the 1970s. During this period the Senate Budget Committee ordinarily attempted to accept guidelines and guidance from the standing committees—in spite of occasional confrontations. However, during the early 1980s when the Republicans controlled the Senate there was a definite decline in accommodation. During this period the Senate Budget Committee was willing to engage in challenges to other standing committees, turf disputes, and the use of reconciliation packages to rewrite both authorization and appropriations bills. The shift from accommodation to confrontation, he concludes, can be at least partially attributed to the fact that Republicans enjoyed greater presidential leadership and sharper partisanship.

While both Reagan's leadership and Republican partisanship declined as the 1980s progressed, the best study of that later period finds that conflict was still central to congressional budgeting from 1982 to 1988. Penner and Abramson [91] show how hostility marked relations between Republicans and Democrats, between members of Congress and the executive branch, and between senators and representatives, and how conflict even frequently boiled over among members of the same party. The fact that each year's cycle dealt with cutbacks generated both antagonisms and defensiveness. Each actor was very much on his or her own, the authors claim, each pursuing the blame game that goes with divided government.

Divided government has also meant that Congress's authorization committees continue to be active in the appropriations process. Such a conclusion was shown most effectively by Irene Rubin [106] in her study of procedures and outcomes relating to three programs: ACTION, the Federal Insecticide, Fungicide and Rodenticide Program (FIFRA), and the Department of Justice. She finds that in all three cases the authorization committees generated significant impacts on appropriations. Among other things, they affected floors and ceilings, engaged in earmarking, limited reprogramming, and provided waivers.

The picture of Congress that emerges from the foregoing discussion of committees and budgeting is one of extreme flux overlaying a blend of centralization and decentralization. In fact, Auten, Bozeman, and Cline [107] have also presented convincing evidence that top-down influences have been combining with bottom-up pressures to the appropriations process at least since 1956. Their work relies on a sequential model utilizing a "budget constraint" to show the top-down aspect.

On balance, Penner and Abramson [91] conclude that today the process is malfunctioning—a condition that they characterize as "broken purse strings." However, they do not believe that the huge deficits were caused by this broken process. Instead, they argue, it has been the deficits themselves that have created the pressures emasculating the process.

Oversight

The next subject in this review of congressional budgeting power is that of oversight. Appropriations committees and subcommittees are ultimately involved in this process, and two distinctions drawn by Ogul [108] help to explain their differing levels of commitment and involvement. First, there are manifest and latent functions to oversight. Latent functions are less immediately obvious and involve such things as constituent service. When they are present to buttress manifest functions, the effect is stronger oversight.

The other distinction involves what Ogul calls opportunity factors and conversion factors. Committees may exercise oversight if the opportunity factors, such as staff and information base, have been provided, but some conversion factor(s) will be necessary for these resources to be channeled into use.

An examination of appropriations politics by LeLoup [109] also contains implications for oversight. In this study of House Appropriations Committee-executive agency relationships we see the sources of conflict. These exist between the program-oriented goals of the agencies and the combination of economy-oversight goals of the Committee. The agencies want the Committee to think in broad, positive terms, while the Committee's own orientation leads it to adopt more particular and negative views regarding what may be unnecessary expenditures.

An orientation can easily result in misplaced oversight priorities, as Robert Art [110] has argued. Relying on over 100 interviews with committee staffers, he has analyzed legislative treatment of the defense budget from 1975 to 1984. His conclusion is that both the authorization and appropriations committees are focusing too much attention on budgetary and programmatic oversight and not enough on policy oversight. The use of oversight for micromanagement purposes is questioned.

One of the classic treatments of oversight is that of Joseph Harris [81]. Years ago, he cataloged the types of actions that an appropriations committee or subcommittee could take to alter effectively the actions of an administrative agency. These include such actions as issuing reports, cutting appropriations to force compliance, and writing restrictions into the legislation itself. Silverman [111] also emphasized the value of oversight as opposed to prospective policy analysis. Its advantages include the availability of a more diverse information base, a greater chance for legislative specialization, and better timing.

In addition to the committees, one other congressional agency is involved in the financial oversight function: the General Accounting Office (GAO). Because of its "watchdog" role, it is given a rather prominent place in the literature. To begin, two very useful books have been written by Mosher and by Brown. The study of Brown [112] is somewhat dated but does cover the basics well: the agency's audit function, investigative activities, and legal work. The uniqueness of Brown's approach is that it proceeds by focusing on GAO interaction with a single executive agency, the Tennessee Valley Authority. Because of the extensive nature of our discussion of the appropriations process above, it is also relevant to note here that Brown includes in his work an examination of the kinds of services the GAO provides to appropriations committees and subcommittees.

Mosher's book [113] is more ambitious. In the first half, it traces the evolution of the GAO from the role of voucher checker to that of program evaluator. Looking at a sweep of almost 60 years, the author refers to the different orientations as comprising a first, second, and third GAO. In an article on the same subject, Rourke [114] presents a similar interpretation. He argues that the GAO has evolved through three separate roles. During its initial 30 years, it focused mainly on voucher audits. This was followed by a period in which the emphasis was on the auditing of managerial efficiency as well as legality. During the 1970s, however, attention shifted to program auditing as the agency moved into cost-benefit and cost-effectiveness analysis.

This reorientation also was noted by Marvin and Hedrick [115], who described from the insider's angle how the GAO had moved into the field of program evaluation. In the process, they present examples of several such evaluations: social services for welfare recipients, the space shuttle, performance contracting, and the Neighborhood Youth Corps.

We are, however, far from unanimity on the question of the desirability of this shift in orientation. Schick [116], for one, believes that the GAO has gone too far and today is not paying enough attention to its original, and more basic, role.

Finally, another study by Mosher [42] compares the GAO and OMB, and we see the two agencies beginning to develop similar orientations. However, the author seems to question whether the GAO has taken on too many oversight-related roles. A small sample includes its work as investigator, critic, evaluator, teacher, rule maker on financial matters, and ombudsman.

Whether one is in favor of, or in opposition to, this broadening of GAO scope, the fact remains that is has aided Congress in expanding its budgetary power. More information regarding program effectiveness and goal attainment is now available. However, this does not guarantee that it will be used. Like the CBO, the GAO is a power resource, not a power center.

An Electoral Connection?

Another way to examine the connection between politics and budgeting is to ask whether elections have an impact on the appropriations process. Perhaps the most extreme characterization of their linkage is a theory known as the political business cycle. It was developed by William Nordhaus [117] and posits the existence of a cycle in a macroeconomic policy corresponding to the electoral cycle. A micro version of this hypothesis has been tested by Kiewiet and McCubbins [118]. The investigators employ an "electoral connection" model to examine appropriations decisions as the responses of reelection-seeking congressmen. Using data from the period 1948–1979, they discovered a pattern in which appropriations are indeed higher during election years. In this study officials thus appear to vote in ways that will maximize the probability of reelection.

This view is also presented in a nonquantitative way by former presidential economic advisor William Niskanen [119]. With echoes of David Stockman, he compares economists and politicians, informing the reader that the role of the policy advisor is to provide information on the potential effects of proposed programs. However, the interest of the politician is in reelection—something that concerns support or opposition to specific policies, rather than the effects of these policies or objective conditions. Shepsle and Weingast [120] state further than this electoral connection politically distorts expenditure policies through two principles: (1) productive inefficiency—targeting expenditures to constituencies— and (2) the distributive tendency—gaining majority support by spreading expenditures broadly. Their evidence, however, is anecdotal.

Of course, not all analysts agree with such interpretations. Golden and Poterba [121] examine public opinion polling and financial data from 1953–1978 and find no evidence for the existence of a political business cycle. Specifically, they assess the importance of electoral cycles and presidential popularity as a way of explaining macroeconomic policy, and find that neither fiscal, monetary, nor transfers policy has any statistically significant relationship to the electoral cycle.

Examining the period 1955–1981, Kamlet and Mowery [122] are similarly unable to confirm any such relationship. A much more modest view of the electoral connection was published by Kiewiet [123], who examined four dimensions of the ways in which people's economic views and concerns affect their votes: the incumbency-oriented hypothesis, the policy-oriented hypothesis, personal experience, and national assessments. Interestingly, he discovered that all four hypotheses were stronger during presidential than during congressional elections.

POLITICS OF THE FEDERAL DEFICIT

The purpose of this chapter has been to present an examination of the politics of federal budgeting. Due to its very nature, the undertaking has been concerned with institutions and processes. However, one substantive problem has become so central to American politics in the late twentieth century that it cannot be divorced from elements of process. Here we refer to the problem of the federal budget deficit—a subject pregnant with politics. In fact, in a very well written book, James Savage [124] assesses how the idea of balancing the budget has influenced American politics for 300 years. This book is a study of the history of the idea of balanced budgets as a symbol. Starting with colonial times and working forward through the Jeffersonians and Hamiltonians to the Keynesians and finally to the Reaganites, he shows how it as signified numerous virtues and a popular desire: to limit the ends and means of national government, to guard states' rights from encroachment, to control corruption, and to promote civic responsibility.

Assessments of the actual, as opposed to the symbolic, effects of deficits have been provided by scores of analysts. Among the more relevant for our purposes are the following. To begin with, Barth et al. [125] have argued quite convincingly that deciding whether deficits really do matter depends very much on one's assumptions and on the data. Empirical results purporting to show the economic effects of deficits are highly sensitive to the time period examined, the selection of dependent and independent variables, and the operational definition of the deficit that is used. However, most analyses of this subject tend to focus on the deficit's negative side. For example, Hoffman and Levy [126] examine its impact on credit, while Miner [127], in a closely related way, looks at its effect on capital formation and the servicing of foreign creditors.

Given the fact that so many have written so ardently about the dangers of excessive debt, how is it that we have survived relatively unharmed? Paul Peterson [128] argues that we have been able to incur huge deficits because the Federal Reserve Board's monetary policy has held down inflation.

To White and Wildavsky [129] the deficit is intimately connected with conceptions of the public interest. Their study of the politics of debt during the Reagan years has resulted in a massive tome whose central theme is that the way in which we deal with the deficit will have a fundamental impact on the quality of our public life. Accordingly, they look at different ideas of the public interest and show how different political actors (in Congress, the executive branch, and among interest groups) have each sought to use the system to further their own goals.

CONCLUSION

American scholars have produced a robust literature on the politics of national budgeting. Basic interpretations have focused on the replacement of the incrementalist theory with a paradigm combining elements of both top-down and bottom-up budgeting. Finally, it appears that solutions to the problem of the deficit will continue to plague scholars—just as they have plagued decision makers—for some time to come.

REFERENCES

1. I. S. Rubin, *New Directions in Budgetary Theory*, State University of New York Press, Albany (1988).
2. R. F. Fenno, *The Power of the Purse*, Little, Brown, Boston (1966).

3. A. Wildavsky, *The Politics of the Budgetary Process*, Little, Brown, Boston (1984).

4. A. Wildavsky, *Budgeting: A Comparative Theory of Budgetary Processes*, Transaction Books, New Brunswick, New Jersey (1986).

5. J. Malachowski, S. Bookheimer, and D. Lowery, The theory of budgetary process in an era of changing budgetary roles FY48–FY84, *Am. Polit. Q.*, *15*(3): 325–354 (1987).

6. B. T. Pitsvada, and R. D. Draper, Making sense of the federal budget the old fashioned way—Incrementally, *Public Admin. Rev.*, (Sept./Oct.): 401–407 (1984).

7. J. F. Plant, Charles E. Lindbloom's "Decision-Making in Taxation and Expenditures," *Public Budget. Fin.*, (Summer): 76–86 (1986).

8. L. LeLoup, The myth of incrementalism: Analytical choices in budgetary theory, *Polity 10*(4): 488–509 (1979).

9. B. Bozeman, and J. D. Straussman, Shrinking budgets and the shrinkage of budget theory, *Public Admin. Rev.* (Nov./Dec.): 509–515 (1982).

10. L. LeLoup, From microbudgeting to macrobudgeting: Evolution in theory and practice, *New Directions in Budget Theory* (I. Rubin, ed.), State University of New York Press, Albany, pp. 19–42 (1988).

11. I. Rubin, Aaron Wildavsky and the demise of incrementalism, *Public Admin. Rev.*, *42*: 78–81 (1989).

12. M. S. Kamlet, and D. C. Mowery, The budgetary base in federal resource allocation, *Am. J. Polit. Sci.*, *24*(4): 804–821 (1980).

13. D. Mowery, M. Kamlet, and J. Crecine, Presidential management of budgetary and fiscal policymaking, *Polit. Sci. Q.*, *95*(3): 395–425 (1980).

14. A. Wildavsky, *The New Politics of the Budgetary Process*, Scott, Foresman, Boston (1988).

15. D. F. Kettl, Expansion and protection in the budgetary process, *Public Admin. Rev.*, (May/June): 231–239 (1989).

16. L. Sigelman, The bureaucrat as budget maximizer: An assumption examined, *Public Budget. Fin.*, (Spring): 50–59 (1986).

17. W. A. Niskanen, *Bureaucracy and Representative Government*, Aldine, Chicago (1971).

18. N. Caiden, The politics of subtraction, *Making Economic Policy in Congress* (A. Schick, ed.), American Enterprise Institute, Washington, D.C., pp. 100–130 (1983).

19. J. L. Sundquist, *The Decline and Resurgence of Congress*, Brookings Institution, Washington, D.C. (1981).

20. D. S. Ippolito, Reform, Congress and the President, *Congressional Budgeting* (W. Wander, F. T. Hebert, and G. W. Copeland, eds.), Johns Hopkins University Press, Baltimore, pp. 133–152 (1984).

21. L. T. LeLoup, *Budgetary Politics*, King's Court Communications, Brunswick, Ohio (1977/1988).

22. Taft Commission, Document No. 854, U.S House of Representatives (1912).

23. H. E. Shuman, *Politics and the Budget: The Struggle Between the President and the Congress*, Prentice-Hall, Englewood Cliffs, New Jersey (1984/1988).

24. L. Fisher, *Presidential Spending Power*, Princeton University Press, Princeton, New Jersey (1975).

25. R. P. Nathan, *The Plot That Failed: Nixon and the Administrative Presidency*, John Wiley & Sons, New York (1975).

26. D. S. Ippolito, *The Budget and National Politics*, Freeman, San Francisco (1978).

27. D. Kinnard, President Eisenhower and the Defense budget, *J. Polit.*, *39*: 595–623 (1977).

28. L. Fisher, *President and Congress, Power and Policy*, Free Press, New York (1972).

29. L. Fisher, Congress, the executive and the budget, *Ann Am. Acad. Polit. Soc. Sci.*, (January): 102–113 (1974).

30. L. Fisher, Reprogramming of funds by the Defense Department, *J. Polit. 36*: 77–102 (1974).

31. M. S. Kamlet, D. C. Mowery, and T. T. Su, Upsetting national priorities? The Reagan administration's budgetary strategy, *Am. Polit. Sci. Rev.*, *82*: 1293–1307 (1988).

32. A. Schick, The budget as an instrument of presidential policy, *The Reagan Presidency and the Governing of America* (L. M. Salamon and M. S. Lund, eds.), Urban Institute Press, Washington, D.C., pp. 91–125 (1984).

33. R. D. Reischauer, The congressional budget process, *Federal Budget Policy in the 1980s* (G. B. Mills and J. L. Palmer, eds.), Urban Institute, Washington, D.C., pp. 385–413 (1984).

34. D. Lowery, S. Bookheimer, and J. Malachowski, Partisanship in the appropriations process: Fenno revisited, *Am. Polit. Q.*, *13*(2): 188–199 (1985).

35. L. LeLoup, and J. Hancock, Congress and the Reagan budgets, *Public Budget. Fin.*, *8*(3): 30–54 (1988).

36. L. LeLoup, After the blitz: Reagan and the U.S. congressional budget process, *Legis. Stud. Q.*, *7*(3): 321–339 (1982).

37. R. W. Hartman, Congress and budget-making, *Polit. Sci. Q.*, *97*: 381–402 (1982).

38. D. A. Stockman, *The Triumph of Politics: How the Reagan Revolution Failed*, Harper & Row, New York (1986).

39. W. Greider, The education of David Stockman, *Atlantic Monthly*, (December): 27–54 (1981).

40. M. D. Hobkirk, *The Politics of Defense Budgeting*, Macmillan, London (1984).

41. L. Berman, *The Office of Management and Budget and the Presidency, 1921–1979*, Princeton University Press, Princeton, New Jersey (1979).

42. F. C. Mosher, *A Tale of Two Agencies: A Comparative Analysis of the GAO and the OMB*, Louisiana State University Press, Baton Rouge (1984).

43. H. Heclo, OMB and the presidency: The problem of "neutral competence," *Public Interest 38*: 80–98 (1975).

44. L. Berman, The Office of Management and budget that almost wasn't, *Polit. Sci. Q. 92*: 281–303 (1977).

45. L. Berman, OMB and the hazards of presidential staff work, *Public Admin. Rev.*, *38*: 520–524 (1978).

46. Zeidenstein (1978).

47. P. M. Benda, and C. H. Levine, OMB and the central management problem: Is another reorganization the answer? *Public Admin. Rev.* (Sept./Oct): 379–391(1986).

48. J. Cooper, and W. West, Presidential power and Republican government: The theory and practice of OMB review of agency rules, *J. Polit. 50*(4): 864–895 (1988).

49. P. M. Benda, and C. H. Levine, The assignment and institutionalization of functions at OMB: Lessons from two cases in work-force management, *New Directions in Budget Theory* (I. Rubin, ed.), State University of New York Press, Albany, pp. 70–99 (1988).

50. P. Bromiley, and J. P. Crecine, Budget development in OMB: Aggregate influences of the problem and information environment, *J. Polit. 42*: 1031–1064 (1980).

51. H. Heclo, Executive budget making, *Federal Budget Policy in the 1980s* (G. B. Mills and J. L. Palmer, eds.), Urban Institute, Washington, D.C., pp. 255–291 (1984).

52. D. G. Mathiasen, The evolution of the Office of Management and Budget under President Reagan, *Public Budget. Fin.*, *8*(3): 3–14 (1988).

53. B. Johnson, From analyst to negotiator: The OMB's new role, *J. Policy Anal. Manage.*, *3*(4): 501–515 (1984).

54. B. Johnson, The OMB budget examiner and the congressional budget process, *Public Budget. Finance*, *9*(1): 5–14 (1989).

55. M. J. Wyszomirski, The de-institutionalization of presidential staff agencies, *Public Admin. Rev.*, (Sept./Oct.): 448–458 (1982).

56. F. Mosher, and M. O. Stephenson, The Office of Management and Budget in a changing scene, *Public Budget. Fin.*, (Winter): 23–41 (1982).

57. L. Reed, The budget game and how to win it, *Wash. Monthly*, *10*: 24–33 (1979).

58. I. S. Rubin, *The Politics of Public Budgeting*, Chatham House, Chatham, New Jersey (1990).

59. I. S. Rubin, *Shrinking the Federal Government*, Longman, New York (1985).

60. J. S. Wholey, Executive agency retrenchment, *Federal Budget Policy in the 1980s* (G. B. Mills and J. L. Palmer, eds.), Urban Institute, Washington, D.C., pp. 295–332 (1984).

61. J. Wanat, Base of budgetary incrementalism, Am. Polit. Sci. Rev., 68: 1221–1228 (1974).
62. J. F. Padgett, Bounded rationality in budgetary research, Am. Polit. Sci. Rev., 74: 354–371 (1980).
63. L. J. Korb, The budget process in the Department of Defense, 1947–77: The strengths and weaknesses of three systems, Public Admin. Rev., 37: 334–346 (1977).
64. J. W. Davis, and R. B. Ripley, The Bureau of the Budget and executive branch agencies: Notes on their interaction, J. Polit. (November): 749–769 (1967).
65. L. T. LeLoup, and W. B. Moreland, Agency strategies and executive review: The hidden politics of budgeting, Public Admin. Rev., 38: 232–239 (1987).
66. I. Sharkansky, Four agencies and an appropriations subcommittee: A comparative study of budget strategies, Midwest J. Polit. Sci., 9: 254–281 (1965).
67. A. Rivlin, Economic Choices 1984, Brookings Institution, Washington, D.C. (1984).
68. J. D. Straussman, Rights-based budgeting, New Directions in Budget Theory (I. Rubin, ed.), State University of New York Press, Albany, pp. 100–123 (1988).
69. R. K. Weaver, Automatic Government: The Politics of Indexation, Brookings Institution, Washington, D.C. (1988).
70. D. Axelrod, A Budget Quartet, St. Martin's Press, New York (1989).
71. D. S. Ippolito, Hidden Spending: The Politics of Federal Credit Programs, University of North Carolina Press, Chapel Hill (1984).
72. J. T. Bennett, and T. J. DiLorenzo, Underground Government: The Off-Budget Public Sector, CATO Institute, Washington, D.C. (1983).
73. R. Fenno, The House Appropriations Committee as a political system: The problem of integration, Am. Polit. Sci. Rev., 56: 310–324 (1962).
74. S. Horn, Unused Power: The Work of the Senate Committee on Appropriations, Brookings Institution, Washington, D.C. (1970).
75. D. M. Fox, Congress and U.S. Military Service budgets in the post-war period: A research note, Midwest J. Polit. Sci. 15: 382–393 (1971).
76. R. D. Thomas, and R. B. Handberg, Congressional budgeting for eight agencies, 1947–1972, Am. J. Polit. Sci., 18: 179–187 (1974).
77. N. W. Polsby, Congress and the Presidency, Prentice-Hall, Englewood Cliffs, New Jersey (1971).
78. R. B. Ripley, Congress: Process and Policy, Norton, New York (1975).
79. I. R. Gist, Appropriations politics and expenditure control, J. Polit. 40: 163–178 (1978).
80. J. F. Manley, The Politics of Finance: The House Committee on Ways and Means, Little, Brown, Boston (1970).
81. J. P. Harris, Congressional Control of Administration, Brookings Institution, Washington, D.C. (1964).
82. J. L. Pressman, House vs. Senate, Yale University Press, New Haven, Connecticut (1966).
83. C. Rudder, Committee reform and the revenue process, Congress Reconsidered (L. C. Dodd and B. I. Oppenheimer, eds.), Praeger, New York (1977).
84. F. Schwengel, Problems of inadequate information and staff resources in Congress, Information Support, Program Budgeting and the Congress (R. L. Chartrand, K. Janda, and M. Hugo, eds.), Spartan, New York, pp. 97–108 (1968).
85. H. Emmerich, and J. McLean, Symposium on budget theory, Public Admin. Rev., 10: 20–31 (1950).
86. D. B. Truman, The Governmental Process, Knopf, New York (1951).
87. A. Kanter, Congress and the Defense budget: 1960–70, Am. Polit. Sci. Rev., 66: 129–143 (1972).
88. W. T. Wander, The politics of congressional budget reform, Congressional Budgeting W. T. Wander, F. T. Hebert, and G. W. Copeland, eds.), Johns Hopkins University Press, Baltimore, pp. 3–30 (1984).
89. J. March, and H. Simon, Organizations, John Wiley & Sons, New York (1958).
90. T. D. Lynch, Public Budgeting in America, Prentice-Hall, Englewood Cliffs, New Jersey (1990).

91. R. G. Penner, and A. J. Abramson, *Broken Purse Strings: Congressional Budgeting, 1974–1988*, Urban Institute Press, Washington, D.C. (1988).

92. A. Schick, *Congress and Money*, Urban Institute, Washington, D.C. (1980).

93. J. P. Pfiffner, *The President, the Budget, and Congress*: *Impoundment and the 1974 Budget Act*, Westview Press, Boulder, Colorado (1979).

94. L. Fisher, The Budget Act of 1974, *Congressional Budgeting* (W. Wander, F. T. Hebert, and G. W. Copeland, eds.), Johns Hopkins University Press, Baltimore, pp. 170–189 (1984).

95. L. Fisher, Ten years of the Budget Act: Still searching for controls, *Public Budget. Fin.*, Autumn: 3–28 (1985).

96. K. A. Shepsle, The congressional budget process: Diagnosis, prescription, prognosis, *Congressional Budgeting* (W. Wander, F. T. Hebert, and G. W. Copeland, eds.), Johns Hopkins University Press, Baltimore, pp. 190–218 (1984).

97. R. G. Penner, eds., *The Congressional Budget Process after Five Years*, American Enterprise Institute, Washington, D.C. (1981).

98. A. Schick, The evolution of congressional budgeting, *Crisis in the Budget Process* (A. Schick, ed.), American Enterprise Institute, Washington, D.C., pp. 3–56 (1986).

99. R. H. Davidson, The congressional budget: How much change? How much reform? *Congressional Budgeting* (W. Wander, F. T. Hebert, and G. W. Copeland, eds.), Johns Hopkins University Press, Baltimore, pp. 153–169 (1984).

100. F. T. Hebert, Congressional budgeting, 1977–1983: Continuity and change, *Congressional Budgeting* (W. Wander, F. T. Hebert, and G. W. Copeland, eds.), Johns Hopkins University Press, Baltimore, pp. 31–50 (1984).

101. G. W. Copeland, Changes in the House of Representatives after the passage of the Budget Act of 1974, *Congressional Budgeting* (W. Wander, F. T. Hebert, and G. W. Copeland, eds.), Johns Hopkins University Press, Baltimore, pp. 51–77 (1984).

102. J. W. Ellwood, Budget reforms and interchamber relations, *Congressional Budgeting* (W. Wander, F. T. Hebert, and G. W. Copeland, eds.), Johns Hopkins University Press, Baltimore, pp. 100–132 (1984).

103. J. W. Ellwood, Budget control in a redistributive environment, *Making Economic Policy in Congress* (A. Schick, ed.), American Enterprise Institute, Washington, D.C., pp. 69–99 (1983).

104. B. I. Oppenheimer, How legislatures shape policy and budgets, *Legis. Stud. Q.*, 8(4): 551–597 (1983).

105. A. Schick, The first five years of congressional budgeting, *The Congressional Budget Process after Five Years* (R. G. Penner, ed.), American Enterprise Institute, Washington, D.C., pp. 3–34 (1981).

106. I. S. Rubin, The authorization process: Implications for budget theory, *New Directions in Budget Theory* (I. Rubin, ed.), State University of New York Press, Albany, pp. 124–147 (1988).

107. G. Auten, B. Bozeman, and R. Cline, A sequential model of congressional appropriations, *Am. J. Polit. Sci.*, 28: 503–523 (1984).

108. M. S. Ogul, *Congress Oversees the Bureaucracy: Studies in Legislative Supervision*, Universityof Pittsburgh Press, Pittsburgh (1976).

109. L. LeLoup, Appropriations politics in Congress: The House Appropriations Committee and executive agencies, *Public Budget. Fin.*, 4: 78–98 (1984).

110. R. J. Art, Congress and the Defense Budget: Enhancing policy oversight, *Polit. Sci. Q.*, 100: 227–248 (1985).

111. E. B. Silverman, Public budgeting and public administration: Enter the legislature, *Public Fin. Q.*, 2: 472–484 (1974).

112. R. E. Brown, *The GAO*, University of Tennessee Press, Knoxville (1970).

113. F. C. Mosher, *The GAO: The Quest for Accountability in American Government*, Westview Press, Boulder, Colorado (1979).

114. J. T. Rourke, The GAO: An evolving role, *Public Admin. Rev.*, 38: 453–457 (1978).

115. K. E. Marvin, and J. L. Hedrick, GAO helps Congress evaluate programs, *Public Admin. Rev.*, 34: 327–333 (1974).

116. A. Schick (1978).

117. W. Nordhaus, The political business cycle, *Rev. Econ, Stud.*, *42*: 169–189 (1975).

118. D. R. Kiewiet and M. D. McCubbins, Congressional appropriations and the electoral connection, *J. Polit.*, *47*: 59–82 (1985).

119. W. Niskanen, Economists and politicans, *J. Policy Anal. Manage.*, *5*(2): 234–244 (1986).

120. K. A. Shepsle and Weingast (1984).

121. D. G. Golden, and J. M. Poterba, The price of popularity: The political business cycle reexamined, *Am. J. Polit. Sci.*, *24*(4): 696–714 (1980).

122. M. S. Kamlet, and D. C. Mowery, Influences on executive and congressional budgetary priorities, 1955–1981, *Am. Polit. Sci. Rev.*, *81*(1): 155–178 (1987).

123. D. R. Kiewiet, *Macroeconomics and Micropolitics*, University of Chicago Press, Chicago (1983).

124. J. D. Savage, *Balanced Budgets and American Politics*, Cornell University Press, Ithaca, New York (1988).

125. J. Barth, G. Iden, and F. Russek, Do federal deficits really matter?, *Contemp. Policy Issues 3*: 79–95 (1984/1985).

126. R. Hoffman, and M. Levy, Economic and budget issues for deficit policy, *Contemp. Policy Iss.*, *3*: 96–114 (1984/1985).

127. J. Miner, The Reagan deficit, *Public Budget. Fin.*, *9*(1): 15–32 (1989).

128. P. Peterson, The new politics of deficits, *Polit. Sci. Q.*, *100*(4): 575–601 (1986).

129. J. White, and A. Wildavsky, *The Deficit and the Public Interest*, University of California Press, Berkeley (1989).

BIBLIOGRAPHY

R. Fair, The effect of economic events on votes for president, *Rev. Econ. Stat.*, *LX*(2): 159–173 (1978).

L. T. LeLoup, The impact of budget reform on the Senate, *Congressional Budgeting* (W. Wander, F. T. Hebert, and G. W. Copeland, eds.), Johns Hopkins University Press, Baltimore, pp. 78 99 (1984).

G. B. Mills, and J. L. Palmer eds., *Federal Budget Policy in the 1980s*, Urban Institute, Washington, D.C. (1984).

A. Schick, ed., *Making Economic Policy in Congress*, American Enterprise Institute, Washington, D.C. (1983).

W. T. Wander, F. T. Hebert, and G. W. Copeland, *Congressional Budgeting*, Johns Hopkins University Press, Baltimore (1984).

A. Wildavsky, Constitutional expenditure limitation and congressional budget reform, *The Congressional Budget Process after Five Years* (R. G. Penner, ed.), American Enterprise Institute, Washington, D.C., pp. 87–100 (1981).

VI

ADMINISTRATIVE CONTEXTS OF BUDGETING AND FINANCE

EDITORIAL INTRODUCTION

Expenditure processes wend their ways—often tortuously—through what we simplistically call "the government." This convenient sim-speak has a rich meaning. In sum, the major activities in the money flow include:

- Authorization
- Appropriation
- Apportionment of appropriations
- Obligations to purchase
- Expenditure
- Renegotiation for a small proportion of government spending
- Audit, both internal to the obligating agency as well as external to it via such overhead agencies as the U.S. General Accounting Office

Typically, several separate administrative or legislative units are involved in each of these activities.

The point of Unit VI is to introduce the reader to seven selections that provide insight about the several "administrative contexts" involved in the expenditure processes. Our focus is necessarily selective, and has two basic thrusts. Thus, Chapters 28 and 29 provide overall perspective on administrative contexts and the kinds of control exercised through them. The other five selections deal with specific administrative functions—accounting, auditing, and so on.

Four Kinds of Management Controls

Unit VI begins with a strong overhead perspective on the expenditure processes, with initial reliance on Fred Thompson's "Matching Responsibilities with Tactics: Administrative Controls and Modern Government." His analysis is rooted in the U.S. Department of Defense, but has a generic applicability to many agencies at all levels of government. Thus, he distinguishes "before-the-fact" controls from "after-the-fact" controls, and he details two examples of each that may serve as models for categorization and analysis in a broad range of public agencies.

Thompson is primarily interested in the "degree of fit": that is, in matching control systems to types of tasks. His motivation is quite direct. Mismatches can be costly—to agencies, to their employees, and to clients/stakeholders alike. Bottom line, a control system poorly matched to the task, precludes responsible and responsive management, in that a poor match implies that the wrong things will be measured exactly or the proper things will go unmeasured.

Execution and Control

Chapter 29 reinforces Thompson's focus on matching responsibilities with tactics. Carol K. Johansen and L. R. Jones join Fred Thompson in detailing "Management and Control of Budget Execution." Their focus is clear: on the highly regulated activities that seek to "control what program managers may and may not do." And their purpose is correspondingly targeted. They seek to "improve understanding of control dynamics, incentives, disincentives, and behavior of the various participants in the budget execution process."

Patently, both their focus and purpose lie close to the heart of PBF. Their key questions involve who is to be controlled, and how, and for what purposes. Johansen, Jones, and Thompson thus set their analysis at *the* critical interface. We can more easily circumscribe this interface than define its specific characteristics. Their target can be conceived as the overlapping of two sets: that zone in which sufficient discretion remains after the key who/how/what choices have been made to respond to the exigencies of reasonable local adaptions to the variable textures of the flow of work; and that zone in which the public interest in sufficient accountability has been achieved.

There will be much controversy as actors set to create the optimum overlay of these two zones, often with cross-purposes and unconscious or hidden agendas playing prominent roles in distorting or camouflaging the realities. Johansen, Jones, and Thompson help by describing those dynamics, as well as by providing useful perspective on how and for what purposes that controversy can be steered a bit by aware and resourceful stakeholders.

Auditing Activities

These activities often have generated schizoid reactions among managers. "Great!" say managers when audits help induce that heightened responsibility required by the often-substantial discretion available to public employees. "Wait a minute," is also a common public managerial reaction. That is, auditing can fixate on catching somebody doing something questionable, at times at disproportionate cost and long after the fact. This fixation can inhibit innovation, preclude timely administrative response, and may even intimidate public employees. Mostly, this fixation makes everybody mad.

Hence, the central role played by Khi V. Thai's "Governmental Auditing," which describes the emerging new balances that seek to avoid both fixation and flaccidity in those central auditing activities.

Thai's essay is extensive, but the subject matter demands nothing less. For example, the U.S. Department of Health and Human Services has the second largest federal auditing staff, which serves more than 1,000 federal installations, over 10,000 units of local government, and 10,000 hospitals and extended-care facilities. In sum, Thai does not focus on exotica. His essay focuses on the power plant of government.

How does Thai structure his approach to this complexity? Three major emphases serve as an introduction. Professor Thai begins with an overview, which touches aspects of the evolution of governmental auditing, of a useful classification of types of governmental auditing, and of the selection of auditors. Then Thai gives detailed attention to auditing standards and procedures. Thai closes with a focus on "the single audit," which is a major way federal officials have tried to become more user-friendly to state and local governments.

Accounting in Two Arenas

PBF tools and theories need to be context specific, at least up to a point, and two contexts get attention in two ways—in Chapter 31, as well as in a brief note about public versus business contexts.

First, C. William Garner details one PBF context in his "An Inquiry into the Feasibility of a National Accounting Policy for Public Schools." Garner conducted an informal survey, respondents to which seemed largely unaware of such a national policy. Subsequently, Garner details how such a national policy has taken form, as well as to how accounting and budgetary practices can influence the public school context.

Second, much of the PBF literature, as well as that in the broader public administration literature, focuses on the kind and character of differences, if any, between business and government arenas. Readers interested in this zesty debate might reasonably consult Anthony [1], among numerous other commentators.

Stripped to essentials, Anthony's argument has dual foci. First, he illustrates some of the major differences between accounting policies and practices in the two arenas. Second, he proposes that at least some of these differences are merely conventional, rather than being somehow inherent in the nature of the two arenas. Anthony illustrates how some greater integration of accounting policies and practices can be accomplished by those willing and able to rise above the conventional.

Contracting and Procurement

Susan A. MacManus also seeks to encompass both the public and business sectors as she focuses on two related sets of activities. Her contribution is revealingly titled "Government Contracting and Procurement: A Critical Process for Both the Public and Private Sectors."

MacManus takes a multimethod approach, as it were. Thus, she employs survey methods to assess the state of opinions about cross-sector buying/selling. In addition, she surveys a great deal of literature to support her assessments of the costs/benefits of cross-sector transactions, as when business practices often permit "substantial performance" while government tends to rely on "strict compliance" to contractual specifications. Finally, MacManus details several useful developments in the "public procurement world" that can facilitate transactions with businesses. Such transactions often will be necessary, and perhaps never more so than in the future that seems to be dawning for all of us.

Capital Assets in Local Government

Gerald J. Miller next directs helpful attention to what often is a proverbial hot potato at all levels of government, given the ongoing alarum about "rebuilding our infrastructure" —cities, schools, utility systems, and the like. The key question is elementally profound and practical: how to arrange for the payment of the costs of adding capital assets.

Miller's "Capital Asset Financing" ranges widely, and is not easy to characterize briefly except as to the great significance of the topic for effective and responsive government. So we editors let Miller set out to meet his own far-reaching ambitions: "to shed light on the institutions which thrive on ambiguity in capital finance, how these institutions operate, and, most important of all, how and what opportunistic strategies the institutions use to finance public sector capital projects."

Enough said, in these introductory notes. Miller will carry on. The task is a central and compelling one.

Capital Budgets at Federal Level

Charles A. Bowsher adds technical and institutional depth to Miller's focus on the financing of capital assets. Bowsher provides a useful review of a long-standing debate in "Pros and Cons of a Separate Capital Budget for the Federal Government."

The balances of pros/cons of a separate capital budget will vary for different observers. For some, the pros will dominate, and Bowsher provides a model of how to develop an argument favoring a separate capital budget. For other observers, that balance will not justify reconfiguring the present unified system, as Bowsher also acknowledges in his balanced contribution. For such observers, consequently, he provides options that provide useful information about capital spending but do not necessarily require fundamental reformatting of the present unified budget. For example, Bowsher proposes that the information about capital budgeting might be provided in a resectioned unified budget.

In sum, Bowsher provides careful readers with a model for highlighting information about capital spending, in both comprehensive as well as incremental modes. Given Miller's appropriate warning in Chapter 33 that capital financing often prefers dark nooks and crannies, the readers' debt to Bowsher is substantial.

REFERENCE

1.　R. N. Anthony, Making sense of nonbusiness accounting, *Harvard Business Rev.*, *58*(5): 83–93 (1980).

28

Matching Responsibilities with Tactics: Administrative Controls and Modern Government

Fred Thompson

Not so long ago, the late Frederick C. Mosher [1, pp. 545–547] observed that in the last generation government has experienced a sea change in its responsibilities and its tactics and concluded that these massive changes have rendered obsolete the traditional administrative controls inherited from our forebears. In a similar vein, Allen Schick [2] noted that these changes have been accompanied by massive growth in the scope and content of rule-bound governance mechanisms: Federal reporting requirements have multiplied; federal auditors scrutinize more closely the accounts of federal agencies, state and local governments, and contractors; and direct controls in the form of rules and regulations have pro liferated. Schick concluded that we cannot afford to go on imposing direct controls over an ever-widening sphere of activities—that new solutions to the problem of administrative governance must be sought. He closed his peroration with a reminder that, in many cases, individuals can be more effectively influenced to serve the citizenry "by inducements which allow them to pursue their own interests than by constraints which try to bar them from behaving as they want" (p. 518).

Remarkably, many of the participants in contemporary debates over government management and operations are unfamiliar with the alternatives to rule-bound governance mechanisms. In this chapter, I describe the four basic management control systems designs[1] that are available for influencing people to advance the policies and purposes of the institutions they serve: (1) outlay budgets, (2) responsibility budgets, (3) fixed-price contracts, and (4) flexible-price contracts. I show how each of these mechanisms can be executed to enforce efficiency in the delivery of services and outline the circumstances under which each has

Source: F. Thompson, "Matching Responsibilities with Tactics: Administrative Controls and Modern Government," Public Administration Review, Vol. 53, No. 4, July/August 1993. American Society for Public Administration. Reprinted with permission from Public Administration Review (c) by the American Society for Public Administration (ASPA), 1120 G Street NW, Suite 700, Washington, DC 20005. All rights reserved.

a comparative advantage over the others. I also show what happens when these designs are misused and overused.

CONTROL SYSTEMS IN GENERAL

The design and implementation of control systems are a ubiquitous problem. They are encountered by engineers, planners, and regulators, as well as management controllers. The purposes of various kinds of control systems differ, as do the details of their execution, but all control system designers face the same key choices: what, where, when, and, in the case of human systems, whom to control. The choice of what and where to control is reasonably self-evident. Management control should be primarily addressed to the behavior of service suppliers (departments and agencies, other levels of government, and contractors), the efficiency with which they produce goods and services, and ultimately the efficiency with which they use the assets at their disposal.

The choice of whom to subject to controls and when to execute those controls is far less self-evident. In the abstract, a control system designer has four sets of options, comprised of two choices of subject and two of timing: (1) The subject may be either an organization or an individual; and (2) controls may be executed either before or after the subject acts.

Before-the-fact controls are intended to prevent subjects from doing undesirable things or to compel them to do desirable things and necessarily take the form of authoritative mandates, rules, or regulations that specify what the subject must do, may do, or must not do. The subjects of before-the-fact controls are held responsible for complying with these commands and the controller attempts to monitor and enforce compliance with them.

After-the-fact controls are executed after the subject acts. Either an organization or an individual decides on and carries out a course of action and, therefore, after some of the consequences of the subject's decisions are known. Because bad decisions cannot be undone after they are carried out, after-the-fact controls are intended to motivate subjects to make good decisions. Hence, subjects are made responsible for the consequences of their decisions, and the controller attempts to monitor those consequences and to see that subjects are rewarded or sanctioned accordingly.

Combining the choice of subject with that of timing, the control system designer must choose among four distinct institutional alternatives: individual responsibility (before-the-fact or after-the-fact) and organizational responsibility (before-the-fact or after-the-fact). In this chapter, I will try to explain the significance of this choice, its relevance to management control, and the economic logic that should guide it.

PRIVATIZATION

The significance of these alternative institutional arrangements is partially reflected in the current debate over the merits of privatizing the delivery of public services. Proponents of privatization imply that we have a choice between rule-governed, often overregulated, monopolistic public bureaucracies, and freely competing private firms. They conclude that the latter will usually be more efficient than the former. If that is the choice, it is difficult to see how privatization could be wrong, since it resolves to a simple question of monopoly or competition. Clearly, provision by competing private firms will almost always be more efficient than provision by a public monopoly except possibly where production of the good or service in question is characterized by increasing returns to scale, a high degree of lumpiness in production or consumption,[2] asset specificities, or the absence of close substitutes.

However, the distinction drawn by proponents of privatization between provision by a public agency and provision by a private entity is inordinately simplistic. It fails to capture the full range of choices available to the management controller. It also fails to reflect all of the factors that are relevant to the choice.

First, although it is true that most goods and services purchased with public money are produced by organizations and not individuals, effective control ultimately presumes individual accountability. The distinction drawn by the proponents of privatization between public and private provision ignores the management controller's capacity to hold managers of public organizations under his jurisdiction personally responsible for their behavior and, thereby, the controller's capacity to influence directly the rewards and sanctions that accrue to those individuals such as salary and opportunities for advancement.

Controllers cannot possibly hold managers personally responsible where their relationship to the supplying organization is at arm's length, and the structure of individual responsibility is veiled by the organizational form. The only way an organization can be rewarded (or punished) is by increasing (or reducing) its revenues. An organization's revenues can affect an individual manager's welfare—but only indirectly.

The difference between holding individuals and organizations accountable or between direct, personal influence and indirect influence is quite straightforward. Take the following example: If the quality of services supplied by a public agency is grossly unsatisfactory, the controller can recommend the dismissal of the agency manager. Where government has an arm's length relationship with a service supplier and the relationship is unsatisfactory, all the controller can do is recommend termination of the relationship. The controller can punish the supplying organization but cannot punish the manager responsible for the failure, although the manager's actions might very well lead the organization's board of directors to do so! Unfortunately, punishing a monopoly (that is, any sole-source supplier) is like cutting off your nose to spite your face; rewarding one is like eating an eclair to celebrate staying on a diet. Consequently, where the supplying organization is a monopoly, the capacity to influence managers directly will have considerable utility, particularly where the controller can stimulate and exploit competition between alternative management teams.

This claim can be verified by reference to the private sector. In the private sector, most real natural monopolies make intermediate products, i.e., goods that are used to produce consumer goods or services. Natural monopoly (decreasing costs as output increases) can usually be attributed to spreading large, lumpy investments in specialized resources—technological know-how, product-specific research and development, equipment—over additional output. Investment in specialized resources often inspires a process called vertical integration ("backward" if initiated by the consumer goods producer, "forward" if initiated by the intermediate goods producer). The new economics of organization tells us that vertical integration occurs because it permits transaction costs to be minimized, in part through the substitution of direct supervision for indirect influence [14].[3]

In the jargon of transaction-cost economics, investment in specialized resources is called "asset specificity." An asset is said to be specific if it makes a necessary contribution to the provision of a good or service and has a much lower value in alternative uses. The corollary of asset specificity is bilateral monopoly, a circumstance that provides an ideal environment for opportunistic behavior on the part of both the intermediate product supplier and the customer.

For example, once an intermediate product producer has acquired a specialized asset, the customer may be able to threaten to switch suppliers to extract discounts from the producer. In that case, the supplier may find it necessary to write off a large part of his or her specialized investment. Or, if demand for the final good increases greatly, the intermediate product supplier may be able to use his or her monopoly power to extort exorbitant prices from his customer. Hence, where the relationship between the intermediate product supplier and the customer is at arm's length, the threat of opportunistic behavior may be sufficient to eliminate the incentive to make what would otherwise be cost-effective investments. Vertical integration can eliminate this threat. Indeed, where the intermediate product producer provides homogeneous goods or services (i.e., outputs that are easily monitored), total production volume is specified, and technologies are mature, vertical integration permits a bilateral monopoly to be governed satisfactorily by unbalanced or two-part transfer prices.[4]

Moreover, the proponents of privatization err in their implicit claim that responsibility can be vested in organizations if, and only if, the organization is private, and in individuals if, and only if, the organization is part of the public sector. The absurdity of this claim becomes clear as soon as it is explicitly stated; it is consistent with neither theory nor practice. For example, many state legislatures base their relationships with public entities such as universities or hospitals on arm's length relationships that are guaranteed by self-denying ordinances, which exempt the managers of these public entities from detailed oversight and direct control [e.g., 24]. Similarly, the recurring procurement fraud cases show that the managers of private entities that supply services to the government can be held directly responsible when their behavior violates federal law.

Finally, most of the proponents of privatization implicitly presume that the services provided to or for government are homogeneous or fungible, which implies that the problem of identifying the most efficient supplying organization or management team resolves to a simple question of price search, an elementary control mechanism that reveals information about the "customer's" demand for the service. In fact, many of the organizations supplying goods or services to or for government supply bundles of more or less heterogeneous products—many of these products are hard to measure and costly to evaluate, some prohibitively so.

CHOOSING BETWEEN ALTERNATIVE INSTITUTIONAL ARRANGEMENTS

The proponents of privatization do, however, make one significant, unexceptionable claim: that the choice of institutional arrangements should depend on the cost and production behavior of the good or service in question. However, they frequently fail to carry this claim to its logical conclusion. At least two factors are relevant to this choice: the ease with which the consequences of operating decisions can be monitored, and the desirability of interorganizational competition.

Most management control theorists believe that where consequences (that is, an organization or responsibility center's outputs) are easily monitored, control should focus on the consequences of the subject's decisions; where they are not, control should focus on their content (inputs). Because consequences are easily monitored where entities produce homogeneous outputs or where a responsibility center within an entity performs fungible activities, it follows that controllers should rely on after-the-fact controls where homogeneous outputs are supplied. In contrast, it follows that they should rely on before-the-fact controls where each item supplied is, from the "customer's" perspective, intrinsically unique. Furthermore, this view has been reinforced by recent findings in transactions costs economics and agency theory.

At the same time, industrial organization theory tells us that interorganizational competition is desirable only where costs are constant or increasing as quantity of output (rate or volume) increases. Where costs decrease as output is increased, monopoly supply is appropriate. Because responsibility can be effectively vested in organizations only where customers or their agents are ultimately indifferent to the survival of one or more of the supplying organizations, this line of reasoning implies that controllers should vest responsibility in organizations only where interorganizational rivalry is practical and likely to be effective—and in individuals, where it is not.

EXECUTION OF ALTERNATIVE CONTROL SYSTEM DESIGNS

These four basic sets of controls are all employed by government. But is each appropriately employed? Before I can answer this question, I must first show how these designs are used and explain the practical logic of their implementation. My discussion will concentrate on the use of before-the-fact controls. This does not mean that I particularly like them. On the contrary, I believe that controllers should resort to before-the-fact control designs only where the cost and production behavior of the good or service in question makes their use the least objectionable alternative available.

I concentrate on the use of before-the-fact controls because it seems to me that their implementation is not well understood, especially by those who most rely on them.[5] Many participants in the policy process believe that before-the-fact controls not only safeguard against abuse but also, by reducing costs, improve mission performance. If failure occurs nevertheless, they tend to believe the solution lies in still more or better rules. One possible explanation for the persistent faith in the efficacy of before-the-fact controls is that its devotees do not understand how hard it is to execute them efficiently. For example, they appear to believe that the subjects of before-the-fact controls will comply with them simply because they are morally obligated to do so. Obviously, however, not everyone is inclined to respect moral authority, to respect the law, or to obey rules.[6] It is necessary to monitor and enforce compliance with rules and to ferret out and punish noncompliance. It is also necessary to specify the content of before-the-fact controls to tell subjects what to do and what not to do in such a way as to find and enforce efficiency, which is no easy matter.

Before-the-fact controls are similar to after-the-fact controls in their reliance on incentives and sanctions for their effectiveness. The difference is that after-the-fact management controls are incentive- or demand-revealing mechanisms, whereas before-the-fact management controls are incentive- or demand-concealing mechanisms. This means that opacity is an essential characteristic of before-the-fact controls. The incentive aspects of before-the-fact controls are thus less clear than are the incentive aspects of after-the-fact controls. This means that their effectiveness is hostage to the skill with which they are executed. It also means that the incentive aspects of before-the-fact controls are easily overlooked, which might help explain why they are not better understood.

AFTER-THE-FACT CONTROL SYSTEM DESIGNS

Through demand-revealing mechanisms, customers (or their agents) declare their willingness to pay for various quantities of goods, services, or activities. Customers transparently reveal a demand schedule that fully expresses their wants and preferences to their suppliers. Then they let suppliers figure out how best to satisfy those wants and preferences. The classic demand-revealing mechanism is the competitive spot market, where customers buy from any number of anonymous firms. When many suppliers are disposed to satisfy customer wants, the customer simply chooses the best price and quantity combination offered—the one that moves him or her farthest down his or her demand schedule. In so doing the customer rewards the organization that is willing to do the most to satisfy his or her preferences and implicitly punishes the rest. For example, the customer might order wheat from a broker at the marker price payable on delivery. In that case, there would be no formal contract. The customer would put no restrictions on the producer. In fact, the customer will probably not even know who grew the wheat. The wheat farmer is nevertheless rewarded for his or her contribution. Government relies on spot markets when, for example, it purchases electrical components off the shelf.

After-the-Fact Controls Transparently Reward Measured Performance

The spot market is by no means the only demand-revealing mechanism that is used to govern relationships between buyers and sellers. Variations are many on the basic theme of reliance on transparent rewards. All of these variations have one common attribute: rewards are provided after operating decisions have been made by the producer, after his or her asset acquisition and use decisions have been carried out and outputs have been monitored. Because they are executed after asset acquisition and use decisions have been carried out, I refer to them as after-the-fact controls.

Closely analogous to spot markets are situations where government uses prospective price mechanisms to reimburse free-standing service providers. The system used by the Health Care Financing Administration to pay hospitals for treating patients is an example. The enrollment-driven funding formulas used by some states to compensate postsecondary institutions for teaching students are another [29]. In both of these instances, the subject is a free-standing organization, and the structure of authority and responsibility within the supplying organization is assumed to be a purely internal matter. The government or its agent, for example, a controller, announces a price schedule and specifies minimum service quality standards (or a process whereby these standards are to be determined) and the time period in which the price schedule will be in effect.

Under prospective pricing, all qualified organizations will be paid a stipulated per-unit price each time they perform a specified service, such as enrolling a full-time equivalent student or treating a heart attack. This means among other things, that the government's financial liability is somewhat open ended. It depends on the quantity of service actually provided, although not directly on the costs incurred by the organizations supplying the service.

Another close relative of the spot market is the fixed-price contract.[7] The government buys from numerous suppliers held at arm's length. Frequent bidding contests are held and orders are shifted among suppliers chosen simply on price.[8] Under a fixed-price contract, government may grant a selected organization a franchise to provide a specified service for a fixed period of time (garbage collection at a military base, for example). When the contract is completed, the government again puts the franchise out to bid to all comers.

Under all of these demand-revealing mechanisms, the government relies upon interorganizational competition, combined in most instances with the profit motive, to motivate service suppliers to produce efficiently and therefore to make wise asset acquisition and use decisions. If interorganizational competition is effective, organizations that don't make wise asset acquisition and use decisions will fall by the wayside.

Demand-Revealing Mechanisms in Vertically Integrated Organizations

In some cases, even where the cost behavior of the service in question renders vertical integration and, therefore, monopoly supply appropriate, demand-revealing mechanisms or after-the-fact controls can still be effectively employed. Where the supplier is part of the same organization as the customer, the organization rewards managers who do the best jobs of satisfying their customer's preferences. This is done in businesses and businesslike public sector organizations by holding a manager responsible for optimizing a single criterion value, subject to a set of specified constraints. This control mechanism is known as responsibility budgeting [5, pp. 365–386; 30].[9] For example, under responsibility budgeting, the manager of a cost center is given the authority to make spending decisions—to acquire and use assets, subject to exogenously determined constraints on the quality and quantity of output—and is held responsible for minimizing costs. Note that, in contrast to other demand-revealing mechanisms, under responsibility budgeting an organization's financial liability will depend upon the costs actually incurred providing the service to the customer and not merely on its quantity or quality.

Under this control system design, the structure of authority and responsibility within the organization is of crucial interest to the management controller. The effectiveness of responsibility budgets depends on the elaboration of well-defined objectives, accurate and timely reporting of performance in terms of those objectives, and careful matching of spending authority and responsibility. Their effectiveness also depends on the clarity and transparency with which individual reward schedules are communicated to responsibility-center managers and the degree of competition between alternative management teams.

BEFORE-THE-FACT CONTROL SYSTEM DESIGNS

Before-the-fact management controls are demand-concealing mechanisms. Their distinguishing attribute is that they are executed before public money is spent. That is, they govern a service supplier's acquisition and use of both short term and long-term assets, which means that the controller retains the authority to preview these decisions. Examples of before-the-fact management control include object-of-expenditure appropriations—these govern the kind of assets that can be acquired by governmental departments and agencies: apportionments, position controls, and the fund and account controls that regulate the rate, timing, and purpose of public spending [2,34,35] and the similar rules and regulations that govern the behavior of private contractors [36,37].

Readers will recognize the combination of before-the-fact controls and individual responsibility in traditional governmental budgets. Most will also recognize the combination of before-the-fact controls and organizational responsibility in the so-called cost-plus contract—the most notorious member of the administered or flexible-price contract family.[10]

Traditional governmental budgets are basically spending plans. To distinguish them from responsibility budgets, I will use the term "outlay budgets." Under outlay budgets, supplying organizations are guaranteed an allotment of funds in return for providing a service for a stipulated period. They usually receive the allotment regardless of the actual quantity or quality of services provided.

Flexible-price contracts are basically production plans. They fully specify product or service characteristics and usually a delivery schedule. Under flexible-price contracts, supplying organizations are guaranteed reimbursement (complete or partial) for any legitimate expense incurred providing the service. Hence, the prices they are paid for providing services are determined retrospectively according to settled cost-accounting standards and the specifics of their contracts.

To say that controllers primarily focus their attention on a supplier's asset-acquisition decisions does not mean, however, that they ignore performance in executing outlay budgets or price in executing flexible contracts. Controllers usually take account of information about the future consequences of a supplier's decisions as well as information on its current and past behavior. Their attention to performance may be tacit, as it is in the execution of traditional line-item budgets, rather than express, as in the execution of performance, program, or zero-base budgets, but the consequences of asset-acquisition decisions usually matter a great deal to controllers. What is crucial is that, under these control systems designs, attention to the performance consequences of spending decisions is necessarily prospective in nature. Controllers will not reveal a demand schedule that fully expresses customer wants and preferences to suppliers or leave it to suppliers to figure out how best to satisfy those wants and preferences.

Even under before-the-fact control systems designs, the service provider, whether a department or an outside contractor, must assume some responsibility for managing output levels and delivery schedules, service quality, or price. Nevertheless, the logic of demand-concealing oversight requires supplier discretion to be carefully restricted. This means that suppliers must be subjected to fairly extensive, fairly detailed before-the-fact controls. A bureau's outlay budget, for example, should clearly identify all the asset acquisitions that it is to execute during the fiscal year, specify their magnitudes, and make it clear who is responsible for implementing each acquisition.

Of course, constraining managerial discretion is not the only function that before-the-fact controls perform. If it were, it would be hard to claim that they ever represented a least-objectionable alternative, let alone explain their widespread use. Rather, as I will explain, constraining managerial discretion is chiefly a means to an end, not an end in itself.

FLEXIBLE-PRICE CONTRACTS

There is a difference in the role that competition plays under fixed- and flexible-price contracts. The difference is not that it takes place before the production of the service in question. (Economists refer to such a competitive regime as competition for the market, to distinguish it from competition in the market.) The recipients of fixed-price contracts often receive exclusive franchises prior to the delivery of services.

The difference between the role played by competition under fixed- and flexible-price contracts is that, under flexible-price contracts, competition cannot be relied upon to keep prices low, let alone to enforce efficiency. Once a flexible-price contract has been signed, the supplier is free to dip into the customer's pocket. Because the supplier is spending somebody else's money, the normal incentives to cost-effectiveness largely disappear. Decisions that affect cost, service quality, or price (i.e., asset acquisition and use decisions) must be made during performance of the contract, but once the contract is signed, the supplier can no longer be fully trusted to make them. This conclusion holds especially where the customer ignores information regarding the performance of incumbent suppliers on earlier contracts or cannot (will not) promise to award future contracts based on good performance. Even where fixed-price contracts are concerned, the refusal to take past performance into account discourages supplier loyalty and eliminates any incentive to improve the quality of the product delivered [38].

Why, then, would a customer ever sign a flexible-price contract? Why not simply write fixed-price contracts? The answer is that a fixed-price contract *is* the mechanism of choice where controllers know precisely what their principals want, and several potential service suppliers know how to meet those preferences. Under those circumstances, service quality attributes offered, promised delivery schedules, and bid price allow us to evaluate proposals satisfactorily. Regrettably, these conditions are likely to obtain only where the service supplied is fairly simple and relatively standard—garbage collection, for example.

Technological Uncertainty and Financial Risk

In other cases, neither the controller nor the service supplier will have enough knowledge of the value of product attributes or production processes prior to performance of the contract to employ a fixed-price contract. It is a simple fact of life that considerable experience is usually required to manage to a narrow range of outcomes; where specialized or unique services are involved, no organization is likely to have the required experience. Consequently, any organization that agreed to produce a unique service, according to a specified schedule, at a fixed price would incur a large financial risk. This risk can be shifted, but it cannot be eliminated.

Government can often bear financial risks better than supplying organizations. This is the usual case where the federal government is concerned, because of the size of the assets it commands and its ability to pool risk. Consequently, the cost to government will often be lower if it assumes a portion of the risk associated with acquisition of the service.[11] Flexible or retrospective pricing is one way for government to assume this risk. Moreover, the preferences of the government may change during performance of a contract. Under a fixed-price contract, it might not be possible to secure desired changes in service attributes if they involve increased costs for the vendor.

My point is that customers should prefer flexible-price contracts to fixed-price contracts where it is cheaper for the customer to deal with uncertainty than it is for the contractor to do so or where the customer is more concerned with the ability of the contractor to provide a product that works than with price. The question is: Can before-the-fact controls be used to ensure that the seller retains an interest in cost effectiveness?

Using Before-the-Fact Controls to Enforce Efficiency Under Flexible-Price Contracts

Execution of a flexible-price contract begins with a fully specified project spending plan detailing work to be performed; personnel, material, and equipment to be used; input quality standards; and scheduled milestones. This plan provides a basis for the enforcement of efficiency through bargaining and negotiations carried on during the performance of the contract.

This process can be compared to a repeated prisoner's dilemma game, in which both parties have a common interest in reaching agreement but also have antagonistic interests with respect to the content of agreements. In this game, the customer tries to get as much as he can at a given price, and the supplier tries to get the highest possible price for providing the service [40]. Bargaining power in a prisoner's dilemma game depends on the information available to each party. In particular, the customer's power is greatest where the customer (or the customer's agent) knows the supplier's true cost schedule but can withhold full information as to his or her preference or demand schedule [41].[12] In a repeated game, the information available to the customer (or his agent) will depend upon his or her ability to control the sequence of moves and countermoves that comprise the game. Public choice theorists refer to this condition as agenda control [42].

Given comprehensive before-the-fact controls, under which changes can be made only with the prior approval of the other party or his or her agent, the party suggesting or initiating a change must necessarily reveal valuable information to the other. This can work to the advantage of the customer or the supplier, or both. For example, consider the following situation:

> [C]ontracts and specifications are drawn for . . . a ship and agreed to. . . . The contractor discovers he can do the welding of some plates less expensively by another means. About that time the client decides that some room on the ship should be larger. . . . The contractor can plead that he cannot easily change the room size; however, if the client will permit the altered welding, maybe a deal can be struck. [43, p. 132].

When flexible-price contrasts are appropriately employed, there is every reason to believe that most change proposals will be initiated by the service supplier. Competition for the market provides an incentive to potential service suppliers to promise more than they can deliver, because contracts are usually awarded to the service suppliers who promise the most. Consequently, very few contract winners can make good on all their promises, especially where their managerial discretion is severely restricted by a full set of before-the-fact controls. This fact will usually become evident to the service supplier during performance of the contract. The service supplier will also learn of the trade-offs between cost, service, quality, and delivery schedule available to it and will eventually want to (or in some cases have to) change promises or plans.

Under a full set of before-the-fact controls, such changes are contingent upon prior approval. To secure that approval, the service supplier must reveal information about its capabilities and tradeoff possibilities. As a result, power to enforce the preferences of the government may over time be passed to the purchasing officer, only if that officer knows what he or she is doing and how to make it happen.

OUTLAY BUDGETS

A similar logic [44] applies where outlay budgets have a comparative advantage—under decreasing costs to scale over an array of specialized or unique services. Outlay budgets can help to keep prices low and to encourage efficiency where large, lumpy investments in specialized resources are needed in order to provide services, where each problem, client, or task performed is in some sense unique and where the most serious problems are supposed to be dealt with first. Many organizational units in government have these attributes. They supply outputs that are heterogeneous, hard to define, and nearly impossible to measure. As a consequence,

> [s]uch bureaus seem always to be near the beginning or end of a comprehensive dismantling and restructuring since there is usually a sense that performance is not all that it might be. The performance of such bureaus can only be improved by budget augmentation. And, of course there are no guarantees in budget augmentation alone [45, p. 43].

Under outlay budgets, the control officer retains the authority to review all significant asset acquisition and use decisions. Presumably, therefore, the officer would like to know as much as possible about alternative choices and their consequences before the manager of an administrative unit decides or acts. That is, the controller would like the service supplier to reveal a comprehensive menu of all possible actions and a price list identifying the minimum cost of performing each action under every possible contingency. But wishes are not horses. There is no way to compel the manager of an administrative unit within an organization to reveal the unit's true production function—even if the manager knows what it is (and in most cases, he or she will not know).

Consequently, the controller must usually settle for a practical approximation of this ideal. Here too, the controller's authority provides a basis for the enforcement of efficiency through bargaining carried on during the execution of the budget. If the controller is skillful, plays his or her cards right, the principals' preferences may be approximated, if not fully satisfied. That is, over time, the manager may be able to compel the supplying organization to address the "most important" problems and to address these problems at a reasonable cost.

The more pressured the unit, the faster its movement. Here too, as with flexible contracts, the impetus for change must come from the operating manager. That is, the responsibility center manager must have an interest in increasing his or her budget. Otherwise, the manager will be indifferent to circumstances in which low-priority problems drain resources from problems that are of greater importance to his or her superiors or legislative sponsors. Furthermore, a full set of before-the-fact controls must be in place. At a minimum, this means that controllers must specify when, how, and where assets are to be employed and how much the subordinate can pay for them. In addition, money saved during the budget period from substituting less costly or more productive assets for more costly or less productive assets must revert to the treasury. Money lost in failed attempts to improve operations must be found elsewhere, and new initiatives requiring the acquisition of additional assets or reallocation of existing assets must be justified accordingly.

These constraints are necessary because they prevent the operating manager from overstating asset requirements in high priority areas to get resources for use elsewhere, thereby creating a precedent for higher levels of support in the lower priority area. They are also necessary to force the operating manager to seek authorization to make changes in spending plans and therefore, to reveal hidden preferences, capabilities, and tradeoff possibilities.

Where these conditions obtain, where a budget maximizer is subject to tight before-the-fact controls, the controller can enforce efficiency during the budget period by requiring affirmative answers to the following questions: Will a proposed change permit the same activity to be carried out at lower cost? Will higher priority activities be carried out at the same cost? Will the proposed asset acquisitions or reallocations of savings support activities that have lower priority than those presently carried out? When operating managers know and understand these criteria, the controllers will approve most changes in spending plans that the managers propose—because managers will propose only mutually advantageous changes.

Paradoxically, to say that before-the-fact controls are needed to reinforce the controller's bargaining power where outlay budgets are called for, does not mean that the controller must administer before-the-fact controls directly.[17] Under certain necessary and sufficient conditions, authority to spend money, transfer funds, and fill positions can be delegated to operating managers. The threat that direct controls might be reimposed can be sufficient to ensure that the operating managers ask the right questions of themselves and get the right answers to those questions before taking action, which should go a long way toward ensuring that the manager's behavior corresponds to the customer's preferences.

The necessary conditions are: reimposition of controls must be a credible threat; the gain to the operating manager from delegation must more than offset the associated sacrifice in bargaining power (the manager of an aging agency in the stable backwaters of public policy, for example, may have nothing to gain from relief from before-the-fact controls, if the price of such relief is a change in business as usual); and the controllers must be confident that their monitoring procedures, including postaudit, will identify violations of "trust."

The sufficient condition is that the controller and the operating manager trust each other.[14] Trust requires mutual respect and understanding and a common sense of commitment to a joint enterprise. In this context, its corollary is a willingness on the part of both the controller and the operating manager to eschew opportunistic behavior that would be costly to the long-term well-being of either the operating unit or the organization as a whole, including a willingness to forego opportunities to exploit events for personal advantage. Trust in a bargaining relationship can be poisoned by a single lapse of honesty or fair dealing; by contempt on the part of one of the parties for the abilities, judgment, or ethical standards of the other; by an excess of zeal or an overtly adversarial or confrontational approach; or by a simple lack of communication. In other words, the kind of trust that is needed to realize the best possible outcomes under a spending budget, or under a flexible-price contract for that matter, can be threatened by the very same conditions that threaten a business partnership or, more familiarly, a marriage.

All long-term buyer–seller relationships must ultimately rely on incentives, even those governed by outlay budgets and flexible-price contracts. As we have seen, the difference is that when these control system designs are employed, the incentives are deeply embedded in the process of budget or contract execution. Consequently, they are often overlooked. External observers fail to understand how they work; they also fail to understand how hard it is to make them work well. Effective execution of demand-concealing control system designs—flexible-price contracts as well as outlay budgets—requires a great deal of skill and savvy on the part of the controller. The skills required to execute demand-concealing control system designs properly are certainly far rarer and more remarkable than are those needed to design and execute after-the-fact controls, for which a modicum of technical expertise will suffice. It usually takes years of training and practical experience, combined with a lot of horse sense, to manage the complexities of bargaining in this context.

THE COSTS OF OVERCONTROL

All long-term buyer–seller relationships rely to a degree on standards and rules. Even, where government uses prospective price mechanisms to reimburse free-standing service providers, quality standards must often be specified and enforced. Demand-concealing control-system designs require considerably higher levels of reliance on before-the-fact controls and also on monitoring and enforcing compliance with them than do demand-revealing designs. At the very least, adoption of one of these control-system designs means that controllers must take steps to ensure that suppliers fairly and accurately recognize, record, and report their expenses. This, in turn, requires careful definition of costs and specification of appropriate account structures, bookkeeping practices and internal controls, direct costing procedures, and the criteria to be used in allocating overheads.

Accurate accounts will not guarantee efficiency. Even if, as is unlikely to be the case, the service supplier's financial and operational accounts completely and accurately present every relevant fact about the operating decisions made by its managers, they will not provide a basis for evaluating the soundness of those decisions. This is because cost accounts can show only what happened, not what might have happened. They cannot show the range of asset acquisition choices and trade-offs the supplier considered, let alone those that should have been considered but were not. As previously noted, under outlay budgets and flexible-price contracts, asset acquisition decisions must be made, but the supplier cannot be trusted to make them efficiently. Consequently, suppliers must be denied some discretion to make managerial decisions.

"How much" is a fundamental question; to what extent should government customers or their agents replace or duplicate the supplier's managerial efforts? It is necessary to pose this question because before-the-fact controls are costly, both in terms of out-of-pocket monitoring and reporting costs and in terms of opportunity costs—benefits lost owing to the customer's inability to exploit fully the supplier's managerial expertise. The government or its agent, the controller, will seldom be more competent to make asset acquisition decisions than the supplier. The answer to this fundamental question is obvious: the minimum necessary, given the motivations of the service suppliers and the incentives confronting them. Sometimes, "the minimum necessary" is a great deal indeed. How much depends on circumstances and the controller's skill in exploiting the opportunities that are created by the supplier's response to institutional constraints.

The problem of figuring out how much constraint is necessary is, perhaps, best expressed in terms of minimizing the sum of the costs that arise out of opportunistic behavior on the part of suppliers (that is, to use the language of public discourse, waste, fraud, and abuse) and the costs of control, both direct and indirect. Economic theory tells us that this optimum is to be found where the marginal costs of controls equal their marginal benefits [49].

The benefits produced by administrative controls are characterized by diminishing marginal returns. This is simply an abstract way of saying that controls that produce the greatest payoffs in terms of waste, fraud, and abuse avoided should be executed first. In contrast, the costs of control (the sum of direct and indirect cost of their execution) are characterized by increasing marginal costs. This assertion is, of course, debatable. So far, as I have been talking about the direct cost of controls—the out-of-pocket search, bargaining, monitoring, and enforcement costs that they impose on buyer and seller alike —it might be more reasonable to presume constant marginal costs. However, it seems to me that the indirect costs of control, those which take the form of stifled initiative, dulled incentives, and duplicative effort [50], do probably increase at an increasing rate as the quantity of controls is increased.

These claims indicate that it almost never makes sense to try to eliminate abuse entirely. If the sum of the costs of opportunistic behavior on the part of suppliers plus the direct and indirect costs of controlling their behavior is minimized, some abuse must remain simply because it would be dreadfully uneconomical to eliminate it.[15] The point is that controls contribute nothing of positive value; their singular purpose lies in helping us to avoid waste. To the extent that they do what they are supposed to do, they can generate substantial savings. It must be recognized, however, that they are themselves very costly.

WHAT DIFFERENCE DOES IT MAKE?

How much more efficient would government be if control-system designs were carefully tailored to circumstances? Unfortunately, I do not have an unambiguous answer for this question. According to the theory outlined here, both the ease of monitoring the consequences of operating decisions and the desirability of interorganizational competition matter. Most empirical studies overlook the distinction between the subject and the timing of controls. Hence, they do not actually relate the cost of supplying services to the choice of governance mechanism. Moreover, I would distinguish the costs of mismatching controls from the costs of overcontrol or micromanagement. The nasty consequences of micromanagement are far more frequently denounced than measured. Nevertheless, the evidence suggests that mismatched controls may add 5 to 20% to the real cost of supplying services—overcontrol can add far more.

Some of this evidence goes to the efficiency of privatizing various services, including custodial services and building maintenance, the operation of day-care centers, fire protection services, hospitals and health care services, housing, postal services, refuse collection, security services, ship and aircraft maintenance, wastewater treatment, water supply, and weather forecasting. Because these are common, homogeneous services that do not require large, lumpy investments in extraordinary assets—indeed, most have direct commercial counterparts—the logic outlined here indicates that they are appropriate candidates for a combination of organizational responsibility and after-the-fact control.

Not surprisingly, the evidence shows that shifting from individual responsibility and after-the-fact controls does reduce the cost of delivering these services. In his evaluation of the navy's commercial activities program, Paul Carrick [54] of the Naval Postgraduate School found that the introduction of competition reduced service cost in 80% of the cases studied, with average savings of nearly 40%—the greater the number of competitors, the greater the average savings. Carrick also found that navy teams won over one-third of the competitions carried out under the Office of Management and Budget Circular A-76, achieving productivity improvements of 13% on average. In these latter instances, the only significant change in governance relations was the shift from a demand-concealing to a demand-revealing control-system design, since the winning in-house teams were usually the incumbent suppliers.

In a second relevant study, Scott Masten, James Meehan, and Edward Snyder [51] carefully analyzed the determinants of control costs, holding production costs constant, in naval shipbuilding. Looking at 74 components (43 "make" items and 31 "buy" items, classified using benchmarks similar to those outlined here) they determined that control costs represented about 14% of total costs (about 13% for make components and 17% for buy components). They also determined that the proper choice of governance mechanism permitted control costs to be substantially reduced. Making the right decisions resulted in control costs that were a third less than if all components had been made internally and half what they would have been if all components had been contracted out.

Several analysts have found that, where appropriate, the substitution of after-the-fact for before-the-fact controls produces similar productivity gains. David J. Harr, for example, reports that replacing standard outlay budgets with responsibility budgets in Defense Logistics Agency depots was associated with efficiency increases of 10 to 25% [52, p. 36; 53, pp. 68–69]. Other analysts make even stronger claims about the significance of the nature and timing of controls. Gordon Chase, for example, asserts that "wherever the product of a public organization has not been monitored in a way that ties performance to reward, the introduction of an effective monitoring system will yield a 50 percent improvement in the product in the short run." [55, p. 16]. Productivity increases of this size are not, in fact, unheard of. One frequently cited example of such an increase is the central repair garage of the New York Sanitation Department, which replaced its standard municipal outlay budget with a well-designed responsibility budget. Robert Anthony claims that this reform increased productivity by nearly 70%—from a high of 143% in the machine repair center to a low of 19% in the motor room [5, pp. 356–357].

William Turcotte's classic matched comparison of two state liquor agencies reports even larger productivity differences caused by the substitution of after-the-fact for before-the-fact controls [56]. The organizations studied by Turcotte ran sizable statewide programs featuring large numbers of local retail sales outlets. Furthermore, both defined their missions in identical terms—maximization of profits from the sale of alcoholic beverages to the public. According to the theory outlined here, this situation called for the use of a rather simple, straightforward responsibility budget to govern local retail sales outlets. One of the states (Turcotte refers to it as state B) did in fact adopt this approach to governance—treating each outlet as a profit center, holding the outlet's manager responsible for meeting a profit target and granting the operational discretion needed to meet it. The other state (Turcotte refers to it as state A) relied on standard outlay budgets and a comprehensive set of before-the-fact controls. Turcotte reports that one consequence of the difference in the control strategies used by the two states is that direct control costs were 20 times higher in state A than in state B. The indirect costs of control were somewhat less disproportionate but absolutely far greater in state A than in state B. Furthermore, individual stores in state B were twice as productive as stores in state A. Operating expenses for each dollar of sales in state A were 150% higher than in state B, administrative expenses were 300% higher, and inventory costs 400% higher.

However, both Anthony and Turcotte appear to conflate the choice of governance arrangements with their intensity. New York's garages and state A's liquor stores were subject not only to the wrong kinds of controls but probably also to an excess of controls. One of the more melancholy properties of before-the-fact controls is their propensity to proliferate—excess controls cause failures, which leads to more controls and then more failure. I would not be surprised if two-thirds of the productivity differences reported here were due to overcontrol.

The evidence also shows some goods are unworthy candidates for after-the-fact controls. The case that has been given the greatest amount of attention by industrial-organization economists is where customers artificially maintain vital suppliers where a single supplier could more efficiently supply the entire market [57]. There is, however, a more interesting case. Consider what can happen when rivals are invited to bid on a fixed-price contract to supply an advanced and, therefore, highly risky or uncertain technology. They will likely respond to such an invitation in one of two ways:

1. If they bid at all, they will bid high to protect themselves against the risk of failure. This means that the price of the service to the customer will be excessively high; or, even worse,

2. One or more of the bidders will underestimate the difficulty of the contract (or overestimate his or her capacity to meet its terms). He or she will often be the low bidder, of course, and win the contract. If the low bidder is not very lucky, the victory will be a curse. When he or she fails to deliver, as mostly happens, or threatens to slide into bankruptcy, the customer may have to step in to rescue project and, in some cases, the contractor as well.

Alas, open-bidding contests tend to select suppliers for their optimism (or their desperation), since the bidder with the most optimistic view of a project's feasibility will usually win the contract. Unfortunately, the most optimistic (or most desperate) bidder is unlikely to have the best understanding of the contract's technical feasibility and may overestimate its feasibility precisely because of his or her incompetence to carry it out! This likelihood probably does not matter very much where all of the bidders have the experience needed to manage to a narrow range of outcomes. In that case, either comparative advantage will trump optimism or, if not, the advantage will usually be borderline. This likelihood is crucial where bidders lack the experience needed to manage to a narrow range of outcomes—as will usually be the case where advanced and, therefore, highly risky technologies are concerned.

Indeed, where a product or service is highly specialized, a single organization is often uniquely qualified to produce it. Identifying the right supplier is, therefore, frequently the key to getting the best product on time and at a reasonable price. In the private sector, this process is often fairly informal. Firms tend to rely on experience and reputation to pick suppliers. A decision to invite a proposal is usually tantamount to a promise to do business. Proposals are more often than not jointly developed.

In the public sector, the process tends to be more formal. Potential suppliers must appear on a list of qualified vendors. Customers must usually request proposals from more than one organization. Requests for proposals (RFP) are supposed to provide detailed explanations of what proposals should include and how they will be evaluated. Evaluations tend to be highly ritualized, with each section of a proposal assigned an explicit numerical score and its overall evaluation based upon the weighted sum of these scores. Only after evaluators have identified the best proposal will the government's representatives engage in *ex parte* conversations with the vendor to work out contractual details and nail down a best and final offer.

Nevertheless, these processes have similar aims and, I believe, more often than not produce similar outcomes.[16] Doubtless, these sham battles are wasteful and add to the costs of executing before-the-fact controls, but the waste is less than when the contract is awarded solely on the basis of price and the winning contractor turns out to be incompetent.

Unfortunately, this happens sometimes. It is generally acknowledged, for example, that the worst defense procurement fiasco in recent memory, Lockheed's default on the C-5A program and the subsequent Department of Defense bailout, occurred because Lockheed misread the difficulty of designing and building the C-5A. Consequently, Lockheed submitted a bid on a fixed-price, total-package procurement contract to design and deliver 150 C-5s that was 50% less than Boeing's, the next highest bid. Evidently, even if Lockheed had known what it was doing, which as it turned out it did not, its bid would have been half-again too low. By the time the Department of Defense and Lockheed discovered the magnitude of their error, they were in too deep to get out [59, pp. 107–117]. Something similar happened recently with the navy's A-12 program. Fortunately, when the A-12 development team got into trouble, the Department of Defense decided the A-12 was expendable and canceled the contract, thereby avoiding the worst aspects of the C-5A case. Nevertheless, this was evidently a near-run thing. In the mid-1980s, Boeing took a bath on a series of fixed-price development contracts that it sought and won despite lack of expertise. Again, fortunately for Boeing and ultimately for the taxpayer, Boeing's civilian profits were sufficient to make good its military losses.

The lesson suggested by the example of the C-5A is that the total costs arising from mismatched controls are asymmetrical in their composition: if other things were equal, it would probably be far more prohibitive to rely on after-the-fact controls where before-the-fact controls are called for than vice versa. This lesson is reinforced by Masten, Meehan, and Snyder's finding [51] that although making "buy" components would have caused control costs to be about 70% higher than they actually were, contracting out "make" items would have caused control costs to increase even more—nearly 200%, from 13% of the total value of the items to over 30%! But other things are not all equal. Not only are after-the-fact controls easier to use, they are also self-limiting. Where the purchaser relies on demand-revealing controls, overcontrol produces negative feedback in the form of higher prices or reduced output that causes controls to be cut back. Before-the-fact controls often produce positive feedback that leads to their multiplication. Hence, their costs are subject to no natural limits.

Carrying Legitimate and Necessary Controls to Self-Defeating Extremes

Organization theorists have long understood that failure induces certain predictable responses and that these responses, in turn, produce certain equally predictable consequences. Pradip N. Khandwalla [60], for example, observes that threatening situations always generate pressures for direct controls: standardization of procedures, institution of rules and regulations, and centralization of authority. Michael Crozier [61] argues that failures to meet expectations almost inevitably produce a cycle of rule making, more failure, and then more rules. Anthony and Young [5] claim that detailed rules result from encrustation: An abuse occurs, someone decides that "there ought to be a law," and a rule is promulgated to avoid the abuse in the future; but such rules often continue after the need for them has passed. No one who has the power to rescind the rule may ever consider "whether the likelihood and seriousness of error is great enough to warrant continuation of the rule" (p. 562). Jack H. Knott and Gary J. Miller [62] observe that stricter rules and tighter oversight often produces positive short-term results, but that they also exacerbate the factors that cause organizational failure. Furthermore, extra supervisors giving more orders and monitoring effort more closely may make subordinates "even more resentful of their status than before, which may make subordinates even more unwilling to trust or cooperate with management. Which leads to more stringent rules, greater reliance on hierarchy, and more hostility on the part of subordinates and on and on" (p. 257). Robert Merton [63; also Marcus, 50] concludes that reliance on rules and regulations reflects a concern with error prevention, and an emphasis on error prevention, rather than measured performance, tends to result in organizational rigidity and ultimately total ineffectiveness.

In other words, the inclination to respond to abuses with calls for more and better rules is normal, as is responding to repeated failure with calls for ever more inflexible and comprehensive rules, greater oversight, and closer supervision.

The propensity to devise inflexible and comprehensive rules is, perhaps, nowhere more irresistible than where military procurement is concerned. Consequently, military procurement generates more than 250 million hours of paperwork a year, 90% of the federal government's procurement paperwork [64, p. 153], and the Department of Defense employs 100,000 men and women, uniformed and civilian, and spends between 5 and 10 billion dollars each year to buy (not to pay for) the weapons, materials, and supplies it uses. Nearly 50,000 of these employees (including 26,000 auditors) are paid to monitor and enforce compliance with before-the-fact controls. As an example of this propensity to devise inflexible and comprehensive standards, consider the MIL-F-1499 (fruitcake), 250 tons of which were recently purchased by the army. To preclude abuses on the part of unscrupulous bakers, to make sure some candied fruits and nuts really were in the fruitcake, to guarantee adequate shelf-life and resistance to handling, and to insure palatability in all the far-flung places of the world where the American Army celebrates Christmas, the specifications for the MIL-F-1499 (fruitcake) were 18 pages long. Plastic whistles take 16 pages of specifications; olives, 17; hot chocolate, 20; chewing gum, 15; condoms, 13; and so on [65, pp. 126–127].

This level of detail may be ludicrous, but it is not evidence of overcontrol. Evidence of overcontrol requires information on the benefits as well as the costs of control.[17] What about the benefits of control? Well, one agency, the Defense Contract Audit Agency, proudly claims that it saved the American taxpayer about $7 billion in 1988 and cost only $1 billion. Its criminal investigations generated an additional $300 million in fines and penalties and cost only $84 million [66, p. 368]. This sounds like a pretty good deal, even if one allows for the source of the claims. However, it is a generally accepted rule of thumb that monitoring and enforcing regulations imposes private costs of about $20 for every dollar spent by the government [67]. Because these costs are ultimately borne primarily by the regulated firm's customers and because in this instance the customer is the Department of Defense, this multiplier implies that Defense Contract Audit Agency regulation imposed costs of $21 billion to save $7 billion, in the first instance, and $1.76 billion to save $300 million in the second—in other words, it cost an average of $3 and $6, respectively, to save $1, which is consistent with marginal costs of $6 and $12! Evidence that marginal costs are greater than marginal benefits, let alone 12 times greater, is prima facie evidence of overcontrol.[18]

There is also evidence that the marginal benefits produced by some before-the-fact controls are actually negative. Alfred A. Marcus, for example, shows that increasing the number of safety rules governing the operation of nuclear power plants, together with greater oversight and closer supervision, actually had the effect of degrading reactor safety [50]. Anecdotal evidence suggests that this is often the case where procurement is concerned, especially where demand-concealing governance mechanisms are called for, but where a plethora of rules deny the controller the authority to trade off costs, schedules, and performance [64].

Finally, excessive reliance on rules often produces organizations that are simultaneously overcontrolled and out of control. Turcotte [56, p. 69], for example, found that the managers of retail stores in state A were subject to may more rules and far stricter executive and legislative oversight than their counterparts in state B, but, even so, were far less responsive to the wishes of their political masters. Evidently, the managers of retail stores in state A were subject to so many rules that none of them mattered very much. Consequently, overcontrol led straightaway to loss of control.

CONCLUSION

Steven Kelman [68, p. 196] argues that one reason for government's excessive reliance on before-the-fact controls is an intellectual failure to understand their high costs, especially the cost they exact in terms of mission performance.[19] If Kelman is correct, then the situation is happy indeed. Intellectual failures are fairly easy to fix. Kelman's diagnosis is also an indictment of many of us in public administration. It implies that in our research, our literature, and our teaching we have failed to show the need for alternatives to traditional controls. The simple fact is that we have not developed governance mechanisms—especially fresh and innovative administrative controls—to match contemporary government's tactics and responsibilities. Many do not even understand that this task should be central to our enterprise.

Fortunately, public administration is changing, albeit slowly. Most students of public administration have accepted Mosher's challenge to look outward more, inward less—to understand a wide variety of institutional arrangements: regulation, incentives in the form of loans and taxes, contracting, and quasi-governmental enterprises. Despite their efforts, however, much of our knowledge remains equivocal. What is the reason for our uncertain progress? Since we have a satisfactory framework for institutional analysis, I believe that it is due largely to an inability to look beyond superficial institutional dissimilarities to their common structural elements—an inability to see that the entire spectrum of institutional arrangements is put together from a common set of materials and that, to design effective institutions, the materials used must fit together harmoniously. This chapter neither promises nor provides a complete answer to the question of how institutions should be put together, let alone a complete parts list. It is, I hope, a step in the right direction.

NOTES

Thanks are owed to several excellent anonymous referees, whose comments materially improved this article, and to my friends and colleagues, G. Marc Choate, Don Homuth, Steven Maser, Aidan Vining, and Aaron Wildavsky for their encouragement and valuable suggestions. Special thanks to my collaborators, L. R. Jones, Naval Postgraduate School, and William M. Zumeta, University of Washington, whose ideas and even words I have shamelessly borrowed. Whatever merits this chapter might have is due in no small measure to their contributions.

1. Several readers have objected to the term "management control," reminding me that managing and controlling are definitely not the same activity [3]. Consequently, I considered using other terms for the organizing concept of this chapter: direction, governance, and, especially, accountability. These seemed too broad for my purposes, however. For example, the entire discipline of accounting is concerned with the functioning of accountability relationships [4, p. ix]; the branch of accounting that is concerned with influencing subordinate behavior is management (or administrative) control [5]. The field of management control like some main currents of public administration traces its intellectual lineage through Chester I. Barnard [6] back to Mary Parker Follett's rule of anticipated reactions [7,8]. Hence, this chapter joins in a debate present at the creation of PAR. I align myself here with Follett's disciples, such as C. J. Friedrich, who believed that "no mere reliance on some traditional device can be counted upon to render the vast public services of a modern government responsible, responsibility will remain fragmentary because of the indistinct voice of the principal whose (expert) agents the officials are supposed to be" [9, p. 20] and against those like Herman Finer [10], who placed full confidence in rule-bound governance mechanisms, which is consistent with the thrust of Martin Landau's seminal works, albeit not his terminology [11,12].

2. Normal goods have continuous and twice-differentiable supply schedules. In contrast, supply of a lumpy good is discrete, perhaps even a single point on the supply schedule. An appendectomy illustrates the concept of lumpiness. A second appendectomy would be useless; half an appendectomy, worse than useless [13].

3. In this chapter, I use the terms transaction cost and control cost interchangeably. Frankly, I prefer the latter. Controls have costs even where transactions fail to occur. The rules governing the disposition of federal lands to private commercial interests provide an example. These rules were intended to protect the public patrimony by making it impossible for corrupt or fraudulent real-estate speculators to profit at the public's expense. They have been proficient in carrying out their purpose. Furthermore, they have done so with little or no direct compliance costs, either to government or to business. This is the case because they are so sweeping that they have prevented almost all transfers of public property to private owners. Consequently, the federal government has not expended resources negotiating property transfers or in monitoring and enforcing compliance with the rules governing these transactions. Neither have business expended resources to comply with these rules.

   However, the failure to transfer federal property to private owners has given rise to substantial indirect or opportunity costs. For example, it is well known that the United States military base structure is millions of acres too large. Yet the rules governing the disposition of federal lands has prevented the transfer of defense facilities to better or higher private uses. Opportunity costs are always somewhat conjectural, but, in this case, they are unquestionably large. It has been estimated that the 5% of the existing military base structure with the highest market value would be worth at least $35 billion and perhaps as much as $90 billion in their best alternative economic uses [15].

   Those who wish to understand better the relevance of transaction cost economics to public administration should see Maser [16], Vining and Weimer [17], and Ferris and Graddy [18], as well as Friedman [19] and Borcherding [20].

4. Vertical integration is, of course, only one way to deal with asset specificity. Some firms invest in specialized resources and own design-specific assets, which they provide to their suppliers. This is called quasivertical integration. It is common in both the automobile and the aerospace industries, and, of course, it is standard procedure for the Department of Defense to provide and own the equipment, dies, and designs that defense firms use to supply it with weapons systems and the like [21]. Other firms that rely on a small number of suppliers or a small number of distributors write contracts that constrain the opportunistic behavior of those with whom they deal. A well-executed contract can approximate the outcome from vertical integration (although such contracts are often very hard to write and, where one of the parties is inclined to exploit the other, prohibitively costly to enforce) without incurring the very real costs of vertical integration. In other cases, desired outcomes can be realized through alliances based on the exchange of hostages (e.g., surety bonds, exchange of debt or equity positions) or just plain old-fashioned trust based on long-term mutual dependence. In Japan, for example, buyer–seller relationships tend to be based on mutual confidence. Toyota relies on a few suppliers that it nurtures and supports. It maintains tight working links between its manufacturing and engineering departments and its suppliers and explicitly eschews opportunistic behavior in the interest of maintaining long-term relationships [22].

    Nevertheless, in one study of vertical integration in the U.S. aerospace industry, Scott Masten [23] unambiguously demonstrated that asset specificity and, therefore, decreasing cost is basic to the make-or-buy decision. Where intermediate products were both complex and highly specialized (used only by the buyer), there was a 92% probability that it would be produced internally; even 31% of all simple, specialized components were produced internally. The probability dropped to less than 2% if the component was not specialized, regardless of its complexity.

5. There is an alternative point of view: political authorities, especially legislators, know exactly what they are doing. They favor administrative controls that are ineffective by design. Friends of this view claim that legislators shun serious policy control and, instead, seek "particularized" control. According to Terry M. Moe [25, p. 140; 26], this perspective's most eloquent booster, legislators "want to be able to intervene quickly, inexpensively, and in ad hoc ways to protect or advance the interests of particular clients in particular matters." Detailed rules that impose rigid limits on an agency's discretion and its procedures help to satisfy this appetite. Moe's logic implies that detailed object-of-expenditure budgets exist, for example, not for historical reasons, but because they are ideally suited to the needs of momentary governing coalitions, which are likely to be far more concerned with who gets public money and where it goes, than with what it buys for the public at large. Perhaps, but I am not convinced—that, however, is another story [15,27].

6. Moreover, many of those who believe in the potency of before-the-fact controls fail to understand that moral authority is all too easily eroded by an oversupply of rules. Moral authority, respect for the law, the inclination to obey rules are of critical importance to the stability and the efficacy of social arrangements. I believe that they are far too important to be frittered away where other mechanisms of social control will suffice. Rather, they ought to be carefully husbanded so that they will be available when and where they are really needed [28].

7. Under a fixed-price contract, the price to the customer should not be affected by the supplier's actual costs of providing a service; under a flexible-price contract, those costs are shared with the customer. The limit is reached in the case of a cost-plus fixed-fee contract, where the customer assumes full responsibility for all legitimate, measured costs.

8. In practice, these price schedules entail all sorts of complex arrangements, including rate, volume, and mix adjustments, as well as inflation adjustments and sometimes default penalties.

9. In the public sector, responsibility budgeting is often called output budgeting. I prefer the former term because it is more widely used in the American management-control literature and also to distinguish it from output-oriented approaches to budget formulation (as opposed to budget

execution, which is the focus of administrative control), such as performance budgeting, PPBS, and ZBB. Examples of governments that have experimented with responsibility budgeting as the term is used here include New Zealand [31,32] and the City of Fairfield, California [33].

10. I generally prefer the term "flexible-price contract," because I am concerned primarily with distinguishing these contracts from fixed-price contracts. Flexible-price contracts comprehend a variety of incentive and cost-sharing contract designs as well as the classic cost-plus contract. In turn, flexible-price contracts are included in the broader category of administered contracts [36].

11. The indifference of government to financial risk is easily exaggerated. Government is not immune to financial risk, otherwise it would never make economic sense for it to rely on outlay budgets [39, p. 503]. Moreover, while it may be true that doing business with government is risky, the risk is mostly unsystematic, and may, therefore, be diversified away. This is especially the case with respect to major defense contractors, whose financial statistics typically exhibit two distinctive characteristics: low price-earnings ratios and even lower betas. According to the capital-asset pricing model, such firms should be far less averse to financial uncertainty than average.

12. This is simply a more formal way of saying that strategic advantage accrues to the party that can best look ahead and reason back. To do so, one must be able to put oneself squarely in the other party's shoes (i.e., one must know the other party's costs under a variety of contingencies). This is one purpose of "should-cost" models. It is also one of the purposes behind selecting agents who have walked in the other party's shoes (promoting trust is another)—purchasing agents in manufacturing plants, for example, are usually recruited from the ranks of industrial salespeople and process engineers and vice versa. The federal government's revolving-door laws enjoin this kind of personnel exchange, however. These laws probably increase the government's power to set an agenda but undoubtedly reduce its ability to understand or use the information which that power confers.

13. This is obviously also the case where flexible-contracts are appropriate. For example, the Department of Defense has a program that designates exemplary production facilities and exempts them from direct oversight.

14. Of course, these conditions also apply where contractual relationships are concerned. According the nearly legendary original manager of Lockheed's Skunk Works, Clarence "Kelly" Johnson, there are 14 rules for running a successful systems-development project, including complete control of the program, small military project offices, specifications agreed to in advance, timely funding, and minimal inspections and reports, but the most important is "mutual trust between the military project officer and the contractor" [46, p. 28]. The significance of trust in bilateral organizational relationships is brilliantly outlined by A. Breton and R. Wintrobe [47]; see also the insightful discussion of these issues by W. T. Gormley [48].

15. See also Williamson [14]; Williamson largely ignores, however, the particular institutional arrangements, including those outlined here, that actually drive costs; see Masten, Meehan and Snyder [51], Harr [52], and Harr and Godfrey [53].

16. Where the customer is authorized to use RPF rather than ITB procedures, the formality described here is probably more apparent than real. Indeed, where a single supplier has an acknowledged technological lead, the law permits the request of a single proposal and a sole-source contract. Even where that is not the case, the purchasing officer probably has a pretty good idea of the identity of the most qualified supplier. The RFP cannot but reflect the purchasing officer's subjective judgments about the importance of various product attributes and the competence of alternative vendors to deliver on their promises. The formality with which proposals are evaluated also serves to insulate him or her from the consequences of choice and, therefore, to protect him or her from the complaints of rebuffed vendors—this is especially important when, as happens in the best of circumstance, things go wrong.

I sympathize with procedures that work to minimize criticism and keep hard-working contracting officers out of trouble. Unfortunately, there is a tendency for the RFP process to swell out of control, particularly where major projects are concerned. These RFPs tend to be very detailed; in response, proposals expand to carload size, and armies of evaluators are needed to score them. This is clearly wasteful. It is also unnecessary. The RFP for the LWF program—the fighter that became the F-16—was only 25 pages long [58, p. 77].

17. The Department of Defense paid $1.50 a pound for the fruitcake, about half the price in civilian markets [66, p. 360].

18. These estimates may seem high, but they are trivial compared to those claimed by William H. Gregory [59, p. 3]. According to Gregory, overcontrol—he uses the term micromanagement, defined as the extension of legitimate and necessary supervision to a self-defeating extreme—increases the cost of military hardware by at least a third and, in some cases, more than doubles it. Unfortunately, he does not explain how he arrived at this conclusion, let alone document it.

19. A great deal of attention has been paid to the congressional predisposition to overcontrol (in this vein, one of the very best analyses remains Ackerman and Hassler [69]. Indeed, the belief that the best way to attack an abuse or to do good is to make a rule prohibiting or requiring some behavior seems to be especially robust on Capitol Hill, perhaps because so many of its denizens are lawyers, who are accustomed by training and professional experience to dealing in mandates. Nevertheless, while I do not deny that Congress too often fails to consider alternatives to before-the-fact controls or that its concern with the details of administration often leads to overcontrol, I would also stress that Congress is not alone in this. These are recurring problems in most organizations. Superiors are nearly everywhere more confident of their own competence than they are of their subordinates'. Most are also far more cognizant of their own decision-making abilities, responsibilities, and prerogatives than they are of their ignorance of the nitty-gritty ramifications of their choices or of the massive paperwork burden that management by fiat imposes upon an organization. One of the major aims of managerial training is overcoming this bias. I hope this chapter will be read in that spirit and not simply as another case of Congress bashing.

REFERENCES

1. F. C. Mosher, "The Changing Responsibilities and Tactics of the Federal Government," *Public Admin. Rev. 40*(November–December):540–547 (1980).

2. A. Schick, "Contemporary Problems in Financial Control," *Public Admin. Rev. 38*(November–December):513–519 (1978).

3. M. Landau and R. Stout, "To Manage Is Not To Control," *Public Admin. Rev. 39*(March–April): 148–156 (1979).

4. Y. Ijiri, *Theory of Accounting Measurement,* Studies in Accounting Research no. 10, American Accounting Association, Sarasota, Fla. (1975).

5. R. N. Anthony and D. Young, *Management Control in Nonprofit Organizations,* 4th ed., Irwin, Homewood, Ill. (1988).

6. C. I. Barnard, *The Functions of the Executive,* Harvard University Press, Cambridge, Mass. (1938).

7. M. P. Follett, "The Psychology of Control," *Psychological Foundations of Business Administration* (H. C. Metcalf, ed.), McGraw-Hill, New York, pp. 148–174 (1927).

8. M. P. Follett, "Control as a Process," *Papers on the Science of Administration,* (Luther Gulick and L. Urwick, eds.), Institute of Public Administration, New York, pp. 159–170 (1937).

9. C. J. Friedrich, "Public Policy and the Nature of Administrative Responsibility." *Public Policy, 1*:3–20 (1940).

10. H. Finer, "Adminstrative Responsibilityin Democratic Government," *Public Admin. Rev. 3*(October):339–347 (1941).

11. M. Landau, "Redundancy, Rationality, and the Problems of Duplication and Overlap," *Public Admin. Rev. 29*(July–August):346–358 (1969).

12. M. Landau, "On the Concept of a Self-Correcting Organization," *Public Admin. Rev. 33*(November–December):533–542 (1973).

13. F. Thompson, "Lumpy Goods and Cheap Riders," *J. Public Policy,* 7(December):427–445 (1987).

14. O. E. Williamson, *The Economic Institutions of Capitalism,* Free Press, New York (1985).

15. F. Thompson, "Why America's Military Base Structure Can't be Reduced." *Public Admin. Rev.* 48(January–February):57–63 (1988).

16. S. M. Maser, "Transaction Costs in Public Administration," In *Bureaucratic and Governmental Reform,* (Donald Calista, ed.), JAI Press, Greenwich, Conn., pp. 55–72 (1986).

17. A. R. Vining and D. L. Weimer, "Government Supply and Government Production Failure: A Framework Based on Contestability," *J Public Policy,* 10(March–April):54–90 (1990).

18. J. M. Ferris and E. Graddy, "Production Costs, Transaction Costs, and Local Government Contractor Choice," *Econ. Inquiry, 19*(Summer):541–554 (1991).

19. L. S. Friedman, "Public Institutional Structure and Resource Allocation: The Analysis of Adjustment," *Res. Public Policy Anal. Manage.* 2:303–325 (1981).

20. T. E. Borcherding, "Some Revisionist Thoughts on the Theory of Public Bureaucracy," *Eur. J. Polit. Econ.* 4:47–64 (1988).

21. K. Monteverde and D. J. Teece, "Appropriable Rents and Quasi-Vertical Integration," *J. Law Econ.* 25:403–418 (1982).

22. Anonymous, "A Guide to Better Buying," *Economist,* October 18:71 (1986).

23. S. E. Masten, "The Organization of Production," *J. Law Econ.* 27:403–417 (1984).

24. G. Blumenstyk, "Fla. Bill Offers Campuses Fiscal Autonomy in Return for Accountability," *Chron. Higher Ed.,* April 24:A22 (1991).

25. T. M. Moe, "The Politics of Structural Choice: Toward a Theory of Public Bureaucracy," *Organization Theory: From Chester Barnard to the Present and Beyond,* (O. E. Williamson, ed.), Oxford University Press, New York (1990).

26. T. M. Moe, "The Politics of Bureaucratic Structure," *Can the Government Govern?* (J. E. Chubb and Paul E. Peterson, eds.), Brookings Institution, Washington, D.C. (1989).

27. L. R. Jones and F. Thompson, "Reforming Regulatory Decision Making: The Regulatory Budget," *Sloan Manage. Rev.* 22(Summer):53–61 (1981).

28. T. R. Tyler, *Why People Obey the Law,* Yale University Press, New Haven, Conn. (1990).

29. L. R. Jones, F. Thompson, and W. M. Zumeta, "The Logic of Budget Execution," *Econ. Ed. Rev.* 6(Spring):44–53 (1986).

30. F. Thompson, "Management Control and the Pentagon: The Strategy-Structure Mismatch," *Public Admin. Rev.* 51(January–February):52–66 (1991).

31. A. Schick, "Budgeting for Results: Recent Developments in Five Industrialized Countries," *Public Admin. Rev. 50*:(January/February):16–33 (1990).

32. F. Goldman and E. Brashares, "Performance and Accountability: Budget Reform in New Zealand," *Public Budgeting and Finance, 11*(Winter):75–85 (1991).

33. C. J. Bellone, "Public Entrepreneurship: New Roles for Local Government," *Urban Anal. Public Manage. 10*(March):71–86 (1988).

34. B. T. Pitsvada, "Flexibility in Federal Budget Execution," *Public Budgeting and Finance, 3*(Spring):17–26 (1983).

35. A. Schick, "Control Patterns in State Budget Execution," *Public Admin. Rev. 24*(June):97–106 (1964).

36. V. Goldberg, "Regulation and Administered Contracts," *Bell J. Econ. 7*(Fall):426–428 (1976).

37. W. E. Kovacic, "The Sorcerer's Apprentice: Public Regulation of the Acquisitions Process," *Arms, Politics, and the Economy,* (R. Higgs, ed.), Holmes & Meier, New York, pp. 104–131 (1990).

38. S. Kelman, *Procurement and Public Management,* AEI Press, Washington, D.C. (1990).

39. D. W. Carlton and J. M. Perloff, *Modern Industrial Organization,* Scott, Foresman-Little, Brown, Glenview, Ill. (1990).

40. G. H. Hofstede, *The Game of Budget Control,* Van Gorcum, Amsterdam (1967).

41. J. Morgan, "Bilateral Monopoly and the Competitive Output," *Q. J. Econ. 63*:370–381 (1949).

42. T. H. Hammond, "Agenda Control, Organizational Structure, and Bureaucratic Politics," *Am. J. Polit. Sci. 30*(May):379–420 (1986).
43. R. Stark and T. Varley, "Bidding, Estimating, and Engineered Construction Contracting," In *Auctions, Bidding, and Contracting* (R. Engelbrecht-Wiggens, et al., eds.), New York University Press, New York, pp. 121–135 (1983).
44. A. Wildavsky and A. Hammond, "Comprehensive vs. Incremental Budgeting in the Department of Agriculture," *Admin. Sci. Q., 10*:321–346 (1965).
45. F. Thompson and W. M. Zumeta, "Control and Controls: A Reexamination of Control Patterns in Budget Execution," *Policy Sci., 13*:25–50 (1981).
46. J. Kitfield, "Black Programs: Too Big to Hide?" *Military Forum, 26*(April):21–28 (1989).
47. A. Breton and R. Wintrobe, *The Logic of Bureaucratic Conduct,* Cambridge University Press, New York (1982).
48. W. T. Gormley, *Taming the Bureaucracy: Muscles, Prayers, and other Strategies,* Princeton Univerity Press, N.J. (1989).
49. A. Breton and R. Wintrobe, "The Equilibrium Size of a Budget-Maximizing Bureau," *J. Polit. Econ. 83*:195–207 (1975).
50. A. A. Marcus, "Responses to Externally Induced Innovation: Their Effects on Organizational Performance," *Strategic Manage. J. 9*(Winter):387–402 (1988).
51. S. E. Masten, J. W. Meehan, and E. A. Snyder, "The Costs of Organization," *J. Law Econ. Organization, 7*(1):1–25 (1991).
52. D. J. Harr, "How Activity Accounting Works in Government," *Management Accounting, 72*: (September):36–40 (1990).
53. D. J. Harr and J. T. Godfrey, *Private Sector Financial Performance Measures and Their Applicability to Government Operations,* National Association of Accountants, Montvale, N.J. (1991).
54. P. M. Carrick, "New Evidence on Government Efficiency," *J. Policy Anal. Manage. 7*(Spring): 518–528 (1988).
55. G. T. Allison, Jr., "Public and Private Management: Are They Fundamentally Alike in All Unimportant Particulars?" *Readings in Public Administration,* (R. T. Golembiewski and Frank Gibson, eds.), 4th ed. Houghton MIfflin, Boston, pp. 1–19 (1983).
56. W. A. Turcotte, "Control Systems, Performance, and Satisfaction in Two State Agencies," *Admin. Sci. Q. 19*(March):60–73 (1974).
57. J. J. Anton and D. A. Yao, "Measuring the Effectiveness of Competition in Defense Procurement," *J. Policy Anal. Manage. 9*(Fall):60–79 (1990).
58. J. McNaugher, *New Weapons Old Politics,* Brookings Institution, Washington, D.C. (1989).
59. W.H. Gregory, *The Defense Procurement Mess,* Lexington Books for the Twentieth Century Fund, Lexington, Mass. (1989).
60. P. N. Khandwalla, "Crisis Responses of Competing versus Noncompeting Organizations," *Studies on Crisis Management* (C. Smart and W. T. Stanbury, eds.), Institute for Research on Public Policy, Montreal, pp. 147–174 (1978).
61. M. Crozier, *The Bureaucratic Phenomenon,* University of Chicago Press, Chicago (1964).
62. J. H. Knott and G. J. Miller, *Reforming Bureaucracy: The Politics of Instutional Choice,* Prentice-Hall, Englewood Cliffs, N.J. (1987).
63. R. Menton, *Social Theory and Social Structure,* Free Press, New York (1957).
64. M. L. Weidenbaum, *Small Wars, Big Defense: Paying for the Military after the Cold War,* Oxford University Press, New York (1992).
65. K. Adelman and N. Augustine, *The Defense Revolution,* ICS Press, San Francisco (1990).
66. J. Dunnigan and J. Nofi, *Dirty Little Secrets,* William Morrow, New York (1990).
67. M. L. Weidenbaum and R. DeFina, *The Cost of Federal Government Regulation of Economic Activity,* American Enterprise Institute, Washington, D.C. (1978).
68. S. Kelman, "The Prescriptive Message," *Public Admin. Rev. 51*(May/June):21–23 (1991).
69. B. A. Ackerman and W. T. Hassler, "Beyond the New Deal: Coal and the Clear Air Act," *Yale Law J. 89*(July):1466–1572 (1980).

29

Management and Control of Budget Execution

Carol K. Johansen
Lewiston/Auburn College, University of Southern Maine, Lewiston, Maine

L. R. Jones
Naval Postgraduate School, Monterey, California

Fred Thompson
Willamette University, Salem, Oregon

INTRODUCTION

Perhaps the most challenging task in budgeting is to execute the budget well so that the best program outcomes are achieved with some degree of efficiency and a genuine concern for the proper use of public funds. Budget execution skill is required to respond to inevitable contingencies that arise to complicate the implementation of programs in the manner planned and according to the promises made in budget formulation. Accountability must be maintained and at the same time uncertainty must be accommodated.

Budget execution typically is highly regulated to control what program managers may and may not do. Controllers are driven by the objective of insuring that budget appropriations in total and by legally segregated account are not overspent by programs [1, Chaps. 7–9]. However, controllers also must be concerned with underexecution. Department and agency budget officers and program managers do not want to underspend and thereby lose claim to resources in the following final year. Central executive budget office controllers do not want programs to execute without good cause, so that money not used in the manner justified in budget formulation may be withdrawn from program managers. Executive controllers want to be able to withdraw funds from programs to protect the integrity of the appropriation process and to reallocate money to areas where it will be spent efficiently in response to client demand. For these reasons, budget execution typically is monitored and controlled carefully both by agency budget staff and central executive budget controllers. Execution also is often monitored closely by legislative oversight committees and their staffs out of a desire to insure that legislative will is implemented faithfully, and also to make sure that benefits are distributed to the clients targeted in the appropriation process [1, p. 288]. Because the electoral fortunes of legislators are tied to some degree to the public perception that they are solving the problems and meeting the demands of their constituents, legislators have considerable interest in budget execution control.

Among the techniques used to control budget execution, variance analysis is probably the most familiar. Controllers and budget officials in government program offices monitor the differences between projected and actual revenues and expenses in total and by account. They monitor revenue and expense rates against allotment controls by quarter, month, week, day—temporal control generally is required by the allotment process. Other variables monitored are purpose of expense relative to budget proposal and appropriation rationale, and location of revenues and expenses by unit and at times by geographical location. Monitoring of actual revenue and expense rates as well as program output and demand, where measurable, also is done to compare current spending to proposals made in the budget for the next year that are under negotiation at the same time as the fiscal year budget is expended. Comparisons are made to historical revenue and spending trends in some instances to better understand how current programs are performing. Budget execution monitoring and control is particularly important toward the end of the fiscal year for the reasons already stated, to avoid both over- and underexpenditure relative to appropriation.

The purpose of the analysis of budget execution control provided in the following sections is to improve understanding of control dynamics, incentives, disincentives, and behavior of the various participants in the budget execution process. The analysis focuses most closely in this regard on the roles of the central executive budget office controller and the program manager. The other purpose served by this analysis is to ask whether there is cause to change the budget execution process as it operates in most public organizations and, if so, what directions change might take. The analysis delineates alternative types of control applied in executing budgets and the rational for employing these different methods. A distinction is drawn between budget execution control intended to influence the behavior and performance of managers of government programs, and controls applied to affect independent private-sector firms that contract to deliver goods or services to the public on behalf of government. The central theme of this analysis is that budget execution control system design should fit the objectives of control and the nature of the entity to be controlled [1, p. 20].

BUDGET EXECUTION CONTROL CHOICES

Research in public finance has paid considerable attention to budget formulation, but has tended to ignore budget execution [2–4]. The reasons for this oversight are understandable: Government budgets are formulated in public, and the issues debated during this stage of the public spending process are dramatic and crucial. On the other hand, budgets are executed in private, and the issues raised in their execution are often mundane. Because of this selective attention, both observers and participants in the public spending process understand program analysis far better than controllership. Consequently, the conduct of program analysis has come to be guided by a fairly coherent set of professional standards. There is agreement on what is good analysis and what is good accounting practice. Although the design and operation of control systems can profoundly influence governmental performance, budget execution controllership is not guided by a coherent set of professional standards. Without appropriate performance standards, budget officers cannot be held accountable for performance of this function. Consequently, control systems are not designed to optimize the quality, quantity, and price of goods and services purchased with public money, but "to facilitate the controller's [other] work" [1, p. 21].

The choice of whom to subject to controls and when to execute those controls is not as easy. The control system designer has at least four options. First, the subject may be either an organization or an individual. Second, controls may be executed before or after the subject acts. The former may be identified as ex ante and the latter as ex post controls [5]. Ex ante controls are intended to prevent subjects from doing wrong things or to compel them to perform well. Necessarily they take the form of authoritative commands or rules that specify what the subject must do, may do, and must not do. Subjects are held responsible for complying with these commands, and the controller attempts to monitor and enforce compliance. In contrast, ex post controls are executed after the subject decides on and carries out a course of action and after some of the consequences of the subject's decisions are known. Since bad decisions cannot be undone after they are carried out, ex post controls are intended to motivate subjects to make good decisions. Subjects are held responsible for the consequences of decisions, and the controller attempts to monitor consequences and rewards or sanctions accordingly. The control system designer may choose between four distinct design alternatives: individual responsibility, ex ante or ex post, and organizational responsibility, ex ante or ex post.

PURPOSE OF EX POST CONTROLS

Ex post financial controls are used to evaluate programs at the level at which they have been funded. They are executed after operating decisions have been made, after asset acquition and use decisions have been carried out and output levels monitored. Examples are those imposed as a result of audit findings, program evaluation, or policy analysis. The most typical of ex post controls are those that are imposed as a result of efficiency or effectiveness analysis. These are rules that are used as mechanisms to enact controls. In this sense all rules are ex ante in that they are imposed prior to spending; however, the distinction for ex post control is the use of rewards or punishment for behavior and performance. Their subject may be either a freestanding organization, such as a private contractor or a quasi-independent public entity, or an individual manager within a government agency.

In the first case, the structure of authority and responsibility within the organization is assumed to be an internal matter. The controller establishes a price schedule and specifies minimum service quality standards or a process whereby these standards are to be determined. This price or cost schedule may entail all sorts of complex arrangements, including rate, volume and mix adjustments, and default penalties. Where one organization can optimally supply the entire market, the controller may grant it a monopoly franchise, for example, in garbage collection for a small town or neighborhood. The significant characteristic of this approach is that a unit price cost schedule remains in effect for a specified time period [6–8]. This means that the government's financial liability will depend on the quantity of service provided and not on the costs incurred by the organizations supplying the service.

Where this budget control system design is employed, for example, where a municipality purchases gasoline at the spot market price or where states commit themselves to pay freestanding organizations such as a university a fixed price for performing a specific service such as enrolling students or treating heart attacks, or where the Air Force buys F-16s for a fixed price, the controller must rely upon interorganizational competition to provide sufficient incentives to service suppliers to produce efficiently and make wise asset acquisition and use decisions. If interorganizational competition is effective, those organizations that don't produce cost-effectively will not survive.

However, even where the declining marginal cost of the service in question makes monopoly appropriate, ex post controls can still be employed. This is done in businesses and businesslike public sector enterprise organizations by holding managers responsible for optimizing a single criterion value, subject to a set of constraints [1]. (The principal mechanism through which this control system design is employed at the federal level is the revolving fund [9,10]). For example, the manager is given the authority to make spending decisions to acquire and use assets, subject to output quality and quantity constraints determined by clients, and is held responsible for minimizing costs. Large private-sector firms produce comprehensive operating reports describing the performance of responsibility centers and programs, but their budgets seldom are very detailed. The logic of ex post control is that the purpose of the budget is to establish performance targets that are high enough to elicit from the organization's managers their best efforts. Such budgets might contain only a single number for each responsibility center—an output quota, a unit-cost standard, a profit, or a return-on-investment target.

Under this approach to budget control, the structure of authority and responsibility within the organization is of interest to the financial controller. The effectiveness of this design depends on the elaboration of well-defined objectives, accurate and timely reporting of performance in terms of objectives, and careful matching of spending authority and responsibility. Its effectiveness also depends upon the clarity with which individual reward schedules are communicated to responsibility center managers and the degree of competition between alternative management teams. Finally, under this approach, the financial liability of government depends on the costs incurred in providing the service and not merely on the quantity or quality of the service provided.

EX ANTE CONTROL OBJECTIVES

In contrast to ex post budget controls, ex ante controls are demand-concealing. Their distinguishing attribute is that the controller retains the authority to make or exercise prior review of spending decisions. Ex ante financial controls are executed before public money is obligated or spent, and governs the service supplier's acquisition and use of assets. Examples of ex ante financial controls include object-of-expenditure appropriations, apportionments, targets, position controls, and fund and account controls that regulate spending by account and the kind of assets that can be acquired by governmental departments and agencies. Such controls also govern the behavior of private contracting entities that supply services to government or to clients on behalf of governments.

Execution of ex ante controls requires assessment of the consequences of asset acquisition decisions. This consideration may be implicit, as it is in the execution of the traditional line-item budget and basic research contracts, or explicit, as in the execution of performance and program budgets and systems development contracts. It is often influenced by information on current and past performance, but the consideration of the consequences of spending decisions is always prospective in nature.

The logic of ex ante control is that constraining managerial discretion is the first purpose of budget execution. Since the degree of constraint will depend upon the detail of the spending plan, as well as the degree of compliance enforced by the controllers, these budgets need to be highly detailed. A department or agency budget must identify all asset acquisitions to be executed during the fiscal year and make it clear who is responsible for implementation.

Under ex ante budget control, service-supplying organizations must be guaranteed an allotment of funds in return for continuously providing a service for a specified period. The service provider will assume some responsibility for managing output levels or delivery schedules, service quality, or price to the government customer. Government is directly responsible for all legitimate costs incurred in the delivery of services, regardless of the actual quantity or quality of the services provided.

An example of ex ante controls is rules that govern how money shall be spent; that is, they are imposed prior to spending, for example, appropriate language controls over movement of dollars within or between appropriation accounts. Controls might result in rules requiring preaudit of employee travel and similar restrictions over other types of employee funding transactions.

EFFECTIVENESS OF EX ANTE CONTROLS

Where a manager seeking to increase his or her budget is tight ex ante controls, the controller can enforce efficiency during the budget period by requiring affirmative answers to the following questions: (1) Will a proposed change permit the same activity to be carried out at a lower cost? (2) Will higher priority activities be carried out at the same cost? (3) Will proposed asset acquisitions or reallocations of savings support activities that have lower priority than those presently carried out? When operating managers are faced with these criteria, they respond appropriately. Controllers approve most changes in spending plans proposed by operating managers because only mutually advantageous changes will be proposed in most circumstances.

However, when line-item or lump-sum appropriations have a comparative advantage, to say that ex ante controls are a necessary means of reinforcing the controllers' bargaining power should not imply that tight ex ante controls always must be administered by them. Under certain conditions, authority to spend money, transfer funds, fill positions, etc. may be delegated to subordinate managers. The threat of reimposition of ex ante controls will be sufficient to insure that the manager's behavior corresponds to the controllers' and elected officials' preferences. In order for such delegation to take place, the following conditions must be present: (1) Reimposition of controls must be a credible treat; (2) the gain to the manager from delegation must more than offset the associated sacrifice in bargaining power—the manager of an agency in the stable backwaters of public policy has little to gain from relief from ex ante controls if the price of such relief is a change in business as usual; and (3) controllers must be confident that their monitoring procedures, including postaudit, will identify violations of "trust."

Clearly, all long-term relationships with private contractors and government goods and service suppliers rely to some degree on ex ante controls. Even the operation of fixed-price contracts requires prior specification of product quality standards and delivery schedules. But flexible-price, cost-plus type contracts and appropriated budgets require considerably higher levels of reliance on ex ante controls and also on monitoring and enforcing compliance. And the cost of tightly held budget execution control is high.

At the very least, adoption of one of the budget execution control systems described herein means that controllers must take steps to ensure that suppliers fairly and accurately recognize, record, and report their expenses. This, in turn, requires careful definition of costs and specification of appropriate account structures, accounting practices and internal controls, direct costing procedures, and the criteria to be used in allocating overheads. Still, accurate accounting does not guarantee efficiency. Even where the service supplier's financial and operational accounts completely and accurately present every relevant fact about the decisions made by its managers, they will not provide a basis for evaluating the sound-ness of those decisions. This is because cost accounts can show only what happened, not what might have happened. They do not show the range of asset acquisition choices and tradeoffs the supplier considered, let alone those that should have been considered but were not.

Under line-item or lump-sum budgets and flexible-price contracts, asset acquisition decisions must be made by the contractor, but the contractor cannot be trusted completely to make them efficiently. Consequently, the contractor must be denied some discretion to make managerial decisions. The fundamental question is, how much must be denied? To what extent should government officials or their controller agents regulate, duplicate, or replace the contractor's managerial efforts?

This question must be addressed because oversight is costly both in terms of monitoring and reporting costs, and also because of the benefits sacrificed due to failure to exploit the contractor's managerial expertise. The controller and the government official will very sel-dom be more competent to make asset acquisition decisions than the contractor. The answer to this dilemma is that controllers and officials should do the minimum necessary, given the incentives faced by and the motivations of the contractor. However, at times, the min-imum necessary is a great deal. This decision depends on circumstance and the controller's skill in exploiting the opportunities created by the contractors response to institutional constraints. In other words, all long-term relationships between government officials and contractors must rely on incentives, even those governed by lump-sum budgets and flexible-price contracts. The difference is that when these control system designs are employed, the incentives are deeply embedded in the process of budget/contract execution.

BUDGET EXECUTION CONTROL DYNAMICS IN THE "REAL WORLD"

Budget execution control should be matched to circumstances: increasing costs and ho-mogeneous outputs imply one kind of design, while decreasing costs and heterogeneous outputs imply another. However, what we observe in practice is that this match is not always achieved. Controllers tend to rely on monopoly supply and ex ante controls [11–14]. This combination cannot be appropriate for every service to which it is applied. Evidence can be marshaled to show that a variety of services might be performed satisfactorily by com-peting organizations, including in air traffic control [15], custodial services and building maintenance [16,17] day-care centers [16], electrical power generation [16], fire protection services [18,19], forest management [20], management of grazing lands [21], hospitals and health care services [22, pp. 106–107], housing [23], postal services [22, p. 108], prisons and correctional facilities [22, pp. 108–109], property assessment [23], refuse collection [24,25], security services [22, pp. 109–110], ship and aircraft maintenance [26; 27, p. 42], urban transit [22, p. 110], and wastewater treatment [22, p. 110]. Furthermore, even when controllers eschew monopoly supply, they frequently fail to fully exploit the benefits of competition. In New York City, for example, with a wide array of ex ante controls, con-trollers often hold competitors to tight output, quality, and service delivery schedules. Per-formance targets that can be met all of the time are not very ambitious.

What accounts for mismatches between how budgets are controlled in practice and the approach advanced here? One explanation is ignorance of consequences on the part of the controllers and elected officials. Also, some of the empirical data required to employ the control criteria outlined here are often unavailable. The most critical gap in this knowledge is how costs vary with output. Definitions and measurements of service outputs and activities also are often inadequate. Insufficient effort has been made to correct this situation in most public organizations. Of the two tasks, getting knowledge about the shape of cost functions is the more difficult. But if we first answer the question, "Cost to do what?," this knowledge can be derived deductively in a manner similar to the methods used in cost accounting and conventional price theory. Cost and supply analysis can yield highly useful information about marginal and average costs. Finally, experimentation with funding and output levels will increase our knowledge of service supply and cost functions [28–30].

The kind of information called for here requires a high level of analytical sophistication in both budget execution and system design, a skill that staff responsible for executing budgets may lack. Indeed, even if controllers had good information on cost and service supply functions, some might not know how to use it. Their experience tends to orient them to the administration of the traditional line-item, object-of-expenditure budget. Effective administration of a lump-sum or line-item appropriation requires no more than a modicum of arithmetical ability combined with a substantial amount of horse sense and bargaining savvy. However, matching control systems design to circumstances requires a practical understanding of applied microeconomics, and financial and managerial accounting. Controllers often fail to understand the ideas outlined here or how to implement alternatives to the line-item appropriations budget—where to exercise judgment and where to exercise specific decision rules. This is demonstrated by the persistent attempt of controllers to employ techniques devised for use within organizations, such as standard costs based on fully distributed average historical costs, to establish per-unit prices for public organizations such as hospitals and universities.

BUDGET EXECUTION REFORM OBSTACLES

Ignorance of options and objectives is not a satisfactory explanation for controller decisions to resist reform. Ignorance can be corrected, and incompetence may be weeded out. If a better match between control system design and circumstances would have a substantial payoff, why hasn't this situation been corrected? One answer regarding the implementation of reform is as follows:

> A large part of the literature on budgeting in the United States is concerned with reform. The goals of the proposed reforms are couched in similar language—economy, efficiency, improvement, or just better budgeting. The President, the Congress and its committees, administrative agencies, even the citizenry are all to gain by some change. However, any effective change in budgetary relationships must necessarily alter the outcomes of the budgetary process. Otherwise, why bother? Far from being a neutral matter of "better budgeting," proposed reforms inevitably contain important implications for the political system, that is, the "who gets what" of governmental decisions. [31, pp. 183–190]

If the controllers and elected officials empowered to determine the methods used in executing budgets are rational, this quote implies that they have a strong interest in maintaining the status quo. To explain the persistent mismatch between budget execution control system designs and practice it is necessary to determine who benefits from the status quo and, therefore, who will oppose the adoption of a more appropriate type of control [32]. Members of Congress, state legislators, city council members, and any politician with a constituency worth cultivating would appear to lose as a result of reforms proposed. As the collective holders of the power of the purse, legislators clearly have the authority to order budgets to be executed in almost any way they like, including the power to delegate this authority to controllers. Efficiency implies an exclusive concern with the supply of goods and services to the citizenry with some indifference as to the means used to supply the goods or even to the identity of the suppliers. However, legislators are frequently as concerned about where public money is spent and who gets it as they are with what it buys [33–36]. Line-item appropriations in general and object-of-expenditure budgets in particular are ideally suited to the satisfaction of legislative preferences with respect to how public money is spent, where it is spent, and who gets it.

Therefore, in order to stimulate reform necessary for the type of control needed, legislative decision makers will have to perceive that changes will enhance rather than diminish their control over spending and budget execution. If legislators were satisfied with directing policy and trusting department and agency officials to execute budgets as directed, then legislators would be more likely to embrace change. Therefore, it is incumbent upon executive agents to increase legislative trust by faithfully executing budgets according to legislative policy preferences. If agency budget directors are effective in demonstrating to legislators that their will has been done, legislative trust probably will increase and legislative micromanagement may decrease.

REFERENCES

1. R. Anthony and D. Young, *Managerial Control in Non-Profit Organizations*, Irwin, Homestead, Ill. (1984).
2. H. Simon, et al., *Centralization vs. Decentralization in Organizing the Controller's Department*, Controllership Foundation, New York (1954).
3. A. Schick, "Control Patterns in State Budget Executions," *Public Admin. Rev.*, *24*: 97–106 (1964).
4. A. Schick, "Contemporary Problems in Financial Control," *Current Issues in Public Administration*, (F. Lane, ed.), 2d ed., St. Martin's Press, New York: 361–371 (1982).
5. J. Demski and G. Feltham, *Cost Determination*, Iowa State University Press, Ames (1967).
6. V. Goldberg, "Regulation and Administered Contracts," *Bell J. Econ.*, *7*: 426–428 (1976).
7. F. Thompson, "How to Stay Within the Budget Using per-Unit Prices," *J. Policy Anal. Manage.*, *4*(1): 72–77 (1984).
8. F. Thompson and G. Fiske, "One More Solution to the Problem of Higher Education Finance," *Policy Anal.*, *3*(4): 78–82 (1978).
9. M. Bailey, "Decentralization Through Internal Prices," *Defense Management* (S. Enke, ed.), Prentice-Hall, Englewood Cliffs, N.J., 337–352 (1967).
10. N. V. Beckner, "Government Efficiency and the Military: Buyer-Seller Relationship," *J. Polit. Econ.*, *68*: 35–57 (1960).
11. F. Thompson and W. Zumeta, "Controls and Controls: A Reexamination of Control Patterns in Budget Execution," *Policy Sci.*, *13*: 25–50 (1981).
12. B. T. Pitsvada, "Flexibility in Federal Budget Execution," *Public Budgeting Finance*, *3*(2): 17–26 (1983).
13. F. Draper and P. T. Pitsvada, "Limitations in Federal Budget Execution," *Government Accountants J.*, *30*: 3 (1981).
14. L. Fisher, *Presidentual Spending Power*, Princeton University Press, Princeton, N.J. (1975).
15. R. Poole, "Air Traffic Control: The Private Sector Option," *Heritage Foundation Backgrounds*, *216* (1982).
16. L. R. Jones, "Municipal Bonds and Public Utility Financing: Municipal Buyouts and Takeovers." *Municipal Finance Journal*, *11*(2): 163–179 (1990); F. Thompson and L. R. Jones, "Reinventing the Pentagon," Jossey-Bass Publishers, San Francisco, CA (1994).
17. C. B. Blankart, "Bureaucratic Problems in Public Choice: Why Do Public Goods Still Remain Public?," *Public Choice and Public Finance* (R. Roskamp, ed.), Cujas, New York: 155–167 (1979).

18. R. Poole, "Fighting Fires for Profit," *Reason*, May: 23–28 (1976).
19. R. G. Smith, "Feet to the Fire," *Reason*, May: 23–29 (1983).
20. S. Hanke, "The Privatization Debate," *Cato J.*, *11*: 656 (1982).
21. S. Hanke, "Land Policy," *Agenda 83* (R. Howill, ed.), Heritage Foundation, Washington, D.C., 65 (1983).
22. S. Hanke, "Privatization: Theory, Evidence, Implementation," *Control of Federal Spending*, (L. Harris, ed.), Academy of Political Science, New York: (1985).
23. R. Poole, *Cutting Back City Hall*, University Books, Baltimore, M.D., 164 (1980).
23. J. Weicker, *Housing*, American Enterprise Institute, Washington, D.C., 80 (1980).
24. E. S. Savas, "Policy Analysis for Local Government," *Policy Anal.*, *3*: 49–77 (1977).
25. J. Bennett and M. Johnson, "Public v. Private Provision of Collective Goods and Services," *Public Choice*, *34*: 55–63 (1979).
26. J. Bennett and M. Johnson, *Better Government at Half the Price: Private Production of Public Services*, Caroline House Ottawa, I.L., (1981).
27. J. Bennett and T. DiLorenzo, "Public Employee Labor Unions and the Privatization of Public Services," *J. Labor Res.*, *4*: 43 (1983).
28. A. Wildavsky, *Budgeting: A Compromise Theory of the Budgetary Process*, Little, Brown, Boston, 118–119 (1975).
29. P. Larkey, *Evaluating Public Programs: The Impact of General Revenue Sharing on Municipal Government*, Princeton University Press, Princeton, N.J. (1979).
30. D. Cothran, "Program Flexibility and Budget Growth," *Western Polit. Q.*, *34*: 593–610 (1981).
31. A. Wildavsky, "Political Implications of Budget Reform," *Public Admin. Rev.*, *21*: 183–190 (1961).
32. J. Zimmerman, "The Municipal Accounting Maze: An Analysis of Political Incentives," *J. Accounting Res.*, *21*: 107–144 (1977).
33. D. Arnold, *Congress and the Bureaucracy*, Yale University Press, New Haven, Conn. (1979).
34. J. Ferejohn, *Pork Barrel Politics*, Stanford University Press, Stanford, Calif. (1974).
35. M. Fiorina, *Congress: Keystone of the Washington Establishment*, Yale University Press, New Haven, Conn. (1977).
36. K. Shepsle and B. Weingast, "Political Preferences for the Pork Barrel," *Am. J. Polit. Sci.*, *25*: 96–111 (1981).

BIBLIOGRAPHY

Barton, D. P., "Regulating a Monopolist with Unknown Costs," *Econometrical*, *50* (1982).
Breton, A., and Wintrobe, R. "The equilibrium size of a budget maximizing bureau". *J. Polit. Econ.* 83:195–207 (1975).
Cheung, S. N. S. "The contractual nature of the firm," *Journal of Law and Economics*, *25* (1983).
Coase, R. "The nature of the firm," *Economica*, *4* (1937).
Fox, R. *Arming America: How the U.S. Buys Weapons*, University Press, Harvard Cambridge, MA (1974).
Hofsted, G. H. *The Game of Budget Control*, Van Gorcum, (1967)
Holstrom, B. "Moral hazard and observability," *Bell J. Econ.* 10 (1979).
Meyerson, R. B. "Incentives compatibility and the bargaining problem," *Econometrica*, *47* (1979).
Mirlees, J. "The optimal structure of incentives and authority within an organization," *Bell Journal of Economics*, *7* (1976).
Mitnick, B. "The theory of agency: The policing "paradox" and regulatory behavior," *Public Choice*, *30* (1977).
Morgan, J. "Bilateral monopoly and the competitive output," *Quarterly Journal of Economics*, *63* (1949).
Peck, M., and Scherer, F. *The Weapons Acquisition Process: An Economic Analysis.* Harvard Business School, Cambridge, MA (1962).

Scherer, F. *The Weapons Acquisition Process*: *Economic Incentives*, Harvard Business School, Cambridge, MA (1964).

Stark, R. "On cost analysis for engineered construction," in R. Englebrecht-Wiggins, M, Shubik, M. and R. Stark, eds., *Auctions, Bidding, and Contracting*, New York University Press, New York (1983).

Stark, R., and Varley, T. "Bidding, estimating, and engineered construction contracting", in R. Englebrecht-Wiggins, M. Shubik, and R. Stark, eds. *Auctions, Bidding, and Contracting*, New York University Press, New York pp. 121–135, (1983).

Thompson, F. "Utility maximizing behavior in organized anarchies," *Public Choice 36* (1981).

Wildavsky, A., and Hammann, A. "Comprehensive versus incremental budgeting in the Department of Agriculture," *Administrative Sciences Quarterly 10*:321–346 (1956).

Williamson, O. *The Economics of Discretionary Behavior*, Prentice-Hall, Englewood Cliffs, N.J. (1964).

Williamson, O. *Markets and Hierarchies*, Free Press: New York, (1975).

30
Governmental Auditing

Khi V. Thai
Florida Atlantic University, Fort Lauderdale, Florida

INTRODUCTION

In the private sector, auditing of financial conditions is a common practice. As it is performed only after manual financial reports are prepared, auditing is considered by some accounting experts as the last stage of an accounting cycle. Schlosser, however, does not agree with this view, and argues that accounting and auditing are two separate processes. While accounting is a process of collecting and preparing financial statements, "auditing is a process of accumulating and evaluating evidence by a competent independent person about quantitative information and established criteria" [1, p. 1.4]. Moreover, as the scope of auditing has expanded to encompass efficiency and program results, auditing is not necessarily carried out at the end of each accounting cycle, but it can be performed at any time as management wishes or law requires. Schlosser classified auditing in the United States into three "branches" or sectors: (1) internal auditing, which is performed by independent auditors within a profit organization; (2) governmental auditing, which is practiced by governments of all levels; and (3) independent auditing, which is provided by certified public accountants to the above sectors. After classifying auditing as just described, Schlosser [1, p. 1.10] stated: "Governmental auditing is the most comprehensive of the three branches of auditing."

Not only the most comprehensive, governmental auditing is the most important of the these sectors as it involves the largest manpower and workload. In the federal government alone, the former U.S. Department of Health and Human Services, with the second largest auditing staff in the federal government, has a workload of more than 1,000 installations, about 550 state agencies, more than 10,000 units of local governments, and about 85 intermediaries and 10,000 hospitals and extended-care facilities under the Medicaid program [2, p. 9.7]. This chapter will provide an overview of governmental auditing, and explore audit procedures and standards in federal as well as state and local governments.

OVERVIEW OF GOVERNMENTAL AUDITING

Evolution of Governmental Auditing

The idea of auditing is as old as organized governments. The evolution of governmental auditing can be traced from two perspectives: authoritative sources, and scope of governmental auditing in the U.S. government.

Authoritative Sources of Auditing

In the early days of the Revolution, accounts were examined by various committees of the Congress itself. As the volume of auditing increased, these committees had to employ persons who were not delegates of the Congress. Later, a Superintendent of Finance was appointed, and delegates ceased examining accounts entirely. When the first Congress met in 1789, the new government had to be organized. Accounting for and controlling public funds proved particularly perplexing. As an evidence, the Congress created, on September 2, 1789, the U.S. Treasury Department. Five key officers—including the Secretary of the Treasury, a Treasurer, a Registrar, an Auditor, and a Comptroller—were appointed, with senatorial approval, to manage the new department. The Secretary was required to plan for the improvement and management of government revenues and to estimate federal receipts and expenditures. The Treasurer had the duties of receiving, keeping, and properly disbursing the public funds and rendering accounts to the Comptroller. The Registrar was charged with accounting and related custodial duties. The Comptroller supervised the adjustment and preservation of accounts, countersigned warrants, and collected debts due to the United States; but his or her principal duty was decide the lawfulness and justice of claims and accounts. Finally, the Auditor was responsible for examining the accounts and certifying the balances to the Comptroller for decision.

To secure more adequate fiscal controls, the Congress added, in 1817, additional auditors and comptrollers to the Treasury Department and established, in 1836, the Office of Auditors of the Treasury for the Post Office Department. In 1894, the Dockery Act abolished all added comptrollers, except the Comptroller of the Treasury, and assigned the Treasury Department's six auditors to examine the accounts of designated departments and to certify balances in the accounts, subject to appeal of the Comptroller.

During the debate on the Act of 1789, James Madison observed that the Comptroller's role had a judicial character that implied direct responsibility to the public, rather than serving at the pleasure of the executive branch. However, the Comptroller remained within the executive branch until 1921 when the Budget and Accounting Act, which acted on James Madison's idea, created the U.S. General Accounting Office (GAO) under the direction of the U.S. Comptroller General. This act shifted audit responsibilities from the executive branch to the legislative branch of government. The U.S. General Accounting Office has been expressly recognized by the Congress as an agency of the Congress.

The GAO was granted authority to audit and settle all public accounts; to settle and adjust all claims by and against the federal government; to prescribe forms systems and procedures for administrative appropriation and fund accounting; and to certify balances in the accounts. Since its creation, the auditing authority of GAO was expanded to government corporations, nonappropriated activities (such as restaurants, concessions, canteens, vending machine operations, and other revenue-producing activities), Postal Office, and funds contributed solely by the U.S. government to international organizations. GAO is also an authoritative auditing standard-setting body of the federal government.

Auditing standards for state and local governments have evolved in a direction different from those of the federal government. While GAO, a governmental agency, has the authority to issue auditing standards for federal agencies, audit standards and requirements for state and local governments come from three different sources.

1. *Federal government requirements*. The GAO, the Office of Management and Budget (OMB), and other federal agencies have issued various audit standards, guidelines, circulars, and other publications that contain important standards, requirements, and guidance for audits of specific federal assistance programs. As required by the Single Audit Act of 1984 and OMB Circular A-110, the GAO audit standards have to be followed by state and local governments that receive federal financial assistance. Moreover, these standards are generally applicable to state and local government audits. Private and not-for-profit accounting and auditing organizations including the American Institute of Certified Public Accountants (AICPA), the Institute of Internal Auditors, and the American Evaluation Association have officially adopted these audit standards.

2. *AICPA auditing standards, interpretations, and guidelines*. In most state governments and some large local governments, there is an independent auditor or auditing office. In some other large local governmental units and a majority of small local governments where a full-time auditor is not necessary, auditing service is usually contracted to public accountants, preferably certified public accountants (CPAs). Due to this practice, AICPA statements on auditing standards (SASs) and statements of position (SOPs) have become an authoritative source of state and local audits. In 1939, AICPA created the Committee on Auditing Procedures to examine into auditing procedure and other related questions. This committee was authorized to prepare "statements of auditing procedures" to guide independent auditors in the exercise of their judgment in the application of auditing procedures. The first statement, under the title of "Codification of Statements on Auditing Procedure," was issued in 1951 and has been regularly revised and published. The name of the committee was changed to the "Auditing Standards and Procedures Committee" in 1972 and then to the Auditing Standards Board in 1978. Also, the name of the AICPA auditing statements was changed from "Statement on Auditing Procedure" to "Statement on Auditing Standards" or SAS. As independent accountants have been significantly involved in state and local government auditing, AICPA has to modify its auditing standards whenever a change in accounting, financial reporting, and auditing standards is made by the Governmental Accounting Standards Board or GASB (an authoritative accounting standard-setting body for state and local governments), GAO, and other federal agencies. For example, in 1987, SAS 52, "Omnibus Statement on Auditing Standards—1987," was issued to amend SAS 5 (July 1975) to recognize statements and interpretations issued by GASB for state and local governments.

   In addition to SASs and SOPs, AICPA also issued in 1974 an audit guide, entitled *Audits of State and Local Governmental Units*, that has been frequently revised to reflect changes in the field of governmental auditing. AICPA revised, in 1995, its *Audits of State and Local Government Units* to incorporate revised audit report wording and certain other changes necessitated by the revised *Government Audit Standards* issued by GAO in 1994.

3. *State government requirements*. Auditing practices vary considerably among state and local governments due to constitutional and statutory requirements and choice, as well as the degree of sophistication of the individual audit staff. In some circumstances, state agencies prescribe accounting systems, financial reports, and au-

dit guidelines and regulations for governmental entities within their jurisdiction. If there are conflicts between state guidelines and those issued by AICPA and GAO, guidelines established by states do not supersede auditing standards issued by AICPA and GAO. In general, in most state governments and some large local governments, there is an independent auditor or auditing office. In some other large local governmental units and those small local governments where a full-time auditor is not necessary, auditing service is usually contracted to public accountants, preferably certified public accountants (CPAs). Due to this practice, auditing standards and procedures imposed on CPAs have had great impacts on auditing of state and local governments.

Scope of Governmental Auditing

Evolution of governmental auditing also has been significant in its scope. Indeed, the scope of governmental auditing has been broadened with the passage of time. Since the formative days of government, auditing has functioned to detect and prevent fraud as well as accounting and legal errors. This objective is performed internally and in the form of preaudit which is an integral part of the internal control system. In order to prevent fraud and detect accounting errors, preaudits or internal controls are necessary to assure that:

- Expenditures are not unreasonable and extravagant.
- Vouchers and payrolls are mathematically accurate.
- Sufficient budget is available.
- There is compliance with financial and legal requirements.

In order to achieve this objective, a sound internal control system is necessary. Limiting internal control to fraud and error prevention and detection has some significant drawbacks. First of all, this type of control does not assure efficiency and effectiveness in governmental operations. For example, it assures the price of office supplies purchased by an agency is recorded accurately, but it does not assure that the supplies were actually needed. Similarly, it assures that payrolls are correctly prepared and paid, but it cannot assure that employees on the payrolls performed efficiently.

Moreover, governments do not operate on the basis of profit making. The lack of profit measurement coupled with limitations of this audit objective has led to a need for audits of economy and performance and program results. As early as the 1920s, the concept of economy and performance audits was endorsed in the Budget and Accounting Act of 1921. Section 312 of this Act stated:

> The Comptroller General shall investiage, at the seat of government or elsewhere, all matters relating to the receipt, disbursement, and application of public funds, and shall make to the President when requested by him, and to Congress at the beginning of each regular session, a report in writing of the work of the General Accounting Office . . . . In such regular report, or in special reports at any time when Congress is in session, he shall make recommendations looking to greater economy or efficiency in public expenditures.

Legislation prior to the Legislative Reorganization Act of 1970 authorized GAO to audit financial transactions, accounts, and financial statements and to review the economy, efficiency, and effectiveness with which executive agencies were spending appropriated funds. The 1970 Act expanded the scope of auditing to audits of program results. Section 204 of the Act stated:

The Comptroller General shall review and evaluate the results of Government programs and activities carried on under existing law when ordered by either House of Congress, or upon his own initiative, or when requested by any committee of the House of Representatives or the Senate, or any joint committee of the two Houses, having jurisdiction over such programs or activities.

In implementing this act and previous acts relating to auditing, the U.S. General Accounting Office (GAO) issued in 1972 "Standards for Audit of Governmental Organizations, Programs, Activities, and Functions." This publication formally prescribed audit standards and procedures that cover not only financial operations but also program results. Its impact on auditing practices was not limited to federal agencies and federal programs governed by state and local governments. The GAO auditing standards and procedures also changed the scope of auditing in state and local governments as well as profit-making organizations. Indeed, many state and local governments issued their own auditing standards based on those of GAO. In the private sector, auditing also made a turn away from detection of fraud and accounting errors in the early twentieth century. In 1912, Montgomery [3, p. 13] stated:

In what might be called the formative days of auditing, students were taught that the chief objectives of an audit were:

1. Detection and prevention of fraud;
2. Detection and prevention of errors; but in recent years there has been a decided change in demand and service. Present-day purposes are:
1. To ascertain actual financial conditions and earnings of an enterprise.
2. Detection of fraud and errors, but this is a minor objective.

Audits of annual financial reports, however, were widely practiced in the private sector only after the 1929 stock market crash, the catalyst that forced improved accounting and financial marketing in the private sector. The 1975 New York City fiscal crisis did the same for the government sector. Indeed, in the public sector, audits of annual financial reports were not a concern of policymakers, investors, and the public until 1975 when New York City was on the verge of bankruptcy. Annual financial statements of New York City were not prepared in such a way that they could show its financial insolvency.

Distorted financial information can be presented in financial statements due to ignorance, personal bias, self-interest, carelessness, or even outright dishonesty. The New York City experience in 1975 has led to a concrete result: Today, most large cities' annual financial statements are audited. Audits of financial statements add some degree of validity to the audited object. The primary objective of this form of auditing is to eliminate distortion of the facts. This will help policymakers to prevent any financial problems.

Recently, in efforts to reduce budget deficits by controlling waste, fraud and inefficiency, the Federal Managers' Financial Integrity Act of 1982 requires the head of each executive agency to report at the end of the fiscal year their compliance with accounting and internal control standards and procedures.

Another reform was made recently, that is, the single audit. The concept of single audit emerged as a result of the rapid expansion of federal grants to and contracts with state and local governments, universities, hospitals, and a host of nonprofit organizations. Before the single audit was endorsed, an organization that received a variety of federal funds from various federal agencies was subjected to numerous different audits. Each audit is performed for a single facet of the organization's operations, such as a research grant, the Food Stamp program, a nursing home, etc. This auditing practice was a waste of resources and time of agencies being audited. The Single Audit Act of 1984 formally required that each audit encompass the entirety of the financial operations of the governmental entity or an agency being audited. The focus of the single audit is on financial and legal compliance. A successful single audit requires careful planning, which includes a list of all grants for which the organization being audited is responsible and material grant agreements.

However, as federal agencies have not been able to prepare annual financial statements and have them audited, among other things, the Congress enacted in 1990 the Chief Financial Officers Act to make federal agencies more accountable by improving their financial management systems, preparing financial statements and having them audited. Moreover, also in 1990, the Federal Accounting Standards Advisory Board was created to develop a basic set of accounting concepts and standards, which need to be issued by OMB and GAO. Subsequent legislation, the Government Performance Management Reform Act and the Government Management Reform Act made performance management the standard of government operations. Internal control has received a greater attention in governmental auditing. In fiscal year 1994, audited financial statements were issued for 124 reporting agencies, and the Congress enacted the Federal Financial Management Act of 1994 to extend the requirement for audited financial statements to all of the 24 largest federal agencies encompassed in the Chief Financial Officers Act and to require an audit of a *government-wide* financial statement starting with fiscal year 1997.

Classifications of Audit

In government, audits can be conducted by internal or external auditors, prior to or after the completion of financial transactions. Moreover, as mentioned earlier, audits can cover only financial operations and legal compliance and/or economy and effectiveness. In other words, there are several types of audits.

Preaudits and Postaudits

On the basis of when the examination is made, audits may be classified as preaudit and postaudit. A preaudit is an examination of financial transactions prior to their completion. This is an integral part of financial internal financial management control. The preaudit achieves the most traditional purpose of auditing: detection and protection of fraud and accounting errors. On the contrary, a postaudit is conducted after transactions and events have occurred.

In the Coast Guard story cited later in this chapter, a good preaudit or internal control system would have been able to avoid that accounting error, and the error would have been detected before the disbursement was made. Some students of public budgeting and financial management may think that even if that error was somehow overlooked in the preaudit a postauditor should have discovered it during his postaudit work. As seen later in this chapter, the postaudit cannot be done for every accounting transaction, and the chance for missing similar errors is high. Therefore, a sound internal financial control system is needed for fraud and error protection and detection.

Financial and Performance Auditing

Another useful and common classification of auditing is the financial audit as opposed to the performance audit, depending on the purpose of auditing. The evolution of governmental auditing analyzed earlier is the result of the search for evaluation of the responsibility and accountability of government officials. Currently, governmental audits cover one or more of the following three major purposes:

- Audits of financial operations and legal compliance, which are to ascertain (a) whether the agency complies with the requirements of applicable laws and regulations including generally accepted accounting principles governing the receipt, disbursement, and application of public funds and (b) whether the agency's financial statements show fully and fairly its financial condition, changes in its financial condition, and revenues and expenditures in conformity with generally accepted accounting principles applied on a basis consistent with that of the preceding year.

- Audits of efficiency and economy of operations, which are to evaluate whether the governmental programs and activities are being carried out in an effective, efficient, and economical manner. Technically, economy deals with cost savings, whereas efficiency implies benefit maximizing.

- Audits of program results, which are to evaluate whether results or benefits of governmental programs and activities are being achieved and whether the established objectives are being met.

An audit having the first purpose is called as a financial and compliance audit, or simply a "fiscal" audit. An audit having either or both of the second and third purposes is called an "operational" or "performance" audit. An audit that extends into all important aspects of an agency's operations is referred to as a "comprehensive" audit. Few governmental audits, however, can be extended into all important aspects of an agency's operations. Rather, an audit focuses on one primary aspect of the comprehensive audit to meet a specific need of policymakers, managers, other governments, investors, and the public, while other aspects of the audit receive secondary attention.

Today, financial and compliance audits are the most widely carried out, although special audits are often directed toward the efficiency and economy of government operations or program results.

Internal and External Audits

Audits may be classified as internal and external on the basis of the relationship of the auditor and the agency being audited. Internal auditing is "an independent appraisal activity within the organization for the review of operations as a service to management. It is management control which functions by measuring and evaluating the effectiveness of other controls" [4, p. 86]. It is conducted by employees of the agency being audited.

On the contrary, external auditing is performed by auditors who are independent of the agency being audited and responsible to the legislative body, the public and other governmental units. There are three groups of external auditors:

- *Independent auditors* elected by the people or appointed by the legislative body. This is the case in the federal government with the Comptroller General of the United States, and most states and few municipalities. They are responsible directly to the people or the legislative body. Election of auditors works well in some jurisdictions, but in some others, auditors with minimal qualifications are elected to the office.

- *Officials of a governmental unit* other than the one being audited, namely, the auditee. In some states, state audit agencies are responsible for auditing their local governmental units.

- *Independent public accountants and auditors.* Most local governments and a few federal agencies and state governments have their audits performed by this group of external auditors. How does a governmental unit select an external auditors? This question is addressed later in the next section.

The internal and external audits are similar in scope, standards, and procedures, as discussed later in this chapter. Moreover, both audits provide the same benefits: constructive recommendations supported by unbiased and relevant information.

Selection of Auditors

Many governments attempt to select an auditor by competitive bidding. The American Institute of Certified Public Accountants and the former National Committee on Governmental Accounting [5, p. 129], in a "Joint Statement on Competitive Bidding for Audit Services in Governmental Agencies" issued in 1955 and revised in 1961, considered competitive bidding inappropriate:

> Competitive bidding . . . is not an effective procedure in arranging for an independent audit. It is not effective for the simple reason that an audit is not something which can be covered by rigid specifications. An audit is a professional service requiring professional independence, skill, and judgment. An independent auditor should have as much latitude as he may find necessary to be assured that the records are in order and that the system of accounts is functioning properly . . .

This statement does not intend to challenge the right of government officials to obtain some estimate of their auditing expenses. Once a governmental agency has decided to engage an independent auditor, it ought to discuss the engagement with the auditor it believes to be the best qualified to render the most satisfactory service. After the independent auditor has surveyed the fiscal records and identified the principal problems, it should be possible to develop an understanding on the scope of his or her audit and on the length of time that will be required for its completion. The independent auditor should then be in a position, if required, to give a reasonable estimate of the cost of the service.

This approach to the selection of an auditor, reflecting a legitimate concern for costs, is perfectly reasonable and acceptable. But no one gains—indeed, everyone is likely to lose—when auditors are selected by competitive bidding on the basis of the lowest possible price. Indeed, audited agencies should select a certified public accountant (CPA) or a CPA firm in whom they have the most confidence, discuss the work to be done, and agree on the basis for the fee. As recommended by the former National Committee on Governmental Accounting [6, p. 128], auditors

> should be selected only on the basis of professional competence and experience. This will not only mean that the auditor should be a certified public accountant authorized to practice in the jurisdiction being audited, but that he should have appropriate experience in the audit of governmental units and a demonstrated high level of attainment in such a professional practice. There must be a clear recognition on the part of both public officials concerned and indepedent accountants that auditing services are truly professional in nature. This being the case, the audit services should be compensated on the basis of professional fees agreed upon in advance of the engagement and not on the basis of competitive bids.

Selection of independent public auditors by competitive bidding decreased significantly in local government since the issuance of the joint statement cited here. This decline, however, has been revised in recent years by the insistence of several federal agencies and many state and local governments on securing audit services on the basis of competitive bidding.

The National Intergovernmental Audit Forum, an organization of federal, state and local government audit executives, recommended:

> Governmental agencies, . . . contracting for audits by other than government employed auditors, should be encouraged to engage public accountants by competitive negotiations that take into consideration such factors as the experience, plans, qualifications and price of the offeror. The weights to be assigned to each factor should be tailored to the particular tasks to be performed. [6, p. 128]

After an auditor has been selected, in order to avoid any misunderstanding of the nature, scope, or other aspects of audit services, a contract should be in written form and should specify, among other things,

- The type and purpose of the audit
- The exact objects to be audited (such as departments, funds, etc.)
- The period the audit is to cover
- Approximate beginning and completion dates and the date of delivery of the report and the number of copies of the report
- The terms of compensation and reimbursement of the auditor's expenses
- The place at which the audit work will be done

Currently, there are two sets of audit standards: the AICPA standards and the GAO standards. The AICPA standards are recognized as being appropriate for financial and compliance audits, but insufficient for the broader scope of governmental auditing. The governmental auditing standards cover not only financial and compliance audits, but also audits of economy and efficiency and program results. The two standards are both effective because the AICPA standards are recognized and incorporated to the GAO audit standards The NCGA recognized both standards in its Statement No. 1. In its revised audit standards for state and local governmental units, the American Institute of Certified Public Accountants, in turn, endorsed the GAO audit standards.

AUDIT STANDARDS AND PROCEDURES

In auditing practices, audit standards must be distinguished from audit procedures. "Standards are guidelines that deal with overall audit quality, while procedures are the actual work that is performed" [7, p. 783]. Standards govern the auditor's judgment in selecting audit procedures. There is no single set of auditing standards applicable to all levels of governments in the United States. Indeed, most local governmental units and some state governments are audited by independent certified accountants, who are guided by AICPA auditing standards. As all state and local governmental units receive federal financial assistance, auditors have to follow audit requirements imposed by the federal government. As mentioned earlier, audit requirements in the federal government are prescribed by two agencies, GAO and the U.S. Office of Management and Budget. Thus, in conducting audits of governments, auditors must comply with both generally accepted auditing standards (GAAS) established by AICPA and generally accepted government auditing standards (GAGAS) established by GAO. Moreover, since the passage of the Single Audit Act of 1984, OMB has prescribed audit guidelines including circular A-128, "Audits of State and Local Governments," Circular A.133, "Audits of Institutions of Higher Education and Other Nonprofit Organizations," and "Compliance Supplement for Single Audits of State and Local Governments." The remaining part of this chapter covers these standards. Thus, in conducting audits of governmental units, auditors must comply with both generally auditing standards established by the American Institute of Certified Public Accountants (AICPA) and generally government auditing standards established by the U.S. General Accounting Office and requirements prescribed by OMB.

Auditing Standards

AICPA Auditing Standards

AICPA issued 10 broad standards of quality for the performance of an audit, established by the AICPA [8, par. 150.02], applying to all audits, whether in the private or public sector:

General Standards.

1. The audit is to be performed by a person or persons having adequate technical training and proficiency as an auditor.
2. In all matters relating to the assignment an independence in mental attitude is to be maintained by the auditor or auditors.
3. Due professional care is to be exercised in the performance of the examination and the preparation of the report.

Field Work Standards.

1. The work is to be adequately planned and assistants, if any, are to be properly supervised.
2. A sufficient understanding of internal control structure is to be obtained to plan the audit and to determine the nature, timing, and extent of the tests to be performed.
3. Sufficient competent evidential matter is to be obtained through inspection, observation, inquiries, and confirmations to afford a reasonable basis for an opinion regarding the financial statements under examination.

Reporting Standards.

1. The report shall state whether the financial statements are presented in accordance with generally accepted principles of accounting.
2. The report shall identify those circumstances in which such principles have been consistently observed in the current period in relation to the preceding period.
3. Informative disclosures in the financial statements are to be regarded as reasonably adequate unless otherwise stated in the report.
4. The report shall either contain an expression of opinion regarding the financial statements, taken as a whole, or an assertion to the effect that an opinion cannot be expressed. When an overall opinion cannot be expressed, the reasons therefore should be stated. In all cases where an auditor's name is associated with financial statements the report should contain a clear-cut indication of the character of the auditor's examination, if any, and the degree of responsibility he is taking.

Many detailed or revised audit standards were set forth in AICPA Statements on Auditing Standards (SASs), and particularly in AICPA's *Audits of State and Local Governmental Units* [9].

Governmental Auditing Standards

There was no comprehensive statement generally accepted government auditing standards prior to issuance of *Standards for Audit of Governmental Organizations, Programs, Activities and Functions* [10] by GAO in 1972. These standards were issued because of the demand of public officials, legislators, and the general public for information on "whether governmental funds are handled properly and in compliance with existing laws and whether governmental programs are being conducted efficiently, effectively, and economically" [10, p. i]. Moreover, the information has to be provided, or at least concurred in, by an independent and objective professional, not by an advocate of the program [10, p. 1]. The GAO audit standards, as stated in the 1994 revised *Government Auditing Standards* [11] are summarized in Table 1.

Basic Premises. As each type of audit can be performed separately, audit contracts should specify which type of audits are to be covered and the auditor's report should indicate which type is audited. GAO [11, pp. 8–10] highlights the objectives of the auditing standards in nine basic premises as follows:

1. The term "audit" includes both financial and performance audits.
2. Public officials and others entrusted with handling public resources (for example, managers of a not-for-profit organization that receive federal assistance) are responsible for applying those resources efficiently, economically, and effectively to

Table 1 GAO Auditing Standards

1. Scope of audit work

Financial audits	Performance audits
Financial statement audits	Economy and efficiency audits
Finance-related audits	Program audits

2. General standards

Qualifications	Due professional care
Independence	Quality control

3. Standards for financial audits

Financial audits	Performance audits
a. Field work standards	a. Field work standards
—Planning	—Planning
—Irregularities, illegal acts, and other noncompliance	Supervision
—Internal controls	— Compliance with laws and regulations
—Working papers	—Management controls
—Financial related audits	—Evidence
b. Reporting standards	b. Reporting standards
—Communications with audit committees or other responsible individuals	—Form
—Reporting compliance with GAGGAS	—Timeliness
—Report on compliance with laws and regulations and on internal controls	— Report contents
—Privileged and confidential information	—Report presentation
—Report distribution	—Report distribution
—Financial related audits	

Source: Ref. 11.

achieve the purposes for which the resources were furnished. This responsibility applies to all resources, whether entrusted to public officials or others by their own constituencies or by other levels of government.

3. Public officials and others entrusted with public resources are accountable for complying with applicable laws and regulations. That responsibility encompasses identifying the requirements with which the entity and the officials must comply and implementing systems designed to achieve that compliance.

4. Public officials and others entrusted with public resources are responsible for establishing and maintaining effective controls to ensure that appropriate goals and objectives are met, resources are safeguarded, laws and regulations are followed, and reliable data are obtained, maintained, and fairly disclosed.

5. Public officials and others entrusted with public resources are accountable both to the public and to other levels and branches of government for the resources provided to carry out government programs and services. Consequently, they should provide appropriate reports to those to whom they are accountable.

6. Audit of government reporting is an important element of public control and accountability. Auditing provides credibility to the information reported by or obtained from management through objectively acquiring and evaluating evidence. The importance and comprehensive nature of auditing place a special responsibility on public officials or others entrusted with public resources who authorize or arrange audits to be done in accordance with these standards. This responsibility is to provide audit coverage that is broad enough to help fulfill the reasonable needs of potential users of the audit report. Auditors can assist public officials and others in understanding the auditors' responsibilities under GAGAS and other audit coverage required by law or regulation. This comprehensive nature of auditing also highlights the importance of auditors clearly understanding the audit objectives, the scope of the work to be conducted, and the reporting requirements.

7. Financial auditing contributes to providing accountability since it provides independent reports on whether an entity's financial information is presented fairly and/or on its internal controls and compliance with laws and regulations.

8. Performance auditing contributes to providing accountability because it provides an independent assessment of the performance of a government organization, program, activity, or function in order to provide information to improve public accountability and facilitate decision making by parties with responsibility to oversee or initiate corrective action.

9. To realize government accountability, the citizens, their elected representatives, and program managers need information to assess the integrity, performance, and stewardship of the government's activities. Thus, unless legal restrictions or ethical considerations prevent it, audit reports should be available to the public and to other levels of government that have supplied resources.

An assumption underlying all the standards is that governments will cooperate in making audits in which they have mutual interests. This is especially true when one government receives funds from several others and each has a continuing need for a financial audit. In these circumstances, audits should be made on an organization-wide basis whenever possible, rather than on a grant-by-grant basis, and in a manner that will satisfy the audit needs of the participating governments.

Scope of Government Audits.   The GAO audit standards widened the scope of governmental auditing to include not only *financial operations* but also "whether governmental organizations are *achieving the purposes* for which programs are authorized and funds are made available, are doing so *economically and efficiently,* and are *complying with applicable laws and regulations*" [10, p. 1]. This scope of auditing has been reaffirmed and grouped into the following four categories in the revised editions of GAO's *Government Auditing Standards*:

- Financial audits, which include two categories: financial statement audits, and financial related audits
- Performance audits, which are two categories: economy and efficiency audits, and program audits

Financial statement audits provide reasonable assurances about whether the financial statements of an audited entity (1) are prepared in conformity with any of several other bases of accounting discussed in AICPA auditing standards, and (2) present fairly the financial position, results of operations, and cash flows in conformity with generally accepted accounting principles [11, p. 13]. Financial related audits may include (1) segments of financial statements, financial information (e.g., statement of revenue and expenses, statement of cash receipts and disbursements, statement of fixed assets), budget requests, and variances between estimated and actual financial performance, and (2) internal controls over compliance with laws and regulations, allegations of fraud, and financial reporting and/or safeguarding assets. Financial related audits determine whether (1) financial information is presented in accordance with established or stated criteria, (2) the audited entity has adhered to specific financial compliance requirements, or (3) the entity's internal control structure over financial reporting and/or safeguarding assets is suitably designed and implemented to achieve the control objectives [11, p. 13].

A performance audit is an objective and systemic examination of evidence for the purpose of providing an independent assessment of the performance of a government organization, program, activity, or function in order to provide information to improve public accountability and facilitate decision-making by parties with responsibility to oversee or initiate corrective action. [11, p. 14]

As mentioned earlier, performance audits consist of two types as explained by GAO [11, pp. 13–14]:

- economy and efficiency audits, determining whether (1) the audited entity is acquiring, protecting, and using its resources economically and efficiently, (2) the causes of inefficiencies or uneconomical practices, and (3) the audited entity has complied with laws and regulations on matters of economy and efficiency; and
- Program audits, determining (1) the extent to which the desired results or benefits established by the legislature or other authorizing body are being achieved; (2) whether organizations, programs, activities, or functions are being operated effectively; and (3) whether the audited entity has complied with significant laws and regulations applicable to the program.

Provision for this broad scope of audit is not intended to imply that all audits are and should be of such an extensive scope, as stated by GAO [11, p. 12]: Auditors may have a combination of financial and performance audit objectives or may have objectives limited to only some aspects of one audit type. It is essential that audit contracts or letters of engagement specify the scope of the audit and that the monitor's report clearly indicate the scope of the audit.

The GAO audit standards apply to audits of all governmental organizations, programs, activities, and functions, as well as internal audits and audits of contractors, grantees, and other external organizations performed by or for a governmental agency, whether they are performed by government auditors, independent public accountants, or others qualified to perform parts of the audit work contemplated under the audit standards. As the AICPA audit standards are appropriate to financial statement audits, but insufficient for the broader scope of governmental auditing, the GAO audit standards incorporate the AICPA audit standards and add additional auditing standards that are unique to governmental auditing.

General Standards.

1. Qualifications: "The staff assigned to perform the audit should collectively possess adequate professional proficiency for the tasks required" [11, p. 18]. In other words, they should have the knowledge and skills necessary for that audit.

2. Independence: "In all matters relating to the audit work, the audit organization and the individual auditors, whether government or public, should be free from personal or external impairments to independence, should be organizationally independent, and should maintain an independent attitude and appearance" [11, p. 22]. This standard is necessary for auditors' impartial opinions, conclusions, judgments, and recommendations. GAO cited two types of impairments under which auditors may not be impartial, or may not be perceived as impartial: personal and external impairments (Table 2).

3. Due professional care: "Due professional care should be used in conducting the audit and in preparing related reports" [11, p. 17]. Auditors should use sound judgment in establishing the scope, selecting the methodology, choosing tests and procedures for the audit, and evaluating and reporting the audit results.

4. Quality control: "Each audit organization conducting audits in accordance with these standards should have an appropriate internal quality control system in place and undergo an external quality control review" [11, pp. 28–29]. The internal quality control system assures that the audit organization (1) has adopted, and is following, applicable auditing standards, and (2) has established, and is following, adequate audit policies and procedures. In addition, the audit organization should have an external quality control review at least once every 3 years by an organization not affiliated with the organization being reviewed in order to assure that the audit organization has an internal quality control system is in place, and established policies and procedures and applicable auditing standards are being followed [11].

Field Work and Reporting Standards. The general audit standards just explained apply to all types of governmental audits. The U.S. General Accounting Office, however, prescribes two sets of field work standards: one for financial audits and another for performance audits. As there is not enough space in this chapter to explain in detail field work and reporting standards for both types of audits, Appendix A contains field work and reporting standards for both types of audits. Those who want to learn more detailed elaborations of these standards need to read the GAO's *Government Auditing Standards* [11].

Audit Committees. GAO [11, p. 49] requires that "auditors should communicate certain information related to the conduct and reporting of the audit to the *audit committee* [author's

Table 2 Circumstances Under Which Auditors May Fail to Be Impartial

Personal impairments	External impairments
Official, professional, personal, or financial relationships that might cause an auditor to limit the extent of the inquiry, to limit disclosure, or to weaken or slant audit findings in any way	External interference or influence that improperly or imprudently limits or modifies the scope of an audit
Preconceived ideas toward individuals, groups, organizations, or objectives of a particular program that could bias the audit	External interference with the selection or application of audit procedures or in the selection of transactions to be examined
Previous responsibility for decision making or managing an entity that would affect current operations of the entity or program being audited	Unreasonable restrictions on the time allowed to complete an audit
Biases, including those induced by political or social convictions, that result from employment in, or loyalty to, a particular group, organization, or level of government	Interference external to the audit organization in the assignment, appointment, and promotion of audit personnel
Subsequent performance of an audit by the same individual who, for example, had previously approved invoices, payrolls, claims, and other proposed payments of the entity or program being audited	Restrictions on funds or other resources provided to the audit organization that would adversely affect the audit organization's ability to carry out its responsibilities
Concurrent or subsequent performance of an audit by the same individual who maintained the official accounting records	Authority to overrule or to influence the auditor's judgment as to the appropriate content of an audit report
Financial interest that is direct, or is substantial though indirect, in the audited entity or program	Influences that jeopardize the auditor's continued employment for reasons other than competency or the need for audit services

Source. Ref. 11.

emphasis] or to the individuals with whom they have contracted for the audit." An audit committee is typically a committee of governing board whose function is "to help select the auditor, monitor the audit process, review results of the audit, assist the governing board in understanding the results of the audit, and to participate with both management and the independent auditor in resolving internal control or other deficiencies, identified during the audit" [12, p. 451]. According to Hay and Wilson [12, p. 452], an audit committee can provide substantial benefit as it:

- Strengthens the stewardship reporting function of the governing board
- Improves communication between the independent auditor and management
- Enhances the auditor's independence by serving as an objective buffer between the auditor and management
- Helps ensures maximum value and benefit from the audit for taxpayers and creditors

Auditing Procedures

As the scope of auditing is broad, it is hardly possible to fully evaluate at one time the performance of a governmental agency's activities in all three types of audits described earlier. Therefore, an audit should begin with a clearly stated objective. After the audit coverage is stated, an efficiently performed audit requires three phases as recommended by the General Accounting Office [13]: survey, review, and report, including recommendations, where appropriate.

Survey Phase

The survey phase of an audit encompasses gathering general working information, studying legislation, and testing management controls.

Gathering General Working Information. An auditor should obtain general working information on all important aspects of the agency being audited or a segment thereof in as short a time as possible. This kind of information will enable the auditor to start organizing the audit work and making plans for preliminary testing and detailed review of controls and activities. Gathering general working information should be done through initial contacts with agency officials who are informed about the general plans and the nature of the audit. Discussions with these officials may lead to obtaining valuable information or identifying troublesome areas.

Some of the sources from which general working information may be readily obtained include:

- Legislative reference files of the General Accounting Office or of the agency being audited
- Budget date submitted to the legislative body
- Printed hearings of legislative committees on authorizations and appropriations or on agency activities and related reports
- Reports prepared by the agency being audited, other governmental agencies, outside consultants, universities, or research organizations
- Reorganization plans
- Historical and informational pamphlets about the agency or its programs
- Agency internal audit, inspection, or other internal reports
- Agency procedural manuals, policy procurements, directories, or regulations

Through initial contacts with agency officials and examination of printed documents, general information such as the following can be compiled:

- History, background, and purposes of the activities or programs being examined
- Organization of the agency such as division of duties and responsibilities, principal delegations of authority, nature, size, and location of field offices, and number of employees
- Types, cost, and location of the assets
- Other financial data such as cost of operations by periods, year-by-year records of income from revenue-producing operations, borrowing authority and operations, if any

The general working information is used in planning succeeding phases of the audit and as source of reference in carrying out the detailed examination work.

Studying Legislation. The pertinent laws and legislative history should be carefully studied to ascertain congressional intent as to:

- The purpose, scope, and objectives of the activity or program being examined
- The manner in which they are to be conducted and financed
- The nature and extent of the agency's authority and responsibility

Limited Testing of Management Controls. The policies established to govern agency activities under examination should be analyzed for conformity with applicable laws and congressional intent and their appropriateness for carrying out authorized activities or programs in an effective, efficient, and economical manner.

The auditor also obtains practical working information on how the agency's system of controls *actually* works by testing the effectiveness and usefulness of controls over specific work activities. This information is useful in identifying possible management weaknesses and other matters on which the expenditure of additional time and effort will be warranted during the review phase.

At completion of the survey phase, the auditor is able to clearly identify important issues and problems to be examined in more depth. Survey information is used to establish specific review objectives, estimate staffing requirements, schedule work at specific locations, prepare work programs, and establish target dates for completion of the review and reporting phases.

Review Phase

This phase consists of the detailed examination or evaluation of specific activities or operations to the extent necessary to achieve the approved objectives of the assignment in accordance with the prescribed auditing standards. Detailed examination or evaluation work includes exploring and developing all pertinent and significant information necessary to properly consider, support, and presenting findings, conclusions, and recommendations.

Report Phase

The results of the audit work should be promptly communicated, either orally or in writing, to the Congress, appropriate congressional committees, or agency officials as a basis for action, where necessary, and for information purposes. Except in very unusual circumstances, some type of external communication should follow every review performed.

Relationship Between Audit Phases

A close relationship exists between all phases of work performed on an audit assignment. The manner and extent to which these phases are carried out and the interrelationships between them vary between assignments, depending on the objectives established in each case, whether the audit is being made for the first time or is a recurring or follow-up assignment, and the significance of the activities or programs to be examined. For example, more survey work would normally be performed on an initial assignment than for one involving activities that have been previously reviewed. In the latter cases, some updating of general information will be required, but complete new surveys should not be necessary.

In all assignments, the nature and objectives of the reporting should be established as soon as possible and all audit work performed so as to meet those requirements adequately and promptly.

Some Underlying Principles

Some basic principles underlying the nature of audit works are summarized next.

Prerequisites for Evaluations of Agency Operations

The starting point in a performance audit is to find out how the agency itself conducts its work and makes its decisions. Without this knowledge, the effectiveness of the agency's methods, policies, or procedures cannot be satisfactorily evaluated.

Emphasis on Opportunities for Improvement

In planning and conducting audits, emphasis should be given to those aspects of agency operations and activities in which opportunities for improvement appear to exist. Thus, auditors need to examine subjects or problems of known or anticipated congressional interest such as management weaknesses as ineffectiveness, inefficiency, waste and extravagance, improper expenditures, and failure to comply with laws or congressional intent. In their reports, auditors should also give recognition to (1) audit work resulting in favorable findings, (2) work sufficiently intensive to enable reporting no significant findings, and (3) general reviews that reveal no indications of weakness warranting closer examination.

Identification of Individuals Responsible for Deficiencies

In developing audit findings and identifying related management weaknesses, auditors should try to determine individuals or organizational units responsible for the agency's deficiency. This information need not be disclosed in audit reports, but should be made available to top agency officials orally or in the letter transmitting copies of the report. On request, or when deemed desirabe, such information should also be disclosed to responsible legislators.

Actions Against Accountable Officers

Although auditors are not empowered to direct changes in agency policies, procedures, and functions, they do possess the power to refuse credit to accountable officers for payments made illegally or improperly from appropriated funds. With this power, they are thus responsible for taking actions against the accountable officer or that officer's surety to enforce recovery of money illegally or improperly paid out.

Violations of Criminal Laws

In performing auditing, auditors may encounter violations of criminal laws that warrant the attention of federal agencies having criminal law enforcement responsibilities. The responsibility for investigating violations of federal criminal laws is vested in the Federal Bureau of Investigation (FBI), except in certain specialized areas where the responsibility is assigned to other agencies. The more important types of federal criminal law violations that may be encountered in audit work and that are subject to referral to the FBI are fraud, false claims, conflict of interest, perjury, bribery, and theft or embezzlement of government funds or property. It is necessary to promptly furnish to the appropriate criminal law enforcement agency all information concerning suspected criminal law violations arising in auditing.

Detection and Prevention of Fraud

The detection of fraud is not a primary reason for an audit. However, the possibilities of fraud in governmental programs and activities should be given full consideration in this type of audit, and any indications of fraud should be investigated to the point where a determination can be made to refer it to the proper criminal law enforcement agency.

THE SINGLE AUDIT

Overview

A major development in governmental auditing was in 1984 when the Single Audit Act was enacted "to improve audits of federal aid programs" [14, p. 1]. Prior to the passage of this act, state and local governments were subjected to numerous audits by various federal and state audit agencies and independent public accountants as each federal aid program had to be audited to ensure that resources provided to a recipient had been used for purposes allowable and that the recipient had compiled with any other legal requirements and agency regulations related to the program. Thus, in order to avoid numerous audits, the single audit approach—that is, *one audit* can satisfy all aspects of many audits done of a governmental unit—was required by Congress by the Single Audit Act of 1984.

The single audit covers the entire operations of a state or local government. Public hospitals and public colleges and universities may be excluded from state and local audits, but they are subjected to statutory requirements and the provisions of OMB's Circular A-110, "Uniform Requirements for Grants to Universities, Hospitals, and other Nonprofit Organizations." Moreover, annual single audits are required for state and local governments that receive, in a fiscal year, a total amount of federal financial assistance of (a) $100,000 or more to have a single audit for that fiscal year; or (b) $25,000 or more, but less than $100,000, to have either a single audit or a series of separate grant program audits for that fiscal year. If a government receives less than $25,000 in any fiscal year, it is exempt from the audit requirements of the Single Audit Act and all other federal audit requirements. Moreover, biennial audits may be accepted for governments that have policy calling for audits less frequent than annual.

One disadvantage of the single audit approach is that the grantor agencies do not receive as much information about the grant programs as they used to when grant-by-grant audits were performed. Thus, some grantor agencies have the right to require such additional work when necessary to fulfill their oversight responsibilities as long as they pay the additional audit costs. Moreover, some grant-by-grant and program-by-program audits are still performed either in addition to the single audit or instead of a single audit under some of the options and exceptions permitted by the Single Audit Act of 1984 [7, p. 790].

The purposes of the single audit, as provided by the Single Audit Act, consist of:

- Improving the financial management and accountability of state and local governments with respect to federal financial assistance programs
- Establishing uniform requirements for audits of federal financial assistance provided to state and local governments
- Promoting the efficient and effective use of audit resources
- Ensuring that the federal government relies upon and uses audit work done pursuant to the Act to the maximum extent practicable

The Single Audit Act also provides for *cognizant federal agencies* to ensure that audits are made and reports are received in a timely manner and in accordance with the requirements of OMB's Circular A-128; provide technical assistance and liaison to state and local governments and independent auditors; coordinate audits made by or for federal agencies; and oversee the resolution of audit findings, among other things. A cognizant agency, assigned by the Director of the Office of Management and Budget, is usually a major grantor.

The scope of single audits consists of (1) financial and performance audits, (2) audit of an entity's internal accounting and other control systems, and (3) audit or an entity's compliance with laws and requirements. In other words, the single audit requirements go beyond those of GAAS and GAGAS to include guidance provided in OMB Circular A-123, OMB Circular A-128, and OMB A-133. "Compliance Supplements for Single Audit of State and Local Governments."

Audit reports, prepared at the completion of the single audit, serve many needs of state and local governments as well as meeting the requirements of the Single Audit Act. They should be made up at least [14, pp. 8–9]:

- The auditor's report on financial statements and on a schedule of federal assistance showing the total expenditures for each federal assistance program
- The auditor's report on the study and evaluation of internal control systems

- The auditor's report on compliance containing (1) a statement of positive assurance with respect to those items tested for compliance, (2) negative assurance on those items not tested, (3) a summary of all instances of noncompliance, and (4) an identification of total amounts questioned as a result of noncompliance

In general, audit reports must state that the audit was made in accordance with GAAS, GAGAS, and the provisions of the Single Audit Act and OMB Circular A-128 or OMB Circular A-133. AICPA [9] illustrated three levels of audit reports, as required by OMB Circular A-128, in Figure 1. The top two levels of Figure 1 consist of three required audit reports in compliance with both AICPA and GAO auditing standards. The bottom level of Figure 1 is comprised of five reports related to the audit of federal financial assistance (FFA).

The costs of single audits are charged to federal assistance programs. State and local governments should follow the federal procurement standards prescribed by Attachment O of the Office of Management and Budget Circular A-102, "Uniform Requirements for Grants to State and Local Governments." These standards provide that federal grant recip-

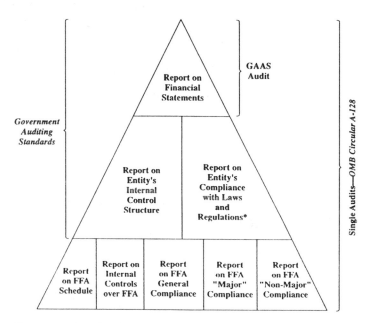

Figure 1 Levels of reporting in governmental single audits.

ients should consider whether it would be more economical to purchase the services from private accounting firms or to enter into intergovernmental agreements for audit services.

Internal Control

As shown in Figure 1, reports on the audited entity's enternal control structure are required by the Single Audit Act, which defines internal controls as a plan of organization and methods and procedures adopted by management to ensure that (1) resource use is consistent with laws, regulations, and policies; (2) resources are safeguarded against waste, loss, and misuse; and (3) reliable data are obtained, maintained, and fairly disclosed in reports. In implementing this requirement, OMB has issued guidelines on internal audits (Circular A-128 and Circular A-133).

In the literature of public budgeting and financial management, a great deal of attention has been given to legislative control of the purse and how to exercise and safeguard that authority. In the federal government, although the Accounting and Auditing Act of 1950 required the head of each federal agency to establish and maintain adequate systems of internal control, little attention had been devoted to how to execute the budget, how to prevent and detect fraud and errors, and how to promote efficiency and effectiveness. Probably recognizing waste and inefficiency in the federal government, President Reagan established in 1982 the Private Sector Survey on Cost Control, known as the Grace Commission, to analyze the operations of federal government including public budgeting and financial management. In 1982, the Federal Managers' Financial Integrity Act was passed to require evaluations and reports on the adequacy of the systems of internal control of each executive agency. In June 1983, the General Accounting Office established and published internal control standards, which were incorporated in Title 2 of the *General Accounting Office Policy and Procedures Manual for Guidance of Federal Agencies*. The Office of Management and Budget issued detailed guidelines in its Circular A-123, "Internal Control Systems," and its booklet entitled "Guidelines for the Evaluation and Improvement of Internal Control Systems in the Federal Government." These documents provide general guidelines and standards for establishing internal control systems of each executive agency, and evaluating and reporting on the adequacy of the agency internal control systems. Moreover, the Single Audit Act of 1984 requires the independent auditor to determine and report on, among other things, whether the organization has internal (accounting and administrative) control systems to reasonably assure that a federal assistance program is in compliance with applicable laws and regulations. Major institutional changes in the early 1990s, including the Chief Financial Officers Act of 1990, the creation of the Federal Accounting Standards Board in 1990, and the Federal Performance and Results Act of 1993, provide the impetus for even greater emphasis on internal control.

Independent auditors are required to obtain an understanding of the internal control structure that is sufficient to plan the audit and assess control risk for the assertions embodied in the financial statements. They must communicate the following matters:

- Identification of the categories of internal control structure
- Description of the scope of their work in obtaining in understanding of the internal control structure and in assessing control risk
- Description of deficiencies in the internal control structure not considered significant enough to be reportable conditions (AICPA, SAS no. 63, p. 18)

GAO has issued two set of audit standards for internal controls: financial control audit standards and management control audit standards.

Financial Control Audit Standards

Field Work Standards.   GAO [11, p. 38] requires that "auditors should obtain a sufficient understanding of internal controls to plan the audit and determine the nature, timing, and extent of tests to be performed." Internal controls focus on controls over (1) compliance with laws and regulations, such as governing bidding for, accounting for, and reporting on grants and contracts, and (2) financial reporting, and/or safeguarding assets. GAO provides four aspects of internal controls important to auditors' judgments:

- Control environment, including management's awareness or lack of awareness of applicable laws and regulations, auditee policy regarding such matters as acceptable operating practices and codes of conduct, and assignment of responsibility and delegation of authority to deal with such matters as organizational goals and objectives, operating functions, and regulatory requirements
- Safeguarding controls constituting a process designed to provide reasonable assurance regarding prevention or timely detection of the entity's assets that could have a material effect on the financial statements
- Controls over compliance with laws and regulations to understand internal controls relevant to financial statement assertions affected by those laws and regulations
- Control risk assessments by (1) identifying internal controls relevant to a specific financial statement assertion, (2) performing tests that provide sufficient evidence for effective controls, and (3) documenting the tests of controls

Auditors should understand these aspects of internal controls to plan the audit and determine the nature, timing, and extent of tests to be performed.

Reporting Standards.   GAO [11, p. 53] requires that "auditors should report . . . reportable conditions in internal controls." Auditors must report deficiencies in internal control systems, including [11, pp. 57–78]:

- *Absence* of (1) appropriate segregation of duties consistent with appropriate control objectives, (2) a sufficient level of control consciousness within the organization, and (3) appropriate reviews and approvals of transactions, accounting entries, or systems output
- *Evidence* of (1) inadequate provisions for safeguarding of assets, (2) failure to safeguard assets from loss, damage, or misappropriation, (3) system failure to provide complete and accurate output consistent with the auditee's control objectives because of misapplication of control procedures, (4) intentional override of internal controls by those in authority to the detriment of the overall objectives of the system, (5) failure to perform tasks that are part of internal controls, (6) significant deficiencies in the design or operation of internal controls that could result in violations of laws and regulations having a direct and material effect on the financial statements, and (7) failure to follow up and correct previously identified deficiencies in internal controls

Management Control Audit Standards

Field Work Standards.   GAO [11, p. 79] requires that "Auditors should obtain an understanding of management controls that are relevant to the audit. When management controls are significant to audit objectives, auditors should obtain sufficient evidence to support their judgments about those controls."

Management is responsible for establishing effective management controls including the plan of organization, methods, and procedures adopted by management to ensure that its goals are met. Auditors can obtain an understanding of management controls through inquiries, observations, inspection of documents and records, or review of other auditors' reports. The procedures auditors perform to obtain an understanding of management controls will vary among audits. Auditors must understand the following types of management controls to determine their significance to the audit objectives [11, pp. 80–81]:

- Program operations. Controls over program operations include policies and procedures that management has implemented to reasonably ensure that a program meets its objectives. Understanding these controls can help auditors understand the program operations that convert efforts to outputs.
- Validity and reliablity of data. Controls over the validity and reliability of data include policies and procedures that management has implemented to reasonably ensure that valid and reliable data are obtained, maintained, and fairly disclosed in reports. Understanding these controls can help auditors (1) assess the risk that data gathered by the entity may not be valid and reliable and (2) design appropriate tests of data.
- Compliance with laws and regulations. Controls over compliance with laws and regulations include policies and procedures that management has implemented to reasonably ensure that resource use is consistent with laws and regulations. Understanding the controls relevant to compliance with those laws and regulations that the auditors have determined are significant can help auditors assess the risk of illegal acts.
- Safeguarding resources. Controls over the safeguarding of resources include policies and procedures that management has implemented to reasonably ensure that resources are safeguarded against waste, loss, and misuse. Understanding these controls can help auditors plan economy and efficiency audits.

Reporting Standards. GAO [11, p. 98] requires that "auditors should report the scope of their work on management controls and any significant weaknesses found during the audit." In a performance audit, auditors may identify significant weaknesses in management controls as a cause of deficient performance.

CONCLUDING REMARKS

GAO [11, p. 8] states, "while not always specified by law, the accountability concept is inherent in the governing process." Governmental officials, legislators, and citizens want to know whether government funds are handled properly and in compliance with laws and regulations and whether governmental units, programs, and services are achieving their purposes and operating economically and efficiently. Governmental auditing helps provide accountability and assist government officials and employees in carrying out their responsibilities.

Audit reports, which are the end products of auditing, contain valuable information about the operations of the agency being audited, and particularly audit recommendations. The usefulness of auditing depends on the effectiveness of actions taken on audit recommendations. Where operating officials disagree with the auditor's recommendations, mechanisms should be established to reconcile the differences or to call for a decision at a higher management level.

Primary responsibility for action and follow-up on audit recommendations rests with management. However, reporting a finding, observation, or recommendation does not mean the end of an auditor's concern with the matter. From time to time auditors should ascertain whether their recommendations have received serious management consideration and whether satisfactory corrective action has been taken.

Finally, governmental audits, particularly through performance audits, should not be viewed only in the context of auditing itself. Audit reports provide useful information for effective budget execution and decision making. Indeed, financial auditing enhances budget execution and decisions as it provides (1) independent reports on whether a governmental entity has complied with laws and regulations including budget appropriations, and (2) an independent assessment of a governmental unit, program, activity, or function. This will help administrators to initiate corrective management and policy actions.

REFERENCES

1. R. E. Schlosser, "The Field of Auditing," *Cashin's Handbook for Auditors* (J. A. Cashin, P. D. Neuworth, and J. F. Levy, eds.), McGraw-Hill, New York: 1.3–1.19 (1986).
2. D. L. Scantlebury, "Federal Government Auditing," *Cashin's Handbook for Auditors* (J. A. Cashin, P. D. Neuworth, and J. F. Levy, eds.), McGraw-Hill, New York: 9.1–9.21 (1986).
3. Robert H. Montgomery, *Auditing Theory and Practice*, The Ronald Press Company, New York (1912).
4. National Council on Governmental Accounting, *Governmental Accounting, Auditing, and Financial Reporting*, Municipal Finance Officers Association, Chicago (1968).
5. American Institute of Certified Public Accountants and National Committee on Governmental Accounting, *Joint Statement on Competitive Bidding for Audit Services in Governmental Agencies*, (1968).
6. National Council on Governmental Accounting, *Governmental Accounting, Auditing and Financial Reporting*, Municipal Finance Officers Association, Chicago (1980).
7. R. J. Freeman and G. D. Shoulders, *Fund Accounting: Theory and Practice*, 5th ed., Prentice Hall, Englewood Cliffs, N.J. (1996).
8. American Institute of Certified Accountants, *Codification of Statements on Auditing Standards*, AICPA, New York (1995).
9. American Institute of Certified Public Accountants, *Audits of State and Local Governmental Units, Revised*, AICPA, New York (1994).
10. U.S. General Accounting Office, *Standards for Audit of Governmental Organizations, Programs, Activities, and Functions*, U.S. GAO, Washington, D.C. (1972).
11. U.S. General Accounting Office, *Government Auditing Standards, 1994 Revision*, U.S. GAO, Washington, D.C. (1994).
12. L. E. Hay and E. R. Wilson, *Accounting for Governmental and Nonprofit Entities*, 10th ed., Irwin, Chicago (1995).
13. U.S. General Accounting Office, *Comprehensive Audit Manual*, U.S. GAO, Washington, D.C. (1978).
14. U.S. Office of Management and Budget, *Circular A-128, Audits of State and Local Governments*, U.S. Office of Management and Budget, Washington, D.C. (1995).

BIBLIOGRAPHY

American Institute of Certified Public Accountants, *Codification of Statements on Auditing Standards*, AICPA, New York (1994).
———, *Guidelines for Financial and Compliance Audits of Federally Assisted Programs*, U.S. GAO, Washington, D.C. (1980).
———, *Inspectors General Find Significant Problems*, U.S. GAO, Washington, D.C. (1985).

31

An Inquiry into the Feasibility of a National Accounting Policy for Public Schools

C. William Garner

This impetus for this inquiry leading to an endorsed documentation of national accounting and budgeting policies in reference to public school districts stemmed from a series of surveys and observations conducted by the author from 1991 to 1994. The information gained from these inquiries indicated that many education administrators and professors were not aware of the meaning of Generally Accepted Accounting Principles (GAAP) and efforts to establish a national accounting policy that would pertain to public school districts. For example, some survey respondents believed the Governmental Accounting Standards Board (GASB) was a federal agency, that all states had the same accounting and budgeting procedures, and the demand for comprehensive financial disclosures would be an improper (even illegal) infringement on the rights of schools.

The deductions gained from the surveys were reinforced by observations made in reference to the implementation of an accounting system based on GAAP for public school districts. Specifically, on July 1, 1993, a double-entry accounting method replaced a single-entry method of accounting used by over 600 public school districts in New Jersey since their creation. In the two years prior to implementation, most administrators were adamantly opposed to changes but were largely uninformed of the reasons for them. Since their implementation, there has been a larger than usual turnover in school business personnel and a number of educators still believe the state did not have a basis for replacing the single-entry method. Yet these new standards of professional practice are likely to be utilized by most state and local governments by the turn of the century, if federal support for them is offered, and if the political consequences of implementation can be tolerated. In any event, the following documented review of the development and status of accounting and budgeting policies, along with an overview of public school finance, was prepared to assist educators in their understanding of the relevant of the evolving business directives.

Source: *Public Budgeting Fin. Manage.*, 8(2): 208–223 (Summer 1996). Copyright © 1996 by Pr-Academics Press.

METHOD OF REVIEW

Contemporary governmental accounting and budgeting in the United States have roots that can be traced to events that occurred before the colonies were founded. Since the creation of the U.S. federal government, the accounting and budgeting policies for state and local governments have had little direct centralized regulation and, as a result, have a great deal of variability. This inquiry, therefore, began with the origin of budgets and double-entry accounting prior to the colonial period and then moved to the framing of the U.S. Constitution, to the events of 1920 and 1921, and to two critical decades of the twentieth century, the 1930s when the Security and Exchange Acts were passed and the 1970s when an effort was made to amend the Security and Exchange Acts, to 1984.

The general method of review was to look at when, where, and why accounting and budgeting policies were implemented and to identify the sources of current governmental budgeting and accounting policies in the United States. The review was then broadened to include the public school movement, particularly in reference to the right of local districts to collect taxes to finance their schools.

THE EVOLUTION OF PUBLIC BUDGET POLICY

The review of the development of budget policy was limited to the English method since the first budget presented to the new federal government of the United States by Alexander Hamilton followed the procedures established by the English government. The first call for a public budget in the English tradition, however, occurred nearly 800 years ago in an effort by the governed to ensure they had opportunities to control the amount of taxes they had to pay. This "first" budget policy was presented in 1215 in England in article 12 of the Magna Carta, meaning Great Charter, which was an important step toward the establishment of a constitutional government [1].

Article 12 of the Magna Carta placed constraints on King John's right to tax nobility by requiring him to obtain approval from his barons before he could levy any special taxes on them. Although the Magna Carta was respected by King John's more immediate successors, but not King John, it was largely ignored by the royal leaders over the sixteenth and seventeenth centuries. In 1689 Parliament recalled the 12th article in order to gain public support for the English Bill of Rights that gave them the authority to set taxes. As a result, in the eighteenth century, when the American colonies began their rebellion, the budget policy in England required a presentation to Parliament through the Chancellor of the Exchequer of the expenditures for the previous year and an estimate of expenditures for the coming year which led to a tax levy. In 1789 when Alexander Hamilton, the first Secretary of the U.S. Treasury and an admirer of the English form of government, presented the first budget to Congress for approval, he presented it in the same manner as did his English counterparts. In doing so, Hamilton set a precedent leading to a law formalizing his procedure [2].

When the framers of the U.S. Constitution provided for a representative form of government with the power to set and collect taxes, they also stipulated in Article I, section 9.7 that "no money shall be drawn from the treasury, but in consequence of appropriations made by law." They also provided as per the English tradition that "a regular statement of the account of receipts and expenditures of all public money shall be published from time to time." The connection between the directives of the Constitution and the individual states is made through article IV, section 4, which holds that every state shall be guaranteed a republican form of government, as opposed to a monarchy or dictatorship. But the Constitution did not set a national budget policy or guidelines such as those expressed in article I, for the state and local governments to follow.

Consequently, the original 13 states, as well as the states that joined the federated government over the nineteenth and twentieth centuries, fashioned their own budget and accounting methods. By 1920 most state governments had adopted a formal budget policy, and in 1921 Congress passed the National Accounting and Budgeting Act requiring the preparation of one national budget. Presently, in the spirit of the democratic form of government, state and local governments have similar budget policies with procedural differences. The basic format for these policies requires that a report of receipts and expenditures for the coming year and a recommended tax levy be presented to the voters or their legally elected representatives for approval. Interestingly, this common policy evolved independent of a specific national directive.

THE DEVELOPMENT OF DOUBLE-ENTRY ACCOUNTING

The single-entry method of accounting, as opposed to the double-entry method, is limited to the maintenance of records of receipts and expenditures for the current fiscal year. This method was used by most state and local governments into the twentieth century, and in some cases is still used by some governments, because it is easy to learn and simple to operate. In addition, it met the needs of early governments since they did not have large sums of money to handle.

On the other hand, the double-entry accounting method is based on an algebraic formula; maintains records of assets, liabilities, and a fund balance as well as the receipts and expenditures of the current year; follows a set of formal procedures to record and process business transactions in order to prepare a set of financial statements; and allows for the accrual of receipts and expenditures. This method, along with a set of funds that segregate activities into independent accounting entities, is proposed for all state and local governments by the GASB. The double-entry method, therefore, provides more information and offers a control for budget receipts and expenditures. Although more complicated, the double-entry method is not difficult to operate or manage because of the availability of user-friendly computer software. Essentially, the bookkeeper has been replaced by the personal computer and a data-entry clerk.

Although some people assume the double-entry method is new, it was used by government managers over 800 years ago. More specifically, the earliest record of the double-entry method was found in the 1211 bank ledgers in Florence, Italy; the first complete set of accounting records was discovered in the treasurer's books dated 1340 for the City of Genoa; and the first book on double entry accounting, *Summa de Arithmetica Geometria Proportioni et Proprotionalita* (*Review of Arithmetic, Geometry, and Proportions*), was written by Luca Pacioli in 1494. One theory is that the double-entry form of accounting, which can be used to accurately record and process a large number of daily business transactions, was developed in the thirteenth century in Italy due to the opening of the trade routes to the Middle East. In addition, the double-entry method has been given partial credit by some historians for the success of the industrial revolution since it provided the means to accurately handle the large number of transactions generated by business and industry [2–5].

Even though the double-entry method was in existence when the United States won its independence, the accounting method of choice by the federal, state, and local governments was (and in some cases still is) the single-entry or budget method of accounting. The initial event that set a rationale for a national accounting policy based on a double-entry method occurred in 1933 and 1934 when the Securities Acts were passed in response to the great economic depression. The purpose of these acts was to develop a means whereby the public would be protected from investing money in profit companies that misrepresented or failed to reveal their financial standing. As a result, the Securities and Exchange Commission (SEC), an independent federal agency, was established in 1934 to oversee the accounting and financial reporting standards for all businesses, nonprofit agencies, and governments.

The SEC determined that rather than having the federal government regulate the accounting practices of private companies and all governments, the accounting profession should set reporting standards and insure compliance with the understanding that the best interests of the public would always be represented. The accounting profession, however, focused its efforts on profit companies, while each state continued to set their own accounting policy. Over the next 50 years, a number of professional associations evolved to make recommendations with respect to business guidelines for nonprofit organizations and state and local governments, including public school districts. Consequently, accounting policies varied from state to state, and in some states from one local government to another and even from one department within a state office to another [1,6].

Although proposals for a national accounting policy for the three levels of government (federal, state, and local) were proposed through the years, not until the succession of financial problems in New York, Cleveland, and Chicago from 1974 to 1980 was a serious effort made by the federal government to pass legislation to amend the Securities Act of 1934. The amendment, introduced by Senator Harrison Williams, would have given the federal government the authority to oversee the financial reporting activities of state and local governments through a standards council. The amendment was not popular and was seen as an assault on federalism. Although this effort failed in the early 1980s, primarily due to the Abscam affair involving Senator Williams, the amendment motivated the accounting profession to find a solution to the problems associated with state and local government accounting policy [7].

During the 1970s and 1980s, another factor contributing to the interest in developing a national accounting policy was the recognition that the number of state and local governments had become extremely large and responsible for collecting and spending a greater amount of public money. For example, in 1982 there were 50 state governments (with many agencies), 3,041 counties, 16,734 townships, 19,076 cities and towns, 28,588 other governmental bodies, and 14,581 school districts, for a total of 82,070 state and local governments [8]. In terms of the gross national product, the expenditures of the federal, state and local governments went from 28% in 1965 to nearly 41% in 1983 with the federal government spending around $1 trillion annually (60–61% of all government spending or 24% of the GNP) and employing around 2.8 million people plus 2.5 million military personnel [9]. In 1986, Conant [10] reported that on the basis of revenue received, 10 states could have been ranked in *Fortune*'s top 50 corporations and 24 in the top 100.

Still another concern was the unusual growth in the size of state governments from 1970 to 1985. For example, they had an increase in the number of people employed from 2.3 million to almost 4 million (an increase of 74%), in budget expenditures from $131.3 billion to $503.4 billion (a growth of 283%), and in revenue receipts from $77.8 billion to $365.3 billion (an increase of 370%) [10].

With respect to local governments, GASB [11] cited a myriad of interesting statistics relating the large amounts of money being spent at the local level. Specifically, in 1984 the transit systems spent $9.4 billion with 48% provided by state and local governments and 10% by the federal government. In 1986 there were 83,550 public schools in the United States serving over 40 million students and spending more than $155 billion (approximately

20% of all state and local expenditures); city governments spent $7.3 billion on fire protection; there were 5,700 community hospitals employing about 3 million people and spending over $130 million; the public assistance programs funded by federal, state and local governments spent over $16 billion and served around 11 million people; and state and local governments spent over $9.4 billion on public health programs. In 1987 all levels of government spent approximately $65 billion on highways with $17 billion on maintenance and operations plus over $7.3 billion for solid waste services; and in 1985–1986 state and local governments spent over $16 billion on water supply and over $13 billion for waste water treatment.

Consequently, in 1984 the Financial Accounting Foundation (FAF) established two national accounting standards boards. The Governmental Accounting Standards Board (GASB) was created to set national accounting policies for all state and local governmental bodies. The Financial Accounting Standards Board (FASB), which was already in existence in 1984, was designated to continue to set accounting policies for all other entities. The standards initially compiled for state and local governments by the GASB included directives of the National Council on Governmental Accounting (NCGA) and the American Institute of Certified Public Accountants (AICPA). In May 1986 the American Institute of Certified Public Accountants (AICPA) passed the AICPA Ethics Rule 203 recognizing the GASB as the standards setting body for state and local governments. In November 1989 the FAF Trustees clarified a jurisdictional division between the GASB and the FASB in terms of a standards hierarchy, and in January 1992 the decision of the FAF Trustees was implemented by the AICPA Auditing and Standards Board by issuing the Statement of Auditing Standards No. 69 [11].

As a result, a national accounting policy for state and local governments was made available. As the GASB acknowledge, however, individual states and some local governments have the legal right to establish their own method of governance even though their practices might not conform to GAAP. In these cases, the GASB [11, Cod. Sec. 1200.110] explains that although a governmental unit may utilize a different accounting method, legal directives may dictate that they must "maintain sufficient supplemental records to permit presentation of financial statements in conformity with GAAP." They continued that since it would be costly, and in some cases impossible, to annually convert financial data generated by one entry method into the statements specified by GAAP, state and local governments would be better off following the accounting procedures and standards of the GASB.

Therefore, the GASB standards do not have the force of law. Rather, the legal directives must come from the individual states. As Richard Roberts [12, p. 3] Commissioner of the Securities and Exchange Commission, pointed out, the "GASB does not enjoy the mantle of an endorsement from a federal regulator as does FASB." Thus, a state or local government may have an accounting system that relies on GAAP, but not be those presented by the GASB. Hence, one source for the confusion!

Indirect support for the implementation of an accounting system based on GAAP (not necessarily those of the GASB) will come from the Securities and Exchange Commission via the Exchange Act 15c2-12 of 1989 that was amended in November 1994 and is to be phased in by 1996. This act requires that sound financial statements be prepared and proper accounting principles (GAAP) be followed by municipalities intending to issue securities or have securities on the open market. Roberts [12] reported that 46 states require, or are in the process of establishing the requirements, that their state government present their financial statements in accordance to GAAP and that a growing majority are relying on those presented by the GASB. Thus, as with a national budget policy, a common national accounting policy may evolve, but without a national directive.

PUBLIC SCHOOL FINANCE

The confusion exhibited by some educators when queried about national accounting and budgeting policies procedures is not surprising in view of the history of public education and school finance. First, some educators do not see the public school district as a local government since by definition governments have the authority to rule, manage and control. In this context, schools are not a government. Second, other public nongoverning entities, such as public libraries, museums, and hospitals, receive their public money from a local, county, or state government. Although school districts are the only public nongoverning body with legal authority to render a tax assessment, educators see themselves more akin to other nongoverning entities not required to make independent public financial disclosures. Third, public schools and the method of financing them evolved because of an omission by the framers of the federal constitution. This omission made education a responsibility of the state governments, which, in turn, eventually transferred the responsibility to their local governments. Because of this shift to the local level, the financing of public education was often a state-local government compromise and the current practices slowly evolved by chance and not by choice.

In the earliest years of the country, education was offered through private schools and some states attempted to offer financial support to these schools by methods carried over from the colonial period. Some states continued the rate bill method, which assessed parents for the education of their children. Unfortunately many parents refused to send their children to school or, since the charges were based on a day-to-day basis, limited the days of schooling to the amount of tuition they could afford. This method was continued by a few states until the beginning of the twentieth century. Other states used the pauper approach, which required parents to publicly declare themselves paupers in order for the state to pay their child's tuition to the private school. Connecticut, in 1795, and later several other states set up education funds that were expected to provide money to schools for an indefinite period. For a number of reasons, the money in these funds did not last as expected [13–15].

The first collection of local tax money was in 1805 for private, and usually sectarian, schools. As a result, for a variety of reasons public budgets and accounting were not considered relevant. For instance, in some towns it would not have been proper to question the church elders. In the first cases when the state offered a community money, they were to match the amount from a local collection. In general, this was not too successful. Free public schools were finally made possible in 1834 in Pennsylvania under the Free School Act. This legislation eliminated the pauper method by permitting (not requiring) districts to collect tax money for local schools. A short time later in 1842, New York legislators gave the New York City Board of Education the authority to set up a system of non-sectarian free schools. The first tax collections were limited to the support of elementary schools and the inclusion of high schools did not become a popular idea until after 1872, when Michigan, in the Kalamazoo Case, declared it to be legal. This obviously contributed to the increase in high school enrollments from 10% of the eligible students in 1900 to 85% by mid-twentieth century. By 1915 all states, except Georgia and Mississippi, had compulsory attendance laws [13–15].

At the turn of the century the most popular method used to raise local revenue was the tax on property. The need to finance two world wars and deal with the Great Depression was likely the reason there were no innovative efforts or startling changes in the financing of public schools during the first half of the twentieth century. After World War II, however, public school enrollments and costs increased dramatically because of the baby boom. There were still no significant changes in the way public schools were financed until the 1960s when federal and state governments determined to reform education by providing a larger share of dollars to local schools [14]. For instance in 1920 state governments provided 16.5% of public school revenues while in 1986 they increased their share to over 50% and the federal government supplied 6.5% [16].

The 1970s began a new era in which a number of legal challenges were aimed at the reduction of educational inequities caused by the unequal availability of local tax dollars, particularly in relation to the needs of students. In particular, the cases focused on the state constitutions that require the state legislature to establish and maintain public schools. The initial ruling in 1973 was made by the New Jersey Supreme Court in *Robinson v. Cahill* that declared the distribution of New Jersey state education dollars violated the state constitution's guarantee of a thorough and efficient education. This case was followed by numerous challenges in other states, although the decisions of the other state courts have been mixed [17].

In these recent legal challenges to the state's system of education, a common denominator has been the failure of the local property tax to adequately finance local schools, especially in poorer communities and rural areas. Guthrie, Garms, and Pierce [16] explain that our country has 50 systems of education, not including the territories, and propose that local property taxes cannot adequately meet the costs of these public school systems. Their position seems to be verified by the successful property tax revolts in four states: California in 1978, Massachusetts in 1980, Oregon in 1990, and Michigan in 1994 [18], and by efforts in other states to find alternatives to the public school system, such as hiring private contractors to run their schools, and passing charter school legislation and the voucher system. Another consequence from the agitation created by the failure to find an acceptable means to finance public schools has been a call for public disclosures of the dollars collected and spent, such as state government officials and local action groups questioning whether or not dollars are being expended properly. Thus, the accounting of school dollars has become a sensitive subject for many educators.

CONCLUSIONS

With respect to budgets, this inquiry suggests the existence of a de facto national budget policy, even for public school districts, most likely stemming from article IV, section 4 of the U.S. Constitution, which guarantees a republican form of government in each state. It is hard to imagine a representative form of government without a budget policy similar to one proposed over 800 years ago. Since budgets must formally interact with the accounting system, budget policies should become more refined and progressive as school officials take greater advantage of the interactions [1].

With respect to accounting, a national policy does not exist for governments, including public school districts. Although the Generally Accepted Accounting Principles are important, school districts may use one of several methods that comply with GAAP and, therefore, have differences in the funds selected, use of accruals, financial statements generated, recording of fixed assets, reporting of earned and unearned income, and so on. Without a national public endorsement from a federal regulator or national authority, attempts to standardize accounting procedures will be met with reservation, especially by the education community. A federal endorsement is problematic since it sets its own accounting standards that, in some cases, do not conform to GAAP. For example, at a workshop conducted for a federal agency, the author had to work with the single entry method used by that agency.

Even though the idea of a national standardized method of accounting may not be popular to some educators, there is ample evidence suggesting the need for a common policy. As the preceding statistics exhibited, the three level of governments (federal, state, and local) have experienced radical growth over the last part of this century. At the same time, they have evolved to create a giant infrastructure. What double-entry accounting did for the industrial revolution can be offered to big government and the infrastructure. For example, a local government regularly receives money from its state or federal government for particular projects or programs. When this occurs, the money must be spent according to the legal definition set forth in the original appropriation and the terms of the contract. Upon completion of the project or program, the expenditures are to be reported to the granting government with a verification by an auditor. The 1994 audits of school districts that installed a GAAP method in 1993 reported that some districts had improperly spent state and federal money appropriated for special education programs. An immediate reaction was to wonder how many times this had occurred in the past and how many times it occurs when audits cannot reveal such transgressions.

At the same time, many school districts have become "big business" operations. For instance, they may sell securities, manage investments, make long-term lease arrangements (both as a landlord and a tenant), generate income from the selling of goods and services, manage income producing capital assets, enter into contracts with private corporations, provide capital financing to nongovernmental third parties, and so on. These big operations require an accounting system that provides school districts with the capability of accurately recording and processing a large number of daily business transactions, the information needed to properly manage debt and investments, and the financial statements that offer investors accurate and reliable information. These ideals are similar to those held when the double-entry method was formed and when the SEC was created.

Further, efforts to equalize educational opportunities for all children are faced with incredible complications when school district budgets range from several million dollars to over $100 million and the value of capital assets in some districts approach $1 billion while in others they are nearly all at their salvage amount. In order to make the best decisions and take the proper actions to reform the education system, state leaders, judges, and legislators need valid financial data that can be compared from school to school, state to state, and year to year. This cannot occur if the method of accounting varies from school to school and the school district policies do not require a full financial disclosure of all money received, including earned and unearned income, and all reserves [19].

Without question, the implementation of a national policy for accounting would require a change in state statutes, the business procedures of school districts, and the jobs of many school officials. These changes, however, could then lead to new arrangements because of the inherent advantages of a GAAP method of accounting and standardization. For example, some state systems of education might be better off if they were financed through an earned income tax at the county level by an elected county board required to make equalized budget allocations to local district boards. In addition, the business operations of some local and county governments and public school districts could be combined. In both cases, the advantages are too numerous to mention, such as the savings of tax dollars, elimination of the property tax, and, at least, a regional equalization of education. Although arguments to such proposals can easily be offered, the quotation by Thomas Jefferson, which appears on the fourth panel in the Jefferson Memorial, makes the more important point. On this panel Jefferson is quoted as saying: "I am not an advocate for frequent changes in laws and constitutions, but laws and institutions must go hand in hand with the progress of the human mind. As that becomes more developed and manners and opinions change, with the change of circumstances, institutions must advance also to keep pace with the times. We might as well require a man to wear still the coat which fitted him when a boy as civilized society to remain ever under the regimen of their barbarous ancestors."

REFERENCES

1. C. W. Garner, *Accounting and Budgeting in Public and Nonprofit Organizations: A Manager's Guide*, Jossey-Bass, San Francisco (1991).
2. M. Chatfield, *A History of Accounting Thought*, Dryden Press, Hinsdale, Illinois (1974).
3. V. Kam, *Accounting Theory*, John Wiley & Sons, New York (1986).
4. G. A. Lee, The Development of Italian Bookkeeping: 1211–1300, *The Development of Double Entry* (C. Nobes, ed.), Garland, New York, pp. 137–155 (1984).
5. B. S. Yamey, The Functional Development of Double Entry Bookkeeping, *The Development of Double Entry* (C. Nobes, ed.), Garland, New York, pp. 333–342 (1984).
6. R. J. Freeman, C. D. Shoulders, and E. S. Lynn, *Governmental & Nonprofit Accounting: Theory & Practice*, 3rd ed., Prentice Hall, Englewood Cliffs, New Jersey (1988).
7. J. L. Chan, The Birth of Governmental Accounting Standards Board: How? Why? *Research in Governmental and Nonprofit Accounting*, Vol. I (J. L. Chan, ed.), JAI Press, Greenwich, Connecticut, pp. 3–32 (1985).
8. D. S. Wright, *Understanding Intergovernmental Relations*, 3rd ed., Brooks/Cole, Monterey, California (1988).
9. E. B. McGregor, Jr., The Evolving Role of the Federal Government, *Handbook of Public Administration* (J. L. Perry, ed.), Jossey-Bass, San Francisco, pp. 11–24 (1989).
10. J. K. Conant, The Growing Importance of State Government, *Handbook of Public Administration* (J. L. Perry, ed.), Jossey-Bass, San Francisco, pp. 25–39 (1989).
11. Governmental Accounting Standards Board, *Codification of Governmental Accounting and Financial Reporting Standards*, Norwalk, Connecticut (1995).
12. R. Y. Roberts, Developing Relations between the SEC and the GASB, *GASB Action Rep.*, *10* (5): 2–3 (1995).
13. A. E. Meyer, *An Educational History of the American People*, 2nd ed., McGraw-Hill, New York (1967).
14. J. D. Pulliam, *History of Education in America*, 2nd. ed., Merrill, Columbus, Ohio (1976).
15. S. A. Rippa, *Education in a Free Society*, 4th ed., Longman, New York (1988).
16. J. W. Guthrie, W. I. Garms, and L. C. Pierce, *School Finance and Educational Policy: Enhancing Educational Efficiency, Equality and Choice*, 2nd ed., Prentice Hall, Englewood Cliffs, New Jersey (1988).
17. W. D. Valente, *Law in the Schools*, 3rd ed., Macmillan, New York (1994).
18. S. D. Gold, *The Outlook for School Revenue in the Next Five Years*, Consortium for Policy Research, Rutgers University, New Brunswick, New Jersey (1995).
19. C. W. Garner, Closing the GAAP Gap: The National Accounting Standards Struggle, *School Business Affairs*, *60*(10): 4–9 (1994).

32

Government Contracting and Procurement: A Critical Process for Both the Public and Private Sectors

Susan A. MacManus

INTRODUCTION

Third-party government involves not merely the contracting out of specified services or acquisition of products. It often involves a real sharing of authority and decision-making, sometimes to a greater degree than is recognized at the outset of a new arrangement [1].

Government needs business and business needs government. From an economic perspective, business can make money from selling to government and government can "make money" through savings generated from contracting out and efficient purchasing. In a time of fiscal stress, it is in the interest of both sectors to do business with each other. The difficulty lies in how to make the public contracting and procurement process acceptable to both purchasing partners. Each sees certain costs and benefits of doing business with the other. Any attempt to reform the public procurement system, which is currently suffering from a bad image both inside and outside government, must begin with an understanding of each "partner's" goals and perspectives.

THE PUBLIC SECTOR'S PERSPECTIVE [2]

The fundamental goals of public purchasing and contracting are competition, conservation of funds, impartiality, and openness. According to the Council of State Governments and the National Association of State Purchasing Officials (NASPO):

Public business is to be offered for competition; bidders are to be treated alike and contracts administered alike, without favoritism; economy and value are basic aims; and the documents used and actions taken are public information [3].

Source: *International Journal of Public Administration*, vol. 15, no. 5 (1992), pp. 1213–1240.

Often these goals are perceived, even by government officials, as conflicting. But few deny the necessity of government buying certain goods and services from the private sector.

Benefits of Purchasing from the Private Sector

A number of studies have identified cost savings as government's primary motive for purchasing goods or services from the private sector. For example, one survey of 1086 cities and counties by the International City Management Association showed that 74% identified cost savings as an advantage of contracting out [4]. Reasons for the private sector's more cost-effective service delivery range from greater competition among suppliers, larger economies of scale, and the profit motive, to more efficient and effective use of labor and new technology [5].

The avoidance of start-up costs in providing a new service is another widely cited cost saving-related advantage of contracting with the private sector. Studies have found that governments tend to turn to the private sector to provide services and facilities that would otherwise not be available due to monetary or legal constraints [6].

Another advantage of private-sector service provision is flexibility. Relying on the private sector permits more rapid reactions to changing service needs and constituent demands and avoids the negative fallout from angry public employees when changes necessitate reductions in the level of service due to fiscal crisis [7]. As Rehfuss notes:

> Private contractors are more flexible. They are not bound to follow civil service rules and regulations in hiring, promoting, or disciplining employees. This reduces costs as well as increasing flexibility, since private employees can be more easily transferred and reassigned to more effective roles. Private employees can also be rewarded more quickly for good performance—a "plus" for morale in these organizations [8].

Risk avoidance is yet another perceived advantage of private-sector provision of goods and services. The skyrocketing costs of insurance and legal services have prompted governments to search for ways of avoiding high risk services [9]. However, case law is emerging that links liability for subcontractor failure to government and increases government responsibility for service specifications, monitoring, and evaluation [10].

Finally, government reliance on the private sector for goods and services is seen as promoting various social and economic objectives.

> [Government] procurement involves much more than buying. The process is used extensively to promote such social and economic objectives as interests of small businesses, use of minority business, fair employment practices payment of fair wages, safe and healthful working conditions, employment of the handicapped, rehabilitation of prisoners, and use of recycled materials [11].

In a number of jurisdictions, purchasing policies also promote goods and services produced locally, in-state or in the United States [12].

Perhaps the most succinct statement of the conditions under which government reliance on the private sector makes the most sense has been made by Rehfuss:

> Times when it is a good idea to contract out [with the private sector] include when the intent is to reduce costs, when the contract can be well monitored, when technical or complex services are required, when benchmark job costs must be set, and when it is important to avoid management or policy constraints [13].

To this list, another key condition must be added: the availability of a number of willing, capable, and competing private-sector suppliers [14].

Costs of Buying From the Private Sector

One large-scale survey of local government officials found that the major obstacles to greater reliance on the private sector are opposition from public employees and elected officials; an insufficient supply of competent private deliverers; lack of evidence of the effectiveness of private alternatives; and bureaucratic and legal constraints [15].

Another large-scale survey of local governments showed that half (51%) of the respondents identified loss of control as the major impediment to greater privatization efforts, followed by government union and employee resistance (46%), politics (42%), lack of belief in the benefits of privatization (37%), lack of awareness of the benefits of privatization (24%), bureaucratic inertia (25%), and hostile public opinion (24%). Also cited were a lack of interest by the private sector (16%), lack of confidence in the private sector (13%), and the need for enabling legislation (8%) [16].

Many governments are hesitant to turn to the private sector where evidence is not clear that there will be either immediate or long-term cost savings. Although some studies have shown that privatization can save money, other studies have come to the opposite conclusion or to no conclusion at all [17]. Valente and Manchester [18] conclude, "It is probably fair to say that for every successful contract there is an unsuccessful one." Studies by the American Federation of State, County, and Municipal Employees (AFSCME) have challenged most of the assertions of privatization proponents [19].

Other studies have questioned whether privatization actually increases competition, especially over time. Fitch summarizes these concerns well by pointing out that (1) intergovernmental competition may be equally effective; (2) competition may diminish the advantages of economies of scale; (3) competition is not always synonymous with integrity or honest workmanship; and (4) competition may increase lobbying efforts on the part of contractors to secure future contracts and may drive up the costs so that no cost savings are generated in the long term [20].

The unreliability of some contractors and the difficulty, legal necessity, and costs of monitoring and evaluating contracts have made privatization less desirable for other governments [21]. Cost overruns, price gouging, and bribery historically have been problems in the defense, construction, and health care arenas, but are not limited to these functional areas [22]. One study estimates the true cost of monitoring "may well exceed 10 percent" [23].

Failures of contracting out are not limited to those involving scandals and corruption. They can include businesses that go bankrupt or businesses that simply cannot deliver a product or service in a quality, timely fashion. Consequently, the costs of failure (new start-up costs, transitional costs, legal costs, and the loss of service) must be considered in any government decision involving privatization [24].

Several other potential problems may emerge from contracting out and deter governments from more efforts in that direction. Some studies have suggested that greater reliance on the private sector reduces citizen participation in government and threatens the foundations of democracy [25]. Another concern is that calculations showing cost savings from privatization frequently fail to determine whether the savings came at the expense of service quality [26]. Relatedly, government officials are often concerned that low bid requirements do not always attract a large pool of high quality bidders.

Critics of privatization also claim there is little evidence that social and economic objectives of government procurement policies have been met to any greater degree through contracting out policies, particularly set-aside programs [27]. Economic development efforts aimed at stimulating creation and expansion of small and minority-owner businesses have not been overwhelming successful. The President's 1990 report on *The State of Small Business* shows that small businesses received only 15% of federal prime contracts (over $25,000), small minority-owned businesses, 3%, and women-owned businesses, 1%. In addition, political and legal backlashes from these "affirmative action" contracting policies (reverse discrimination lawsuits) have increasingly made governments reticent to contract out [28].

In summary, the long list of concerns about contracting out has made governments more cautious in increasing their reliance on the private sector, but the perceived fiscal benefits have often outweighed the costs. Governments are more likely to conclude that the benefits of buying from the private sector outweigh the costs. The reverse is more often the case among businesses.

THE PRIVATE SECTOR'S PERSPECTIVE [29]

A business's primary goal in selling to any entity—government, another business, or an individual—is to make as large a profit as possible. As noted earlier, one of government's goals is to buy a good/service at the lowest cost (which translates into a smaller profit margin for the competing firms). Thus from the outset, it is apparent that the goals of the two purchasing partners are somewhat counter to each other, although when a business itself is the purchaser, its goals are similar to government's.

The Benefits of Selling to Government

The opportunity to make a profit is the major benefit of selling to government. The importance of this motive is predictable in a capitalistic economy and should not automatically be regarded as unethical or undesirable.

In some instances, businesses have been created specifically to meet the unique product and service needs of the public sector, such as defense-related items. Several of the federal government's largest suppliers sell over half of their products/services to the federal government. However, the vast majority of government contracts (measured in terms of numbers, not total dollars) go to medium-sized and small firms [30].

For many businesses, government is just another customer, not their primary customer. There are a number of reasons why these businesses find government a desirable buyer. Preeminent may be the fact that government will pay its bills—eventually [31]. Unlike private-sector customers, governments rarely refuse to pay their bills, although they may not be as prompt as businesses would like.

Businesses that have sold to government for quite some time may find that government contracts are a fairly predictable revenue source, far less elastic than the private sector [32]. More-established businesses may also have less difficulty in getting through the government procurement maze and may be less intimidated by it than newly established firms. More-established firms most likely have less difficulty in meeting government surety requirements such as bid, performance, or payment bonds. Established firms also are more likely to benefit from reputations for delivering goods and services of high quality in prompt fashion. For the new firm, the advantages of contracting with government may be the opportunity to get established, expand its business, and make a profit [33].

In other instances, businesses sell to government because they genuinely believe "that private sector know-how and private sector efficiency [can] save the government and taxpayers a lot of money" [34]. Business owners are taxpayers, too!

For other firms, the incentive to sell to government comes from their interactions with elected officials and their perceptions about the liabilities of refusing to sell to government. For example, a firm may place itself on the vendor list and compete for contracts at the request of an elected official for fear that failure to compete for government businesses may have negative consequences in the regulatory arena (e.g., loss of tax incentives).

Another factor that may influence a firm's willingness to sell to government is the availability of detailed, yet easy to follow, guides and/or help sessions describing how to complete the necessary forms to get certified (if necessary), how to compete for government business, and delineating who makes the purchasing decision. Without such help, many small firms often are unwilling to invest the time and energy it takes to sell to government.

A survey of 3,282 businesses of all sizes, industrial classifications, and ownership characteristics, located in 30 states and the District of Columbia, asked why corporations did, or would like to do, business with government [35]. The vast majority (61%) said they sell to government because they "are confident payment will be received"; 33% see government revenue as "a predictable revenue source"; and 10% see government business as attractive because of its volume, its potential for helping them establish and expand their business, and as their reward for offering a high-quality product or service at a good price. Nearly one-fourth see government as their primary market because their firm "produces a service/commodity that is primarily used by government." Nine percent, mostly new, small, or minority-owned firms, see selling to government as offering them "a chance to get established."

A sizeable proportion of businesses report that they sell to the public sector because they have become familiar with its rules and processes. Forty-one percent say they sell to government because "they have been doing business with the same government for years"; 22% identify "good relations with the government's purchasing office"; 15% cite the fairness of purchasing policies; and 11% see government purchasing procedures as efficient and easy to follow.

Still other firms do business with government because they have been enticed to do so by government purchasing practices designed to broaden the vendor pool. Some 12% report they were actively "recruited by the government purchasing staff" to sell to government; 7% identify participation in a government minority business enterprise program as a reason; 7% identify small business enterprise program participation as a reason. However, the businesses most likely to acknowledge that they were recruited by a government purchasing staff are older, larger, more established firms.

The "Costs" of Selling to Government

Statistics show that only a small proportion of American businesses sell to government. One account estimates that less than 2% of U.S. businesses sell to the federal government [36]. The proportion of businesses selling to state and local governments is probably somewhat higher, although we found no estimate of this figure in our research.

There are a number of reasons why businesses are reluctant to sell to government [37]. One oft-cited reason is that businesses see public sector purchasing and contracting practices as different, more difficult, and potentially more "risky" from a liability perspective. One legal scholar specializing in public contract law argues that "government contracts differ markedly from customary business contracts for three reasons—the laws, the specifications, and the performance standards" [38].

The laws require businesses selling to government to make various certifications and representations about the way they do business. They must document their level of compliance with federal equal-opportunity, environmental protection, and drug-free work place laws; federal wage, health, and safety standards; and federal goals for subcontracting with small or minority-owned firms [39]. These certification requirements can result in "substantial costs to contractors: extraordinary amounts of time, energy and effort [are] involved in preparing such certifications [40].

Unquestionably, government procurement has become more time-consuming as a consequence of greater government regulation in reaction to "painful headlines decrying criminal indictments over contractors' possession of confidential bid information, allegations of bribery and influence peddling, and charges of poor contractor technical performance, mischarging, or the like" [41]. But should a firm fail to accurately certify compliance with the federal requirements, it faces both civil and criminal sanctions [42].

Businesses are frequently disenchanted with the seeming inflexibility and inefficiency created by government's rigid adherence to, and interpretation of, standard specifications. According to one attorney, "The law holds that the government is entitled to receive exactly what's in the specifications. In some instances, contract specifications are outmoded, leading contractors to assume they can substitute more up-to-date parts and techniques. Not so. In federal contracts, no changes are permitted unless the contract is specifically modified" [43].

The sheer volume of specifications to wade through is sometimes enough to deter a business from selling to government. One study estimates that 50% of small high-technology defense contractors drop out of competition for government contracts or go out of business completely due largely to bureaucratic regulations [44].

Businesses are often baffled by the government's failure to abide by the legal principle of "substantial performance" which governs ordinary private commercial transactions. Instead of allowing a contractor to substitute a cheaper part upon certification that the product complies with the specifications, the federal government adheres to a standard of strict compliance.

Some businesses avoid selling to the government because of government's bad reputation for not paying its bills in a timely fashion in spite of federal, state, and local prompt payment laws [45]. According to one account, "Winning [a government contract] may turn out to be only half of the battle. When it comes to getting paid on time, companies selling goods and services to the government have faced lousy odds" [46]. For many businesses, especially small, newly established ones, slow reimbursements can put a severe cash flow strain on their operations and even cause bankruptcy.

Small and newly established firms, particularly those operating on the margin as is commonly the case, also see a number of other government requirements as deterrents to selling to government. They perceive bid, performance, and payment bonds to be unaffordable. They may also avoid selling to any government which has a "paper heavy" procurement process [47].

It is also frustrating if the procurement process itself is not well delineated. Not knowing which government agency official has the major responsibility for a specific purchasing decision or not knowing precisely which agency or officials will actually use the service/product can deter businesses from trying to sell to government. They would rather sell in the private sector where their potential market is more easily identifiable.

A number of firms that have never done business with government before (and many that have) perceive the government procurement process to be highly political and noncompetitive, wrought with sole-source contracts. Even in competitive bidding situations, some feel that bid specifications are written so specifically as to produce limited competition among potential suppliers. Others feel just the opposite—that specifications are written too generally and imprecisely, effectively giving too much latitude to government officials to choose the supplier.

Extensive media coverage of dishonest business deals between government and certain private-sector firms has given all public procurement a bad reputation. Some firms perceive that government rarely "cleans house" and gets rid of incompetent or corrupt business suppliers. They also doubt the utility and objectivity of government protest or appeals procedures for unsuccessful bidders.

Firms specializing in high-tech goods and services are critical of the Office of Federal Procurement Policy for being "slow to introduce guidelines to protect them from losing proprietary information to the government and the commercial market." "The government often gives information supplied by one company to other companies during the course of [system or product] development; when such data is proprietary and developed through private financing, its release usually destroys its commercial value" [48].

Firms selling new products or services frequently become frustrated by the reluctance of public sector purchasers to consider something different. This phenomenon is sometimes known as "bureaucrats' fear of high tech" [49]. It has been most common with respect to telecommunications and electronic products and services.

Business leaders also complain about what they perceive to be a growing animosity toward them from government personnel, particularly at the federal level. One observer lamented, "The apparent skepticism of numerous government personnel and Congress about contractor conduct, motives, integrity, and business practices makes the entire business environment for government contractors much more unpleasant on a day-to-day basis than it ought to be" [50].

A survey of defense-related firms in the mid-1980s found that 70% of them identified the paperwork associated with government procurement (pre- and post-bid) as a major problem in dealing with government. Fifty-seven percent cited government bidding methods, particularly the excessive bid package documentation requirements, as problematic. Nearly one-third identified "low profitability" as a deterrent to contracting with the Department of Defense. Thirteen percent mentioned technical data rights problems as a reason for not doing business with DOD. One third pointed to the uncooperative attitude of government personnel as a major problem in selling to government [51].

A more broad based survey of businesses identified the following as the 10 most common problems: slow payment cycles (44%); narrowly written bid specifications (35%); difficulty making contact with the actual user of the product/service (32%); too much paperwork for the application (29%); too much competition pushing prices too low to compete (28%); confusion over who is responsible for making a specific purchasing decision (27%); reluctance to consider new products/services (26%); bid specifications written too generally (24%); too much paperwork once contract is received (24%); and inordinate delays between bid closing and the actual contract decision (24%) [52]. The rank ordering of these problems and the proportions of firms citing them as common varied considerably across different categories of firm characteristics.

Approximately 10% of the respondents to the survey just cited identified something in the "Other" category. Responses to this open-ended category generally fell into two major categories: (1) deficiencies of government purchasing personnel (unavailability; incompetence; lack of objectivity; inability to make a decision; failure to distribute information to vendors in a comprehensive, timely fashion); and (2) deficiencies related to procurement procedures and rules (lack of concern for slow/nonpayment of subcontractors by prime contractors, unrealistic inspection procedures, the lack of procedures to recruit new vendors, favoritism in the letting of contracts, graft and fraud, inefficient and unfair change policies and procedures, large and unrealistic insurance requirements, bidder-fee requirements, fixed-price contracts).

Previous research has shown that many of these "Other" problems can be traced to the relatively low ranking of the purchasing function in most governments (in comparison with budgeting, accounting, debt management, cash management, and risk management). Low salaries, high turnover, lack of specialized training, and a tendency for the chief purchasing official to be excluded from the primary financial management decision-making loop have all contributed to the image problem confronting many public procurement divisions or departments [53].

The bad image of public purchasing agencies is not limited to the private sector. A 1991 survey of the employees of the City of Clearwater, Florida, showed that over three-fourths believe that purchasing decisions take too long and end up costing the city more money [54]. Those who view the process most negatively are employees in the direct service delivery functions where new equipment and technology are most critical (e.g., those in service and professional/technical positions; and employees in the police, fire, gas, and general services—administration, building and maintenance, energy, and fleet maintenance—work groups; (see Table 1). While the results are not generalizable, it is likely they are not atypical.

In the survey of 3,282 businesses cited earlier, the respondents identified more "negatives" than "positives" about doing business with government. However, in spite of the negatives, a large proportion of these businesses reported they still would like to sell to government. The most desirable customers are general-purpose local governments (counties and cities), followed by the state government, and school districts. The federal government is rated most negatively, although only 13% of the businesses surveyed reported they would not like to sell to the federal government [55]. Nonetheless, the general image of government as a customer is not as good as it could be.

When asked to assess how businesses like themselves view various aspects of the public procurement process, 52% said "businesses like mine" do not generally believe that government purchasing practices attract first-rate vendors to compete for contracts; 60% do not believe that government purchasing practices result in purchases of goods and services at the lowest cost; and 49% do not think public procurement practices are fair and impartial.

A random survey of small businesses from a business directory (rather than from a government vendor list) reflects this more pessimistic attitude, especially among small business owners. Forty-two percent said they have no interest in selling to any government. Of those who were interested enthusiasm was greatest for selling to a city government (48%), followed by state government (35%), county government (32%), the federal government (29%), and a school district (23%). There was less enthusiasm for selling to any type of special district government, primarily because the functions of these governments are more specialized and less understood by the average small business owner [56].

For many private-sector firms, especially smaller ones, the liabilities of selling to government outweigh the benefits. This poses special problems for procurement policymakers since newer, smaller, and minority-owned firms are projected to be a majority of all U.S. businesses by the year 2000 [57]. Higher proportions of these firms say they frequently have difficulty competing with large firms, or are in situations where competition from other firms pushes prices too low for them to compete. Higher proportions of these firms are also likely to see the current system as somewhat closed; they are more likely to cite sole-source contracts, inadequate procedures for protests and appeals, and political favoritism as problematic. In the future, such information might well include opportunities to

Table 1 Government Employees' Views of Public Purchasing: Inefficient and Costly

Employee background	Purchasing decisions take too long and cost city money[a] (n = 719)
All employees	76.5%
By job function	
Service	80.1%
Clerical/clerks	65.1
Professional/technical	83.7
Managerial/administrative/ supervisory	63.1
By work group	
Administrative/support[b]	66.7%
Administrative services[c]	51.4
Fire	82.2
Gas	88.2
General services[d]	82.9
Library	70.0
Marine	54.6
Parks & recreation	60.0
Planning & development	56.5
Police	92.7
Public works[e]	71.4

[a] Respondents were asked to respond to this statement: "Purchasing decisions generally take too long, which ends up costing the city more money."
[b] Administrative/support work group includes personnel in City Manager's office, Economic Development, Internal Audit, Affirmative Action, Legal, City Clerk, Personnel, and Public Information.
[c] Administrative services work group includes personnel in Office of Management and Budget, Finance, Risk Management, Data Information Services, Purchasing, and Utility Customer Support.
[d] General services work group includes personnel in Administration, Building and Maintenance, Energy, and Fleet Maintenance.
[e] Public works work group includes personnel in Engineering, Environmental Management, Pollution Control, Sanitation/Solid Waste, Sewers/Streets/Infrastructure, Storm Water, Transportation, and Water.
Source: Ref. 54 (n = 954).

sell to foreign governments, as U.S. governments at all levels (federal, state, local) expand their economic development activities to foreign soils.

FUTURE DEVELOPMENTS IN THE PUBLIC PROCUREMENT WORLD

This review of the public and private sector's cost-benefit analyses of public contracting and procurement opportunities and practices, and a look forward at the political and economic environments likely to encompass each during this decade, leads us to forecast 10 developments that will yield a vastly different public procurement world by the year 2000. Without a doubt, continued pressures on governmental entities to do more with less and the growing size and political and legal clout of minority and women business owners will be the major forces affecting many of these changes. It is probable that many of the changes will occur first at the state and local government level. Public policy analysts have long noted the tendency in the United States for major innovations to emerge at the grassroots level and spread upward—and outward.

Expansion of Current Vendor Pools

If the trend toward more contracting out continues (as most experts expect it to), vendor pools will be enlarged. The projected growth and character of the small business sector will mandate a revision of current vendor recruitment efforts. To date these efforts have not significantly increased the number of small, minority, or women-owned firms in government vendor pools. The difficulty will be in designing recruitment strategies that will attract a wider range of firms to compete for government business without violating the fairness principle of purchasing. The growing size of the government marketplace (both at home and abroad) will increasingly become a factor in attracting more vendors.

Adoption of Common Forms/Procedures for Getting/Staying on Vendor Lists

The multiplicity of vendor registration and certification procedures existing even among governments within the same metropolitan area makes little sense and is a major deterrent to firms competing for government business. In this decade, we are likely to see more intergovernmental sharing and pooling of vendor lists. There is already evidence of this at the state level as state purchasing officials are already engaging in discussions about how to promote cooperative and coordinated *interstate* purchasing ventures.

"Mainstreaming" of Purchasing into the Financial Management System

It is increasingly apparent that many of the shortcomings of current public purchasing systems can be traced to the "secondary" involvement of top-level purchasing officials in the financial management decision-loop. To counter this, and to repair the negative image of government as a buyer, the purchasing function will be given more preeminence in many governments' organizational charts. The purchasing function will gain an equal footing with budgeting, accounting, investment management, risk management, and debt administration.

More Rigorous Training Requirements for Purchasing Personnel

To date, the purchasing staffs of many governments are inadequately trained in many of the highly legalistic and technical dimensions of procurement. Already there are signs that during this decade, job skill requirements for purchasing personnel at all levels will be upgraded, along with salaries, to reduce the amount of turnover and to attract more qualified persons to the area. Participation in professional certification programs will become imperative and purchasing will become a more preeminent element in Masters of Public Administration and Masters of Business Administration curricula.

Greater Use of Public-Private Task Forces to Reform Procurement Policies and Practices

As the quote by Kull at the beginning of this chapter indicates, to be effective, the purchasing process must involve input from both "business" partners. Government procurement officials must do a better job of explaining how and why public purchasing differs from business procurement. For example, government must show how certain seemingly onerous aspects of public procurement (e.g., lengthy testing, inspection, or auditing procedures) frequently protect businesses and individuals. Businesses must accept that public procurement is different, then help governments design better forms and procedures that recognize the unique goals of public purchasing but do not deter businesses from participating in the process.

Greater Use of Surveys to Identify Specific Problem Areas

Similar to increases in the use of citizen and client surveys, governments will turn to surveys of the private sector and of their own employees (as we have done here) to identify shortcomings of the procurement process and to formulate reform strategies.

Expansion of the Auditing Section of Procurement Departments

Public frustrations with current government procurement systems often emanate from widely publicized media accounts of unethical or incompetent behavior by government contractors who have "ripped off" the government and its taxpayers. In many cases, a shortage of trained performance auditors and contract specialists has accounted for a government's inability or delay in uncovering such improprieties. This is related to the relatively low esteem of the purchasing function. Both situations will improve in the 1990s, as governments implement more aggressive public relations, information, and marketing strategies—learning from their private-sector counterparts the essentiality of such activities in restoring public confidence in a "product."

Extension of Bidding/Contract Monitoring and Evaluation Requirements and Procedures to Subcontractors

One of the major complaints of small businesses and minority-owned firms has been the government's propensity to ignore subcontractors in their procurement processes and to focus primarily on prime contractors. This practice undoubtedly will change in this decade and will be a key element in efforts to enlarge vendor pools and to make them more representative of newly emerging firms.

Greater Efforts to Include Quality Dimensions to Cost Estimates

Business and government employees alike constantly complain of the long-term costs of making purchasing decisions exclusively on the basis of the price of a good or service, with little or no consideration of quality. While quality is a hard concept to quantify, it is likely that public/private-sector task forces can, and will, develop some mutually acceptable measures of quality, such as repair costs, down time, employee satisfaction ratings, etc., that can at least be considered in contract negotiations. Already governments are increasing their reliance on Request for Proposal bid acquisition methodologies. RFPs, in addition to price, allow procurement officers the latitude to consider contractor and product performance and other qualitative elements. It is also likely that governments will increasingly share information about qualitative measures with each other lest they all continue to suffer from intensifying taxpayer animosity toward government in general.

More Tension and Litigation over "Protectionism" in Public Procurement

Local preference policies and set-aside programs will remain at the center of controversy in this decade, whether the government involved is federal, a state, or a local government.

Any government that does not "favor" local industries or target certain industries and ownership groups in its procurement policies may be pictured by its critics as deterring economic development. At the same time, such efforts may not necessarily yield the taxpayers of that jurisdiction the best buy for their tax dollars. This age-old dilemma of public procurement is likely to intensify by the year 2000. Intergovernmental competition for foreign business opportunities for local firms will add to this problem.

In summary, there is reason to expect that public purchasing and contracting practices will be considerably different by the year 2000. This forecast is based upon two projections. First, it is highly likely that the structure of the private sector will be vastly different, due to a markedly different pattern of business ownership, reflecting significant changes in the nation's socioeconomic profile. Second, there is substantial evidence that fiscal and political pressures on governments at all levels will continue to intensify thereby increasing the need to rely more on the private sector for goods and services.

NOTES AND REFERENCES

This research was funded by the Lynde and Harry Bradley Foundation. The author wishes to thank the Foundation for its support and the City of Clearwater, Florida, for its permission to cite results of an employee survey.

1. D. C. Kull, "Reflections on Third-Party Government," *Bureaucrat*, *18*(Winter): 41 (1989–90).
2. Council of State Governments and the National Association of State Purchasing Officials, *State and Local Government Purchasing*, 3rd ed., Council of State Governments, Lexington, Ky., p. 7 (1988).
3. Much of this discussion is condensed from S. A. MacManus, *Doing Business with Government*, Paragon House, New York (1992).
4. I. T. David, "Privatization in America," *Municipal Year Book 1988*, International City Management Association, Washington, D.C. (1988).
5. For example, see E. S. Savas, *Privatizing the Public Sector: How to Shrink Government*, Chatham House, Chatham, N.J. (1982); E. B. Berenyi and B. J. Stevens, "Does Privatization Work? A Study of the Delivery of Eight Local Services," *State and Local Government Rev.*, *20*(Winter): 11–20 (1988); and J. D. Donahue, *The Privatization Decision: Public Ends, Private Means*, Basic Books, New York (1989).
6. J. A. Rehfuss, *Contracting Out in Government: A Guide to Working with Outside Contractors to Supply Public Services*, Jossey-Bass, San Francisco (1989); T. Renner, "Trends and Issues in the Use of Intergovernmental Agreements and Privatization in Local Government," *Baseline Data Report*, *21*(November/December): 1–15 (1989); and Ref. 4.
7. J. Straussman and J. Farie, "Contracting for Social Services at the Local Level," *Urban Interest*, *3*(Spring): 43–49 (1981).
8. Rehfuss (see note 6), pp. 22–23.
9. J. Muzychenko, "Local Governments at Risk: The Crisis in Liability Insurance," *The Municipal Year Book 1987*, International City Management Association, Washington, D.C., pp. 3–7 (1987).
10. L. F. Del Duca, P. J. Falvey, and T. A. Adler, *State and Local Government Procurement: Developments in Legislation and Litigation*, American Bar Association, Chicago (1986); M. H. Flener, "Legal Considerations in Privatization and the Role of Legal Counsel," *Public Sector Privatization: Alternative Approaches to Service Delivery* (L. L. Finley, ed.), Quorum Books, New York, pp. 141–152 (1989); B. A. Kinosky, "Commentary: Another Perspective on *Boyle v. United Technologies Corporation*," *National Contract Manage. J.*, *23*(Summer): 77–83 (1989).
11. P. V. Farrell, ed. *Alijan's Purchasing Handbook*, 4th ed., McGraw-Hill, New York (1982).
12. R. J. Zee, *Summary of Preferences In-State and for Cities Over 500,000 Population* (*As of August 1988*), National Institute of Governmental Purchasing, Falls Church, Va. (1989); National

Institute of Governmental Purchasing, *Results of the 1989 Procurement Survey*, NIGP, Falls Church, Va. (1989).

13. Rehfuss (note 6), pp. 2–3.

14. H. P. Hatry and E. Durman, *Issues in Competitive Contracting for Social Services*, National Institute of Governmental Purchasing, Falls Church, Va. (1985); K. Chi, *Privatization and Contracting for State Services: A Guide*, Council of State Governments, Lexington, Ky. (1988).

15. E. Morley, "Patterns in the Use of Alternative Service Delivery Approaches," *Municipal Year Book 1989*, International City Management Association, Washington, D.C., pp. 33–44 (1989).

16. Ref. 4.

17. H. P. Hatry, "Privatization Presents Problems," *National Civic Review*, 77(March–April): 112–117 (1988); Donahue (note 5).

18. C. F. Valente and L. D. Manchester, "Rethinking Local Services: Examining Alternative Deliver Systems," *Management Information Service Special Report*, no. 12, International City Management Association, Washington, D.C., p. 1 (1984).

19. American Federation of State, County, and Municipal Employees (AFSCME), *Passing the Bucks*, AFSCME, Washington, D.C. (1983).

20. L. C. Fitch, "The Rocky Road to Privatization," *Am. J. Econ. Sociol.*, 47(January): 1–14 (1988).

21. J. R. Pack, "Privatization of Pubic Sector Services in Theory and Practice," *J. Policy Anal. Manage.*, 6(Summer): 523–540 (1987).

22. P. E. Starr, "The Limits of Privatization," In *Prospects for Privatization*, (S. H. Hanke, ed.), Academy of Political Science, New York, pp. 124–137 (1987).

23. Rehfuss (note 6), p. 45.

24. R. W. Bailey, "Uses and Misuses of Privitization," (S. H. Hanke, ed.), pp. 138–152; L Manchester, "Alternative Service Delivery Approaches and City Service Planning," In *Public Sector Privatization: Alternate Approaches to Service Delivery* (L. L. Finley, ed.), pp. 13–24.

25. D. R. Morgan and R. E. England, "The Two Faces of Privatization," *Public Admin. Rev.*, 48 (November/December): 979–987 (1988); R. C. Moe, "Exploring the Limits of Privatization," *Public Admin. Rev.*, 47(November/December): 453–460 (1987).

26. Ref. 22.

27. J. D. Hanrahan, *Government by Contract*, Norton, New York (1983); J. F. Magnotti, Jr., "The Small Business Administration's Pilot Program: A Study in Frustration," *Nat. Contract Manage. J.*, 20(Summer): 61–65 (1986); D. E. Black, "Socioeconomic Contract Goal Setting Within the Department of Defense: Promises Still Unfilled," *Nat. Contract Manage. J.*, 22(Winter): 67–82 (1989); T. A. Cantor, "The Small Business in the Federal Marketplace—A Study of Barriers," *J. Small Business Manage.*, 27(January): 74–77 (1989); S. A. MacManus, "Minority Business Contracting With Local Government," *Urban Affairs Q.*, 25(March): 455–473 (1990).

28. C. H. Davis and D. D Jackson, "The Sunset of Affirmative Action? *City of Richmond v. J. A. Croson Co.*," *National Black Law J.*, 12: 73–87 (1990); M. F. Rice, "Government Set Asides, Minority Business Enterprises, and the Supreme Court," *Public Admin. Rev.*, 51(March/April): 114–122 (1991); D. D. Scherer, "Affirmative Action Doctrine and the Conflicting Messages of Croson," *Univ. Kansas Law Rev.*, 38(Winter): 281–341 (1990).

29. This discussion is condensed from S. A. MacManus, *Doing Business with Government* (see note 3).

30. *Government Executive*, 21(May): 30–31 (1989); H. Holtz, *The $100 Billion Market: How to Do Business with the U.S. Government*, AMACON, New York (1980).

31. D. E. Gumpert and J. A. Timmons, "Penetrating the Government Procurement Maze," *Harvard Business Rev.*, 60(May/June): 14–20 (1982).

32. Ref. 36.

33. Ref. 31.

34. Ref. 31.

35. Business names and addresses were obtained from the vendor mailing and registration lists of the Hillsborough County, Florida, and Harris County, Texas, Purchasing Departments. Surveys

were mailed in the spring and summer of 1989 to 9,040 businesses. The response rate was 36.3%.

36. Holtz (see note 3).
37. S. A. MacManus, "Why Businesses Are Reluctant to Sell to Governments," *Public Admin. Rev.*, *51*(July/August): 328–344 (1991).
38. B. J. Shillito, in J. E. Bahls, "A Demanding Customer," *Nation's Business*, *78*(March): 29–30 (1990).
39. E. M. Meyers, "Regulation of Federal Contractors' Employment Patterns," *Public Admin. Rev.*, *49*(January/February): 52–60 (1989).
40. A. R. Yuspeh, "Stop Picking on Contractors," *Government Executive*, *21*(May): 40 (1989).
41. W. H. Gregory, "The Defense Procurement Mess," *Internal Auditor*, *47*(April): 49 (1990).
42. J. J. Graham, "Corporate Criminal Liability of the Public Contractor—Are Guidelines Needed?" *Nat. Contract Manage. J.*, *21*(Winter): 9–20 (1988).
43. W. R. Lucas, in Bahls (see note 38), p. 30.
44. L. B. Hoshower, "How Regulatory Ambiguity Frustrates Defense Contractors," *Financial Executive*, *5*(September/October): 54–57 (1989).
45. R. A. Donnally and M. W. Stone, "The Prompt Payment Act in 1987: Collecting From Uncle Sam," *Nat. Contract Manage. J.*, *21*(Summer): 45–55 (1987); Coalition for Prompt Pay, *Guide to Getting Paid Promptly by State and Local Agencies*, Coalition for Prompt Pay, Fairfax, Va. (1989).
46. L. Reynolds, "When Government Says 'The Check's in the Mail,'" *Manage. Rev.*, *78*(June): 53 (1989).
47. D. V. Lamm, "Why Firms Refuse DOD Business: An Analysis of Rationale," *National Contract Management Journal*, *21*(Winter): 45–55; MacManus, Ref. 3.
48. M. L. Goldstein, "Uncle Sam: A Tough Customer," *Government Executive*, *21*(May): 15–16 (1989).
49. M. Lewyn, "Revolt of Uncle Sam's Paper Pushers," *Business Week*, *31*(October 30): 156 (1989).
50. Ref. 48, p. 12.
51. Lamm,
52. Ref. 37.
53. S. A. MacManus and S. A. Watson, "Procurement Policy: The Missing Element in Financial Management Education," *Int. J. Public Admin.*, *1/2*: 155–179 (1990).
54. S. A. MacManus, J. Benton, J. L. Daly, and D. Rahm, *City of Clearwater Employee Survey*, Institute of Government, University of South Florida, Tampa, May 30 (1991).
55. Ref. 3.
56. A mail questionnaire was sent in July 1989 to 500 businesses randomly selected from the *Contacts Influential Marketing Information Directory*, which lists local businesses in Hillsborough and Pinellas, Florida, counties. This survey was intended to solicit the opinions of businesses not on any official government vendor mailing or registration lists. The response rate was 20%.
57. D. V. Lamm, "Why Firms Refuse DOD Business: An Analysis of Rationale," *National Contract Management Journal*, *21*(Winter): 45–55.

33
Capital Asset Financing

Gerald J. Miller
Rutgers University—Newark, Newark, New Jersey

Understanding the capital financing process in state and local government proves difficult in the face of the ambiguity surrounding the multiplicity of actors involved, the lack of agreement about what they do, various types of borrowings, and the economic variables that have effect, particularly interest rates. Moreover, the area has attracted controversy regularly. In fact, a few organizations have become issues themselves because their attempts to control ambiguity backfired [1, 2]. Thus, what little observers agree upon regularly gets upset by the controversies that often defy ready explanation. The purpose of this chapter is to shed light on the institutions that thrive on ambiguity in capital finance, how these institutions operate, and, most important of all, how and what opportunistic strategies the institutions use to finance public sector capital projects

We turn next to a brief overview of the

1. Setting in which capital project financing takes place, and then to
2. An explanation of the form of institutionalization that takes place to permit opportunistic strategies to emerge,
3. A description of the process of mobilizing bias that underlies opportunistic strategies, and
4. A classification of capital investment strategies that provide opportunities to mobilize bias, construct reality, and rationalize ambiguous events

SETTING

In the description of actual roles and behaviors in financing strategy formulation and implementation here, we discuss the market making efforts that go into creating a bond sale. Financing strategies emerge from a set of people who form a team; this semipermanent institutional form has responsibility for bargaining the major parts of the investment strategy with bargaining positions developed over short or long periods of development through direct and indirect contact [3, 4]. Strategy implementation may best be described as the mobilization of bias through the classification of information. Classification emerges out of the efforts of those directly involved in the sales and the larger network of financing market participants of which they are a part.

INSTITUTIONALIZATION OF ROLES OF MEMBERS OF A TEAM

Capital financing suggests either a principal-agent model of strategy formulation [5] or an interorganizational network model that behaves as a political economy [6]. The principal agent model is straightforward. Strategy requires principals formulating strategy (public agency managers) to choose among projects of different rates of return and levels of risk, in order to exploit targeted capital markets. These projects will convert resource and tax base contributions to a higher performing portfolio of assets. The strategy may be implemented by employing agents such as financial advisors, legal counsel, accountants, and other consultants. These agents provide the analyses of what measures will connect the project to a capital market that can finance it in return for the government's promise to repay with a stream of revenue directly or indirectly connected to the project itself.

On the other hand, the strategies that emerge in financing capital improvements may actually result from substantial interaction among many parties, all of which have relatively insular views about the specific strategic and tactical moves to be made to insured success in financing. In fact, the insularity or the lack of it that the individual organizations (again the public agency, financial advisors, legal counsel, accountants and other consultants) bring to the bond sale team makes bargaining, rather than mere principal-agent computation, possible.

The bargaining may be the only accountability mechanism available, and it is one the principal-agent model overlooks. That is, the agency model forces the reformer to blame public managers and to promote efforts to rein them in, not realizing how dependent the public manager is on the information and bargaining that goes on among the larger network of members—the public agency manager as well as financial advisors, legal counsel, accountants, and other consultants. In order to achieve efficiency, to encourage creativity, and to serve the public interest, the network approach argues that pressure has to be exerted on all team members either by stabilizing their relationships or by making the members less insular in their views.

How is this set of members a network rather than a set of agents doing the bidding of a principal? Assume a simplistic situation, momentarily, a small group of organizations consisting of a financial advisor, an accounting firm, and a law firm. The three are richly joined in the following ways:

1. The law firm acts as corporation counsel to the other two organizations.
2. The accounting firm audits the transactions of the other two organizations; moreover, auditors have been recruited and have joined the financial advising firm from time to time as principals.
3. The three organizations are active in the new-issue market for municipal securities with all other possible participants, and they serve together as a team for a bond sale for a public agency issuer.

The public agency becomes the beneficiary of knowledge about changes made by Congress in tax laws relating to municipal debt, about specific needs for information by credit rating agencies, and about new debt structures that may be designed to appeal to specific segments of the market at specific points in the business cycle. The richly joined network ultimately results in the group's ability to adjust to complex and changing environments when working together on a government capital financing project.

The stability or instability of a team across financings can have consequences for the government employing them to help issue debt and the public manager becoming a team member. Consider a more complex example. Assume that among a population of law firms that act as municipal bond counsel, the firms tend, as a matter of each one's practice, to differ in their approach to interpreting the law as it regards various creative capital financing structures, some firms being indulgent, others strict. Assume, furthermore, that in a population of accounting firms asked to forecast the revenue stream that would generate principal and interest payments for various creative capital financing structures, some firms would tend to be liberal, others tight. Finally, assume that among a population of financial advisors, the same sort of variation would exist among opinions about the applicability and marketability of debt strictures.

Random selection of a combination of these firms by an issuer would yield a team advising the issuer to take a particular course of action, one in which the knowledge each advisor had, as well as the expectation each had of the other's interpretation and its effect on the market for the issue, would play a part. The result would produce a bargain in which a security configured in a unique way was rated and sold.

Now assume a second random selection of firms by an issuer and a second sale. What knowledge or desire for following that implicit strategy does the second team have about the configuration of the first security? What keeps the second team from relying on the first team's correct or incorrect interpretation of what happened? In the end does stability or instability on the team cause the second sale to "miss the market"? Thus either stability and instability on the team will lead to consistency and success or it will lack creativity and lead to disaster.

Network Stability: Good or Bad?

The literature on stability and instability in such situations is not conclusive. Consider first the evidence favoring network stability. Stability evolves through the work of linking-pin organizations that have extensive and overlapping ties to different parts of a network. Functionally, the links may be thought of as communications channels between organizations, resource conduits among network members, and even models to be imitated by other organizations in the population. Thus, an accounting firm might channel information about a reporting standard from rating agencies to bond issuers; the firm might direct clients to financial advisors the firm's members respect as a result of previous bond sales or the firm itself, through one or more of its many services might serve as a model for a municipal finance office. The strength of the network lies in its duplicative links:

> The ultimate predictor of network [success] is the probability of a link failing, given that another has failed. This, in turn, is a function of the probability of any one link failing and two networks characteristics: the duplication of linkages and the multiplicity of linkages between any two organizations. [7, p. 391]

Such hypotheses find confirmation in the literature on public management. Landau [8] argues that redundancy tends to ensure performance. Golembiewski [9] has argued that, in symbiotic interrelationships, duplication works to prevent the exercise of vetoes by power subunits. Lastly, research suggests that the major result of stability is adaptability. Networks that are richly joined provide for greater opportunity for trial and error and the spread of innovation [7, pp. 393–397].

The small group literature provides further evidence that one might generalize to debt management networks. Some qualities can compensate for the lack of cohesion in financing teams, a problem some point to as compounding and others as remedying the insularity that grows as the same members continually work with each other [10–12].

One of these compensating qualities is heterogeneity. Hoffman [13] has shown that group members with heterogeneous backgrounds tend to work together more effectively, up to a point, because of the greater diversity of information they bring. Because permanent group membership tends to lead to a homogenizing of views [14, 15], diversity might counter that tendency. Diversity implies turnover, however. Trow [16] suggests that turnover leads to a short-run decline in performance as the group undergoes reorganization. In a review of the literature on turnover, Hom, Griffith, and Carson [17] found that negative consequences included productivity or service losses, opportunity costs, disrupted work routines, and reduced retention among stayers. On the positive side, they found that turnover displaced poor performers and led to an infusion of new knowledge and technology by replacements. In fact, they argued that among research and development teams excessive group longevity decreased performance [17, p. 543].

> Given criticality of external technical knowledge and new ideas, long-term R&D teams become ineffective because they increasingly rely on customary work patterns and insulate themselves from outside information that threatens comfortable, predictable work habits. [Moreover,] long-tenured executive teams followed more persistent company strategies that mirrored industry norms, whereas short-tenured teams adopted more novel strategies deviating from industry patterns.

In the reviewers' view, lengthy group membership reduces team performance.

A second quality compensating for either too much to too little cohesion in financing teams is equality of status or, even more likely, settled status. Research shows that groups are more productive when members can avoid status struggles, are relatively stable, or because the method of cost sharing or surplus sharing is settled [18].

Why Stability or Insularity Matters

The question of how stability, turnover, and status matter in the bond sale process is a major controversy at present, especially in the arguments surrounding the reform of the municipal securities market [2, 19]. The question is one of more competition in the selection of team members in a bond sale versus less. Instilling competition and mitigating the consequences of what results, the instability and turnover among team members, lies at the heart of present reforms. Perhaps, then, attention should focus on what methods encourage team members' joint contributions to lead to preferred outcomes, outcomes I call "learning." Let met explain.

The process of issuing debt involves four steps. First, initiation of a sale rests on the choice of the market. Which investors will/should buy the securities? Tax laws, the economic cycle, and the habitual purchasing practices of individuals and institutions combine in various ways. They create choices based on the probability that legislators, interest rates, and consumers will behave with reasonable predictability.

The second step in the process involves structuring a debt issue to confront two problems: the predilections of the market chosen and the capacity of the issuer. The market choices put a premium on accuracy, but the ability of the issuer to manage the debt provided in the structure sets limits.

Third, the structure directly connects the market with the issue and the issuer through disclosure. What facts will be disclosed, and, more important, what interpretation will be presented for these facts, in the major document for disclosing information, the offering statement, and the presentations to credit ratings agencies?

The final step is the sale, at which time all parties decide the price of the issue. The sale confirms the assumptions made by the team about the structure of the issue and the level of demand for the quantity provided. From another point of view, it becomes a confirming piece of information about supply and demand, or whether the team "learned."

What factors might encourage learning? I would expect that the number of links among members of the team would lead to stability, and stability, in turn, would lead either to insularity or to learning and adaptation. An expectations approach helps to understand richly linked organizations in the bond team context. That is, in doing their assigned tasks, each member of the bond team must be guided by expectations of the behavior of others. The financial advisor cannot select a market unless the advisor can expect to have counsel's positive legal interpretation of the structure that would most likely follow the selection of that market. The advisor also cannot select a market without the expectation that the accountant will interpret the various issuer capacities in such a way as to support the structure the market suggests. No decision made by any member of the team, in the end, can be made in a vacuum without the knowledge of what the other members are likely to do. Otherwise, the decisions made by the members form an endless iteration—a loop—in which market choice forces structure and disclosure but that does not sell, leading to a second issue, a new market, and a new structure and interpretations wedded to the previous issue's structure, confounding this new market and structure.

One solution to the problem of expectations is to live with the short-term chaos that accompanies individuals getting organized. Another solution might exist in a richly linked network of organizations. Rich links lead to the knowledge of likely behavior under varying circumstances. Assumptions at extremely general levels are shared or at least made widely known through large numbers of activities in which the linked organizations jointly participate. Rich links also provide multiple avenues for the testing of expectations under widely varying conditions. For example, legal interpretations that a bond counsel is likely to submit may be expected based on the legal interpretations the bond counsel has traditionally issued in the capacity of the corporate counsel, as the earlier illustration depicted

If rich links lead to shared expectations of behavior, these links contribute either to insularity or to learning. Consider the argument for specific types of teams in municipal finance. The negotiated rather than the competitive sale involves the sort of stability and exploitation of existing rich links among potential members of a team. Negotiated sales require the issuer to choose precisely those members who have apparently learned the market as well as each other in terms of the market. A negotiated sale provides an opportunity to choose the market (especially when the sale is privately placed), opening the way or creating the need for innovation (craft work rather than routine technology) in the type of issue structure chosen. The negotiated sale also provided incredible overlap and duplication in the work involved.

Such rich links and the opportunities provided by the negotiated sale invite learning. Stigler [20] indicated that buyers and sellers accumulate information from their experience in the market place that allows them to obtain more favorable conditions in each successive transaction. More specifically, Bland [21] found that issuers using multiple, negotiated sales received more favorable terms through each successive sale up to a certain point. Leonard's review of bond sales research [19] tends to confirm Bland's findings. Bland concluded "that local governments with previous bond market experience are capable of assembling a management team that can negotiate an interest rate comparable to what the most sought after competitive issues obtain" [21, p. 236].

In opposing negotiated sales, proponents of competition point out that competitive sales lead to lower interest costs when the issuer does not have experience gained through repeated sales in the market and thus little cumulative knowledge of market dynamics [22]. Implicit in these arguments is the view that the team, under no real competitive pressures, turns inward and becomes less creative and more interested in pursuing pet structures to increase their own profits. Little interest is shown in lowering the government's interest costs. These proponents of competition set the lack of turnover as the cause. The wealth of links engendered by a larger, unstable network is jettisoned in favor of the stability that encouraged short-term learning.

To recap, a network's being stable or unstable depends on the wealth of links among its members. The greater the number of possible links, the greater the opportunities for learning. The greater the amount of learning, the greater the chance for innovation and adaptation.

Efficient Markets

Finally, we turn to the notion of efficient markets, the broader goal of all participants in the sale of municipal securities. An efficient market is one that allocates scarce capital among competing uses, and assigns appropriate prices (interest payments to the issuer and bond prices and yields to the investor) to structures at particular levels of repayment capacity. Under what conditions does the number of rich links lead to market efficiency?

The answer lies in the reiteration of our model with one significant addition. Network effectiveness develops through duplicative links among organizations in a network. Rich links open opportunities for learning. Learning leads to greater adaptability. Greater adaptability, of course, leads to better guesses about which market to choose under what conditions. Moreover, adaptability helps shape disclosure, telling what to disclose to what market to provide its participants evidence of levels of risk and levels of reward.

MOBILIZING BIAS

We have considered here the team involved in the sale of municipal securities, a fairly large group of experts involved in either of two types of sale: guaranteed debt and nonguaranteed debt (for the distinction, see Ref. 23). Guaranteed debt is that which the full taxing power of a governmental unit supports. Non guaranteed debt is usually secured by the repayment capacity of a revenue stream, such as a sales tax or fees from the sale of water. Guaranteed debt sales have become ever more tightly regulated by state constitutions and legal codes. As a result, these securities have become homogenous, commodity-like structures, requiring little distinction among advisors in their structuring. They rely for distinction on the credit worthiness of their issuers, as interpreted by rating agencies, and the point in the business cycle at which they are sold.

Ambiguity and Risk

A nonguaranteed sale has become the place where advisors may actually use their creative talents. Because revenue streams may lack history as a basis for forecasting, "the market" must rely on an advisor to depict their earning capacity. Legal interpretations may also be required. Moreover, the market itself has to be analyzed to determine likely purchasers of the securities both initially and in the secondary market.

Such ambiguity comes in at least four forms and is normally depicted as "risk." First, economic risk entails the ups and downs of the business cycle and the effect of those changes on interest rates. Second, market risks reflect the sources of demand for municipal securities. Third, legal risk may involve accurately depicting local, state, and federal law regarding securities offerings as well as foreseeing the strategic necessity to forestall litigation or, at the very least, unfavorable court judgments. Fourth, the default risk is best known and is the calculated potential of a borrower to repay principal and interest in a timely manner.

The bond sale teams' major responsibility lies in coping with these risks. The team does so by mobilizing bias, by identifying, exchanging, and classifying the bases for ambiguity and the coping mechanisms appropriate to them that are formed out of team members' biases. These biases respond to concerns of those outside the immediate circle of bond sale team participants, avoid opposition inside and outside, and advance each member's own interests. We discuss this mobilization of bias as three stages: (1) organizing responsibility for sensing risk and opportunity, (2) exchanging this information, and (3) classifying it in ways that dictate action.

Information and Sensing

The ambiguity or risk that attaches to a municipal securities offering leads to both strategic and tactical necessities. Most of these can be classed as coping mechanisms for dealing with uncertainty or, more simply, efforts at pooling available information. The issuer forms a team to pursue a securities offering, and this team pools information.

The team in a nonguaranteed debt sale forms out of three basic groups of advisors: those whose efforts are made toward informing the issuer of the market and of the economic conditions constraining the offering, those who inform the underwriter/investor of the law, and those who inform the issuer and the bond buyers of the financial condition of the issuer. *On Economic and Market Risk.* The financial advisor usually leads the effort to inform the issuer of economic and, especially, market conditions. The financial advisor determines how broad a market can be attracted to a sale and when the sale might take place to minimize interest costs or what might be done to negotiate a private placement. The determination of the market leads directly to the structuring of the security, influencing fundamentally its various features [24]. The financial advisor may also be the underwriter—the buyer of the securities from the issuer for resale—if the sale is a negotiated one between issuer and underwriter, rather than a competitive one or a private placement.

On Legal Risk. The bond counsel leads the effort to inform the structuring of the security in terms of applicable law for the underwriter/issuer. Many regard bond counsel as the primary representative of investors, assuring them that the issuer will not default on an obligation by pleading legal defects in the procedures used to authorize or issue the bonds. Yet, Petersen observes [25, p. 4] that "additional roles of bond counsel in preparing transactions for market and [for] disclosure are extensive, flexible, and subjects of professional debate." Very clearly, one such additional role is that of creative thinker, assuring one and all that new financing techniques are not burdened by the means and ends of traditional financing. Such roles blur the traditional view of the counsel as an overseer for investors, and, as a way to add focus, the bond counsel may be assisted by counsel for an underwriter in a negotiated sale as well as counsel for any other party, including the issuer, if the structure's complexity demands it.

On Default Risk. Third, the auditor or accounting specialist (CPA) informs the team members and potential bond buyers of the issuer's financial condition, in terms of the structure of the security. For example, the CPA reports the issuer's financial status, as depicted through financial reports. If the revenue stream underlying the security must be forecast, the CPA may also verify the assumptions and calculations made to confirm the stream's contribution to the issuer's ability to repay principal and interest. While others, such as consulting engineers, management specialists, and other experts, may join in the pooling of information on the issuer's financial status or the project being financed, the CPA remains the primary data source for determining default risk.

Exchange of Information

The pooling of information that will be used later in characterizing the risk of the issuer comes through consultation and advice and disclosure.

Consultation and Advice.   Foremost among the expected traits of the financial advisor, bond counsel, and CPA is that of consultant. Looking at a vast number of important projects and the impenetrable future of the market for debt, the issuer relies on these sources of expertise. Yet these advisors must rely on each other as well, since the risks each deals with have implications for those of the others. To illustrate with the most obvious, the CPA's study of default risk has much to say about the financial advisor's opinion about timing of the sale: the greater the default risk, the greater the wait for periods of high market demand for securities of all levels of quality. Likewise, legal advice will confine the range of permissible debt structures, and that will, in turn, limit the market potential of the issue from the financial advisor's point of view.

The Public and the Press.   Information provided to reduce interest rate, market, legal, or default risk may also come from the larger public, including the press. Certainly, the financial press has a great deal to say about default risks, as experience with defaulting bond issuers suggests. However, this press, as well as contact in more direct ways, serves to publicize and realize new debt structures, interest rate cycles, and litigation issues. The larger world of everyday securities practice, therefore, poses its own information constraints and opportunities for the bond sale team.

Disclosure.   While the information and advice from financial and legal advisors come with contact, and credit ratings may result from interviews and on-site inspections conducted by these agencies, the primary vehicle for information exchange is a process called disclosure. Therefore, economic and market information are implied, legal information is directly opined, and financial condition information related to default risk is analyzed in the process of disclosure among team members, between the team and the credit rating agency, and among the team, credit-raring agencies, intermediaries, and investors.

Three separate areas of information are disclosed primarily through the production of a document, the official statement (OS). The OS is both official—the issuer's authorization of interpretations made on its behalf by the team members—and a "direct exposition of information concerning the offering" [25, p. 5].

Other items of disclosure usually emerge in annual financial reports that are becoming common among issuers. These establish trends beyond those elaborated in the OS as well as providing information to secondary market traders in years subsequent to the initial issue.

In summary, the disclosure of the structure of the security and the legal status and repayment capacity of the issuer present the market with essential data regarding risk and reward. With these data, theoretically, the new-issue market for municipal securities may achieve efficiency by allocating scarce capital among competing uses, assigning appropriate prices (interest payments to the issuer and bond prices and yields to the investor) to structures at particular levels of repayment capacity.

Classification of Information

Actually, however, the new-issue market must depend on classifications of these data that will permit interpretation. With the data collected and pooled through disclosure, the various parties classify it in straightforward ways, forcing interpretation. Three significant methods of classification usually emerge: the offering's structure, the legal tax class of the issue, and the credit rating.

The Offering's Structure.   The debt structure may vary in terms of economic condition or budget requirements.

Structure and Interest Rates.   The economic conditions prompting a particular debt structure usually require attention to the sale date, and that date is a matter of long-range rather than short-range planning. With the average business cycle for the last 135 years lasting 3 years from peak to peak, the optimum sale date is one in which the peak of the cycle has passed and a contraction is in progress. Therefore, predicting the peak of a cycle is a means of forecasting the sale date at which interests costs will be lowest.

Predicting the peak of a cycle has its problems. For example, no cycle has ever lasted the same length of time as any other. Most of the time the structure must adjust to the vagaries of the yield curve.

Experience (and almost every money and banking textbook) reveals that short-term interest rates are a product of and influential agent in business cycles. As economic expansion takes place, short-term interest rates (1 month to 20 years) rise relative to long-term rates (21–30 years). As economic contraction takes place, these short-term rates fall in relation to longer term ones.

To some extent supply and demand for money can help explain the phenomena. In expansions, firms find demand for their goods and services increasing and try to borrow money to expand and meet such demand. These firms effectively bid up the price (the interest rate) of a relatively fixed supply of money. The reverse occurs as a contraction takes place; less demand for goods and services reduces a firm's need to borrow to expand. Midway through peak and trough, demand and supply for money balance, and short-term rates nearly equal long-term ones as firms refinance short-term loans with long-term ones (paying off short-terms ones increases the money supply, borrowing long-term decreases it).

For issuers of debt, obviously, troughs have advantages for borrowing. If revenues permit, timing sales for troughs yields lower interest costs. Such countercyclical policies may not be feasible, however, so structuring an issue to take advantage of the yield curve may present the best alternative. At expansionary peaks, selling middle- to long-term debt may yield lower interests costs than would short-term debt, while troughs provide the opportunity for lower costs through short-term debt.

Structure and Issuer Budget Requirements.   Besides the classification of information in terms of interest rates, the bond team categorizes strategies in terms of the issuer's budget constraints. The issuer's budget for debt service may guide the development of debt-structuring strategies that account for the cash flow requirements and cash available.

Three patterns of bond repayment series, known as serial maturities, have wide use: an equal annual series of bond payments, equal annual debt service patterns, and irregular maturities in which the budgeted debt service from existing as well as new debt issues is the same across future years. These patterns are illustrated in Table 1.

The three patterns have different budget purposes. The equal annual maturity pattern spreads repayment over the life of the facility being financed, matching what is paid to what amount of the useful life of the facility is exhausted. This strategy makes sense in ensuring that the facility is paid for at the same rate as it is used. The strategy also ensures that the community residents who gain the benefit of the facility pay for it. That is, those using the facility in year 20 pay for their fair share of its cost just as do those using it in year 1.

Table 1 Maturity Patterns for Serial Bonds That Consider Budgetary Timing

	Pattern A: Equal annual maturity		
Year	Principal	Interest	Total debt service
1	$ 40,000	$ 12,000	$ 52,000
2	40,000	9,600	49,600
3	40,000	7,200	47,200
4	40,000	4,800	44,800
5	40,000	2,400	42,400
	$200,000	$ 36,000	$236,000

	Pattern B: Equal annual debt service		
Year	Principal	Interest	Total debt service
1	$ 35,000	$ 12,000	$ 47,000
2	37,500	9.900	47,400
3	40,000	7,650	47,650
4	42,500	5,250	47,750
5	45,000	2,700	47,700
	$200,000	$ 37,500	$237,500

	Pattern C: Equal annual debt service over two issues			
Year	Old debt service	New principal	New interest	New total debt service
1	$ 47,000	$ 250	$ 15,690	$ 62,940
2	47,400	250	15,675	63,325
3	47,650	250	15,660	63,560
4	47,750	250	15,645	63,645
5	47,700	500	15,630	63,830
6		48,000	15,600	63,600
7		50,000	12,720	62,720
8		52,000	9,720	61,720
9		55,000	6,600	61,600
10		55,000	3,300	58,300
	$237,500	$261,500	$499,000	$625,240

The equal annual debt service and irregular maturity (level total) make predictable, if not exactly even, calls on budgets. Such level debt service makes budgeting more stable since the amount budgeted changes very little from year to year.

In addition to the various level debt structures, issuers may accelerate retirement of bonds or set up sinking funds for retirement of term bonds. A revenue-producing facility that exceeds revenue productivity forecasts can illustrate accelerated retirement. Having more funds on hand than anticipated, a public enterprise, such as a toll road, might choose to repay bonds ahead of schedule rather than invest in short-term securities or prepay other expenses. Bond issue legal documents, or indentures, however, govern accelerated retirement so that bondholders can anticipate the actual yields and prices of bonds when initially offered.

Sinking funds also often provide advantages. The issuer simply contributes amounts to an investment fund before the maturity date of the bond. These amounts are invested to yield the difference between the contribution and the principal and interest required to be paid the investor upon maturity. While federal tax reform has limited the utility of some of these sinking funds, the sinking fund approach has obvious budget appeal, since it can reduce budget commitments

Structure and the Tax Classes Affecting the Market Strategy of the Issuer. While interest rates influence those who have an interest in buying municipal securities, much concern also exists in specifically what well-known classes of bond buyers want. Most of these concerns relate to tax-exempt income and the favorability of federal, state, and local tax law in encouraging these purchases.

Recalling the three goals of investing as safety, liquidity, and yield, we can recognize the part that a tax-exempt investment will play in forming an investment decision by individuals, fire and casualty insurance companies, and commercial banks, the traditional mainstays of the municipal market.

For individuals, all these goals are served. The tax bracket of the individual determines the actual tax-equivalent yield, but an individual in the highest tax bracket will receive the highest after-tax yield. The yield for this buyer is comparable to the best corporate securities, for each of which the principal is relatively safe. With the expansion of municipal bond funds, even liquidity may be achieved.

For insurance companies, yield and, to a lesser extent, safety are important. For these insurance companies, premium income, in a period of low underwriting losses, can gain a high yield with lower grade, long-term nonguaranteed securities. In any case, the investment of funds set aside for reserves against losses demands yield as well as safety. Such investments increase the yields for insurance companies for the same reason as individuals and preserve the safety required of these reserves. Federal tax reform has had a large impact on the attractiveness of tax-exempt securities to insurance companies, but on observer notes that "with more profits to shelter and fewer options, . . . property and casualty insurance companies should be good customers for tax-exempts" [26, pp. 3–11].

For commercial banks, federal tax reform efforts have reduced demand for tax-exempt income (yield) considerably. Except for "public purpose" bonds or nonprofit organization bonds issued by government units in annual amounts less than $10 million, banks will gain less income from municipal securities than from taxable, corporate ones. Public purpose bonds are those already well known: general obligation or guaranteed securities and nonguaranteed or revenue bonds in which private-sector involvement represents less than 10% of the use of the bond proceeds. Nonprofit bonds are those for public authorities generally as well as universities and hospitals and governmentally owned airports, docks and wharves, and solid waste facilities. In the case of both public purpose and nonprofit bonds sold by small, under $10 million a year issuers, commercial bands may deduct from their taxes 80% of the interest they earn.

Classification of Information Through the Credit Ratings. The ultimate classifier of information on municipal securities, and that pertaining to risk, comes from credit-rating agencies. By considering the security's structure, the legal interpretation affixed to it, and the financial status if the issuer—as well as relevant economic and managerial information—the agencies determine, essentially, the likelihood that the issuer will repay principal and interest as scheduled.

When referring to the credit rating agencies, we refer to three such organizations: Standard and Poor's Corporation, Moody's Investors Service, and Fitch Investors Service. Standard and Poor's (S&P) is the most diversified of the three agencies, providing credit ratings as only one among many information services. Moody's is the oldest and largest. Fitch is the smallest and newest.

Each one's process is basically the same. The issuer submits information relating to the financial, economic, and organizational condition of the issuer. More specific information is submitted on the debt being sold. In the view of an expert in these agencies, their use of this information is to establish "credit quality, the likelihood that bonds will pay interest and principal in full and on time" [25, p. 8].

When the agency receives the information, the agency begins a review process that is basically a municipal comparison in nature. The analyst, given the issuer data, initially compares them to those in S&P's own database, which consists of revenue, expenditure, and debt statistics on all previous issues rated by S&P.

These data are analyzed and presented to a rating committee. The committee includes the analyst and other experts in the particular region and type of financing. The rating committee members, almost all of whom are senior to the analysts, also use their experience for comparing the issuer they are rating with others.

Finally, each agency assigns a rating symbol indicating credit quality. These symbols are compared in Table 2. The speculative debt issues are those from Ba/BB to D. Investment-grade debt is that rated from Baa/BBB up to Aaa/AAA.

What credit ratings relate to is a corporate secret held closely by the ratings agencies, although ratings correlates are a matter of regular conjecture, argument, and even research. The agencies indicate that ratings are a mixture of quantitative analysis subjective views, and judgment [27]. Research on Moody's ratings suggests the predominant importance of the total economy—a variable largely out of the control of a local decision maker attempting to increase creditworthiness. One researcher using Moody's ratings observed that only economic variables show an real discriminating ability [28, p. 20].

Creditworthiness, it seems, may be a condition determined by national economic trends. Moreover, the wealth of data required by the agencies, as well as the local decision making control of financial management that this implies, may not guide ratings.

Table 2 Bond Rating Symbols and Meaning

Moody's	S&P	Fitch	Meaning
Aaa	AAA	AAA	Highest quality; extremely strong ablility to repay principal and interest
Aa	AA	AA	High grade; margins of protection are not as large; long-term risks somewhat larger
A, A-1[a]	A	A	Upper medium grade; neither highly protected nor poorly secured
Baa, Baa-1[a]	BBB	BBB	Medium grade; neither highly protected nor poorly secured
Ba	BB	BB	Have speculative elements
B	B	B	Lack characteristics of desirable investment
Caa	CCC	CCC	Poor standing
Ca	CC	CC	Speculative in a high degree; default probable
C	C	C	Bonds for which interest not now being paid
Con	D	DDD,DD,D	Default; payment in arrears

[a]The hyphenated ratings of A-1 and Baa-1 used by Moody's indicate that those credits are considered to be the better quality credits in the respective categories. An added plus or minus sign attached to Standard & Poor's and Fitch ratings indicates that a credit is considered to be in the upper or lower segment of the rating category.

The effect of the ratings on borrowing costs is substantial, nevertheless. Aguila and Holstein [29, p. 39] compared a AA rated and an A rated issue and found the difference to amount to about 10% more for the lower rated issue.

For investors, the ratings signal the amount of risk in timely payment of principal and interest, but not *when* to sell to avoid risk. For this reason, bond salespeople routinely warn investors not to smugly ignore the news in hopes that the ratings agencies are correct (see Ref. 30, p. 479–480, for an example). Bond analysts have recommended that investors take a very close and skeptical view of ratings agencies. "In many cases, by the time a rating has been lowered on a given credit, you've already lost the bulk of your money," the *Wall Street Journal* quoted a tax-exempt fund manager [31]. The *Journal* continued, "In fact, when a rating service finally gets around to downgrading an issue, that may be a good time to buy."

In summary, this outline of activity involved in implementing capital investment strategies has deliberately highlighted the range of discretion involved in a team's attempt to participate in an efficient market. Such discretion must exist to take account of the vast uncertainty with which an issuer must contend. The team must often guess, but at all times, it must develop strategies that cope with phenomena that are dynamic and unpredictable.

CLASSIFICATION OF OPPORTUNISTIC STRATEGIES FOR CAPITAL INVESTMENTS

There are an infinite number of variations among financing strategies from which communities may choose when funding capital improvements, and most cities can find one that fits their own unique legal, economic, financial, and political constraints. This is sometimes a matter of imitation of other communities and sometimes it is a matter of true innovation. Thus, innovation per se is not the prime reason for choosing a particular strategy. What is the prime reason?

The answer, we argue, lies in the idea advanced earlier that public managers themselves do not decide what reality is. Instead, managers participate with others in a team in which a bargain suiting the interests of the team members results in constructing a reality that all members find particularly useful. This reality is constructed to cope with an uncertain environment outside the members' organizations involved in issuing bonds; the choices made about investment strategies create stability, and sometimes promote innovation.

This section offers a classification of ways team members sought stability in its description of the ways state and local government financial managers reacted to uncertainty in capital financing activities over the last 20 years. The period has had a breathtaking volatility when viewed from its end. Merely reciting the financial condition of New York City at the beginning, middle, and end of the period—near default in 1975, embarking on major service increases and capital improvements with large surpluses in 1985, suffering a period of stress with a downgrade of its bonds' credit rating in 1995—perhaps portrays the bust to boom to bust character of many, if not all, state and local governments during this period.

As a matter of surprise to on one, the bust–boom–bust characteristics New York City exhibit are mirrored in interest rate swings. Rates have swung from double digits in the late 1970s to some of the lowest single digits seen since World War II in the 1990s.

The reaction communities have made to such instability can be described as coping and their coping strategies as prevention, absorption and information [32, p. 217].

Preventive strategies reduce the probability of shocks occurring so that resources flowing to the organization do not vary widely.

Absorption strategies adjust to events in making a given financial system operate within new and changing confines. Offsetting the effects of variations in resources, particularly the ravages of inflation and interest rate increases, shock absorbers exist to hedge against change, to adjust to the variations in interest rates, and to level consumer demand.

Information strategies deal with uncertainty in capital financing by forcing a reinterpretation of reality on the part of the strategizing organization or by the larger world. This often entails reinterpreting the agenda of issues that frame the need for investment [33].

This section catalogs each coping strategy, briefly explaining and illustrating it.

Coping by Prevention

Prevention efforts have attempted to forestall uncertainty. Generally, managers aim these efforts at reducing the probability of shocks occurring so that resources flowing to the organization do not vary widely. State and local financial managers have followed four basic strategies to prevent excessive variability: diversifying, merging, leveraging, and securitizing.

Diversifying

Diversification in state and local governments has applied primarily to revenue sources. The search for alternative revenues to the property tax at the local government level and to the income tax at the state level has become one of the clearest trends of the last two decades. The results of the search for alternatives have yielded a trend: user fees and other benefit-based revenues have become a major area of growth for state and local governments. In terms of capital asset financing, the revenue stream that results from the user fee may be pledged to repay bonds. These capital financings then support the activity charging the user fee.

Merger

Two major types of mergers have entered the scene to provide much preventive potential for financial managers.

Horizontal Mergers. Mergers with the private sector have gained a great deal of use as well as notoriety. "Privatization" of public functions has a substantial following and applies to almost any activity in which former public functions are shared with private-sector or profit-oriented groups. In capital finance, communities have demanded and received equity positions in private-sector projects financed with tax exempt bonds involving such projects as downtown redevelopment and particularly downtown hotel development.

Vertical Mergers. Mergers with other levels of government, intergovernmental sharing of responsibility, is not new but has taken on new characteristics. In capital finance, the creation of bond banks among governments with small capital financing needs takes advantage of the size preference in bond issues in which larger issues receive more attention. States also provide assistance to communities in marketing bonds. State guarantees of localities' bonds also merges the state's greater knowledge and presence in the bond market with localities' poorer credit ratings and substantial needs.

Leveraging

With newer revenue sources based on an income stream, similar to an annuity, a government can leverage these streams, or borrow based on them by using them as pledges of collateral. Such an approach amounts to simple nonguaranteed bond financings or revenue bonds; however, newer methods in which various revenue streams act together as leverage provide the potential for new and more reliable sources of capital financing funds.

One of the best examples of leveraging various revenue streams has occurred in New Jersey. Through the New Jersey Turnpike Authority, the state's Transportation Trust Fund gains $12 million a year to restore transportation infrastructure. The state's three toll roads earmark a portion of revenues for the trust, a combined total of $25 million yearly over a 20-year period to service and repay bond issues financing repair work. These funds are added to existing federal and state appropriations that further guarantee the repayment of bonds.

Securitizing

Traditionally, communities have financed limited-benefit capital improvements through pledges of receivables. For example, paving a residential street often has depended upon the willingness of the residents to pledge monthly repayments for the work. If the pledges emerged, the local government issued bonds with that revenue stream securing it.

Private sector borrowers call this procedure "securitization of assets." Involving an illiquid loan or lease agreement such as a tax lien, the securitization process transforms the asset into a liquid security.

The prevention of uncertainty through design of systems that increase the potential pool of resources and the willingness to use the resources has marked state and local government finance. Diversification and merger have gained new life. New techniques, such as leveraging and securitizing, have future value. Yet, present needs require a great deal of absorption of uncertainty.

Coping by Absorption

Action during a period of uncertainty often occurs as absorption activities. Absorbing uncertainty means adjusting to it by making a given financial systems operate within new and changing confines. Offsetting the effects of variations in resources, particularly the ravages of inflation and interest rate swings, uncertainty absorption tactics and strategies used by state and local government financial managers come in several forms. At least four groups of shock absorbers exist: hedging programs to deal with interest rate risk exposure; new financial instruments that move with the changes in interest rates but also allow bondholders the opportunity to sell the security if necessary; advance refunding programs to convert relatively high interest rate debt service to lower rates as interest rates fall; and programs that entice an ever-larger group of investors into the market to maintain demand.

Hedging to Absorb Uncertainty

Hedging involves the use of futures or options contracts or both to anticipate movements in interest rates. Futures contracts are agreements to deliver or receive cash or securities at a specified time or place. Options give investors the right, but not the obligation, to buy or sell something, such as a futures contract or a security, at a specified time or place. Hedging strategies have developed as futures and options markets have offered new products. Basic hedging involves the purchase of a futures contract, or an option on a physical or futures contract, to guard or "lock in" an interest rate.

Absorbing Uncertainty with New, Rate-Sensitive Debt Products

The fastest growing, and the most often used, method of absorbing uncertainty today has emerged as "creative capital finance" activities. The nature and type of these "creative" techniques have changed as quickly as the volatile trends affecting both borrowers/issuers and lenders/securities holders. These techniques span all dimensions that exist to describe capital financing: short- and long-term, interest-sensitive and -insensitive, borrower-tilted and lender-tilted, general and specific use oriented, and relatively more tax-weighted versus less.

For example, floating or variable-rate financing allows the bond buyer to receive an interest payment on bonds that changes with prevailing interest rates in the larger market. The bond issuer, in other words, opts for the equivalent of an adjustable-rate home mortgage. The rate floats within agreed upon levels, and at points agreeable to both the buyer and seller, the floating rate can be fixed for the remainder of the bond repayment period.

Absorbing Uncertainty Through Advance Refunding

The concept of refinancing an existing indebtedness is a long-established practice utilized not only by state and local governments but also by corporations and individuals to reduce interest costs. New, relatively lower interest rate debt replaces debt issued at relatively higher interest rates.

Advance refunding programs, most frequently, are used to reduce debt service costs, with the most common refunding process involving issuing the refunding bonds at an interest rate that is lower than the rate of the refunded bonds. However, an advance refunding may also be employed to restructure debt payments or to update overly restrictive bond indenture covenants. Therefore, refunding has several characteristics: (1) It is a "clean" swap of the outstanding bonds with the refunding bonds; (2) outstanding bonds would immediately cease to have any pledge of revenues; (3) the yearly debt service reduction may, if desired, begin immediately; and (4) the holders of the outstanding bonds would have, as security for the outstanding bonds, a portfolio of qualifying securities.

Leveling Demand Through New Bond Buyers

One major source of variation that state and local governments had to absorb in the last decade lay in changes in demand due to changes in types of bond holders. In fact, as banks and insurance companies, due to tax law changes and their own low profits, stopped buying bonds, individuals and households began buying more. Significant new forms of securities have emerged to take advantage of these new buyers, such as unit trusts, zero-coupon bonds, bonds with warrants, and, especially, mutual bond funds. In mutual funds, bond buyers purchase shares in a fund that fund mangers continually "restock" to achieve higher yields. The shareholder holdings are liquid even to the point of permitting limited check writing to liquidate holdings.

Thus, uncertainty absorption activities of state and local government financial managers have led to the use of hedging programs to deal with interest rate risk exposure; new financial instruments that move with the changes in interest rates but also allow bondholders the opportunity to sell the security if necessary; advance refunding programs to convert relatively high interest rate debt service to lower rates as interest rates fall; and programs that entice an ever-larger group of investors into the market to maintain demand.

Coping by Information

Not only does the network political economy play a major part in the social construction of reality through the imagery of prevention and absorption activities, but they also operate more fundamentally through information strategies. That is, from activities that act to reinterpret the agenda of work or the roles of those involved, additional dimensions of a reality network members can agree on are constructed.

Thus, a third method of dealing with the ambiguity of project finance has emerged as a reinterpretation of the agenda of issues [33]. Agenda setting in the policymaking process encompasses the simple act of identifying a problem, thereby setting in motion the apparatus for solving it. The apparatus involves various institutional arrangements that act to aggregate resources.

The last, full national issue-attention cycle neared its waning moments at the beginning of the 1975–1995 period that I have chosen for study. That is, the civil rights/urban disorders cycle of the late 1970s had exhausted itself to be replaced by the fiscal crisis, and, now, by the infrastructure crisis.

The fiscal crisis actually combined two issues, city financial emergencies and tax limitation. The financial emergency side began with New York City's 1975 crisis. The tax limitation movement was ignited by the passage of an expenditure cap law in 1976, ultimately spreading with California's Proposition 13 in 1978.

In a sort of policy dialectic, the fiscal crisis gave way to a new issue-attention cycle of the 1980s and early 1990s, infrastructure problems and their repair and replacement. Fiscal crisis solutions tended to lead ultimately to proposals for higher taxes. Tax limitation and antigovernment solutions barred the rise in taxes. In the standoff or vacuum, the opportunity arose for resetting the agenda.

With the opportunity for agenda-setting came the opportunity for someone or some group not on either side to synthesize the proposals. Infrastructure provided the obvious candidate for synthesis, and public financial managers and investment bankers became the obvious issue entrepreneurs. The direct consequence of the fiscal problem was the declining facilities cities had to support. At the heart of the tax limitation/antigovernment movement was the question of the redistribution of wealth.

The infrastructure movement could solve both sides' greatest fear: that economic problems were not getting solved. Economic problems of cities might not get solved through infrastructure replacement, but the multiplier effect of government spending on infrastructure would have an ameliorative effective (and those standing for reelection might have something to distribute). Economic problems of individuals might not be solved by infrastructure, but the new emphasis might produce productivity improvements and spark economic expansion (and to the middle class blunt the redistribution of wealth carried on through social programs).

Likewise, infrastructure joined heretofore sparring institutions. Infrastructure repair could join federal departments: Transportation for roads, bridges, and mass transit; Housing and Urban Development for general purpose development and public administration professionalism; and Environmental Protection for sewer and water systems. These departments, with infrastructure dominating the agenda, might appear to be doing what they intended—something "new," "innovative," or "pioneering"— even if it involved the most standard, traditional, and mundane of activities and dealt with mere "upgrading of existing services." The infrastructure issues would also get the departments out of the "social engineering" morass and make managers responsive to the rising Sunbelt coalition of public officials.

The trick of getting infrastructure off and running in the face of tax limitation movements and federal budget contraction turned out to be financing. Who would pay for such a massive group of construction projects? Direct taxation or pay-as-you-go as well as direct federal aid having been eliminated, the only alternatives left were long-term debt. Seeing such a demand, investment bankers and financial managers literally reshaped public capital financing as well as short-term cash management.

The entire "rebuilding America's cities' movement, as well as the budding "good schools" movement, represent agenda setting of a high order. Forces at work have reshaped the policy agenda, focusing direct attention on an issue other than tax limitation and blurring the deflate-the-government debate. The essential truth, however, lies in the notion that public financial managers have coped with uncertainty by information strategies, by seizing the initiative and resetting debate on policy in such a way that uncertainty may be absorbed or adjusted to in traditional, agreed-upon ways.

REFERENCES

1. J. Leighland, and R. Lam, *WPP$$: Who is to Blame for the WPPSS Disaster*, Ballinger, Cambridge, Mass. (1986).
2. G. J. Miller, "Debt Management Networks," *Public Admin. Rev.*, *53*(1): 50–58 (1993).
3. G. J. Miller, "Coping with Uncertainty," *Int. J. Public Admin.*, *7*(4): 451–495 (1985).
4. A. M. Sbragia, "Politics, Local Government, and the Municipal Bond Market," *The Municipal Money Chase: The Politics of Local Government Finance* (A. M. Sbragia, ed.), Westview, Boulder, Colo. (1983).
5. K. M. Eisenhardt, "Agency Theory: An Assessment and Review," *Acad. Manage. Rev.*, *14*(1): 57–74 (1989).
6. G. J. Miller, *Government Financial Management Theory*, Marcel Dekker, New York (1991).
7. H. E. Aldrich and D. A. Whetten, "Organization-Sets, Action-Sets, and Networks: Making the Most of Simplicity," *Handbook of Organizational Design* (P. D. Nystrom and W. H. Starbuck, eds.), Vol. L, Oxford University Press, New York (1981).
8. M. Landau, "Redundancy, Rationality, and the Problem of Duplication and Overlap," *Public Admin. Rev.*, *29*: 346–358 (1969).
9. R. T. Golembiewski, "Accountancy as a Function of Organization Theory," *Accounting Rev.*, *39*(April): 333–342 (1964).
10. M. E. Shaw, and L. M. Shaw, "Some Effects of Sociometric Group upon Learning in a Second Grade Classroom," *J. Social Psychol.*, *57*: 453–458 (1962).
11. M. M. Sukurai, "Small Group Cohesiveness and Detrimental Conformity," *Sociometry*, *38*: 234–242 (1975).
12. J. K. Murnighan, and D. E. Conlon, "The Dynamics of Intense Work Groups: A Study of British String Quarters," *Admin. Sci. Q.*, *36*: 165–186 (1991).
13. R. L. Hoffman, "Group Problem Solving," *Advances in Experimental Social Psychology* (L. Berkowtiz, ed.), Vol. 2, Academic Press, New York, pp. 99–132 (1966).
14. M. Sherif, "A Study of Some Social Factors in Perception," *Arch. Psychol. 27*: 187 (1935).
15. L. Festinger, "Informal Social Communication," *Psychol. Rev.*, *57*: 271–292 (1950).
16. D. B. Trow, "Membership Succession and Team Performance," *Hum. Relations*, *13*(August): 259–269 (1960).
17. P. W. Hom, R. W. Griffith, and P. P. Carson, "Turnover of Personnel," *Handbook of Public Personnel Administration* (J. Rabin, T. Vocino, W. B. Hildreth, and G. J. Miller, eds.), Marcel Dekker, New York, pp. 531–582 (1995).
18. H. Moulin, *Axioms of Cooperative Decision Making*, Cambridge University Press, Cambridge (1989).
19. P. A. Leonard, "Negotiated Versus Competitive Bond Sales: A Review of the Literature," *Municipal Finance J.*, *15*(2): 12–36 (1994).
20. G. J. Stigler, "The Economics of Information," *J. Polit. Econ.*, July/August: 706–738 (1961).
21. R. L. Bland, "The Interest Cost Savings from Experience in the Municipal Bond Market," *Public Admin. Rev.*, *45*: 233–237 (1985).
22. R. W. Forbes and J. E. Petersen, *Local Government General Obligation Bond Sales in Pennsylvania: The Cost Implications of Negotiation vs. Competitive Bidding*, Government Finance Research Center, Municipal Finance Officers Association, Washington, D.C. (1979).
23. E. Sharp, "The Politics and Economics of New City Debt," *Am. Polit. Sci. Rev.*, *80*: 1271–1288 (1986).
24. L. L. Moak, *Municipal Bonds, Planning, Sale and Administration*, Government Finance Officers Association, Chicago (1982).

25. J. E. Petersen, "Information Flows in the Municipal Securities Market: A Preliminary Analysis," unpublished manuscript, Government Finance Research Center, Government Finance Officers Association, Washington, D.C. (1988).

26. J. E. Petersen, *Tax Exempts and Tax Reform: Assessing the Consequences of the Tax Reform Act of 1986 for the Municipal Securities Market*, Government Finance Officers Association, Chicago (1987).

27. Standard and Poor's Corporation, *S&P's Municipal Finance Criteria*, McGraw-Hill, New York (1989).

28. S. R. Willson, "Credit Ratings and General Obligation Bonds: A Statistical Alternative," *Government Finance Rev.*, 2(3): 19–22 (1986).

29. P. R. Aguila, Jr., and C. L. Holstein, "The Cost of a Rating Downgrade," *Government Finance Review*, 5(1): 38–39 (1989).

30. G. J. Miller, "Capital Investment and Budgeting," *Handbook of Public Budgeting* (J. Rabin, ed.), Marcel Dekker, New York, pp. 419–502 (1992).

31. T. Herman, "Downgrading the Credit-Rating Services," *Wall Street Journal*, June 23: C1 (1989).

32. D. J. Hickson, C. R. Hinings, C. A. S. Lee, R. E. Schneck, and J. M. Pennings, "A Strategic Contingencies Theory of Intraorganizational Power," *Admin. Sci. Q.*, 16: 216–229 (1971).

33. J. W. Kingdon, *Agendas, Alternatives and Public Policies*, Little, Brown, Boston (1984).

34

Pros and Cons of a Separate Capital Budget for the Federal Government

Charles A. Bowsher

OBJECTIVES, SCOPE, AND METHOD

Because of recent interest in the idea of a separate capital budget, the Chairman and Ranking Minority Member of the Senate Committee on Environment and Public Works asked us to examine the advantages and disadvantages of the federal government using such a budget. The committee's request for this analysis and for an explanation of our previously stated position serves as the basis for this report.

We clarify the basic needs a separate capital budget would serve, present and analyze the potential advantages and disadvantages of using a separate federal capital budget, and then consider three options for improving information on capital expenditures within the current unified budget.

When analyzing the advantages and disadvantages of a separate capital budget for the United States, one must examine its hypothetical attributes because the federal government has never used such a system. Thus, such an exercise could be highly speculative were it not for the controlled use of evidence and arguments that have bearing on this issue. Ideally, comparative data might be used in lieu of historical experience. Capital budgeting in the state and local governments and in the private sector might serve to exemplify the sorts of opportunities and drawbacks its adoption by the federal government would provide. Analogies cannot be pushed too far, however, especially when the differences between existing capital budgeting systems and that of a potential federal equivalent are greater than the similarities. Comparative analysis, then, can help us to identify important budgeting practices but cannot determine their appropriateness in the federal setting. . . .

In the absence of relevant historical data, other approaches must be used. All budgeting systems are designed to serve specific purposes. Among the most basic of these purposes is the allocation of resources, using a process and corresponding documentation that allows the allocation to be sufficiently visible to permit effective decisionmaking and oversight.

Source: GAO Report PAD-83-1, September 22, 1983.

So, when analyzing the advantages and disadvantages, we focused part of our analysis on the question, would it be easier to allocate federal resources under a separate capital budget or the current unified budget?

In developing an alternative to a separate capital budget, we further divided the purposes of the budget into two parts to direct our analysis. First, a government's budget and its supporting documentation should fully disclose both the costs and the purposes of programs. Second, the display and analysis of capital expenditures within the context of the current unified budget should facilitate congressional decisionmaking and oversight. The options considered represent differing levels of commitment to augmenting the treatment of capital in the budget.

The visibility of decisions within any capital budgeting system is highly dependent on the definition of capital assets it employs. Also, how federal capital assets are defined directly affects whether or not there will be a budget surplus or deficit. . . .

Notwithstanding the nonempirical character of our topic, we did consult relevant literature and data bases. To learn about existing capital budgeting systems, we reviewed diverse published materials on planning, budgeting, and accounting practices. Our experience, knowledge, and judgment about the federal policymaking process have been used to assess the relevance of comparative information and analyses. Some of our data comes from a GAO capital budget record. . . [1].

ADVANTAGES AND DISADVANTAGES OF A SEPARATE FEDERAL CAPITAL BUDGET

Measured in terms of the dollars it spends or lends for capital assets, the federal government can be said to play a major role in our nation's public facilities. Measured in terms of those assets directly managed through federally run programs, that role is considerably smaller. The federal government directly or indirectly finances or encourages billions of dollars worth of capital acquisitions over which it has minimal or no control. Federal grants-in-aid, loans, loan guarantees, and tax expenditures (revenue losses attributable to provisions of the federal income tax laws encouraging certain activities) constitute sources of funds and incentives for acquiring capital assets whose ownership and management are controlled by state and local governments, businesses, and private individuals. Regardless of how successfully these organizations and individuals have controlled federally financed assets, the accountability to the U.S. taxpayer requires that a government budget fully disclose how economic resources are allocated to meet a legislatively defined range of needs. The display of capital asset resource allocations in a separate capital budget is one way of employing descriptive categories and analytical discussions to provide a maximum amount of meaningful information to both citizens and decision makers. However, whether or not a separate federal capital budget is the best way to handle capital investment decisions is a question open to debate. The adoption of a separate federal capital budget has a number of advantages and disadvantages. Some of them are discussed in the following sections.

Advantages

The advocates of a separate federal capital budget believe that if a separate federal capital budget were adopted, it would provide a way for allocating capital investment dollars in a manner consistent with federal policy and program objectives, even though ownership of capital assets is vested in nonfederal sectors. They also believe that it is a highly desirable vehicle for tracking and controlling the allocation of capital investment resources.

They argue that such a budget would

- Serve as a national strategy for coordinating the many federal capital investment programs and assessing their effect on public facilities and on public and private sector capital formation
- Help focus public attention on the amount and condition of capital assets owned and/or financed by the federal government
- Help change public perceptions of the relationship between long-term borrowing for capital assets and its effect on the federal debt
- Help provide a way to distribute the costs of long-term capital projects equitably among present and future users through depreciation or some other adjustment formula

Serve as a National Investment Plan

In the same way that it serves state and local governments, federal decision makers would find that a capital budget establishes a useful planning process because it would focus on proposed long-term projects, their estimated costs, and their anticipated national benefits. . . .

To a large extent, we are simply not aware of the full scope and nature of the federal government's contribution to public facilities and other capital investments. Diverse methods of financing, while useful in tailoring programs to meet policy objectives, tend to obscure the dimensions of the federal role, especially when they do not result in measurable direct outlays from the Treasury, as is the case with tax expenditures and loan guarantees [2]. While a separate capital budget would not necessarily resolve this problem, it could improve both the disclosure and planning of the various types of more direct federal outlays used for capital investment purposes. . . .

Focus Attention on Federal Assets and Their Condition

A capital budget would help focus public attention on the government ownership and/or financing of assets that produce long-term benefits. As in the private sector, government managers commonly make capital expenditures because they expect a future return in the form of increased services, benefits, or income for citizens. These capital expenditures represent collective investment and increase the nation's assets. The value and stream of benefits derived from these assets decrease, however, if they are not adequately maintained. Also, the costs of owning and using capital assets increase over time. Thus, maintenance is a critical component of long-term capital investment strategy.

Presently, reliable information on the condition and maintenance costs of federal capital assets is not available governmentwide. A separate capital budget would provide a stimulus for acquiring this needed data. It would also help to illuminate the degree of federal responsibility being assumed for maintaining assets financed by grants-in-aid and loans but owned and managed by state and local governments. Bridges, highways, and wastewater treatment facilities are among the capital assets built with substantial federal funding but whose maintenance costs fall on the budgets of state and local governments.

Change the Public's Perception of Debt Financing

Given the long-term benefits provided by capital assets, a case is sometimes made for treating a federal deficit incurred to acquire these assets differently from one incurred for current expenditures. Borrowing to finance current expenditures requires extended payments for present benefits. Although there may be sound economic reasons for doing so, this practice makes it appear that the government is spending beyond its means. In contrast, using long-term debt to finance capital projects requires extended payments for extended benefits. Such borrowing exchanges the extended repayment of loaned monetary assets for the future services of tangible capital assets. Thus, deficits resulting from borrowing to acquire capital assets is accompanied by an increase in the nation's assets. A separate capital budget could be used to highlight the distinction between the two forms of debt and shape public awareness of the federal deficit's composition as well as its absolute magnitude. Nonetheless, we believe that an inflexible rule requiring the debt financing of capital assets is not a necessary or useful requirement of a separate capital budget.

Increase Intergenerational Equity

It is often claimed that a separate capital budget that employs debt financing of capital assets contributes to increased equity between those who pay for and those who use these assets. If the life of the loan used for a capital acquisition approximates the service life of the asset acquired, then each generation pays for the amount of capital it actually uses. However, debt financing of capital assets could occur without the need for a separate capital budget.

Disadvantages

Whatever benefits a separate capital budget might provide, serious practical problems are associated with its adoption by the federal government. Opponents of this budget system argue that it has the potential to

- Impose constraints on countercyclical fiscal policy measures if capital investment were financed by long-term debt
- Require what may be extensive and costly changes in the current federal budget process with little direct evidence of the potential benefits from doing so
- Introduce greater complexity and increased opportunity for manipulation into the framework of budget categories because of the need to define and decide what should be classified as a capital asset and, if required, how that asset should be depreciated
- Shift the focus of the budget away from broad questions of resource allocation to meet functionally defined national needs to narrower questions of public investment and how it is to be financed

Constrain Countercyclical Fiscal Policy

The effect a separate capital budget would have on federal fiscal policies used to counter short-term swings in the economy depends on the specific characteristics that are built into a dual budget system, such as how capital and operating expenditures are separated, whether or not assets are depreciated, and how capital assets are financed.

Although there is no technical requirement that restricts the acquisition of assets by debt financing alone, the assumption that the adoption of a separate federal capital budget would require this method to be used is what gives credibility to claims about its effects on fiscal policy. Three reasons might be advanced to justify this assumption: (1) Debt financing would be desirable for increasing equity between those who pay for and those who use capital assets; (2) debt financing capital expenditures would smooth the fluctuations in large federal outlays; (3) a separate capital budget might be adopted along with a balanced budget requirement, which would require balancing current expenditures with current tax receipts and financing capital outlays through long-term debt.

The actual validity of the three reasons is less important than their persuasiveness in linking debt financing with the adoption of a separate federal capital budget. If such a link were successfully made, then the consequences of debt financing for fiscal policy should be closely examined.

Were the federal government to use long-term borrowing for the bulk of its capital expenditures, the flow of one type of federal outlay would be made independent of short-term changes in economic conditions. To a greater extent, capital acquisitions would be planned and financed to meet long-term capital needs, not to play a role in the short-term stabilization of the economy. Insulating capital outlays from serving the requirements of fiscal policy would necessarily increase the burdens on expenditures from the operating budget, tax policy, and monetary policy to act as instruments of overall economic policy. If a balanced operating budget were also a requirement of an adopted dual budgeting system, the corresponding constraints imposed on current outlays and tax receipts would make the task of stabilization even more reliant on monetary policy [3]. How these potential consequences are viewed depends on the amount of federal economic stabilization deemed both necessary and desirable.

Disrupt the Budget Process

The adoption of a separate capital budget is quite likely to unpredictably disrupt the existing budget process. A dual budget would more than likely require some changes in institutional structure, shifts in responsibility, and modifications of the budget cycle's timing. The need to relate aggregate debt, tax, and spending limits to two separate budgets—capital and operating—would introduce greater complexity into the already complicated budget process. . . .

Complicate Budget Categories

Establishing a dual budgeting system requires the ability to distinguish between capital and operating expenditures and assumes that it is possible to clearly and unambiguously define capital assets. But, even among those public- and private-sector organizations that use capital budgets, no definitions of capital assets are universally accepted. . . . Whether or not the federal operating budget were in balance would depend upon what is included in the definition of capital. Although any budgeting system can potentially be subject to manipulation and while strong oversight and accounting controls can minimize the occurrence of abuse, the complexity associated with defining Federal capital assets remains.

The problems of definition also interact with the question of how capital assets, once defined, should be treated within a dual budgeting system. More specifically, should federal capital assets be subject to depreciation, how should it be handled in the budget, and what are the consequences of doing so [4]?

Shift the Purpose of the Budget

The primary purpose of the unified budget is to allocate resources based on policy decisions made by the President and the Congress. To reflect the major areas of the government's responsibility, budget authority and outlays are organized in accordance with 17 functional categories designed to present the costs of policy choices without regard to the jurisdictions of specific federal agencies. Although the yearly flow of federal resources is a necessary concern of the budget process and is expressed in the budget documents, of even greater significance is the way those resources meet the basic needs of society and the economy as categorized in functional terms. The overriding objective of policy is to ensure that these diverse needs of society are considered in making budget decisions.

A dual budgeting system could result in treating policy and functional needs as secondary to the type of expenditure—capital investment or operating expense. Capital and current expenses present different technical problems to a resource manager and, consequently, could be separated to ensure optimal financial treatment of each. With a separate capital budget, the acquisition of assets could be more carefully managed, but the policy implications of financial decisions could be blurred. The allocation of resources for capital is not separable, in a policy sense, from the host of related operating expenditures with which it is joined to execute federal government programs.

A functional breakdown of expenditures in the unified budget presupposes that the primary policy goal of the budget—the satisfaction of different types of needs in society through the allocation of resources—will take precedence over the specific technical means used to achieve it. The possible financing of social and other non-capital programs with current revenues or of financing capital acquisitions through long-term debt has little bearing on how each type of expenditure is judged in policy terms. Programs are viewed as a unified whole regardless of the mix of capital and noncapital resources required for their implementation. In contrast, unless programs are wholly capital or operating, a dual budget dissects the individual programs by their operating and capital segments. Since these parts would appear in two separate budgets, capital assets' contribution to achieving either program goals or broader functional goals may be obscured. . . .

OPTIONS FOR PROVIDING CAPITAL INVESTMENT INFORMATION WITHIN THE UNIFIED BUDGET

Any budgeting system used by the federal government should disclose the full range of government programs and their associated costs, indicate the purposes and needs these programs are intended to serve, and suggest the nature and size of budgetary commitments that extend beyond a single budget year. These criteria and the desire to increase the information on federal capital investments that is available for making budget decisions do not automatically entail adopting a separate capital budget. Many of the disadvantages of a dual budgeting system presented in our analysis might be avoided by considering alternative displays of budget information more closely tailored to the nature and range of federal responsibilities. The following three options describe proposals for increasing the comprehensiveness with which federal capital expenditures can be examined.

Option I: Display Capital Investments Separately in a Resectioned Unified Budget

The need for more comprehensive information on the size and composition of federal capital investments can be partially satisfied by collecting and prominently displaying capital investment data in the unified budget. Although the format in the budget documents would be altered, the fundamental purposes of the unified budget would still be served. Specifically, the budget functional categories used to aggregate outlays and budget authority across agency lines could continue to show how federal policies serve national needs. . . .

Option 2: Prepare a New Infrastructure and Capital Investment Analysis

A new "infrastructure and capital investment analysis" is one way of providing capital investment data within the current budget. In addition to its prospective role for presenting aggregate data on federal capital investment, it could also be used to reveal some of the policy implications of current capital investment levels. To ensure that this approach has adequate visibility in the budget documents, it could include a descriptive analysis in Part 3 of the budget –Budget Program and Trends—and tabular budget data in a new special analysis.

The descriptive analysis in Part 3 of the budget could discuss federal capital investment policy and policy changes, programs, trends, and major problem areas. Two new special analysis tables could be prepared, one covering investment in existing assets and the other covering investment in new additions to public facilities.

For existing assets, the first analysis could show the past year's outlays, current year estimates and budget year estimates at current policy levels, and budget year outlays under the administration's proposed policy.

The second analysis would cover additions to the existing stock of assets. It would show investment for the past year, the current year, and the budget year under current policy; budget year investment under the administration's proposed policy; and expected additions to the capital stock. Thus, this analysis and the one on existing public facilities would enable policymakers and decision makers to determine whether to expand the capital stock or to maintain the existing capital stock according to national needs and policy.

Both of the proposed analyses could be prepared using the budget functional format that is designed to relate federal policies to the satisfaction of national needs. Major programs would follow the functional categorization. This would allow the decision makers to focus on areas of investment priorities and allocation of scarce budgetary resources. It would also be possible to distinguish between direct federal investment where assets are owned and maintained by the federal government and those investments that are not owned and maintained by the federal government.

Preparing infrastructure and capital investment analysis tables would require the agencies to prepare and maintain an inventory and condition assessment against which projected spending authority and outlays could be judged. In this regard, certain complexities would have to be resolved; capital investment is not quite analogous to providing beneficiaries with a constant stream of services. Capital projects have discrete life cycles: There will always be new starts, ongoing efforts, completions, and disposals of existing assets. Also, federal investment in capital assets involves both outlays for assets owned and maintained by the federal government and grants to state and local governments for assets owned and maintained by them. . . .

Option 3: Improve the Special Analyses of the Budget

The collection of better data on federal capital investments and their display in the Special Analyses, which constitute a companion volume to the President's budget proposals, is a third option. It is the easiest to carry out but has less potential impact than the other two. . . .

EXISTING CAPITAL BUDGETING PRACTICES

Many organizations are bound by operational or legal constraints that dictate the use of capital budgets. Businesses, for example, must separate current expenses from capital outlays to determine net profit or loss. Most state and local governments distinguish between capital and operating expenses because they are required by law to present balanced operating budgets. Often, businesses and governments use capital budgets as plans for determining the need for and nature of capital assets, as well as their cost, timing of acquisition, and methods of financing. The federal government, however, treats capital asset outlays in the same manner as current operating expenses because it is not bound by any of the constraints that would require it to separate the capital and operating portions of the national budget.

Business Accounting and Capital Budgeting Practices

Business accounting practices are designed to portray accurately the magnitude of the firm's current operations, the value of its assets, and the extent of its indebtedness. Creditors, stockholders, and government agencies require information concerning these three factors. Consequently, businesses typically report data on their revenues, expenses, profits, tax liabilities, assets owned, depreciation, and equity and bond issues. Many of these data and the structure of the budget and financial statements in which they appear are not relevant to many of the purposes and responsibilities of the federal government.

Unlike the federal government, business firms usually do not deduct total capital outlays from current revenues in computing a "bottom line." Rather, capital expenses are shown as a series of operating charges representing the annual depreciation of capital assets and the cost of borrowing. Businesses charge depreciation in order to allocate proportionately the investment costs of depreciable assets to each accounting period during which the asset was used in the production of goods and services and to recognize the decline of service potential. Annual depreciation for tax purposes is determined using the Internal Revenue Code. Depreciation for accounting purposes may be determined on a basis more consistent with the estimated life of the asset.

Many businesses draw up separate capital budgets that show large capital outlays scheduled to be made in future years, the proposed means to finance them, and their expected benefits. In this regard, the purpose of the capital budget is to help evaluate the need for and nature, cost, and timing of acquiring and financing long-lived assets. This is similar to the capital budgeting practices of state and local governments.

State and Local Governments' Accounting and Capital Budgeting Practices

State and local governments use capital budgets as plans for acquiring and financing capital items. Frequently, capital items are distinguished and separated from the operating budget because of a legal requirement to balance operating budgets. However, they are not identical to business models. Generally, strict business-type accounting methods are not used. Usually, except for self-supporting enterprise funds, state and local governments do not draw up business-type balance sheets of assets and liabilities, nor do they provide an estimate of asset depreciation. This makes it impossible to compute their net worth or determine whether their stock of assets is increasing or decreasing. Where depreciation is used, the productive life of an asset is often defined the same as in business accounting practices.

Capital budgets have become an essential part of the financial plans of state and local governments. Although the definition of capital varies substantially, many capital budgets summarize each capital item's need, cost, method of financing, and, in some cases, its anticipated contribution to the community. Used in this way, the capital budget is a good way of displaying proposed capital projects—such as schools, sewer and water systems, public parks, and the like—and focusing the public's attention on a very important segment of government operations.

Capital budgets have also become an effective means of carrying out the long-term projects of state and local governments. For the purpose of obtaining borrowed funds, capital budgets are indispensable because state and local governments

- Often operate under legislative constraints that restrict borrowing and taxing ability (mandatory debt ceilings, requirements to balance the budget, limitations on tax rates and what can be taxed)
- Must meet solvency criteria set by investment bankers to gain access to financial markets [5].

Separate budgeting for capital and operating expenses can and has caused coordination problems for state governments. One state developed its capital budget independent from its operating agencies. This resulted in the construction of facilities that were unplanned and even unwanted by the agencies that had to operate them. However, many states are recognizing this oversight and are improving their capital planning techniques. Operating and capital budgets are now often contained in the same document or handled as companion documents within a coordinated timetable. The recognized interdependence of capital assets and their operations has increased this type of coordination.

Many of the reasons that a capital budget is useful to state and local governments do not apply to the federal government. These include the fact that the federal government

- Does not need a capital budget to preserve its credit rating and obtain access to the financial market
- Is not, in its ability to borrow, affected by asset acquisition, as in the case of municipal governments
- Is not subject to the solvency criteria investment bankers enforce on local governments

Instead, the federal government makes capital investment decisions within the boundaries set by aggregate debt limits, spending ceilings for each of the functional areas within the budget, and targeted levels of taxation. Collectively, these components of the budget process provide a major means of discipline for fiscal policy

CAPITAL BUDGETING CONCEPTS AND THEIR IMPLICATIONS

How capital items are defined determines the percentage of total outlays that can be included in a capital budget. Varied definitions of capital assets can affect the respective sizes of capital and operating budgets and directly influence the size of the federal deficit.

What Is a Capital Expenditure?

Because there is lack of agreement on what should be classified as capital, organizations use various classifications. Different organizations using different definitions of capital items and capital budget totals showing large fluctuations from year to year complicate assessing the real costs of capital investment. Comparing yearly totals may be misleading because of irregular rates of new acquisitions or major rehabilitation of capital assets, and totals aggregated for more than one organization may be misleading because of the varying capital investment definitions used by different organizations. Under a dual budget system, it is often argued that the operating budget should be balanced, and thus the incentive is strong to define capital as broadly as possible.

Generally, businesses define capital expenditures according to accounting principles and tax regulations. However, there is still some variation among businesses as to what is counted as a capital item. As a matter of prudence, state and local governments restrict capital expenditures to tangible assets, but their definitions of this term also vary widely.

For the federal sector, limiting the definition of capital to federally owned nonmilitary tangible assets would be very restrictive. . . . Using this definition would give only a partial picture of the federal government's contribution to asset formation. The federal government plays various roles in stimulating capital investment. It directly builds and maintains infrastructure, such as bridges and roads, and helps state and local governments do the same through grants-in-aid. The federal government also helps individuals and businesses with capital investments by making direct loans and by guaranteeing loans obtained from private sources. Frequently discussed but probably the least direct stimulus to capital investment provided by the federal government is the use of tax incentives, such as tax credits and accelerated depreciation allowances.

Direct federal programs, grants-in-aid, loans, loan guarantees, and tax expenditures have diverse effects when they contribute to the building of infrastructure and the stimulation of private sector capital formation. It is difficult to identify the scope and intensity of the federal role even in those areas where that role seems to be the most straightforward. Although direct federal programs and grants-in-aid, for example, often produce highly visible public facilities—highways, mass transit systems, wastewater treatment plants, and the like—the benefits of these projects for the private sector of the economy are often unmeasureable. Not only do private corporations depend upon public facilities for the conduct of commerce and industry, but their own decisions to invest in new capital may be influenced—in some cases decisively—by federal investments either projected or current.

Notwithstanding the virtues of adopting a broadly based definition of capital investment, it is important to note the potential pitfalls in doing so. Any departure from defining capital investments in terms of tangible assets clears the way for a wide range of expenditures, each possessing a legitimate claim to be classified as developmental or capital forming. The problem is: Where does one stop? Exactly what should be called capital is a policy choice and depends on how the Congress chooses to use the budget. Keeping a capital budget free from manipulation requires a precise and consistently used definition of capital [6]. It is worth noting, however, that unified budgets can be similarly abused through the use of off-budget items.

Alternative Definitions

Assets are defined as "probable future economic benefits obtained or controlled by a particular entity as a result of past transactions or events [7]." But classifying an item as an asset does not solve the problem of defining which items to capitalize. Tangible assets run the range from supplies to buildings, yet no one would dispute treating supplies as current and buildings as capital expenditures. What is not clear is how to treat the assets that fall between these extremes.

Deciding which assets to capitalize is largely a matter of judgment and depends on the asset's life, value, and frequency of procurement. To place an asset in the capital category, it must have a service life longer than the fiscal period, usually 1 year. Beyond this, the distinction between operating and capital items lies in the perceived role of an item in relation to other items being classified and, generally, whether the item is a recurring or nonrecurring expenditure. What would be considered a capital item for a small municipality might be regarded as too insignificant to be similarly classified by a large city, a state, or the federal government. Furthermore, most of the time only nonrecurring expenditures are considered capital.

Despite the inherent problems of classification, specific criteria for defining capital must be established before a capital budget can be used at the national level. For the federal government, criteria could take numerous forms, such as the nature of the asset, the asset's ownership, or the asset's relationship to accomplishing agency and program goals. Using these criteria, it is necessary to determine whether the definition of capital

- Should be restricted to only tangible assets or broadened to include research and development expenditures and financial assets
- Should include only civilian assets or also military assets
- Should include only federally owned assets or also those assets totally or partially financed by the federal government but not federally owned, or
- Should be restricted to those major items needed to accomplish an agency's primary mission as opposed to those items that provide administrative support

Whether or not capital investments used for defense purposes should be included in a capital budget raises an issue meriting closer attention. Defense assets are often highly specialized in the purposes they serve, may be highly expendable for the same reason, and may also be subject to rapid and unpredictable technological obsolescence. It is commonly believed that defense assets are not productive in the same way as are the capital assets of the private sector or of federal civilian agencies. These grounds could be used to justify excluding defense investments from a capital budget.

One way of arguing for including defense assets in a capital budget is to consider which of these assets are potentially transferable for civilian federal or private-sector use. Only transferable defense assets would then be capitalized. The primary difficulty with this approach is the arbitrary assumption upon which it is based. Many capital assets, regardless of the sector of society that uses them, are highly specialized, vulnerable to premature deterioration and subject to technological obsolescence. When private-sector or civilian federal assets are considered in these terms, little justification would seem to exist for no longer regarding broad categories of "rapidly depreciable" assets as capital investments. Insofar as an asset has a projected useful life in excess of 1 year and is expected to deliver a stream of future benefits, a cogent argument can be made for treating it as capital. So viewed, defense assets can be regarded quite appropriately as capital investment, although there may be other reasons for their exclusion from a capital budget. . . .

NOTES AND REFERENCES

1. U.S. General Accounting Office, "Federal Capital Budgeting: A Collection of Haphazard Practices," PAD-81-19, February 26 (1981).
2. Tax expenditures and loan guarantees, for example, are not direct outlays from the Treasury. It is difficult to assess how much capital investment can be attributed to these two vehicles of financing on the basis of information provided in the current unified budget. Nevertheless, tax expenditures provide powerful and, in large measure, uncontrollable (entitlements) incentives for private investment in a diversity of capital assets. At the same time, they represent sizeable amounts of revenue foregone by the federal government. Loan guarantees also make the purchase of capital assets possible without the need for direct federal expenditures. In addition, they influence private credit markets in ways not fully described in the unified budget.
3. These comments refer to the fiscal policy choices available to federal decision makers under differing sets of requirements for the functioning of a dual budgeting system. In the absence of legislative changes to the contrary, the automatic stabilizers of the economy, such as unemployment insurance and the taxation of large marginal increases in profits, would still continue to operate.
4. Depreciation (the method of allocating the net cost of a tangible capital asset over the estimated useful life of the asset in a systematic and rational manner) of federal capital assets is being addressed in a separate GAO study and will not be discussed in detail in this report. . . .

5. Between 1972 and 1977, debt financing of state and local capital outlays declined from slightly over one-half to slightly over one-third of totals for this type of expenditure. There has been a corresponding, although not uniform, increase in reliance upon federal grants-in-aid for capital financing, which in 1977 reached a 21-year high of 47%. User fees, short-term debt, and accumulated reserves are also sources of capital investment funds. See U.S. Department of Commerce, *A Study of Public Works Investment in the United States*, April, Vol. I, Ch. 4. (1980).
6. New York City is a prime example of how a capital budget can be manipulated. GAO has conducted several reviews (PAD-77-1, GGD-78-13, and GGD-80-5) of New York City's fiscal crisis. These, as well as a study entitled *The Future of New York City's Capital Plant*, prepared by the Urban Institute, showed that New York included in its capital budget many expenditures that, in strict municipal accounting terms, are generally operating costs. These included funds for manpower training and vocational education, code enforcement, repair programs, purchase of motor vehicles, and lease payments. By listing these expenditures as capital, the city removed them from a severely constrained operating budget and made them eligible for bond financing. In fiscal year 1975, which was the onset of New York's fiscal crisis, these expenditures exceeded 50% of the capital budget.
7. Financial Accounting Standards Board, "Statement of Financial Accounting Concepts No. 3," December (1980).

VII

BEHAVIORAL CONTEXTS OF BUDGETING AND FINANCE

EDITORIAL INTRODUCTION

The study of human behavior always wrestles with two contradictory strains. For genetic reasons, as well as philosophical ones in Western civilizations, the uniqueness of the individual gets attention. However, if people do differ in significant ways, many people are also similar in particulars. Most people in fact behave similarly under enough conditions that one would be foolish to insist in principle on the unmodified uniqueness of the individual. Such behavioral similarities in no way deny that people are also unique in an ultimate sense.

PBF thus cannot avoid being in the differences/similarities business, as the selections that follow show in various ways. By way of introductory support, note only that budgets set goals. Immediately, then, the budget maker is involved in balancing the differences and similarities of those people subject to the budget. Will Charlean best respond to a "tight" budget and work energetically and with intelligence even though the budget is realistically unattainable? Or does Sam work best when he experiences the success of "bringing a project in under budget," and the more so the better, even though that is a slam dunk? So the "looser" Sam's budget, the better.

Bringing People Up Front

Chris Argyris's "What Budgeting Means to People" goes right to the heart of important differences and similarities. Basically, Argyris finds that those specially charged with responsibility for budgeting or finance are likely to see PBF in different ways than those performing other activities. For example, Argyris compares the perceptions of the two types of organization members concerning this theme: What are the uses of budgets? As might be expected, budgeting personnel see their activity as crucial and strategic. Budgeting is "the watchdog": Persons in that activity closely identify with top management because they supply the data required for overhead control. Foremen tend toward a different view. Budgets tend to complicate the foreman's job of dealing with individual cases, and budgeting personnel often appear uninformed and pretentious, and sometimes even malicious.

These differences in perceptions suggest the delicacy of the relations of budgeting and finance personnel with other organization members, especially because perceptual differences are reinforced by a family of issues that can reduce effectiveness. Patently, for example, budgeting and finance personnel monitor money. Since money is the lifeblood of all organizations, both business and government, budgeting and finance often will be where the heated action is.

Similar Models, Different Individual Motivation

Hal G. Rainey provides another perspective on differences/similarities in his "Work Motivation." Basically, he provides an extended catalog of the several ways in which the behavioral sciences have tried to distinguish what individuals need and, hence, what stimuli they will respond to in order to get what they need or want. In McClelland's theory, for example, individuals are seen as desiring some blend of three "needs"—for achievement, for affiliation, and for power. The most effective motivational system, by extension, will be the one that best relates to an individual's particular profile on such needs and that best permits meeting those needs. What motivational system would be next best? You just work yourself down the list, keeping in mind that individuals often will differ in the values they assign to each of three McClelland "needs."

The basic lesson for PBF is direct. As much as possible, PBF policies and practices should facilitate a "best fit," or a "good fit," with both the different and similar features of the profiles of people involved. Good fit, or better, will generate the most motivation. Failing in the effort to achieve a good fit, PBF policies and practices will generate costs that will variously constrain individual and collective performance. See also Chapter 8.

The PBF reader should have a good time in assessing the need-satisfying potential of a range of budgetary and accounting tools, techniques, and theories. Rainey describes some simple models, and others with substantial complexity. But they all can be put in the service of assessing degree of fit.

Expectancy Theory and Differences/Similarities

J. Ronen and J. L. Livingstone provide detailed counterpoint to Rainey in their "An Expectancy Theory Approach to the Motivational Impacts of Budgets." For present purposes, expectancy theory can be expressed in terms of dual concerns: the probability that effort will be reflected in performance at work, and the probability that effective performance will be rewarded in ways that the individual values. This done, Ronen and Livingstone essentially focus on the new question: What kinds of budgeting processes will lead to which kinds of effects, given expectancy theory? More specifically, they focus on five major assumptions that often have been made about the budgeting process:

- The budget should be set at a reasonably attainable level.
- Managers should participate in budget making.
- Managers should operate on the principle of management by exception, "loose" about implementation but "tight" about policies and standards.
- Personnel should be rewarded/punished only for activities within their control, with the caveat that system features are major contributors to most problems.
- Dimensions of performance that cannot be conveniently measured in monetary terms are outside the PBF domain.

In assessing these assumptions, Ronen and Livingstone raise a host of important questions—for example, concerning levels of aspiration. What happens to the performance of any individual who settles on a level of aspiration that is easy to achieve? Or simply impossible? And do some people habitually overestimate or underestimate their actual performance? With what consequences in each case? Such questions imply great challenges to the behavioral sciences, and far outstrip the available answers in theory or practice. But such are the questions that daily confront budgeters and financial officers.

Fortunately, some useful behavioral benchmarks exist. For example, individuals tend to decrease their levels of aspiration in response to consistent failure. That generalization does not hold for all individuals under all conditions, but the generalization constitutes a reasonable bet. Hence, budgets ought not be so demanding that they preclude success, for example. If budgets are impossibly tight, individuals will tend to reject them because those budgets unavoidably require that an individual will fail psychologically, even if that person "does a great job." As a practical consequence, levels of aspiration may be lowered by an approach that seeks to raise them too much. At the same time, "easy" budgets may also lower levels of aspiration.

Behavioral Perspectives on Budgeting

The several preceding selections, in various ways, urge the value of balance in PBF activities. V. Bruce Irvine provides another guiding synthesis in his "Budgeting: Functional Analysis and Behavioral Implications." Essentially, Irvine tries to bring together that which is often separate: the findings of behavioral sciences, and the professional literatures dealing with budgeting, accounting, and finance. Irvine distinguishes the functional versus dysfunctional aspects of budget systems, basically, and seeks to detail how various findings about human behavior can increase the former and decrease the latter. His useful general model synthesizes these findings, which relate to participation, types of organization structures, and motivation, among numerous other features.

Behavioral Perspectives on Accounting

To conclude Unit VII, Edwin H. Caplan adds an overview concerning another central PBF activity in "Behavioral Assumptions of Management Accounting." Caplan begins with a dictum that some will find hard to accept: that the "management accounting function is essentially a behavioral function." Beyond that, he charts the here → there development necessary to exploit that basic proposition. "Here" Caplan defines in terms of the behavioral assumptions underlying "traditional management accounting," and "there" involves the behavioral assumptions derived from "modern organization theory" that Caplan prescribes should be built into a new form of management accounting. Of course, that "new form" represents the ultimate "there" of the required development.

We remain a long distance from where Caplan would like PBF to reach. But the map Caplan provides seems both clear and direct.

35
What Budgeting Means to People

Chris Argyris

One of the most common of the factory supervisors' attitudes about budgets was that budgets were used as a pressure device to increase production efficiency. Many cases were cited to support this point. Finance people also admitted that budgets helped "keep people on the ball" by raising their goals and increasing their motivation. The problem of the effects of pressure applied through budgets seems to be the core of the budget problem.

THE CAUSES OF PRESSURE

Employees and front-line supervisors believe that the cause for pressure from the top is due to top management's belief that most employees are basically or inherently lazy. Employees and front-line supervisors also feel that top management believes that employees do not have enough motivation of their own to do the best possible job.

The interviews with top management officials revealed that the employees' beliefs were not totally unfounded, as a few quotations from some of the top management (both line and finance) make clear:

> I'll tell you my honest opinion. Five percent of the people work, ten percent of the people think they work. And the other eighty-five percent would rather die than work.

> I think there is a need for more pressure. People need to be needled a bit. I think man is inherently lazy and if we could only increase the pressure, I think the budget system would be more effective.

Such feelings, even if they are never overtly expressed toward employees, filter through to the employees in very subtle ways. Budgets represent one of the more subtle ways. Once

Source: "Budget Pressure: Some Causes and Consequences," in C. Argyris, *The Impact of Budgets on People*, Controllership Foundation, New York, pp. 14–22 (1954). Reprinted with permission of author and publisher.

the employees sense these feelings exist in top management, they may become very resentful.

THE EFFECTS OF PRESSURE

How do people react to pressure? In three of the plants studied factory supervisors felt they were working under pressure and that the budget was the principal instrument of pressure. Management exerts pressure on the workforce in many ways, of which budgets is but one. Budgets, being concrete, seem to serve as a medium through which the total effects of management pressure are best expressed. As such they become an excellent point of focus for studying the effect of pressure on people in a working organization.

THE CREATION OF GROUPS

An increase in tension, resentment, suspicion, fear, and mistrust may not be the only result of ever-stronger management pressures transmitted to supervisors, and in turn, to employees. We know, from psychological research, that people can stand a certain amount of pressure. After this point is passed, it becomes intolerable to an individual. We also know that one method people have to reduce the effect of the pressure (assuming that the employees cannot reduce the pressure itself) is to join groups. These groups then help absorb much of the pressure and the individual is personally relieved.

The process of individuals joining groups to relieve themselves of pressure is not an easy one. It does not occur overnight. The development of a group on such a basis seems to have the following general stages of growth.

> *First*, the individuals "feel" the pressure. They are not certain, but they sense an increase in pressure.
>
> *Second*, they begin to see definite evidences of the pressure. They not only feel it, they can point to it.
>
> Since they feel this pressure is on them personally, they begin to experience tension and general uneasiness.
>
> *Next*, the people usually "feel out" their fellow workers to see if they sense the pressure.
>
> Finding out that others have noted the pressure, the people begin to feel more at ease. It helps to be able to say, "I'm not the only one."
>
> *Finally*, they realize that they can acquire emotional support from each other by becoming a group. Furthermore, they can "blow their top" about this pressure in front of their group. Gradually, therefore, the individuals become a group because in becoming a group they are able to satisfy these needs:

1. A need to reduce the pressure on each individual.
2. A need to get rid of tension.
3. A need to feel more secure by belonging to a group which can counteract the pressure.

In short, a new, cohesive group has developed to combat management pressure. In a sense, the people have learned that they can be happier if they combine against this management pressure.

Suppose now that top management, aware of the tensions which have been generated and the groups which have been formed, seeks to reduce the pressure. The emphasis on budgets is relaxed. Perhaps even the standards are "loosened." Does this then destroy the group? After all, its primary reason for existence was to combat the pressure. Now, the pressure is gone. The group should eventually disintegrate.

The answer seems to be that the groups continue to exist!

The evidence for this is not as conclusive as it should be. Therefore, the following explanation should be considered primarily in the realm of inference and conjecture rather than scientific fact.

These factors seem to operate to keep the group in existence:

1. There is a "time lag" between the moment management announced the new policy and the time the workers put it into effect.

2. The individuals have made a new and satisfactory adjustment with each other. They have helped to satisfy each other's needs. They are, as the social scientist would say, "in equilibrium" with each other. Any attempt to destroy this balance will tend to be resisted even if the attempt represents an elimination of a "bad" or unhealthy set of conditions. People have created a stable pattern of life and they will resist a change in this pattern.

3. The individuals fear pressure will come again in the future. Because of this feeling, they will tend to create unreal conditions or to exaggerate existing conditions so that they can rationalize to themselves that pressure still exists and, therefore, the need for the group also exists.

PRESSURE ON FRONT-LINE SUPERVISORS

But what about the foreman? Strong pressures converge upon him. How does he protect himself from these pressures?

He cannot join a group against management, as his workforce does. For one reason, he probably has at least partially identified himself with management. For another reason, he may be trying to advance in the hierarchy. Naturally, he would not help his chance for advancement if he joined a group against management.

The evidence of the previous chapters seems to indicate that the line supervisor cannot pass all the pressure he receives to his employees. Time and time again the factory supervisors stated that passing the pressure down would only create conflict and trouble which would lead to a decrease in production.

The question arises, where does the pressure go? How do the supervisors relieve themselves of at least some of the pressure? There is evidence to suggest at least three ways in which pressure is handled by the supervisors:

1. Interdepartmental strife. The foremen release some of the pressure by continuously trying to blame fellow foremen for the troubles that exist. "They are," as one foreman expressed it, "trying to throw the dead cat in each other's backyard."

    In three plants observed, much time was spent by certain factory supervisors in trying to lay the blame for errors and problems on some other department.

2. Staff versus factory strife. The foremen released much of the pressure by blaming the budget people, production control people and salesmen for their problems. The data already presented concerning factory supervisors' attitudes towards budget people substantiate this point.

3. "Internalizing" pressure. Many supervisors who do not express their feelings about the pressure have in reality "internalized" it and, in a sense, made it a part of

themselves. Such damming up of pressure seemed to be expressed in the following ways:

(a) Supervisor A is quiet, relatively nonemotional, seldom expresses his negative feelings to anyone, but at the same time he works excessively. Supervisor A can be found working at his desk long after the others have gone home. As one supervisor expressed it, "That guy works himself to death."

(b) Supervisor B is nervous, always running around "checking up" on all his employees. He usually talks fast, gives one the impression that he is "selling" himself and his job when interviewed. He is forever picking up the phone, barking commands and requesting prompt action.

Both of these types (or a combination of these types) are expressions of much tension and pent up emotions that have been internalized. People working under such conditions finally are forced to "take it easy," or they find themselves with ulcers or a nervous breakdown.

But that is not the end of the problem. Constant tension leads to frustration. A frustrated person no longer operates as effectively as he was accustomed. He finds that he tends to forget things he used to remember. Work that he used to do with pleasure, he now delegates to someone else. He is no longer able to make decisions as fast as he did months ago. Now he finds he has to take a walk or get a cup of coffee—anything to get "away from it all."

SUCCESS FOR BUDGET SUPERVISORS MEANS FAILURE FOR FACTORY SUPERVISORS

Students of human relations agree that most people want to feel successful. We observe people constantly defining social and psychosocial goals, struggling to meet them, and as they are met, feeling successful.

Finance and factory supervisors are no exception. The typical finance supervisor does his work as best he can. He hopes and expects just praise of this work from his supervisor. Most of his success comes, therefore, from his superior's evaluation. It is the "boss" who will eventually say "well done," or recommend a promotion. In other words, a finance supervisor measures his success on his job, to a substantial degree, by the reactions of his superior.

The situation is the same for the factory supervisor. He also desires success. Like the finance supervisor, much of his success also derives from the comments and behavior the "boss" exhibits. In short, the factory supervisor is also oriented toward the top for an evaluation of how well he is doing his job.

What is the task of a good and successful finance supervisor? The reader will recall that the finance people perceive their task as being the watchdog of the company. They are always trying to improve the situation in the plant. As one finance supervisor said, "Always, there is room to make it better." And finally, the reader will recall the statement that, "The budget man has made an excellent contribution to this plant. He's found a lot of things that were sour. You might say a good budget man . . . lets top management know if anything is wrong."

In other words, their success derives from finding errors, weaknesses, and faults that exist in the plant. But, when they discover these errors, weaknesses, and faults, they also single out a "guilty party" and implicitly, at least, accuse him of failure. This is true because in finding weaknesses, errors or faults in a certain department, one is at the same time telling the factory supervisors that "things aren't going along as well as they could be." This, naturally, gives many factory supervisors a feeling of failure.

To be sure, such an occurrence will not make every supervisor feel he has failed. Some supervisors do not worry much about their job. Therefore, we find that the supervisor who really feels the failure is the one who is highly interested in doing a good job.

REPORTING SHORTCOMINGS OF THE FOREMAN

The way in which these shortcomings are reported is also important:

Assume that finance man A discovers an error in foreman B's department. How is this error reported? Does the finance man go directly to the factory foreman? In the plants studied the answer, usually, is "no."

The finance man cannot take the "shortest" route between the foreman and himself. For one reason, it may be a violation of policy for a staff man to go directly to a line man. But, more important (from a human point of view), the staff man derives his success when his boss knows he is finding errors. Therefore, his boss would never know how good a job finance man A is doing unless it came to this attention. In short, perhaps because of organizational regulations but basically because much success in industry is derived from above, the finance person usually takes his findings to this own boss, who in turn gives it to his, and so on up the line and across and down into the factory line structure.

Taking the long way around has at least one more positive value for finance people. The middle and top management finance people also derive some success in being able to go to the plant manager and point to some newly discovered weaknesses in the factory. Therefore, not only one man obtains feelings of success, but all interested people up the entire finance structure obtain some feeling of satisfaction.

But, how about the factory people? The answer seems evident. They experience a certain sense of "being caught with their pants down."

Finally, to add insult to injury, the entire incident is made permanent and exhibited to the plant officials by being placed in some budget report which is to be, or has been, circulated through many top channels.

EFFECTS OF FAILURE ON PEOPLE

One might ask: What effects does this kind of failure have upon an individual? If they were insignificant, obviously we would not be concerned. Such is not the case. Feelings of failure can have devastating effects upon an individual, his work and his relationships with others.

Lippitt and Bradford, reporting on some ingenious scientific experiments conducted on the subject of success and failure, state that people who fail tend to:

Lose interest in their work.

Lower their standards of achievement.

Lose confidence in themselves.

Give up quickly.

Fear any new task and refuse to try new methods or accept new jobs.

Expect failure.

Escape from failure by daydreaming.

Increase their difficulty in working with others.

Develop a tendency to blame others, to be overcritical of others' work and to develop troubles with other employees.

On the other hand, people who succeed tend to:

Raise their goals.

Gain greater interest in the activity in which they are engaged.

Gain greater confidence in their ability in the activity.

Increase their persistence to future goals.

Increase their ability to cooperate and work.

Increase their ability to adapt readily to new situations.

Increase their emotional control.

In summary, we should point out that finance people aren't inherently "out to get them" as factory people in the plants described them. Rather, they are placed in a social organization where the only way in which they can receive success is to place someone else in failure.

36
Work Motivation

Hal G. Rainey

Motivation is one of the central topics in the social sciences, and work motivation plays a similarly central role in organizational behavior (OB). Work motivation has received as much intensive theoretical development as any topic in OB. As with other major concepts, such as power, leadership, and attitude, scholars have exhaustively debated the proper definition of motivation, and have reported thousands of studies bearing on the topic.

Also as with other major concepts, reviewers of all this work often express disappointment over the weak validation of most of the theories and wonder whether or not we have really learned much [1]. Yet the disappointments are in relation to very high standards that implicitly call for a comprehensive, well-validated theory of motivation. While the research has not yet produced one, each of the well-known theories reviewed here adds valuable insights to our understanding of motivation.

In addition, the dilemmas that scholars face translate into challenges for practitioners in organizations. The problems we have in both precisely defining motivation, and clearly encompassing it in a theory, are reflected in the challenges in measuring and assessing motivation in organizations and in establishing effective incentive systems [2,3]. As illustrated in examples in the sections that follow, the theories of motivation can aid in the analysis of motivational issues in organizations; therefore scholars and well-informed practitioners need to be aware of the conceptual and theoretical backgrounds that the theory and research on motivation provide.

This chapter summarizes that conceptual and theoretical background, as well as some of the practical implications of the theoretical contributions, and some of the motivational techniques used in organizations. The chapter first reviews efforts to define and measure motivation, pointing out that challenges and controversies have caused motivation to become more of an umbrella concept referring to a set of concepts and issues than a single variable with a precise operational definition. Then the chapter describes the most prominent theories of motivation and the research and debates about their validation and conception.

Source: Robert T. Golembiewski, ed., *Handbook of Organizational Behavior*, Marcel Dekker, New York, pp. 19–39 (1993).

The chapter then summarizes some of the more recent statements about directions for motivation theory. Regardless of whether or not researchers produce well-validated theories, managers and professionals have to try to motivate people in organizations, so the chapter ends with a description of some of the procedures that organizations use to enhance motivation.

THE MEANING AND MEASUREMENT OF MOTIVATION

Everyone feels familiar with the concept of motivation, yet scholars struggle with its definition. Reviews have unearthed some 140 distinct definitions [4,5]. The term derives from the Latin word *motus*, a form of the verb *movere*, to move, from which also derive such words as motor and motif [6]. By motivation, we mean the degree to which a person is moved or aroused to expend effort to achieve some purpose. Work motivation refers to how much a person tries to work hard and well—to the arousal, direction, and persistence of effort in work settings.

Motivation theorists have also sought to clarify distinctions between motivation and other major concepts. For example, they distinguish general work motivation from affective and attitudinal states such as work satisfaction [7]. They usually define job satisfaction as a matter of affect and attitude, of how one feels about the job and various facets of it, sometimes including behavioral components such as whether or not one intends to quit. Some people express satisfaction, without displaying motivation to perform well. Highly motivated people may express dissatisfaction in certain ways because of their high standards or because they believe they deserve better rewards than they get.

Motivation researchers have also struggled with different ways of measuring motivation, none of which provides an adequately comprehensive measurement. For example, the typical definition of motivation already noted—the willingness and tendency to exert effort toward successful work performance—raises complications about what we actually mean by motivation. Is it an attitude or a behavior, or both? Must we observe a person exerting effort? Does it suffice to have the person tell us that she or he is working hard or trying as hard as possible?

As Table 1 shows, researchers have tried to measure motivation in different ways, which imply different answers to these questions. Some researchers have taken the course of asking people about their behavior and attitudes (entries 1 through 4 in Table 1), while at least one study (entry 5; ref. 8) has tried to develop measures based on observations by a person's co-workers. Interestingly, the literature on organizational behavior and psychology provides very few measures of general work motivation. One of the few available general measures, Patchen's (ref. 9; entry 1 in Table 1), relies on questions about how hard one works and how often one does some extra work. Although researchers have reported successful use of this scale [10], one study using this measure found that managers responding to the questions tend to give very high ratings of their own work efforts. The vast majority reported that they work harder than others in their organization. They gave such high self-ratings that there was little difference among them, and so it was difficult to test for the determinants of those differences [11].

These results underscore the problems of asking people about their motivation, and often reflect the cultural emphasis on hard work and effort that leads some people to report that they work hard whether or not they do. More likely, many people also want to think that they work hard, and feel that they do. Yet what does it mean to work hard and exert effort? By what standard? Compared to what? One of the Patchen items refers to working harder than others in the organization. In the study mentioned earlier [11], in reporting very

Table 1 Questionnaire Items Used to Measure Work Motivation

1. Job motivation [9]

On most days on your job, how often does time seem to drag for you?

Some people are completely involved in their job; they are absorbed in it night and day. For other people their job is simply one of several interests. How involved do you feel in your job?

How often do you do some extra work for your job that isn't really required of you?

Would you say that you work harder, less hard, or about the same as other people doing your type of work at (name of organization)?

2. Job involvement (*short form*; [65])

The major satisfaction in my life comes from my job.

I'm really a perfectionist about my work.

I live, eat, and breathe my job.

I am very much involved personally in my work.

Most things in life are more important than work.

3. Intrinsic motivation [66]

When I do my work well, it gives me a feeling of accomplishment.

When I perform my job well, it contributes to my personal growth and development.

I feel a great sense of personal satisfaction when I do my job well.

Doing my job well increases my feeling of self-esteem.

4. Reward expectancies [11]

Producing a high quality of work increases my chances for higher pay.

Producing a high quality of work increases my chances for a promotion.

5. Peer evaluations of a person's work motivation [8,14]

Dimensions for peer ratings of a fellow employee's work motivation

    Team attitude

    Task concentration

    Independene/self-starter

    Organizational identification

    Job curiosity

    Persistence

    Professional identification

high levels of motivation in this sense, most of the managers in the study were reporting that they worked harder than the others. Consider an organization in which everyone works harder than everyone else. The thought is humorous because it calls to mind Garrison Keillor's fictional town of Lake Wobegone, where all the children are above average.

Researchers also employ scales of job involvement, and intrinsic or internal work motivation, such as the examples in Table 1 (entries 2 and 3; see also ref. 10). Researchers in organizational behavior define intrinsic work motives or rewards as those that are mediated within the worker, such as psychic rewards deriving directly from the work itself. Extrinsic rewards are externally mediated, and exemplified by salary, promotion, and other rewards that come from the organization or work group. As the examples indicate, the questions on intrinsic motivation ask about an increase in feelings of accomplishment, growth, and self-esteem through work well done. Measures such as these assess important work-related attitudes, but they do not ask directly about work effort or direction; rather, they infer that if one feels this way when doing good work, one must be motivated to exert effort.

Similarly, researchers and consultants sometimes use items derived from expectancy theories of work motivation, described in a later section, as proxy measures for motivation.

As shown in Table 1, these questions resemble those for intrinsic motivation described above, but often refer to extrinsic rewards such as pay and promotion. Again, these questions do not ask people directly about the level and directions of their work effort, and infer that perceiving such connections between work performance and rewards enhances motivation. Such items have been widely used by consultants in their assessments of organizations, and in huge surveys of federal employees for assessments of the civil service system and its reform [12,13]. In this sense, both these procedures and the intrinsic motivation scales also implicitly acknowledge the limitations of asking people to report their levels of motivation and effort.

If one cannot very well ask the people themselves, one can ask others around that person for their observations about that person's motivation, as did Landy and Guion (ref. 14; entry 5 in Table 1). They had peers rate individual managers on the dimensions listed in Table 1. Significantly, their research indicated that peer observers disagree a lot on the same focal case. This method obviously requires considerable time, resources, and organizational access to administer, which probably explains why other researchers have not used this very interesting approach. As indicated earlier, most definitions of motivation mention that it involves direction as well as amplitude of effort. As the Landy and Guion conception shows, however, the issue of direction becomes quite complex, and one can demonstrate motivation along many directions.

As an additional example of the different outcomes or directions on which motivation can concentrate, one of the classic distinctions in the theory of management and organizations concerns the difference between the motivation to join an organization and stay in it on the one hand, and the motivation to work hard and well within it on the other. These two motivations have related, but fairly distinct, determinants. Chester Barnard, and later James March and Herbert Simon, in books widely acknowledged as the most prominent contributions to the field, analyzed this distinction. You might get people to shuffle into work every day, rather than quit, but they can display keen ingenuity at avoiding doing what you ask them to do if they do not want to do it. Currently, management experts widely acknowledge Barnard's prescience in seeking to analyze the ways in which organizational leaders must employ a variety of incentives, including the guiding values of the organization, to induce cooperation and effort [15,16].

Rival Influences on Performance

Writers on work motivation also point out that motivation alone does not determine performance. Ability figures importantly in performance, obviously, such that a person may display high motivation but insufficient ability, or have such immense ability that the person performs well with little effort or apparent motivation. The person's understanding of the task influences performance, as do the behaviors of leaders or co-workers that can confuse or clarify, guide or misdirect. These and other factors can also interact with motivation in determining performance, and in intricate ways. A person may gain motivation by feeling greater ability to perform, or lose motivation through the frustrations of lacking the ability to perform well. Alternatively, one may lose motivation for a task that one has mastered completely and that then fails to provide a challenge or sense of growth. As we will see, the major theories try in various ways to capture some of these intricacies.

Motivation as an Umbrella Concept

All these complexities have moved the concept of motivation into the status of an umbrella concept that refers to a general topic rather than a precisely defined and measured research variable [7]. Considerable research and theorizing about motivation continue, but usually employing the term as referring to a general concept incorporating many variables and issues [e.g., 17–19]. Locke and Latham [20], for example, present a model of work motivation that does not include within it a concept or variable labeled motivation. Motivation currently appears to serve as an implicit theme overarching research on a variety of related topics. These include organization identification and commitment, leadership practices, job involvement and intrinsic work motivation, organizational climate and culture, and characteristics of work goals.

THEORIES OF MOTIVATION

No theory explains motivation comprehensively, then, but each contributes an important component of a well-developed conception of motivation and its determinants and outcomes. The theories are diverse, and not easily classified, but one conventional classification distinguishes between content theories and process theories. Content theories are concerned with analyzing the particular needs, motives, or rewards that motivation theories should contain. Process theories concentrate more on the psychological or behavioral processes in motivation, often with no designation of the important rewards and motives. The distinction does not classify perfectly, since most of the theories include some attention to both process and content. Consult more elaborate typologies of motivation theories [3] for more careful distinctions, but this dichotomy serves well enough for introducing the major theories.

Content Theories

Maslow's Need Hierarchy
Abraham Maslow [21] proposed a theory of human needs or motives that receives attention in every review of work motivation literature. Interestingly, while researchers on work motivation have shown diminished acceptance of Maslow's approach as an adequate theory of motivation, it continues to influence important intellectual developments [e.g., 22].

Maslow argued that human motives or needs follow a hierarchy of prepotency, as he put it, involving the levels listed in Table 2. The lower order needs, beginning with physiological needs, dominate human motivation and behavior until they are satisfied. Then needs at the next higher level dominate, and so on up the hierarchy. Once one has satisfied hunger and the need for sleep, one becomes more concerned with safety and security. Next, needs for social and love relationships dominate. With those needs reasonably satisfied, needs for esteem dominate. The highest order need, for self-actualization (see Table 2), appeals widely to people searching for a way to express this ultimate human motive for fulfilling one's potential.

In later writings Maslow [23] further developed his ideas about self-actualization, and its association with work, duty, and group or communal benefits. He sharply rejected conceptions of self-actualization as self-absorbed concern with one's personal emotional salvation or satisfaction, especially through merely shedding inhibitions or social controls. In contrast to some gurus of encounter techniques, Maslow insisted that genuinely self-actualized persons achieve this ultimate mode of satisfaction through hard-working dedication to a duty, form of work, or mission, which serves higher values than one's simple self-satisfaction, and which benefits others or society. Genuine personal contentment and emotional salvation, he argued, come as by-products of such dedication. In this later discussion, Maslow [23] depicts the levels of need not as separate steps or phases from which one successively departs. Rather, he treats them as cumulative phases of a growth toward

Table 2 Categories of Needs and Values Employed in Selected Content Theories

Maslow's Need Hierarchy

Physiological needs. Needs for relief from hunger, thirst, and sleepiness, and for defense from the elements.

Safety needs. Needs to be free of the threat of bodily harm.

Social needs. Needs for love, affection, and belonging to social units and groups.

Esteem needs. Needs for sense of achievement, confidence, recognition, and prestige.

Self-actualization needs. The need to become everything one is capable of becoming, to achieve self-fulfillment, especially in some area of endeavor or purpose (such as motherhood, artistic creativity, or a profession).

Herzberg's Two-Factor Theory

Hygiene factors	*Motivators*
Company policy and administration	Achievement
Supervision	Recognition
Relations with supervisor	The work itself
Working conditions	Responsibility
Salary	Growth
Relations with peers	Advancement
Personal life	
Relations with subordinates	
Status	
Security	

McClelland: Need for Achievement, Power, and Affiliation[a]

Need for achievement: The need for a sense of mastery over one's environment and successful accomplishment through one's own abilities and efforts, a preference for challenges involving moderate risk, clear feedback about success, and ability to sense personal responsibility for success. Purportedly stimulates and facilitates entrepreneurial behavior.

Need for power: A general need for autonomy and control over oneself and others, which can manifest itself in different ways. When blended with degrees of altruism and inhibition, and low need for affiliation, can facilitate effectiveness at management.

Need for affiliation: The need to establish and maintain positive affective relations or "friendship" with others [38, p. 160].

Adams: The Need for Equity

The need to maintain a balance between one's contributions to an organization and one's returns and compensations from it, which is equitable or fair, as compared to the balance maintained by others in the organization to whom one compares oneself. The need to feel that one is not overcompensated or undercompensated for one's contributions to the organization.

[a]McClelland and other researchers of these concepts do not provide concise or specific definitions of the need concepts. These definitions summarize the apparent meaning of the concepts.

self-actualization, a motive that grows out of satisfaction of social and esteem needs and also builds on them.

As described later, Maslow's ideas have had a significant impact on many social scientists, but his model has received little reverence from empirical researchers attempting to validate it. Researchers attempting to devise measures of the needs and to test the theory have not confirmed the existence of a five-step hierarchy. Studies have tended to find a two-step hierarchy, in which lower level employees show more concern with material and security rewards. Higher level employees place more emphasis on achievement and challenge [1]. Of course these studies may fail to support the theory simply because of limitations of our ability to operationalize and test the concepts and dynamics of the theory. For example, as implied by the findings mentioned, the tests often compare lower level to higher level employees, and this provides only a static assessment of a process that the theory treats as dynamic. In addition, since the concept of self-actualization is quite complex, questionnaire items in the studies may be too limited or simplified to capture this complexity.

More important, scholars point to theoretical problems with Maslow's model, as did Maslow himself. He said that more than one need may determine behavior, that some needs may disappear, and even that some behavior is not determined by needs. Others offer their generous assistance in pointing out such limitations. Locke and Henne [24] emphasize ambiguities in the behavioral implications of need deprivation. Need deprivation may induce discomfort, but it does not tell the person what to do about it, and therefore the behavioral implications of the theory remain amorphous. Locke and Henne also criticize the hazy concept of self-actualization as an impediment to developing and testing the theory.

Still, for those less concerned with empirical verification than with face validity, Maslow's theory retains a strong plausibility and attractiveness. Maslow contributed to a growing recognition of the importance of motives for growth, development, and actualization among members of organizations [25, pp. 193–197]. The current influence of his ideas have followed some interesting paths. For example, in his analysis of leadership, James MacGregor Burns [22] drew on Maslow's concepts of a hierarchy of both needs and higher order needs such as self-actualization. Burns observed that *transformational* leaders—that is, leaders who bring about major transformations in society—do not engage in simple exchanges of benefits with their followers. Rather, they elicit higher order motives in the population, including forms of self-actualization motives tied to societal ends, with visions of a society transformed in ways that fulfill such motives. As a political scientist, Burns concentrated on political and societal leaders, but writers on organizational leadership have acknowledged his influence in recent writings about transformational leadership in organizations [26,27]. In addition, Maslow's [23] later writings on self-actualization in work settings foreshadow many aspects of the discussion of the management of organizational mission and culture, empowerment of workers, and highly participative forms of management [16,25,28,29].

McGregor: Theory X and Theory Y

Douglas McGregor's [30] arguments about theories X and Y also reflect the influence of Maslow's views and highlight the general penetration into management thought of an emphasis on higher-order needs. McGregor argued that industrial management in the United States reflected the dominance of a theory of human behavior, theory X, which assumed that workers had fundamental needs for direction and control. Since workers lack the capacity for self-motivation and self-direction, managers must structure organizations and incentive systems to closely control, reward, and punish workers. McGregor called for wider acceptance of theory Y, the theory that workers have strivings akin to those Maslow described as higher order needs—for growth, development, interesting work, and self-actualization. Theory Y should guide practice, McGregor argued. Managers and organizations must take steps to employ participative management styles, decentralized decision-making, revised performance evaluation procedures that emphasize self-evaluation and objectives set by the employee, and job enlargement to make jobs more interesting and responsible. McGregor's ideas offered only the rudiments of a theory, and researchers do not currently pursue it or treat it as such. Nonetheless his ideas have influenced the thinking of managers seeking change and reform in many organizations [e.g., 31]. His general theme served as one of the important influences on admonitions about empowering middle managers and employees, as well as on related directions in organization and management thought.

Herzberg: Two-Factor Theory

Frederick Herzberg [32] proposed one of the best-known analyses of motivational issues in his two-factor theory, which also emphasized the importance of higher order needs in motivating individuals in organizations. From multiple studies involving about 2000 respondents in numerous occupational categories, he and his colleagues concluded that two major factors influence individual motivation in work settings: "motivators" and "hygiene factors." The absence or insufficiency of hygiene factors can contribute to dissatisfaction with the job, but the presence of hygiene factors does not stimulate high levels of satisfaction. As suggested by the examples in Table 2, hygiene factors are extrinsic both to the work itself and to the individual, involving organizational, group, or supervisory conditions, or externally mediated rewards such as salary. While hygiene factors can only prevent dissatisfaction, motivators produce a heightened level of satisfaction and increased motivation. As Table 2 indicates, motivators are intrinsic to the job and include interest and enjoyment of the work itself, as well as a sense of growth, achievement, and fulfillment of other higher order needs.

Herzberg concluded that motivators provide the real sources of stimulation and motivation for employees. Hygiene factors can only prevent dissatisfaction; they cannot really stimulate and enhance motivation. Therefore managers must avoid negative techniques of controlling and directing employees, and should arrange job settings to provide for the growth, achievement, recognition, and other needs represented in the motivators. Such procedures as human relations training do not usually solve the problem, he warned. It takes careful job enrichment programs that design jobs to make the work itself interesting, and to give the worker the sense of control, achievement, growth, and recognition that produces high levels of motivation.

Herzberg's work sparked controversy among experts and researchers. He and his colleagues developed their evidence by asking people to describe events on their jobs that led to feelings of extreme satisfaction, and events that led to extreme dissatisfaction. Most of the reports of instances of great satisfaction mentioned the intrinsic and growth factors. Herzberg labeled these motivators in part because the respondents often mentioned their connection to better performance. The reports of dissatisfaction tended to concentrate on the hygiene factors.

Researchers using other methods of generating evidence, however, did not isolate the same two types of factors [1]. Critics argued that when asked to describe an event that made them feel highly motivated, people might hesitate to report great satisfaction over pay or some improvement in physical working conditions. Instead, in what social scientists call a social desirability effect, they might attempt to provide more high-minded answers. On the other hand, when describing an instance leading to dissatisfaction, they might try to attribute bad outcomes to external conditions such as company policies or supervisory behaviors, thereby defending themselves and their self-esteem.

In addition, some researchers raised questions about the conceptual clarity of the two factors and the questions that Herzberg used to assess them. Critics also questioned Herzberg's conclusions about the effects of the two factors on individual behavior. Lawler [33], for example, cited Herzberg as one of a number of researchers who understated the importance of pay in organizations. Lawler found that numerous surveys highlighted the importance of various rewards. Survey respondents tended to rank pay fairly high—about third overall. Lawler pointed out that pay can serve as an indicator of achievement, recognition, and increased responsibility, and therefore can overlap with intrinsic rewards.

Herzberg and his colleagues responded that many of the attempts to test their theory did not provide accurate and fair tests. Nevertheless, the critiques of the theory, and the inability to reproduce the two factors with alternative methods, appear to be responsible for a decline in interest in the theory. Locke and Henne [24], for example, find no recent attempts to test the theory, and conclude that theorists no longer take it seriously. Whether or not the particular elements of this theory have been rejected, the idea of restructuring work to make it interesting, and to provide satisfaction of motives for growth and fulfillment, continues to receive serious attention among many practicing managers and organizational researchers.

McClelland: Needs for Achievement, Power, and Affiliation

David McClelland's theory about motivations for achievement, power, and affiliation (the desire for friendly relations with others) has elicited thousands of studies [e.g., 24,34,35]. The need for achievement (hereafter, n Ach), the central concept in his theory, refers to a motivation—a "dynamic restlessness" [34, p. 301]—to achieve a sense of mastery over one's environment, through success at achieving goals and outcomes through one's own cunning, abilities, and efforts. He originally argued that motivation for achievement in this pattern was characteristic of persons attracted to managerial and entrepreneurial roles, although he later narrowed its application to predicting success in entrepreneurial roles [1].

McClelland measured n Ach through a variety of procedures, including the thematic apperception test (TAT). The TAT involves showing a standard set of pictures to individuals who then write brief stories about what is happening in each picture. One typical picture shows a boy sitting at a desk in a classroom reading a book. A respondent identified as low in n Ach might write a story depicting the boy as daydreaming, while someone high in n Ach might write a story about how hard the boy was studying to do well on a test, and how anxiously the boy wanted to do well. Similarly, McClelland drew on analyses of the achievement-oriented content of fantasies that people reported, and the stories that people tell to children in different societies. Researchers also measured n Ach through questionnaires asking about such matters as occupational and work role preferences, about the role of luck in outcomes, and about preferences for activities such as stamp collecting or racing another person.

McClelland's [34] conception of n Ach involved the motivation to achieve in a particular pattern. Persons high in this need, he said, tend to choose reasonably challenging goals and moderate risks in which outcomes are fairly clear and accomplishment reflects success through one's own abilities. Persons successful in certain roles, such as research scientists who have to wait for a long time for success and recognition, would have a motivation to achieve, but not in this particular pattern on which McClelland focused. As one example of the nature of this motive, McClelland [34] cited the performance of children and students in experiments in which they chose how to behave in games of skill. In a series of experiments, researchers had children and students participate in a ringtoss game. The participants chose how far from the target peg they would stand in trying to throw the ring onto it. The high n Ach participants tended to stand at intermediate distances from the peg, not too close but not too far away. McClelland interpreted this as a reflection of their desire to achieve on the basis of their own skills. Standing too close made success too easy, and did not satisfy the desire to have a sense of accomplishment and mastery. Standing too far away, however, made success a gamble, a matter of a lucky throw. The high n Ach participants chose a distance that would reflect success through their own skills. McClelland [34] also offered evidence of other characteristics of persons with high n Ach, such as physical restlessness and particular concern over the rapid passage of time and aversion to wasting time.

Some of McClelland's more ambitious ideas related n Ach to success in business activities and the success of nations in economic development [34,36]. He analyzed the achievement orientation in folk tales and children's stories in various nations, and produced some evidence that cultures high in n Ach themes in such stories also showed higher rates of economic development. He has also claimed successes in training managers in business firms in less-developed countries to increase their n Ach and thereby to enhance the performance of their firm [36]. He suggested more achievement-oriented fantasizing and thinking as a means of improving the economic performance of nations. Others have also used achievement motivation training with apparent success in enhancing the motive and increasing entrepreneurial behaviors [37, p. 67].

As noted already, McClelland [38] later concluded that n Ach induced entrepreneurial behaviors, rather than directing a person toward success in managerial roles. He argued, however, that his conceptions of power motivation and need for affiliation did indeed apply to successful management (although there is much less empirical research about these needs to support or refute his claims). McClelland concluded that the most effective managers develop through a set of stages into a stage in which they have high power motivation, but with an altruistic orientation and a concern for group goals. This stage also involves a low need for affiliation, however, since too strong a need for friendship with others can hinder a manager.

Reviewers vary in their assessments of the state of this theory. Some rather positive assessments [37] contrast with others who focus only brief attention on it [1], or who criticize it harshly [24]. Locke and Henne characterize the body of research as chaotic. They also complain that the domain of the theory has become confused, since McClelland has narrowed the focus of n Ach to entrepreneurial behaviors even though the overwhelming proportion of the numerous empirical studies have not focused on entrepreneurs. Currently, one finds little very recent research on the theory in major management or organizational journals. Regardless of its current prestige among scholars, however, this theory adds another very plausible element to a well-developed perspective on motivation. Individuals do apparently vary in the general level and pattern of the internal motivation for achievement and excellence they bring to work settings.

Equity Theory

J. Stacy Adams [39,40] developed a theory about a motive for equity in organizations that has received much attention. He drew on a body of research in psychology about the need for cognitive balance and consistency (our need to feel that our various beliefs and attitudes are consistent with each other and not conflicting). He also drew on research about social comparison processes (our tendency to assess ourselves and our status by comparing ourselves to others whom we accept as referents). He theorized that in their work, people want to feel equitably compensated. People have a need for a sense of equity, and are uncomfortable with indications inconsistent with that need—that is, with evidence that they are inequitably compensated. They compare their own exchanges with the organization to the exchanges between the organization and other employees. If a person senses that he or she receives treatment that is inequitable in relation to the others, he or she will be motivated to reduce the inequity. His or her other efforts to maintain or restore a sense of equity will have important influences on subsequent behavior.

Although here classified as a content theory because of its emphasis on the equity motive, the theory contains much detail on the processes involved in perceptions of inequity and their effects on behavior. People assess equity by comparing themselves to one or more other persons in the organization. One assesses the balance between one's own "inputs" (contributions such as effort, experience, and credentials; longevity; and successful accomplishments) and one's "outcomes" (returns or compensations from the organization and the work, such as pay, benefits, and enjoyment). One compares this balance to that of the other person, the referent. One experiences inequity if the other person's balance is more favorable or unfavorable. If the other person gets more good outcomes for the same level of inputs, one feels inequity in the sense of undercompensation; the other person is getting more rewards for the same contributions. If the other person gets the same or lower levels of good outcomes, but makes more and better contributions, one feels inequity in the sense of overcompensation; the other person does better but gets less for it.

Adams argued that individuals will be motivated to reduce or avoid inequity in either the form of over- or undercompensation. The person may respond to inequity in various ways: by altering inputs or outcomes, mentally distorting one's inputs and outcomes, acting on the referent person (such as pressuring the person to produce more or less), or leaving through transferring or quitting. Adams's discussions of the theory offer some propositions about choices among these responses; for example, some inputs are costly and require effort, so individuals will be slow to respond by increasing them. Individuals will be less likely to change or distort inputs and outcomes that are very important to their self-esteem. People will quit only at high levels of inequity, and at lower levels of inequity will tend toward more limited responses such as absenteeism.

Adams also proposed and tested some relatively precise hypotheses about responses to inequity under well-specified circumstances, such as piece rate versus hourly rate pay systems. He predicted that a person overcompensated (compared to a referent other) in a piece rate system will try to produce fewer pieces, but of higher quality. A person overcompensated at an hourly rate, however, will strive to produce more outputs. A person undercompensated in a piece rate system will strive to produce more outputs, to bring his or her total compensation up to that of the referent person. A person undercompensated on an hourly basis will slow down and reduce production.

Adams and others have tested hypotheses such as these, but reviews of this research agree that the empirical studies have produced a mixture of supporting and disconfirming studies [1,37,41]. The hypotheses about overpayment tend to receive support, but not other hypotheses. The research that successfully supports the hypotheses about overpayment has usually taken place in laboratory settings, in experiments with college students working under clearly defined pay systems for clearly defined tasks. Occasional studies outside the laboratory setting have, for example, examined baseball players' performances after pay changes with inconclusive results [24].

Critiques of the theory and research typically point out that most of the research consists of laboratory experiments using pay, thus leaving questions about implications for non-laboratory settings and rewards other than pay. This also reflects the problem that formulations and tests of the theory have not taken into account many factors, such as individual differences and how individuals choose referents. As a result, some of the most recent efforts to extend the theory point out that individuals may vary in sensitivity to inequity and preferences concerning its levels [42]. More important, equity theory has trouble overcoming problems cited in a critique by Weick [43] years ago, which pointed out that the theory leaves a lot of ambiguities in its concepts and predictions. Important issues such as which of the various inputs and outcomes a person will focus on, how a person will respond to inequity, and how a person chooses and maintains referents, have never been well clarified through hypotheses and tests. This explains why Miner [37] observed that although personnel managers and others have been concerned with equity issues for a long time, Adams's equity theory has apparently led to no applications in industry.

As with previous theories, however, even pending the success of this specific formulation, equity researchers deal with a crucial issue in organizations. Equitable treatment obviously figures significantly in organizations as an influence on many members. As racial and ethnic diversity have become more important issues in organization and management, the issue looms even larger.

Process Theories

Another group of theories concentrates more on the psychological and behavioral processes in motivation than on attempting to specify the major needs and values that influence motivation. This dichotomy is somewhat procrustean, in that all the theories to some extent deal with both content and process. What we here call process theories place relative emphasis on how various goals, values, needs, or rewards—often not specified in the theory itself—operate with other factors to determine motivation.

Expectancy Theory

For some years the expectancy theory of work motivation in various formulations elicited about as much optimism as any of the theories. Researchers appeared to hope that this departure would provide a fairly well-elaborated theory with predictive capacity. Although such matters are difficult to assess, the theory may well continue to be the most prominent and well-regarded among motivation researchers. Even so, it has taken its full share of criticism. Expectancy theory draws on the classic observation, attributable to various psychologists and philosophers in the past, that humans seek to do what they think is most likely to maximize desirable results and to minimize bad results. Yet those developing the theory sought to refine this point in ways that would aid clarification and analysis of work motivation. Table 3 illustrates an early formulation of this theory in the literature of organizational psychology by Vroom [44], as well as a more recent version of the theory reflecting revisions caused by criticisms of Vroom's use of mathematical assumptions and symbols.

The mathematical formula provides a shorthand or symbolic expression of some of the intricacies that elaborate the classic observation mentioned above. It posits that an individual will be more strongly motivated to engage in a behavior as he or she perceives stronger probabilities ("expectancies") that the behavior will lead to valued outcomes and avoid bad ones. Vroom used the term *valence* to refer to the values of outcomes. Valences can be positive or negative, as in the case of positively and negatively valent atomic particles. Valence connotes both attraction (when positive) and repulsion (when negative); thus, the outcomes of the behavior are conceived as having positive or negative scores or assessments in the perception of the individual.

In effect, the formula posits that an individual will consider the outcomes that will result from the behavior and assign a probability to each outcome—the expectancy that it will result from the behavior. Then the individual will multiply, or weight, each of these probabilities by its positive or negative valence, and sum up the products of all these multiplications (i.e., the algebraic sum). So, if the person feels that the behavior has a high

Table 3   Formulations of Expectancy Theory

A Formulation Similar to Vroom's Early Version:

$$F_i = \Sigma\ (E_{ij} \times V_j)$$

where
  F = the force acting on an individual to perform act i
  E = the expectancy, or perceived probability, that act i will lead to outcome j
  V = the valence of outcome j

and

$$V_j = \Sigma\ (V_k \times I_{jk})$$

where
  V = the valence of outcome
  I = the instrumentality of outcome j for the attainment of outcome k

A Formulation Similar to Various Revised Formulations:

$$\text{Motivation} = f[E\ I \times E\ II(V)] = f[(E \rightarrow P) \times [(P \rightarrow O)(V)]]$$

where
  E I = (E → P) = expectancy I, the perceived probability that a given level of work effort will
        result in a given level of performance
  E II = (P → O) = expectancy II, the perceived probability that the level of performance will lead
        to attainment of outcome j
  V = the valence of outcome j

probability of leading to a very good outcome, this will mean the multiplication of a high expectancy times a high positive valence; the product will be a high positive addition to the sum of all the expectancy-times-valence products. If the person also senses a high probability of another outcome, but a very negatively valent one, this will lead to a very negative product when the two are multiplied. This negative product is then subtracted from the high positive product for the outcome just described (i.e., the algebraic sum of the products is taken).

In other words, if a behavior is very likely to lead to some very desirable results (more pay, more interesting work), but also very likely to lead to some undesirable results (more overtime work, more stress), one's motivation to engage in the behavior will depend on just how desirable or undesirable one considers the results, and one's sense of the likelihood of each result. Following the implications of the formula, if the probabilities of the bad outcomes are low, the negative scores in the summation go down. If the probabilities of the good results go up, the positive scores in the summation go up. The theory, then, conceives of motivation as involving this joint consideration of outcomes, their probabilities, and their positive or negative values.

The theory appeared to offer an advancement in conceiving and analyzing motivation. One could hope to apply it by asking employees to express their perceptions about the probabilities of outcomes from important work behaviors, express their positive or negative valuations of those outcomes, and develop a score for each employee indicating that person's motivation. In addition, influences on that level of motivation could be examined by looking at the expressed probabilities and valences of various outcomes. There rapidly followed a number of studies applying and testing the theories, reporting some early apparent successes and inducing optimism [45].

Also fairly rapidly, however, problems in applying and validating the theory mounted, along with questions and criticisms. Many contributed to this elaborate discussion, and their numerous points do not summarize easily [1,7,37,46,47].

Researchers found the component constructs hard to clearly define and operationalize. One has trouble identifying and expressing all the relevant "outcomes" sought by the different people in an organization, as well as measuring with questionnaires or other means their perceived probabilities and their positive and negative values. A researcher might try to get employees to rate the expectancy of getting each of a standard set of rewards (such as "a pay raise") on a numerical scale, and then rate the valence of that reward on another scale (say, from +5 to −5), and then multiply the ratings together and sum the products. These proved to be rather cumbersome and imprecise ways of measuring the constructs. Often the summated score would not correlate very highly with other measures of motivation, effort, or work satisfaction. Some studies found one of the components, such as expectancies, to be a stronger predictor than the full model [46,47].

Other theorists pointed to dubious postulates of the theory. The theory posits that people perform extensive and complex mathematics in their heads in a highly rational pattern. Critics pointed out that our minds do not work that way, especially in complex situations involving uncertainty and so many criteria that such calculative faculties would be overloaded [46]. Defenders of the theory responded that the theory was simply a model generally approximating the mental processes leading to motivation, and did not require strict application of all mathematical postulates to have value. For example, people may do some rough unconscious calculations of this sort for a small set of salient outcomes [7]. Still, critics effectively attacked the mathematical form of the model, pointing out that multiplying E and V together required the assumption that they were independent quantities. Yet we know that our expectations about obtaining rewards can influence the values we attach to those rewards. Prestige products that seek to gain allure from their high prices illustrate this point. So do "sour grapes" responses in which persons say they do not want something because they cannot have it.

All these problems soon deflated any dramatic hopes for the theory, and theorists set about developing revised versions, such as the one in Table 3. The later versions typically removed mathematical procedures such as multiplying E's and V's [1,7]. They tend to state the theory as a general conceptual framework without clear postulates as to how the component constructs are supposed to be combined. Newer formulations also distinguish between expectancy I (E I), the probability that effort will lead to performance, and expectancy II (E II), the probability that the level of performance will lead to valent outcomes. The more recent versions also add other variables to the framework, such as task clarity and self-esteem, which can influence E I, and organizational evaluation and compensation procedures, which can influence E II.

For all the discussion of their limitations, expectancy theory constructs have served as a foundation for a prominent theory of leadership—the path-goal theory. Many studies have found that versions of expectancy theory predict self-reported effort fairly well, especially when valences and expectancies are also self-reported [18]. Theorists attempting to further develop motivation theories typically employ expectancy theory concepts [17,18,48].

Expectancy models also can be helpful in analyzing motivational issues. For example, in some cases organizations have attempted pay-for-performance schemes for middle managers, only to encounter problems when most of the managers got high evaluations, but there was too little money for raises. Only a very small proportion of the managers got a significant raise (high E I, but low E II). In another case, salesmen complained about an incentive system in a major corporation, because the very high performers got large bonuses, and the vast majority felt that they could never get one (high E II, but low E I). The corporation reformed the system to equalize pay. Analyzing such systems using the more recent versions of expectancy theory, in terms of E I and E II and their determinants, appears to be a useful way to try to foresee such problems [49, p. 137].

In addition, researchers on expectancy theory developed questionnaire items about reward expectancies that are frequently used in research and organizational assessments. For example, they have been included in very large surveys of federal employees [50]. These items ask employees or managers for their level of agreement with statements such as these: I will get a pay raise if I do high-quality work. If I perform well, I will increase my chances for a promotion. (See also the intrinsic motivation items in Table 1.) Regardless of controversies over the adequacy of expectancy theory as a general theory of motivation, many researchers and managers consider such perceptions about reward expectancies very important.

While research on expectancy theory has attenuated, it still receives attention in texts as one of the best versions of a motivation theory [e.g., 1,41]. As noted earlier, recent efforts to advance motivation theory incorporate expectancy theory concepts. The theory clearly covers important dimensions of work motivation.

Operant Conditioning Theory and Behavior Modification

Theorists have also drawn on operant conditioning theory as a basis for analysis of work motivation. Operant theory derives from what psychologists have called the "behaviorist" school in psychology, of which B. F. Skinner served as one of the most prominent members. Behaviorism gained its label because of the emphasis of its proponents on the observation of the overt behaviors of animals and humans, without hypothesizing what goes on inside them. This reflects a classic debate in psychology, in which some of the theorists argued that motivation and learning theories should include hypothetical constructs referring to what goes on within the organism. For example, some of them employed the concept of "incentive" to refer to the internal cognition that corresponds to an external attraction, such as the incentive within a rat to learn to negotiate a maze, in the form of some cognitive vision or depiction of the reward at the end of the maze.

Behaviorists such as Skinner rejected the use of such internal constructs, arguing that one cannot observe them scientifically and that they add only confusing speculation to the analysis of motivation. Skinner argued that one can scientifically analyze only overtly observable behaviors. He and other behaviorists recognized the existence of thought, emotion, and other internal states, but regarded such states as products of the external forces—reinforcements and punishments—that shape behavior. (Actually, behaviorists vary in the degree to which they include references to cognition in their theories. Especially in recent years, psychologists have worked toward a reconciliation of operant behaviorism with cognitive concepts. See Refs. 51, 52.)

Skinner and other researchers developed numerous concepts and observations about how external conditions influence animals in learning and acquiring behaviors. Skinner studied the contingencies of reinforcement, the conditions that cause behaviors to be reinforced. In this terminology, a reinforcement is any condition that increases the probability of occurrence of a behavior. A pigeon pecks a light bulb when it comes on, and we give it a pellet of food, and it shows an increased tendency to peck the light bulb when it comes on. We have reinforced the behavior. The terms and the example are significant. Many of us would use such terms as learning and reward in this instance, but the behaviorists' terminology is cleansed of the cognitive implications of such terms [53, p. 64]. All we can infer is that the behavior increased, not that the pigeon learned something or experienced some inner sense of reward. Also, this example shows that this body of theory developed out of research on laboratory animals, a detail that feeds later criticisms of the approach as manipulative and applicable mainly to simplified situations unlike those common in complex organizations.

The term *operant conditioning* stems from a revision Skinner and others made in older versions of stimulus-response psychology. Skinner [53, p. 65] pointed out that we animals do not develop behaviors simply in response to stimuli. We emit behaviors as well, and our behaviors operate on our environments, generating consequences. We repeat or drop the behaviors depending on the consequences. We acquire behaviors or extinguish them in response to the conditions or contingencies of reinforcement.

Skinner and others carefully studied how contingencies of reinforcement influence acquisition and extinction of behaviors. They pointed out, for example, that one can train a pigeon to turn in a circle when a light comes on, first by reinforcing the behavior of turning slightly when the light comes on. The pigeon will acquire that behavior, and one can then reinforce a larger turn, and so on until the pigeon is turning full circle when the light comes on. This interest in shaping behaviors provided the foundations for later developments in *behavior modification* techniques in therapeutic, educational, and managerial applications.

The operant conditioning theorists developed concepts and principles that influenced later efforts to apply this type of theory in management. They distinguished between types of reinforcement. *Positive reinforcement* applies a stimulus that increases the behavior on which it is made contingent. We receive payment for taking an action, and our tendency to take that action increases. *Negative reinforcement* increases the behavior on which it is made contingent through removal of the stimulus or condition. We find that a bright light in our eyes or a very loud noise is removed when we take an action, so the probability that we will take that action increases when we encounter the stimulus again. Both types of reinforcement increase contingent behaviors. Reinforcing properties of a stimulus can extend or generalize to other stimuli. Primary reinforcers such as food play a role in the development of secondary reinforcers such as pay, which develop their reinforcing properties through association with the primary reinforcers. For example, a very young child shows little more attraction to paper money than to other scraps of paper until its connection to food and other reinforcements is established.

Operant extinction decreases a behavior through removal of a reinforcement that had been contingent on it. We have trained a pigeon to turn in a circle when a light comes on, and we stop feeding it when it does so, and eventually it stops responding to the light. *Punishment* is one means of attempting extinction, and Skinner defined punishment as removal of a positive reinforcer or application of a negative reinforcement [53, p. 185]. Yet this definition does not distinguish between punishment and negative reinforcement, and Skinner found himself having to refer to the "aversive" nature of the stimuli used in punishment (p. 186). Thus, in spite of his rejection of references to internal states in animals and humans, he came close to having made some assumptions about needs and values within the organism.

Operant theorists also distinguish between various patterns of reinforcement. One can apply reinforcements on a fixed or variable schedule, and a ratio or interval schedule [1, p. 193; 41, p. 153; 53]. A *fixed schedule* applies the reinforcement on a regular basis, after a fixed period of time, or a fixed number of repetitions of the behavior. A *variable schedule* varies the time period or number of repetitions. A *ratio schedule* applies reinforcements according to a designated ratio of reinforcements to responses, such as once for every five repetitions. An *interval schedule* applies reinforcement after a designated time interval. The categories can be combined. A fixed-interval schedule reinforces after a fixed period of time—a weekly paycheck. A variable-interval schedule follows a variable period of time—a bonus every so often. A fixed-ratio schedule reinforces a fixed proportion of responses, as in piece-rate pay scales that pay a certain amount for a certain number of units produced. A variable-ratio schedule reinforces after a varying number of responses, as in praise from a supervisor for a particular behavior, which the supervisor gives after varying numbers of repetitions.

In their research, operant conditioning theorists developed principles concerning reinforcement, some of which help clarify a number of motivational issues and have interesting implications. For example, they typically point out that positive reinforcement provides the most efficient means of influencing behavior. They typically take a very negative view of punishment as less efficient and effective in shaping behavior [53, p. 182ff]. They point out that a behavior is acquired most rapidly through a low, fixed-ratio reinforcement schedule—a reinforcement after each occurrence of the behavior, for example, or after every other occurrence. Yet a behavior reinforced with that schedule will extinguish more rapidly once reinforcement terminates.

Intermittent schedules, such as a high-variable interval or variable-ratio schedule (reinforcing after long, varying periods or after many responses on a varying ratio), require more time for acquisition of the behavior, but extinction occurs more slowly when the reinforcements cease. This leads some behavior modification proponents [51,54] to prescribe such managerial techniques as not praising a desired behavior constantly, but on a varying basis after a number of repetitions. They might also prescribe a periodic bonus program to supplement a weekly paycheck, on the argument that the regular check will lose its reinforcing properties over time, while the bonus program will act as a variable-interval reinforcement procedure, thus strengthening the probability of sustained long-term effort. They also have useful suggestions about incremental shaping of behaviors by reinforcing successively larger portions of a desired behavior—as with the circling pigeon described earlier. Operant theorists have described successful correction of various problem behaviors through such procedures as the correction of anorexic behaviors through reinforcement of incremental steps toward eating [55,56].

Organizational Behavior Modification.   These kinds of prescriptions provide examples of those offered by practitioners of organizational behavior modification (hereafter, OB Mod), which applies versions of operant conditioning theory in organizations. Actually, many people have used the term behavior modification in a variety of ways that often range quite afield from behaviorist psychology and operant conditioning theory. Most motivation theorists, however, regard OB Mod as the effort to apply principles from operant conditioning theory in organizations.

Organizational behavior modification often involves approaches such as these: measuring and recording desirable and undesirable behaviors to establish baselines, determining the antecedents and consequences of the behaviors, determining a strategy for using reinforcements and punishments—such as praise and pay increases—to apply to the behaviors, applying them with some of the considerations of scheduling them mentioned, and assessing behavioral change. A number of field studies of such projects have reported successes in improving employee performance, attendance, and safety procedures [1]. A highly successful effort by Emery Air Freight, for example, received much attention [51,57]. That project involved having employees monitor their own performance, setting performance goals, and using feedback and positive reinforcements such as praise and time off.

Yet controversy over explanations of the success of this project reflect more general controversies about OB Mod. Critics have argued that the Emery example, as well as other applications of OB Mod, do not succeed because they apply operant conditioning principles, but because they involve such steps as setting clear performance goals and making rewards contingent upon them [58]. These are valuable steps, but they hardly offer any distinctive or original insights deriving from operant conditioning theory. More generally, while one can point to ways in which operant conditioning theory would lead to different hypotheses and prescriptions from expectancy theory, in practice and research they often lead to very similar hypotheses and procedures. Other criticisms of operant theory and OB Mod focus on the questionable ethics of the emphasis on manipulation and control of people, its apparent applicability mainly to relatively simplified conditions amenable to relatively clear measurement, and even then the practical difficulties of all the measuring and reinforcement scheduling required.

For their part, proponents of OB Mod point to the successful applications, of course. Advocates of operant conditioning theory counterattack on the ethical implications of their approach by arguing that they cut through a lot of obfuscating fluff about values and internal states and move right to the issue of correcting bad behaviors and augmenting good ones. Do you want smokers to be able to stop, anorexics to eat, or workers to follow safety precautions, or do you not? Similarly, OB Mod advocates claim that their approach succeeds in developing a focus on desired behaviors (getting Joe to come to work on time), as opposed to attributions about attitudes ("Joe has a bad attitude"), and an emphasis on strategies for positive reinforcement of the desired behaviors [51].

Social Learning Theory Revisions of OB Mod. Also reflecting the limitations of operant conditioning theory and OB Mod are some recent efforts to revise those theories in light of social learning theory [52]. Social learning theory represents a blending of operant conditioning theory with more recognition of internal cognitive processes. It gives attention to forms of learning and behavioral change that are not tied tightly to some external reinforcement.

For example, individuals obviously learn by modeling their behaviors on those of others and through vicarious experiences. If one sees another person burned by a hot object, one does not need to touch the object to know to avoid it. Humans also engage in anticipation, mental rehearsal and imagery, and self-rewarding behaviors (praising oneself). Applications of such processes to organizational settings have mainly involved the development of frameworks and prescriptions for leadership and self-improvement, with a few studies suggesting that the sorts of techniques already mentioned can improve performance [54,59].

While interesting and apparently useful to developing leadership and motivation in organizations, these extensions are unlikely to satisfy the critics of OB Mod [24]. On balance, operant conditioning theory and OB Mod appear to represent a minority position among work motivation theorists, with most theorists not convinced of their value for theory development, but with a fairly impressive number of reports of successful applications in organizations [1].

Goal-Setting Theory

Edwin Locke and his colleagues have advanced a theory of goal setting that reviewers acknowledge as the most successful work motivation theory in gaining validation through well-designed research [1,37]. Relatively simple, the theory [60; 24, pp. 17–20] holds that difficult specific goals lead to higher task performance than easy and/or vague goals or no goals (e.g., "do your best"). Difficult goals enhance performance by directing attention and action, mobilizing effort, increasing persistence, and by motivating the search for effective performance strategies. Commitment to the goals, and feedback about performance against the goals, are also necessary for higher performance, but do not in themselves stimulate it without difficult specific goals. Research findings also indicate that participation in goal setting does not enhance commitment to the goal, but commitment increases with the expectancy of success in attaining the goal, as well as in the value of the goal. Also, money may lead to the setting of higher goals and higher goal commitment, and individual differences do show strong relations to the effectiveness of goal setting.

Locke and Latham [60] contend that assigning difficult specific goals enhanced performance by way of the goals' influence on an individual's personal goals and his or her self-efficacy. Self-efficacy refers to a person's sense of capability or efficacy in accomplishing outcomes [61]. Assigned goals influence personal goals through a person's acceptance of and commitment to them. They influence self-efficacy by providing a sense of purpose and standards for evaluating performance, and they create opportunities for accomplishing lesser and proximal goals that build a sense of efficacy. Earley and Lituchy [62] report evidence supporting this explanation.

Many studies support the basic tenets of the theory about the enhancement of task performance through difficult specific goals. Locke and Henne [24] argue that occasional disconfirmations are all explainable by reference to artifacts of the research designs or other interpretations. Other reviewers mount few criticisms of the theory. One reason for the success of the theory, however, may be its compactness and relatively narrow focus [1]. The theory and research concentrate on task performance, a very important issue, and offer very useful conclusions about enhancing it. The research tends to concentrate on relatively clear and simple task settings, amenable to the setting of specific goals, yet some of the prominent contributions to organization theory in recent decades, such as contingency theory and garbage can models of decision-making, have concerned those settings in which clear, explicit goals are quite difficult to specify. The implication of these contributions is that in many of the most important settings, such as high-level strategy development teams, clear, specific goals may be impossible or dysfunctional. For example, might a specific, difficult set of goals in a complex task setting drive attention away from important goals not included in the goal set?

Relatedly, important issues surround what might be called *goal validity*. The goals may be specific and difficult, but what if they are not valid indicators of what ought to be accomplished? Some writers on public administration and public policy assert that too often goal clarification in public bureaucracies leads to specification of procedural goals rather than valid impact goals. For example, one might state the goal of having a record of the client intake interview in the file within 1 hour after the interview rather than a goal pertaining to improvement of the client's quality of life. Some of the research on goal setting does focus on relatively complex task settings [60], but further clarification of the domain of applicability of the theory would be very valuable. In the meantime, the value of specific, difficult goals for work tasks seems well established.

Theoretical Forays: Integration and Separation

This issue of domain of applicability, together with the obvious balkanization of motivation theory into the separate theories just reviewed, brings us to the consideration of where motivation theory should go from here. Reviewers tend to agree that motivation theory is in a disorderly state [4], although they disagree in their level of optimism about the amount we have learned about motivation [3; 1, p. 306]. Proposals and initiatives for the further development of motivation theory emphasize either the integration of existing theories, or the separateness of theories while recognizing how each theory is useful, or some degree of both.

Those emphasizing separateness call for the development of middle-range theories to apply to different settings or dependent variables. Pinder [1] argues that the effort to develop and evaluate the existing motivation theories as general, universal theories is fruitless. He proposes the development of a typology of motivational settings (the motivational attributes of a work setting), combined with a typology of motivational types (the motivation-related attributes of individuals in a work group). He suggests development of middle-range theories for application within such setting/type categories. Apparently, he intends that these new theories would draw on existing theories. Somewhat similarly, Landy and Becker [4] reject the quest for universal theory and contend that the existing theories should be treated as middle-range theories, applicable to different combinations from a set of dependent variables (choice, effort, satisfaction, performance, and withdrawal). They also call for some integration of theories that apply to similar sets of these variables.

Others concentrate more on such integration, with varying levels of comprehensiveness. Katzell and Thompson [3] report an effort to develop a framework integrating all the existing theories. Both Klein [17] and Evans [48] propose models of motivation that integrate elements of expectancy and goal-setting theory, with elements of other psychological theories, such as control and attribution theory. Similarly, there has been a good deal of attention to the integration of goal-setting theory and expectancy theory [4,24,60]. Klein [17] proposes a feasibility theory of motivation, which emphasizes the availability of resources for task performance, bringing in need theory and drawing on expectancy theory.

Probably because of the success of goal-setting theory, there appears to be a particularly strong trend toward inclusion and analysis of goal concepts in theories, and to integrate these and other cognitive concepts such as those from the social learning theory approach described earlier [20,60,61,63,64].

These attempts to assess the distinct attributes of motivation theories or to partially integrate different theories provide reasonable prospects for progress in the development of fairly distinct middle-range theories.

MOTIVATION PRACTICE AND TECHNIQUES

As mentioned at the outset, in spite of the travails of the theorists, organization requires motivated members, and one finds in organizations numerous approaches to the problem. In addition to some of the procedures described in earlier sections, Table 4 provides a description of many of the general techniques, several of which have a large literature devoted to them. As with other dimensions of management and organization, real-world practice often reflects theory only loosely, and places highest priority on pragmatism. Far from making theory and expert knowledge irrelevant, however, the practices of organizations often justify the apparently obvious advice of the theorists and experts, since organizations typically have trouble achieving desirable motivational strategies [2]. For example,

Table 4 Methods Commonly Used to Enhance Work Motivation in Organizations

- *Improved performance appraisal systems.* Reforms involving the use of group-based appraisals (ratings for a work group rather than an individual), appraisals by a member's peers, and other approaches mentioned below.

- *Merit pay and pay-for-performance systems.* A wide variety of procedures for linking a person's pay to performance [67].

- *Bonus and award systems.* Offer one-time awards for instances of excellent performance or other achievements.

- *Profit sharing and gain-sharing plans.* Involve sharing profits with members of the organization, usually possible only in business organizations, for obvious reasons. Employee stock ownership plans are roughly similar as a means of rewarding employees when the organization does well.

- *Management by objectives and other performance-targeting procedures.* Organizations of all types have tried MBO programs, which involve evaluating people on the basis of stated work objectives. Superiors work with subordinates on developing objectives for their work, thus enhancing communication. That person's performance appraisal then concentrates on those objectives. This focuses the person's attention on the most important outcomes of work, gives the person more say in what he or she does, and enhances decentralization and autonomy, since agreement on the objectives provides a basis for allowing the person to go ahead and work his or her way, rather than through constant directions by the boss. The most elaborate MBO programs involve mapping broad organizational objectives down through more specific objectives at the different levels of the organization. Organizations also use a wide variety of "performance-targeting" procedures emphasizing productivity or performance targets for groups.

- *Participative management and decision making.* Involve a sustained commitment to engage in more communication and sharing of decisions through teams, committees, task forces, general meetings, open door policies, and one-to-one exchanges.

- *Work enhancement: job redesign, job enlargement, and rotation.* Usage varies, but job redesign usually means changing jobs to enhance control and interest for the people doing the work. Job enlargement, or "horizontal loading," involves giving a person more different tasks and responsibilities at the same skill level. Job restructuring or "vertical loading" involves giving a person more influence over decisions normally made by superiors, such as work scheduling, or more generally to enlarge the employee's sense of responsibility by giving him or her control of a more complete unit of work output (work teams that build an entire car as a team, or case workers who handle all needs of a client). These approaches may involve job sharing and rotation among workers, and various team-based approaches.

- *Quality of work life (QWL) programs and quality circles (QCs).* Organizations of all types have tried QWL programs, which typically involve efforts to enhance the general working environment of an organization through representative committees, surveys and studies, and other procedures improving the work environment. Quality circles, used successfully in Japanese companies, are teams that focus more directly on improving the quality of work processes and products.

- *Organizational development interventions.* Organizational development (OD), employed widely in the public and private sectors, applies behavioral science techniques to improving communication, conflict resolution, and trust.

surveys find that fewer than one-third of employees in organizations feel that their pay is based on performance [3]. For these reasons, just as theorists will go on seeking ways to unravel the complexities of work motivation, members of organizations will go on trying to find ways to enhance it in their work settings.

REFERENCES

1. C. C. Pinder, *Work Motivation*, Scott, Foresman, Glenview, Illinois (1984).
2. S. Kerr, On the folly of rewarding A, while hoping for B, *Classic Readings in Organizational Behavior* (J. S. Ott, ed.), Brooks/Cole, Pacific Grove, California, pp. 114–126 (1989).
3. R. A. Katzell and D. E. Thompson, Work motivation: Theory and practice, *Am. Psychologist*, *45*: 144–153 (1990).
4. F. J. Landy and W. S. Becker, Motivation theory reconsidered, *Research in Organizational Behavioral*, vol. 9 (L. L. Cummings and B. M. Staw, eds.), JAI Press, Greenwich, Connecticut, pp. 1–38 (1987).
5. P. R. Kleinginna and A. M. Kleinginna, A categorized list of motivation definitions with a suggestion for a consensual definition, *Motiv. Emotion*, *5*: 263–292 (1981).
6. R. M. Steers and L. M. Porter, eds., *Motivation and Work Behavior*, McGraw-Hill, New York (1987).
7. J. P. Campbell and R. D. Pritchard, Motivation theory in industrial and organizational psychology, *Handbook of Industrial and Organizational Psychology* (M. D. Dunnette, ed.), Wiley, New York (1983).
8. R. M. Guion and F. J. Landy, The meaning of work and the motivation to work, *Org. Behav. Hum. Perform.*, *7*: 308–339 (1972).
9. M. Patchen, D. Pelz, and C. Allen, *Some Questionnaire Measures of Employee Motivation and Morale*, Institute for Social Research, Ann Arbor, Michigan (1965).
10. J. D. Cook, S. J. Hepworth, T. D. Wall, P. B. Warr, *The Experience of Work*, Academic Press, London (1981).
11. H. G. Rainey, Public agencies and private firms: Incentive structures, goals, and individual roles, *Administration and Society*, *15*: 207–242 (1983).
12. U.S. Office of Personnel Management, *Federal Employee Attitudes, Phase I*, U.S. Office of Personnel Management, Washington D.C. (1979).
13. U.S. Office of Personnel Management, *Federal Employee Attitudes, Phase II*, U.S. Office of Personnel Management, Washington D.C. (1980).
14. F. J. Landy and R. M. Guion, Development of scales for the measurement of work motivation, *Organizational Behavior and Human Performance*, *5*: 93–103 (1970).
15. O. E. Williamson, *Organization Theory: From Chester Barnard to the Present and Beyond*, Oxford University Press, New York (1990).
16. T. J. Peters and R. H. Waterman, *In Search of Excellence*, Harper and Row, New York (1982).
17. H. J. Klein, An integrated control theory model of work motivation, *Acad. Manage. Rev.*, *14*: 150–172 (1989).
18. J. I. Klein, Feasibility theory: A resource-munificence model of work motivation and behavior, *Acad. Manage. Rev.*, *15*: 646–665 (1990).
19. U. Kleinbeck, H. H. Quast, H. Thierry, and H. Hartmut, eds., *Work Motivation*, Lawrence Erlbaum Associates, Hillsdale, New Jersey (1990).
20. E. A. Locke and G. P. Latham, Work motivation: The high performance cycle, *Work Motivation* (U. Kleinbeck et al., eds.), Lawrence Erlbaum Associates, Hillsdale, New Jersey, pp. 3–26 (1990).
21. A. H. Maslow, *Motivation and Personality*, Harper and Row, New York (1954).
22. J. M. Burns, *Leadership*, Harper and Row, New York (1978).
23. A. H. Maslow, *Eupsychian Management*, Richard D. Irwin, Homewood, Illinois (1965).

24. E. A. Locke and D. Henne, Work motivation theories, *International Review of Industrial and Organizational Psychology* (C. L. Cooper and I. Robertson, eds.), John Wiley and Sons, New York, pp. 1–35 (1986).

25. R. T. Golembiewski, *Men, Management, & Morality*, Transaction, New Brunswick, New Jersey (1989).

26. B. M. Bass, *Leadership and Performance Beyond Expectations,* Free Press, New York (1985).

27. W. Bennis and B. Nanus, *Leaders: The Strategies for Taking Charge*, Harper and Row, New York (1985).

28. P. Block, *The Empowered Manager*, Jossey-Bass, San Francisco (1987).

29. R. T. Golembiewski, *Humanizing Public Organizations*, Lomond, Mount Airy, Maryland (1985).

30. D. McGregor, *The Human Side of Enterprise*, McGraw-Hill, New York (1960).

31. D. P. Warwick, *A Theory of Public Bureaucracy*, Harvard University Press, Cambridge, Massachusetts (1975).

32. F. Herzberg, One more time: How do you motivate employees? *Harvard Business Rev.*, *46*: 36–44 (1968).

33. E. E. Lawler, *Pay and Organizational Effectiveness*, McGraw-Hill, New York (1971).

34. D. C. McClelland, *The Achieving Society*, Free Press, New York (1961).

35. J. W. Atkinson and J. O. Raynor, *Motivation and Achievement*, Winston, Washington, D.C. (1974).

36. D. C. McClelland and D. G. Winter, *Motivating Economic Achievement*, Free Press, New York (1969).

37. J. B. Miner, *Theories of Organizational Behavior*, Dryden Press, Hinsdale, Illinois (1980).

38. D. C. McClelland, *Power: The Inner Experience*, Irvington, New York (1975).

39. J. S. Adams, Towards and understanding of inequity, *J. Abnormal Soc. Psychol.*, *67*: 422–436 (1963).

40. J. S. Adams, Inequity in social exchange, *Advances in Experimental Social Psychology*, vol. 2 (L. Berkowitz, ed.), Academic Press, New York, pp. 267–299 (1965).

41. J. R. Gordon, *Organizational Behavior.* Allyn and Bacon, Boston (1991).

42. R. C. Huseman, J. D. Hatfield, and E. W. Miles, A new perspective on equity theory: The equity sensitivity construct, *Acad. Manage. Rev.*, *12*: 232–234 (1987).

43. K. E. Weick, The concept of equity in the perception of pay, *Admin. Sci. Q.*, *11*: 414–439 (1966).

44. V. H. Vroom, *Work and Motivation*, Wiley, New York (1964).

45. H. G. Heneman and D. P. Schwab, Evaluation of research on expectancy theory predictions of employee performance, *Psychol. Bull.*, *78*: 1–9 (1972).

46. O. Behling, C. Schriesheim, and J. Tolliver, *Present Trends and New Directions in Theories of Work Effort*, Journal Supplement Abstract Service of the American Psychological Association (1973).

47. T. Connolly, Conceptual and methodological issues in expectancy models of work performance motivation, *Acad. Manage. Rev.*, *1*: 37–47 (1976).

48. M. G. Evans, Organizational behavior: The central role of motivation, *Yearly Review of Management* (J. G. Hunt and J. D. Blair, eds.), *J. Manage.*, *12*: 203–222 (1986).

49. H. G. Rainey, *Understanding and Managing Public Organizations*, Jossey-Bass, San Francisco (1991).

50. U.S. Office of Personnel Management (1983).

51. R. Kreitner and F. Luthans, A social learning approach to behavioral management: Radical behaviorists "mellowing out," *Organizational Behavior* (J. Gordon, ed.), Allyn and Bacon, Boston, pp. 59–72 (1987).

52. A. Bandura, *Social Learning Theory*, Prentice Hall, Englewood Cliffs, New Jersey (1978).

53. B. F. Skinner, *Science and Human Behavior*, Macmillan, New York (1953).

54. F. Luthans and R. Kreitner, *Organizational Behavior Modification: An Operant and Social Learning Approach*, Scott, Foresman, Glenview, Illinois (1985).

55. A. Bandura, *Principles of Behavior Modification*, Holt, Rinehart and Winston, New York (1969).

56. W. M. Sherman, *Behavior Modification*, Harper and Row, New York (1990).
57. W. F. Dowling, At Emery Air Freight: Positive reinforcement boosts performance, *Org. Dynam.*, 2: 41–50 (1973).
58. E. A. Locke, The myth of behavior modification in organizations, *Acad. Manage. Rev.*, 2: 543–553 (1977).
59. C. C. Manz and C. P. Neck, Inner leadership: Creating productive thought patterns, *Acad. Manage. Executive*, V: 87–95 (1991).
60. E. A. Locke and G. P. Latham, *A Theory of Goal Setting and Task Performance*, Prentice Hall, Englewood Cliffs, New Jersey (1990).
61. A. Bandura, Self-regulation of motivation and action through internal standards and goal systems, *Goal Concepts in Personality and Social Psychology* (L. A. Pervin, ed.), Lawrence Erlbaum Associates, Hillsdale, New Jersey, pp. 19–86 (1989).
62. P. C. Earley and T. R. Lituchy, Delineating goal and efficacy effects: A test of three models, *J. Appl. Psychol.*, 76: 81–98 (1991).
63. L. A. Pervin, ed., *Goal Concepts in Personality and Social Psychology*, Lawrence Erlbaum Associates, Hillsdale, New Jersey (1989).
64. M. E. Tubbs and S. E. Ekeberg, The role of intentions in work motivation: Implications for goal-setting theory and research, *Acad. Manage. Rev.*, 16: 180–199 (1991).
65. Lodahl and Kejner (1965).
66. Lawler and Hall (1970).
67. E. E. Lawler, *Strategic Pay*, Jossey-Bass, San Francisco (1990).

37

An Expectancy Theory Approach to the Motivational Impacts of Budgets

J. Ronen and J. L. Livingstone

In this chapter we discuss the implications of budgets for motivation and behavior in the context of expectancy theory as developed in the psychology of motivation. We argue that propositions from expectancy theory can be used to integrate and accommodate the fragmented research findings on budget and behavior in the accounting literature. We discuss how the expectancy model reconciles what might appear to be contradictory findings from prior studies.

THE FUNCTIONS OF BUDGETS

Budgets serve three decision-making functions: planning, control, and motivation. Budgets aid planning in that they incorporate forecasts which reflect the anticipated consequences of different combinations of plans (actions) made by management and the relevant uncontrollable events that may occur in the environment. Budgets also serve the planning function through being utilized as a tool for sensitivity analysis, which includes the examination of how slight changes in management plans affect the consequences (budgets). Many budgets could be thus generated as a result of alternative plans so that the most desirable plan could then be chosen.

The control function is typically a feedback process whereby information about past performance (both anticipated and actual) is provided to those who "control," to be utilized by them for making decisions. As a motivational tool, the budget conveys information to the subordinate about expectations of superiors regarding what constitutes successful task performance and the consequent reinforcement contingencies. These characterizations of the control and motivation processes probably apply whether the budget is imposed on subordinates, whether developed through the participation of the "controlled," or whether they result from a dynamic, interlevel bargaining process over goals and resource allocations [1].

Source: *The Accounting Review*, *50*(4): 671–685 (1975).

The three functions of budgets are interdependent. The motivational effect must be explicitly considered in planning and control. Similarly, knowledge by subordinates of superiors' plans and control styles has motivational effects. Furthermore, the budgeting process is likely to cause subordinates to bargain for increases in the resources they command. This may result in dysfunctional budgetary slack [1, 2].

THE DYSFUNCTIONAL ASPECTS OF BUDGETS

Budgetary slack is not the only potential dysfunctional aspect of budgets. The literature is filled with exhortations to consider the behavioral effects of standards and budgets on motivation and, consequently, on performance [3–6]. These effects could be either dysfunctional or positive. Many articles deal specifically with the behavioral impacts of budgets on employees; some base their conclusions on generalizations from the psychological literature, and others show findings from empirical experiments [7–9]. Mostly, these discussions were launched in terms of specific principles taken from various areas of psychology such as aspiration level, participation, and attitude change.

To gain better understanding and insight into how these behavioral effects are created, we propose the expectancy model as a unifying framework within which the effects could be analyzed. While the universal usage of budgets implies that their benefits are perceived to exceed the possible dysfunctional effects, the latter can be minimized if the budget's behavioral impacts are better understood.

By choosing the expectancy model (a description of the model appears later) as a framework, we do not wish to imply that it accurately describes behavior even though some recent progress has been made.[1] Rather, we view it as a framework that facilitates the generation of hypotheses about the behavioral effects of budgets. The testing of these hypotheses would indicate whether subordinates' behavior is consistent with the model.

In the following section we describe the expectancy model. After that, we reinterpret the budget's behavioral implications discussed in the literature within the expectancy framework.

THE EXPECTANCY MODEL

The expectancy model is viewed as underlying the superior–subordinate budget relationship in two respects: (1) as the model according to which the subordinate's motivation to perform the task is influenced via the budget and (2) as the model which the superior regards as determining the subordinate's motivation (it is assumed that the superior can and may affect the subordinate's motivation via the budget in accordance with the expectancy model).[2]

The particular expectancy model version that we use in this chapter is the one advanced by House [10], which in turn is derived from the path–goal hypotheses advanced by Georgopoulos, Mahoney, and Jones [11] and from previous research supporting the class of expectancy models of motivation [12–19]. The basic tenet of expectancy theory is that an individual chooses his behavior on the basis of (1) his expectations that the behavior will result in a specific outcome and (2) the sum of the valences, i.e., personal utilities or satisfaction that he derives from the outcome. A distinction is made [13] between valences that are intrinsic to behavior itself (such as feelings of competence) and those that are the extrinsic consequences of behavior (such as pay). Behavior that is intrinsically valent is also intrinsically motivational because the behavior leads directly to satisfaction, whereas extrinsic valences are contingent on external rewards.

House's formulation can be expressed as follows:

$$M = IV_b + P_1 \left(IV_a + \sum_{i=1}^{n} P_{2i} EV_i \right) \qquad i = 1, 2, \ldots, n$$

where

M = motivation to work

IV_a = intrinsic valence associated with successful performance of the task

IV_b = intrinsic valence associated with goal-directed behavior

EV_i = extrinsic valences associated with the i-th extrinsic reward contingent on work goal accomplishment

P_1 = the expectancy that goal-directed behavior will accomplish the work goal (a given level of specified performance); the measure's range is $(-1, +1)$

P_{2i} = the expectancy that work goal accomplishment will lead to the i-th extrinsic reward; the measure's range is $(-1, +1)$

The individual estimates the expectancy P_1 of accomplishing a work goal given his behavior. For the estimate he considers factors such as (1) his ability to behave in an appropriate and effective manner and (2) the barriers and support for work goal accomplishment in the environment. Also, he estimates the expectancy P_2 that work goal accomplishment will result in attaining extrinsic rewards that have valences for him such as the recognition of his superiors of his goal accomplishment. He also places subjective values on the intrinsic valence associated with the behavior required to achieve the work goal IV_b, the intrinsic valence associated with the achievement of the work goal IV_a, and the extrinsic valences associated with the personal outcomes that accrue to him as a result of achieving the work goal EV_i.

The superior can affect the independent variables of this model:

1. He partially determines what extrinsic rewards (EV_i) follow work goal accomplishment, since he influences the extent to which work goal accomplishment will be recognized as a contribution and the nature of the reward (financial increases, promotion, assignment of more interesting tasks or personal goals, and development).

2. Through interaction, he can increase the subordinate's expectancy (P_2) that rewards ensure work goal accomplishment.

3. He can, through his own behavior, support the subordinate's effort and thus influence the expectancy (P_1) that the effort will result in work goal achievement.

4. He may influence the intrinsic valences associated with goal accomplishment (IV_a) by determining factors such as the amount of influence the subordinate has in goal setting and the amount of control he is allowed in the task-directed effort. Presumably, the greater the subordinate's opportunity to influence the goal and exercise control, the more intrinsically valent is the work goal accomplishment.

5. The superior can increase the net intrinsic valences associated with goal-directed behavior (IV_b) by reducing frustrating barriers, by being supportive in times of stress, and by permitting involvement in a wide variety of tasks and being considerate of the subordinate's needs [10].

Three classes of situational variables that determine which particular superior behaviors are instrumental in increasing work motivation were hypothesized by House and Dessler [20]:

1. *The needs of the subordinate*: The subordinate views the superior's behavior as legitimate only to the extent that he perceives it either as an immediate source of satisfaction or as instrumental to his future satisfaction. For example, subordinates with high needs for social approval find warm, interpersonal superior behavior immediately satisfying and therefore legitimate. On the other hand, subordinates with high need for achievement desire clarification of path–goal relationships and goal-oriented feedback from superiors. The perceived legitimacy of the superior's behavior is thus partially determined by the subordinate's characteristics.

2. *Environmental demands*: When the task is routine and well defined, attempts by the superior to clarify path–goal relationships are redundant and are likely to be viewed as superfluous, externally imposed control, thus resulting in decreased satisfaction. Also, the more dissatisfying the task, the more the subordinate resents behavior by the superior directed at increasing productivity and enforcing compliance with organizational procedures.

3. *The task demands subordinates*: The superior's behavior is assumed to be motivational to the extent that it helps subordinates cope with environmental uncertainties, threat from others, or sources of frustration. Such behavior is predicted to increase the subordinate's satisfaction with the job content and to be motivational to the extent that it increases the subordinate's perceived expectancies that effort will lead to valued rewards.

THE RELATION BETWEEN THE EXPECTANCY MODEL AND THE ACCOUNTING BUDGETING PROCESS

Budgets have long been recognized as a managerial tool of communication between superiors and subordinates with respect to the parameters of the task. As a tool of communication, the budgets are perceived by subordinates as an aspect of their superior's attitudes toward them, the task and the work environment.

First, the budgets reflect management's expectations about what constitutes successful task performance; implicit in this is the promise of extrinsic rewards for the subordinates if the budget is accomplished. The imposition by management of a particular budget implies that its accomplishment will be recognized by management because it is in accordance with what management views as desirable goal attainment. To the extent that subordinates value the superior's recognition of their accomplishment, the budget communication constitutes a specification of the potential level of some of the extrinsic valences associated with work-goal accomplishment (EV_i). The budgeting process, when coupled with subordinate knowledge of the external reinforcement contingencies (i.e., the set of rewards contingent on effective performance), clarifies the set of external valences associated with work goal accomplishment or at least helps the subordinate to subjectively assess these valences.

Second, the perceived difficulty of the budget affects the expectancy of the subordinate that his effort would lead to budget achievement. Thus, the content of the budget also serves as an input for the subordinates to formulate their P_1 expectancies. Comparison of past levels of performance with past budgets generates a record of deviations which clearly influences P_1.

Third, the degree to which superiors were consistent or inconsistent in delivering the contingent rewards following budget accomplishment may induce the subordinates to revise their estimates of P_{2i}. Also, the degree to which superiors show recognition of past accomplishments will affect the subordinate's expectation of the level of future extrinsic valences (EV_i) associated with work goal accomplishment.

The budget may also fulfill the role of providing structure to an ambiguous task as well as coordinating activities, so that merely working toward accomplishment of the budget provides satisfaction. To the extent that the budget content facilitates the derivation of this satisfaction, the budget also affects the intrinsic valence associated with the goal-directed behavior (IV_b).

Thus, the budgeting process can crucially affect the parameters of the expectancy model. Consequently, we can gain insights into the effect on motivation—the dependent variable in this model—by examining the effects of the budgets on the independent variables of the model, such as the subordinate's expectations, perceived valences, etc. Such an examination should increase the likelihood of identifying the psychological mechanisms underlying the effects of budgets on work motivation. Among the psychological states of subordinates that deserve exploration are the subordinate's intrinsic job satisfaction, his expectancies that effort leads to effective performance, and his expectancies that performance leads to reward.

In the next section, it is shown that reinterpretation of previous experimental and other empirical investigations regarding the effects of budget on behavior makes it possible to integrate and reconcile the otherwise fragmented findings cited in the literature within the expectancy model framework.[3]

INTEGRATION OF PRIOR STUDIES WITHIN THE EXPECTANCY FRAMEWORK

It is useful to reconcile prior findings and assumptions regarding impacts of budgets by focusing on the underlying behavioral assumptions assumed (although not necessarily valid) by accountants in the budgetary process:

1. The budget should be set at a reasonably attainable level.
2. Managers should participate in the development of budgets for their own functions in the organization.
3. Managers should operate on the principle of management by exception.
4. Personnel should be charged or credited only for items within their control.
5. Dimensions of performance that cannot be conveniently measured in monetary terms are outside the budgetary domain.

The possible invalidity of these assumptions has been extensively discussed in the accounting literature. The generalizations offered can be summarized as follows.

Achievement of budgeted performance may not satisfy the needs of the subordinates, who thus need not be motivated by the budget. Also, the individual's goals and the organization's goals may not be identical. For an individual to internalize or accept the budget, he must believe that achieving it will satisfy his needs better than not achieving it. A goal that an individual has internalized is known as his aspiration level—the performance level that he undertakes to reach (see, e.g., Ref. 5). The probability that an individual will internalize the budget is influenced by his expectations of what he is able to achieve [21], his past experience of success in reaching budgeted goals, and the priority that he assigns to the need for a sense of personal achievement.

These assumptions are now closely examined in an attempt to show how the expectancy model can be used to integrate findings and assertions related to them within a cohesive framework.

The Assumption That Standards Should Be Reasonably Attainable

Summary of Existing Studies. The assumption implies that as long as the standards do not exceed what is reasonably attainable, the subordinate will internalize them. If too tight, presumably the subordinate will regard the budget as unrealistic and either cease to be motivated or be negatively motivated by it. Thus, while loose standards (as opposed to reasonably attainable standards) will lead to slackening of effort, tight standards could be perceived as unrealistic and therefore fail to motivate personnel, except perhaps in a negative direction [22]. For example, Stedry [8] suggested that under certain conditions performance could be improved if management would impose unattainable standards on subordinates. Under laboratory conditions, he found that his measurements of the subjects' aspiration levels were influenced by the level at which the imposed standards were set. He also found that performance that was significantly different from the aspiration level led to an adjustment of the aspiration level in the direction of the performance level that was actually achieved. Thus, he suggested that standards be changed from period to period so that they are met some of the time and are slightly above the attainable level the rest of the time. Hofstede [23] also found that motivation is highest when standards are difficult to reach but are not regarded as impossible.

Other discussions and evidence in the literature support these findings. When an individual barely achieves the level of aspiration, he is said to have subjective feelings of success; subjective feelings of failure follow nonachievement of the level of aspiration [24]. In particular, Child and Whiting [25] argue that (1) success generally raises the level of aspiration, failure lowers it; (2) the probability of rise in level of aspiration is positively correlated with the strength of success or failure; (3) changes in the level of aspiration partially depend on changes in the subject's confidence in his ability to attain goals; and (4) failure is more likely than success to lead to avoidance of setting a level of aspiration.

From their review of the literature, Becker and Green [5] conclude that "level of aspiration not only describes a goal for future attainment but also it partially insures that an individual will expend a more than minimal amount of energy, if necessary, to perform at or above the level." Indeed, although not in a business budgeting setting, Bayton [26] found that higher performance followed higher level of aspiration in testing the performance of 300 subjects on seven arithmetic problems. Also, Cherrington and Cherrington [7] experimentally found that when supervisors imposed either a minimum or a specific standard of performance, the subordinate's estimate of their performance (level of aspiration) was higher than when supervisors imposed either lenient minimum standards of performance or imposed none at all. They also found that the higher estimates of performance also were followed by higher actual performance. Cherrington and Cherrington's findings seem somewhat to contradict some of Stedry's [8] results. In Stedry's study, one group was first given the standard and then asked to indicate its own goal for performance in the subsequent period. The second group was asked to indicate its goals *before* it knew what the experimental manager's goals were. The group setting its personal goals first set higher goals and performed better than the group which was informed of management's goals first, although it must be noted that in Cherrington and Cherrington's study high estimates and performance were achieved when the group also formulated its estimates before knowledge of the supervisor's imposed minimums. Thus, in a sense, the situation is not unsimilar to Stedry's except that revision of the estimate after knowledge of the supervisor's higher standards proved to be beneficial.

Reconciliation with the Expectancy Model. In terms of the expectancy model, the conclusion that standards regarded as impossible are not motivational or negatively motivational can simply be explained by the fact that P_1, the expectancy that goal-directed behavior would lead to work goal accomplishment, was low or even negative and, to show this more clearly, Stedry's conclusions are examined in light of the expectancy model.

As indicated, Stedry found that his measurement of the subject's aspiration levels was influenced by the level at which the imposed standards were set. The results of the Cherringtons' study partially confirm Stedry's results in that the experimental group's estimate of their performance was highest under nonparticipation conditions, i.e., when high minimum standards were imposed. If the aspiration level is taken to reflect the level which the subordinate sets out to achieve, then it is understandable that (within limits) the higher the imposed standards by superiors, the higher would be the aspiration level. In comparison with other levels of attainment, P_{2i}, the expectancies that work goal accomplishment will lead to extrinsic valences would be higher the nearer the performance level is to the imposed standard. Thus, if the subordinate's task is viewed as a selection among different aspiration levels, it is only natural that he will choose the aspiration level that maximizes the dependent variable M in the model.

However, if the imposed standards are too high, the aspiration level will lag behind since, although P_{2i} will increase, P_i, the expectancy that goal-directed behavior will lead to work goal accomplishment is likely to be negatively correlated with the perceived difficulty of attaining the standard.

The assessment of P_1 is also likely to be affected by feedback on past performance; P_1 will tend to be positively correlated with prior levels of performance and consequently the dependent variable and the aspiration level will tend to move in the same direction as performance. This "expectancy model" induced observation could explain Stedry's other finding that performance which differed significantly from the aspiration level led to the latter's adjustment in the direction of the performance level actually achieved.

It is particularly important and interesting to relate the level of aspiration conceptualization of the budgeting process with the expectancy approach. The expectancy model's dependent variable—motivation to exert effort in the task—is a direct function of the expected valences. The model's underlying assumption is that the higher the expectation of valences, the greater the effort the subordinate is likely to exert and, thus, the higher the performance level. In other words, the subordinate's effort exerted in task performance is assumed to change along a continuum as a function of the expectation of valences.

Level of aspiration, on the other hand, is operationally defined as "the goal one explicitly undertakes to reach," where "maximum effort will be exerted to just reach an aspiration goal" [5]. According to this view, effort is seen not as a continuum but as changing discretely where the level of aspiration goal of performance is that for which a maximum—a specifically defined amount of effort—is spent in order to derive the subjective feeling of success. If we attempt to interpret the meaning of the level of aspiration within the expectancy framework, it seems that it corresponds to the performance level consciously chosen by the subordinate (among alternative performance levels) so as to maximize the expectation of valences—the value of the expectancy equation. That is, the subordinate behaves as if he computes the expected values associated with different performance levels, which clearly depend on the model's parameters (P_1, P_2, IV_b, IV_a, and EV_i) and selects the one that maximizes M as the level of aspiration. The implications of this relationship between the level of aspiration and the expectancy model's dependent variable to the specification of desirable attributes of the budgetary process could be far reaching.

Participation

Summary of Existing Studies.   Participation means that decisions affecting a manager's operations are, to some extent, jointly made by the manager and his superior. As such, it is more than mere consultation by which the superior informs himself of the manager's views but makes the decisions himself. The participation of subordinates in budgeting setting is usually regarded as effective in getting subordinates to internalize the standards embodied in the budgets and thus in achieving goal congruence [27].

The role of participation can perhaps be best understood in the context of group dynamics. Aspiration levels are said partially to depend on the levels of aspiration prevailing in the groups to which the individual belongs [28]. The amount of influence that group members are said to have on the individual's aspiration level depends on the group's cohesiveness, i.e., the degree to which individual members value their group membership.

The value of group membership to an individual derives from the degree to which the individual believes that group membership will help him attain his own goals [29, 30]. Perceived value of membership seems to be correlated with the likelihood that different members in the group will have similar goals—thus the individual's likelihood of continued membership in the group. The relationship between the two appears to be reciprocal. Similarity of goals among the group's members will make membership in the group more attractive. On the other hand, if membership in the group is highly valued, the individual will tend to assimilate the group's goal to be able to maintain the valued membership. As a result of valuing his own membership and his desire to maintain it, the individual will tend to reject goals that he believes conflict with those prevailing in the group and accept those that appear to be consistent with the group's goals [29, 30].

Thus, participation does not seem to automatically produce congruence between the group's goal and that of the firm. Conditions may be such that a more authoritarian managerial style will be more effective in raising the aspiration levels of subordinates. Becker and Green [5] describe these conditions in greater specificity. This position could be summarized as follows: If greater interaction of individuals leads to greater group cohesiveness, and if this cohesiveness plus some incentive to produce either at higher or lower levels are positively correlated, then participation can be an inducement for higher or lower levels of performance. Also, if participation at an upper level generates positive attitudes on the part of supervisors, then they will try to induce higher individual and group aspirations in the subgroup which will hopefully lead to higher rather than lower levels of performance.

There is also some evidence that participation improves morale. Coch and French [31] found a much lower turnover rate, fewer grievances about piece rates, and less aggression against the supervisor as individual participation in planning job changes increased. Vroom [32] argues that participation makes employees feel more a part of the activities and less dominated by a superior, more independent, and thus improves their attitude toward the job. But while participation enhanced satisfaction, it did not necessarily increase productivity. Or at least the results are ambiguous. Literature to date shows no direct correlation between participation and improved productivity [e.g., 7, 31, 33].

Personality variables can also affect the relation between participation and performance. For example, Vroom emphasizes the affective consequences of the degree of consistency between a person's performance and his self-concept: persons were found to perform better on tasks perceived to require highly valued ability or intelligence which they believed themselves to possess [32].

Reconciliation with the Expectancy Model.   It was indicated that participation tends to increase performance if interaction of individuals leads to greater group cohesiveness and if the group norms are such that they are conductive to higher levels of production. These particular effects of participation can be accommodated within the expectancy model. A group is cohesive when the individual members value their acceptance within the group. Participation in the context of a cohesive group would be a process of reaching consensus within the group on the desirable standards of performance within the group. Once such a consensus has been reached as a result of the group's participation, it would be viewed by the individual as reflecting the group's own norm. Striving to attain that goal would therefore increase the individual's likelihood of maintaining his acceptance in the group. In terms of the expectancy model, the existence of a cohesive group of which the subordinate is a member enhances the extrinsic valence associated with work goal accomplishment. With the attainment of the goal, the individual achieves not only the extrinsic and intrinsic valences that exist in the absence of a group context, but, in addition, he maintains his acceptance in a cohesive group which can be regarded as an extrinsic valence associated with goal accomplishment.

In addition, participation may create intrinsic valences that are absent in nonparticipative environments. These intrinsic valences may be due to a tendency for individuals to become "ego-involved" in decisions to which they have contributed, as would be the case in participative decision making. A similar process is suggested by evidence that participation by a single person in decision making with a superior affects the subsequent performance of that person [34].

Thus, only when groups are cohesive and their norms support the organization would participation be likely to increase motivation and hence the aspiration level and hence performance. When groups are not cohesive, no additional valence is introduced and therefore motivation is not likely to be increased, although participation may increase group cohesiveness, as stated above. In fact, participation in certain environments can lead to negative results as related, for example, by Shillinglaw [35] The introduction of participative budgeting in a large electrical equipment factory years ago was received coldly by most of the first level supervisors. The reason offered was that foremen were reluctant to accept the risk of censure for failure to achieve targets that they had set themselves [9]. In terms of this expectancy model, this phenomenon can be explained in terms of the effect of undesired participation on IV_b. Since participation under this environment induced anxiety and thus a decrement in the intrinsic valence associated with goal-directed behavior, motivation and performance were likely to decline.

Management by Exception

Summary of Existing Studies.   The fact that accountants and managers emphasize deviations (we use this term instead of variances) in accounting reports implies that, by and large, attention is merited when significant deviations are observed and not when standards are met. Such a system, however, may be perceived as emphasizing failure with only exceptional success attracting management attention. The response to favorable deviations not requiring corrective actions often seems to be weaker than that to unfavorable deviations. As a result, subordinates may be led to view the system as punitive rather than as informative. This may lead to defensiveness, overcautious behavior, and other dysfunctional effects [36]. This suggests that effort should be made to emphasize positive as well as negative aspects of performance to provide "positive reinforcement" [37].

Reconciliation with the Expectancy Model. In terms of the expectancy model, it is easy to predict the effect of these practices. Nonreinforcement or mere attainment of the budget will tend to decrease P_{2i}, the expectancy goal that accomplishment leads to extrinsic valences. The same effect would be produced by relative nonreinforcement of performance that is superior to the budget. On the other hand, punitive response to unfavorable deviations, while it may accomplish some results since subordinates have no alternatives, may also result in resistance, sabotage, and other kinds of conflict. Punishment is known to have generally negative effects [30]. The Cherringtons' [7] finding that only appropriate reinforcement contingencies (i.e., when subordinates can control the performance on which rewards are contingent) were motivational can also be explained in terms of the effect on P_{2i}.

The Controllability Criterion

Summary of Existing Studies. Controllability refers to the ability of the subordinate to make decisions and execute them in his attempt to accomplish specified goals or a budget. A distinction must be made between *actual* control and *perceived* control. The motivational variable of interest is perceived control, which may differ from the actual degree of control that the subordinate can apply to a task. Personality as well as sociological factors can affect the degree of deviation between perceived control and actual control [38].

It is generally asserted that only controllable activities in the budget should constitute the basis for evaluation and reinforcement of the subordinate. For example, according to Vroom [34].:

> The effectiveness of any system in which rewards and punishments are contingent on specified performance outcomes appears to be dependent on the degree of control which the individual has over these performance outcomes. The increment in performance to be expected from an increase in the extent to which the individual is rewarded for favorable results and/or punished for unfavorable results is directly related to the extent to which the individual can control the results of his performance.

Several sources can contribute to the lack of control over results which appears from existing evidence to reduce the effectiveness of organizationally administered reward–punishment contingencies. The first source is the existence of interpersonal and interdepartmental interdependencies within the formal organization. The jointness of the inputs in terms of subordinate's effort makes it extremely difficult to measure and assess a particular subordinate's contribution to the results. In such an interdependence setup, only the effort of a group as a whole can be adequately evaluated and each person has but partial control over the group's outcome.

The second source for lack of control is the operation of "chance" events that perturb the otherwise one-to-one relationship between the subordinate's efforts and his accomplishments. States of nature that are beyond his control affect the results of his effort. The existence of these "chance" events is partially a function of the nature of the task itself. Shooting at a fast-moving target, for example, is subject to far more external and uncontrollable events than performing a standard manufacturing operation.

The degree of skill of a subordinate to perform a job constitutes a third source of lack of control over results. While the degree of skill tends to be inversely related to the incidence of "chance" events, the two variables (skill and chance) are usefully viewed as distinct from each other [38]. The degree to which "chance" factors affect performance depends on the skill of the performer as well as on the nature of the task. Thus, a very competent and skillful performer may still fail because the task is subject to many external perturbances, and at the same time an unskilled worker may fail to perform effectively even if his task is highly structured and subject to no external disturbances.

As indicated above, the perceived and not the actual degree of control is the variable of interest from the standpoint of predicting motivation and performance. And, as suggested, perceived control may differ from actual control, and the difference can depend on personality variables such as degree of achievement motivation, risk-taking behavior, as well as on cultural variables such as black vs. white, etc. [39–41].

Reconciliation with the Expectancy Model.   Using the expectancy model, it can be explained why only activities in the budget that are perceived as controllable by the subordinate should constitute the basis for evaluation and reinforcement. Only activities that are perceived as controllable are likely to be associated with a relatively high P_1. In addition, performing tasks that are perceived as controllable could be associated with higher intrinsic valences [42].

Unfortunately, since it is difficult to discriminate finely between controllable and noncontrollable activities, dysfunctional decisions may result:

1. Excluding from the evaluation basis activities that are partially controllable but classified as uncontrollable will direct the subordinate not to exert effort in those activities and eventually to jeopardize the accomplishment of the organization's goals. When basically controllable activities are excluded from the evaluation basis, the dependent variable M of the expectancy model operates on only some of the activities that are instrumental to the firm's overall goal attainment and it bypasses other beneficial activities.

2. Including in the evaluation basis activities that are perceived by the subordinate as noncontrollable can result in lowering his expectancy that effort will lead to work accomplishment, i.e., P_1.

Also, the intrinsic valence associated with goal accomplishment may decrease if the task is perceived as partially beyond the subordinate's control. Under both cases, the subordinate's motivation to exert effort in his performance will tend to decrease.

The Exclusion of Criteria That Are Not Easily Measured in Monetary Terms

Summary of Existing Studies.   Because of the difficulty of measuring nonmonetary dimensions of performance, the accounting structure usually restricts itself to reporting financial performance. As a result, managers may be motivated to emphasize the things that are measured to the neglect of those that are not. One suggested solution to this problem is the development of a composite measure of performance, with each dimension assigned a weight in proportion to top management's perceived priority. But this solution is deficient because the weighting schemes are implicit, difficult to translate into numerical form, and possibly nonstable over time. However, a useful step is said to be to identify the major dimensions of performance, whether measurable or not, so that they could be incorporated into the performance review process. The motivational problem involved is that the subordinates lack knowledge of the precise managerial reward structure and the weighting schemes implicit in the evaluation system.

Reconciliation with the Expectancy Model.   The exclusion of nonmonetary criteria from the evaluation basis can be interpreted in terms of the expectancy model as motivating subordinates on the basis of only one dimension. In other words, the dependent variable

M is characterized by only one dimension—the maximization of monetary profits. Since the work goal accomplishment that is expected to secure extrinsic rewards EV_i is only defined by the criterion of maximizing monetary profits, the kinds of effort spent by the subordinate in the task will be only directed to that, and other objectives will be neglected.

Using the expectancy model, the subordinate can be motivated to spend effort to accomplish nonmonetary objectives if these are formally introduced into the control system by (1) making extrinsic rewards contingent on their accomplishment, (2) facilitating their accomplishment through task clarification, i.e., through increasing P_1, and (3) attempting to make the accomplishment of the nonmonetary criteria intrinsically valent to the subordinate.

As suggested by Vroom [34], one of the conditions needed to improve productivity by making effective performance on a task instrumental to the attainment of organizationally mediated rewards or the avoidance of punishments is that

> there is no conflict, either actual or perceived, between those behaviors necessary to attain a short term reward (for example, higher wages this week) and those required to avoid a longer term punishment (for example, a tightening of standards). [34]

However, merely introducing the nonmonetary criteria into the expectancy model through the explicit specification of effective performance via the budget does not in itself facilitate the attainment of goal congruence, unless the importance attached by top management to the attainment of various criteria is also made explicit to subordinates and internalized by them. If the weights to be attached to the criteria that are implicit in management's preference function are not made explicit to the subordinate, he may impose his own preference ordering on the criteria. That may not coincide with the management's preference ranking. In this case, goal congruence will not be attained in spite of the incorporation of the nonmonetary criteria into the model.

SUMMARY AND CONCLUSIONS

The literature on the effects of budgets on behavior is quite fragmentary and draws upon many diverse and partial areas of behavioral science. We have shown that this is the case for five general assumptions made in accounting with respect to budgets and behavior. These assumptions are

1. That standards should be reasonably attainable
2. That participation in the budgeting process leads to better performance
3. That management by exception is effective
4. That noncontrollable items should be excluded from budget reports
5. That budgetary accounting should be restricted to criteria measurable in monetary terms

We then introduced an expectancy model of task motivation within which, with some refinement, it was possible both to reconcile the fragmentary and contradictory past research findings and to explain the five assumptions in a consistent manner. To summarize, the following relations between the assumptions and variables in the expectancy model were discussed:

- Standards: P_1, P_2 (expectancies of performance and of reward)
- Participation: IV_a, IV_b, EV_i (intrinsic and extrinsic valences)
- Exception management: P_2
- Controllability: P_1, IV_a
- Monetary criteria: P_1, EV_i

We examined not only the budget's impact on behavior per se, but also the effects of the superior's responses contingent on given levels of budget achievement on the part of the subordinate. Thus, the administration of extrinsic rewards contingent on successful budget achievement and the facilitation of intrinsic values are both related to the budgeting process and affect the subordinate's performance. As a result, the expectancy model could be also used as a framework for evaluating the effect of the accounting reports that compare actual performance with the budget on the subordinate's future performance.

Of course, there is a wealth of other relations which fall outside the immediate scope of this chapter. The literature of expectancy theory is large, rich in empirical research, and fast growing. We recognize that the expectancy theory and its assumptions have come under criticism and that tests of the model's predictive ability have produced ambiguous results (see note 1). Nonetheless, progress in the testing and the operationalization of the model has apparently been made.[4]

Further research should be concerned with the derivation of testable hypotheses that apply the expectancy framework to the budgeting process as well as with further improving the predictive validity of the model through better operationalization of its variables. Also, the moderating effects of situational variables that are part of the working environment on the relation between budgets and motivation should be explored and tested. These situational aspects include variables such as the needs of subordinates, the environmental pressures and demands with which subordinates must cope to accomplish work goals and satisfy their needs, and the task demands of subordinates.

Motivation, the dependent variable in the expectancy model, can be used as an indication of the probability that the task will be performed, given the ability of the subordinate. In other words, the probability that a task will be performed is a function of motivation and ability. To the superior it is important to assess this ability in order both to evaluate the merit of competing activities and to allocate effectively people to tasks. Hypotheses generated and tested within an expectancy framework should be helpful toward that end.

NOTES

1. Indeed, the model has been found wanting with respect to its description power (see, e.g., [43]). But there is some recent evidence of progress (see note 4).
2. Clearly, motivation is only one variable that is likely to affect performance. Others are the subordinate's general ability as well as specific skills. To improve the subordinate's performance, the superior may choose to initiate training programs or take other actions to enhance the subordinate's skill, in addition to affecting his motivation.
3. Cherrington and Cherrington [7] tested experimentally the effect of various conditions of budget participation and reinforcement contingencies on performance and on psychological states of subordinates such as satisfaction with job and perceived superior consideration. However, they did not test an expectancy model per

se but merely investigated the effects of their manipulated conditions in the context of reinforcement and operant conditioning theory.

4. Reviews of empirical studies in nonbudget contexts which were designed either to test directly the expectancy model or to provide an inferential basis for assessing the model's validity indicate some empirical support for the relationships stipulated by the expectancy theory [20, 44–46]. In fact, Kopelman [46] observed coefficients of correlation between the model's independent variables and performance indicators as high as .53. Furthermore, operational tools for measuring the model's parameters are available [47].

REFERENCES

1. M. Schiff and A. Y. Lewin, "The Impact of People on Budgets," *Accounting Rev.*, April: 259–268 (1970).
2. O. E. Williamson, *The Economics of Discretionary Behavior: Managerial Objectives in a Theory of the Firm*, Prentice Hall, Englewood Cliffs, N.J., pp. 28–37 (1964).
3. C. Argyris, *The Impact of Budgets on People*, Controllership Foundation (1952).
4. G. Benston, "The Role of the Firm's Accounting System for Motivation," *Accounting Rev.*, April: 351–353 (1963).
5. S. Becker and D. Green, "Budgeting and Employee Behavior," *J. Business*, October: 392–402 (1962).
6. M. Usry, "Solving the Problem of Human Relations in Budgeting," *Budgeting*, Nov.–Dec: 4–6 (1968).
7. D. J. Cherrington and J. O. Cherrington, "Appropriate Reinforcement Contingencies in the Budgeting Process," Presented at the Accounting Empirical Research Conference, University of Chicago, May (1973).
8. A. Stedry, *Budgetary Control and Cost Behavior*, Prentice Hall, Englewood Cliffs, N.J. (1960).
9. A. Stedry and E. Kay, "The Effects of Goal Difficulty on Performance: A Field Experiment," *Behav. Sci.*, 2: 459–470 (1966).
10. R. J. House, "A Path-Goal Theory of Leader Effectiveness," *Admin. Sci. Q.*, 16(3): 321–338 (1971).
11. B. S. Georgopoulos, G. M. Mahoney, and N. W. Jones, "A Path Goal Approach to Productivity," *J. Appl. Psychol.*, 41: 345–353 (1957).
12. J. W. Atkinson, "Toward Experimental Analysis of Human Motivation in Terms of Motives, Expectations and Incentives," *Motives in Fantasy, Action and Society* (J. W. Atkinson, ed.), Van Nostrand, New York, (1958).
13. J. Galbraith and L. L. Cummings, "An Empirical Investigation of the Motivational Determinants of Past Performance: Interactive Effects Between Instrumentality, Valence, Motivation and Ability," *Organizational Behav. Hum. Perform.*, 237–257 (1967).
14. G. Graen, "Instrumental Theory of Work Motivation: Some Empirical Results and Suggested Modifications," *J. Appl. Psychol.*, 53: 1–25 (1969).
15. E. E. Lawler, "A Correlation Causal Analysis of the Relationship Between Expectancy Attitudes and Job Performance," *J. Appl. Psychol.*, 52: 462–468 (1968).
16. E. E. Lawler, *Pay and Organizational Effectiveness: A Psychological Perspective*, Wiley, New York (1971).
17. E. E. Lawler and J. K. Suttle, "Expectancy Theory and Job Behavior," *Organizational Behav. Hum. Perform.*, 9: 482–503 (1973).
18. L. Porter and E. E. Lawler, *Managerial Attitudes and Performance*, Irwin-Dorsey, Chicago (1967).
19. V. H. Vroom, *Work and Motivation*, Wiley, New York (1964).

20. R. J. House and G. Dessler, "The Path-Goal Theory of Leadership: Some Post Hoc and A Priori Tests," Paper presented at the Second Leadership Symposium: Contingency Approaches to Leadership, Southern Illinois University, Carbondale, April (1973).

21. T. Costello and S. Zelking, *Psychology in Administration: A Research Orientation*, Prentice Hall, Englewood Cliffs, N.J. (1963).

22. National Association of Accountants, *How Standard Costs Are Used Currently*, New York, pp. 8–9 (1948).

23. G. H. Hofstede, *The Game of Budget Control*, Koninklijke Van Corcum, Assen, The Netherlands, pp. 152–156 (1967).

24. K. Lewin, T. Dembo, L. Festinger, and P. Sears, "Level of Aspiration," *Personality and Behavior Disorder* Vol. 1 (J. McV. Hunt, ed.), Ronald Press, pp. 338–378 (1944).

25. J. L. Child and J. W. M. Whiting, "Determinants of Level of Aspiration: Evidence from Everyday Life," *The Study of Personality* (H. Branch, ed.), Wiley, New York, pp. 145–158 (1954).

26. J. A. Bayton, "Inter-relations Between Levels of Aspiration, Performance, and Estimates of Past Performance," *J. Exp. Psychol.*, *33*: 1–21 (1943).

27. G. A. Welsch, *Budgeting: Profit Planning and Control*, 3rd ed., Prentice Hall, Englewood Cliffs, N.J., pp. 17, 22–23 (1971).

28. K. Lewin, "The Psychology of a Successful Figure," *Readings in Managerial Psychology* (H. S. Leavitt and L. R. Pondy, eds.), University of Chicago Press, Chicago pp. 25–31 (1964).

29. E. Caplan "Behavioral Assumptions of Management Accounting," *Accounting Rev.*, July: 476–509 (1966).

30. V. H. Vroom, "Some Psychological Aspects of Organizational Control," *New Perspectives in Organizational Research* (Cooper, Leavitt, and Shelly, eds.), Wiley, New York (1961).

31. L. Coch and J. R. P. French, "Overcoming Resistance to Change," *Hum. Relations, 1*: 512–532 (1948).

32. V. H. Vroom, *Some Personality Determinants of the Effect of Participation*, Prentice Hall, Englewood Cliffs, N.J. (1960).

33. J. R. P. French, E. Kay, and H. H. Meyer, *A Study of Threat and Participation in a Performance Appraisal Situation*, General Electric Co. (1962).

34. V. H. Vroom, "Industrial Social Psychology," *Handbook of Social Psychology*, Addison Wesley, Boston (1970).

35. G. Shillinglaw, *Cost Accounting, Analysis and Control*, 3rd ed., Irwin, Homewood, Ill. (1972).

36. L. R. Sayles and M. K. Chandler, *Managing Large Systems: Organizations for the Future*, Harper & Row, New York (1971).

37. J. G. Birnberg and R. Nath, "Implications of Behavioral Science for Managerial Accounting," *Accounting Rev.*, July: 478 (1967).

38. N. T. Feather, "Valence of Outcome and Expectation of Success in Relation to Task Difficulty and Perceived Locus of Control," *J. Personality Social Psychol.*, *7*: 372–386 (1967).

39. H. M. Lefcourt, "Risk Taking in Negro and White Adults," *J. Personality Social Psychol.*, *2*: 765–770 (1965).

40. J. B. Rotter, S. Liverant, and D. P. Crowne, "Growth and Extinction of Expectancies in Chance Controlled and Skill Tasks," *J. Psychol.*, *52*: 151–177 (1961).

41. J. P. Sutcliffe, "Random Effects as a Function of Belief in Control," *Aust. J. Psychol.*, *8*: 128–139 (1956).

42. J. Ronen, "Involvement in Tasks and Choice Behavior," *Organizational Behav. Hum. Perform.*, *2*: 28–43 (1974).

43. S. Kerr, R. J. Klimoski, J. Tolliver, and M. A. Von Glinow, "Human Information Processing and Problem Solving," Paper presented at the Workshop in Behavioral Accounting, Annual Meeting of the American Institute for Decision Sciences, Atlanta, Ga., Oct. 30 (1974).

44. G. Dessler, "A Test of the Path-Goal Theory of Leadership," Doctoral dissertation, Bernard M. Baruch College, City University of New York (1973).

45. R. J. House and M. A. Wahba, "Expectancy Theory as a Predictor of Job Performance, Satisfaction and Motivation: An Integrative Model and a Review of the Literature," Paper presented

at the American Psychological Association Meeting, Hawaii, August (1972); Working Paper 72-21, Faculty of Management Studies, University of Toronto (1972).

46. R. Kopelman, "Factors Complicating Expectancy Theory Prediction of Work Motivation and Job Performance," Paper presented at the meeting of the American Psychological Association (1974).

47. R. J. House, "Some Preliminary Findings Concerning a Test of the Path Goal Theory of Leadership," Unpublished manuscript, University of Toronto, April (1972). R. J. House, *Notes on Questionnaires Frequently Used by or Developed by R. J. House*, Faculty of Management Studies, University of Toronto, July (1972).

38

Budgeting: Functional Analysis and Behavioral Implications

V. Bruce Irvine

Many of those who have written about budgets have emphasized the problems resulting from typical budgeting systems. Little enthusiasm has been voiced for the practical effectiveness of budgets as a means of obtaining the optimal benefits of which such a device is capable.

A more positive approach might result from a consideration of the control and motivational effects of budgets on the behavior of people. But any analysis of the reactions of these people (supervisors, foremen, laborers) to control devices (such as budgets) has received little attention as a specific subject in the literature of the past decade. The studies reported have usually concentrated attention on improving the usefulness of budgets from a top management viewpoint and have deemphasized the subordinate positions. Also, many of the studies have been conducted by behavioral scientists and have not been incorporated into accounting and management thought and teaching. Consequently, although accountants and management are aware that their actions have behavioral implications, they have not thoroughly understood what these are. The result is uncertainty, confusion, and indecision when human problems do arise.

The purpose of this chapter is to make a functional analysis of budgeting toward the goal of maximizing long-run profits (considered to be the present value of the owner's net worth). An analysis of reactions of the employees on whom budgets are primarily exercised rather than a purely management viewpoint analysis will be used to develop basic propositions. Human behavioral aspects of budgets, therefore, become a very relevant factor in this approach. After investigation of why employees react as they do, the usefulness of budgets in view of such reactions and the implications of suggestions for making budgets

Source: Condensation of a thesis submitted for R.I.A. qualification to the Society of Industrial Accountants of Saskatchewan. Reprinted from an article appearing in *Cost and Management* by V. Bruce Irvine, March/April 1970 issue, with permission of The Society of Management Accountants of Canada.

more successful and acceptable can be considered within particular situations facing modern day business.

DEFINITIONAL AND TECHNICAL CONSIDERATIONS

A functional analysis considers the various consequences of a particular activity and determines whether or not these consequences aid in the achievement of the organization's objective. According to Merton [1], the consequences of an activity are functional if they increase the ability of a given system to achieve a desired goal. A consequence is dysfunctional if it hinders the achievement of the goal. Consequences of an activity may also be classified as manifest (recognized and intended by the participants in the system) or latent (neither intended nor recognized). Decisions based only on manifest consequences may often be incorrect because of latent consequences.

A budget is a device intended to provide greater effectiveness in achieving organizational efficiency. To be effective, however, the functional aspects must outweigh the dysfunctional aspects. Whether or not this will be true depends on many factors, which will be discussed and summarized in a model of the elements of budgeting.

First it is necessary to understand what a budget is. Although formal definitions of a budget exist, a definition is not always the most relevant aspect of a concept.

Amitai Etzioni distinguishes between two types of models in organizational analysis [2]. The survival system consists of activities which, if fulfilled, allow a system to exist. Budgets are not part of such a system. Organizations in the past have functioned and in the future will function without the help of budgets. Budgets can be classified within an effectiveness system. These "define a pattern of interactions among the elements of the system which would make it more effective in the service of a given goal" [3].

A budget, as a formal set of figures written on a piece of paper, is, in itself, merely a quantified plan for future activities. However, when budgets are used for control, planning, and motivation, they become instruments which cause functional and dysfunctional consequences, both manifest and latent, which determine how successful the tool will be.

Budgets mean different things to different people according to their different points of view. Accountants see them from the preparation aspect, managers from the implementation aspect, and behavioral scientists from the human implication aspect. All of these viewpoints must be melded together if budgets are to obtain the best functional results.

There are many types of budgets. The major purpose of having budgets, the type of organization using a budget, the personalities of people handling the budget, the personal characteristics of people subject to budget direction, the leadership style of the organization, and the method of preparing a budget are all factors accounting for budget type and style.

The technical procedures involved in the preparation and use of budget figures are similar for most organizations. People make estimates (standards) of what they expect should reflect future events. These estimates are then compared to what actually happened and the differences (variances) are studied.

THE FUNCTIONAL ASPECTS OF BUDGET SYSTEMS

In what specific way do budgets make management action more efficient and effective in maximizing the present value of the owner's worth?

Basically, a budget system enables management to more effectively plan, coordinate, control, and evaluate the activities of the business. These are functional, manifest consequences in terms of their desirability.

Planning means establishing objectives in advance so that members of the organization will have specific, activity-directed goals to guide their actions. Budgets are quantitative plans for action. As such, they force management to examine the available resources and to determine how these can be used efficiently.

The point that budgets require this clarification and concrete quantification of ideas is not usually recognized directly by budgeting people as a benefit. As such, it could be considered functional and latent.

The planning aspect of budgeting has other latent functions. Planning requires that the plans be communicated to those involved in carrying them out. Communication is enhanced by distributing the budget to those responsible for various parts of it.

A budget makes lower level managers more aware of where they fit into an organization. Their budget indicates what is expected of them and that they have a goal towards which their activities are to be directed.

With a budget, junior (new) members of an organization have a better idea of where the company is going and are made to feel that the business is concerned about their future. This can affect both their own future plans and the company's recruitment policy and turnover problems.

When a person is given an objective, he is more likely to feel that he is part of the organization and that the upper echelons are interested in his work. Conversely, top management is likely to become more interested in, and aware of, the activities of lower level employees.

These latent, functional consequences of budgets create interest and, possibly, enthusiasm, which increase morale and could result in greater efficiency and initiative.

Planning of departmental activities must be coordinated so that bottlenecks do not occur and interdepartmental strife can be limited. A budget system can assist in this coordination. By basing organizational activity on the limiting factor (such as sales, production, working capital), a comprehensive budget coordinating all of the firm's activities can be approved by top management and the controller. Such a budget permits these people to bring together their overall knowledge of the firm's abilities and limitations. By using budgets to coordinate activities, the organization is more likely to operate at an optimal level, given the constraints on its resources.

The control consequences are among the more important aspects of budgeting. Because a budget plan exists, decisions are not merely spontaneous reactions to stimuli in an environment of unclarified goals. The budget provides relevant information to a decision maker at the time he must choose between alternatives. Therefore, a budget implicitly incorporates control at the point of the decision. However, provision for taking advantage of unforeseen situations should certainly be allowed even though a budget is violated.

A second type of control can be derived from budgets. A comparison of actual with budgeted performance after decisions have been made reveals to management the performance of the organization as a whole and of the individual responsible members.

A comparison merely reveals discrepancies. The action which is taken as a result of variances is in the hands of management. But the investigation of why these are variances, whether or not they are controllable, and the resulting control procedures is stimulated by the budgeting process. The result is the discovery of methods to save costs, improvement in the firm's efficiency, and better future planning.

Control of both types is important to top management because it cannot maintain personal contact with those in the lower management ranks. Devices such as budgets, employment contracts, job descriptions, and rules are therefore necessary to direct subordinate behavior. In general, control is based on the assumption that individuals are motivated by their own security needs to fulfill the plans and obey the rules. To the extent that this is true, the benefits to be derived from the control aspects of budgeting can be deemed functional and manifest.

These benefits could be obtained only in the ideal situation where budgets work as they are intended to work. The theoretical benefits make budgets very appealing devices, but the practical problems of implementing and using them greatly affect their usefulness. Most of the problems arise from the difficulty of convincing people to accept and use a budget. Mechanical problems also exist. These difficulties create many possibilities for dysfunctional consequences to occur with the result that some functional consequences become difficult, if not impossible, to attain.

DYSFUNCTIONAL ASPECTS OF BUDGET SYSTEMS

Any system which involves motivation and control of individuals has dysfunctional aspects, simply because human behavior cannot be predicted or controlled with certainty. Frequently, activities by management to obtain desired functional results will actually lead to dysfunctional consequences. Management must understand why such a reversal can occur so that existing problems can be solved or an environment created which prevents problems arising.

This section will indicate how results of a budget system can be dysfunctional in nature. The basic approach will be to analyze the deterrents to achieving particular functional results. Within a particular organization, the dysfunctional aspects must be considered in relation to the functional aspects in order to evaluate the worthiness of a budget system. Obviously, if the dysfunctional consequences of an action outweigh the functional aspects, management should delete the activity. Because each business is unique, no attempt can be made to state that certain activities will be dysfunctional or functional in every situation.

Because factors which can lead to dysfunctional consequences are complex, each will be analyzed separately although it is realized that they are usually interrelated.

The Term "Budget"

The first dysfunctional consequence of a budget system results from the name itself. Traditionally, budgets have carried a negative connotation for many:

> Some of the words historically associated with the term budget are: imposed, dictated by the top, authorized. And what are the original purposes of control—to reduce, to eliminate, to increase productivity, to secure conformance, to assure compliance, to inform about deviation. An historical meaning of budget is to husband resources—to be niggardly, tight, Scrooge-like [4].

If attitudes expressing such beliefs are not eliminated at the start, the budget will never get off the ground. One method of eliminating this problem is to refrain from calling the activity "budgeting."

Organizational Arrangements of Authority and Responsibility

If a budget system is to be used to control and evaluate personnel, the persons involved must possess responsibility and authority over what is being assigned to them. Consequently a large and/or decentralized organization would probably have a greater potential use for budgeting than a small, highly centralized business.

Centralized organizations may simply use budgets to plan and coordinate future activities. Because responsibility, control, and authority rest with the top executives in such a business, any attempt to reward, punish, or hold lower level employees responsible for variances would achieve nothing beneficial and would probably cause resentment. Any negative feelings on the part of those who follow directives in carrying out operations would likely lead to less than optimal achievement of organizational objectives. Therefore, even though budgets can be used to improve planning and coordination, assignment of control responsibilities where there is no power to carry out those responsibilities could easily create dysfunctional, latent consequences.

On the other hand, overemphasis on departmentalization can also have dysfunctional, latent effects:

> Budget records, as administered, foster a narrow viewpoint on the part of the user. The budget records serve as a constant remainder that the important aspect to consider is one's own department and not one's own plant [5].

Overemphasis on one's own department can lead to considerable cost in work-hours, money, and interpersonal relations when responsibility for variances, particularly large ones, is being determined. The result is a weakening of cooperation and coordination between departments.

Role Conflict Aspects of Budgeting

Status differences or, more accurately, role conflict between staff and line personnel are an important source of dysfunctional consequences. The problems created affect budget usefulness directly and also indirectly through their effect on communication, motivation, and participation. The basic difficulties arise because of differences in the way budget staff people and line personnel understand the budgeting system and each other.

From Table 1 [6] it can be seen how important budgets and the budget staff are in the supervisor's or foremen's working world. Ninety-nine percent of the supervisors and foremen questioned in four companies stated that the budget department was either first or second in importance of impact on the performance of their activity.

From the supervisor's and foremen's follow-up comments, it was readily apparent that the budget department's influence was not only significant, it was usually considered troublesome as well. Why should this be so? Some suggested reasons are:

1. Line employees see budgets as providing results only and not the reasons for those results. Any explanation of variances by the financial staff, such as failure to meet expected production or inadequate use of materials, prove grossly insufficient. Causes behind these explanations still have to be determined before the supervisors and foremen could consider budget reports as being useful to them or presenting a fair appraisal of their activities to top management.

Table 1 Responses to the Request "Name the Departments Affecting Your Actions Most" Asked of Supervisors and Foremen Individually in Four Firms [6]

	Most affect	Second most affect	Total
Production control	55%		
Budget department	45%	54%	99%

2. Budgets are seen as emphasizing past performance and as a device for predicting the future. Supervisors and foremen are basically concerned with the present and with handling immediate problems. Budget figures would often be ignored in order to solve present difficulties.

3. Supervisors and foremen apparently see budgets as being too rigid. In some cases, budget standards have not been changed for 2 or 3 years. Even if they now meet such a budget, they often would not be performing efficiently. Budget people would then adjust the budget. In such cases, those working under a budget would not really know what was expected of them until after they had submitted their cost reports and had received a control report.

4. Supervisors and foremen would also resent the opposite treatment of constantly changing a budget in the belief that increased efficiency would result. Such a procedure would lead them to believe, and often justly so, that budgets were unrealistically set. Budget men would be seen as individuals who could never be satisfied as they would raise the budget if a person made or came close to his previous budget. This would only result in frustration for the supervisor or foreman. The feeling that the company executives did not believe in the supervisor's own desire to do a good job could easily be implied when budgets are continually changing.

5. Thoughts about budgets are further aggravated when foremen and supervisors receive budget reports on their performance in a complicated format with an analysis that is incomprehensible to them. Supervisors felt that the job of budget people was to be critical and that the use of jargon and specialized formats enabled them to justify their criticism of others without too much debate.

Whether or not these criticisms are logical and rational is not important. The point is that such feelings can and do exist. If the budget is regarded as merely emphasizing history, being too rigid, unrealistic, unattainable, and unclear and if budget people are seen as overconcerned with figures, unconcerned with line problems, and cut off by a language of their own, there can be no doubt that the effectiveness of a budget system would deteriorate.

The problems are compounded if the budget personnel's attitude is unconducive to overcoming these opinions. Budget people should see their jobs as examining, analyzing, and looking for new ways to improve plant efficiency. They should also think of a budget as an objective that should fairly challenge factory personnel. Since it cannot be assumed that line personnel subscribe to or even recognize these ideas, the ideas should be impressed upon them directly through adequate budget introduction and education. Moreover, the effective use of budgets cannot be forced on supervisors and foremen; it must be accepted by them. This can only be accomplished if budget people try to work constructively with line people as compatriots rather than commanders. This accord is usually very difficult to bring about. Often budget people will not even attempt it or simply give up on it because of lack of success. They conclude, correctly or incorrectly, that the line personnel's unsatisfactory use of budgets is due to their lack of education, understanding, and interest.

Given this unwillingness to buck line opposition by the budget personnel and the line's viewpoint of budgeting as a hindrance to their performance, a classic role conflict is created. The optimal benefits possible from budgeting cannot be obtained in such an environment.

Argyris also determined how foremen and supervisors felt the potential dysfunctional results of budgeting could be overcome. Suggestions dealt mainly with improving the outlook of budget men. According to the line personnel, budgeting people should be taught that budgets are merely opinions, not the "be-all and end-all." They should also be taught, it was felt, that line employees are not inherently lazy, that budget men should learn to look at a problem from another's point of view, and that they are not superior to supervisory people. Also suggested were the use of timely and understandable reports to foremen and supervisors, the practice of conferring with people who have variances so that the budget report indicates the real cause to top management, and the setting of realistic budgets.

The problems arising are not, however, entirely the fault of the budget staff. Supervisors and foremen must put more effort into understanding the budget figures, they must not be continually suspicious of budgets, and they should use budgets in performing their duties. Most important, they should alter their outlook toward budgeting. Budgets must be realistic and fair, but also foremen and supervisors should realize that the budget is designed to help them achieve the standards management expects of them.

How can these requirements be achieved? An educational program involving foremen, supervisors, middle and upper management, and budget personnel could help to clarify the different viewpoints and promote understanding of each other's objectives and difficulties. Such a program should precede the introduction of a budgeting system and continue after the system has been introduced.

Budgets and Nonmanagement People

The involvement of laborers (nonmanagement personnel) in the budgeting process presents both functional and dysfunctional possibilities. Often, front-line supervisors who have a budget to meet do not use it as a device to spur their subordinates. According to the comments reported by Argyris, they fear that workers would look upon such action unfavorably and that no benefit would be received.

The proposition that workers would not respond to budgetary pressures is challenged by W. F. Whyte:

How do workers see budgets? They often recognize that management people are worried about costs, but with the foremen afraid to put the cost situation to them, they remain uninvolved in the struggle [7].

Since workers generally have not been directly involved in budgetary systems, the question of whether or not such involvement would be functional is unresolved.

Motivational Aspects of Budgeting

The most controversial area of budgeting concerns its motivational implications.

The budget makes available information for comparison of expected with actual performance. When such an evaluation of performance is known to result in rewards and punishments, people are expected to be motivated to do their best. Let us examine this assumption and its possible functional or dysfunctional consequences.

Argyris states that budgets are principal instruments for creating pressure which motivates individuals [8]. Budgets can also be seen as creating more pressure than they actually do. This pressure illusion is due to the fact that the budget is a concrete, quantitative instrument and managers and supervisors, feeling pressure from more abstract sources, place the blame for it on the concrete budget.

Factors directly related to budget pressure are budget "pep" talks (A), red circles around poor showings (B), production and sales derives using budgets (C), threats of reprimand (D), and feelings of failure if budgets are not met (E). These can all be considered as functional and manifest in terms of their motivational intent.

There are, however, counteracting effects which can be dysfunctional and latent in terms of budget effectiveness. These factors include informal agreements among managers and/

or supervisors (V), fear of loss of job if efficiency increases but cannot be maintained (W), union agreements against speed-ups (X), performance abilities of individual employees (Y), and abilities of work teams as a whole (Z).

Equilibrium is attained when:

$$A + B + C + D + E = V + W + X + Y + Z$$

Management, by increasing one or more of the components on the left-hand side of the relationship or by adding additional ones, can increase productivity. This increase is matched by an increase in tension, uneasiness, resentment, and suspicion on the part of the employees. This pressure increase is absorbed by joining groups which are strongly cohesive against top management and budget people. Again equilibrium is attained but each time pressures are increased by top management, they must become more intense as resistance is higher.

When and if management feels that the pressures are detrimental to the organization, it may attempt to reduce the causes on the left-hand side of the equation. This does not result in decreased antimanagement feeling because the groups have developed into relatively permanent social units and the individuals feel the pressures may occur again. Therefore, in the long run, increasing pressures may be very dysfunctional because of these latent features.

The rational way for management to approach this problem would be to concentrate its activities on reducing the forces that decrease efficiency rather than on increasing the factors that tend to increase efficiency.

Other dysfunctional ways of relieving motivational pressure could easily exist:

1. Interdepartmental strife could occur. A manager, supervisor, of foreman could try to blame the variances on someone else. This would result in concentrated effort by individuals to promote only the cause of their own departments. The personal rivalries thus caused and the lack of cooperation among departments could mean decreased efficiency for the company in achieving its overall goals.

2. Another type of strife develops when the line employees blame the staff employees for their predicaments and absolve themselves of the responsibility for the variances. Budget people become scapegoats for problems and salesmen are blamed for incorrect predictions of orders that make the production process unstable.

3. An individual may internalize the personal pressure he feels. By not outwardly showing his problems, he would build up tension within himself. Eventually, frustration would develop and he would perform less efficiently in the long run.

4. If internal means of relieving pressure are used, manipulation of activities may result. Reporting sizable variances when one knows he will be over his budget may allow him to shift his costs so that he will easily make his budget in the next period. Saving easy jobs until just before the end of a budget period may enable a person to achieve the stipulated goal.

The point is that in the short run increasing motivational pressure through budgets may be functional, but in the long run it may also be very dysfunctional.

Andrew C. Stedry postulates additional concepts concerning motivation through budgeting [9]. Through experiment, Stedry developed the findings shown in Figure 1.

The level of costs for which a person will strive (aspired costs) will be conceived by the individual in relation to past experience, confidence in personal skills, expectation of future difficulties, and feelings about the budget costs. Aspired and budget costs do not

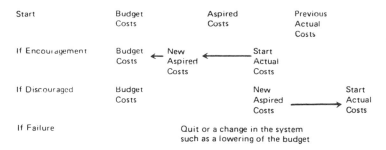

Figure 1   Simplified model of Stedry's motivational relationships involving aspirations.

necessarily (or usually) coincide. The aspired costs are what the individual sets for himself. The budget costs are set by top management. When actual costs are compared to these two costs, the reaction of the employees depends on the discrepancies involved:

1.   Other things being equal, aspiration levels will move relative to the actual costs depending on the degree of discrepancy.
2.   A person will be encouraged if the discrepancy between actual costs and aspired costs is not greater than an amount known as the discouragement point. Aspirations would be set higher on the next period of performance measurement.
3.   A person will be discouraged if the discrepancy is greater than the discouragement point but less than a failure point. In this case, aspirations would move downward.
4.   If the discrepancy is greater than the failure point, the system would cease to exist or a new one would be needed. Otherwise the individual concerned would resign.

Stedry concludes that management should set high, unattainable budgets to motivate individuals to achieve the greatest efficiency. "Unattainable" would have to mean that the discrepancy between aspired costs, formulated after the high budget was presented, and actual costs could not exceed the discouragement point. Such a policy would mean that individuals receiving separate budgets would be manipulated in accordance with the variances in the size of their discouragement points.

This may sound all right in theory but in practice the reactions of employees could make this a dangerous proposition for long-run efficiency. If individuals found out that they were the subjects of outright manipulation, they could become rebellious and ignore future budgets whether they were fair or not. Other management control devices would probably be considered with unwarranted suspicion. Moreover, how is management going to determine the aspiration level and discouragement point of each individual, a necessary requirement for setting "personal" budgets? The use of individual budget standards would also have to be kept confidential. Otherwise, the resentment that employees would feel might lead them to resist all budgeting attempts and even to leave the organization.

Stedry's study suggests that participation in budget preparation is not as beneficial as having management set the budget. He points out, however, that participation may be desirable where low budgets are given as managers, supervisors, and foremen would likely feel that they are capable of achieving greater efficiency and would say so.

Stedry's study is limited in that long-run results were not extensively examined. Also, the nature of his "laboratory" data leads to serious questions as to whether real business world conditions were reproduced [10]. However, his research on the reactions of lower level management to budgets does help to explain the behavior of these people. The study also indicates how management can improve a budgeting process where budgets are being ignored or causing personnel problems because it shows why such situations exist.

Another consequence of budgetary motivation which has received little emphasis involves "a fear of failure" on the part of the individual. The failure to meet a budget or at least come close to it when it is accepted and fairly determined and when other members of a person's reference group are successful represents a potential loss of status within both the group and the organization. A person's self-concept is also deflated in such circumstances.

The fear of such a loss may be a stronger motivating factor for a person to achieve his budget than any of the other pressures mentioned. Fear of failure, then, is a very powerful functional consequence of budgeting systems and, quite likely, is latent.

One of the major benefits of budgeting is motivation, explicitly incorporated in the use of standards. Budgets should reflect a goal which people can strive for and achieve. To provide maximum motivation for employees, management should judge failure to achieve an objective in the context of the situation causing failure and not merely in terms of a figure circled in red. All members of the organization must be aware of this basic principle.

Participation in Budgeting

In a participatory system of budgeting, preparation of budget schedules would start at the lower levels of the hierarchy and move upward. As it moved upward, various people would make additional suggestions and some eliminations until the schedules reached the controller and top management. These people would analyze it and see that it was a coordinated plan in accordance with organizational goals before final approval would be given. Movement up and down the hierarchy could be made if drastic changes were necessary. By reciprocal communications, people would know why changes were justified and could constructively criticize them if they desired.

Behavioral scientists and accountants generally believe that such a system would be an improvement on imposed budgets. The functional, manifest results claimed for this system are:

1. It would have a healthful effect on interest, initiative, morale, and enthusiasm.
2. It would result in a better plan because the knowledge of many individuals is combined.
3. It would make all levels of management more aware of how their particular functions fit into the total operational picture.
4. It would increase interdepartmental cooperation.
5. As a result of their direct involvement in the planning function, it would make junior management more aware of the future with respect to objectives, problems, and other considerations.

It is possible to achieve these benefits through successful participation. There are, however, factors that have a significant impact on whether or not participation can lead to successful results.

One essential requirement is that participation be legitimate. If participation is allowed but top management continually changes the budgeted figures resulting from participation, legitimate participation does not exist. This might better be described as a form of "pseudoparticipation." The supposed "participants" would likely resent such a policy and the consequences would be dysfunctional. This is borne out by the studies of V. H. Vroom, who found that productivity was higher when participation was viewed as legitimate, but lower when it was viewed as not legitimate [11].

Other factors limiting the usefulness of budget participation are:

1. Personality differences of managers as reflected in their leadership style are important. Aggressive managers can put forth their demands more strongly than meek ones. Subordinates would view the latter as not looking out for their interests and antagonism between subordinates and their superior, and managers themselves, could easily develop.

2. An autocratic, centralized organization would have little use for a participation policy, whereas a democratic, decentralized organization would likely benefit from, and almost require, a participation policy.

3. Those allowed participation rights must be positively oriented toward the objectives of the firm. Only if the group is cohesive in thought and desire toward, and understands, the plan can participation policy be functional.

4. The cultural setting of an organization and the background of employees should be considered. People in rural areas or with a rural background are more inclined to accept assigned tasks. In such an atmosphere, a participation policy would probably meet with little response.

Studies have been carried out showing that participation in any situation is not necessarily useful for increasing efficiency [12]. Other studies have reported that when a nonparticipative group became participative and was compared with an existing nonparticipative or participative group, the former never caught up in terms of performance with the latter two groups. These studies imply that the introduction of a participation policy for a formerly nonparticipative group would not likely lead to increased efficiency and may even result in decreased efficiency. If this conclusion is accepted, a group should be endowed with the right to participate only when the group is created or the budget system is being implemented and not after either has previously been directed through decisions made by superiors.

The most severe criticism offered against participation is that the increased morale which supposedly results does not necessarily result in increased efficiency. Is high morale a cause of increased efficiency or is greater efficiency a cause of high morale, or is there some intervening variable which must be present if a true causal relationship is to exist? Group cohesiveness seems to be the most significant of possible variables that have been examined although other variables are obviously involved. Figure 2 shows postulated relationships that could develop using group cohesiveness with regard to subordinate thoughts toward management.

As those participating in a budget (foremen and up) would be management-oriented, at least to some extent, they would probably have a positive approach to management activities and objectives. The previous discussion on role conflict situations shows, however, that negative attitudes toward budgeting are quite possible.

If the group is antimanagement or antibudget, a participation policy would be of little use. Supervisors may even propose ridiculously low standards and upper management would be forced to revise them. Pseudoparticipation would exist and likely result in the increase of negative attitudes toward management or budgeting.

If the atmosphere is favorable for allowing participation, group cohesiveness toward management and budgeting should be maintained and enhanced if possible. Group discussions led by an able management person to inform *and* listen to supervisors, foremen, and

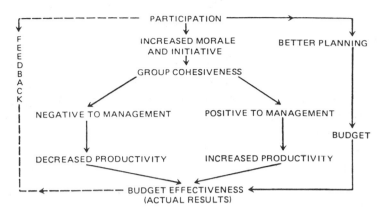

Figure 2 Participation and budgets.

other management people could probably aid in implementing the budget. By listening to and taking action on suggestions made by the group, he would be able to indicate his and top management's sincerity in gaining successful participation in the budgeting system.

Undoubtedly, the evidence on the effectiveness of participation in budgeting is mixed. Supporters of participation readily admit that it is by no means a panacea for achieving the full motivational potential of the budget. The fact is that participation is not a segregated aspect of management but embraces several technical and behavioral concepts which make it more or less useful in different organizations. The organization's particular situation with regard to the development of these concepts must be recognized and thoughtfully considered when contemplating or evaluating a participation policy.

It should be noted that even if productivity does not increase directly through participation, better planning and increased morale and initiative may of themselves justify such a policy.

Communication Aspects of Budgeting

Researchers on control and motivation generally agree that information on planned and actual results should be communicated to the employee whose performance is being measured.

Nevertheless, many budget departments merely communicate the results to management with the result that the employee does not know how he has done until he is called up to discuss his performance report. Consequently, the individual may ignore the budget and perform without a guide, hoping for the best.

When results are communicated as rapidly as possible, an employee's mistakes can be associated with his recent actions and he is likely to learn more from the experience than if reports are received long after the action has been taken. This learning would likely result in improved performance on future budgets.

When reports given to management employees are timely, reasonably accurate, and understandable, functional consequences are more likely to occur than if the opposite exists. Figure 3 summarizes the effect of the communication system on the behavior of line people.

Employee Group Behavior and Its Effects on Budgeting

Peter Blau's study on the use of statistical measures in evaluating employee performance has implications for evaluating and understanding budgeting [13]. The study examined the

Figure 3 The importance of the communication factor when using budgets to control and motivate employees.

effect of group cohesiveness, in the sense of willingness to cooperate among members, and the resulting productivity in different situations.

His findings showed that the group which cooperated was more productive than the group which did not cooperate but competed individually among themselves. He also discovered that highly competitive individuals in the latter group were more productive than any individual in the cooperative group. Blau's hypothesis was that a paradox existed: "The resulting paradox is that competitiveness and productivity are inversely related for groups but directly related for individuals in the competitive group" [14].

In terms of the achievement of organizational objectives, the implication is that cooperative cohesiveness among group members assigned a particular task is most desirable. When this is achieved, cooperation will result in each member helping others in the group, even though it may result in a decrease in the performance record of the assisting individual

Applying this to budgeting, the suggestion is that individual performance should not be the ultimate objective in the eyes of top management or employees. Rewards and punishments should not be based entirely on an individual's performance as compared to the plan. The budget reports should be only one of many factors used for evaluation and superiors should recognize this fact. The result would be a decline in individual competition and greater cooperation toward the achievement of a goal. This environment could eliminate possible dysfunctional consequences. Group cohesiveness will be greatly affected by the leadership style of the group's superior. Whether he believes in rigidity or flexibility, whether he is authoritative or democratic, and the freedom granted him by the organizational structure and policies, will influence the way he controls his subordinates.

Mechanical Consideration of Budgeting

Dysfunctional consequences can arise from the mechanical aspects of budgeting.

Budgeting systems cost money to install and continue. These costs must always be considered when evaluating the worthiness of a system.

It must also be remembered that budgets are merely estimates or predictions. As such, they could be incorrect or inappropriate because of economic, technical, and environmental changes. The estimating procedure itself may be inappropriate. If budgets are thought of as a goal rather than a means of reaching the goal, the emphasis on budgets cannot help but carry dysfunctional consequences, particularly when the estimates have been incorrectly computed.

A final mechanical problem involves the assignment of costs to the person deemed responsible for them. There is always a strong possibility that costs assigned to one person may have been caused by another. The subsequent bickering and ill-feeling would obviously be dysfunctional.

Budgets must be capable of flexibility. This is fundamentally the result of management attitudes and not inherent in the budget itself. Management must recognize that forced adherence to a plan could cause decisions to be made that are not in the long-run interest of the business. Unforeseen opportunities may arise which were not planned. A decision resulting in a significant, unfavorable variance on the short-range plan may be the best alternative in terms of long-range profitability. Failure to take advantage of such situations may result in adherence to the budget but also in dysfunctional consequences in terms of achieving the objectives of budgeting.

Alternatively, failure to adhere to budget figures when they are correct, merely to protect the individuals involved or their superiors, must also be avoided. Such an attitude would destroy one of the cornerstones of a successful budgeting system.

GENERAL MODEL OF THE CONSEQUENCES OF A BUDGETING SYSTEM

Figure 4 summarizes the factors which must be considered when determining the functional and dysfunctional consequences possible from a budgeting system.

The square immediately outside the budget square indicates the potential benefits to be derived from a successful budgeting system. These benefits are functional to the more efficient achievement of an organization's goal of making profit. The next surrounding square indicates many of the factors which can aid or prevent the achievement of the desired benefits. The descriptive model is arranged so that the effects of various environmental circumstances and managerial policies (participation, motivational intentions, organization structure, etc.) can be immediately related to a particular benefit (planning). The square at the top of the diagram includes factors which are not specifically related to any one particular benefit but which have an important influence on the success or failure of the overall budget system.

The points mentioned in the peripheral square and the top square cannot be clearly identified as either functional or dysfunctional. The relationship of these points to the benefits of budgeting depends on the particular circumstances.

CONCLUSION

The model which has been developed to point out the functional possibilities of budgeting and to identify the sources of possible dysfunctional consequences represents a summary of relevant findings and statements by behavioral scientists, accountants, and managers.

Budgeting is only one type of control technique used by top management. Many of the propositions developed are equally applicable to other types of quantitatively oriented control techniques.

The points developed in this chapter should be considered by any organization using or contemplating the introduction of a budgeting process. The importance of each point will vary, however, according to the particular organization, its strategy, history, organizational structure, reasons for using the system, the personalities involved, the leadership style of individuals in responsible positions, the general attitudes of employees toward the organization and control devices, the cohesiveness of reference groups working on and with the budget, and the personal attitudes of employees regarding the justification of, and methods of achieving, organizational goals.

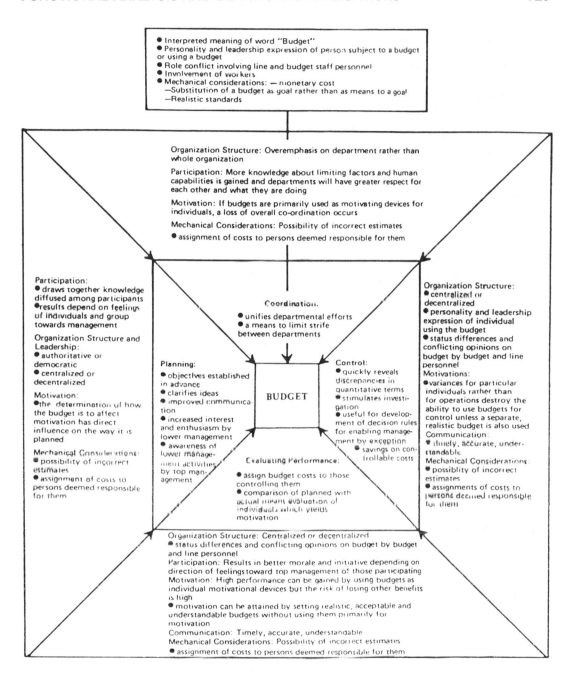

Figure 4 General model of the factors to consider when determining the functional and dysfunctional aspects of introducing and using a budgeting system.

The major proposition suggested is that a budgeting system designed to accomplish the designated benefits is something more than a series of figures. Its organization, implementation, and degree of success are significantly related to the behaviorally oriented problems that can easily arise. Management methods for solving these problems cannot be generalized into a specific set of rules. Definite rules can seldom cover the particular developments of unique situations. Therefore, only general aspects of budgeting systems with emphasis on behavioral topics have been considered.

The only absolute conclusion that can be proposed is that the human factors involved are generally more difficult to identify and deal with and more serious in nature than the development of quantifying and figure determination techniques. Accountants and managers must recognize this fact if they expect to perform their functions adequately.

NOTES AND REFERENCES

1. R. Merton, A paradigm for functional analysis in sociology, *Sociological Theory: A Book of Readings* (L. Coser and B. Rosenberg, eds.), Macmillan, New York, pp. 458–467 (1957).
2. A. Etzioni, Two approaches to organizational analysis: A critique and a suggestion, Bobbs-Merrill Reprint Series in the Social Sciences 8-80. Reprinted by permission of *Administrative Science Quarterly*, 5:257–278 (1960).
3. Etzioni, p. 272.
4. D. Green, Jr., Budgeting and accounting: The inseparable Siamese twins, *Budgeting*, Nov.:11 (1965).
5. Chris Argyris, *The Impact of Budgets on People*, Ithaca, N.Y., p. 23. Prepared for the Controllership Foundation at Cornell University (1952).
6. The source of this figure and study is Argyris, *The Impact of Budgets on People*, a summary of comments and statements, pp. 10–12.
7. W. F. Whyte, *Men at Work*, Irwin and Dorsey Press, Homewood, Ill., p. 495 (1961).
8. Argyris, *The Impact of Budgets on People*.
9. A. C. Stedry, *Budget Control and Cost Behavior*, Prentice-Hall, Englewood Cliffs, N.J. (1960).
10. S. Becker and D. Green, Jr., Budgeting and employee behavior, *J. Business*, 35 (1962). These are among the authors who debate the practical application of Stedry's conclusions.
11. A. C. Stedry, Budgeting and employee behavior: A reply, *J. Business*, 37:198 (1964).
12. Stedry, p. 196; also. N. Morse and E. Reimer, The experimental change of a major organizational variable, *J. Abnormal Soc. Psychol.*, 52:120–129 (1956); and J. R. P. French, Jr., E. Kay, and H. H. Meyer, *A Study of Threat and Participation in a Performance Appraisal Situation*, General Electric Co., New York (1962).
13. P. M. Blau, Cooperation and competition in a bureaucracy, Bobbs-Merrill Reprint Series in the Social Sciences, S-28. Reprinted by the permission of the *American Journal of Sociology*, 59 (1964).
14. Blau, p. 530.

39

Behavioral Assumptions of Management Accounting

Edwin H. Caplan

Accounting has been closely associated with the development of the modern business organization. Thus, we might expect accountants to show a strong interest in recent contributions to organization theory which increase our understanding of the business firm and how it functions. An examination of accounting literature, however, suggests that (despite the steadily increasing flow of accounting articles and texts incorporating the words "management" and "decisions" in their titles) accountants have been relatively unconcerned with current research in organization theory. Although the past few years have witnessed the beginnings of an effort to bridge this gap, much still remains to be done [1]. This chapter attempts to demonstrate that an understanding of behavioral theory is relevant to the development of management accounting theory and practice.

The discussion to be presented here may be summarized as follows:

1. The management accounting function is essentially a behavioral function and the nature and scope of management accounting systems are materially influenced by the view of human behavior which is held by the accountants who design and operate these systems.
2. It is possible to identify a "traditional" management accounting model of the firm and to associate with this model certain fundamental assumptions about human behavior. These assumptions are presented in Table 1.
3. It is also possible to postulate behavioral assumptions based on modern organization theory and to relate them to the objectives of management accounting. A tentative set of such assumptions appears in Table 2.
4. Research directed at testing the nature and validity of accounting assumptions with respect to human behavior in business organizations can be useful in evaluating and perhaps improving the effectiveness of management accounting systems.

Source: *The Accounting Review*, *41*(3): 496–509 (1966). References have been renumbered.

Table 1 Behavioral Assumptions of "Traditional" Management Accounting Model of the Firm

Assumptions with Respect to Organization Goals
A. The principal objective of business activity is profit maximization (economic theory).
B. This principal objective can be segmented into subgoals to be distributed throughout the organization (principles of management).
C. Goals are additive—what is good for the parts of the business is also good for the whole (principles of management).

Assumptions with Respect to the Behavior of Participants
A. Organization participants are motivated primarily by economic forces (economic theory)
B. Work is essentially an unpleasant task which people will avoid whenever possible (economic theory).
C. Human beings are ordinarily inefficient and wasteful (scientific management).

Assumptions with Respect to the Behavior of Management
A. The role of the business manager is to maximize the profits of the firm (economic theory).
B. In order to perform this role, management must control the tendencies of employees to be lazy, wasteful, and inefficient (scientific management).
C. The essence of management control is authority. The ultimate authority of management stems from its ability to affect the economic reward structure (scientific management).
D. There must be a balance between the authority a person has and his responsibility for performance (principles of management).

Assumptions with Respect to the Role of Management Accounting
A. The primary function of management accounting is to aid management in the process of profit maximization (scientific management).
B. The accounting system is a "goal allocation" device which permits management to select its operating objectives and to divide and distribute them throughout the firm, i.e., assign responsibilities for performance. This is commonly referred to as "planning" (principles of management).
C. The accounting system is a control device which permits management to identify and correct undesirable performance (scientific management).
D. There is sufficient certainty, rationality, and knowledge within the system to permit an accurate comparison of responsibility for performance and the ultimate benefits and costs of that performance (principles of management).
E. The accounting system is "neutral" in its evaluations—personal bias is eliminated by the objectivity of the system (principles of management).

MANAGEMENT ACCOUNTING AS A BEHAVIORAL PROCESS

The management of a business enterprise is faced with an environment—both internal and external to the firm—that is in a perpetual state of change. Not only is this environment constantly changing, but it is changing in many dimensions. These include physical changes (climate, availability of raw materials, etc.), technological changes (new products and processes, etc.), social changes (attitudes of employees, customers, competitors, etc.), and financial changes (asset composition, availability of funds, etc.).

An important characteristic of "good" management is the ability to evaluate past changes, to react to current changes, and to predict future changes. This is consistent with the view that management is essentially a decision-making process and the view that accounting is an information system which acts as an integral part of this decision-making process. It is inconceivable, however, that any workable information system could provide data relative to all, or even a substantial portion, of the changes occurring inside and outside of the organization. There are several reasons for this. Many changes—particularly those

Table 2 Some Behavioral Assumptions from Modern Organization Theory

Assumptions with Respect to Organization Goals

A. Organizations are coalitions of individual participants. Strictly speaking, the organization itself, which is "mindless," cannot have goals—only the individuals can have goals.

B. Those objectives which are usually viewed as organizational goals are, in fact, the objectives of the dominant members of the coalition, subject to whatever constraints are imposed by the other participants and by the external environment of the organization.

C. Organization objectives tend to change in response to (1) changes in the goals of the dominant participants, (2) changes in the relationships within the coalition, and (3) changes in the external environment of the organization.

D. In the modern complex business enterprise, there is no single universal organization goal such as profit maximization. To the extent that any truly overall objective might be identified, that objective is probably organization survival.

E. Facing a highly complex and uncertain world and equipped with only limited rationality, members of an organization tend to focus on "local" (i.e., individual and departmental) goals. These local goals are often in conflict with each other. In addition, there appears to be no valid basis for the assumption that they are homogeneous and thus additive—what is good for the parts of the organization is not necessarily good for the whole.

Assumptions with Respect to the Behavior of Participants

A. Human behavior within an orgaization is essentially an adaptive, problem-solving, decision-making process.

B. Organization participants are motivated by a wide variety of psychological, social, and economic needs and drives. The relative strength of these diverse needs differs between individuals and within the same individual over time.

C. The decision of an individual to join an organization, and the separate decision to contribute his productive efforts once a member, are based on the individual's perception of the extent to which such action will further the achievement of his personal goals.

D. The efficiency and effectiveness of human behavior and decision making within organizations is constrained by (1) the inability to concentrate on more than a few things at a time, (2) limited awareness of the environment, (3) limited knowledge of alternative courses of action and the consequences of such alternatives, (4) limited reasoning ability, and (5) incomplete and inconsistent preference systems. As a result of these limits on human rationality, individual and organizational behavior is usually directed at attempts to find satisfactory—rather than optional—solutions.

Assumptions with Respect to Behavior of Management

A. The primary role of the business manager is to maintain a favorable balance between (1) the contributions required from the participants and (2) in the inducement (i.e., perceived need satisfactions) which must be offered to secure these contributions.

B. The management role is essentially a decision-making process subject to the limitations on human rationality and cognitive ability. The manager must make decisions himself and must effectively influence the decision premises of others so that their decisions will be favorable for the organization.

C. The essence of management control is the willingness of other participants to *accept* the authority of management. This willingness appears to be a nonstable function of the inducement–contribution balance.

D. Responsibility is assigned from "above" and authority is accepted from "below." It is, therefore, meaningless to speak of the balance between responsibility and authority as if both of these were "given" to the manager.

Table 2 Continued

Assumptions with Respect to the Role of Accounting

A. The management accounting process is an information system whose major purposes are (1) to provide the various levels of management with data which will facilitate the decision-making functions of planning and control and (2) to serve as a communications medium within the organization.

B. The effective use of budgets and other accounting control techniques requires an understanding of the interaction between these techniques and the motivations and aspiration levels of the individuals to be controlled.

C. The objectivity of the management accounting process is largely a myth. Accountants have wide areas of discretion in the selection, processing, and reporting of data.

D. In performing their function within an organization, accountants can be expected to be influenced by their own personal and departmental goals in the same way other participants are influenced.

---

that occur in the external environment—are simply not available to the information system of the firm. These changes represent "external unknowns" in a world of uncertainty and limited knowledge. Further, a substantial number of changes that occur within the firm itself may not be perceived by the information system. Thus, there exist internal as well as external unknowns.

Even if accountants were aware of all the changes which are taking place—or if they could be made aware of them—they still would not be able to reflect them all within their information system. There must be a selection process, explicit or implicit, which permits the gathering and processing of only the most critical information and facilitates the screening out of all other data. In the first place, many items of information would cost more to gather and process than the value of the benefits they would provide. Also, an excessive flow of data would "clog" the system and prevent the timely and efficient passage and evaluation of more important information [2]. Therefore, only a certain, very limited, set of data (i.e., observations about changes) can be selected for admission into the system. The essential point to be noted here is that decisions regarding what information is the most critical, how it should be processed, and who should receive it are almost always made by accountants. In addition, they are often directly involved, as participants, in the management decision-making process itself.

In carrying out these activities, accountants utilize a frame of reference that is, in effect, their view of the nature of the firm and its participation. The operation of their system requires them to be constantly abstracting a selected flow of information from the complex real world and using this selected data as the variables in their "model" of the firm. It seems clear that accountants exercise choice in the design of their systems and the selection of data for admission into them. It also seems clear that the entire management accounting process can be viewed from the standpoint of attempting to influence the behavior of others. It follows, therefore, that they must perform these functions with certain expectations with respect to the reactions of others to what they do. In other words, their model of the firm must involve some set of explicit or implicit assumptions about human behavior in organizations.

THE "TRADITIONAL" VIEW OF BEHAVIOR

Once it has been demonstrated that the management accounting function does by necessity involve assumptions about behavior, the next task is to identify these assumptions. Our investigation is complicated by the fact that nowhere in the literature of accounting is there a formal statement of the behavioral assumptions of the management accounting model of the firm. It is necessary, therefore, to attempt to construct such a statement. We begin with the premise that present-day management accounting theory and practice are the product of three related conceptual forces, namely, industrial engineering technology, classical organization theory, and the economic "theory of the firm." An examination of the literature of management accounting suggests that accountants may have avoided the necessity of developing a behavioral model of their own by borrowing a set of assumptions from these other areas. If this thesis is valid, an appropriate point to begin the search for such assumptions is by an examination of the assumptions of these related models. Since much of the engineering view appears to be incorporated in the classical organization theory model [3], it can probably be eliminated from this analysis without significant loss. Further, it appears that classical organization theory and economics do not represent two completely different views of human behavior, but rather that they essentially share a single view.

The following paragraphs will attempt to demonstrate that—with the exception of the modern organization theory concepts of recent years—there has been a single view of human behavior in business organizations from the period of the industrial revolution to the present and that management accounting has adopted this view without significant modification or serious question as to its validity.

The Economic Theory of the Firm

It has been suggested that, from the beginnings of recorded history, the traditional determinant of human behavior in organization has been either custom or physical force [4]. As long as this was the case, there was no real need for an organization theory or economic theory to explain how and why human beings worked together cooperatively to accomplish common goals. However, the changing structure of society, which accompanied—and to an extent caused—the industrial revolution, destroyed much of the force of these traditional determinants of behavior. The new entrepreneurial class of the eighteenth century sought not only a social philosophy to rationalize its actions, it also sought practical solutions to the immediate problems of motivating, coordinating, and controlling the members of its organizations. The second of these needs resulted in the development of the classical organization theories which will be discussed in the following section. The first need, that is, the quest for a rationalization, ultimately led to the incorporation of the economic theory of the firm into the logic of the industrial society.

The economic theory of the firm can be summarized as follows. The entrepreneur is faced with a series of behavior alternatives. These alternatives are limited by the economic constraints of the market and the technological constraints of the production function. Within these constraints he will act in such a way as to maximize his economic profit. This behavior is facilitated by the personality characteristic of complete rationality and the information system characteristic of perfect knowledge. Finally, the individual so described is one who is entirely motivated by economic forces. A more subtle elaboration of this last point is the view that leisure has value and that a person will not work except in response to sufficient economic incentives. Thus, the classical economist specifically assumed that man was essentially "lazy" and preferred to minimize his work effort [5].

Most modern economists would agree that the classical theory of the firm is based on several rather severe abstractions from the real world of business enterprise [6]. Nevertheless, despite these criticisms, there can be little doubt that it has had a substantial influence on the development of management philosophy and practice. The explanation of human behavior offered by economists, that is, economic motivation and profit maximization, was incorporated into the patterns of thought of the merging industrial community, where it not only became established in its own right but also provided the philosophical and psychological foundations of the scientific management movement.

Classical Organization Theory

At the turn of the century, Frederick W. Taylor began a major investigation into the functioning of business organization which became known as the scientific management movement. Taylor's approach combined the basic behavioral assumptions of the economic theory of the firm with the viewpoint of the engineer seeking the most effective utilization of the physical resources at his disposal. He was concerned with people primarily as "adjuncts to machines" and was interested in maximizing the productivity of the worker through increased efficiency and reduced costs. Implicit in this approach was the belief that if men who might otherwise be wasteful and inefficient could be instructed in methods of achieving increased productivity and at the same time be provided with adequate economic incentives and proper working conditions, they could be motivated to adopt the improvements, and the organization would benefit accordingly [7].

March and Simon have noted that the ideas of the scientific management movement are based predominantly on a model of human behavior which assumes that "organization members, and particularly employees, are primarily *passive instruments*, capable of performing work and accepting directions, but not initiating action or exerting influence in any significant way [8].

The scientific management movement flourished and rapidly became an important part of the business enterprise scene; in fact, for many years it virtually dominated this scene. Furthermore, even a brief glance at current management literature and practices should satisfy the reader that most of Taylor's views are still widely accepted today. Newer theories of management may have supplemented but they have never entirely replaced the scientific management approach.

The work of Taylor and his scientific management successors led them into detailed studies of factory costs and provided an important stimulus for the development of modern cost and management accounting. Administrative management theory further contributed to this development through its emphasis on control and departmental responsibility and accountability. Finally, all of this occurred within the overall setting provided by the economic theory of the firm. In summary, it seems clear that with respect to both its philosophy and techniques, much of contemporary management accounting is a product of, and is geared to, these classical theories. This is what is referred to here as the traditional management accounting model of the firm.

A Tentative Statement of the Behavior Assumptions Underlying Present-Day Management Accounting

It should now be possible to draw together the several strands of the preceding discussion and attempt to postulate some of the fundamental behavioral assumptions that appear to underlie the traditional management accounting model. These assumptions were presented in Table 1. The parenthetical notations note the major conceptual sources of the assumptions. In some cases, there appears to be a considerable overlapping of sources; however, since this is not crucial to the present investigation, the notations have been limited to the primary or most significant area.

SOME BEHAVIORAL CONCEPTS OF MODERN ORGANIZATION THEORY

The preceding paragraphs were concerned with an effort to identify a set of behavioral assumptions which could be associated with current theory and practice in management accounting. We will now attempt to develop an alternative set of behavioral assumptions for management accounting—one that is based on concepts from modern organization theory.

Of the several different modern organization theory approaches, the "decision-making model" of the firm has been selected for use here. The basis for this choice is the close relationship which appears to exist between the decision-making model and the information system concept of management accounting discussed earlier. The decision-making approach to organization theory effectively began with the writings of Chester I. Barnard, particularly in *The Functions of the Executive*, and was further developed by Simon and others [9]. The model is primarily concerned with the organizational processes of communication and decision making. While drawing heavily on sociology and psychology, it is distinguished from these organization theory approaches by its emphasis on the decision as the basic element of organization.

Organizations are viewed as cooperative efforts or coalitions entered into by individuals in order to achieve personal objectives which cannot be realized without such cooperation. These individuals are motivated to join the organization and contribute to the accomplishment of its objectives because they believe that in this way they can satisfy their personal goals. It is important to note that these personal goals include social and psychological, as well as economic, considerations. Thus, the survival and success of the organization depends on the maintenance of a favorable balance between the contributions required of each participant and the opportunities to satisfy personal goals which must be offered as inducements to secure effective participation.

It is common practice to speak of organization goals; however, to be completely precise, it is the participants who have goals. The organization itself is mindless and therefore can have no goals. In the sense that it is used here, the term "organization goals" is intended to mean the goals of the dominant members of the coalition subject to those constraints which are imposed by other participants and by the external environment. This view implies an organizational goal structure which is in a constant state of change as the environment and the balances and relationships among the participants change. Under such circumstances, it seems meaningless to talk of a single universal goal such as profit maximization. To the extent that any long-run overall objective might be identified, it appears that this objective would have to be stated in very broad and general terms, such as the goal of organization survival.

The decision-making process is usually described as a sequence of three steps: (1) the evoking of alternative courses of action, (2) a consideration of the consequences of the evoked alternatives, and (3) the assignment of values to the various consequences [10].

It has been suggested that any behavioral theory of rational choice must consider certain limits on the decision maker [11]. These include his (1) limited knowledge with respect to all possible alternatives and consequences, (2) limited cognitive ability, (3) constantly changing value structure, and (4) tendency to "satisfice" rather than maximize. Rational behavior, therefore, consists of searching among limited alternatives for a reasonable solution under conditions in which the consequences of action are uncertain.

The behavioral concepts which flow from the decision-making model have a number of interesting implications. For example, authority is viewed as something which is accepted from "below" rather than imposed from "above" [12]; in other words, there must be a *decision to accept* authority before such authority can become effective. Further, human activity is considered to be essentially a process of problem-solving and adaptive behavior—a process in which goals, perception, and abilities are all interrelated and all continually changing.

To summarize the decision-making model, the basic element of organization study is the decision. The objective of managerial decision making is to secure and coordinate effectively the contributions of other participants. This is accomplished by influencing, to the extent possible, their perception of alternatives and consequences of choice and their value structures, so that the resulting decisions are consistent with the current objectives of the dominant members of the organization.

While the theorists of the decision-making school have paid substantial attention to behavioral concepts, the literature does not appear to contain a detailed and complete statement of their underlying behavioral assumptions. Accordingly, it becomes necessary, as it was with the traditional accounting model, to abstract and formulate a set of assumptions. The modern organization theory assumptions presented in Table 2 represent an attempt by the present writer to identify and extend the behavioral assumptions of the decision-making model in terms of the management accounting function.

BASIC CONFLICTS BETWEEN THE BEHAVIORAL ASSUMPTIONS OF TRADITIONAL MANAGEMENT ACCOUNTING AND MODERN ORGANIZATION THEORY

An examination of the two sets of behavioral assumptions developed above suggests a number of interesting questions. Answers to these questions. however, can only be found through extended empirical analysis. Thus, whatever value attaches to the foregoing discussion appears to relate to its possible contribution in providing a theoretical framework for future empirical research. This research might be designed to explore such questions as the following:

1. What behavioral model provides the most realistic view of human behavior in business organizations? (Accountants should, perhaps, be willing to accept the research findings of organization theorists regarding this question.)
2. Is it possible to draw any general conclusions about the view of behavior actually held by accountants (and managers) in practice?
3. What, if any, are the major differences in the behavioral assumptions of the views in 1 and 2 above?
4. What, if any, are the consequences for the organization and its participants of the differences in the behavioral assumptions of the views in 1 and 2?
5. Is it possible to design management accounting systems which are based on a more realistic view of behavior, and would such systems produce better results than present systems?

Lacking empirical evidence, any attempt to investigate the implications of the differences between the two views of behavior discussed in this chapter must be considered highly speculative. We might, however, examine briefly a few of the major differences in order to illustrate the nature of the problem. Let us assume for the moment that the decision-making model represents a more realistic view of human behavior than the traditional management accounting model. Let us further assume that the traditional model is a reasonably accurate summary of actual management accounting views in practice. Under these circumstances, what are some of the consequences for business organizations of the use of accounting systems based on the traditional management accounting model of behavior?

Assumptions with Respect to Organization Goals

In comparing these two sets of assumptions, the most immediately apparent difference concerns the relative simplicity and brevity of the traditional accounting assumptions as contrasted to those of the organization theory model. This should not be particularly surprising since such a difference seems to be consistent with the general philosophies of the two models. There can be little doubt that the view of human behavior associated with the scientific management movement and classical economics is much less complicated than the behavioral outlooks of modern organization theory. In fact, the principal conflict between modern and classical organization theories appears to rest precisely on this issue. Since traditional management accounting is closely related to the classical models, it seems reasonable to expect that it will also tend toward a relatively simple and uncomplicated view of behavior. For example, with respect to organization goals, the behavioral assumptions of the accounting model focus on a single universal objective of business activity. The organization theory assumptions, on the other hand, suggest a much broader and rather imprecise structure of goals.

The traditional management accounting view of organization goals, which appears to be directly related to the theory of the firm of classical economics, may be summarized as follows: The principal objective of business activity is the maximization of the economic profits of the enterprise; the total responsibility for the accomplishment of that objective can be divided into smaller portions and distributed to subunits throughout the organization; the maximization by each subunit of its particular portion of the profit responsibility will result in maximization of the total profits of the enterprise.

The entire structure of traditional management accounting appears to be built around this concept of profit maximization and the related (but quite different) idea of cost minimization. Management accountants have, for the most part, limited the scope of their systems to the selection, processing, and reporting of data concerning certain economic events, the effects of which can be reduced—without too many complications—to monetary terms. This approach is justifiable only if the particular class of events under consideration can be viewed as *the* critical variables affecting the organizations. Thus, accountants have been able to rationalize the importance of the data flowing through their systems by relating these data and their use directly to the assumed goal of profit maximization. However, the classical economic view of profits as the universal motivating force of business enterprises has come under substantial attack in recent years. This attack has been based on two general issues. First, questions have been raised concerning the adequacy of economic profits as the sole significant explanation for what takes place within an organization. Second, it has been suggested that limitations on the decision-making process result in behavior which is best described as satisficing rather than maximizing.

It should be particularly emphasized that the recognition of a more complex goal structure does not mean that economic profits can be ignored. Obviously, business firms cannot survive for any extended period of time without some minimum level of profits.

What is the practical implications of these observations? How would management accounting change if accountants did not concentrate exclusively on profit maximization?

The traditional accounting assumption with respect to the divisibility and additivity of the responsibility for the accomplishment of organization goals seems to warrant some additional comment. Research in organization theory has indicated that individual members of an organization tend to identify with their immediate group rather than with the organization itself. This tendency appears to encourage the development of strong subunit loyalties and a concentration on the goals of the subunit even when these goals are in conflict with the interests of the organization. The usual departmental budgeting and accounting techniques, by which management accountants endeavor to measure the success of the various subunits within an organization in achieving certain goals, are based on the assumption that profit maximization or cost minimization at the departmental level will lead to a similar result for the firm as a whole. Thus, accounting reports tend to highlight supposed departmental efficiencies and inefficiencies. Reports of this type seem to encourage departmental activities aimed at "making a good showing" regardless of the effect on the entire organization. It appears to be common for departments within an organization to be in a state of competition with each other for funds, recognition, authority, and so forth. Under such circumstances, it is not very likely that the cooperative efforts necessary to the efficient functioning of the organization as a whole will be furthered by an accounting system which emphasizes and, perhaps, even fosters interdepartmental conflicts.

The tendency for intraorganizational conflict appears to be further compounded by some of the common management accounting techniques for the allocation and control of costs. For example, in some organizations with relatively rigid budgeting procedures, it appears to be a normal practice for departments to deliberately attempt to use up their entire budget for a given period in order to avoid a reduction in the budgets of succeeding periods. Another example is the emphasis often placed on the desirability of keeping costs below some predetermined amount. In such cases, it is likely that, even though a departmental expenditure would be extremely beneficial to an organization, it will not be undertaken if such action would cause the costs of that department to exceed the predetermined limit.

CONCLUSIONS

This chapter has attempted to postulate a set of behavioral assumptions which could be associated with the theory and practice of "traditional" management accounting. The resulting set of 15 assumptions represents an accounting adaptation of what might be termed the classical view of human behavior in business organizations. This view emphasizes such concepts as profit maximization, economic incentives, and the inherent laziness and inefficiency of organization participants. It is a model which is structured primarily in terms of the classical ideas of departmentalization, authority, responsibility, and control. The accounting process which has emerged in response to the needs presented by this classical model appears to treat human behavior and goals essentially as given. Further, the generally accepted measure of "good" accounting seems to be one of relevance and usefulness in the maximization of the money profits of the enterprise.

In addition, we have examined a set of behavioral assumptions based on research in modern organization theory. It seems clear that a management accounting system structured around this second set of behavioral assumptions would differ in many respects from the accounting systems found in practice and described in the literature.

One should not infer that the traditional assumptions considered here are completely invalid. The very fact that they have endured for so long suggests that this is not the case. It should at least be recognized, however, that in many respects the extent of their validity may be subject to question. Also, it is not argued that all accountants limit themselves at all times to this traditional view. Rather, the two sets of behavioral assumptions discussed might be considered as extreme points on a scale of many possible views. The significance of the traditional point on such a scale appears to be twofold: (1) It is likely that the traditional model represents a view of behavior which is relatively common in practice, and (2) this view seems to underlie much of what is written and taught about accounting.

If the modern organization theory model does ultimately prove to be a more realistic view of human behavior in business organizations, there is little doubt that the scope of management accounting theory and practice will need to be expanded and broadened. In particular, accountants will have to develop an increased awareness and understanding of the complex social and psychological motivations and limitations of organization participants. What is urgently needed, and what we have had very little of in the past, is solid empirical research designed to measure the effectiveness with which management accounting systems do, in fact, perform their functions of motivating, explaining, and predicting human behavior.

NOTES AND REFERENCES

1. See, for example, R. T. Golembiewski, "Accountancy as a Function of Organization Theory," *Accounting Rev.*, April: 333–341; and J. J. Willingham, "The Accounting Entity: A Conceptual Model," *Accounting Rev.*, July: 543–552 (1964).

2. See also the "capacity problem" discussed by Anton. See H. R. Anton, *Some Aspects of Measurement and Accounting*, Working Paper No. 84, Berkeley, Calif., Center for Research in Management Science, University of California (1963).

3. One of the earliest, and perhaps the best, example of this consolidation can be found in the work of Taylor. See F. W. Taylor, *Scientific Management*, Harper & Brothers, New York (1911).

4. R. L. Heilbroner, *The Worldly Philosophers*, rev. ed., Simon and Schuster, New York, pp. 7–8 (1961).

5. This assumption is the basis for the "backward bending" labor supply curve found in the literature of economics.

6. See, for example, A. G. Papandreou, "Some Basic Problems in the Theory of the Firm," *A Survey of Contemporary Economics*, Vol. 2 (B. F. Haley, ed Irwin, Homewood, Ill., pp. 183–219 (1952).

7   J. G. March and H. A. Simon, *Organizations*, Wiley, New York, pp. 12ff. (1958).

8. March and Simon, *Organizations*, p. 6.

9. C. I. Barnard, *The Function of the Executive*, Harvard University Press, Cambridge, Mass. (1938); H. A. Simon, *Administrative Behavior*, Wiley, New York (1947); J. G. March and H. A. Simon, *Organizations*; and R. M. Cyert and J. G. March, *A Behavioral Theory of the Firm*, Prentice Hall, Englewood Cliffs, N.J. (1963). The preceding works represent the principal theoretical sources for the decision-making model discussed here.

10. March and Simon, *Organizations*, p. 82.

11. Simon, *Administrative Behavior*, pp. xxv–xxvi.

12. D. McGregor, *The Human Side of Enterprise*, McGraw-Hill, New York, pp. 158–160 (1960).

VIII
ORGANIZATIONAL CONTEXTS OF BUDGETING AND FINANCE

EDITORIAL INTRODUCTION

PBF activities are at the heart of any collective enterprise, and the influence is mutual. Let us put the essential point directly, if perhaps too simply. The style and efficiency with which PBF activities are carried out will have clear impacts on the host organization. At the same time, the properties of organizations will influence—and at times even determine—how PBF activities are performed.

Unit VIII focuses on the latter point, and with ample justification since the point often gets neglected. Units VI and VII set the table for the focus here, as it were. In contrast, much literature focuses on the impact of PBF activities on how organizations function. Indeed, much of that literature complains about that impact. Unit VIII seeks to establish a bit better balance.

Accountancy and Organization Theory

The basic proposition in Chapter 40 has three components but is nonetheless direct: accountancy developed in the context of a long-dominant model for organizing work, usually called the bureaucratic model; massive forces are encouraging modifications of that model for organizing work, and even root-and-branch replacements for it; and, consequently, accountancy must change in order to serve that emerging model, no matter how formidable the resistances to change.

Robert T. Golembiewski's "Accountancy as a Function of Organization Theory" simplifies the situation in the service of analysis, contrasting a single alternative model with the bureaucratic structure. The alternative model seeks to permit the more human use of human beings, and in that basic sense encourages the building into PBF activities of those behavioral features especially emphasized in the previous two units.

Chapter 40 has two major attractions, despite its focus on only two structural forms. First, the alternative model is consistent with a wide range of research that permits substantial confidence in its usefulness. Recent summaries of that evidence are available [1]. In addition, the alternative model increases the probability that PBF activities can succeed as operating officials succeed, as opposed to encouraging the former to try to catch the latter doing something wrong. Earlier units provide chapter and verse concerning how PBF activities, as reinforced by the traditional model of work, can fall into that self-defeating rut.

A Retrospective Look, After a Quarter Century

It pays to look back, if only to check on whether earlier positions are still serviceable. And that is what Chapter 41 does concerning Chapter 40. The overall judgment: The position in Chapter 40 still holds, far more than less. That is the substance of Robert T. Golem-biewski's "Progress, Persisting Trends, and Future Challenges: Accountancy as a Function of Organization Theory."

This retrospective does not propose that little has happened during the past two or three decades. So what does the summary just given intend, more specifically? Things have changed in some regards relevant to the preceding selection, but much remains as it was, or has gotten worse. In addition, the tensions surrounding the poor fit of emerging structural models with traditional PPF assumptions, policies, and practices seem to be growing, and rapidly. So the ante has been raised, even sharply. In that sense, one crucial matter *has* changed in connection with the basic organization structure in which PBF activities will be imbedded in the future that is cascading down on us: More than ever, we need to get moving on adapting PBF to postbureaucractic structures, policies, and procedures.

Structures for Implementing Programs

Richard F. Elmore nicely extends the illustrative but limited analysis in the two preceding selections. His "Organization Models of Social Program Implementation" builds on the view that different structural models can be observed in different organizations, despite the dominance of the bureaucratic model. Elmore selects four types for detailed description:

- A *systems management model*, which represents the mainstream view of policy analysis.
- A *bureaucratic process model*, which is common in most organizations.
- An *organizational development model*, which assumes the possibility of a substantial commonality of interests reflected in a substantial congruence of individual needs and organization demands.
- A *conflict-and-bargaining model*, which focuses on how individuals "with divergent interests coalesce around a common task."

Elmore's work does not draw specific implications for PBF, but his basic point seems clear enough. Traditional PBF philosophy and policies will differently fit the four types Elmore isolates. His illustrative emphasis on the implementation of social programs also can without violence be extended to numerous considerations raised in the selections already introduced. Thus, the organization development model seems best suited to an emphasis on employee involvement and participation, as well as to the meeting of individual needs. No doubt, also, the bureaucratic model probably would rank lowest of the four structural alternatives in those regards.

Size as a Critical Variable

John M. Stevens and Josephine M. LaPlante utilize an analytic microscope, as it were, in contrast to the emphasis on macro features in the last several selections. These two re-searchers focus on the variable of size, as they attempt to gain perspective on "Shaping State-Based Financial Policy in an Era of Change: A Policy and Research Perspective on City Size."

Perhaps even more so than in most selections in this volume, the delight here is in the details. So readers are encouraged to have a good go at the text, tables and all. The basic point is clear enough: Size may be a significant variable in determining whether alternative PPF philosophies and practices will fit well or poorly.

Two facts, especially, contribute to the required motivation to cope with a detailed text. First, Stevens and LaPlante are inspired by "an unprecedented relinquishing of federal responsibility for domestic programs," and that devolution has not stopped with the Reagan administration. Indeed, given the policy debates of the fourth year of the Clinton presidency, we probably have not yet seen the flood tide of such planned devolution. There seems far more of such public program localizations in our future, in short, which provides a heightened motive to read Chapter 43, and aggressively.

Second, size does seem a relevant variable in the Stevens and LaPlante data. This suggests the need for a fine-tuned sense of how PBF activities can be tailored to local settings, and perhaps beyond the insights consistent with Chapters 40, 41, and 42.

PBF Activities and Change

To judge from the Stevens and LaPlante data, even if there were no other clues available, change seems prominent on the PBF agenda. Convenient but limited perspective is provided by Robert T. Golembiewski's "Two Superoptimum Solutions in a Cutback Mode." Cutbacks are never any fun, he acknowledges, but cutbacks or right-sizing are unavoidable; still, there are many ways to skin those particular cats. Golembiewski illustrates two such approaches, in the context of the line of research and application labeled organization development, or OD.

Basically, OD seeks to collapse time and reduce the adverse consequences of change, whether the basic challenge is growth or downsizing. Much theory and experience reinforce the bare bones of the two illustrations in Chapter 44 [2].

Focus on Strategy

W. Bartley Hildreth provides a capstone perspective, for present purposes, on the multiple contexts associated with PBF. His title, "Financing Strategy," suggests this comprehensive focus. Most observers will agree that PBF needs strategic planning; but, to put Hildreth's major thesis in a nutshell, he also proposes that it is more essentially the case that strategic planning needs finance.

How does Hildreth go about developing his mind-expanding approach? To begin, he solidly roots his analysis in "cultural environments," as he distinguishes between the individuating characteristics of fiscal *and* managerial environments. Basically and in useful detail, then, Hildreth urges against a unitary view. In sum, one size definitely does not fit all organizations. Why? Many variations in both fiscal and management environments are possible, and substantial tailoring is necessary to develop these variations.

Further, Hildreth usefully distinguishes and illustrates a fulsome portfolio for financing strategy. He identifies eight elements in that portfolio.

- Budgeting
- Multiyear planning
- Accounting policy
- Tax policy
- Debt policy
- Credit policy

- Priority determination
- Performance measurement

This range of coverage clearly explains the earlier labeling of "Financing Strategy" as a capstone selection. Hildreth provides a common context for much of the substance of this book of readings. And he also outlines a useful template for helping readers develop a total PBF sense suited to their own organizational conditions and stages of understanding.

REFERENCES

1. R. T. Golembiewski, *Practical Public Management*, Marcel Dekker, New York (1995).
2. R. T. Golembiewski, Organization development and change in the public sector, *Handbook of Public Administration* (ed. J. L. Perry), Jossey-Bass, San Francisco, pp. 511–526 (1996).

40

Accountancy as a Function of Organization Theory

Robert T. Golembiewski

Modern accountancy is ineluctably the product of a wide variety of environmental factors that shaped its tools and approach. This truism can prove very useful. For example, common opinion has it that significant changes in the scope and methods of accountancy must be made. The truism heading this paragraph, then, requires this important qualification: Any lasting changes in accountancy will depend in significant respects upon understanding these environmental factors and upon changing or eliminating them, where possible.

An earlier article "Organization Theory and New Accountancy: One Avenue of Revolution" [1] —developed this point of view by considering one major environmental determinant that has left a deep impress upon accountancy. The present chapter attempts to satisfy numerous requests to present the argument in which both theorists and practitioners in accountancy will have a more convenient opportunity for study and comment. Mere repetition, of course, seldom has much to recommend it. Therefore, this chapter takes a different approach to demonstrating the importance of organization theory to accountancy, and to outlining how structural innovation can contribute fruitfully to the present reevaluation of the scope and methods of accountancy. The reader reasonably may move from this piece to the more detailed argument of the original article, and thence to the massive literature on behavior in organizations that underlays both analyses [2].

PURPOSES, PROCEDURES, AND PROBLEMS OF ACCOUNTANCY: SOME HERITAGES OF THE TRADITIONAL THEORY OF ORGANIZATION

The purposes, procedures, and problems of contemporary accountancy can be approached in useful ways as a function of the traditional theory of organization. Figure 1 facilitates

Source. Public Budgeting and Financial Management, *1*(1): 99–118 (1989). Citation style of original retained in this reprint. Originally published in *The Accounting Review*, *39*: 333–341 (1964). Reprinted with permission.

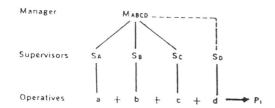

Figure 1 Organizing a simple set of operations in terms of the traditional theory of organization. ―― Command relations; - - - - advisory relations.

making this point in detail. This figure depicts the conventional organization of three "line" processes A, B, and C, and of one "staff" service D. Symbolically, the contributions of A + B + C + D combine to yield product P_1. Note also that M designates the managers, and that each S refers to a first-line supervisor.

Figure 1 may be drawn with assurance and confidently taken to be a simplified analog of the kind of structure usually encountered in practice. For Figure 1 is based upon the well-known "principles" of the traditional theory of organization that guide most attempts at organizing. These "principles" include such propositions:

1. That work must be specialized in terms of functions at upper levels of organization and in terms of processes at lower levels.
2. That authority must be delegated by a single head to a sharply limited number of subordinates.
3. That supervision must be detailed and continuous.

The effects of these "principles" of organizing are clearly reflected in the purposes, procedures, and problems of accountancy. Some of the senses in which this is the case will be sketched below. For convenience, the emphasis will be upon internal reporting, as opposed to public accounting or the preparation of materials for annual reports and the like.

Purposes of Internal Reporting

Raising the question of the purposes of internal reporting easily could get out of hand. For the enumeration of such purposes is limited only by the ingenuity of the commentator. Let us keep tight rein on ingenuity here by restricting our attention to the several kinds of questions which a full-fledged system of internal reporting should be able to handle successfully. These questions, then, serve conveniently to outline the purposes of internal reporting. Following Simon and his collaborators [3], three types of questions may be taken to outline the full rage of challenges facing internal reporting:

1. Score-card questions: "Am I doing well or badly?"
2. Attention-directing questions: "What problems should I look into?"
3. Problem-solving questions: "Of the several ways of doing the job, which is the best?"

The quoted illustrative questions, of course, are those that a "line" manager might ask himself and those that an internal accountant could help answer.

Procedures for Internal Reporting

These purposes of internal reporting, as it were, provide destinations rather than routes. These are numerous procedures that might be employed to achieve these purposes, that is. In general, however, the procedures actually employed have tended toward a stereotypic pattern. This fact does not reflect the rigid requirements of optimum efficiency in organizations. In fact, the stereotypic approach often significantly curbs efficiency, as will be demonstrated. The stereotypy of the procedures developed in pursuit of the major purposes of internal reporting, rather, reflects the domineering guidance of the "principles" of the traditional theory of organization and of the structure sketched in Figure 1.

The argument of this introductory paragraph is an important one, of course, and requires careful support. To this end, let the focus be upon one major procedural element that pervades so much of the practice of internal reporting in today's business and government agencies, the "line–staff" concept. I have elsewhere analyzed in some detail the classical "staff" model [4]. This classical model was dubbed the "neutral and inferior instrument" (NII) concept, for it prescribes that the "staff" man is outside the line of command, that he merely provides neutral advice or expertise, and so on. This terse characterization suffices for present purposes.

The NII concept of "staff" all but monopolizes the field in prescribing relations in contemporary organizations [5]. Evidence of the impact of this procedural device upon internal accounting is common, for example. Illustratively, and consistent with the NII model, the internal accountant commonly does not report "across" to a lower level "line" official at his own level. In contrast, he reports *up* his own "staff" hierarchy of one or more superiors, the "staff" superior then reports *over* to the appropriate higher level "line" official, and the latter in turn communicates *downward* to the "line" official directly concerned, the communication going through one or more levels of intermediate "line" supervision. More generally, much of the content of the role of the accountant engaged in internal reporting is defined in terms of the NII model [6].

The NII "staff" model did not just happen, of course. In all relevant particulars, it evidences the influence of the traditional theory of organization. Consider but a few factors that establish the point. At the very least, the NII model fits exactly such "principles" of the traditional theory of organization as specialization by function. In its crudest form, that model requires that the "line" specialize in "doing." "Thinking," or "planning," or some such, is reserved to the "staff."

Relatedly, only the NII model avoids a challenge to the unity of command underlying the traditional theory of organization. For the classical "staff" model claims both neutrality and inferiority, and both are necessary if the "principles" are to be respected.

This suggests the weakness of the NII model. Not that logical consistency with the "principles" was the only support of the NII model. That model was aided and abetted by the vigorous complaints of "line" officials around the turn of the century about sharing their authority with the new "staff" specialists. As Dale and Urwick [7] described these complaints and their consequences:

> So the fur flew, and harassed chief executives in business after business were driven into a hysteria of assurances that staff specialists were not meant to do what they had manifestly been hired to do. The line managers were solemnly told that the staff men were "purely advisory" and that no one need take their advice if they did not want to.

Convenience, that is, proved a powerful reinforcement for logical consistency. Both together, however, hardly constitute scientifically desirable criteria for a "staff" model.

Problems of Internal Reporting

Internal reporting has suffered from this molding of procedures to the traditional theory of organization. In sum, the derived procedures proved inadequate to meet the three broad purposes of internal reporting as well as to surmount the mensural and motivational difficulties created by the traditional theory of organization. That is, the three purposes impose requirements different enough—*when the traditional theory of organization is respected*—that they tend to frustrate efforts designed to achieve all of them. Thus Simon and his co-workers noted the tendency of controller's departments to fulfill admirably one or another of the three purposes of internal reporting, while others receive less effective attention [8].

The point here may be supported by outlining the demands of fulfilling each of the three purposes of internal reporting. Score-card questions, to begin, have attracted the lion's share of attention in organizations, and with substantial reason. For the traditional theory of organization requires that an undue importance be placed on score-card data. Referral to Figure 1 helps explain this bias of the traditional theory. Simply, three "line" processes A, B, and C are involved in the production of item P_1. A "staff" service D—internal reporting, let us say—provides valuable service toward the same end. Therefore, crudely, $A + B + C + D = P_1$.

There are motivational and mensural problems aplenty in this simple formulation. Let us forsake comprehensiveness, and attempt to make the most of a single datum. That is, only M_{ABCD} oversees enough of the operations to make reasonable decisions on nontrivial matters related to production of P_1. Understandably, then M_{ABCD} will place great emphasis on score-card data. Many difficulties are implied and encouraged thereby. Three particular difficulties deserve spotlighting.

First, the traditional theory of organization encourages a separatism of the several units of organization while it requires that the efforts of each must be delicately integrated into a common flow of work. This works at cross-purposes, patently. Thus the units headed by S_A, S_B, S_C, and S_D have only tenuous responsibilities for P_1, the volume and the quantity of which is of obvious significance. The enduring interests of each of these units is more or less rooted in their own particular process or function. It could hardly be otherwise. For the traditional theory of organization stresses them, and individuals are paid to be interested in them. The difficulty, of course, is that total performance commonly comes off the loser in the effort to mesh such particularistic interests.

This phenomenon of separatism in organizations has been observed often, and it has been analyzed in telling detail [9]. We may, therefore, assume the incidence and significance of such organizational separatism and concentrate on its effects. When things go awry, as they often will, this situation obtains: M_{ABCD} will place increasingly great emphasis on score-card data; the individual supervisors will strive all the more mightily to have their own particular function or process appear in a good light, whatever this means for the total flow of work; and accountants will be forced to apply increasingly great pressure to unearth crucial data or to gain some measure of agreement about the allocation of costs. All this is natural enough, given the traditional theory of organization. But the dynamics tend to be self-defeating.

Second, these unfortunate dynamics do not reflect man's consistent and pervasive perversity. Rather, the traditional theory of organization tends to create an environment within which little better can be expected. Thus the traditional theory of organization forces the accountant to handle score-card questions that are at least very difficult, if that theory does not create an ersatz complexity that makes impossible and nonarbitrary assignments of costs to individual organization units. These score-card questions, in the bargain, have great relevance for the lower "line," and great reliance often is placed in them by the upper "line." This outlines an unfortunate condition, and certainly one not likely to exhibit man at his cooperative best. The assignment of the cost of an error to A or B or C, for example, illustrates the kind of issues on which the mischief of the traditional theory is most patient [10]. Matters are delicate enough under the best of circumstances. Consider only one awkward feature of the traditional theory. Each "line" supervisor has a relatively large organization unit, all of whose members are bound by the tie of performing the same function or process. This datum implies the possibility of an organization unit waging substantial political warfare if it feels disadvantaged in the assignment of costs. Relevantly, a single unit in a structure like that in Figure 1 can disrupt the total flow of work. Ample evidence demonstrates that this leverage does not always go unutilized [11].

The role of "staff" in such jostling for power must be conflicted. Let it not be said that the accountant always shrinks from the effort of developing the power necessary to play the game with some success [12]. An accounting unit hardly could meet the rigorous demands of the traditional theory of organization otherwise. Short of settling for a program of nagging obstructionism or of desperate devotion to minutiae, the effort to develop power—to be taken seriously by others in an organization—must be a constant one. The common reliance of the upper "line" upon internal reporting, in addition, simplifies matters for the accountant via "having the boss's ear." But note that this effort must remain a source of conflict for the "staff" man, even if it is successful. For the NII model does not legitimate such an active role, necessary though it may be. The "line," therefore, can seriously question the legitimacy of "staff's" exercise of power. And "staff" might feel guilty enough about its own efforts to resort to more or less elaborate subterfuges to assuage its discomfort. These conditions are not well designed to induce favorable working relations between "line" and "staff."

Third, score-card data often must be used in attempts to force the integration of operations complicated by the traditional theory of organization. Particularly because of the separatism by functions and processes prescribed by that theory, great demands are placed upon internal reporting as a means of goading cooperative effort or of assigning responsibility in its absence. This punitive motivational use of such data makes mensuration very difficult. For example, it can easily force organization units into a greater resort to devices of self-protection, thereby worsening the separatism already endemic to the traditional theory of organization and thereby increasing the difficulties of meaningful internal reporting. As Worthy perceptively put the matter [13], respecting the "principles" eliminates

> "natural" standards of performance, and management is forced to exercise considerable ingenuity in inventing controls which it can use for administrative purposes. Unfortunately, contrived controls such as these, so far from facilitating interdivisional cooperation (which is one of their purposes) often become themselves a source of conflict. The individual supervisor or executive is under strong compulsion to operate in such a manner as to make a good showing in terms of the particular set of controls to which he is subject, and often he does so only at the expense of effective collaboration across divisional lines.

This brief analysis is capable of terse summary. Score-card questions in an organization patterned after the classical theory have a punitive bias. Or to say almost the same thing, they tend to induce mechanisms of defense and self-protection. The point is crucial, for these products of generating score-card data outline just the conditions that make it very difficult to meet the other purposes of internal accounting. The point may be put in another way. Given the general acceptance of the traditional theory of organization, the collection of score-card data must preoccupy internal reporting. And to the degree that this is in fact true of any accounting unit, the less likely is that unit to prove effective in handling attention-directing questions or problem-solving questions.

These are not merely logical surmises, be it noted. Relevant research leaves much to be desired. But this conclusion seems generally appropriate to the question of whether internal reporting should develop in the direction of more elaborate periodic score-card reports or toward strengthening special studies: "Further development of staff and facilities for special studies is a more promising direction of progress than elaboration of periodic accounting reports" [14]. This conclusion reflects both a potential usefulness and a relatively unfilled need.

If this analysis is near the mark, then, merely calling for emphasis on attention-directing questions and problem-solving questions must prove abortive. For the traditional theory of organization remains undisturbed, with all that implies. Tersely, the procedures appropriate for score-card questions under the traditional theory ill suit the requirements of the two former types of questions. The same is true of the tone of relations commonly induced in seeking score-card data, and perhaps of the personality characteristics appropriate for the effort under the traditional theory of organization. It might seem reasonable, as an alternative, to assign responsibility for each of the three purposes of internal reporting to separate units. This possibility is not considered here. Thus, among other consequences, it aggravates organizational separatism, raises jurisdictional questions, and invites overlap and duplication of effort. Moreover, for our purposes, this alternate approach is not very instructive, although it might be the best accommodation possible under specific practical conditions.

This position may be supported parsimoniously. Consider attention-directing questions. Thus, Simon and his collaborators note that they require "direct and active channels of communication with the operating executives at those points in the organization where operations are being measured." The implied argument needs to be developed only briefly to suggest how the search for score-card data under the traditional theory of organization often fouls the delicate relations Simon sketches. The NII model of "staff," needless to say, greatly complicates just the kind of communication required, if the burdens of "up, over, and down" reporting do not in fact result in a hardening of the communicative arteries. Relatedly, the punitiveness and defensiveness that characterize so much of internal reporting do not provide much encouragement for the kind of interaction required by attention-directing questions. Finally, the separatism fostered by the traditional theory of organization and the NII model does not predispose the component units of an organization to the continuing and sensitive cooperation required by the use of internal reporting to indicate the specific problems that "line" personnel might keep in mind [15].

Much the same, if perhaps more pointedly, might be written of problem-solving questions. They draw on a wide variety of information, including accounting data. They also require a high degree of mutual confidence, intimate knowledge of the needs of the affected units of an organization, and cooperative and continuing relations that permit timely studies. The traditional theory of organization, in general, would not be likely to do tender service to this catalog of prerequisites.

TOWARD A NEW ORGANIZATION THEORY

These few paragraphs sketch some dismal probabilities for cooperative effort, to be sure. Despair, however, is not necessarily in order. Indeed, it has proved possible for men of persistence and inventiveness to avoid the difficulties posed by the traditional theory of organization while meeting the full range of purposes of internal reporting. Guest, for example, provides an interesting record of just such a case of the fruitful cooperation of a new plant manager, his comptroller, and other "line" and "staff" officials in an organization that had suffered grievously from the full list of maladies sketched above [16]. Even in this case, however, some participants were pessimistic. They felt a new era of good feeling would pass quickly with the transfer of the plant manager, who induced and sustained the changes by his skillful handling of men.

It would be foolish, of course, to place our hopes in managerial supermen. The good intentions of the vast majority of us are combined with lesser talents. Structural innovation can provide the continuing reinforcement of good intentions and average talents, however. Figure 2 sketches such a structure for the simplified set of processes considered in Figure 1. Notice that the focus in Figure 2 is upon what may be called "administrative entities," each of which contains all of the elements necessary for producing P_1. Figure 1, in contrast, stresses individual processes and functions. In this sense, a Figure 2 structure may be characterized as holistic, or integrational; a Figure 1 structure may be considered as particularistic, or fragmentary. To illustrate, each supervisor in Figure 2 controls all of the organizational elements necessary for P_1. The individual supervisors in Figure 1, however, each oversee only individuals performing a single activity required for P_1.

The unorthodox structure in Figure 2 is not merely an alternative to the traditional structure. It has been approached in numerous practical situations. Indeed, some aspects of the figure have been stressed by accountants as of great importance in the more effective use of accounting data for managerial control [17], although such stress is not commonplace. Any organization with strong tendencies toward decentralization, moreover, will have important points of similarity with Figure 2. More or less typically, to illustrate, an accounting service (like D in Figure 2) will report directly to the "line" official at its level (S_1, for example) rather than upwards to unit D at headquarters. There are many variations in practice on the basic pattern, but their purpose is the same: to reduce time lags between observation and remedial action and to reduce the punitiveness both associated with the "up, over, and down" pattern of "line–staff" relations consistent with the traditional theory of organization [18].

The several advantages of the structure in Figure 2 have been outlined in detail elsewhere. Here consider only one crucial sense in which internal reporting is facilitated. Thus, the managerially significant measure of performance (e.g., variance from standard cost of the units headed by S_1, S_2, and S_3) is also a relatively simple accounting task. The more difficult task of determining the costs to be assigned A, B, C, or D within any unit of organization, moreover, is less significant. For a supervisor's status no longer will depend directly upon whether the charges go to A or B or C, as is the case in a Figure 1 structure. In addition, no supervisor will be threatened by the internal accountant's handling of this

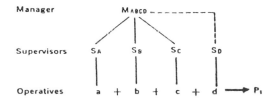

Figure 2 Organizing a simple set of operations in terms of an unorthodox theory of organization. —— Command relations; - - - - advisory relations.

more difficult task. For the results of such inquiry can help the supervisor in more effectively managing the total administrative entity for which he is responsible. In a Figure 1 structure, in stark contrast, the results of such an inquiry inherently imply punishment of supervisors for imperfections in a total flow of work, of which any supervisor controls but a part, and for which he often has no clear and unambiguous responsibility. There is a world of difference between the two structures in this particular, needless to note.

There are other convenient features of the structure in Figure 2. Thus, much of the pressure is taken off internal reporting—and off accountants!—because it is not used as a goad to superior (or more likely acceptable) performance. For now the units headed by the three supervisors can be compared in terms of simple and meaningful measures of performance.

Thus, the relative value of the efforts of units headed by S_A, S_B, S_C, and S_D in Figure 1 can be approached only via arbitrary and often troublesome conventions that are all too vulnerable to sharp dealing. Moreover, these conventions often act as ceilings on performance, a happenstance that motivated one student to argue for the use of bogus budgets so as to avoid limiting efforts [19]. In addition, developing or changing these conventions often will prove difficult and seem arbitrary, in that these conventions are not tied to the demands of work in any clear and direct way. The meaningful competition of the several comparable units in a Figure 2 structure, in pleasing oppositeness, should operate so as to induce an upward orientation in what is considered an acceptable level of performance. The "pressure," in a real sense, is sustained and yet seems natural in that it derives directly from work.

Consider also that a Figure 2 structure reduced the intensity of the force field within which internal reporting must take place. Any single unit in a Figure 1 structure, to approach the point, can exercise considerable power. Thus, the unit headed by S_A, for example, could seriously disrupt the total flow of work. Indeed, output by one unit would disadvantage only members of that unit. Output would fall at most by $1/N$, where N is the total number of similar autonomous units. Realistically, units in a Figure 2 structure would hesitate to punish only themselves, a fact that reduces the probability of resistance by an obstreperous unit of organization.

Simple structure variations, that is to say, can have profoundly different consequences for behavior.

Such description might be extended, but it would come to the same point. The structure in Figure 2 is very congenial to filling the three purposes of internal reporting. Score-card questions, that is, are neither so crucial, nor so subject to arbitrary allocations, nor so likely to adversely color the relations of accountants and others, as Figure 1 structures. This of itself makes more probable a telling emphasis on attention-directing questions and problem-solving questions.

But the argument need not be made by default. More positively, the accountant "d" in the unit headed by S_1 patently has a continuing relationship with the several processes necessary to produce P_1; moreover, he has a direct stake in the successful performance of his unit. He is no longer an organizational "outsider" with interests quite different from those of the unit served, as in Figure 1 structures. He can communicate directly with the official at just the point at which operations are being measured. And it is definitely in the interest of accountant "d" to draw quick attention to opportunities to improve operations, to know and to anticipate needs, and to help study alternate ways of meeting them. For shoddy work will be subject to facile comparison with the performance of other units. The implied enlargement of the job of accountant "d," in addition, also is attractive [20].

This merely sketches the positive argument, of course. But it suffices to demonstrate that, following Figure 2, it is possible to challenge the full range of purposes of internal accounting with more optimism than one can muster when considering the traditional theory of organization.

SUMMARY

Internal reporting serves as a case in point of the intimate senses in which accountancy is a function of organization theory. The traditional theory of organization has the effect of directing attention to but one of the purposes of internal reporting, the asking of score-card questions, and this at great cost to cooperative effort. An unorthodox theory of organization does not suffer from the same liabilities to the same degree. Of particular significance, this unorthodox theory of organization facilitates asking attention-directing questions and problem-solving questions that must receive a growing proportion of the attention of the accountant engaged in internal reporting, and this if only because electronic data processing will increasingly eliminate much of the accounting time heretofore devoted to score-card questions.

Therefore, it seems appropriate that organization theory receive considerable attention by members of the accounting profession, which is presently in the throes of rethinking its scope and methods. For an inappropriate organization structure can frustrate the most worthy of intentions and, in any case, any fundamental changes in accountancy will require changes in the traditional theory of organization.

NOTES AND REFERENCES

1. R. T. Golembiewski, "Organization Theory and the New Accountancy: One Avenue of Revolution," *Q. Rev. Econ. Business*, 3: pp. 29–40 (1963).
2. Much of this literature is reviewed and synthesized in the author's *Organizing Men and Power: Patterns of Behavior and "Line-Staff" Models*, Rand McNally, Chicago: (1967).
3. H. A. Simon, H. Guetzkow, G. Kozmetsky, and G. Tyndall, *Centralization vs. Decentralization in Organizing the Controller's Department*, Controllership Foundation, New York, pp. 3–4 (1954).
4. R. T. Golembiewski, "Toward the New Organization Theories: Some Notes on 'Staff,'" *Midwest J. Polit. Sci.*, 5: pp. 237–259 (1961).
5. D. E. McFarland, *Cooperation and Conflict in Personnel Administration*, American Foundation for Management Research, New York: p. 18 and Table 19, p. 73 (1962).
6. See, for example, D. S. Brown, "The Staff Man Looks in the Mirror," *Public Admin. Rev.*, 23: pp. 67–73 (1963); and C. Argyris, *The Impact of Budgets on People*, Controllership Foundation, New York: (1952).
7. E. Dale and L. Urwick, *Staff in Organization* New York, p. 165 (1960).
8. Simon, et al., *Centralization vs. Decentralization*, pp. 3–4.
9. J. G. March and H. A. Simon, *Organizations*, John Wiley & Sons, New York, especially pp. 36–47 (1958); and E. D. Chapple and L. R. Sayles, *The Measure of Management*, Macmillan, New York, especially pp. 18–45 (1961).
10. For a case in point, see Argyris, *The Impact of Budgets*, pp. 17–19.
11. Chapple and Sayles, *The Measure of Management*, pp. 89–97.
12. M. Dalton, *Men Who Manage*, John Wiley & Sons, New York, particularly chap. iii (1959).
13. J. C. Worthy, "Some Aspects of Organization Structure in Relation to Pressure on Company Decision-Making," *Proceedings of the Fifth Annual Meeting of the Industrial Relations Research Association* (L. R. Tripp, ed.), IRRA Publication No. 10, p. 77 (1953).

14. Simon et al., *Centralization vs. Decentralization*, p. 4.
15. On this point, see Argyris' analysis of interviews with budget officers in his *The Impact of Budgets on People*, chap. i.
16. R. H. Guest, *Organizational Change*, Irwin, Homewood, Ill., Irwin-Dorsey Series in Behavioral Science in Business (1962).
17. Consult, for example, R. N. Anthony, *Management Accounting: Text and Cases*, Irwin, Homewood, Ill., 2d ed., especially pp. 320–333 (1960).
18. Harry D. Kolb, "The Headquarters Staff Man in the Role of a Consultant," *Organization Theory in Industrial Practice*, John Wiley & Sons, New York, pp. 143–146 (1962).
19. A. C. Stedry, *Budget Control and Cost Behavior*, Prentice-Hall, Englewood Cliffs, N.J., especially pp. 17, 41–42, and 71 (1960).
20. For numerous examples of the efficacy of job enlargement, see G. Friedmann, *The Anatomy of Work*, Free Press, Glencoe, Ill., pp. 40–67 (1961).

41

Progress, Persisting Trends, and Future Challenges: Accountancy as a Function of Organization Theory

Robert T. Golembiewski

Commenting on a piece of my own work that was published nearly a quarter century ago engages two opposing forces. On the one hand, it is growthful to reflect on and to learn from one's omissions and commissions—whether of exuberance or timidity. So energies mobilize to trash the past, or at least put it in an appropriately diminished perspective. On the other hand, it is also nice to have got it correct the earlier-time-around. Indeed, getting-it-right has much to recommend it, and not only for those bucking for guru status. All of us have our unexpected learning experiences—that is, mistakes or gaffes appropriately responded to—but most of us have a definite upper limit on our tolerance for snatching victory from the jaws of defeat. So, energies also mobilize to see the past as progress, or at least as a solid prologue to that progress.

A recent rereading of "Accountancy as a Function of Organization Theory"—first published in 1964 and reprinted in several other places over the years—induces both sets of forces in me, and about in equal measure. In some senses, then, "Accountancy" is still just about right, if mostly in a somber and even nagging way. In other senses, however, "Accountancy" is dated and (if ardent) in some particulars a bit like the college freshman embarking on life armed mostly with the perspective of *Catcher in the Rye*.

SOME PERSISTING TRENDS, PERHAPS HEIGHTENED

How does "Accountancy" get it about right? The overall description there strikes about the appropriate tone, I conclude—not only for then, but still more rather than less for now. Put another way, the prescriptions for what needed doing then seem to apply about as well today.

In an important sense, indeed, today's needs to reform accountancy practices may be more pressing than they were then. For that was a more optimistic time, and some of the

Source: Public Budgeting and Financial Management, 1(1): 119–131 (1989).

brave initiatives of those days have withered, or at least been pruned substantially. Consider Pilegge's recent review [1] of the line-item budget, which got severely beaten about in the two decades or so preceding the mid-1970s. To suggest the full catalog of particulars, the line-item budget was seen as mindless, irrational, shortsighted, fragmented, and conservative [2]. Yet, the line-item survives and, indeed, may be in for a reemphasis. Why? Pilegge [3] cites four factors undergirding this invigorated reemergence, with a focus on the public sector: a lack of trust by legislators in administrators, which he sees as still great and perhaps growing; the related concept of narrow accountability, as reinforced by the efforts of auditors and accountants; the impact of cutback of management on budgeting and finance, with the line items conveniently targeting objects for attack; and the "failure" (Pilegge's emphasis) of the budgetary reforms of the 1960s and the 1970s, which has led to today's disinclination for "big reforms" [4].

Surveying what now still needs to be done with respect to improving accountancy and finance as contributors to effective management, then, one gets a sense of *deja vu*. Indeed, an escalated intensity of need seems to have occurred, even as the pattern remains the same in important particulars.

Hence, I propose, the four basic changes I saw as necessary in the 1960s still ring true today, and each relates basically to the persistence of what "Accountancy" calls the "traditional theory of organization" (see Figure 1 in selection 40). Let me quote loosely from "Accountancy's" predecessor [5], and the reader can judge how those words of the 1960s go with today's music.

I concluded then, and reinforce it now, that no basic improvement is in the cards unless and until four changes occur in the role of accountancy vis-à-vis management, and all the changes relate to the structure of Figure 2 (in selection 40) and to its associated dynamics. Both are emphasized in "Accountancy," of course.

Overall, there seems ample reason to move toward the type of structure in Figure 2, both in general and from the perspective of the accountant, even though such a move will have its costs. Fortunately, no radical changes in accounting tools seem to be required to take initial advantage of the Figure 2 structure. However, considerable innovation by the accountant will be required in what may be called the "style" in which these tools are employed, whether or not basic structural change occurs.

Four points suggest the nature of the innovation required in matters of style. First, the *tone of relations* will change radically. The principles rest on a basic distrust of people, as reflected in the limited span of control and in staff monitoring of the line. Under the principles the relations of accountants and the line commonly take on the appearances of a dignified game of hide-and-seek, if not something worse [6]. The antipathy derives from such factors as the punitive role of the accountant under the principles, where staff success often requires catching the line in a mistake or failure. Derivative costs are great, even if one considers only the improbability of effective communication under threatening conditions. Improvement in the tone of relations, then, can pay significant dividends. In one case, for example, less strained relations had mutually beneficial consequences for the line and for accountants. Accounting officials received more reliable and appropriate information from the line, and reciprocated by adding a new system of internal reports for plant use when they learned of the inappropriateness for the line of many of the reports that plant accountants were responsible for compiling for company headquarters [7].

Tense relations between accountants and the "line" are supported by significant forces: certainly by experience, probably by training, and perhaps even by personality selection. Structural change away from the principles will not necessarily overcome these forces despite change's many attractive features. However, movement toward a Figure 2 structure can help change the tone of relations.

Second, significant changes in gross *interaction patterns* seem required. The accountant has strong tendencies to be "upward oriented"—as in reporting, for example—in part because of the acceptance of the principles which require that most action be taken toward the top of any hierarchy. In Figure 1, for example, only M_{ABC} oversees enough operations to make reasonable decisions concerning a complete flow of work. Therefore, massive upward reporting is both reasonable and necessary in a Figure 1 structure. In Figure 2, however, S_1 might make many reasonable decisions concerning a complete flow of work. And, under some conditions, many decisions might be further delegated to those employees who perform some integrated set of operations. Interaction "across" or "downward" becomes more necessary under the unorthodox theory of organization.

This point about structure $\leftrightarrow$ style dynamics is both elemental and profound. Its impact was felt earliest at executive levels, and perhaps most dramatically in the so-called divisional structure [8]. More recently, the lesson has been applied at workaday levels of the line organization—as in job rotation, job enrichment, cross-training, and autonomous groups [9]. The message has not structurally penetrated middle levels of staff services in corresponding degree, however.

These changes in interaction patterns imply substantial psychological reorientations, and correspondingly great resistance to change [10]. The advantages of a Figure 2 structure will encourage such changes, but they will hardly provide complete answers to such questions: Just how does a bright young person make oneself known in an organization without being very aggressive in upward contacts, as in discovering and reporting on lower level irregularities? Such questions highlight the necessity of comprehensive programs of performance evaluation and employee development, whether or not structural change occurs.

Third, modifications or even elimination of *traditional line–staff relations* may be expected. Thus, particularly in decentralized organizations, clarity has grown about the general inappropriateness for many operating purposes of the "up, over, and down" pattern of reporting consistent with the traditional concept of staff as "purely advisory." The inappropriateness has diverse facets. Consider only that subordinate line officials will be reticent about volunteering information that later may be used as a basis for disciplining them. Zest for gathering such information inheres in the elemental fact that it can be the vehicle for bringing reward and advancement to staff persons. Consequently many organizations have sought to develop norms or structural arrangements intended to encourage subordinate line officials to reveal information because it will be used to help them. For example, "traveling internal auditors" in General Electric reported directly and only to the local manager, apparently in all cases short of a gross violation of a major company policies. The conscious attempt is to provide a service—*as defined by the line official* who alone determines what should be done about the auditor's findings—while sharply reducing the punitive aspects implicit in upward reporting.

If the present analysis is correct, profound changes in the style of providing accounting services will be required as integrative relationships grow in significance and as organizations move toward Figure 2 structures. For example, much of the accountant's self-concept is defined in terms of the traditional staff concept, if often implicitly so. In addition, staff persons may reflect deeply ingrained attitudes, if not basic orientations to life. Thus, one senior accounting official notes that: "Maybe I am the eternal pessimist. I see all the problems. You know, line people accentuate the positive. As for me, I unfortunately—no, I don't say unfortunately, because that's my job . . . I accentuate the negative" [11]. Many of the tensions experienced by accountants and other staff officials also derive from the awkward character of the traditional staff concept [12]. New role content and getting it communicated and accepted will have a high priority, in all the cases, and others as well.

Fourth, the *accountant's role in "management by crisis"* must decline. The point needs some stage setting.

Basically, the principles encourage awkward social and psychological identifications, as reflected in the common complaint that "the departments are the only reality around here; the company hardly exists for our operating executives." This complicates the integration of the various partial contributions in the several horizontal flows of work. The accountant has suffered for his sincere efforts to work within the environment conditioned by the structure sketched in Figure 1. Because of suborganization loyalties and the "tallness" of the structure prescribed by the principles, the reports of the accountant can become pawns in the process of "keeping the pressure on." Operating supervisors, consequently, come to perceive such reports as punitive and therefore resist them. This hardly facilitates work. Moreover, time is often lost in the "up, over, and down" pattern of reporting consistent with the traditional staff concept, as well as in the accountant's penchant for exactness that is necessary for some purposes. Hence, the common charge that accounting reports are ancient history as far as the operating official is concerned.

Ironically, the high-pressure approach often will prove self-defeating. Thus, existing research reveals a strong association of high pressure and low output, rather than the Hi–Hi pattern implied by the "keep the pressure on" school of thought. In fact, something less than 10% of the cases in one study were of the Hi–Hi pattern, with high pressure associated with low output in nearly 90% of the cases [13]. This is a poor showing indeed for the taxing efforts that the traditional theory of organization requires of the accountant.

Crisis as a way of life in organizations may be used to suggest both the payoffs and the costs of "artificial pressure" generated to integrate operations. In a training session, Argyris noted to a number of executives that he was struck by two facts: their dislike of crises, and their periodic creation of crises to motivate effort. The response of the executives is illuminating: "Someone: We hate them, but we love them. A Lot of People: Yes, yes, this is true. This is us" [14].

This love-hate reaction to crisis is not difficult to understand. Positively, crisis aids in forcing the integration of operations, while traditional structures encourage subunit interests and loyalties that can fragment the flow of work as they serve its separate component activities. However, the resort to crisis sets in motion some self-defeating dynamics. Thus, there is a great danger that organization members will become so conditioned as to wait until a crisis is fomented before they take action, and greater and greater crises may be required to induce the same effort.

Relatedly, reliance on crises can encourage extreme submissiveness to superiors. This understandable adaptive behavior by the subordinate may have disquieting effects. For example, subordinates might strive to protect themselves by encouraging their superiors to make even trivial decisions. This reasonable protective strategy of subordinates will add considerably to executive workload, while it decreases the probability that subordinates will develop consensus about the decisions they must implement and skills/attitudes relevant to prudent risk-taking. The consequences feature a further resort to crisis.

Moreover, crisis implies the frequent use of what might be called "zero-sum games." A superior's order that two departments settle which should bear the cost of an error, for example, sets up a zero-sum game. Such an order may induce action, but it also will tend to increase interpersonal conflict and interdepartmental rivalry. In an organization patterned after the principles, of course, crisis then would add to the problems of integrating operations while it aimed to force the integration of operations impeded by the traditional theory of organization. Reasonably, such circular effects lead to observations that life in some organizations is "a rat-race."

Finally, frequent resort to crisis encourages what might be called "preventive organizational politics." The prime strategy is to increase one's status and/or to deflate the status of others, thereby improving one's bargaining position for the inevitable day when worse comes to worst. The many tactics suitable for manufacturing impressions and gaining power have been summarized rigorously in Goffman's [15] analysis of the dramaturgical aspects of life in organizations. These tactics patently do not have the one-way effect of increasing organization effectiveness, although they are often useful for wooing superiors.

SOME REAL PROGRESS

Although these four recommendations can be made with as much force today as two decades ago, this does not merely signal just another case of the more things change, the more they stay the same. This space permits only illustration, but four major positive developments suggest the broader range of affirmative things that have occurred recently to accounting and financial services that buffer the impact of traditional organization theory.

First, the widening use of the various forms of team building [16] has contributed substantially to inducing the kind of changes in the style of relationships prescribed above. The success rates of such interventions are quite high [17], moreover. In most cases, team-building efforts seek to "fill the gaps" in traditional organization structures. In a few cases, team-building experiences have been used to augment and reinforce basic structural change. In either case, team building emphasizes regenerative interaction—higher trust, openness, and owning, as well as lower risk. As "Accountancy" suggests, the principles of organization theory encourage degenerative interaction. The principles rest on a substantial mis trust or distrust, and counterproductively raise the risk of interacting and serve to restrict openness and owning [18].

Second, various approaches have sought to increase the service versus control component of staff activities. See the next two points for introductions to comprehensive efforts of this kind. More modest efforts include dedicating a specific person as (for example) "production's woman (or man) in budgeting." The up side of such arrangements includes the development of mutual identifications and working relationships, with the down side featuring possible collusive efforts bred of familiarity. In more extended cases, staff resources are housed in the units they serve, often with dual reporting relationships —a "direct line" to the unit head, and a "strong dotted line" to the head of the staff activity in question.

Third, the tendencies above are strongly increased in so-called "high-involvement organizations" [19]. Here, the almost-unrelieved focus is simultaneously on creating a strong and inclusive "operating culture," which helps reduce fragmenting or divisive features. The underlying model rejects the principles of traditional organization theory, in sum.

In such organizations, traditional line/staff concepts have very limited usefulness. Relatedly, hierarchy has a sharply reduced place, with participation and consensual forms of decision making gaining greater prominence. In addition, role boundedness gives way to problem solving in the team effort. All in all, the traditional principles of organization theory and conventional line/staff relationships play a much diminished role in such settings.

Fourth, "chunking" has become not only more fashionable [20] but also more common. Chunking refers to making "several small units" out of one large one, so as to achieve a more workable scale, greater identification with more self-contained units, and sharper definitions of missions and roles. In contrast, the principles have an orientation toward aggregation—toward making one large organization out of several smaller units. The twain do not meet comfortably very often, and they encourage (even require) very different concepts of line/staff relationships. Under the principles, overhead control and centralized patterns dominate. For chunking to really happen, more complex and mixed patterns have to evolve, and "authority" becomes a many-splendored thing. The matrix form represents the most complex form of such nontraditional structures [21], but less demanding integrative structures also exist [22].

Chunking and its concomitants do not constitute a ride in the park, of course. Particularly touchy are those situations in which major team-building efforts have been undertaken in conventionally structured organizations and where participants "got it all together," despite the fragmenting tendencies of their structure. When chunking occurs in such cases, typically in response to substantial growth, these initial efforts may have to be dismantled and the "old" relationships changed. The "chunked" units tend to quickly develop strong identities of their own, and these can variously tug against, or even rupture, the hard-won gains appropriate under conditions of smaller total organization size and lesser product/ service diversity. Complex emotional dynamics can be unleashed [23].

REFERENCES

1. J. C. Pilegge, "The Line-Item Budget: Ubiquitous and Indestructible," *Discussion Pieces*, The Barnard Society (1988).
2. A. Wildavsky, "Budgetary Reform in An Age of Big Government," *Contemporary Public Administration* (T. Vocino and J. Rabin, eds.), Harcourt Brace Jovanovich, New York, 261–291 (1981).
3. Pilegge, "The Line-Item Budget," 3–8.
4. A. Schick, "Micro-budgetary Adaptations to Fiscal Stress in Industrial Democracies," *Public Admin. Rev.*, *48*: 523–533 (1988).
5. R. T. Golembiewski, "Organization Structure and the New Accountancy: One Avenue of Revolution," *Q. Rev. Econ. Business*, *3*: 29–40 (1963).
6. M. Dalton, *Men Who Manage*, Wiley, New York (1959).
7. R. H. Guest, *Organizational Change*, Dorsey and Irwin, Homewood, Ill. (1962).
8. A. D. Chandler, *Strategy and Structure*, MIT Press, Cambridge, Mass. (1962).
9. A. F. Alber, "Job Enrichment Programs Seen Improving Employee Performance, but Not Without Cost," *World Work Rep*, *3*: 8–10 (1978).
10. P. R. Lawrence, *The Changing of Organizational Behavior Patterns*, Harvard University Press, Cambridge, Mass. (1958).
11. R. T. Golembiewski and A. Kiepper, *High Performance and Human Costs*, Praeger, New York, 141 (1988).
12. R. T. Golembiewski, *Organizing Men and Power*, Rand McNally, Chicago (1967).
13. R. Likert, *New Patterns of Management*, McGraw-Hill, New York, 20, 45 (1961).
14. C. Argyris, *Interpersonal Competence and Organizational Effectiveness*, Dorsey Press, Homewood, Ill., 119 (1962).
15. E. Goffman, *The Presentation of Self in Everyday Life*, Doubleday, Garden City, N.Y. (1959).
16. W. Dyer, *Team Building*, Addison-Wesley, Reading, Mass. (1977, 1987).
17. R. T. Golembiewski, C. W. Proehl, Jr., and D. Sink, "Success of OD Applications in the Public Sector: Toting-Up the Score for A Decade, More or Less," *Public Admin. Rev.*, *41*: 679–682 (1981); R. T. Golembiewski, C. W. Proehl, Jr., and D. Sink, "Estimating the Success of OD Applications," *Training Dev. J.*, *72*: 86–85 (1982).
18. R. T. Golembiewski, *Approaches to Planned Change*, Vol. 1, Marcel Dekker, New York (1977).

19. For example, D. N. T. Perkins, V. F. Nieva, and E. E. Lawler III, *Managing Creation*, Wiley, New York (1983); and Golembiewski and Kiepper (1988).
20. T. J. Peters and R. H. Waterman, Jr., *In Search of Excellence*, Harper & Row, New York (1982).
21. S. M. Davis and P. R. Lawrence, *Matrix*, Addison-Wesley, Reading, Mass. (1977).
22. R. T. Golembiewski, "Why Theory and Practice Should Emphasize Purpose, and How to Do So," *A Centennial History of the American Administrative State* (R. C. Chandler, ed.), Free Press, New York, 433–474 (1987).
23. R. T. Golembiewski, R. C. Chandler, ed.), *Approaches to Planned Change*, Vol. 2, Marcel Dekker, New York, 189–190 (1979).

42

Organization Models of Social Program Implementation

Richard F. Elmore

I will develop four organizational models representing the major schools of thought that can be brought to bear on the implementation problem. The *system management model* captures the organizational assumptions of the main-stream, rationalist tradition of policy analysis. Its point of departure is the assumption of value-maximizing behavior. The *bureaucratic process model* represents the sociological view of organization, updated to include recent research by students of "street level bureaucracy" that bears directly on the analysis of social program implementation. Its point of departure is the assumption that the essential feature of organizations is the interaction between routine and discretion. The *organizational development model* represents a relatively recent combination of sociological and psychological theory that focuses on the conflict between the needs of individuals and the demands of organizational life. Finally, the *conflict and bargaining model* addresses the problem of how people with divergent interests coalesce around a common task. It starts from the assumption that conflict, arising out of the pursuit of relative advantage in a bargaining relationship, is the dominant feature of organization life.

The most important aspect of these models, however, is not that they represent certain established traditions of academic inquiry. As we shall see, their major appeal is that each contains a common sense explanation for implementation failures. And each explanation emphasizes different features of the implementation process.

The format of the discussion will be the same for each model. I will first present a list of four propositions that capture the essential features of each model. The first proposition states the central principle of the model; the second states the model's view of the distribution of power in organizations; the third states the model's view of organizational decision making; and the fourth gives a thumbnail sketch of the implementation process from the perspective of the model. I will then discuss how these assumptions affect the analyst's perception of the implementation process. In Allison's words, I will develop "a dominant

Source: *Public Policy*, 26(2): 185–228 (1978). Copyright © 1978 John Wiley & Sons, Inc. Reprinted by permission of the publisher. References have been renumbered.

inference pattern" that serves to explain why certain features of the implementation process are more important than others and to predict the consequences of certain administrative actions for the success or failure of implementation efforts. Finally, I will draw some examples from the current case literature on social program implementation that demonstrate the strengths and weaknesses of each model.

Some readers will no doubt chafe at the idea that highly complex bodies of thought about organizations can be reduced to a few simple propositions. My defense is that this is an exercise in the *application* of theory, not an exercise in theory building. The premium is on capturing the insights that each model brings to the problem, not on making the theory more elegant or defensible. I have tried mightily to avoid creating straw men. Each model is offered as a legitimate analytic perspective.

MODEL I: IMPLEMENTATION AS SYSTEMS MANAGEMENT

Propositions

1. Organizations should operate as rational value maximizers. The essential attribute of rationality is goal-directed behavior; organizations are effective to the extent that they maximize performance on their central goals and objectives. Each task that an organization performs must contribute to at least one of a set of well-defined objectives that accurately reflect the organization's purpose.

2. Organizations should be structured on the principle of hierarchical control. Responsibility for policymaking and overall system performance rests with top management, which in turn allocates specific tasks and performance objectives to subordinate units and monitors their performance.

3. For every task an organization performs there is some optimal allocation of responsibilities among subunits that maximizes the organization's overall performance on its objectives. Decision making in organizations consists of finding this optimum and maintaining it by continually adjusting the internal allocation of responsibilities to changes in the environment.

4. Implementation consists of defining a detailed set of objectives that accurately reflect the intent of a given policy, assigning responsibilities and standards of performance to subunits consistent with these objectives, monitoring system performance, and making internal adjustments that enhance the attainment of the organization's goals. The process is dynamic, not static; the environment continually imposes new demands that require internal adjustments. But implementation is always goal-directed and value-maximizing.

A frequent explanation for failures of implementation is "bad management." We generally mean by this that policies are poorly defined, responsibilities are not clearly assigned, expected outcomes are not specified, and people are not held accountable for their performance. Good management, of course, is the opposite of all these things, and therein lies the crux of the systems management model. The model starts from the normative assumption that effective management proceeds from goal-directed, value-maximizing behavior. Organizations are thought of as problem-solving "systems"—functionally integrated collections of parts that are capable of concerted action around a common purpose [1].

Integration presupposes the existence of a controlling and coordinating authority. In the systems management model, this authority is called the "management subsystem," "the source of binding pronouncements and the locus of the decision-making process" [2]. It provides "a means of insuring role performance, replacing lost members, coordinating the several subsystems of the organization, responding to external changes and making decisions about how all these things should be accomplished" [3]. Hierarchical control is the single most important element ensuring that organizations behave as systems.

The translation of policy into action consists of a deliberate, stepwise process in which goals are elaborated into specific tasks. Robert Anthony's discussion of planning and management control gives a succinct statement of the transition from policy to operations:

> Strategic planning is the process of deciding on objectives, on resources used to obtain these objectives, and on the policies that are to govern acquisition, use and disposition of these resources. . . . Management control is the process by which managers assure that resources are obtained and used effectively and efficiently in the accomplishment of the organization's objectives . . . [and] operational control is the process of assuring that specific tasks are carried out effectively and efficiently [4].

These functions are distributed in descending order from the highest to lowest levels of the organization. Taken together, they describe a general set of decision rules for the optimal allocation of resources, tasks, and performance criteria among subunits of an organization.

For all its emphasis on hierarchical control, one would expect that the systems management model would make little or no allowance for the exercise of lower level discretion by subordinates carrying out policy directives. In fact, this is not quite the case. The problem of subordinate discretion figures prominently in the literature of systems management. Understandably, the issue arose in a very visible way during the initial attempts to apply systems analysis to national defense planning. Defense planners found almost immediately that the ability of the management subsystem to control the performance of subunits was limited by the enormous complexity of the total system. Hence, a great deal hinged on discovering the correct mix of hierarchical control and subordinate discretion. Hitch and McKean call this process *suboptimization*, which they define as an "attempt to find optimal (or near optimal) solutions, but to subproblems rather than to a whole problem of the organization in whose welfare or utility we are interested" [5]. In organizational terms, suboptimization consists of holding subunits responsible for a certain level of output but giving subunit managers the discretion to decide on the means of achieving that level. In business parlance, these subunits are called "profit centers"; in the public sector they have been called "responsibility centers." Suboptimization provides a means of exercising hierarchical control by focusing on the output of subunits rather than on their technically complex internal operations.

In practice, suboptimization raises some very complex problems—selecting appropriate criteria of subunit performance, accounting for the unintended consequences, or spillovers, of one unit's performance on another's, and choosing the appropriate aggregation of functions for each subunit [6]. But the notion of suboptimization gives the systems management model a degree of flexibility that is not often appreciated by its critics. It is *not* necessary to assume that all organizational decisions are centralized in order to assume that organizations are functionally integrated [7]. If the outputs of delegated decisions are consistent with the overall goals of the organization, then there is room for a certain degree of latitude in the selection of means for achieving those outputs.

A great deal of behavior in organizations can be explained by examining devices of control and compliance. Some are easy to identify, some blend into the subtle social fabric of organizations. One common device is what Herbert Kaufman calls the "preformed decision." He argues that "organizations might disintegrate if each field officer made entirely independent decisions," so organizations develop ways of making decisions for their field officers "in advance of specific situations requiring choice":

> [Events] and conditions in the field are anticipated as fully as possible, and courses of action [for each set of events and conditions] are described. The field officer then need determine only into what category a particular instance falls; once this determination is made, he then simply follows a series of steps applicable to that category. Within each category, therefore, the decisions are "preformed." [8]

Much of the work of high-level administrators in the implementation process consists of anticipating recurrent problems at lower levels of the system and attempting to program the behavior of subordinates to respond to these problems in standardized ways.

But not all devices of control are so obvious. In a casual aside, Robert Anthony remarks that "the system [of management controls] should be so constructed that actions that operating managers take in their perceived self-interest are also in the best interests of the whole organization" [9]. An important ingredient of control, then, is to be found in the way people are socialized to organizations. Social psychologists Katz and Kahn observe that all organizations have "maintenance subsytems" for recruitment, indoctrination, socialization, reward, and sanction that "function to maintain the fabric of interdependent behavior necessary for task accomplishment"[10]. These devices are the basis for "standardized patterns of behavior required of all persons playing a part in a given functional relationship, regardless of personal wishes or interpersonal obligations irrelevant to the functional relationship"[11]. In plain English, this means that organizations often require people to put the requirements of their formal roles above their personal preferences. The effect is to enhance the predictability and control of subordinate behavior in much the same way as preformed decisions and suboptimization. The difference is that instead of shaping decisions, it is the decision *makers* who are shaped.

The major appeal of the systems management model is that it can be readily translated into a set of normative prescriptions that policy analysts can use to say how the implementation process ought to work. From the model's perspective, effective implementation requires four main ingredients: (1) clearly specified tasks and objectives that accurately reflect the intent of policy; (2) a management plan that allocates tasks and performance standards to subunits; (3) an objective means of measuring subunit performance; and (4) a system of management controls and social sanctions sufficient to hold subordinates accountable for their performance. Failures of implementation are, by definition, lapses of planning, specification, and control. The analysis of implementation consists of finding, or anticipating, these breakdowns and suggesting how they ought to be remedied.

Analysis is made a good deal easier in this model by virtue of the fact that organizations are assumed to operate as units; a single conception of policy governs all levels of an organization. Success or failure of the organization is judged by observing the discrepancy between the policy declaration and subordinate behavior. The analyst focuses on the "clarity, precision, comprehenesiveness, and reasonableness of the preliminary policy," on "the technical capacity to implement," and on "the extent to which the actual outputs of the organization have changed in the expected direction after the introduction of the innovation" [12]. But in order for this conception of analysis to make any sense in organizational terms, one must first assume that policymakers, administrators, and analysts have a common understanding of policy and have sufficient control of the implementation process to hold subordinates accountable to that understanding.

A great deal would seem to depend, then, on whether organizations can actually be structured on the assumptions of the systems management model. The empirical evidence is suggestive but hardly conclusive. Herbert Kaufman, who has made a career of studying administrative compliance and control, concludes his classic study of the U.S. Forest Service with the observation that the "over-all performance comes remarkably close to the goals set by the leadership" [13]. This was accomplished using a set of management controls and social sanctions that closely approximate the systems management model. The net results is that "the Rangers want to do the very things that the Forest Service wants them to do, and are able to do them, because these are the decisions and actions that become second nature to them as a result of years of obedience" [14]. Much the same conclusions is reported by Jeremiah O'Connell in his study of the implementation of a major reorganization of a large insurance company. He sets out to demonstrate the effectiveness of an implementation strategy based on "unilateral" action by top management and on "economic values" [15]. The reorganization plan was a pristine example of suboptimization:

> Managers will have line responsibility for the accumulated results every week of a unit composed of seven to ten men. . . . Line responsibility makes each . . . manager accountable for determining the use of his personal time. His record will be the combined record of his agency unit. On this record his performance will be evaluated, he will be recognized, and he will be compensated [16].

O'Connell argues that the plan had its intended effect of putting "the best resources possible in the most promising markets," hence presumably increasing company profits [17].

The distinctive feature of both these cases is strong management control in the presence of wide geographic dispersion, which suggests that large organizations can approximate the ideal of value-maximizing units. But neither example comes from the literature on social program implementation, and in the existing literature there are no examples that come close to approximating the ideal. One explanation for this is that the literature records only failures. Another is that social programs are characterized by chronically bad management. If we could find successful examples of implementation, one could argue, they would manifest all the essential attributes of the systems management model. This is an empirical question that requires more evidence than we presently have.

But there are at least two other explanations for the lack of systems management examples in the implementation literature, and both point to weaknesses in the model. The first is that the model completely disregards a basic element common to all cases of social program implementation: federalism. Regardless of how well organized an agency might be, its ability to implement programs successfully depends, to some degree, on its ability to influence agencies at other levels of government. In both of the examples cited above, the implementing agent is a direct subordinate of management; he is selected, indoctrinated, rewarded, and penalized by the same people who articulate policy. Where more than one agency is involved in the implementation process, the lines of authority are much more blurred. It is not uncommon for implementors of social policy to be responsible to more than one political jurisdiction—to the federal government for a general declaration of policy and certain specific guidelines, and to a state or local unit for myriad administrative details. These jurisdictional boundaries are a permanent fixture of the American federal system; they exist not to enhance the efficiency of implementation but to protect the political prerogatives of state and local government. Insofar as it equates "success" of implementation with outcomes that are consistent across all levels of government, the systems management model is antifederalist. A good example of this antifederalist bias is Herbert Kaufman's study of management control in nine federal agencies. Six of the agencies in Kaufman's sample administered their own programs; three agencies administered programs through units of state and local government. Kaufman recognized the distinction, but chose to treat it as analytically unimportant:

> In the case of inter-governmental programs, we opted to treat the recipients of bureau-administered funds as though they were the subordinates of the administering agencies in order to sharpen the comparisons . . . between feedback practices in direct and intergovernmental administration, and we found this artificial convention useful even though it exaggerated some seeming shortcomings in some of the bureaus [18].

Not surprisingly, Kaufman found that the two weakest agencies, in terms of his criteria of administrative feedback, were those that administered intergovernmental programs in areas where functions were understood to be primarily state and local—the Law Enforcement Assistance Administration and the U.S. Office of Education [19]. Far from an indictment of internal management in these agencies, his analysis turns out to be an unintentional affirmation of the strength of federalism in the face of administrative efficiency. The systems management model, then, fails to account for the weakness of management control across jurisdictional boundaries.

The second possible explanation for the lack of systems management examples in the literature on social program implementation is perhaps that the model is not intended to describe reality. Recall that all propositions on which the model is based are normative; they describe how organizations *ought* to function, not necessarily how they actually do. The distinction is not as disingenuous as it sounds. We frequently rely on normative models to help us evaluate performance, diagnose failure, and propose remedies, even though we understand perfectly well that they have very little descriptive validity. We do so because they provide useful ways of organizing and simplifying complex problems. In this sense, the test of a model is not whether it accurately represents reality, but whether it has some utility as a problem-solving device. The major utility of the systems management model is that it directs our attention toward the mechanisms that policymakers and high-level administrators have for structuring and controlling the behavior of subordinates.

It is dangerous, however, to focus on the normative utility of the model to the exclusion of its descriptive validity. To say that the model simplifies in useful ways is not the same thing as saying that the implementation process should be structured around the model. This is a mistake that policy analysts are particularly prone to make, and it involves a peculiar and obvious circularity. If the fit between model and reality is poor, the argument goes, then the model should be used to restructure reality. Only then, the analyst concludes triumphantly, can it be determined whether the model "works" or not. A special form of this argument claims that social programs fail because policies are poorly specified and management control is weak. To the extent that we remedy these problems we can predict a higher ratio of successes to failures. The problem with this argument is that the definition of success is internal to the model and it may or may not be shared by people who are actually part of the process. The systems management model will almost certainly "work" if everyone behaves according to its dictates. If we could make value-maximizers of all organizations, then we could no doubt prove that all organizations are value-maximizers. But the point is that participants in the implementation process don't necessarily share the norms of the model. And it is this fact that leads us to search for alternative models.

MODEL II: IMPLEMENTATION AS BUREAUCRATIC PROCESS

Propositions

1. The two central attributes of organizations are discretion and routine; all important behavior in organizations can be explained by the irreducible discretion exercised by individual workers in their day-to-day decisions and the operating routines that they develop to maintain and enhance their position in the organization.

2. The dominance of discretion and routine means that power in organizations tends to be fragmented and dispersed among small units exercising relatively strong control over specific tasks within their sphere of authority. The amount of control that any one organizational unit can exert over another—laterally or hierarchically—is hedged by the fact that as organizations become increasingly complex, units become more highly specialized and exercise greater control over their internal operations.

3. Decision making consists of controlling discretion and changing routine. All proposals for change are judged by organizational units in terms of the degree to which they depart from established patterns; hence, organizational decisions tend to be incremental.

4. Implementation consists of identifying where discretion is concentrated and which of an organization's repertoire of routines need changing, devising alternative routines that represent the intent of policy, and inducing organizational units to replace old routines with new ones.

We reach instinctively for bureaucratic explanations of implementation failures. "There was a major change in policy," we say, "but the bureaucracy kept right on doing what it did before." Or alternatively, "When the bureaucracy got through with it, the policy didn't look anything like what we intended." Bureaucracy was not always a pejorative term; for Max Weber, it was a form of organization that substituted impersonal, efficient, and routinized authority for that based on personal privilege or divine inspiration. Lately, though, bureaucracy has become an all-purpose explanation for everything that is wrong with government. We use terms like "the bureaucracy problem" [20] and "the bureaucratic phenomenon" [21] to describe behavior of public officials that is "inefficient, unresponsive, unfair, ponderous, or confusing" [22].

When we look behind these characterizations, the problems of implementing policies in bureaucratic settings can be traced to two basic elements: discretion and routine. As bureaucracies become larger and more complex, they concentrate specialized tasks in subunits. With specialization comes an irreducible discretion in day-to-day decision making; the ability of any single authority to control all decisions becomes attenuated to the point where it ceases to be real in any practical sense. In the words of Graham Allison, factored problem solving begets fractionated power [23]. With the growth of discretion also comes the growth of routine. Individuals and subunits manage the space created by discretion so as to maintain and enhance their position in the organization. They create operating routines in part to simplify their work but also to demonstrate their specialized skill in controlling and managing their assigned tasks. Individuals and subunits resist attempts to alter their discretion or to change their operating routines—in other words, they resist hierarchical management—because these things are a concrete expression of their special competence, knowledge, and status in the organization. The central focus of the bureaucracy problem, according to J. Q. Wilson, is "getting the front-line worker—the teacher, nurse, diplomat, police officer, or welfare worker—to do the right thing" [24]. The job of administration is, purely and simply, "controlling discretion" [25].

The standard techniques of hierarchical management—budget and planning cycles, clearance procedures, reporting requirements, and evaluation systems—are the means by which high-level administrators attempt to structure the behavior of subordinates. To the front-line worker, though, these techniques are often incidental to the "real" work of the organization. The front-line worker's major concern is learning to cope with the immediate pressures of the job, and this requires inventing and learning a relatively complex set of work routines that go with one's specialized responsibility. This split between high-level administrations and front-line workers accounts for the quizzical, sometimes skeptical, look one often gets from teachers, social workers, and other front-line workers when they're asked about the implementation of policy. "Policy?" they reply, "We're so busy getting the work done we haven't much time to think about policy."

The bureaucratic process model, then, traces the effect of lower level discretion and routinized behavior on the execution of policy. The central analytic problem is to discover where discretion resides and how existing routines can be shaped to the purposes of policy. The major difference between systems management and bureaucratic process models is that the former assumes that the tools of management control can be used to program subordinate behavior, while the latter posits the existence of discretion and operating routines as means by which subordinates resist control. The systems management model assumes that the totality of an organization's resources can be directed at a single, coherent set of purposes—that organizations can be programmed to respond to changes in policy. The bureaucratic process model assumes that the dominant characteristic of organizations is resistance to change—not simply inertia (the tendency to move in one direction until deflected by some outside force), but, as Donald Schon observes, "dynamic conservatism" (the tendency to fight to remain the same) [26]. In the systems management model one assumes that given the right set of management controls, subunits of an organization will do what they are told; in the bureaucratic process model, one assumes that they will continue to do what they have been doing until some way is found to make them do otherwise.

In the implementation of social programs, new policies must typically travel from one large public bureaucracy to another, and then through several successive layers of the implementing agency before they reach the point of impact on the client. Whether or not the policy has its intended effect on the client depends in large part on whether the force of existing routine at each level of the process operates with or against the policy.

It is frequently at the final stage of this process—the point of delivery from agency to client—that the forces of discretion and routine are most difficult to overcome. This problem is the central concern of students of "street-level bureaucracy." The growth of large public service agencies has created a distinguishable class of bureaucrat—one who shoulders virtually all responsibility for direct contact with clients, who exercises a relatively large degree of discretion over detailed decisions of client treatment, and who therefore has considerable potential impact on clients [27]. From the client's perspective, the street-level bureaucrat *is* the government. Clients seldom, if ever, interact with higher level administrators; in fact, most public service bureaucracies are deliberately designed to prevent this. Because of the frequency and immediacy of the contact between street-level bureaucrats and their clients, it is usually impossible for higher level administrators to monitor or control all aspects of their job performance. Consequently, a significant distance opens up between the street-level bureaucrat and his superiors. This distance breeds autonomy and discretion at lower levels of the organization. The distinctive quality of street-level bureaucracy is the "discretion increases as one moves down the hierarchy" [28].

But this concentration of discretion at lower levels has a paradoxical quality. For while street-level bureaucrats occupy the most critical position in the delivery process, their working conditions are seldom conducive to the adequate performance of their jobs. More often than not, they find themselves in situations where they lack the organizational and personal resources to perform their jobs adequately, where they are exposed regularly to physical or psychological threat, and where there are conflicting and ambiguous expectations about how they ought to perform their work [29]. Social service delivery jobs are among the most stressful in our society. Street-level bureaucrats are expected to treat clients as individuals, but the high demand for their services forces them to invent routines for mass processing. High-level administrators and policymakers are preoccupied with the way policy is expressed in legislation, regulations, and guidelines. But the major concern for the street-level implementor is how to control the stress and complexity of day-to-day work. Out of this concern grows a whole set of informal routines that students of street-level bureaucracy call "coping mechanisms."

Learning to cope with the stresses of service delivery means learning to rely on simple, standardized sources of information to clients—case histories, employment records, permanent school records, test scores, eligibility forms, and the like. It means developing a facility for classifying and labeling people simply and quickly—"an alcoholic parent," "a broken family," "a history of drug abuse," "violence-prone and resistant to authority," "can't hold a job," and so on. It means developing one's "faculties of suspicion" in order to spot people who pose a threat either to oneself or to the system one is administering. And it means using the formal procedures of the organization to strike an impersonal distance between oneself, as an individual, and the client [30]. All these mechanisms have the effect of reducing and controlling the stress and uncertainty of daily work, and for this reason they figure prominently in the implementation of social policy. On the other hand, they are not typically included in the policymaker's or the high-level administrator's definition of "policy." More often than not, they're either ignored or regarded as external to the implementation process.

Concentrating on formal declarations of policy at the expense of informal coping routines means that "even the most imaginative manipulations of goals, structure, staff recruitment, training and supervision may . . . represent only superficial changes . . . rather than the fundamental reforms hoped for" [31]. From the perspective of the bureaucratic process model, major shifts in policy have little or no effect until they reach the final transaction between service giver and client. The elaborate superstructure of regulations, guidelines, and management controls that accompany most social programs tend to have weak and unpredictable effects on the delivery of social services because street-level bureaucrats and their clients develop strong patterns of interaction that are relatively immune to change. Implementation failures, from this point of view, are the results of a failure on the part of policymakers to understand the actual conditions under which social services are delivered.

Empirical evidence demonstrating the effect of organizational routines on the implementation of social policy, while not extensive, is certainly compelling. Probably the first serious attempt to document the street-level effect of a major shift in policy was Miriam Johnson's study of how national manpower policy influenced the operation of local employment service offices in California [32].

The major advantage of the bureaucratic process model is that it forces us to contend with the mundane patterns of bureaucratic life and to think about how new policies affect the daily routines of people who deliver social services. Policymakers, analysts, and administrators have a tendency to focus on variables that emphasize control and predictability, often overlooking the factors that undermine control and create anomalies in the implementation process. Bureaucratic routines operate against the grain of many policy changes because they are contrived as buffers against change and uncertainty; they continue to exist precisely because they have an immediate utility to the people who use them in reducing the stress and complexity of work. Failing to account for the force of routine in the implementation of policy leads to serious misperceptions.

Walter Williams argues that most implementation problems grow out of a division of labor between what he calls the "policy and operations spheres" [33]. In the policy sphere, people tend to focus on global issues and general shifts in the distribution of power among governmental units. Consequently, when the responsibility for implementation shifts to the operations sphere there is little in the way of useful guidance for implementors. The limited case literature on the role of bureaucratic routines bears out this observation. The unresponsiveness of large public bureaucracies to new policy initiatives is more often than not attributable to a failure to connect the "big ideas" of policymakers with the mundane coping mechanisms of implementors.

Unlike the systems management model, the bureaucratic process model does not give any clear-cut prescriptions for improving the implementation process. About the only normative advice offered by students of street-level bureaucracy is the rather weak suggestion that "bureaucratic coping behaviors cannot be eliminated, but they can be monitored and directed" by rewarding "those that most closely conform to preferred public objectives [and] discouraging objectionable practices" [34]. What this prescription overlooks is that coping routines derive their appeal and resilience from the fact that they are rooted in the immediate demands of work: They are, then, almost generically immune to hierarchical control. It's difficult, within the context of the bureaucratic process model, to think of ways to change street-level behavior in a predictable fashion. But, as we shall see in the following section, it's not at all different to solve this problem when we adopt the perspective of another model.

The utility of the bureaucratic process model shouldn't hang entirely on its limited normative power, although, since its major advantages are descriptive, it captures a very common pattern of implementation failure, in which hierarchical controls generated by top management to alter the behavior of subordinates, or by one government agency to structure the behavior of another, simply fail to affect the important street-level transactions that determine the success of a policy.

MODEL III: IMPLEMENTATION AS ORGANIZATIONAL DEVELOPMENT

Propositions

1. Organizations should function to satisfy the basic psychological and social needs of individuals—for autonomy and control over their own work, for participation in decisions affecting them, and for commitment to the purposes of the organization.

2. Organizations should be structured to maximize individual control, participation, and commitment at all levels. Hierarchically structured bureaucracies maximize these things for people in upper levels of the organization at the expense of those

in lower levels. Hence, the best organizational structure is one that minimizes hierarchical control and distributes responsibility for decisions among all levels of the organization.

3. Effective decision making in organizations depends on the creation of effective work groups. The quality of interpersonal relations in organizations largely determines the quality of decisions. Effective work groups are characterized by mutual agreement on goals, open communication among individuals, mutual trust and support among groups members, full utilization of members' skills, and effective management of conflict. Decision making consists primarily of building consensus and strong interpersonal relations among group members.

4. The implementation process is necessarily one of consensus building and accommodation between policymakers and implementors. The central problem of implementation is not whether implementors conform to prescribed policy but whether the implementation process results in consensus on goals, individual autonomy, and commitment to policy on the part of those who must carry it out.

Another frequent explanation of implementation failures is that those who implement programs are seldom included in decisions that determine the content of those programs. The closer one gets to the point of delivery in social programs, the more frequently one hears the complaint that policymakers and high-level administrators don't listen to service deliverers. What grates most on the sensibilities of teachers, social workers, employment counselors, and the like is the tacit assumption in most policy directives that they are incapable of making independent judgments and decisions—that their behavior must be programmed by someone else. It's difficult for persons who see themselves as competent, self-sufficient adults to be highly committed to policies that place them in the role of passive executors of someone else's will.

The prevailing theories of organizational behavior represented by the systems management and bureaucratic process models encourage and perpetuate this pathology. Hierarchy, specialization, routine, and control all reinforce the belief that those at the bottom of the organization are less competent decision makers than those at the top. High-level administrators can be trusted to exercise discretion while those at the bottom must be closely supervised and controlled. Policy is made at the top and implemented at the bottom; implementors must set aside their own views and submit to the superior authority and competence of policymakers and high-level administrators.

Not surprisingly, this view has become increasingly difficult to defend as the work force has become more professionalized and better educated. It's now relatively clear that there are basic conflicts between the individual's need for autonomy, participation, and commitment and the organization's requirement of structure, control, and subordination. Concern for this conflict has led some to posit a "democratic alternative" to established theories of organization [35]. The label we attach to this alternative is "organizational development." A number of schools of thought coexist within this tradition, but we will concentrate primarily on the work of Chris Argyris, who has spent an unusually large amount of effort specifying the assumptions on which his view is based.

Argyris begins with the observation that what we define as acceptable adult behavior outside organizations directly contradicts what's acceptable inside. On the outside, adults are defined as people who are self-motivating, responsible for their own actions, and honest about emotions and values. Inside organizations, adults are expected to exhibit dependency and passivity toward their superiors, they resort to indirection and avoid taking responsibility as individuals, and they are forced to submerge emotions and values [36]. Resolving this tension requires a fundamentally different kind of organization and a different theory of organizational behavior. Rational or bureaucratic theories of organization stress abstract, systemic properties—structure, technology, outputs—at the expense of the social and psychological needs of individuals [37]. The reasonable alternative is a theory that begins from the needs of individuals rather than the abstract properties of organizations. Such a theory leads "not only to a more humane and democratic system but to a more efficient one" [38].

The essential transactions of organizational life occur in face-to-face contacts among individuals engaged in a common task, that is, in work groups. Organizational effectiveness and efficiency depend more than anything else on the quality of interpersonal relations in work groups. As stated earlier, effective work groups are characterized by agreement on goals, open communication, mutual trust and support, full utilization of member skills, and effective management of conflict [39]. The cultivation of these attributes requires a special kind of skill, which Argyris calls "interpersonal competence" to distinguish it from the purely technical competence that comes from the routine performance of a task. Individuals are interpersonally competent when they are able to give and receive feedback in a way that creates minimal defensiveness; to give honest expression to their own feelings, values, and attitudes; and to remain open to new ideas [40]. The trappings of bureaucracy and rational decision-making routines, management controls, objectified accountability— undermine interpersonal competence and group effectiveness, encouraging dependence and passivity while penalizing openness and risk taking. Hence, "the very values that are assumed to help make [an organization] effective may actually . . . decrease its effectiveness [41].

Nowhere in the literature on organizational development is there a simple composite of the well-structured organization. It's fair to infer from the theory, though, that an effective organization would have at least the following features: Most responsibility for decisions would devolve to lower levels of the organization; the focus of organizational activity would be the work group, formed of people engaged in a common task; and information —statements of purpose, evaluative judgments, and expressions of needed changes— would be readily exchanged without negative social consequences at all levels of the organization. All these features originate from the simple assumption that people are more likely to perform at their highest capacity when they are given maximum control over their own work, maximum participation in decisions affecting them, and hence maximum incentives for commitment to the goals of the group.

The organizational development model gives quite a different picture of the implementation process than either the systems management or bureaucratic process models. In the systems management model, implementation consists of the skillful use of management controls to hold subunits accountable for well-defined standards of performance. In the bureaucratic process model, implementation consists of changing the formal and informal work routines of an organization to conform with a declaration of intent. In both instances, *policy is made at the top and implemented at the bottom.* But in the organizational development model the distinction is much less clear. If major responsibility is actually devolved to work groups at lower levels of the organization, it makes very little sense to think of policy as flowing from top to bottom. More about this in a moment.

Implementation failures are not the result of poor management control or the persistence of bureaucratic routines, but arise out of a lack of consensus and commitment among implementors. The features of the implementation process that matter most are those that affect individual motivation and interpersonal cooperation, not those that enhance hierarchical control. Success of an implementation effort can be gauged by looking at the extent to which implementors are involved in the formulation of a program, the extent to which they are encouraged to exercise independent judgment in determining their own behavior, and the extent to which they are encouraged to establish strong work groups for mutual support and problem solving.

Empirical evidence on the underlying assumptions of the organizational development model is relatively scarce.

The real significance of the organizational development model is that it effectively turns the entire implementation process on its head. It reverses what we instinctively regard as the "normal" flow of policy, from top to bottom. The message of the model is, quite bluntly, that the capacity to implement originates at the bottom of organizations, not at the top. In each of the two previous models the central problem was how policymakers and high-level administrators could shape the behavior of implementors using the standard devices of hierarchical control. What the organizational development model suggests is that these devices explain almost none of the variation in implementation outcomes. The factors that do affect the behavior of implementors lie outside the domain of direct-management control—individual motivation and commitment, and the interaction and mutual support of people in work groups. Hence, the closer one gets to the determinants of effective implementation, the further one gets from the factors that policymakers and administrators can manipulate. The result is that, in terms of the effective structure of organizations, *the process of initiating and implementing new policy actually begins at the bottom and ends at the top.* Unless organizations already have those properties that predispose them to change, they are not likely to respond to new policy. But if they have those properties, they are capable of initiating change themselves, without the control of policymakers and administrators. The role of those at the top of the system, then, is necessarily residual; they can provide resources that implementors need to do their work, but they cannot exert direct control over the factors that determine the success or failure of that work.

If one accepts this view, the important business of implementation consists not of developing progressively more sophisticated techniques for managing subordinates' behavior but of enhancing the self-starting capacity of the smallest unit. The organizational capacity to accept innovations necessarily precedes the innovations themselves, so one can't expect individuals to respond to new policies unless they are predisposed to do so. But once this predisposition exists, it is no longer practical to think of imposing changes from above. The only conception of implementation that makes sense under these conditions is one that emphasizes consensus building and accommodation between policymakers and implementors. Mutual adaptation exists not because it is a pleasing or democratic thing to do, but because it is the only way to ensure that implementors have a direct personal stake in the performance of their jobs. This is what the advocates of organizational development mean when they say that more democratic organizations are also the more efficient ones.

The organizational development model focuses on those aspects of an organization's internal structure that enhance or inhibit the commitment of implementors. The chief determinants of success are the sort of microvariables identified by the Rand analysts: material development by implementors, strong interpersonal and professional ties among implementors, nonmanipulative support by high-level administrators, and explicit reliance on incentives that elicit individual commitment from implementors rather than those designed to enforce external conformity. To the extent that the implementation process actually becomes these things, it is neither accurate nor useful to think in terms of a single declaration of policy that is translated into subordinate behavior. Policy does not exist in any concrete sense until implementors have shaped it and claimed it for their own; the result is a consensus reflecting the initial intent of policymakers and the independent judgment of implementors.

The organizational development model also forces us to recognize the narrow limits of one organization's capacity to change the behavior of another. When an agency at one level of government attempts to implement policy through an agency at another level, the implicit assumption is that the former controls factors that are important in determining the performance of the latter. The organizational development model suggests that those factors that have the greatest influence on the success or failure of implementation are precisely the ones over which external agencies have the least control. The maximum that one level of government can do to affect the implementation process is to provide general support that enhances the internal capacity of organizations at another level to respond to the necessity for change, independent of the requirements of specific policies. So to the extent that the implementation process actually took the shape of the model, the federal government, for example, would invest most of its resources not in enforcing compliance with existing policies, but in assisting state and local agencies to develop an independent capacity to elicit innovative behavior from implementors.

The most powerful criticism of the organizational development model comes, surprisingly, from its strongest supporters. The bias of the model toward consensus, cooperation, and strong interpersonal ties leads us to ignore or downplay the role of conflict in organizations. The model, one of its advocates argues, "seems most appropriate under conditions of trust, truth, love, and collaboration. But what about conditions of war, conflict, dissent, and violence?" "The fundamental deficiency in models of change associated with organization development," he concludes, is that they "systematically avoid the problem of power, or the *politics* of change" [42]. The same criticism may be leveled, to one degree or another, against each of the three models discussed thus far, because none directly confronts the issue of what happens in organizations when control, routine, and consensus fail. A wide range of implementation problems can be understood only as problems of conflict and bargaining.

MODEL IV: IMPLEMENTATION AS CONFLICT AND BARGAINING

Propositions

1. Organizations are arenas of conflict in which individuals and subunits with specific interests compete for relative advantage in the exercise of power and the allocation of scarce resources.

2. The distribution of power in organizations is never stable. It depends exclusively on the temporary ability of one individual or unit to mobilize sufficient resources to manipulate the behavior of others. Formal position in the hierarchy of an organization is only one of a multitude of factors that determine the distribution of power. Other factors include specialized knowledge, control of material resources, and the ability to mobilize external political support. Hence, the exercise of power in organizations is only weakly related to their formal structure.

3. Decision making in organizations consists of bargaining within and among organizational units. Bargained decisions are the result of convergence among actors with different preferences and resources. Bargaining does not require that parties agree on a common set of goals, nor does it even require that all parties concur in

the outcome of the bargaining process. It only requires that they agree to adjust their behavior mutually in the interest of preserving the bargaining relationship as a means of allocating resources.

4. Implementation consists of a complex series of bargained decisions reflecting the preferences and resources of participants. Success or failure of implementation cannot be judged by comparing a result against a single declaration of intent because no single set of purposes can provide an internally consistent statement of the interests of all parties to the bargaining process. Success can only be defined relative to the goals of one part to the bargaining process or in terms of the preservation of the bargaining process itself.

Social programs fail, it is frequently argued, because no single unit of government is sufficiently powerful to force others to conform to a single conception of policy. With each agency pursuing its own interest, implementation does not progress from a single declaration of intent to a result, but is instead characterized by constant conflict over purposes and results and by the pursuit of relative advantage through the use of bargaining. This diversity of purpose leads some participants to characterize programs as "failures" and some to characterize them as "successes," based solely on their position in the bargaining process. Conflict and bargaining occur both within and among implementing agencies. Single organizations can be thought of as semipermanent bargaining coalitions, and the process of moving a declaration of policy across levels of government can be understood as bargaining among separate organizations.

Bargaining can be explicit or tacit. We tend to associate the notion of bargaining only with direct confrontations between well-defined adversaries—labor negotiations, arms limitation talks, and peace negotiations, for example. But many forms of bargaining, especially those in implementation, occur without direct communication and with an imperfect understanding by each party of the others' motives and resources [43]. Seen in this light, implementation becomes essentially a series of strategic moves by a number of individual units of government, each seeking to shape the behavior of others to its own ends.

The key to understanding bargaining behavior is recognizing that conflict implies dependency. Even the strongest adversaries must take account of their opponents' moves when they formulate a bargaining strategy. "The ability of one participant to gain his ends," Schelling observes, "is dependent to an important degree on the choices or decisions that the other participant will make." Furthermore, "there is a powerful common interest in reaching an outcome that is not enormously destructive of values to both sides" [44]. In implementation, as in all important bargaining problems, parties with strongly divergent interests are locked together by the simple fact that they must preserve the bargaining arena in order to gain something of value. Failure to bargain means exclusion from the process by which resources are allocated. But the mutual advantage that accrues to participants in bargaining has little or nothing to do with their ability to agree explicitly on the goals they're pursuing or their means for pursuing them. Mutual advantage results only from the fact that by agreeing to bargain they have preserved their access to something of value to each of them.

Lindblom uses the general term "partisan mutual adjustment" to characterize the variety of ways in which individuals with divergent interests coordinate their actions. The common element in all forms of bargaining behavior, he argues, is that "people can coordinate with each other without someone's coordinating them, without a dominant purpose, and without rules that fully prescribe their relations to each other" [45]. This point is essential for understanding the usefulness of the conflict-and-bargaining model in the analysis of social program implementation. The model permits us to make conceptual sense of the implementation process without assuming the existence of hierarchical control, without asserting that everyone's behavior is governed by a predictable set of bureaucratic routines, and without assuming that concerted action can proceed only from consensus and commitment to a common set of purposes. In short, the model provides a distinct alternative to the limiting assumptions of the previous three. Implementation can, and indeed does, proceed in the absence of a mechanism of coordination external to the actors themselves, such as hierarchical control, routine, or group consensus.

Bargained decisions proceed by convergence, adjustment, and closure among individuals pursuing essentially independent ends. Allison makes this point when he says that "the decisions and actions of governments are . . . political resultants . . . in the sense that what happens is not chosen as a solution to a problem but rather results from compromise, conflict, and confusion of officials with diverse interests and unequal influence" [46]. The term *resultant*, appropriated from physics, emphasizes the idea that decisions are the product of two or more converging forces. The mechanism of convergence depends on what Schelling calls "interdependence of expectations." Parties to the bargaining process must predicate their actions not only on predictions of how others will respond but also on the understanding the others are doing likewise. So bargaining depends as much on shared expectations as it does on concrete actions.

> The outcome is determined by the expectations that each player forms of how the other will play, where each of them knows that their expectations are substantially reciprocal. The players must jointly discover and mutually acquiesce in an outcome or a mode of play that makes the outcome determinate. They must together find "rules of the game" or together suffer the consequences [47].

In concrete terms, this means that much of the behavior we observe in the implementation process is designed to shape the expectations of other actors. An agency might, for example, put a great deal of effort into developing an elaborate collection of rules and regulations or an elegant system of management controls, knowing full well that it doesn't have the resources to make them binding on other actors. But the *expectation* that the rules *might* be enforced is sufficient to influence the behavior of other actors. The important fact is not whether the rules are enforced or not, but the effect of their existence on the outcome of the bargaining process.

The outcomes of bargaining are seldom "optimal" in any objective sense. More often than not, they are simply convenient temporary points of closure. Asking "what it is that can bring . . . expectations into covergence and bring . . . negotiations to a close," Schelling answers that "it is the intrinsic magnetism of particular outcomes, especially those that enjoy prominence, uniqueness, simplicity, precedent, or some rationale that makes them qualitatively differentiable" from other alternatives [48]. In other words, the result of bargaining is often not the best nor even the second or third best alternative for any party; all parties can, and frequently do, leave the bargaining process dissatisfied with the result. As long as an opportunity to resume bargaining remains, there is seldom a single determinant result; all resolutions are temporary. So one should not expect the mechanisms of bargaining to lead teleologically from a single purpose to a result.

The real structure of organizations, then, is to be found in their bargaining processes rather than in their formal hierarchy or operating routines. Notions of top and bottom have very little meaning. Formal position is a source of power, but only one of many, and it does not necessarily carry with it the ability to manipulate the behavior of subordinates.

Many other sources of power—mastery of specialized knowledge, discretionary control over resources, a strong external constituency, and so on—can be used to enhance the bargaining position of subordinates relative to superiors, and vice versa. No simple rules can be set forth for determining the distribution of power in organizations. Stability, if it exists at all, is the short-term product of bargaining on specific decisions.

This view leads to a conception of implementation considerably different from any of the other models. One understands the process by focusing on conflict among actors, the resources they bring to the bargaining process, and the mechanisms by which they adjust to each others' moves. Most important, the distinguishing feature of the conflict-and-bargaining model is that *it doesn't rest on any assumptions about commonality of purpose.* In each of the previous models, it was possible to say that successful implementation was in some sense dependent on a common conception of policy shared by all participants in the process. In the systems management model, agreement was the product of management control; in the bureaucratic process model, it resulted from incorporation of a new policy into an organization's operating routines; and in the organizational development model, it resulted from consensus among policymakers and implementators. But in the conflict-and-bargaining model, the outcomes of implementation are temporary bargained solutions —resultants—that reflect no overall agreement on purposes.

Success or failure of implementation is therefore largely a relative notion, determined by one's position in the process. Actors who are capable of asserting their purposes over others, however temporarily, will argue that the process is "successful." Those with a disadvantage in the bargaining process will argue that the process is "unsuccessful." It is entirely possible for the process to proceed even when all actors regard it as unsuccessful because the costs of refusing to bargain may exceed the costs of remaining in a disadvantageous bargaining relationship. Under these circumstances, the only objective measure of success or failure is the preservation of the bargaining process itself. So long as all parties agree to bargain and mutual benefit is to be gained from bargaining, preservation of the bargaining arena constitutes success. Regardless of the level of conflict in social programs, all actors have an interest in maintaining the programs as long as they deliver benefits that are not otherwise accessible.

The empirical evidence on conflict and bargaining in social program implementation is abundant. The implementation of federal educational programs provides some of the best examples because the process occurs in a system whereby power is radically dispersed across all levels of government.

The extremely diffuse and fluid nature of organizational relationships in the field of education has led Karl Weick to characterize educational organizations as "loosely coupled systems" [49]. Although conflict and bargaining do not figure prominently in Weick's model, the characteristics of loosely coupled systems that he identified lead to the same conclusions as the conflict-and-bargaining model. The lack of structure and determinancy, the absence of teleologically linked events, the dispersion of resources and responsibilities, and the relative absence of binding regulation all add up to the kind of system in which concerted action is possible only through tacit or explicit bargaining among relatively independent actors.

NOTES AND REFERENCES

1. This account of the systems management model is drawn from the following sources: D. Katz and R. Kahn, *The Social Psychology of Organizations*, Wiley, New York: (1966); W. Baumol,

Economic Theories and Operations Analysis, 3rd ed., (Prentice-Hall, Englewood Cliffs, N.J.: (1972); R. Anthony, *Planning and Control Systems: A Framework of Analysis*, Boston: Harvard Graduate School of Business Administration, Boston (1965); C. W. Churchman, *The Systems Approach*, Delta, New York: (1968); and C. Hitch and R. McKean, *The Economics of Defense in a Nuclear Age*, Harvard University Press, Cambridge, Mass.: (1963).

2. Katz and Kahn, *The Social Psychology of Organizations*, p. 79.

3. Katz and Kahn, *The Social Psychology of Organizations*, p. 203. Cf. Churchman, *The Systems Approach*, p. 44.

4. Anthony, *Planning and Control Systems*, pp. 16–18.

5. Hitch and McKean, *The Economics of Defense in a Nuclear Age*, pp. 128–129, 396–402. Their choice of the term *suboptimization* is perhaps unfortunate because to most of us it communicates the meaning "less than optimal," which is quite opposite from the meaning they wish to convey. It is clear from their discussion that they intend the term to mean "optimizing at lower levels." Some writers, however, insist on using the term to mean less than optimal. See, e.g., Anthony, *Planning and Control Systems*, p. 35. Two other sources in which the term is used consistently with the meaning of Hitch and McKean are Baumol, *Economic Theories and Operations Analysis*, p. 395n, and R. Zeckhauser and E. Schaefer, "Public Policy and Normative Economic Theory," *The Study of Policy Formation*, (R. Bauer and K. Gergen, eds.), Free Press, New York, pp. 73–76 (1968). A more recent treatment of suboptimization in policy analysis may be found in E. S. Quade, *Analysis for Public Decisions*, Elsevier, New York, pp. 95–98 (1975).

6. Hitch and McKean, *The Economics of Defense in a Nuclear Age*, p. 129.

7. Nor is it necessary to assume, as Graham Allison does, that a "rational" model of decision making is one that treats all decisions as if they were the product of a single decision maker (Graham T. Allison, *The Essence of Decision*, Little, Brown, Boston (1971) 3, 28, 36). Most theories of rational choice encourage this view by using stock phrases like "the decision maker's problem," "the decision maker's preference," etc. In organizational terms, though, the important issue is not whether the peculiar fiction of the single, value-maximizing decision maker can be maintained, but whether it is possible to construct a set of organizational controls sufficient to integrate subunits of an organization into a functional whole. This is a point of difference between Allison's discussion and mine. In his rational actor model (*Essence of Decision*, pp. 10–38), he treats all decisions as the product of a single decision maker, and this makes it very easy to criticize the model. My intention is to demonstrate that a substantial body of theory treats organizations as rational, value-maximizing units but does not depend on the fiction of the single decision maker.

8. H. Kaufman, *The Forest Ranger: A Study of Administrative Behavior*, Johns Hopkins University Press, Baltimore, p. 91 (1960).

9. Anthony, *Planning and Control Systems* p. 45.

10. Katz and Kahn, *The Social Psychology of Organizations*, p. 40.

11. Katz and Kahn, *The Social Psychology of Organizations*, p. 40.

12. W. Williams, "Implementation Analysis and Assessment," *Social Program Implementation* (W. Williams and R. F. Elmore, eds.), Academic Press, New York, 281–282 (1976).

13. Kaufman, *The Forest Ranger*, p. 203.

14. Kaufman, *The Forest Ranger*, p. 228.

15. J. O'Connell, *Managing Organizational Innovation*, Irwin, Homewood, Ill., p. 10 (1968).

16. O'Connell, *Managing*, pp. 72 and 74.

17. O'Connell, *Managing*, p. 13.

18. H. Kaufman, *Administrative Feedback: Monitoring Subordinate's Behavior*, Brookings Institution, Washington, D.C., p. 17 (1973).

19. Kaufman, *Administrative Feedback*, p. 68.

20. J. Q. Wilson, "The Bureaucracy Problem," *Public Interest*, 6 (winter): 3–9 (1967).

21. M. Crozier, *The Bureaucratic Phenomenon*, University of Chicago Press, Chicago (1964).

22. J. Q. Wilson, *Varieties of Police Behavior*, Atheneum, New York, p. 1 (1973).

23. Allison, *Essence of Decision*, p. 80.

24. Wilson, *Varieties of Police Behavior*, pp. 2–3.

25. Wilson, *Varieties of Police Behavior*, p. 9; see also pp. 64ff.

26. D. Schon, *Beyond the Stable State*, Random House, New York, p. 32 (1971).

27. M. Lipsky, "Toward a Theory of Street-Level Bureaucracy," *Theoretical Perspectives on Urban Politics* (W. Hawley and M. Lipsky, eds.), Prentice Hall, (Englewood Cliffs, N.J.), p. 197 (1976).

28. Wilson, *Varieties of Police Behavior*, p. 7.

29. Lipsky, "Toward a Theory of Street-Level Bureaucracy," pp. 197–198.

30. Lipsky, "Toward a Theory," pp. 201ff.

31. R. Weatherly, "Toward a Theory of Client Control in Street-Level Bureaucracy," unpublished paper, School of Social Work, University of Washington, p. 5 (1976).

32. M. Johnson, *Counter Point: The Changing Employment Service*, Olympus, Salt Lake City, Utah (1973).

33. W. Williams, "Implementation Problems in Federally Funded Programs," in Williams and Elmore (eds.), *Social Program Implementation*, pp. 20–23.

34. R. Weatherly and M. Lipsky, "Street-Level Bureaucrats and Institutional Innovations," p. 196.

35. See, e.g., Katz and Kahn, *The Social Psychology of Organizations*, Katz, Daniel and Robert L. Kahn (eds.), Wiley, New York, pp. 211; (1978).

36. C. Argyris, *Personality and Organization: The Conflict Between System and Individual*, Harper, New York, pp. 53ff. (1957).

37. C. Argyris, *The Applicability of Organizational Sociology*, Cambridge University Press, London (1972).

38. W. Bennis, *Organization Development: Its Nature, Origins, and Prospects*, Addison-Wesley, Reading, Mass., p. 28 (1969).

39. Bennis, *Organizational Development*, p. 2, quoting D. McGregor, *The Professional Manager*, McGraw-Hill, New York, (1967).

40. C. Argyris, *Interpersonal Competence and Organizational Effectiveness*, Irwin, Homewood, Ill., p. 42 (1962).

41. C. Argyris, *Integrating the Individual and the Organization*, Wiley, New York, p. 138 (1964).

42. Bennis, *Organization Development*, p. 77; emphasis in original.

43. An elegant account of tacit bargaining and coordination is given in T. Schelling, *The Strategy of Conflict*, Oxford University Press, New York, (1963).

44. Schelling, *The Strategy of Conflict*, pp. 5–6.

45. C. Lindblom, *The Intelligence of Democracy: Decision Making Through Mutual Adjustment*, Free Press, New York, p. 3 (1965). In the interest of economy of expression, I have taken some liberties with Lindblom's terminology. Lindblom actually develops no fewer than 12 distinguishable types of partisan mutual adjustment, based on different assumptions about the ability of parties to determine the effect of their actions on others, the level of communication among parties, their ability to use conditional threats, and their ability to elicit behavior using unilateral action (pp. 33–84). I have equated bargaining with partisan mutual adjustment, where in Lindblom's scheme bargaining is one particular type of partisan mutual adjustment involving the use of conditional threats and promises (pp. 71ff).

46. Allison, *Essence of Decision*, p. 162.

47. Schelling, *The Strategy of Conflict*, pp. 106–107.

48. Schelling, *The Strategy of Conflict*, p. 70; Lindblom, *The Intelligence of Democracy*, pp. 205–225.

49. K. Weick, "Educational Organizations as Loosely Coupled Systems," *Admin. Sci. Q.*, *21*: 1–18 (1976).

43

Shaping State-Based Financial Policy in an Era of Change: A Policy and Research Perspective on City Size

John M. Stevens and Josephine M. LaPlante

Observers of federalism have been witnessing an unprecedented relinquishing of federal responsibility for domestic programs as the Reagan administration has worked to implement the President's philosophy of governance. Two complementary paths have been followed by Washington to implement decentralization: policy actions in selected arenas and an absence of policy initiatives in others. Where there have been policy directives from Wash ington, such as in the case of the Community Services Block Grant, a thrusting of respon- sibility for fiscal decision making upon the states, but with reduced funding levels, has resulted. Where a need for policy has been identified, such as in the case of the condition of elementary and secondary education in the United States, the President has acknowledged the problem and then deftly placed the responsibility for its resolution with the states and local governments. The net impact has been a spiraling of the states' responsibility for fiscal management and oversight [1].

Whether all or only part of the federal funding channeled to the states for distribution will be passed through to local governments and how the determination of the allocations is made in each state is a subject of concern [1,2]. Important questions, often related to the size of the governmental unit, have been raised about the capability of the states and localities to manage under new policies and increased responsibility [3,4]. Among these, the most critical are questions related to local jurisdictions' abilities to finance current or expanded levels of service. The inability of many educational systems to attract and retain teachers, particularly in the areas of science, math, and bilingual education, has led to efforts to implement minimum salary levels in many states. The resultant financial burdens upon the states and local school districts of upgrading elementary and secondary education prom- ises to be enormous.

Source: *Policy Studies Rev.*, 7(1): 61–76 (1987), with permission. The authors wish to express their appreciation to Professor Robert McGowan of the University of Denver for his contribution to the early data collection phase of this study.

While many of the states are on one hand welcoming the opportunities which accompany the changing face of federalism because it means an increased control over their own affairs, even the most "home rule" oriented states and localities are plagued by worries as the implications of Reagan's definition of intergovernmental relations are tackled. "Who will pay and how" is a resounding concern, despite reported state financial surpluses. The need to ensure equity and accountability will challenge policymakers as they strive to develop mechanisms to meet the new demands of the increasing state and local responsibility [5].

Since the time of New York City's near financial collapse in the mid 1970s, states have been urged to undertake a variety of financial management policy initiatives ranging from changes in restrictions on local government taxing and borrowing to outright assumption of more costly local functions [6,7]. Nevertheless, state action has been slow in coming [8–10]. The dual impetus of the federal divestiture of domestic responsibilities and a local outcry for more responsive fiscal and financial management policies have recently prompted some states to reassess their roles, and it can be safely assumed that others will follow [2].

THE STATES AND MUNICIPAL FINANCES

MacManus [6] underscores the importance of the relationship of states with finances of their localities: "State governments supervise the financial activities of their municipalities. States determine where cities get their money, how cities borrow money, how cities spend money, and how cities manage their financial affairs. States have the legal power to regulate municipal finance by virtue of their superior constitutional position." Research conducted for the period of the early to late 1970s has demonstrated links between state regulation and municipal financial conditions. For example, municipalities which had restrictions on property taxes were more likely to diversify their tax structures, resulting in better fiscal viability; municipalities with few state restrictions on nonproperty tax-raising ability became less dependent on outside aid [6]. MacManus underscores the critical relationship between states and their local governments when she notes, "Because the very existence of cities is a product of state authorization through grants of incorporation rights and charter approvals, it should come as no surprise that municipalities depend on state governments for the powers they need to maintain their fiscal health" [7, p. 1].

States differ markedly on the restrictions they place upon their local jurisdictions to raise various types of revenues and also levels of revenues and expenditures. Currently, many states grant differential tax-raising authority to large and small jurisdictions. Whether because of a perceived need on the part of lawmakers for larger cities to have more flexibility in raising revenues or because of a conservatism toward smaller jurisdictions who might "get in over their heads," the bias is generally toward fewer restrictions on larger municipalities. Non-property taxing authority, including the right to levy sales and income taxes, is often reserved for large cities when allowed at all. Millage rates, the allowed tax per dollar of assessed valuation, varies by city size in some states [6, p. 152]. Municipal borrowing restrictions vary by state and often by city size within states. The impacts of these differences upon smaller communities under a reduced federal presence is becoming a source of concern.

THE STATES AND THE POLICY GAP

The roles individual states will play as they move to fill the vacuum left by the federal withdrawal and whether their paths of action will be successful are of critical importance yet difficult to predict [1]. Early evidence on the decentralization of the Community Services Block Grants shows that overall states are not moving to make up lost federal funds [11]. Broadnax [12, p. 233] raised concerns which have become even more important as the full implications of the transfer of "power" back to the states are realized.

> Will it be all that much simpler for states to cope with the variations between jurisdictions than it was for the Federal government? Remember, the scaling down of the size of the jurisdictional interaction required to promulgate and execute rules and regulations will not necessarily carry with it a proportionate scaling down of the issues to be addressed and resolved.

In the past, the development of federal policies was in some respects simpler, because categorical and often block grants were designed within specific functional areas (housing, health, social services) and for particular jurisdictional size groupings (large cities, small cities, rural). Despite this, researchers have not found the federal decisions to be optimal [13]. The small luxury of narrow and definite criteria evaporates as broad-based policies aimed at improving or at least stabilizing local governments' fiscal viability and ensuring adequate response to citizens' needs become the major objectives of state-based policy-making. Policies of states which affect the finances of their local governments are neither easily agreed upon nor free of value judgments. Questions which have long fueled the school finance debate, including the "proper" objectives of state aid and the composition of the "correct" formula for its disbursal, promise to raise controversy in the arena of noneducational aid as more attention focuses on state assistance and financial management policies. Issues which have troubled policymaking in the complex and narrow arenas of finance can only intensify when both differing functions and characteristics of local governments are the targets of policymaking.

IMPLICATIONS OF JURISDICTION SIZE

While the focus of research on finances has typically been upon the larger cities, there is a growing recognition that small communities and rural areas may be particularly hard pressed to finance change [1,14,15]. Questions related as to what differences exist between smaller and larger communities are not new. However, questions concerning jurisdiction size which have occupied researchers through the years are still unresolved where they relate to fiscal capability and needs [4,14]. Assumptions about differences and similarities between large and small jurisdictions are being challenged, yet as Cigler [4] points out, research on fiscal conditions of smaller local governments has been slow to emerge and lacks a coherent theoretical framework.

Several recent efforts highlight some of the issues and evidence associated with small city and nonmetropolitan policy in the 1980s. In their study of budgeting in small jurisdictions, Sokolow and Honadle [16] found evidence of differences in the ways in which smaller governments budget. They suggest that attempts to improve budgeting should work within "existing resources and arrangements" (p. 382). Other studies have also begun to pinpoint what may be important behavioral differences in responses to demands and perceived financial circumstances, with smaller jurisdiction size linked to less flexibility. In his study of budget retrenchment in two small Ohio cities, Weinberg [17] found important evidence related to small city financial condition and decision making which suggests that size plays a key role in determining retrenchment behavior. He also found that small cities may be "at a disadvantage in making cuts or raising revenues when compared with larger cities which have more fiscal flexibility" (p. 56). Weinberg notes that not all large cities have fiscal flexibility and some have very little. Weinberg further admits the difficulty inherent in generalizing beyond such a small sample, but concludes by emphasizing the need for more research on differences between large and small jurisdictions using larger samples (p. 56).

At first glance, there appears to be a wealth of information available on fiscal conditions and stress contained in the voluminous literature on large cities which should be easily transferable to smaller governments. However, two major barriers hamper efforts to extend what is already known about fiscal problems based upon research in large cities to small cities and nonmetropolitan governments. First, while federal reports and analytical research efforts suggest that certain urban or metropolitan problems and their probable causes have been identified, little in the way of either a theory of financial condition or a consensus on constructive policy approaches has emerged. In her systematic evaluation of small city and rural local government policy issues, Cigler [4] points out that:

> The 1980s have demonstrated that the rhetoric and conceptions about rural and small town America that dominated research and policy discussions for many years are outdated. The decade of the 70s produced a unique historical trend: a reversal in the movement of people from rural to urban areas in virtually all regions of the nation. . . . Wide disparities within and among communities suggest the need for rethinking the theoretical foundations for policymaking. (p. 540)

This assessment is also supported by Bahl [18], who stipulates the specification of both a theoretical model and clearly defined criteria to assess the financial condition of local governments.

Thus, a direct transfer of "knowledge" about large city fiscal conditions to smaller governments is hampered by both theoretical and methodological concerns. More importantly, gaps in knowledge about significant differences in underlying characteristics related to stress and financial condition preclude the assumption that even if a "proper set of indicators of fiscal viability" were available for large cities [18] that they can be extended to cover small cities. Reeder [14] posits that fiscal efforts, capacity, and trend analysis are the most promising areas for further research on small local governments and further argues that such efforts are a prerequisite to effective administration of federal and state assistance.

THIS STUDY: APPROACH AND OBJECTIVES

Since much of what is now known about small city and nonmetropolitan fiscal indicators is tentative with theory and research models vague, the approach taken in this research effort is considered exploratory but focused on the key needs: longitudinal, readily comparable data on small city versus larger city financial characteristics. Two objectives of this chapter are to examine the impact of size and answer three basic research questions about the associations between governmental size and financial indicators. Three research questions considered essential to answering the ongoing issues and improving the foundation for further research on small governments and state based financial policy for formulating are advanced:

Research Question I: Are financial indicators related to the size of local government?

Research Question II: What patterns and trends in the financial indicators and size associations occurred over the 14-year study period for the 167 local governments?

Research Question III: What are the policy and research implications of the findings?

Methods and Data

Various financial indicators from 1966, 1970, 1973, 1977, and 1980 for 167 local governments in Pennsylvania are analyzed. By considering data from local governments in one state, problems associated with interstate comparison such as the influence of differing political characteristics, assignments of functions, and tax and revenue raising limitations, other statutory requirements and economic climate can be minimized. This research design and approach complements and builds upon previous studies which have examined two [17], seven [19], and 12 [16] local governments.

Data on the financial indicators for Pennsylvania cities of 10,000 residents and over were obtained from the Pennsylvania Department of Community Affairs (DCA) detailed local financial records. Local governments in Pennsylvania are required to submit comprehensive budget, tax, revenue, expenditure, and information on an annual basis to the DCA. Much of the data are used for state reporting rather than analytical purposes. The indicators used in this study were created from the basic financial data to correspond to measures found in the financial management and analysis literature.

Most of the financial indicators used in this study, including intergovernmental revenue, police and fire expenditure levels, number of employees, debt, debt service, property value, and taxes, are standard measures broadly used in the local finance literature or adapted from the Financial Trend Monitoring System [20]. Other variables used are based upon recent studies of financial indicators in local government and include fiscal capacity, funds flow, and capital burden. The measure of fiscal capacity used here is the ratio of assessed value to population and represents a local government's ability to raise revenue. Funds flow is a measure of the difference between revenues and expenditures and reflects potential inability to balance the budget or meet required service levels. Capital burden is a ratio of capital expenditures to total expenditures, and debt to revenue and debt to assessed value are ratios used to assess the relationship between funding or capacity and the degree of explicit expenditure obligation not easily controllable. Some of the variables or indicators used in previous large city research are not available for smaller jurisdictions because many are not collected systematically in Pennsylvania at present, or were not previously collected, preventing sufficient continuity over time. Nevertheless, indicators collected by DCA or computed from the basic data available meet the research need for consistent and reliable data, in addition to allowing for an important look at trends over time not seen in past research. One other external "objective" measure, bond rating, is used because it can provide an additional perspective on overall financial condition of the smaller versus larger governments, and it is widely considered in drawing conclusions about fiscal viability.

The literature includes very few explicit or specific judgments about the relationships between financial indicators and size, but implies that they are different in larger than smaller cities and that larger cities are more likely to exhibit signs of burden. Smaller cities in turn are thought to be in less financial difficulty, but provide generally lower levels of service.

Means and their changes over time for various financial indicators are examined for both small and large cities to assess whether and what kinds of systematic differences emerge. One-way analysis of variance is then used over the five data points in the 1966–1980 period to determine whether observed differences in the financial indicators are significant and whether important differences persist over time. The statistical technique of analysis of variance compares variances between two groups to determine the probability that the two populations from which the sample is drawn actually have the same mean. The F distribution is used to determine whether the difference observed between two groups is statistically significant. Larger F values coupled with low probabilities indicate a significant difference does exist between the two categories, in this case large versus small cities.

To further explore the relationships between size and financial indicators indicative of fiscal condition, other relationships will also be investigated. These supplemental analyses will be performed using regression and the logarithm of population to deal with the argument that the over and under 50,000 categories found in the existing literature may appear arbitrary. Because this study is considered exploratory, and the models of fiscal stress in the literature somewhat tenuous, certain individual indicators of financial condition such as tax, debt, interest and intergovernmental aid will be used in the regression analysis.

RESULTS

Table 1 presents the mean values of selected financial indicators by local government size over the period from 1966 to 1980. Examination of the patterns and trends over time reveals some notable difference between small and large cities, yet the differences appear to diminish over the period. Per capita taxes as well as per capita federal and state aid are both higher in large cities. Both small and large communities had large intergovernmental revenue increases during the period 1966 to 1980. Per capita debt, one sign of fiscal burden, is also much higher in larger cities, although the proportion of and to total revenue has generally increased over time in both large and small cities. The debt to revenue ratio has declined over time in both large and small cities, but far more notably in large cities so that the ratios in large and small cities have become much more similar.

The differences seen between large and small cities for the financial indicators shown in Table 1 appear to be substantial and support the "conventional wisdom" about city size. Yet there is evidence of increasing similarity in a number of categories. Nevertheless, it must be kept in mind that these findings are based on averages of the variables for numerous

Table 1 Mean Values of Various Financial Indicators by City Size Category, 1966–1980

Financial indicator	1966	1970	1973	1977	1980
Per capita taxes					
Small cities[a]	$32.70	$44.35	$48.55	$ 66.89	$ 88.33
Larger cities[b]	48.87	74.80	83.49	202.43	148.75
Per capita aid					
Small cities	$ 1.41	$ 2.52	$16.81	$ 27.46	$ 34.98
Larger cities	3.43	11.38	45.85	73.84	82.86
Per capita debt					
Small cities	$15.53	$26.86	$23.68	$ 27.68	$ 32.27
Larger cities	43.81	57.80	69.14	68.30	97.76
Debt to revenue ratio					
Small cities	0.28	0.36	0.21	0.20	0.17
Larger cities	0.79	0.83	0.36	0.29	0.28
Aid to revenue ratio					
Small cities	0.03	0.03	0.16	0.17	0.17
Larger cities	0.07	0.09	0.23	0.25	0.23

[a]Cities with 1980 populations under 50,000.
[b]Cities with 1980 populations above 50,000.

localities. To more carefully study these broad findings, a disaggregated approach, one-way analysis of variance is used.

Analysis of Variance

The relationships between small and large cities for each of the variables is investigated using one-way analysis of variance with the results presented in three separate tables. Indicators are grouped by their primary attribute (i.e., revenue related [capacity], debt related, or specific financial indicator variables). The analysis of variance for the revenue-related financial indicators for the small and large local governments over the time period from 1966 to 1980 provides some findings conforming to the traditional view (see Table 2). There are also interesting results that require further examination. Some indicators appear to vary not only by size, but change across the years and sometimes in unexpected directions. Per capita taxes and per capita state and federal aid show distinct differences between small and large cities over the entire time period. This is not unexplained, since tax levels and aid are both related to total expenditures. The federal and state aid to revenue ratio straddles the line over time, with a definite difference determined in the 1970s but

Table 2 Revenue-Related Financial Indicators, Two-Group Analysis of Variance for Equality of Means, Small and Large Cities

Financial indicator	1966	1970	1973	1977	1980
Per capita taxes					
F-statistic[a]	6.40	15.15	20.90	19.09	32.71
(Prob)[b]	(.012)	(.000)	(.000)	(.000)	(.000)
n	164	165	164	165	167
Non-real-estate tax burden					
F-statistic	1.50*	0.07*	0.37*	0.81*	3.03
(Prob)	(.215)	(.788)	(.692)	(.369)	(.083)
n	165	165	164	165	167
Per capita federal and state aid					
F-statistic	3.73	22.63	18.60	27.43	16.27
(Prob)	(.055)	(.000)	(.000)	(.000)	(.000)
n	164	165	164	165	167
Federal and state aid to revenue ratio					
F-statistic	0.94*	8.30	3.21	6.30	2.64
(Prob)	(.333)	(.004)	(.043)	(.013)	(.106)
n	165	165	164	165	167
Fiscal capacity					
F-statistic	0.40*	5.47	1.41*	9.38	0.65*
(Prob)	(.529)	(.021)	(.247)	(.002)	(.421)
n	164	165	164	165	167

[a]The first line for each indicator reports the F-statistic under the hypothesis of equality of means.
[b]The second line reports the probability of getting an F-statistic larger than that reported, given that the hypothesis holds.
*F-statistic is not significant; null hypothesis of equality of means accepted.

dwindling again in 1980. Fiscal capacity, measured here by assessed value, is the most sporadic. The pattern may reflect problems in measurement, since assessment practices can vary widely even within one state. It is important to note that the low level of relative difference between small and large in fiscal capacity does not support the conception that small communities are "better off" than large.

Taken together, these financial indicators related to revenues may indicate a diverse sequence of any number of influences on small and large governments that are related to or "caused" by uncontrollable demands not amenable to service changes or the adoption of user based revenues such as fees and charges. Small local governments may also be more subject to conservative community attitudes about the role of government, and the provision of public services, or as Weinberg [17] suggests, reduced flexibility. Some findings could be interpreted as consistent with the belief that large or urban governments are "inefficient" and require more taxes and intergovernmental aid. However, care must be taken when attempting to compare expenditures for revenues of small and large governments, because both the range of services and their individual compositions vary dramatically in different jurisdictions, whether of similar size or not. Aggregate revenue and expenditures amounts can tell us little about the quantity, quality, or relative efficiency of public services in the respective size categories of cities.

Other financial indicators that may represent differences in patterns between large and small local governments are expenditure based. Researchers have previously used debt, public safety (police and fire), and capital expenditures as indicators, and related measures are analyzed here. Since absolute police and fire expenditures would be larger in metropolitan areas simply because of the larger numbers of persons to be served, the figures are adjusted by population to somewhat more accurately reflect the units of service offered. Results shown in Table 3 indicate clearly that there is a significant difference over the entire 14 years with 1973 representing the greatest difference. This result reinforces the idea that "central cities" face demand or cost of service factors, including density, high proportions of poor, and high daytime population, that necessitate higher expenditure levels. On the other hand, public services such as highways and direct client service types of functions face higher costs of provision in very small jurisdictions because of low density, which may not be adequately captured by using cities of over 10,000 in population.

Capital burden, a ratio of capital to total expenditures, only exhibits one moderate difference ($p \le .10$) in 1966. The differences in 1970, 1973, and 1977 and 1980 are insignificant. This finding generally contradicts the usual idea of bigger cities facing high infrastructure costs. However, the *composition* of the capital expenditures is unknown and may reflect quite different situations.

Two other fiscal indicators, employees per 1,000 population and funds flow (revenues minus expenditures), demonstrate some mixed results. As expected, the ratio of employees per 1,000 residents is significantly greater in the larger cities for 1966 through 1980 than small, no doubt largely due to the greater range of services offered in large cities. However, the funds flow measure difference is barely significant.

A final indicator of financial health used here is bond rating. This measure is based upon Standard and Poor's bond rating system wherein higher values denote a determination of greater credit worthiness and financial viability. No data were available for 1966, and data for only 48 cases of the 167 could be obtained for 1970 and 53 for 1973. For 1977 and 1980, the means showed that the ratings were higher for the largest cities. However, with the exception of 1980, the analysis of variance results indicate no significant difference between large and small cities.

Table 3 Selected Other Financial Indicators, Two-Group Analysis of Variance for Equality of Means, Small and Large Cities

Financial indicator	1966	1970	1973	1977	1980
Funds flow					
F-statistic[a]	NA	14.16	4.15	12.78	3.37
(Prob)[b]	NA	(.000)	(.017)	(.000)	(.068)
n	NA	165	164	165	167
Employees per 1,000					
F-statistic	5.25	9.60	9.60	21.65	18.39
(Prob)	(.023)	(.000)	(.000)	(.000)	(.000)
n	164	164	164	165	165
Per capita public safety expenditure					
F-statistic	13.41	7.46	33.94	11.20	13.84
(Prob)	(.000)	(.007)	(.000)	(.001)	(.000)
n	167	167	166	167	167
Capital burden					
F-statistic	2.61	0.09*	0.76*	0.11*	0.11*
(Prob)	(.000)	(.000)	(.000)	(.000)	(.000)
n	167	167	166	167	167
Bond rating					
F-statistic	NA	2.26*	1.69*	0.18*	32.24
(Prob)	NA	(.139)	(.194)	(.670)	(.000)
n	NA	47	52	67	167

[a]The first line for each indicator reports the F-statistic under the hypothesis of equality of means.
[b]The second line reports the probability of getting an F-statistic larger than that reported, given that the hypothesis holds.
*F-statistic is not significant; null hypothesis of equality of means accepted.

Table 4 presents the ANOVA results on debt related financial indicators. Debt has been one of the most consistent indicators of fiscal stress found in the literature on large cities and reflects a long-term claim against current and future resources. All of the debt-related financial indicators generally exhibit significant differences between large and small cities which would be predicted based upon previous research and the functions performed in each size group. However, it is noteworthy that although no conclusive pattern exists, the debt to revenue ratio difference between small and large cities revealed by the F values has declined considerably since 1966, with 1973 and 1977 showing no real difference and 1980 very little. Per capita debt and debt to assessed value also show evidence of diminishing differences between small and large governments through the 1970s with a resurgence in 1980.

Regression Analysis

Though there is very little consensus or generally accepted theory related to general indices of fiscal stress [18], one way to supplement the explanatory power of the previous analysis is to investigate the effects of population size on select, individual indicators of potential financial difficulty. The purpose of the use of analysis of variance is to assess differences related to size. However, regression analysis may increase our understanding of the rela-

Table 4 Debt-Related Financial Indicators, Two-Group Analysis of Variance for Equality of Means, Small and Large Cities

Financial indicator	1966	1970	1973	1977	1980
Debt revenue ratio					
F-statistic[a]	14.91	8.47	2.07*	0.46*	3.38
(Prob)[b]	(.000)	(.004)	(.130)	(.497)	(.068)
n	154	165	165	165	167
Per capita debt					
F-statistic	24.60	5.95	8.28	5.38	18.76
(Prob)	(.000)	(.015)	(.022)	(.022)	(.000)
n	164	165	164	165	167
Debt-to-assessed value					
F-statistic	7.31	NA	3.57*	6.40	11.50
(Prob)	(.008)	NA	(.170)	(.012)	(.000)
n	167	NA	166	167	167
Interest burden					
F-statistic	1.40*	14.65	3.36	1.40*	16.52
(Prob)	(.238)	(.000)	(.037)	(.234)	(.000)
n	167	167	166	167	167

[a]The first line for each indicator reports the F-statistic under the hypothesis of equality of means.
[b]The second line reports the probability of getting an F-statistic larger than that reported, given that the hypothesis holds.
*F-statistic is not significant; null hypothesis of equality of means accepted.

tionships between size and financial indicators over time. Several of the debt, tax, grant, and expenditure indicators used in the previous analysis will be used as dependent variables and the log of population will be used as a predictor of the eight measures over the base 14-year period.

Overall, the results of the F-test and variance accounted for from the regression analysis presented in Table 5 illustrate that the influence of size on the selected indicators of financial stress is not uniform. Only in the case of police and fire expenditures, interest burden, and employees per capita is there more than one dependent measure by which the variance accounted for is more than ten percent. Though there are many statistically significant relationships, many of the results would be difficult to interpret substantively. For example, the debt to revenue, debt to assessed value, and interest burden measures exhibit some expected relationships with population size; however, they are not consistent or compelling support for a strong argument that size is the major influence on these indicators of financial stress.

With the other variables where there are moderate levels of variance accounted for (police/fire expenditures, employees per capita, and interest burden in 1966), there appears to be a size dynamic at work. It is logical to assume that expenditures on public safety (especially police in the local governments being used here) and public employees will increase with population. Yet, these same relationships do not hold for capital burden, non-real-estate tax burden, or even federal and state grants measures.

Table 5 Summary of *F*-Test and Variance Accounted for, Results for Regression Analysis of Log of Population on Financial Indicators

Financial indicator	F-Value, significance, and variance accounted for				
	1966	1970	1973	1977	1980
Debt to revenue	4.4[a] (.04)	15.8[c] (.11)	n.s.	n.s.	3.9[c] (.03)
Grant to revenue	n.s.	15.4[c] (.09)	12.6[c] (.07)	14.6[c] (.08)	n.s.
Non-real-estate tax burden	n.s.	n.s.	n.s.	n.s.	n.s.
Debt to assessed value	n.s.	15.9[c] (.09)	8.8[b] (.05)	11.0[b] (.06)	14.9[c] (.08)
Interest burden	54.9[c] (.25)	13.3[c] (.07)	30.8[c] (.16)	n.s.	29.4[c] (.15)
Employees per capita	9.3[c] (.06)	33.2[c] (.07)	39.8[c] (.19)	28.2[c] (.14)	n.s.
Capital burden	n.s.	n.s.	n.s.	n.s.	n.s.
Police/fire expenditures	53.1[c] (.25)	54.5[c] (.25)	62.8[c] (.27)	56.5[c] (.25)	70.7[c] (.30)

[a,b,c]Significant at $p \leq$ .05, .01, and .001, respectively.

Note: The variance accounted for (R^2) in the statistically significant cases is presented in parentheses.

CONCLUSIONS AND IMPLICATIONS OF FINDINGS

The Reagan administration's efforts to set responsibility for policymaking and financing of many governmental functions closer to the point of delivery has resulted in an unparalleled transfer of control to the states and local governments. Over the years, states have been urged to assume a stronger leadership role in the overall direction of financial activities within their borders. Numerous policy actions ranging from changes in current restrictions on taxing and borrowing to outright assumption of more costly local functions have been suggested [7]. There can be little doubt that under the current intergovernmental situation the pressure on the states to develop and implement policy will escalate. The differences revealed in this study between large and smaller cities indicate that they *do* differ in some regards, but not necessarily along the expected dimensions. In addition, and more importantly, the small and large communities studied are becoming more similar. Lack of coherent, state-based policies to explicitly deal with the changing needs of smaller communities could seriously threaten their future financial viability as they struggle to adapt to both endogenous and exogenous fiscal challenges.

Broad-based policy aimed at improving or at least stabilizing local governments' fiscal conditions and effectively and equitably allocating and managing resources must encompass a heterogeneous group of governmental units of various sizes with differing complements of functions, population compositions, and financial abilities. The results of this research underscore the fact that structuring policies which meet key criteria will be aided by a clear understanding of underlying distinctions among units which make their circumstances different than other units or groups.

Given the unique characteristics of each local government, one might conclude that there are far more differences than similarities, and thus each unit should be treated individually. Since that option is not efficient or possible, nor even necessarily desirable, what is needed is a framework for policy that can recognize any important differences which set groups or subgroups of local governments apart from the bulk of governmental units within a state. In this way, the parts are less likely to suffer because only the whole was considered. In times of relative munificence when "side payments" are possible, it is neither as difficult nor necessary that policy meet a workable, comprehensive set of standards. Today, with continued scarcity, the luxury of mistakes which are later ameliorated by additional outlays of funds is something which no level of government can long afford.

This research has focused on community size as one characteristic among several which may legitimately demand differential policy, not because "special" policy is necessarily demanded, but rather because special, negative policy is apt to be implemented by *default* as continued attention on the fiscal plights of large communities prevents (by time constraints) study and decisions from being made regarding smaller communities. Questions have been raised concerning the ability of smaller communities to meet new fiscal challenges both because of their relatively smaller tax bases and managerial capability. Despite this, the assumption that smaller communities are essentially different from large because larger cities face such a complex range of problems still persists. The results of this study show that for cities in the 10,000–50,000 population bracket, this assumption may be based more on myth than reality. While small, affluent communities do exist, they coexist with small communities with limited wealth but increasing costs.

While the results of this research give challenge to historical assumptions and research findings on city size, a study of communities below 10,000 in population might also be revealing. Including this category of communities in this study would have given an important basis of comparison, but lack of data and the poor reliability of available data prevented their inclusion. Smaller jurisdictions, particularly the smallest jurisdictions in some states, face more stringent revenue-raising restrictions. Yet, they already are confronted by implicit and revenue restrictions because of the limitations of small size. Smaller communities may have quite homogeneous populations; if the characteristic of homogeneity is poverty, property tax increases not only hit hard but may be impossible. Taxes which can easily be avoided through mobility such as a sales tax or even various fees are not realistic, and have the additional complicating potential of backfiring (e.g., driving away tourists or shoppers altogether).

Growth may particularly burden a smaller community's existing service system's capacity. For example, a recent study of fiscal impacts of growth on rural jurisdictions in Idaho found that in one community the fiscal impact of new high-rise condominiums was actually negative, rather than the positive projected, in part because the buildings were too tall for existing fire equipment [21, p. 134]. In addition, research through the years has indicated the existence of U-shaped cost functions for many common municipal services, where the highest unit costs are seen at the extreme low and high ends of population size.

SUGGESTED FURTHER RESEARCH

As noted by Cigler [4] and Bahl [18], the research and policy models related to financial condition require further development of a theoretical framework, relevant methodology, sound databases, and substantive knowledge about fiscal indicators for policy development. These findings support the existence of systematic, underlying differences in local governments of varying sizes which lead to different, but not necessarily superior or inferior, outcomes. Structuring of a generally acceptable set of indicators for policy development will also require the recognition of similar influences among units to allow comparison across jurisdictions. In the process of comparing and monitoring performance of effectiveness, unique circumstances may be identified and their most likely impact projected.

The results of this study indicate that it is unlikely that one set of fiscal indicators could be used to adequately assess all sizes of local governments. Different economic, political, and decision-making dynamics are clearly at work in large and small or even subgroups of the jurisdictions. However, common patterns and categories of variables do exist and form an important foundation for further refinement of the elements within those size categories. Consensus on general principles and operational definitions of measures such as debt, fiscal capacity, tax effort, intergovernmental aid, and related indicators does not exist, but will be needed to draw together empirical research into an integrated approach to policy formulation at one or more levels of government.

The results of this study underscore the need for financial policy models to be legitimated by research as well as for an increased level of and more focused effect to extend and refine the study of fiscal conditions. The development of a framework for study is necessary to determine whether causal mechanisms related to community size exist. This would include a judgment and understanding of which variables are important to each group of governments, how specific variables may differentially affect jurisdictions of varying sizes, and what causal, policy, and feedback processes may be at work. Further, explicit comparisons between different levels of small as well as between large and small and metropolitan and nonmetropolitan governments are needed to fully distinguish potential impacts of economic, industrial, demographic, and higher level government policy changes.

Policy relevant financial indictors should meet the requirements of researchers who are providing the foundations for further research, methodology, and theoretical developments. Financial policy models have to address the diversity and complexity facing practitioners and policymakers at federal and state levels who have the responsibilities for allocating scarce resources across levels and units of government as well as determining the parameters within which local taxing and spending policy must be made. Where differences between classes of local governments and subgroups of classes are systematic and different enough to warrant potentially separate policy consideration, development of relevant financial indicators and measures of both financial conditions and efficiency will be critical. Effective research and policy models have to be targeted to develop equitable and efficient federal and state financial policies in the evolving and increasingly turbulent intergovernmental fiscal system.

Further research on smaller communities is needed. The results of this study and the recommended research directions and policy efforts do not in any way minimize the fiscal problems of large local governments, or take priority over other issues facing the states and their local governments. However, the findings *do* underscore the importance of investigating and clarifying underlying assumptions and criteria upon which financial, state and federal policy is based.

REFERENCES

1. T. Luce and J. R. Pack, "State Support under the New Federalism," *Policy Anal. Manage.*, *3*: 339–358 (1984).
2. C. L. Bradbury, H. F. Ladd, M. Perrault, and A. Reschovsky, *National Tax Journal*, *37*: 151–170 (1984).
3. B. W. Honadle, *Public Administration in Rural and Small Jurisdictions*, Garland, New York (1983).
4. B. A. Cigler, "Small City and Rural Governance: The Changing Environment," *Public Administration Review*, *44*(6): 540–544 (Nov/Dec 1984).

5. D. E. Shalala, "Government's Role—More Losses Ahead," *National Civic Review, 71*: 142–143 (1982).

6. S. A. MacManus, "State Government: The Overseer of Municipal Finance," *The Municipal Money Chase* (A. Sbragia, ed.), West Virginia Press, Boulder, CO, pp. 135–183 (1983).

7. D. E. Shalala, "Using Financial Management to Avert Financial Crisis," *Govern. Fin., 8*: 17–21 (1979).

8. Advisory Commission on Intergovernmental Relations. *State-Local Relations Bodies: State ACIRs and Other Approaches* (1981, March).

9. Advisory Commission on Intergovernmental Relations. *ACIR Annual Report* (25th ed.) (1983a).

10. Advisory Commission on Intergovernmental Relations. *1981 Tax Capacity of the Fifty States.* (1983b September).

11. General Accounting Office. *Community Service Block Grant: New State Role Brings Program and Administration Changes*, HRD-84-76 (1984).

12. W. D. Broadnax, "The New Federalism: Hazards for State and Local Governments?" *Policy Studies Rev., 1*: 231–235 (1981).

13. F. Teitelbaum, "The Relative Responsiveness of State and Federal Aid to Distressed Cities," *Policy Studies Rev.*, November: 309–322 (1981).

14. R. J. Reeder, *Nonmetropolitan Fiscal Indicators: A Review of the Literature*, Economic Research Service, U.S. Department of Agriculture, Washington, D.C. (1984).

15. R. J. Reeder, *Rural Government: Raising Revenue and Feeling the Pressure*, Economic Research Service, U.S. Department of Agriculture, Washington, D.C. (1985).

16. A. Sokolow & B. W. Honadle, "How Rural and Local Governments Budget," *Public Admin. Rev.*, September/October: 373–383 (1984).

17. M. Weinberg, "Budget Retrenchment in Small Cities: A Comparative Analysis of Wooster and Athens, Ohio," *Public Budget. Fin., 4*: 46–57 (1984).

18. R. W. Bahl, *Financing State and Local Government in the 1980s*, Oxford University Press, New York (1984).

19. A. Sokolow, "Population Growth and Administration Variations in Small Cities," *Policy Studies Rev.*, 72–85 (1982).

20. S. M. Groves, W. M. Godsey, and M. A. Shulman, "Financial Indicators for Local Government," *Public Budgeting Fin., 3*: 5–19 (1981).

21. S. M. Smith, G. E. Morousek, and D. Blayney, "Managing the Costs of Growth in Rural Communities," *State Local Govern. Rev., 16*: 130–135 (1984).

44

Two Superoptimum Solutions in a Cutback Mode

Robert T. Golembiewski

Various forms of the alternative resolution of problems have appeared in recent years, and Nagel [1] adds to them the fertile notion of "superoptimum solutions." His focus is on public controversies, and he urges attention to that form of resolution whereby participants—who are potential combatants—all "come out ahead of their initial best expectations" [2]. Generically, superoptimum solutions can involve:

1. Achieving some goal objectively beyond that considered the best attainable.
2. Resolving policy disputes involving apparently intractable positions in opposition, such as liberal and conservative goals and priorities.
3. Resolving adjudicative or rule-applying controversies.
4. Enabling all sides to a controversy to add substantially to the values received from a solution.

Terms like "superoptimum solutions" should be used sparingly, and always carefully. Here, the usage denotes a solution that is arguably "better" than a body of experience would lead one to expect. Moreover, this analysis adds the requirement that qualifying solutions must rest on a theoretic base of general applicability which helps solve relatively targeted problems without creating other and less tractable problems.

The purpose here is to expand a bit on the superoptimum solution genre. Policy disputes will not be at issue. The focus will be on alternative patterns of interaction and their products, in contrast to Nagel's basic emphasis on public policy. Two brief case studies constitute the present vehicle for this illustration of how one can usefully expand the sense of superoptimum solutions. Both case studies deal with the management of cutback situations—adverse personnel actions required by obdurate economic conditions. Typically, cutback results in no-win or lose/lose resolutions, and the present purpose is to illustrate how an alternative model of interaction can help avoid such somber outcomes.

Source: Public Budgeting and Financial Management, 4(1): 231–254 (1992).

DOUR DYNAMICS OF COMMON CUTBACKS

Cutback management is much with us nowadays, in all arenas, and hunkering down seems the general order of the day. Native cunning encourages caution, closedness, avoidance, and more than a little whistling in the dark. Few people can tolerate the experience, let alone grow from it or relish it, despite some brave talk about eliminating the deadwood or about becoming lean and mean. Bluntly, cutback sets a proverbial tiger loose in the streets, and neither theory nor experience suffice to manage those often-powerful forces. Even "adequate" solutions are rare.

Beta Plant illustrates the typical case of "resolution." An old facility in the so-called rust belt had seen its best days, and even the good ones. Management decided to close the plant, relocate whatever personnel possible, and deal with the others gently and as generously as possible. Employees resisted, however, and especially that substantial proportion of them approaching retirement. Many present employees had opened the plant over two decades ago. Just a bit more time would suit them just fine.

A reluctant management agreed to stretch out the plant closing, in real appreciation for past good works under trying circumstances. Management also realized a demonstration of reasonableness might defang possible union resistance.

This strategy had some surprising effects. For example, management expected a substantial attrition of personnel as well as a leisurely end-of-game play by those remaining. Both would exacerbate the several and growing inefficiencies of Alpha as a worksite for doing what a changing technology demanded. Management was surprised, at times pleasantly: The stretch-out was put to good use for planning that paid dividends, and management even had the time to commission a study of the plant-closing. Curiously to management, however, only a few employees left. More curious still, the remaining employees began setting an almost continuous succession of monthly production records.

These surprises to management imply they had an unreliable model of the human effects of the plant closing, and strange events reinforced this conclusion. Despite constant and orchestrated announcements to the contrary, researchers found that a growing proportion of employees came to believe that "management can't close a going concern." In fact, the proportion of such true believers actually peaked in the last survey before the closing, in the month of the *highest production ever*. Employees paid little apparent attention to the schedule for closing, which was widely disseminated. Moreover, most workshop sessions for out-placement experiences had to be canceled because of insufficient attendance, despite the fact that they were on "company time."

Hence the closing came like a bolt out of the blue to many employees, and some suffered strong reactions. Indeed, over the next year so many ex-employees became suddenly unavailable for the study—either because of illness or death, or due to a sudden unwillingness to have anything to do with Beta—that research on the aftermath of the plant closing was canceled.

TOWARD A VALUE-GUIDED TECHNOLOGY FOR CUTBACK

These typical outcomes can be minimized by a standard technology-cum-values. The line of "action research" labeled organization development (or OD) had begun to accumulate theory and experience relevant to the cutback mode [3], and some derivative applications can reasonably claim superoptimum status. In general, adverse personnel actions have strong lose/lose components for both employees and the employing organization. In specific cases, in contrast, OD provides a normatively based technology for extracting some aspects of win/win gold from the lose/lose dross characteristic of cutback.

The purpose here is to illustrate two such cases of superoptimum solutions in cutback situations—when individual needs were met to a greater degree than is usual under conditions of stringent organization demands. The two contexts are not exotic and, if in distinct ways, commonly reflect how OD values and approaches can be helpful in cutback.

The two cases also differ in significant ways. The first case is labeled "unfolding" in that it relies on rudimentary structure and basically trusts the processes and values of OD and thus, in the OD vernacular, "lets things happen" within the context of these processes and values.

The second case may be labeled "articulated." It relies on a detailed design, applied in several different contexts by different teams of facilitators, which seeks to encourage relatively specific outcomes while also enlarging the normal range of choices for both individuals and organizations in cutback situations. In contrast to the first case, the second has an inclination to "make things happen."

Organizational Town Meeting as Unfolding Design

The first case derives from the "oil patch," from the petroleum/gas exploration business, which is infamous for its boom-and-bust cycles. The specific locus is the Canadian headquarters of a multinational firm, which had grown to several hundred employees in a short period of time under the stimulus of high oil prices. The case involves gently guided participative responses to a budget crunch, and relevant description can be summarized by three emphases. In turn, following sections detail a start-up OD effort in the organization, describe a cutback response congruent with that OD effort, and review the superoptimum features of that response.

Critical Prework Toward Regenerative Systems

From start-up, the management team sought to develop a model organization, and devoted considerable time and resources to building a high-involvement culture—responsive *and* lean [4]. The creation of "regenerative interaction" [5] constitutes *the* key feature of this culture. Figure 1 depicts how combinations of four variables can generate contrasting mod-

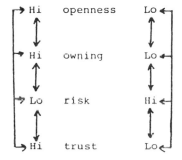

```
Regenerative   Degenerative
Interaction    Interaction


  Hi   openness    Lo

  Hi   owning      Lo

  Lo   risk        Hi

  Hi   trust       Lo
```

Figure 1 Two models for interaction and selected consequences.

els of interpersonal and group interaction. Two extreme combinations of those variables induce "regenerative" and "degenerative" interaction.

The component variables can be briefly described, with details available elsewhere [6]. One can be open without owning, as in this common statement: "They, but I can't tell you who, really dislike what you did on project X." Risk refers to the objective threat in some environment, and trust refers to the degree of confidence one has in colleagues that things will come out okay.

Figure 1 presents one other crucial piece of information. It depicts some common consequences attributed to the degenerative condition which motivate avoiding it, whenever possible and even where awkward. More or less, an opposite set of consequences explains why major resources can be justified for moving toward regenerative interaction, and for maintaining it.

Some probable consequences of degenerative interaction are:

Communication and decision-making procedures become increasingly burdened.

Persons become less effective in isolating and resolving substantive issues.

The amount of unfinished business sharply increases.

Persons feel diminished interpersonal competence and psychological failure and they fail to solve problems that stay solved without creating other problems.

Persons become dependent and over-cautious, and respond by "tattling" activities, by preoccupation with being "safe," or by "don't rock the boat" attitudes.

Organization norms restricting owning and openness are reinforced or developed.

Tendencies toward fragmentation of organization units are enhanced, particularly as the basic organizing model uses functional departmentalization, which is usually the case.

An Unhappy and Unexpected Learning Opportunity

The regenerative system got an early challenge—an unexpected and unwelcome learning opportunity to test the strength and reaction time of the organization. Progress toward the culture building was advanced but still ongoing when the price of oil experienced a double shock—both Canadian policies and those of the oil-rich Arabian states depressed prices, suddenly and sharply. The prime consequence? An organization in a sharply growing mode was "tasked" by corporate to cut payroll by 20%. (This simplifies a bit: Expenses also had to be cut. But the present description serves well enough.)

The general manager (GM) put it directly. "We are on our way to Camelot, and the world intrudes on our plans."

During the morning the GM learned of the bad news, he also decided on a strategy, in collaboration with his management team and an OD consultant. "Decided" is too formal a description of the process, however: "We kind of reflexed into the decision," in the GM's words. After contacting corporate officials to assess degrees of local "wriggle room," this rationale and design came to dominate the team's discussion:

Well, we could go into the common mode—meet behind closed doors, try to keep the lid on things, and draw up the master plan for the fates of others.

But what the hell? That gets us tied in knots, encourages inevitable rumors, and risks losing precisely those people we want most to keep.

Above all, that's out-of-sync with the culture we've been building.

So, let's have a kind of organizational town meeting—bring everybody together, beginning tomorrow morning, first thing. We'll lay out what we know, and decide our common fate.

The "town meeting" began the next morning, with little encumbering structure. The GM led a series of guided discussions that relied heavily on many small "buzz groups" to permit simultaneous expressions of opinion, brainstorming, and so on, concerning individual issues. The town meeting spent the first 90 minutes or so in four basic kinds of activities:

- *Ventilation*: how individuals felt about the "tasking."
- *Corporate boundaries*: 20% payroll savings, any way, within certain time constraints.
- A *needs assessment*: a discussion of priorities, given the "task."
- *General strategies*: a half-dozen were evaluated—across-the-board cut, etc.—but a participative strategy was the consensus choice.
- *Options available to individuals*: early retirement, educational leave, and so on.

In each activity, a brief input was followed by discussion or evaluation in buzz groups with shifting memberships, and then reports were made to the total assembly, where discussion continued until repetition set in. Then the process moved on.

An "aha!" experience came early. The motto became: "Let's do it our way, in our diverse ways." A voice rang out: "All those interested in working 4 days a week meet over in the northwest corner." Pretty soon, 8 or 10 "gaggles" were clustered here and there in the large auditorium—for early retirement, educational leave, a few persons considering voluntary separations, and so on. To make a longer story very short, the firm soon had its 20% savings, basically before the day was over.

It did not all just occur, of course, as five points demonstrate. Paramountly, the early work toward regenerative interaction fueled the effort, which required unusual openness and trust. Moreover, early on, a steering committee was established to coordinate the several personnel actions to assure that priorities could be met. In addition, a sophisticated Human Resources information system permitted quick turnaround on many details. Further, some decisions were left until the following week—as persons checked with a relevant other, such as about planning to have a child; as part-time teaching opportunities at the local business schools were canvassed; and so on. Finally, some decisions applied for only 6 months, although most were for a year. So the associated details and risk would remain until much time had passed. Normal attrition was expected to provide sufficient flexibility for returning to the *status quo ante* after the contracted periods.

Aspects of Superoptimum Solution

No real-time data gathering was attempted in this case, but many follow-up interviews and a master's project permit substantial confidence that the organizational town meeting generated major aspects of a superoptimum solution.

Four points illustrate the support for this conclusion. First, an unwelcome task was accomplished with a preponderance of win/win for both management and employees. In both cases, the design sought to empower, with a direct motivation. As Slaby notes succinctly: "A feeling of powerlessness goes hand in hand with a sense of unfairness" [7].

Such empowering covered a substantial range, and especially for employees for whom choices appeared in many forms. Some employees had only a limited choice, to be sure—as to decide on whether or not to reduce their work week, usually with some costs either way. Other employees took fuller advantage of the unfortunate opportunity to do things that might ordinarily have been delayed, or even forfeited: begin a degree program, develop a business on a full- or part-time basis, or have a baby. In one case, an employee with marginal performance appraisals was empowered to seek greater clarity of his chances to succeed in the organization. The result? The individual began a program to remedy certain deficiencies in skills and knowledge, and negotiated a reduction in work hours.

Second, on very definite balance, awkward consequences were avoided. Thus management avoided playing God. This is energy-depleting at best, and at worst often comes to be seen as arbitrary and procrustean. Relatedly, no "survivor's mentality" developed, and this avoids variable but tricky potential for later mischief. Perhaps most of all, the town meeting largely avoided the several debilitations of a top-down effort: an intended secrecy, but often vitiated by rumors if not serious leaks; a dribbling away of morale; people leaving in disgust; possible posturing if not toadying for favored treatment; and so on.

Win/win was not universal, of course. In a few cases, to choose a prime example, some employees were seen as "not doing what they could," and active efforts were made to surface such issues as they occurred. An external consultant encouraged and facilitated such confrontations, with major multiple going-in presumptions: that individuals would differ in what they "could do"; that consequently any tendencies for a norm of "equal shares" should be resisted; but that in any case colleagues were better off if suspicions of slacking were raised even if all could not be settled. Several employees also played similar facilitative roles, operating on the same assumptions.

Third, and perhaps paramountly, the town meeting design both legitimated and drew strength from the culture of regenerative interaction. The style was applied in a tough case, and risking its loss was not only affirming but also heightened the probability of the persistence of a regenerative style. Reliance on regenerative interaction, and its persistence under adversity, perhaps best reflect a superoptimum solution in this case. Degenerative interaction is more common in organizational cutback, where avoiding lawsuits may seem the most desirable goal.

Fourth, some may propose that this approach "wasted time" and hence cannot be "adequate," let alone superoptimum, but I do not believe this is true even in the short-run when one contrasts the town meeting with the typical cutback scenario. There, ideally after top-secret discussions, those to be let go are informed close to a normal time-out boundary—for example, noon on a Friday, or the afternoon before a holiday. People are given the afternoon to clear out their desk, with the apparent expectation that the succeeding weekend or vacation provides sufficient emotional distance for both those remaining and the "unbuckled." The more likely short-run reality has very different features. Management's decision making is likely to be extended, and even tumultuous; rumors will overstate the dimensions of the cutback, if anything; and an exodus is likely, with the most mobile people being the first to leave, and the departures have been known to be so numerous or so strategic that an organization has at one and the same time been conducting a cutback as well as numerous personnel searches.

In the long run, moreover, the typical scenario does not promise benign effects. Let us be selective. For example, attempting to distance one's self and others from the immediate pain by quick shuffles very often will increase the long-run pain for all, as in later concerns about the justice of it all. Absent the information on which the original cutback was based, in addition, survivors may fear the other shoe will soon drop. Moreover, the fantasies underlying the typical cutback scenario probably will not mirror reality in important particulars, as Sutton [8] and others have shown. For example, people's productivity does not necessarily deteriorate sharply if they are given substantial notice of an adverse personnel action, which represents the quintessential fear that typically rationalizes sudden personnel separations.

Demotion Experience as Articulated Design

This section describes a second example of a superoptimum solution via OD under cutback conditions, and the label "articulated" has multiple denotations. Basically, unlike the first case, the design is substantially programmed and comes closer to "making things happen" than to "allowing things to happen" [9,10]. Moreover, this second design of a superoptimum solution via OD under cutback conditions design has been applied several times, beginning in 1971 when a national marketing organization had to sharply reduce its employment even as the national economy was booming. In addition, several teams of facilitators have applied the design, and in several decades. Various pre- versus post-test measures also have estimated effects, and the overall results have been positive in all applications [11,12]. Finally, the demotion design was first used with organizational members who had substantial prior experience with OD values and approaches [13], but some subsequent applications involved no prework. The effects have been similar.

So the demotion design has a generic OD kinship with the town meeting just illustrated, but the two differ in many respects. The town meeting was held only once, with one facilitator. Moreover, only postintervention data are available for the town meeting, and those come largely from interviews. In addition, the town meeting design rested on substantial prior experience with OD values, while the demotion design seems to profit from such experiences but has been applied successfully without them.

Elements of OD Design for Demotion

The initial demotion design was motivated by an unsuccessful effort to add to the product line of a pharmaceutical firm, which resulted in a major cutback that was long delayed by hopeful marketing executives. Among other actions, the original decision envisioned releasing 13 district managers of salespersons, all of whom had been satisfactory performers for periods of time—often 5–10 years. Management found the decision unpalatable—both in humanistic terms as well as in a loss of valuable experience that could be tapped later if sales permitted—but executives saw no reasonable alternative. For example, demotion was seen by them as both unusual and beset with insurmountable difficulties for employer and employee. Demoted managers would suffer loss of income and important perks in "picking up the bag" again, and the required changes in attitude and behaviors were seen as beyond the reach of the ex-managers as well as of management.

However, a team of OD intervenors persisted in advocating a "demotion experience" for all willing ex-managers, and management relented. Most managers accepted the offer of demotion, and only 2 of 13 opted for a generous separation package. The willing ex-managers, along with two facilitators, met at a central location several days after the adverse personnel action.

The demotion design occurred over 2 days. Essentially, it was rooted conceptually in avoiding condition I and approaching condition II below:

I. Imaginings triggered by demotion + relative aloneness + relative helplessness = increases in anxiety, hostility and depression, all associated with poor coping
II. Imaginings triggered by demotion + community + mastery = more effective coping, as reflected in reductions in initial anxiety, hostility, and depression

Details of the design are available elsewhere [14,15], but several dominant themes economically suggest its character;

1. Choice was emphasized throughout the design, so as to maximize involvement, commitment, and ownership.

2. The first half of the design focused on building and utilizing a sense of community among the demotees: They shared reactions, feelings, hopes, and fears; they recounted how they dealt with news of the demotions, as in telling spouses; and they practiced ways of talking about their demotion to relevant others—customers, peers, and so on.

3. The second half of the design dealt with establishing relationships between demotees and their new supervisors, who in cases were chosen by individual demotees. Pairs discussed sales philosophies, reviewed territories, and so on.

Effects were estimated via pre- and postmeasures on the Multiple Affect Adjective Checklist (MAACL), as well as by the long-run performance of the demotees.

Four points summarize the results of several applications of the demotion design. First, the MAACL measures three important affects—hostility, anxiety, and aggression—and the demotions not only seem to have sharply increased the levels of all three, but apparently maintained those elevated levels over the interval between the receipt of the news about the option and arrival at the training site. How high is high? Norms from other populations exposed to the MAACL imply that the population of demotees score "high" but not "unusually high," with the latter referring to decompensations implying the need for clinical intervention. Specifically, perhaps 10% of demotees' scores attain the top 2% of a standardization sample, with an additional 20% of the scores approaching that level. The demotees' pretest scores average very much higher than their new managers, with all differences typically being statistically significant.

Second, the two-day demotion experience typically has a major impact on the three MAACL measures for the demotees, and almost always in the expected direction. Specifically, as Table 1 shows for the original application, there were 33 total paired-comparisons of MAACL scores for individuals—11 demotees on 3 MAACL scales. Twenty-six show reductions, and 3 indicate no change. One demotee did resent the "hand-holding," however.

Table 1 Summary of MAACL Scores, Days 1, 2, and 45, in One Application

	Mean scores, by administrations			t-test for differences between pairs of means		
	1	2	3	1 vs. 2	1 vs. 3	2 vs. 3
A. Demotees						
Anxiety	9.8	7.5	6.5	*	*	*
Depression	17.8	14.8	13.6	*	*	*
Hostility	9.5	7.2	7.2	*	*	NS
B. Managers						
Anxiety	6.3	5.3	4.6	*	*	NS
Depression	9.8	9.5	9.5	NS	NS	NS
Hostility	5.1	5.3	5.7	NS	NS	NS

*Designates a statistically significant difference at or beyond $p = .5$.
Note: NS designates a random difference.

Significantly, the participating managers seem to suffer no major adverse effects during the intervention, as far as the MAACL measures are concerned. See B in Table 1.

The MAACL reductions tend to persist. For the initial application, as Table 1 shows, no major regressions in MAACL scores occurred throughout the long posttest, which followed the short posttest by about a month. Not only were all short posttest reductions maintained for demotees, but anxiety and depression also decreased significantly between the second and third administrations of the MAACL.

Fourth, interviews with participants typically reveal no broader adverse effects over time. Several (but not all) applications of the demotion design include a series of interviews—shortly after the experience and extending over several years in one case. In the initial application, a third of the participants were repromoted during a 3- to 4-year interval, and the population as a whole in the interval experienced no work difficulties beyond normal company experience. All but one of the demotees continued employment, and he died of causes unrelated to work.

Aspects of a Superoptimum Solution

The demotion design has numerous attractive features, on balance, and these qualify it as a superoptimum solution in a situation that is usually a "downer" for all, and dire for some. Five perspectives suggest how the demotion design can improve this general state of affairs, although it cannot eliminate the sting of the personnel action felt by management as well as the demotees.

First, the demotion design increases the range of alternatives for both management and the demotees. Thus management can tangibly express its appreciation for a job satisfactorily performed in the past, and valuable experience may be husbanded for economic recovery. Moreover, the decisions by ex-managers relevant to separation/demotion give them real choices—not only about staying on or accepting generous separation settlements, but also about possibly moving closer to relatives or children and even in choosing their new supervisor.

In a critical sense, choice is at the heart of OD, and an enriched set of possibilities increases the chances that real psychological ownership of decisions will result. Hence one can expect greater commitment to make a success of the adaptations required from all by the decisions.

Second, of course, not just *any* choices will do: A choice that involves a probable failure has little to recommend it. The growing experience with the demotion design increases confidence that it presents reasonable, informed, and attainable choices. For both management and employees, in sum, experience indicates that the demotion design can help in the numerous adjustments that both supervisors and demotees must make in a workable demotion. A key factor may be that all applications of the demotion design of which I have knowledge involve people who were satisfactory performers, or better, in the role from which they were demoted.

Third, relatedly, the demotion design increases the mutual control by all participants in a difficult situation. Major elements of coercion remain for both major sets of actors, of course, but their diminution seems a definite consequence of the design. This generalization applies least to the new supervisors of the demotees, several of whom report they agreed to participate with faint heart. This may explain the significant decrease in anxiety over time for the managers in Table 1. By hypothesis, confirmed by interviews, the managers may have experienced sharply elevated anxiety when they initially learned of the demotion experience, which the pretest picks up. Evidence like that reviewed above may help managers in dealing with this up-front anxiety, ostensibly associated with facing the demotees and perhaps triggered by a conviction that demotions tend to be difficult or impossible for all.

Fourth, the design seems to have positive implications for the survivors of a cutback. In a significant sense, as interviews generally confirm, the demotion design seems to be viewed by many as a significant sign of a general organizational resolve to be "people oriented," and this implies enhanced commitment by all and removes a potential block to performance.

Fifth, the apparent palliative effects of the demotion design constitute a major reason for proposing superoptimum status. Of course, the MAACL scores suggest the stressful character of the adverse personnel action. What we know about their consequences motivates substantial efforts to moderate the stressful situations and their aftermath. Stress effects can be mundane, if troublesome [16], but those effects also can even unleash dangerous assaults on our immunological systems [17].

However, the demotion design does not ease all problems associated with adverse personnel actions. Thus not all cutbacks permit demotion, although even close observers will be surprised at its incidence in today's human resources administration [18,19]. Moreover, the initial application of the demotion design did attract some early unfavorable attention [20], essentially on ethical grounds. The major issue: Who is the client? Clearly, the management was the initiating client, and some observers worried that this might leave the demotees unrepresented and thus potentially disadvantaged.

The issue and related ones are consequential, and the reader can consult the literature for efforts to address them [21]. Consider the answer of our consulting team to the question: Who is the client? We viewed our "client" in multiple and shifting terms, as moderated by our sense of an effective organization. Consequently, top management *was* our client. During the demotion experience, the demotees became the focal client and management understood the privileged status of off-site discussions.

DISCUSSION

These two candidates for superoptimum solution do double-duty. They illustrate a technology-cum-values, usually called organization development or OD, and they support the usefulness of Nagel's seminal metaphor. Three points add useful detail supporting these broad conclusions.

First, the two micro case studies rest on a broadly applicable approach to superoptimum solutions—via inducing aspects of regenerative interaction between people and groups. This augments Nagel's original list of "procedures," which include [22] generating new or novel policy alternatives; proposing new goals; bringing in a third-party; and so on. The OD approach often involves a third party—a change agent or intervenor—but adds to Nagel's list a focus on useful interpersonal and intergroup processes and interaction that can enrich and enliven exchanges between people.

This focus on models of interaction is at once narrow, and yet ubiquitous in application. Thus regenerative interaction might well facilitate policy development, whenever. For example, I hear—but do not know for certain—that the Camp David accords rested on the conscious effort to induce regenerative interaction by a skilled facilitator. And Nagel rightly highlights Camp David as illustrating a superoptimum solution.

Second, the two cameos also add a useful sense of reproducibility of approaches to superoptimum solutions. Both cases involve the induction of aspects of regenerative interaction, via techniques that typically "work" [23]. Moreover, the demotion design has been replicated—by different intervenors, in several settings, at various times. These two senses of reproducibility add to the appeal of superoptimum solutions, which can in part rest on foundations in addition to flashes of insight about (for example) new or novel policies.

Third, the two case studies serve to highlight the challenge inherent in the concept of superoptimum solutions. Their *basic* definition —as referring to situations from which participants "come out ahead of their initial *best* expectations"—constitutes a dynamic target. To illustrate, efforts to build regenerative systems are no longer rare, but neither are they usual. That situation may well change. Certainly, the trend line of reliance on OD is sharply up over the last two decades. Today's superoptimum solution, in short, can become tomorrow's initial best expectation, or even a commonplace expectation. And so the continual search for superoptimum solutions will be motivated by its own successes.

REFERENCES

1. S. S. Nagel, "Super-Optimum Solutions in Public Controversies," *Futures Res. Q.*, (1989).
2. Nagel, "Super-Optimum Solutions," p. 11.
3. R. T. Golembiewski, *Approaches to Planned Change*, Vol. 2, Marcel Dekker, New York (1979).
4. R. T. Golembiewski and A. Kiepper, *High Performance and Human Costs*, Praeger, New York (1988).
5. R. T. Golembiewski, *Approaches to Planned Change*, Vol. 1, Marcel Dekker, New York (1979).
6. R. T. Golembiewski, *Approaches to Planned Change*.
7. A. E. Slaby, *Aftershock*, Villard Books, New York (1989).
8. R. I. Sutton, "Managing Organizational Death," *Human Resource Manage.*, 22: 391–412 (1983).
9. R. T. Golembiewski, S. B. Carrigan, W. R. Mead, R. Munzenrider, and A. Blumberg, "Toward Building New Work Relationships," *J. Appl. Behav. Sci.*, 8: 135–148 (1972).
10. R. T. Golembiewski, "The Demotion Design," *National Productivity Rev.*, 2: 63–70 (Winter 1982–83).
11. R. T. Golembiewski, et al., "Toward Building New Work Relationships."
12. R. T. Golembiewski, et al., "The Demotion Design."
13. R. T. Golembiewski, S. B. Carrigan, and A. Blumberg, "More On Building New Work Relationships," *J. Appl. Behav. Sci.*, 9: 26–28 (1973).
14. R. T. Golembiewski, et al., "Toward Building New Work Relationships."
15. R. T. Golembiewski, et al., *Approaches to Planned Change*, Vol. 1, pp. 196–201.
16. R. T. Golembiewski and R. Munzenrider, *Phases of Burnout*, Praeger, New York (1988).
17. Slaby, *Aftershock*.
18. F. H. Goldner, "Demotion in In Industrial Management," *Am. Sociol. Rev.*, 30: 714–724 (1965).
19. D. T. Hall and L. A. Isabella, "Downward Movement and Career Development," *Organizational Dynamics*, 14: 5–23 (1985).
20. R. E. Walton and D. P. Warwick, "The Ethics of Organization Development," *J. Appl. Behav. Sci.*, 9: 681–699 (1973).
21. R. T. Golembiewski, *Public Administration as a Developing Discipline*, Marcel Dekker, New York (1978).
22. Nagel, pp. 12–15.
23. R. T. Golembiewski, *Approaches to Planned Change*, Vol. 1.

45

Financing Strategy

W. Bartley Hildreth

Hugo Wall School of Urban and Public Affairs, Wichita State University, Wichita, Kansas

Strategic management seeks to shape and steer the direction of an organization. It is about choices—choices related to markets, tasks, technology, structure, processes, and resources. This chapter explores financial resource choices and the degree to which they help advance strategic initiatives. Fundamentally, financial resources permit organizational managers to acquire raw materials, to retain personnel, and to deploy assets in the production of goods and services. The strategic importance of financial choices extends beyond raising prices or cutting expenses—tactics common to organizations in all sectors of the economy. Financial choices, instead, power strategic management and serve as the indicators of success or failure.

Financing is a strategic decision. Based on an intensive study of decision making by selected top corporate executives, Donaldson and Lorsch [2, p. 6] defined strategy as the "stream of decisions over time that reveal management's goals for the corporation and the means they choose to achieve them."[1] Financial strategy relates to the

> subset of corporate goals for which management can be held accountable, and which is concerned with the financial condition and performance of the corporate entity and with the related decisions and actions of management involving the acquisition, custody, and disposition of corporate funds. [2, p. 35].

Strategic decisions exhibit spatial, size, and temporal qualities. These characteristics were highlighted by Hickson and others [3, p. 27] in a 10-year study of decision making in organizations. They concluded that strategic decisions "are those made at the top about the bigger matters." Furthermore, "(a) strategic decision is one in which those who are

---

Source: This essay is a revised version of Hildreth [1].

involved believe will play a bigger rather than a smaller part in shaping what happens for a long while afterwards" [3, p. 27].

Organizational strategies are hostage to financing questions, tempering the most sophisticated and skilled strategist. Simply stated, without economic resources, most strategic plans gather dust on a shelf [4]. As Cleverley [5, p. 181] states about health care organizations: "A strategic plan is not valid if it is not financially feasible, and a financial plan is of little value if it does not reflect the strategic decisions reached by management and the board." This requires the identification, allocation, and mobilization of resources along a strategic path.

This chapter isolates the dominant paradigms of financial choice in both business and government—each termed a unitary model for this discussion. Although the two unitary models differ, each obfuscates more complex financial choices. The mitigating influences of fiscal and managerial cultures illustrate the imprecision of a unitary model to adequately describe financial choices. An alternative model of financing strategy is advanced, at least for government. Due to the complexity of public-sector financial decision making a portfolio model is employed to capture the range of strategic choices available to accomplish the desired organizational results.

UNITARY MODELS

Both business and government alike follow a limited model of financial decision making. In business the unitary goal is to maximize shareholders' wealth. For government, the parallel unitary goal is to balance the budget. Each unitary model defines the results and structures the choice processes. In fact, the utility of a financial choice is determined by its contribution to the unitary goal. The following subsections define the two models.

The Unitary Model of a Firm

Modern financial theory posits that the rational economic behavior of the firm dictates a unitary goal—to maximize shareholders' wealth. The optimal decision results from a comparison of financing choices in relation to the bottom-line question: Which option maximizes the wealth of owners? Accepting this theoretical paradigm permits mathematical tests of strategic options [6, 7]. The primary measurement tool is the return on investment, or the rate of return on investments compared to the cost of capital [2, p. 39].

In financing strategy, the primary choice is between debt and equity. The value of the firm, however, is independent of the choice of the financing instrument [8]. By incurring debt to finance strategic decisions, a firm obtains a stock of current funds based on the expectation that future cash flow will more than offset the debt repayment terms (or debt service). The capital financing choice is measured, in part, by the ratio of total debt to owners' equity. As an alternative to debt, the firm could obtain the resources by altering ownership interests. The selling of more shares of ownership dilutes the ownership interests of current equity holders, however. Given that shareholders expect not only dividend payments, but also increasing levels over time, measures such as earnings per share and growth in earnings per share dominate [9]. The costs of equity represents the expected return from dividends and price appreciation.

According to the unitary theory, strategic decisions influence the firm's financial performance, which in turn influences its market value. The simplicity of the model has, until recently, escaped some corporate managers. With the growth in the size and frequency of hostile takeovers, corporate executives have renewed their interest in the market value of individual business units. Thus, strategic decisions such as acquisitions and mergers are evaluated in terms of the creation of increased shareholder value [10]. In summary, the unitary model is the dominate basis for studying the economic behavior of a firm, including strategic management.

The Unitary Model of Government

A balanced budget is both a legal requirement and a political necessity for most governments. A budget links revenues and expenditures, thus seemingly encapsulating all that is needed to understand the governmental entity's financial strategy.

A balanced budget is a matter of definition. The traditional presumption is that the budget is balanced at each stage from executive submission to legislative enactment and at the end of the fiscal period. The legal measurement, however, may be taken at any one of the three stages. Furthermore, budgets may meet the measurement goal based on liberal interpretations of the decision choices. For example, an executive's budget proposal balanced on the assumption that a new (or increased) tax will gain legislative approval may satisfy the requirements of a single balanced budget rule—that is, that the executive must submit a balanced budget—but fail to represent the probability that the tax will actually be enacted into law.

A myopic focus on the balanced budget rule has become enticing of late. Calls for a balanced federal budget engender much vitriol, especially given the long history of large unbalanced budgets submitted by Presidents from both parties and subsequently adopted by a Congress of the opposite party. Yet there appears to be bipartisan political interest in reaching a balanced budget by 2002. Despite this recent reassertion of a goal, it appears that financial strategy has followed a route different from one based solely on the balanced budget target. If the stabilization function of the budget [11] is appropriate policy, then the balanced budget goal is more flexible than fixed. Thus, the ability and willingness to maintain fidelity to a unitary model of governmental finance is subject to debate.

CHALLENGE TO UNITARY MODELS: THE CULTURAL ENVIRONMENT

Strategy is not conducted in a vacuum. An organization's external environment imposes a shifting mix of demands and pressures. Laws change, markets fluctuate, and competitors gain advantages, among numerous other scenarios. Organizations must cope with their internal environments too. The internal environment is not value neutral. Fundamentally, the environment is comprised of actors, or stakeholders, who influence organizational actions—both positively and negatively.

This section highlights two arenas of so-called cultural influences on financial choices. The first area examined is fiscal culture, a market metaphor. To business the market is dominative. To government, the parallel concern is the fiscal culture—thus the subsection title. The second area is the organizational or "internal" culture, a widely observed phenomenon in both business and government alike. As viewed here, the limits on an organization's financial activities relate both to the internal culture and to its surrounding fiscal culture.

Fiscal Culture

Strategic choices emerge as powerful requirements in a competitive environment. Businesses compete for market share and value. All types of organizations—business, government, and nonprofit organizations—compete for capital. A particular organization's set of strategies is conditioned by the changing, competitive market [12,13].

An organization's strategic capacity depends on its ability to "generate resources from its day-to-day activities, and . . . its capacity to acquire strategic support from aggregates and entities within its environment" [14,p. 228]. For example, governmental decisions influence a firm's strategic choices through differentiation in factors such as regulations and taxation.

A government's strategic capacity begins with its overarching fiscal culture. In applying a cultural analogy, Wildavsky [15, p. 336] posits that "different regimes cause different budgetary behaviors." According to Wildavsky [15], regime decisions relate to the wealth of the area. Wealth is defined as economic resources that can be converted into capital, including natural resources, human skills, etc. Individuals create wealth. A political preference to tax the wealth must exist before government can mobilize resources. Without the political preference to tax, budgetary poverty results. As to a balanced budget, Wildavsky [15, p. 434] says that "the essential relationships between revenue and expenditure vary with the type of regime."

Straussman [16] relates financial choices to the fiscal climate, a factor tempering the fiscal culture. He notes that strategies vary with the fiscal climate; fiscal climates range from an unrestrained climate to a deteriorating and worsening one. As the climate changes, modifications in the fiscal institutions emerge, as in new taxes or the imposition of spending constraints.

In summary, organizational decisions are premised on conceptions about the fiscal environment. The more insensitive the organization is to the fiscal culture, the more the financial risk. Financing strategies constructed on such an ill-considered foundation is likely to prove difficult to sustain.

Managerial Culture

Of emerging concern is the impact of organizational culture, or "the shared attitudes, values, beliefs, and customs of members" [17, p. 301]. As such, organizational culture can foster, retard, or mitigate effective strategic choices [18].

Cultural biases intrude in strategy making. Strategic choices are affected, since "important decisions are often matters of judgment based on past experiences and shared assumptions about likely future events" [2, p. 164]. Plus, research suggests that an external orientation enhances strategic interests [19].

The area of finance is prone to this criticism. Miller, Rabin, and Hildreth [20, p. 94] contend that the "value base of financial managers favors control." Ellsworth [21, p. 172] points out that "the risk preferences and beliefs of the CEO [chief executive officer] and CFO [chief financial officer] are seldom questioned. Unchallenged, these benefits remain unchanged and become enshrined in financial structure policies." Ellsworth [21, p. 173] cautions that when individual value-based policies "become institutionalized, they can influence the definition and expression of the company's unique corporate character and sense of purpose, and determine the company's attitude toward risk, growth, and, in some cases, the kind of business in which the firm chooses to compete and its strategy within those businesses."

An indicator of the impact of managerial culture in business is the power of individual preferences over strategic decision making. For example, top managers, according to Donaldson and Lorsch [2], prefer internal financing over debt or equity. By limiting the distribution of excess income to equity owners through the payment of dividends, financial resources are freed for strategic initiatives. Myers [22, p. 585] observes a pecking order—"the preference for internal finance" ranks highest, but "if external financing is sought" then the "preference [is] for debt over equity." Myers [22, p. 582] is quick to note that internal financing of strategy is not necessarily in conflict with a focus on increasing shareholders' wealth.

Managers may have goals that conflict with the organization. For corporate managers, shareholders' wealth maximization may be supplanted by other conceptions. The incentive to manage a larger organization—asset growth—may be as strong as increasing profits [6, 23]. This line of reasoning is termed managerial capitalism. It reflects the view that control is separated from ownership. In fact, the premise is that managers avoid financing decisions that subject them to the "discipline of the capital market" [22, p. 582].

The centralization of decisions fuels managerial capitalism. Donaldson [24, p. 38], calls it "purchasing power for the future: the anticipated flows of unspecialized funds feeding into a single business entity for its exclusive use and benefit." He elaborates by stating that "management may be expected to prefer, all other things being equal, that corporate net funds flows be as large as possible, as soon as possible, and as certain as possible, because these spendable funds confer the power to plan and to execute action." Thus, "the magnitude, timing, and certainty of the flows of funds" are important.

The "growth of government" literature points out several related cautions. Politicians are considered rational economic actors. Thus, in the "politics for profit" reasoning, politicians rationally trade votes to accumulate political capital. This translates into institutional power and enhances the probability of reelection. In a related manner, the power of the bureaucracy to control information, and the incentive to accumulate ever increasingly larger (incremental) shares of "wealth," combine to promote the growth of government [25].

In sum, the environment—both managerial and fiscal—mitigates and complicates financial strategy, especially any attempt to place absolute fidelity to a unitary model of financial strategy. In this regard, an alternative model is advanced—a portfolio model.

THE FINANCING STRATEGY PORTFOLIO

Organizational strategies affect the ability to provide goods and services. At least in government, a range of financing strategies is available [26]. Elements of the financing strategy portfolio include:

- Budgeting
- Multiyear planning
- Accounting policy
- Tax policy
- Debt policy
- Credit policy
- Priority determination
- Performance measurement

Each of the portfolio choices are reviewed, but not in priority order. Rather, the order helps isolate the strategic implications of each. While the primary focus of the discussion is on governmental finance, factors relevant to corporate finance are sometimes included to indicate possible generic aspects of many of the strategic financial choices.

Budgeting

Budgets are more than just mechanisms to define the balanced budget rule—the unitary model of governmental finance. Budgets are recurring and integral aspects of management strategy. The budgeting process allocates scarce resources during a fiscal period; it helps to ration resources. Fundamentally, a budget is a "process of transforming a series of programming decisions into an operating plan for the constituent parts" of an organization [27, pp. 783–784]. In fact, the budget provides financial details down to the department or expense center level [28, p. 750]. Budgeting has the opportunity to represent what Donaldson and Lorsch [2, p. 6] calls the "stream of decisions" leading to organizational goals. To some observers, however, budget decisions "are more about the locked-in distribution of power between interests than about the direction in which the organization is to go" [3, p. 158].

Budgeting serves a fundamental role in government: It is a legal instrument for defining revenue levels and disclosing spending plans. Thus, many of the strategic policy and programming decisions emerge from, and are a part of, the budgeting process [29, 30].

Given that most governmental jurisdictions budget on a yearly basis, it is feasible to make a yearly assessment of priorities. Yet practice confirms that current budgets reflect past budgets. In moderate fiscal climates, this practice means the initiation of limited program enhancements, the reduction of some programs, and the retention of most programs at levels only marginally different from prior funding cycles. The budget theory that incorporates this view is incrementalism [15, 31].

Efforts to improve the utility of the budgeting process have led to several significant budget reforms. According to Grizzle [32], the theory of budget reform is that budget formats influence budget deliberations, which in turn influence budget allocations. While evidence of the format–deliberation relationship is strong, the literature is weak on proving the deliberation–allocation linkage, according to Grizzle [32]. Still, the point is clear: The choice of a budget format may promote or impede strategic uses of the budget.

Each budget format has strategic implications. Line-item budgeting has limited utility for strategic direction other than control due to its narrow focus on the commodities purchased. Program budgeting offers a positive thrust by allowing decision makers to focus on larger goals irrespective of artificial limits imposed by historical artifacts—the organizational structure created over time. Thus, the budget forces attention to goals and programs—strategic metaphors—instead of commodities. Performance budgeting, especially when married with program budgeting, encourages measurement of intended strategies. While efforts thus far have been rather crude, outcome-oriented performance measurement initiatives now are taking hold at federal, state, and local levels. As a variant, PPBS—planning, programming, and budgeting systems—focus on policy choices over time with the added capability of incorporating performance indicators.

Zero-base budgeting (ZBB) offers a slight improvement to the program/performance combination. By structuring a series of alternative service packages, each with program and performance characteristics, decision makers can select various levels for funding consideration. For example, the city of Milwaukee designed its strategic budget system on the principles of ZBB. Each decision unit had to formulate a budget for at least three different levels of expenditures—minimum, reduced, and current. To reduce the budget during a tough fiscal climate, each decision unit's budget was assessed against six factors [33, p. 19]:

The size of each decision unit's budget
Productivity

The impact of deferred maintenance

The impact of revenue-generating capacity

The nature of each decision unit's functions

The proper funding sources for each function

These factors show the financing linkages to the ZBB options. In ZBB, the prioritizing of program service levels is a plus for choice making. While the advocates of ZBB inferred great advantages to this reform, the results fell sort of the expectations.

Strategic budgeting is the dominant element in the financing of public-sector strategy. The public budget is central and controlling due to its allocation role, yet the public budget as commonly structured and employed is only one tool—albeit the most visible—among a portfolio of fiscal choices.

Multiyear Planning

Organizations plan for the future. Some do it more deliberately than others. As a concept and framework, strategic management helps define the purpose and structure of such planning. Planning extends beyond a single year, yielding a multiyear perspective. A review of the strategic importance of multiyear planning proceeds by first reviewing its purpose, then its structure.

Purpose

Most organizations have an indefinite life. Only members of a small subset of organizations adopt ex ante, or intended, task-limiting or time-specific life spans.[2] Even then, organizations can defy intended strategies, as the transformation of the March of Dimes shows. Upon successfully achieving its single goal of eliminating polio, a revised goal of reducing birth defects permitted the March of Dimes organization to have a broader and longer-lasting claim to organizational life.

Some organizations fail due to emergent, or unintended, results. Small businesses are especially vulnerable during their first few years. For other firms, while the test marketing of a new product may fail, organizational life is seldom at severe risk unless the proposed product comprises a major share of the product line or corporate value is diminished. Ownership may change, however, and with it there may be a revision of corporate strategy.

The vast majority of organizations continue to exist in one form or another despite mergers, acquisitions, and reorganizations. The buying and selling of a distinct company or product line is all too common. Governmental agencies are seldom permitted to fail or go out of existence; rather an agency's program is merged into another agency's set of programs [34]. By the time a public program is formally recognized in law and funding, requiring as it does political consensus, the program's likely path is more toward expansion, rather than decline. However, changes in the fiscal or managerial culture can interrupt this path.

To expect organizational continuity beyond a single year requires attention to choices, both past and current. This requires an assessment of past strategic choices and the resulting economic transactions. Past choices influence the organization's future, as do current choices. Sensitivity to alternative scenarios of the environment is critical. Fundamentally, organizations make choices with the future in mind. The past is easier to deal with—the economic results are reflected in assets, liabilities, and equity: the balance sheet. Lost opportunities are not recorded. Thus, strategic decisions about the future must consider the implications of a lost opportunity as well as an opportunity taken.

The accumulation of prior taxing and spending decisions narrows contemporary and future choices. Tax options are foreclosed; spending alternatives are limited. As the deficit reduction debate at the national level demonstrates, past decisions temper current policy options. This is not to suggest that significant departures from past trends are precluded; it only recognizes the low probability given stable fiscal and managerial cultures.

In government, one legislative session cannot bind the actions of a subsequent session. Only the constitution can limit the actions of a legislative session. Thus, a law mandating specific spending in the current year cannot bind future legislative sessions from changing the base law. An exception occurs when one legislative session sanctions a legally enforceable agreement to incur a long-term liability, such as to borrow money. Future legislatures are bound to honor debt repayment terms. Future options are limited. Labor contracts and entitlement programs with cost-of-living adjustments (COLAs) also bind future policymakers; to eliminate a COLA is seen as an attempt to break a bond of faith with current and future recipients, as those who attempt to delimit the Social Security program all too frequently are reminded. So, the past constrains current choices. The purpose of multiyear planning is to bring the choices, and their implications, to the forefront of decision making.

Structure

Multiyear planning consolidates two concepts: long-range planning and multiyear budgeting. While both enhance an organization's strategic plan by expressing future expectations and paths to accomplish goals [28, p. 750], there are conceptual differences. As developed in the private sector, long-range planning represents plans or programs to attain corporate strategy [35, pp. 32–33]. The conversion of strategic plans into specific programs is at the heart of long-range planning. Multiyear budgeting is a logical extension; it specifies expected financial results within a narrow time frame. Often more tactical than strategic, a multiyear budget provides a baseline or referent against which to assess actual results.

Multiyear baselines have become institutionalized in government. The Congressional Budget and Impoundment Control Act of 1974 mandated the preparation and submission to Congress of a current services budget. The President's current services budget was designed to provide "a baseline for measuring the fiscal impact of policy changes proposed in the President's budget" [36, p. 2]. Program costs were to be expressed in real terms (adjusted for inflation), taking into account expected changes in service activity (such as the number of clients) based on current law. During the mid-1980s, however, the President's Office of Management and Budget (OMB) incorporated new initiatives in defense spending within the current services base, effectively masking the difference between current and new policy [36, p. 7]. In contrast, the officially nonpartisan Congressional Budget Office (CBO) implemented the baseline concept to assess the budgetary impact of economic, programmatic, and policy changes.

The use of baselines has radically changed the budgetary debate. In practice, budgetary savings are said to occur when actual spending falls short of the projected baseline, even if the spending actually increases over past levels. Instead of programmatic differences, out-year deficit estimates define the current year's budget debate [37].

In state and local governments, legal structures force a type of multiyear planning. Specifically, budgets generally have to be balanced; revenues must equal expenditures. A balanced budget rule provides some limited protection against one year's overspending jeopardizing the following year's budget. The balanced budget rule loses some of its constraining power when estimated revenues define allowable expenditure levels, without a prohibition on end-of-year deficits. In such a situation, spending can be pushed into a new year and/or revenue estimates can be highly optimistic at the time of budget preparation.

Multiyear financial planning in local government is often imposed following financial emergencies [38]. Following its brush with near default in 1975, New York City adopted state-required financial planning guidelines. The city prepared 4-year "rolling" financial plans; with the passing of each fiscal year, the city added a new year as the fourth future year covered in the financial plan. For each covered year, the plan detailed revenues, expenditures, sources of capital, and cash flow. Explicit steps were required to fill the gaps between revenues and expenditures [39].

The most frequent application of multiyear planning in local government is the capital improvements program. This permits priorities in the scheduling of major, costly capital improvements. The choices related to infrastructure improvements rebound to local economic advantage or disadvantage [40]. For most state and local governments, capital budgeting is their only experience with formal multiyear budgeting.

A key focus in multiyear planning is the concept of the fund balance. A fund balance is the amount of resources remaining unallocated and unreserved after accounting for all uses of funds. A political jurisdiction's fund balance policy is a matter of credit quality, with market attention now focused on a fund balance standard set at roughly 5% of yearly source of funds. What the market actors say and what they do may vary, however. In one empirical test, both a positive and a negative fund balance translated into higher costs of borrowing! Giroux and Apostolou [41] suggested that their results might reflect the market's dissatisfaction over a jurisdiction's inability to balance its budget: A penalty is given for either deficits or positive fund balances (often termed a "surplus").

In summary, fiscal choices have an impact for more than a single year. The goal of a balanced budget is more easily achieved when a multiyear focus is disregarded—just push the problem into the future. Thus, multiyear planning influences strategic decisions.

Accounting Policy

Financial transactions reflect an organization's economic activity. Accounting concepts permit consistent handling of all economic transactions to make financial history beneficial for current and future decisions. Strategic choices relate to the utilization of accounting concepts to promote external disclosure and internal control.

External Disclosure

The financial performance of an organization affects internal as well as external stakeholders. In response, the organization has a responsibility for accurate representation and timely disclosure of its financial results. Accurate reports offer little value if they are not disclosed. To maximize disclosure, an organization must consider the content and methods by which data are presented. Heading the list of choices facing an organization is its intent to follow the protocols known as generally accepted accounting principles (GAAP). For a growing subset of organizations this option is moot because of controlling tax and securities laws or capital market entry requirements (to satisfy debtholder demands). Publicly traded firms are required to follow GAAP. Other firms follow the same principles due to lender requirements.

Organizations must reveal periodically their financial performance. Quarterly earnings reports influence the share value of publicly traded firms; yearly financial reports give the past year's results along with future plans (and assumptions) for the upcoming year. Yearly audits of governmental jurisdictions attest to financial stewardship as well as to the jurisdiction's basic financial condition.

The first level of disclosure is the basis of accounting. A minimum form of disclosure reflects all cash sources and uses during a reporting period. This approach belies the serious distortions caused by a cash-based financial report—such as not recognizing bills incurred but still outstanding, or the prepayment of a future year's operating expenses.

Rejecting the vagaries of cash accounting, GAAP emphasizes the need to reflect all economic transactions affecting current period activities. In accrual accounting, revenues are recognized when earned, and expenses are recognized when consumed, regardless of when ordered or paid. GAAP provides a detailed, and ever growing, set of protocols to guide the accomplishment of maximum disclosure. Currently, GAAP for governments permits a modified form of accrual accounting for general public services. Under this modified form, most expenditures are recognized when incurred, but revenues are recorded when received in cash. Only revenues that are both measurable and available are susceptible to accrual. There is some room for interpretation in applying revenue accruals.

A second level of disclosure requires the proper recognition of the organization's full scope of responsibility. This requires the identification and inclusion of all subsidiaries plus units that may appear to be separate but that operate under the effective control of the parent organization. The objective is to disclose all linkages that might have a call on the parent organization's resources. In a discussion of strategic management this is important given the propensity of governments to create "quasi-private" organizations to facilitate the accomplishment of public policy (such as economic development authorities, bond finance conduit agencies, fee-for-use turnpike authorities, etc.). While these types of units are termed "off-budget" or "public enterprises" for policy reasons, the true distinction is not as precise or clear, due to the parent's contingent liability or responsibility. These labels mask economic, political, or leadership umbilical cords. Accounting policy forces the combination, at least for financial disclosure purposes, of all parent and clearly related subsidiary units.

Data presentation in the financial statements may or may not reflect the combination of parent and subsidiary units into a single set of numbers, a third level of disclosure concern. The accounting entity is the circumscribed area of interest that establishes the boundaries within which financial transactions, events, and balances are recorded and reported upon. For a corporation, the accounting entity is easy to define: The entire business, including all subsidiaries, is the accounting entity. Operational accountability dominates in this case.

For governmental jurisdictions, however, more importance is placed on dollar accountability—the accounting for sources and uses of financial resources. The accounting entity is the *fund*, such as the General Fund. A fund is an accounting entity with a set of self-balancing accounts. Therefore, the reporting entity is broader than the accounting entity. The primacy of the fund as the accounting entity is not inconsistent with the organizational scope of responsibility as the reporting entity; the accounting entity and the reporting entity are two separate levels of accounting focus.

A fourth disclosure issue relates to debt financing (reviewed later in more detail). Publicly traded firms must file debt offering documents with the U.S. Securities and Exchange Commission (SEC). By law, the SEC cannot dictate the form and content of a state or local debt offering document, but the SEC enjoys remedial powers when investors are subjected to fraudulent disclosures.

In summary, to maximize disclosure requires the inclusion and reporting of all financial transactions affecting the value and viability of an organization. Financial policy that undermines the integrity of disclosure is likely to reduce investor (or taxpayer) long-term support, threatening organizational (or political) continuity.

Management Control

Accounting affects strategy by enhancing management control. Beyond the generation of reports showing variances between planned and actual results, accounting policy can help structure production choices by revealing the cost of a product or activity [42]. The linkage of accounting and strategy was clearly stated by Cooper and Kaplan [43, p. 97]:

> Indeed, activity-based costing is as much a tool of corporate strategy as it is a formal accounting system. Decisions about pricing, marketing, product design, and mix are among the most important ones managers make. None of them can be made effectively without accurate knowledge of product costs.

The need for accounting by program and product is clear for private firms given their need to track each product, but not-for-profit organizations have some experience with these systems. Hospitals, for example, have shifted their operational activities to capture relevant information by product line. Managers must plan and control by product-line differentiation; the financial health of health-care organizations now rests on such decisions.

As governments deal with an increasingly scarce fiscal environment, they turn to service charges and user fees to recover the costs of services. The pressure builds for a more accurate product- and activity-based accounting system. Otherwise, governments will be at a disadvantage in designing products to meet service demands at a price to recover all costs. Furthermore, the new emphasis on reengineering government depends upon a clear sense of what it takes to adequately perform a particular service, including procedural steps and the costs of each service.

In summary, the strategic importance of accounting policy relates to the disclosure of relevant financial information to external stakeholders and the improvement of accounting systems to more effectively set the price of activities, products, and services. Without attention to accounting policy, grand strategy may impose an indeterminable financial liability.

Tax Policy

To finance public services, governments obtain income through official coercion or monopoly sales. A tax is a coercive payment since there is a responsibility to pay even though the taxpayer may not agree with its imposition for use, much less receive noticeable service benefits. The selling of services and products by government is enhanced by the near monopoly most public organizations have in the geographic market. For example, sewer collection and treatment services are generally priced as a product but no alternative sewer services are allowed (laws prohibit raw sewage disposal); thus, true market pricing is unobtainable.

Fundamentally, taxes are imposed to fund the government, yet other criteria dominate economic discussions [44]. Tax choices turn on the debate as to who incurs the burden to pay the tax and the impact that the tax will have on the taxpayers and the economy in general. Specific tax methods affect some citizens but not all; thus, taxes discriminate in incidence. Plus, taxation can intrude unnecessarily into economic choices, thus upsetting market efficiency.

Our Constitutional framework protects citizens against undesired taxation, at least if the majority votes to change their representatives. Tax revolts occur, but infrequently. More commonly, public officials heed the warnings. One strategic response is the selection of taxing schemes with varying degrees of fiscal illusion, whereby taxpayers underestimate their tax liability.

A government's ability to tax—its taxing capacity—is restricted not only by the law, but by the tax base. As will be elaborated later, economic development strategy is reviewed here as a tax-base strategy. The shifting of economic wealth from manufacturing to a service economy introduces the need for "tax tailoring" [45].

Taxation choices at one level of government are constrained by taxes imposed by other governments; this is termed tax source separation. Citizens incur tax liabilities to numerous taxing jurisdictions, including the municipality in which they reside and the one they work in, as well as the school district, the county, the state, and the national government, not to mention the special "off-budget" taxing districts proliferating at the local level (such as utility districts, road districts, etc.).

The tax and revenue policies of a governmental unit reflect an accumulation of decisions over time. Rarely do governments reassess entire revenue portfolios. Instead, incremental rate or base changes are made. After reviewing many state tax reform initiatives, Gold [46, p. 1] concluded that "the immediate results . . . in terms of altered policy have been rather meager. Significant tax reform is not easily achieved." At the national level, one only has to read David Stockman's [47] account of the 1981 income tax reduction program to get an introduction to the political hurdles in tax reform. As income tax reform in 1986 proves, reform is possible, nevertheless [48].

Tax effort and tax capacity measures are often used in the evaluation of an individual tax or the full tax portfolio. Tax capacity measures the amount of revenue obtainable if the political jurisdiction imposed a nationally uniform set of tax rates to a common set of tax bases. By employing a standard tax rate, the revenue yield varies with the tax base. Tax effort, in contrast, is the actual tax burden placed on the tax base. This measures the extent to which the political jurisdiction exploits its potential tax base. Taken together, the tax capacity and tax effort afford a comparative perspective on local tax choices.

Governments are increasingly treating "citizens not as clients, but as customers" [49, p. v]. One manifestation of this new focus is the emphasis given to charges for specific services. Pricing decisions, such as for enterprise operations, are strategic decisions. A government enterprise provides measurable private benefits—water to a given business, access to an airplane at a public airport, parking space in a public garage, or tee time at a public golf course. Inadequate pricing decisions can result in general tax subsidies for services that really provide a private benefit, not a public benefit. A financially troubled enterprise threatens the financial stability of the general government.

An examination into nonoperating revenues is also important. For example, pension investment practices influence operating budgets. Corporations have been known to acquire another firm, only to pay for the acquisition by raiding the excess pension assets contained in the overfunded defined contribution pension plan of the acquired firm. Even governments have exploited pension funds, self-insurance funds, trust funds, dedicated accounts, and windfall receipts to provide operating fund relief [50].

In a theoretical argument, Levi [51] contends that rulers seek to maximize revenue. In some situations this requires accepting lower revenue returns in early years in order to maximize a higher return over time. Thus, rulers may provide incentives to production by permitting the ruled to keep more of what they produce. Higher production over time yields higher revenues, thus achieving the rational goal of revenue maximization.

Stimulating economic growth has enormous political, social, and economic benefits, termed here a tax strategy. Investments strengthening the economic base yield higher returns in the future, including governmental revenue. Public economic development initiatives take advantage of a range of the financing strategy portfolio, including debt policy (borrowing money with general credit), credit policy (direct loans to businesses), budget subsidies, and tax abatement [52]. Ann O. Bowman [52, p. v] concludes that "Economic development activism . . . is associated with positive economic performance." Yet governments differ in their economic development incentives. Rubin and Rubin [53, p. 55] show that "the cities that are poorest—that have the poorest citizens and the highest unemployment rates— are the ones that are spending the most money on expensive and possibly ineffective economic development incentives." Regan [54] implies a similar problem by his call for the evaluation of accomplishments versus the costs of such programs. Despite these protestations, Levi's rational model has its applications in contemporary economic development initiatives.

Debt Policy

Debt policy relates to the borrowing of money with the requirement to satisfy (pay) the obligation in the future. The obligation may be an external or an internal debt. When an organization acquires funds from the capital markets, it incurs an external obligation to repay the funds, with interest. This is the more visible debt due to market assessments of the ability, and willingness, to repay the debt. Similarly, when an organization delays or defers a valid payment obligation, it creates also a debt. One set of short-term obligations is termed accounts payable, where a purchase is made on credit. More significantly for our purposes is the set of obligations termed internal debt. The distinguishing characteristic of this "internal debt" is that such debt is owed to employees. This section explores both external and internal debt.

External Debt

Organizations borrow money to generate a stock of funds to finance currently defined needs that exceed current or expected cash flows [55]. Debt financing generates a stock of funds to build facilities, to buy equipment, or to finance other activities that enhance longer term opportunities. Debt repayment is spread out over time, thus minimizing the impact on cash flow. In some situations sufficient cash is available yet borrowing occurs. For instance, if future expected rates to borrow funds (the interest rate) significantly exceed current rates, then borrowing to initiate immediate capital investments may prove more economically sound than deploying cash or delaying investments.

Debt creation carries an obligation to repay the debt according to a specified time schedule, at least for any organization with long-term plans. The infusion of debt proceeds enhances liquidity until the proceeds are expended. Later, during debt repayment, the cash crunch occurs.

The choice of financing method, or capital structure, as it is called, is a critical strategic decision. In corporate finance, capital structure is measured as the proportion of debt to equity. For a firm, the basic financing options are to borrow funds (to incur debt) or to increase ownership interests (to increase equity capital). The firm chooses between debtholders and equity owners. A firm's leverage increases as its debt to equity ratio increases. As leverage increases, the firm is more vulnerable to economic shocks but less vulnerable to takeovers, all other things considered. To Sandberg et al. [56, p. 23], a major "component of a company's strategic posture is the borrowing plan it adopts to support its operating activities."

Governments face parallel capital structure decisions. The option is either to finance on a pay-as-you-go basis with taxes or to borrow funds, thereby creating debt [57]. A pay-as-you-go approach does not entail the same dilution of ownership concerns as it does for private corporations. Still, debt creation forces residents and taxpayers to pay the bill even if the benefits derived from the debt proceeds are exhausted long before the end of the repayment period [58].

In terms of public borrowing, there are basically two forms—general obligation debt and revenue debt. General obligation debt involves the political jurisdiction pledging its full taxing powers as collateral for the borrowed capital. Thus, a local government pledges to levy a property tax sufficient to pay debtholders; if default occurs, debtholders have a preferred standing in state court to enforce the tax levy. A state government, in turn, pledges its general taxing powers (sales, income, etc.) as collateral.

Revenue debt for a government is similar to corporate debt. The assurance of repayment is normally tied to the cash flow from the project being financed with the debt. The probability of repayment is inextricably tied to the soundness of the project (or the flow of revenue from an earmarked tax source). In return for capital, the debt issuer gives up management discretion as specified in the contractual agreement—termed the trust indenture. This takes the form of an agreement to maintain specified reserves, impose appropriate rates, and follow certain procedural details. Failure to meet the requirements imposed by the trust indenture can result in loss of control over the project [59].

Scarce capital requires rationing. A ranking system structures the selection process. A viable economic basis for comparing projects is to rely on the payoff of each project in terms of net present value—the discounting of a future stream of benefits and costs into current terms. However, this relates more to capital budget decisions than to debt policy.

Internal Debt

The nomenclature of internal debt conveys the lack of a market transaction. In fact, the debt is owed to employees as future pension or cash entitlements, for example. As a mechanism for deferring or creating a contingent liability, this involves deferring into the future an obligation yielding current fiscal advantages. Internal debt commonly takes the form of allowing employees to accumulate, without limit, unused sick and annual leave time. Employees earn a claim on future resources that can be cashed in at retirement (or exit). Therefore current labor costs are pushed into future years. The result is a current budget allocation decision with significant long-term debt implications.

In summary, debt practices promote balanced budgets by pushing costs into the future. While debt to employees and debt to external bondholders rest on different market orientations, each constitutes fiscal choices with implications for strategic management.

Credit Policy

An organization creates a real or potential call on its resources by extending its credit to others. In its application in government, the jurisdiction "acts much like a bank, raising funds or directing their flow to provide credit on terms it specifies to borrows it selects" [60, p. 1]. By exploiting credit policy, organizations seek to advance policy or program goals in equal or better ways than through normal budget expenditures. A major reason is that the cost of credit may be hidden while the cost of a budget grant or subsidy is more visible and open to debate.

There are four forms of credit. First, a government can enter into a direct loan with an individual or organization. In such an arrangement, the government provides a certain amount of funds in return for specified considerations, usually a repayment schedule. Direct loans require a direct expenditure of funds. The government, as a credit issuer, assumes the burden of adopting criteria to evaluate credit applicants; lax criteria presage more defaults, while stringent criteria lead to few participants—a delicate policy choice.

In the second form of credit—a guaranteed loan—government guarantees payment of the principal owed in a private loan. A government credit guarantee facilitates the transaction by holding the lender harmless from default risk. While incurring a processing cost, the government faces limited outlays except when the borrower defaults on repayment to the lender. In a default, the government first pays off the loan, then seeks repayment directly from the borrower.

A third form of credit is the government's creation and sponsorship of a financial intermediary mechanism to facilitate the financing of selected economic activities. For example, the U.S. government created federally chartered organizations such as the Federal National Mortgage Association (or Fannie Mae) to buy individual mortgages from financial institutions in order to package the individual mortgages into large-denomination, tradable securities. While the U.S. government does not guarantee payment of Fannie Mae's debts, it is a legal device created by Congress to provide certain public benefits. Conceivably, the U.S. government will not allow its financial intermediary to default, thus adding a form of default guarantee. A similar set of state-level intermediaries is the conduit bond financing units that account for a large volume of the municipal bond market.

A fourth form of credit is when one level of government, such as the federal government, allows a subordinate level, such as state and local governments, to borrow money on a preferred basis in comparison to other borrowers. Federal tax laws permit purchasers of state and local government securities (municipal bonds) to receive interest payments that are considered exempt for most federal income tax purposes. As a result, state and local governments borrow at rates cheaper than the federal government. Plus, they "have used this low-cost financing to establish their own financial institutions, which make below-market-rate loans to favored borrowers" [60, p. 4]. The cost of this interest subsidy falls on the federal government through the loss of tax revenue.

Credit programs have strong political advantages, yet the subsidy cost is often hidden. The subsidy cost of a credit program is measured by determining [61, p. 14]:

1. The difference between the interest the government will pay to borrow funds to make the loans and the interest income it will receive from borrowers
2. The estimated amount of future loan defaults based on prior experience with similar types of loans
3. The estimated cost of administering the loan program

The federal government took a major step in 1990 to improve the budgeting of credit programs. An estimated subsidy cost, defined by a net present-value basis, is used in the budget. This makes it easier to focus on the budgetary impact of credit policy.

State and local governments are generally considered small users of credit policy. Without adequate disclosure, it is difficult to confirm or deny this hypothesis. An innovation that indicates some use of credit policy is the practice of state treasurers applying state treasury balances as collateral to buy-down interest rates on private loans. Local governments have extended credit for so-called public–private economic development partnerships, agreeing to accept a limited or passive return on the investment [54]. In another example, unexpendable trust funds, such as the Texas School Permanent Fund, act as a credit guarantee on the debt issued by local school districts [62]. Thus, state and local governments are not adverse to using credit policy to enhance their financing of strategy. In fact, creative strategies for stimulating economic growth rely greatly on credit policy [63].

Upon determining the subsidy cost of credit, several strategies are possible. If the subsidy cost of a loan program exceeds the perceived benefits, the governmental unit can reduce program activity, change the program to a lower cost option, or institute structural changes. To reduce program activities involves cutting the supply—either ending the program or reducing its scope. Another reduction strategy focuses on demand by restricting eligibility rules and increasing up-front services charges. Another structural change is to sell loan assets, in effect making an illiquid asset into liquid asset.

In summary, a clear liability occurs when the government agrees to loan money to others; there is an initial outlay plus the possibility that the principle will not be repaid. A less clear allocation of resources occurs when a governmental unit agrees to guarantee payments on a loan between two private parties (for example, a farmer and a banker). In such cases, the only government outlay is if the borrower defaults; otherwise, the government is only out the processing cost of the transaction. Regardless of the form of credit, there is a cost to the government. Thus, deliberate strategies for handling credit are needed, including a linkage between credit policy and debt policy, since both involve long-term liabilities. Furthermore, the strategic advantages of credit policy over direct budget allocations weaken the balanced budget rule.

Priority Determination

Organizations face limits in the financing of programs, activities, and projects. The effect is a rationing or prioritizing of all the funding opportunities. This section introduces the conceptual issue, as well as strategic options in priority determination.

Making priorities relates to decision theory. Rational-comprehensive decision theory suggests that all alternatives are explored in terms of benefits and costs to reach a stated goal. According to this logic, alternatives are ranked from top to bottom, with the top project exhibiting the highest benefits at the lowest costs.

Incremental theory, an alternative decision-making theory, posits that financial outcomes are best understood as historical artifacts [64]. The theory suggests that the past is the best guide to the future. Complex environments render all but marginal changes too costly in terms of organization risk, measured by political and resource continuity. Thus, the highest ranked items exhibit high consensus; the costs may outweigh the calculable benefits.

In government, the priorities of a community are often thought to arise out of elections. Of the candidates seeking election, each with a professed set of priorities, electors select the candidate whose preferences best fit their own, or so goes the theory. Modern political behaviorists take issue with this hypothesis. Some participants have more influence than others in the choice function. Furthermore, structuring the decision-making process to favor some interests is a frequent complaint. An annual priority-setting sequence with established rules governing the involvement of all relevant participants contrasts greatly with organizational elites meeting surreptitiously to dictate priorities.

An organization facing resource decline or slower than expected growth faces difficult fiscal choices, including revenue enhancements, spending cuts, and/or productivity improvements. Incremental theory often dominates during cutback periods, but couched in terms such as across-the-board cuts [65, 66]. All too frequently, the opportunity to follow a more rational determination of priorities—cutting the lowest priority programs first—is squandered.

As earlier reviewed in the section on budgeting strategy, the budget format can facilitate the clarification of program priorities. Furthermore, multiyear planning enhances the identification of strengths, weaknesses, opportunities, and threats—all useful in developing organizational priorities.

In summary, priority determination is important in financing strategy. Managers must adapt the organization's unique attributes to meet the fiscal realities, or else face replacement.

Performance Measurement

The theory of strategic management posits a positive relationship between strategic behavior and performance. Purposeful action—as called for by strategic management—presupposes certain results. To King [67, p. 85], "objectives and strategies . . . specify performance expectations for the organization." The time and attention required by strategic management is of little, if any, value, if the results make no difference or are random. Strategic management asserts a proactive role for managers.

The desired results may involve interim benchmarks as well as final-stage outcomes. Traditionally, the desired result is a product or service valued by the client—the ingredient for repeat business as well as organization growth and continuity. The price mechanism is the measurement tool. Thus, measuring performance relates to financial results. And, since the financial statements disclose year-end results, one sugestion is to have government accounting standards require the incorporation of service efforts and accomplishment within the yearly audit [68].

The measurement of financial goals is critical for judging the results of overall organizational strategy. As earlier quoted, Donaldson and Lorsch [2, p. 35] defined financial goals as a "subset of corporate goals for which management can be held accountable, and which is concerned with the financial condition and performance of the corporate entity and with the related decisions and actions of management involving the acquisition, custody, and disposition of corporate funds." The accountability issue is central.

For a publicly traded corporation, an aggregate measure of economic value is the stock price, capturing as it does the expectations of future earnings potential. For noncorporate forms of organizations, the amount of retained earnings, the satisfaction of clients to the services rendered, and the degree to which the services are distributed in a fair and equitable manner all provide somewhat parallel measures. For example, an extensive literature on urban service distribution has significantly enhanced our understanding of the impact of service delivery rules on the levels and distribution of urban services [69, 70]. The linkage of financial data to service delivery patterns is an inadequately explored research area, however.

An organization's performance influences future strategic decisions—the feedback function at work. To E. H. Bowman [71, p 334], performance is the "context that drives process to change content." Performance is the contextual antecedent: It triggers changes in strategic momentum. Poor past performance translates into inferior borrowing opportunities, lower debt ratings, and poor client relations. That organization's economic viability is at risk.

SUMMARY

A single framework of financial strategy has its limitations. The financing of strategy is tempered by the influences of fiscal and managerial cultures. To reflect the need for a broader view of governmental financial strategy, this chapter introduced the portfolio model of financing strategy. As employed here, the portfolio is comprised of choices related to budget allocations, multiyear planning, accounting, taxation debt, and credit policies, as well as priority determination and performance measurement.

Financing of strategy often gets short shrift in the strategic measurement literature. According to Myers [72, p. 129], "much of the literature of strategic planning seems extremely naive from a financial point of view." Myers concludes [72, p. 136] that "strategic planning needs finance." This chapter has presented a preliminary structure for understanding the range of financial choices called for in strategic management. Further refinement of the portfolio of financial strategy is warranted and is this author's continuing focus of research.

NOTES

1. As Donaldson and Lorsch [2, p. 6] reveal, the "stream of decisions" concept is attributed to Mintzberg [73] and others.
2. The concept of intended (and emergent) strategy is from Mintzberg [73].

REFERENCES

1. W. B. Hildreth, "Financing Strategy," *Handbook of Strategic Management* (J. Rabin, G. J. Miller, and W. B. Hildreth, eds.), Marcel Dekker, New York, pp. 279–300 (1989).
2. G. Donaldson and J. W. Lorsch, *Decision Making at the Top: The Shaping of Strategic Direction*, Basic Books, New York (1983).
3. D. J. Hickson, et al., *Top Decisions: Strategic Decision-Making in Organizations*, Jossey-Bass, San Francisco (1986).
4. S. Smith, III and J. E. Walsh, Jr., *Strategies in Business*, John Wiley and Sons, New York (1978).
5. W. O. Cleverley, *Essentials of Health Care Finance*, 2nd ed., Aspen, Rockville, Md. (1986).
6. S. L. Barton and P. J. Gordon, "Corporate Strategy: Useful Perspective for the Study of Capital Structure?," *Acad. Managem. Rev., 12*: 67–75 (1987).
7. R. A. Bettis, "Modern Financial Theory, Corporate Strategy, and Public Policy: Three Conundrums," *Acad. Manage. Rev., 8*: 406–415 (1983).
8. F. Modigliani and M. Miller, "The Cost of Capital, Corporation Finance and the Theory of Investment," *Am. Econ. Rev., 48*: 261–297 (1958).
9. R. R. Ellsworth, "Capital Markets and Competitive Decline," *Harvard Business Rev., 63*: 171–183 (185).
10. B. C. Reimann, *Managing for Value: A Guide to Value-Based Strategic Management*, Planning Forum, Oxford, Ohio (1987).
11. R. A. Musgrave and P. B. Musgrave, *Public Finance in Theory and Practice*, 3rd ed., McGraw-Hill, New York (1980).
12. M. E. Porter, *Competitive Strategy*, Free Press, New York (1980).
13. M. E. Porter, *Competitive Advantage: Creating and Sustaining Superior Performance*, Free Press, New York (1985).
14. R. T. Lenz, "Strategic Capability: A Concept and Framework for Analysis," *Acad. Manage. Rev., 5*: 225–234 (1980).
15. A. Wildavsky, *Budgeting: A Comparative Theory of Budgetary Processes*, 2nd ed., Transaction, New Brunswick, N.J. (1986).
16. J. D. Straussman, "A Typology of Budgetary Environments," *Admin. Society, 11*: 216–226 (1979).
17. G. A. Walter, "Culture Collusions in Mergers and Acquisition," *Organizational Culture* (P. J. Frost et al., eds.), Sage, Beverly Hills, Calif., pp. 301–314 (1985).
18. G. Donaldson, "Financial Goals and Strategic Consequences," *Harvard Business Rev., 63*: 57–66 (1985).
19. G. Bruton and W. B. Hildreth, "Strategic Public Planning: External Orientations and Strategic Planning Team Members," *Am. Rev. Public Admin., 23*: 307–318 (1993).
20. G. J. Miller, J. Rabin, and W. B. Hildreth, "Strategy, Values, and Productivity," *Public Productivity Rev., 43*: 81–96 (1987).
21. R. R. Ellsworth, "Subordinate Financial Policy to Corporate Strategy," *Harvard Business Rev., 61*: 170–182 (1983).
22. S. C. Myers, "The Capital Structure Puzzle," *J. Finance, 39*: 575–592 (1984).
23. M. McComas, "Atop the Fortune 500: A Survey of C.E.O.'s," *Fortune, 113*: 29 (1986).
24. G. Donaldson, *Strategy for Financial Mobility*, Harvard Business School Press, Boston (1969).

25. E. S. Savas, *Privatization: The Key to Better Government*, Chatham House, Chatham, N.J. (1987).
26. U.S. General Accounting Office, *Managing the Cost of Government: Building an Effective Financial Management Structure*, Government Printing Office, Washington, D.C. (1985).
27. M. R. Mathews, "Preparing the Annual Budget," *Controller's Handbook* (S. R. Goodman and J. S. Reece, eds.), Dow Jones-Irwin, Homewood, Ill., pp. 782–811 (1978).
28. L. M. Murray, "Long-Range Business Planning Systems," *Controller's Handbook* (S. R. Goodman and J. S. Reece, eds.), Dow Jones-Irwin, Homewood, Ill., pp. 749–765 (1978).
29. J. B. Olsen and D. C. Eadie, *The Game Plan: Governance with Foresignt*, Council of State Planning Agencies, Washington, D.C. (1982).
30. S. Walter and P. Choate, *Thinking Strategically: A Primer for Public Leaders*, Council of State Planning Agencies, Washington, D.C. (1984).
31. J. R. Gist, "Decision Making in Public Administration," *Handbook of Public Administration* (J. Rabin, W. B. Hildreth, and G. J. Miller, eds.), Marcel Dekker, New York, pp. 225–251 (1989).
32. G. A. Grizzle, "Does Budget Format Really Govern the Actions of Budgetmakers?," *Public Budgeting & Fin.*, 6: 60–70 (1986).
33. H. W. Maier, "A System for Strategic Budgeting and Resource Management," *Intergovern. Perspect.*, 14: 18–21 (1988).
34. H. Kaufman, *Are Government Organizations Immortal?*, Brookings Institution, Washington, D.C. (1976).
35. L. G. Blatz, "The Controller as a Corporate Strategist," *Controller's Handbook* (S. R. Goodman and J. S. Reece, eds.), Dow Jones-Irwin, Homewood, Ill., pp. 32–41 (1978).
36. U.S. General Accounting Office, *Budget Issues: The President's Current Services Budget*, Government Printing Office, Washington, D.C. (1986).
37. N. Caiden, "The New Rules of the Federal Budget Game," *Public Admin. Rev.*, 44: 109–188 (1984).
38. W. B. Hildreth, "State Supervision of Municipal Financial Emergencies," presented at National Conference, Urban Affairs Association, Akron, Ohio (1987).
39. C. Brecher and J. M. Hartman, "Financial Planning," *Setting Municipal Priorities, 1988* (C. Brecher and R. D. Horton, eds.), New York University Press, New York, pp. 202–244 (1982).
40. M. A. Pagano and R. J. T. Moore, *Cities and Fiscal Choices*, Duke University Press, Durham. N.C. (1985).
41. G. A. Giroux and N. G. Appostolou, "The Market Reaction to the Information Content of Municipal Surplus/Deficit Ratios," *Public Budgeting Fin. Manage.*, 3: 487–514 (1991).
42. H. T. Johnson and R. S. Kaplan, *Relevance Lost: The Rise and Fall of Managerial Accounting*, Harvard Business School Press, Boston (1987).
43. R. Cooper and R. S. Kaplan, "Measure Costs Right: Make the Right Decisions," *Harvard Business Rev.*, 66: 96–103 (1988).
44. J. J. Minarik, *Making Tax Choices*, Urban Institute Press, Washington, D.C. (1985).
45. A. E. Merget and S. Robinson, *Where Will The Money Come From?*, Academy for State and Local Government, Washington, D.C. (1986).
46. S. D. Gold, *Reforming State Tax Systems*, National Conference of State Legislatures, Denver, Colo. (1986).
47. D. Stockman, *The Triumph of Politics*, Harper and Row, New York (1986).
48. T. J. Conlan, M. T. Wrightson, and D. R. Beam, *Taxing Choices: The Politics of Tax Reform*, Congressional Quarterly, Washington, D.C. (1990).
49. K. Neels and M. Caggiano, *The Entrepreneurial City*, Rand Corporation, Santa Monica, Calif. (1984).
50. W. B. Hildreth, "The Politics of a Windfall: Allocating Special Offshore Oil and Gas Receipts in Four Southern States Facing Fiscal Retrenchment," *Int. J. Public Admin.*, 11: 581–600 (1988).
51. M. Levi, *Of Rule and Revenue*, University of California Press, Berkeley (1988).
52. A. O. Bowman, *The Visible Hand: Major Issues in City Economic Policy*, National League of Cities, Washington, D.C. (1987).

53. I. S. Rubin and H. J. Rubin, "Economic Development Incentives: The Poor (Cities) Pay More," *Urban Affairs Q.*, *23*: 37–62 (1987).
54. E. V. Regan, *Government, Inc.: Creating Accountability for Economic Development Programs*, Government Finance Officers Association, Washington, D.C. (1988).
55. W. B. Hildreth, "State and Local Governments as Borrowers: Strategic Choices and the Capital Market," *Public Admin. Rev.*, *53*: 41–49 (1993).
56. C. M. Sandberg, W. G. Lewellen, and K. Stanley, "Financial Strategy: Planning and Managing The Corporate Leverage Position," *Strategic Manage. J.*, *8*: 15–24 (1987).
57. D. Methé, J. Baesel, and D. Shulman, "Applying Principles of Corporate Finance in the Public Sector," *Public Management* (J. L. Perry and K. Kraener, eds.), Mayfield, Palo Alto, Calif., pp. 243–255 (1983).
58. A. Breton, "The Theory of Local Government Finance and the Debt Regulation of Local Governments," *Public Finance*, *32*: 16–28 (1977).
59. W. B. Hildreth, "The Anatomy of a Municipal Bond Default," *Handbook of Debt Management* (G. J. Miller, ed.), Marcel Dekker, New York (1996).
60. B. P. Bosworth, A. S. Carron, and E. H. Rhyne, *The Economics of Federal Credit Programs*, Brookings Institute, Washington, D.C. (1987).
61. F. D. Wolf, "Federal Government Credit Activities and How They Relate to Loan Sales," testimony to President's Commission on Privatization (1987).
62. R. L. Bland, "The Interest Cost Savings from Municipal Bond Insurance: The Implications for Privatization," *J. Policy Anal. Manage.*, *6*: 207–219 (1987).
63. J. I. Chapman, *Long-Term Financial Planning: Creative Strategies for Local Government*, International City Management Association, Washington, D.C. (1987).
64. C. Lindblom, "The Science of Muddling Through," *Public Admin. Rev.*, *19*: 78–88 (1959).
65. C. H. Levine and I. Rubin, *Fiscal Stress and Public Policy*, Sage, Beverly Hills, Calif. (1980).
66. C. H. Levine, "Police Management in the 1980s: From Decrementalism to Strategic Thinking," *Public Admin. Rev.*, *45*: 691–699 (1985).
67. J. P. King, "The Role of Evaluation in Strategic Planning: Setting Performance Expectations at a State Mental Health Authority and a State Institution of Higher Education," *Performance and Credibility: Developing Excellence in Public and Nonprofit Organizations* (J. S. Wholey, M. A. Abramson, and C. Bellavita, eds.), Lexington Books, D.C. Health, Lexington, Mass., pp. 83–92 (1986).
68. N. G. Apostolou, R. C. Brooks, and W. B. Hildreth, "Research and Trends in Governmental Accounting and Reporting," *Public Budgeting Fin. Manage.*, *15*: 1121–1148 (1995).
69. B. D. Jones, S. Greenburg, and J. Drew, *Service Delivery in the City*, Longman, New York (1980).
70. W. E. Lyons, D. Lowery, and R. H. DeHoog, *The Politics of Dissatisfaction: Citizens, Services and Urban Institutions*, M. E. Sharpe, Armonk, N.Y. (1992).
71. E. H. Bowman, "Generalizing About Strategic Change: Methodological Pitfalls and Promising Solutions," *Organizational Strategy and Change* (J. M. Pennings et al., eds.), Jossey-Bass, San Francisco, pp. 319–335 (1985).
72. S. C. Myers, "Finance Theory and Financial Strategy," *Interfaces*, *14*: 126–137 (1984).
73. H. Mintzberg, "Patterns in Strategy Formation," *Manage. Sci.*, *24*: 934–948 (1978).

IX

TECHNICAL CONTEXTS OF BUDGETING AND FINANCE

EDITORIAL INTRODUCTION

Any system of PBF controls of necessity rests on a technology of policies, practices, and tools; it could not be otherwise. This concluding unit introduces a number of such techniques or technical features. The range is broad. Exemplars include the commonplace as well as the exotic, and selections stress definitions as well as details. Other units help do some of the heavy work. For example, Chapter 45, introduced in Unit VIII, considers both isolated techniques and also their complicated combinations in subsystems or systems of financial controls.

Decision Making in PBF

A pervasive orientation in PBF has emphasized decision making generally, and specifically the variant proposed by Nobel laureate Herbert A. Simon. This motivates the front-and-center consideration by Robert T. Golembiewski of "Simon's *Administrative Behavior* as Intent and Content " This selection highlights a critical dysjoint in Simon's central work.

The bottom line of Chapter 46 is that Simon went 1-for-2, which is super for baseball but less adequate for analysis. Specifically, Simon's work had a clear *intent*—to provide a core for public administration that would anchor the field, as well as provide a platform of ideas from which extensions of the field could be attempted. Simon's *Administrative Behavior* provided the major statement expressing this intent and, overall, Simon provided an approach that attracted much attention. As *content*, however, *Administrative Behavior* was not adequate to provide the methodological foundations on which a research-based field could build. That, at least, is the argument presented by "Simon's *Administrative Behavior* as Intent and Content."

An Update About *Administrative Behavior*

This selection updates Chapter 46, and sees no reason to retract that opinion of twenty-plus years ago. The focus here is on the third edition of *Administrative Behavior*, whose core text remains unchanged from the original volume published two decades earlier, more or less. But the third edition's introductory materials substantially augment the original text, which otherwise remains as it was; Golembiewski details four major features of those front materials that, on definite balance, reinforce the opinion expressed in Chapter 46. That is the essence of Chapter 47—"Updating the Approach to *Administrative Behavior* as Intent and Content."

Politics Dominates Analysis

The late Aaron Wildavsky powerfully draws attention to the power of economic ideas while at the same time proposing that "political rationality" should not surrender to "economic rationality." In his view of the right order of things, political rationality should dominate over "pure efficiency" as well as "mixed efficiency." In fact, both versions of efficiency "take for granted the existing structure of the political system and work within its boundaries." Neglecting that fact not only is inelegant and misleading, Wildavsky argues, but also is dangerous.

Wildavsky beards the lion in its den, as it were, writing during the heyday of analysis. "The Political Economy of Efficiency: Cost-Benefit Analysis, Systems Analysis, and Program Budgeting" was originally published in 1966. And Wildavsky targets three of the primary manifestations of the spirit of economic analysis that dominated in that period, with an emphasis on the basic fact that technique should serve purpose, rather than be seen as a substitute for it. Wildavsky also seems suspicious that—with "systems" meaning so many different things to so many observers—it may not mean anything specific to anyone.

An Update About the "Political Economy of Efficiency"

Wildavsky looks back in this contribution, and he is of two minds in assessing his work of 22 years earlier, introduced in the preceding selection. This duality is clear in the title of his update: "The Political Economy of Efficiency Has Not Changed, But the World Has and So Have I."

Broadly, Wildavsky's update reflects elements of "continue" and "start." As for Chapter 48, he proposes that we continue its basis emphasis on the fact that politics does, and should, determine the normative framework within which analysis does, and should, take place. At the same time, Wildavsky in Chapter 49 urges a critical startup that does not appear in the earlier selection: He emphasizes the cultural bases of the values and preferences that can and should provide context for economic analysis. He explains:

> By cultural, I mean . . . that the independent variables are ways of life made up of people who share values justifying social relationships. There are no disembodied values without social relations to defend and no relations without those who prefer them offering justifications. These cultures are plural . . . but not infinite in number.

Pros and Cons of Analysis

James R. Schlesinger at once agrees with Wildavsky, and yet would tether the latter's analysis in some regards. Schlesinger's basic concern is both elemental and fundamental. To be sure, he urges that—even in 1968—analysis often was oversold. At the same time, Schlesinger worries about an overreaction: that the overselling has less costly consequences than the reaction against the overselling.

Schlesinger's "Uses and Abuses of Analysis" signals his search for a middle ground. Like Mother Nature, he proposes, most people dislike being fooled or duped. And this explains the strong reaction to the overselling of "analysis." But another matter remains: saving the baby while throwing away only the bathwater. In short, Schlesinger urges that "analysis" has real advantages, on balance, and proposes that we should not forfeit that definite balance simply to punish past overexuberances of those who should have known better.

Why Forecasts Differ

Following Schlesinger, then, let balance prevail. Stephen K. McNees does that job for us in his "Why Do Forecasts Differ?" Simply, there are great forecasts, good ones, and real "bummers." These should be distinguished, McNees proposes, but forecasting need not be rejected because some of its exemplars do not measure up.

There are many reasons why such differences occur, McNees establishes. He focuses on a panel of five commonly used econometric models, comparing them in terms of their relative efficacies in predicting historical events. In these comparisons, McNees is able to generate a working knowledge abut the relative impacts of several factors: For example, what are the relative effects of the models as well as of the modelers on the efficacy of predictions? Models differ in their technical features, of course. But they also differ in the input assumptions as well as in the judgmental adjustments made by the modelers.

Cost-Benefit Analysis as Technique and as Value-Loaded

Robert C. Zinke continues the effort to seek balance concerning evaluations of PBF tools and techniques in his "Cost-Benefit Analysis and Administrative Legitimation." The tool has been proposed as an attractive one for making decisions via public hierarchies that once were left to market forces, and that tool constituted a major feature of the PPB approach emphasized in Unit I and elsewhere. Zinke tackles the issue of how and why cost-benefit analysis can be legitimated in administrative and regulatory processes. To this end, Zinke stresses the universality of possible applications of the technique, and also reviews the pro/con arguments relevant to its legitimacy.

Zinke does not rush to judgment, but he well summarizes the yeastiness of the existing debate about whether and when cost-benefit analysis can supplant or reinforce capitalist economic theories in legitimating administrative decisions. Zinke details the key questions that must be answered to justify this legitimation, and concludes that this capability does not yet exist.

Microperspective can be given to the inherently political character of tools for managerial analysis and application. In a selection not reprinted here, Harry Levinson [1] draws spritely and even humorous attention to "Management by Whose Objectives?" but his basic points apply broadly to managerial control as well as to budgeting, finance, and accounting. Levinson's specific referent is management by objectives, or MBO.

Experience with MBO has been mixed, and space restrictions here limit us to two points. First, Levinson raises a philosophical issue with motivational implications. He proposes that a kind of "jackass fallacy" underlies most MBO efforts: the incorrect (to him) view that most or all employees respond only to a narrow range of motivators—the proverbial carrot and stick. The consequences Levinson emphasizes deserve careful attention, for they are often unintended and usually serious. This constitutes a very bad combination.

Second, MBO is difficult to apply in organizations that are conventionally structured. See also Chapters 40 and 41. Broadly, clear and meaningful objectives are difficult to define and monitor where work is departmentalized by major functions—for example, as personnel or human resources, finance, operations, and so on. This form of departmentation encourages separation and fragmentation rather than the wholistic flows of work congenial to MBO.

Behavior of Budget Analysts

PBF activities always involve people, both as recipients as well as appliers of tools and techniques. In this sense, Katherine G. Willoughby provides detailed insight about one critical aspect of a technical context: What goes on in the minds of budget analysts as they go about contributing to decisions about how to spend public monies? She details a research design and results relevant to a dichotomy introduced earlier: that between rationalists and incrementalists. The whole of her work is reported in "Decision-Making Orientations of State Government Budget Analysts: Rationalists or Incrementalists?"

Why do we editors recommend this selection to readers? Let us sample only. Basically, Willoughby reflects the kind of research that can add content relevant to deciding between the contentions common in the PBF literature. Moreover, her results suggest that practice tends to reflect a more complicated pattern than inspires so much of the debate in PBF literature.

A Closing Integration: "Hard" Variety

PBF can be seen, overall, as an uneasy alliance between the "hard" and the "soft," "the numbers" and qualitative aspects. And so it should be, we editors propose. At the same time, "the numbers" have tended to dominate. And, we editors believe, this can get both people and institutions out of kilter.

The "soft stuff," the nonquantitative, has tended to dominate in this reader, however, and hence the closing piece—Chapter 54, which details one way to deal with a ubiquitous PBF problem, from a quantitative perspective. Most readings in this volume emphasize the mixed character of PBF analysis, and some even see it as by-guess-and-by-golly.

Aman Khan provides this technical closing for Unit IX in his "Capital Rationing, Priority Setting, and Budget Decisions: An Analytic Guide for Public Managers." The mathematics may be daunting, but they are not formidable. And Khan is careful to spell out both the uses and limitations of his approach, as well as to emphasize that he seeks to provide only a guide for managers, rather than some alleged technocratic quick fix.

REFERENCE

1. H. Levinson, Management by whose objectives?, *Harvard Business Rev.*, *48*(7): 125–134 (1970).

46

Simon's *Administrative Behavior* as Intent and Content

Robert T. Golembiewski

The twin foci here for the methodological review of the decision-making schema in *Administrative Behavior* are "intent" and "content." By way of preview, Simon's intent was the global one of providing new direction and vocabulary for approaching administrative study. That Simon achieved his intention in significant ways could hardly be in doubt. Massive bibliographies testify to the incredible industry devoted to manifold aspects of decision making [1]; and much of that industry either has been supplied by Simon [2] or was in some measure motivated by his seminal contribution. Moreover, the decision-making approach has significantly influenced this diverse range of disciplines and research areas: public administration; international relations [3]; community power, as in the issue orientation of Robert A. Dahl, and diverse mathematical and statistical specialties [4]. Dill appropriately notes that "Decision-making is one of the major functions that administrators (or managers or executives) perform. It is accepted by many, in fact, as *the* central activity in management and as a key subject for attention in management training" [5].

The approach to *Administrative Behavior* as "intent" may be summarized in a revealing way. Even his harshest critics acknowledge Simon's important role—if they usually accord primacy to Chester I. Barnard—in establishing the centrality of decision making as a focus for the study of administration. For example, Storing allows that:

> The most significant recent contributions to the study of administration have undoubtedly been made by Herbert A. Simon. He was one of the first to popularize the vocabulary of decision-making which, it is scarcely an exaggeration to say, is the native tongue of a growing body of students. If the approach to administrative problems which this vocabulary is intended to facilitate has not yet replaced the traditional one, it seems likely to dominate the field for many years. [6]

The position here, in addition, is that in crucial senses Simon's decision-making schema did not realize its "intent" because of significant problems with its methodological "con-

Source: Public Budgeting and Financial Management, 3(1): 209–271 (1991).

tent." Two variations of our orientation can be distinguished here briefly. One variation emphasizes that while (and perhaps, because) it strives so hard to achieve its comprehensive intent, the content of Simon's approach is general and unspecific and diffuse. Thus William Gore—certainly no unreconstructed critic of Simon, he—suggests the difficulties with the overly wide sweep of the typical formulation of the decision-making approach. To this effect, for example, he notes that "Research indicates that decision-making is an ubiquitous concept, referring variously to change, to a choice, to a climate of opinion, to a condition of agreement, to communication, or to a vaguely-felt state of affairs which—like ice—melts in the hands of anyone who stops to examine it" [7].

A second variation of decision making as "content" goes even further. It grants something to *Administrative Behavior*, but not much. This variation agrees only with one of Simon's own evaluations of the volume. "I suppose that I might claim some sort of prophetic gift," he noted, "in having incorporated in the title and subtitle three of the currently most fashionable words in social science—'behavior,' 'decision-making,' and 'organization' " [8].

Our complex approach to *Administrative Behavior* as intent and content deals only with the methodological issues raised but not resolved by the volume. Our rationale is straightforward. First, that volume is a major historical source of the emphasis upon decision making, and the usefulness of its methodological dicta consequently assumes enormous significance.

Second, we shall eschew textual analysis here. That job has already been done in exhaustive fashion [9]. Moreover, Simon's forte is not careful analytical development.

Third, despite many major shifts in his opinion Simon has allowed the basic methodology of *Administrative Behavior* to stand. Thus he has noted that he had enough of the methodological debate about "facts and values in decision-making" which has been emphasized "all out of proportion to its importance in the book as a whole." But a central chapter on the issue stands without change in a reissue of the volume, and its emphasis is still acknowledged in context "to be a very fundamental one" [10]. Similarly, Simon's major shift from Administrative Man as "maximizing" to "satisficing" is one of these changes. Krislov expressed the consequence pithily. Speaking of Lindblom's "incrementalism," Krislov noted that: "Simon . . . is in the interesting position of being both Lindblom's chief opponent and his John the Baptist" [11].

ADMINISTRATIVE BEHAVIOR AS INTENT: DEFINING A "CENTER" FOR THE DISCIPLINE OF PUBLIC ADMINISTRATION

The sweep of *Administrative Behavior* qua intent might be illustrated variously, but we shall do the expedient thing and concentrate on the volume's redefinition of the scope of public administration. The argument has seldom been made at length, in part because Simon almost casually tosses off his redefinition of the scope of public administration. Finally, Landau has developed a detailed argument of the nature and value of Simon's effort at redefinition [12]. Landau's argument will be relied on heavily in this section, although neither the insight about the disciplinary implications of Simon's position [13] nor a positive evaluation of that position [14] is unique to Landau.

Simon's effort at redefining the scope of public administration came as a consequence of a concern that the disciplinary area, "that lusty young giant of a decade ago" in Landau's words, "may now 'evaporate' as a field" [15]. The prime difficulty was widely perceived as the lack of an organizing focus for research. Its major consequences are a lack of coherence and a lack of cumulative relevance. If a healthy discipline "has a solid center as well as an active circumference," following Waldo, the state of public administration was disturbing. "I have a nagging worry of late," Waldo confessed, "a fear that all is not as healthy as it should be at the center of the discipline" [16].

Simon's *Administrative Behavior* in a major sense was a sharp reaction to the spiraling out from definiteness to vagueness of the scope of public administration. But the reaction was too late and too little. That spiraling out predated Simon's emergence as an influential in political science; and it continued after Simon—not unrelatedly—began to seek his vision of the good research life in the applied social sciences under the organization tent of industrial administration. Simon's volume, that is, attempted to stop the progression of public administration through four major stages that led to the contemporary condition. The four stages differed both in scope and content and sometimes radically so. They are:

1. The *analytic* distinction of "politics" from "'administration," interpreted as ideal categories or functions of governance.
2. The *concrete* distinction of "politics" from "administration," interpreted as having a real locus in the legislative and executive and in the "neutral civil service," respectively [17].
3. The internal differentiation and analysis of the components of "administration," based upon the concrete distinction of "politics" and "administration" [18], as represented by such efforts as early work in "human relations" on the behavioral side and scientific management on the mechanical.
4. The orientation toward "public policy," in which "politics" and "administration" are said to commingle in the real world, which commingling has a real locus in the executive and in the civil service [19].

The definition of public administration's disciplinary province progressively became less precise as the discipline moved historically through these four major stages. The point may be approached by defining Phase 1 in some detail to serve as our bench mark. Frank Goodnow's *Politics and Administration* [20] provides our basic source. The analytical province of public administration is clear in Phase 1, although the real locus of the appropriate phenomena is not specified. That is, wherever they occur, the phenomena of concern in public administration are defined as those activities of governance that possess "internal" criteria of correctness. In Goodnow's words, these activities include "semi-scientific, quasi-judicial and quasi-business or commercial activity." These activities have "little if any influence on the [political] expression of the true state will," and consequently require little if any "external" control as (for example) by representative legislatures. "External" means of control are appropriate only when no "internal" criteria of success exist, that is, when some measure of the consensus about the degree of correctness must perforce suffice.

Goodnow's distinction is analytically clear, even though students respecting it still face the universal problem of determining which specific phenomena fall within that analytical province. That is, administration might be found anywhere and everywhere. And anywhere and everywhere students of public administration would seek out their phenomena and cope with them: in the executive or legislative or judicial branches; at state or local or federal levels; in matters both great and small. Not that all real loci were equally likely to produce phenomena of politics or of administration. Goodnow's obscure terminology sometimes gets in the way of his argument on the matter of concrete locus. But if we give him the benefit of an inept usage or two, he consistently conceives of the three branches of federal government as having different loadings of politics and administration. The legislative branch qua concrete locus is mostly politics, for example, and the lower bureaucratic levels

are largely administration. Whatever the loading in a real locus, however, public administration is concerned with the administration component wherever it appears.

Because they were analytically clear, Goodnow's two concepts permitted easy differentiation of the provinces of public administration and political science. Their focus, that
is, was on different classes of behaviors. As Landau noted, Goodnow's two major distinctions "referred to a different class of behavior and each presented a different set of problems." The total operations of government, however, cannot be assigned completely to
different agencies of government which perform them. Landau put the matter in these terms:
"The empirical processes of politics were far too complex to be discharged by any single
governmental body and, similarly, administrative functions could not be deemed exclusive
to any specific agency" [21].

Goodnow's analytical distinction is a difficult one with which to live, a conclusion
irrefutably supported by the plain fact that few scholars (including Goodnow) ever did so
consistently. The magnitude of these difficulties may be indicated economically. For example, any discipline with a "generalist" orientation to its real locus faces acute practical
difficulties. And it is just such a generalist orientation which Goodnow urged for public
administration. In terms of their real locus, most disciplines are "specialist" oriented. Goodnow's definition of public administration, consequently, would require that students of
administration confront specialists in (for example) legislatures in a competition to claim
some of the latter's real locus. This neglects a simple fact: A subtle analytical distinction
is no match for a distinction based on concrete locus, for a variety of reasons. In
addition, Goodnow's distinction certainly would cut off students of public administration
from significant issues of governance. Some students identified with public
administration—particularly given its intimate connections with political science—would
resist thus being separated from phenomena of learned concern to them. Analytical distinctions are fragile barriers indeed against such resistance. This is an acute practical consideration, even though the purpose of any analytical distinction is to isolate some phenomenal areas from others.

Such perceived difficulties set the consensus in public administration moving, and that
movement did not stop until the field was defined so as to swallow virtually the whole of
political science. Of course, this did not happen in one fell swoop. But it happened quickly.
The eyes of students of public administration were bigger than their stomachs, and those
were bullish days indeed among disciplinary adherents. This characterization helps us understand important components of the disciplinary history which we will summarize in
thumbnail fashion: why ambitions were so expansive; why the pace of pushing forward the
scope of the discipline was so rapid; and why a kind of dyspepsia persists after scholars
forced their specialty to attempt to swallow too much too quickly.

Phase 2 of the moving consensus about the boundaries of public administration is at
once definite about the locus of relevant phenomena and indiscriminate about its focus.
Thus the locus of public administration is restricted to the executive and the governmental
bureaucracy. But within that real locus the discipline knows no analytical limits in Phase
2. Everything is its meat. Administrative case law and administrative behavior, for example,
are put cheek by jowl at a common trough in Phase 2. In contrast, Phase 1 has a sharp
analytical focus, but its locus is unspecified.

The difficulties with Phase 2 are manifold and significant, both practically and conceptually. First, a real locus is given to the analytical distinction between politics and administration. This left proponents of this definition of the field with no defense against the
correct charge—and it was leveled time after interminable time—that "things are not that

way" within the executive and its bureaucracy. That politics and administration in fact are really intermixed in this real locus thus became a datum to be "discovered" in the post-World War II period. Second, Phase 2 cuts off the field of specialization from relevant phenomena in other real loci. The rapidly obsolescing—but still very real—isolation of business administration from public administration stands as perhaps the most unfortunate of the products of Phase 2's defining the discipline in terms of a specific locus. This left many scholars out of intimate touch with the revolutionary developments that have taken place of late in our many schools of business [22]. Third, in its emphasis upon locus rather than focus, Phase 2 assumes that where phenomena occur is more significant than what the phenomena are. This seems a procrustean basis for differentiation.

The gross magnitude of the disciplinary expansionist tendencies became manifest in Phase 3, in a negative sort of way. In sum, Phase 3 had a short reign as king-of-the-mountain, although it was glorious while it lasted. Both the briefness and the brilliance of Phase 3 had a similar root: the narrow scope of the definition of the area of concern. Indeed, Phase 3 may be characterized as concerned largely with the "internal" analysis of the components of administration. As such Phase 3 was sharply honed. It gave Goodnow's basic distinction a concrete locus, and it dealt with but a narrow spectrum of phenomena within its locus.

Phase 3's simultaneous restriction of locus and narrowing of focus provoked mixed reactions. On the one hand, when Gulick proposed his famous mnemonic word POSDCORB [23] derived from the first letters of purported administrative functions, public administration was by consensus at the top of the heap in terms of competence in handling the problems of large-scale organizations. A rash of published and unpublished work spanning the period between the Great Depression and World War II established this superiority definitely, for example, over what was going on in business administration [24].

One of the most lasting monuments of Phase 3, in this sense, is Gulick and Urwick's *Papers on the Science of Administration* [25]. Some of the work in this symposium was so much fancy embroidery, but the foundations have withstood the test of time. Early work on human relations also was part of Phase 3's behaviorally oriented work, as was the more established and technically oriented "scientific management" that had such a major impact on public administration between the two World Wars.

However, success in the limited disciplinary area prescribed by Phase 3 proved no match for the allures of a far broader scope for public administration. In part, this was due to a common feeling among students that had "'gone about as far as they could go" with Phase 3. The senses in which this work was merely a solid introduction for what could be done became clear only in the late fifties, and then largely outside of public administration. That is, guardianship of Phase 3 passed essentially into the hands of researchers in our numerous schools of business and departments of industrial administration, where fantastic advances have been made in mathematical and behavioral extensions of administration differentiated "internally." Public administration—which started it all—became largely a bastard child at a family outing featuring a feast of managerial research. An increasing number of students trained in political science and public administration, but with particular interests in administration, did the reasonable if difficult thing.

Rather than running out of track in exploiting "internal" administration, however, students chafed at the narrow confines of Phase 3. And perhaps the state of political science—as then a very junior member of the social sciences, still professionally delicate, and threatened by the secession of such fields as public administration and international relations [26]— placed a premium on the solidarity implied in a congruent definition of the scope of political science and public administration. Consensus moved rapidly to Phase 4, whatever the explanation, to what is generally called the *public policy approach*. The emphasis can be dated accurately enough as a post-World War II phenomenon [27].

Students of public administration may have made a gross mistake in leaving the narrow definition of their field in Phase 3. But at least they made that mistake almost unanimously; they made it in high spirits and in delicious awareness of their past successes; and their redefinition of their field was consistent with their training and affiliations in political science. The public-policy approach of Phase 4 builds around variations on this theme: "As a study, public administration examines every aspect of government's efforts to discharge the laws and to give effect to public policy" [28]. There is no mistaking the change, certainly. In surveying changes in the concepts of the scope of the field of public administration, for example, Landau concludes that "the sharpest change to be seen, of course, [is] between the definitions of the 1930's and those of the 1950's" [29]. Indeed, except for transdisciplinary ambitions, Phase 4 is the end of the line. Landau put the point sharply: "The field of public administration is left with an imprecise and shifting base, indistinguishable from political science. [In Phase 4], public administration is neither a subfield of political science, nor does it comprehend it; it simply becomes a synonym" [29].

Like most revolutions, however, the public-policy approach had roots firmly (if unconsciously) in the past. All limits of real locus and analytic focus were swept aside by some of the more exuberant versions of Phase 4's definition of the scope of the discipline, that is. In most cases, however, parallelisms with Phases 2 and 3 seem clear. Thus both orthodoxy and neo-orthodoxy emphasize the same real locus—the executive as an institution. And both distinguish internal (administrative) and external (political) areas within the executive, although public policyers argue that if politics and administration really are separable in any real locus, it is only at lower bureaucratic levels than most orthodox adherents assumed [30]. Public policy advocates rushed into the future, as it were, with both feet solidly planted in the past.

Disciplinary ambition had its clear costs, in any case. Landau stresses that the public-policy definition of the scope of public administration "challenges the integrity of the 'field.'" The "rigidities of the politics–administration dichotomy" needed correction, he observes, but the public policyers provided the correction only by defining away the problem. Their definition of scope, Landau continues, is "so extensive as to provide little meaning." Indeed, he notes, the public policyers "make it virtually impossible to specify an area of [governmental] activity that cannot be considered within [their] scope." The public-policy redefinition of the field, that is, fails a primary test: It does not designate clearly the phenomenal field of interest, and its locus is as wide as all political science. Landau pushes the point even farther. "In the effort to define the field," he concludes, "the field evaporates" [31].

Disciplinary history provides ample support for Landau's position. With but a scattering of notable exceptions that seek to define scope and method for public administration [32], the matter tends to be shrugged off. Consider Mosher's response to these central questions: Is public administration a field? Is public administration a discipline? Mosher clearly carried the public-policy banner into battle, although he ostensibly refrained from the definitional fray:

> Public administration cannot debark any sub-continent as its exclusive province—unless it consists of such mundane matters as classifying budget expenditures, drawing organization charts, and mapping procedures. In fact, it would appear that any definition of this field would be either so encompassing as to call

forth the wrath or ridicule of others, or so limiting as to stultify its own disciples. Perhaps it is best that it not be defined. It is more an area of interest than a discipline, more a focus than a separate science [33].

If directly given, this response implied significant costs for public administration as a distinct area of inquiry rather than being a proud area of specialization. Public administration must somehow find its "chief satisfaction in providing a way of looking at government" [34]. This offers but a niggardly and vague opportunity, if indeed it is not the death-rattle of a once-virile area of specialization.

A younger Herbert Simon was not disposed to give up the discipline's ghost so easily. *Administrative Behavior* was published just as the mass of specialists in public administration were gathering momentum for their rush into Phase 4. And Simon left no doubt as to his hunches and feelings about what was happening around him. He opted for Phase 3, as specifically defined in terms of his decision-making schema.

Simon clearly foresaw that the public-policy redefinition of the scope of public administration implied the end of the golden days of Phase 3, whose fuller flowering he correctly perceived as being just around the disciplinary corner [35]. Unfortunately for Simon, at least, he was a little too far ahead of the research that would substantiate his hopes. As it was, his argument was an easy target [36]. And he also correctly but ineffectually warned that the public-policy orientation set scholars in pursuit of multiple analytical will-of-wisps, thereby destroying that "center" so vital to a healthy discipline. Simon held out little promise for the success of the effort, but he thought he knew what success in public-policy terms required: "nor can it stop when it has swallowed the whole of political science: It must attempt to absorb economics and sociology as well" [37]. The maw of the public-policy approach, that is, was cavernous.

Simon did more than point with alarm, however, he provided an alternative definition of scope of public administration in terms of focus. As Landau observed, Simon's contribution was "all the more significant in the face of the general disorganization which has occurred. Simon was trying to redefine public administration so as to give it a 'solid center,' a standard of relevance, a set of operating concepts—to make it, in short, a 'field' of inquiry. This was the function of the decision-making scheme" [38].

A brief description of Simon's decision-making schema will serve dual ends. The description will sketch the scope of public administration he proposed as an alternative to the public-policy orientation; and it will outline the senses in which Simon attempted to sharpen Goodnow's analytical distinction between politics and administration. Simon saw "deciding" rather than "doing" as the heart of administration, and decision-making involves both factual and ethical elements. "Facts" and "values" differ fundamentally; the former may be validated by empirical tests, and the latter are imperatives beyond empirical proof or disproof. In Simon's terms, "different criteria of 'correctness' . . . must be applied to the ethical and factual elements in a decision" [39].

The basic distinction between factual and ethical elements is analytic, as Simon recognizes. Reality does not always divide so neatly. Given that behavior in organizations is purposive at multiple levels, an "end" in some immediate means–end linkage may be a "means" in some more distinct means–end linkage. Simon's decision rule for applying his analytical distinction is this then: As far as decisions lead to the selection of "fine goals," they are considered to be "value judgments" beyond empirical validation. When decisions implement any final goals, they are "factual judgments" [40].

Major parallels were drawn by Simon between his schema and Goodnow's analytical distinction of Politics and Administration. Basically, Simon argued that Goodnow's development of his two central concepts was too ragged to support inquiry. When Goodnow was written and read, one still faced the challenge of distinguishing a policy decision from an administrative decision. "Apparently it has been assumed that the distinction is self-evident," Simon observed, "so self-evident as hardly to require discussion" [41].

Simon took advantage of the open opportunity to provide the required discussion of politics and administration in terms of his decision-making schema. Goodnow had proposed that politics and administration be distinguished analytically in terms of different criteria of correctness. Administrative issues are beyond politics in that they "do not require external control because they possess an internal criterion of correctness," embracing as they do the "fields of semi-scientific, quasi-judicial, quasi-business or commercial activity" which all have "little if any influence on the expression of the state will" [42]. Political issues, in contrast, are value-loaded and beyond scientific standards. Simon sees a transparent parallel here with his decision-making schema. "The epistemological position of [*Administrative Behavior*] leads us to identify [Goodnow's] internal criteria with the criterion of factual correctness," he spelled out the matter, "and the group of decisions possessing this criterion with those that are factual in nature" [43]. "If it is desired to retain the terms 'politics' and 'administration,' " Simon concluded, "they can best be applied to a division of the decisional functions that follow these suggested lines. While not identical with the separation of 'value' from 'fact,' such a division would clearly be dependent upon the fundamental distinction" [44]. Significantly, Simon also carefully and consciously preserves the analytical flavor of Goodnow while recognizing the problems of application to any real locus. He notes:

> Democratic institutions find their principal justification as a procedure for the validation of value judgements. There is no "scientific" or "expert" way of making such judgments, hence expertise of whatever kind is no qualification for the performance of this function. If the factual elements in decision could be strictly separated, in practice, from the ethical, the proper roles of representative and expert in a democratic decision-making process would be simple. For two reasons this is not possible. First, as has already been noted, most value judgments are made in terms of intermediate values, which themselves involve factual questions. Second, if factual decisions are entrusted to the experts, sanctions must be available to guarantee that the experts will conform, in good faith, to the value judgments that have been democratically formulated. [45]

ADMINISTRATIVE BEHAVIOR AS CONTENT: SOME METHODOLOGICAL DIFFICULTIES WITH SIMON'S DECISION-MAKING SCHEMA

Why Simon's attempt at the redefinition of the scope of public administration should be such a neglected portion of so prominent a volume as *Administrative Behavior* cannot be explained simply, and we shall not attempt the full, complex demonstration. Rather, our economical analysis will stress a few major methodological difficulties with Simon's decision-making schema. Some of these difficulties do in fact explain the general neglect of Simon's redefinition of disciplinary scope, and all of them would have bedeviled any students of public administration who accepted the schema as their jumping-off point for empirical analysis. Broadly, content inadequacies implied limits on achieving Simon's intent.

These methodological difficulties illustrate the inadequacies of *Administrative Behavior* as "content." In sum, that volume ill equipped students of public administration for empirical inquiry. Four methodological problem areas will receive attention here. We shall stress the confusion of types of theory in *Administrative Behavior*; its inadequate and ambiguous attention to operational definition; the significance of the phenomena neglected by the decision-making schema; and the narrow definition of decision making implicit in *Administrative Behavior*.

The following may seem a particularly academic exercise, but it does not lack a firm rationale. True enough, Simon's specification of politics and administration in terms of types of decisions was not generally accepted as a redefinition of the scope of public administration, even when it was perceived as such. Thus Sayre writes caustically of "prophets" such as Simon who have "presented a new administrative science" but whose "claims . . . have not been widely accepted" in public administration or political science [46]. But this hardly destroys Simon's great impact, even upon his sworn disciplinary enemies. For Simon must bear the massive responsibility of all those who contribute a major book for any age. They help form the language, and thus the patterns of thought, of the reading masses. Indeed, Simon consciously expressed just such a central goal. His desire in *Administrative Behavior* was to develop adequate "linguistic and conceptual tools," thereby striking for the analytical jugular. For such linguistic and conceptual tools can become "the shaper of ideas, the program and guide for the individual's mental activity, for his analysis of impressions, for his synthesis of his mental stock in trade" [47].

There is a grave responsibility for writer and reader in all of this subtle business, and that responsibility provides rationale aplenty for us. For once they achieve any vogue at all, such linguistic and conceptual tools can be called back only with enormous difficulty by even the most careful author. Less reserved polemicists riding in the wake of an analytical dreadnaught like Simon, as they inevitably do, have less motivation and less power to do the job. Alice in *Through the Looking Glass* had to face the implicit responsibility more squarely and immediately than most, but she illustrates the present point:

> "The cause of lighting," Alice said very decidedly, for she felt quite sure about this, "is the thunder—no, no!" she hastily corrected herself, "I meant the other way."
>
> "It's too late to correct it," said the Red Queen; "When you've once said a thing, that fixes it, and you must take the consequences."

Ample evidence demonstrates that Simon has long since left far behind all but the vestiges of *Administrative Behavior*. But once he said the thing, that fixed it, and the consequences must be faced.

Confusion of Types of Theory

Herbert Simon proposed a science of administration divorced from values, but his approach leans heavily for its support on what is purportedly excluded. Or at least many observers in public administration saw this unseemly dependence. These observers consequently rejected Simon's argument as analytical sleight-of-hand, and rather unpolished sleight-of-hand at that. And with the rejection of his argument, many observers also rejected out of hand the possibility of a science of administration.

The paradox of the forceful rejection of, and the abject dependence upon, values requires illustration and amplification. The only possible "science of administration" is absolutely value free, according to Simon, and that can be our starting point. "Propositions about administrative processes will be scientific in so far as truth and falsehood, in the factual sense," he notes, "can be predicated of them." Nor does Simon take any chance that the point will escape even the most casual reader. "Conversely," he notes, "if truth or falsehood can be predicated on a proposition concerning administrative processes, then that proposition is scientific" [48]. Consistently, Simon denies that the "science of administration contains an essential ethical element." Indeed, given his framework, it logically cannot contain any ethical element. "If this were true," he instructs, "a science of administration would be impossible for it is impossible to choose, on an empirical basis, between ethical alternatives" [49].

Many were willing to take Simon at his word, and conclude that a science of administration was impossible. For they saw no way of excluding "an essential ethical element" from the study of administration. And Simon left them no alternative but to deny—as he said they must—the possibility of a science of administration.

That Simon's methodological position rather than a science of administration was impossible may be established by backing into the demonstration. That is, given the inevitable imprecision of any argument, Simon's position is defensible under (but only under) three conditions. Let us describe these conditions, demonstrate that they are very restrictive, and describe how they are violated even by Simon.

First, Simon's prescription for science of administration applies tolerably well to what may be designated as the progress toward, and the development of, conclusions in *empirical theories*. In this phase of scientific effort, clearly, no values but the values of the scientific process itself ought intrude.

But scientific effort has other significant phases and—although Simon neglects them—they are in significant respects value loaded. The choice of a subject for study, for example, is value loaded. We do not deal with trifles. A major inelegancy of Simon's adumbration of a science of administration rejects the crucial relevance of values to these phases of the scientific process: the choice of research problems; the treatment of materials and experimental subjects; the application of the canons of scientific procedure, which are "values" rather than "facts"; and the use of results.

The exclusion of values from a science of administration is awkward, then. Research could never begin in their absence, that is, nor could it proceed, nor could anything be done with the results of empirical research [50].

Second, Simon's description of a science of administration is more tolerable if nothing is ever to be done with the results of empirical investigations. This is a faint concession, indeed, and unacceptable even to Simon. For any specific empirical datum might be put to many uses, depending on the values of the user. In our terms, several *goal-based, empirical* theories might be developed within a "science of administration." The neglect of this point is of some moment, since Simon's "science" is clearly meant to be put to "practical" use. But logic wins out in this case. Since a science of administration must be value free, according to Simon, there patently can be no room in it for goal-based, empirical theories whose bases rest in preferential goals or values. Many students of public administration found logic in this case difficult to square with what they felt was one unavoidable emphasis in *their* discipline.

Third, Simon's position is defensible if and only if he can and does abide by his own limits for a science of administration. That is, recall that his science of administration is restricted to those propositions whose truth or falsity may be established empirically. There will be many administratively relevant propositions that fit this definitional mold. But many will not, and not all of these are trivial cases.

Ample evidence indicates Simon's unwillingness and inability to respect his own boundaries. It is difficult to judge what proportion of relevant phenomena fall inside or outside of Simon's boundaries for a science of administration. Substantial considerations suggest, however, that Simon's science will be considerably less extensive than the phenomena we normally think of as "administrative." Indeed, some observers go so far as to suggest that Simon's decision-making schema excludes all but low-level phenomena, and does not include most low-level phenomena at that. Moreover, even Simon seemed to chafe within his own confines. Thus a trick with means–ends analysis—which Simon has abandoned of late—is necessary to give *Administrative Behavior* even the reduced analytical room it has. Simon attributes a greater "factual component" to some proximate ends as they mediate "higher-level" goals, thereby admitting more data to his science of administration [51]. Indeed, Simon implies that the process can be extended indefinitely by recognizing "more final goals" and then "still-more final goals." And all this without admitting values to his science of administration! Dwight Waldo's complaint is appropriate: "In reply to any question concerning [values], the logical positivist [like Simon] points to an escalator that ascends and ascends but never arrives anywhere" [52].

There are fragile elements indeed in Simon's treatment of values. But let us accept Simon's own condition for the relative appropriateness of that treatment, and add one condition of our own. His decision-making schema must be restricted to nonvaluational data, as he notes, and in the process must encompass a broad enough range of phenomena to permit speaking of a science of administration. In addition—and Simon is not very insistent on the point—the decision-making schema must at once encourage and permit the incorporation of a range of "factual data" beyond those explicitly treated by Simon.

Even Simon does not respect these variably restrictive conditions which define the relative appropriateness of his science of administration. The point is clearest in his original emphasis on "the structure of human rational choice" and on "a theory of rational choice in order to be able to understand the influences that come to bear upon decision-making in an organizational environment" [53]. In its most unencumbered form, then, Simon is interested not in an empirical theory of what-is-related-to-what in organizations. Rather, from the start, his focus is upon one of the innumerable goal-based, empirical theories, relevant for administration, specifically that one whose focus is "human rational choice." That is, Simon's basic argument is not of this form: X is related to Y under conditions a, b, and c. Simon's basic underlying formulation is this,

> If increased rationality in decision-making is the goal—and it is so obvious to me that I can conceive of a science of administration in no other terms—then a, b, c . . . are some of the factors that foster intended rationality and d, e, f . . . are some factors which must be eliminated or whose incidence must be reduced because they limit the rationality of organizational actors. [54]

This unacknowledged but basic emphasis on goal-based, empirical theory particularly prompted the earlier observation that Simon at once rejected and was dependent upon values in his science of administration. In sum, the maximization of "human rational choice" is the value toward which Simon's attention is directed.

For an author as complex as Simon, every position has its multiple qualifications and exceptions. But we need shrink little if any from the bold position sketched above. Simon's preoccupation with a base value—and certainly not the only conceivable base value, nor even a clearly defined one—may be established directly. Thus Storing notes with interest that Simon uses the "term 'efficiency' . . . most commonly . . . in connection with the values and opportunity costs as viewed by the managerial group in an organization, rather than the values and opportunity costs as assessed by employees or some other group" [55].

This orientation is reasonable, but it squares poorly with the dictum that, in adopting that orientation, one is free of values.

But we are not content with debater's points. Consider a broader range of evidence supporting Simon's monolithic drive to gain the best of all possible worlds in relation to values. He clearly and often enough says that his heart is with intended rationality, and he implies that the rest of administrative reality can take care of itself. As one major consequence, the "limits of rationality were defined . . . largely as residual categories" [56] in *Administrative Behavior*, as Simon notes in the introduction to the reissue of the volume, although he does little with this product of 10 years of perspective. The omission is a truly remarkable one in any purportedly empirical theory. To a similar point, Simon in the same place acknowledges that during "the past several years"—and in sharp contrast with *Administrative Behavior*—he attempted "to construct a model of rational choice that would incorporate the actual properties of human beings [as well as] some of the formal clarity of the economic model" [57]. This is truly notice of a monumental neglect in a purported science of administration.

Such omissions of mountainous realities in *Administrative Behavior*, in addition, were not likely to be spotlighted by Simon's methodology. Indeed, Simon's clear bias is to deny to Nature the phenomena omitted from his model. This is a curious posture for a scientist, but Simon often assumes that posture. More or less consistently, his basic press is articulated in such terms:

> An important fact to be kept in mind is that the limits of rationality are variable limits. Most important of all, consciousness of the limits may in itself alter them. Suppose it were discovered in a particular organization, for example, that organizational loyalties attached to small units had frequently led to a harmful degree of intra-organizational competition. Then, a program which trained members of the organization . . . to subordinate loyalties toward the smaller group to those toward the larger, might lead to a very considerable alteration of the limits [of rationality]. [58]

That Simon pushes this position to unreasonable extremes is made clear in his explanation that "propositions about behavior, in so far as it is rational, do not involve propositions about the psychology of the person who is behaving." He acknowledges the apparent paradox, but dismisses it. Given a system of values, that is, Simon argues that "there is only one course of action which an individual can rationally pursue." And that one course is the one which permits maximum attainment of the applicable system of values. "Psychological propositions," Simon concludes, therefore are "needed only to explain why . . . behavior, in any given instance, departs from the norm of rationality" [59]. With the implicit assumption that the science of administration deals only with rational behavior, "psychological propositions" have a narrow province indeed in Simon's science.

Here again Simon succumbs to his own vocabulary and chooses to impose it on reality. His rationale may be sketched. Simon's decision-making schema is to deal with data without dependence on values. He claims the emphasis on "rational choice" meets this condition. That is, the individual rational actor in behaving makes no value choices, for "there is only one course of action which an individual can rationally pursue." The individual, in sum, acts out of logical necessity, not preferential choice. Neglecting the question of what this line of argument means in any but very simple choice decisions, its motivation seems clear enough. It avoids some embarrassing questions about values, but only at the expense of throwing out "propositions about the psychology of the person who is behaving." An empirical theory could not be so cavalier.

That Simon cannot live with the three conditions above also may be suggested indirectly, thereby demonstrating the methodological weaknesses of *Administrative Behavior* from another point of view. For example, the more Simon attempts to inject reality-based elements into the original model of *Administrative Behavior*, the less integral and meaningful is the model. This is curious indeed, given that the decision-making model is tied so tightly to the "facts." The opposite effect is the expected one.

The inability of Simon's model to increasingly absorb reality will be illustrated here and at a number of points. Consider only the case of "satisficing" versus "maximizing" man. *Administrative Behavior* leans heavily on the latter, and for a necessary reason. Since maximizing man weights *all* factors and compares *all* alternative outcomes in decision-making, the relevance of value elements is sharply reduced. Such a reduction is crucial for Simon's argument. Indeed, there may be "only one course of action" which maximizing man can rationally pursue, which case is the one particularly dear to Simon. Maximizing man need not puzzle greatly about what he values, that is, because he has the computational skills to compare any alternative against every other alternative.

But maximizing man is a rare bird indeed, as Simon's introduction to his second edition notes. Thus it is not really possible for Simon to whistle his way through what is, for his argument, the graveyard of values. Although the body of *Administrative Behavior* remains undisturbed by the note, Simon's introduction of "satisficing man" who does "not have the wits to maximize" [60] vitally undercuts the argument of that volume. Note just a few of the difficulties that satisficing man implies for Simon's treatment of values. If administrative man seeks the alternative that is "good enough" rather than a one-best alternative, this patently and enormously increases the importance of those values which Simon has defined out of his science of administration. A train of problems cries for attention, but Simon does not recognize them and his science must be poorer for that fact. Storing puts one of the questions incisively. He noted that:

> "Satisficing" is a new name for an old idea. It is sensible to say that a rational man seeks a course of action that is good enough; and that is surely preferable to saying that he seeks the unique best way. But Simon gives scarcely any systematic consideration to what would seem to be the next question, the one that points to the basis on which we distinguish more or less rational behavior in ordinary life: good enough for what? [61]

In brief, the admission of satisficing man has two crucial consequences for the place of values in Simon's analysis. One consequence is direct; the other implied. Admitting valuational man qua satisficer sharply narrows the real locus to which, on Simon's own accounting, his science of administration can apply. For example, Simon acknowledges [62] that satisficing man will depend in major ways on the institutional values of his organization in choosing a decision that is good enough. But these "ethical elements" have been defined out of a science of administration. Moreover, indirectly, if satisficing man utilizes a drastically simplified model of an incredibly diverse real world, what of the canons of "internal correctness" which might serve to discipline the decision-making of maximizing man? Storing pithily expresses the challenge to value analysis spotlighted by Simon's admission of satisficing man, the challenge that faced even maximizing man but less dramatically. Satisficing determines by fiat what is "good enough." Here is revealed "with a startling clarity what was always implicit in Simon's conception of rationality—the absolute subservience of 'rationality' to nonrational preferences" [63], or to values. Strong though Storing's statement is, it does not lack firm support. The fascination in contemporary discussions with "levels of aspiration" provides a case in point. Decision making is commonly rooted in the differential levels of aspiration of relevant actors and—although the point does not receive great emphasis—this ties decision making firmly into considerations of value.

These and other considerations establish that Simon cannot operate consistently within his own boundaries for a science of administration, and they also imply the inappropriateness of the decision-making schema as a methodologically viable definition of a disciplinary core for public administration. A viable discipline of public administration should provide for active research in empirical theory, goal-based empirical theory, and value analysis. *Administrative Behavior* provides guidance only for the first of these necessary emphases, and at best does so only in clumsy ways. Other specific examples of the methodological clumsiness of Simon's schema even for empirical theory will be of immediate concern.

Awkward Approaches to Operational Definition

Commonly, and unfairly, the decision-making schema is criticized because of its incompleteness or its generality. These criticisms impose standards on Simon other than his own, however, Clearly enough, Simon has described his own ambitions in more limited terms. Thus he is predisposed "to construct tools" for the study of administration, "adequate linguistic and conceptual tools for realistically and significantly describing . . . administrative organization—describing it, that is, in a way that will provide the basis for scientific analysis of the effectiveness of its structure and operation" [64]. He prefaced the original edition of *Administrative Behavior* with this disclaimer:

> These conclusions do not constitute a "theory" of administration, for except for a few dicta offered by way of hypothesis, no principles of administration are laid down. If any "theory" is involved, it is that decision-making is the heart of administration, and that the vocabulary of administrative theory must be derived from the logic and psychology of human choice. [65]

If Simon cannot reasonably be taken to task for incompleteness, however, raising the question of the probability that his "linguistic and conceptual tools" will generate an empirical theory is appropriate. Simon's confusion of types of theory, adumbrated above, does not encourage optimistic estimates of this probability. The attention given to operational definition in *Administrative Behavior* further deepens this pessimism.

Operational definition is at the heart of empirical research, but operational definition is at best of only surface interest to Simon. Early on, Simon does acknowledge that the "first task of administrative theory is to develop a set of concepts that will permit . . . description." And he affirms that these concepts "to be scientifically useful, must be operational" [66]. Beyond this early point, however, reservations about Simon's handling of the matter of operational definition are in order. Several factors particularly encourage caution.

First, Simon gives but meager attention to operational definition. This is suggestive, but certainly not damning. Second, the attention actually accorded operational definition presents significant ambiguities that permit little optimism about their successfully sustaining empirical inquiry. Thus Simon explains that concepts "must be operational," which he explains requires that "their meanings must correspond to empirically observable facts or situations" [67]. This implies a concreteness that is inappropriate, if indeed the explanation has any meaning at all. Moreover, it sets up an awkward criterion for judging whether concepts are operational.

That we should expect the worst of the ambiguities in Simon's treatment of operational definition can be established directly. Matters only get more confused when Simon notes that his "definition of 'authority' . . . is an example of an operational definition." Referring to that definition (15 pages earlier, suggestively) helps only to establish the fugitive character of Simon's meaning. "A subordinate may be said to accept authority," we are told, "whenever he permits his behavior to be guided by a decision reached by another, irrespective of his own judgment as to the merits of that decision" [68]. The example permits no definite construction, however. Thus if the criterion for an operational definition is whether the phenomenon referred to has empirical counterparts, then Simon's definition of authority is operational. But this is a very permissive criterion indeed. It also has multiple additional liabilities: It excludes few or no concepts; it gives no hint of how one scientifically chooses between two operational definitions, as Simon conceives them; and it is innocent of the complications attending operational definition in empirical inquiry.

Let us be more specific. If we conceive of an operational definition as one providing predictively useful measurements, one can at least entertain doubts about Simon's approach. Thus Simon's example implies no specific ways in which measurements of "acceptance of authority" can be made. Indeed, that problem is not raised. Apparently, "acceptance of authority" is assumed to be an easily defined condition. Even if Simon could measure the phenomenon, moreover, there is every reason to believe that attempts to verify predictions based on Simon's notion of authority would yield mixed results [69]. That is, at least three combinations can be formed of the two components of Simon's approach to authority: acceptance of authoritative orders; judgment by the acceptance of authoritative orders; and judgment by the acceptor of the merits of the order. These three combinations are:

1. Acceptance, irrespective of judgment
2. Acceptance, judgment supporting
3. Acceptance, judgment rejecting

That these three combinations will yield homogeneous consequences is an extreme presumption. That only the first of them is useful for describing reality is similarly presumptuous.

Significance of the Phenomena Neglected

There is little hope that a clarification of operational issues, even were it brought off, would remedy matters. Tersely, Simon is quite selective of the data admitted to his study-universe. This picking and choosing on nonempirical grounds stands in marked contrast to the bias toward comprehensiveness in empirical theory and goal-based, empirical theory.

A brief comparison of two approaches to decision making helps make the present point. Students of group dynamics, for example, have had a strong interest in decision making in a variety of applied areas. In accordance with their empirical bias, variations in decision making were explained in terms of a network of theory that was comprehensively extended to such levels of phenomena as the demands of specific kinds of decisions; the specific properties of the large organizations within which specific decisions were made; the properties of decision makers; the characteristics of the social atmosphere within which decisions were made; and so on. The dynamics of the process may be chained to a few words. This was the dialetic of the group dynamicists: to achieve increasingly accurate prediction, and this by specifying an increasingly wide range of conditions which reduce the amount of unpredictable variance in tests of hypotheses.

Simon works in an opposed direction, apparently from contrary assumptions. His dialectic in *Administrative Behavior* is to increase the clarity and the simplicity of his model by *a priori* exclusion of major classes of phenomena of significance in any organization. Given his definition of a science of administration, of course, Simon is justified in excluding whatever phenomena he wishes. The plain fact is this, however. As he excludes phenomena, so does the content of his science of administration dwindle.

The danger of starving his science of administration does not deter Simon from really phenomenal exclusions of phenomena. Rationales vary in Simon, but the consequence is uniform. In the introduction to his 1957 reissue, that is, Simon notes that he treats very wide phenomenal areas as "residual categories." Because the "model of economic man was far more completely and formally developed," he informs us, treatment by *Administrative Behavior* of "the actual properties of human beings" was "very incomplete." The explanation makes some sense, up to a point. But some massive omissions by Simon are nonetheless puzzling. For example, much of Lewin's pioneering work with choice—certainly an area of relevance for any approach to human decision making—was available to Simon. Indeed, that work had roots in studies published long before Simon began his work on *Administrative Behavior*. No matter how compelling any rationale for exclusion might be, it does nothing to enhance the decision-making schema. At best, any rationale helps make the volume's inadequacies understandable.

The inadequacies of omission of the two editions of *Administrative Behavior*, however, tend to be interpreted by Simon as virtues. Thus "unavailable" behavioral data are excluded, as a methodological rule rather than as an unfortunate necessity. Thus Simon defends the "paradoxical statement" that "propositions about human behavior, in so far as it is rational, do not ordinarily involve propositions about the psychology of the person who is behaving." Paradoxical the statement is for someone dealing with a science of administration. But it could not be avoided, given Simon's emphasis on rational behavior, his professed preoccupation with empirical theory, and his patent neglect of actual behavioral properties.

No good case could be made for the "paradoxical statement," given these conflicting elements in Simon. And no good case is made: Simon's argument limps badly. He notes correctly that "In any given situation, and with a given system of values, there is only one course of action which an individual can rationally pursue" [70]. But winning a point by logical definition was paid for by the narrowing of the scope of *Administrative Behavior* to a veritable phenomenal pinpoint. For the obvious next question is: Just how much behavior anywhere is rational in this sense? And the answer is: Precious little. Indeed, Simon himself acknowledges the point when he introduces "satisficing man," which concept does not even make a pretense that "there is only one course of action which an individual can rationally pursue."

Decision Making$_1$, Decision Making$_2$, . . . Decision Making$_3$

This section builds toward three conclusions. Simon's emphasis on rational decision making, first, has the effect of shrinking drastically the scope of his science of administration. Second, Simon's methodology is such as to inhibit forceful efforts designed to remedy this condition. Third, the act of deciding tends to be seen by Simon as too definite, if not too dramatic, and as discontinuous.

Considerable detail is necessary to flesh out these three conclusions. In terms now fashionable, to approach the task of detailing our argument for one point of view, Simon emphasized a "closed system." In a closed system, individual actors have more or less full factual and value inputs which can be exhaustively manipulated and in which all alternative outcomes can be compared. Lindblom has generically classified closed systems as examples of the rational-comprehensive model of decision making [71]. Table 1 summarizes the properties of the rational-comprehensive model.

An alternative "open system" of decision making contrasts sharply with closed systems. Some of the particular points of contrast are expressed by Wilson and Alexis in these terms:

Table 1 Two Contrasting Models of Decision Making

Rational-comprehensive model	Successive limited comparisons model
1a. Clarification of values or objectives distinct from and usually prerequisite to empirical analysis of alternative policies.	1b. Selection of value goals and empirical analysis of the needed action are not distinct from one another but are closely intertwined.
2a. Policy formulation is therefore approached through means–end analysis: First the ends are sought.	2b. Since means and ends are not distinct, means–end analysis is often inappropriate or limited.
3a. The test of a "good" policy is that it can be shown to be the most appropriate means to desired ends.	3b. The test of a "good policy" is typically that various analysts find themselves directly agreeing on a policy (without their agreeing that it is the most appropriate means to an agreed objective).
4a. Analysis is comprehensive; every important relevant factor is taken into account.	4b. Analysis is drastically limited: (i) Important possible outcomes are neglected. (ii) Important alternative potential policies are neglected. (iii) Important affected values are neglected.
5a. Theory is often heavily relied upon.	5b. A succession of comparisons greatly reduces or eliminates a reliance on theory.

Source: From Ref. 71, p. 81, used with permission.

(1) predetermined goals are replaced by some unidentified structure which is approximated by an aspiration level.

(2) all alternatives and outcomes are not predetermined; neither are the relationships between specific alternatives and outcomes always defined.

(3) the ordering of all alternatives is replaced by a search routine which considers fewer than all alternatives.

(4) the individual does not maximize but seeks to find a solution to "satisfy" an aspiration level. [72]

More broadly, open-system analysis stresses the subtle and continuous character of decision making. In this sense, Barnard epitomized open-system analysis when he observed that "most executives decisions produce no direct evidence of themselves and . . . knowledge of them can only be derived from the accumulation of indirect evidence" [73]. Such a notion is foreign to Simon, which only spotlights his preoccupation with low-level decision making and the apparently "firm" facts associated with it. Lindblom has designated an open model as a successive limited approximations model of decision-making. Table 1 details the major properties of that model.

Closed system analysis is increasingly seen as analytically sterile. As two students conclude [74]: "There is a growing disenchantment with 'closed' decision models in economic and management science circles." One supporting datum must suffice to explain this change of taste. Closed-system analysis is appropriate largely for "programmed" (= simple and recurring) decisions. Even Simon seems convinced. He has argued that heuristic problem solving—the muddling through characteristic of open-system analysis—is not susceptible to resolution through logic. Moreover, heuristic problem solving is said to characterize much—if not most—problem solving by managers. Appropriately, Wilson and Alexis conclude that "most vital decisions are non-recurring. 'Search' is required to find feasible alternatives," they continue. "And often this search must not be constrained by the bounds of some preferred solution. Problem-solving requires a flexible and dynamic framework. Organizations grow and thus have growing aspirations; and changes occur in definition of what are organizational problems and of what constitute acceptable solutions. The future of 'open' decision models, in light of these straws in the wind, seems highly promising" [75]. Finally, Simon's recent emphasis on "satisficing man" reflects his own movement toward open-system analysis [76].

The methodology of *Administrative Behavior* but weakly supports Simon's new emphasis on open-system analysis. For open-system analysis requires the empirical investigation of "a complex mixture of many elements—[man's] culture, his personality, and his aspirations . . . the limitations of human cognition and the complexity of man's total environment" [77]. In our terms, that is, open-system analysis requires the development of a comprehensive empirical theory. And this effort, in turn, rests upon a supporting methodology. That methodology's role is multiple. It enforces an appreciation of the complexity of man's total environment; it provides the framework for cumulative work through nominal and operational definitions; and it requires a clarity about types of theories and about their uses and limitations.

The methodological press of *Administrative Behavior*, however, is ill suited to meet these requirements of open-system analysis. It serves only a narrowly construed science of administration. Given these properties, patently, that volume and its methodology could hardly serve either as a vehicle for exploiting open-system analysis or as a viable definition of the scope and method of public administration.

ADMINISTRATIVE BEHAVIOR AS CONTENT: TECHNICAL PREOCCUPATION AND INSTITUTIONAL NEGLECT

The issues raised by *Administrative Behavior* also can be painted on a broader canvas of contrasting approaches to administrative reality. That volume and its methodology tend toward one extreme, and in doing so that volume reflects a special case of the neglect of relevant phenomena. Two consequences of this neglect are particularly noteworthy for our purposes. The volume's extreme approach to administrative reality severely limits its usefulness, both generally as a primer for the scientific study of administration and specifically as a definition of scope for Public Administration.

Philip Selznick's *Leadership in Administration* poses a view of administrative reality sharply opposed to Simon's, and his treatment will provide a contrast with *Administrative Behavior*. Selznick basically distinguishes two contrasting views of administrative life: organization engineering, and institutional leadership. At best, *Administrative Behavior* qualifies as a treatise on the former. This is clear from Selznick's description of organizing engineering:

> When the goals of the organization are clear-cut, and when most choices can be made on the basis of known and objective technical criteria, the engineer rather than the leader is called for. His work may include human engineering to smooth

personal relations, improve morale, or reduce absenteeism. But his problem remains one of adapting known qualities through known techniques to predetermined ends.

From the engineering perspective, the organization is made up of standardized building blocks. These elements, and the ways of putting them together, are the stock-in-trade of the organization engineer [78].

Organization engineering has a range of limitations in comprehending administrative reality that have clear analogues in *Administrative Behavior*. The basic bond is the highly programmed nature of organization engineering and the closed system analysis of that volume. More specific similarities are illustrated by Simon's description of the ultimate in science. "What is a scientifically-relevant description of an organization?" he asks. "It is a description that, so far as possible, designates for each person in the organization *what* decisions that person makes, and the influences to which he is subject in making each of these decisions" [79].

Organization engineering has its value, but it has significant limitations in both practice and analysis. In practice, some—but only some—administrative activities approach a closed system. To them, of course—but only to them—organization engineering is an appropriate approach. However, and here is the greater mischief, extending such a limited approach into a methodological guide for the analysis of administrative phenomena has substantial costs. Radical separation of fact and value in practice—based upon the useful analytical distinction between what is desired and what exists—causes particular grief. As Selznick explained:

> Like other forms of positivism, this position in administrative theory raises too bright a halo over linguistic purity. Pressing a complex world into easy dichotomies, it induces a *premature* abandonment of wide areas of experience to the world of the aesthetic, the metaphysical, the moral. Let us grant the premise that there is an ultimately irreducible nonrational (responsive) element in valuation, inaccessible to scientific appraisal. This cannot justify the judgment in a particular case that the anticipated irreducible element has actually been reached. [80]

Selznick's point is not one of delicate logic. The point is often boldly (if not grossly) reflected in work ostensibly dedicated to exploring the real world. For example, Simon hastily discarded vast areas of experiential data in the process of developing his science of administration. Moreover, he felt it necessary to develop rationales to exclude those experiential data forevermore.

We may summarize the present point by using methodological terms. Science *inter alia* requires hypothetical statements of covarying factors, of the effects of nominal independent variables on dependent variables. An important part of validating such hypotheses involves attempting their extension to increasingly wider phenomenal areas by specifying intervening variables and testing for their effects. Terseness and accuracy go hand in hand in Simon's case. He neglected to specify and to provide for the test of intervening variables, in the overwhelming majority of cases. Moreover, he also commonly defined out of existence potentially significant intervening variables that could have helped in estimating the usefulness of his model.

Simon's methodological inelegance may be demonstrated easily. We rely on Selznick to sketch one vast phenomenal area neglected by Simon, saving for later the demonstration of how Simon in fact excluded that area from his analysis. Selznick has left a slim volume reflecting his concerns with "institutional leadership," which he sees as necessary in all but completely programmed organizations and as particularly vital when "we must create a structure uniquely adapted to the mission and role of the enterprise. This adaptation goes beyond a tailored combination of uniform elements; it is an adaptation in depth, affecting the nature of the arts themselves" [81].

To create such a structure, in effect, is to infuse technical structures with values, to make social organizations out of technical structures. Organization engineering must give way to institutional leadership in the process. Products of this process are familiar to all students, as illustrated by technically identical units of organization that have distinctive commitments to program, method, or clientele. These pervasive commitments become so intimate a part of organizational life that they influence if not determine a wide range of decisions at many levels. They give "organizational character" to technical operations, and they reflect an organization's "distinctive competence." As Selznick concluded:

> The terms "institution," "organization character," and "distinctive compe-tence" all refer to the same basic process—the transformations of an engineered, technical arrangement of building blocks into a social organism. This transition goes on unconsciously and inevitably wherever leeway for evolution and *adaptation* is allowed by the system of technical controls; and at least some such leeway exists in all but the most narrowly circumscribed organizations. [82]

If such processes of institutionalization are significant in organizations—and that cannot be disputed—*Administrative Behavior* has significant liabilities in its presentation both of a framework for administration and of a definition of scope and method for public admin-istration. To be sure, Simon may not completely disregard institutional leadership. But he could hardly give it less attention. We may parsimoniously rest our case on two pieces of evidence. First, as Stark correctly notes, "the word leadership itself cannot be found in the heading of a single chapter, chapter section, chapter subsection, or anywhere in the index" of *Administrative Behavior* [83]. Given the vast dimensions of the then-existing literature on leadership—and it was overwhelming in 1957 if it was only mountainous in 1947—the omission is truly startling. Here, again, is an example of the premature exclusion of data about which Selznick wrote. Within Simon's framework, the exclusion may be due to the fact that leadership patently implies valuational elements. But so much the worse for that framework. As the still burgeoning literature on leadership demonstrates, much empirical work can be done with leadership even though many aspects of relevant phenomena are value loaded [84].

Second, the press of Simon's *Administrative Behavior* permits little confidence that the processes of institutionalization will receive attention. Recall Simon's position that a "sci-entifically relevant description of an organization" is one that "designates for each person in the organization what decisions that person makes, and the influences to which he is subject in making each of these decisions." Such "influences" might include leadership and its diverse forms, but *Administrative Behavior* does not urge that inclusion.

Properly construed, then, any science of administration must encompass institutional leadership. We may outline briefly how our own methodological guidelines could do the job. Any empirical theory, first, would have to attempt to treat empirically the total fact—value mix associated with leadership. For example, specific styles of supervision can be shown generally to produce specific existential outcomes [85]. This is clearly an empir-ical task, and cannot be shunned simply because both specific styles of supervision and specific outcomes raise issues of value. Briefly, our methodology avoids two dangers: (1) It does not encourage or require the premature exclusion of phenomenal areas like leadership that are value loaded; and (2) our methodological guidelines—involving operational definition and so on—restrain observers anxious to report seeing what they prefer.

Any science of administration also must generate diverse goal-based, empirical theories. One goal-based, empirical theory would have such components, among others:

Goal: To increase the amount of "supportive" supervision.

Required empirical conditions:

1. To select supervisors who are low scores on the Adorno F scale and who are not "authoritarians of the left" [86].
2. To select subordinates with appropriate personality predispositions for such supervisory style, as above.
3. To departmentalize around "flows of work" rather than functions or processes.

The list might be extended significantly, as it has been elsewhere [87]. Such goal-based empirical theories are necessary for practical applications. Moreover, such theories help sharpen many evaluative issues. For example, one might highly value the goal of fostering a "supportive" supervisory style. The specification of necessary empirical conditions and ways of achieving them might well modify such clear preferences. For example, even from the brief list above, some individuals may be concerned with what happens to subordinates who do not have personality characteristics appropriate for a supportive supervisory style. And one's valuation of likely ways of handling deviant cases may encourage modification of the original goal of increasing the amount of supportive supervision. And these are but simplistic examples of the universe relevant to the fact–value mix in administrative reality that any science of administration must encompass.

SIMON'S "DECISION MAKING" AS INTENT AND CONTENT: A SUMMARY STATEMENT

There is no completely satisfactory methodological summary of Simon's complex effort, but like his new administrative man we shall be satisfied with less than a whole loaf. Our straightforward strategy is to focus on the classification of Simon's effort in *Administrative Behavior*. Is it a major step toward an empirical theory? Or a goal-based, empirical theory? Or is it a variant of utopian theory dealing with a phenomenal area of contemporary popularity?

The preceding analysis permits some boldness in approaching one aspect of this classification. Very definite reservations prevent us from regarding the decision-making schema as a success in developing method or results appropriate for empirical theory or goal-based, empirical theory. The evidence will not be remarshaled, but no other position squares with Simon's exclusion of vast phenomenal areas. Further, the exclusion was not only analytically convenient—which is reasonable—but it was made in terms which preclude or hinder the subsequent admission of those phenomena.

The same point can be usefully made in a different way. Consider Meehan's trio of standards for evaluating empirical theory. Any such theory must be evaluated in terms of:

1. Its explanatory power, which depends on the range of data it includes, on the comprehensiveness of the phenomena it seeks to explain, and on the significance of those phenomena;
2. The esthetic and psychological satisfaction the theory affords; and

3.   Its usefulness to a particular discipline at a particular point in time [88].

Simon's decision-making schema scores low on Standard 1 for, even using the loosest criteria, it explains little. Indeed, Simon has stressed his emphasis on developing a vocabulary and a method rather than on enumerating theoretical propositions of predictive and explanatory power. As for Standard 2, the present analysis should reflect some of the significant senses in which the decision-making schema provides little aesthetic or psychological satisfaction, that is, if one's baseline for judgment is defined in terms of the methodology of empirical science. The decision-making schema has proved useful to a variety of disciplines, at their present level of development; that is, it scores highest on Standard 3.

A second aspect of the classification of Simon's work permits less boldness. That is, the fact that the decision-making schema falls short of standards for an empirical theory does not establish that it is an exercise in utopian theory. Nonetheless, the schema does have some resemblance to a utopian model. The schema's formal and deductive character, for example, suggests that it was logically developed from a (presumably) poorly articulated set of assumptions and goals. And the deductions often triumph over reality. On the other hand, the schema is rooted in some significant phenomenal data, and it does assert a claim to its usefulness for scientific purposes as a picture of the administrative world. Those data and that claim must be honored.

A specific choice need not be really made in classifying *Administrative Behavior*, however. For the volume is complex enough and inconsistent enough to reflect significant strains of all three types of theory distinguished above. Meehan expresses the sense of this "yes, but" kind of theory in appropriate terms. He calls such a theory a "quasi-theory." It does not reflect the conscious rigor and verbal precision of what we have called utopian theory; neither does it respect the methodology of empirical theory; and all the while it rather tends more toward the former than toward the latter. As Meehan described a quasi-theory, it

refers to any intellectual construction that is a useful tool for the . . . theorist, though it cannot meet the standards [relevant for empirical theory.] In particular, quasi-theories serve as aids to classification, exploration, and discovery. . . . Actually, constructions of this sort are widely used in political science, though more often than not they are simply referred to as "theories." Max Weber's "Ideal Types," the postulational structures suggested by Talcott Parsons, the mathematical theory of games . . . and so on all fall into this category. The structures range from a fairly simple classification system to complex mathematical networks. . . . They do not "explain," in the strict sense of the terms, but they can be very useful indeed in theory. [89]

NOTES AND REFERENCES

1. For one example, see W. J. Gore and F. S. Silander, "A Bibliographical Essay in Decision Making," *Admin. Sci. Q.*, *4*(June): 97–121 (1959).
2. Herbert Storing tells us, on this point, that Simon's bibliography contains an article, book review, or comment for every two months of his professional career. Simon also has averaged a book every two years. See "The Science of Administration," in H. Storing (ed.), *Essays on the Scientific Study of Politics*, Holt, Rinehart & Winston, New York, p. 123n (1962).
3. R. C. Snyder, H. W. Bruck, and B. M. Sapin (eds.), *Foreign Policy Decision Making*, Free Press, Glencoe, Ill. (1962).

4. By way of ultimate selectivity, see R. Schlaifer, *Probability and Statistics for Business Decisions*, McGraw-Hill, New York (1959); and *A Comprehensive Bibliography on Operations Research*, Wiley, New York (1958).

5. W. R. Dill, "Administrative Decision-Making," *Concepts and Issues in Administrative Behavior* (S. Mailiek and E. H. Van Ness, eds.), Prentice-Hall, Englewood Cliffs, N.J., p. 29 (1962).

6. Storing, *Essays*, p. 65.

7. Gore, *op. cit.*, p. 50.

8. Simon, *Administrative Behavior*, p. ix.

9. Storing, *Essays*.

10. Simon, *Administrative Behavior*, pp. xxxiv, 45.

11. S. Krislov, "Organizational Theory: Freedom and Constraint in a Large-Scale Bureaucracy," *Empathy and Ideology: Aspects of Administrative Innovation* (C. Press and A. Arian, eds.), Rand McNally, Chicago, p. 50 (1967).

12. M. Landau, "The Concept of Decision-Making in the Field of Public Concepts and Issues," (Mailick and Van Ness, eds.), pp. 1–28.

13. Much of the reaction against Simon by "public policyers," for example, was motivated by a correct view of what it was that Simon's argument implied.

14. R. T. Golembiewski, "The Small Group, Public Administration, and Organization," Ph.D. dissertation, Yale University (1958).

15. Landau, "The Concept of Decision-Making," p. 2.

16. D. Waldo, *Perspectives on Administration*, University of Alabama Press, University (1956).

17. W. F. Willoughby, *Government of Modern States*, Appleton-Century, New York, pp. 219–221 (1936).

18. M. E. Dimock, "The Study of Administration," *Am. Polit. Sci. Rev.*, *30* (February): 28–40 (1937).

19. J. Pfiffner and R. V. Presthus, *Public Administration*, 3rd ed., Ronald Press, New York, p. 5 (1953).

20. F. Goodnow, *Politics and Administration*, Macmillan, New York (1900).

21. Landau, "The Concept of Decision-Making," p. 17.

22. Unfortunately for public administration, the estrangement was near its peak during the period when business administration was well along in attempting to set its own house in order. As massive evidence of this self-scrutiny, see R. A. Gordon and I. F. Howell, *Higher Education for Business*, Columbia University Press, New York (1959); and F. Pierson, *The Education of American Businessmen: A Study of University College Programs in Business Administration*, Carnegie Corporation, New York (1959). Relatedly and in sharpest contrast, the Committee for the Advancement of Teaching of the American Political Science Association took a more casual approach to their disciplinary state of affairs in the report *Goals for Political Science* (1951). James W. Fesler—as moderate and fair a reviewer as might be found—concluded that the report had "little more than distinguished authorship to recommend it" ["Goals for Political Science: A Discussion," *Am. Polit. Sci. Rev.*, *45*: 1000 (1951).] Other observers are more direct, if anything: A. Somit and J. Tannenhaus, *The Development of American Political Science: From Burgess to Behavioralism*, Allyn and Bacon, Boston, p. 188 (1967), for example, conclude that "the very triteness and superficiality of the volume made it important."

23. The mnemonic word represents Planning, Organizing, Staffing, Directing, Coordinating, Reporting, and Budgeting; L. Gulick "Notes on the Theory of Organization," *Papers on the Science of Administration* (L. Gulick and Urwick, eds.), Institute of Public Administration, New York, p. 13 (1937).

24. The most prominent mass of such materials may be attributed to the President's Committee on Administrative Management, including its *Report with Special Studies* (Washington, D.C.: Government Printing Office, 1937). On this crucial part of our administrative history, including its major and minor actors, see B. D. Karl, *Executive Reorganization and Reform in the New Deal*, Harvard University Press, Cambridge, Mass. (1963). Acknowledgment of the superiority of this

work over that in business administration, for example, is a dominant theme of Gordon and Howell, *Higher Education for Business.*

25. Gulick and Urick, *Papers on the Science of Administration.*
26. A. Somit and J. Tannenhaus, *The Development of Political Science: From Burgess to Behavioralism,* Allyn and Bacon, Boston, pp. 147–148 (1967).
27. A prominent dating-point is provided by P. Appleby, *Policy and Administration,* University of Alabama Press, University (1949).
28. M. E. Dimock, G. O. Dimock, and L. W. Koenig, *Public Administration,* Rinehart, New York, p. 12 (1953).
29. Landau, "The Concept of Decision-Making," p. 9.
30. H. Stein, "Preparation of Case Studies," *Am. Polit. Sci. Rev., 45:* 479–487 (1951).
31. Landau, "The Concept of Decision-Making," p. 9.
32. D. Waldo, *The Study of Administration,* Doubleday, Garden City, N.Y., especially pp. 1–14 (1955).
33. F. C. Mosher, "Research in Public Administration," *Public Admin. Rev., 16:* 177 (1956).
34. R. Martin, "Political Science and Public Administration," *Am. Polit. Sci. Rev., 46:* 672 (1952).
35. H. A. Simon, "A Comment on "The Science of Public Administration,'" *Public Admin. Rev., 7:* 200–203 (1947). Most of this "flowering" has occurred in the behavioral sciences and in schools of business and industrial administration, not the least of which in the Carnegie Institute of Technology, with which Simon has been associated since 1949. Within public administration, work consistent with Phase 3 has been more rare and less noted. One exception is J. D. Millet, *Management in the Public Service,* McGraw-Hill, New York (1954).
36. R. A. Dahl, "The Science of Public Administration: Three Problems," *Public Admin. Rev., 7:* 1–11 (1947).
37. Simon, "A Comment on 'The Science of Public Administration,' " p. 202.
38. Landau, "The Concept of Decision-Making," p. 15.
39. Simon, *Administrative Behavior,* p. 240.
40. Simon, *Administrative Behavior,* p. 21.
41. Simon, *Administrative Behavior,* p. 54.
42. Goodnow, *Politics and Administration,* p. 85.
43. Simon, *Administrative Behavior,* p. 55.
44. Simon, *Administrative Behavior,* p. 58.
45. Simon, *Administrative Behavior,* pp. 56–57.
46. W. S. Sayre, "Premises of Public Administration," *Public Admin. Rev., 17:* 194 (1958).
47. B. L. Whorf, "Science and Linguistics," *Language, Thought, and Reality* (J. B. Carrol, ed.), Wiley, New York, p. 212 (1956).
48. Simon, *Administrative Behavior,* p. 249.
49. Simon, *Administrative Behavior.*
50. See especially Chapter II of R. T. Golembiewski, W. Welsh, and W. Crotty, *A Methodological Primer for Political Scientists,* Rand McNally, Chicago (1969).
51. Simon, *Administrative Behavior,* p. 21.
52. D. Waldo, "Replies and Comment," *Am. Polit. Sci. Rev., 46:* 503 (1952).
53. Simon, *Administrative Behavior,* p. xiii.
54. The bias becomes more explicit in J. G. March and H. A. Simon, *Organizations,* Wiley, New York (1958), in their chapter on the limits of cognitive rationality.
55. Storing, *Essays,* p. 104.
56. Simon, *Administrative Behavior,* pp. xxiv–xxv.
57. Simon, *Administrative Behavior,* p. xxv.
58. Simon, *Administrative Behavior,* p. 41.
59. Simon, *Administrative Behavior,* p. 149.
60. Simon, *Administrative Behavior,* p. xxiv.
61. Storing, *Essays,* pp. 115–116.
62. Simon, *Administrative Behavior,* p. 198.

63. Storing, *Essays*, p. 71.
64. Simon, *Administrative Behavior*, p. xlv.
65. Simon, *Administrative Behavior*, p. xlvi.
66. Simon, *Administrative Behavior*, p. 37.
67. Simon, *Administrative Behavior*, p. 37.
68. Simon, *Administrative Behavior*, p. 22.
69. R. T. Golembiewski, *The Small Group: An Analysis of Research, Concepts and Operations*, University of Chicago Press, Chicago, especially pp. 97–104 (1962).
70. Simon, *Administrative Behavior*, p. 149.
71. C. E. Lindblom, "The Science of 'Muddling Through,' " *Public Admin. Rev.*, *19*: 79–85 (1959).
72. C. Z. Wilson and M. Alexis, "Basic Frameworks for Decisions," *J. Acad. Manage.*, *5*: 162 (1962).
73. C. I. Barnard, *The Functions of the Executive*, Harvard University Press, Cambridge, p. 193 (1938).
74. Wilson and Alexis, "Basic Frameworks for Decisions," p. 164.
75. Wilson and Alexis, "Basic Frameworks for Decisions."
76. Simon, *The New Science of Management Decision*, p. 21.
77. Wilson and Alexis, "Basic Frameworks for Decisions," p. 160.
78. P. Selznick, *Leadership in Administration*, Row, Peterson, Evanston, Ill., p. 137 (1957).
79. Simon, *Administrative Behavior*, p. 37.
80. Selznick, *Leadership in Administration*, p. 81.
81. Selznick, *Leadership in Administration*, pp. 138–139.
82. Selznick, *Leadership in Administration*, p. 139.
83. S. Stark, "Creative Leadership," *J. Acad. Manage.*, *6*: 166–167 (1963).
84. Golembiewski, *The Small Group*, especially pp. 128–144.
85. R. T. Golembiewski, *Men, Management and Morality*, McGraw-Hill, New York (1965). Reprinted by Transaction (1989).
86. The test apparently does not discriminate "authoritarians of the left" from "authoritarians of the right." See E. A. Shils, "Authoritarianism: "Right' and 'Left,' " especially pp 24–49, *Studies in the Scope and Method of "The Authoritarian Personality"* (R. Christie and M. Jahoda, eds.), Free Press, Glencoe, Ill. (1954).
87. Golembiewski, *Men, Management, and Morality*, especially pp. 161–202.
88. E. J. Meehan, *The Theory and Method of Political Analysis*, Dorsey Press, Homewood, Ill., p. 157 (1965).
89. Meehan, *The Theory and Method of Political Analysis*, p. 161. For a related view, see J. N. Roseman, "The Premises and Promises of Decision-Making Analysis," *Contemporary Political Analysis* (J. C. Charlesworth, ed.), Free Press, New York, pp. 189–192 (1967).

47

Updating the Approach to *Administrative Behavior* as Intent and Content

Robert T. Golembiewski

It has been over 20 years since the publication, in almost exactly the form of the preceding chapter, of the selection now titled "Simon's *Administrative Behavior* as Intent and Content" [1]. I find the selection about as serviceable then as now, which I trust does not simply mean that I have not learned much in that interval. It pleases me to see the piece reprinted, and I hope it serves those readers who did not cut their analytic teeth on the original source. Indeed, that original source—a book titled *A Methodological Primer for Political Scientists*—had classically bad timing. After spritely sales and several printings in the year or so following publication, the book's theme ran into the explosion in political science of *the* theme of the times. The emphasis on "relevance" won, hands-down, over methodological considerations, and retained that primacy for a decade or so. So the resurrection of the selection here has an especial relevance to me.

But what factors legitimate using valuable newsprint for these prefatory comments? The question stands in particular need of a direct response because it has been only a short time since I edited a long symposium on *Administrative Behavior*, on the occasion of its fortieth anniversary [2]. There, also, I provide a substantial introduction [3] which seeks to tell it like it is with respect to my long fascination with that volume, as well as with its mimeographed predecessor [4] that I stumbled across on some late-night foray into the Sterling Library at Yale.

Perhaps no convincing answer exists for why the present introduction should see the light of printed day, but I can provide a satisficing response (to rely on Simon's terminology). Here, I shall reflect on two new sources in addition to the text of the first and second editions of *Administrative Behavior*, on which the preceding selection focuses. These two new sources bear directly on the original argument, and contribute to it. Source number 1 is the third edition of *Administrative Behavior* [5], which is much expanded over its two predecessors and which became available just about the time that *A Methodological Primer* was going out of print. Source number 2 is the Simon/Argyris debate of some years ago

Source: *Public Budgeting and Financial Management*, *3*(1): 191–208 (1991).

in the *Public Administration Review* [6], which also substantially postdates the *Primer*. These two sources provide the most fulsome opportunities for Simon to variously modify or change the text and sense of *Administrative Behavior*. And his decisions in those two sources, in turn, encourage this look at "Content and Intent" to consider whether any changes in it are required.

From one perspective, these two sources may be said to provide little legitimation for extended comments here, or for substantial modifications of my original views reprinted in the preceding selection. Basically, Simon sticks with a winner. He does add six chapters in the third edition of *Administrative Behavior*, but all were previously published and are (to my eye) only gently articulated with the bulk of the text, which remains as it was in the first two editions. Indeed, except for some attention to interpersonal differences and roles, these new materials relate to that original text only in that all fall within the general rubric of "decision making," broadly defined. Depending upon one's tastes, this testifies either to the comprehensiveness of *Administrative Behavior* or to its abstract and extremely pliable quality. As to the central and original text, in any case, Simon stands pat. He observes [7]:

> In this third edition, as in the second, the text of the original work . . . is kept intact, for there is essentially nothing in it that I wish to retract. *Administrative Behavior* has served me as a useful and reliable port of embarkation for voyages of discovery into human decision-making: the relation of organization structure to decision-making, the formalized decision-making of operations research and management science, and in more recent years, the thinking and problem-solving activities of individual human beings.

Despite this lack of general encouragement, I review those two new sources and here report my sense of new or heightened perspectives on *Administrative Behavior* to which the preceding selection is insensitive, or of which it is unaware. After all, Simon does acknowledge his intent to considerably augment the original text [8], and that may provide grist for the present mill. Let me refer to this augmented sense of *Administrative Behavior* as "notes."

There are seven of these notes, in total, and they variously relate to my original thoughts on Simon's *Administrative Behavior* as "Intent and Content."

NOTES SUGGESTED BY THE THIRD EDITION

The new materials in Simon's third edition motivate three "notes." They follow, in no particular order.

First, the introduction for me heightens the sense of a central tension in *Administrative Behavior*, which Simon locates in the "core" of the book—Chapters IV and V. To rely on his own words [9],

> These chapters propose a theory of human choice or decision-making that aims to accommodate both those rational aspects of choice that have been the principal concern of economists and those properties and limitations of the human decision-making mechanisms that have attracted the attention of psychologists and practical decision-makers.

Perhaps I was not listening with sufficient empathy before, but this passage seems to me to put more tersely and clearly than earlier explanations *the* basis for the degree and character of the attention that has been devoted to *Administrative Behavior*. Simon's intended combination draws attention, if not ire, from both of two often-opposed camps. This puts Simon either in the middle of a crossfire, or in a crucial linkage role between disciplines, or both. In sum, all three positions attract great attention, and I believe it arguable that *Administrative Behavior* at various times occupies each of the three positions.

The view in the preceding selection of this central tension has two main features. Thus *Administrative Behavior* focuses on the cognitive aspects of human behavior, rather than the broadly social. Hence the general neglect in that book of behavioral themes that were breaking on an otherwise receptive world during the period of all three editions—the climate studies of Lewin, Lippitt, and White, the group emphases, and so on. So Simon does not provide the intended balance. Far from it, in fact.

Moreover, the preceding selection proposes that the economics/psychology accommodation does not get support from Simon's methodology. More sharply, in this view, the attempted accommodation not only encourages a basic methodological confusion between types of theories but that accommodation also involves methodological incompatibles. To paraphrase the preceding selection, Simon's content is not, and cannot be, adequate to his intent with respect to empirical work. This reflects a serious discrepancy between the reach and the grasp of *Administrative Behavior*.

Second, the most recent edition of *Administrative Behavior* also directs augmented attention to factors that seek to increase the specificity of the volume, both empirical as well as conceptual. See the emphasis on role and decision premises. These at once seek a greater flexibility and applicability, and yet undercut the thrust of Simon's original argument.

Consider Simon's reemphasis on "premises" in the introduction to the third edition. He observes [10]: "It is therefore the *premise* (and a large number of these are combined in every decision) rather than the whole *decision* that serves as the smallest unit of analysis." So he despairs of answering *the* question that most people pose: Who really made the decision? Simon permits no doubt [11]: "Such a question is meaningless—a complex decision is like a great river, drawing from its many tributaries the innumerable component premises of which it is constituted."

The preceding selection has no argument with this augmented emphasis, but the degree of insistence on it only increases the dissonance with the basic thrust of *Administrative Behavior*. At numerous places in the original text, a counterthrust dominates the later augmentations. For example, Simon observes [12], "The behavior of a rational person can be controlled, therefore, if the value and factual premises upon which he bases his decisions are specified for him. This control can be complete or partial."

The preceding selection has serious quarrels with such dissonance inducers. If Simon intends such generalizations as normative, *the* issue is which *specific premises should be controlled*, even if all premises could be controlled. If Simon intends such generalizations as empirical, on the other hand, I have serious doubts as to their validity—certainly for people as the behavioral sciences have come to know them, and no doubt even for the "rational person" to whom Simon alludes. The general sense of behavioral research is that at least some, and probably many, premises cannot be specified for us over the long run in the absence of two (to me) unacceptable concomitants: major repression by others; and periodic expressions (if not explosions) of general discontent whose ill-fated management requires scapegoats and purges [13].

The preceding selection highlights such dissonance inducers in the first and second editions of *Administrative Behavior*, and the third edition increases their number and severity. In general, Simon tries to increase the empirical content of the third edition [14] but, to the degree that he succeeds, he contributes to the kind of dissonance inducing illustrated above. In the terms of the preceding selection, *Administrative Behavior* provides an awkward methodological context for Simon's later augmentations, and often raises serious imprecisions concerning which theoretical realms are being addressed.

Third, and finally for present purposes, the third edition of *Administrative Behavior* clearly—and for the first time, as I read the several editions of the book—articulates why the volume cannot be neglected, content aside, by the broad array of students of organization and administration. In the new introduction, Simon proposes an exclusive province for *a* theory of organization or administration: "It is precisely in the realm where human behavior is *intendedly* rational, but only *limited* so [sic], that there is room for a genuine theory of organization and administration" [15]. As Simon sees it, the thesis of his two "core" chapters relates to this exclusive circumscription: "*The central concern of administrative theory is with the boundary between the rational and the nonrational aspects of human social behavior.*" So Simon's theory—and *perforce*, of everyone else doing "genuine" work—is "the theory of intended and bounded rationality—of the behavior of human beings who *satisfice* because they have not the wits to maximize" [16].

So other students have only three choices: accept *Administrative Behavior* and do what it prescribes; reject it; or neglect it. The third alternative is not really open, given the volume's historic place. The first two alternatives ineluctably draw attention to *Administrative Behavior*.

The preceding selection rejects Simon's exclusionist posture. In opposition, perhaps the basic point of dispute between the selection and *Administrative Behavior* derives from the fact that the former admits—indeed, encourages—many theories of organization and administration:

- One progressively comprehensive empirical theory, which over the entire developmental period will synthesize numerous theoretical fragments of variable reach-and-grasp into burgeoning networks.
- Multiple goal-based, empirical theories, each of which proposes to detail how specific goals can be achieved, given the existing knowledge of empirical regularities.
- Numerous possible utopian theories, each of which begins with a set of assumptions and axioms and proceeds by logical analysis.

As noted, the preceding selection judges *Administrative Behavior* as providing no sound methodological basis for empirical efforts. In the introduction to the third edition of *Administrative Behavior*, Simon highlights the additional disattractor that only one theory of organization and administration can exist.

A brief review of some of my own work suggests the sense in which I see Simon's highlighted exclusionism as severely limiting. My efforts focus on developing *a* goal-based, empirical theory whose normative focus is on increasing responsible freedom in organizations [17, 18]. The emphasis is on "a"—as in one, or a single example—of that theoretical genre. Quite self-consciously, the approach I favor seeks to develop a growing panel of interventions—a technology to change with values, if you will—which can with substantial success rates generate high employee satisfaction as well as meet organization needs such as high productivity [19–21]. In the process of elaborating this goal-based, empirical theory, it often proves necessary to develop empirical theory fragments, as for defining contextual features so as to permit more precise fitting of interventions to them. One such theory fragment deals with psychological burnout—operationally defining it, tracking its covariants, and remedying it, among other things [22–24].

The preceding selection does not see *Administrative Behavior* as supporting such a specific developmental line of effort, or any set of them. The implied paradox invites overstatement, but it goes something like this: We are all with *Administrative Behavior*, if in very general and often harshly qualified senses; and hence no one is doing its empirical work, except in very general senses.

NOTES SUGGESTED BY SIMON/ARGYRIS DEBATE

The debate between Argyris and Simon also provides new perspectives on the preceding selection. Four themes will have to suffice for present purposes, but a longer list could be generated easily.

First, Simon's previously quoted passage about the intended accommodation of economics and psychology [25] helps explain the ideational impasse between Argyris and Simon reflected in their stalemate of a debate, which approximates an exchange of heavy barrages aimed at positions each participant denies holding. The one is too much the economist for the other; and that other, in turn, is too much the student of individual and group behavior for his debating opponent.

Put in another elemental way, Argyris argues within the context of a relatively specific goal-based, empirical theory—that theory whose values emphasize human needs, and whose empirical theory fragments for meeting those needs emphasize the centrality of choice and participation. This is far more than Simon can give, however. To him, human behavior and needs constitute less the core of the matter *than limits* on the corpus of economic thought to which Simon seeks to accommodate.

That twain can never meet, and do not meet in the pages of the *Public Administration Review*.

The preceding selection does not explicitly deal with the intended accommodation of economics and psychology, but that selection clearly has a socio-psychologic bias. No more than Argyris, then, can it share common ground with *Administrative Behavior* on that issue. As noted earlier, "Intent and Content" also distances itself from Argyris' position in several central particulars.

Second, relatedly, the Simon/Argyris debate highlights a kind of engine/caboose issue. For Argyris, human needs are the basic engine, and their frustration is seen as causing huge mischief for people and for their employing organizations. Viewed positively, he sees organizational sensitivities to these human needs as generating positive outcomes in satisfaction and productivity. For Simon, although extremes have to be avoided in such judgments because of the protean quality of *Administrative Behavior*, these human needs are more caboose. *Administrative Behavior* encourages a focus on limits to achieving organizational goals and efficiency, rather than on human potentials to be engaged and enriched. Speaking of Simon and others, Argyris concludes on this important point: "They suggest that the present theories are based on a concept of man, indeed a morality, that leads the scholar to conduct research that is, intentionally or unintentionally, supportive of the status quo" [26]. Speaking only of *Administrative Behavior*, Argyris relatedly but more directly notes the "central and dominant role [of management] in designing and controlling human behavior." This bias leads Argyris to wonder, and to answer his own query [27]:

> How can Simon imply that some employees would not resist—indeed resent—having their nervous systems so directly managed? The answer is that the conception of indoctrination as a rational and psychologically benign process is possible if man is viewed as being intendedly rational.

Here, again, the central issue derives from *Administrative Behavior's* methodological posture. Simon and Argyris focus on different goals and assumptions, which would pose real problems even if both were self-consciously developing goal-based, empirical theories. Matters are far from that situation. In effect, for example, Simon proposes that there is only one kind of "genuine" theory of organization and management. And Argyris unsuccessfully urges him to look at one other theoretical approach, at least.

The preceding selection, as explained earlier, takes a differentiated view of theory types. It proposes two basic points in opposition to *Administrative Behavior*: There are numerous possible goal-based, empirical theories; and *Administrative Behavior* does not provide suitable methodological content if its intent involves either empirical theory or goal-based empirical theories. Hence, while the preceding selection and my other work also distance themselves from *Administrative Behavior*, I take a more limited position than Argyris. To explain, Argyris proposes that need-serving approaches get substantial attention, per se. I see myself as more pragmatic. I seek specific need-serving interventions that *also* have a demonstrated capability of serving organizational needs, on clear average. In that sense, I am tethered: I incline toward Argyrian values, but I emphasize the need to respond to Simon's test of those values, as developed in the third point which follows.

Third, *the* basic issue of human nature surfaces in the Argyris/Simon debate, if briefly. Argyris stresses the importance of normative or value statements in theories about human behavior in organizations, consistent with his focus on a goal-based, empirical theory. For him, "one reply" to the question of where this normative view would come from is that it can derive from the "desired potentialities of man," building on such "growth psychology" as that of Masow [2]. Simon is not impressed by such "pleas for sweeping social change," however. Rather, he counters with a plea of his own that advocates like Argyris "provide us with empirical evidence to support the postulates about human nature—and particularly about its mutability and malleability—upon which their advocacy rests" [29].

The preceding selection gives no attention to this central issue, except by drawing attention to the need to root goal-based, empirical theories in values or normative statements. Personally, however, I find the polarization proposed in the title of Simon's rejoinder—rational or self-actualizing?—to be more confusing than helpful. Directly, is that apposition meant to be normative or empirical? Simon asks Argyris to provide empirical data, as noted, but it seems to me perfectly appropriate to see self-actualization as a statement of *one* normative preference, which Argyris does. As such, it could generate one goal-based, empirical theory concerning how to maximize the probability of achieving those "desired potentialities," given what we know about the world. I do not much like self-actualization as a goal. It *is* imprecise, although I do not go as far as Simon in portraying self-actualization as "usually swaddled and stifled by layers of social and psychological encumbrance" [30]. We have not yet found the precisely right conceptual and operational combination for measuring human needs and their satisfaction, to be sure, but the several growth psychologies seem to me to point us in a generally useful direction.

Fourth and finally, the debate surfaces a form of is/ought. Argyris sees *Administrative Behavior* as purely descriptive rather than normative, and proposes that this runs a serious risk. His charge? Describing behavior can legitimate it or, at the very least, can make it more difficult to test competing theories, especially (I add) when the describer has the status of a Nobel laureate, as Simon does [31].

Simon sees this as Argyris' "most serious charge" [32], and responds with corresponding intensity.

The preceding selection tends to be less generous to *Administrative Behavior* than Argyris in the passage referred to immediately above. It sees the content of that volume as "descriptive" only if that term is used very generally, and qualified severely in the bargain.

Oppositely, indeed, the selection sees the volume as *impeding description* of the kind required for cumulative empirical research, even as the volume obviously has motivated much discussion.

A concluding caveat is in order. To be factual, Argyris withdraws in another place the generosity referred to above. He observes: "Simon's brilliant *Administrative Behavior* would never have become a classic if people judged its contribution on the basis of empirical scientific evidence" [33]. Substantially, that is what the selection reprinted above attempts to establish, if in its own complex and qualified ways. Perhaps it is a debater's point, but Simon nowhere provides the kind of evidence he asks of Argyris. Nor can Simon's methodological posture ever generate that evidence, the preceding piece emphasizes.

NOTES AND REFERENCES

1. R. T. Golembiewski, W. Welsh, and W. Crotty, *A Methodological Primer for Political Scientists*, Rand McNally, Chicago, pp. 191–225 (1969).
2. R. T. Golembiewski (ed.), "Perspectives on Simon's *Administrative Behavior*," *Public Admin. Q.*, Part 1, *12*: 257–384 (1988) and Part 2, *12*: 349–483 (1989).
3. R. T. Golembiewski, "Perspectives on Simon's *Administrative Behavior*," pp. 259–274.
4. H. A. Simon, *Administrative Behavior*, Illinois Institute of Technology, Chicago (1945). Mimeoed.
5. H. A. Simon, *Administrative Behavior*, Free Press, New York (1976).
6. C. Argyris, "Some Limits of Rational Man Organizational Theory," *Public Admin. Rev.*, *33*: 253–267 (1973); H. A. Simon, "Organization Man: Rational or Self-Actualizing?," *Public Admin. Rev.*, *33*: 346–353 (1973); and C. Argyris, "Organization Man: Rational *and* Self-Actualizing," *Public Admin. Rev.*, *33*: 354 (1973).
7. Simon, *Administrative Behavior*, p. ix.
8. Simon, *Administrative Behavior*, p. ix ff.
9. Simon, *Administrative Behavior*, p. ix.
10. Simon, *Administrative Behavior*, p. xii.
11. Simon, *Administrative Behavior*, p. xii.
12. Simon, *Administrative Behavior*, p. 223.
13. R. T. Golembiewski, *Men, Management, and Morality*, Transaction, New Brunswick, N.J. (1989).
14. Simon, *Administrative Behavior*, especially, pp xxii–xxv, xxxv–xxxviii, and 309–314.
15. Simon, *Administrative Behavior*, p. xxviii.
16. Simon, *Administrative Behavior*, p. xxviii.
17. R. T. Golembiewski, *Humanizing Public Organizations*, Lomond, Mt. Airy, Md. (1985).
18. R. T. Golembiewski and A. Kiepper, *High Performance and Human Costs*, Praeger, New York (1988).
19. R. T. Golembiewski, C. W. Proehl, Jr., and D. Sink, "Success of OD Applications in the Public Sector," *Public Admin. Rev.*, *41*: 679–682 (1981).
20. J. M. Nicholas, "The Comparative Impact of Organization Development Interventions on Hard Criteria Measures," *Acad. Manage. Rev.*, *7*: 531–542 (1982).
21. R. T. Golembiewski and B. C. Sun, "Enriching Work and Empowering Employees," *J. Health Hum. Resources Admin.*, (in press).
22. R. T. Golembiewski, R. F. Munzenrider, and J. G. Stevenson, *Stress in Organizations*, Praeger, New York (1986).
23. R. T. Golembiewski and R. F. Munzenrider, *Phases of Burnout*, Praeger, New York (1988).
24. R. T. Golembiewski, R. Hilles, and R. Daly, "Some Effects of Multiple OD Interventions on Burnout and Worksite Features," *J. Appl. Behav. Sci.*, *23*: 295–314 (1987).

25. Simon, *Administrative Behavior*, p. ix.
26. Argyris, "Some Limits," p. 253.
27. Argyris, "Some Limits," p. 255.
28. Argyris, "Some Limits," pp. 264–266.
29. Simon, "Organization Man," p. 346.
30. Simon, "Organization Man," p. 350.
31. Argyris, "Some Limits," p. 254.
32. Simon, "Organization Man," p. 350.
33. Argyris, "Organization Man," p. 354.

48

The Political Economy of Efficiency: Cost-Benefit Analysis, Systems Analysis, and Program Budgeting

Aaron Wildavsky

There was a day when the meaning of economic efficiency was reasonably clear.

An objective met up with a technician. Efficiency consisted in meeting the objective at the lowest cost or in obtaining the maximum amount of the objective for a specified amount of resources. Let us call this "pure efficiency." The desirability of trying to achieve certain objectives may depend on the cost of achieving them. In this case the analyst (he has graduated from being a mere technician) alters the objective to suit available resources. Let us call this "mixed efficiency." Both pure and mixed efficiency are limited in the sense that they take for granted the existing structure of the political system and work within its boundaries. Yet the economizer, he who values efficiency most dearly, may discover that the most efficient means for accomplishing his ends cannot be secured without altering the machinery for making decisions. He not only alters means and ends (resources and objectives) simultaneously but makes them dependent on changes in political relationships. While he claims no special interest in or expertise concerning the decision apparatus outside of the market place, the economizer pursues efficiency to the heart of the political system. Let us call this "total efficiency." In this vocabulary, then, concepts of efficiency may be pure or mixed, limited or total.

A major purpose of this chapter is to take the newest and recently most popular modes of achieving efficiency—cost-benefit analysis, systems analysis, and program budgeting—and show how much more is involved than mere economizing. *Even at the most modest level of cost-benefit analysis, I will try to show that it becomes difficult to maintain pure notions of efficiency. At a higher level, systems analysis is based on a mixed notion of efficiency. And program budgeting at the highest levels leaves pure efficiency far behind its over-reaching grasp into the structure of the political system. Program budgeting, it turns out, is a form of systems analysis, that is, political systems analysis.*

Source: *Public Budgeting and Financial Management*, *1*(1): 1–41 (1989).

These modes of analysis are neither good for nothing nor good for everything, and one cannot speak of them as wholly good or bad. It is much more useful to try to specify some conditions under which they would or would not be helpful for various purposes. While such a list could not be exhaustive at this stage, nor permanent at any stage (because of advances in the art), it provides a basis for thinking about what these techniques can and cannot do. Another major purpose of this chapter, therefore, is to describe cost-benefit and systems analysis and program budgeting as techniques for decision-making. I shall place particular stress upon what seems to me the most characteristic feature of all three modes of analysis: the aids to calculation designed to get around the vast areas of uncertainty where quantitative analysis leaves off and judgment begins.

COST-BENEFIT ANALYSIS

One can view cost-benefit analysis as anything from an infallible means of reaching the new Utopia to a waste of resources in attempting to measure the unmeasureable. [1]

The purpose of cost-benefit analysis is to secure an efficient allocation of resources produced by the governmental system in its interaction with the private economy. The nature of efficiency depends on the objectives set up for government. In the field of water resources, where most of the work on cost-benefit analysis has been done, the governmental objective is usually postulated to be an increase in national income. In a crude sense, this means that the costs to whomever may incur them should be less than the benefits to whomever may receive them. The time streams of consumption gained and foregone by a project are its benefits and costs.

The aim of cost-benefit analysis is to maximize "the present value of all benefits less that of all costs, subject to specified restraints" [2]. A long view is taken in that costs are estimated not only for the immediate future but also for the life of the project. A wide view is taken in that indirect consequences for others—variously called externalities, side effects, spillovers, and repercussion effects—are considered. Ideally, all costs and benefits are evaluated. The usual procedure is to estimate the installation costs of the project and spread them over time, thus making them into something like annual costs. To these costs are added an estimate of annual operating costs. The next step involves estimating the average value of the output by considering the likely number of units produced each year and their probable value in the market place of the future. Intangible, "secondary," benefits may then be considered. These time streams of costs and benefits are discounted so as to obtain the present value of costs and benefits. Projects whose benefits are greater than costs may then be approved, or the cost-benefit ratios may, with allowance for relative size, be used to rank projects in order of desirability.

Underlying Economic and Political Assumptions

A straightforward description of cost-benefit analysis cannot do justice to the powerful assumptions that underlie it or to the many conditions limiting its usefulness. The assumptions involve value judgments that are not always recognized and, when recognized, are not easily handled in practice. The limiting conditions arise partly out of the assumptions and partly out of severe computational difficulties in estimating costs, and especially benefits. Here I can only indicate some major problems.

Cost-benefit analysis is based on superiority in the marketplace [3], under competitive conditions and full employment, as the measure of value in society. Any imperfection in the market works against the validity of the results. Unless the same degree of monopoly were found throughout the economy, for example, a governmental body that enjoys monopolistic control of prices or outputs would not necessarily make the same investment decisions as under free competition. A similar difficulty occurs when the size of a project is large in comparison to the economy, as in some developing nations. The project itself then affects the constellation of relative prices and production against which its efficiency is measured. The assumption based on the classical full employment model is also important because it gives prices special significance. Where manpower is not being utilized, projects may be justified in part as putting this unused resource to work.

The economic model on which cost-benefit analysis depends for its validity is based on a political theory. The idea is that in a free society the economy is to serve the individual's consistent preferences revealed and rationally pursued in the market place. Governments are not supposed to dictate preferences nor make decisions.

This individualist theory assumes as valid the current distribution of income. Preferences are valued in the market place where votes are based on disposable income. Governmental action to achieve efficiency, therefore, inevitably carries with it consequences for the distribution of income. Projects of different size and location and composition will transfer income in different amounts to different people. While economists might estimate the redistributive consequences of various projects, they cannot, on efficiency grounds, specify one or another as preferable. How is this serious problem to be handled?

Cost-benefit analysis is a way of trying to promote economic welfare. But what welfare? No one knows how to deal with interpersonal comparisons of utility. It cannot be assumed that the desirability of rent supplements versus a highway or dam can be measured on a single utility scale. There is no scientific way to compare losses and gains among different people or to say that the marginal loss of a dollar to one man is somehow equal to the gain of a dollar by another. The question of whose utility function is to prevail (the analyst versus the people involved, the upstream gainers versus the downstream losers, the direct beneficiaries versus the taxpayers, the entire nation or a particular region, and so on) is of prime importance in making public policy.

The literature on welfare economics is notably unable to specify an objective welfare function [4]. Ideally, actions would benefit everyone and harm no one. As an approximation, the welfare economist views as optimal an action that leaves some people better off and none worse off. If this criterion were applied in political life, it would result in a situation like that of the Polish Diet in which anyone who was damaged could veto legislation. To provide a way out of this impasse, Hicks and Kaldor proposed approval of decisions if the total gain in welfare is such that the winners could compensate the losers. But formal machinery for compensation does not ordinarily exist and most modern economists are highly critical of the major political mechanism for attempting to compensate, namely, log-rolling in Congress on public works projects [5]. It is a very imperfect mechanism for assuring that losers in one instance become winners in another.

Another way of dealing with income distribution is to accept a criterion laid down by a political body and maximize present benefits less costs subject to this constraint. Or the cost-benefit analyst can present a series of alternatives differing according to the individuals who pay and prices charged. The analyst must not only compute the new inputs and outputs, but also the costs and benefits for each group with whom the public authorities are especially concerned. No wonder this is not often done! Prest and Turvey are uncertain whether such a procedure is actually helpful in practice [6].

Income redistribution in its most extreme form would result in a complete leveling or equality of incomes. Clearly, this is not what is meant. A more practical meaning might be distributing income to the point where specific groups achieve a certain minimum. It is also possible that the operational meaning of income redistribution may simply be the transfer of some income from some haves to some have-nots. Even in the last and most minimal sense of the term it is by no means clear that projects that are inefficient by the usual economic criteria serve to redistribute income in the desired direction. It is possible that some inefficient projects may transfer income from poorer to richer people. Before the claim that certain projects are justified by the effect of distributing income in a specified way can be accepted, an analysis to show that this is what actually happens must be at hand.

Since the distribution of income is at stake, it is not surprising that beneficiaries tend to dominate investment decisions in the political arena and steadfastly refuse to pay for what they receive from government tax revenues. They uniformly resist user charges based on benefits received. Fox and Herfindahl estimate that of a total initial investment of $3 billion for the Corps of Engineers in 1962, taxpayers in general would pay close to two-thirds of the costs [7]. Here, greater use of the facilities by a larger number of beneficiaries getting something for nothing inflates the estimated benefits which justify the project in the first place. There may be a political rationale for these decisions, but it has not been developed.

In addition to redistributing income, public works projects have a multitude of objectives and consequences. Projects may generate economic growth, alleviate poverty among some people, provide aesthetic enjoyment and opportunities for recreation, improve public health, reduce the risks of natural disaster, alter travel patterns, affect church attendance, change educational opportunities, and more. No single welfare criterion can encompass these diverse objectives. How many of them should be considered? Which are susceptible of quantification? The further one pursues this analysis, the more impassable the thicket.

Limitations in the Utility of Cost-Benefit Analysis

One possible conclusion is that at present certain types of cost-benefit analysis are not meaningful. In reviewing the literature on the calculus of costs and benefits in research and development, for example, Prest and Turvey comment on "the uncertainty and unreliability of cost estimates . . . and . . . the extraordinarily complex nature of the benefits" [8].

Another conclusion is that one should be cautious in distinguishing the degree to which projects are amenable to cost-benefit analysis.

> When there are many diverse types of benefits from a project and/or many different beneficiaries it is difficult to list them all and to avoid double counting. This is one reason why it is so much easier to apply cost-benefit analysis to a limited purpose development, say, than it is to the research and development aspects of some multi-purpose discovery, such as a new type of plastic material. . . . It is no good expecting those fields in which benefits are widely diffused, and in which there are manifest divergences between accounting and economic costs or benefits, to be as cultivable as others. Nor is it realistic to expect that comparisons between projects in entirely different branches of economic activity are likely to be as meaningful or fruitful as those between projects in the same branch. The technique is more useful in the public-utility area than in the social-services area of government [9].

If the analysis is to be useful at all, calculations must be simplified [10]. The multiple ramifications of interesting activities can be taken into account only at the cost of introducing fantastic complexities. Prest and Turvey remark of one such attempt, that "This system . . . requires knowledge of all the demand and supply equations in the economy, so is scarcely capable of application by road engineers" [11]. They suggest omitting consideration where (1) side effects are judged not terribly large or where (2) concern for these effects belongs to another governmental jurisdiction [12].

If certain costs or benefits are deemed important but cannot be quantified, it is always possible to guess. The increasing use of recreation and aesthetic facilities to justify public works projects in the United States is disapproved by most economists because there can be a vast, but hidden, inflation of these benefits. For example, to attribute the same value to a recreation day on a reservoir located in desert miles from any substitute source of water as to a day on an artificial lake in the heart of natural lake country is patently wrong. Economists would prefer to see recreation facilities listed in an appendix so that they can be taken into account in some sense, or, alternatively, that the project be presented with and without the recreation facilities, so that a judgment can be made as to whether the additional services are worth the cost [13].

Economists distinguish between risk, where the precise outcome cannot be predicted but a probability distribution can be specified, and uncertainty, where one does not even know the parameters of the outcomes. The cost-benefit analyst must learn to live with uncertainty, for he can never know whether all relevant objectives have been included and what changes may occur in policy and in technology.

It is easy enough to cut the life of the project below its expected economic life. The interest rate can be raised. Assumptions can be made that costs will be higher and benefits lower than expected. All these methods, essentially conservative, are also highly arbitrary. They can be made somewhat more systematic, however, by sensitivity analysis in which length of life, for instance, is varied over a series of runs so that its impact on the project can be appraised.

Lessening uncertainty by hiking the interest or discount rate leads to greater difficulties, for the dominance of "higher" criteria over economic analysis is apparent in the frustrating problem of choosing the correct interest rate at which to discount the time streams of costs and benefits essential to the enterprise. Only an interest rate can establish the relationship between values at different periods of time. Yet people differ in preferences for the present versus the intermediate or long-run value. Moreover, the interest rate should also measure the opportunity cost of private capital that could be used to produce wealth elsewhere in the economy if it had not been used up in the form of tax income spent on the project under consideration. Is the appropriate rate the very low cost the government charges, the cost of a government corporation like TVA that must pay a somewhat higher rate, the going rate of interest for private firms, or an even higher rate to hedge against an uncertain future? As Otto Eckstein has observed, "the choice of interest rates must remain a value judgment" [14].

If the efficiency of a project is insensitive to interest costs, then these costs can vary widely without mattering much. But Fox and Herfindahl discovered that if Corps of Engineer projects raised their interest (or discount) rate from $2\frac{5}{8}$ to 4, 6, or 8%, then 9, 64, and 80% of their projects, respectively, would have had a benefit-cost ratio of less than unity [15]. This single value choice among many has such large consequences that it alone may be decisive.

The Mixed Results of Cost-Benefit Analysis

Although cost-benefit analysis presumably results in efficiency by adding the most to national income, it is shot through with political and social value choices and surrounded by uncertainties and difficulties of computation. Whether the many noneconomic assumptions and consequences actually result in basically changing the nature of a project remains moot. Clearly, we have come a long way from pure efficiency, to verge upon mixed efficiency.

Economic analysts usually agree that all relevant factors (especially nonmarket factors) cannot be squeezed into a single formula. They therefore suggest that the policymaker, in being given the market costs and benefits of alternatives, is, in effect, presented with the market value he is placing on nonmarket factors. The contribution of the analyst is only one input into the decision, but the analyst may find this limited conception of his role unacceptable to others. Policymakers may not want this kind of input; they may want *the* answer, or at least an answer that they can defend on the basis of the analyst's legitimized expertise.

The dependence of cost-benefit analysis on a prior political framework does not mean that it is a useless or trivial exercise. Decisions must be made. If quantifiable economic costs and benefits are not everything, neither would a decision maker wish to ignore them entirely. The great advantage of cost-benefit analysis, when pursued with integrity, is that some implicit judgments are made explicit and subject to analysis. Yet, for many, the omission of explicit consideration of political factors is a serious deficiency.

The experience of the Soil Conservation Service in lowering certain political costs may prove illuminating. For many years the service struggled along with 11 major watershed projects involving big dams, great headaches, and little progress. Because the watersheds were confined to a single region, it was exceedingly difficult to generate support in Congress, particularly at appropriations time. The upstream–downstream controversies generated by these projects resulted in less than universal local approval. The SCS found itself in the direct line of fire for determining priorities in use of insufficient funds.

Compare this situation with the breakthrough which occurred when SCS developed the small watershed program. Since each facility is relatively inexpensive, large numbers can be placed throughout the country, markedly increasing political support. Agreement on the local level is facilitated because much less land is flooded and side payments are easier to arrange. A judicious use of cost-benefit analysis, together with ingenious relationships with State governors, places the choice of priorities with the states and yet maintains a reasonable level of consistency by virtue of adherence to national criteria. Errors are easier to correct because the burden of calculation has been drastically reduced and experience may be more easily accumulated with a larger number of small projects.

Consider the situation in which an agency finds it desirable to achieve a geographical spread of projects in order to establish a wider base of support. Assume (with good reason) that cost-benefit criteria will not permit projects to be established in some states because the value of the land or water is too low. One can say that this is just too bad and observe the agency seeking ways around the restriction by playing up benefits, playing down costs, or attacking the whole benefit-cost concept as inapplicable. Another approach would be to recognize that federalism—meaning, realistically, the distribution of indulgences to state units—represents a political value worth promoting to some extent and that gaining nationwide support is important. From this perspective, a compromise solution would be to except one or two projects in each state or region from meeting the full requirement of the formula, though the projects with the highest benefit-cost ratio would have to be chosen. In return for sacrificing full adherence to the formula in a few instances, one would get enhanced support for it in many others.

Everyone knows, of course, that cost-benefit analysis is not the messiah come to save water resources projects from contamination by the rival forces of ignorance and political corruption. Whenever agencies and their associated interests discover that they cannot do what they want, they may twist prevailing criteria out of shape: Two projects may be joined so that both qualify when one, standing alone, would not. Costs and benefits may be manipulated, or the categories may be so extended that almost any project qualifies. On the other hand, cost-benefit analysis has some "good" political uses that might be stressed more than they have been. The technique gives the responsible official a good reason for turning down projects, with a public-interest explanation the Congressman can use with his constituents and the interest-group leader with his members.

This is not to say that cost-benefit analysis has little utility. Assuming that the method will continue to be improved, and that one accepts the market as the measure of economic value, it can certainly tell decision makers something about what they will be giving up if they follow alternative policies. The use of two analyses, one based on regional and the other on national factors, might result in an appraisal of the economic costs of federalism.

The burden of calculation may be reduced by following cost-benefit analysis for many projects and introducing other values only for a few. To expect, however, that the method itself (which distributes indulgences to some and deprivations to others) would not be subject to manipulation in the political process is to say that we shall be governed by formula and not by men.

Because the cost-benefit formula does not always jibe with political realities—that is, it omits political costs and benefits—we can expect it to be twisted out of shape from time to time. Yet cost-benefit analysis may still be important in getting rid of the worst projects. Avoiding the worst where one can't get the best is no small accomplishment.

SYSTEMS ANALYSIS

The good systems analyst is a "chochem," a Yiddish word meaning "wise man," with overtones of "wise guy." His forte is creativity. Although he sometimes relates means to ends and fits ends to match means, he ordinarily eschews such pat processes, preferring instead to relate elements imaginatively into new systems that create their own means and ends. He plays new objectives continuously against cost elements until a creative synthesis has been achieved. He looks down upon those who say that they take objectives as given, knowing full well that the apparent solidity of the objective will dissipate during analysis and that, in any case, most people do not know what they want because they do not know what they can get.

Since no one knows how to teach creativity, daring, and nerve, it is not surprising that no one can define what systems analysis is or how it should be practiced. E. S. Quade, who compiled the RAND Corporation lectures on systems analysis, says it "is still largely a form of art" in which it is not possible to lay down "fixed rules which need only be followed with exactness" [16]. He examined systems studies to determine ideas and principles common to the good ones, but discovered that "no universally accepted set of ideas existed. It was even difficult to decide which studies should be called good" [17].

Systems analysis is derived from operations research, which came into use during World War II when some scientists discovered that they could use simple quantitative analysis to get the most out of existing military equipment. A reasonably clear objective was given, and ways to cut the cost of achieving it could be developed, using essentially statistical models. Operations research today is largely identified with specific techniques: linear programming; Monte Carlo (randomizing) methods; gaming and game theory. While there is no hard and fast division between operations research and systems analysis, a rough separation may perhaps be made. The less that is known about objectives, the more they conflict, the larger the number of elements to be considered, the more uncertain the environment, the more likely it is that the work will be called a systems analysis. In systems analysis there is more judgment and intuition and less reliance on quantitative methods than in operations research.

Systems analysis builds models that abstract from reality but represent the crucial relationships. The systems analyst first decides what questions are relevant to his inquiry, selects certain quantifiable factors, cuts down the list of factors to be dealt with by aggregation and by eliminating the (hopefully) less important ones, and then gives them quantitative relationships with one another within the system he has chosen for analysis. But crucial variables may not be quantifiable. If they can be reduced to numbers, there may be no mathematical function that can express the desired relationship. More important, there may be no single criterion for judging results among conflicting objectives. Most important, the original objectives, if any, may not make sense.

It cannot be emphasized too strongly that a (if not the) distinguishing characteristic of systems analysis is that the objectives are either not known or are subject to change. Systems analysis, Quade tells us, "is associated with that class of problems where the difficulties lie in deciding what ought to be done—not simply how it do it—and honors go to people who . . . find out what the problem is" [18]. Charles Hitch, the former Comptroller of the Defense Department, insists that

> learning about objectives is one of the chief objects of this kind of analysis. We must learn to look at objectives as critically and as professionally as we look at our models and our other inputs. We may, of course, begin with tentative objectives, but we must expect to modify or replace them as we learn about the systems we are studying—and related systems. The feedback on objectives may in some cases be the most important result of our study. We have never undertaken a major system study at RAND in which we are able to define satisfactory objectives at the beginning of the study [19].

Systems analysts recognize many good reasons for their difficulties in defining problems or objectives. Quade reaches the core: "Objectives are not, in fact agreed upon. The choice, while ostensibly between alternatives, is really between objectives or ends and non-analytic methods must be used for a final reconciliation of views" [20]. It may be comforting to believe that objectives come to the analyst from on high and can be taken as given, but this easy assumption is all wrong. "For all sorts of good reasons that are not about to change," says Hitch, "official statements of national objectives (or company objectives) tend to be nonexistent or so vague and literary as to be non-operational" [21]. Objectives are not only likely to be "thin and rarified," according to Wohlstetter, but the relevant authorities "are likely to conflict. Among others there will be national differences within an alliance and within the nation, interagency, interservice, and intraservice differences" [22].

Moreover, even shared objectives often conflict with one another. Deterrence of atomic attack might be best served by letting an enemy know that we would respond with an all-out, indiscriminate attack on his population. Defense of our population against death and destruction might not be well served by this strategy [23], as the Secretary of Defense recognized when he recommended a city-avoidance strategy that might give an enemy some incentive to spare our cities as well. Not only are objectives large in number and in conflict with one another, they are likely to engender serious repercussion effects. Many objectives, like morale and the stability of alliances, are resistant to quantification. What is worth doing depends on whether it can be done at all, how well, and at what cost. Hence, objectives really cannot be taken as given; they must be made up by the analyst. "In fact," Wohlstetter declares, "we are always in the process of choosing and modifying both means and ends" [24].

Future systems analysts are explicitly warned not to let clients determine objectives. A suggestive analogy is drawn with the doctor who would not ignore a patient's "description of his symptoms, but . . . cannot allow the patient's self diagnosis to override his own professional judgment" [25]. Quade argues that since systems analysis has often resulted in changing the original objectives of the policy-maker, it would be "self-defeating to accept without inquiry" his "view of what the problem is" [26].

I have stressed the point that the systems analyst is advised to insist on his own formulation of the problem because it shows so closely that we are dealing with a mixed concept of efficiency.

Adjusting objectives to resources in the present or near future is difficult enough without considering future states of affairs which hold tremendous uncertainty. Constants become variables; little can be taken for granted. The rate of technological progress, an opponent's estimate of your reaction to his latest series of moves based on his reaction to yours, whether or not atomic war will occur, what it will be like, whether we shall have warning, whether the system we are working on will cost anything close to current estimates and whether it will be ready within five years of the due date—on most of these matters, there are no objective probabilities to be calculated.

An effective dealing with uncertainty must be a major goal of systems analysis. Systems analysis is characterized by the aids to calculation it uses, not to conquer, but to circumvent and mitigate some of the pervasive effects of uncertainty. Before a seemingly important factor may be omitted, for example, a sensitivity analysis may be run to determine whether its variation significantly affects the outcome. If there is no good basis for calculating the value of the factor, arbitrary values may be assigned to test for extreme possibilities. Contingency analysis is used to determine how the relative ranking of alternatives holds up under major changes in the environment, say, a new alliance between France and Russia, or alternations in the criteria for judging the alternatives, such as a requirement that a system work well against attacks from space as well as earth. Contingency analysis places a premium on versatility as the analyst seeks a system that will hold up well under various eventualities even though it might be quite as good for any single contingency as an alternative system. Adversary procedures may be used to combat uncertainty. Bending over backwards to provide advantages for low ranking systems and handicaps for high-ranking systems is called a fortiori analysis. Changing crucial assumptions in order to make the leading alternatives even, so that one can judge whether the assumptions are overly optimistic or pessimistic, is called break-even analysis [27]. Since all these methods add greatly to the burden of calculation, they must be used with some discretion.

A variety of insurance schemes may also be used to deal with uncertainty. In appraising what an opponent can do, for instance, one can assume the work, the best, and sheer inertia. In regard to the development of weapons, insurance requires not one flexible weapon but a variety of alternatives pursued with vigor. As development goes on, uncertainty is reduced. Consequently, basic strategic choice involves determining how worthwhile paying for the additional information is by developing rival weapons systems to the next stage. The greater the uncertainty of the world, the greater the desirability of having the widest selection of alternative weapons to choose from to meet unexpected threats and opportunities. Alchian and Kessel are so wedded to the principle of diversified investment that they "strongly recommend this theorem as a basic part of systems analysis" [28].

As a form of calculation, systems analysis represents a merger of quantitative methods and rules of thumb. First, the analyst attempts to solve the problem before he knows a great deal about it. Then he continuously alters his initial solution to get closer to what he intuitively feels ought to be wanted. Means and ends are continuously played off against one another. New objectives are defined, new assumptions made, new models constructed, until a creative amalgam appears that hopefully defines a second best solution, one that is better than others even if not optimal in any sense. In the famous study of the location of military bases conducted by Albert Wohlstetter and his associates at the RAND Corporation, widely acknowledged as a classic example of systems analysis, Wohlstetter writes:

> The base study . . . proceeded by a method of successive approximations. It com-pared forces for their efficiency in carrying a payload between the bases and targets without opposition either by enemy interceptors or enemy bombers. Then, it intro-duced obstacles successively: first, enemy defenses; then enemy bombardment of our bombers and other elements needed to retaliate. In essence, then, the alternative systems were tested for their first-strike capability and then they were compared for their second-strike capacity. And the programmed system performed in a dras-tically different way, depending on the order in which the opposing side struck. In the course of analyzing counter-measures and counter-counter-measures, the enemy bombardment turned out to be a dominant problem. This was true even for a very much improved overseas operating base system. The refueling base system was very much less sensitive to strike order. It is only the fact that strike order made such a difference among systems contemplated that gave the first-strike, second-strike distinction an interest. And it was not known in advance of the analysis that few of the programmed bombers would have survived to encounter the problem of penetrating enemy defenses which had previously been taken as the main obstacle. The analysis, then, not only was affected by the objectives considered, it affected them. [29]

The advantage of a good systems study is that by running the analysis through in theory on paper certain disadvantages of learning from experience may be avoided.

If the complexity of the problems encountered proved difficult in cost-benefit analysis, the burdens of calculation are ordinarily much greater in systems analysis. Many aspects of a problem simply must be put aside. Only a few variables can be considered simulta-neously. "Otherwise," Roland McKean tell us, "the models would become impossibly cumbersome, and . . . the number of calculations to consider would mount in the thousands" [30]. Formulas that include everything may appear more satisfactory but those that cannot be reduced "to a single expression are likely to convey no meaning at all" [31]. Summing up their experience, Hitch and McKean assert that:

> analyses must be piecemeal, since it is impossible for a single analysis to cover all problems of choice simultaneously in a large organization. Thus comparisons of alternative courses of action always pertain to a part of the government's (or cor-poration's) problem. Other parts of the over-all problem are temporarily put aside, possible decisions about some matters being ignored, specific decisions about oth-ers being taken for granted. The resulting analyses are intended to provide assis-tance in finding optimal, or at least good, solutions to sub-problems: in the jargon of systems and operations research, they are sub-optimizations. [32]

Although admitting that much bad work is carried on and that inordinate love of num-bers and machines often gets in the way of creative work [33], practitioners of systems analysis believe in their art. "All of them point out how the use of analysis can provide some of the knowledge needed, how it may sometime serve as a substitute for experience, and, most importantly, how it can work to sharpen intuition" [34]. Systems analysis can increase explicitness about the assumptions made and about exclusions from the analysis. The claim is that systems analysis can be perfected; sheer intuition or unaided judgment can never be perfect.

Yet there is also wide agreement that systems analysts "do philosophy" [35], that they are advocates of particular policy alternatives. What Schelling calls "the pure role of expert advisor" is not available for the analyst who "must usually formulate the questions themselves for his clients" [36]. Beyond that, Wohlstetter argues that systems analysts can perform the function of integrating diverse values. New systems can sometimes be found that meet diverse objectives [37]. The politician who gains his objectives by inventing policies that also satisfy others, or the leader of a coalition who searches out areas of maximum agreement, performs a kind of informal systems analysis.

All these men, however, work within the existing political structure. While cost-benefit analysis may contain within it implicit changes in existing governmental policies, it poses no direct challenge to the general decision-making machinery of the political system. Program budgeting is a form of systems analysis that attempts to break out of these confines.

PROGRAM BUDGETING

It is always important, and perhaps especially so in economics, to avoid being swept off one's feet by the fashions of the moment. [38]

So this new system will identify our national goals with precision. [39]

On August 25, 1965, President Johnson announced that he was asking the heads of all federal agencies to introduce "a very new and revolutionary system" of program budgeting. Staffs of experts set up in each agency would define goals using "modern methods of program analysis." Then the "most effective and the least costly" way to accomplish these goals would be found [40].

Program budgeting has no standard definition. The general idea is that budgetary decisions should be made by focusing on output categories like governmental goals, objectives, end products or programs instead of inputs like personnel, equipment, and maintenance. As in cost-benefit analysis, to which it owes a great deal, program budgeting lays stress on estimating the total financial cost of accomplishing objectives. What is variously called cost-effectiveness or cost-utility analysis is employed in order to select "alternative approaches to the achievement of a benefit already determined to be worth achieving" [41].

Not everyone would go along with the most far-reaching implications of program budgeting, but the RAND Corporation version, presumably exported from the Defense Department, definitely does include "institutional reorganization to bring relevant administrative functions under the jurisdiction of the authority making the final program decisions." In any event, there would be "information reporting systems and shifts in the power structure to the extent necessary to secure compliance with program decisions by the agencies responsible for their execution [42]. Sometimes it appears that comprehensiveness—simultaneous and complete examination of all programs and all alternatives to programs every year—is being advocated.

Actually, comprehensiveness has been dropped (though not without regret) because "it may be too costly in time, effort, uncertainty, and confusion" [43]. There exists considerable ambivalence as to whether decisions are implicit in the program categories or merely provide information to improve the judgment of governmental officials.

Programs are not made in heaven. There is nothing out there that is just waiting to be found. Programs are not natural to the world; they must be imposed on it by men. No one can give instructions for making up programs. There are as many ways to conceive of programs as there are of organizing activity [44], as the comments of the following writers eloquently testify:

> It is by no means obvious . . . whether a good program structure should be based on components of specific end objectives (e.g., the accomplishment of certain land reclamation targets), on the principle of cost separation (identifying as a program any activity the costs of which can be readily segregated), on the separation of means and ends (Is education a means or an end in a situation such as skill-retraining courses for workers displaced by automation?), or on some artificially designed pattern that draws from all these and other classification criteria. [45]

> Just what categories constitute the most useful programs and program elements is far from obvious. . . . If one puts all educational activities into a broad package of educational programs, he cannot simultaneously include school lunch programs or physical education activities in a Health Program, or include defense educational activities (such as the military academies) in the Defense Program. . . . In short, precisely how to achieve a rational and useful structure for a program budget is not yet evident. [46]

> In much current discussion it seems to be taken for granted that transportation is a natural program category. But that conclusion is by no means obvious. [47]

> A first question one might ask is whether, given their nature, health activities merit a separate, independent status in a program budget. The question arises because these activities often are constituents of, or inputs into, other activities whose purpose or goal orientation is the dominating one. Outlays by the Department of Defense for hospital care, for example, though they assist in maintaining the health of one segment of the population, are undertaken on behalf of national defense, and the latter is their justification. [48]

The difficulties with the program concept are illustrated in the space program. A first glance suggests that space projects are ideally suited for program budgeting because they appear as physical systems designed to accomplish different missions. Actually, there is a remarkable degree of interdependence between different missions and objectives—pride, scientific research, space exploration, military uses, etc.—so that it is impossible to apportion costs on a proper basis. Consider the problem of a rocket developed for one mission and useful for others. To apportion costs to each new mission is purely arbitrary. To allocate the cost to the first mission and regard to the rocket as a free good for all subsequent missions is ludicrous. The only remotely reasonable alternative—making a separate program out of the rocket itself—does violence to the concept of programs as end products. The difficulty is compounded because the facilities that have multiple uses like boosters and tracking networks tend to be very expensive compared to the items that are specific to a particular mission [49]. Simple concepts of programs evaporate upon inspection.

Political realities lie behind the failure to devise principles for defining programs. As Melvin Anshen puts it, "The central issue is, of course, nothing less than the definition of the ultimate objectives of the Federal government as they are realized through operational decisions." The arrangement of the programs inevitably affects the specific actions taken to implement them. "Set in this framework," Anshen continues, "the designation of a schedule of programs may be described as building a bridge between a matter of political philosophy (what is government for?) and . . . assigning scarce resources among alternative governmental objectives" [50].

Because program budgeting is a form of systems analysis (and uses a form of cost-benefit analysis), the conditions that hinder or facilitate its use have largely been covered in the previous sections. The simpler the problem, the fewer the interdependencies, the greater the ability to measure the consequences of alternatives on a common scale, the more costs and benefits that are valued in the market place, the better the chances of making effective use of programs. Let us take transportation to illustrate some of the conditions in a specific case.

Investments in transportation are highly interdependent with one another (planes versus cars versus trains versus barges, etc.) and with decisions regarding the regional location of industry and the movements of population. In view of the powerful effects of transportation investment on regional employment, income, and competition with other modes of transport, it becomes necessary to take these factors into account. The partial equilibrium model of efficiency in the narrow sense becomes inappropriate and a general equilibrium model of the economy must be used. The combination of aggregative models at the economy-wide level and interregion and interindustry models that this approach requires is staggering. It is precisely the limited and partial character of cost-effectiveness analyses, taking so much for granted and eliminating many variables, that makes them easy to work with for empirical purposes. Furthermore, designing a large-scale transportation system involves so close a mixture of political and economic considerations that it is not possible to disentangle them. The Interstate Highway Program, for example, involved complex bargaining among federal, state, and local governments and reconciliation of many conflicting interests. The development of certain "backward" regions, facilitating the movement of defense supplies, re-distribution of income, creating countervailing power against certain monopolies, not to mention the political needs of public officials, were all involved. While cost-utility exercises might help with small segments of the problem, J. R. Meyer concludes that, "Given the complexity of the political and economic decisions involved, and the emphasis on designing a geographically consistent system, it probably would be difficult to improve on the congressional process as a means of developing such a program in an orderly and systematic way" [51].

On one condition for effective use —reorganization of the federal government to centralize authority for wide-ranging programs—proponents of program budgeting were markedly ambivalent. The problem was that responsibility for programs was scattered throughout the whole federal establishment and decentralized to state and local authorities as well. In the field of health, for example, expenditures were distributed among at least twelve agencies and six departments outside of Health, Education, and Welfare. A far greater number of organizations were concerned with American activities abroad, with natural resources and with education. The multiple jurisdictions and overlapping responsibilities did violence to the concept of comprehensive and consistent programs. It "causes one to doubt," Marvin Frankel wrote, "whether there can exist in the administrative echelons the kind of overall perspective that would seem indispensable if Federal health resources are to be rationally allocated" [52]. To G. A. Steiner it was evident that "The present 'chest of drawers' type of organization cannot for long be compatible with program budgeting" [53]. W. Z. Hirsch declared that "if we are to have effective program budgeting of natural resources activities, we shall have to provide for new institutional arrangements" [54]. Yet the inevitable resistance to wholesale reorganization would be so great that, if it were deemed essential, it might well doom the enterprise. Hence, the hope was expressed that translation grids or crossover networks could be used to convert program budget decisions back into the usual budget categories in the usual agencies. That is what was done in Defense, but that Department had the advantage of having most of the activities it is concerned with under the Secretary's jurisdiction.

Recognizing that a conversion scheme was technically feasible, Anshen was aware that there are "deeply frustrating" issues to be resolved. "The heart of the problem is the fact that the program budget in operation should not be a mere statistical game. Great strategic importance will attach to both the definition of program structure and content and the establishment of specific program objectives (including magnitude, timing, and cost)" [55]. The implications of program budgeting, however, went far beyond specific policies.

It will be useful to distinguish between policy politics (which policy will be adopted?), partisan politics (which political party will win office?), and system politics (how will decision structures be set up?). Program budgeting is manifestly concerned with policy politics, and not much with partisan politics, although it could have important consequences for issues that divide the nation's parties. *My contention is that the thrust of program budgeting makes it an integral part of system politics.*

As conceived in the 1960s, program budgeting contained an extreme centralizing bias. Power is to be centralized in the Presidency (through the Budget Bureau) at the national level, in superdepartments rather than bureaus within the executive branch, and in the federal government as a whole instead of state or local governments. Note how W. Z. Hirsch assumes the desirability of national dominance when he writes: "These methods of analysis can guide Federal officials in the responsibility of bringing local education decisions into closer harmony with national objectives" [56]. G. A. Steiner observes that comprehensiveness may be affected by unrestricted federal grants-in-aid to the states because "such a plan would remove a substantial part of Federal expenditures from a program budgeting system of the Federal government" [57]. Should there be reluctance on the part of state and local officials to employ the new tools, Anshen states "that the Federal government may employ familiar incentives to accelerate this progress" [58]. Summing it up, Hirsch says that "It appears doubtful that a natural resources program budget would have much impact without a good deal of centralization" [59].

Within the great federal organizations designed to encompass the widest ramifications of basic objectives, there would have to be strong executives. Cutting across the subunits of the organization, as was the case in the Department of Defense, the program budget could only be put together by the top executive. A more useful tool for increasing his power to control decisions vis-à-vis his subordinates would be hard to find [60].

Would large-scale program budgeting benefit the Chief Executive? President Johnson's support of program budgeting could in part have stemmed from his desire to appear frugal and also be directed at increasing his control of the executive branch by centralizing decisions in the Bureau of the Budget. In the case of foreign affairs, it was not at all clear whether it would have been preferable to emphasize country teams, with the budget made by the State Department to encompass activities of the other federal agencies abroad, or to let Commerce, Agriculture, Defense, and other agencies include their foreign activities in their own budgets. Program budgeting unleashed great struggles of this kind in Washington. (An especially intriguing possibility was that the Bureau of the Budget might have preferred to let the various agencies compete, with the Bureau coordinating (that is, controlling) these activities through a comprehensive foreign affairs program devised only at the Presidential level.)

Yet it was never entirely clear that Presidents would have welcomed all the implications of program budgeting. It is well and good to talk about long-range planning; it is another thing to tie a President's hands by committing him in advance for five years of expenditures. Looking ahead is fine but not if it means that a President cannot negate the most extensive planning efforts on grounds that seem sufficient to him [61]. He may wish to trade some program budgeting for some political support.

In any event, that all decisions ought to be made by the most central person in the most centralized body capable of grabbing hold of them is difficult to justify on scientific grounds. We see what has happened. First pure efficiency was converted to mixed efficiency. Then limited efficiency became unlimited. Yet the qualifications of efficiency experts for political systems analysis are not evident [62].

We would have been in a much stronger position to predict the consequences of program budgeting if we had known (1) how far toward a genuine program budget the Defense Department had gone and (2) whether the program budget had fulfilled its promise. To the best of my knowledge, not a single study of this important experiment was undertaken (or at least published) before the decision was made to spread it around the land. On the surface, only two of the nine program categories used in the Defense Department appeared to be genuine programs in the sense of pointing to end purposes or objectives. Although strategic retaliation and continental defense appeared to be distinct programs, it was difficult to separate them conceptually; my guess is that they were, in fact, considered together. The third category—general-purpose forces—was presumably designed to deal with (hopefully) limited war anywhere in the world. According to Arthur Smithies, "The threat is not clearly defined and neither are the requirements for meeting it. Clearly this program is of a very different character from the other two and does not lend itself as readily to analysis in terms either of its components or of its specific contribution to defense objectives" [63].

What about the program called airlift and sealift? These activities support the general-purpose forces. Research and development is carried on presumably to serve other defense objectives, and the same is true for the reserve forces.

No doubt the elements that make up the programs comprise the real action focus of the budget, but these may look less elegant when spread into thousands of elements than they do in nine neat rows. When one hears that hundreds of program elements are up for decision at one time [64], he is entitled to some skepticism about how much genuine analysis can go into all of them. Part of the argument for program budgeting was that by thinking ahead and working all year around it would be possible to consider changes as they came up and avoid the usual last minute funk. Both Hitch [65] and Novick [66] (the RAND Corporation expert on defense budgeting) report, however, that this had not worked out. The services hesitated to submit changes piecemeal, and the Secretary wanted to see what he was getting into before he acted. The vaunted five-year plans were still in force but their efficacy in determining yearly decisions remained to be established.

One good operational test would be to know whether the Department's systems analysts actually used the figures from the five year plans in their work or whether they went to the services for the real stuff. Another test would have been whether or not the later years of the five-year projections turned out to have any future significance, or whether the battle was really over the next year that is to be scooped out as part of the budget. From a distance, it appeared that the services had to work much harder to justify what they were doing. Since McNamara's office had to approve changes in defense programs, and he could insist on documentation, he was in a strong position to improve thinking at the lower levels. How much this was due to McNamara himself, to his insistence on quantitative estimates, or to the analytic advantages of a program budget cannot be determined now. It is clear that a program budget, of which he alone was master, helped impose his will on the Defense Department.

It should also be said that there are many notable differences between decision making in defense and domestic policy that would render suspect the transmission of procedures from one realm to the other. The greater organizational unity of Defense, the immensely large amounts of money at stake, the extraordinarily greater risks involved, the inability to share more than minimal values with opponents, the vastly different array of interests and perceptions of the proper roles of the participants, were but a few of the factors involved.

The Armed Services and Appropriations Committees in the defense area, for example, were normally most reluctant to substitute their judgment on defense for that of the President and the Secretary of the Department. They did not conceive it to be their role to make day to day defense policy, and they were apparently unwilling to take on the burden of decision. They therefore accepted a budget presentation based on cavernous program categories even though these were so arranged that it was impossible to make a decision on the basis of them. If they had asked for and received the discussion of alternative actions contained in the much smaller program elements on which McNamara based his decisions, they would have been in a position to take the Department of Defense away from its Secretary.

There is no reason whatsoever to believe that a similar restraint would be shown by committees that deal with domestic policies. It is at least possible that the peculiar planning, programming, and budgeting system adopted in Defense could not have been repeated elsewhere in the federal establishment.

Political Rationality

> Political rationality is the fundamental kind of reason, because it deals with the preservation and improvement of decision structures, and decision structures are the source of all decisions. Unless a decision structure exists, no reasoning and no decisions are possible. . . . There can be no conflict between political rationality and . . . technical, legal, social, or economic rationality, because the solution of political programs makes possible an attack on any other problem, while a serious political deficiency can prevent or undo all other problem solving. . . . Nonpolitical decisions are reached by considering a problem in its own terms, and by evaluating proposals according to how well they solve the problem. The best available proposal should be accepted regardless of who makes it or who opposes it, and a faulty proposal should be rejected or improved no matter who makes it. Compromise is always irrational; the rational procedure is to determine which proposal is the best, and to accept it. In a political decision, on the other hand, action never is based on the merits of a proposal but always on who makes it and who opposes it. Action should be designed to avoid complete identification with any proposal and any point of view, no matter how good or how popular it might be. The best available proposal should never be accepted just because it is best; it should be deferred, objected to, discussed, until major opposition disappears. Compromise is always a rational procedure, even when the compromise is between a good and a bad proposal. [67]

We are witnessing the beginning of significant advances in the art and science of economizing. Having given up the norm of comprehensiveness, economizers are able to join quantitative analysis with aids to calculation of the kind described by Lindblom in his strategy of disjointed incrementalism [68].

Various devices are employed to simplify calculations. Important values are omitted entirely; others are left to different authorities to whose care they have been entrusted. Here, sensitivity analysis represents an advance because it provides an empirical basis to justify neglect of some values. Means and ends are hopelessly intertwined.

The real choice is between rival policies that encapsulate somewhat different mixes of means and ends. Analysis proceeds incrementally by successive limited approximations. It is serial and remedial as successive attacks are made on problems. Rather than waiting upon experience in the real world, the analyst tries various moves in his model and runs them through to see if they work. When all else fails, the analyst may try an integrative solution reconciling a variety of values to some degree, though meeting none of them completely. He is always ready to settle for the second or third best, provided only that it is better than the going policy. Constrained by diverse limiting assumptions, weakened by deficiencies in technique, rarely able to provide unambiguous measures, the systems, cost-benefit, and program analysis is nonetheless getting better at calculating in the realm of efficiency. Alas, he is an imperialist at heart.

In the literature discussed above there appears several times the proposition that "the program budget is a neutral tool. It has no politics" [69]. In truth, the program budget was suffused with policy politics, made up a small part of President Johnson's partisan politics, and tended towards system politics. How could men account for so foolish a statement? It must be that they who make it identify program budgeting with something good and beautiful, and politics with another thing bad and ugly. McKean and Anshen speak of politics in terms of "pressure and expedient adjustments," "haphazard acts . . . unresponsive to a planned analysis of the needs of efficient decision design." From the political structure they expect only "resistance and opposition. corresponding to the familiar human disposition to protect established seats of power and procedures made honorable by the mere facts of existence and custom" [70]. In other places we hear of "vested interests," "wasteful duplication," "special interest groups," and the "Parkinson syndrome" [71].

Not so long ago less sophisticated advocates of reform ignored the political realm. Now they denigrate it. And, since there must be a structure for decision, it is smuggled in as a mere adjunct of achieving efficiency. Who is to blame if the economic tail wags the political dog? It seems unfair to blame the evangelical economizer for spreading the gospel of efficiency. If economic efficiency turns out to be the one true religion, maybe it is because its prophets could so easily conquer

It is hard to find men who take up the cause of political rationality, who plead the case for political man, and who are primarily concerned with the laws that enable the political machinery to keep working. One is driven to a philosopher like Paul Diesing to find the case for the political:

> The political problem is always basic and prior to the others. . . . This means that any suggested course of action must be evaluated first by its effects on the political structure. A course of action which corrects economic or social deficiencies but increases political difficulties must be rejected, while an action which contributes to political improvement is desirable even if it is not entirely sound from an economic or social standpoint. [72]

There is hardly a political scientist who would claim half as much. The desire to invent decision structures to facilitate the achievement of economic efficiency does not suggest a full appreciation of their proper role by students of politics.

A major task of the political system is to specify goals or objectives. It is impermissible to treat goals as if they were known in advance. "Goals" may well be the product of interaction among key participants rather than some "deus ex machina" or (to use Bentley's term) some "spook" which posits values in advance of our knowledge of them. Certainly, the operational objectives of the Corps of Engineers in the Water Resources field could hardly be described in terms of developing rivers and harbors.

Once the political process becomes a focus of attention, it is evident that the principal participants may not be clear about their goals. What we call goals or objectives may, in large part, be operationally determined by the policies we can agree upon. The mixtures of values found in complex policies may have to be taken in packages, so that policies may determine goals as least as much as general objectives determine policies. In a political situation, then, the need for support assumes central importance. Not simply the economic, but the *political* costs and benefits turn out to be crucial.

A first attempt to specify what is meant by political costs may bring closer an understanding of the range of requirements for political rationality [73]. Exchange costs are incurred by a political leader when he needs the support of other people to get a policy adopted. He has to pay for this assistance by using up resources in the form of favors (patronage, log-rolling) or coercive moves (threats or acts to veto or remove from office). By supporting a policy and influencing others to do the same, a politician antagonizes some people and may suffer their retaliation. If these hostility costs mount, they may turn into reelection costs—actions that decrease his chances (or those of his friends) of being elected or reelected to office. Election costs, in turn, may become policy costs through inability to command the necessary formal powers to accomplish the desired policy objectives.

In the manner of Neustadt, we may also talk about reputation costs, that is, not only loss of popularity with segments of the electorate, but also loss of esteem and effectiveness with other participants in the political system and loss or ability to secure policies other than the one immediately under consideration. Those who continually urge a President to go all out—that is, use all his resources on a wide range of issues—rarely stop to consider that the price of success in one area of policy may be defeat in another. If he loses popularity with the electorate, as President Truman did, Congress may destroy almost the whole of his domestic program. If he cracks down on the steel industry, as President Kennedy did, he may find himself constrained to lean over backwards in the future to avoid unremitting hostility from the business community.

A major consequence of incurring exchange and hostility costs may be undesirable power-redistribution effects. The process of getting a policy adopted or implemented may increase the power of various individuals, organizations, and social groups, which later will be used against the political leader. The power of some participants may be weakened so that the political leader is unable to enjoy their protection.

The legitimacy of the political system may be threatened by costs that involve the weakening of customary political restraints. Politicians who try to suppress opposition, or who practice election frauds, may find similar tactics being used against them. The choice of a highly controversial policy may raise the costs of civic discord. Although the people involved may not hate the political leader, the fact that they hate each other may lead to consequences contrary to his desires.

The literature of economics usually treats organizations and institutions as if they were costless entities. The standard procedure is to consider rival alternatives (in consideration of price policy or other criteria), calculate the differences in cost and achievement among them, and show that one is more or less efficient than another. This typical way of thinking is sometimes misspecified. If the costs of pursuing a policy are strictly economic and can be calculated directly in the marketplace, then the procedure should work well. But if the costs include getting one or another organization to change its policies or procedures, then these costs must also be taken into account [74]. Perhaps there are legal, psychological, or other impediments that make it either impossible or difficult for the required changes to be made. Or the changes may require great effort and result in incurring a variety of other costs. In considering a range of alternatives, one is measuring not only efficiency but also the cost of change.

Studies based on efficiency criteria are much needed and increasingly useful. My quarrel is not with them as such, at all. I have been concerned that a single value, however important, could triumph over other values without explicit consideration being given these others. I would feel much better if political rationality were being pursued with the same vigor and capability as is economic efficiency. In that case I would have fewer qualms about extending efficiency studies into the decision-making apparatus.

My purpose has not been to accuse economizers of doing what comes naturally. Rather, I have sought to emphasize that economic rationality, however laudible in its own sphere, ought not to swallow up political rationality—but will do so, if political rationality continues to lack trained and adept defenders.

ACKNOWLEDGMENTS

I am more than ordinarily indebted to the people who have improved this paper through their comments. Win Crowther, John Harsanyi, John Krutilla, Arthur Maas, Arnold Meltsner, Nelson Polsby, William Riker, and Dwight Waldo saved me from errors and contributed insights of their own. The responsibility for what is said is entirely my own.

The paper, written while the author was a Research Political Scientist at the Center for Planning and Development Research, University of California, Berkeley, was originally presented at a conference on public policy sponsored by the Social Science Research Council.

Citation style of original retained in this reprint. Originally published in Volume 26, Number 4, *Public Administration Review*, December, 1966, pp. 292–310.

NOTES AND REFERENCES

1. A. R. Prest and R. Turvey, "Cost-Benefit Analysis: A Survey," *Economic J, LXXV:* pp. 683–675 (1965). I am much indebted to this valuable and discerning survey. I have also relied upon: O. Eckstein, "A Survey of the Theory of Public Expenditure Criteria," *Public Finances: Needs, Sources, and Utilization*, National Bureau of Economic Research. Princeton University Press, New York, pp. 439–504 (1961); I. K. Fox and O. C. Herfindahl, "Attainment of Efficiency in Satisfying Demands for Water Resources," *Am. Econ. Rev.*, May: 198–206 (1965); C. J. Hitch, *On the Choice of Objectives in Systems Studies*, RAND Corporation, Santa Monica, Calif. (1960); J. V. Krutilla, "Is Public Intervention in Water Resources Development Conducive to Economic Efficiency," *Natural Resources J.*, January: 60–75 (1966); J. V. Krutilla and O. Eckstein, *Multiple Purpose River Development*, Johns Hopkins Press, Baltimore (1958); R. N. McKean, *Efficiency in Government Through Systems Analysis with Emphasis on Water Resources Development*, New York (1958).
2. Prest and Turvey, "Cost-Benefit Analysis," p. 686.
3. In many important areas of policy such as national defense it is not possible to value the product directly in the market place. Since benefits cannot be valued in the same way as costs, it is necessary to resort to a somewhat different type of analysis. Instead of cost-benefit analysis, therefore, the work is usually called cost-effectiveness or cost-utility analysis.
4. A. Bergson, "A Reformulation of Certain Aspects of Welfare Economics," *Q. J. Econ.*, February (1938); N. Kaldor, "Welfare Propositions and Interpersonal Comparisons of Utility," *Econ. J.*,

pp. 549–552 (1939); J. R. Hicks, "The Valuation of Social Income," *Economica,* pp. 105–124 (1940); I. M. D. Little, *A Critique of Welfare Economics,* Oxford (1950); W. J. Baumol, *Welfare Economics and the Theory of the State,* Cambridge (1952); T. Scitovsky, "A Note of Welfare Propositions in Economics," *Rev. Econ. Studies,* pp. 98–110 (1942); J. E. Meade, *The Theory of International Economic Policy,* Vol. II: *Trade and Welfare,* New York (1954).

5. For a different view, see J. M. Buchanan and G. Tullock, *The Calculus of Consent: Logical Foundations of Constitutional Democracy,* University of Michigan Press, Ann Arbor (1962).

6. Prest and Turvey, "Cost-Benefit Analysis," p. 702. For a contrary view, see A. Maas, "Benefit-Cost Analysis: Its Relevance to Public Investment Decisions," *Q. J. Econ., LXXX:* 208–226 (1966).

7. Fox and Herfindahl, "Attainment of Efficiency," p. 200.

8. Prest and Turvey, "Cost-Benefit Analysis," p. 727.

9. Prest and Turvey, "Cost-Benefit Analysis," pp. 729, 731.

10. D. Braybrooke and C. Lindblom, *A Strategy for Decision,* New York (1963).

11. Prest and Turvey, "Cost-Benefit Analysis," p. 714.

12. Prest and Turvey, "Cost-Benefit Analysis," p. 705.

13. See J. L. Knetch, "Economics of Including Recreation as a Purpose of Water Resource Projects," *J. Farm Econ.,* December: 1155 (1964). No one living in Berkeley, where "a view" is part of the cost of housing, could believe that aesthetic values are forever going to remain beyond the ingenuity of the quantifier. There are also costs and benefits, such as the saving and losing of human life, that can be quantified but can only be valued in the market place in a most peculiar (or ghoulish) sense. See B. Weisbrod, *The Economics of Public Health; Measuring the Economic Impact of Diseases,* Philadelphia (1961), for creative attempt to place a market value on human life. Few of us would want to make decisions about public health by use of this criterion, not at least if we were the old person whose future social value contribution is less than his cost to the authorities.

14. Eckstein, "A Survey," p. 460.

15. Fox and Herfindahl, "Attainment of Efficiency," p. 202.

16. E. S. Quade, *Analysis for Military Decisions,* Chicago, p. 153 (1964).

17. Quade, *Analysis for Military Decisions,* p. 149.

18. Quade, *Analysis for Military Decisions,* p. 7.

19. Hitch, *On the Choice of Objectives,* p. 19.

20. Quade, *Analysis for Military Decisions,* p. 176.

21. Hitch, *On the Choice of Objectives,* pp. 4–5.

22. A. Wohlstetter, "Analysis and Design of Conflict Systems," in Quade, *Analysis for Military Decisions,* p. 121.

23. See G. H. Snyder, *Deterrence and Defense,* Princeton, N.J. (1961).

24. Wohlstetter, "Analysis and Design," p. 122.

25. Quade, *Analysis for Military Decisions,* p. 157. Quade attempts to soften the blow by saying that businessmen and military officers know more about their business than any one else. But the import of the analogy is clear enough.

26. Quade, *Analysis for Military Decisions,* pp. 156–157.

27. H. Kahn and I. Mann, *Techniques of Systems Analysis,* RAND Corporation, Santa Monica, Calif. (1957), believe that "*More than any single thing,* the skilled use of a fortiori and break-even analyses separate the professionals from the amateurs." They think that convincing others that you have a good solution is as important as coming up with one.

28. A. A. Alchian and R. A. Kessel, *A Proper Role of Systems Analysis,* RAND Corporation, Santa Monica, Calif. p. 9 (1954).

29. Wohlstetter, "Analysis and Design," pp. 125–26.

30. R. N. McKean, "Criteria," in Quade, *Analysis for Military Decisions,* p. 83.

31. Quade, *Analysis for Military Decisions,* p. 310.

32. C. J. Hitch and R. N. McKean, *The Economics of Defense in the Nuclear Age,* Harvard University Press, Cambridge, Mass., p. 161 (1961).

33. See C. H. Hitch on "Mechanitis—putting . . . machines to work as a substitute for hard thinking," in "Economics and Operations Research: A Symposium, II," *Rev. Econ. Stat.,* August: 209 (1958).
34. Quade, *Analysis for Military Decisions,* p. 12.
35. Quade, *Analysis for Military Decisions,* p. 5.
36. T. C. Schelling, "Economics and Operations Research: A Symposium V. Comment," *Rev. Econ. Stat.,* August: 222 (1958).
37. Wohlstetter, "Analysis and Design," p. 122.
38. Prest and Turvey, "Cost-Benefit Analysis," p. 684.
39. D. Novick, ed., *Program Budgeting,* Harvard University Press, Cambridge, Mass., p. vi (1965).
40. Novick, *Program Budgeting,* pp. v–vi.
41. Alan Dean, quoted in D. Novick, *ibid.,* p. 311.
42. R. N. McKean and N. Anshen in Novick, *Program Budgeting,* pp. 286–287. The authors say that this aspect of program budgeting is part of the general view adopted in the book as a whole.
43. A. Smithies, in Novick, *Program Budgeting,* p. 45.
44. A look at the classic work by L. Gulick and L. Urwick, *Papers on the Science of Administration,* Columbia University Press, New York (1937), reveals considerable similarity between their suggested bases of organization and ways of conceptualizing programs.
45. N. Anshen in Novick, *Program Budgeting,* pp. 19–20.
46. G. A. Steiner in Novick, *Program Budgeting,* p. 356.
47. A. Smithies in Novick, *Program Budgeting,* p. 41.
48. M. Frankel in Novick, *Program Budgeting,* pp. 291–220. I have forborne citing the author who promises exciting discussion of the objectives of American education and ends up with fascinating programs categories like primary, secondary, and tertiary education.
49. See the excellent chapter by M. A. Margolis and S. M. Barro, in Novick, *Program Budgeting,* pp. 120–145.
50. Novick, *Program Budgeting,* p. 18.
51. J. R. Meyer in Novick, *Program Budgeting,* p. 170. This paragraph is based on my interpretation of his work.
52. M. Frankel in Novick, *Program Budgeting,* p. 237.
53. Novick, *Program Budgeting,* p. 348.
54. Novick, *Program Budgeting,* p. 280.
55. Novick, *Program Budgeting,* pp. 358–59.
56. Novick, *Program Budgeting,* p. 206.
57. Novick, *Program Budgeting,* p. 347.
58. Novick, *Program Budgeting,* p. 365.
59. Novick, *Program Budgeting,* p. 280.
60. See my comments to this effect in *The Politics of the Budgetary Process,* Boston, p. 140, (1964). For discussion of some political consequences of program budgeting, see pp. 135–142.
61. See W. H. Brown and C. E. Gilbert, *Planning Municipal Investment: A Case Study of Philadelphia,* University of Pennsylvania Press, Philadelphia (1961), for an excellent discussion of the desire of elected officials to remain free to shift their commitments.
62. It may be said that I have failed to distinguish sufficiently between planning, programming, and budgeting. Planning is an orientation that looks ahead by extending costs and benefits or units of effectiveness a number of years into the future. Programming is a general procedure of systems analysis employing cost-effectiveness studies. In this view program budgeting is a mere mechanical translation of the results of high level systems studies into convenient storage in the budgetary format. No doubt systems studies could be done without converting the results into the form of a program budget. This approach may have a lot to be said for it and it appears that it is the one that is generally followed in the Department of Defense in its presentations to Congress. But if the systems studies guide decisions as to the allocation of resources, and the studies are maintained according to particular program categories and are further legitimatized by being given status in the budget, it seems most unlikely that programming will be separated

from budgeting. One is never sure whether too much or too little is being claimed for program budgeting. If all that program budgeting amounts to is a simple translation of previous systems studies into some convenient form of accounting, it hardly seems that this phenomenon is worth so much fuss. If the program categories in the budget system are meaningful, then they must be much more than a mere translation of previously arrived at decisions. In this case, I think that it is not my task to enlighten the proponents of program budgeting, but it is their task to make themselves clear to others.

63. A. Smithies in Novick, *Program Budgeting,* p. 37.
64. See U.S. House Appropriations Committee Subcommittee on Department of Defense Appropriations for Fiscal 1965, 88th Congress, 2nd Session, IV, p. 133. McNamara asserted that some 652 "subject issues" had been submitted to him for the fiscal 1965 budget.
65. C. Hitch, *Decision Making for Defense,* University of California Press, Berkeley (1965).
66. Novick, *Program Budgeting,* p. 100.
67. P. Diesing, *Reason in Society,* Urbana, Ill., pp. 198, 203–204, 231–232 (1962).
68. Braybrooke and Lindblom, *A Strategy for Decision.* See also Lindblom, *The Intelligence of Democracy,* New York (1965).
69. M. Anshen in Novick, *Program Budgeting,* p. 370.
70. Novick, *Program Budgeting,* p. 289.
71. Novick, *Program Budgeting,* p. 359.
72. Diesing, *Reason in Society,* p. 228.
73. I am indebted to John Harsanyi for suggestions about political rationality.
74. In the field of defense policy, political factors are taken into account to the extent that the studies concentrate on the design of feasible alternatives. In the choice of overseas basing, for example, the question of feasibility in relation to treaties and friendly or unfriendly relationships with other countries is considered. Thus it seems permissible to take into account political considerations originating outside of the country, where differences of opinion and preferences among nations are to some extent accepted as legitimate, but apparently not differences internal to the American policy.

49

The Political Economy of Efficiency Has Not Changed, But the World Has and So Have I

Aaron Wildavsky

Reading "The Political Economy of Efficiency" for the first time in over a decade, I am pleasantly surprised to find myself still in agreement with it. Nuances aside, I could say (and, no doubt have said) it again without going against what I believed over two decades ago [1]. This momentary feeling of satisfaction, however, was almost instantly replaced by a sense of wonder at the dramatic change in ideas and practices that a mere 22 years has wrought in things that then seemed self-evident to everyone who studied cost-benefit analysis, systems analysis, program budgeting, and political rationality. Who would have imagined that the same people that thought these forms of analysis to be too conservative, because of their bias against radical change, would themselves bias analysis against any change whatsoever? Who, caught up in the passions of the sixties, would have supposed that planning, programming, budgeting systems (PPBS) would fall from sight, never, ever heard of again in budgetary matters? Nor did I imagine, picking up Paul Diesing's idea of political rationality, that I would later think this daring thought too limited, believing as I do now that there is more than one kind of political rationality. In the spirit of the old "Political Economy of Efficiency," whose classifications appear to me, by and large, to have held up, my retrospective view shall be presented under two categories— how the world has changed, and how my ideas about the world have changed.

HOW THE WORLD HAS CHANGED

Once upon a time the few advocates of laissez-faire were customarily overrun by advocates of economic redistribution who deliberately kept the discount (or interest) rate used in figuring cost-benefit ratios way below the market rate, so as to expand the production of governmental "pork," otherwise known as Rivers and Harbors legislation. This still happens, but the odds have changed and the discount rate has gone up. The cause lies within the rise of the environmental movement. Environmentalists have figured out that the higher

---

Source: Public Budgeting and Financial Management, 1(1): 43–53 (1989).

the discount rate, the fewer the projects that can be authorized (because their cost-benefit ratios would be negative), the less disruption there will be to the physical environment. Aside from time altering political forces and perceptions of interest, this tale tells us that it is usually not instruments of policy that political forces accept or reject but the consequences of the employment of these instruments, an observation that will hold us in good stead as we continue showing what a difference a decade (or two) makes.

There was a time when, as one of the few critics of program budgeting, I feared being consumed by being tempted to talk ad infinitum about it. No doubt some of PPBS's promoters felt the same way. How, then, explain its virtual disappearance, at least at the federal level within the United States?

Actually, a more sweeping observation is in order. It is not merely PPB but related budgetary forms, such as ZBB (zero-base budgeting), that have disappeared. Nor is it only these forms of budgeting but the most basic notions of analysis that have gone along with PPB. What happened?

Political dissensus has driven out analysis [2]. When the question is not "what for" but "how much," not "is this expenditure worthwhile compared to others" but "how will spending impact the deficit," not "how will the budget affect the economy" but "will the deficit be reduced at higher or lower levels of taxing and spending," there is either no room or no need for analysis. As partisan and policy polarization proceeds—in Congress the parties disagree about how much revenue shall be raised and who will pay, as well as how much will be spent and on what—the problem to be solved is "who will win," not "what ought to be done." It is not the deficit itself, therefore, that is the effective center of attention, but whether it will be balanced by making government bigger or smaller. Since how the deficit is reduced matters more than reducing it, and the parties cannot agree, there is stalemate. When size matters more than content, there is no need for analysis. Nor is there much room for analysis when the question routinely asked is "how much for defense versus how much for domestic?" As "The Political Economy of Efficiency" makes clear, such questions are too aggregated (analysis means decomposition) and too philosophical to be subjected to analysis. Rather, the old union song, with its refrain of "Whose side are you on?" calls for commitment, not discussion. It has been a long time since budget discussion included such previously worthwhile and standard items as how the budget might affect economic management.

From this I conclude that when budgeting does become part of "system politics," that is, when the most far-reaching aspects of PPBS dissolve into "what kind of government and society we should have," the system drives out the planning, programming, and budgeting. It has taken time to see that PPBS is a contradiction in terms: when it is systematic, it self-destructs.

Though the disappearance of program budgeting stands to reason, if the analysis in "The Political Economy of Efficiency" is correct, taking the benefits out of cost-benefit analysis has left me astounded. While I did wish to deny that cost-benefit (or any other form of) analysis could (or should) be done without value judgments [3], I thought the effort to make explicit the considerations involved in balancing the helpful and harmful aspects of a project or a policy [4], quantitatively where appropriate, was a good thing that could be made better [5]. How else consciously decide than by weighing the pros and cons? But that was before I came across government policy and the advocacy of so-called safety groups in regard to the dangers stemming from technology.

It took me longer than it should have, I confess, so great was my astonishment that government policy and private advocacy in regard to new products, substances, and practices came down essentially to the position that if harm is done (the cost side), no amount of benefit can compensate for it, so the offending thing must be forbidden. Since there is almost nothing that doesn't harm someone, somewhere, yet health and safety continue to improve, astonishment soon gave way to concern, which ended with the writing of *Searching for Safety* [6].

Leaving aside the aspects of risk covered in that book—"trial without error" or "no trials without guarantees against harm"—applying the same principle would destroy all forms of policy analysis. "No, you must not" would replace "maybe we might." If there is no balance to be struck between positive and negative effects, there is no point in analysis, that is, in disciplined thought.

Try applying this "only costs count" to areas of life about which you, the reader, are well informed. No hospital in the world (think of iatrogenic or hospital-caused diseases) could stay open were this criterion applied. Ask AIDS sufferers if they would like a criterion of "no trials without prior guarantees against error" applied to them. They know better. That is why they seek to suspend regulations that apply to the rest of the population. Most vaccines would have to be prohibited. If the principle that "no benefits need apply" is not counter to reason, nothing is.

Another name for counting costs but not benefits would be "reactionary incrementalism." Where concepts of incrementalism (or piecemeal social engineering à la Popper) are concerned, the major argument against them was that moving by small steps from the status quo was too conservative. Perhaps. What, then, is one to say about the "one-hit" theory of cancer causation, where a molecule of a cancer-causing substance is deemed sufficient to kill and the offending material fit for prohibition? Where once incremental moves might have been too slow, now they are so fast they must be stopped from moving at all. Again, we see that where there's a will, there's a way to obtain the desired result, even if ancient verities have to be turned upside down: Toward a bad cause, any movement is too fast, apparently, while toward a good one, no movement is fast enough. What was that about principles of decision making?

HOW MY IDEAS ABOUT THE WORLD HAVE CHANGED

Knowing what has come after makes it a lot easier (no doubt, too easy) to see the connections with what went before. So I see, or imagine, indications of my current interest in cultural-functional explanation in "The Political Economy of Efficiency."

By cultural, I mean (following Mary Douglas) that the independent variables are ways of life, made up of people who share values justifying social relationships. There are no disembodied values without social relations to defend and no relations without those who prefer them offering justifications. These cultures are plural (more than one exits in a country or large organization) but not infinite in number. Functions come in because the consequences of these cultures also play a part in maintaining them. People who adhere to a way of life learn to want what they want by internalizing their desired social relationships. By constructing their institutions, people teach one another which preferences will keep their culture-mates together and simultaneously weaken opposing cultures. This is the essence of cultural rationality—strengthening your way and weakening rival ways [7]. If cultures were without functions, we could not explain why anyone could persuade others to want to live that way because there would be nothing they could do with each other that would add to the prospects of their staying together [8].

As I reread myself saying "Programs are not natural to the world; they must be imposed on it by men. . . . There are as many ways to conceive of programs as there are of organizing activity" [9], I see a prototype of "The Social Construction of Definitions" [10], in which meanings are seen as products of social interaction. Without understanding that the individual is a social construct, a cultural-functional theory in which individuals internalize their preferred social relations, which they then use to interrogate their environment so as to determine their preferences, would be impossible. Perhaps this is what I meant when I wrote that "Goals may well be the product of interaction among key participants rather than some 'deus ex machine' or (to use Bentley's term) some 'spook' which posits values in advance of our knowledge of them" [11].

It is true that "The politician who gains his objectives by inventing policies that satisfy others, or the leader of a coalition who searchers out areas of maximum agreement, performs a kind of informal systems analysis" [12]. What came with cultural theory was an understanding of what the possible values (derived from the cultures) might be that had to be satisfied. This made it easier to do such empirical analyses as how Reagan's tax reform (said to be politically unfeasible) passed, why Nixon's family assistance program failed, and how Moses' behavior altered as the political cultures to which the Hebrew people adhered changed over time [13].

In highlighting the difficulty of making interpersonal comparisons of preferences, I then stated what should have been self-evident but was not: "The question of whose utility function is to prevail . . . is of prime importance in making public policy" [14]. But how many and what kind are these utility functions? Suppose there is a forceful act of leadership. If the act is undertaken by a duly appointed or elected leader, people who believe in hierarchy, where authority inheres in position, will be pleased. But if this is an act that restricts individual initiative or one in which a leader overstays his appointed time, individualists, who seek to substitute self-regulation for authority, will object. Should this act reduce differences in resources among people, egalitarians may well favor it. But they will repulse repetition of such forceful leadership because they believe that leadership implies followership and is thus a prima facie instance of inequality [15]. For much the same reasons, hierarchists think apathy is functional, individualists think there must be an inadequate payoff, and egalitarians claim it shows rejection of an exploitative establishment. Saying utilities or preferences differ is one thing; being able to explain or predict how they will differ in order to support different ways of life is another [16].

In the seminal source from which I quoted words of wisdom about political rationality, Paul Diesing wrote that in regard to politically rational decisions "compromise is always a rational procedure, even when the compromise is between a good and a bad proposal" [17]. This is true, I now believe from the perspective of cultural theory, but only if the organization one has in mind makes it rational (by furthering the purposes of the members) to value compromise. In a large and inclusive hierarchy, for instance, adjudicating the relative positions of the numerous statuses is a sine qua non of survival. Decision making is already so cumbersome that intransigence might well lead to breakdown. That is why these hierarchies (think of broad-based political parties) becomes tissues of evasions. Of course, compromise is the essence of competitive individualism, in which some bargain is often better than none. The connection between capitalism and democracy likely comes about because individualism is the only culture whose adherents value competition. Among egalitarians, however, compromise may well be life-threatening. The structure of egalitarian cultures (with their strong group boundaries and weak internal prescription) leads them to adopt equality of condition as their guiding norm. Any departure from that would threaten their reason for being. Hence egalitarians often identify compromise with corruption. Giving in on this principle, to them, means giving up all their principles. Whether or not certain compromises are desirable depends on analysis not undertaken here. I merely wish to observe that while it may be politically rational for people adhering to certain cultures to compromise, it may well be politically irrational for others, differently structured, to give an inch.

I still agree, even more strongly than before, that "Political rationality is the fundamental kind of reason, because it deals with the preservation and improvement of decision structures, and decision structures are the source of all decisions. Unless a decision structure exists, no reasoning and no decisions are possible" [18]. Only now I think there are several, not just one, kinds of political rationality. If we conceive of rationality as a relationship between means and ends, when we change the objectives—from maintaining differences (as in hierarchies), to increasing differences (as in individualism) to diminishing differences (as in egalitarianism)—we necessarily alter the behavior a reasonable person would judge efficacious in achieving these disparate goals.

REFERENCES

1. This is far from true for everything. Recently, for instance, I responded to a similar request for a retrospective view of "The Two Presidencies," a thesis that has generated many followup articles pro and con. Now it is apparent that while the thesis was true in the 1950s, it may not have been true in earlier decades and is certainly not true now. Here the interest lies in why the "Two Presidencies" thesis held at one time but not at others.
2. This story is told in much greater depth and detail in my *The New Politics of the Budgetary Process*, Scott Foresman/Little Brown College Division, Glenview, Ill./Boston (1988).
3. "Although cost-benefit analysis presumably results in efficiency by adding the most to national income, it is shot through with political and social value choices and surrounded by uncertainties and difficulties of computation" ("The Political Economy of Efficiency," p. 297).
4. "The great advantage of cost-benefit analysis, when pursued with integrity, is that some implicit judgments are made explicit and subject to analysis" ("The Political Economy of Efficiency," p. 297)
5. "These modes of analysis are neither good for nothing nor good for everything, and one cannot speak of them as wholly good or bad. It is much more useful to try to specify some conditions under which they would or would not be helpful for various purposes" ("The Political Economy of Efficiency," p. 293).
6. A. Wildavsky, *Searching for Safety*, Transaction Press, New Brunswick, N.J. (1988).
7. See A. Wildavsky, "Choosing Preferences By Constructing Institutions: A Cultural Theory of Preference Formation," *Am. Polit. Sci. Rev.*, *81*: 3–21 (1987); and M. Douglas and A. Wildavsky, *Risk and Culture*, University of California Press, Berkeley (1982).
8. See M. Thompson and A. Wildavsky, *The Foundations of Cultural Theory* (manuscript in progress); and R. Ellis and A. Wildavsky, "Cultural Functionalism: A Historical Comparison," paper prepared for the XIVth World Congress of the International Political Science Association, August 28–September 1, Washington, D.C. (1988).
9. "The Political Economy of Efficiency," p. 302.
10. A. Wildavsky, typescript, August 1988.
11. "The Political Economy of Efficiency," p. 308.
12. "The Political Economy of Efficiency," p. 302.
13. See D. Coyle and A. Wildavsky, "Requisites of Radical Reform: Income Maintenance versus Tax Preferences," *J. Policy Anal. Manage. 7*: 1–16 (1987); and A. Wildavsky, *The Nursing Father: Moses As a Political Leader*, University of Alabama Press (1985).
14. "The Political Economy of Efficiency," p. 294.
15. See A. Wildavsky, "A Cultural Theory of Leadership," *Leadership from Political Science Perspectives* (B. D. Jones, ed.), University Press of Kansas, Lawrence.

16. See A. Wildavsky, "Frames of Reference Come from Cultures: A Predictive Theory," *The Relevance of Culture* (M. Freilich, ed.), Bergin & Garvey, South Hadley, Mass. (1988).

17. "The Political Economy of Efficiency," p. 307.

18. P. Diesing, *Reason in Society*, Urbana (1962); quoted in "The Political Economy of Efficiency," p. 307.

50

Uses and Abuses of Analysis

James R. Schlesinger

The Subcommittee's invitation to assess the role that analysis may play in governmental decision making is gratifying for a number of reasons. In its current stocktaking, the Subcommittee is accomplishing something of a turnabout: the analysis of systems analysis. This evaluation takes place at a critical time. Like other offspring in American life, analysis has been absorbed into an environment which has been at once both too permissive and too resentful. There is ample evidence that such a pattern is beneficial to neither the offspring nor the environment. Currently there is a risk that reactions against what may be termed the exuberance of certain claims and activities of analysis could result in the discarding of the substantial benefits that analysis does offer. I shall be attempting to bring out the instances of undue gullibility as well as undue skepticism, but in so doing I should perhaps make my own position clear. My attitude has long been one of two-and-a-half cheers for systems analysis. I recognize—and have emphasized—its limitations. I will make no excuses for offenses committed in its name. But despite the limitations and distortions, I remain an unabashed, if qualified, defender of the value of analysis in policy formation.

In the pages that follow I shall deal with some salient issues regarding the role of analysis: its relation to decisions and decision makers, its functioning in a political environment where conflicting objectives exist, and its utility for improving the resource allocation process.

THE AUTHORITY OF ANALYSIS

Systems analysis has been variously defined. In the most ambitious formulation it has been described as "the application of scientific method, using that term in its broadest sense." Certain attributes of science—objectivity, openness, self-correctability, verifiability, etc.—are alleged to apply to systems analysis. Would that it were so, but realistically speaking such assertions must be rejected. Even for science—as those who are familiar

Source: U.S., Congress, Senate, Committee on Government Operations, *Planning-Programming-Budgeting*, 80th Cong., 2nd sess., U.S. Government Printing Office, Washington, D.C., pp. 125–136 (1968).

with the history of scientific investigations will recognize—this represents a rather romanticized view. In science, however, competition takes the form of establishing hypotheses regarding the workings of the natural order. Evidence and experiments are reproducible, and institutions and personalities consequently play a smaller long-run role. In scientific investigations the search for truth is by and large unfettered. By contrast, in the search for preferred policies such encumbrances as social values and goals, constraints, institutional requirements (both broad and narrow) pertain. Truth becomes only one of a number of conflicting objectives and, sad to relate, oftentimes a secondary one.

An alternative definition described systems analysis as "quantified common sense." By some expositors this definition has been treated as the equivalent of the earlier one, but is really quite distinct. However high the regard in which common sense, quantitative or otherwise, is held in the American community, it never has been regarded as synonymous with scientific method. Nonetheless, the definition is far more apt. Common sense, for example, will accept that within a complicated bureaucratic structure distortions inevitably creep into the process of acquiring and organizing evidence. What one sees depends upon where one sits—an earthy way of describing what is more elegantly referred to as cognitive limits. It may be inferred that a systems analysis shop attached to the Office of the Secretary of Defense (OSD) will be quite responsive to the perceptions and prejudices of the Secretary and the institutional requirements of his Office. This should be no more surprising than that the Operations Analysis shop at Omaha will be influenced by the doctrine, present activities, and aspirations of the Strategic Air Command.

In the early years of the introduction of the PPB into the Department of Defense, faith in the ease with which scientific objectivity could be attained tended to be high in OSD. For Service staffs, this was a rather painful period, for rather invidious distinctions were drawn regarding *their* objectivity. In recent years an enormous change has taken place regarding the nature of the analytical dialogue. Undoubtedly this new attitude reflects experience and the growing awareness that past decisions and past commitments limit the openness and the freshness with which the OSD staff can address issues in controversy.

This new realism has been reflected in a number of ways. Especially in private appraisals, analysis has been justified with increasing frequency and frankness as part of an adversary proceeding. But such an interpretation is symptomatic of a substantial change. Whatever the merits of an adversary procedure—and these are substantial where there exist clashes of interests and goals and where evidence is difficult to unearth—no one has ever suggested that adversaries seek to be wholly objective. One may hope that the result will be the eludication of the best possible case for and the best possible case against. But, unfortunately, the emphasis tends to shift to a search for the winning argument as opposed to the correct conclusion. In view of the uneven distribution of debating skills, one cannot fail to have qualms about the probable outcomes. One senior official has observed, only half facetiously, that experience in debate is the most valuable training for analytical work.

Acceptance of the tug-of-war concept, as opposed to the objective-scholar concept, of analysis has coincided with recognition of an even greater limitation on analysis as a guide to policymaking. In recent years it has been recognized in public statements (as well as the textbooks) that analysis is not a scientific procedure for reaching decisions which avoid intuitive elements, but rather a mechanism for sharpening the intuitions of the decision maker. Once again this is right. No matter how large a contribution that analysis makes, the role of the subjective preferences of the decision maker remains imposing. Analysis is, in the end, a method of investigating rather than solving problems. The highest strategic objectives, the statement of preferences or utility, must in large part be imposed from outside. Poor or haphazard analysis may contribute to poor decisions, but good analysis by itself cannot insure correct decisions. This implies two things. First, whatever the complex of decisions, legitimate differences of opinion will persist. Second, disagreement with the decisions should not automatically cast doubt on either the role of analysis in general or on the quality of specific analyses. These must be examined in and of themselves.

To be sure, the judgment of the decision makers regarding major objectives and what is or is not important is likely to feed back and influence the analysis. This is not always true, but there are strong pressures to make it come true. Studies are driven by the underlying assumptions, and these may be imposed directly or indirectly from above. Specific terms of reference may indicate which scenarios are acceptable, which unacceptable, and which contingencies should or should not be considered. It is perfectly appropriate, if not obligatory, for the analyst to point out deficiencies in study assumptions or terms of reference. Yet, many will lack the perception or the inclination, while others would regard such action as personally imprudent. In these cases the analysis will only play back to the decision maker a more sharply defined version of what was already implicit in his assumptions. The role of analysis then becomes not so much to *sharpen* the intuitions of the decision maker as to *confirm* them.

Under these circumstances analysis is not being used in its most fruitful form, that of raising questions. But analysis is a tool that can be used in a variety of ways. Much depends upon how the decision maker decides to employ it. Considerable fear has been expressed that analysis will usurp the decision-making role, that the decision maker will become passive, and let analysis (implicitly) make the decisions. This is possible; it is also improper. But whether the decision maker will control the tool rather than letting it run away with him strikes me as a less important question than whether he will employ it properly in another sense. Will the decision maker tolerate analysis—even when it is his own hobby horses which are under scrutiny?

How many hobby horses are there?

Are they off limits to the analysts?

Dr. Enthoven has quite properly objected to the canard that analysis is somehow responsible for what are regarded as the mishaps of the TFX decisions, pointing out that the new procedures were only tangentially involved. A more penetrating question, it seems to me, is: Why did the analysts steer away from the issue?

A slightly different issue arises in the case of Vietnam. Numerous blunders are alleged to be chargeable to analytic errors. But analysis has been employed in the Vietnamese context in only the most cursory fashion. In this context neither the high level civilian or the military authorities have been eager to exploit the full potentials of analysis. Once again, rather than blaming analytic efforts for the failures, the appropriate question should be: Why has analysis been so little employed?

An acquaintance, who has been deeply involved in analytic activities in one of the Departments, recently commented to me on his experiences. Analysis he felt had been relevant in only a small proportion of the decisions. Half the time a decision had been foreclosed by high-level political involvement: a call from the White House, interest expressed by key Congressmen or Committees. In an additional 30% of the cases, the careers of immediate supervisors were involved. Analysis could not influence the recommendations; it could serve only as an irritant. But, he argued, in something like 20% of the issues, analysis was unfettered and contributed to much improved overall results. This was only the experience of one individual. In other cases the proportions might be quite different. The point is that analysis should be judged on the basis of the only minority of cases in which its influence is in some sense instrumental. Analysis is an useful tool, but it is only a tool. It would be a mistake to turn over a new proverbial leaf—and generally find fault with tools rather than craftsmen.

PRACTITIONERS VERSUS INSTRUMENTS

Accepting that analysis only sharpens the intuitions of decision makers, that its powers may be curtailed by unquestioned (or question-begging) assumptions or by imposed terms of reference, and that it is increasingly viewed as a contest between adversaries permits us to be more realistic about analysis in a number of ways. The inflated claims, periodically made in its behalf, may be rejected—along with the misplaced criticisms made in response. Questioning of decisions is turned into questioning of decision makers' judgments rather than the role of analysis. And analysis itself can be employed more effectively in clarifying the underpinnings of policies, thereby creating the potential for designing more effective ones. We should understand that analysis provides no formula for solving problems, no prescription for sensible policies. It cannot and should not be employed to "demonstrate" that one's own policies are so right and those of others, so wrong.

What analysis provides is an exercise in logical coherence, hopefully with knowledge of and respect for the underlying technical, economic, and organizational data. Coherence does not insure the "correctness" of policy. In fact, an incoherent policy will sometimes be closer to correct than a coherent one. But the incoherence itself scarcely makes a contribution. It is almost invariably a source of waste, and typically of policy muddles.

Analysis may make a contribution, but we should be very clear what it cannot do. It does not provide an instant cure for pigheadedness. In fact, it does not provide an instant cure for anything—not because of its theoretical deficiencies, but because it has to be employed by people and by organizations with divergent goals and views and with stringently limited information about actual conditions.

It is a mistake to identify analysis with the particular judgments, prejudices or arguable decisions of some of its major proponents. Especially is this so when analysis has been employed as a weapon of political conflict. The political process being what it is, it is hardly advisable to admit error in public; that would prove too costly. Human emotions being what they are, it is also unlikely that error will be admitted in private. This does not gainsay the value of analysis before policy commitments are made—or when they are being seriously reconsidered. What it does say is that we should avoid tying analysis to the personal proclivities of the particular individuals who were instrumental in introducing it into government. To do so may be flattering to the individuals. Some may even be inclined to treat their own attitudes and commitments as synonymous with analysis. It would be a serious error for others to accept this view. Disciplined, orderly thought is the characterization given to analysis, but disciplined, orderly thought suggests certain traits: reflectiveness, self-criticism, and the willingness to reconsider past commitments without self-justification. However rarely or frequently encountered in the general human population, these are not traits characteristic of the action-oriented, incisive individuals who reach policymaking positions. Questioning and self-doubt lead to Hamlet-like decision makers.

Analysts themselves may be self-doubting, bemused by uncertainties, frightening candid, but different tactics have been required of the missionaries who have proselytized in behalf of analysis. I do not need to develop this point at any length. It should be plain, for example, that the actual decision to introduce analysis on a government-wide basis (as previously within the DOD) required an act of judgment and courage passing beyond the confines of analysis. Some analysts found the manner in which analytical procedures were instituted disquieting. This no doubt reflects a certain naivete on their part regarding political processes. But analysis was introduced rather suddenly. There was little advance preparation, little attempt to assess resource availability or calculate short-run costs. There was no "program definition phase." What occurred was that the political conditions were ripe [1], and the opportunity was seized—for analysis.

I have perhaps belabored the distinction between analysis and judgment and the fact that the act of deciding occurs in the nonanalytical phase. These matters need to be emphasized right now. It is important that analytical procedures in the DOD or elsewhere *not* be identified with particular sets of policies, decisions, or individuals. If analysis comes to be confused with the idiosyncrasies of a few dominant personalities, there is some risk that it will disappear along with its original proponents. Its potential benefits for U.S. policy would then be lost for some time to come.

Admittedly there have been overstated claims, planted stories, and an impression generated among the *cognoscenti* of a new, scientific means for grinding out decisions. Admittedly the limitations appeared in the footnotes and not in the fanfare. But these are just the accoutrements of attention-getting. Analysis itself should scarcely be discarded on these grounds. Even if some decision makers or analysts have failed to display the mental elasticity that analysis in principle demands, this is only a reflection of the human condition. Why throw the baby out with the bathwater?

PAYOFFS

What is the baby? I seem to have devoted most of my attention to the reasons for refraining from that last half cheer for analysis, and virtually no attention to the reasons for the two and one-half cheers. In part this is due to the excellent set of papers and comments that the Subcommittee has published. Therein the potential benefits of program budgeting and analysis are fully presented. Lengthy reiterations of either the potential advantages or the accomplishments seem unnecessary. However, there are some points on which I should like to add a few words.

First, analysis has great value in turning debates over resource allocation toward the realities and away from simple statements of noble purpose. Analysis is not scientific method. Neither will it necessarily be objective in an organizational context. Yet, within the adversary relationship, analysis at least focuses the debate on what particular systems can accomplish and what numbers are required. The emphasis is on the real rather than the symbolic function of weapon systems. Disappointed as many in the Services have been with major policy decisions of the OSD, I believe most knowledgeable officers would agree that the new methods have been beneficial in this respect.

Second and closely related, analysis is oriented toward outputs rather than toward inputs. In this way expenditures can be tied to specific goals, and those expenditures which satisfy primarily the traditions or well-being of individual agencies are brought into question. There are difficulties with goal or output orientation, particularly since we so frequently lack complete understanding of the mechanism that ties inputs to outputs. But the orientation is correct. The government structure is subdivided into agencies that typically concentrate on inputs. Dams, warships, trees, post offices, bombers, nuclear power, supersonic transportation, and, I may add, research expenditures are often treated as ends in themselves—with little examination as to how these instruments serve public purposes. Conscious output orientation, with as much quantitative backup as possible, points in the right direction. It forces agencies to shift attention from their beloved instruments and to explain the goals they serve rather than the functions they perform—and this at a level more practical than the usual rhetoric of noble purpose.

Third, the attempt is made to design systems or policies with practical budgetary limits in mind. The time-honored gap between the planners and the budgeteers has been widely discussed, along with the difficulties it causes. There is little point in plans too costly to be implemented or systems too expensive to be bought in the requisite quantity—if some reduction in quality will provide a feasible and serviceable, if less ideal, posture. (Here we are discussing capabilities and postures which would be effective, if bought—keeping in mind that so many expensive proposals serve little purpose at all.)

Fourth, an attempt is made to take spillovers into account and to achieve better integration between the several Services and Commands. Once again, this is more easily said than done. For example, we are belatedly becoming aware of the spillovers and the integration problems between the strategic offensive force under Air Force management and the new Sentinel system under Army control. This indicates that the attempt to take spillovers into account has not been overwhelmingly successful, but the goal is a correct one. The nation would not wish to duplicate SAC's capabilities for SACEUR or the Polaris force for CINCSAC.

Fifth, the attempt is made to take into account the long-run cost implications of decisions. Perhaps, it is more appropriate to say . . . the attempt *should* be made. There has been a certain inconsistency on this account. The costs of some systems have been carefully investigated, before a choice is made. For other (preferred) systems this has not been the case. The Program Definition Phase was originally introduced to insure that technology was in hand and the long-run costs considered before force structure decisions were made. Yet, curiously, in the programmed forces for the '70s our strategic forces are scheduled to become increasingly dependent on MIRVed vehicles, even though the technology is not yet in hand and we have only an inkling of the ultimate costs. The appropriate review of alternatives and hedges did not take place. But this represents, not a criticism of the objective, but a plea for more consistency in its pursuit. It hardly negates the desirability of the careful weighing of alternatives with the long-run cost implications taken into account.

These attributes and precepts of analysis seem unexceptionable.

They are.

An appropriate inference is that many of the complaints couched in terms of "too much analysis" or "the errors of analysis" should be altered into "better and more consistent analysis." In this connection, an editor and friend recently suggested a paper on the impact of systems analysis: "not the general appraisals, we've had enough of that; tell us whether systems analysis has every really been employed in the Department of Defense." An exaggeration perhaps, but as the MIRVing case suggests, analytic techniques have not been consistently applied.

Bernard Shaw observed somewhere that the only trouble with Christianity was that it had never really been tried. An epigram is at best a half truth, designed as someone has commented to irritate anyone who believes the other half. In DOD systems analysis has at least been tried. But there is an element in Shaw's remark that needs to be taken into account. In assessing the success of analysis, both the incomplete implementation and the resistance should be kept in mind.

BUDGETS

Military posture is determined in large measure by the total volume of resources the society is willing to divert from nondefense to defense uses. Yet, understanding the determinants of this resource flow presents a most perplexing problem. No good mechanism or rationale exists for deciding what diversion is proper. Some analysts have shied away from the problem arguing that the main objective should be the efficient employment of whatever resources are provided. A limited feel for appropriate diversion may be obtained by asking such questions as how much more is needed for defense than is needed for other purposes. In principle, senior policymakers may find it no harder to decide on allocation between damage limiting and urban renewal than between damage limiting and assured destruction. They will certainly find it no easier. For a number of practical reasons, they may find it far harder actually to bring about such a resource shift.

The amorphousness of this decision area combined with the repudiation of what were regarded as the rigidities of the Eisenhower years led to some bold words in 1961: There would be no *arbitrary* budget limits; in addition, every proposal would be examined on its own merits. These guidelines have since been regularly reasserted—with perhaps somewhat falling conviction. Originally they might be attributed to sheer enthusiasm; now they can only be taken as either propaganda or self-deception.

However, no matter the source, they will not stand up to *analysis*.

At any time there exists a rough political limit on defense expenditures. For members of this Subcommittee—in fact for any practicing politician—such an assertion will seem like a truism. Something like a consensus develops regarding proper levels of defense expenditures—and in the absence of external shocks this sum will not be substantially augmented. Of course, the *arbitrary* limit is always the *other fellow's*. One's own limit is only proximate and is wholly reasonable. Yet, defense expenditures do tend to become stabilized for years within rather narrow limits. Inevitably, new pressure for funds leads to the sacrifice of programs previously desirable on their own merits. That is as simple as arithmetic.

The only time that budget limits are not pressing (and more or less arbitrary) is when, as during the early Kennedy years, a political decision has been made that much more can be spent on defense. After a brief period of exuberance, the old constraints reappear. The decision does not have to be announced by the President or the Budget Bureau. The Secretary of Defense may get a feel for what is feasible, or he may be trusted to bring in a reasonable figure. But within a rather narrow range he will face a limit, which he may not transcend without either creating a minor fiscal crisis or straining his own credit with the President of the United States.

Save in the rare periods of budgetary relaxation, this, rightly or wrongly, is the way the system works. There is no point in kidding oneself. One may erect a facade intended to demonstrate that there are no arbitrary budget limits and each proposal is examined on its own merits. The pretense can be partially successful, but only because the criteria for choice are so imprecise. Standards can be made increasingly stringent, yet no one can prove how large was the role of budgetary pressures.

Nonetheless, no one should be deceived. What happens is that various alternatives and hedges are discarded; Programs become less pressing and are stretched out. The practices are well known from the bad, old meat-axe days. Under budgetary pressure (arbitrary or not) it is truly remarkable how many options one discovers one can do without. Multiple options just become less multiple. Before uncertainties are resolved, commitments are made and hedge programs are terminated. In the well-advertised adversary relationship, the negotiator-analysts become much harder to persuade. If they are not directly instructed, *they know.*

These are not hypothetical possibilities. With the intensification of budgetary pressures stemming from the Vietnamese war, there has, for example, been a wholesale slaughter of programs in the strategic area. It is important not to be misled regarding the critical role of budgetary pressures—and thus come to believe that so many programs, previously regarded as meritworthy, have suddenly lost their merit. Otherwise, we might gradually come to believe that we are doing far better than is actually the case. One should remain aware that the decimation of a program has long-run postural implications. That is, after all, the message that PPB attempts to convey.

These are elementary propositions. I do not dwell on certain theoretical problems and inconsistencies bearing on the relationship of overall defense spending to the optimality of programs. Suffice it to say that the *quality* of what one buys depends upon how much one wants to spend. This connection between level of demand and cost-effectiveness creates a dilemma in that *neither* the character of the programs nor the size of the budget can be determined initially. But that is a theoretical nicety, the direct consequences of which may not be of major importance.

The vital point is the way in which budgetary limits may control force posture and therefore strategy. Shifting sands seems the best way to characterize the strategic rationales of recent years. In 1961 the suicidal implications of massive retaliation were underscored: The United States would be faced with a choice between humiliation or holocaust. Interest then developed in damage-limiting and coercion. But there has been little willingness to invest money in either. Since 1965 the merits of Assured Destruction have been emphasized—with little attention paid to the suicidal implications found so distressing in prior years. The principal rationale for the current emphasis on Assured Destruction reflects certain recently developed notions of arms control. It clearly falls within the province of the decision makers to adopt a strategy of measured response to any Soviet buildup with the long-term objective of preserving U.S. Assured Destruction capabilities. One should note, however, that to accept this particular guide to action implies that the buildup of the Minuteman force in 1961–62 was a mistake. These newer arms control criteria may be the preferred ones, but they rest on the judgments and intuitions of the decision makers. They certainly do not emerge by themselves from analysis.

May one infer that the oscillations in strategy have something to do with budget limits, or in this case something more specific: a preconception regarding how much this nation should spend on the strategic forces? I find the conclusion irresistible. The evidence antedates the current phase-down in the face of the Soviet buildup. Once again, these lie within the decision maker's prerogatives, but particular beliefs regarding budget limits or the "adequacy" of specific strategies should not be attributed to, much less blamed on, analysis.

A USEFUL IF OVERSOLD TOOL

Whatever resources are made available to defense (or any other mission), choices will have to be made.

Allocative decisions inevitably are painful; many claimants will be sorely disappointed. Few will find fault with their own proposals, almost all with the machinery for selection.

Any procedures for allocation will be criticized—even in a hypothetical case in which the conceptual basis is unarguable and no errors are made. Analysis provides the backup for a selective process. What does it contribute? How does it compare with real-world alternatives—not with mythical alternatives in which all claimants get their requests and no one is disappointed?

It has been emphasized that analysis cannot determine the appropriate strategy. It can shed light on costs and trade-offs. But the choice to press arms control or arms competition or to rely on tactical nuclears or nuclear firebreaks must be determined by the decision maker sustained primarily by hope, conviction, and prayer. Even if a decision could be demonstrated as correct at a given moment in time, there is the certainty that objectives will change over time. For these higher level problems analysis is an aid, but a limited aid. The toughest problems, dominated as they are by uncertainties and by differences in goals, do not yield to analysis.

Happily many problems are more mundane and more tractable. Where analysis has proved its highest value is in uncovering cases of gross waste: points at which substantial expenditures may contribute little to any stated objective. It might be thought that a problem of diminishing returns exists for analysis in that the cases of gross misuse of resources are likely to be uncovered at an early stage. Thus, as the opportunity for major savings through elimination of irrational forms of waste theoretically recedes, analysis would be forced into the more ambiguous areas in which strategic choices become intimately involved. In some cases, where information is readily available and objectives and conditions relatively unchanging, this could prove to be true. The very success of analysis would then undermine near-term expectations of additional returns. However, in defense this turns out to be irrelevant, since the problems are so volatile and information so difficult to unearth.

To say that analysis works best in cases of gross waste should not be taken to imply that analysis accomplishes little. The simple cases involving so-called dominant solutions may involve billions of dollars. The volume of government resources that may be lavished on the care and feeding of white elephants is simply staggering.

Here we have "quantified common sense" in its most direct form. In bureaucracies, units at all levels are concerned with organizational health. Rather than making the hard choices, the tendency is strong to maintain morale by paying off all parties. Analysis provides a means for coping with this problem. The big issues may not be directly involved, though they are likely to be dragged in by the proponents of particular programs.

Should the assessment of analysis be much influenced by the annoyance felt by those whose proposals have failed the tests? Certainly not in the general case. No more than should the decision makers be permitted to hide their judgments behind the camouflage of analysis, should the patrons of doubtful proposals be encouraged to argue that acceptance would and should have come—if *only* analysis had not been employed. Budgets are limited and hard choices must be made. If nobody were annoyed analysis would not be doing its job —of questioning both routinized practices and blue-sky propositions. Disappointment is unavoidable. The question is not the existence of annoyance, but to strive to annoy in the right way and for the right reasons.

In this light it may be desirable to examine the issue of the generalist versus the specialist which has been touched upon in the Hearings. In the nature of things specialists become committed to particulars: a piece of hardware, a technological criterion, a disciplinary blind spot. It is a case of suboptimization run wild. Proponents of specific capabilities or gadgets tend to become monomaniacs. In a sense that is the way they should be: totally dedicated to their tasks. But one does not turn to them for detached judgments. There is no substitute for the *informed* generalist. There is a recognizable risk that the superficiality of the generalist may match the monomania of the specialist. However, that need not be the case. Although the generalist's knowledge cannot match that of the specialist in detail, analysis can once again play a useful role, by permitting the organization for the generalist of more specialized information than he alone could master.

How does this relate to the limits of the analyst's role? Two distinctions should be kept in mind: that between the technical specialist and the analytical generalist and that between the analyst and the decision maker. The analyst's tools are not circumscribed by discipline or even by subject matter. But general tools are not immediately convertible into broad policies. Many analysts are, in some sense, specialists in the use of general tools. Being a good analytical generalist does not necessarily imply possession of such additional qualities as breadth, judgment, and political attunement. These latter qualities are what many have in mind when they speak of the generalist as policymaker.

CONCLUSION

In closing I should like to underscore three points.

First, the position of the decision maker employing analysis is somewhat ambiguous. For tactical purposes this ambiguity may be deliberately augmented. Intermittently he may choose to stress *analysis* or *judgment*, and to shift hats according to the tactical requirements of the moment. His policy judgments may be obscured or defended by cryptic references to detailed analyses which allegedly force the policy conclusions. On the other hand, if any limitations or inadequacies in the analyses should come to light, these can be waved away with the reminder that all issues are ultimately matters for the decision maker's judgment.

Moreover, the pattern is in reality far more complicated than the standard exposition in which the analyst produces an *objective* study, and the decision maker's judgment enters at a later stage erected on the foundation of these objective results. That makes the analytical and judgmental stages seem clean-cut. Few studies are that pure. The decision maker's judgments quite typically are dumped in at an early stage in the form of guidance, assumptions, and terms of reference. The more political a study, the less likely is it to be pure. In fact, the process can be (and has been) far more corrupted, when questionable (phony) numbers are introduced. Since judgment and analysis are thoroughly intertwined in all but a few studies, the attempt of decision makers to shift roles by referring to fundamental analyses should be treated with some skepticism. The decision maker should not be permitted to escape the full burden of responsibility by the invocation of analysis.

The temptation for those who have introduced analytical techniques into the government to treat their own positions or careers as identical with analysis is understandable. No outsider should yield to the same temptation. The roles and even the temperaments of decision maker and analyst are quite distinct. The confusion tends to disguise the heavy personal burden borne by the decision maker. More important, if analysis is treated as synonymous with particular decisions or personalities, there is a risk that it will be throttled or abandoned after their departure. From the standpoint of public policy this would be a major loss.

Second, we should avoid the erroneous belief that the performance or potential power of analysis will be uniform in all contexts. If a town is considering building a bridge, a number of difficult analytical problems must be addressed: Does demand warrant construction, where should the bridge be built, what should be its capacity, and so on. But once these questions are resolved the engineer falls back on a solid technical base. By contrast, for such goals as deterrence, assured destruction, controlled nuclear warfare, damage limiting, to say nothing of welfare benefits, we fall back, not on a firm technical base, but on what may be scientific mush. The distinction is not always appreciated. The difficulty is sometimes dealt with by referring euphemistically to *the model problem*. But our ability to formulate models depends upon our knowledge of the mechanics of the real world. For many problems our knowledge is meager, and the proffered models are misleading or downright erroneous. The lack of good models in many problem areas simultaneously limits the power of analysis, while increasing the burden placed on judgment. In treating analysis as a uniformly efficient problem-solving technique, the variability of analysis, which reflects the variability of the knowledge base, is ignored.

Though analysis is a powerful tool, specific analyses vary greatly in quality. Some are little more than trash. But we need to discriminate, rather than to reject analysis in toto. At the present time there is some risk that we will do the latter. In an address some years ago Secretary Enthoven observed: "My general impression is that the art of systems analysis is in about the same stage now as medicine during the latter half of the 19th century; that is, it has just reached the point at which it can do more good than harm." That was a frank and realistic, if somewhat pessimistic, assessment of the state of the *art*. Scientifically speaking, there are numerous blind spots in medicine. Yet, most of us ultimately are inclined to accept the doctor's diagnosis, if not his advice. Quite plainly at the present time Congress and the public are having second thoughts regarding how much trust to put in systems analysis. No doubt it is necessary to develop a greater ability to discriminate. Nonetheless, I suggest that policy will benefit substantially from the analysts' diagnoses.

Third, there is little doubt that analysis has been oversold. That strikes me as a rather standard result in matters political. But the reaction against the overselling could be more costly than the overselling itself. Analysis is a powerful instrument: With it our batting average has been far higher than without it. Analysis is also an adaptable instrument. The McNamara regime has in many respects been a highly personalized one. Its performance should not be taken as defining the limits of this flexible tool. Admittedly, analyses vary substantially in quality. Each should be taken with a large grain of salt. On the other hand, if one does not demand too much of it, analysis will prove to be a most serviceable instrument.

NOTE

1. This episode suggests why the politician in his role may find analysis both incomplete and frustrating. Analysis deals in a rather abstract way with resource usage and efficient allocations. It does not deal with the attitudinal issues of support-generation, coalition gathering, or with timing which are so important in the political context.

51
Why Do Forecasts Differ?

Stephen K. McNees

Experts typically have a wide variety of views on the future economic environment. Insofar as their views are based on explicit, systematic methods of assessing economic information, we can say forecasts differ because forecasters use different models. However, even if everyone used the same model, all forecasts would not be identical. First, most models are conditional; the predicted outcome depends on the specific input assumptions a forecaster uses to solve the model. A single model can generate an infinite number of forecasts, depending on what assumptions are made. Second, forecasters have different beliefs about the degree to which the predictive value of all information can be fully captured by a formal model. Some econometricians place their faith solely in their model and regard judgmental adjustments of their models as "unscientific" and more likely than not to be counterproductive. Other forecasters, typically those whose models have evolved, or even dissolved, are more open to the possibility that special events that cannot be formally modeled from historical data can still have predictive values. Differences in these attitudes affect the extent to which mechanically generated forecasts are modified.

Most forecasts, in other words, reflect a complex interaction among three elements: (1) a model, (2) the conditioning information or input assumptions used to generate a model forecast, and (3) the model user's attempts to incorporate extra model information through judgmental adjustments.

Unfortunately, little is known about the relative importance of these elements. This chapter addresses three kinds of questions:

1. What are the relative roles of the model and the modeler in generating a forecast? To what extent do forecasts reflect judgments by the forecaster in the form of input assumptions and judgmental adjustments?

2. Why do ex ante forecasts differ? Clearly, different forecasters use different models. In addition, individual forecasters adopt different assumptions about future mac-

Source: *New England Economic Review*, Jan./Feb. 1989, published by the Federal Reserve Bank of Boston. This article is based on a chapter from *Econometric Model Comparison* (L. R. Klein, ed.), Oxford University Press, New York (1989).

roeconomic policy and economic developments in the rest of the world. Forecasters also have different philosophies about how much to override the mechanically generated model results with their own judgment. Do these differences in assumptions and adjustments increase the dispersion of forecasts, exaggerating differences among models, or do they decrease the dispersion of forecasts, masking larger differences in what the models would predict on the basis of a common set of assumptions and adjustments?

3. What are the sources of forecast errors? Do modelers' adjustments help or hurt forecast accuracy? When, in particular, have they helped and when have they hurt? Does lack of knowledge about future input variables impair forecast accuracy? Or, as some previous research indicates, can modelers somehow compensate for the deficiencies of their models through judicious choice of forecast assumptions?

AN OVERVIEW

This chapter compares model solutions based on different sets of conditioning information. In general, a model can be thought of as a conditional statement about the relationship between inputs (Xs) and outputs (Ys), or $Y = f(X)$.

The most frequently observed model solution, the ex ante published forecast, or ($Y^{P,i}$), is the model solution based on the individual forecaster's expected values of the input variables (EX) and any judgmental adjustments (Ad) he chooses to make.

$$Y^{P,i} = f(EX^i) + Ad^i \tag{1}$$

The mechanically generated forecast, $Y^{m,i}$, is the solution of the model based on the individual modeler's input assumptions and a fixed, predetermined rule for adjustments based on the pattern of recent residuals,

$$Y^{m,i} = f(EX^i) + Rule^i \tag{2}$$

A comparison of the published and mechanical forecasts, (1) and (2), measures the importance for Y forecasts of the nonroutine adjustments made in generating the published forecast.

The conditional model forecast, $Y^{C,i}$ is the model solution based on a common input assumption, $E\overline{X}$, as well as the rule,

$$Y^{C,i} = f(E\overline{X}) + Rule^i \tag{3}$$

Note that the individual modeler has no influence on the conditional model forecast, above and beyond that of constructing the model and the explicit adjustment rule. A rule, once it has been formalized, can properly be regarded as part of the model, as some models already include some form of residual adjustment in their estimation procedures. A comparison of the conditional model forecast and the mechanical forecast, (2) and (3), constitutes a measure of the role of the modeler's individual input assumptions relative to common assumptions. In fact, models employ many different kinds of input assumptions, a matter pursued more fully below.

The ex post forecast, $Y^{ep,i}$, is the model solution based on the actual values of the input assumptions, X, which are of course not observed until after the forecast period has ended.

$$Y^{ep,i} = f(X) + Rule^i \tag{4}$$

A comparison of the conditional model forecast and the ex post model solution, (3) and (4), reveals the importance of the knowledge of the actual values of the input variables relative to the common values that were assumed before the fact. The difference between the ex post model solution and the actual historic outcome will be regarded as the model error, the discrepancy between the actual value of Y and the value that the model indicates conditioned on the actual historic input information.

In summary, comparisons of model solutions based on varying sets of input information provide measures of the relative importance of the various factors that are blended together to generate a model-based forecast: the judgmental adjustments, the modeler's assumptions, and the model per se.

MODEL ADJUSTMENT PROCEDURES

Most forecasters adjust their mechanically generated, "pure model" results to try to account for a multitude of considerations outside of their formal model or its inputs. These factors can range from the mundane—for example, the incoming high-frequency data indicate that the forecast of lower-frequency data is likely to be wrong—to the purely subjective—the results look "unreasonable" for no stated reason—to the nefarious—the results are manipulated to induce the forecast user to adopt a certain course of action. Because the rationales for these adjustments are seldom documented, different commentators characterize adjustments in different ways.

Conceptually, forecasters could be asked to document their motives for each adjustment and these could be categorized to assess the extent to which the adjustments are "scientific," that is, grounded in theory or evidence. Because the object of this exercise is to compare models rather than various forms of judgment, for the purpose of this exercise the participants decided to permit only adjustments that could be written down explicitly in the form of a predetermined rule based on observed residuals. Each modeler was permitted to devise the rule for his own model, or even a different rule for each equation in the model, but it was agreed that the rules, once adopted, would not be changed over time. With no room for individual discretion, once these adjustment rules were formulated, adopting this convention amounts to redefining the model as the model plus the appended adjustment rules. Except for published forecasts, all forecasts examined below employ the adjustment rule and no adjustments.

INPUT ASSUMPTIONS

Even if there were only one model, it would be a challenge to understand how that model performed and the inputs used to generate forecasts with that model. In fact, because there are numerous alternative models and one wishes not only to understand each but to contrast and compare them, comparisons must confront the fact that model outcomes (Ys) are conditioned on the assumed values of the input variables (Xs) used to solve the model. This fact poses a dilemma: (1) On the one hand, Ys based on *any* Xs other than their actual values cannot be compared to the actual Ys to assess the model's accuracy. Counterfactual values of Xs can either increase or decrease discrepancies between the model solution and the actual outcome. To isolate the performance of a model defined as a conditional statement, the model must be solved with the actual Xs.

Ex ante forecasts intermingle the quality of the model with the skills of the model user in selecting future values of input assumptions. A clever model user may compensate for a deficient model by judicious choice of inputs. A foolish model user could confound even a perfect model by providing unreliable inputs. Ex ante forecast accuracy therefore does not provide a clear comparison of models as conditional statements. This is the reason why early model comparisons focused on ex post simulations, where none of the error can be attributed to counterfactual Xs. (2) On the other hand, different models are conditional on different, nonoverlapping, sometimes even logically inconsistent, input information sets. Due to these differences in their "degree of exogeneity," comparisons of ex post simulations can be difficult to interpret. Models that require large amounts of input enjoy an informational advantage from the actual values of these additional variables in an ex post simulation.

The first step in this exercise was to examine the input assumption (or "exogenous variable") set of each participating model [1]. That examination confirmed that models differ greatly in the informational input they require. Even when all models embody the same broad concept, such as "monetary policy" or economic growth outside the United States, typically each model uses a different specific measure of that concept. Complete standardization would therefore require supplementary procedures for reconciling alternative concepts and measures. Without building a supermodel to encompass all individual models, complete standardization across fairly similar models is virtually impossible. When different models adopt logically inconsistent assumptions, standardization becomes literally impossible.

Despite such differences, all of these models contain similar types of input assumptions [2]. For example, all participating models employ some assumptions about fiscal and monetary policy. The most obvious standardization of input assumptions is to solve each model on a common set of policy assumptions. With regard to fiscal policy, all models were constrained to follow common paths of nominal federal expenditures and were requested to introduce no changes in the tax code beyond those that had already been legislated.

Standardization for monetary policy was more difficult because of the lack of a consensus on the appropriate instrument to represent monetary policy. Rather than attempt to resolve this long-standing controversy, forecasts were generated under two alternative monetary policy assumptions—a given path of M1 and also a given path of short-term interest rates (the federal funds rate, or, for some models, identical changes in the Treasury bill rate).

All these models are also conditioned on input assumptions about economic developments in the rest of the world (ROW). These models vary greatly in the extent to which their external sectors are developed and disaggregated. A complete model of the world economy might require information on ROW macro policies, and perhaps the world price of oil, providing extensive linkages between these and the U.S. economy. At the other extreme, some models were developed essentially as closed models of the U.S. economy, excluding all these linkages and treating only real exports and import prices as input variables. The appropriate standardization for the world model would require other modelers to develop the additional linkages between foreign economies and the U.S. economy. This could be expected to change the character of these models. In order to "let the models be models," standardization for the ROW was made on the basis of the "lowest common denominator"—the closed economy model with the least developed external sectors. Specifically, the closed economy forecasts are all based on the same assumptions about the path of real exports and the import price deflator. Auxiliary assumptions were provided on the world price of oil, ROW real growth, and ROW inflation rates to help the more open economy models conform to the common external assumptions.

This exercise did not attempt to standardize across all input assumptions but only for two different, important types of assumptions: macroeconomic policy and external sector. Extending the notation introduced earlier, the published forecast ($Y^{P,i}$) becomes:

$$Y^{P,i} = f(EP^i, EX^i, EO^i) + Ads^i i \tag{1a}$$

Here EP^i, EX^i, and EO^i are, respectively, the individual forecaster's policy assumptions, external sector assumptions, and other input assumptions. The mechanical forecast becomes:

$$Y^{m,i} = f(EP^i, EX^i, EO^i) + Rule^i \tag{2a}$$

The conditional model forecast now consists of two parts: the open economy forecast,

$$Y^{o,i} = f(\overline{EP}, EX^i, EO^i) + Rule^i \tag{3a}$$

and the closed economy forecast,

$$Y^{c,i} = f(\overline{EP}, \overline{EX}, EO^i) + Rule \tag{3b}$$

A comparison of the mechanical forecast with the open economy forecast, (2a)–(3a), measures the impact of the individual modeler's macro policy assumptions relative to the common assumption. A comparison of the open economy forecast with the closed economy forecast, (3a)–(3b), illustrates the importance of the individual modeler's treatment of the external sector relative to the common assumption. Even the mechanical model solution with common policy and external sector assumptions depends on the modeler's assumptions about other input variables. It, like all ex ante forecasts, does not isolate the role of the model as a conditional statement. The model is isolated only in an ex post simulation:

$$Y^{ep,i} = f(P, X, O) + Rule \tag{4}$$

when P, X, and O are actual values.

In principle, any values could be used as the common core input assumptions. In fact, some combinations of input variables may be economically or politically infeasible. One way to try to avoid such inconsistencies would be to employ one individual's assumptions as the common ones. This would ensure that the common assumptions were consistent in at least one individual's eyes. In this case, the common input assumptions imposed on the models were a simple average among several forecasters, only some of whom participated in this project. Under this approach, the results measure the impact of an individual modeler's assumptions relative to "the" consensus view that is prevailing among forecasters generally.

THE PRELIMINARY RESULTS

The array of data collected so far is a rich one, covering 21 variables, each over an eight-quarter horizon for as many as eight models under as many as six sets of input assumptions. Some models participated in the early rounds, but subsequently dropped out for a variety of reasons. Other models joined the project after the first two rounds had been completed. The results presented here cover the five models that participated in the six sets of forecasts conducted in 1987 and early 1988. The results focus on two of the most important variables, the real GNP growth and the inflation rate, over three horizons—the first year, the second year, and the first two years.

Recall that the models were simulated under two alternative representations of monetary policy—a common M1 path and a common short-term interest rate path. The dispersion among the real GNP forecasts was smaller under the common M1 assumption than under the common interest rate assumption, while the dispersion of the inflation rate forecasts was about the same. The rest of this chapter deals only with the common interest rate path representation of monetary policy because one of the regularly participating models does not contain an M1 variable.

The results are grouped into three sections—forecast dispersion, forecast decomposition, and error decomposition—that correspond to the three questions posed in the introduction to this chapter.

Forecast Dispersion

The answer to the question "Why do forecasts differ?" depends critically on the variable of interest. For example, while real GNP forecasts differ primarily because the underlying models differ, mechanically generated model predictions of the inflation rate based on common assumptions are somewhat more similar than published inflation rate forecasts. (See Table 1.) This result reflects the differential impacts of individual forecasters' assumptions relative to common "consensus" assumptions and adjustments of their model forecasts.

Forecasters' choices of external assumptions have had a negligible impact on the dispersion of their real growth forecasts but a major impact on the dispersion of their inflation rate forecasts. This reflects both the diversity of opinion about future import prices and the different sensitivities across models to changes in import prices.

In contrast, the individual forecasters' choices of policy assumptions had a fairly small impact on the dispersion of their inflation rate forecasts over a two-year horizon, but a major impact on the dispersion of their real GNP forecasts. This result can be interpreted as illustrating the modeler's role as an implicit reaction function or policy rule that tends to push real GNP back toward a satisfactory path. Specifically, if a model exhibits particularly weak (strong) real growth, the modeler is likely to employ more stimulative (restrictive) macroeconomic policy assumptions in his forecast. It is interesting to note that the implicit policy rule emphasizes stabilizing real GNP growth, not the inflation rate, at least over a two-year horizon.

Table 1 Sources of Forecast Dispersion (Ranges, Annual Growth Rates)

	(1) 1st Year	(2) 2nd Year	(3) Two Years
Real GNP			
Closed	3.4	3.6	2.7
Policy	2.8	3.4	2.5
Mechanical	2.6	2.5	1.8
Published	1.3	2.6	1.4
Inflation rate			
Closed	1.7	2.3	1.8
Policy	2.6	3.0	2.8
Mechanical	2.9	3.3	3.1
Published	2.0	2.4	2.1

Note: Closed, mechanical forecasts with common policy and external sector assumptions. Policy, mechanical forecasts with common policy assumptions. Mechanical, mechanical forecasts with individual assumptions. Published, forecasts with individual assumptions and adjustments.

The forecasters' adjustments virtually always work to make the forecasts more similar. Their importance is relatively large for the dispersion of inflation rate forecasts and of real GNP forecasts in the first, though not the second, year of the forecast period. This tendency of convergence toward the consensus may reflect a greater reluctance to rely on the model as the model deviates further from the consensus. The consensus view, for example, may be the most likely outcome and the model an indicator of the most likely deviation from the mode. For real GNP, the tendency to adjust the forecast toward the consensus reinforces the unifying impact of individual policy assumptions, so that published forecasts are far more similar than mechanical model forecasts are far more similar than mechanical model forecasts based on common assumptions. For the inflation rate, the unifying adjustments serve to offset the diverging impact of individual external sector assumptions, so that the dispersion of published forecasts is about the same as the dispersion of standardized model forecasts.

Forecast Decomposition

These data also help to measure the relative roles of the model and the modeler in generating a forecast. In Table 2 the modeler's role is decomposed into three parts: the impact of external sector assumptions, measured as the difference between the forecast based on

Table 2 Importance of Three Forms of Forecasters' Judgment; Mean Absolute Change (Percentage Points)

	Real GNP			Inflation rate		
	External sector assumptions (1)	Policy assumptions (2)	Adjustments (3)	External sector assumptions (4)	Policy assumptions (5)	Adjustments (6)
First year						
Model 1	.7	?	.4	.5	0	.9
Model 2	.3	1.0	1.1	.4	.8	1.1
Model 3	.3	1.1	0	.8	.1	0
Model 4	1.5	1.1	.7	.6	.5	.8
Model 5	.4	.2	.8	0	0	.6
Mean	.6	.7	.6	.5	.3	.7
Second year						
Model 1	.9	.3	.6	.4	0	.9
Model 2	.1	1.2	.9	1.0	1.1	1.8
Model 3	.6	.3	0	.9	.2	0
Model 4	1.4	.9	.8	.7	.5	1.5
Model 5	.8	.3	.7	.1	0	.9
Mean	.8	.6	.6	.6	.4	1.0
Two years						
Model 1	.8	.3	.4	.4	0	.9
Model 2	.2	.7	.6	.7	.9	1.5
Model 3	.2	.7	0	.8	.1	0
Model 4	.4	.4	.6	.7	.5	1.2
Model 5	.5	.2	.7	.1	0	.7
Mean	.4	.5	.5	.5	.3	.9

common policy assumptions and the forecast based on common assumptions for both policy and the external sector; the impact of policy assumptions, measured as the difference between the forecast based on common policy assumptions and the one based on the modeler's individual policy assumptions; and the impact of adjustments, measured as the difference between the published and mechanical forecasts. We focus on the mean *absolute* differences rather than the mean differences to avoid equating a forecaster who never makes adjustments (for example, model 3) with a forecaster whose upward adjustments just happen to be as large as his downward adjustments. The results vary by both model and variable. For real GNP over a two-year horizon, adjustments were most important for models 4 and 5, policy assumptions for models 2 and 3, and external sector assumptions for model 1. For these five models taken as a group, each of these three forms of modeler's judgment is roughly equally important for each of the forecast horizons examined.

For the inflation rate, adjustments have the largest impact on the forecasts of four of the five models. The only exception was model 3, which was never adjusted and where the external sector assumptions were the most important form of judgment embodied in the inflation forecast. Differences in policy assumptions had relatively little impact on the inflation rate forecasts except for model 2.

Combining the information on forecast dispersion with the information on the impact of assumptions and adjustments suggests a stylized description of the forecasting process: (1) When different models are solved initially with "consensus" values of external sector and policy assumptions, real growth forecasts differ by more than 3 percentage points and inflation rate forecasts by less than 2 percentage points. (2) When the modelers impose their individual assumptions, real growth forecasts converge (reflecting a real-growth-stabilizing implicit policy rule) but inflation rate forecasts diverge further. (3) Judgmental adjustments are imposed to narrow forecast dispersion, offsetting the divisive impact of individual assumptions on the inflation rate and reinforcing the converging impact on real growth forecasts.

The mean absolute deviation of the published real GNP forecasts from the average or "consensus" published forecast is about half as large as the deviation of "pure model" forecasts based on common assumptions. In contrast, the mean absolute deviation of the published inflation forecasts from the consensus forecast is about the same as the deviation of "pure model" forecasts based on common "consensus" assumptions. The net effect of the individual modelers' assumptions and adjustments is to draw their real GNP forecasts together—the forecasts are more similar than the models. The *net* effect is essentially nil for their inflation rate forecasts—the dispersion among published forecasts—is similar to the dispersion among models, once the role of the individual modeler has been minimized.

Over this period the models, as a group, based on common consensus assumptions, generated higher forecasts of both real growth and inflation rates than the published forecasts. About half of the difference was due to adjustments, the other half due to the individual modelers' nonconsensus assumptions.

Error Decomposition

All of the preceding information describes the evolution of individual ex ante forecasts and the dispersion of those forecasts. We have seen how the forecasters' judgments affect their forecasts and the disparity among forecasts. This section describes two forecast periods for which the actual outcome is now known. This enables us to examine not only how judgments affect the forecasts but also whether they aid or impair the accuracy of the forecast.

Figure 1 shows the quite general tendency to overestimate real GNP from 1986:I to 1987:IV, especially early in the period. For models 1 and 3, the extent of overestimation

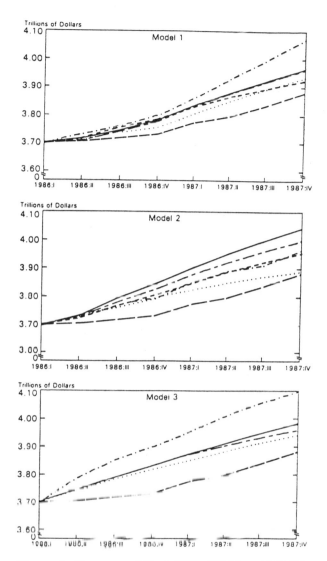

Figure 1 Forecasts of Real GNP, 1986:I to 1987:IV. – – – Published, ... Mechanical, ———
Policy, — – Closed, – · – Ex Post, — — Actual. Published: forecast with individual assumptions
and adjustments. Mechanical: mechanical forecast with individual assumptions. Policy: mechanical
forecast with common policy assumptions. Closed: mechanical forecast with common policy and
external sector assumptions. Ex post: simulations using actual values of exogenous variables.

was greater with the actual values of exogenous variables than with any set chosen ex ante.
The forecaster's own ex ante assumptions led to slightly better forecasts than did imposing
consensus assumptions. For model 2, the overestimation was worse with the common, ex
ante assumptions and less with the forecaster's individual assumptions than with their actual
values. For models 1 and 2, the published, adjusted forecasts were less accurate than the
mechanically generated forecasts.

Figure 2 shows forecasts of the deflator for personal consumption expenditures over
the same period. The ex ante forecasts from models 1 and 3 tended to underestimate the

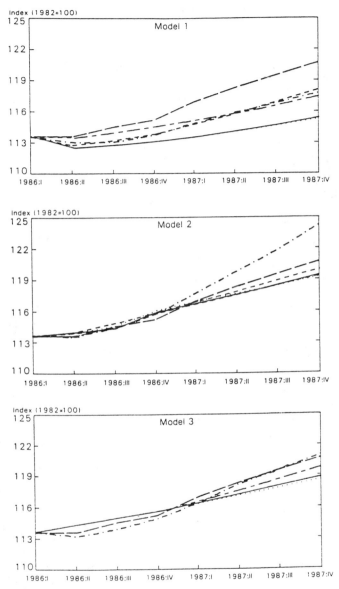

Figure 2 Forecasts of the personal consumption deflator, 1986:I to 1987:IV. – – – Published, ... Mechanical, —— Policy, — – Closed, – · – Ex Post, —— Actual. See Fig. 1 for explanation of key.

price level. The ex ante forecast of model 2 was quite accurate. Using the actual values of the exogenous variables, the model 1 forecast remained too low, the model 2 forecast started to overestimate, and model 3's forecast became highly accurate. The proprietor of model 2 was able to offset his model's deficiencies to give "the right forecast for the wrong reasons." In contrast, model 3's ex ante error was solely attributable to the modeler's ex ante choice of assumptions; the model as a conditional statement was on track.

Figures 3 and 4 graph the ex ante forecasts, ex post simulations, and actual data for the period from 1986:III through 1988:II. Figure 3 shows that all these forecasts tracked real GNP fairly closely. While the ex post forecasts of model 1 were somewhat better than its ex ante forecasts, the ex post forecasts of model 3 were somewhat worse. The adjustments to models 1 and 2 improved their forecasts, particularly early in the period.

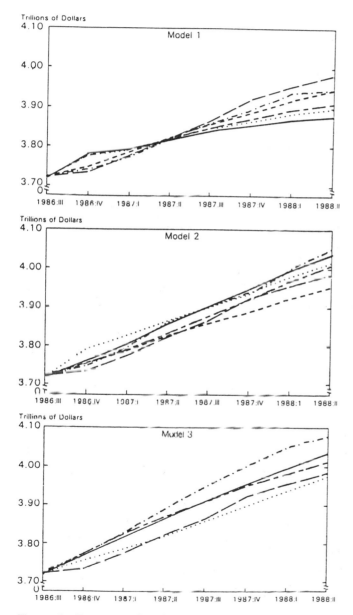

Figure 3 Forecasts of real gross national product, 1986:III to 1988:II. – – – Published, ... Mechanical, ——— Policy, –– – Closed, – · – Ex Post, —— Actual. See Fig. 1 for explanation of key.

Figure 4 shows the inflation forecasts over the same period. Ex ante, model 1 forecasts were quite accurate, the forecasts of models 2 and 3 were too low. However, with actual values of the exogenous variables, the forecasts of models 2 and 3 were quite accurate and model 1's forecast was slightly too high.

SUMMARY AND CONCLUSIONS

The chapter opened by posing three questions. This conclusion summarizes the limited evidence that has been presented.

1. Although the importance of judgment adjustments varies among individual models, for the models as a group the choices of macro policy assumptions and external sector assumptions, relative to consensus assumptions, are as important to real GNP forecasts and nearly as important to inflation forecasts as are modelers' judgmental adjustments (Table 2).

2. The reason for the dispersion among forecasts depends critically on the variables analyzed. The differences between the modeler's individual policy assumptions and the consensus assumptions tend to narrow differences in real GNP forecasts. Differences between individual and consensus external sector assumptions tend to increase the disparity among inflation forecasts. Model adjustments seem to narrow the dispersion among forecasts of both real GNP and the price level.

3. Judgmental adjustments can either help or hurt. This evidence shows instances of both "good" judgment and "bad" judgment, depending primarily on which forecast period is examined. The adjustments hurt the real GNP forecasts of models 1 and 2 in the first forecast period, but helped in the second period, especially for model 2 in the short term. Adjustments had little impact on the inflation forecasts. The sole exception is for model 1 in the first round, when adjustments improved the inflation forecast at the same time they hurt the real GNP forecasts. This evidence is not consistent with the widespread belief that mechanically generated forecasts are wildly inaccurate compared to adjusted forecasts. It is consistent, however, with the view that judgmental adjustments can either help or hurt. Other evidence, covering longer periods, does suggest that adjustments do tend to help on average over time, but very little is known about when adjustments are likely to hurt and when they are likely to help.

4. Consensus ex ante assumptions do not necessarily produce a more accurate forecast than individual assumptions. Two very different concepts of a model coexist. To some, the main virtue of using a model is that it gives the same answer to a precise question regardless of who poses the question. A model can be viewed as a disembodied system or formula like the laws of the natural sciences, totally independent of who uses it. From this perspective, there is no particular reason to believe that the person who built a model will necessarily be more skilled in formulating ex ante assumptions to generate a model-based forecast. If the model and the forecast assumptions were totally independent, there is no particular reason to think the model builder's individual assumptions would produce a more accurate forecast than any other feasible set of assumptions, such as the consensus assumptions.

Others tend to think of models, at least in a forecasting context, as tools the forecaster can use to enhance his skills. Just as not all craftsmen use the same kind of tools and not all athletes use the same brand of equipment, the performance of the model and the modeler

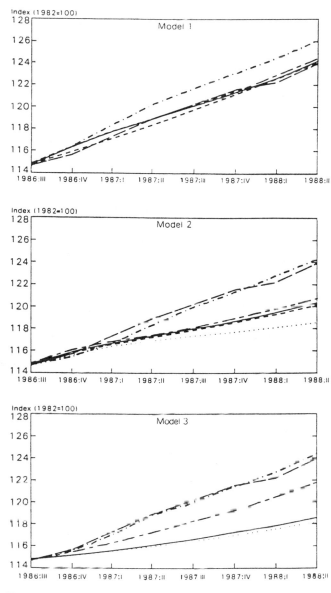

Figure 4 Forecasts of personal consumption deflator, 1986:III to 1988:II. – – – Published, ...
Mechanical, —— Policy, — – Closed, – · – Ex Post, —— Actual. See Fig. 1 for explanation of
key.

are not independent and the two must be viewed as a team. Under this view, a model
builder is in the best position to know the particular characteristics of his model and would,
therefore, be especially capable of selecting ex ante assumptions to generate more accurate
forecasts. Any externally imposed assumptions, such as the ad hoc consensus assumptions,
would be less likely to be compatible with a specific model.

The evidence provides some insight into which of these perspectives is the more fruitful. Fortunately, these data are fairly clear across models and forecast periods. Unfortu-

nately, the results differ depending on which variable is examined. Individual assumptions tend to produce more accurate real GNP forecasts than the common or consensus assumptions, reflecting perhaps the forecasters' implicit policy reaction function which attaches major importance to stabilizing real GNP. In contrast, the common consensus assumptions tended to produce more accurate inflation forecasts than the modeler's own individual assumptions. This result is more consistent with the traditional view of a model as independent of the model user. The individual's unique knowledge of the model is not particularly helpful for generating accurate inflation forecasts, at least over a two-year horizon.

5. Model (ex post) accuracy versus forecast accuracy cannot be predicted on the basis of the evidence presented here. Forecast errors may either overestimate or underestimate the deficiency of a model viewed as a conditional relationship between input and output variables.

The input assumptions chosen ex ante to generate a forecast are bound to be counterfactual. To the extent that the actual assumptions enhance accuracy, the forecast error overstates the deficiency in the conditional model. In practice, much evidence suggests that the counterfactual (ex ante) assumptions work to offset model deficiencies—that ex post model solutions, those based on actual input assumptions, are typically inferior to the ex ante forecast. These results are consistent with the view in Lucas [1] that conditional models are flawed but that the model users can somehow offset these model deficiencies and generate reliable ex ante forecasts.

The limited evidence on this issue presented here is extremely mixed. For model 3, the ex post forecasts of real GNP were distinctly inferior to the ex ante real GNP forecasts, but the inflation forecasts were clearly superior. For model 1, the ex post real GNP forecasts were distinctly inferior in the first forecast but somewhat superior in the second period, when ex post inflation rate simulations were inferior to the ex ante. The results for model 2 are even more ambiguous, except for the inflation rate in the second forecast period where the ex post simulation was more accurate than the ex ante forecasts. This evidence, in other words, does not provide support for either extreme position on the relative accuracy of ex post and ex ante forecasts.

As noted at the outset, these conclusions are based on a very limited number of observations and may well not hold in the future. The experiment is an ongoing one, to try to determine under what circumstances the conclusions hold and when they do not. In addition, future research on this topic should examine more variables and perhaps include more models. Much more experience will be required to understand why forecasts differ and to evaluate the reasons for their differences.

NOTES

1. The five models participating were those of Data Resources, Inc. of Lexington, MA; Fairmodel, Macro Inc.; Center for Econometric Model Research, Indiana University; Research Seminar in Quantitative Economics, University of Michigan; Allen Sinai at The Boston Company Inc.

2. Using what appears to be a more heterogeneous group of models, Wallis et al. (1986) argue that differences in the degree of exogeneity are of little practical importance for comparisons of models of the United Kingdom's economy. Accordingly, they consistently find differences in exogenous variable assumptions account for little of the differences among forecasts.

REFERENCE

1. R. E. Lucas, Jr., "Econometric Policy Evaluation: A Critique," *The Phillips Curve and Labor Markets* (Carnegie-Rochester Conferences on Public Policy 1) (K. Brunner and A. H. Meltzer, eds.), American Elsevier, New York, pp. 19–46 (1976).

BIBLIOGRAPHY

M. K. Evans, Y. Haitovsky, and G. I. Treyz, "An Analysis of Forecasting Properties of U.S. Econometric Models," *Econometric Models of Cyclical Behavior,* (B. G. Hickman, ed.), National Bureau of Economic Research, New York (1972).

Y. Haitovsky and G. I. Treyz, "Forecasts with Quarterly Macroeconomic Models, Equation Adjustments, and Benchmark Predictions: The U.S. Experience." *Rev. Econ. Stat.*, *54*: 317–25 (1972).

K. F. Wallis, ed., *Models of the UK Economy: A Review by ESRC Macroeconomic Modelling Bureau*, vols. 1–4, Oxford University Press, New York (1984–1987).

52

Cost-Benefit Analysis and Administrative Legitimation[1]

Robert C. Zinke

Since the mid-1970s, regulatory processes have undergone a "crisis of legitimacy," reflecting larger doubts about the administrative process as a whole. Given the conflicting demands and doubts raised by critics, regulatory reformers have sought new or refined methodological tools to generate rules and regulations. Of the methodological approaches developed and advocated by regulatory reformers to overcome the crisis of legitimacy, cost-benefit decision-making techniques have become the most popular and widely accepted. As Meier [2, p. 287] recently noted: "Cost-benefit analysis is perhaps the most intuitively attractive reform proposed for regulation. Nothing could make more sense than to issue regulations only if the regulation provided more benefits than costs. Cost-benefit analysis has been the cornerstone of regulatory reform efforts of the last three presidents."

Cost-benefit analysis, as a regulatory reform approach, has gained acceptance on the basis that scientific objectivity and economic rationality in regulatory decision making will restore administrative legitimacy. Underlying this view is the assumption that "administrative legitimacy" refers to the ability of administrative institutions to implement and enforce public policies and programs in a way that gains the support of the majority of citizens. This assumption underlies the use of cost-benefit analysis in regulatory and administrative decision making. It has also generated, in part, intense debate and discussion regarding the desirability and applicability of cost-benefit approaches to regulatory reform.

Source: *Policy Studies Journal*, *16*(1): 63–88 (1987).

[1]Much of this paper draws from the author's unpublished doctoral dissertation: *Cost-Benefit Analysis and Administrative Decision Making: A Methodological Case-Study of the Relation of Social Science to Public Policy*, Graduate School of Public Administration, New York University, February 1984 [1].

Cost-benefit analysis has been a focal point of dispute in several court cases, and the subject of heated debates in Congress.[2] In addition, it has been a central issue in controversies surrounding the Reagan Administration's "deregulation" of the American economy through the use of Executive Orders and administrative rulemaking.[3]

This paper examines the legitimation assumptions underlying cost-benefit approaches to regulatory reform. It explores the implications of those assumptions and argues that cost-benefit approaches tend to further undermine the legitimacy of administrative and regulatory processes. The primary issue surrounding cost-benefit analysis is the arbitrariness with which it is imposed, and not the merits or demerits of the technique itself. By arguing that cost-benefit approaches restore the legitimacy of administrative and regulatory processes by making decisions more scientifically objective and economically efficient, proponents of the technique already assume, or have decided arbitrarily, that social scientific and economic criteria represent the most salient grounds on which public policies should be judged and the exercise of administrative power justified. In democratic societies, however, it is the normative political conditions under which public policy deliberations take place that determine the legitimacy of policies. Knowledge, or claims to knowledge, alone do not suffice as legitimations of the use of power.

ADMINISTRATIVE LEGITIMACY AND THE EMERGENCE OF COST-BENEFIT APPROACH TO REGULATORY REFORM

O'Toole [6] argues that an "orthodoxy of reform" has remained an integral part of administrative thought since the turn of the century. Nowhere has the reform tradition been more evident than the area of regulatory theory and practice. Since the late 1880s, critics have raised doubts about either the constitutionality or the viability of using administrative agencies to enforce regulatory policies. Some argued that the reform tradition failed to produce significant changes in regulatory policy. They began to link the failure of regulatory reform efforts with a "recurring sense of crisis" regarding "the legitimacy of American administrative institutions as a whole" [7, p. 7]. Dubnick and Gitelson [8] argued, for example: "In spite of all the efforts devoted to understanding and dealing with problems associated with regulation, we seem no more informed today than we were at the turn of the century and no more capable of making significant changes in regulatory programs than we were when reforms were first contemplated."

Based on a perceived crisis of legitimacy, a variety of newly refined analytical and theoretical perspectives gained attention. Cost-benefit analysis, around since the early 1900s, became the most important of these approaches. As Paris and Reynolds [9, p. 111] pointed out, cost-benefit analysis:

> seems to combine empirical predictions of the results of proposed policy alternatives with normative evaluations of positive and negative consequences (costs and benefits). It is one of the few approaches within the broad economic tradition that has been extensively developed at both the theoretical and applied levels. . . . There is also a vast literature addressing the measurement problems associated with cost-

---

[2]See *American Textile Manufacturers Institute, Inc., et. al. v. Raymond J. Donovan*, 49 *Law Week* 4720 (June 16, 1981); *American Iron and Steel Institute v. O.S.H.A.*, 577 F.2d 825 (1978). For examples of debates in Congress, see refs. 3 and 4.

[3]See for example, ref. 5.

benefit analysis and assessing the costs and benefits of actual policy proposals. Government agencies frequently undertake or commission cost-benefit studies. Cost-benefit analysis is clearly very important to contemporary policy arguments.

COST-BENEFIT ANALYSIS AND ITS CLAIMS TO RESTORE ADMINISTRATIVE LEGITIMACY

At its most basic level, cost-benefit analysis builds on the commonsense notion that decision makers should systematically examine the advantages and disadvantages of the possible decisions they could or might make. As Gramlich [10, pp. 2–3] argues: "It may be couched in fancy terms, such as the Johnson Administration's Planning Programming and Budgeting System (PPBS). It may be worshipped as yet another herald of the Age of Technology, or feared and rejected because it tries to put dollar amounts on underlying values. But ultimately, something like it must necessarily be employed in any rational decision." Specifically, "cost-benefit analysis is a way of setting out the factors which need to be taken into account in making certain economic choices" [11, p. 685]. Since the early 1900s, this approach can and has been applied to public investment decisions to deal with such matters as "whether or not a particular project is worthwhile, which is the best of several alternative projects, or when to undertake a particular project." In addition, it has been used to evaluate proposed law changes, changes in regulations or rulemaking, and proposed price control policies [11, p. 685].

Regulatory reformers point to three general arguments for cost-benefit decision making techniques: (1) They improve the rationality of regulatory decisions, (2) they reduce the level of unnecessary conflict surrounding regulatory and administrative processes, and (3) they are useful for all types of policymaking.

Improved Rationality of Regulatory Decisions

The conception of "rationality" underlying arguments for cost-benefit analysis derive from common economic and legal assumptions about individual decision making in market societies, and from social scientific assumptions concerning the need for verifiable and replicable data in analytical studies. Traditionally, "rational behavior" has referred to instrumental modes of thought in decision making, where alternative courses of action are systematically examined and weighed to find the most efficient means to achieve a given end [12, p. 26]. One of the strongest proponents of this view, Murray Weidenbaum, testified before Congress that when used by government agencies, cost-benefit analyses "have provided some basis for ranking and comparing projects and choosing among alternatives," and that "the overriding value of benefit-cost analysis has been in demonstrating the importance of making relatively objective economic evaluations of essentially political actions and perhaps narrowing the area in which subjective factors dominate." Thus, he notes, "If economically inefficient programs are approved, at least government decision makers know the price that is being paid for those actions [13].

Weidenbaum's remarks suggest that cost-benefit analysis allows—or even requires —government agencies to reduce the consideration of "subjective political factors" in favor of "objective economic evaluations" in their decision-making processes. At this point the scientific canons of empirical verification and replication enter in the discussion.

Cost-benefit proponents assume that the use of social-scientific research criteria insures that any incorrect or fraudulently presented data can be detected by citizens as long as the methods for data collection and the decision-making criteria are made available and known to citizens. Agency decisions can be independently inferred from the data disclosed by the agency. Stokey and Zeckhauser [14, p. 135] allude to these assumptions when they argue that "If presented in a professional manner, they [cost-benefit techniques] lend themselves to the introduction of alternative sets of assumptions that enable the policy maker *and his critics* to see whether different conclusions would emerge. Thus, an important contribution of cost-benefit analysis is the information it provides to the political process."

Generally, the proponents' arguments suggest that the required use of cost-benefit analysis improves decision-making rationality in administrative agencies since it permanently incorporates economic and social-scientific canons into regulatory processes.

Reduction of Conflict Surrounding Administrative and Regulatory Processes

The claim that cost-benefit analysis helps reduce unnecessary conflict surrounding regulatory and administrative processes derives from two related sets of claims: cost-benefit approaches seek to establish "realistic" compromises in policy disputes, rather than "idealistic" but "impractical" consensual agreements; and the use of cost-benefit analysis brings bureaucratic decision-making criteria "back in line" with the most widely held principles in society.

Cost-benefit proponents suggest that real, "objective interests" exist and must be taken into account in public policy decisions, and that cost-benefit analysis helps both decision makers and citizens see these interests. For example, Leonard and Zeckhauser [15], acknowledging that policy decisions should conform with any social consensus of opinion, argue that decision processes which require "explicit consent" are unworkable and unrealistic because of the full-discussion requirements. They suggest that cost-benefit analysis provides a "second best" solution to the problem by allowing analysts and policymakers to identify the point at which a compromise or settlement can be reached without a full discussion:

> We believe that the benefit-cost criterion is a useful way of defining "hypothetical consent" for centralized decisions affecting individuals with widely divergent interests: hypothetically, if compensation could be paid, all would agree to the decision offering the highest net benefits. [15, p. 6]

Some proponents further suggest that cost-benefit analysis helps minimize possible negative public reaction by allowing decision makers to anticipate any questions regarding the legitimacy of public policies or programs and make necessary alterations. Arguing for "social cost-benefit analysis," Luft [16, p. 260] contends that, "In these times when the 'silent majority' is no longer silent, it is imperative that the decision-maker be provided with information that identifies implementation problems and predicts individual reactions prior to undertaking a project."

In essence, the arguments of Leonard and Zeckhauser and Luft suggest that cost-benefit analysis resolves policy disputes through prior analysis and elimination of potential issues reflecting hidden or latent conflicts. By assuring the public that the "neutral" criteria of cost-benefit analysis are used in decision making, these proponents suggest, conflicts that disrupt the administrative legitimation of public policies and programs can be avoided.

At this point, a second major assumption regarding conflict resolution emerges. According to proponents, cost-benefit decision making techniques conform with the "implicit consensus" in American society that all public policy decisions be based on voluntary agreements between individuals, either in the marketplace or in constitutionally-established policy making institutions. Pointing to a "problem of governmental encroachment on U.S. business," Weidenbaum [17, pp. 9–10] argues:

> the concern with the future of our economic system may be seen as a reflection of a more basic desire to maintain and strengthen the free and voluntary society of which the economy is a vital but only a constituent part. Boiled down to its essence, economic freedom is inseparable from political freedom.

Bureaucratic institutions, according to cost-benefit proponents, must base their rules and regulations, when possible, on voluntary agreements between themselves and those citizens and groups who are affected by administrative actions. Cost-benefit analysis helps administrative agencies use voluntary agreements to implement policies and programs by providing larger, more neutral grounds on which "regulatory agreements" can be based. Edwards [18, pp. 34–35] implicitly refers to these assumptions:

> Cost-benefit analysis attempts to reflect a broader consensus of values in the "valuation" function than other approaches. It seeks values or priorities from the society as a whole rather than from specific decision makers. Cost-benefit analysis is based on the assumption that the prices of goods and services determined in an open market adequately reflect the priorities, preferences, and values of the society for those goods and services.

> Ultimately, cost-benefit proponents suggest that conflict reduction rests with the ability of administrators to implement public policies without creating conflict-laden issues regarding policymaking processes in general. According to proponents, cost-benefit analysis helps administrators avoid conflict by allowing them to find the point of "hypothetical consent" at which both regulators and those who are affected by regulatory actions can come to compromise settlements.

The Universality of Cost-Benefit Decision-Making Techniques

An underlying theme in the previous arguments concerns the general applicability of cost-benefit analysis to all types of policies. At a deeper level, proponents claim cost-benefit analysis is relevant and a appropriate in all decision-making contexts. Lave [119, pp. 3–4] argues that "government decisions in general and regulatory decisions in particular can be improved by subjecting the alternatives to benefit-cost analysis." This view has led other proponents to claim that cost-benefit analysis reflects a "natural" decision-making logic used by all decision makers whether they are aware of it or not. James C. Miller argues that administrative agencies "have an implicit benefit-cost framework" and that "although on many occasions the full array of benefits and costs and how they are weighted is not described for the public in adequate detail, nevertheless the very fact that decisions are made reveals that some assessment and weighing takes place [13]. Similarly, John McAdams [20, p. 94] contends that "in practice" any political decision regarding the allocation of funds among competing programs "is almost certain to be the result of a cost-benefit analysis which is implicit, covert, and indeed even unconscious."

On the basis of arguments similar to these, Charles Schultz suggests that public policy makers rely on a "natural marketplace of ideas" to decide what courses of action to follow, and he implies that cost-benefit analysis can be used to calculate political as well as economic marginal constraints:

> Because values conflict among different groups and among themselves, securing the agreement necessary to pursue one line of action must often reduce the

opportunity to pursue other lines of action . . . These costs dictate a set of efficiency criteria for political decisions equally as real and valid as the resource costs which lead to the efficiency criteria of systematic costs analysis.[4]

Proponents suggest that just as knowledge of economics helps private-sector decision makers optimize their opportunities for profit making and for goods and services acquisition in the marketplace, so cost-benefit analysis helps policymakers "maximize" the public interest pursued in policymaking processes: "Economists can provide these decision makers (elected officials) with information via benefit-cost analysis and analysis of the distributional impact of regulations, leaving the final decision to society's representatives. These individuals are better able to make objective decisions with such information on the impacts of the actions they contemplate" [22, pp. 359–360].

Methodologically, the assumptions and arguments outlined imply that the "objective interests" of rationality, guiding the formulation and the use of cost-benefit analyses, are separate from the political interests attached to the "subjective" views of participants in policy disputes. Cost-benefit analysis is assumed to be a "neutral," nonpolitical technique that does not presuppose any particular course of action. As Weidenbaum [22, p. 63] argues, "Benefit/cost analysis is a neutral concept; the same weight is given to a dollar of costs as to a dollar of benefit. There is no advance assurance that a benefit/cost approach will support a given regulation or that it will condemn it."

For proponents, the "methodological neutrality" of cost-benefit analysis serves as the unifying link between the improvement of rationality in decision making and the reduction of political and legal conflict. The technique is appropriate for all types of policy situations and circumstances because it reflects a "natural" logic of decision making. In short, the use of cost-benefit analysis restores legitimacy to the administrative process through its reliance on a decision-making logic that any "rational" citizen can understand and accept.

THE COST-BENEFIT CONCEPTION OF "LEGITIMACY"

The claims made for cost-benefit approaches derive from a particular, underlying conception of "legitimacy," and they reflect basic a priori assumptions regarding the nature of the relation of social science to public policy.

Cost-benefit analysis, as a regulatory reform approach, has emerged in response to the view that public demands for efficient and effective governmental action should be reconciled with the legal and constitutional traditions of our society, thus restoring administrative legitimacy. Underlying this view is the assumption that "administrative legitimacy" refers to the ability of administrative institutions to implement and enforce public policies and programs in a way that gains the support of the majority of citizens. Here, the legitimation of political institutions represents a communication, or "learning," process, and the level of public support for a policy or program represents an accurate indicator of the level of legitimacy accorded governmental institutions by citizens. From this perspective, parties engaged in policy discussions are really seeking to "discover" the point at which a social consensus can ideally be reached. A given policy can then be explained in such a way that all citizens can understand what the policy is seeking to do and why it is necessary; citizens will be able to see the "objective necessity" of the policy, and understand that, given the circumstances and the existing balance of power among competing interests, it was the

---

[4]Quoted by Alan Williams [21, p. 65].

only possible course of action that could be taken [15]. Ultimately, from this perspective, it is the knowledge produced and distributed by administrative decision makers which either succeeds or fails in legitimating public policies and programs.[5]

The conception of "legitimacy" outlined above hinges on an a priori assumption regarding the methodological relation of social science to public policymaking. Gunnell has suggested that traditional social science approaches to social reform assume that social science is related to policy in much the same way that theory is related to practice, and that theory is related to practice in the same way that thought relates to action:

> The view is that the mind reasons and the body executes and that theory is the primary faculty of the mind. It is assumed that "knowing how," or intelligent action, depends on "knowing that," or having access to true propositions or correct rules of procedure . . . The assumption is that there is a "given" or logical link between theory and rational practice and that the former is the precondition of the latter. [24, p. 35]

Similarly, Rein [25, p. 362] argues that the traditional social science concern to link social science with public policy stems from the epistemological assumption that knowledge exists independently of action and that the function of social science analysis is to "translate" knowledge of empirical realities into "workable" public policies. Traditionally, social scientists have assumed that the "logical link between theory and practice" should translate into *empirically observable connections* between social science research and public policy [25]. These assumptions underly the use of cost-benefit analysis in regulatory and administrative decision making. They have also generated, in part, intense debate and discussion regarding the desirability and applicability of cost-benefit approaches to regulatory reform.

THE COST-BENEFIT DEBATE: ARGUMENTS AND COUNTERARGUMENTS

Despite claims that cost-benefit analysis restores administrative legitimacy, the use of the technique for public policy and regulatory decision making has come under attack on at least three levels of argument: scientific, moral, and political.

On scientific grounds, critics question the status of cost-benefit analysis as "hard" value-free science. First, the critics argue, cost-benefit analysis has often not been conducted in any systematic way, such that (1) the assumptions underlying cost-benefit studies are made explicit; (2) all the evidence used in the analysis is comprehensively presented; and (3) the results of the analysis are adequately communicated and specified for independent replication in other analyses [26,27]. A second criticism on scientific grounds centers on the question of whether analyses are conducted fairly and objectively. Here, conflict of interest charges have been levied at those who conduct the analyses [28]. Finally, a third criticism centers on the precision of analysts in their calculations of enumerated costs and benefits. Given the fact that analysts must often rely on "shadow prices" and uncertain discount rates of future market values of costs and benefits, the figures arrived at by analysts are often unreliable and imprecise in measuring the factors which are valued [29]. In this regard, one Congressional study concluded that "when subjective valuation is unavoidable, benefit/cost analysis is neither neutral nor objective" [29, p. 515]. Generally, the critics

---

[5]For a full discussion of traditional social science approaches to legitimation, see Paul D. Rosen [23, pp. 75–95].

charge, cost-benefit analysis is open to abuse and fraud by those who utilize it in making policy decisions.

On moral and ethical grounds, opponents of cost-benefit analysis argue that the least-cost, net-worth test of public programs reflects the moral principles of utilitarianism. On the basis of this philosophical association, critics argue that (1) the normative assumptions underlying the use of cost-benefit techniques are morally deficient, and (2) as a set of normative principles to be followed in resolving policy questions, cost-benefit criteria are not appropriate for certain types of decisions.

Concerning the inadequacy of the ethical assumptions underlying cost-benefit techniques, critics often point to the arguments against utilitarianism posited by moral philosophers. Alasdair MacIntyre [30], for example, argues that the ethical stance of utilitarianism and the use of cost-benefit analysis in public and private bureaucracies reflect the same "central errors and distortions." Among his complaints, MacIntyre argues that no scale of measurement exists that allows incommensurable activities or values to be compared, weighed, or ranked against one another; accordingly, before a utilitarian test is performed, the decision maker must adopt a framework that provides a "prior scheme of values by means of which goods and evils, pleasures and pains, benefits and harms are to be ranked" [30, p. 269]. The most common example of this difficulty involves the valuation of human life. MacIntyre notes that each of the various methods for calculating the value of human life produces different valuations, and hence:

> The range of possible different answers to one and the same question that you can extract from the same techniques of cost/benefit analysis makes it clear that all the mathematical sophistication and rigor that may go into the modes of computation may be undermined by the arbitrariness (relative to the mathematics) of the choice to adopt one principle for quantifying [the value of life] rather than another. [30, p. 272]

Overall, MacIntyre suggests that cost-benefit approaches are morally deficient because the ethical stance of utilitarianism, underlying these approaches, allows decision makers and analysts to ignore the moral positions they take when they enter into analytical and decision making processes.

With such criticisms in mind, other critics have gone on to argue that cost-benefit criteria are inapplicable in certain policymaking situations. Steven Kelman [31, p. 33], for instance, argues that "In environmental, safety, and health regulation, there may be many instances where a certain decision might be right even though its benefits do not outweigh its costs," and that there may be "good reasons to oppose efforts to put dollar values on non-marketed benefits and costs." In such policy areas, he concludes, "it is not justifiable to devote major resources to the generation of data for cost-benefit calculations or to undertake efforts to 'spread the gospel' of cost-benefit analysis further."

Overall, the criticisms at the moral level of debate focus on the "technical feasibility and limits" of cost-benefit analysis and on the "appropriateness of this technique to certain classes of problems and the value implications of its use in the analysis of these problems" [32, p. 200].

On political grounds, critics charge that "increasing the use of cost-benefit analysis changes the nature of decision making," and that "it closes off opportunities for public debate, and substitutes control by a new breed of "experts" who subtly manipulate the evaluation so that it conforms to the procedures of the market-place" [33]. These charges are based on three interrelated arguments: (1) Cost-benefit analysis is not a value-free, neutral technique, (2) the use of social science techniques in public-policymaking, generally, serves particular class interests in society, and (3) cost-benefit analysis imputes a normative, substantive content to public policymaking.

Regarding the charge that cost-benefit analysis is not value-free or neutral, Tribe [34] argues that cost-benefit techniques (as well as the policy sciences in general) are inherently ideological. He suggests that the social science adherence to the objectivist ideals is itself a normative stance which "may substantively structure the characteristics and the conclusions of a given mode of thought," and which "distorts the perspective afforded by the policy sciences" [34, p. 78].

The critics also charge that the model of knowledge utilization underlying cost-benefit approaches reflects particular class interests in society. Weiss argues that social science researchers, rather than being "disinterested bystanders," often exude a desire to increase the social status and prestige of their disciplines, gain a greater voice in swaying public policy, and make public policy according to their own beliefs and values [35, p. 7].

Other scholars suggest that the "knowledge-should-inform-action" perspective represents the view of business decision makers, and that advocating this view implicitly or explicitly supports traditional capitalist conceptions of the social function of knowledge. Deshpande found that private-sector decision makers "seem to react to specific research studies in a stimulus-response manner," and that the main goal of social science research produced for business decision making was to "provide knowledge for action rather than for understanding or enlightenment" [36, pp. 317–330]. Leiss [37] suggests that the "knowledge-for-action" view derives from the political concerns of early capitalist societies to maintain social stability, and at the same time, "retain(s) the principle of self-interest as the only source of obligation in society." According to Leiss, liberal political theory, as it developed in the seventeenth century, sought to promote the "inculcation of rational self-interest (individuals properly instructed in the principles of reason)," and to justify the ascendance to power of those who "could demonstrate a capacity for the rational understanding of their interests." From this perspective, knowledge is seen as a commodity, and "those who are able to organize or manage the use of this commodity will derive individually the material benefits of it" [37, pp. 178–179].

Finally, critics charge, cost-benefit techniques impute a substantive content to policymaking. Writers such as Byrne [32], Hoos [38], Self [39], Lilienfeld [40], and Wildavsky[41] argue that at best, these techniques serve to reinforce the ideological tenets of market capitalism and, at worst, serve to undermine democratic ideals in favor of what critics term an "administrative state." Wildavsky argues that cost-benefit analysis seeks its validity from the political theory that "in a free society the economy is to serve the individuals' consistent preferences revealed and rationally pursued in the marketplace," and that "governments are not supposed to dictate preferences or make policies." According to Wildavsky [41, p. 58], "This individualist theory assumes as valid the current distribution of income. Preferences are valued in the marketplace where votes are based on disposable income."

Hoos [38] suggests that the systems framework in which social cost-benefit analysis has been conceived has "encouraged emphasis on the wrong questions and provided answers the more dangerous for having been achieved through 'scientific' or 'rational' means." This has resulted in "a systematic foreclosing of promising avenues toward possible improvement and reform." Thus, "Cost-benefit ratios, program budgeting and other procedures have forced preoccupation with only limited and arbitrarily delineated facets of public affairs, with the objective more likely to be bureaucratic self-justification than the general social welfare [38, p. 32, p. 242].

On the basis of these arguments, Byrne [32, pp. 204–205] contends that the conditions required to make cost-benefit methods operational, and policymaking "objective," "would require a profound transformation in the basis of governance." In the world envisioned by cost-benefit approaches, effective public policy must eliminate citizen participation since citizens could only "contaminate" the realization of "objective values" with "subjective assessments of their idiosyncratic circumstances." Here, "government" represents a "consumptive good." "Citizens" are nothing more than "glorified consumers" who merely decide "whether and to what degree they are satisfied with the products of governance;" they have "no responsibility for the production of governance or even overseeing its production." According to Byrne [32, pp. 204–205], the worlds projected by cost-benefit proponents "call for the abandonment of rule by consent in favor of the rule of reason":

> The replacement of consent with reason as the foundation of governance is intended to dispense with the inefficiency and irrationality of politics, but in fact it dispenses with democracy in favor of the administrative state. The issues that normally give rise to questions of democratic participation and consent are simply without salience in the transformed world of cost-benefit analysis. Indeed, the ideals of democracy could not be tolerated in the new world and only its veneer would survive the transformation.

The arguments of the critics point to growing bodies of literature in the areas of the utilization of knowledge and the philosophy of social science which question traditional assumptions underlying cost-benefit analysis regarding the relation of knowledge to action.

EXPLORATIONS IN THE UTILIZATION OF KNOWLEDGE

Findings in the area of knowledge utilization suggest that attempts to fully incorporate cost-benefit analysis into the policy process will probably fail. Basic problems stand in the way of direct translations of social science research into policymaking: (1) There exist inherent barriers to the application of research to policy issues; (2) there are diverse meanings attached to terms such as "using research" and "knowledge utilization"; and (3) knowledge is often produced only in response to certain guiding interests in society and derives its status as "knowledge" from those interests.

Scholars have identified a host of factors which act as inherent barriers to the direct application of research in policymaking. First, the organizational–institutional context in which knowledge is used may limit the extent of utilization of social science research. In addition, given differences and changes in conceptual paradigms and theoretical frameworks, policymakers may hesitate to adopt or accept only one piece of research as authoritative [42–44].

How the use of knowledge is defined also poses a problem. Scholars in the field have identified a variety of ways in which policymakers and administrators use knowledge [35, pp. 11–16]. The multiplicity of knowledge utilization models leads some scholars to argue that knowledge and action should be seen as two poles on a continuum, from more passive "fact gathering" to more action "control" oriented uses of scientific research. This framework, as Bulmer suggests, avoids "the misleading and unsatisfactory dichotomy between 'basic' and 'applied' research, doing greater justice to the complexity of the actual patterns of influence between social science research and policy" [45, p. 206].

Finally, it appears that any conception of the production of knowledge and its use reflects the social and political interests of society and is embedded in basic cultural structures and institutions. Rein [25, p. 362] has argued: "Knowing and acting are linked when people's livelihood and social position depend on the social importance of theory. That theory precedes and should influence action is an idea which supports a socially defined group in society and, in this sense, is a class interest. Ideas are set forth as the stock in trade of various occupational groups, including both academics and policymakers."

In this vein, Holzner and Marx [46, pp. 122–123] refer to "epistemic communities" composed of members who share a common framework for understanding the world and share "a mode of knowing characteristic of themselves." For such communities, "particular knowledge-related criteria take precedence over other criteria of judgment," and their status "in the social structure has much to do with the manner in which the community can achieve autonomy and maintain its particular frame of reference."

Taking the epistemic community as a point of departure, Crable [47] argues for the conception of "knowledge-as-status." From this perspective, "knowledge" refers to "an argumentative claim, the status of which is the consensual, but not timeless, acceptance by the most competent judge(s) of the claim." According to Crable [47, pp. 250, 262]:

> What is considered "knowledge" in a particular field will progress, digress, regress, and so forth on the basis of the analysis of the reasons for and against the change. Those reasons will be advanced and analyzed in a rhetorically epistemological way. Knowledge-as-status is conferred—and altered—through socially and academically argumentative processes.

Overall, the findings in the knowledge utilization literature suggest that the relation of social science to public policy is more complex than what many mainstream social scientists have assumed. Indeed, they point to deeper, methodological, epistemological issues.

EXPLORATIONS IN THE PHILOSOPHY OF SOCIAL SCIENCE

In the philosophy of social science, where the problem of relating knowledge to action has reached critical proportions, the findings suggest that (1) scientific naturalism, underlying the cost-benefit position, represents only one of several epistemological frameworks competing for acceptance among social science philosophers; and (2) an adequate theory of social and political reform must be based on the insights of each of these competing frameworks.[6]

A larger methodological controversy underlies the cost-benefit debate. Cost-benefit approaches are grounded on the epistemological tenets of neo-positivism and scientific naturalism, the main heirs of logical positivism.[7] At the level of the philosophy of social science, however, the neo-positivist/scientific naturalist position has created renewed controversy concerning positivist tenets taken as a whole.

Bernstein [48] identifies three alternative frameworks that raise questions concerning scientific naturalism: analytical philosophy, social phenomenology, and "critical" social theory. Analytical philosophers (such as Winch, Louch, and Taylor) have argued that the

---

[6]Much of the discussion in this section derives from Richard J. Bernstein [48].

[7]These include: (1) "*the unity of the scientific method*," which asserts the method's applicability to both the natural and the social sciences; (2) individually observed cases of social phenomenon can be subsumed and explained under "hypothetically proposed *general laws*"; (3) the belief that "*the relation of theory to practice is primarily technical*," allowing for the manipulation of natural conditions to achieve social goals and objectives; and (4) the belief that only scientific knowledge is *testable*, that is, it can be refuted with further observation (outlined in [49]).

use of any language presupposes the validity of an underlying ideology. As Bernstein [48, pp. 138, 141] notes, the analytical philosophers have increased our awareness "that human beings are self-interpreting creatures, and that these interpretations are constitutive of what we are as human beings." Their works have "helped us to see how limiting and constraining are the framework assumptions of mainstream social science."

Social phenomenology, as set forth in the works of Husserl [50], Schutz [51], and Berger and Luckman [52], emphasizes the necessity of studying social phenomena to identify the structural rules of interaction, constitutive of human behavior. The phenomenological critique of the scientific naturalist position focuses on the perspective that naturalist frameworks force on individual social scientists. As Schutz argues, naturalism takes the "life-world" for granted: "Naturalists do not account for the way which this social reality is constituted and maintained, in what ways it is intersubjective, or how actors in their common-sense thinking interpret their own actions and the actions of others" [48, p. 138]. The result is that positivists and naturalists "objectify" reality; that is, they prematurely close off investigations of certain aspects of reality which are problematic or questionable [52].

The third alternative position focuses on the need for critical social theory—that is, theory which moves beyond existing realities and points the way toward the literation of people from past and contemporary thought forms. To be critical, social theory must enable policy analysts to be "self-reflective" concerning the value interests they serve or promote. This does not mean that researchers merely recognize the value assumptions they implicitly or explicitly draw on, but also that they promote "processes of self-reflection and self-understanding . . . among those to whom the theory is directed, thereby dissolving reified power relations and resistances" [48, p. 215].

Critical theorists emphasize that the relation of theory to practice is not technical in orientation; rather the relation is "prudential," based on practical considerations of the contexts in which scientific, or any other kind of theoretical knowledge, is applied. "Practical discourse directed toward political action cannot be reduced to technical control or the technical application of theoretical knowledge, for this distorts human social life and the medium of communicative action" [48, p. 219].

Critical theory does not argue that a science of society is impossible, but rather that it is one-sided. In this sense, the debate concerning cost-benefit approaches to policymaking is misguided; the underlying issue is not a question of whether one technique or methodological position is better than another. As Bernstein [48, p. 235] argues:

> In the final analysis we are not confronted with exclusive choices: *either* empirical theory *or* interpretative theory *or* critical theory. Rather, there is an internal dialectic in the restructuring of social and political theory: when we work through any one of these moments, we discover how the others are implicated. An adequate social and political theory must be *empirical, interpretive, and critical.*

The considerations in the philosophy of social science suggest that many "logics" and "modes of reasoning" are available to public policymakers, and that any reform measure based on a *single* logic is unlikely to gain full acceptance or legitimacy since one mode of reasoning alone cannot meet the varying demands of different policy contexts. On the basis of these considerations, policy scholars such as Fischer and Forester have developed critical-theory frameworks that integrate the empirical and the normative modes of reasoning. The frameworks can be used by decision makers in different policy contexts [53; 54, pp. 23–31].

Cost-benefit analysis may provide valuable data or serve as the basis for empirical arguments, but it represents only one of many perspectives that policy makers must consider.

In addition, the assumptions of universality underlying the cost-benefit framework may require reformulation. White's recent arguments regarding research in public administration apply equally to policy research: "Insofar as the criteria of validity, testability, and causality are derived from the orthodox models of explanation and theory, they need to be rethought in light of the developments in the philosophy of science, and they should not be imposed on all research situations" [55, pp. 15–24].

Most cost-benefit policy reforms appear to arbitrarily place the empirical, traditional economics component of social research above the normative and the critical perspectives and seek to have this component imposed on administrative decision makers at the expense of the other perspectives. (The Reagan Administration's attempt to impose cost-benefit criteria on regulatory decision making under Executive Order 12291 exemplifies this single-emphasis approach.) Yet, as Forester [54, p. 30] suggests, single-logic reform strategies such as those offered by cost-benefit proponents are likely to fail. "If practical strategies are context dependent and contexts in practice vary widely, always changing, then rational action and decision making will fail in a technical search for a one-best recipe."

COST-BENEFIT ANALYSIS AND THE NORMATIVE, CONTEXTUAL DIMENSION OF "LEGITIMACY"

Attempts to impose cost-benefit analysis in policy contexts where cost-benefit criteria are inappropriate raise questions regarding the sincerity of reformers in truly solving the problems to which the technique is to be applied. Such attempts may serve to further delegitimate the decision-making processes of administrative institutions.

The critics' concern rests with the contextual *conditions* under which parties to policy discussions agree or might agree to use cost-benefit analysis in the determination of a policy consensus. Those who suggest that cost-benefit approaches fail to meet *scientific* standards really argue that the use of the technique to legitimate public policies relies on the "aura" surrounding scientific pursuits to justify goals or values which cannot be scientifically proven. Thus, its use misleads policy discussants. On *moral* grounds, criticisms that the technique contains technical limitations (such as the problem of valuing human life) and that its use is not appropriate in handling certain types of policy issues underscore the way in which value commitments go unexamined by policy discussants themselves. Finally, on *political* grounds, criticisms regarding the ideological basis of cost-benefit analysis suggest that the success of the technique in conflict reduction depends upon the "domination" of social interests with a stake in social scientific modes of decision making rationality over other interests with stakes in alternative "logics."

Generally, the criticisms against cost-benefit approaches appeal to a conception of legitimacy that involves more than just the development of a "technical index of the politics of domination" to determine the extent to which citizens accept and support public policies [23, p. 85]. The criticisms appeal to a conception that can be invoked as a standard to judge the reasons set forth for using administrative institutions to justify public policies and programs at all. Under this alternative conception, as Habermas points out, the *"claim to legitimacy* is related to the social-integrative preservation of a normatively determined social identity," and *"legitimations* serve to make good this claim, that is, to show how and why existing (or recommended) institutions are fit to employ political power in such a way that the values constitutive for the identity of the society will be realized" [56, pp. 182–183]. When cost-benefit arguments are used to legitimate the administrative exercise of power, the normative conditions under which cost-benefit based decisions should be accepted as true and relevant to the specific policy issues at hand must be spelled out before such decisions are implemented by administrative agencies.

By arguing that cost-benefit approaches restore the legitimacy of administrative and regulatory processes by making decisions more scientifically objective and economically efficient, proponents of the technique already assume, or have decided arbitrarily, that social scientific and economic criteria represent the most salient grounds on which public policies should be judged and the exercise of administrative power justified.

The concerns of the critics suggest that knowledge and action are separate domains of experience. Instead, the relations of social science to policy, and of knowledge to action, depend upon the normative conditions under which the relations themselves have been formed. As Habermas [56, pp. 187–188] contends:

> Today it is neither ultimate nor penultimate grounds that provide legitimation. Whoever maintains this is operating at the level of the Middle Ages. Only the rules and communicative presuppositions that make it possible to distinguish an accord or agreement among free and equals from a contingent or forced consensus have legitimating force today. Whether such rules and communicative presuppositions can best be interpreted and explained with the help of natural law constructions and contract theories or in the concepts of a transcendental philosophy or a pragmatics of language or even in the framework of a theory of the development of moral consciousness is secondary in the present context.

The arbitrarinesses with which cost-benefit criteria are imposed on administrative decision processes represents the real, primary issue underlying the cost-benefit debate, not the merits or demerits of the technique itself.

CONCLUSIONS AND IMPLICATIONS

The growth of social science's role in public policymaking took place in the context of increasing pressures on the state to curb the excesses of capitalism, and in response, the state began to take on many of the functions once left to the market mechanism [57–59]. In the past, capitalist theories of the state served to define and legitimate the exercise of power by political institutions. Indeed, it was on the basis of traditional economic theory that the original establishment of modern administrative institutions at the turn of the century was justified [60]. Today, it appears that capitalist economic theories which once seemed to legitimate administrative institutions have just as easily been used to delegitimate those same institutions. The rise of cost-benefit analysis and other social scientific approaches to administrative reform appear to have corresponded to the new theoretical mood toward administrative institutions. Thus, the answer to the question of whether administrative institutions can or should justify public policies and programs with economic and social scientific modes of discourse in policy debates appears to be that they can and they should. But it remains to be seen under what normative conditions the answer to this question has been implicitly or explicitly agreed to. Have cost-benefit and other social-scientific decision-making techniques been adopted under conditions where "equal parties" have acted "freely" in the agreement to use these techniques? Or has the agreement been "forced," based on (1) communicative distortions due to prior ideological commitments, (2) misunderstandings on the part of those who have adopted the techniques, or (3) "systems of domination" which have precluded the discussion of certain problematic questions and issues from arising? From the perspective of "legitimation-as-justification," implicit in the argument of cost-benefit critics, the crisis of administrative legitimacy stems from the apparent failure of most contemporary, mainstream theorists, practitioners, and reformers to answer these questions. As Ackerman [61, p. 373] asserts, "it is only the failure to answer the question of legitimacy that conclusively establishes the illegitimacy of an exercise of power."

REFERENCES

1. R. C. Zinke, "Cost-Benefit Analysis and Administrative Decision Making: A Methodological Case-Study of the Relation of Social Science to Public Policy," unpublished doctoral dissertation, Graduate School of Public Administration, New York University (1984).

2. K. J. Meier, *Regulation: Politics, Bureaucracy, and Economics*, St. Martin's Press, New York (1985).

3. "All Sides Seek Scapegoats: Regulatory Reform Measure Collapses at End of Session," *Congressional Quarterly*, December 13 (1980).

4. "Administration Takes Sweeping Action: Reagan, Congress Planning Regulatory Machinery Repair," *Congressional Quarterly*, March 7 (1981).

5. "OMB Accused of 'Backdoor' Policy Role," *Washington Post*, July 29 (1981).

6. L. J. O'Toole, "American Public Administration and the Idea of Reform," *Admin. Society*, 16(2): 141–166 (1984).

7. J. O. Freedman, *Crisis and Legitimacy: The Administrative Process and American Government*, Cambridge University Press, New York (1978).

8. M. Dubnick and A. R. Gitelson, "Regulatory Policy Analysis: Working in a Quagmire," *Policy Studies Rev.*, 1(3): 423–435 (1982).

9. D. C. Paris and J. F. Reynolds, *The Logic of Policy Inquiry*, Longman, New York (1983).

10. E. M. Gramlich, *Benefit-Cost Analysis of Government Programs*, Prentice-Hall, Englewood Cliffs, N.J. (1981).

11. A. R. Prest and R. Turvey, "Cost-Benefit Analysis: A Survey," *Econ. J.*, December: 683–735 (1965).

12. M. Weber, In *Economy and Society*, Vol I (G. Roth and C. Wittich, eds), University of California Press, Berkeley (1978).

13. U.S. Congress, House Committee on Interstate and Foreign Commerce, *Use of Cost-Benefit Analysis By Regulatory Agencies, Joint Hearings*, Presentation to the Subcommittee on Oversight and Investigations and the Subcommittee on Consumer Protection and Finance, 96th Congress, 1st Session, Serial No. 96-157, Government Printing Office, Washington, D.C., pp. 339, 366 (1979).

14. E. Stokey and R. Zeckhauser, *A Primer for Policy Analysis*, W. W. Norton, New York (1978).

15. H. B. Leonard and R. J. Zeckhauser, "Cost-Benefit Analysis Defended," *Rep. for Philosophy and Public Policy*, 3(3) 6 (1983).

16. H. S. Luft, "Benefit-Cost Analysis and Public Policy Implementation: From Normative to Positive Analysis," *Reaching Decisions in Public Policy and Administration* (R. D. Bingham and M. E. Ethridge, eds.), Longman, New York, p. 260 (1982).

17. M. L. Weidenbaum, *The Future of Business Regulation: Private Action and Public Demand*, American Management Association, New York (1979).

18. L. Edwards, "Cost-Benefit Analysis," *Bureaucrat*, Spring: 34–35 (1981).

19. L. B. Lave, *The Strategy of Social Regulation: Decision Frameworks for Policy*, Brookings Institution, Washington, D.C. (1981).

20. J. McAdams, "The Anti-Policy Analysts," *Policy Studies J.*, 13(1): 91–101 (1984).

21. W. Williams, "Benefit-Cost Analysis: Bastard Science? And/or Insidious Poison in the Body Politic?" *Benefit-Cost and Policy Analysis 1972*, Aldine, Chicago (1973).

22. M. L. Weidenbaum, *Business Government, and the Public*, 2nd ed., Prentice Hall, Englewood Cliffs, N.J. (1981).

23. P. D. Rosen, "Legitimacy, Domination, and Ego Displacement," *Conflict and Control* (A. J. Vidich and R. M. Glassman, eds.), Sage, Beverly Hills, Calif., pp. 75–95 (1979).

24. J. G. Gunnell, "Social Scientific Knowledge and Policy Analysis: A Critique of the Intellectualist Model," *Problems of Theory in Policy Analysis* (P. M. Gregg, ed.), D. C. Heath, Lexington, Mass., p. 35 (1976).

25. M. Rein, "Methodology for the Study of the Interplay between Social Science and Social Policy," *Int. Social Sci. J.*, *32*(2): 361–368 (1980).

26. U.S. Government Accounting Office, *Better Analysis of Uncertainty*, Report submitted to the Congress by the Comptroller General, PAO-78-67, June 2, Government Printing Office, Washington D.C., p. 8 (1978).

27. U.S. Congress, House Committee on Interstate and Foreign Commerce, *Cost-Benefit Analysis: The Potential for Conflict of Interest*, Hearings by Subcommittee on Oversight and Investigations, April 17, June 17, August 22, September 24, and September 30, 1980, Serial No. 96-218, Government Printing Office, Washington, D.C., p. 423 (1980).

28. U.S. Congress, House Committee on Interstate and Foreign Commerce, *Cost-Benefit Analysis: Wonder Tool or Mirage?* Report by the Subcommittee on Oversight and Investigations, 96th Congress, 2d Session, Committee Print 96-IFC62, Government Printing Office, Washington, D.C., pp. 11–12 (1980).

29. U.S. Congress, House Committee on Interstate and Foreign Commerce, *Federal Regulation and Regulatory Reform*, Report to Subcommittee on Oversight and Investigations, 96th Congress, 2nd Session, Government Printing Office, Washington, D.C. (1979).

30. A. MacIntyre, "Utilitarianism and Cost/Benefit Analysis: An Essay on the Relevance of Moral Philosophy to Bureaucratic Theory," *Ethical Theory and Business* (T. L. Beauchamp and N. E. Bowle, eds.), Prentice-Hall, Englewood Cliffs, N.J., pp. 266–275 (1979).

31. S. Kelman, "Cost-Benefit Analysis: An Ethical Critique," *Regulation*, January/February: 33–40 (1981).

32. J. Byrne, "A Critique of Beauchamp and Braybrooke-Schotch," *Ethical Issues in Government* (N.E. Bowle, ed.), Temple University Press, Philadelphia: pp. 220–205 (1981).

33. "The Cost-Benefit Swindle Puts Dollar Signs on Human Health," *In These Times*, May 13–19 (1981).

34. L. H. Tribe, "Policy Science: Analysis or Ideology?," *Philos. Public Affairs*, *2*(1): 66–110 (1972).

35. C. H. Weiss, ed., *Using Social Research in Public Policy Making*, D. C. Heath, Lexington, Mass., pp. 7–16 (1977).

36. R. Deshpande, "Action and Enlightenment Functions of Research: Comparing Private- and Public-Sector Perspectives," *Knowledge*, *2*(3): 317–330 (1981).

37. W. Leiss, "The Social Function of Knowledge in the Liberal Tradition," *Liberalism and the Modern Polity* (M. J. Gorgas McGrath, ed.), Marcel Dekker, New York, pp. 178–179 (1978).

38. I. R. Hoos, *Systems Analysis in Public Policy: A Critique*, University of California Press, Berkeley (1972).

39. P. Self, *Econocrats and the Policy Process*, Westview Press, Boulder, Colo. (1975).

40. R. Lilienfeld, *The Rise of Systems Theory: An Ideological Analysis*, John Wiley and Sons, New York (1978).

41. A. Wildavsky, "The Political Economy of Efficiency: Cost-Benefit Analysis, Systems Analysis, and Program Budgeting," *Political Science and Public Policy* (A. Ranney, ed.), Markham, Chicago (1968).

42. P. D. Uliassi, "Research and Foreign Policy: A View From Foggy Bottom," *Using Social Research in Public Policy Making* (C. H. Weiss, ed.), D. C. Heath, Lexington, Mass. (1977).

43. P. L. Rosen, "Social Science and Judicial Policy Making," *Using Social Research in Public Policy Making* (C. H. Weiss, ed.), D. C. Heath, Lexington, Mass. (1977).

44. D. A. Dreyfus, "The Limitations of Policy Research in Congressional Decision Making," *Using Social Research in Public Policy Making* (C. H. Weiss, ed.), D. C. Heath, Lexington, Mass. (1977).

45. M. Bulmer, "Applied Social Research: A Reformulation of 'Applied' and 'Enlightenment' Models," *Knowledge*, *3*(2): 187–210 (1981).

46. B. Holzner and J. H. Marx, *Knowledge Application: The Knowledge System in Society*, Allyn and Bacon, Boston (1979).
47. R. E. Crable, "Knowledge-As-Status: On Argument and Epistemology," *Commun. Monog., 49*: 249–262 (1982).
48. R. J. Bernstein, *The Restructuring of Social and Political Theory*, University of Pennsylvania Press, Philadelphia (1978).
49. T. McCarthy, *The Critical Theory of Jurgen Habermas*, MIT Press, Cambridge, Mass. (1981).
50. E. Husserl, *The Crisis of European Sciences and Transcendental Phenomenology*, Northwestern University Press, Evanston, Ill. (1970).
51. A. Schutz, *On Phenomenology and Social Relations: Selected Writings* (H. Wagner, ed.), University of Chicago Press, Chicago (1970).
52. P. L. Berger and T. Luckmann, *The Social Construction of Reality*, Anchor Books, New York (1967).
53. F. Fischer, *Politics, Values,* and Public Policy: *The Problem of Methodology*, Westview Press, Boulder, Colo. (1980).
54. Forester, "Bounded Rationality and the Politics of Muddling Through," *Public Adminis. Rev.*, January/February: 23–31 (1984).
55. J. White, "On the Growth of Knowledge in Public Administration," *Public Admin. Rev.*, January/February: 15–24 (1986).
56. J. Habermas, *Communication and the Evolution of Society*, Beacon Press, Boston (1979).
57. D. Hart and W. Scott, *Organizational America*, Houghton Mifflin, Boston (1979).
58. B. Gross, *Friendly Fascism*, M. Evans, New York (1980).
59. F. F. Piven and R. A. Cloward, *The New Class War*, Pantheon, New York (1982).
60. A. E. Kahn, *The Economics of Regulation: Principles and Institutions*, Vols. 1 and 2, John Wiley & Sons, New York (1970).
61. B. A. Ackerman, *Social Justice in the Liberal State*, Yale University Press, New Haven, Conn. (1980).

BIBLIOGRAPHY

Y. Dror, "Social Science Meta-Policy: Some Concepts and Applications," *Public Science and Government* (A. B. Cherns, R. Sinclair, and W. 1. Jenkins, eds.), Tavistock, London, p. 230 (1972).
Y. Dror, *Public Policymaking Reexamined*, Chandler, Scranton, Pa (1968).
M. J. Falco, *Truth and Meaning in Political Science*, Charles F. Morrill, Columbus, Ohio (1973).

53

Decision-Making Orientations of State Government Budget Analysts: Rationalists or Incrementalists?

Katherine G. Willoughby

INTRODUCTION

Our understanding of human cognitive process remains inadequate as long as we are unable to accurately predict individual or group choice in any given situation. Development of the perfect predictive equation of such human behavior is so alluring because it implies the ability to determine outcomes, or future events. Concerning the decision-making practices of public officials, knowledge of this sort suggests the ability to influence public policy. This research develops a model of behavior for a specific public servant involved in a familiar and required task which ultimately is reflected in state-level public policy. While the model is far from perfect, it does clarify the information-processing task of this public employee and lends insight into the expected behavior of those responsible for the management of taxpayers' dollars.

This study takes advantage of social judgment theory to analytically illustrate the budgetary judgments of state government budget analysts. One hundred and thirty-one analysts from the central budget offices of 10 Southern states participated in the project, which required direct administration of a questionnaire. The survey instrument included a decision-making exercise which asked for analysts' judgments regarding 40 hypothetical state agency budget requests. Each request was represented by seven cues or criteria which have been consistently referred to by public budgeters as important when making spending decisions. Participants were also asked questions about their job title, work background, education, and personal characteristics.

Results from this study indicate that most analysts depend upon two or, at most, three factors when making budgetary recommendations to their governor. More importantly, the results underscore the role of the governor in state government budget development as well as indicate the actual integration of rational decision aids in the budget process. For ex-

Source: Public Budgeting and Financial Management, 5(1): 67–114 (1993).

ample, while gubernatorial direction is weighted most heavily by a predominant number of analysts completing the questionnaire, specific analytical information does provide a healthy influence to almost three quarters of those surveyed. Somewhat surprisingly, incremental data serves as an important decision cue for only 11% of the participating analysts.

RESEARCH PURPOSES

There are several purposes for conducting this research. First, dissatisfaction with traditional considerations of budgetary behavior provided the impetus for this project. Past research can be characterized by expenditure determinant studies, surveys of the personal and professional aspects of budget players, or case studies involving a specific budgetary situation [1]. In particular, the incrementalist–rationalist debate is fueled by studies which focus on yearly appropriation changes and their relationship to past budgetary behavior.

Many scholars dispute the adequacy of such research. Data availability is often problematic, as is accommodation to analysis when the variable of interest is termed "budgetary behavior" [2]. Schick [3] points out that the routines implicit in incremental theory are disrupted in an age of fiscal instability. Likewise, LeLoup [4] suggests that adherence to an incrementalist perspective simplifies a truly intricate process. Padgett's [5] analysis of federal budgetary data also confirms the notion that budgetary behavior is a more complicated endeavor than traditionally described. He finds that "[public budgeting] is much more responsive to political, bureaucratic, and technical dynamics, on a routine even if constrained basis, than the theory of process incrementalism would lead one to believe [6].

Bretschneider et al. [7] concur with these scholars that the concept of incrementalism is too restrictive an explanation of budgetary decision making. They promote the application of controlled experimental design to the study of such behavior in order to fully comprehend public budgeters' methods of information processing. While these authors acknowledge that engaging budgeters in decision-making simulations may simplify an otherwise complex endeavor, they note that results can provide "useful insights" about the types of information actually used by decision makers concerning budgetary matters [8].

In this case, social judgment theory serves as the foundation necessary to "capture" mathematically the organizing principles of state-level budget analysts. The decision-making exercise included in the questionnaire is a simulation which engages the active participation of these budgetary experts in a familiar decision-making task. The behavioral approach to this research represents a movement from pure description of past actions to direct analysis of the information processing activity of budgeters.

The incrementalist–rationalist debate suggests a second purpose of this study—to distinguish between different types of information used by public budgeters when making spending decisions. While a great deal of literature exists concerning the importance and use of productivity analysis and performance measures in the public sector, very little research directly assesses the usefulness of analytical measures to those responsible for making decisions about the allocation of public funds [9]. Reformers have traditionally promoted rational methods of decision making as a means to improved budgetary decision making. Nevertheless, research indicates that such factors are often overshadowed by the political considerations of budget players [10]. In fact, Klay [11] finds that the characteristics of budgetary process provide disincentives concerning the use of "rational" measures by public budgeters. Specifically, he cites type of funding, environmental conditions, nonexistent reward systems, and inadequate integration of the development and use of such measures as reasons why public budgeters turn to traditional and political cues when making spending decisions.

The model employed in this study, and the method of analysis chosen, allow for the mathematical distinction among analytical (or rational), traditional, and political criteria regarding their use by state government budget analysts. Rather than ask these budgeters which factors they take into consideration when making spending decisions, this research provides a measure of the influence of certain types of information on these public employees when involved in a given decision-making situation.

A third purpose of this project is to investigate the decision-making practices of an important, but rarely studied, public employee. Especially during the latter half of the 20th century, gubernatorial budget powers have been so enhanced as to provide a substantial advantage in terms of influence to those employed in the central budget offices of state governments [12]. Polivka and Osterholt [13] point out that governors draw much of their strength from their budget powers and, in turn, their budget staff. Essentially, by virtue of their position as budget office staff, state government budget analysts have become increasingly powerful players in the money game [14].

In fact, the governor, his budget staff, and the existence of the executive budget together form an "arsenal" considered vital to agency budget success, as measured by level of appropriation. This trio was listed as a major factor in appropriations by 48% of the state budget officials from five Western states interviewed by Duncombe and Kinney [15]. Additionally, the authors point out that "very few respondents" separately categorized the influence of the three elements of the arsenal. That is, participants in their survey did not distinguish the governor from budget staff or the existence of the executive budget in terms of influencing agency appropriations from year to year. Such results are indicative of the very real power enjoyed by budget staff in conjunction with their chief executive officer concerning development and subsequent passage of the budget [16].

It seems strange then, that despite such a strong role in determining budgetary outcome, executive budget staff, and especially budget analysts, remain largely ignored in research pertaining to state government in particular, and to the field of public budgeting in general [17]. Specifically, public budgeting literature has been remiss in terms of investigating the decision-making patterns of these powerful budget players. For instance, while research on the national level successfully illustrates the changing role and influence of budget examiners employed in the Office of Management and Budget [18], none exists concerning the decision-making practices of those in similar positions at any level of government. As one analyst from the present study commented,

> It is surprising that so little research has focused on [state government] budget analysts, considering how powerful they really are in determining final appropriations. Analysts in this state are very powerful employees concerning budgetary matters [19].

Perhaps the unelected status of this employee and/or the visibility of the position vis-à-vis the state budget office director have contributed to the dearth of information regarding the decision practices of such an important person in state budget process.

MODELS OF DECISION MAKING IN A BUDGETARY CONTEXT

An understanding of the decision-making context of the state government budget analyst is a necessary precursor to the presentation of the research method and model. The different criteria used by budget officials at any level of government when making allocation decisions fall within several decision-making paradigms of public budgeting and administration which reflect normative and behavioral models of human judgment. Most relevant to the behavior of the state government budget analyst are (1) the rational or bureaucratic model, (2) the incremental or coalition model, and (3) the power or political model [20]. The first approach exemplifies normative theory of human behavior as mechanistic [21]. Decisions are based on universalistic criteria (objective data). Goals are clearly articulated; alternative actions to reach goals and the consequences of alternatives are known. Decision making is a deliberative, sequential process toward efficiency [22].

However, as Caiden [23] suggests regarding public budgeting, "Choice among alternatives often arises intuitively or is negotiated, rather than made in any technical way." Incrementalism provides a second model within which the analyst's decision making can be understood. This approach recognizes the limitations of the human brain, as well as the lack of information concerning means and ends. This model proposes that many decisions in the public sector involve value judgments. Where there is disagreement over values, simplifying heuristics are used to reduce conflict and reach a decision. Present policies are those which have been agreed upon in the past and therefore serve as a good starting point when making decisions about the future. In budgetary matters, decisions center around changes to the current appropriation or the base. The result of bargaining among decision makers (partisan mutual adjustment) is marginal change in the base (current policy or appropriation) [24].

A third approach accepts certain aspects of the second model yet emphasizes the role of power in directing decisions [25]. This approach also recognizes the existence of bargaining strategies when conflicts among values present themselves. However, it emphasizes that "what decisions will be made is to be found in examining who has power to apply in a particular decision context" [26]. Further, regarding resource allocation in the organization, subunit power plays a strong role in determining final budget outcomes [27]. The criteria which are important in making decisions within this framework are particularistic rather than universalistic; the final decision reflects the biases of the most powerful decision maker.

The Analyst's Decision Criteria

These perspectives illuminate different criteria upon which the analyst bases decisions regarding departmental requests. In the analyst's world, the separate criteria manifest themselves accordingly: Universalistic criteria can include performance data in the form of workload and efficiency measures of department operation and output. Incremental or "heuristic" criteria can include measures of change in the status quo (for example, percent change in present request from current budget). Particularistic criteria can be measured in terms of influence relationships, specifically, the reputation of the department head (trustworthiness of expressed needs compared to actual spending), department interests compared to gubernatorial and legislative agendas, and level and type of public support for department programs and services.

Incrementalism, the Analyst, and Use of Criteria

Traditionally, state budgetary process has been conceptualized by the incremental model; earmarked revenues, uncontrollable expenditures, a balanced budget requirement, and debt limits necessitate adherence to precedent which facilitates agreement on spending decisions within a particular time frame [28]. In this setting, the governor favors the role of administrative manager and the budget process serves as his or her "most institutionalized, persistent and readily available management tool" [29]. The analyst is usually portrayed as a budget conserver, in contrast to department heads who are portrayed as budget claimers

[30]. While agency administrators pursue a growth strategy which involves protecting their base (appropriations for current programs) and garnering a fair share of any budget surplus, the chief executive officer (and also his staff) pursues a conservative strategy of balancing the budget by bringing requested spending in line with expected revenues [31].

In developing spending plans, the analyst considers the current request in relation to actual spending (or adherence to the base). While universalistic and particularistic criteria come into play in formulating a request, heuristic criteria are most helpful to the analyst and promote continued incrementalism—the resulting spending decisions provide for marginal growth in annual appropriations [32].

RESEARCH METHOD: THEORY AND APPLICATION

This section presents a theoretical understanding of the research method and model. Application of social judgment theory is outlined which takes advantage of the information related to the analyst's decision context considered in this study. Subsequent sections will relay data source and analytical techniques prior to the presentation of results and concluding comments.

Theory

Social judgment theory provides a decompositional and integrative approach to the study of decision making. A decompositional approach is different from traditional, compositional methods of analysis. Rather than have subjects rate criteria and then sum the criteria to obtain an overall rating or policy judgment, social judgment analysis requires the inference of the relative importance of criteria from an overall rating provided by the subject [33]. The approach is integrative because it requires subjects to perceive multiple cues and discern their importance when making a decision or judgment.

Social judgment theory and analysis arose from the work of Brunswik [34], who conceptualized the decision process as a "lens model" with individual judgment, proximal cues, and a distal state (goal). The relationship of individual judgment to a final goal or policy orientation is influenced by proximal cues. Further, there exists a "zone of ambiguity" between judgments and goals. This theory considers decision making a probabilistic process of adapting to the environment. The use of cues is functional; not all cues are needed, and some are more dependable than others [35].

The zone of ambiguity can be defined by several measures: (1) the weight or importance placed on each cue by the individual, (2) the form of the functional relationship between each proximal cue and the distal state [36], and (3) the organizing principle of the individual. The organizing principle is the individual's integration of the cues to reach the distal state (that is, a subject's judgment policy) [37].

Research Model and Theoretical Application

Using the lens model interpretation of human judgment process and considering the decision cues relevant to analysts' budgetary decisions in this study, the research model in Figure 1 was developed.

In this study, the lens model is transformed. Individual judgment is an analyst's recommendation regarding each of 40 hypothetical state agency budget request profiles. Proximal cues are the criteria traditionally depended upon by these budgeters when making judgments regarding specific budget requests. Distal state is the analyst's overall judgment policy or decision-making orientation which reflects individual dependence on and useful-

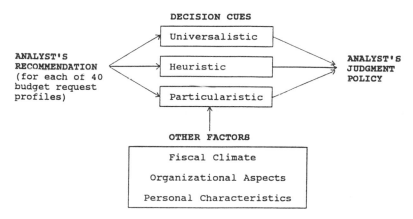

Figure 1 The research model.

ness of cues. An analyst's organizing principle can be analytically represented by a multiple regression equation:

$$\hat{Y} = b_1X_1 + b_2X_2 + \cdots + b_nX_n + c$$

where $\hat{Y}$ is the predicted judgment policy, b the weight and functional direction, there are $1 - n$ of each cue, X_{1-n} is the datum for each cue, and c is constant value [38].

According to this model, the independent variables include the decision cues, the fiscal climate of each state government, organizational aspects of each budget office, and the personal characteristics of each analyst. Judgment policy is dependent upon an analyst's particular weighting of the specified criteria in his or her fiscal, organizational, and personal setting. Thus, the dependent variable is the analyst's decision-making orientation or "spending" policy.

The analysis requires the development of hypothetical budget requests through criteria definition and scoring. The cues have been developed from the literature regarding public budgeting and decision making, and the role of the budget analyst in state government budgetary process. Table 1 defines the suggested cues of relevance to the budget analyst when reviewing agency and department budget requests [39]. The 40 profiles included in the simulation were randomly generated by the Policy PC software package from Executive Decision Services, Inc., of Albany, New York. Examples of profiles included in the simulation presented to participating analysts are illustrated in Figure 2 [40]. Analysts provided their judgments in the form of strength of recommendation to the governor concerning inclusion of each request in the total budget package (scaled from 1, very weak recommendation for inclusion, to 20, very strong recommendation for inclusion).

Using social judgment analysis to conceptualize mathematically the decision-making orientation of each analyst, a multiple regression equation is developed which incorporates the cues relevant to the decision task of interest. The equation is further modified by adding squared terms in order to account for curvilinear relationships which may exist between any cue and an analyst's spending policy. The model becomes:

$$\hat{Y} = b_{11}X_1 + b_{12}X_1^2 + \cdots + b_{71}X_7^2 + b_{72}X_7^2 + c$$

where $\hat{Y}$ is the analyst's predicted spending policy, b_{11-71} the regression coefficients for the value of cues, WORKLOAD to SUPPORT, respectively, b_{12-22} the regression coefficients

Table 1 Criteria Relevant to State Government Budget Analysts When Reviewing State Agency Budget Requests for Fiscal Year 3

Universalistic/rational criteria:

WORKLOAD: the degree of increase or decrease in the volume of work or number of clients served by the agency from FY1 through FY2

-10 = significant decrease in volume of work or number of clients served from FY1 through FY2

0 = no change in workload

$+10$ = significant increase in volume of work or number of clients served from FY1 through FY2

EFFICIENCY: the degree to which workload measures indicate increased or decreased efficiency of agency performance from FY1 through FY2

-10 = significant decrease in efficiency of agency performance from FY1 through FY2

0 = no change in efficiency

$+10$ = significant increase in efficiency of agency performance from FY1 through FY2

Heuristic/traditional criteria:

ACQUISITIVENESS: the degree to which this request reflects an increase over the agency's current budget

0 = request equals agency's current budget

$+10$ = request is a significant increase over agency's current budget

Particularistic/political criteria:

GOVERNOR'S AGENDA: the degree of importance that this agency's policy goals and objectives are to the governor's fiscal and policy agenda for FY3

-10 = agency's goals and objectives are high on the governor's agenda—governor is seeking cuts in this agency's budget

0 = agency's goals and objectives are not on the governor's agenda—governor is seeking no change in this agency's budget

$+10$ = agency's goals and objectives are high on the governor's agenda—governor is seeking to increase this agency's budget

LEGISLATURE: the degree of importance that this agency's policy goals and objectives are to the agenda of important members of the state legislature

-10 = agency's goals and objectives are high on the agenda of important legislators—legislators are seeking cuts in this agency's budget

0 = agency's goals and objectives are not on the agenda of important legislators—legislators are seeking no change in this agency's budget

$+10$ = agency's goals and objectives are high on the agenda of important legislators—legislators are seeking to increase this agency's budget

AGENCY HEAD REPUTATION: the degree of trustworthiness of the agency director in terms of past requests compared to actual spending practices

-10 = agency head has reputation for padding requests

0 = agency head is new to position—submitting budget for the first time

$+10$ = agency head has reputation as fully trustworthy in terms of equating requests with true spending needs

SUPPORT: the degree to which client groups and constituents outside of state government are interested in the agency's programs and services

-10 = public support is active and negative

0 = public support is nonexistent

$+10$ = public support is active and positive

```
┌─────────────────────────────────────────────────────────────────────┐
│  BUDGET REQUEST #1         (-max)      (min)        (+max)            │
│                            -10 . . . . 0 . . . . +10                  │
│                                                                       │
│  WORKLOAD                               XXXXX          ( 4)           │
│  EFFICIENCY                             XXXXXXXXX       ( 8)           │
│  ACQUISITIVENESS                        XXXXXXXXXXX     (10)           │
│  GOVERNOR'S AGENDA                      X              ( 0)           │
│  LEGISLATURE                            XXX           ( 2)            │
│  AGENCY HEAD REPUTATION                 XXXXXXXXXXX     (10)           │
│  PUBLIC SUPPORT                         XXXXXXXXXX      ( 9)           │
│                                                                       │
│  STRENGTH OF RECOMMENDATION:  _____                                 │
└─────────────────────────────────────────────────────────────────────┘


┌─────────────────────────────────────────────────────────────────────┐
│  BUDGET REQUEST #2         (-max)      (min)        (+max)            │
│                            -10 . . . . 0 . . . . +10                  │
│                                                                       │
│  WORKLOAD                    XXXXXXX                   (-6)           │
│  EFFICIENCY                             X              ( 0)           │
│  ACQUISITIVENESS                        XXXXXXX        ( 6)           │
│  GOVERNOR'S AGENDA                      XXXXXXXXX      ( 8)           │
│  LEGISLATURE                            XXX           ( 2)            │
│  AGENCY HEAD REPUTATION      XXXXXXX                   (-6)           │
│  PUBLIC SUPPORT                         X              ( 0)           │
│                                                                       │
│  STRENGTH OF RECOMMENDATION:  _____                                 │
└─────────────────────────────────────────────────────────────────────┘
```

Figure 2 Hypothetical state agency budget requests: Examples of those included in decision-making simulation presented to analysts participating in the 1988 State Government Budget Analysts Project.

for the square of the values of cues, WORKLOAD to SUPPORT, respectively, X_{1-7} the scored cues, WORKLOAD to SUPPORT, respectively, X_{1-7}^2 the square of the scored cues, WORKLOAD to SUPPORT, respectively, and c is a constant value.

Analysts' weightings of cues are exhibited by their numerical judgments concerning the 40 hypothetical budget requests presented in the simulation. Different weightings of criteria across separate budget requests should indicate distinct patterns of dependence—analysts consistently relying more heavily on universalistic criteria when making spending decisions can be termed rational or bureaucratic in orientation; heavier reliance on heuristic criteria implies a traditional or incremental orientation; and greatest reliance on particularistic criteria suggests a political or power orientation. Based upon the knowledge of the role of the budget analyst vis-à-vis the governor, and traditional theory regarding the usefulness of heuristic criteria to such an employee when developing budgetary recommendations, it is hypothesized that the majority of analysts will manifest political and incremental orientations—that is, that they will weigh these cues most heavily when making spending decisions.

This chapter considers the influence of the decision cues alone. Subsequent research will address the influences of the other factors mentioned by studying the differences between group means of cues weightings across fiscal and organizational environments, and across analysts of different age, sex, and educational and work backgrounds.

DATA SOURCE

Group administration of the survey instrument facilitated the collection of data used in this study. The researcher visited the central budget office of each participating state government in the fall of 1988 to administer the questionnaire to all eligible analysts. The state governments included in this survey represent the Southern region of the United States, including Alabama, Florida, Georgia, Kentucky, Louisiana, Mississippi, North Carolina, South Carolina, Tennessee, and Virginia.

To be considered eligible for inclusion in this research project, an analyst must have been employed by the budget office through one budget cycle, or for at least one full year. Also, analysts were only included if their primary responsibility is the review of state government agency and department budget requests prior to submission to the governor. Ineligible analysts included those employed less than one year with their budget office, or those involved strictly in capital outlay, special policy analyses and evaluation, management review, econometrics, or specially requested data gathering and statistical analyses. Table 2 illustrates the completion rate by state for this survey [41].

DATA ANALYSES

Data collected were analyzed on both an individual and group level. The statistical procedures involved are listed below:

1. A multiple correlation coefficient or predictability score (multiple R), calculated for each analyst, provides a measure of the comparability of an analyst's predicted judgment policy with his or her actual budgetary recommendations. Multiple R provides an indication of both the fit of the model to an analyst's actual behavior, and the consistency with which the analyst makes recommendations.

2. Multiple regression provides the predictive equation for the spending policy of each analyst. Regression coefficients are standardized to indicate the relative influence of each cue to each analyst. Standardized coefficients, or beta weights, provide a

Table 2 Completion Rate by State for Budget Analysts Survey

State	Total number of analyst positions	Number eligible	Number completing questionnaire	%
Alabama[a]	9	9	9	100
Florida[b]	38	28	23	82
Georgia	39	19	18	95
Kentucky[c]	14	14	14	100
Louisiana[d]	21	18	15	83
Mississippi	7	6	6	100
North Carolina	13	12	8	67
South Carolina[e]	13	10	10	100
Tennessee[f]	22	6	6	100
Virginia	35	30	22	73

[a]Questionnaires completed include that of the Deputy Budget Officer who also serves as an analyst.
[b]Questionnaires completed include those of Division Directors.
[c]Questionnaires completed include those of two Deputy Directors.
[d]Questionnaires completed include those of State Budget Managers from each division within the state budget office.
[e]Questionnaires completed include that of the Director of Budget Development.
[f]Questionnaires completed include those of Division Directors.

measure of the percentage of variability in an analyst's judgment policy that can be explained by each cue. Relative weights are standardized beta weights.

3. Function forms provide graphic illustration of the "idealized functional relation-ships" between cue values and each analyst's judgments [42]. These graphs illus-trate the manner in which an analyst takes advantage of particular cues and are interpreted in conjunction with relative weights.

4. The principal components method of factoring with varimax rotation was used for parsimony—to reduce from 40 the number of judgments used to group analysts according to specific decision-making orientations. Examination of the scree plot and eigenvalues suggests a seven-factor solution.

5. Cluster analysis of the factor scores calculated for each analyst produced eleven groups of analysts. The Ward method of clustering was used. Mean weights were then calculated for each group.

RESULTS

Results from this project are promising in terms of the application of method in future research as well as providing an interesting contribution to the literature regarding public budgetary behavior, specifically at the state government level. As noted above, data analyses were carried out in stages, moving from individual to group consideration.

Predictability scores provide an indication of the "goodness of fit" of the mathematical model as well as a measure of the consistency with which analysts made their spending recommendations. Predictability scores fall between zero and one, the predictive qualities of the arithmetic model improving as multiple R approaches one. Scores from .70 to .90 are common in judgment research, with those above .80 considered "good" [43]. The mean predictability score for all analysts in this study is .88. Approximately 70% of analysts' scores fall at .86 or above, which signifies: (1) that the mathematical model used to represent analysts' spending policies is quite good, and (2) that analysts generally were consistent in their judgments across the 40 request profiles.

Examination of weights and function forms provides a more detailed analysis of the decision-making behavior of the subjects. Figure 3 illustrates weights and function forms for three analysts, all of whom take greatest advantage of the political cues. The predict-ability score for each analyst is printed directly under the function forms. Weights are found in the lower right corner of the function forms, which illustrate the manner in which an analyst utilized each cue.

Case number 31 provides an instance where an analyst depends almost completely upon gubernatorial direction when making spending recommendations. That is, the weight of 59 for GOVSAGENDA suggests that 59% of the variability in this analyst's judgments can be explained by his or her consideration of this cue. Case number 20, however, rep-resents an analyst who takes advantage of several political cues—both gubernatorial and legislative direction, as well as public support (weights of 27, 29, and 28, respectively). Like the previous analyst and his or her use of GOVSAGENDA, case number 20 takes advantage of these cues in a positive, linear fashion. Case number 108 illustrates the func-tion forms for an analyst who takes greatest advantage of both agency head reputation and gubernatorial direction (weights of 26 and 25, respectively). Notice that this analyst seems to utilize AGHEADREP in a slightly curvilinear fashion.

While the use of political cues on the part of analysts was generally in a positive, linear fashion, those taking greater advantage of the heuristic cue, ACQUISITIVE, illustrate very

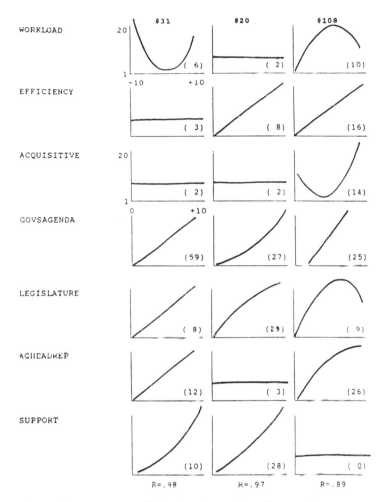

Figure 3 Judgment policies for three selected respondents.

different patterns of influence. Figure 4 represents the weights and function forms for three analysts who consider acquisitiveness of the request rather heavily when making spending recommendations to their governor.

Case numbers 4 and 110 take advantage of this cue in a curvilinear fashion, though in opposite manners. For case number 4, requests above current budget result in weaker recommendations for inclusion in the total budget package to a point, after which rather large requests compared to current budget are considered positively and result in a stronger recommendation for inclusion in the total budget package.

Case number 110, however, views some increase from current budget positively, yet after a certain point very large requests are treated negatively, resulting in weaker recommendations for inclusion in the total budget package. Case number 124 takes advantage of this cue in a negative, linear fashion, conferring weaker recommendations as requests increase compared to current budget.

The results discussed thus far indicate the complexity and uniqueness of information processing exhibited on the part of state-level budget analysts engaged in a necessary and

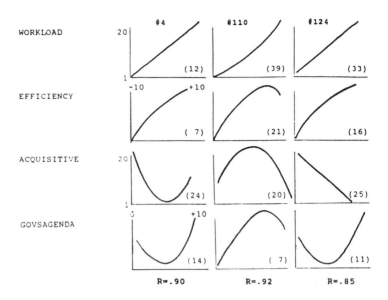

Figure 4   Judgment policies for three selected respondents.

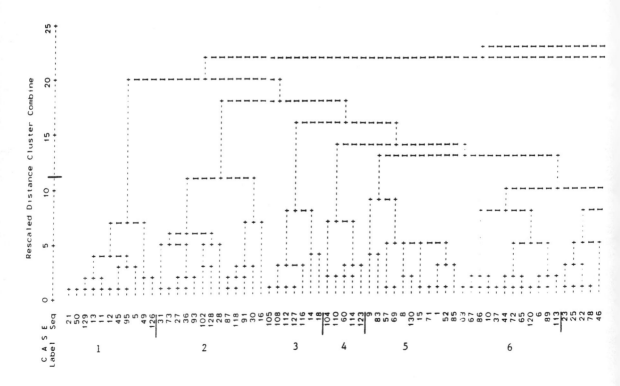

Figure 5   Dendrogram using Ward method.

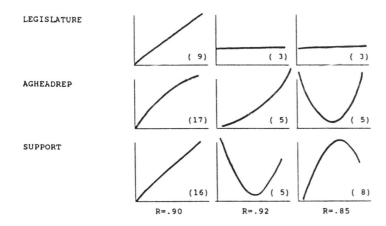

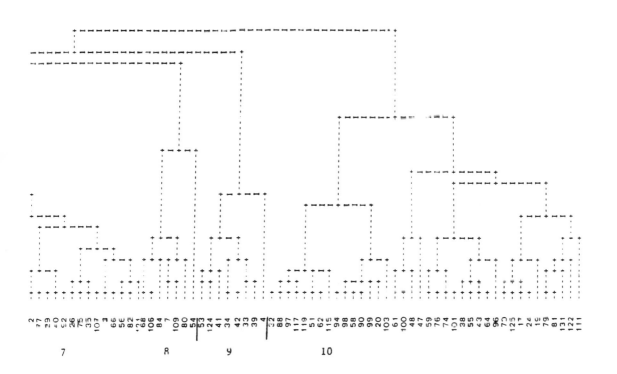

Table 3 Mean Weights of Budgetary Cues by Group[a]

Group	Cue[b] 1	2	3	4	5	6	7	Total number of analysts
1	18	14	10	25	12	12	9	11
2	16	8	8	41	11	9	7	13
3	11	16	12	24	10	21	5	7
4	38	15	11	13	8	8	6	5
5	20	15	14	18	8	16	8	11
6	15	22	8	25	10	13	7	12
7	17	17	11	24	12	12	7	19
8	12	18	17	22	8	14	9	7
9	24	10	32	11	9	6	7	8
10	8	13	8	27	18	12	14	15
11	12	26	7	22	9	11	12	23
Average cue weights (total):	17	16	13	23	11	12	8	131

[a]Mean weights were calculated for each group of analysts exhibited in Figure 5. For example, the mean weights for Group 1 are found directly under the cue numbers beside Group 1. The information on that line (18, 14, 10, 25, 12, 12, 9) indicates the mean percent of variability in an analyst's judgment policy that can be explained by each cue. For analysts in Group 1, gubernatorial direction (GOV-SAGENDA) accounts for 25% of the variability in an analyst's judgment policy. The mean weights for each group sum to 100 (may not be exact due to rounding). The last column in this table indicates how many analysts are included in the group. The first, second, and sometimes third heaviest weighted cues in each group are highlighted to more easily distinguish between the groups.

[b]Cue numbers correspond to the following as defined in Table 1 and as represented in Figure 1: 1-WORKLOAD, 2-EFFICIENCY, 3-ACQUISITIVENESS, 4-GOVERNOR'S AGENDA, 5-LEGISLATURE, 6-AGENCY HEAD REPUTATION, 7-PUBLIC SUPPORT.

familiar decision task. Specific examination of the weights in Figures 3 and 4 also illustrate clear distinctions across analysts concerning the usefulness of certain cues when making budgetary decisions. For instance, whereas those analysts represented in Fig. 3 exhibit political orientations, those in Fig. 4 exhibit traditional, or traditional/bureaucratic orientations. Case numbers 110 and 124 in particular, weigh the cues WORKLOAD, EFFICIENCY, and ACQUISITIVE most heavily, and afford the political cues very little weight when making their spending recommendations.

The data illustrated in Figs. 3 and 4 is available for all 131 analysts and provides a wealth of information concerning individual use of cues represented in the simulation. However, it is instructive to consider if analysts can be grouped according to their cue weightings. This was carried out using the factor and cluster procedures of SPSSX. Figure 5 illustrates the dendrogram produced using the Ward method of clustering [44]. Case and group numbers are listed along the bottom of the graph. Group numbers correspond to those found in Table 3.

A variety of decision-making structures are exhibited in Table 3. It is interesting to note that while 64% of the analysts weigh the cue, GOVSAGENDA, most heavily, 90% weigh the cue most heavily or equally heavy with at least one other cue. Also, while only 30% of the analysts weigh the rational cues, WORKLOAD or EFFICIENCY, heaviest, 83% exhibit a spending policy which reflects some influence from either one or both of these cues (see Groups 1, 2, 4–9, and 11 in Table 3)

Other interesting aspects to these results include the fact that the heuristic cue, ACQUISITIVE, is weighed heaviest by a mere six percent of the analysts surveyed. This cue comes into play in budgetary recommendations as the third highest weighted cue for only seven other analysts. And finally, only 18 analysts apply predominant weight to just one cue, as opposed to considering two or more cues rather heavily (see Groups 2 and 4 in Table 3).

These results are exciting for several reasons. First, the multiple correlation coefficients are extremely encouraging—suggesting that simulations of this kind can adequately model the decision-making task of certain experts. Of course, the choice and number of criteria, and their definition are crucial aspects to the development of an appropriate simulation for the subjects of interest.

Second, considering the analysts individually, the function forms graphically illustrate that it is important to distinguish not only cue weights, but the manner in which cues are utilized. As noted in Figure 4, analysts can apply similar weightings to cues, yet consider the information in a different linear or curvilinear fashion.

A third implication of this research concerns the groups produced by the cluster analysis. The variation in decision structures manifested on the part of the analysts suggests that these budgeters cannot be labeled strictly rationalist, traditionalist, or politico. For instance, 73% of the analysts in this study utilized GOVSAGENDA and either WORKLOAD or EFFICIENCY as the first and second most heavily weighted cue when making budgetary recommendations to their governor (see Groups 1, 2, 5–8, and 11 in Table 3). This implies that for almost three-quarters of the analysts, their relationship with the governor by virtue of their position as budget staff does not necessarily preclude their consideration of rational aids to decision making.

Finally, it is somewhat curious that so few analysts indicated heavy or moderate weighting of the cue ACQUISITIVE. Such results lend credence to arguments that adherence to traditional routines and heuristics is weakened as fiscal climate, organizational setting, and technological capabilities change [45]. Future research will address the influences of these other factors. Specifically, discriminant analysis will be used to determine if significant differences exist across groups depending upon these independent variables.

CONCLUSION

This study probes what is most important to state government budget analysts when making decisions about how to spend public money. Social judgment analysis provides the means of discovering the structure of the decision process of these budgeters, as well as the consistency with which they adhere to such structure. Ultimately, the focus of this investigation answers a call for research by Abney and Lauth [46] regarding the relationship between values and public policy decision making. Specifically, these authors note that "the role of rational values in state government decision making [remains] largely unexamined" [47].

Certainly, in the area of budgetary decision making, there has been a persistent movement to enhance rational practices of allocation in an effort to suppress traditional and/or political methods of spending. The implication is that "parochial" and not analytical interest on the part of public budgeters lends itself to inequitable public policy. Thus, the results of this investigation should be very encouraging to reformers. That is, it is rare that the budgeter of interest in this case considers only one type of cue when making spending recommendations. In fact, this study determines that most analysts take healthy advantage of both GOVSAGENDA and at least one analytical cue when making budgetary recommendations to their chief executive officer. While analysts favor gubernatorial direction when examining agency budget requests, they also take advantage of rational measures of performance before making their final spending decision. The "mixed-value" adherence of these budget players suggests that they realize the usefulness of rational aids to decision making, yet recognize the reality of political relationships (and particularly, gubernatorial direction) and their influence on final spending plans.

ACKNOWLEDGMENTS

I would like to acknowledge the assistance of the 10 state government budget directors who agreed to participate in this project and afforded time to their analysts to complete the questionnaire. Special thanks to the following for their assistance in scheduling administration of the survey instrument as well as for their time during interviews regarding the organizational and financial status of their office and state: Dr. Allen J. Barwick, Mr. Ronald J. Carson, Mr. George N. Dorn, Jr., Ms. Jane C. Driskell, Mr. Robert Harper, Mr. J. Lamar Harris, Mr. Jerry Lee, Ms. Karen McFarland, Mr. Charles Rowe, Mr. Bill Rowland, Ms. Jean Shaw, and Mr. Bill Smith. I am especially grateful to all of the analysts participating in this project, particularly as regards their interest and enthusiasm for this research effort.

NOTES AND REFERENCES

1. J. P. Crecine, "A Computer Simulation Model of Municipal Budgeting," *Manage. Sci.*, *13*: 812 (1967); see also L. T. LeLoup, "The Myth of Incrementalism: Analytical Choices in Budget Theory," *Polity*, *10*: 488–509 (1978).

2. M. S. Kamlet and D. C. Mowery, unpublished paper; "A Comparative Analysis of Congressional and Executive Budgetary Priorities," in J. White, "Much Ado About Everything: Making Sense of Federal Budgeting," *Public Administration Rev.*, *45*: 627 (1985), M. S. Kamlet and D. Mowery, "The Budgetary Base in Federal Resource Allocation," *Am. J. Polit. Sci.*, *24*: 804–821 (1980); H. J. Tucker, "Budgeting Strategy: Cross-Sectional Versus Longitudinal Models," *Public Admin. Rev.*, *41*: 644–649 (1981).

3. A. Schick, "Incremental Budgeting in a Decremental Age," *Policy Sci.*, *16*: 1–25 (1983).

4. LeLoup, "The Myth of Incrementalism."

5. J. F. Padgett, "Bounded Rationality in Budgetary Research," *Am. Polit. Sci. Rev.*, *74*: 354–372 (1980).

6. Padgett, "Bounded Rationality," p. 370.

7. S. Bretschneider, J. J. Straussman, and D. Mullins, "Do Revenue Forecasts Influence Budget Setting? A Small Group Experiment," *Policy Sci.*, *21*: 305–325 (1988).

8. Bretschneider et al., "Do Revenue Forecasts Influence," p. 309.

9. T. P. Lauth, "Budgeting and Productivity in State Government: Not Integrated but Friendly," *Public Productivity Rev.*, *41*: 21–32 (1987); see also S. B. Botner, "Utilization and Impact of Microcomputers in State Central Budget Offices," *Public Budgeting Fin.*, *7*: 99–108 (1987); S. B. Botner, "The Use of Budgeting/Management Tools by State Governments," *Public Admin. Rev.*, *45*: 616–620 (1985); G. H. Cope, "Local Government Budgeting and Productivity: Friends or Foes?," *Public Productivity Rev.*, *41*: 45–57 (1987); G. A. Grizzle, "Linking Performance to Funding Decisions: What is the Budgeter's Role," *Public Productivity Rev.*, *41*: 33–44 (1987); R. D. Lee, Jr., "Centralization/Decentralization in State Government Budgeting," *Public Budgeting Fin.*, *1*: 76–79 (1981); T. H. Poister and R. P. McGowan, "The Use of Management Tools in Municipal Government: A National Survey," *Public Admin. Rev.*, *43*: 215–223 (1984); T. H. Poister and G. Streib, "Management Tools in Municipal Government: Trends Over the Past Decade," *Public Admin. Rev.*, *49*: 240–248 (1989); J. R. Ramsey and M. M. Hackbart, "Impacts of Budget Reform: The Budget Office Perspective," *State Local Govern. Rev.*, *14*: 10–15 (1982); J. R. Ramsey and M. M. Hackbart, "Budgeting: Inducements and Impediments to Innovations," *State Govern.*, *52*: 65–69 (1979).

10. See M. Connelly and G. L. Tompkins, "Does Performance Matter? A Study of State Budgeting," *Policy Studies Rev.*, *8*: 288–289 (1989); T. J. Anton, *The Politics of State Expenditures in Illinois*, University of Illinois Press, Urbana, Ill. (1966); O. A. Davis, M. A. H. Dempster, and A. Wildavsky, "A Theory of Budgetary Process," *Am. Polit. Sci. Rev.*, *60*: 529–547 (1966).

11. W. E. Klay, "Management Through Budgetary Incentives," *Public Productivity Rev.*, *41*: 59–71 (1987).

12. G. Abney and T. P. Lauth, "The Executive Budget in the States: Normative Idea and Empirical Observation," *Policy Studies J.*, *17*: 5–6 (1989).

13. L. Polivka and B. J. Osterholt, "The Governor as Manager: Agency Autonomy and Accountability," *Public Budgeting Fin.*, *5*: 91–104 (1985).

14. See also P. Bromiley and J. P. Crecine, "Budget Development in OMB: Aggregate Influences of the Problem and Information Environment," *Politics*, *42*: 1031–1064 (1980); and Lee, "Centralization/Decentralization."

15. S. Duncombe and R. Kinney, "The Politics of State Appropriation Increases: The Perspectives of Budget Officers in Five Western States," *J. State Govern.*, *59*: 117 (1986).

16. See also P. M. Benda and C. H. Levine, "OMB and the Central Management Problem: Is Another Reorganization the Answer?," *Public Admin. Rev.*, *46*: 379–391 (1986); and G. E. Hale, "Executive Leadership Versus Budgetary Behavior," *Admin. Society*, *9*: 169–190 (1977).

17. Cope, "Local Government Budgeting"; and J. J. Gosling, "The State Budget Office and Policy Making," *Public Budgeting Fin.*, *7*: 51–65 (1987).

18. See, for example, B. Johnson, "The OMB Budget Examiner and the Congressional Budget Process," *Public Budgeting Fin.*, 9: 5–14 (1989); B. Johnson, "OMB and the Budget Examiner: Changes in the Reagan Era," *Public Budgeting Fin.*, 8: 3–21 (1988); and B. Johnson, "From Analyst to Negotiator: The OMB's New Role," *J. Policy Anal. Manage.*, 3: 501–515 (1984).

19. Interview with state government budget analyst, Monday, September 12, 1988, at 2:00 p.m.

20. F. S. Hills and T. A. Mahoney, "University Budgets and Organizational Decision Making," *Admin. Sci. Q.*, 23: 454–465 (1978); A. J. Meltsner and A. Wildavsky, "Leave City Budgeting Alone: A Survey, Case Study and Recommendations for Reform," *Financing the Metropolis—Public Policy in Urban Economics* (J. P. Crecine, ed.), Sage, Beverly Hills, Calif., pp. 311–355 (1970); J. Pfeffer and G. R. Salancik, "Organizational Decision Making as a Political Process: The Case of a University Budget," *Admin. Sci. Q.*, 19: 135–151 (1974); J. Pfeffer and G. R. Salancik, "The Bases and Uses of Power in Organizational Decision Making: The Case of a University," *Admin. Sci. Q.*, 19: 453–473 (1974).

21. See R. M. Cyert, H. A. Simon, and D. B. Trow, "Observation of a Business Decision," *J. Business*, 29: 237–248 (1956); R. M. Hogarth and M. W. Reder, "Perspectives from Economics and Psychology," *J. Business*, 59: S185–S207 (1986); H. A. Simon, "Rationality in Psychology and Economics," *J. Business*, 59: S209–S224 (1986); H. A. Simon, "The Decision-Making Schema: A Reply," *Public Admin. Rev.*, 18: 60–63 (1958).

22. J. M. Pfiffner, "Administrative Rationality," *Public Admin. Rev.*, 20: 125–132 (1960).

23. N. Caiden, "The Boundaries of Public Budgeting: Issues for Education in Tumultuous Times," *Public Admin. Rev.*, 45: 489 (1985).

24. R. M. Cyert and J. G. March, *A Behavioral Theory of the Firm*, Prentice Hall, Englewood Cliffs, N.J. (1963); C. E. Lindblom, "The Science of Muddling Through," *Public Admin. Rev.*, 19: 79–88 (1959).

25. J. V. Baldridge, *Power and Conflict in the University*, John Wiley and Sons, New York (1971).

26. Pfeffer and Salancik, "Organizational Decision Making," p. 136.

27. C. Perrow, *Complex Organizations*, 2nd ed., Foresman, Glenview, Ill. (1979).

28. S. K. Howard, *Changing State Budgeting*, Council of State Governments, Lexington, Ky., pp. 58–67 (1973); I. Sharkansky, "Agency Requests, Gubernatorial Support and Budget Success in State Legislatures," *Am. Polit. Sci. Rev.*, 62: 1220–1231 (1968).

29. S. K. Howard, "Governors, Taxpayer Revolts, and Budget Systems," *State Govern.*, 52: 134 (1979).

30. Meltsner and Wildavsky, "Leave City Budgeting Alone."

31. R. C. Elling, "Bureaucrats and Bucks: The Dynamic of State Budgeting," *Politics in the American States: A Comparative Analysis* (V. Gray, H. Jacob, and K. N. Vines, eds.), Little, Brown, Boston, pp. 269–274 (1983).

32. Meltsner and Wildavsky, "Leave City Budgeting Alone."

33. G. A. Grizzle, "Priority-Setting Methods for Plural Policymaking Bodies," *Admin. Society*, 17: 331–359 (1985).

34. E. Brunswik, *Perception and the Representative Design of Experiments*, University of California Press, Berkeley (1956).

35. K. R. Hammond, J. Rohrbaugh, J. Mumpower, and L. Adelman, "Social Judgment Theory: Applications in Policy Formation," *Human Judgment and Decision Processes* (M. R. Kaplan and S. Schwartz, eds.), Academic Press, New York, pp. 1–27 (1975).

36. Function forms can be linear or curvilinear. A positive, linear relationship would indicate the more of the criterion (cue), the better; a negative, linear relationship would indicate the less of the criterion the better; a U-shaped, curvilinear relationship would indicate that small and large amounts of the criterion are valued by the subject, while moderate amounts are not; an inverted, U-shaped, curvilinear relationship would indicate that up to a point (moderate), the more of the criterion, the better. Any amount of the criterion over that moderate amount however, is not as valued by the subject and, in fact, from that point on, less of the criterion is better; L. Adelman, T. R. Stewart, and K. R. Hammond, "A Case History of the Application of Social Judgment Theory to Policy Formulation," *Policy Sci.*, 6: 141 (1975).

37.   Past research indicates that social judgment analysis has been applied successfully in the public arena, though not concerning state budgetary decision-making, per se. The method has been useful regarding the priority-setting of citizen groups and public policy makers as well as the evaluation of research by editorial board members in the field of public administration. See Adelman, Stewart, and Hammond, "A Case History"; Grizzle, "Priority-Setting Methods"; K. R. Hammond, R. M. Hamm, J. Grassia, and T. Pearson, "Direct Comparison of the Efficacy of Intuitive and Analytical Cognition in Expert Judgment," *IEEE Trans. Systems, Man, Cybernet.*, *17*: 753–770 (1987); T. R. Stewart and L. Gelberd, "Analysis of Judgment Policy: A New Approach for Citizen Participation in Planning," *Am. Inst. Planners J.*, January:33–41 (1976); and J. W. Whorton, Jr., J. A. Feldt, and D. D. Dunn, "Exploring the Values Underlying Evaluation of Research: A Social Judgment Analysis," *Knowledge Society Int. J. Knowledge Transfer*, *1*: 40–55 (1988–1989). The procedure has also been used to model the acquisition decisions of executives employed in private business; M. J. Stahl and T. W. Zimmerer, "Modeling Strategic Acquisition Policies: A Simulation of Executives' Acquisition Decisions," *Acad. Manage. J.*, *27*: 369–383 (1984).

Similar methodology was used in a study of the performance-related judgments of 229 public managers by Huber et al. These authors recognize the implications of the use of simulation concerning the external validity of results. Yet, they note that, "the realism of the materials, the expertise of the subjects, and the controlled manipulation of independent variables" provides a good "first effort" at understanding human judgment; V. L. Huber, M. A Neale, and G. B. Northcraft, "Judgment by Heuristics: Effects of Ratee and Rater Characteristics and Performance Standards on Performance-Related Judgments," *Organizational Behav. Hum. Decision Processes*, *40*: 165 (1987).

A more recent example of the analysis of expert judgment regarding hypothetical decision scenarios in a budgetary context is exhibited in the work of Bretschneider et al. Their experiment required subjects (graduate students in business or public administration at Syracuse University) to provide a "maximum expenditure ceiling" for a hypothetical city. Subjects were given specific policy roles and information concerning the past accuracy of revenue forecasts in addition to revenue, expenditure, and demographic information about the city. Results from their study confirm that budgetary role greatly influences the decisions of budgeters (in this case, potential budgeters). Additionally, they were able to mathematically illustrate the "usefulness" of certain types of information on the part of subjects. Their results indicate the usefulness of "objective" data to subjects when making spending decisions. This experiment provides an interesting model of the information processing "structures" of future public and private employees (Bretschneider et al., "Do Revenue Forecasts Influence")

38.   Adelman, Stewart, and Hammond, "A Case History"; J. Rohrbaugh and P. Wehr, "Judgment Analysis in Policy Formation: A New Method for Improving Public Participation," *Public Opin. Q.*, *42*: 521–532 (1978).

39.   Every cue except ACQUISITIVENESS is scored on a scale from   10 to +10 in each of the 40 hypothetical budget request profiles. ACQUISITIVENESS is scored from 0 (request equals agency's current budget) to +10 (request represents significant increase over agency's current budget) as it is rare that agency administrators request less than current year funding.

40.   Budget request number 1 represents a request from an agency that has moderately increased its volume of work (in terms of service provided or number of clients served); also, the agency has substantially increased its efficiency of operation. The agency director is asking for a significant increase over the agency's current budget. The agency's policy goals and objectives are not part of the governor's policy agenda, and are only slightly more important to the most significant decision-makers in the state legislature. This agency's director has a good reputation as being trustworthy regarding matching budget requests with actual needs. Finally, this agency generates positive public support for its programs and/or services.

Budget request number 2 represents a request from an agency that has experienced a decrease in workload from FY1 through FY2. No change has been made regarding efficiency of operation. This agency's director is asking for an increase over current budget (though not as large an increase as represented in budget request number 1). This agency's policy goals and objectives are high on the governor's agenda (the governor is seeking to increase this agency's budget), though such objectives are less significant to important members of the legislature. The agency's director has a reputation for padding budget requests, and no public support, positive or negative, exists regarding the agency's programs and/or services.

41. The reasons for drop-off from the number of eligible to the number completing the questionnaire include absence of analysts due to sickness, vacation, required attendance at agency hearings or other meetings, or prior commitments which conflicted with the administration of the questionnaire by the researcher. In the case of Tennessee, which had very few analysts eligible to participate in the project, this state underwent great turnover and expansion of their budget office in 1988. Over two-thirds of the analysts employed at the time of the administration of the questionnaire had not been through one complete budget cycle, or had been employed in the budget office as an analyst for less than one year.

42. *Policy PC Reference Manual, Executive Decision Services, Incorporated*, Albany, N.Y., p. III-7 (1986).

43. T. R. Stewart, "Judgment Analysis: Procedures," *Human Judgment: The SJT View* (B. Brehmer and C. R. B. Joyce, eds.), Elsevier, Amsterdam, pp. 41–74 (1988).

44. Several methods of cluster were used in order to provide the clearest and most representative illustration of groups. Average linkage between groups and single linkage (nearest neighbor) methods recognized fewer clusters than did the Ward method, namely groups similar to numbers 1, 3–5, and 9 in Table 3. The Ward method further differentiated several of the groups recognized by the first two methods of clustering.

45. See J. Chapman, "Fiscal Stress and Budget Activity," *Public Budgeting Fin.*, *2*: 83–87 (1982); Duncombe and Kinney, "The Politics of State Appropriation Increases"; S. A. MacManus and B. P. Grothe, "Fiscal Stress as a Stimulant to Better Revenue Forecasting and Productivity," *Public Productivity Rev.*, *4*: 387–400 (1989); A. Schick, "Micro-Budgetary Adaptations to Fiscal Stress in Industrialized Democracies," *Public Admin. Rev.*, *48*: 523–533 (1988); J. D. Straussman, "A Typology of Budgetary Environments," *Admin. Society*, *11*: 216–226 (1979); and D. Tarschys, "From Expansion to Restraint: Recent Developments in Budgeting," *Public Budgeting Fin.*, *6*: 25–37 (1986), for discussions of changing budgetary relationships and decision-making patterns in periods of financial decline in the public arena. Similarly, consult Botner, "The Use of Budgeting/Management Tools"; Cope, "Local Government Budgeting"; Gosling, "The State Budget Office"; Grizzle, "Linking Performance"; Lauth, "Budgeting and Productivity"; Lee, "Centralization/Decentralization"; Polivka and Osterholt, "The Governor as Manager"; Ramsey and Hackbart, "Impacts of Budget Reform" and "Budgeting"; and D. C. Stone, "Orchestrating Governor's Executive Management," *State Govern.*, *58*: 33–39 (1985), concerning the influences of organizational setting and informational capabilities on public decision-makers.

46. G. Abney and T. P. Lauth, *The Politics of State and City Administration*, SUNY Press, New York (1986).

47. Abney and Lauth, *The Politics of State and City Administration*, p. 106.

54

Capital Rationing, Priority Setting, and Budget Decisions: An Analytical Guide for Public Managers

Aman Khan

Texas Tech University, Lubbock, Texas

Capital budgeting in government, as in the private sector, is a long, involved, and complex undertaking. Much of this complexity arises from the fact that there are more demands for capital projects and improvement activities than the available funds can permit. This discrepancy between the demands for capital investment on one hand and the availability of funds on the other is commonly known as a "capital rationing" problem [1]. An important consideration in capital rationing is the need to rank or prioritize numerous requests for capital projects the public officials receive each year from various operating agencies. Prioritization provides an ordering of projects relative to one another and makes resource allocation easier.

Traditionally, the capital rationing problem in government has been addressed through ad hoc measures and occasionally using decision techniques, such as benefit-cost analysis [2]. Although attractive as a decision tool, benefit-cost analysis has an inherent weakness in that it requires one to convert all goals to a common numerical measure, such as dollar values in order to produce a B-C ratio. Where nonmonetary goals are involved, benefit-cost analysis produces a less than adequate result. Furthermore, it does not provide any mechanism by which public officials can compare proposals from one agency or from one service area to proposals from another [3]. This is not a problem for a capital project that has been mandated by the courts or a project for which all of the funds come from external earmarked sources. Projects do not compete with other projects in such cases. A great majority of projects, however, involve a match, or liens, on future government expenditures and, as such, compete with each other as candidates for funding [4].

NEED FOR EFFICIENT DECISION TOOLS

In recent years, various mathematical programming techniques have been suggested as an alternative to benefit-cost analysis [5]. Mathematical programming techniques, such as linear programming with multiple goals, provide a better measure since they can take into consideration both monetary and nonmonetary goals as constraints [6]. However, unlike benefit-cost analysis, mathematical programming techniques lack the capability for ranking or prioritizing capital projects. Since prioritization involves both economic and noneconomic factors, they are often considered external to a programming problem. Nevertheless, it is an important part of the capital rationing problem, one that needs more attention than has been given in the capital budgeting literature. Besides, given an appropriate methodology, it is not difficult to show that the priorities derived from such methodologies can be easily integrated within a programming framework to improve the quality of solution [7].

This chapter discusses a simple yet attractive technique called the Constant Sum Method (CSM) and shows its potential as an operational tool for ranking capital projects. Unlike benefit-cost analysis, the CSM does not assume the existence of a common measuring unit among diverse criteria and is both flexible and less complicated to use. Originally developed by Metfessel [8] in the 1940s and subsequently expanded by Guilford [9], the CSM was designed to deal with measurement problems involving non-quantifiable variables that require human judgment. The present discussion is based in part on the works of Kocaoglu [10] and Bell [11], who have further improved the method for dealing with complex problems involving multiple criteria or attributes.

The attractiveness of CSM as a decision tool lies in its ability to compare both discrete alternatives and their attributes. The comparison task is not restricted to any particular class of compared entities. The entities can be activities, elements, utilities, attributes, or whatever else may be appropriate. It requires the decision maker to provide fundamental comparisons between elements taken pairwise (in all possible combinations) and to construct a tabular matrix containing those comparisons expressed as numerical ratios. The final product is a vector of normalized relative weights which summarize the judgments of the decision maker who initially assigned the weights.

STRUCTURE OF THE METHOD

The CSM derives its name from the procedures employed for collecting judgments. When given an assessment problem having n activities, the decision maker must provide numerical judgments about the relative standing of each activity. To relieve the decision maker from the difficulty of judging n activities simultaneously, especially as n becomes large, he or she is asked to judge only two activities at a time. For each pair of activities, the decision maker is asked to allocate 100 points in proportion to the relative importance of each activity. Thus each comparison bears a constant sum of 100 points.

When a decision maker is asked to make constant sum comparisons, the allocation of points to the activity is proportionate to their respective weights. For example, point allocations of 75 and 25 denote a 3 to 1 weight ratio. The constant sum allocation describes a ratio relationship. There are two reasons for using a ratio scale: One, the method relies upon the ratio values when creating relative weight estimates. Two, by expressing comparisons as ratios one avoids the use of measurement units, which is particularly important for activities or attributes that do not have clearly recognized units.

The Basic Structure

To obtain a complete set of information, the CSM requires one to judge all of the pairwise combinations. The number of possible combinations among n activities, taken two at a time, is given by the well-known combinatorial expression: $n!/\{2!(n - 2)!\} = n(n - 1)/2$.

Once all of the pairwise constant sum comparisons have been made, the information is examined using a sequence of three matrices, namely M1, M2, and M3 to organize and process the data. One can represent each comparison as $c\{a(i): a(j)\}$, where i and j are the comparing activities. The constant-sum constraint is then $c(i,j) + c(j,i) = 100$. The M1 matrix contains this raw comparison data in a square array of order n. The cell defined by the jth column and ith row contains the point score of the jth activity when it was compared with the ith activity:

$$M1(i,j) = c(i,j) \tag{1}$$

Since an activity is always identical to itself, one naturally defines the diagonal cells $M1(i,j) = 100$. Whereas the M1 matrix merely stores the constant-sum data in its raw form, the M2 matrix is used to contain the comparison in ratio form. When i and j are compared so that $c(i,j) = 80$ and $c(j,i) = 20$, then it follows that 80/20 is the ratio of activity j's weight to activity i's weight:

$$M2(i,j) = c(i,j)/c(j,i) \tag{2}$$

Thus each element of the M2 matrix shows the ratio of the column activity's weight to the row activity's weight. It may be important to include that $M2(i,i) = 1$ and that $M2(i,j) = 1/M2(j,i)$. Matrix M2 is a reciprocal matrix.

Once these data have been structured in ratio form in matrix M2, the calculations for matrix M3 begins. Each value in the M3 matrix is calculated by dividing the corresponding value in the M2 matrix by its right-hand neighbor. This division provides an estimate of the ratio of the jth activity's weight to the $(j + 1)$-th activity's weight:

$$M3(i,j) = M2(i,j)/M2(i,j + 1) \tag{3}$$

The M3 matrix columns are labeled using the names of the attributes whose relative weight ratios appear in the columns. The ratios in each column are formed using judgments associated with the intermediary attributes whose names label each row.

Typically, the estimate for the ratio of the weight of the jth attribute to that of its successor varies from row to row due to inconsistencies in the decision maker's judgments. For this reason, the CSM uses the average ratio estimate for each column in the M3 matrix. The averages for the columns of the M3 matrix can be used to derive an estimate of the relative weight vector. If one scales the activities by letting, say, column $a(j) = 1$ of a 9×9 matrix, where j stands for the 9th column, then

a8 = a9(a8/a9)
a7 = a8(a7/a8)
a6 = a7(a6/a7)
$$\vdots$$
a1 = a2(a1/a2)

To make further comparisons convenient, the sum of these weights is normalized to produce an estimate of relative weights for the M3 matrix. This, in a way, constitutes the basic structure of the method.

A SIMPLE ILLUSTRATIVE EXAMPLE

To illustrate the method, we now present a simple example of a capital rationing problem for a hypothetical government involving nine projects, three criteria, and a global objective that aims at generating long-term growth and development for the government. The three criteria, which vary in characteristics and focus, are political attractiveness (C1), size of capital requirement (C2), and return on investment (C3). It is important to note that if one has to judge the merit of the projects in terms of these criteria, one may find several projects competing for the same position. In other words, a project may be ranked as number one when viewed from the point of view of political attractiveness, but may not rank as high when considered in terms of return on investment. This is where methods, such as CSM, become extremely useful in deciding how best to select a project or allocate resources when faced with multiple choices that are not readily comparable.

Table 1 lists these criteria and the nine projects for our hypothetical problem. Of the three criteria, C2 and C3 seem to be more amenable to quantification than C1, the criterion of political attractiveness. Consider the criterion of political attractiveness: It simply means the appeal a government decision will have (in this case involving a capital project) on the population it serves. It reflects the degree of constituent support for this decision. Obviously the greater the appeal, the stronger will be the support, although translating this appeal vis-à-vis political attractiveness in precise numerical terms will not be an easy exercise. At the same time, it is important to recognize that quantitative criteria are not necessarily precise and can have considerable uncertainty in the analysis. Capital investments, by their very nature, require some assurances about the future. Although costs and returns can be measured with accuracy for the past as well as the present, there is no guarantee that they can be measured with the same level of accuracy for the future. Quantitative criteria do not always provide better measures of accuracy.

The preceding logic also holds good for the nine projects presented in Table 1. Let us assume that these projects represent the choices expressed by various agencies and departments within the government, such as expanding the Southside commercial strip or extending the East–West speedway to Bayshore. Although the primary objective of these projects is to help generate long-term growth, their contributions to this goal cannot be measured in equal monetary terms. For instance, expanding the commercial strip would improve the economic conditions by attracting new businesses, but it would also create problems of traffic congestion and public safety, and would place additional burden on other governmental services. Likewise, expanding the Central Library may not produce

Table 1   Capital Investment Goal/Objective, Criteria, and Projects

---

Global goal/objective [G]: Generate long-term growth and development
Decision criteria [C]:
  C1: Political attractiveness
  C2: Size of capital requirements
  C3: Return on investments
Specific projects [P]:
  P1: Expand the Central Library
  P2: Expand the Southside commercial strip
  P3: Construct a temporary prison facility
  P4: Expand the District-5 health center
  P5: Extend the East–West Speedway to Bayshore
  P6: Renovate the Administrative Building
  P7: Refurbish the Northside Recreation Center
  P8: Replace the water treatment facility
  P9: Renovate the Civic Center

---

exactly the same kind of results as constructing a temporary prison facility, or renovating the Civic Center, especially if the government and the citizen are equally committed to crime prevention.

ANALYSIS OF CHOICES AMONG CRITERIA

We now proceed to apply the method to our hypothetical example. We do it in two stages: First, we compare the three criteria with one another relative to the global objective of generating long-term growth. The rationale for this is quite simple: While all our criteria or attributes are desirable, they may not be of equal importance to the government given its goals and objectives. Therefore, one needs to know which of these criteria are more important with respect to the global objective so that it will allow the decision maker(s) to prioritize the projects and allocate resources consistent with this choice. Second, we compare the projects with respect to each of the three criteria in order to derive a series of rankings of these projects. That is, for each criterion we will have one set of rankings, and for all three criteria we will have three such sets of rankings. Having done this, we then summarize these rankings by constructing a "composite ranking" of the projects. The composite ranking provides the final ordering of the projects.

A Single Decision Maker

We begin with a single decision maker and by asking our decision maker which of the three criteria is more important to the long-term growth and development and, hence, should be given greater attention. (Since this is a hypothetical problem, we will make certain assumptions for making comparison between the choices that would seem reasonable in this context). The choices or judgments provided by our decision maker are presented in Table 2. Note that the judgments are based on random, pairwise comparison of these attributes. Randomizing the comparisons is necessary in order to eliminate any bias that may result from sequential shift in judgments.

Matrices 1, 2, and 3 present the weights based on pairwise comparisons of the three criteria. According to M1, political attractiveness received a much higher ranking than the remaining two criteria. This has an intuitive appeal. In recent years, public support for increased government activities has declined. Governments at all levels are currently under pressure to improve their internal operations as well as their relationship with external political environment. With declining public support and privatization gaining momentum, governments must pay full attention to public response to their decisions and must make every effort to improve the quality of their services to remain competitive with private sector operations and, more importantly, to regain the support and confidence of the tax-payers. This is especially true for capital planning and investment decisions where voter

Table 2 Random Comparison of Judgments on Criteria

C3:C1	45:55
C2:C1	40:60
C3:C2	60:40

Note: For a 3×3 matrix, the number of elements to be compared is: $n(n - 1)/2 = 3(3 - 1)/2 = 3$.

approval is frequently required to generate the financial resources necessary for funding long-term projects and programs.

G	M1 Matrix C1	C2	C3	G	M2 Matrix C1	C2	C3	G	M3 Matrix C1/C2	C2/C3
C1	100	40	45	C1	1.00	0.67	0.82	C1	1.49	0.82
C2	60	100	60	C2	1.49	1.00	1.50	C2	1.49	0.67
C3	55	40	100	C3	1.22	0.67	1.00	C3	1.83	0.67
							Average:		1.60	0.72

In order to determine the relative weight of our criterion vector, we now use the averages for the columns of the M3 matrix. As noted previously, we achieve this by scaling the criteria by letting, say, A3 = 1.0, so that we have the following relative weights:

C2 = C3(C2/C3) =   (1)(0.72) = 0.72
C1 = C2(C1/C2) = (0.72)(1.60) = 1.15

The sum of these weights is then normalized to yield an estimate of the relative weights for the M3 matrix:

1.15 + 0.72 + 1.00 = 2.87
[C1]   [C2]   [C3]
0.40 + 0.25 + 0.35 = 1.00
[R1]   [R3]   [R2]

The vector of relative weights shows political attractiveness (0.40) as the number one criterion in the decision affecting capital investments, followed by return on investment (0.35), and the size of capital requirements (0.25).

However, the calculation of the relative weights does not end here because the relative weights estimated from the M3 matrix depend on the order in which the criteria are arranged. If, instead of the order 1, 2, 3, one were to arrange the criterion data such that the columns were ordered 3, 2, 1, then the criterion relative weights would differ somewhat. To account for this variation, and recognizing that no column order is necessarily a best order, the results of the M3 matrix are computed using all possible permutations of the criterion columns. The results of these permutations are presented in Table 3. As the table shows, the average relative weight of the permutations did not change the initial ordering of our criterion vector. In fact, they came out to be almost the same.

Multiple Decision Makers

Up to this point, we have considered a single decision maker. Let us assume that there is more than one decision maker whose judgments are just as important and who may not quite agree with the judgments of the first decision maker. Thus we need to find out the level of inconsistency or disagreement the two decision makers have on their choices of these criteria. We can easily use the standard Root Mean Square (RMS) for this purpose:

$$d(1,2) = \sqrt{\left[(1/n) \left(\sum_{i=1}^{n} [w1(i) - w2(i)]^2 \right) \right]}$$

Table 3 M3 Matrix Based on Permutations

Criterion order	Normalized weights		
	C1	C2	C3
1 2 3	0.40	0.25	0.35
1 3 2	0.40	0.25	0.35
2 1 3	0.40	0.25	0.35
2 3 1	0.38	0.28	0.34
3 1 2	0.41	0.26	0.33
3 2 1	0.41	0.26	0.33
Average:	0.40	0.26	0.34

where $d(1,2)$ stands for the level of disagreement between decision-makers 1 and 2, and $w(i)$ represents the weight on the ith criterion.

Suppose the vector of relative weights, as given by the second decision maker, is $(0.35 \quad 0.30 \quad 0.35)$, where each component of this vector corresponds to the components of the first decision maker's weight vector. To calculate the disagreement or inconsistency between the two decision makers, we take the square of the difference between the components of the vector. The differences are:

$$w1(1) - w2(1) = 0.40 - 0.35 = +0.05; (0.05)^2 = 0.0025$$
$$w1(2) - w2(2) = 0.25 - 0.30 = -0.05; (-0.05)^2 = 0.0025$$
$$w1(3) - w2(3) = 0.35 - 0.35 = \quad 0.00; (0.00)^2 = 0.0000$$

The disagreement, $d(1,2)$, is calculated using the square root of $[(0.0025 + 0.0025 + 0.0000)/3]$, the mean squared difference, which is 0.0408. The RMS appears to be low, suggesting that the decision makers in general do not disagree much in their judgments of the criteria considered in this example, although the second decision maker ranked return on investment equally with political attractiveness. Ideally, the lower the value of d, the better is the agreement or consistency. As a general rule, any value of d equal to or less than 0.04 is considered a good measure of consistency [12].

There are certain advantages of using RMS type measures. For one, they are easy to compute. In addition, they are found in numerous statistical problems, including multicriteria–multiattribute type situations. However, when more than two decision makers are involved, a better alternative would be to process each decision maker's judgments and obtain the average for the group. This group average can be presented as a proposed consensus viewpoint or at least a reasonable compromise viewpoint. Alternatively, the M1 matrices can be averaged before applying the constant-sum calculations. This second option yields results that are virtually identical to the average of the individual results. Since the second option drops information about the variance among the estimators, it is usually used as a time saver.

ANALYSIS OF CHOICES AMONG PROJECTS

With the rankings for each criterion thus derived, we can now continue with our analysis. The next step is to rank the projects by each of the criteria. We do so by taking a pair of projects at a time and asking the decision maker which of these two projects would he or she consider more important with respect to a given criterion and continue the process until the comparisons for all pairs of projects are exhausted. The normalized weights based on the judgments provided by our hypothetical decision maker for the various projects are presented next.

Criterion C1: Political Attractiveness

[P1]   [P2]   [P3]   [P4]   [P5]   [P6]   [P7]   [P8]   [P9]
0.15 + 0.08 + 0.19 + 0.07 + 0.09 + 0.05 + 0.16 + 0.10 + 0.11 = 1.00
[R3]   [R7]   [R1]   [R8]   [R6]   [R9]   [R2]   [R5]   [R4]

This ranking places the construction of a temporary prison facility as the number one priority. There are two simple explanations for this: One, maintaining law and order has a general appeal and, as such, is politically more attractive than any other project. Two, let us further suppose that the government under consideration presently has two prisons that are overcrowded and badly in need of rehabilitation. A temporary facility will produce immediate relief and significantly contribute to the government's crime prevention program. Refurbishing the Northside recreation center, which serves as the principal hub for all youth programs, and expanding the Central Library were ranked a close second and third, respectively. Renovating the Civic Center, which is the central place for all social and cultural activities, was ranked fourth. It is interesting to note that these are popular projects and garnering public support for them will be considerably easier than for any other project that does not have similar appeal.

Criterion C2: Size of Capital Requirements

[P1]   [P2]   [P3]   [P4]   [P5]   [P6]   [P7]   [P8]   [P9]
0.20 + 0.03 + 0.09 + 0.17 + 0.04 + 0.08 + 0.14 + 0.10 + 0.12 = 1.00
[R1]   [R8]   [R6]   [R2]   [R9]   [R7]   [R3]   [R5]   [R4]

Size of capital requirements plays a vital role in all investment decisions. Given a choice, most governments would prefer not to disregard any proposal. But governments do not have unlimited funds and, as a result, there is often a tendency to consider as many proposals as the available funds would allow. While this may keep the competing agencies satisfied, it creates a problem in that meritorious projects that produce longer term benefits, but cost more, can easily get deferred, if not completely deleted. A simple way to overcome this is to group the projects according to the size of their capital requirements and to select a desired number of projects from each group. This procedure is particularly effective when the number of projects is large and the projects differ in size and characteristics. Projects that were ranked high, according to this criterion, are the Central Library, District-5 health center, Northside recreation center, the Civic Center, and the water treatment facility, in that order.

Criterion C3: Return on Investment

[P1]   [P2]   [P3]   [P4]   [P5]   [P6]   [P7]   [P8]   [P9]
0.07 + 0.21 + 0.14 + 0.08 + 0.18 + 0.05 + 0.06 + 0.10 + 0.11 = 1.00
[R7]   [R1]   [R3]   [R6]   [R2]   [R9]   [R8]   [R5]   [R4]

Governments must think of projects as investments for the future. Projects that create jobs, generate increased revenue, or leverage private investments should be given high priority.

Accordingly, the Southside commercial strip and the East–West speedway were ranked as number one and number two in the priority ranking. These projects are important to the government and can be expected to keep the economy revitalized and competitive for many years to come. The temporary prison facility and the Convention Center were ranked third and fourth, respectively. Both of these projects are also important here since they can complement the economic growth of the government by lowering its crime rate and by bringing in additional income through various social and cultural activities. Renovating the administrative building was placed last in keeping with the current political trend in the sense that most taxpayers would give a higher weight or priority to projects that would generate income, insure public health, and provide safety. The benefit that would result from the renovation of the administrative building, although has merit from the point of the government, does not have the same public appeal as the rest.

The Composite Ranking

It becomes apparent from the priorities just presented that our projects do not have exactly the same order of preference for different criteria. Yet from a decision-making point of view, it is important that these preferences are somehow aggregated into a single, coherent set. In other words, we need to synthesize these differences in such a way as to be able to derive a final ranking of the projects. In order to achieve this, we expand the method by constructing a matrix where each column of this matrix represents a vector of preferences for the projects, and then multiply the matrix by the vector of criterion weights (since the projects were evaluated by each of these criteria) to derive a "composite" or "final" ranking of the projects.

$$
\begin{bmatrix}
0.15 & 0.20 & 0.07 \\
0.08 & 0.06 & 0.21 \\
0.19 & 0.09 & 0.14 \\
0.07 & 0.17 & 0.08 \\
0.09 & 0.04 & 0.18 \\
0.05 & 0.08 & 0.05 \\
0.16 & 0.14 & 0.06 \\
0.10 & 0.10 & 0.10 \\
0.11 & 0.11 & 0.11
\end{bmatrix}
\begin{bmatrix}
0.40 \\
0.25 \\
0.35
\end{bmatrix}
=
\begin{bmatrix}
0.1345 \\
0.1205 \\
0.1475 \\
0.0985 \\
0.1090 \\
0.0575 \\
0.1200 \\
0.1000 \\
0.1125
\end{bmatrix}
\begin{matrix}
R2[P1] \\
R3[P2] \\
R1[P3] \\
R8[P4] \\
R6[P5] \\
R9[P6] \\
R4[P7] \\
R7[P8] \\
R5[P9]
\end{matrix}
$$

According to the composite vector, temporary prison facility came out on top (0.1475), followed by the Central Library (0.1345), the Southside commercial strip (0.1205), and so on. The final ranking seems to have fitted well with the overall preferences for projects based on the criteria used in this example.

EXTENSION OF THE METHOD

An important factor in considering this method as a decision tool is that it can be easily extended to show how the scarce resources of a government could be allocated in keeping with the priorities of the decision makers or those involved in making investment decisions. A good example will be a linear programming formulation of the problem with the priorities incorporated so that the available resources could be allocated in an optimal fashion. Thus a typical linear programming formulation for a standard six-year capital budget allocation problem with established priorities and costs associated with each of the nine capital projects will look like the following:

$$\text{Maximize } z = \sum_{j=1}^{9} w(j)x(j)$$

$$\text{s.t.} \sum_{j=1}^{9} c(jt)x(j) \leq b(t)$$

$$0 \leq x(j) \leq 1$$

where z is the objective function representing the global objective of the government in our hypothetical example, the $x(j)$'s represent the projects under consideration, and the $w(j)$'s represent the weight assigned to each project j; $j = 1, 2, \ldots, 9$. The expression $c(jt)$ represents the cost of the jth project in year t, while the notation $b(t)$ represents the budget availability in year t; $t = 1, 2, \ldots, 6$. Finally, as characteristic of linear programming problems, the model assumes a fractional achievement of projects that is acceptable to the government. If fractional achievement is not acceptable, alternative methodologies such as integer programming could be used. On the other hand, if one is using a goal programming solution, the results obtained from the CSM could very easily be used as preemptive priorities for the deviational variables in the objective function.

EVALUATION OF METHOD APPLICATION

Like most analytical tools, the CSM has its strengths and weaknesses. Let us first consider its strengths before discussing the weaknesses: (1) The Constant Sum Method offers a useful aggregation procedure for multicriteria–multiattribute type problems by breaking them down into their constituent components, such as goals, objectives, criteria, projects, programs, and the like; (2) if performed before data gathering, it can significantly help the process by identifying the relevant information to be collected; and (3) it is relatively easy to use in spite of the fact that it does involve some technical computations. At the operational level, the CSM's single-most contribution is the utilization of a ratio scale that avoids the use of a common measure, particularly when the attributes do not have clearly recognizable units. Thus the priorities, derived from the method, serve as the basic units, which can be used for a variety of other problems, such as human resource management with budget constraints, energy conservation, conflict resolution, health facilities planning, and so on.

The method is not without its problems, however. The first is related to thoroughness of the prioritization analysis: Decision makers can spend a lot of time on aspects of a problem that, in retrospect, may not be quite as important. Ideally, if the decision makers could have only one goal or criterion, much unnecessary work could be avoided by concentrating on that goal or criterion rather than an entire set of goals, objectives, and criteria. This would not only save time but would also improve the quality of solution.

A second weakness is really a neutral characteristic of the method. There is no guarantee that a single answer will emerge. The method does not provide an alternative to deal with ties that may occur in the normalized vector. Too many ties can lead to imprecise decision. This is not so much a problem of the method itself as much as it is of the complexity of the real world the method is trying to address.

A final disadvantage is again a problem common to these types of methods, in general. One must be familiar with the problem or the issue to provide judgments in a consistent manner. As the problem gets larger and becomes more complex, it would require much more intricate detail on goals, objectives, criteria, and so on than one would ordinarily be willing to consider. Unless one is quite conversant with the problem, one might not have enough interest or the commitment to deal with the detail involved. On balance, however, the strengths of CSM far outweigh its weaknesses.

CONCLUSION

Capital rationing in government is a common, but serious problem that must concern all public officials. Decision makers must understand the gravity of their decisions when confronted with the task of rebuilding bridges, constructing new plants to purify water, building better roads to take the commuters to work, investing in neighborhood commercial and inner-city industrial areas in order to create jobs and tax revenues, and restoring libraries, recreation centers, and parklands to full public use. These are complex tasks, but to meet these challenges, especially when funds are limited, a government must direct its energy and resources to the most pressing needs—those that would insure health and safety of its residents, those that would improve its internal operations, and those that would promise economic growth. Decision tools, such as CSM can be of immense help in this regard by providing a rational approach for making choices that would best reflect these needs as well as suggesting the most efficient way to achieve them.

NOTES AND REFERENCES

1. J. D. Forsyth and D. C. Owen, "Capital Rationing Methods," *Capital Budgeting Under Conditions of Uncertainty* (R. L. Crum and F. G. J. Derkindersen, eds.), Martinus Nijhoff, Boston, pp. 213–235 (1981). Also see S. Schmidt, *The Capital Budgeting Decision*, McMillan, New York, pp. 191–196 (1988).
2. A. Khan, "Capital Budgeting Practices in Large US Cities," *Engineering Economist* 33(1): 1–13 (1987). Also see A. Millar, "Selecting Capital Investments for Local Governments," *Capital Projects* (J. Matzer, Jr., ed., ICMA, Washington, D.C., pp 81–99 (1989); J. R. Aronson and E. Schwartz, "Capital Budgeting," *Management Policies in Local Government Finance*, ICMA, Washington, D.C., pp. 433–461 (1987).
3. R. L. Trosper, "Multicriterion Decision Making in a Tribal Context," *Policy Studies J.*, 16(4): 826–842 (1988). Also see J. A. Vogt, "Budgeting Capital Outlays and Improvements," *Budget Management* (J. Rabin et al., eds.), Carl Vinson Institute of Government, University of Georgia, Atlanta, pp. 128–143 (1983).
4. H. P. Hatry, *Guide to Setting Priorities for Capital Investment*, Urban Institute Press, Washington, D.C. (1988).
5. H. M. Weingartner, "Capital Rationing: *n* Authors in Search of a Plot," *J. Fin.*, 92: 1403–1431 (1977).
6. S. M. Lee, "Capital Budgeting for Multiple Objectives," *Financial Management 3*: 58–66 (1974). Also see A. Khan, "Evaluating Capital Programs and Budget Decisions: A Goal Programming Application," *J. Manage. Sci. Policy Anal.*, 6(2): 57–69 (1989); J. P. Ignizio, *Linear Programming in Single and Multiple Objective Systems*, Prentice-Hall, Englewood-Cliffs, N.J. (1982); R. E. Steuer, *Multiple Criteria Optimization: Theory, Computation, and Application*, John Wiley and Sons, New York (1986).
7. T. L. Saaty, *Analytic Hierarchy Process*, McGraw-Hill, New York (1980). For a simpler exposition of the method, see also T. L. Saaty, *Decision Making for Leaders*, Lifetime Learning, Belmont, Calif. (1982).
8. M. Metfessel, "A Proposal for Quantitative Reporting of Comparative Judgments," *J. Psychol.* 24: 229–235 (1947).

9. J. P. Guilford, *Psychometric Methods*, McGraw-Hill, New York, pp. 214–220 (1954).
10. D. F. Kocaoglu, "A Systems Approach to Resource Allocation Process in Police Control," unpublished Ph.D. thesis, School of Engineering, University of Pittsburgh (1976).
11. T. R. Bell, *A Consistency Measure for Constant-Sum Method*, unpublished master's thesis, Department of Industrial Engineering, University of Pittsburgh (1980).
12. For further discussion on the subject, see Refs. 10 and 11.

Author Index

Subject Index

About the Editors

ROBERT T. GOLEMBIEWSKI is a Research Professor of Political Science and Management at the University of Georgia, Athens. The author, coauthor, editor, or coeditor of over 50 books, including the *Handbook of Organizational Behavior*, the *Handbook of Organizational Consultation*, *Public Personnel Update*, *Public Administration as a Developing Discipline* (in two parts), and *Practical Public Management* and the author or coauthor of more than 600 professional papers, he serves on the editorial boards of 12 journals, including the *International Journal of Public Administration* (all titles, Marcel Dekker, Inc.). An International Consultant to governments, businesses, and universities, Dr. Golembiewski received the A.B. degree (1954) from the Woodrow Wilson School of Public and International Affairs, Princeton University, New Jersey, and the M.A. (1956) and Ph.D. (1958) degrees in political science from Yale University, New Haven, Connecticut. He is the only winner of four major prizes for management researchers: the McGregor Award for Excellence in Applications of the Behavioral Sciences; the Waldo Award in public administration; the Irwin Award in business; and the NASPAA/ASPA Research Award in public policy.

JACK RABIN is Professor of Public Administration and Public Policy at The Pennsylvania State University—Harrisburg, Middletown. Previously, he was Associate Professor and Chair in the Graduate Program in Human Services Administration at Rider College in Lawrenceville, New Jersey. He serves as editor/coeditor of six journals: the *International Journal of Public Administration* (Marcel Dekker, Inc.), *Public Administration Quarterly*, the *Journal of Health and Human Services Administration*, the *Journal of Public Budgeting, Accounting, and Financial Management*, the *Journal of Management History*, and *Public Administration and Management: An International Journal*. Dr. Rabin is author, editor, or coeditor of 23 books, including the *Handbook of Public Budgeting*, the *Handbook of Public Personnel Administration*, the *Handbook of Public Sector Labor Relations*, *Politics and Administration*, *Managing Administration*, *State and Local Government Administration*, the *Handbook of Information Resource Management*, the *Handbook on Human Services Administration*, the *Handbook of Public Administration*, and the *Handbook of Strategic Management* (all book titles, Marcel Dekker, Inc.). Dr. Rabin, moreover, was a consultant in budgeting and strategic planning in the Executive Office of the President of the United States. He also serves as executive editor of the Public Administration and Public Policy series (Marcel Dekker, Inc.). Dr. Rabin received the Ph.D. degree (1972) in political science from the University of Georgia, Athens.